www.bedfordstmartins.com/bedguide

Integrated with the text. *The Bedford Guide* and its companion Web site work together to help you become a better writer. Look for marginal references throughout the book to guide you to the Web site. Once you're on the site, you can search for information by the book's contents or by keywords from the marginal references.

the richest resource a
...necessary when you are
...an instructor hands you a subject that seems to have noth
do with you, your memory is the first place to look. Suppose you h
write a psychology paper about how advertisers play on consumers'
Begin with what you remember. What ads have sent chills down your
What ads have suggested that their products could save you from a p
social blunder, a lonely night, or a deadly accident! All by itself, me
may not give you enough to write about, but you will rarely go wrong
start by jotting down something remembered.

Learning from Other Writers

Here are two samples of good writing from recall — one by a profes
writer, one by a college student.

As You Read

1. Is the perspective of the essay that of a child or an adult? How do you know
2. What does the author realize after reflecting on the events recalled?
   the realization come soon after the experience or later, when the wri
   amines the events from a more mature perspective?
3. How does the realization change the individual?

Russell Baker
The Art of Eating Spaghetti

The only thing that truly interested me was writing, and I knew
sixteen-year-olds did not come out of high school and become w
I thought of writing as something to be done only by the rich. It was s
viously not real work, not a job at which you could earn a living. Still,
begun to think of myself as a writer. It was the only thing for wh
seemed to have the smallest talent, and, silly though it sounded when
people I'd like to be a writer, it gave me a way of thinking about m
which satisfied my need to have an identity.

The notion of becoming a writer had flickered off and on in my
since the Belleville days, but it wasn't until my third year in high schoo
the possibility took hold. Until then I'd been bored by everything assoc

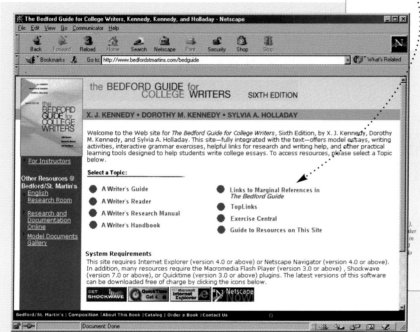

Practical support for each part of the book. Want to read more writing samples or get help with revising your paper? Need to find readings from online sources? Interested in creating a schedule for your research project? From the home page for *The Bedford Guide,* you can access useful resources to supplement whatever part of the book you're using. You can also get to *TopLinks* — a database of links to the best sites on the Web for writing papers on popular culture, body image, and other topics — and *Exercise Central,* a huge bank of online editing exercises with immediate feedback and personal scorecards.

Other resources for writers. Need practice searching the Web? Have questions about integrating sources? Want to see more sample papers and projects? The English Research Room, Research and Documentation Online, and the Model Documents Gallery provide fast help.

X. J. Kennedy, Dorothy M. Kennedy, and Sylvia A. Holladay

the BEDFORD GUIDE for COLLEGE WRITERS

SIXTH EDITION

with Reader, Research Manual, and Handbook

Bedford / St. Martin's   Boston ◆ New York

FOR BEDFORD/ST. MARTIN'S

Developmental Editors: Michelle M. Clark, Maura Shea, Amanda J. Bristow, Genevieve Hamilton
Production Editor: Karen S. Baart
Senior Production Supervisor: Catherine Hetmansky
Marketing Manager: Brian Wheel
Editorial Assistant: Erin Durkin
Production Assistants: Kerri Cardone, Courtney Jossart
Copyeditor: Paula Woolley
Text Design: Claire Seng-Niemoeller
Cover Design: Anna George
Cover Art: © PhotoDisc, Inc. 2001
Composition: Monotype Composition Company, Inc.
Printing and Binding: R.R. Donnelley & Sons Company

President: Charles H. Christensen
Editorial Director: Joan E. Feinberg
Editor in Chief: Karen S. Henry
Director of Marketing: Karen Melton
Director of Editing, Design, and Production: Marcia Cohen
Managing Editor: Elizabeth M. Schaaf

Library of Congress Control Number: 2001095136

Manufactured in the United States of America.

6   5   4   3   2   1
f   e   d   c   b   a

For information, write: Bedford/St. Martin's, 75 Arlington Street, Boston, MA 02116
(617-399-4000)

ISBN: 0–312–39632–5 (Instructor's Annotated Edition)
      0–312–26014–8 (hardcover Student Edition)
      0–312–39292–3 (paperback Student Edition)

ACKNOWLEDGMENTS

Julia Alvarez, "I Want to Be Miss América," from *Something to Declare* (Chapel Hill, North Carolina: Algonquin Books of Chapel Hill, 1998). Copyright © 1998 by Julia Alvarez. Reprinted with the permission of Susan Bergholz Literary Services, New York.

Russell Baker, "The Art of Eating Spaghetti," from *Growing Up.* Copyright © 1982 by Russell Baker. Reprinted with the permission of NTC/Contemporary Publishing Group, Inc.

Dave Barry, "From Now On, Let Women Kill Their Own Spiders," from *The Miami Herald* (February 12, 1999). Copyright © 1999 by Dave Barry. Reprinted with the permission of the author.

Judy Brady, "I Want a Wife," from *Ms.* (December 1971). Reprinted with the permission of the author.

Ian Bruce, "Commercial Fisherman," from *Gig: Americans Talk about Their Jobs at the Turn of the Millennium,* edited by John Bowe, Marisa Bowe, and Sabin Streeter. Copyright © 2000 by John Bowe, Marisa Bowe, and Sabin Streeter. Reprinted with the permission of Crown Publishers, a division of Random House, Inc.

Elinor Burkett, "Unequal Work for Unequal Pay," from *The Baby Boon: How Family-Friendly America Cheats the Childless.* Copyright © 2000 by Elinor Burkett. Reprinted with the permission of The Free Press, a division of Simon & Schuster, Inc.

Acknowledgments and copyrights are continued at the back of the book on pages A-43–44, which constitute an extension of the copyright page. It is a violation of the law to reproduce these selections by any means whatsoever without the written permission of the copyright holder.

Preface: To the Instructor

The *Bedford Guide for College Writers* has always emphasized learning by doing, helping students improve their writing through practice and feedback. Over time, however, we have increasingly recognized the value of experience with skills not only for writing but also for reading and thinking. Effective writers, like seasoned musicians, depend upon integrated skills when they "perform." Musicians master the mechanics of a particular instrument — the keys of the piano, for instance, or the strings of the cello — but also must read the musical notes for a piece and deliver a compelling interpretation during each performance. Similarly, writers must skillfully craft ideas into words, but the best writers are both critical readers — of their own work and the work of others — and critical thinkers who scrutinize their processes, their premises, and their prose every step of the way. The sixth edition of *The Bedford Guide* gets writers writing, reading, and thinking right away.

The Bedford Guide continues to offer four coordinated composition books integrated into one convenient text. A single volume offers a process-oriented rhetoric, a thematically arranged reader, a full research manual, and a comprehensive handbook — all of the textbooks you and your students will need for a thorough writing course. (*The Bedford Guide* is available in two other versions as well: as three books in one, without a handbook, and as two books in one, a rhetoric and a reader.) For the sixth edition, we have streamlined the coverage, redesigned the book, added new material on visual rhetoric and document design, and developed a suite of electronic tools to help you as you teach composition with *The Bedford Guide*.

Overview of The Bedford Guide

BOOK ONE: *A Writer's Guide*

This first book is a process-oriented rhetoric with readings; it addresses all of the traditional assignments and topics typically covered in the first-year writing course. For convenience, the rhetoric is divided into four parts.

Part One, "A College Writer's Processes," is new to this edition. The chapters in Part One introduce students to processes for writing (Chapter 1), reading (Chapter 2), and critical thinking (Chapter 3) — essential skills for meeting college expectations. Each chapter presents an overview of the process along with several activities. Part Two, "A Writer's Situations," contains the main assignment chapters, which are structured according to a typical writing process. If followed sequentially, these chapters move students gradually into the rigorous analytical writing that will comprise most of their college writing. The rhetorical situations in Part Two include recalling an experience (Chapter 4), observing a scene (Chapter 5), interviewing a subject (Chapter 6), comparing and contrasting (Chapter 7), explaining causes and effects (Chapter 8), taking a stand (Chapter 9), proposing a solution (Chapter 10), evaluating (Chapter 11), and writing from critical reading (Chapter 12).

Each of the chapters in Part Two begins with "Learning from Other Writers"—two model essays, one by a professional and one by a student writer. Next, students are whisked into an assignment in "Learning by Writing." As they navigate the writing situation, students are guided by suggestions for generating ideas, planning, drafting, developing, revising, and editing. "Learning by Writing" also features checklists for discovery, revision, editing, and peer response, as well as tips for writing with a computer and for collaborative learning. Revised "Facing the Challenge" boxes alert students to the most critical part of each assignment and give them strategies for coping effectively with it. Each chapter concludes with "Applying What You Learn," linking the writing situation with other courses across the curriculum and with professional and personal writing situations.

Part Three, "Special Writing Situations," supports students' efforts in three additional situations: responding to literature, writing in the workplace, and writing for assessment. Chapter 13, "Responding to Literature," guides students through writing an analysis of a literary work. This chapter includes a glossary of terms for analyzing the elements of literature and a section on specific strategies for writing about literature—synopsis and paraphrase. Chapter 14, "Writing in the Workplace," helps students with their personal and professional business writing—letters, memoranda, e-mail, and résumés. Chapter 15, "Writing for Assessment," discusses essay examinations, timed writings, and portfolios.

Part Four, "A Writer's Strategies," is a convenient resource for approaching all aspects of writing. The first five chapters explain and exemplify the stages of the writing process: generating ideas (Chapter 16), planning (Chapter 17), drafting (Chapter 18), developing (Chapter 19), and revising and editing (Chapter 20). Marginal annotations in the assignment chapters (4–12) direct students to these later chapters, which collectively serve as a writer's toolbox. Part Four also includes two new chapters, "Strategies for Designing Your Document" (Chapter 21) and "Strategies for Understanding Visual Representations" (Chapter 22).

BOOK TWO: *A Writer's Reader*

A Writer's Reader offers provocative content and clear models, accompanied by apparatus that moves students smoothly from reading and thinking to writing. Thirty-three brief prose selections—fifteen new—are arranged according to five themes: families (Chapter 23), men and women (Chapter 24), popular culture (Chapter 25), the workplace (Chapter 26), and body image (Chapter 27). The thematic arrangement, which helps students find something to write about, is unique in a textbook of this kind. The reader mixes the works of new and familiar writers who are culturally and professionally diverse. Here you can find perennial favorites like E. B. White's "Once More to the Lake" and Judy Brady's "I Want a Wife" alongside essays by engaging contemporary writers such as Veronica Chambers, Dave Barry, Amy Tan, and Stephen King. Readings are also coordinated with *A Writer's Guide* and serve as models of the writing situations assigned there; a new rhetorical table of contents helps students see these connections. Introduced by a biographical headnote, each reading is followed by questions on meaning, writing strategies, critical reading, vocabulary, and connections to other selections; journal prompts; and suggested writing assignments, one personal and one analytical. These questions move students from reading carefully for both thematic and rhetorical elements to applying new strategies and insights in their own writing.

BOOK THREE: *A Writer's Research Manual*

A Writer's Research Manual is the most comprehensive research guide in a combination textbook. All of the essential information that students need is here, in chapters reorganized and updated to reflect the new reality of research: planning and managing the research project (Chapter 28); finding sources in the library, on the Internet, and in the field (Chapter 29); evaluating sources and taking notes (Chapter 30); writing the research paper (Chapter 31); and documenting sources (Chapter 32). *A Writer's Research Manual* is the only research section in a combination textbook to emphasize planning and project management and to include so extensive a selection of documentation models — ninety-four in MLA style and forty-five in APA style. In fact, this book within a book can hold its own against research guides offered separately.

BOOK FOUR: *A Writer's Handbook*

With thorough coverage of all the standard topics, reference tabs, highlighted rules, boxed charts, and ESL guidelines, *A Writer's Handbook* looks and works like a conventional handbook. It also includes forty-eight exercise sets for practice in and out of class. Answers to half of the questions in each set are provided in the back of the book so that students can check their understanding.

QUICK EDITING GUIDE

Newly revised, this resource (which is included in all versions of *The Bedford Guide*) gives special attention to the most troublesome grammar and editing problems. The "Quick Editing Guide" also includes basic guidelines for manuscript format and documentation of sources. Editing checklists in *A Writer's Guide* include cross-references to the "Quick Editing Guide."

New to the Sixth Edition

The revisions in this new edition reflect trends in the field of composition and incorporate the suggestions of a host of users and reviewers. Together they create a truly flexible, integrated textbook. The sixth edition is a stronger whole because of the changes we have made both globally and within each of the four books.

ALL FOUR BOOKS

We wanted the sixth edition of *The Bedford Guide* to be easy to use, both for students and their instructors. To make it so, we have streamlined the content, improved the design, and integrated with the text a comprehensive array of electronic tools.

A Thoroughly Streamlined Text.   Recognizing that students today benefit from quick comprehension and easy reference, the sixth edition is streamlined to offer all the coverage of a full four-in-one text without added bulk. In all chapters, more concise explanations and well-designed charts, checklists, and illustrations make essential material more accessible.

A New Four-Color Design and Clear Cross-Referencing System.   The new design features references in the margins to other material in the text and on the book's companion Web site; redesigned editing checklists; and

---

Sample page reproduction:

For more strategies for generating ideas, see Chapter 16.

A WRITER'S GUIDE

recalled a childhood trip when she had to adjust to meeting new relatives and discovered the complexities of change.

Another recalled competing with a classmate who taught him a deeper understanding of success.

Learning by Writing

GENERATING IDEAS

For more strategies for generating ideas, see Chapter 16.

You may find that the minute you are asked to write about a significant experience, the very incident will flash to mind. Most writers, though, will need a little time for their memories, recent or long ago, to surface. Often, when you are busy doing something else — observing the scene around you, talking with someone, reading about someone else's experience — the activity can trigger a recollection. When a promising one emerges, write it down. Perhaps, like Russell Baker, you found success only when you ignored what you thought you were supposed to do in favor of what you really wanted to do. Perhaps, like Robert Schreiner, you learned from a painful experience.

For more on brainstorming, see pp. 260–62.

Try Brainstorming.   When you brainstorm, you just jot down ideas, coming up with as many as you can. You can start with a suggestive word or phrase — disobedience, painful lesson, childhood, peer pressure — and list under it whatever ideas occur through free association. You can also use the questions in the following checklist:

DISCOVERY CHECKLIST

___ Did you ever break an important rule or rebel against authority? Did you learn anything from your actions?

___ Did you ever succumb to peer pressure? What were the results of going along with the crowd? What did you learn?

___ Did you ever regard a person in a certain way and then have to change your opinion of him or her?

___ Did you ever have to choose between two equally attractive alternatives? How might your life have been different if you had chosen differently?

___ Have you ever been appalled by witnessing an act of prejudice or insensitivity? What did you do? Do you wish you had done something different?

For more on freewriting, see pp. 263–64.

Try Freewriting.   You might also spend ten or fifteen minutes freewriting — simply writing without stopping. If you think you have nothing to say, write "I have nothing to say" over and over, until ideas come. They will come. After you are finished, you can circle or draw lines between related items, considering what main idea connects events.

Keyboarding words onto a screen and using the edit menu to copy, cut, or paste can give you a sense that your writing is fluid and can be manipulated to answer the writing task. You may start generating ideas by brainstorming, freewriting, answering some of the reporter's questions, outlining a chronology, or writing directly about the experience you recall. Some students find it helpful to write out notes or guidelines in bold type to remind themselves about their tasks and their assignment's challenges. Just as your teacher will encourage you to find and develop your own writing processes, you should actively create your own online writing space to support these processes.

WRITING WITH A COMPUTER

Try a Reporter's Questions.   Once you recall an experience you want to write about, ask "the five W's and an H" that journalists find useful in their work:

- Who was involved?
- What happened?
- Where did it take place?
- When did it happen?
- Why did it happen?
- How did the events unfold?

Any one of these questions can lead to further questions — and to further discovery. Take, for instance, Who was involved? If others were involved in the incident, you might also ask, What did they look like? What did they do or say? (Might their words supply a lively quotation?) What information would a reader need to appreciate their importance to your story? Or take the question What happened? You might also ask, What were your thoughts as the event took place? At what moment did you become aware that the event was no ordinary experience?

For more on using a reporter's questions, see p. 231.

Check Other Sources of Information.   Because the memory drops as well as retains, you may want to check your recollections against those of a friend or family member who was there. Did you keep a diary or a journal at the time? Was the experience public enough (such as a riot or a blizzard) to have been recorded in a newspaper or a magazine? If so, perhaps you can refresh your memory and rediscover details or angles that you had forgotten.

PLANNING, DRAFTING, AND DEVELOPING

Now, how will you tell your story? If the experience is still fresh in your mind, you may be able simply to write a draft, following the order of events, and shaping your story as you go along. If you decide to plan before you write, here are some additional suggestions.

For more strategies for planning, drafting, and developing papers, see Chapters 17, 18, and 19.

boxes that call attention to collaborative projects, peer response strategies, and tips for writing with computers. The layout of each assignment chapter (4–12) makes it easy for students to focus first on the assignment and then to access, as needed, the resources in each chapter — model essays, writing checklists, cross-references, computer advice, and collaborative help.

Innovative Technology Offerings.   The sixth edition is supported by a number of useful and flexible media products designed to help you to teach — and your students to succeed in — the first-year writing course. Marginal annotations throughout the text guide you in using these tools along with the text. For details about each of these tools, see "Electronic Media" on page xvi.

Companion Web site   Research Assistant

Writing Guide Software   *Comment*

Exercise Central   *e-Content for Online Learning*

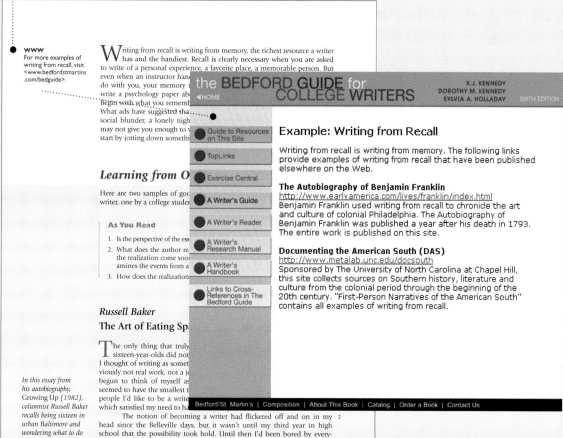

www
For more examples of writing from recall, visit <www.bedfordstmartins.com/bedguide>.

Writing from recall is writing from memory, the richest resource a writer has and the handiest. Recall is clearly necessary when you are asked to write of a personal experience, a favorite place, a memorable person. But even when an instructor han... do with you, your memory i... write a psychology paper ab... Begin with what you remem... What ads have suggested tha... social blunder, a lonely nigh... may not give you enough to ... start by jotting down somethi...

Learning from O...

Here are two samples of goo... writer, one by a college stude...

As You Read

1. Is the perspective of the ess...
2. What does the author re... the realization come soo... amines the events from a ...
3. How does the realization...

Russell Baker

The Art of Eating Sp...

The only thing that truly ... sixteen-year-olds did not ... I thought of writing as somet... viously not real work, not a je... begun to think of myself as ... seemed to have the smallest t... people I'd like to be a write... which satisfied my need to ha...

In this essay from his autobiography, Growing Up (1982), columnist Russell Baker recalls being sixteen in urban Baltimore and wondering what to do with his life.

The notion of becoming a writer had flickered off and on in my head since the Belleville days, but it wasn't until my third year in high school that the possibility took hold. Until then I'd been bored by everything associated with English courses. I found English grammar dull and

36

the BEDFORD GUIDE for COLLEGE WRITERS

X.J. KENNEDY
DOROTHY M. KENNEDY
SYLVIA A. HOLLADAY   SIXTH EDITION

◀HOME

- Guide to Resources on This Site
- TopLinks
- Exercise Central
- A Writer's Guide
- A Writer's Reader
- A Writer's Research Manual
- A Writer's Handbook
- Links to Cross-References in The Bedford Guide

Example: Writing from Recall

Writing from recall is writing from memory. The following links provide examples of writing from recall that have been published elsewhere on the Web.

The Autobiography of Benjamin Franklin
http://www.earlyamerica.com/lives/franklin/index.html
Benjamin Franklin used writing from recall to chronicle the art and culture of colonial Philadelphia. The Autobiography of Benjamin Franklin was published a year after his death in 1793. The entire work is published on this site.

Documenting the American South (DAS)
http://www.metalab.unc.edu/docsouth
Sponsored by The University of North Carolina at Chapel Hill, this site collects sources on Southern history, literature and culture from the colonial period through the beginning of the 20th century. "First-Person Narratives of the American South" contains all examples of writing from recall.

Bedford/St. Martin's | Composition | About This Book | Catalog | Order a Book | Contact Us

A WRITER'S GUIDE

Writing, Reading, and Thinking More Closely Connected.   A new Part One, "A College Writer's Processes," brings together three essential, integrated skills necessary for college and workplace success—writing, reading, and critical thinking. The three chapters in Part One provide overviews of these and, more importantly, useful activities to get students writing, reading, and thinking right away. In addition, "As You Read" questions now preceding the professional and student essays in Part Two, "A Writer's Situations," help sharpen critical reading skills and relate reading to writing.

ACTIVITY: READING ANALYTICALLY

Think back to something you have read recently that helped you make a decision, perhaps a newspaper article, a magazine article, an electronic posting, or a college brochure. How did you analyze what you read, breaking the information into parts? How did you synthesize it, combining it with what you already knew? How did you evaluate it, judging its significance for your decision?

New Focus on Visual Literacy.   A new chapter, "Strategies for Understanding Visual Representations," helps students to read visual texts—advertisements, photographs, paintings, cartoons, and other images. In addition, each assignment chapter in Part Two of *A Writer's Guide* opens with an image whose theme suggests the writing situation covered in the chapter. Each of these images is coupled with a critical reading activity.

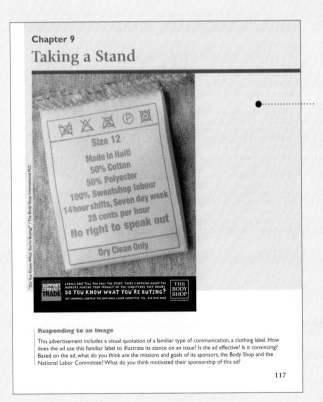

Chapter 9

Taking a Stand

Size 12
Made in Haiti
50% Cotton
50% Polyester
100% Sweatshop labour
14 hour shifts, Seven day week
28 cents per hour
No right to speak out

Dry Clean Only

SUPPORT COMMUNITY TRADE — LABELS ONLY TELL YOU HALF THE STORY. THERE'S NOTHING ABOUT THE WORKERS MAKING YOUR PRODUCT OR THE CONDITIONS THEY ENDURE. **DO YOU KNOW WHAT YOU'RE BUYING?** GET INFORMED: CONTACT THE NATIONAL LABOR COMMITTEE. TEL. 212 242 3002 — THE BODY SHOP

Responding to an Image

This advertisement includes a visual quotation of a familiar type of communication, a clothing label. How does the ad use this familiar label to illustrate its stance on an issue? Is the ad effective? Is it convincing? Based on the ad, what do you think are the missions and goals of its sponsors, the Body Shop and the National Labor Committee? What do you think motivated their sponsorship of this ad?

117

New Introduction to Document Design.
Instructors want students to become not
only competent readers of verbal and visual
texts but also competent creators of these
texts. A full chapter on document design
offers basic guidelines for formatting papers
and using images and other design elements
to create documents that are both rhetori-
cally sound and visually effective.

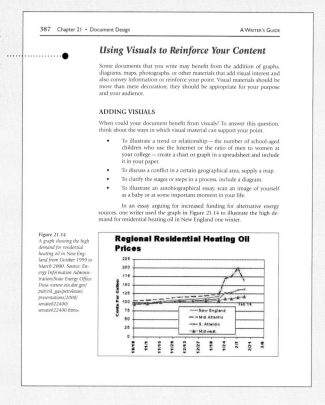

**More Support for the Most Chal-
lenging Writing and Thinking
Skills.** The popular "Facing the
Challenge" section in each assignment chapter (4–12) has been
streamlined to alert students more
effectively to the most critical part
of the assignment and to supply
strategies for meeting it.

Facing the Challenge: Writing from Recall

**The major challenge writers confront when they write from recall is to
focus their essays on a main idea.** When writing about a familiar — and
often powerful — experience, writers often have difficulty deciding how to
present that experience to readers. On the one hand, it is tempting to include every detail that comes to mind. On the other hand, because the experience is so familiar, it is easy to overlook details that would make the story's
relevance clearer to the reader.

If you are not certain of your *purpose* in writing about a particular event —
what you want to show readers about your experience — your narrative is
likely to read like a laundry list of details. Instead, you want to connect
events clearly around a main idea. You want to select details that work together to convey the significance of your experience. To help you to decide
what to show your readers, respond to each of the following questions in a
nutshell (no more than two or three sentences):

- What was important to you about the experience?
- What did you learn from it?
- How did it change you?

Once you have decided on your main point about the experience, you
should select those details that will best illustrate that point and show readers why the experience was important to you.

Applying What You Learn:
Some Uses of Recalling Experience

In College Courses.   Virtually every paper, no matter what it sets out to accomplish, stands to benefit from vivid examples and illustrations that you recall.

• Recalling a relevant personal experience to lead into a subject can engage your readers' interest and provide a springboard for your investigation, analysis, explanation, or argument. Your recollections of visiting or living in another country might introduce a sociology paper on cultural differences or a psychology paper on adaptation to change.

• Your recollection of events and experiences may provide the foundation for the reflective journal you keep during an internship or clinical experience.

In the Workplace.   You will also use memory as you tackle writing tasks on the job.

• Recalling past successes or failures can demonstrate compelling reasons for adopting proposals you offer. If your department's method of disseminating information has caused problems in the past, recalling those problems in detail would support your argument for changing the information management system.

• Records that recall data can be valuable in resolving problems, satisfying customers or clients, or investigating causal chains. Asking employees to compile and analyze a list of customer complaints can lead to meaningful changes in a product or service.

In Your Community.   In your private life, not only is your memory the source for personal writing such as journals, diaries, or correspondence, it also provides the basis for much of your writing as an involved member of your community.

• Relevant details are critical in correspondence to reso[lve]
purchase you made or a service you engaged. Recou[nt]
makes your claim clear and credible.

• Your personal experiences can lend enormous impa[ct]
changes in city plans, school policies, or governmen[t]
child has been hurt by her school's policy of social p[romotion]
her embarrassment and frustration at falling behind
alert school board members to the problems inherent

A Stronger Emphasis on Applying Writing Skills.   Understanding the applications of academic skills can help to motivate students. "Applying What You Learn" concludes each assignment chapter with cross-curricular, professional, and civic or community applications of writing skills.

A WRITER'S READER

New Readings on Provocative Topics. Two new chapters—"Body Image" and "The Workplace"—offer current readings that will get students talking, thinking, and writing. *A Writer's Reader* features thirty-three selections in all; fifteen are new to this edition.

New Focus on Critical Reading of Images.   Each thematic chapter opens with an image and a visual exercise—a series of prompts designed to help students "read" and write about the image and think critically about the chapter's theme.

Chapter 27

Body Image

Amanda and Her Cousin Amy, Valdese, NC, © Mary Ellen Mark

Responding to an Image

The two girls in this photograph are each responding to a "look" they've seen in the media. As objectively as possible, write a detailed description of the girls, including their clothes, hairstyles, facial expressions, posture, and other physical characteristics. What word or short phrase might you use to describe the relationship of each girl with the camera that is pointed at her? Use your descriptions to compare and contrast the two girls, discussing how each girl is (or is not) responding to cultural expectations about body image.

501

SAMPLE SCHEDULE

- *Week One:* If you are not assigned a topic, start thinking about an interesting general subject. Take an overview of your topic by searching your library database and the Internet.
- *Week Two:* Begin narrowing your topic to a workable research question. Conduct a preliminary search on your research question. Start your working bibliography and your research archive.
- *Week Three:* Begin your research in earnest. Locate and evaluate your most promising sources. Take notes.
- *Week Four:* Continue narrowing your research, identifying promising sources, evaluating them as you go along, and taking efficient notes.
- *Week Five:* Begin your preliminary outline, and state your thesis. Continue to update your bibliography and research archive, putting your sources in the order in which you think you might use them.
- *Week Six:* Refine your thesis statement. Start your first draft.
- *Week Seven:* Complete your first draft. Begin thinking about ways to revise and improve it. Seek feedback from a peer editor.
- *Week Eight:* Revise and edit your draft. Check that you have used quotations properly and consistently. Carefully go over your documentation. Finally, proofread the entire paper, checking for any errors.

A WRITER'S RESEARCH MANUAL

New Emphasis on Managing a Research Project. A full chapter on planning and project management as well as new coverage throughout the research manual help students to take control of their research processes. Students are encouraged to create a schedule for their project, keep a working bibliography, maintain a research archive, and actively manage their project from beginning to end.

A WRITER'S HANDBOOK

Easier Access to Basic Grammar Help. Marginal grammar definitions help students understand basic grammar terms without flipping around in the text.

More Opportunities for Practice. With four hundred exercise items, one hundred of which are new, students can practice the skills they need to communicate clearly. For additional practice, students can visit *Exercise Central,* an online bank of editing activities with items developed especially for *The Bedford Guide.*

transitive verb: A verb that must have an object to complete its meaning: Alan *hit* the ball.

WWW
For more practice, visit *Exercise Central* at <www.bedfordstmartins.com/bedguide>.

on the floor all day." *Lay,* a transitive verb, always requires an object: "*Lay* that pistol down."

The same distinction exists between *sit* and *set.* Usually, *sit* is intransitive: "He *sits* on the stairs." *Set,* on the other hand, almost always takes an object: "He *sets* the bottle on the counter." There are, however, a few easily memorized exceptions. The sun *sets.* A hen *sets.* Gelatin *sets.* You *sit* on a horse. You can *sit* yourself down at a table that *sits* twelve.

■ Exercise 3-1

Using Irregular Verb Forms

Underline each incorrectly used verb in the following sentences, and substitute the verb's correct form. Some sentences may be correct. Answers for the lettered sentences appear in the back of the book. Example:

> We have already <u>drove</u> eight hundred miles, and we still have a long way to go to reach Oregon.

> We have already driven eight hundred miles, and we still have a long way to go to reach Oregon.

a. In those days, Benjamin wrote all the music, and his sister sung all the songs.

b. After she had eaten her bagel, she drank a cup of coffee with milk.

c. When the bell rung, darkness had already fallen.

d. Voters have chose several new representatives, who won't take office until January.

e. Carol threw the ball into the water, and the dog swum after it.

Ancillaries

The Bedford Guide for College Writers, sixth edition, is accompanied by a full ancillary package that offers instructors and students a wide array of useful resources. Providing flexibility and support for experienced and beginning instructors alike, this package includes a variety of supplements, all newly revised and updated, to help you tailor your course to your students' needs.

Instructor's Annotated Edition of *The Bedford Guide for College Writers* puts information that busy instructors need right where they need it: on the page of the book itself. The marginal annotations offer teaching tips, last-minute activities, vocabulary glosses, additional assignments, and cross-references to other ancillaries.

Practical Suggestions for Teaching with *The Bedford Guide for College Writers*, by Dana Waters of Dodge City Community College, Sylvia A. Holladay, and Phillip Sipiora of the University of South Florida, helps instructors plan and teach their composition course. This text includes practical advice on designing an effective course, sample syllabi, pop quizzes, chapter-by-chapter support (including answers to all exercises), and suggestions for using the electronic media package.

(reproduced sample page at left:)

42   Chapter 4 • Recalling an Experience   A WRITER'S GUIDE

On the other side of the drift was a sight that I doubt 5 I will ever forget. There was a shallow, snow-covered ditch on the leeward side of the drift and it was into this ditch that the rabbits had fallen, at least what was left of the rabbits. The entire ditch, in an area about ten feet wide, was spattered with splashes of crimson blood, pink gobbets of brain, and splintered fragments of bone. The twisted corpses of the rabbits lay in the bottom of the ditch in small pools of streaming blood. Of both the rabbits, only the bodies remained, the heads being completely gone. Stumps of vertebrae protruded obscenely from the mangled bodies, and one rabbit's hind legs twitched spasmodically. I realized that my cousin must have made a mistake and loaded the rifle with hollow-point explosive bullets instead of solid ones.

I shouted back to the pickup, explaining the situation, 6 and asked if I should bring them back anyway. My grandfather shouted back, "No, don't worry about it, just leave them there. I'm gonna toss these jacks by the side of the road anyway; jackrabbits aren't any good for eatin'."

Looking at the dead, twitching bodies I thought only of 7 the incredible waste of life that the afternoon had been, and I realized that there was much more to being a hunter than knowing how to use a rifle. I turned and walked back to the pickup, riding the rest of the way home in silence.

QUICK START
Have each student write a letter to Schreiner about his essay. (See For Group Learning, p. 46.) Discuss how the comments might make the writer feel and how they could be made more helpful.

RESOURCES
See *Practical Suggestions,* Ch. 7, for help with using these questions.

Questions to Start You Thinking

Meaning

1. Where in the essay do you first begin to suspect the writer's feelings about hunting? What in the essay or in your experience led you to this perception?
2. How would you characterize the writer's grandfather? How would you characterize his cousin?
3. How did the writer's understanding of himself change as a result of this hunting experience?

Writing Strategies

4. How might the essay be strengthened or weakened if the opening paragraph were cut out? Without this paragraph, how would your understanding of the author and his change be different?
5. Would Schreiner's essay be more or less effective if he explained such as paragraph what he means by "much more to being a hunter"
6. What are some of S...

...mine what gives a person authority or expertise. To help students ask questions that will prompt recall about the problem, have them role-play an interview during class. Then have them write a report on their understanding of the people they interviewed.

3. Organize an oral-history project in which each student interviews an older person who has been successful in the career or profession the student wants to enter. Assign an essay in which students define the critical issues in their profession by incorporating what they learned from the people they interviewed.

> *Here's an Idea . . .*
>
> Ask students to write a letter to Robert G. Schreiner about his essay, "What Is a Hunter?" Then have them discuss in groups how they would feel and react if they received those comments about their own work. Are the suggestions specific enough to be helpful? Would any of the comments make them angry or defensive? How might the comments be phrased to make them more helpful or more palatable to the writer? These discussions will make students aware of how their comments need to be specific but supportive in order to be helpful. For more about collaborative learning, see Chapter 2 of this manual.

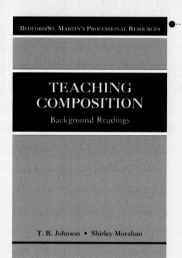

Teaching Composition: Background Readings, edited by T. R. Johnson of the University of New Orleans and Shirley Morahan of Northeast Missouri State University, is an anthology of articles on composition and rhetoric covering theory, research, and pedagogy. Its thirty-one readings are professional resources selected to help novice instructors get the most out of a composition textbook as they develop their own teaching techniques. Introductions and suggested activities connect the readings to the writing course.

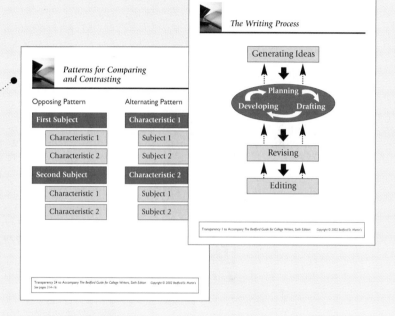

Transparency Masters to Accompany *The Bedford Guide for College Writers*, by Sylvia A. Holladay, provides supplemental examples of writing strategies, visual representations of rhetorical and grammatical concepts, and other materials useful for classroom discussion.

NEW

Study Skills for College Writers, by Laurie Walker of Eastern Michigan University, offers helpful tips and strategies for managing time, taking notes, taking tests, and accessing college resources. This value-priced supplement is full of activities designed to help underprepared students improve their study skills.

PREPARATION

The best way to prepare for a test is little by little, day by day. It is easier, less stressful, and more productive to study for tests in this incremental, methodical fashion than to cram.

Cramming may be better than not studying at all, but not much better. It increases anxiety and decreases stamina, the energy your brain needs to function at its best. If you have been studying little by little, day by day, the time you might otherwise spend cramming would be better spent getting an extra hour of sleep. Attend class faithfully, take notes, review your notes, and read all assigned material. Reread, whenever possible.

Try It!

Working backward from your exam date, construct a three- or four-day study schedule. Write down specific hours and specific tasks. Consider inviting a classmate or two to join you for one or two of these times. Be sure to set — and meet — a reasonable goal for each session.

Electronic Media

The Bedford Guide is accompanied by a comprehensive array of media products to help you teach everything from writing different kinds of essays to conducting research to understanding grammar and usage.

The Companion Web Site offers a convenient home base for students and instructors using *The Bedford Guide.*

❶ Students can access more writing activities and models, take additional grammar and usage quizzes, and follow carefully chosen links to useful Web sites for research and writing help.

❷ Instructors can access a rich array of resources, such as sample syllabi, supplemental course materials, and password-protected reports on students' exercise activity.

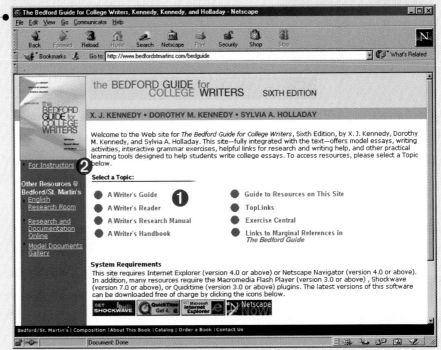

Writing Guide Software provides flexible support for the writing process by transforming the pedagogy of *The Bedford Guide* into an interactive tutorial system for writing college papers. The software's personalized Error Log and link to *Exercise Central* ensure that students practice grammar and usage skills in the context of their own writing.

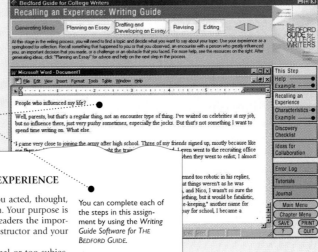

You can complete each of the steps in this assignment by using the *Writing Guide Software for THE BEDFORD GUIDE.*

THE ASSIGNMENT: RECALLING A PERSONAL EXPERIENCE

Write about one specific experience that changed how you acted, thought, or felt. Use your experience as a springboard for reflection. Your purpose is not merely to tell an interesting story but to show your readers the importance of that experience for you. Your audience is your instructor and your classmates.

We suggest you pick an event that is not too personal or too subjective. Something that happened to you or that you observed, an encounter

Exercise Central, the largest collection of editing exercises available online, offers students additional practice items for each topic in A Writer's *Handbook* — with immediate and helpful feedback.

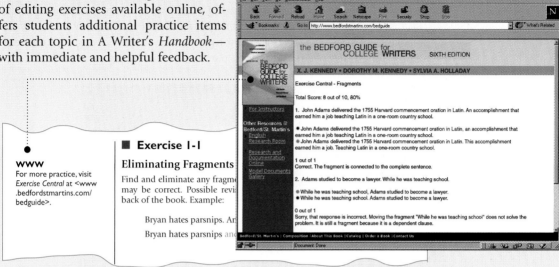

www
For more practice, visit *Exercise Central* at <www.bedfordstmartins.com/bedguide>.

■ **Exercise 1-1**

Eliminating Fragments

Find and eliminate any fragme[...] may be correct. Possible revi[...] back of the book. Example:

    Bryan hates parsnips. Ar[...]

    Bryan hates parsnips and [...]

RESEARCH CHECKLIST

Evaluating Sources — Print and Electronic

www
For help with evaluating sources, use *Research Assistant Hyperfolio,* a software tool available with *The Bedford Guide.*

——— What is the purpose of the publication or Web site? Is it to sell a product or service? To inform? To publish new research? To shape opinion about a particular issue or cause?

——— Who is the intended audience? Experts in the field or novices? The general public or people with a particular bias? How does this audience affect the tone and evidenc[...]

——— Who is the author of the [...] about the author's creden[...] thor's bias or point of vie[...]

——— Is your material a primar[...] source (an analysis of p[...] does it use sound evider[...] more if you looked at the[...]

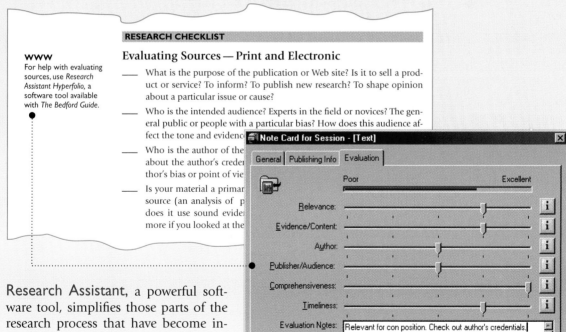

Research Assistant, a powerful software tool, simplifies those parts of the research process that have become increasingly complex with the advent of the Web: collecting, evaluating, organizing, and citing sources found both online and off.

Comment, a Web-based tool, allows students and instructors to use the Web to share and respond to writing — and to integrate references to *The Bedford Guide* directly into their annotations. Ideal for peer review, *Comment* lets student reviewers read one another's papers online and add comments of any length to specific sentences, paragraphs, or the paper as a whole.

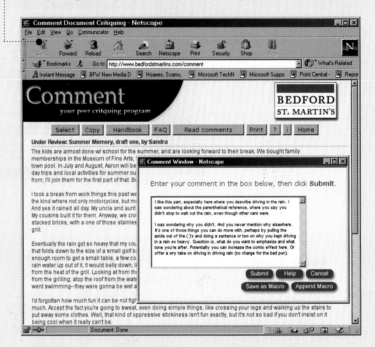

e-Content for Online Learning, an e-Pack for *WebCT* or *Blackboard,* helps instructors tailor their own online learning environment using content from *The Bedford Guide* and a host of powerful course management and communication tools.

Thanks and Appreciation

Working on the sixth edition of *The Bedford Guide for College Writers* has been a giant collaborative writing project, different only in scope from those assigned to the students for whom we write. Many individuals have contributed significantly to our project, and we extend our sincerest thanks to all of them.

COLLEAGUES

First off, thanks to our colleagues across the country who took time and care to review the fifth edition and previous editions, to respond to our questionnaires, to participate in a focus group, and to send us their suggestions gleaned from experience with students. For this we thank Dr. Ted Allder, University of Arkansas Community College at Batesville; Patricia Allen, Cape Cod Community College; Steve Amidon, University of Rhode Island; David Auchter, San Jacinto Junior College; Stuart Barbier, Delta College; Randolph A. Beckham, Germanna Community College; Pamela J. Behrens, Alabama A&M University; Carmine J. Bell, Pasco Hernando Community College; Kay Berg, Sinclair Community College; Joan Campbell, Wellesley College; Tom Casey, El Paso Community College; Dr. Steve Cirrone, Tidewater Community College; Susan Romayne Clark, Central Michigan University; Jane Corbly, George Peabody College for Teachers; Dr. Carolyn Craft, Longwood College; Sheilah Craft, Marian College; Mary Cullen, Middlesex Community College; Fred D'Astoli, Ventura College; Patricia Ann Delamar, University of Dayton; Irene Duprey-Gutierrez, University of Massachusetts, Dartmouth; Sandy Fuhr, Gustavus Adolphus College; Dr. Daniel Gonzales, Louisiana State University; Sherry F. Gott, Danville Community College; Robert Grindy, Richland Community College; Jefferson Hancock, San Jose State University; Johnnie Hargrove, Alabama A&M University; Judy Hatcher, San Jacinto College Central; Elaine Hays, University of Rhode Island; Marita Hinton, Alabama A&M University; Tom Hodges, Amarillo College; Patricia Hunt, Catonsville Community College; Barbara Jensen, Modesto Junior College; Jean L. Johnson, University of North Alabama; Ted Johnston, El Paso Community College; Andrew Jones, University of California at Davis; Cynthia Kellogg, Yuba College; Dr. Yoon Sik Kim, Langston University; Kaye Kolkmann, Modesto Junior College and Merced Community College; Sandra Lakey, Pennsylvania College of Technology; Norman Lanquist, Eastern Arizona College; Colleen Lloyd, Cuyahoga Community College; Dr. Stephen Ma, University of Alberta; Susan Peck MacDonald, California State University at Long Beach; Jennifer Madej, Milwaukee Area Technical College; Janice Mandile, Front Range Community College; Gerald McCarthy, San Antonio College; Jenna Merritt, Eastern Michigan University; Dr. Elizabeth Metzger, University of South Florida; Libby Miles, University of Rhode Island; Sandra Moore, Mississippi Delta Community College; Cleatta Morris, Louisiana State University at Shreveport; Sheryl A. Mylan, Stephen F. Austin State University; Dr. Clement Ndulute, Mississippi Valley State University; Peggy J. Oliver, San Jacinto College South; Mike Palmquist, Colorado State University; Laurel S. Peterson, Norwalk Community Technical College; Kenneth E. Poitras, Antelope Valley College; Michael Punches, Oklahoma City Community College; Patrice Quarg, Cantonsville Community College; Dr. Jeanie Page Randall, Austin Peay State University; Joan Reteshka, Sewickley Academy; Kira Roark, University of Denver; Dawn Rodrigues, University of Texas at Brownsville; Ann Westmoreland Runsick, Gateway Technical College; Dr. Susan Schurman, Ventura College; Patricia C. Schwindt, Mesa Community College; Elizabeth Smart, Utah State University; Ognjen Smiljanic, Eastern Michigan University; Scott R. Stankey, Anoka-Ramsey Community College; Leroy Sterling, Alabama A&M University; Dean Stover, Gateway Community

College; Ronald Sudol, Oakland University; Darlene Summers, Montgomery College; David Tammer, Eastern Arizona College; Dave Waddell, California State University at Chico; Laurie Walker, Eastern Michigan University; Dana Waters, Dodge City Community College; Patricia South White, Norwich University; Jim Wilcox, Southern Nazarene University; and Dr. Valerie P. Zimbaro, Valencia Community College.

CONTRIBUTORS

The sixth edition could not have been completed without the help of numerous individuals. Karla Saari Kitalong (University of Central Florida) contributed two outstanding chapters to the rhetoric — one on document design and one on understanding visual texts; she also wrote "Responding to an Image" activities to accompany the images throughout the text. Laurie Walker (Eastern Michigan University) revised the collaborative learning boxes and prepared *Study Skills for College Writers*, a useful new student supplement. Will Hochman (Southern Connecticut State University) revised and wrote new computer tips, and Valerie Duff wrote headnotes for many selections in *A Writer's Reader*. The sixth edition is much more lively thanks to the art research of Martha Friedman and Nicole Simonsen. Carolyn Lengel contributed handbook content for the text and for *Exercise Central*, an online bank of practice items that accompanies *The Bedford Guide*. A special thanks to Dana Waters (Dodge City Community College) for writing editorial apparatus for *A Writer's Reader*, revising the "Applying What You Learn" feature in each assignment chapter, judiciously editing the annotations in the *Instructor's Annotated Edition*, and calling on her expertise and experience as she revised *Practical Suggestions*. Once again, T. R. Johnson (University of New Orleans) edited *Background Readings*. Joanne Diaz (Boston University) thoughtfully adapted content for the *Writing Guide Software*, and Linda Scott helped with manuscript preparation.

STUDENT WRITERS

We offer sincere thanks to all the students who have challenged us over the years to find better ways to help them learn. In particular we would like to thank those who granted us permission to use their essays in the sixth edition. Focused as this textbook is on student writing, student essays are the linchpin of *A Writer's Guide*. The writings of Robert G. Schreiner, Sandy Messina, Tim Chabot, Yun Yung Choi, Heather Colbenson, Jonathan Burns, and Thaddeus Watulak were included in earlier editions as well as this one. New to the sixth edition are the writings of Sarah E. Goers, Dawn Kortz, Ryan Miday, and Clay McCuistion.

EDITORIAL

At Bedford/St. Martin's two particular individuals merit special recognition. President Charles H. Christensen and Editorial Director Joan E. Feinberg have provided unstinting encouragement and inspiration from the beginnings of this book. We deeply appreciate their creative guidance and perceptive advice; their continuing faith in our work has buoyed us through long hours at the computer screen.

The editorial effort behind this edition was truly a team endeavor. Editor Michelle Clark managed all aspects of the project, keeping us on track and, most importantly, on schedule. She edited the rhetoric and the handbook with skill and insight and oversaw the development of the writing guide software and the companion Web site. Maura Shea lent her experience to the project just in time to get the manuscript into production. Amanda Bristow edited and refreshed *A Writer's Reader*, managed the art program, and developed the *Instructor's Annotated Edition* and *Practical Suggestions*. Genevieve Hamilton ambitiously edited the research manual and worked with several of our new student writers. She also developed *Study Skills for College Writers*, a new student ancillary, and the companion Web site. Erin Durkin edited *Teaching Composition: Background Readings* and managed other details too numerous to count. And Marcia Muth, editor extraordinaire, helped us to streamline the text and harmonize a number of dissonant voices. The sixth edition certainly would not exist without her wisdom and diligence. Karen Henry, Editor in Chief, was largely responsible for guiding this team through the many twists and turns of the development process.

Other members of the Bedford staff contributed greatly to the sixth edition. Many thanks and heartfelt appreciation go to Karen Baart, whose exacting eye, careful hand, and great patience shepherded the book through production. Kerri Cardone and Courtney Jossart provided invaluable assistance. Marcia Cohen, Elizabeth Schaaf, and John Amburg were immensely helpful in overseeing production, as was Senior Production Supervisor Catherine Hetmansky. Tony Perriello produced the *Writing Guide Software*. Karen Baart, Deborah Baker, Courtney Jossart, and Kendra LeFleur guided the production of the print ancillaries. Donna Dennison oversaw the impressive redesign of the book's cover, giving us a new look that still preserves the integrity of *The Bedford Guide*. Karen Melton and Brian Wheel coordinated the marketing of the book, while its promotion was ably handled by Hope Tompkins, Paige Sampara, and Terry Govan. Sandy Schechter and Martha Friedman cleared permissions. We are grateful for Paula Woolley's copyediting and for Claire Seng-Niemoeller's tasteful and exciting redesign of the book's interior. Thanks are also due to proofreaders Helaine Denenberg and Janet Cocker.

Finally, we thank our friends and families for their unwavering patience, understanding, and encouragement.

How to Use The Bedford Guide for College Writers

Just as you may be unsure of what to expect from your writing course, you may also be unsure of what to expect from your writing textbook. You may even be wondering how any textbook can improve your writing. In fact, a book can't make you a better writer, but practice can, and *The Bedford Guide for College Writers* guides your practice. This text offers help — easy to find and easy to use — for writing the essays most commonly assigned in a first-year composition course.

Underlying *The Bedford Guide* is the idea that writing is a necessary and useful skill in and beyond the writing course. What this book also provides is help with writing for other college courses, writing on the job, and writing as a member of a community. In other words, the skills you will learn throughout this book are transferable to other areas of your life, making *The Bedford Guide* both a time-saver and a money-saver.

The following sections describe how you can get the most out of this text. *The Bedford Guide* is designed so that you can move quickly and easily to the section you need. And once you are there, several key features can help you to improve your writing by guiding your practice. Let us show you what we mean.

Finding Information in The Bedford Guide

It's easy to find what you need when you need it in *The Bedford Guide*. Each of the tools described here will direct you to useful information — fast.

Brief List of Contents.   Open the book to the inside front cover. At a glance you can see a list of the topics within *The Bedford Guide*. If you are looking for a specific chapter, this brief list of contents is the quickest way to find it.

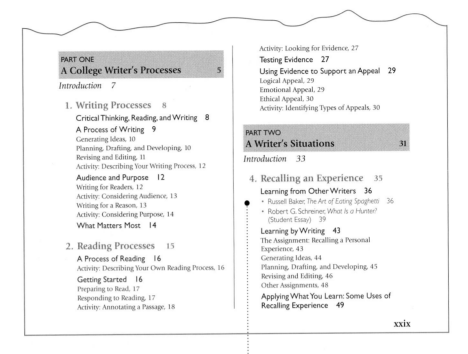

PART ONE
A College Writer's Processes   5

Introduction   7

1. **Writing Processes**   8
    Critical Thinking, Reading, and Writing   8
    A Process of Writing   9
    Generating Ideas, 10
    Planning, Drafting, and Developing, 10
    Revising and Editing, 11
    Activity: Describing Your Writing Process, 12
    Audience and Purpose   12
    Writing for Readers, 12
    Activity: Considering Audience, 13
    Writing for a Reason, 13
    Activity: Considering Purpose, 14
    What Matters Most   14

2. **Reading Processes**   15
    A Process of Reading   16
    Activity: Describing Your Own Reading Process, 16
    Getting Started   16
    Preparing to Read, 17
    Responding to Reading, 17
    Activity: Annotating a Passage, 18

Activity: Looking for Evidence, 27
Testing Evidence   27
Using Evidence to Support an Appeal   29
Logical Appeal, 29
Emotional Appeal, 29
Ethical Appeal, 30
Activity: Identifying Types of Appeals, 30

PART TWO
A Writer's Situations   31

Introduction   33

4. **Recalling an Experience**   35
    Learning from Other Writers   36
    • Russell Baker, *The Art of Eating Spaghetti*   36
    • Robert G. Schreiner, *What Is a Hunter?* (Student Essay)   39
    Learning by Writing   43
    The Assignment: Recalling a Personal Experience, 43
    Generating Ideas, 44
    Planning, Drafting, and Developing, 45
    Revising and Editing, 46
    Other Assignments, 48
    Applying What You Learn: Some Uses of Recalling Experience   49

xxix

Detailed List of Contents.   Beginning on page xxix, the longer, more detailed list of contents breaks down the topics covered within each chapter of the book. Use this part of the book to find a specific part of a chapter. For example, if you have been assigned to read Russell Baker's "The Art of Eating Spaghetti," a quick scan of the detailed contents will show you that it begins on page 36.

Rhetorical List of Contents.   This list, which begins on page xxxvii, includes all of the readings in *The Bedford Guide,* organized by writing strategy. You can use this list to help you locate additional examples of a particular kind of writing such as comparison and contrast or cause and effect.

Index.   An index is a complete list of a book's contents in alphabetical order. Turn to page I-1 when you want to find all of the information available in the book for a particular topic. This example shows you all of the places to look for help with your thesis.

Thesis, 596, 604
    causes and effects and, 110
    concluding with restatement of, 293–94
    developing, 213–14
    in essay answers, 246
    proposals with, 148
    refining, 585–86
    source evaluation and, 575, 576
    statements of, 95
    stating, 271–75, 293–94, 586, 596, 602
    using, 275
    working, 272–73, 538

Guide to the Handbook.   The inside back cover helps you to see at a glance the entire contents of *A Writer's Handbook*. Turn to this guide when you need help editing your essays. It gives exact page numbers for each handbook topic, such as "sentence fragments."

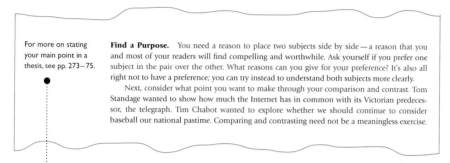

For more on stating your main point in a thesis, see pp. 273–75.

Find a Purpose.   You need a reason to place two subjects side by side—a reason that you and most of your readers will find compelling and worthwhile. Ask yourself if you prefer one subject in the pair over the other. What reasons can you give for your preference? It's also all right not to have a preference; you can try instead to understand both subjects more clearly.

Next, consider what point you want to make through your comparison and contrast. Tom Standage wanted to show how much the Internet has in common with its Victorian predecessor, the telegraph. Tim Chabot wanted to explore whether we should continue to consider baseball our national pastime. Comparing and contrasting need not be a meaningless exercise.

Marginal Cross-References.   You can find additional information quickly by using the references in the margins—notes on the sides of each page that tell you exactly where to turn in the book or on the Web site for more help or for other activities related to what you are reading. Handbook pages include key definitions in the margin.

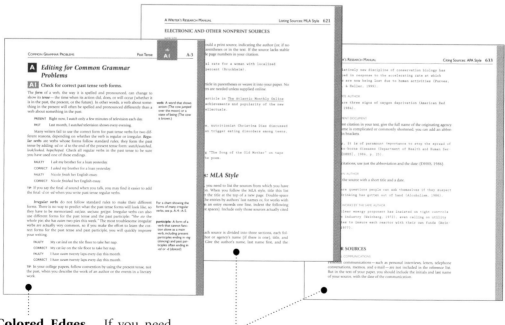

Colored Edges.   If you need help as you edit your essay, turn to the "Quick Editing Guide" on the pages with the dark blue edge.

If you are writing a research paper and are looking for guidelines for MLA documentation, check the pages with the brown edge. If you need to find APA guidelines, check the pages with the green edge.

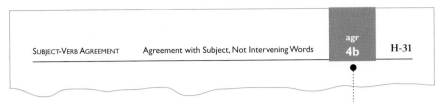

SUBJECT-VERB AGREEMENT   Agreement with Subject, Not Intervening Words   **agr** **4b**   H-31

Colored Tabs.   Your instructor may use correction symbols, such as "agr" for subject-verb agreement, to indicate areas in your draft that need editing. Blue tabs in *A Writer's Handbook* link these common correction symbols with explanations, examples, and exercises related to the particular editing problem. The example above shows a page from handbook Chapter 33, section 4, on subject-verb agreement.

Answers to Exercises.   As you complete the exercises in the handbook, you will want to know if you're on track. Turn to pages A-36–A-41 in the back of the book to find the correct answers to the lettered exercises.

Becoming a Better Writer by Using **The Bedford Guide**

The Bedford Guide includes readings, checklists, computer tips, and other help you can use to complete each writing assignment.

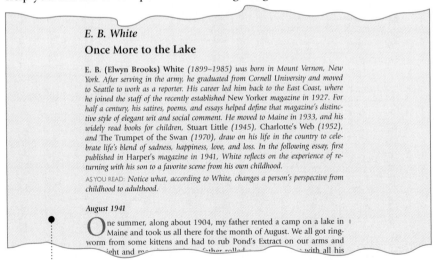

E. B. White
Once More to the Lake

E. B. (Elwyn Brooks) White *(1899–1985) was born in Mount Vernon, New York. After serving in the army, he graduated from Cornell University and moved to Seattle to work as a reporter. His career led him back to the East Coast, where he joined the staff of the recently established* New Yorker *magazine in 1927. For half a century, his satires, poems, and essays helped define that magazine's distinctive style of elegant wit and social comment. He moved to Maine in 1933, and his widely read books for children,* Stuart Little *(1945),* Charlotte's Web *(1952), and* The Trumpet of the Swan *(1970), draw on his life in the country to celebrate life's blend of sadness, happiness, love, and loss. In the following essay, first published in* Harper's *magazine in 1941, White reflects on the experience of returning with his son to a favorite scene from his own childhood.*

AS YOU READ: *Notice what, according to White, changes a person's perspective from childhood to adulthood.*

August 1941

One summer, along about 1904, my father rented a camp on a lake in
    Maine and took us all there for the month of August. We all got ring-
worm from some kittens and had to rub Pond's Extract on our arms and
    ight and m̶ . . . . . . f̶ther rolled . . . . . . with all his

Model Readings. *The Bedford Guide* is filled with examples of both professional and student essays to help you as you write your own. Model essays are located on the blue-shaded pages in *A Writer's Guide* and in *A Writer's Reader*. With each essay, you'll find an informative note about the author, helpful prereading questions, definitions for difficult words, and suggestions for writing.

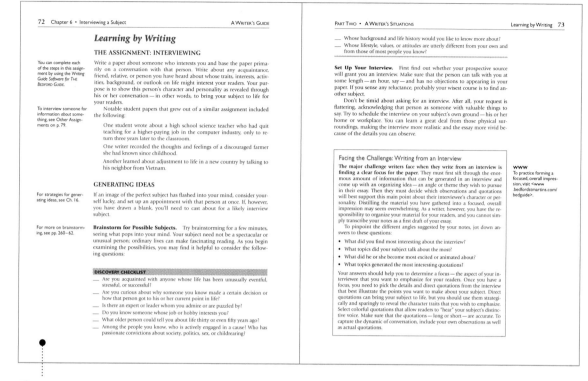

Clear Assignments. The "Learning by Writing" section in Chapters 4 to 12 presents the assignment for the chapter and guides you through the process of writing that type of essay. The "Facing the Challenge" box in each of these sections helps you through the most complicated step in the assignment.

Computer Advice. Each "Writing with a Computer" box offers handy tips for using technology wisely as you write your paper.

As a genre, the college composition has certain typical visual features, such as double spacing, one-inch margins, and left-justified text. You can easily apply these features to your papers by creating a template to use for all papers with the same specifications.

First, format your paper the way you want it to look. Then, create a template that you can access any time you create a new document. Depending on your word processor, you will follow a sequence like the following:

1. Create a duplicate copy of your formatted file.
2. Delete all of the text in the document.
3. Save this file as a document template.
4. Give the template a name, such as "English paper" or "Paper form."

The format for this paper will be stored in a folder for document templates. The template will be called whatever you named it when you saved it. When you create a new file, this template will be among your choices. You won't have to recreate the format every time; simply select the template.

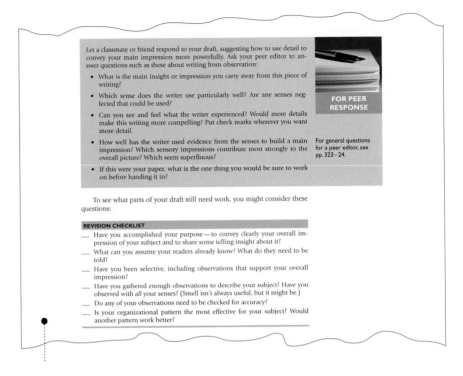

Let a classmate or friend respond to your draft, suggesting how to use detail to convey your main impression more powerfully. Ask your peer editor to answer questions such as these about writing from observation:

- What is the main insight or impression you carry away from this piece of writing?
- Which sense does the writer use particularly well? Are any senses neglected that could be used?
- Can you see and feel what the writer experienced? Would more details make this writing more compelling? Put check marks wherever you want more detail.
- How well has the writer used evidence from the senses to build a main impression? Which sensory impressions contribute most strongly to the overall picture? Which seem superfluous?
- If this were your paper, what is the one thing you would be sure to work on before handing it in?

FOR PEER RESPONSE

For general questions for a peer editor, see pp. 323–24.

To see what parts of your draft still need work, you might consider these questions:

REVISION CHECKLIST

___ Have you accomplished your purpose—to convey clearly your overall impression of your subject and to share some telling insight about it?

___ What can you assume your readers already know? What do they need to be told?

___ Have you been selective, including observations that support your overall impression?

___ Have you gathered enough observations to describe your subject? Have you observed with *all* your senses? (Smell isn't always useful, but it might be.)

___ Do any of your observations need to be checked for accuracy?

___ Is your organizational pattern the most effective for your subject? Would another pattern work better?

Helpful Checklists.   Easy-to-use checklists help you to discover something to write about, get feedback from a peer, and revise and edit your draft.

Applying What You Learn.   You can apply the writing skills that you learn using *The Bedford Guide* to writing in other college courses, at your job, in your community, and in your everyday life. The "Applying What You Learn" section at the end of Chapters 4 through 12 shows how you might use different kinds of writing—for example, using observation to write a case study on the job or using evaluation to assess a public service in your community.

Contents

Preface: To the Instructor *v*

How to Use The Bedford Guide for College Writers *xxiii*

Rhetorical Contents *xxxvii*

A WRITER'S GUIDE

Introduction: Writing in College 3

PART ONE
A College Writer's Processes 5

Introduction 7

1. Writing Processes 8
   Critical Thinking, Reading, and Writing 8
   A Process of Writing 9
   Generating Ideas, 10
   Planning, Drafting, and Developing, 10
   Revising and Editing, 11
   Activity: Describing Your Writing Process, 12
   Audience and Purpose 12
   Writing for Readers, 12
   Activity: Considering Audience, 13
   Writing for a Reason, 13
   Activity: Considering Purpose, 14
   What Matters Most 14

2. Reading Processes 15
   A Process of Reading 16
   Activity: Describing Your Own Reading Process, 16
   Getting Started 16
   Preparing to Read, 17
   Responding to Reading, 17
   Activity: Annotating a Passage, 18

   Reading on a Literal Level 19
   Knowing, Comprehending, and Applying, 19
   Reading on an Analytical Level 20
   Analyzing, Synthesizing, and Evaluating, 20
   Activity: Reading Analytically, 21

3. Critical Thinking Processes 22
   A Process of Critical Thinking 22
   Using Critical Thinking 23
   Activity: Thinking Critically to Solve a Problem, 24
   Supporting Critical Thinking with Evidence 25
   Types of Evidence, 25
   Activity: Looking for Evidence, 27
   Testing Evidence 27
   Using Evidence to Support an Appeal 29
   Logical Appeal, 29
   Emotional Appeal, 29
   Ethical Appeal, 30
   Activity: Identifying Types of Appeals, 30

PART TWO
A Writer's Situations 31

Introduction 33

4. Recalling an Experience 35
   Learning from Other Writers 36
   • Russell Baker, *The Art of Eating Spaghetti* 36
   • Robert G. Schreiner, *What Is a Hunter?* (Student Essay) 39
   Learning by Writing 43
   The Assignment: Recalling a Personal Experience, 43
   Generating Ideas, 44
   Planning, Drafting, and Developing, 45
   Revising and Editing, 46
   Other Assignments, 48
   Applying What You Learn: Some Uses of Recalling Experience 49

5. **Observing a Scene**   51

   Learning from Other Writers   52
   - E. B. White, *Here Is New York*   52
   - Sandy Messina, *Footprints: The Mark of Our Passing* (Student Essay)   54

   Learning by Writing   57
   The Assignment: Observing a Scene, 57
   Generating Ideas, 58
   Planning, Drafting, and Developing, 60
   Revising and Editing, 60
   Other Assignments, 62

   Applying What You Learn: Some Uses of Observing a Scene   63

6. **Interviewing a Subject**   65

   Learning from Other Writers   66
   - Monica Yant Kinney, *Mining for Humor*   66
   - Dawn Kortz, *Listen* (Student Essay)   68

   Learning by Writing   72
   The Assignment: Interviewing, 72
   Generating Ideas, 72
   Planning, Drafting, and Developing, 76
   Revising and Editing, 78
   Other Assignments, 79

   Applying What You Learn: Some Uses of Writing from an Interview   80

7. **Comparing and Contrasting**   81

   Learning from Other Writers   82
   - Tom Standage, *The Victorian Internet*   82
   - Tim Chabot, *Take Me Out to the Ball Game, but Which One?* (Student Essay)   86

   Learning by Writing   90
   The Assignment: Comparing and Contrasting, 90
   Generating Ideas, 90
   Planning, Drafting, and Developing, 93
   Revising and Editing, 96
   Other Assignments, 97

   Applying What You Learn: Some Uses of Comparing and Contrasting   98

8. **Explaining Causes and Effects**   100

   Learning from Other Writers   101
   - William Severini Kowinski, *Kids in the Mall: Growing Up Controlled*   101

   - Yun Yung Choi, *Invisible Women* (Student Essay)   105

   Learning by Writing   108
   The Assignment: Explaining Causes and Effects, 108
   Generating Ideas, 109
   Planning, Drafting, and Developing, 111
   Revising and Editing, 112
   Other Assignments, 115

   Applying What You Learn: Some Uses of Explaining Causes and Effects   115

9. **Taking a Stand**   117

   Learning from Other Writers   118
   - Suzan Shown Harjo, *Last Rites for Indian Dead*   118
   - Thaddeus Watulak, *Affirmative Action Encourages Racism* (Student Essay)   121

   Learning by Writing   124
   The Assignment: Taking a Stand, 124
   Generating Ideas, 125
   Planning, Drafting, and Developing, 130
   Revising and Editing, 132
   Recognizing Logical Fallacies, 134
   Other Assignments, 136

   Applying What You Learn: Some Uses of Taking a Stand   136

10. **Proposing a Solution**   138

   Learning from Other Writers   139
   - Wilbert Rideau, *Why Prisons Don't Work*   140
   - Heather Colbenson, *Missed Opportunities* (Student Essay)   142

   Learning by Writing   145
   The Assignment: Proposing a Solution, 145
   Generating Ideas, 146
   Planning, Drafting, and Developing, 148
   Revising and Editing, 150
   Other Assignments, 153

   Applying What You Learn: Some Uses of Proposals   154

11. **Evaluating**   156

   Learning from Other Writers   157
   - Bill McKibben, *The Frog Factor*   157
   - Clay McCuistion, *Coffee Odyssey* (Student Essay)   160

Learning by Writing 165
The Assignment: Writing an Evaluation, 165
Generating Ideas, 165
Planning, Drafting, and Developing, 168
Revising and Editing, 169
Other Assignments, 170

Applying What You Learn: Some Uses of Evaluating 171

12. **Reading Critically** 173

Learning from Other Writers 174
- Ellen Goodman, *Kids, Divorce, and the Myth* 175
- Ryan Miday, Times *Series Delved Successfully into Race* (Student Essay) 177

Learning by Writing 180
The Assignment: Reading Critically, 180
Generating Ideas, 181
Planning, Drafting, and Developing, 184
Revising and Editing, 186
Other Assignments, 188

Applying What You Learn: Some Uses of Writing from Critical Reading 188

PART THREE
Special Writing Situations 191

Introduction 193

13. **Responding to Literature** 194

Literary Analysis 194
Learning from Other Writers, 194
- Shirley Jackson, *The Lottery* 195
- Jonathan Burns, *The Hidden Truth: An Analysis of Shirley Jackson's "The Lottery"* (Student Essay) 203
Analyzing the Elements of Literature: A Glossary of Terms, 206
Learning by Writing, 209

Strategies for Writing about Literature: Synopsis and Paraphrase 216
Learning from Other Writers: Synopsis, 216
- Jonathan Burns, *A Synopsis of "The Lottery"* (Student Example) 217
Learning by Writing: Synopsis, 219
- Kate Chopin, *The Story of an Hour* 219
Learning by Writing: Paraphrase, 221

Other Assignments for Writing about Literature 222

14. **Writing in the Workplace** 224

Guidelines for Writing in the Workplace 224
Know Your Purpose, 225
Keep Your Audience in Mind, 225
Use an Appropriate Tone, 226
Present Information Carefully, 226

Business Letters 227
Format for Business Letters, 229

Memoranda 231
Format for Memoranda, 232

Electronic Mail 233
Format for E-mail, 234

Résumés and Application Letters 234
Résumés, 234
Application Letters, 236

15. **Writing for Assessment** 239

Essay Examinations 239
Preparing for the Exam, 239
Learning from Another Writer, 240
Generating Ideas, 241
Planning: Recognizing Typical Exam Questions, 242
Drafting: The Only Version, 245
Revising: Rereading and Proofing, 247

Short-Answer Examinations 248

Timed Writings 248
Types of Topics, 249

Writing for Portfolio Assessment 250
Understanding Portfolio Assessment, 251
Tips for Keeping a Portfolio, 252

PART FOUR
A Writer's Strategies 257

Introduction 259

16. **Strategies for Generating Ideas 260**

Finding Ideas 260
Brainstorming, 260
Freewriting, 263
Keeping a Journal, 265
Asking a Reporter's Questions, 267

Getting Ready   268
Setting Up Circumstances, 268
Preparing Your Mind, 270

17. Strategies for Planning   271

Stating and Using a Thesis   271
Discovering Your Thesis, 272
How to State a Thesis, 273
How to Use a Thesis, 275

Organizing Your Ideas   275
Grouping Your Ideas, 276
Outlining, 279

18. Strategies for Drafting   285

Making a Start Enjoyable   285
Restarting   287
Paragraphing   287
Using Topic Sentences   288
Kinds of Topic Sentences, 289
Writing an Opening   291
Kinds of Openings, 291
Writing a Conclusion   293
Kinds of Conclusions, 293
Achieving Coherence   296
Devices That Create Coherence, 296

19. Strategies for Developing   300

Giving Examples   301
Providing Details   303
Defining   305
Analyzing   307
Dividing and Classifying   310
Analyzing a Process   312
Comparing and Contrasting   314
Identifying Causes and Effects   316

20. Strategies for Revising and Editing   319

Re-viewing and Revising   319
Revising for Purpose, 320
Revising for Audience, 320
Revising for Structure, 321
Working with a Peer Editor, 323

Stressing What Counts   324
Stating First or Last, 325
Cutting and Whittling   326
Editing and Proofreading   331

21. Strategies for Designing Your Document   335

Understanding Four Basic Principles of Document Design   338
Principle 1: Know Your Readers, 338
Principle 2: Satisfy Your Reader's Expectations, 339
Principle 3: Consider Your Reader's Constraints, 342
Principle 4: Remember Your Purpose, 342

Creating an Effective Design for Your Document   342
Choosing Fonts, 343
Preparing Lists, 346
Using White Space Strategically, 347
Using Headings and Alignment, 349
Using Repetition Purposefully, 351

Using Visuals to Reinforce Your Content   354
Adding Visuals, 354
Crediting Sources, 355
Arranging Visuals and Text in Your Document, 355

22. Strategies for Understanding Visual Representations   358

Using Strategies for Visual Analysis   359
Seeing the Big Picture   359
Prominent Element, 360
Focal Point, 360

Observing the Characteristics of an Image   361
Cast of Characters, 361
Story of the Image, 363
Design and Arrangement, 363
Artistic Choices, 364

Interpreting the Meaning of an Image   369
General Feeling or Mood, 369
Sociological, Political, Economic, or Cultural Attitudes, 370
Language, 370
Signs and Symbols, 372
Themes, 372

A WRITER'S READER

Introduction: Reading to Write 377

23. Families 378

- E. B. White, *Once More to the Lake* 379

  The author reflects on the impact of taking his son to visit a favorite scene from his own childhood.

- Amy Tan, *Mother Tongue* 385

  A Chinese American writer examines the effects of her mother's imperfect English on her own experience as a daughter and a writer.

- Gerald Early, *Black like . . . Shirley Temple?* 391

  A summer of watching Shirley Temple movies prompts this African American writer to consider how his daughters handle growing up in America.

- Anna Quindlen, *Evan's Two Moms* 394

  A Pulitzer Prize–winning columnist examines the controversy surrounding same-sex marriages.

- John McPhee, *Silk Parachute* 397

  Reflecting on his relationship with his mother, this essayist focuses on the many gifts she gave him, including a silk parachute.

  PAIRED ESSAYS

  Noel Perrin, *A Part-Time Marriage* 400

  This writer takes a wry look at a postdivorce arrangement and current ideas about marriage.

  Stephanie Coontz, *Remarriage and Stepfamilies* 404

  A sociologist proposes solutions to the problems that stepfamilies face as they redefine what a family should be.

24. Men and Women 411

- Judy Brady, *I Want a Wife* 412

  Considering the hard work of a wife leads the author to an unusual conclusion.

- Scott Russell Sanders, *The Men We Carry in Our Minds* 415

  The author explains why, as a working-class male, he had difficulty understanding the deep grievances of women he knew in college.

- Emily Prager, *Our Barbies, Ourselves* 420

  A journalist analyzes what the American infatuation with Barbie tells us about ourselves.

- Joy Harjo, *Three Generations of Native American Women's Birth Experience* 423

  A Native American writer reflects on the childbearing experiences of her mother, her daughter, and herself.

- Dave Barry, *From Now On, Let Women Kill Their Own Spiders* 428

  By identifying with the frustrations of both men and women, this humor columnist pokes fun at the inevitable miscommunication between the genders.

  PAIRED ESSAYS

  Deborah Tannen, *Women and Men Talking on the Job* 431

  A linguist claims that understanding the different communication styles of women and men sheds light on gender conflict in the workplace.

  Nicholas Wade, *How Men and Women Think* 437

  If research uncovers differences between the brains of men and women, according to this journalist, we may have to face some "impolitic truths."

25. Popular Culture 442

- Stephen King, *Why We Crave Horror Movies* 443

  A popular horror fiction writer examines why people enjoy being frightened.

- Veronica Chambers, *The Myth of Cinderella* 446

  A journalist considers a new interpretation of Cinderella's story and its impact on women, especially African American women.

- Phyllis Rose, *Shopping and Other Spiritual Adventures in America Today* 450

  Most Americans shop for reasons other than necessity, according to the author.

- Jay Chiat, *Illusions Are Forever* 453

  This Internet company chairman discusses the effects of advertising on consumers and claims that ads shape a person's perception of reality.

  PAIRED ESSAYS

  Ellen Goodman, *How to Zap Violence on TV* 456

  A popular newspaper columnist examines the treatment of violence on television.

  Mike Males, *Public Enemy Number One?* 459

  Responding to critics such as Ellen Goodman, the author defends the media against charges of contributing to youth violence.

26. The Workplace 466

• Joe Robinson, *Four Weeks Vacation* 467

The editor of a travel-adventure magazine examines the implications of the rising American obsession with work, comparing America's work ethic with that of other countries.

• Steve Olson, *Year of the Blue-Collar Guy* 473

A construction worker offers a tribute to blue-collar workers in America.

• Jane Smiley, *The Case against Chores* 476

Taking an untraditional stance on childhood chores, this critically acclaimed author highlights how chores may teach children the wrong lesson about work.

• Katherine S. Newman, From *No Shame in My Game* 479

An anthropologist known for her research on city life and the working poor examines the often overlooked skills required of the "unskilled" worker.

• Ian Bruce, *Commercial Fisherman* 485

This boat captain shares his experiences as an Alaska salmon fisherman, explaining why, despite all its dangers, he loves his work.

PAIRED ESSAYS

Anne Finnigan, *Nice Perks — If You Can Get 'Em* 489

A journalist identifies the three main obstacles workers encounter in trying to use the family-friendly benefits offered by their employers.

Elinor Burkett, *Unequal Work for Unequal Pay* 495

This reporter questions the fairness and usefulness of family-friendly benefits offered by some corporations, arguing that not enough employees benefit from such programs.

27. Body Image 501

• Julia Alvarez, *I Want to Be Miss América* 502

An English professor reflects on how growing up on the outskirts of white American culture has affected her life.

• Garry Trudeau, *My Inner Shrimp* 507

This cartoonist and writer recalls the difficulty of being short as a teenager, an experience that haunts him even as a six-foot-tall adult.

• Marisa Kula, *Victoria's Not-So-Secret Strategy* 510

In a critical examination of the Victoria's Secret catalog, this writer considers how women's body images are shaped by the fantasies of men.

• Alicia Potter, *Mirror Image* 514

Treating what is no longer exclusively a women's issue, this freelance writer looks at men's increasing obsession with body image due to standards set by the media.

PAIRED ESSAYS

Lisa Jervis, *My Jewish Nose* 519

An author shares her personal experience of resisting the pressures to alter one's ethnic appearance in order to conform to societal ideals of beauty.

Janice Turner, *Cutting Edge* 524

This journalist posits that more men are opting for plastic surgery to keep a competitive edge in a corporate world that judges by appearances.

A WRITER'S RESEARCH MANUAL

Introduction: The Nature of Research 531

28. Planning and Managing Your Research Project 533

Planning Your Project 534
The Assignment: Writing from Sources, 534

Generating Ideas and Forming a Research Question 535
Choosing Your Territory, 535
Taking an Overview, 536
Stating Your Question, 537
Making a Preliminary Search, 539
Using Keywords and Links, 539

Managing Your Project 541
Creating a Schedule, 541
Starting a Working Bibliography, 542
Starting a Research Archive, 544
Keeping Track of Your Electronic Searches, 545

29. Finding Sources in the Library, on the Internet, and in the Field   546

Searching the Library   **546**
Using the Online Catalog, 547
Consulting Databases: Periodical Indexes and Bibliographies, 552

Using Other Library Resources   **555**
Consulting Reference Materials, 556
Locating Special Materials, 558

Using the Web for Research   **559**
Conducting Advanced Electronic Searches, 559
Finding Online Texts and Discussions, 563

Finding Sources in the Field   **564**
Interviewing, 564
Observing, 565
Using Questionnaires, 565
Corresponding, 568
Attending Public and Online Events, 568

30. Evaluating Sources and Taking Notes   570

Evaluating Sources   **570**
What Is the Purpose? 571
Who Is the Intended Audience? 572
Who Is the Author? 573
Is This a Primary or a Secondary Source? 574
Who Is the Publisher? 575
How Sound Is the Evidence? 575
Is the Source Up-to-Date? 576
Is the Source Relevant to Your Research? 576
Are Your Field Sources Useful and Reliable? 576

Taking Notes   **577**
Recording Information, 577
Taking Better Notes, 578
Avoiding Plagiarism, 579
Quoting, Paraphrasing, Nutshelling, 579

31. Writing Your Research Paper   584

Planning and Drafting   **584**
Moving from Notes to Outline to Draft, 584
Incorporating Source Material: Quoting, Paraphrasing, Nutshelling, 588
Avoiding Plagiarism, 592
Beginning and Ending, 595

Revising and Editing   **596**

Documenting Sources   **598**

Citing Sources in Your Text, 599
Listing Sources at the End, 599
Other Assignments, 599

Applying What You Learn: Some Uses of Research   **600**

A Sample Research Paper   **601**
• Sarah E. Goers, *Is Inclusion the Answer?*   602

32. Documenting Sources   615

Citing Sources: MLA Style   **616**
Printed Sources: Nonfiction Books, 616
Printed Sources: Literature, 618
Printed Sources: Reference Books and Periodicals, 619
Electronic and Other Nonprint Sources, 621

Listing Sources: MLA Style   **621**
Books, 621
Parts of Books, 624
Reference Books, 625
Periodicals, 625
Other Printed Sources, 627
Internet and Electronic Sources, 627
Other Nonprint Sources, 630

Citing Sources: APA Style   **631**
Printed Sources, 631
Other Sources, 633

Listing Sources: APA Style   **634**
Books, 634
Periodicals, 636
Other Printed Sources, 637
Internet and Electronic Sources, 637
Other Nonprint Sources, 639

A WRITER'S HANDBOOK

Introduction: Grammar, or The Way Words Work   *H-3*

33. Grammatical Sentences   H-5
   1. Sentence Fragments   **H-5**
   2. Comma Splices and Fused Sentences   **H-10**
   3. Verbs   **H-14**
   4. Subject-Verb Agreement   **H-31**

5. Pronoun Case   H-36
6. Pronoun Reference   H-40
7. Pronoun-Antecedent Agreement   H-44
8. Adjectives and Adverbs   H-46
9. Shifts   H-52

34. Effective Sentences   H-57

10. Misplaced and Dangling
    Modifiers   H-57
11. Incomplete Sentences   H-60
12. Mixed Constructions and Faulty
    Predication   H-64
13. Parallel Structure   H-68
14. Coordination and
    Subordination   H-71
15. Sentence Variety   H-78

35. Word Choice   H-81

16. Appropriateness   H-81
17. Exact Words   H-86
18. Bias-Free Language   H-90
19. Wordiness   H-94

36. Punctuation   H-96

20. End Punctuation   H-96
21. The Comma   H-98
22. The Semicolon   H-108
23. The Colon   H-110
24. The Apostrophe   H-113

25. Quotation Marks   H-116
26. The Dash   H-120
27. Parentheses, Brackets, and the
    Ellipsis Mark   H-122

37. Mechanics   H-127

28. Abbreviations   H-127
29. Capital Letters   H-130
30. Numbers   H-134
31. Italics   H-136
32. The Hyphen   H-139
33. Spelling   H-142

APPENDICES

Quick Editing Guide   A-1

A. Editing for Common Grammar Problems   A-3
B. Editing to Ensure Effective Sentences   A-12
C. Editing for Common Punctuation
   Problems   A-14
D. Editing for Common Mechanics
   Problems   A-17
E. Editing for Common Format Problems   A-23

A Glossary of Troublemakers   A-29

Answers for Lettered Exercises   A-37

Index   *I-1*

Rhetorical Contents

(in order of appearance)

Argument

Suzan Shown Harjo, *Last Rites for Indian Dead*   118

Thaddeus Watulak, *Affirmative Action Encourages Racism*   121

Wilbert Rideau, *Why Prisons Don't Work*   140

Heather Colbenson, *Missed Opportunities*   142

Anna Quindlen, *Evan's Two Moms*   394

Noel Perrin, *A Part-Time Marriage*   400

Judy Brady, *I Want a Wife*   412

Dave Barry, *From Now On, Let Women Kill Their Own Spiders*   428

Deborah Tannen, *Women and Men Talking on the Job*   431

Ellen Goodman, *How to Zap Violence on TV*   456

Mike Males, *Public Enemy Number One?*   459

Joe Robinson, *Four Weeks Vacation*   467

Steve Olson, *Year of the Blue-Collar Guy*   473

Elinor Burkett, *Unequal Work for Unequal Pay*   495

Marisa Kula, *Victoria's Not-So-Secret Strategy*   510

Comparing and Contrasting

Sandy Messina, *Footprints: The Mark of Our Passing*   54

Tom Standage, *The Victorian Internet*   82

Tim Chabot, *Take Me Out to the Ball Game, but Which One?*   86

Clay McCuistion, *Coffee Odyssey*   160

Dave Barry, *From Now On, Let Women Kill Their Own Spiders*   428

Deborah Tannen, *Women and Men Talking on the Job*   431

Nicholas Wade, *How Men and Women Think*   437

Veronica Chambers, *The Myth of Cinderella*   446

Anne Finnigan, *Nice Perks—If You Can Get 'Em*   489

Definition

Robert G. Schreiner, *What Is a Hunter?*   39

Thaddeus Watulak, *Affirmative Action Encourages Racism*   121

Gerald Early, *Black like . . . Shirley Temple?*   391

Noel Perrin, *A Part-Time Marriage*   400

Judy Brady, *I Want a Wife*   412

Phyllis Rose, *Shopping and Other Spiritual Adventures in America Today*   450

Steve Olson, *Year of the Blue-Collar Guy*   473

Katherine S. Newman, *From No Shame in My Game*   479

Ian Bruce, *Commercial Fisherman*   485

Janice Turner, *Cutting Edge*   524

Description

Russell Baker, *The Art of Eating Spaghetti*   36

Robert G. Schreiner, *What Is a Hunter?*   39

E. B. White, *Here Is New York*   52

Sandy Messina, *Footprints: The Mark of Our Passing*   54

Dawn Kortz, *Listen*   68

Clay McCuistion, *Coffee Odyssey*   160

E. B. White, *Once More to the Lake*   379

Julia Alvarez, *I Want to Be Miss América*   502

Division and Classification

E. B. White, *Here Is New York*   52

Stephanie Coontz, *Remarriage and Stepfamilies*   404

Emily Prager, *Our Barbies, Ourselves*   420

Jane Smiley, *The Case against Chores*   476

Janice Turner, *Cutting Edge*   524

Evaluating

Bill McKibben, *The Frog Factor*   157

Clay McCuistion, *Coffee Odyssey*   160

Ellen Goodman, *Kids, Divorce, and the Myth*   175

Ryan Miday, *Times Series Delved Successfully into Race*   177

Emily Prager, *Our Barbies, Ourselves*   420

Stephen King, *Why We Crave Horror Movies*   443

Veronica Chambers, *The Myth of Cinderella*   446

Jay Chiat, *Illusions Are Forever*   453

Ellen Goodman, *How to Zap Violence on TV*   456

Joe Robinson, *Four Weeks Vacation*   467

Jane Smiley, *The Case against Chores*   476

Anne Finnigan, *Nice Perks — If You Can Get 'Em*   489

Example

Sandy Messina, *Footprints: The Mark of Our Passing*   54

Tom Standage, *The Victorian Internet*   82

Dave Barry, *From Now On, Let Women Kill Their Own Spiders*   428

Ellen Goodman, *How to Zap Violence on TV*   456

Joe Robinson, *Four Weeks Vacation*   467

Steve Olson, *Year of the Blue-Collar Guy*   473

Katherine S. Newman, From *No Shame in My Game*   479

Marisa Kula, *Victoria's Not-So-Secret Strategy*   510

Alicia Potter, *Mirror Image*   514

Explaining Causes and Effects

William Severini Kowinski, *Kids in the Mall: Growing Up Controlled*   101

Yun Yung Choi, *Invisible Women*   105

Bill McKibben, *The Frog Factor*   157

Ellen Goodman, *Kids, Divorce, and the Myth*   175

Amy Tan, *Mother Tongue*   385

Noel Perrin, *A Part-Time Marriage*   400

Stephanie Coontz, *Remarriage and Stepfamilies*   404

Emily Prager, *Our Barbies, Ourselves*   420

Stephen King, *Why We Crave Horror Movies*   443

Veronica Chambers, *The Myth of Cinderella*   446

Jay Chiat, *Illusions Are Forever*   453

Ellen Goodman, *How to Zap Violence on TV*   456

Mike Males, *Public Enemy Number One?*   459

Joe Robinson, *Four Weeks Vacation*   467

Elinor Burkett, *Unequal Work for Unequal Pay*   495

Garry Trudeau, *My Inner Shrimp*   507

Alicia Potter, *Mirror Image*   514

Lisa Jervis, *My Jewish Nose*   519

Interviewing a Subject

Monica Yant Kinney, *Mining for Humor*   66

Dawn Kortz, *Listen*   68

Amy Tan, *Mother Tongue*   385

Gerald Early, *Black like . . . Shirley Temple?*   391

Alicia Potter, *Mirror Image*   514

Janice Turner, *Cutting Edge*   524

Narration

Russell Baker, *The Art of Eating Spaghetti*   36

Robert G. Schreiner, *What Is a Hunter?*   39

Dawn Kortz, *Listen*   68

E. B. White, *Once More to the Lake*   379

John McPhee, *Silk Parachute*   397

Ian Bruce, *Commercial Fisherman*   485

Julia Alvarez, *I Want To Be Miss América*   502

Garry Trudeau, *My Inner Shrimp*   507

Lisa Jervis, *My Jewish Nose*   519

Observing a Scene

E. B. White, *Here Is New York*   52

Sandy Messina, *Footprints: The Mark of Our Passing*   54

Dawn Kortz, *Listen*   68

E. B. White, *Once More to the Lake*   379

Phyllis Rose, *Shopping and Other Spiritual Adventures in America Today*   450

Steve Olson, *Year of the Blue-Collar Guy*   473

Proposing a Solution

Wilbert Rideau, *Why Prisons Don't Work*   140

Heather Colbenson, *Missed Opportunities*   142

Noel Perrin, *A Part-Time Marriage*   400

Stephanie Coontz, *Remarriage and Stepfamilies*   404

Joe Robinson, *Four Weeks Vacation*   467

Reading Critically

Bill McKibben, *The Frog Factor*   157

Ellen Goodman, *Kids, Divorce, and the Myth*   175

Ryan Miday, *Times Series Delved Successfully into Race*   177

Jonathan Burns, *The Hidden Truth: An Analysis of Shirley Jackson's "The Lottery"*   203

Jay Chiat, *Illusions Are Forever*   453

Mike Males, *Public Enemy Number One?*   459

Elinor Burkett, *Unequal Work for Unequal Pay*   495

Recalling an Experience

Russell Baker, *The Art of Eating Spaghetti*   36

Robert G. Schreiner, *What Is a Hunter?*   39

E. B. White, *Once More to the Lake*   379

Amy Tan, *Mother Tongue*   385

Gerald Early, *Black like . . . Shirley Temple?*   391

John McPhee, *Silk Parachute*   397

Scott Russell Sanders, *The Men We Carry in Our Minds*   415

Joy Harjo, *Three Generations of Native American Women's Birth Experience*   423

Jane Smiley, *The Case against Chores*   476

Julia Alvarez, *I Want To Be Miss América*   502

Garry Trudeau, *My Inner Shrimp*   507

Lisa Jervis, *My Jewish Nose*   519

Taking a Stand

Suzan Shown Harjo, *Last Rites for Indian Dead*   118

Thaddeus Watulak, *Affirmative Action Encourages Racism*   121

Anna Quindlen, *Evan's Two Moms*   394

Ellen Goodman, *How to Zap Violence on TV*   456

Mike Males, *Public Enemy Number One?*   459

Joe Robinson, *Four Weeks Vacation*   467

Elinor Burkett, *Unequal Work for Unequal Pay*   495

A Writer's
Guide

Contents

Introduction: Writing in College   **3**

Part One: A College Writer's Processes

Introduction   7
1. Writing Processes   8
2. Reading Processes   15
3. Critical Thinking Processes   22

Part Two: A Writer's Situations

Introduction   33
4. Recalling an Experience   35
5. Observing a Scene   51
6. Interviewing a Subject   65
7. Comparing and Contrasting   81
8. Explaining Causes and Effects   100
9. Taking a Stand   117
10. Proposing a Solution   138
11. Evaluating   156
12. Reading Critically   173

Part Three: Special Writing Situations

Introduction   193
13. Responding to Literature   194
14. Writing in the Workplace   224
15. Writing for Assessment   239

Part Four: A Writer's Strategies

Introduction   259
16. Strategies for Generating Ideas   260
17. Strategies for Planning   271
18. Strategies for Drafting   285
19. Strategies for Developing   300
20. Strategies for Revising and Editing   319
21. Strategies for Designing Your Document   335
22. Strategies for Understanding Visual Representations   358

Introduction:
Writing in College

As a college writer you probably wrestle with the question What should I write? You may feel you have nothing to say or nothing worth saying. Sometimes your difficulty lies in understanding the requirements of a particular writing situation, sometimes in finding a topic, and sometimes in uncovering enough information about the topic you have chosen. Perhaps you, like many other college writers, have convinced yourself that professional writers are different in some way, that they have some special way of thinking or looking at the world or discovering ideas for writing. But they have no magic. In reality, what they have is experience and confidence, the products of lots of practice writing.

In *The Bedford Guide for College Writers,* we want you to become a better writer by actually writing. To help you do so, we'll give you a lot of practice throughout the book. We'll also supply useful advice about writing processes, situations, and strategies to help you build your skills and confidence. Because writing and learning to write are complex and many-faceted tasks, each part of *A Writer's Guide* is devoted to a different aspect of writing.

Part One, "A College Writer's Processes."   This part introduces processes for writing, reading, and thinking critically — essential skills for meeting college expectations.

Part Two, "A Writer's Situations."   The nine chapters in Part Two form the core of *The Bedford Guide* and are supported by the three other parts in this section of the book. Each chapter in this part presents a writing situation and then guides you as you write a paper in response. You'll develop skills in recalling, observing, interviewing, comparing and contrasting, explaining causes and effects, taking a stand, proposing a solution, evaluating, and reading critically.

Part Three, "Special Writing Situations."   This part leads you through three special situations that most students encounter at one point or another — writing about literature, writing in the workplace, and writing for assessment.

Part Four, "A Writer's Strategies."   Part Four is packed with advice, tips, and activities that you can use whenever you need to generate ideas, plan, draft, develop, revise, edit, and proofread your writing. You will also find strategies for designing documents and analyzing visual images.

Together, these four parts contribute to a seamless whole, much like the writing process itself. Read them at a leisurely pace, study them when you need help, browse through them for ideas, or turn to them in a pinch. They will guide you as you write — and as you become a more skillful and confident writer.

PART ONE

A College Writer's Processes

Introduction

Your composition course may be one of your first college classes. For this reason, the course will both introduce you to college expectations and equip you with the skills that you need to meet these expectations. You may already feel confident that you will meet this challenge successfully, that your past education and experiences have prepared you well for higher education. On the other hand, like many students, you may feel worried about your skills or uncertain about what will be expected and how you will fare in the academic world. In either case, *The Bedford Guide for College Writers* will give you concrete advice to help you succeed.

You already know a good deal about what college instructors expect. Like other teachers you've had, they will require you to come to class, contribute to discussions, and hand in your assignments. But they hope and expect that you will do far more than this—that you will engage fully in what's sometimes called "the college experience." The richness of this experience depends on your active response to the intellectual exchanges, resources, and opportunities that surround you in college. Sometimes this environment seems intimidating, and you may feel that you are simply drifting with the current and passively absorbing ideas as they flow through your college classrooms. But you can learn how to ask questions about your writing, your reading, and your thinking—and how to navigate your own voyage of discovery.

As you undertake the process of becoming a well-educated person, your college instructors will expect you to show how you have grown as a writer, a reader, and a thinker. More specifically, they will want you to write thoughtful, purposeful papers, appropriately directed to your audience. They will want you not only to rely on your own ideas but also to read the writings of others, to ask questions about what you read, and to conduct research in complex disciplines, sometimes using and documenting many sources. And they will expect you to think critically and to support your points as you write, integrating your own ideas and conclusions with those drawn from your reading. The first three chapters in this book briefly introduce the processes—writing, reading, and thinking critically—that will help you meet these essential academic expectations.

Chapter 1

Writing Processes

You are already a writer with long experience. In school you have taken notes, written book reports and term papers, answered exam questions, perhaps kept a journal. In community meetings you have recorded minutes, and on the job you've composed memos. You've e-mailed friends, made shopping lists, maybe even tried your hand at writing poetry. All this experience is about to pay off for you.

Unlike parachute jumping, writing in college is something you go ahead and try without first learning all there is to know. In truth, nothing anyone can tell you will help as much as learning by doing. In this book our purpose is to help you to write better, deeper, clearer, and more satisfying papers than you have ever written before and to learn to do so by actually writing. Throughout the book we'll give you a lot of practice — in writing processes, patterns, and strategies — to build confidence. And we'll pose various writing situations and say, "Go to it!"

Critical Thinking, Reading, and Writing

In college you will add new techniques to what you already know about writing, and you will perform challenging writing tasks that expand your skills. You may be asked not only to recall an experience but also to reflect upon its significance. Or you may be asked to go beyond summarizing varied positions about an issue by presenting your own position or proposing a solution. Above all, you will be reading and thinking critically — not just stacking up facts but analyzing what you discover, deciding what it means, and weighing its value.

In your composition course, you can view each writing task as a problem to solve, often through careful reading and objective thinking. You will need to read — and write — actively, engaging with the ideas of others. At the same time, you will need to think critically, purposefully analyzing and judging those ideas. To help you assess whether you are achieving what you have in mind, you will use criteria — models, conventions, principles, standards. As you write and rewrite, you can evaluate what you are doing by considering specific questions:

For more on reading critically, see Ch. 2. For more on thinking critically, see Ch. 3.

- Have you made your point clear?
- Are your ideas arranged logically?
- Does each thought follow from, support, or add to the preceding thought?
- Will the connections among ideas be clear to a reader?
- Have you provided enough evidence to convince your readers?
- Is your tone appropriate?

In large measure, learning to write well is learning what questions to ask as you write. Throughout *A Writer's Guide*, we include questions and suggestions designed to help you write, read, and think critically as you accomplish your writing tasks and reflect on your own processes.

A Process of Writing

Writing can seem at times an overwhelming drudgery, worse than scrubbing floors; at other moments, a sport full of thrills — like whizzing downhill on skis, not knowing what you'll meet around a bend. Surprising and unpredictable though the writing process may seem, nearly all writers do similar things:

You can complete each of these steps for any essay you write using the *Writing Guide Software for THE BEDFORD GUIDE*.

- They generate ideas.
- They plan, draft, and develop their papers.
- They revise and edit.

These three activities form the basis of most effective writing processes, and they lie at the heart of each chapter in Part Two, "A Writer's Situations." These activities aren't lockstep stages: you don't always proceed in a straight line. You can skip around, taking up parts of the process in whatever order you like, or work on several parts at a time, or circle back over what you have already done. For example, while gathering material, you may feel an urge to play with a sentence until it clicks. Or while writing a draft, you may decide to look for more material. You may find yourself leaping ahead, crossing out, backtracking, adjusting, questioning, testing a fresh approach, tinkering, polishing — and then in the end looking up unfamiliar punctuation and spell-checking the tricky words.

GENERATING IDEAS

For strategies on generating ideas, see Ch. 16.

The first activity in writing—finding a topic and something to say about it—is often the most challenging and least predictable. Each chapter in Part Two includes a section called "Generating Ideas," which is filled with examples, questions, and checklists designed to trigger ideas and associations that will help you begin the chapter's writing assignment.

Discovering What to Write About.   Finding a topic is not always easy, but you may discover an idea while talking with friends, riding your bike, or staring out the window. Often a topic lies near home, in a conversation you remember or an everyday event you recall. Of course, a particular writing assignment may seem to hold no personal interest for you. In that case, your challenge is to make the topic your own by finding a slant that does interest you. Find it, and words will flow.

Discovering Material.   You'll need information to back up your ideas—facts and figures, reports and opinions, examples and illustrations. How do you find such material to make your ideas clear and convincing to your readers? Luckily you have numerous sources at your fingertips. You can recall your own experience and knowledge, you can observe things around you, you can converse with others who are knowledgeable, you can read enlightening materials that draw you to new thoughts and information, and you can think critically about all these sources around you.

PLANNING, DRAFTING, AND DEVELOPING

After discovering a topic and figuring out what you want to say about it, you will plan your paper, write a draft, and then develop your ideas further. Each chapter in Part Two has a section entitled "Planning, Drafting, and Developing," designed to help you through these stages of the writing process for the assignment studied in that chapter.

For planning strategies, see Ch. 17.

Planning.   Having discovered a burning idea to write about (or at least a smoldering one) and some material to back it up with (but maybe not enough yet), you will sort out what matters most. If right away you see one main point for your paper, try to state that point. Test various ways of expressing it, maybe "Parking in the morning before class is annoying" or "Campus parking is a big problem." Next, arrange your ideas and material in a sensible order that will make your one point clear. To discover that order, you might group and label the ideas you have generated, or you might analyze the main idea, breaking it down into its parts: "Campus parking is a problem for students because of the long lines, inefficient entrances, and poorly marked spaces." But if no one main point emerges quickly, don't worry. You may find one while you draft—that is, while you write an early version of your paper.

Drafting.   When your ideas first start to flow, you want to welcome them — lure them forth, not tear them apart — or they might go back into hiding. Don't be afraid to take risks at this stage: you'll probably be surprised and pleased at what happens, even though your first version will be rough. Writing takes time; a paper usually needs several drafts and may require a revised plan, especially for an unfamiliar or complicated subject. You may even throw out your first attempt and start all over if a stronger idea or a better arrangement hits you.

For drafting strategies, see Ch. 18.

Developing.   As you draft, you will weave in explanations, definitions, illustrations, and evidence to make your ideas clear. For example, you may need to define an at-risk student, illustrate the problems faced by a single parent, or supply statistics about hit-and-run accidents. If you realize you don't have enough specific support for your main idea, you can use strategies for developing ideas — or return to strategies for generating ideas. You can expect to keep discovering ideas, having insights, and drawing conclusions while you draft. By all means, welcome them, and work them in if they fit.

For strategies on developing ideas, see Ch. 19. For strategies on generating ideas, see Ch. 16.

REVISING AND EDITING

You might hope that your work is done once you have a draft, but for most writers, revising begins the work in earnest. Revising means both reseeing and rewriting, making major changes so that your paper accomplishes what you want it to. When you have a well-developed and well-organized draft, you are ready to edit: to correct errors and improve wording. Each chapter in Part Two has a "Revising and Editing" section, which focuses on these final stages of the writing process. In this section you will find a revision checklist, an editing checklist, and a suggestion for working with a peer.

For revising and editing strategies, see Ch. 20.

Revising.   Revision is more than just changing words: you sometimes revise what you know and what you think. Such changes may take place while you're writing or at any moment when you pause to reread or to think. You can then shift your plans, decide what to put in or leave out, move sentences or paragraphs around, connect ideas differently, or express them better. Perhaps you'll decide to add costs to a paper on parking problems; perhaps you'll switch your attention to teenage fathers instead of mothers if you are writing about teen parenthood.

    If you put aside your draft for a few hours or a day, you can reread it with fresh eyes and a clear mind. As humorist Leo Rosten has said, "You have to put yourself in the position of the negative reader, the resistant reader, the reader who doesn't surrender easily, the reader who is alien to you as a type, even the reader who doesn't like what you are writing." Other students can also help you — sometimes more than a textbook or an instructor can — by responding to your drafts as engaged readers.

For editing advice, see the "Quick Editing Guide" (the dark-blue-edged pages).

Editing.   Editing means refining the details and correcting any flaws that may stand in the way of your readers' understanding and enjoyment. Don't edit too early, though, because you may waste time on some part that you later revise out. In editing, you usually accomplish these repairs:

- Get rid of unnecessary words.
- Choose livelier and more precise words.
- Rearrange words in a clearer, more emphatic order.
- Combine short, choppy sentences, or break up long, confusing sentences.
- Add accurate transitions for continuity of thought.
- Check grammar, usage, and punctuation.

Proofreading.   Near the end of your labors, you'll proofread your paper, taking a last look, checking correctness, and catching doubtful spellings or word-processing errors.

ACTIVITY: DESCRIBING YOUR WRITING PROCESS

Describe your writing process. How do you get started? How do you keep writing? What process do you go through to reach a final draft? Do your steps ever vary depending upon the type of writing you're doing? What step or strategy in your writing process would you most like to change?

Audience and Purpose

At any moment in the writing process, two questions are worth asking: Who is my audience? Why am I writing?

WRITING FOR READERS

Your audience, or your readers, may or may not be defined in your assignment. Consider the following examples:

ASSIGNMENT 1   Discuss the advantages and disadvantages of home schooling.

ASSIGNMENT 2   In a letter to parents of school-aged children, discuss the advantages and disadvantages of home schooling.

Notice how the first assignment differs from the second. Because the first leaves the audience undefined, you can assume that your primary readers would be your instructor and your classmates. Writing for these readers will give you practice in writing for more general or public audiences. If your assignment defines an audience, as in the second example, you will need to think carefully about how to approach those readers and what to assume about their relationship to your topic. For example, what points would you include in a discussion aimed at parents? How would you organize your ideas? Would you discuss advantages first? Or disadvantages? Consider how your approach might be different if the assignment read this way:

> ASSIGNMENT 3   In a letter to public school teachers, discuss the advantages and disadvantages of home schooling.

When you analyze your audience carefully — reflecting on what they know, believe, and value — you can aim your writing toward them with a better chance of hitting your mark.

Use these critical questions to help you consider your audience:

- Who are your readers? What is their relationship to you?
- What do your readers already know about this topic? What do you want them to learn?
- How much detail will they want to read about this topic?
- What objections are they likely to raise as they read? How can you anticipate and overcome their objections?
- What's likely to convince them?
- What's likely to offend them?

For more on revising for audience, see pp. 320–21

You'll also want to ask similar questions about audience when you revise your essay.

ACTIVITY: CONSIDERING AUDIENCE

Write a short paragraph describing in detail a "worst" event — your worst date, worst dinner, worst car repair, or some similar catastrophe. Then revise that paragraph so that your audience is a person involved in the event — the person who went on that date with you, cooked or served the dinner, worked on your car. Now revise the paragraph once again — this time writing to a person you plan to date soon, a cook at a restaurant you want to try, or a repair person working at another garage. Compare the three paragraphs. How are they similar? How do they differ?

WRITING FOR A REASON

Usually a college writing assignment has a clear-cut purpose. Every assignment in this book asks you to write for a definite reason. For example, in Chapter 4 you'll be asked to recall a memorable experience in order to explain its importance for you; in Chapter 9, to take a stand on a controversy in order to convey your position and persuade readers to respect it. Be careful not to confuse the sources and strategies you are asked to apply in these assignments with your ultimate purpose for writing. "To compare and contrast two things" is not a very interesting purpose; "to compare and contrast two household products, two Web sites, or two poems *in order to explain their differences*" implies a real reason for writing. In most college writing, your ultimate purpose will be to explain something to your readers or to convince your readers of something.

To sharpen your concentration on your reason for writing, ask yourself from the start: What do I want to do? And, in revising, Did I do what I meant to do? You'll find that these are very practical questions. They'll help you slice out irrelevant information and remove other barriers to getting your paper where you want it to go.

ACTIVITY: CONSIDERING PURPOSE

Return to the three paragraphs you wrote for the last activity (p. 13). Write a sentence or two summing up your purpose in writing each paragraph. Given these three purposes, how might you revise your paragraphs?

What Matters Most

Like a hard game of basketball, writing a college paper is strenuous. Without getting in your way, we want to lend you all possible support and guidance. So, no doubt, does your instructor, someone closer to you than any textbook writers. Still, like even the best coaches, instructors and textbook writers can improve your game only so far. Advice on how to write won't make you a better writer. You'll learn more and have more fun when you take a few sentences to the hoop and make points yourself. After you sink a few baskets, you will increase your confidence in your ability and find the process of writing a bit easier.

Chapter 2
Reading Processes

What's so special about college reading? Don't you just pick up the book, start on the first page, and keep on going? Certainly this approach works for much reading, and you probably have been reading this way ever since you met *The Cat in the Hat*. Reading from beginning to end works especially well when you just want to find out what happens next, as in a thriller or a romance, or what to do next, as in a cookbook. On the other hand, much of what you read in college — whether textbooks, scholarly articles, books, research reports, or the papers of your peers — is complicated and challenging. Dense material like this may require special reading strategies such as rereading, identifying main points, or annotating key passages. And, most importantly, college reading often requires closer reading and deeper thinking — in short, a process for reading critically.

Reading critically is a useful skill. For assignments in this course alone, you will need to evaluate essays by professionals and students to assess their strengths and weaknesses. If you do research about any topic, you will need to discover what your sources say, how you might use their information, and whether they are reliable. Critical reading is important in other courses, too. For example, you might scrutinize a sociology report on violent children not only for the soundness of its argument but also for its assumptions and implications. On the job, you may be required to make certain that your product meets technical specifications, while in the community, you may want to respond to a proposal for a property tax hike. Whenever you write based on critical reading, you explain what is going on in the text and then go further, making your own point based on its ideas.

For more on basing a paper on critical reading, see Ch. 12.

A Process of Reading

Reading critically means approaching whatever you read in an active, questioning manner. It is an essential college-level skill, and it changes reading from a spectator sport to a contact sport. You no longer sit in the stands, watching graceful skaters glide by. Instead, you charge right into a rough-and-tumble hockey game, gripping your stick and watching out for your teeth.

For more on critical thinking, see Ch. 3.

Critical reading, like critical thinking, is not a specialized, isolated activity. It is a continuum of strategies that thoughtful people use every day to grapple with new information, to integrate it with existing knowledge, and to apply it to problems in daily life and in academic courses. Many readers do similar things:

- They get ready to do their reading.
- They read on a literal level.
- They read on an analytical level.

Educational expert Benjamin S. Bloom[1] identified six levels of cognitive activity: knowledge, comprehension, application, analysis, synthesis, and evaluation. Each level becomes more complex and demands higher thinking skills than the previous one. The first three levels are literal skills. When you show that you know a fact, comprehend its meaning, and can apply it to a new situation, you demonstrate your mastery over one of the building blocks of thought. The other three levels — analysis, synthesis, and evaluation — are critical skills. These skills take you beyond the literal level: you break apart the building blocks to see what makes them work, recombine them in new and useful ways, and judge their worth or significance.

ACTIVITY: DESCRIBING YOUR OWN READING PROCESS

How do you read a magazine or newspaper or popular novel? What are your goals when you do this kind of reading? What's different about reading the material assigned in college? What techniques do you use for reading assignments? How might you make your college reading more effective? Do you use any strategies that might help your classmates, especially in classes with a lot of reading?

Getting Started

College reading is active reading. Before you read, think ahead about what you are reading, why you are reading, and what you hope to do with the reading. Also think ahead about how to approach the reading process — how to make the most of the time you spend reading.

---

[1] Benjamin S. Bloom, et al., *Taxonomy of Educational Objectives, Handbook 1: Cognitive Domain* (New York: McKay, 1956).

PREPARING TO READ

Thinking about Your Purpose.   Naturally enough, your overall purpose for doing most college reading is to be successful in your courses. When you begin to read an assignment, ask questions like these about your immediate purpose:

- What does your instructor expect you to learn from this assignment?
- Do you need to memorize the details of the content, find the main points, or look for connections among ideas?
- How does this reading build on, add to, contrast with, or otherwise relate to other reading assignments in the course?

Planning Your Follow-Up.   When your instructor assigns a specific essay, chapter, or article, or a reading of your own choosing about a certain topic, he or she probably expects something to follow the reading. Consider what you will need to do after you read the material:

- Do you need to be ready to discuss the reading during class?
- Will you need to mention it or analyze it during an examination?
- Will you need to write an essay or paper about it or its topic?
- Do you need to find its main points? Sum it up? Compare it? Question it? Spot its strengths and weaknesses? Draw useful details from it?

Skimming the Text.   Before you engage in a thorough, active reading of a text, begin by skimming it — reading only enough to give you an idea of the content and organization of the material. If the reading has a table of contents or subheadings, read those first to understand what the material covers and how it is organized. Read the first paragraph and then the first and last sentences of each paragraph that follows. If the material has any illustrations or diagrams, read the captions.

RESPONDING TO READING

Keeping a Reading Journal.   A reading journal is an excellent place to record not just what you read but how you respond to it. It helps you read critically and also builds a reservoir of ideas for your follow-up writing. You can use a special notebook or computer file to record reactions each time you read. Your responses to readings might address questions like these:

- What is the subject of the reading? What is the author's stand?
- What does the writer take for granted? What assumptions — stated or unstated — does he or she begin with?
- What evidence supports the writer's main points?
- Do you agree with what the writer has said? Do his or her ideas clash with your ideas or question something you take for granted?

For advice on keeping
a writer's journal, see
Ch. 16.

- What conclusions can you draw from the reading? Has the writer failed to tell you something you wish you knew?
- Has something you read opened your eyes to new ways of looking at the subject?

Annotating the Text.   Writing notes on the page (or on a photocopy if the material is not your own) is a useful way to trace the author's points, question them, and add your own comments as they pop up. The following example shows how a reader might annotate the opening of Judy Brady's essay "I Want a Wife."

For the complete essay,
see pp. 412–14.

I belong to that classification of people known as wives. I am

Why capitals? Looks like a job title! — A Wife. And, not altogether incidentally, I am a mother.

Not too long ago a male friend of mine appeared on the scene — *Assumes women always get custody* — fresh from a recent divorce. He had one child, who is, of course, with his ex-wife. He is looking for another wife. As I thought about him while I was ironing one evening, it suddenly occurred to me that

Main idea — I, too, would like to have a wife. Why do I want a wife?   *Asks Q. & answers it*

I would like to go back to school so that I can become economically independent, support myself, and, if need be, support those dependent upon me. I want a wife who will work and send me to school. And while I am going to school I want a wife to take care of — *Repeats pattern*

Sounds sarcastic — my children. I want a wife to keep track of the children's doctor and dentist appointments. And to keep track of mine, too.

ACTIVITY: ANNOTATING A PASSAGE

For another example of
an annotated passage,
see p. 183.

Annotate the following paragraph, the next in Judy Brady's essay "I Want a Wife."

I want a wife who will take care of *my* physical needs. I want a wife who will keep my house clean. A wife who will pick up after my children, a wife who will pick up after me. I want a wife who will keep my clothes clean, ironed, mended, replaced when need be, and who will see to it that my personal things are kept in their proper place so that I can find what I need the minute I need it. I want a wife who cooks the meals, a wife who is a *good* cook. I want a wife who will plan the menus, do the necessary grocery shopping, prepare the meals, serve them pleasantly, and then do the cleaning up while I do my studying. I want a wife who will care for me when I am sick and sympathize with my pain and loss of time from school. I want a wife to go along when our family takes a vacation so that someone can continue to care for me and my children when I need a rest and change of scene.

Reading on a Literal Level

To read critically, you must engage with a piece on both a literal level and an analytical level. As the diagram on this page shows, each skill acts as a foundation for the next. When you read on the literal level, you are aware of the information the text is presenting, you comprehend what the fact or idea means, and you are able to apply it. For example, suppose you read in your history book a passage about Franklin Delano Roosevelt (FDR), the only American president elected to four consecutive terms of office.

KNOWING, COMPREHENDING, AND APPLYING

Becoming Aware of the Information.   Once you read the passage, even if you have little background in American history, you know and can recall the information it presents about FDR and his four terms in office.

Comprehending the Information.   To comprehend the information, you need to know that a term for a U.S. president is four years and that *consecutive* means "continuous." Thus, FDR was elected to serve sixteen years as president.

Applying the Information.   To apply this knowledge, you think of other presidents — George Washington, who served two terms; Grover Cleveland,

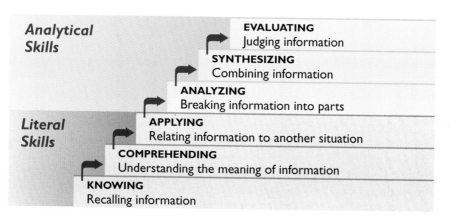

Figure 2.1   *Literal and Analytical Reading Skills
The information in this figure is adapted from Benjamin S. Bloom, et al.,* Taxonomy of Educational Objectives, Handbook 1: Cognitive Domain *(New York: McKay, 1956).*

who served two terms but not consecutively; Jimmy Carter, who served one term; and Bill Clinton, who served two terms most recently. Then you realize that being elected to four terms is quite unusual.

When you read literally, you decode the words in the passage, figure out the meaning, and connect the information to what you already know. Even a good literal reading of a passage requires active reading and thinking.

Reading on an Analytical Level

After mastering a fact or passage on the literal level, you need to read on the analytical level, probing deeply into the meaning beneath the surface. First you analyze the information, looking at its parts and considering its implications from various angles. Then you gather related material and synthesize all of it, recombining it to achieve new insights. Finally, you evaluate the significance of the information.

ANALYZING, SYNTHESIZING, AND EVALUATING

Analyzing.   To return to the example above, once you have literally understood that Franklin Delano Roosevelt was elected to four terms of office as president, you can start asking questions about this information to scrutinize it from various angles. As you analyze, you select a principle for analysis depending on your purpose. Then you use this principle to break something into its components or parts. For example, you might analyze FDR's tenure in office in relation to the political longevity of other presidents. Why is FDR the only president who has been elected to serve four terms? What circumstances during his terms of office contributed to three reelections? How is FDR different from other presidents?

Synthesizing.   To answer your questions, you may have to read more or review material you have read in the past. What you discover may lead to even more questions. After gathering information about FDR's reelections, you begin synthesizing — recombining information, pulling together all the facts and opinions, identifying the evidence accepted by all or most sources, examining any controversial evidence, and drawing whatever conclusions reliable evidence seems to support. For example, it would be logical to conclude that the special circumstances of the Great Depression and World War II contributed to FDR's four terms. On the other hand, it would not be logical to conclude that Americans reelected him out of pity because he was a victim of polio.

Evaluating.   Finally, you evaluate your newly found knowledge to determine its significance, both to your understanding of depression-era politics and to your assessment of the soundness of your history book's approach. At this point, you might ask yourself, Why has the book's author chosen to make this point? How does it affect the rest of the author's presentation? Does this author seem reliable? And you may also have formed your own opinion about FDR's reelections based on your critical reading and the evidence you have gathered. For instance, you might conclude that FDR's four-term presidency is understandable in light of the events of the 1930s and 1940s, that the author has mentioned this fact to highlight the unique political atmosphere of that era, and that, in your opinion, it is evidence neither for nor against FDR's excellence as a president.

ACTIVITY: READING ANALYTICALLY

Think back to something you have read recently that helped you make a decision, perhaps a newspaper article, a magazine article, an electronic posting, or a college brochure. How did you analyze what you read, breaking the information into parts? How did you synthesize it, combining it with what you already knew? How did you evaluate it, judging its significance for your decision?

www
For additional critical reading activities, visit <www.bedfordstmartins.com/bedguide>.

Chapter 3
Critical Thinking Processes

*C*ritic, from the Greek word *kritikos,* means "one who can judge and discern"—in short, someone who thinks critically. College will have given you your money's worth if it leaves you better able to judge and discern—to determine what is more and less important, to make distinctions and recognize differences, to generalize from specifics, to draw conclusions from evidence, to grasp complex concepts and get to the bottom of things, to judge and choose wisely. The effective thinking that you will need in college, on the job, and in your daily life is active and purposeful, not passive and ambling. It is critical thinking.

A Process of Critical Thinking

You use critical thinking already to solve problems and make decisions every day. Suppose you don't have enough money both to pay your college tuition and to buy the car you need. You have to analyze your situation and decide what to do. First, you might pin down the causes of your financial strain. Have you had a medical emergency or lost your job? Have you spent a lot of money on a trip to the Bahamas? Has tuition increased?

If the cause is higher tuition, that's a cost you can't control. Given that, you can see three options: do without a car, decrease your tuition expenses, or get more money. To eliminate the need for a car, can you catch rides with a friend or relative? Can you use public transportation? To decrease your tuition costs, can you take fewer courses? Can you get a loan from the bank, the college, or a family member? (If so, can you repay it without sacrificing other things you need?) Can you get another job to bring in more money? (If so, can you still keep up your studies?)

Figure 3.1
Critical Thinking
Processes in Action

? Problem

You can't afford both your college tuition and the car you need.

Solution

❶ IDENTIFY CAUSES

Causes in your control:
Expensive vacation?

Causes out of your control:
Medical emergency?
Job loss?
Tuition increase?

❷ ANALYZE OPTIONS		**❸ SYNTHESIZE AND EVALUATE**
Do without a car	*(how?)*	• Get rides with family or friends? • Take public transportation?
Decrease your tuition	*(how?)*	• Take fewer courses?
Get more money	*(how?)*	• Get a loan from the bank? • Get a loan from the college? • Get a loan from a family member? • Get another job?

❹ DRAW A LOGICAL CONCLUSION

Apply for a short-term loan for tuition so that you can buy the car.
Repay the loan with earnings from work.

After evaluating your choices, you conclude the most logical solution is a short-term loan for tuition so that you can use the money you have to buy a car. You make your case to the financial aid officer — showing that you are a serious student with a B average, that you have a job that pays enough to repay the loan, and that you have proven you can work and go to college at the same time. When you receive the loan, your problem is solved.

Using Critical Thinking

Using critical thinking, you've explored your problem step by step and reached a reasonable solution. Critical thinking, like critical reading, draws on a cluster of intellectual strategies and skills. It requires complex analysis, synthesis, and evaluation. *Analysis* is the breaking down of information into its elements and parts. As a reader, you will analyze the information in

For more on critical reading, see Ch. 2.

articles, reports, and books to grasp the facts and concepts they contain. As a writer, you will analyze events, processes, structures, and ideas to understand them fully and explain them to readers. *Synthesis* is putting together elements and parts to form new wholes. As a researcher, you will synthesize information from several sources you have read, integrate this synthesized material with your own thoughts, and convey the unique combination to others through writing. Finally, *evaluation* means judging according to standards or criteria. When you evaluate something you have read, you determine standards for judging, apply them to the passage, and arrive at a conclusion about the significance or value of the information. When you as a critic evaluate something in writing, you must convince readers that your standards are reasonable and that the subject being evaluated either does or does not meet those standards.

These three activities — analysis, synthesis, and evaluation — are the core of critical thinking. They are not new to you, but applying them rigorously in college-level reading and writing may be. When you approach college reading and writing tasks, instructors will expect you (and you should expect yourself) to do the following:

- Think through a topic or problem critically.
- Read relevant sources of information critically.
- Write, presenting information and arguments that will pass critical scrutiny.
- Think critically — about your own thinking, reading, and writing skills.

Sometimes your assignments, like those in this class, will give you explicit opportunities to use your reading and thinking skills. For example, the writing tasks in Part Two of this book ask you to develop and apply these skills in various situations. Other times, you'll simply dive into an assignment without considering whether you're analyzing at one moment or synthesizing at the next. At such times, you'll be concentrating on your destination, where you want to go in your paper and what your assignment or course requires. Later you can look back on your route as a critical thinker, reconsidering the curves in the road and the scenery along the way — thinking critically about your own skills.

ACTIVITY: THINKING CRITICALLY TO SOLVE A PROBLEM

With classmates, identify a common problem for students at your college — juggling a busy schedule, parking on campus, making a class change, joining a social group, or some other issue. Working together, use critical thinking to explore the problem and identify possible solutions.

Supporting Critical Thinking with Evidence

As you write a paper, you try to figure out what you need to achieve, what position you want to take, and how to get your readers to follow your logic and accept your points. Your challenge, of course, is not just to think actively and clearly yourself but also to demonstrate your thinking to others, to persuade them to pay attention to what you say. And sound evidence is what critical readers want to see.

Sound evidence supports your points or assertions, substantiating them for readers. It also bolsters your stance as a credible writer, demonstrating the merit of your position. When you write, you need to find enough appropriate evidence to make your case. You need to marshal it to clarify, explain, and support your ideas. You need to weave evidence and assertions together into a clearly reasoned explanation or argument. And as you do so, you need to select and test your evidence so that it will convince your readers.

TYPES OF EVIDENCE

What is evidence? It is anything that demonstrates the soundness of a claim. Facts, statistics, firsthand observations, and expert testimony are four reliable forms of evidence. Other evidence might include examples, illustrations, details, and opinions. But some kinds of evidence weigh in more heavily than others: readers might discount your memories of livestock care on the farm where you spent your childhood summers unless you can show that your memories are representative or that you are an expert on the subject. Personal experience may strengthen an argument but generally is not sufficient as the sole support. If you are in doubt about the type of evidence an assignment requires, ask your instructor whether you should use sources or rely on personal experience and examples.

Facts.   Facts are statements that can be verified objectively, by observation or by reading a reliable account. They are usually stated dispassionately: "If you pump the air out of a five-gallon varnish can, it will collapse." Of course, we accept many of our facts based on the testimony of others. For example, we believe that the Great Wall of China exists although we may never have seen it with our own eyes.

Sometimes people say that facts are true statements, but truth and sound evidence may be confused. Consider the truth of the following statements:

The tree in my yard is ten feet tall.   *True* because it can be verified

A kilometer is 1,000 meters.   *True* using the metric system

The speed limit on the highway is sixty-five miles per hour.	*True* according to law
Fewer fatal highway accidents have occurred since the new exit ramp was built.	*True* according to research studies
My favorite food is pizza.	*True* as an opinion
More violent criminals should receive the death penalty.	*True* as a belief
Murder is wrong.	*True* according to value judgment

Some would claim that each of these statements is true, but when you think critically, you should avoid treating opinions, beliefs, judgments, or personal experience as true in the same sense that verifiable facts and events are true.

Statistics.   Statistics are facts expressed in numbers. What portion of Americans living at or below the poverty level are children? According to statistics compiled by the U.S. Department of Health and Human Services and the Census Bureau in 1999, children comprise 38 percent of the poor but only 26 percent of the total population.

Most writers, without trying to be dishonest, interpret statistics to help their causes. The statement "Fifty percent of the populace have incomes above the poverty level" might substantiate the fine job done by the government of a developing nation. Putting the statement another way — "Fifty percent of the populace have incomes below the poverty level" — might use the same statistic to show the inadequacy of the government's efforts.

Even though a writer is free to interpret a statistic, statistics should not be used to mislead. On the wrapper of a peanut candy bar, we read that a one-ounce serving contains only 150 calories. The claim is true, but the bar weighs 1.6 ounces. Gobble the whole thing — as you are more likely to do than to eat 62 percent of it — and you'll ingest 240 calories, a heftier amount than the innocent statistic on the wrapper suggests. Because abuses make some readers automatically distrust statistics, use figures fairly when you write, and make sure they are accurate. If you doubt a statistic, compare it with facts and statistics reported by several other sources. Distrust a statistical report that differs from every other report unless it is backed by further evidence.

Expert Testimony.   By experts, we mean people with knowledge gained from study and experience of a particular field. The test of an expert is whether his or her expertise stands up to the scrutiny of others who are knowledgeable in that field. An essay by basketball player Michael Jordan explaining how to play offense or by economist John Kenneth Galbraith setting forth the causes of inflation carries authority, while a piece by Galbraith on how to play basketball would not be credible. Also consider whether the expert has any bias or special interest that would affect reliability. Statistics on cases of lung cancer attributed to smoking might be better taken from government sources than from the tobacco industry.

Firsthand Observation.   Firsthand observation is persuasive. It can add life and concrete reality to abstract or complex points. You might support the claim "The Meadowfield waste recycling plant fails to meet state safety and sanitation guidelines" by recalling your own observations: "When I visited the plant last January, I was struck by the number of open waste canisters and by the lack of protective gear for the workers who handle these toxic materials daily."

For more on observation, see Ch. 5.

As readers, most of us tend to trust the writer who declares, "I was there. This is what I saw." Sometimes that trust is misplaced, though, and you should always be wary of a writer's claim to have seen something that no other evidence supports. Ask yourself, Is this writer biased? Is he or she an expert? Might the writer have (intentionally or unintentionally) misinterpreted what he or she saw? Of course, your readers will scrutinize your own firsthand observations, too; take care to reassure them that your observations are unbiased and accurate.

ACTIVITY: LOOKING FOR EVIDENCE

Using the issue you explored with classmates for the activity on page 24, what would you need to support your identification, explanation, or solution of the problem? Working with classmates, identify the kinds of evidence that would be most useful. Where or how might you find such evidence?

Testing Evidence

As both a reader and a writer, you should always think critically about evidence, testing and questioning it to see whether it is strong enough to carry the weight of the writer's claims. Evidence is useful and trustworthy when it satisfies these requirements:

WWW
For additional practice in testing evidence, visit <www.bedfordstmartins.com/bedguide>.

It is **accurate**. A writer assumes all responsibility for facts and figures in an essay. Are they accurate? Can you check doubtful information against published sources, reports by others, or reference works? Have you copied figures or quoted facts correctly?

It is **reliable**. To decide whether you can trust the evidence, you'll need to evaluate its source and check the writer's credentials. Do some reading to compare information in one source with that in another. If an important point rests on an opinion or information from an expert, check to see that the person is respected as an authority in the field.

It is **up-to-date**. Facts and statistics, such as population figures or scientific research, from ten-year-old sources may be out of date. Use information from the latest sources in what you write, and check that what you read contains up-to-date source material, as well.

It is **to the point**. Evidence must back the exact claim a writer makes—no matter how interesting an unrelated fact or opinion may be. Sometimes a writer will leap from evidence to conclusion without reason, and the result is a *non sequitur* (Latin for "it does not follow"): "Benito Mussolini made the trains run on time. He was one of the world's leading statesmen." The evidence about trains doesn't support a judgment on Mussolini's statesmanship.

It is **representative**. Any examples should be typical of all the things included in the claim. If a writer wants to support the claim that students on campus are generally well informed about their legal rights, she should talk not just to prelaw majors but also to nursing, engineering, marketing, or other majors. Perhaps most writers, in the heat of persuading, can't help unconsciously stacking the evidence in their own favor, but the best writers don't deliberately suppress contrary evidence. A writer promoting package tours of India, "an attractive land of sumptuous wealth and splendor," might use the Taj Mahal and a luxury hotel as evidence but ignore the slums of Bombay and Calcutta. The result might be effective advertising but not a full, faithful, or critically sound view.

For information on mistakes in thinking called logical fallacies, see pp. 134–36.

It is **not oversimplified**. Some writers fall into supplying a too-easy explanation for a vast and complicated phenomenon: "Of course our economy is in trouble. People aren't buying American-made cars." Evidence may support both statements, but the second is insufficient to account for the first: there is much more to the economy than the auto industry alone. Evidence should be clear, but it may not be simple. It needs to address the complexities of the case.

It is **sufficient** and **strong enough** to back the claim and persuade your readers. How much evidence a writer should use depends on the claim. It takes less evidence to claim that a particular intersection needs a traffic signal than to claim that the Department of Transportation needs reorganizing. How much evidence a writer needs may depend, too, on how much readers already know. A group of readers all from Washington, D.C., and its vicinity will not need much evidence to be persuaded that the city's modern Metro transit system is admirably efficient, but more evidence may be needed to convince readers from out of town. When writing, try to imagine yourself in a reader's place. What does that person believe or feel? What questions would he or she ask? What other evidence might you supply to support other points or answer likely objections? But mere quantity is not enough. One piece of vivid and significant evidence—such as the memorable firsthand testimony of a reliable expert—may be more valid and persuasive than a foot-high stack of statistics.

Using Evidence to Support an Appeal

One way to select evidence and to judge whether it is appropriate and sufficient is to consider the types of appeal — logical, emotional, and ethical. Most effective arguments work on all three levels, using all three types of appeals. As a writer, you will usually want to make sure that you have evidence that supports all three. As a reader, you will want to make sure that the author has not relied too heavily on any one type of appeal.

LOGICAL APPEAL

When writers use a logical appeal, they appeal to the reader's mind or intellect. The logical appeal relies on evidence that is factual, objective, clear, and relevant. Critical readers expect logical evidence to support major claims and important statements. For example, if a writer were arguing for term limits for legislators, she wouldn't want to base her argument on the evidence that some long-term legislators weren't reelected last term (irrelevant) or that the current system is unfair to young people who want to get into politics (not logical). Instead, she might argue that the absence of term limits encourages corruption and then use evidence of legislators who became indebted to lobbyists or special-interest committees by taking campaign contributions from them and then sided with these groups in key legislative votes.

EMOTIONAL APPEAL

When writers use an emotional appeal, they appeal to the reader's heart. They choose language, facts, quotations, examples, and images that will evoke emotional responses. Of course, convincing writing does touch readers' hearts as well as their minds. Without this heartfelt tug, a strict logical appeal may seem cold and dehumanized. If a writer were arguing against hunting seals for their fur, he might combine statistics about the number of seals killed each year and the overall population decrease with a vivid description of baby seals being slaughtered. Some writers, however, use emotionally loaded words and overly sentimental examples to manipulate readers — to arouse their sympathy, pity, or anger in order to convert them to the writer's position without any logical evidence. Readers are likely to be alienated by dishonest emotional appeals. Instead of basing an argument against a particular political candidate on pitiful images of scrawny children living in roach-infested squalor, a good writer would report the candidate's voting record on issues that affect children. When reading, be wary of anyone who tugs on your heartstrings without giving you hard facts as well.

ETHICAL APPEAL

When writers use an ethical appeal, they call on the reader's sense of fairness and trust. They select and present evidence in a manner that will make the audience trust them, respect their judgment, and believe what they have to say. The best logical argument in the world falls flat when readers don't take the writer seriously. How can you use an ethical appeal to establish your credibility as a writer? First you need to establish your credentials in the field through experience, such as a job, travel, or relevant reading or interviews that helped you learn about the subject. If you are writing about environmental pollution, tell your readers that your allergies have been irritated by chemicals in the air. Identify medical or environmental experts you have contacted or whose publications you have read. You can demonstrate your knowledge of the subject through the information you present, the experts and sources you cite, and the depth of understanding that you convey. Further, you can establish a rapport with your readers by indicating values and attitudes that you share with them and by responding seriously to the arguments of the opposition. Finally, you can use language that is precise, clear, and appropriate in tone. As a reader, you're likely to be most swayed by authors who have managed to do all these things successfully. Be careful, however, not to let a strong ethical appeal manipulate you into believing someone who doesn't also offer hard evidence for claims.

ACTIVITY: IDENTIFYING TYPES OF APPEALS

Bring to class the editorial or opinion page from a newspaper or newsmagazine. Read some of the letters or articles. Identify the types of appeals used by each author to support his or her point.

PART TWO

A Writer's Situations

Introduction

In Part Two, we present a sequence of writing situations that require you to use processes for writing, reading, and thinking critically. The nine writing assignments — recalling an experience, observing a scene, interviewing a subject, comparing and contrasting, explaining causes and effects, taking a stand, proposing a solution, evaluating, and reading critically — are arranged roughly in order of increasing complexity — that is, according to the level of critical reading and thinking required. Some require analysis — breaking something down into its components to understand it better. Others require synthesis — combining information from various sources with your own ideas and conclusions in order to achieve a new perspective. The most complex task, evaluating, can incorporate several of the other critical strategies. Let's look at these writing situations in more detail.

Recalling an Experience.   Recalling an event depends on your richest resource as a writer — your memory. Chapter 4 guides you in focusing and shaping your writing from memory so that you can present recollections effectively and convey their importance to your readers.

Observing a Scene.   Observation relies on using your senses to see, hear, smell, touch, and taste what's around you. Chapter 5 helps you select and arrange compelling details in order to convey your insights about what you have observed.

Interviewing a Subject.   Interviewing brings the freshness of conversation, the liveliness of exchange with someone else, and the informed viewpoint of an expert to your writing. Chapter 6 encourages you to bring the subject of an interview to life as you distill the impression and information gained during your interview.

Comparing and Contrasting.   Comparing and contrasting focuses on the similarities and differences of two (or more) items or groups. Chapter 7 guides you first in analyzing each item and then in lining up the characteristics of each, side by side, to determine how they are alike and how they are different. Most importantly, because effective comparison and contrast points out likenesses and differences for some significant purpose, you will convey your conclusion about how each alternative operates or which alternative is preferable.

Explaining Causes and Effects.   As you focus on an action, event, or situation, identifying causes means ferreting out roots and origins. Determining effects means figuring out results. Sometimes as you analyze, you will find a chain of causes and effects: a situation causes specific effects, which in turn cause other effects. Chapter 8 helps you to analyze and explain causes, effects, or both in order to support an overall point that helps you and your readers understand the issue better.

Taking a Stand.   When you take a stand, you argue for one side or another of an issue. Chapter 9 helps you develop your position in a controversy and present your opinion so that readers will respect it even if they do not agree with you. You may come to a debate with strong views, or you may develop a position while looking into the matter. In either case, once you reach a clear position, you will present your case persuasively to your readers using solid, pertinent evidence — facts, statistics, expert opinion, and direct observation.

Proposing a Solution.   Proposing a solution requires not only taking a stand but also presenting a feasible solution to the problem at hand. Chapter 10 helps you identify a problem and then propose a convincing, workable solution. You will use two main methods of persuading readers that the problem should be solved as you recommend: showing readers why the problem matters to them and supplying evidence to support your solution.

Evaluating.   Evaluating means judging: deciding whether your subject is good or bad, effective or ineffective. As Chapter 11 explains, you will identify, implicitly or explicitly, specific criteria for judging your subject, whether it is an idea, a presentation, a product, or a work of art. Once your standards are clear, whether based on your personal preferences or the views of experts in the field, you can analyze your subject to see how well it meets the criteria you propose. As you explain your judgment, you will also try to persuade your readers that your view is reasonable.

Reading Critically.   When you read critically, you engage with a written passage in order to understand it at both a literal level and an analytical level. Chapter 12 presents the skills involved in this essential college-level activity and guides you as you write a paper based on critical reading, first explaining what is going on in the text you have read and then making your own point based on its ideas.

Taken together, these nine chapters present many of the writing situations you will encounter in other college courses and in your career. Use the processes outlined in these chapters as resources when you meet unfamiliar writing situations or need to marshal appropriate evidence for essays.

Chapter 4
Recalling an Experience

Fairfield Porter, *The Screen Porch,* 1964. Oil on canvas. 79 ¹/₂ × 79 ¹/₂ in. (201.9 × 201.9 cm.). Collection of Whitney Museum of American Art. 77.1.41. Photograph Copyright © 2001: Whitney Museum of American Art. Photography by Geoffrey Clements.

Responding to an Image

In your view, who might the four people in the picture be? Where are they, and what are they doing? Why are they there? When did this scene take place: What was the approximate year and the season of the year? What emotions can you detect in each person's facial expression and body language? Does this image remind you of an experience that you have had? Write about your experience—or about a possible explanation of events in this picture—using as much vivid detail as you can.

Writing from recall is writing from memory, the richest resource a writer has and the handiest. Recall is clearly necessary when you are asked to write of a personal experience, a favorite place, a memorable person. But even when an instructor hands you a subject that seems to have nothing to do with you, your memory is the first place to look. Suppose you have to write a psychology paper about how advertisers play on consumers' fears. Begin with what you remember. What ads have sent chills down your back? What ads have suggested that their products could save you from a painful social blunder, a lonely night, or a deadly accident? All by itself, memory may not give you enough to write about, but you will rarely go wrong if you start by jotting down something remembered.

Learning from Other Writers

WWW
For more examples of writing from recall, visit <www.bedfordstmartins.com/bedguide>.

Here are two samples of good writing from recall — one by a professional writer, one by a college student.

As You Read

As you read these essays, ask yourself the following questions:

1. Is the perspective of the essay that of a child or an adult? How do you know?
2. What does the author realize after reflecting on the events recalled? Does the realization come soon after the experience or later, when the writer examines the events from a more mature perspective?
3. How does the realization change the individual?

Russell Baker

The Art of Eating Spaghetti

In this essay from his autobiography Growing Up *(1982), columnist Russell Baker recalls being sixteen in urban Baltimore and wondering what to do with his life.*

The only thing that truly interested me was writing, and I knew that sixteen-year-olds did not come out of high school and become writers. I thought of writing as something to be done only by the rich. It was so obviously not real work, not a job at which you could earn a living. Still, I had begun to think of myself as a writer. It was the only thing for which I seemed to have the smallest talent, and, silly though it sounded when I told people I'd like to be a writer, it gave me a way of thinking about myself which satisfied my need to have an identity. 1

The notion of becoming a writer had flickered off and on in my head since the Belleville days, but it wasn't until my third year in high school that the possibility took hold. Until then I'd been bored by everything associated with English courses. I found English grammar dull and baffling. I hated the 2 assignments to turn out "compositions," and went at them like heavy labor, turning out leaden, lackluster paragraphs that were agonies for teachers to read and for me to write. The classics thrust on me to read seemed as deadening as chloroform.

When our class was assigned to Mr. Fleagle for third-year English I antici- 3 pated another grim year in that dreariest of subjects. Mr. Fleagle was notorious among City students for dullness and inability to inspire. He was said to be stuffy, dull, and hopelessly out of date. To me he looked to be sixty or seventy and prim to a fault. He wore primly severe eyeglasses, his wavy hair was primly cut and primly combed. He wore prim vested suits with neckties blocked primly against the collar buttons of his primly starched white shirts. He had a primly pointed jaw, a primly straight nose, and a prim manner of speaking that was so correct, so gentlemanly, that he seemed a comic antique.

I anticipated a listless,° unfruitful year with Mr. Fleagle and for a long 4 time was not disappointed. We read *Macbeth*. Mr. Fleagle loved *Macbeth* and wanted us to love it too, but he lacked the gift of infecting others with his own passion. He tried to convey the murderous ferocity of Lady Macbeth one day by reading aloud the passage that concludes

> . . . I have given suck, and know
> How tender 'tis to love the babe that milks me.
> I would, while it was smiling in my face,
> Have plucked my nipple from his boneless gums. . . .

The idea of prim Mr. Fleagle plucking his nipple from boneless gums was too much for the class. We burst into gasps of irrepressible snickering. Mr. Fleagle stopped.

"There is nothing funny, boys, about giving suck to a babe. It is the — 5 the very essence of motherhood, don't you see."

He constantly sprinkled his sentences with "don't you see." It wasn't a 6 question but an exclamation of mild surprise at our ignorance. "Your pronoun needs an antecedent, don't you see," he would say, very primly. "The purpose of the Porter's scene, boys, is to provide comic relief from the horror, don't you see."

Late in the year we tackled the informal essay. "The essay, don't you see, 7 is the . . ." My mind went numb. Of all forms of writing, none seemed so boring as the essay. Naturally we would have to write informal essays. Mr. Fleagle distributed a homework sheet offering us a choice of topics. None was quite so simpleminded as "What I Did on My Summer Vacation," but most seemed to be almost as dull. I took the list home and dawdled until the night before the essay was due. Sprawled on the sofa, I finally faced up to the grim task, took the list out of my notebook, and scanned it. The topic on which my eye stopped was "The Art of Eating Spaghetti."

This title produced an extraordinary sequence of mental images. Surging 8 up out of the depths of memory came a vivid recollection of a night in

---

listless: Lacking energy or enthusiasm.

Belleville when all of us were seated around the supper table — Uncle Allen, my mother, Uncle Charlie, Doris, Uncle Hal — and Aunt Pat served spaghetti for supper. Spaghetti was an exotic treat in those days. Neither Doris nor I had ever eaten spaghetti, and none of the adults had enough experience to be good at it. All the good humor of Uncle Allen's house reawoke in my mind as I recalled the laughing arguments we had that night about the socially respectable method for moving spaghetti from plate to mouth.

Suddenly I wanted to write about that, about the warmth and good feel- 9 ing of it, but I wanted to put it down simply for my own joy, not for Mr. Fleagle. It was a moment I wanted to recapture and hold for myself. I wanted to relive the pleasure of an evening at New Street. To write it as I wanted, however, would violate all the rules of formal composition I'd learned in school, and Mr. Fleagle would surely give it a failing grade. Never mind. I would write something else for Mr. Fleagle after I had written this thing for myself.

When I finished it the night was half gone and there was no time left to 10 compose a proper, respectable essay for Mr. Fleagle. There was no choice next morning but to turn in my private reminiscence° of Belleville. Two days passed before Mr. Fleagle returned the graded papers, and he returned everyone's but mine. I was bracing myself for a command to report to Mr. Fleagle immediately after school for discipline when I saw him lift my paper from his desk and rap for the class's attention.

"Now, boys," he said, "I want to read you an essay. This is titled 'The Art 11 of Eating Spaghetti.' "

And he started to read. My words! He was reading *my words* out loud to 12 the entire class. What's more, the entire class was listening. Listening attentively. Then somebody laughed, then the entire class was laughing, and not in contempt and ridicule, but with openhearted enjoyment. Even Mr. Fleagle stopped two or three times to repress a small prim smile.

I did my best to avoid showing pleasure, but what I was feeling was pure 13 ecstasy at this startling demonstration that my words had the power to make people laugh. In the eleventh grade, at the eleventh hour as it were, I had discovered a calling. It was the happiest moment of my entire school career. When Mr. Fleagle finished he put the final seal on my happiness by saying, "Now that, boys, is an essay, don't you see. It's — don't you see — it's of the very essence of the essay, don't you see. Congratulations, Mr. Baker."

For the first time, light shone on a possibility. It wasn't a very heartening 14 possibility, to be sure. Writing couldn't lead to a job after high school, and it was hardly honest work, but Mr. Fleagle had opened a door for me. After that I ranked Mr. Fleagle among the finest teachers in the school.

Questions to Start You Thinking

Meaning

1. In your own words, state what Baker believes he learned in the eleventh grade about the art of writing. What incidents or statements help identify this lesson for readers? What lesson, if any, did you learn from the essay?

reminiscence: Memory.

2. Why do you think Baker included this event in his autobiography?

3. Have you ever changed your mind about something you had to do, as Baker did about writing? Or about a person, as he did about Mr. Fleagle?

Writing Strategies

4. What is the effect, in paragraph 3, of Baker's many repetitions of the words *prim* and *primly*? What other devices does Baker use to make vivid his characterization of Mr. Fleagle? Why do you think the author uses so much space to portray his teacher?

5. What does the quotation from *Macbeth* add to Baker's account? Had the quotation been omitted, what would have been lost?

6. How does Baker organize the essay? Why does he use this order?

STUDENT ESSAY

Robert G. Schreiner
What Is a Hunter?

What is a hunter? This is a simple question with a relatively straightforward answer. A hunter is, according to <u>Webster's New Collegiate Dictionary</u>, a person who hunts game (game being various types of animals hunted or pursued for various reasons). However, a second question is just as simple but without such a straightforward answer: What characteristics make up a hunter? As a child, I had always considered the most important aspect of the hunter's person to be his ability to use a rifle, bow, or whatever weapon was appropriate to the type of hunting being done. Having many relatives in rural areas of Virginia and Kansas, I had been exposed to rifles a great deal. I had done extensive target shooting and considered myself to be quite proficient in the use of firearms. I had never been hunting, but I had always thought that since I could fire a rifle accurately I would make a good hunter.

One Christmas holiday, while we were visiting our grandparents in Kansas, my grandfather asked me if I wanted to go jackrabbit hunting with him. I eagerly accepted, anxious to show off my prowess° with a rifle. A younger cousin of mine also wanted to come, so we all went out into the garage, loaded two .22 caliber rifles and a 20-gauge shotgun, hopped

In this college essay, Robert G. Schreiner uses vivid details to bring a significant childhood event to life.

1

2

prowess: Superior skill.

into the pickup truck, and drove out of town. It had snowed the night before, and to either side of the narrow road swept six-foot-deep powdery drifts. The wind twirled the fine crystalline snow into whirling vortexes° that bounced along the icy road and sprayed snow into the open windows of the pickup. As we drove, my grandfather gave us some pointers about both spotting and shooting jackrabbits. He told us that when it snows, jackrabbits like to dig out a hollow in the top of a snowdrift, usually near a fencepost, and lie there soaking up the sunshine. He told us that even though jackrabbits are a grayish brown, this coloration is excellent camouflage in the snow, for the curled-up rabbits resemble rocks. He then pointed out a few rabbits in such positions as we drove along, showing us how to distinguish them from exposed rocks and dirt. He then explained that the only way to be sure that we killed the rabbit was to shoot for the head and, in particular, the eye, for this was on a direct line with the rabbit's brain. Since we were using solid point bullets, which deform into a ball upon impact, a hit anywhere but the head would most likely only wound the rabbit.

My grandfather then slowed down the pickup and told us 3
to look out for the rabbits hidden in the snowdrifts. We eventually spotted one about thirty feet from the road in a snow-filled gully. My cousin wished to shoot the first one, so he hopped out of the truck, balanced the .22 on the hood, and fired. A spray of snow erupted about a foot to the left of the rabbit's hollow. My cousin fired again, and again, and again, the shots pockmarking the slope of the drift. He fired once more and the rabbit bounced out of its hollow, its head rocking from side to side. He was hit. My cousin eagerly gamboled into the snow to claim his quarry.° He brought it back holding it by the hind legs, proudly displaying it as would a warrior the severed head of his enemy. The bullet had entered the rabbit's right shoulder and exited through the neck. In both places a thin trickle of crimson marred the gray sheen of the rabbit's pelt. It quivered slightly and its rib cage pulsed with its labored breathing. My cousin was about to toss it into the back of the pickup when my grandfather pointed out that it would be cruel to allow the rabbit to

vortex: Rotation around an axis, as in a whirlwind.   **quarry:** Prey.

bleed slowly to death and instructed my cousin to bang its
head against the side of the pickup to kill it. My cousin
then proceeded to bang the rabbit's head against the yellow
metal. Thump, thump, thump, thump; after a minute or so my
cousin loudly proclaimed that it was dead and hopped back
into the truck.

The whole episode sickened me to some degree, and at the 4
time I did not know why. We continued to hunt throughout the
afternoon, and feigning boredom, I allowed my cousin and
grandfather to shoot all of the rabbits. Often, the shots
didn't kill the rabbits outright so they had to be killed
against the pickup. The thump, thump, thump of the rabbits'
skulls against the metal began to irritate me, and I was
strangely glad when we turned around and headed back toward
home. We were a few miles from the city limits when my grandfather slowed the truck to a stop, then backed up a few
yards. My grandfather said he spotted two huge "jacks" sitting in the sun in a field just off the road. He pointed them
out and handed me the .22, saying that if I didn't shoot
something the whole afternoon would have been a wasted trip
for me. I hesitated and then reluctantly accepted the rifle.
I stepped out onto the road, my feet crunching on the ice.
The two rabbits were about seventy feet away, both sitting
upright in the sun. I cocked and leveled the rifle, my elbow
held almost horizontal in the military fashion I had learned
to employ. I brought the sights to bear on the right eye of
the first rabbit, compensated° for distance, and fired. There
was a harsh snap like the crack of a whip and a small jolt to
my shoulder. The first rabbit was gone, presumably knocked
over the side of the snowdrift. The second rabbit hadn't
moved a muscle; it just sat there staring with that black
eye. I cocked the rifle once more and sighted a second time,
the bead of the rifle just barely above the glassy black orb
that regarded me so passively. I squeezed the trigger. Again
the crack, again the jolt, and again the rabbit disappeared
over the top of the drift. I handed the rifle to my cousin
and began making my way toward the rabbits. I sank into powdery snow up to my waist as I clambered to the top of the
drift and looked over.

compensate: Counterbalance.

On the other side of the drift was a sight that I doubt 5 I will ever forget. There was a shallow, snow-covered ditch on the leeward side of the drift and it was into this ditch that the rabbits had fallen, at least what was left of the rabbits. The entire ditch, in an area about ten feet wide, was spattered with splashes of crimson blood, pink gobbets of brain, and splintered fragments of bone. The twisted corpses of the rabbits lay in the bottom of the ditch in small pools of streaming blood. Of both the rabbits, only the bodies remained, the heads being completely gone. Stumps of vertebrae protruded obscenely from the mangled bodies, and one rabbit's hind legs twitched spasmodically. I realized that my cousin must have made a mistake and loaded the rifle with hollow-point explosive bullets instead of solid ones.

I shouted back to the pickup, explaining the situation, 6 and asked if I should bring them back anyway. My grandfather shouted back, "No, don't worry about it, just leave them there. I'm gonna toss these jacks by the side of the road anyway; jackrabbits aren't any good for eatin'."

Looking at the dead, twitching bodies I thought only of 7 the incredible waste of life that the afternoon had been, and I realized that there was much more to being a hunter than knowing how to use a rifle. I turned and walked back to the pickup, riding the rest of the way home in silence.

Questions to Start You Thinking

Meaning

1. Where in the essay do you first begin to suspect the writer's feelings about hunting? What in the essay or in your experience led you to this perception?
2. How would you characterize the writer's grandfather? How would you characterize his cousin?
3. How did the writer's understanding of himself change as a result of this hunting experience?

Writing Strategies

4. How might the essay be strengthened or weakened if the opening paragraph were cut out? Without this paragraph, how would your understanding of the author and his change be different?
5. Would Schreiner's essay be more or less effective if he explained in the last paragraph what he means by "much more to being a hunter"?
6. What are some of Schreiner's memorable images?

Learning by Writing

THE ASSIGNMENT: RECALLING A PERSONAL EXPERIENCE

Write about one specific experience that changed how you acted, thought, or felt. Use your experience as a springboard for reflection. Your purpose is not merely to tell an interesting story but to show your readers the importance of that experience for you. Your audience is your instructor and your classmates.

You can complete each of the steps in this assignment by using the *Writing Guide Software* for *The Bedford Guide.*

We suggest you pick an event that is not too personal or too subjective. Something that happened to you or that you observed, an encounter with a person who greatly influenced you, a decision that you made, or a challenge or an obstacle that you faced will be easier to recall (and to make vivid for your readers) than an interior experience like a religious conversion or falling in love.

Some memorable student papers have recalled experiences both heavy and light:

> One writer recalled guitar lessons with a teacher who at first seemed harsh but who turned out to be a true friend.

> Another student recalled a childhood trip when everything went wrong and she discovered the complexities of change.

> Another recalled competing with a classmate who taught him a deeper understanding of success.

Facing the Challenge: Writing from Recall

The major challenge writers confront when they write from recall is to focus their essays on a main idea. When writing about a familiar — and often powerful — experience, writers often have difficulty deciding how to present that experience to readers. On the one hand, it is tempting to include every detail that comes to mind. On the other hand, because the experience is so familiar, it is easy to overlook details that would make the story's relevance clearer to the reader.

If you are not certain of your *purpose* in writing about a particular event — what you want to show readers about your experience — your narrative is likely to read like a laundry list of details. Instead, you want to connect events clearly around a main idea. You want to select details that work together to convey the significance of your experience. To help you decide what to show your readers, respond to each of the following questions in a nutshell (no more than two or three sentences):

- What was important to you about the experience?
- What did you learn from it?
- How did it change you?

Once you have decided on your main point about the experience, you should select those details that will best illustrate that point and show readers why the experience was important to you.

WWW
To practice generating details and focusing an essay, visit <www.bedfordstmartins.com/bedguide>.

GENERATING IDEAS

For more strategies for generating ideas, see Ch. 16.

You may find that the minute you are asked to write about a significant experience, the very incident will flash to mind. Most writers, though, will need a little time for their memories to surface. Often, when you are busy doing something else — observing the scene around you, talking with someone, reading about someone else's experience — the activity can trigger a recollection. When a promising one emerges, write it down. Perhaps, like Russell Baker, you found success only when you ignored what you thought you were supposed to do in favor of what you really wanted to do. Perhaps, like Robert Schreiner, you learned from a painful experience.

For more on brainstorming, see pp. 260–62.

Try Brainstorming.   When you brainstorm, you just jot down ideas, coming up with as many as you can. You can start with a suggestive word or phrase — *disobedience, painful lesson, childhood, peer pressure* — and list under it whatever ideas occur through free association. You can also use the questions in the following checklist:

DISCOVERY CHECKLIST

___ Did you ever break an important rule or rebel against authority? Did you learn anything from your actions?

___ Did you ever succumb to peer pressure? What were the results of going along with the crowd? What did you learn?

___ Did you ever regard a person in a certain way and then have to change your opinion of him or her?

___ Did you ever have to choose between two equally attractive alternatives? How might your life have been different if you had chosen differently?

___ Have you ever been appalled by witnessing an act of prejudice or insensitivity? What did you do? Do you wish you had done something different?

Try Freewriting.   You might also spend ten or fifteen minutes freewriting — simply writing without stopping. If you think you have nothing to say, write "I have nothing to say" over and over, until ideas come. They will come.

WRITING WITH A COMPUTER

Keyboarding words onto a screen and using the Edit menu to copy, cut, or paste can show you that your writing is fluid and can be manipulated to answer the writing task. You may start generating ideas by brainstorming, freewriting, answering some of the reporter's questions, outlining a chronology, or writing directly about the experience you recall. Some students find it helpful to write out notes or guidelines in bold type to remind themselves about their tasks and their assignment's challenges. Just as your teacher will encourage you to find and develop your own writing processes, you should actively create your own online writing space to support these processes.

After you are finished, you can circle or draw lines between related items, considering what main idea connects events.

For more on freewriting, see pp. 263–64.

Try a Reporter's Questions.   Once you recall an experience you want to write about, ask "the five *W*'s and an *H*" that journalists find useful in their work:

For more on using a reporter's questions, see pp. 267–68.

- Who was involved?
- What happened?
- Where did it take place?
- When did it happen?
- Why did it happen?
- How did the events unfold?

Any one of these questions can lead to further questions — and to further discovery. Take, for instance, Who was involved? If others were involved in the incident, you might also ask, What did they look like? What did they do or say? (Might their words supply a lively quotation?) What information would a reader need to appreciate their importance to your story? Or, take the question What happened? You might also ask, What were your thoughts as the event took place? At what moment did you become aware that the event was no ordinary experience?

Check Other Sources of Information.   Because the memory drops as well as retains, you may want to check your recollections against those of a friend or family member who was there. Did you keep a diary or a journal at the time? Was the experience public enough (such as a riot or a blizzard) to have been recorded in a newspaper or a magazine? If so, perhaps you can refresh your memory and rediscover details or angles that you had forgotten.

PLANNING, DRAFTING, AND DEVELOPING

Now, how will you tell your story? If the experience is still fresh in your mind, you may be able simply to write a draft, following the order of events, and shaping your story as you go along. If you decide to plan before you write, here are some additional suggestions.

For more strategies for planning, drafting, and developing papers, see Chs. 17, 18, and 19.

Establish a Chronology.   Retelling an experience is called *narration*, and the simplest way to organize the information is chronologically — relating events in the order in which they occurred. If you are uncertain just when to start or stop, stick to the essentials, and write in chronological order.

For examples of time markers and other transitions, see p. 297.

Sometimes you can start an account of an experience in the middle and then, through *flashback*, fill in whatever background a reader needs to know. Richard Rodriguez, for instance, begins *Hunger of Memory* (Boston: David R.

Godine, 1982), a memoir of his bilingual childhood, with an arresting sentence:

> I remember, to start with, that day in Sacramento, in a California now nearly thirty years past — when I first entered a classroom, able to understand about fifty stray English words.

The opening hooks our attention. In the rest of his essay, Rodriguez fills us in on his family history, on the gulf he came to perceive between the public language (English) and the language of his home (Spanish).

For more on providing details, see pp. 303–05.

Show What Happened.   How can you best make your recollections come alive for your readers? Look again at Russell Baker's account of Mr. Fleagle teaching *Macbeth* and at the way Robert G. Schreiner depicts his cousin putting the wounded rabbits out of their misery. These two writers have not merely told us what happened; they have *shown* us, by creating scenes that we can see in our mind's eye. As you tell your story, zoom in on at least two or three such specific scenes. Show your readers exactly what happened, where it occurred, what was said, who said it. Use details and words that appeal to all five senses — sight, sound, touch, taste, and smell.

REVISING AND EDITING

For more revising and editing strategies, see Ch. 20.

After you have written an early draft, put it aside for a day or two — or a few hours if your deadline is looming. Then read it over carefully. Try to see everything through the eyes of one of your readers, noting both the pleasing parts and the confusing spots. Revise to ensure that you've expressed your thoughts and feelings clearly and strongly in a way that will reach your readers; edit to ensure that no distracting weaknesses in grammar or expression remain.

Focus on a Main Idea.   As you read over the essay, ask yourself: What was so important about this experience? Why is it so memorable? Will readers be able to discern why this experience was a crucial one in your life? Ask

FOR GROUP LEARNING

Learning to Be a Peer Editor

To practice peer response before trying your skills on a classmate's paper, select any student-written paper from this book's table of contents and write a short but detailed letter to the writer. Tell the writer what is effective and ineffective about the essay, and explain why. Get together with others in your class who chose the same paper, and compare comments. What did you notice in the essay? What did you miss that others noticed? As you will see, several people can notice far more than one individual can.

again how your life has been different ever since. Be sure that the difference is genuine and specific, reflecting the incident's real impact on you. In other words, be sure that your essay is focused on a single main idea or thesis.

For more about a thesis, see pp. 271–75.

Use Concrete Detail.   Ask whether you have succeeded in making the events come alive for your readers by recalling them in sufficient concrete detail. Be specific enough that your readers can see, smell, taste, hear, and feel what you experienced. Notice again Robert Schreiner's focus in his second paragraph on the world outside his own skin: his close recall of the snow, of the pointers his grandfather offered about the habits of jackrabbits and the way to shoot them. As you revise, you may well recall more vivid details to include.

For more about providing details, see pp. 303–05.

Follow a Clear Sequence.   Will the story you tell be easy for readers to follow? Have you consistently followed a logical sequence of events? Have you indicated transitions clearly? Readers will follow you through your essay more readily if you give them a good idea of where they're going.

For more on transitions, see pp. 296–98.

Revise and rewrite until you know you've related your experience and its impact as well as you can. Here are some useful questions about revising your paper:

REVISION CHECKLIST

___ Have you fulfilled your purpose by showing why this experience was important and by demonstrating how it changed your life?

___ How have you engaged readers so that they will want to keep reading? Will they find your paper dramatic, instructive, or revealing? Will they see and feel what you experienced?

___ Why do you begin your narration as you do? Is there another place in the draft that would make a better beginning?

___ If the events are not in chronological order, is the paper's organization easy to follow?

___ Does the ending provide a sense of finality?

___ Do you stick to the point? Is everything relevant to your main idea or thesis?

___ Do you portray any people? If so, is their importance clear? Do you provide enough detail to make them seem real, not just shadowy figures?

___ Does any dialogue have the ring of real speech? Read it aloud. Try it on a friend.

After you have revised your recall essay, edit and proofread it. Check carefully for problems with grammar, word choice, punctuation, and mechanics — and then correct any problems you find. Here are some questions to get you started:

For more editing and proofreading strategies, see Ch. 20.

For more help, turn to
the dark-blue-edged
pages, and find the
"Quick Editing Guide"
section noted here.

EDITING CHECKLIST

—— Have you used correct verb tenses and forms throughout?   A1
When you present a sequence of past events, is it clear what
happened first and what happened next?

—— Is your sentence structure correct? Have you avoided writing   A6, A7
fragments and run-on sentences?

—— When you use transitions and other introductory elements to   C1
connect events, have you placed any needed commas after them?

—— In your dialogue, have you made sure that commas and periods   C3
are inside the closing quotation mark?

—— Have you spelled everything correctly, especially the names   D1, D2
of people and places? Have you capitalized names correctly?

When you have made all the changes you need to make, print out a
clean copy of your paper — and hand it in.

OTHER ASSIGNMENTS

1. Choose a person outside your immediate family who had a marked effect on your life, either good or bad. Jot down ten details that might
   help a reader understand what that person was like. Consider the person's physical appearance, way of talking, and habits as well as any
   memorable incidents. When your list is finished, look back to "The Art
   of Eating Spaghetti" to identify the kinds of detail Baker uses in his portrait of Mr. Fleagle, noting any kinds of detail you might add to your
   list. Then write a paper in which you portray that person, including
   those details that help explain his or her impact on you.

**FOR PEER
RESPONSE**

For general questions
for a peer editor, see
pp. 323–24.

Have a classmate or friend read your draft and suggest how you might present
the main idea about your experience more clearly and vividly. Ask your peer
editor questions such as these about writing from recall:

- What do you think the writer's main idea or message is? Why was this experience significant to him or her?

- What emotions do the people in the essay feel? How did *you* feel while
  reading the essay?

- Where does the essay come alive? Underline images or descriptions that
  seem especially vivid.

- If this were your paper, what is the one thing you would be sure to work
  on before handing it in?

2. Write a paper in which you remember a place you were once fond of—your grandmother's kitchen, a tree house, a library, a locker room, a clubhouse, a vacation retreat. Emphasize why this place was memorable. What made it different from every other place? Why was it important to you? What do you feel when you remember it?

3. Write a paper in which you recall for your readers some traditional ceremony, ritual, or observation familiar to you. Such a tradition can pertain to a holiday, a rite of passage (confirmation, bar or bat mitzvah, graduation), a sporting event, a family custom. Explain the importance of the tradition to you, making use of whatever information you recall. How did the observation or custom originate? Who takes part? How has the tradition changed through the years? What does it add to the lives of those who observe it?

Applying What You Learn: Some Uses of Recalling Experience

In College Courses.   Virtually every paper, no matter what it sets out to accomplish, can benefit from vivid examples and illustrations that you recall.

- Recalling a relevant personal experience to lead into a subject can engage your readers' interest and provide a springboard for your investigation, analysis, explanation, or argument. For example, your recollections of visiting or living in another country might introduce a sociology paper on cultural differences or a psychology paper on adaptation to change.

- Your recollection of events and experiences may provide the foundation for the reflective journal you keep during an internship or clinical experience.

- Your personal experience can add authority to the judgments and conclusions you offer in your academic writing assignments. In a paper for an anthropology course, you might recall your impressions of visiting the Anasazi ruins at Mesa Verde. In a paper for a human development course, you might include memories of caring for your grandmother.

In the Workplace.   You will also use recall as you tackle writing tasks on the job.

- Recalling past successes or failures can provide compelling reasons for adopting proposals you offer. If your department's method of distributing information has caused problems in the past, recalling those problems in detail would support your argument for changing the information management system.

- Detailed records that recall data can be valuable in resolving problems, satisfying customers or clients, or investigating causal chains. For instance, you might compile and analyze a list of customer complaints that could lead to meaningful changes in a product or service.
- Recalling past contacts with customers or clients can remind them of your company's valuable product or service and help to personalize your letters, e-mail messages, or other contacts with them.

In Your Community.   In your private life, your memory is not only the source for personal writing, such as journals, diaries, or correspondence, but also the basis for much of your writing as an involved member of your community.

- Your personal experiences can lend enormous impact to an appeal for changes in city plans, school policies, or government funding. If your child has been hurt by her school's policy of social promotion, recalling her embarrassment and frustration at falling behind her classmates can alert school board members to the problems inherent in such a policy.
- Recalling and recording how you have organized or implemented plans for a group activity can save time and improve the event the next time around.
- Relevant details are critical in correspondence to resolve a dispute over a purchase you made or a service you engaged. Recounting such details makes your claim clear and credible.

Chapter 5
Observing a Scene

John Storey/Timepix

Responding to an Image

A scene like this one might look and feel very different to different observers. Depending on each observer's emotions, background, and experience, certain details might stand out as important. In this image, who is the observer? Make a list of the details that might be important for this observer. Although visual details are obviously central, feel free to describe sound, smell, and touch, as well as any emotions that might come into play. Next, identify a second person who might be observing this scene. Which details might matter most to this other observer? In what ways are your two lists of details similar or different?

The terrain of New York is such that a resident sometimes travels farther, in the end, than a commuter. Irving Berlin's journey from Cherry Street in the lower East Side to an apartment uptown was through an alley and was only three or four miles in length; but it was like going three times around the world.

Questions to Start You Thinking

Meaning

1. What does White mean when he says there are "roughly three New Yorks"?

2. According to White, which of the New Yorks is the greatest? Why? What does this opinion suggest about White's own view of the city?

3. How, according to White, is the commuter like a bird? How effective is this analogy?

4. Explain what White means when he says, "The terrain of New York is such that a resident sometimes travels farther" than the commuter.

Writing Strategies

5. How does White use observation in his essay?

6. In paragraph 1, what concrete examples does White give of those who come to New York? What examples does he use in paragraph 2 to show what commuters never see?

7. Look at the order in which White presents the natives, commuters, and settlers. Is this organization effective? Why or why not?

STUDENT ESSAY

Sandy Messina

Footprints: The Mark of Our Passing

Submitted for an assignment in both first-year composition and environmental biology, Sandy Messina's essay looks closely at the relationships among the desert, its inhabitants, and humans.

No footprints. No tracks. No marks. The Navajo° leave no footprints because their shoes have no heels to dig into the earth's womb. They have a philosophy--walk gently on mother earth; she is pregnant with life. In the spring, when the earth is ready to deliver, they wear no shoes at all.

As I walk across the desert, I watch my shoes etch the sand dune. There they are following me: the telltale prints left on the brown earth. Each footprint has a story to tell, a story of change, a story of death. Many lives are marked by our passing. Our steps can bring death to the life of a flower, the life of a forest, the life of a friendship. Some of our passages can bring death to the life of a nation.

Navajo: Native American group indigenous to the Southwestern region of the United States.

I see my prints dug deeply into the spawning° grounds 3
of the desert lavender, the evening primrose, the desert sun-
flower, and the little golden gilia. Life destroyed. Birth
aborted. There under each mark of my passing is death. The
fetuses--seeds of desert color, spring glory, trapped just
below the surface waiting parturition°--crushed into life-
lessness. Man walks heavily on the earth.

He tramples across America, leaving giant footprints 4
everywhere he goes. He fills swamps, furrows hillsides, forms
roads, fells trees, fashions cities. Man leaves the prints of
his lifelong quest to subdue the earth, to conquer the
wilderness. He pushes and pulls and kneads the earth into a
loaf to satisfy his own appetites. He constantly tugs at the
earth, trying to regulate it. Yet man was not told to regulate, restrict, restrain the Garden of Eden but to care for
it and allow it to replenish itself.

I look at my own footprints in the sand and see nearby 5
other, gentler tracks. Here on the sandy hummock I see
prints, soft and slithery. The snake goes softly on the
earth. His willowy form causes no tyranny.° He has no need to
prove his prowess: he graciously gives warning and strikes
only in self-defense. He doesn't mar the surface of the earth
by his entrance, for his home is found in the burrows of the
other animals.

The spidery prints of the roadrunner, as he escapes with 6
a lizard dangling from his beak, show that he goes mercifully
on the earth. He does not use his power of flight to feed off
wide distances but instead employs his feathers to insulate
his body from high temperatures. He takes sustenance from the
earth but does not hoard or store it.

The wood rat scrambles over the hillock to burrow be- 7
neath the Joshua tree. His clawed plantigrade feet make sensitive little marks. He is caring of the earth. He doesn't
destroy forage but browses for food and eats cactus, food no
other animal will eat. His home is a refuge of underground
runways. It even provides protection for his enemy the snake,
as well as for himself, from the heat of the day. He never
feels the compulsion to be his own person or have his own

spawning: Fertile, productive.   **parturition:** Childbirth.   **tyranny:** Absolute power,
often cruel or unjust.

space but lives in harmony with many other animals, under the
Joshua tree.

   The Joshua tree, that prickly paragon° that invades the   8
desolation of desert, welcomes to its house all who would
dwell there. Many lives depend on this odd-looking creature,
the Joshua tree. It is intimately associated with the moth,
the lizard, the wood rat, the snake, the termite, the woodpecker, the boring weevil, the oriole. This spiky fellow is
hospitable, tolerant, and kind on the earth. He provides a
small world for other creatures: a world of pavilion, provision, protection from the harsh desert.

   Unlike the Navajo's, my prints are still there in the   9
sand, but not the ruthless furrows I once perceived. My mus-
ings over nature have made my touch on the earth lighter,
softer, gentler.

   Man too can walk gently on the earth. He must reflect on   10
his passing. Is the earth changed, bent and twisted, because
he has traveled there, or has he considered nature as a symphony he can walk with, in euphony? He need not walk heavily
on the earth, allowing the heat of adversity and the winds of
circumstance to destroy him. He can walk gently on the earth,
allowing life to grow undisturbed in seeming desert places
until it springs forth.

Questions to Start You Thinking

Meaning

1. According to Messina, how is her way of walking across the earth different
   from the Navajo way?

2. How has the process of observing her own footprints changed the writer's
   behavior? How would she change the behavior of the rest of us?

Writing Strategies

3. Why doesn't Messina plunge right in and immediately report her observations? Of what use to her essay is her first paragraph?

4. Paragraph 3 isn't observation, but what does Messina accomplish in it?
   With paragraphs 4, 5, and 6, the writer returns to observing — for what purpose? What is the function of paragraphs 7–8? Of 9–10?

5. What specialized words suggest that this essay was written for readers familiar with biology (her instructor and other students)? Would any of the
   jargon, or technical terminology, interfere with Messina's communication of
   her ideas to general readers?

paragon: Model of excellence.

Learning by Writing

THE ASSIGNMENT: OBSERVING A SCENE

Observe a place near your campus, home, or job and the people who frequent this place. Then write a paper in which you describe the place, the
people, and their actions so as to convey the spirit of the place and offer
some insight into the impact of the place on the people.

>   This assignment is meant to start you observing closely. Go somewhere
> nearby, and station yourself where you can mingle with the people there.
> Open your senses — all of them, so that you see, smell, taste, hear, and feel.
> Jot down what you immediately notice, especially the atmosphere and how
> it affects the people there. Take notes in which you describe the location, the
> people, and the actions and events you see. Then use your observations to
> convey the spirit of the scene. What is your main impression of the place?
> Of the people there? What is the relationship of the people to the place? Re-
> member, your purpose is not only to describe what you see but also to ex-
> press thoughts and feelings connected with those sights.

You can complete each of
the steps in this assign-
ment by using the *Writing
Guide Software for THE
BEDFORD GUIDE.*

Facing the Challenge: Observing a Scene

**The major challenge writers face when they write from observation is to
include compelling details that fully convey to readers the main impression of a scene.** As we experience the world, we are constantly bombarded
by sensory details, but our task as writers is to choose details that will make
a subject come alive for readers. For example, describing a tree as "a big tree
with green leaves" is too vague to help readers envision the tree or show
them what is unique about it.

Use the following questions to help you notice sensory details as a
writer:

- What colors, shapes, and sizes do you see?
- What tones, pitches, and rhythms do you hear?
- What textures, grains, and physical features do you feel?
- What fragrances and odors do you smell?
- What sweet, spicy, or other tastes do you sense?

After carefully observing and recording the sensory details that define the
scene, ask two more questions:

- What overall main impression do these details establish?
- Which specific details will best show the spirit of this scene to a reader?

Your answers will help you decide which details to include in your paper
and which to leave out.

WWW
To practice choosing
details, visit <www
.bedfordstmartins.com/
bedguide>.

Three student writers wrote about these observations:

One student, who works nights in the emergency room of a hospital, observed the scene and the community of people that abruptly forms on the arrival of an accident victim (doctors, nurses, orderlies, the patient's friends or relatives, the patient himself or herself).

Another observed a bar mitzvah celebration that reunited a family for the first time in many years.

Another observed the activity in the bleachers in a baseball stadium before, during, and after a game.

GENERATING IDEAS

For more strategies for generating ideas, see Ch. 16.

Setting down observations might seem a cut-and-dried task, not a matter of discovering anything. But to many writers it is true discovery. Here are some ways to generate the observations you'll need for your paper.

For more on brainstorming, see pp. 260–62.

Do Some Brainstorming.   First, you need to find a scene to observe. What places interest you? Which are memorable? Get out your pencil, and start brainstorming — listing rapidly and at random any ideas that come to mind. Here are a few questions to help you start your list:

DISCOVERY CHECKLIST

___ Where do people gather for some event or performance (a stadium, a theater, an auditorium)?

___ Where do people get together to participate in some activity (a church, a classroom)?

___ Where do people form crowds while they are obtaining something or receiving a service (a shopping mall, a dining hall or student union, a dentist's waiting room)?

___ Where do people go for recreation or relaxation (a party, a video arcade, a ballpark)?

___ What events do people gather at (a fire, a wedding, a graduation)?

Get Out and Look.   If no subject on your list strikes you as compelling, plunge into the world, and see what you will see. You might go to a city street or a country hillside, a college building or a campus lawn, a furiously busy scene — a shopping mall, an airport, a fast-food restaurant, a student hangout — or one in which only two or three people are sunbathing, walking dogs, or throwing Frisbees. Stand off in a corner for a while, and then mix in with the group to obtain different viewpoints on the scene.

For more on journal keeping, see pp. 265–66.

Record Your Observations.   Sandy Messina's essay "Footprints: The Mark of Our Passing" began as a journal entry. In her biology course, Sandy was asked to keep a specialized journal in which to record her thoughts and observations on environmental biology. When she looked back over her observations of a desert walk, a subject stood out — one deep enough for a paper for her English course as well.

Your notes on a subject — or tentative subject — can be taken in any old order or methodically. To draw up an "observation sheet," fold a sheet of paper in half lengthwise. On the left make a column labeled "Objective" and impartially list exactly what you see, like a zoologist looking at a new species of moth. Then on the right make a column labeled "Subjective" and list your thoughts and feelings about what you observe. The quality of your paper will depend in large part on the truthfulness and accuracy of your observations. If possible, keep looking at your subject while you write. An observation sheet inspired by a trip to a beach might begin in this way:

Objective	Subjective
Two kids toss a red beach ball while a spotted dog runs back and forth trying to intercept it.	Reminds me of when I was five and my beach ball rolled under a parked car. Got stuck crawling in to rescue it, had to be dragged free. Never liked beach balls after that.
College couples on dates, smearing each other with sunscreen.	Good way to get to know each other!
Middle-aged man eating a foot-long hot dog. Mustard drips on his paunch. "Hell! I just lost two percent!"	Guy looks like a business executive, but today he's a slob. Who cares? The beach brings out the slob in everybody.

Your notes in column one of an observation sheet will trigger more notes in column two. As your list grows, write on one side of your paper only: later you can spread your notes out and look at them all in one glance. Even in the sample observation sheet made at the beach, a main impression is starting to take shape. The second and third notes both suggest that the beach is where people come to let their hair down.

Include a Range of Images.   Have you captured not just sights but sounds, touches, odors? A memorable *image*, or evocation of a sense experience, can do wonders for a paper. In his memoir *Northern Farm* (New York: Rinehart, 1948), naturalist Henry Beston observes a remarkable sound: "the voice of ice," the midwinter sound of a whole frozen pond settling and expanding in its bed.

> Sometimes there was a sort of hollow oboe sound, and sometimes a groan with a delicate undertone of thunder. [. . .] Just as I turned to go, there came from below one curious and sinister crack which ran off into a sound like the whine of a giant whip of steel lashed through the moonlit air.

PLANNING, DRAFTING, AND DEVELOPING

For more strategies, see Ch. 17 on planning and Ch. 19 on developing.

After recording your observations, look over your notes. If you have made an observation sheet, circle whatever looks useful. Maybe you can rewrite your notes into a draft, throwing out details that don't matter, leaving those that do. Maybe you'll need a plan to help you organize all the observations, laying them out graphically or in a simple scratch outline. In either case, you'll need to organize sensibly and select details that help convey your main impression.

Consider Your Purpose.   What main insight or impression do you want to get across? Answering this question will help you decide which details to include and which to omit. Focusing on purpose will also help you avoid a dry recitation of observed facts.

For more organization strategies, see pp. 275–84.

Use a Sensible Method of Organization.   How do you map out a series of observations? Your choice will depend on your purpose in writing. One simple way is to proceed *spatially*. In observing a landscape, you might move from left to right, from top to bottom, from near to far, from center to periphery. Or you might see a reason to move *from the most prominent feature to the least prominent*, beginning with a sketch of an artist's busy, confident hands or the action under a basketball hoop.

You might also move *from specific details to a general statement of an overall impression*. In describing Fisherman's Wharf in San Francisco, you might start with souvenir sellers, tour boats loading passengers, and the smell of frying fish and go on to say, "In all this commotion, a visitor senses the vitality of the wharf." Or you could move *from common, everyday features to the unusual features you want to stress*. After starting with the aroma of frying fish and the cries of gulls, you might go on, "Yet this ordinary scene attracts visitors from afar: the Japanese sightseer, perhaps a fan of American prison films, making a pilgrimage by tour boat to Alcatraz." However you organize, be sure to add transitions—words or phrases that guide the reader from one point to the next.

For transitions that mark place or direction, see p. 297.

REVISING AND EDITING

For more revising and editing strategies, see Ch. 20.

Your revising, editing, and proofreading will all be easier if you have taken accurate notes on your observations. But what if, when you look over your draft, you find that you don't have enough detail? If you have any doubts, go back to the scene, and take more notes to flesh out your draft. Professional journalists often make such follow-ups.

Let a classmate or friend respond to your draft, suggesting how to use detail to convey your main impression more powerfully. Ask your peer editor to answer questions such as these about writing from observation:

FOR PEER RESPONSE

- What is the main insight or impression you carry away from this piece of writing?

- Which sense does the writer use particularly well? Are any senses neglected that could be used?

- Can you see and feel what the writer experienced? Would more details make this writing more compelling? Put check marks wherever you want more detail.

- How well has the writer used evidence from the senses to build a main impression? Which sensory impressions contribute most strongly to the overall picture? Which seem superfluous?

- If this were your paper, what is the one thing you would be sure to work on before handing it in?

For general questions for a peer editor, see pp. 323–24.

To see what parts of your draft still need work, you might consider these questions:

REVISION CHECKLIST

___ Have you accomplished your purpose — to convey clearly your overall impression of your subject and to share some telling insight about it?

___ What can you assume your readers already know? What do they need to be told?

___ Have you been selective, including observations that support your overall impression?

___ Have you gathered enough observations to describe your subject? Have you observed with *all* your senses? (Smell isn't always useful, but it might be.)

___ Do any of your observations need to be checked for accuracy?

___ Is your organizational pattern the most effective for your subject? Would another pattern work better?

After you have revised your observation essay, edit and proofread it. Check carefully for problems with grammar, word choice, punctuation, and mechanics — and then correct any problems you find. If you have added more details while revising, consider whether they have been sufficiently blended with the ideas already there.

Here are some questions to get you started when editing and proofreading your observation paper:

For more editing and proofreading strategies, see Ch. 20.

For more help, turn to the dark-blue-edged pages, and find the "Quick Editing Guide" section noted here.

EDITING CHECKLIST

___ Is your sentence structure correct? Have you avoided writing   A6, A7
fragments and run-on sentences?

___ Have you used an adjective whenever describing a noun or   A5
pronoun? Have you used an adverb whenever describing a verb,
adjective, or adverb? Have you used the correct form when
comparing two or more things?

___ Is it clear what each modifier in a sentence modifies? Have you   B1
created any dangling or misplaced modifiers?

___ Have you used parallel structure wherever needed, especially in   B2
lists or comparisons?

FOR GROUP LEARNING

Reading Your Writing Aloud

Try reading your draft aloud to your group. Rehearse your reading beforehand, and deliver it with feeling. Ask your audience to stop you when something isn't clear. Have a pencil in hand to mark such problems or ask someone else to note them for you. After you've finished reading aloud, ask for reactions. (Or ask your listeners any of the questions in the peer response checklist on page 61.) Have someone in your group record the most vital suggestions and reactions that your draft provokes. If possible, audiotape your reading and the reactions. Review both the written notes and the taped comments when you revise.

WRITING WITH A COMPUTER

When you write an observation, you will want to use modifiers (adjectives or adverbs) to qualify other words so that your observations are clear. However, intensifying prose with adverbs like *very* and *really* or adjectives like *beautiful* and *great* may confuse readers because these words are vague rather than concrete and precise. Read your draft aloud, and note any vague or imprecise modifiers you have used. Then, use the Find function in your word processor's Edit menu to help you locate all of the places in your paper where you have used *really*, for example, or another potentially vague modifier. As you find each modifier, ask, "Is it specific enough?" and "Will it guide my reader carefully through my way of seeing?" Delete any weak modifiers, or replace them with more specific words.

OTHER ASSIGNMENTS

1. To develop your powers of observation, follow Sandy Messina's example. Go for a walk, recording your observations in two or three detailed paragraphs. Let your walk take you through either an unfamiliar scene or a familiar scene worth a closer look than you normally give

it (such as a supermarket, a city street, an open field). Avoid a subject so familiar that you would struggle to see it from a fresh perspective (such as a dormitory corridor or a parking lot). Sum up your impression of the place, including any opinion you form through your close observations.

2. Try this short, spontaneous writing exercise. Begin the assignment immediately after class, and turn it in the same afternoon.

> Go to a nearby public place — burger joint, library, copy center, art gallery — and select a person who catches your eye, who somehow intrigues you. Try to choose someone who looks as if she or he will stay put for a while. Settle yourself where you can observe your subject unobtrusively. Take notes, if you can do so without being observed yourself.
>
> Now, carefully and tactfully (we don't want any fistfights or lawsuits) notice everything you can about this person. The obvious place to start would be with physical characteristics, but focus on other things too. How does the person talk? Move? What does the person's body language tell you?
>
> Write a paragraph describing the person. Pretend that the person is going to hold up a bank ten minutes from now, and the police will expect you to supply a full and accurate description.

3. The perspective of a tourist, an outsider alert to details, often reveals the distinctive character of places and people. Think of some place you have visited as an outsider in the past year, and jot down any notable details you recall. Or spend a few minutes as a tourist right now. Go to a busy spot on or off campus and record your observations of anything you find amusing, surprising, puzzling, or intriguing. Then write an essay on the unique character of the place.

Applying What You Learn:
Some Uses of Observing a Scene

In College Courses. Observing and accurately recording your observations is critical to your success in many courses besides English, especially those that involve labs, field trips, or practica that prepare you for your career.

- Students in the social sciences — sociology, criminal justice, psychology, anthropology — often take field trips requiring them to observe behavior closely and report their observations. Similarly, students in the humanities or fine arts may be expected to observe and record their impressions of a play, concert, exhibit, or historical site.

- Classes in health, childcare, or education may include clinical or field observations.

- Science classes — biology, anatomy, physics, or chemistry — may call for lab reports, recording observations of experiments conducted in the laboratory.

In the Workplace.   In many careers and professions, observing and analyzing what you've seen provide valuable information and lend credibility to your writing.

- If you choose a career in nursing, teaching, or social work, you will probably write case studies based on observation, sometimes for publication, sometimes for reference.

- Journalists must draw on what they observe to report news events accurately or write feature articles. During interviews, body language, tone of voice, and surroundings are often as revealing as the words spoken by the subject.

- Many careers will require you to make field observations and report your findings to your superiors. Architects and engineers observe at a building site; biologists and conservationists observe animals in the wild; astronomers observe movement in the night sky.

In Your Community.   Observation is a primary resource for your writing as an active member of your community.

- Vivid observations in an editorial or proposal calling for resolution of a neighborhood problem — a dangerous intersection, a poorly lighted park, a run-down building — will make the hazards real and immediate for your readers.

- Joining the planning group for a community project, such as a sports arena or a performing arts center, may require you to observe facilities in other communities and report back on your findings. Observing another community's festival or celebration also can provide ideas and identify logistical details for planning an event in your own community.

- You may find it necessary to report to authorities what you've observed at the site of an accident or a crime.

Chapter 6
Interviewing a Subject

Responding to an Image

You may or may not have heard of Laurie Anderson, but suppose you have been assigned to interview her. What does a careful examination of this photograph of her suggest? What might you say about her personality, for example, or her relationship to the photographer? What do you suppose she does for a living? What do her hairstyle, clothing, and facial expression suggest? What do you think the photographer finds interesting about Laurie Anderson?

Don't know what to write about? Go talk with someone. Meet for half an hour with an anthropology professor, and you probably will have plenty of material for a paper. Just as likely, you can get a paper's worth of information from a ten-minute exchange with a mechanic who relines brakes. Both the mechanic and the professor are experts. But even people who aren't usually considered experts may tell you things you didn't know and provide you with material.

As this chapter suggests, you can direct a conversation by asking questions to elicit what you want to find out. You do so in that special kind of conversation called the *interview*. An interview is a conversation with a purpose — usually to help you understand the other person or to find out what the other person knows.

Learning from Other Writers

WWW
For more examples of writing based on interviews, visit <www .bedfordstmartins.com/ bedguide>.

Here are two essays whose writers talked to someone and reported the conversations, using direct quotations and telling details to reveal engaging personalities.

As You Read

As you read these essays, ask yourself the following questions:

1. Was the conversation reported from an informal discussion or planned as an interview? Does the writer report the conversation directly or indirectly?

2. What does the conversation show about the character and personality of the individual speaking? What does it show about the author who is listening?

3. Why do you think the writer draws on conversation?

Monica Yant Kinney
Mining for Humor

Philadelphia Inquirer staff writer Monica Yant Kinney published her impressions of the comedic writer Jim Brogan in the 2000 alumni magazine of Notre Dame University.

The tools of the trade are modest: a spiral notebook and a Bic pen. After that, it's a lot of sitting. Thinking, waiting, remembering, hoping that a moment that made you giggle will at least make the tourists from Topeka grin.

It's not like there's a magical funny well from which a comic can draw jokes like water. If there is, could somebody please let Jim Brogan know? He's been doing it the hard way for more than twenty-five years.

Brogan has been called the "funniest guy you've probably never heard of." He's done stand-up everywhere, even starred in his own sitcom for a nanosecond. He is also the man who has helped select and sharpen Jay Leno's *Tonight Show* monologue every night for the last eight years — a job that has earned Brogan the ill-fitting title of L.A.'s premier "joke scientist."

Comedy isn't science. It's a lanky fifty-one-year-old guy in jeans and glasses talking about the tuna fish sandwiches his mom packed him as a kid. It's Brogan poking fun at his Catholicism and the fact that — despite a fat Hollywood paycheck and scads of famous friends — he's still kind of an oddball.

Brogan's comedy is much like his friend Jerry Seinfeld's, which is to say 5 that both men are storytellers who delight in sharing the absurdities of life night after night with a crowd of two-drink-minimum strangers.

Unlike many of his contemporaries, Brogan doesn't swear on stage. "We 6 call that 'humor helper,'" he sniffs, "relying on language to pump a weak joke up. In the long run, that really limits what you can do."

In Brogan's world of wonderfully wacky observations, there are no lim- 7 its. He writes jokes about putting his hand down [a] garbage disposal and worrying that he might "flip out and turn on the switch." He admits that while he still shops at Payless Shoes, "I'd rather pay more."

Much of the time, he's making it up as he goes along, improvising with 8 his audience in a form of pure, interactive entertainment you'll never find staring at a computer screen.

> *Brogan:* So, what do you do for a living?
> *Audience Member:* Nothing.
> *Brogan:* That's nice, but how do you know when you're done?

Brogan found humor in a strange place. The summer before his senior 9 year at Notre Dame, he dropped out of Army ROTC — in part out of fear of being sent to Vietnam. Seeking a release from the stress of his decision, he read *Enjoyment of Laughter*. In the book was a chapter about academics who studied humor and babies.

"What they found was: You had to smile, so they knew you weren't 10 threatening. Then you hold something out, the baby reaches for it, and then you take it away. That made them laugh," Brogan recalls.

It's no different in front of a roomful of grown-ups at the Improv in 11 New York, The Comedy Underground in Seattle, or Snickerz in Fort Wayne, Indiana.

"You're friendly to the audience. You hold something out for them, they 12 reach for it, and then you take it away," Brogan explains. "That's the closest thing to defining comedy that I can think of."

The opposite of comedy? It's excruciating,° humiliating personal agony, 13 if you wrote the joke that bombs. If someone else did, well, it's still painful and embarrassing, but at least it's not entirely your fault.

"I once did a television pilot about driving around the streets of Los 14 Angeles in a tank," Brogan recalls. "They thought it would be so hilarious. We went through the drive-through at Burger King. No one paid any attention. It didn't seem to be that funny."

Being funny for a living is still a job. Brogan works the *Tonight Show* gig 15 from 2 P.M. through dinnertime. He performs stand-up three or four times a week between 7 P.M. and 10 P.M. Every night from 10:30 P.M. on, Brogan is perched on Leno's couch, dissecting hundreds of jokes, contenders° for the next night's monologue.

excruciating: Intensely painful.   **contender:** Competitor.

The later they go, the more risks they take. The joke about the radio-   16
active goat on the loose in New Mexico seemed hilarious to Leno and Brogan one morning at 5:30 A.M. Of course, it tanked on TV.

The routine, the repetition — it isn't so different from a lawyer filing briefs   17
or a teacher following a lesson plan. Except, of course, for the bright lights, big
smiles, and thunderous applause that come at the end of Brogan's work day.

"When you find a joke that works, it's such a difficult nugget to have   18
mined out of a huge mound of dirt. You created it, you wrote it, you tried it
on stage and it worked. It's a delight, it's joy," he confides.

"But to me, it's mostly relief — relief that what I thought was funny actu-   19
ally is."

Questions to Start You Thinking

Meaning

1. How does Jim Brogan define comedy?

2. Kinney tells us that "Brogan doesn't swear on stage" (paragraph 6). What
   explanation does Brogan give for this? What does he call swearing in a comedy routine?

3. Kinney says when Jay Leno and Brogan work on Leno's monologue, "the
   later they go, the more risks they take" (paragraph 16). What does she mean
   by this? Is this her own assessment, or is it Brogan's?

Writing Strategies

4. Kinney's interview focuses, of course, on Jim Brogan. Where do you see Kinney in this essay? Would the essay be more or less effective if the reader saw
   more of the writer?

5. What is Kinney's thesis? What do the last two paragraphs contribute to the
   thesis? What do they contribute to your impression of Jim Brogan?

6. Find places where Kinney uses Brogan's own words. Where does she paraphrase? Is her choice effective? Why or why not?

STUDENT ESSAY

Dawn Kortz

Listen

*Dawn Kortz, a student
at Dodge City Com-
munity College, cre-
ates a lively portrait
of an elderly man.*

Mic-Leo's Café--named after the two sisters that own it,   1
Mickey and Lee--is tucked into a corner of the Eckles Build-
ing, a former department store located in downtown Dodge
City, Kansas. The first time I saw the café, I fell in love.
It is decorated in warm tones of green and burgundy, with
plants in almost every corner. The tables are of every shape,

size, and color imaginable, giving the room a cozy, comfortable feeling. Warm sunlight wafts through the café during business hours through the large plate windows that make up the front of the café. The people that come to Mic-Leo's Café are, for the most part, regulars--folks we all know by name. In the mornings the local businessmen and farmers can be seen gathering around the tables, drinking coffee, and sharing stories of grandchildren, politics, and golf. Among these regulars is Emmett Sherwood, who taught me how to appreciate the past.

I first met Emmett when I began working at Mic-Leo's Café as a part-time waitress trying to earn some extra money for college. Emmett, a grandfatherly man, has a gift for making everyone around him laugh with his colorful personality and stories. Interested in Emmett and how much of Dodge City's history he has lived through, I arrange to meet with him at the café early one afternoon. As we settle ourselves into a quiet corner I take notice of the deliberate, professional way that Emmett is dressed. It is obvious from his clothing that he is from another generation. Unlike my generation, which believes comfort is the most important quality in clothing, Emmett dresses for style. Today, like every other day, he is wearing dress slacks and a starched white shirt and tie. When I ask him about his clothing and why he wears a tie every day, he replies, "Going to town requires dignity." The only casual thing Emmett is wearing is his signature bright red beret. The red color matches Emmett's bright personality. Everyone who knows Emmett recognizes him by his hat.

I can tell that Emmett is excited to have a captive audience listen to his stories by the eagerness with which he accepts my invitation for this interview. As we begin to talk, I notice the far-off look in his eyes, as if he is trying to remember the old days, his youth, and how the city he loves looked when he first arrived. After each of us is served a cup of steaming coffee, Emmett begins by telling me he was born in Oklahoma but grew up in St. Johns, Kansas. As a young man of fourteen, he became attracted to the big city and in 1920 moved to Dodge City, Kansas, where he was married, raised a family, and continues to live.

Emmett points out the window and shows me where, on   4
Saturdays, the farmers would come to town and set up open-air
markets for the town folks to trade for baked goods, produce,
and eggs. "For me," he says, "going shopping at Wal-Mart
can't compare to the feeling I got when I dressed up to go to
town, see friendly folks, and help my neighbor." Emmett
fondly remembers the 1920s as a time of growth for the nation
and for Dodge City and as a happy, carefree time. With a
smile and a mischievous twinkle, Emmett remembers the saloons
and harlot houses--and especially the popular Harvey House
restaurant where the waitresses wore black and white outfits
which "sported the shortest skirts anyone in Dodge had seen
until then." He blushes and his voice drops to a hush as he
recalls this detail. He recovers and goes on to describe
Front Street, the only street at the time to be paved with
the distinctive red brick that now covers most of downtown.
Front Street was the center of business for Dodge City; the
Eckles Building, too, is located here. Emmett explains that
all of the most prominent establishments were located in the
downtown square, including the famous O'Neal Hotel. Emmett
glows as he remembers the dances and shows he saw there, but
his eyes glaze over as he recounts the fire that destroyed
the beautiful, majestic building.

I ask Emmett what Dodge City was like during the Great   5
Depression. Emmett recalls with sadness families and children
that he knew then. Many went hungry while the men went to
look for jobs, sometimes even leaving the state in search of
an opportunity. Other men, who before the depression worked
in stores, were forced to work fields for local farmers for
enough food to feed their families. "I am lucky to have always had a decent job and a place to sleep," Emmett says
reflectively. "People these days think they need so much;
they're wrong." Emmett's words are especially meaningful in
today's material world.

The time after World War II was important for Dodge   6
City. Emmett remembers it as a period of economic boom when
everyone had a renewed sense of pride in the United States.
After the war ended, the communities came together to celebrate the return of their fathers, sons, and husbands. For

the first time in history, it was common for women to work outside of the home, and Emmett remarks, "We never could get them back home!" I know he is teasing by his smile.

As we wind down our interview, coffee cups sitting cold   7
and empty, I thank Emmett for taking the time to talk. The café has emptied, and the sun has started going down--leaving a chill in the air. As Emmett slowly rises to leave, stretching his weak back from the long period of inactivity, I appreciate his age for the first time. As he walks down the sidewalk toward his car, he turns and with a tip of his head waves good-bye.

Today, when I look around the city in which I live, I   8
realize that what I see is not what Dodge City has always been. Emmett has given me a new appreciation of the past. He has instilled in me the importance of history--my family history, my town's history, my country's history, and my world's history. Every day when he comes into Mic-Leo's and I serve him coffee, I remember our talk, and I can only hope that there are others like Emmett sharing their life stories with people of another generation. I also hope that there are more people of my generation willing to take the time to listen.

Questions to Start You Thinking

Meaning

1. What is the main point of Kortz's essay?

2. What kind of man is Emmett Sherwood? How does Kortz feel about him?

3. How is Emmett's history the history of Dodge City? Is an interview an effective method of relating the history of a place? Why, or why not?

Writing Strategies

4. Why does Kortz begin her essay with a description of Mic-Leo's Café? What sensory details does she use to create the scene for a reader? How does Kortz's description serve as a frame for her conversation with Emmett?

5. What details does Kortz use to describe Emmett? What senses does she draw on? Does she provide enough detail for you to form a clear image in your head?

6. Where is Kortz's thesis statement? Is it stated or implied? How effective is this placement?

7. How much of what Emmett says does Kortz quote directly? Why does she choose to quote directly rather than paraphrase in these places? Would her essay be stronger if she used more of Emmett's own words?

Learning by Writing

THE ASSIGNMENT: INTERVIEWING

You can complete each of the steps in this assignment by using the *Writing Guide Software for THE BEDFORD GUIDE.*

Write a paper about someone who interests you and base the paper primarily on a conversation with that person. Write about any acquaintance, friend, relative, or person you have heard about whose traits, interests, activities, background, or outlook on life might interest your readers. Your purpose is to show this person's character and personality as revealed through his or her conversation—in other words, to bring your subject to life for your readers.

Notable student papers that grew out of a similar assignment included the following:

To interview someone for information about something, see Other Assignments on p. 79.

> One student wrote about a high school science teacher who had quit teaching for a higher-paying job in the computer industry, only to return three years later to the classroom.

> One writer recorded the thoughts and feelings of a discouraged farmer she had known since childhood.

> Another learned about adjustment to life in a new country by talking to his neighbor from Vietnam.

GENERATING IDEAS

For strategies for generating ideas, see Ch. 16.

If an image of the perfect subject has flashed into your mind, consider yourself lucky, and set up an appointment with that person at once. If, however, you have drawn a blank, you'll need to cast about for a likely interview subject.

For more on brainstorming, see pp. 260–62.

Brainstorm for Possible Subjects.   Try brainstorming for a few minutes, seeing what pops into your mind. Your subject need not be a spectacular or unusual person; ordinary lives can make fascinating reading. As you begin examining the possibilities, you may find it helpful to consider the following questions:

DISCOVERY CHECKLIST

___ Are you acquainted with anyone whose life has been unusually eventful, stressful, or successful?

___ Are you curious about why someone you know made a certain decision or how that person got to his or her current point in life?

___ Is there an expert or leader whom you admire or are puzzled by?

___ Do you know someone whose job or hobby interests you?

___ What older person could tell you about life thirty or even fifty years ago?

___ Among the people you know, who is actively engaged in a cause? Who has passionate convictions about society, politics, sex, or childrearing?

___ Whose background and life history would you like to know more about?

___ Whose lifestyle, values, or attitudes are utterly different from your own and from those of most people you know?

Set Up Your Interview.   First find out whether your prospective source will grant you an interview. Make sure that the person can talk with you at some length — an hour, say — and has no objections to appearing in your paper. If you sense any reluctance, probably your wisest course is to find another subject.

Don't be timid about asking for an interview. After all, your request is flattering, acknowledging that person as someone with valuable things to say. Try to schedule the interview on your subject's own ground — his or her home or workplace. You can learn a great deal from those physical surroundings, making the interview more realistic and the essay more vivid because of the details you can observe.

Facing the Challenge: Writing from an Interview

The major challenge writers face when they write from an interview is finding a clear focus for the paper. They must first sift through the enormous amount of information that can be generated in an interview and come up with an organizing idea — an angle or theme they wish to pursue in their essay. Then they must decide which observations and quotations will best support this main point about their interviewee's character or personality. Distilling the material you have gathered into a focused, overall impression may seem overwhelming. As a writer, however, you have the responsibility to organize your material for your readers, and you cannot simply transcribe your notes as a first draft of your essay.

To pinpoint the different angles suggested by your notes, jot down answers to these questions:

- What did you find most interesting about the interview?
- What topics did your subject talk about the most?
- What did he or she become most excited or animated about?
- What topics generated the most interesting quotations?

Your answers should help you to determine a focus — the aspect of your interviewee that you want to emphasize for your readers. Once you have a focus, you need to pick the details and direct quotations from the interview that best illustrate the points you want to make about your subject. Direct quotations can bring your subject to life, but you should use them strategically and sparingly to reveal the character traits that you wish to emphasize. Select colorful quotations that allow readers to "hear" your subject's distinctive voice. Make sure that the quotations — long or short — are accurate. To capture the dynamic of conversation, include your own observations as well as actual quotations.

WWW
To practice forming a focused, overall impression, visit <www.bedfordstmartins.com/bedguide>.

Ask a classmate to read the questions you plan to use in your interview and then to respond to the following:

- Are the questions appropriate for the person who will be interviewed?
- Will the questions help gather the information you are seeking?
- Are any of the questions unclear? How could you rephrase them?
- Do any of the questions seem redundant? Irrelevant?
- What additional questions might you ask?

Prepare Questions.   The interview will go better if you have prepared questions in advance. Questions about the person's background, everyday tasks, favorite activities, hopes, and aspirations are likely to encourage your subject to open up. Asking your subject to do a little imagining may elicit a revealing response. (If your house were on fire, what are the first objects you'd try to save? If you had your life to live over, what would you do differently?)

You can't find out everything about the person you're interviewing, but you should focus on whatever aspect of that person's life will best reveal his or her personality. Good questions will enable you to lead the conversation where you want it to go, get it back on track when it strays too far, and avoid awkward silences. For example, if you were to interview someone with an unusual occupation or hobby, you might ask questions like these:

- How long have you been a park ranger?
- How did you get involved in this work?
- How have you learned about the physical features and ecological balance in your park?
- What happens in a typical day on the job?
- Has this job changed your life or your concerns in any way?
- What are your plans and hopes for the future?

One good question can get some people talking for hours, and four or five may be enough for any interview, but we believe it's better to prepare too many than too few. You can easily skip any that seem irrelevant during the interview.

For more on using observation, see Ch. 5.

Be Flexible and Observant.   Sometimes a question won't interest your subject as much as you'd hoped it would. Or the person may seem reluctant to answer, especially if you're unwittingly trespassing into private territory, such as someone's love life. Don't badger. If you wait silently for a bit, you might be rewarded. But if the silence persists, just go on to the next question. Anytime the conversation heads toward a dead end, you can always steer it back: "But to get back to what you were saying about . . ."

WRITING WITH A COMPUTER

Reporters transcribe conversations and interviews into computer files so that they can work easily with their research. After you have conducted your interview, try to type in the exact conversation from the tape or at least as much of the interview as possible from your notes. If you have recorded the conversation on tape and also made notes, combine them in a single computer file, but use bold to distinguish your notes. Don't edit the conversation transcript and original notes until you have saved the complete document with a descriptive file name.

Open a new file when you begin your first draft. As you quote and summarize your subject's words and ideas in your draft, you can return to your transcript and notes to check his or her own wording. In this way you will be able to refine your interview while maintaining your original research in the first file. The Window menu in your word processor lets you go back and forth between two open files so that you can copy and paste quotations into your draft. Be sure to add quotation marks to indicate exact words from the interview.

If the discussion is moving in a worthwhile direction, don't be a slave to your questions. Sometimes the question that takes the interview in its most rewarding direction is the one that simply grows out of something the subject says or your inquiries about some distinctive item in the subject's environment. Observing your subject's clothing, expressions, mannerisms, and equipment may also suggest unexpected facets of his or her personality. For example, Kortz describes both the café and Emmett's clothing as she introduces his character.

Decide How to Record the Interview.   Many interviewers use only paper and pen or pencil so that they can take notes unobtrusively. Even though they won't be able to write down everything the person says, they want to look the subject in the eye and keep the conversation lively. As you take notes, be sure to record exact details on the scene — names and dates, numbers, addresses, surroundings, physical appearance, whatever. Also take time to jot down memorable words just as the speaker says them. Put quotation marks around them so that when you transcribe your notes later, you will know that they are a direct quotation.

A telephone interview may sound easy, but you won't be able to duplicate the lively interplay you can achieve face-to-face. You'll miss observing the subject's possessions and environment, which so often reveal personality, or seeing your subject's smiles, frowns, or other body language. Meet with your subject if at all possible.

Many professionals advise against using a tape recorder because it may inhibit the subject and make the interviewer lazy about concentrating on the subject's responses. Too often, the objections go, it tempts the interviewer simply to quote the rambling conversation from the tape without shaping it into good writing. If you do bring a tape recorder to your interview, be sure that the person you're talking with has no objections. Arm yourself with a pad of paper and a pen or pencil just in case the recorder malfunctions or the tape runs out. And don't let your mind wander. Perhaps the best practice is to tape-record the interview but at the same time take notes. Write down the main points of the conversation, and use your tape as a backup to check the accuracy of your notes or to expand an idea or quotation.

As soon as the interview ends, rush to the nearest desk or table, and write down everything you remember but were unable to record. Do this while the conversation is still fresh in your mind. The questions you prepared for the interview will guide your memory, as will any notes you took while your subject talked.

PLANNING, DRAFTING, AND DEVELOPING

For more strategies for planning, drafting, and developing, see Chs. 17, 18, and 19.

After your interview, you may have a good notion of what to include in your first draft, what to emphasize, what to quote directly, what to summarize. But if your notes seem a confused jumble, what should you do? Inevitably, much of what you collected will be garbage, useless information. As you plan, you have to identify what is most valuable and then throw out the rest.

For strategies using examples and details, see Ch. 19.

Evaluate Your Material.   Remember that your purpose in this assignment is to reveal your subject's character and personality through his or her conversation. Start by making a list of those details you're already pretty sure you want to include. As you sift your material, you may find it useful to consider these questions:

What part of the conversation gave you the most insight into your subject's character and circumstances?

Which direct quotations reveal the most about your subject? Which are the most amusing, pithy, witty, surprising, or outrageous?

Which objects in the subject's environment provide you with valuable clues about his or her interests?

What, if anything, did your subject's body language reveal? Did it suggest discomfort, pride, self-confidence, shyness, pomposity?

Did tone of voice or gestures tell you anything about the person's state of mind?

How can you summarize your subject's personality?

Is there one theme that runs through the material you have written down? If so, what is it?

For more on grouping ideas, see Ch. 17.

If you have a great deal of material and if, as often happens, your conversation tended to ramble, you may want to emphasize just one or two things about your subject — a personality trait, the person's views on one particular topic, or the influences that shaped those views. If such a focus is not immediately evident, try grouping your details to help you discover one.

Have a classmate or a friend read your draft and suggest how to make the portrait more vivid, complete, and clear. Ask your peer editor to answer questions such as these about writing from an interview:

- Does the beginning of the essay make you want to know the person portrayed? If so, how has the writer interested you? If not, what gets in your way?

- What seems to make the person interviewed interesting to the writer?

- What is the writer's dominant impression of the person interviewed?

- Does the writer include any details that contradict or are unrelated to the dominant impression or insight?

- Do the quoted words or reported speech of the person interviewed "sound" real to you? Does anything quoted seem at odds with the overall impression of the person?

- Would you leave out any of the conversation the writer used? Mark anything you would omit.

- Do you have questions about the subject that aren't answered in the paper?

- If this were your paper, what is the one thing you would be sure to work on before handing it in?

FOR PEER RESPONSE

For general questions for a peer editor, see pp. 323–24.

Focus on a Dominant Impression. Most successful portraits focus on a single dominant impression of the interview subject. If you had to characterize your subject in a single sentence, how would you describe him or her? See if you can state a single main impression that you want to convey about your subject. Then eliminate anything that doesn't contribute to this view.

Bring Your Subject to Life. At the beginning of your paper, can you immediately frame the person you interviewed? A quotation, a bit of physical description, a portrait of your subject at home or at work can bring the person instantly to life in your reader's mind. Kinney, for example, notes Jim Brogan's notebook and pen in her first sentence.

From time to time you'll want to quote your subject directly. Be as accurate as possible, and don't put into quotation marks anything your subject didn't say. Sometimes you may want to quote a whole sentence or more, sometimes just a phrase. Keep evaluating and selecting your quotations until they all convey the essence of your subject.

Double-Check Important Information. You may find yourself unable to read your hasty handwriting, or you may discover that some crucial bit of information somehow escaped you when you were taking notes. In such a case, telephone the person you interviewed and have specific questions

For more on using quotations, see C3 in the "Quick Editing Guide" (the dark-blue-edged pages).

FOR GROUP LEARNING

Conducting a Collective Interview

Let your whole class or just your writing group interview someone with special knowledge or expertise that you want to learn about. Public figures often visit schools and are accustomed to facing the questions of a whole class. Or someone on campus might be willing to discuss a problem that interests your group. Before you meet with your subject, plan the interview:

- What do you want to find out?
- What lines of questioning will you pursue?
- What topic will each student ask about?
- How much time will each group member have to ask a series of questions?
- Who will take notes?

Preview each other's questions to avoid duplication. Ask open-ended, rather than yes/no, questions to encourage a more interesting discussion. Your group's end result can be many individual papers or one collaborative paper based on the group's review of the interview notes and a fair division of drafting and revising responsibilities.

ready so that you will not take much time. You may also want to read back to your subject any direct quotations you intend to use in your final paper, so that he or she can confirm their accuracy.

REVISING AND EDITING

For more revising and editing strategies, see Ch. 20.

As you read over your first draft, keep in mind that your purpose was to make the person you interviewed come alive for your reader. Remember, too, that most successful papers of this kind focus on a single dominant impression and that readers will be interested in your observations and insights. This checklist may help you revise your work.

REVISION CHECKLIST

___ Are the details focused on a dominant impression you want to emphasize? Are all the details in your paper relevant to this impression?

___ Do the parts of the conversation you've reported reveal the subject's unique personality, character, or mood? Do you show what your subject cares most about?

___ Should your paper have a stronger beginning? Is your ending satisfactory?

___ Should some quotations be summarized or indirectly quoted? Should some of what you summed up be emphasized by adding specific quotations?

___ When the direct quotations are read out loud, do they sound as if they're coming out of the mouth of the person you're portraying?

___ Have you included revealing details about the person's surroundings, personal appearance, or mannerisms?

___ Have you added a few of your own observations and insights?

___ Does any of your material strike you now as irrelevant or dull?

If your portrayal still lacks life and focus, you may want to skim over your notes or listen again to selected parts of your tape recording. Do additional details seem worth putting in after all? Is there anything you now wish you had asked your interview subject? It may not be too late to add new material.

After you have revised your essay, edit and proofread it. Check carefully for problems with grammar, word choice, punctuation, and mechanics — and then correct any problems you find. Here are some questions to get you started when editing and proofreading your paper:

For more editing and proofreading strategies, see Ch. 20.

EDITING CHECKLIST

___ Is it clear what each pronoun refers to so that the *he*'s and *she*'s are not confusing? Does each pronoun agree with (match) its antecedent?	**A4**
___ Have you used the correct case for all your pronouns (*he* versus *him*)?	**A3**
___ Is your sentence structure correct? Have you avoided writing fragments and run-on sentences?	**A6, A7**
___ Have you used quotation marks, ellipses (to show the omission of words), and other punctuation correctly in all your quotations?	**C3**

For more help, turn to the dark-blue-edged pages, and find the "Quick Editing Guide" section noted here.

OTHER ASSIGNMENTS

1. Interview someone from whom you think you can learn a lot, possibly someone whose profession interests you or whose advice can help you solve a problem or make a decision. Your purpose will be to gather and communicate information, not to characterize the person you interview.

2. Write a paper based on an interview with at least two members of your extended family about some incident that is part of your family lore. If different people's accounts of the event don't always agree, combine them into one vivid account, noting that some details may be more trustworthy than others. Give credit to your sources. The paper that results might be worth saving for younger relatives.

3. After briefly questioning fifteen or twenty students on your campus to find out what careers they are preparing for, write a short essay summing up what you find out. What are their reasons for their choices? Are most students intent on earning money or on other pursuits? How many want lucrative careers because they have to pay back college loans? Provide some quotations to flesh out your survey. From the information you have gathered, characterize your classmates. Are they materialists? Idealists? Practical people?

Applying What You Learn: Some Uses of Writing from an Interview

In College Courses. Often you will find yourself interviewing people not because you are interested in their personalities but because they can contribute valuable insights into what you are studying.

- In a human development course, you might interview people at various stages of the life cycle — asking about the transition from student life to the working world, about parenthood, or about widowhood or retirement.

- History students may interview people who have firsthand knowledge of an event or era they are studying — a veteran of the Vietnam War, a farmer who remembers a major drought, a woman who participated in the famous Selma to Montgomery civil rights march.

- Education students may interview classroom teachers to gain an understanding of the demands and rewards of teaching.

In the Workplace. Interviewing is a useful tool, too, for writing on the job.

- Journalists rely on interviews with "informed sources" to give readers the complete story; conversely, political figures, authors, or actors often use interviews to air their opinions.

- Businesses interview customers to gain feedback on a product or service so they can better meet consumer demands. Interviewers compile and report results from broad, general surveys or from fewer, more extensive interviews.

- In circumstances that require investigation, professionals conduct interviews to gather evidence — insurance adjusters who are settling a claim, lawyers who are preparing a case, medical researchers who are tracking a disease.

In Your Community. As a citizen of the larger community, you will find conversation can provide the support you need in many writing tasks.

- Interviewing experts can help you make informed evaluations of community proposals. If county commissioners propose raising taxes to build a new sewage treatment center, you might talk to a waste water management expert about the merits of the plan.

- Information from experts can support your own position on an issue. For example, an official of the department of transportation might substantiate the benefits of a bypass to relieve traffic congestion in your neighborhood.

- Interviewing the missionary group speaking at your church is a good way to create a flyer or pamphlet seeking support for the group's work.

Chapter 7
Comparing and Contrasting

Rhymes with Orange by Hilary Price, © 2001

Responding to an Image

The humor in this cartoon hinges on the reader's understanding of contrasting cultural stereotypes. List ways that the cartoon compares and contrasts different cultural stereotypes. Then, list as many characteristics of each stereotype as you can. Write a one-sentence summary of each point of view that the cartoon suggests.

Which city — Dallas or Atlanta — has more advantages and more draw-backs for a young single person thinking of settling down to a career? As songwriters, how are Sarah McLachlan and Cheryl Crow similar and dissimilar? Such questions invite answers that set two subjects side by side.

When you compare, you point out similarities; when you contrast, you discuss differences. When you write about two complicated subjects, usually you will need to do both. Considering Mozart and Bach, you might find that each has traits the other has — or lacks. Instead of concluding that one is great and the other inferior, you might conclude that they're two distinct composers, each with an individual style. On the other hand, if your main purpose is to judge between two subjects (as when you'd recommend moving either to Dallas or to Atlanta), you would look especially for positive and negative features, weigh the attractions of each city and its faults, and then stick your neck out and make your choice.

Learning from Other Writers

WWW
For more examples of writing based on comparing and contrasting, visit <www.bedfordstmartins.com/bedguide>.

In this chapter you will be asked to write a paper setting two subjects side by side, comparing and contrasting them. Let's see how other writers have used these familiar habits of thought in writing.

As You Read

As you read these essays, ask yourself the following questions:

1. What two (or more) items are compared and contrasted? Does the writer use comparison only? Contrast only? A combination of the two? Why?
2. What is the purpose of the comparison and contrast? What idea does the information support or refute?
3. How does the writer organize the essay? Why?

Tom Standage
The Victorian Internet

Tom Standage, science correspondent for the Economist, compares the telegraph with the Internet to examine the bold claims made for new technology.

Although it has now faded from view, the telegraph lives on within the 1 communications technologies that have subsequently built upon its foundations: the telephone, the fax machine, and, more recently, the Internet. And, ironically, it is the Internet — despite being regarded as a quintessentially° modern means of communication — that has the most in common with its telegraphic ancestor.

Like the telegraph network, the Internet allows people to communicate 2 across great distances using interconnected networks. (Indeed, the generic

quintessentially: Perfectly embodying something.

82

term *internet* simply means a group of interconnected networks.) Common rules and protocols° enable any sort of computer to exchange messages with any other — just as messages could easily be passed from one kind of telegraph apparatus (a Morse printer, say) to another (a pneumatic tube). The journey of an e-mail message, as it hops from mail server to mail server toward its destination, mirrors the passage of a telegram from one telegraph office to the next.

There are even echoes of the earliest, most primitive telegraphs — such 3 as the optical system invented by Chappe — in today's modems and network hardware. Every time two computers exchange an eight-digit binary number, or byte, they are going through the same motions as an eight-panel shutter telegraph would have done two hundred years ago. Instead of using a codebook to relate each combination to a different word, today's computers use another agreed-upon protocol to transmit individual letters. This scheme, called ASCII (for American Standard Code for Information Interchange), says, for example, that a capital "A" should be represented by the pattern 01000001; but in essence the principles are unchanged since the late eighteenth century. Similarly, Chappe's system had special codes to increase or reduce the rate of transmission, or to request that garbled information be sent again — all of which are features of modems today. The protocols used by modems are decided on by the ITU, the organization founded in 1865 to regulate international telegraphy. The initials now stand for International Telecommunication Union, rather than International Telegraph Union.

More striking still are the parallels between the social impact of the tele- 4 graph and that of the Internet. Public reaction to the new technologies was, in both cases, a confused mixture of hype and skepticism.° Just as many Victorians believed the telegraph would eliminate misunderstanding between nations and usher in a new era of world peace, an avalanche of media coverage has lauded the Internet as a powerful new medium that will transform and improve our lives.

Some of these claims sound oddly familiar. In his 1997 book *What Will* 5 *Be: How the New World of Information Will Change Our Lives,* Michael Dertouzos of the Laboratory for Computer Science at the Massachusetts Institute of Technology wrote of the prospect of "computer-aided peace" made possible by digital networks like the Internet. "A common bond reached through electronic proximity may help stave off future flareups of ethnic hatred and national breakups," he suggested. In a conference speech in November 1997, Nicholas Negroponte, head of the MIT Media Laboratory, explicitly declared that the Internet would break down national borders and lead to world peace. In the future, he claimed, children "are not going to know what nationalism is."

The similarities do not end there. Scam artists found crooked ways to 6 make money by manipulating the transmission of stock prices and the results of horse races using the telegraph; their twentieth-century counterparts

protocol: Customs or etiquette of a given means of communication.   **skepticism:** A doubting or questioning attitude.

have used the Internet to set up fake "shop fronts" purporting to be legitimate providers of financial services, before disappearing with the money handed over by would-be investors; hackers have broken into improperly secured computers and made off with lists of credit card numbers.

People who were worried about inadequate security on the telegraph 7 network, and now on the Internet, turned to the same solution: secret codes. Today software to compress files and encrypt° messages before sending them across the Internet is as widely used as the commercial codes that flourished on the telegraph network. And just as the ITU placed restrictions on the use of telegraphic ciphers, many governments today are trying to do the same with computer cryptography, by imposing limits on the complexity of the encryption available to Internet users. (The ITU, it should be noted, proved unable to enforce its rules restricting the types of code words that could be used in telegrams, and eventually abandoned them.)

On a simpler level, both the telegraph and the Internet have given rise 8 to their own jargon and abbreviations. Rather than plugs, boomers, or bonus men, Internet users are variously known as surfers, netheads, or netizens. Personal signatures, used by both telegraphers and Internet users, are known in both cases as sigs.

Another parallel is the eternal enmity° between new, inexperienced users 9 and experienced old hands. Highly skilled telegraphers in city offices would lose their temper when forced to deal with hopelessly inept operators in remote villages; the same phenomenon was widespread on the Internet when the masses first surged online in the early 1990s, unaware of customs and traditions that had held sway on the Internet for years and capable of what, to experienced users, seemed unbelievable stupidity, gullibility,° and impoliteness.

But while conflict and rivalry both seem to come with the online terri- 10 tory, so does romance. A general fascination with the romantic possibilities of the new technology has been a feature of both the nineteenth and twentieth centuries: Online weddings have taken place over both the telegraph and the Internet. In 1996, Sue Helle and Lynn Bottoms were married online by a minister 10 miles away in Seattle, echoing the story of Philip Reade and Clara Choate, who were married by telegraph 120 years earlier by a minister 650 miles away. Both technologies have also been directly blamed for causing romantic problems. In 1996, a New Jersey man filed for divorce when he discovered that his wife had been exchanging explicit e-mail with another man, a case that was widely reported as the first example of "Internet divorce."

After a period of initial skepticism, businesses became the most enthusias- 11 tic adopters of the telegraph in the nineteenth century and the Internet in the twentieth. Businesses have always been prepared to pay for premium services like private leased lines and value-added information — provided those services can provide a competitive advantage in the marketplace. Internet sites routinely offer stock prices and news headlines, both of which were available over a hundred years ago via stock tickers and news wires. And just as the tele-

---

encrypt: To convert a message into a code.   **enmity:** Deep-seated, usually mutual, hatred.   **gullibility:** Tendency to be fooled.

graph led to a direct increase in the pace and stress of business life, today the complaint of information overload, blamed on the Internet, is commonplace.

The telegraph also made possible new business practices, facilitating the 12 rise of large companies centrally controlled from a head office. Today, the Internet once again promises to redefine the way people work, through emerging trends like teleworking (working from a distant location, with a network connection to one's office) and virtual corporations (where there is no central office, just a distributed group of employees who communicate over a network).

The similarities between the telegraph and the Internet — both in their 13 technical underpinnings and their social impact — are striking. But the story of the telegraph contains a deeper lesson. Because of its ability to link distant peoples, the telegraph was the first technology to be seized upon as a panacea.° Given its potential to change the world, the telegraph was soon being hailed as a means of solving the world's problems. It failed to do so, of course — but we have been pinning the same hope on other new technologies ever since.

In the 1890s, advocates of electricity claimed it would eliminate the 14 drudgery of manual work and create a world of abundance and peace. In the first decade of the twentieth century, aircraft inspired similar flights of fancy: Rapid intercontinental travel would, it was claimed, eliminate international differences and misunderstandings. (One commentator suggested that the age of aviation would be an "age of peace" because aircraft would make armies obsolete, since they would be vulnerable to attack from the air.) Similarly, television was expected to improve education, reduce social isolation, and enhance democracy. Nuclear power was supposed to usher in an age of plenty where electricity would be "too cheap to meter." The optimistic claims now being made about the Internet are merely the most recent examples in a tradition of technological utopianism that goes back to the first transatlantic telegraph cables, 150 years ago.

That the telegraph was so widely seen as a panacea is perhaps under- 15 standable. The fact that we are still making the same mistake today is less so. The irony is that even though it failed to live up to the utopian claims made about it, the telegraph really did transform the world. It also redefined forever our attitudes toward new technologies. In both respects, we are still living in the new world it inaugurated.

Questions to Start You Thinking

Meaning

1. What technology does Standage refer to as the "Victorian Internet"?

2. In what ways are the Internet and the telegraph similar? How are they different?

3. What ironies does Standage find in the story of the telegraph? How does he apply these ironies to other technologies?

panacea: A cure for all diseases, evils, and difficulties.

4. Does Standage feel the utopian claims made by proponents of the telegraph and other technologies were entirely without justification? What similarities does he see between the Victorians' expectations of their technology and modern society's expectations of the Internet?

Writing Strategies

5. Restate in your own words the thesis of Standage's essay. Where does he place it? Is this the most effective placement?

6. Find the topic sentence of each paragraph. What pattern has Standage used to organize his essay? What would be the advantages or disadvantages of a different organizational pattern?

7. What kinds of support does Standage use for each of his main points? Is the kind of support he uses for each point effective? Is it adequate?

STUDENT ESSAY

Tim Chabot

Take Me Out to the Ball Game, but Which One?

Student Tim Chabot compares and contrasts baseball and basketball, asking which sport deserves the title of America's national pastime.

For much of the twentieth century, baseball has been considered the national pastime of the United States. Hank Aaron, home runs, and hot dogs seem as American as Thanksgiving. Many American presidents, from Eisenhower to Clinton, have participated in the tradition of a celebrity throwing out the first ball on opening day of a new baseball season. But in the 1990s, baseball stars are being eclipsed by the stars of another game invented in America--basketball. Michael Jordan and Shaquille O'Neal, basketball greats and household names, have become more famous than any current pitcher or home run king. In addition, the 1994 to 1995 baseball strike has pushed the sport further out of the limelight as the public has become disillusioned with the greed of both players and managers. The strike has raised a question in the minds of many: Should baseball continue to be considered our national pastime, or should basketball take its place?

Both sports are very popular with American sports fans. In addition, both games attract fans of all races--white, African American, Asian American, Hispanic--and all classes, rich and poor, educated and uneducated. Baseball has become a national treasure through its appeal to a wide, wide audience. At a Saturday afternoon game, men, women, grandparents, and kids of all ages wait to catch a fly ball. The appeal of

basketball is growing, the sport having become popular in
urban and rural areas, on high school and college campuses.
Both sports are played in quite a variety of locations. Baseball games occur on neighborhood sandlots as well as official
diamonds. Basketball requires little space and equipment, so
pickup basketball games occur in almost every neighborhood
park and virtually anywhere that a hoop can be rigged up.

Although both sports are popular with American fans,   3
attending a baseball game is quite different from attending
a basketball game. Baseball is a family-oriented spectator
sport. Because of the widely diverse baseball fans with varied attention spans, attending a baseball game is like going
to an open-air carnival, and the game itself is only one of
the many spectacles. If fans are bored with the game, they
can listen to the vendors hawking ice cream, watch a fight
brewing in the bleacher seats, stand in line to buy peanuts
or hot dogs, participate in "the wave," or just bask in the
sun. Only diehard fans keep a constant eye on the game itself
because there are frequent breaks in the play.

In contrast, the central spectacle of any basketball arena 4
is definitely the game itself. Few distractions to entertain a
casual fan occur, except for cheerleaders for college teams.
Basketball arenas are always indoors, and the games are usually at night, creating an atmosphere that is urban and adult.
The constant motion of the sport rivets° attention to the game
itself. Attending a basketball game can be compared to an exciting night on the town, while watching a baseball game is
like relaxing with the family in the backyard.

The pace of the two games is also quite different. The   5
leisurely pace of a baseball game contributes to its popularity because it offers relaxation to harried Americans. Each
batter may spend several minutes at the plate, hit a few foul
balls, and reach a full count of three balls and two strikes
before getting on base, hitting a routine pop fly, or striking
out. While batters slow things down by stepping out of the box
to practice their swing, pitchers stall the play by "holding
the runners on" to prevent stolen bases. The substitution of
relief pitchers suspends the game and gives spectators an opportunity to purchase junk food or memorabilia. In games in

rivets: Commands or fixes attention to.

which star pitchers duel, the audience may see only a few men on base in nine innings and a very low score. Also, the tradition of the seventh-inning stretch underscores baseball's appeal to a person who wants to take it easy and relax.

On the other hand, the quick pace of basketball has contributed to its popularity in our fast-paced society. Players run down the court at sometimes exhausting speed for a "fast break," successful baskets can occur merely seconds apart, each team may score as many as one hundred points a game, and the ball changes sides hundreds of times, as opposed to every half-inning in baseball. Games can be won or lost in the few seconds before the final buzzer. Basketball players are always in motion, much like American society. The pounding excitement of basketball appeals to people who play hard as well as work hard.   6

These two sports require different athletic abilities from the players. Although baseball games are slow-paced, the sport places a premium on athletic precision and therefore showcases strategy and skill rather than brute physical strength. The choice of a pitch, the decision to bunt or to steal a base, and the order of batters are all careful strategic moves that could affect the outcome of the whole game. Baseball has been called the "thinking person's game" because of its emphasis on statistics and probabilities. Although mental strategy and dexterity° are emphasized, physical strength is important, too. A strong arm obviously increases the power of a player's throw or of his swing, and speed is essential in running bases. But intimidating physical ability is not necessarily a required element to become a major league player, and even out-of-shape players can become stars if their bats are hot. The importance of skill over brawn has contributed to baseball's popularity not merely as a spectator sport but also as a sport in which millions of Americans participate, from Little League to neighborhood leagues for adults.   7

Unlike baseball, basketball emphasizes physical power, stamina, and size since jumping high, running fast, and just being tall with long legs and big hands usually contribute to a player's success. Skill and dexterity are certainly necessary in executing a slam dunk or dribbling past a double team,   8

dexterity: Skill in using the hands or body.

but these skills are usually combined with physical strength.
In order to be a successful rebounder, a player needs to be
extremely aggressive and occasionally commit fouls. Many more
injuries occur on basketball courts than on baseball fields.
Perhaps the physical power and intimidation required in basketball have led to the media's focus on individual players'
star qualities. Magic, Bird, Jordan, and Shaq are icons° who
have taken the place of baseball stars of previous generations
like Joe DiMaggio, Ted Williams, and Babe Ruth. Furthermore,
in the international arena of the Olympics, basketball came to
be seen as a symbol of American strength and power, as the
1992 Dream Team demolished all of its opponents.

    If the rest of the world now equates basketball with   9
America, should we consider it to be our true national pastime? The increasing popularity of basketball seems to reflect the change in American society in the past few decades,
a change to a more fast-paced and aggressive culture. But
basketball doesn't yet appeal to as diverse an audience as
does baseball, and thus it doesn't seem to deserve to be
called a national phenomenon--yet. Until kids, women, and
grandparents are as prevalent at a Lakers game as are young
males, baseball will retain its title as the national pastime. But when the leisurely pace of the baseball game grinds
to a halt because of players' strikes, impatient fans may
turn to the exciting speed of basketball to rejuvenate their
faith in American sports.

Questions to Start You Thinking

Meaning

1. In what specific ways does Chabot claim that baseball and basketball are similar? In what ways are these two sports different? Do the similarities outweigh the differences, or vice versa?

2. Can you think of other ways these two sports are similar and different?

3. As a result of comparing and contrasting baseball and basketball, what conclusion does Chabot arrive at? Does he convince you of his conclusion?

4. Would you nominate another sport, say soccer or ice hockey, for the national pastime? If so, why?

Writing Strategies

5. What is Chabot's thesis? Where does he state it? Why there?

icon: Image or symbol.

6. How does Chabot organize his essay?

7. What transitional devices does Chabot use to indicate when he is comparing and when he is contrasting?

Learning by Writing

THE ASSIGNMENT: COMPARING AND CONTRASTING

You can complete each of the steps in this assignment by using the *Writing Guide Software for THE BEDFORD GUIDE.*

Write a paper in which you compare and contrast two items for the general purpose of enlightening readers about both subjects. The specific points of similarity and difference will be important, but you will go beyond them to draw a conclusion from your analysis. This conclusion, your thesis, needs to be more than "point A is different from point B" or "I prefer subject B to subject A." You will need to explain why you have drawn your conclusion. You'll also need to provide specific supporting evidence to explain your position and to convince your readers of its soundness. You may choose two people, two kinds of people, two places, two objects, two activities, or two ideas, but be sure to choose two you care about. You might write an impartial paper that distinctly portrays both subjects, or you might demonstrate why you favor one over the other.

Among the most engaging student papers we've seen in response to similar assignments are these:

An American student compared and contrasted her home life with that of her roommate, a student from Nigeria. Her goal was to understand more deeply Nigerian society and her own.

A student who was interested in history compared and contrasted millennial fears for the years 1000 and 2000, considering whether popular responses had changed.

Another writer compared and contrasted conditions at two city facilities, making a case for a revised funding formula.

GENERATING IDEAS

For strategies for generating ideas, see Ch. 16.

Find Two Subjects.   Pick subjects you can compare and contrast purposefully. An examination question may give them to you, ready-made: "Compare and contrast ancient Roman sculpture with that of the ancient Greeks." But suppose you have to find your subjects for yourself. You'll need to choose things that have a sensible basis for comparison, a common element. There is probably no point in comparing and contrasting moon rocks and stars, but it makes sense to bring together Dallas and Atlanta *as cities to consider settling in* or Montel Williams and Rosie O'Donnell *as television talk show hosts*. Besides sharing a common element, the subjects should have enough in common to compare but should differ enough to throw each other into sharp relief. A comparison of sports cars and racing cars might reveal much, but a comparison of sports cars and oil tankers would probably reveal little.

Try generating a list or brainstorming. Let your mind skitter around in search of pairs that go together. Have you experienced, seen, discussed, or read anything lately that suggests a suitable subject? You might find the following questions useful as you look for a topic:

For more on brainstorming, see pp. 260–62.

DISCOVERY CHECKLIST

—— Do you know two people who are strikingly different in attitude or behavior (perhaps your parents or two brothers, two friends, two teachers)?

—— Can you think of two groups of people who are both alike and different (perhaps two teams or two clubs)?

—— Have you taken two courses that were both valuable to you although they were quite different?

—— Can you describe two places where you have lived or visited? Do you prefer one over the other?

—— Can you recall two events in your life that shared similar aspects but turned out to be quite different (perhaps two sporting events or two romances or the births of two children)?

—— Can you compare and contrast two holidays or two family customs? What would be your point in setting this pair side by side?

—— Are you familiar with two writers, two artists, or two musicians who seem to have similar goals but quite different accomplishments?

You can also play the game of *free association,* jotting down a word and whatever it brings to mind. What comes to mind when you write *mothers? Fathers* perhaps. *Democrats? Republicans. New York? Los Angeles. King Kong? Godzilla.* Or whatever.

Facing the Challenge: Comparing and Contrasting

The major challenge that writers face when they compare and contrast two subjects is determining their purpose. Writers who skip this step run the risk of having readers ask, "So, what's the point?" After all, an essay that presents brilliant points of similarity and difference between the films of Oliver Stone and those of Stanley Kubrick will be ineffective if the reader is unclear about the purpose of the comparison. Do you want to argue that one director is more skilled than the other? Or perhaps you want to show how they treat love or war differently in their films? Keep in mind that you need to have a clear and compelling reason for comparing and contrasting. Consider the following questions as you determine your primary purpose:

• Do you want to inform your readers about these two subjects in order to provide a better understanding of the two?

• Do you want to persuade your readers that one of the two subjects is preferable to the other?

Asking what you want to demonstrate, discover, or prove *before* you begin to draft will help you to write a more effective comparison and contrast essay.

WWW
To practice choosing the most effective organizational pattern, visit <www.bedfordstmartins.com/bedguide>.

**WRITING WITH
A COMPUTER**

After deciding on the items you will compare, open a file and record everything you know about item A. Identify as many aspects of the item as possible so that you get most of what you know onto the screen. Then hit the Return key four or five times to create plenty of white space, and describe item B in the same way.

After you have written about each item, go back to item A, and look for features that can be used as headings to group details into logical categories. List these headings, but not any specific details, in the space you created with your Return key. Do the same for item B. As you list each heading for item B, move your cursor next to the most similar heading under item A, and type in the item B heading next to it. You can now see that the pairs of headings have much in common. If the headings do not correspond exactly, consider rephrasing them so that they more effectively link similar groups of details for both items. Whether you write a subject-by-subject or point-by-point essay, the common features you have identified will help you structure your essay around logical comparisons.

Once you have a list of pairs, put a star by those that seem promising. Ask yourself what similarities immediately come to mind. What differences? Can you jot down several of each? Are these striking, significant similarities and differences? If not, move on until you discover a workable pair.

For more on stating your main point in a thesis, see pp. 273–75.

Find a Purpose.   You need a reason to place two subjects side by side — a reason that you and most of your readers will find compelling and worthwhile. Ask yourself if you prefer one subject in the pair over the other. What reasons can you give for your preference? It's also all right not to have a preference; you can try instead to understand both subjects more clearly.

Next, consider what point you want to make through your comparison and contrast. Tom Standage wanted to show how much the Internet has in common with its Victorian predecessor, the telegraph. Tim Chabot wanted to explore whether we should continue to consider baseball our national pastime. Comparing and contrasting need not be a meaningless exercise. Try instead to think clearly and pointedly in order to explain an idea about which you care.

Limit the Scope of Your Paper.   If you propose to compare and contrast Japanese literature and American literature in 750 words, your task is probably impossible. But to cut down the size of this subject, you might compare and contrast, say, a haiku of Bashō about a snake with a short poem about a snake by Emily Dickinson. This topic you could cover adequately in 750 words.

Explore Each Member of Your Pair.   As you examine in depth each of your two subjects, your goal is twofold: you want to analyze each using a similar approach so that you have a reasonable basis for comparison and contrast, and you want to find the details and examples that you'll need to support your points.

If you are considering two events, procedures, or processes, try asking a reporter's questions — five *W*'s (who, what, where, when, why) and an *H* (how). Make two columns so you can write your answers for your pair opposite each other. If you are considering two events from the past, try using conversation to generate material: discuss what happened at each event with someone else who was there. Ask both people the same questions so that you can compare and contrast the same points without gaps in your information. Or if you want to contrast a public perception with what goes on behind the scenes, talk to someone who has been in the situation.

For more on using a reporter's questions, see pp. 267–68.

You can also try reading. If you are not sure whether a pair of possible subjects will work or you do not know quite enough about them for a full essay, go to the library. Read a few articles about the subjects to test the possibilities. You may want to pick a new pair and start again, or you may find you've made a good choice after all.

For more on interviewing, see Ch. 6.

PLANNING, DRAFTING, AND DEVELOPING

As you start writing your paper, remind yourself once more of your goal in comparing and contrasting the two subjects. What is it you want to demonstrate, argue, or find out? Then consider how some planning can help speed the job of writing. For one thing, even a rough scratch outline enables you to keep track of all the points you want to make, which easily may be lost or confused as you move from subject to subject. An outline will also help you figure out whether you need to come up with more specific details about your subjects. You can make an outline in your head, of course, but it is probably easier to keep track of things on paper.

For more on planning, drafting, and developing, see Chs. 17, 18, and 19. For more on outlines, see pp. 279–84.

Use the Opposing Pattern of Organization. In comparing and contrasting, two ways of organizing are possible. The first way is the *opposing pattern* of *subject by subject.* You state all your observations about subject A and then do the same for subject B. As an example, in Chapter 15 of *Educational Policies in Crisis: Japanese and American Perspectives* (New York: Praeger, 1986), the book's editors, William K. Cummings and others, use the opposing pattern to compare and contrast how the two countries think about education. For each country, they cover similar points, first the attitude toward career opportunities and then the attitude toward educational institutions.

For another example using the opposing pattern, see p. 315.

More salient, however, than these structural characteristics is the way that the two nations think about education. The United States fosters a myth of limitless opportunity. Football players can earn more than corporation presidents, and the local shoe store of today has the possibility of becoming one of *Fortune*'s Top 100 in 20 years. School is but one of several routes to success. For the individual who seeks the educational route, being a late bloomer is not necessarily an obstacle to upward mobility. Thus even when they enter college, many Americans have poorly developed intellectual skills. Most Americans are also relaxed about choosing their educational institutions, believing that what happens outside school and later in life may

Subject A: American attitude

Point 1: Careers

Point 2: Educational institutions

Shift to Subject B:
Japanese attitude

Point 1: Careers

Point 2:
Educational institutions

have more influence on their chances for success than what takes place in school. In contrast with the American belief in limitless opportunity, the Japanese assign great importance to a small number of career choices in the central government bureaucracy and the top corporations. They rank other careers in descending order and assume that an individual's educational performance will determine where he or she ends up in this hierarchy. Most Japanese parents seek to manage the lives of their children, from a surprisingly young age, so that the children will have the best chances of entering the top careers. Because admission to a prestigious university is known to be essential for gaining access to these attractive careers, parents are deeply concerned with the educational performance of their children. They exert every effort to ensure that their children earn good grades and enter the best schools. The large number of parents sharing this common belief results in severe academic competition. In contrast to Americans, Japanese children develop from an early age a realistic sense of the opportunities they can expect as they grow up.

This opposing pattern of organization is workable for a single paragraph or a short essay, but for a long essay or a more complicated subject, it has a drawback: readers might find it difficult to remember all the separate information about subject A while reading about subject B.

For another example using the alternating pattern, see p. 314.

Use the Alternating Pattern of Organization.   There's a better way to organize most longer papers: the *alternating pattern* of *point by point*. Working by this method, you take up one point at a time, applying it first to one subject and then to the other. Tim Chabot uses this pattern of organization to lead the reader along clearly and carefully, looking at each subject before moving on to the next point. His outline might have looked like the following:

FOR PEER RESPONSE

You may want a classmate or friend to respond to your draft, suggesting how to present your two subjects more clearly. Ask your peer editor to answer questions like these about comparison and contrast:

- In what ways does the introduction make you want to read the entire essay?

- What is the point of the comparison and contrast of the two subjects? Is it stated in the essay, or is it implied?

- Is the essay organized by the opposing pattern or by the alternating pattern? Is the pattern appropriate for the subjects, or would the other pattern work better?

- Are the same categories discussed for each item? If not, should they be?

- Are there enough details for you to understand the comparison and contrast? Put a check where more details or examples would be useful.

- If this were your paper, what is the one thing you would be sure to work on before handing it in?

For general questions for a peer editor, see pp. 323–24.

Thesis: Despite the popularity of basketball in the 1990s, baseball should
continue to be considered our national pastime.

For more on outlines, see pp. 279–84. For Tim Chabot's full paper, see pp. 86–89.

   I. Similarities of fans

      A. Appeal to diverse groups

         1. Baseball

         2. Basketball

      B. Varied locations

         1. Baseball

         2. Basketball

  II. Difference in atmosphere at game

      A. Baseball as a diverse family-oriented spectator sport

         1. Many distractions

         2. Frequent breaks in play

      B. Basketball as game-focused sport

         1. Few distractions

         2. Constant game activity

 III. Difference in pace of game

      A. Leisurely pace of baseball

         1. Slow batters

         2. Stalling pitchers

         3. Substitution of relief pitchers

         4. Low score

         5. Seventh-inning stretch

      B. Quick pace of basketball

         1. Fast players

         2. High scores

         3. Frequent changes of sides

         4. Constant motion

 IV. Different athletic abilities of players

      A. Baseball as a mental game

         1. Emphasis on athletic precision

            a. Strategy

            b. Skill

            c. Decision-making

         2. Physical strength less important

      B. Basketball as a physical game

         1. Emphasis on physical power

            a. Jumping high

            b. Running fast

            c. Being tall and big

            d. Being aggressive

         2. Importance of skill and dexterity

FOR GROUP LEARNING

Comparing and Contrasting Yourself with a Partner

Work with a partner to develop a single comparison and contrast essay for assignment 3 on page 98. Decide together what the focus of your essay will be: Your family backgrounds? Your hobbies? Your career goals? Your study habits? Your taste in music or clothes? Your political beliefs? Then each partner should work alone to generate a detailed analysis of himself or herself, given this focus. Come together again to compare your analyses, to decide how to shape the essay, and to draft, revise, and edit the paper.

For more on transitions, see pp. 296–98.

Add Transitions.   Once your essay is organized, you can bring cohesion to it through effective transitional words and phrases — *on the other hand, in contrast, also, both, yet, although, finally, unlike.* Your choice of transitional phrases will depend on the content of your paragraphs, but make sure that your transitions are varied and smooth. Jarring, choppy transitions will distract attention from your main point. While your task is to compare and contrast two distinct subjects, your ultimate goal is to produce a unified essay, each part of which works to support a meaningful thesis.

REVISING AND EDITING

For more revising and editing strategies, see Ch. 20.

Reconsider your purpose when you begin to review your draft. If your purpose is to illuminate two subjects impartially, ask yourself whether you have given your reader a balanced view even if you say more about one than the other. Obviously it would be unfair to set forth all the advantages of Oklahoma City and all the disadvantages of Honolulu and then conclude that Oklahoma City is superior to Honolulu on every count.

For more on outlines, see pp. 279–84.

Of course, if you love Oklahoma City and can't stand Honolulu, or vice versa, go ahead: don't be balanced; take a stand. Even so, you will want to include the same points about each city and to admit, in all honesty, that Oklahoma City has its faults. One useful way to check your comparison and contrast for either balance or thoroughness is to make an outline of your first draft and then give the outline a critical squint.

Make sure, too, as you go over your draft, that you have escaped a monotonous drone: A does this, B does that; A has these advantages, B has those. Comparison and contrast is a useful method, but it needn't result in a paper as symmetrical as a pair of sneakers. Revising and editing give you a chance to add any lively details, varied transitions, interesting later thoughts, dashes of color, and finishing touches that may occur to you.

For strategies for increasing coherence, see pp. 296–99.

In critiquing your draft as you rewrite, this checklist may prove handy:

REVISION CHECKLIST

— Does your introduction present your topic and main point clearly? Is it interesting enough to make a reader want to read the whole essay?

— Is your reason for doing all the comparing and contrasting unmistakably clear? What do you want to demonstrate, argue for, or find out? Do you need to reexamine your goal?

— Have you chosen to write about the *major* similarities and differences?

— Have you used the same categories for each item? In discussing each feature, do you always look at the same thing?

— Have you come to a conclusion about the two? Do you prefer one over the other? If so, is this preference (and your reasons for it) clear? Have you treated both fairly?

— Does your draft look thin for lack of evidence? If so, how might you develop your ideas?

— Have you avoided a boringly mechanical, monotonous style ("On one hand, . . . now on the other hand")?

After you have revised your comparison and contrast essay, edit and proofread it. Check carefully for problems with grammar, word choice, punctuation, and mechanics — and then correct any problems you may find. Here are some questions to get you started editing and proofreading your paper:

For more editing and proofreading strategies, see Ch. 20.

EDITING CHECKLIST

— Have you used comparative forms (for two things) and superlative forms (for three or more) correctly for adjectives and adverbs?   A5

— Is your sentence structure correct? Have you avoided writing fragments and run-on sentences?   A6, A7

— Have you used parallel structure in your comparisons and contrasts? Are your sentences as balanced as your ideas?   B2

— Have you used commas correctly after introductory phrases and other transitions?   C1

For more help, turn to the dark-blue-edged pages, and find the "Quick Editing Guide" section noted here.

OTHER ASSIGNMENTS

1. Listen to two different recordings of the same piece of music as performed by two different groups, orchestras, or singers. What elements of the music does each performer stress? What contrasting attitudes toward the music do you detect? In an essay, compare and contrast these versions.

2. Write an essay in which you compare and contrast the subjects in any of the following pairs for the purpose of throwing light on both. In a short

paper, you can hope to trace only a few similarities and differences, but don't hesitate to use your own observations, go to the library, or interview a friendly expert if you need material.

> Women and men as single parents
> Living at home and living away from home
> The coverage of a world event on a television newscast and in a newspaper
> The state of AIDS research at two moments in time — ten years ago and today
> The styles of two athletes playing in the same position (two pitchers, two quarterbacks, two goalies)
> English and another language
> Your college and a rival college
> Two differing views of a current controversy
> Northern and southern California (or two other regions)
> The experience of watching a film on a VCR and in a theater
> Two similar works of architecture (two churches, two skyscrapers, two city halls, two museums)

3. In an essay either serious or nonserious, for the purpose of introducing yourself to other members of your class, compare and contrast yourself with someone else. You might choose either a real person or a character in a film, a TV series, a novel, or a comic strip, but you and this other person should have much in common. Choose a few points of comparison (an attitude, a habit, or a way of life), and deal with each.

Applying What You Learn: Some Uses of Comparing and Contrasting

In College Courses.   College instructors know that distinguishing subtle similarities and differences between two subjects requires close attention, so they frequently ask students to demonstrate that understanding by comparing and contrasting.

- You would use comparing and contrasting if you were asked to "evaluate" the relative merits of Norman Rockwell and N. C. Wyeth in an art history course.
- A question that asks you to "consider" the consequences of doing business as a small corporation and doing business as a partnership calls for comparison and contrast.
- When you are asked to "describe" a subject, comparing or contrasting it with a similar, more familiar subject might be the best way to accomplish the task. If your instructor asks you to write a paper describing the

funeral customs in medieval England, comparing and contrasting them with modern traditions could give your readers a frame of reference.

In the Workplace.   In the world of work, you will constantly be comparing and contrasting the products or services of one company with those of another, the merits of one proposal with those of another, or the benefits of option A with the benefits of option B.

- Health professionals compare methods of treatment, the side effects of drugs, or the usefulness of various kinds of health-care equipment to help providers determine what is best for their patients.

- When you recommend a new procedure for your department, you will want to emphasize its strong points by comparing and contrasting it with the existing procedure.

- When hiring personnel, organizations compare and contrast applicants' management style, work experience, educational levels, and personal attributes.

In Your Community.   Comparing and contrasting is an effective method of analyzing alternatives in your community life as well.

- The advantages of one option over another quickly become apparent when you compare or contrast them, whether you want to choose a childcare provider, a fitness center, or an apartment.

- You can create an effective pamphlet urging voters to support building a new elementary school in your community by contrasting the costs and benefits of a new building with those of a renovated one.

- If you were appointed to recommend a resort for your organization's annual conference, you would want to compare and contrast accommodations, meeting facilities, food services, and dates of availability in your report for the executive board.

Chapter 8
Explaining Causes and Effects

Global Warming by Peter Fend, © 2001

Responding to an Image

This photograph has been altered and colorized for emphasis. Carefully examine the selection and arrangement of the photograph's elements and the addition of colors and type styles. How do these features suggest a cause-and-effect relationship? Based on your examination of the image, do you think it means just what it shows or something other than that?

When a house burns down, an insurance company assigns a claims adjuster to look into the disaster and answer the question Why? He or she investigates to find the answer — the *cause* of the fire, whether lightning, a cooking mishap, or a match that someone deliberately struck — and presents it in a written report. The adjuster also details the *effects* of the fire — what was destroyed or damaged, what repairs will be needed, how much they will cost.

Often in college you are asked to act and think like the insurance adjuster, tracing causes or identifying effects. To do so, you have to gather information to marshal evidence. Effects, by the way, are usually easier to identify than causes. Results of a fire are apparent to an onlooker the next day, although its cause may be obscure. For this reason, seeking causes and effects may be an uncertain pursuit, and you are unlikely to set forth definitive explanations with absolute certainty.

Learning from Other Writers

The following essays explore causes and effects, each examining a different culture.

WWW
For more examples of writing that explains causes and effects, visit <www.bedfordstmartins.com/bedguide>.

As You Read

As you read these essays, ask yourself the following questions:

1. Does the writer explain causes? Or effects? Or both? Why?

2. Does the writer perceive and explain a chain or series of causal relationships? If so, how are the various causes and effects connected?

3. What evidence does the writer supply? Is the evidence sufficient to clarify the causal relationships and to provide credibility to the essay?

William Severini Kowinski
Kids in the Mall: Growing Up Controlled

> Butch heaved himself up and loomed over the group. "Like it was different for me," he piped. "My folks used to drop me off at the shopping mall every morning and leave me all day. It was like a big free baby-sitter, you know? One night they never came back for me. Maybe they moved away. Maybe there's some kind of a Bureau of Missing Parents I could check with."
> –Richard Peck, *Secrets of the Shopping Mall*, a novel for teenagers

From his sister at Swarthmore, I'd heard about a kid in Florida whose mother picked him up after school every day, drove him straight to the mall, and left him there until it closed — all at his insistence. I'd heard about a boy in Washington who, when his family moved from one suburb to an-

William Severini Kowinski examines some of the underlying reasons for "mall culture" in this excerpt from his book The Malling of America *(1985).*

other, pedaled his bicycle five miles every day to get back to his old mall, where he once belonged.

There stories aren't unusual. The mall is a common experience for the 2 majority of American youth; they have probably been going there all their lives. Some ran within their first large open space, saw their first fountain, bought their first toy, and read their first book in a mall. They may have smoked their first cigarette or first joint or turned them down, had their first kiss or lost their virginity in the mall parking lot. Teenagers in America now spend more time in the mall than anywhere else but home and school. Mostly it is their choice, but some of that mall time is put in as the result of two-paycheck and single-parent households, and the lack of other viable° alternatives. But are these kids being harmed by the mall?

I wondered first of all what difference it makes for adolescents to experi- 3 ence so many important moments in the mall. They are, after all, at play in the fields of its little world and they learn its ways; they adapt to it and make it adapt to them. It's here that these kids get their street sense, only it's mall sense. They are learning the ways of a large-scale artificial environment: its subtleties and flexibilities, its particular pleasures and resonances,° and the attitudes it fosters.

The presence of so many teenagers for so much time was not something 4 mall developers planned on. In fact, it came as a big surprise. But kids became a fact of mall life very early, and the International Council of Shopping Centers found it necessary to commission a study, which they published along with a guide to mall managers on how to handle the teenage incursion.

The study found that "teenagers in suburban centers are bored and 5 come to the shopping centers mainly as a place to go. Teenagers in suburban centers spent more time fighting, drinking, littering, and walking than did their urban counterparts, but presented fewer overall problems." The report observed that "adolescents congregated in groups of two to four and predominantly at locations selected by them rather than management." This probably had something to do with the decision to install game arcades, which allow management to channel these restless adolescents into naturally contained areas away from major traffic points of adult shoppers.

The guide concluded that mall management should tolerate and even 6 encourage the teenage presence because, in the words of the report, "The vast majority support the same set of values as does shopping center management." *The same set of values* means simply that mall kids are already pre-programmed to be consumers and that the mall can put the finishing touches to them as hard-core, lifelong shoppers just like everybody else. That, after all, is what the mall is about. So it shouldn't be surprising that in spending a lot of time there, adolescents find little that challenges the assumption that the goal of life is to make money and buy products, or that just about everything else in life is to be used to serve those ends.

Growing up in a high-consumption society already adds inestimable 7 pressure to kids' lives. Clothes consciousness has invaded the grade schools,

viable: Effective or practical.   resonance: A profound and lasting impact.

and popularity is linked with having the best, newest clothes in the currently acceptable styles. Even what they read has been affected. "Miss
[Nancy] Drew wasn't obsessed with her wardrobe," noted the *Wall Street
Journal*. "But today the mystery in teen fiction for girls is what outfit the
heroine will wear next." Shopping has become a survival skill and there is
certainly no better place to learn it than the mall, where its importance is
powerfully reinforced and certainly never questioned.

The mall as a university of suburban materialism, where Valley Girls   8
and Boys from coast to coast are educated in consumption, has its other lessons in this era of change in family life and sexual mores° and their economic and social ramifications.° The plethora of products in the mall, plus
the pressure on teens to buy them, may contribute to the phenomenon that
psychologist David Elkind calls "the hurried child": kids who are exposed to
too much of the adult world too quickly, and must respond with a sophistication that belies their still-tender emotional development. Certainly the
adult products marketed for children — form-fitting designer jeans, sexy tops
for preteen girls — add to the social pressure to look like an adult, along
with the home-grown need to understand adult finances (why mothers
must work) and adult emotions (when parents divorce).

Kids spend so much time at the mall partly because their parents allow   9
it and even encourage it. The mall is safe, it doesn't seem to harbor any unsavory activities, and there is adult supervision; it is, after all, a controlled
environment. So the temptation, especially for working parents, is to let the
mall be their babysitter. At least the kids aren't watching TV. But the mall's
role as a surrogate mother may be more extensive and more profound.

Karen Lansky, a writer living in Los Angeles, has looked into the subject 10
and she told me some of her conclusions about the effects on its teenaged
denizens of the mall's controlled and controlling environment. "Structure is
the dominant idea, since true 'mall rats' lack just that in their homelives," she
said, "and adolescents about to make the big leap into growing up crave more
structure than our modern society cares to acknowledge." Karen pointed out
some of the elements malls supply that kids used to get from their families,
like warmth (Strawberry Shortcake dolls and similar cute and cuddly merchandise), old-fashioned mothering ("We do it all for you," the fast-food slogan), and even home cooking (the "homemade" treats at the food court).

The problem in all this, as Karen Lansky sees it, is that while families 11
nurture children by encouraging growth through the assumption of responsibility and then by letting them rest in the bosom of the family from the
rigors° of growing up, the mall as a structural mother encourages passivity
and consumption, as long as the kid doesn't make trouble. Therefore all
they learn about becoming adults is how to act and how to consume.

Kids are in the mall not only in the passive role of shoppers — they also 12
work there, especially as fast-food outlets infiltrate the mall's enclosure. There
they learn how to hold a job and take responsibility, but still within the same

mores: Moral principles or codes of conduct.   **ramifications:** Consequences stem-
ming from an initial plan, act, or process.   **rigors:** Harsh difficulties.

value context. When *CBS Reports* went to Oak Park Mall in suburban Kansas City, Kansas, to tape part of their hour-long consideration of malls, "After the Dream Comes True," they interviewed a teenaged girl who worked in a fast-food outlet there. In a sequence that didn't make the final program, she described the major goal of her present life, which was to perfect the curl on top of the ice-cream cones that were her store's specialty. If she could do that, she would be moved from the lowly soft-drink dispenser to the more prestigious ice-cream division, the curl on top of the status ladder at her restaurant. These are the achievements that are important at the mall.

Other benefits of such jobs may also be overrated, according to Laurence D. Steinberg of the University of California at Irvine's social ecology department, who did a study on teenage employment. Their jobs, he found, are generally simple, mindlessly repetitive, and boring. They don't really learn anything, and the jobs don't lead anywhere. Teenagers also work primarily with other teenagers; even their supervisors are often just a little older than they are. "Kids need to spend time with adults," Steinberg told me. "Although they get benefits from peer relationships, without parents and other adults it's one-sided socialization. They hang out with each other, have age-segregated jobs, and watch TV."   13

Perhaps much of this is not so terrible or even so terribly different. Now that they have so much more to contend with in their lives, adolescents probably need more time to spend with other adolescents without adult impositions, just to sort things out. Though it is more concentrated in the mall (and therefore perhaps a clearer target), the value system there is really the dominant one of the whole society. Attitudes about curiosity, initiative, self-expression, empathy, and disinterested learning aren't necessarily made in the mall; they are mirrored there, perhaps a bit more intensely — as through a glass brightly.   14

Besides, the mall is not without its educational opportunities. There are bookstores, where there is at least a short shelf of classics at great prices, and other books from which it is possible to learn more than how to do sit-ups. There are tools, from hammers to VCRs, and products, from clothes to records, that can help the young find and express themselves. There are older people with stories, and places to be alone or to talk one-on-one with a kindred spirit. And there is always the passing show.   15

The mall itself may very well be an education about the future. I was struck with the realization, as early as my first forays into Greengate,[1] that the mall is only one of a number of enclosed and controlled environments that are part of the lives of today's young. The mall is just an extension, say, of those large suburban schools — only there's Karmelkorn instead of chem lab, the ice rink instead of the gym: It's high school without the impertinence of classes.   16

Growing up, moving from home to school to the mall — from enclosure to enclosure, transported in cars — is a curiously continuous process, without   17

---

[1] Greengate Mall in Greensburg, Pennsylvania, where Kowinski began his research on malls [Eds.].

much in the way of contrast or contact with unenclosed reality. Places must tend to blur into one another. But whatever differences and dangers there are in this, the skills these adolescents are learning may turn out to be useful in their later lives. For we seem to be moving inexorably° into an age of pre-planned and regulated environments, and this is the world they will inherit.

Still, it might be better if they had more of a choice. One teenaged girl   18 confessed to *CBS Reports* that she sometimes felt she was missing something by hanging out at the mall so much. "But I'm here," she said, "and this is what I have."

Questions to Start You Thinking

Meaning

1. According to Kowinski, what do teenagers seek at the mall?

2. In paragraph 6, Kowinski quotes a study concluding that mall management and teens share "the same set of values." What are the values they share? What is the effect of these values on teenagers?

3. How do mall experiences shape the kinds of adults these teens become?

4. Kowinski compares the mall experience to high school. In what ways is it similar to high school? How is it different?

Writing Strategies

5. What is the thesis of Kowinski's essay? Where do you find it?

6. Kowinski examines both negative and positive effects of mall life on teens. In which paragraphs do you find negative effects? Where does he include positive effects? How well does this organization work?

7. Does Kowinski's essay deal predominantly with causes or effects? Where and to what degree does he examine each of these? How would his essay change if he limited his focus to only causes or only effects?

8. Kowinski begins his essay with a quotation from Richard Peck's *Secrets of the Shopping Mall.* Is this an effective beginning? Why or why not? In what other ways might he have begun his essay?

STUDENT ESSAY

Yun Yung Choi
Invisible Women

For me, growing up in a small suburb on the outskirts of   1 Seoul, the adults' preference for boys seemed quite natural. All the important people that I knew--doctors, lawyers, po-licemen, and soldiers--were men. On the other hand, most of the women that I knew were either housekeepers or housewives

Yun Yung Choi examines the adoption of a new state religion in her native Korea and the effects of that adoption on Korean women.

inexorably: Incapable of being stopped or deterred.

whose duty seemed to be to obey and please the men of the
family. When my teachers at school asked me what I wanted to
be when I grew up, I would answer, "I want to be the wife of
the president." Because all women must become wives and mothers, I thought, becoming the wife of the president would be
the highest achievement for a woman. I knew that the birth of
a boy was a greatly desired and celebrated event, whereas the
birth of a girl was a disappointing one, accompanied by the
frequent words of consolation for the sad parents: "A daughter is her mother's chief help in keeping house."

These attitudes toward women, widely considered the con-   2
tinuation of an unbroken chain of tradition, are, in fact,
only a few hundred years old, a relatively short period considering Korea's long history. During the first half of the Yi
dynasty, which lasted from 1392 to 1910, and during the Koryo
period, which preceded the Yi dynasty, women were treated almost as equals with many privileges that were denied them
during the latter half of the Yi dynasty. This turnabout in
women's place in Korean society was brought about by one of
the greatest influences that shaped the government, literature, and thoughts of the Korean people--Confucianism.°

Throughout the Koryo period, which lasted from 918 to   3
1392, and throughout the first half of the Yi dynasty, according to Laurel Kendall in her book View from the Inner
Room, women were important and contributing members of the
society and not marginal and dependent as they later became.
Women were, to a large extent, in command of their own lives.
They were permitted to own property and receive inheritances
from their fathers. Wedding ceremonies were held in the
bride's house, where the couple lived, and the wife retained
her surname. Women were also allowed freedom of movement--
that is, they were able to go outside the house without any
feelings of shame or embarrassment.

With the introduction of Confucianism, however, the   4
rights and privileges that women enjoyed were confiscated.
The government of the Yi dynasty made great efforts to incorporate into society the Confucian ideologies, including the
principle of agnation. This principle, according to Kendall,

Confucianism: Ethical system based on the teachings of Chinese philosopher Confucius
(551–479 B.C.)

made men the important members of society and relegated°
women to a dependent position. The government succeeded in
Confucianizing the country and encouraging the acceptance of
Confucian proverbs such as the following: "Men are honored,
but women are abased." "A daughter is a 'robber woman' who
carries household wealth away when she marries."

The unfortunate effects of this Confucianization in the   5
lives of women were numerous. The most noticeable was the
virtual confinement of women. They were forced to remain un-
seen in the anbang, the inner room of the house. This room
was the women's domain, or, rather, the women's prison. Outside, a woman was carried through the streets in a closed
sedan chair. Walking outside, she had to wear a veil that
covered her face and could travel abroad only after nightfall. Thus, it is no wonder that Westerners traveling through
Korea in the late nineteenth century expressed surprise at
the apparent absence of women in the country.

Women received no formal education. Their only schooling   6
came from government textbooks. By giving instruction on the
virtuous° conduct of women, these books attempted to fit
women into the Confucian stereotype--meek, quiet, and obedi-
ent. Thus, this Confucian society acclaimed particular women
not for their talent or achievement but for the degree of
perfection with which they were able to mimic the stereotype.

A woman even lost her identity in such a society. Once   7
married, she became a stranger to her natal° family, becoming
a member of her husband's family. Her name was omitted from
the family chokpo, or genealogy book, and was entered in the
chokpo of her in-laws as a mere "wife" next to her husband's
name.

Even a desirable marriage, the ultimate hope for a   8
woman, failed to provide financial and emotional security for
her. Failure to produce a son was legal grounds for sending
the wife back to her natal home, thereby subjecting the woman
to the greatest humiliation and to a life of continued shame.
And because the Confucian ideology stressed a wife's devotion
to her husband as the greatest of womanly virtues, widows
were forced to avoid social disgrace by remaining faithfully

relegated: Reduced to a less important position.   **virtuous:** Moral, honorable.
natal: Relating to one's birth.

unmarried, no matter how young they were. As women lost their rights to own or inherit property, these widows, with no means to support themselves, suffered great hardships. Thus, as Sandra Martielle says in Virtues in Conflict, what the government considered "the ugly custom of remarriage" was slowly eliminated at the expense of women's happiness.

This male-dominated system of Confucianism is one of the surviving traditions from the Yi dynasty. Although the Constitution of the Republic of Korea proclaimed on July 17, 1948, guarantees individual freedom and sexual equality, these ideals failed to have any immediate effect on the Korean mentality that stubbornly adheres to its belief in the superiority of men. Women still regard marriage as their prime objective in life, and little girls still wish to become the doctor's wife, the lawyer's wife, and even the president's wife. But as the system of Confucianism is slowly being forced out of existence by new legal and social standards, perhaps a day will come, after all, when a little girl will stand up in class and answer, "I want to be the president."

9

Questions to Start You Thinking

Meaning

1. What effect does Choi observe? What cause does she attribute it to?

2. What specific changes in Korean culture does Choi attribute to the introduction of Confucianism?

3. What evidence do you find of the writer's critically rethinking an earlier belief and then revising it? What do you think may have influenced her to change her belief?

Writing Strategies

4. What does Choi gain by beginning and ending with her personal experience?

5. Where does Choi use the strategy of comparing and contrasting? Do you think this is effective?

Learning by Writing

THE ASSIGNMENT: EXPLAINING CAUSES AND EFFECTS

You can complete each of the steps in this assignment by using the *Writing Guide Software for THE BEDFORD GUIDE.*

Pick a disturbing fact or situation that you have observed, and seek out the causes and effects to help you and your readers understand the issue better. In your essay, you may limit your ideas to the causes *or* the effects, or you may include both but emphasize one more than the other. Yun Yung Choi uses the last approach when she briefly identifies the cause of the status of

Korean women (Confucianism) but spends most of her essay detailing the effects of this cause.

The situation you choose may have affected you and people you know well, such as the limited number of scholarships available for college students, the difficulty of working while going to school, or divorce in the family. It might have affected people in your city or region — a small voter turnout in a city or county election, decaying bridge supports, or pet owners not using pooper-scoopers. It may affect society at large — economic upheavals in other countries, drunk driving, or the high cost of health care. It might be gender or racial stereotypes on television, unsavory language in music lyrics, spouse abuse, teenage suicide, pollution, the shortage of male elementary school teachers, or the effects of using dragnets for ocean fishing. Don't think you must choose an earthshaking topic to write a good paper. On the contrary, you will do a better job if you are personally familiar with the situation you choose.

Papers written in response to this assignment have included the following:

One student recollected her observations of the hardships that Indians in rural Mexico face and cited these as one cause of the recent rebellions there.

Another analyzed the negative attitudes of men toward women in the company where she worked and the resulting tension among workers. She identified some of the effects as inefficiency and low production.

A third contended that buildings constructed in Miami are not built to withstand hurricane-force winds. One reason he cited is the inadequate city inspection system.

GENERATING IDEAS

Find a Topic.   What familiar situation would be informative or instructive to explore? This assignment leaves you the option of writing from personal experience, from what you know or can find out, or from a combination of the two. Begin by letting your thoughts wander over the results of an undesirable situation. Has the situation always been this way? Or has it changed in the last few years? Have things gotten better or worse?

For more strategies for generating ideas, see Ch. 16.

The ideas in the following list may help you search your memory:

> **DISCOVERY CHECKLIST**
> ___ Has a difficult situation resulted from a change in your life (a new job; a fluctuation in income; personal or family upheaval following death, divorce, accident, illness, or good fortune; a new school)?
> ___ Has the environment changed (due to air pollution, a flood or a storm, a new industry, the failure of an old industry)?
> ___ Has a disturbing situation been caused by an invention (the computer, the VCR, the television, the ATM, the cell phone)?
> ___ Do certain employment trends cause you concern (for women in management, for blacks in the military, for white males in nursing)?

____ Is a situation in your neighborhood, city, or state causing problems for you (traffic, pollution, population, health care)?

For more on brainstorming, see pp. 260 – 62.

When your thoughts begin to percolate, jot down a list of likely topics. Then choose the idea that you care most about and that promises to be neither too large nor too small. A paper confined to the causes of a family's move from New Jersey to Montana might be only one sentence long: "My father's company transferred him." But the subsequent effects of the move on the family might form the basis of an interesting essay. On the other hand, you might need hundreds of pages to study all the effects of gangs in urban high schools. Instead, you might consider just one unusual effect, such as gang members staking out territory in the parking lot of a local school.

List Causes and Effects.   Your choice tentatively made, write for ten or fifteen minutes, identifying likely causes and effects. Look first for *immediate causes* — those evident and close at hand that clearly led to the situation. Then look for *remote causes* — underlying, more basic reasons for the situation, perhaps causes that came earlier. The immediate cause of unemployment in a town might be a factory closing, but the more remote cause might be foreign competition, against which the local company couldn't survive. Other causes might be contributing, related, or even hidden factors. When looking for effects, also consider both *immediate* consequences and more distant *remote* effects.

WWW
To practice limiting (or *narrowing*) a subject, visit <www.bedfordstmartins .com/bedguide>.

Facing the Challenge: Causes and Effects

The major challenge writers face when they explore causal relationships is to limit the subject. When you explore a given phenomenon — from teenage drug use to the success of your favorite band — devoting equal space to all possible causes and effects will either overwhelm your readers or put them to sleep. Instead, you need to decide what you want to show your readers — and then emphasize the causal relationships that will help achieve this purpose.

Once you can articulate your thesis as a cause-and-effect relationship, you are ready to decide which part of the relationship — cause or effect — to stress and how to limit your ideas to strengthen your overall point. If you are writing an essay about your parents' divorce, for example, you may be tempted to discuss all the possible *causes* for their separation and then analyze all the *effects* it has had on you. Your readers, however, won't want to know about every single argument your parents had as you explore the causes of their divorce. Both you and your readers will have a much easier time if you make some decisions about your focus:

• Do you want to focus on *causes* or *effects*?
• Which of your explanations are most and least effective?
• How can you emphasize the points that are most important to you?
• Which relatively insignificant or irrelevant ideas can you omit?

Try making separate lists of causes and effects and, next to each item, noting your evidence for it. You can then tell from a glance at your list exactly where you need to generate more material. Star or underline any causes and effects that stand out as major ones. A way to rate the items on your list is to ask, How significant is this cause? Would the situation not exist without it? (This major cause deserves a big star.) Or would the situation have arisen without it, for some other reason? (This minor cause might still matter but be less important.) Has this effect had a resounding impact? Is it necessary to explain the results adequately?

PLANNING, DRAFTING, AND DEVELOPING

Yun Yung Choi's "Invisible Women" follows a clear plan. The essay was written from a brief scratch outline that simply lists the effects of the change:

For Choi's complete essay, see pp. 105–08.

For more about informal outlines, see pp. 279–81.

Intro — Personal anecdote

  – Tie with Korean history

  – State thesis: This turnabout in women's place in Korean society was brought about by one of the greatest influences that shaped the government, literature, and thoughts of the Korean people — Confucianism.

Comparison and contrast of status of women before and after Confucianism

Effects of Confucianism on women

  1. Confinement
  2. Little education
  3. Loss of identity in marriage
  4. No property rights

Conclusion: Impact still evident in Korea today but some hints of change

The paper makes its point: it identifies Confucianism as the reason for the status of Korean women and details four specific effects of Confucianism on women in Korean society. And it shows that cause and effect are closely related: Confucianism is the cause of the change in the status of Korean women, and Confucianism has had specific effects on Korean women.

For strategies for stating your main point in a thesis, see pp. 271–75.

Organize Causes and Effects.   The main part of your paper — showing how the situation came about (the causes) or what followed as a result (the effects) or both — more than likely will follow one of these patterns:

I. The situation	I. The situation	I. The situation
II. Its causes	II. Its effects	II. Its causes
		III. Its effects

You can begin planning your paper by grouping the causes and effects and then classifying them as major or minor. If, for example, you are writing about the reasons more college students accumulate credit card debt now than they did a generation ago, you might list (1) easy credit, (2) high credit limits, and (3) compulsive buying. On reflection you might decide that

For more planning strategies, see Ch. 17.

compulsive buying — especially of CDs, videos, vinyls, software, games, and electronic equipment — is a major cause and that the availability of credit actually is a minor one. You could then organize the causes from least important to most important, emphasizing the major one by giving it more space and the final place in your essay.

Introduce the Situation.   When you draft the first part of your paper, describe the situation you want to explain in no more than two or three paragraphs. Make clear to your readers which task — explaining the causes of the change, explaining the effects, or explaining both — you intend to accomplish. Instead of doing this in a flat, mechanical fashion ("Now I am going to explain the causes of this situation"), you can announce your task casually, naturally, as if you were talking to someone: "At first, I didn't realize that keeping six pet cheetahs in our backyard would bother the neighbors." Or, you might tantalize your readers as one writer did in a paper about her father's sudden move to a Trappist monastery: "The real reason for Father's decision didn't become clear to me for a long while."

REVISING AND EDITING

For more revising and editing strategies, see Ch. 20.

Because explaining causes and effects takes hard thought, you'll want to set aside plenty of time for rewriting. As Yun Yung Choi approached her paper's final version, she faced the problem of making a smooth transition from recalling her own experience to probing causes.

(emphasize that everyone thinks that) ——→ *widely*

, a relatively short time, considering Korea's long history

[tell when]

These attitudes toward women, ~~which I once~~ believed to be the continuation of an unbroken chain of tradition, are, in fact, only a few hundred years old. During the first half of the Yi dynasty, which lasted from 1392 to 1910, and during [the Koryo period,] women were treated almost as equals, with many privileges that were denied them during the latter half of the Yi dynasty. This upheaval in women's place in Korean society was brought about by one of the greatest influences that shaped the government, literature, and thoughts of the Korean people: Confucianism. Because of Confucianism, my birth was not greeted with joy and celebration but rather with these words of consolation: "A daughter is her mother's chief help in keeping house." *(Belongs in opening paragraph)*

You can use the Table menu in your word processor to help you assess the importance of causes and effects. Open a file, and go to the Table menu. Select "Insert Table" and enter "4" when asked for the number of columns. Label the columns "Major Cause," "Minor Cause," "Major Effect," and "Minor Effect." Divide up your causes and effects accordingly, making appropriate entries under each heading. You can create additional rows automatically as you make each entry by placing your cursor at the end of the table and hitting the Return key. Each box should expand automatically to fit whatever you type into it. Using a table will help you think about how your causes and effects relate as well as how to order and limit your points.

WRITING WITH A COMPUTER

In revising a paper that traces causes, effects, or both, you might consider questions like these:

REVISION CHECKLIST

—— Have you shown your readers your point in presenting causes or effects?

—— Is your explanation thoughtful, searching, and reasonable?

If you are tracing causes,

—— Have you made it clear that you are explaining causes?

—— Have you left out any significant causes?

—— Have you given enough evidence to convince readers that the causal relationships are valid, not just guesses?

—— Have you claimed remote causes you can't begin to prove? Or made assertions but offered no proof?

—— Have you oversimplified by assuming only one small cause for a large phenomenon or assuming that one thing caused another just because the one preceded the other?

For more on evidence, see pp. 25–28. For mistakes in thinking called logical fallacies, see pp. 134–36.

If you are determining effects,

—— Have you made it clear that you are explaining effects?

—— What possible effects have you left out? Are any of them worth adding?

—— Have you given sufficient evidence that these effects have occurred?

—— Could any effect have resulted not from the cause you describe but from some other cause?

After you have revised your cause-and-effect essay, edit and proofread it. Check carefully for problems with grammar, word choice, punctuation, and mechanics—and then correct any problems you find. Here are some questions to get you started when editing and proofreading your paper:

For more editing and proofreading strategies, see Ch. 20.

EDITING CHECKLIST

For more help, turn to the dark-blue-edged pages, and find the "Quick Editing Guide" section noted here.

—— Have you used correct verb tenses and forms throughout? When you describe events in the past, is it clear what happened first and what happened next?   **A1**

—— Is your sentence structure correct? Have you avoided creating fragments when filling in additional causes or effects? (Check revisions carefully, especially those beginning *"Because . . ."* or *"Causing . . . ."*) Have you avoided writing run-ons when trying to integrate additional ideas smoothly?   **A6, A7**

—— Do your transitions and other introductory elements have commas after them, if these are needed?   **C1**

FOR PEER RESPONSE

For general questions for a peer editor, see pp. 323–24.

Let a classmate or friend read your draft, considering how you've analyzed causes or effects. Ask your peer editor to answer questions such as the following:

If the writer explains causes,

- Does the writer explain, rather than merely list, causes?
- Do the causes seem logical and possible?
- Have other causes occurred to you that the writer might consider? If so, list them.

If the writer explains effects,

- Do all the effects seem to be results of the situation the writer describes?
- Have other effects occurred to you that the writer might consider? If so, list them.

For all cause-and-effect papers,

- What is the writer's main point? Does the explanation of causes or effects help the writer accomplish the purpose of the essay?
- Is the order of supporting ideas clear and useful? Can you suggest a better organization?

For more on evidence, see pp. 25–28. For mistakes in thinking called logical fallacies, see pp. 134–36.

- Are you convinced by the logic used in the draft? Do you see any logical fallacies?
- Point out any causes or effects you find hard to accept.
- Does the writer supply enough evidence and detail to convince you? Put stars where more evidence is needed.
- If this were your paper, what is the one thing you would be sure to work on before handing it in?

Explaining the News

In class or in your writing group, tell aloud a two-minute story that you invent to explain the causes behind any surprising event reported in the morning's news. Either realistic explanations or tall tales are acceptable, but be sure to prepare some brief notes about your story in advance. Invite the others to comment on it, and, with their reactions in mind, set down your story on paper to turn in at the next class. In writing it down, embellish and improve on your story as much as you wish. If your group wants to videotape its version of the news, select an anchor, decide on the order of your stories, and rehearse first. Invite your whole class to watch and evaluate your video.

FOR GROUP LEARNING

OTHER ASSIGNMENTS

1. Pick a change that has taken place during your lifetime, and seek out its causes and effects to help you and your readers understand that change better. By "change," we mean a noticeable, lasting transformation produced by an event or series of events. The change might be one that has affected only you, such as a move to another location, a decision you made, or an alteration in a strong personal opinion or belief. It might be a change that has also affected other people in your neighborhood or city (a new zoning law), in a region (the growth of a new industry such as high technology), or in society at large (general access to the Internet). Or it might be a new invention, a medical breakthrough, or a deep-down shift in the structure or attitudes of society.

2. Explore your own motives and explain your reasons for taking some step or for doing something in a routine way.

3. Read one newspaper or magazine article that probes the causes of some contemporary problem: the shortage of reasonable day-care options, for instance, or the low academic scores of American students compared with those of students in other developed countries. Can you suggest additional causes that the article writer seems to have ignored? Write an essay in which you argue either that the author has done a good job of explaining the causes of this problem or that he or she has not.

Applying What You Learn: Some Uses of Explaining Causes and Effects

In College Courses.   Both writing assignments and examination questions often pose problems in causality.

- One or two paragraphs that explore the causes of a phenomenon or its effects might add depth to a paper assigned on almost any subject — a sociology paper about the increase in teenage pregnancy or a literature paper on characteristics of romanticism in American fiction.

- Exam questions may call for you to define causes ("Trace the causes of the decline of foreign automobile sales in America") or survey effects ("What economic effects were immediately evident when Prohibition was repealed in 1933?").

- Instructors in many of your courses will require you to write about causal relationships. In a speech pathology course, you might investigate the effects of head trauma, fetal alcohol syndrome, or learning disabilities.

In the Workplace.   Causal relationships are the driving issues of the workplace. Understanding causes and effects can make the critical difference between success or failure.

- Advertising agencies carefully examine causes and effects to determine what strategies will convince consumers to buy, buy, buy. Political strategists use similar techniques to garner votes.

- Environmental engineers and consultants prepare reports on the effects of specific working conditions on employee productivity.

- State department officials and military officers analyze international relations and issue causality reports—the possible consequences of an impending war between Pakistan and India, the effects of a military coup in South America, or the causes of genocide in Rwanda.

In Your Community.   Understanding the reasons a problem exists in your community or the likely results of a proposed action will allow you to add your voice to those in the community who wish either to maintain the status quo or to initiate beneficial changes.

- Your professional or civic organization may respond to a controversy by drafting a policy statement outlining the consequences of a current or proposed practice and making clear the organization's stance.

- Images of the long-term effects of dumping in your city's landfill can help build a persuasive poster campaign urging recycling.

- A letter to your school board sharing evidence of the effects of a dress code on student behavior in other school districts can assist board members in making the most enlightened decision and the one most beneficial to your child.

Chapter 9
Taking a Stand

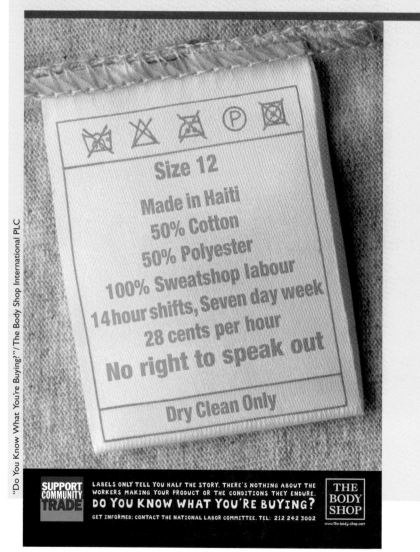

Responding to an Image

This advertisement includes a visual quotation of a familiar type of communication, a clothing label. How does the ad use this familiar label to illustrate its stance on an issue? Is the ad effective? Is it convincing? Based on the ad, what do you think are the missions and goals of its sponsors, the Body Shop and the National Labor Committee? What do you think motivated their sponsorship of this ad?

Both in class and outside of class, you'll hear controversial issues discussed — prayer in the schools, Internet copyright issues, health care. In some fields of study, experts don't always agree, and issues remain controversies for years. Taking a stand in response to these issues will help you understand the controversy and clarify what you believe.

Writing of this kind has a twofold purpose — to state an opinion and to win your readers' respect for it. What you say might change a reader's opinion; then again, it might not. But if you fulfill your purpose, a reader at least will see good reasons for your thinking the way you do. In taking a stand, you do three things:

- You state what you believe and give reasons with evidence to support your position.
- You enlist your readers' trust.
- You consider and respect what your readers probably think and feel.

Learning from Other Writers

WWW
For more examples of writing that takes a stand, visit <www .bedfordstmartins.com/ bedguide>.

Let's look at two essays in which the writers take a stand effectively on issues of importance to them.

As You Read

As you read these essays, ask yourself the following questions:

1. What stand does the writer take? Is it a popular opinion, or does it break from commonly accepted beliefs?
2. How does the writer appeal to readers?
3. How does the writer support his or her position? Is the evidence sufficient to gain your respect? Why, or why not?

Suzan Shown Harjo
Last Rites for Indian Dead

As a result of persuasive efforts such as Suzan Shown Harjo's essay, the Native American Graves Protection and Repatriation Act was passed in 1990.

What if museums, universities, and government agencies could put your dead relatives on display or keep them in boxes to be cut up and otherwise studied? What if you believed that the spirits of the dead could not rest until their human remains were placed in a sacred area? 1

The ordinary American would say there ought to be a law — and there 2 is, for ordinary Americans. The problem for American Indians is that there are too many laws of the kind that make us the archeological property of the United States and too few of the kind that protect us from such insults.

Some of my own Cheyenne relatives' skulls are in the Smithsonian In- 3
stitution today, along with those of at least 4,500 other Indian people who
were violated in the 1800s by the U.S. Army for an "Indian Crania Study." It
wasn't enough that these unarmed Cheyenne people were mowed down by
the cavalry at the infamous Sand Creek massacre; many were decapitated
and their heads shipped to Washington as freight. (The Army Medical Museum's collection is now in the Smithsonian.) Some had been exhumed°
only hours after being buried. Imagine their grieving families' reaction on
finding their loved ones disinterred° and headless.

Some targets of the Army's study were killed in noncombat situations 4
and beheaded immediately. The officer's account of the decapitation of the
Apache chief Mangas Coloradas in 1863 shows the pseudoscientific nature
of the exercise. "I weighed the brain and measured the skull," the good doctor wrote, "and found that while the skull was smaller, the brain was larger
than that of Daniel Webster."

These journal accounts exist in excruciating detail, yet missing are any 5
records of overall comparisons, conclusions, or final reports of the Army
study. Since it is unlike the Army not to leave a paper trail, one must wonder
about the motive for its collection.

The total Indian body count in the Smithsonian collection is more than 6
19,000, and it is not the largest in the country. It is not inconceivable that the
1.5 million of us living today are outnumbered by our dead stored in museums, educational institutions, federal agencies, state historical societies, and
private collections. The Indian people are further dehumanized by being exhibited alongside the mastodons and dinosaurs and other extinct creatures.

Where we have buried our dead in peace, more often than not the sites 7
have been desecrated. For more than two hundred years, relic-hunting has
been a popular pursuit. Lately, the market in Indian artifacts has brought
this abhorrent activity to a fever pitch in some areas. And when scavengers
come upon Indian burial sites, everything found becomes fair game, including sacred burial offerings, teeth, and skeletal remains.

One unusually well-publicized example of Indian grave desecration oc- 8
curred two years ago in a western Kentucky field known as Slack Farm, the site
of an Indian village five centuries ago. Ten men — one with a business card
stating "Have Shovel, Will Travel" — paid the landowner $10,000 to lease dig-
ging rights between planting seasons. They dug extensively on the forty-acre
farm, rummaging through an estimated 650 graves, collecting burial goods,
tools, and ceremonial items. Skeletons were strewn about like litter.

What motivates people to do something like this? Financial gain is the 9
first answer. Indian relic-collecting has become a multimillion-dollar industry. The price tag on a bead necklace can easily top $1,000; rare pieces fetch
tens of thousands.

And it is not just collectors of the macabre° who pay for skeletal re- 10
mains. Scientists say that these deceased Indians are needed for research that

---

exhumed: Dug up out of the earth.   **disinterred:** Taken out of a place of burial.
macabre: Gruesome, ghastly.

someday could benefit the health and welfare of living Indians. But just how many dead Indians must they examine? Nineteen thousand?

There is doubt as to whether permanent curation of our dead really 11 benefits Indians. Dr. Emery A. Johnson, former assistant Surgeon General, recently observed, "I am not aware of any current medical diagnostic or treatment procedure that has been derived from research on such skeletal remains. Nor am I aware of any during the thirty-four years that I have been involved in American Indian . . . health care."

Indian remains are still being collected for racial biological studies. 12 While the intentions may be honorable, the ethics of using human remains this way without the full consent of relatives must be questioned.

Some relief for Indian people has come on the state level. Almost half 13 of the states, including California, have passed laws protecting Indian burial sites and restricting the sale of Indian bones, burial offerings, and other sacred items. Rep. Charles E. Bennett (D-Fla.) and Sen. John McCain (R-Ariz.) have introduced bills that are a good start in invoking the federal government's protection. However, no legislation has attacked the problem head-on by imposing stiff penalties at the marketplace, or by changing laws that make dead Indians the nation's property.

Some universities — notably Stanford, Nebraska, Minnesota, and Seattle — 14 have returned, or agreed to return, Indian human remains; it is fitting that institutions of higher education should lead the way.

Congress is now deciding what to do with the government's extensive 15 collection of Indian human remains and associated funerary objects. The secretary of the Smithsonian, Robert McC. Adams, has been valiantly° attempting to apply modern ethics to yesterday's excesses. This week, he announced that the Smithsonian would conduct an inventory and return all Indian skeletal remains that could be identified with specific tribes or living kin.

But there remains a reluctance generally among collectors of Indian re- 16 mains to take action of a scope that would have a quantitative impact and a healing quality. If they will not act on their own — and it is highly unlikely that they will — then Congress must act.

The country must recognize that the bodies of dead American Indian 17 people are not artifacts to be bought and sold as collector's items. It is not appropriate to store tens of thousands of our ancestors for possible future research. They are our family. They deserve to be returned to their sacred burial grounds and given a chance to rest.

The plunder of our people's graves has gone on too long. Let us rebury 18 our dead and remove this shameful past from America's future.

Questions to Start You Thinking

Meaning

1. What is the problem Harjo identifies? How extensive does she show it to be?
2. What is Harjo's position on this issue? Where does she first state it?

valiantly: Bravely.

3. What evidence does Harjo present to refute the claim that housing skeletal remains of Native Americans in museums is necessary for medical research and may benefit living Indians?

Writing Strategies

4. What assumptions do you think Harjo makes about her audience?

5. What types of evidence does Harjo use to support her argument? How convincing is the evidence to you?

6. How does Harjo use her status as a Native American to enhance her position? Would her argument be as credible if it were written by someone of another background?

7. How does she appeal to the emotions of the readers in the essay? In what ways do these strategies strengthen or detract from her logical reasons?

8. Why does Harjo discuss what legislatures and universities are doing in response to the situation?

STUDENT ESSAY

Thaddeus Watulak
Affirmative Action Encourages Racism

Racism: discrimination or prejudice based on race. That's the dictionary definition of the word. By that, or any other reasonable definition, affirmative action is easily the most racist institution in America today. From its inception° affirmative action was at best misguided, and it is today the single largest obstacle to good race relations in this country.

How is affirmative action racist? Let's say a firm sees two almost equally qualified candidates for the same position, one white and one black. If the white guy is hired because he's white, then the company has broken the law and is considered terribly immoral. If the black guy is hired because he's black, not only is the firm considered morally righteous, but it will probably qualify for some kind of government subsidy.° Let's go back to the dictionary for a second. Discrimination: action or policies based on prejudice or partiality. Both possibilities in this imaginary scenario clearly show partiality based on race; both are clearly racist. Yet one is the official policy of our government, a

Thaddeus Watulak, a student at Johns Hopkins, published his essay as an opinion piece in the university's online newsletter on March 26, 1998.

1

2

---

inception: Beginning.   **subsidy:** Financial aid paid to a private party by the government.

government supposedly founded on the principle that all men
are created equal.

Not only does affirmative action require discrimination   3
based on race; it also ignores our status as individuals. The
notion that the white race should be punished for, or at
least forced to make amends for, supposed racial crimes
against minority races is as racist a proposition as anything
from the darkest days of Jim Crow.° No one alive today has
ever been a slave or owned a slave; there are no legitimate
parties for reparations° there. The people of our generation
have grown up in a society utterly devoid of legal discrimination against minorities of any kind.

Just what crimes are we supposed to be making amends   4
for? The usual answer is that it's our racial crimes of the
past. Well, frankly, I feel responsible only for actions that
I have taken or directly sanctioned. When the city of Rome
starts granting preferential treatment to Tunisians to make
up for the razing of Carthage, I'll think about reconsidering. Even then I don't think I'll quite understand why a
dirt-poor, just naturalized Australian immigrant should
legally be discriminated against in favor of the scion of an
old-money American family who happens to be Hispanic.

Affirmative action also has some rather unpleasant   5
racist assumptions hiding behind it. The clear implication
that minorities could not adequately get ahead without special considerations seems just a touch bigoted. Personally,
I'd be a bit insulted if an employer said they understood
since I grew up in Vermont I couldn't possibly do as well as
those cosmopolitan New Yorkers and that they'd take that into
consideration when they decided whether or not to give me a
job. I'd also be a bit upset if I applied to law school and
was told that since I have brown hair I wasn't expected to
have a high LSAT score. All that kind of treatment does is
make the recipients question whether or not they really
earned their accomplishments.

I honestly believe that all people, whether they are in   6
the majority or the minority in their particular region, have
the same inherent capacity to succeed given a level playing

Jim Crow: Laws that legalized segregation by sanctioning "separate but equal" facilities
for blacks and whites.   reparations: Compensation.

field. A white kid in inner-city L.A. is just as disadvantaged as his black and Latino neighbors. The minority student at Harvard who had a tutor as a child before going off to a top-rated prep school is just as much a member of the privileged elite as any of her classmates. Using the term minority as a kind of shorthand for poor and disadvantaged is not only terribly insulting, but it also obscures the real problems in this country.

Finally, not only is affirmative action essentially racist, and not only does it rely on racial stereotypes, but it also reinforces racist attitudes in our society that are based on these stereotypes. First, as already noted, the debate on affirmative action tends to portray minorities as kind of poor and disadvantaged second-class citizens. This trend can't help but boomerang by reinforcing the ghetto stereotypes held about minority groups. Second, nothing can further embitter the closet racist more than the belief, encouraged by the existence of affirmative action programs, that minorities promoted above him have not really earned their positions. Perhaps most significant for the continuance of racist attitudes, affirmative action polarizes society along racial lines and encourages an "us versus them" attitude.   7

Affirmative action is an essentially racist policy that generates only more racism. It is past time that society moved beyond this stumbling block and took the next halting steps toward Dr. King's dream of a truly colorblind society.   8

Questions to Start You Thinking

Meaning

1. What claims does Watulak make to support his general position that affirmative action is racist in both its premises and its effects?

2. What does Watulak claim are "unpleasant racist assumptions" hiding behind the policy of affirmative action?

3. What does Watulak's concluding allusion ("Dr. King's dream of a truly colorblind society") mean?

Writing Strategies

4. What impression of Watulak do you get from reading his paper? What kind of person do you think he is? Would you like to meet him?

5. How does Watulak use the issue of class to support his argument that affirmative action promotes racist attitudes and practices?

6. What kind of support does Watulak use to back up his claims about affirmative action? Do you find his argument effective? Is his evidence sufficient and appropriate for this kind of paper? Why, or why not?

7. Where and how does Watulak consider the attitudes of readers who might be the beneficiaries of affirmative action? Does he do enough to reach out to them?

8. What is Watulak's tone? What are the benefits and drawbacks of the tone he uses? How effective is it when he includes personal anecdotes and opinions such as "Personally, I'd be a bit insulted . . ."?

Learning by Writing

THE ASSIGNMENT: TAKING A STAND

You can complete each of the steps in this assignment by using the *Writing Guide Software for THE BEDFORD GUIDE.*

Find a controversy that rouses your interest. It might be a current issue or a long-standing one, such as "In our public schools, should the teaching of creationism, the Biblical explanation for the origin of species, be given the same amount of classroom time as Darwin's theory of evolution?" or "Do intercollegiate sports on campus enhance the educational purpose of college or detract from it?" Your purpose in this paper isn't to try to solve a large social or moral problem but to make clear where you stand on an issue and to persuade your readers to respect your position, perhaps even to accept it. To do so effectively, you must first know exactly where you stand and why. As you reflect on your topic, you may change your position, but don't shift positions in the middle of your essay.

Assume that your readers are people who may or may not be familiar with the controversy, so provide some background or an overview to give them a clear understanding of the situation. Furthermore, your readers may not have taken sides yet or may hold a position different from yours. To be effective, you must also consider their views and choose strategies that will enlist their support.

Here are brief summaries of a few good papers that take a stand, written by students at several colleges:

A student who pays her own way through college countered the opinion that working full- or part-time during the school year provides a college student with valuable knowledge. Citing her own painful experience, she maintained that a student who can devote full time to her studies is far better off than a student who must work.

Another writer attacked his history textbook's portrayal of Joan of Arc on the grounds that the author had characterized Joan as "an ignorant farm girl subject to religious hysteria."

A member of the wrestling team argued that the number of weight categories in competitive wrestling should be increased because athletes who desperately overtrain to qualify for the existing categories often damage their health.

Facing the Challenge: Taking a Stand

The major challenge writers face when they take a stand on an issue is to gather sufficient evidence to support their position. To encourage readers to respect your opinions, even if they don't agree with you, you must do enough research to anticipate their objections or possible counterarguments. Once you understand other possible views, you'll have a better idea of the evidence you'll need to support your position. Otherwise, the only readers you'll convince will be those who agreed with you in the first place.

If you rave emotionally about an issue—insulting people whose opinions differ from yours by dismissing their concerns as ignorant—you will convince no one. Instead, you must win your audience's regard by demonstrating a knowledge of and respect for opposing viewpoints. You needn't be wishy-washy or avoid strongly expressing your own position. Rather, carefully considering opponents' views enables you to strengthen your own argument by finding evidence that addresses their concerns.

To anticipate and find evidence to counter other arguments, list groups that might have strong opinions on your topic. Then try putting yourself in the shoes of a member of each group by writing a paragraph on the issue from *her* point of view.

- What would her opinion be?
- On what grounds might she object to your argument?
- How can you best address her concerns and overcome her objections?

This exercise will show you where you need to find additional evidence to support your claims.

WWW
To practice testing evidence, visit <www.bedfordstmartins.com/bedguide>.

GENERATING IDEAS

For this assignment, you will need to select an issue on which to take a stand, develop a clear position, and assemble evidence that supports your view.

For more strategies for generating ideas, see Ch. 16.

Find an Issue.   The topic for this paper should be an issue or controversy that's interesting to both you and your readers. Try brainstorming a list of possible topics. If you can't get started, look at the headlines of a newspaper or newsmagazine or Web site, review the letters to the editor, consult the indexes to *CQ Researcher* or *Opposing Viewpoints* in the library, listen to a news broadcast, talk with your friends, or consider topics raised in class. If you keep a journal, look over your entries to see what has perplexed or angered you.

For more on brainstorming, see pp. 260–62. For more on keeping a journal, see pp. 265–66.

At this stage, many writers find it useful to pose the issue as a question—a question that will be answered through the position they take. Remember that you need to find a topic that allows different stands. The question "Is sexism bad?" is probably not going to lead to a strong paper because most rational, reasonably educated readers would agree that sexism is a bad thing, whatever the vague word *bad* really means here. However, a question like "Should we fight sexism by eliminating sexist stereotypes in advertising?" is more fruitful because it focuses on a clearly debatable topic.

Once you have a list of possible topics, drop those that seem too broad or complex or those that you don't know much about. Weed out anything that looks as if it might not hold your interest or that of your readers. From your new, shorter list, pick the issue or controversy for which you think you can make the strongest argument.

Do Some Preliminary Exploring.   Once you have an issue in mind, you may need to do a little investigating—both to understand the topic better and to make sure that you really can and want to take a stand on it.

As he strove to discover ideas for his paper, Thaddeus Watulak kept a free-flowing journal. Many of the ideas he wrote down never actually made it into his final draft. Still, when he began writing, he had more than enough material to choose from.

> 10/18/98
>
> Topic: Effectiveness of affirmative action
> — Has it really helped racism in this country?
> — What have been the real consequences of this policy?
>
> 10/22/98
>
> Those students talking about affirmative action in the cafeteria sounded really angry. "Another way white people are discriminated against." "Punishing us for something we didn't do." What do most people think about when they hear about a.a.? Can a.a. possibly be fair?
>
> 10/23/98
>
> Why do people only care about race? What about the difference between poor and rich? Someone could be black but have loads of resources—money, good schools, caring parents. Someone else could be white but have almost nothing. Why should race be the only consideration?

For more on developing a thesis, see Ch. 17.

State Your Position.   You can help focus your view by stating it in a sentence—a thesis, or statement of the stand you are taking. If you phrased your topic as a question, answer that question. Your position needs to be one that invites continued debate, so stick your neck out a little. "Minority students constitute 3 percent of our school's population" isn't a stand; it's a fact. "Minority students are underrepresented at our school" or—even better—"Our school should increase its minority population" is a strong position that can be argued.

Consider the Types of Claims You Can Use.   If you're unsure what sort of evidence your position would need, consider the issue in terms of the three general types of claims—claims that require substantiation, claims that provide evaluation, and claims that endorse policy.

Making a Claim

Hold a meeting at which each member of your writing group writes out, in one complete sentence, the core claim or position he or she will support. Drop all these "position statements" into a hat, with no names attached. Then, draw and read each aloud in turn. For each position proposed, invite group members to suggest useful supporting evidence, counterevidence, and possible sources for both. Ask the group's recorder to list suggestions on a separate page for each claim. Finally, match up writers with claims, and share reactions to the discussion. If this activity causes you to alter your stand, be thankful: it will be easier to revise now than to revise later.

FOR GROUP LEARNING

CLAIMS OF SUBSTANTIATION. These require examining and interpreting information in an effort to resolve disputes about facts or circumstances, causes or effects, the applicability of definitions, or the extent of a problem, as in these examples:

- Certain types of cigarette ads, such as the once-popular Joe Camel ads, significantly encourage smoking among teenagers.

- Rather than being a major problem, police brutality in this country is a distorted perception based on a few well-publicized exceptions to the rule.

- On the whole, bilingual education programs actually help students learn English faster than total immersion.

CLAIMS OF EVALUATION. These claims consider the rightness or wrongness, appropriateness or inappropriateness, worth or lack of worth involved in certain issues, as seen in these examples:

- Research using fetal tissue is unethical in a civilized society.

- English-only legislation promotes cultural intolerance in our society.

- Keeping children in foster care for years, instead of releasing them for adoption, is wrong.

CLAIMS OF POLICY. Claims of policy challenge or defend approaches for achieving generally agreed upon goals, as in the following:

- The federal government should support the distribution of clean needles to reduce the rate of HIV infection among intravenous drug users.

- Denying illegal immigrant children enrollment in American public schools will reduce the problem of illegal immigration.

- Underage teenagers accused of murder should be tried as adults.

Consider Your Audience as You Develop Your Claim. The nature of your audience might influence the type of claim you choose to make. For example, suppose you wish to promote the distribution of free condoms in high school and your audience consists of conservative parents. The following claim of evaluation might anger them: "Because it saves lives and prevents unwanted pregnancies, distributing free condoms in high school is our moral duty." If you assume that most conservative parents oppose dispensing free condoms because they believe it would promote immoral sexual behavior, your claim seems to accuse the parents themselves of immorality for not agreeing with your position. Thus, this claim seems counterproductive.

A claim of substantiation might work better with these parents, using the issue of effectiveness as a common ground. Most parents, after all, want to protect their children from harmful consequences, no matter what. This thesis might gain a more receptive response: "Distributing free condoms in high school is an effective way of reducing the pregnancy rates and the incidence of STDs, especially the spread of AIDS, without necessarily leading to a substantially higher rate of sexual activity among teenagers." Notice that this claim also attempts to deflate the main fear parents probably have about free condom distribution in high school. While your position on free condoms remains the same, you are far more likely to achieve your purpose — to persuade, not alienate.

School administrators, on the other hand, might be better swayed with a claim endorsing policy. Most of them want to do what's right, but they don't want hordes of outraged parents banging down the school doors. They might be more inclined to consider your position if you stated it this way: "Distributing free condoms in high school to prevent unwanted pregnancies and the spread of STDs, including AIDS, is best accomplished in the context of a voluntary sexual education program that strongly emphasizes abstinence as the primary preventative."

These three types of claims may also be used as support for a position. Stating supporting claims as supporting points can provide topic sentences to help your reader follow your line of reasoning. In "Affirmative Action Encourages Racism," for example, Thaddeus Watulak uses topic sentences that are claims; these help the reader see the subpoints he's trying to make through his examples. "Affirmative action also has some rather unpleasant racist assumptions hiding behind it" and "I honestly believe that all people, whether they are in the majority or the minority in their particular region, have the same inherent capacity to succeed given a level playing field" are two such topic sentences.

For more on selecting and testing evidence, see Ch. 3.

For more on logical fallacies, see pp. 134–36.

Assemble Evidence.   Your claim stated, you'll need evidence to support it. What is evidence? It is anything that demonstrates the soundness of your position and the points you make in your argument — facts, statistics, observations, expert testimony, illustrations, examples, and case studies. Of course, evidence must be used carefully to avoid defending logical fallacies — common mistakes in thinking — and making statements that lead to wrong conclusions.

One logical fallacy that often crops up in position papers is the misuse of examples (claiming proof by example or using too few examples). Because two professors you know are dissatisfied with state-mandated testing programs, you can't claim that all or even most professors are. Even if you surveyed more professors at your school, you could speak only generally of "many professors." To claim more, you might need to conduct scientific surveys, access reliable statistics in the library or on the Internet, or solicit the views of a respected expert in the area.

If you are having trouble thinking of types of evidence, consider the following questions:

DISCOVERY CHECKLIST

___ What experiences in your own life have shaped your opinions?

___ What have you observed, or what might you observe, that would support your stand?

___ What expert might you interview?

___ What reading might you do?

___ What precise information do you want to find?

The three most important sources of evidence are these:

1. *Facts, including statistics.*   Facts are statements that can be verified by objective means; statistics are facts expressed in numbers. Facts usually form the basis of a successful argument.
2. *Expert testimony.*   By experts, we mean people with knowledge of a particular field gained from study and experience.
3. *Firsthand observation.*   Your own observations can be a persuasive source of evidence, if you can assure your readers that your account is accurate.

For more about forms of evidence, see pp. 25–27.

Record Evidence.   For this assignment, you will need to record your evidence in written form. Take notes in a notebook, on index cards, or on the computer. Be sure to note exactly where each piece of information comes from. Keep the form of your notes flexible so that you can easily rearrange them as you plan your draft.

Test and Select Evidence.   Now that you've collected some evidence, you need to sift through it to decide which pieces of information to use. Evidence is useful and trustworthy when it is accurate, reliable, up-to-date, to the point, representative, not oversimplified, and sufficient and strong enough to back the claim and persuade your readers. You may find that your evidence supports a position different from the one you intended to state. Is it possible that you could find some facts, testimony, and observations that would support your original position after all? Or should you rethink your original position?

For more on testing evidence, see pp. 27–28.

Most effective arguments take opposing viewpoints into consideration and refute them whenever possible. Do you know the arguments and evidence on the other side of the issue? Do you know who supports these arguments? Do you have evidence or reasons that you can use to show why these arguments are weak, only partially true, misguided, or just plain wrong? In your final paper, you will want to acknowledge these counterarguments and try to rebut them effectively. As you begin to put together your argument, consider your readers' points of view. What are their attitudes, interests, and priorities? What do they already know about the topic? What do they expect you to say? Ask yourself whether your evidence is appropriate and sufficient to convince them.

PLANNING, DRAFTING, AND DEVELOPING

For more strategies for planning, drafting, and developing, see Chs. 17, 18, and 19.

Reassess Your Position.   Now that you have looked into the issue, what is your current position? If necessary, revise the thesis that you formulated earlier. Then summarize your reasons for holding this view, and list your supporting evidence.

For more on outlines, see pp. 279–84.

Organize Your Material.   Arrange your notes into the order you think you'll follow, perhaps making an outline. One useful pattern is the classical form of argument:

1. Introduce the subject to gain the readers' interest.
2. State your main point or thesis.
3. If useful, give the historical background or an explanatory overview of the situation.
4. Provide evidence to support your position.
5. Refute the opposition.
6. Reaffirm your main point.

In some situations, especially when you expect readers to be hostile to your position, you may want to take the opposite approach: refute the opposition to weaken it first, then replace those views by building a logical chain of evidence that leads to your main point, and finally state your position. If you state your position too early, you might alienate resistant readers or make them defensive. Of course, you can always try both approaches to see which one works better. Note also that some papers will be mostly based on refutation (countering opposing views) and some mostly on confirmation (directly supporting your position). Others might even alternate refutation and confirmation rather than separating them.

Define Your Terms.   To prevent misunderstanding, make clear any unfamiliar or questionable terms used in your thesis. If your position is "Humanists are dangerous," give a short definition of what you mean by *humanists* and by *dangerous* early in the paper.

Attend to Logical, Emotional, and Ethical Appeals. The logical appeal engages readers' intellect; the emotional appeal touches their hearts; the ethical appeal draws on their sense of fairness and reasonableness. A persuasive argument usually operates on all three levels.

For more on appeals, see pp. 29–30.

To use the *logical appeal,* you need to make sure that your reasoning is clear and your evidence is sound. Don't claim more than you can demonstrate, and do demonstrate everything that you claim. Much of the advice we've given so far on testing and selecting evidence will help you construct a sound logical appeal.

To use the *emotional appeal,* select examples and language that will influence how your readers feel about the issue. A well-chosen image — a father accidentally shooting his son who unexpectedly arrives home from college at 3 A.M. — may win more support than a truckload of statistics on accidental killings. Be careful not to overdo it, though: your argument will fall flat if you tug too hard on readers' heartstrings. Emotions should support the logical appeal but never replace it.

To use the *ethical appeal* in a paper taking a position, you must spell out your beliefs and give attention to beliefs opposing yours. If you declare, "I am against eating red meat because it contains fats and chemicals known to be harmful," you assert a position and then provide evidence for it. The reader who responds, "That's right. I'm a vegetarian myself," is likely to see the soundness of your position. But even the reader who responds, "Oh, I don't know. A hamburger never killed anyone!" may warm to your view if you consider his or her possible assumptions that a burger is delicious, that red meat supplies needed protein, and that the chemicals haven't been proved dangerous. You should consider these assumptions seriously, maybe even agree with some of them, but then set forth in a reasonable way your

As you plan a paper taking a stand, try using three columns to write about your logical, emotional, and ethical appeals. Begin a new file by going to the Format menu and selecting "Columns." When your word processor asks you to select the number of columns, click on "3." Begin the first column with the heading "Logical Appeals." In this column write the claims and support that rely on reasoning and sound evidence. When you have completed as much as you can in this column, create the next column, generally by going to the Insert menu, clicking on "Break," selecting "Column break," and clicking "OK." Begin your second column with the heading "Emotional Appeals." Here, note the claims and support that may affect readers' emotions. Now create a third column, headed "Ethical Appeals." Record here the claims and support showing that your beliefs are based on values and that you also understand the values of opposing points of view. To move back and forth between columns, simply move your cursor. As you reread each column, you can begin to consider how to relate your claims and support across columns, how to organize your ideas persuasively, and how best to merge or separate your logical, emotional, and ethical appeals.

WRITING WITH A COMPUTER

own view. By spelling out your assumptions and by imagining those of a dissenting reader, you will win respect, if not agreement.

As part of the ethical appeal, you should establish your credentials, if you have any, and those of your experts. If you are writing about euthanasia, for example, establish the fact that you have witnessed the lingering death of a grandparent.

If you quote an expert who has outstanding credentials, you may easily be able to insert them: "Lewis Thomas, former chancellor of the Memorial Sloan-Kettering Cancer Center..." If you have talked to experts and are convinced of their authority, state why you believe that they can be trusted: "During my interview with Mr. Dworshak, he showed me six model wind tunnels he has built, testifying to his extensive knowledge of aeronautics."

For more on logical fallacies, see pp. 134–36.

Consistently demonstrate that you are a rational, trustworthy, and caring individual who will express yourself, relate to your reader, and handle your topic respectfully. A skeptical reader is unlikely to take you seriously if you stoop to name-calling, misrepresentations of the other side, logical fallacies, and emotional excess.

For pointers on documenting sources, see E2 in the "Quick Editing Guide" (the dark-blue-edged pages).

Credit Your Sources.   As you write, make your sources of evidence clear. One simple way to do so is to incorporate your source into the text: "According to an article in the December 10, 2000, issue of *Time*" or "According to my history professor, Dr. Harry Cleghorn..."

REVISING AND EDITING

When you're writing a paper taking a stand, you may be tempted to fall in love with the evidence you've gone to such trouble to collect. Taking out information is hard to do, but if it is irrelevant, redundant, or weak, the evidence won't help your case.

As you revise, here are some questions to consider:

REVISION CHECKLIST

____ Is your main point clear? Do you stick to it rather than drifting into contradictions?

____ Does your view convince you? Or do you think you need still more evidence?

____ Have you tried to keep in mind your readers and what would appeal to them? Have you answered what are likely to be their major objections?

____ Have you defined all necessary terms and explained all your points clearly?

____ Is your tone suitable for your readers? Are you likely to alienate them, or, at the other extreme, do you sound weak or apologetic?

____ Might your points seem stronger if arranged in a different sequence?

____ Have you unfairly omitted any evidence that would hurt your case?

For more revising and editing strategies, see Ch. 20.

____ In rereading your paper, do you have any excellent, fresh thoughts? If so, make room for them.

After you have revised your argument, edit and proofread it. Check carefully for problems with grammar, word choice, punctuation, and mechanics—and then correct any problems you find. Wherever you have given facts and figures as evidence, check for errors in names and numbers. This advice may seem trivial, but there's a considerable difference between "10,000 people" and "100,000 people." Here are some questions to get you started editing and proofreading:

For more editing and proofreading strategies, see Ch. 20.

EDITING CHECKLIST

___ Is it clear what each pronoun refers to? Does each pronoun agree with (match) its antecedent? Do pronouns used as subjects agree with their verbs? Carefully check sentences making broad claims about *everyone, no one, some, a few,* or some other group identified by an indefinite pronoun.   **A4**

___ Have you used an adjective whenever describing a noun or pronoun? Have you used an adverb whenever describing a verb, adjective, or adverb? Have you used the correct form when comparing two or more things?   **A5**

___ Have you set off your transitions, other introductory elements, and interrupters with commas, if these are needed?   **C1**

___ Have you spelled and capitalized everything correctly, especially names of people and organizations?   **D1, D2**

___ Have you correctly punctuated quotations from sources and experts?   **C3**

___ Have you documented your sources as directed by your teacher?   **E2**

For more help, turn to the dark-blue-edged pages, and find the "Quick Editing Guide" section noted here.

Enlist several other students to read your draft critically and tell you whether they accept your arguments. For a paper in which you take a stand, ask your peer editors to answer questions such as these:

FOR PEER RESPONSE

• Can you state the writer's claim?

• Do you have any problems following or accepting the reasons for the writer's position? Would you make any changes in the reasoning?

• How persuasive is the writer's evidence? What questions do you have about that evidence? Can you suggest some good evidence the writer has overlooked?

• Has the writer provided enough transitions to guide you through the argument?

• Has the writer made a strong case? Are you persuaded to his or her point of view? If not, is there any point or objection that the writer could address to make the argument more compelling?

• If this were your paper, what is the one thing you would be sure to work on before handing it in?

For general questions for a peer editor, see pp. 323–24.

RECOGNIZING LOGICAL FALLACIES

Logical fallacies are common mistakes in thinking that may lead to wrong conclusions or distort evidence. Here are a few of the most familiar logical fallacies.

Non Sequitur.   From the Latin, "It does not follow," this fallacy is the error of stating a claim that doesn't follow from your first premise (the statement you begin with): "Jenn should marry Mateo. In college he got all A's."

Oversimplification.   This fallacy is evident when a writer offers easy solutions for complicated problems: "If we want to do away with drug abuse, let's sentence every drug user to life imprisonment." (Even users of aspirin?)

Post Hoc Ergo Propter Hoc.   Meaning "after this, therefore because of this," this fallacy assumes a cause-and-effect relationship where none exists even though one event preceded another in time. Many superstitions result from *post hoc* reasoning: neither seeing a black cat nor strolling under a ladder causes misfortune.

Allness.   The allness fallacy means stating or implying that something is true of an entire class of things. Instead of saying "Students enjoy studying" (which implies that all students enjoy all types of studying all the time), qualify: "Some students enjoy studying math." Be wary of allness words — *all, everyone, no one, always, never.*

Proof by Example (or Too Few Examples).   An example can illustrate or clarify, but it does not prove: "Armenians are great chefs. My neighbor is Armenian, and, boy, can he cook!" This type of overgeneralizing is the basis of much prejudice. Be sure you have sufficient evidence — enough examples, a large enough sample — to draw a conclusion.

Begging the Question.   A writer who begs the question sets out to prove a statement already taken for granted, often simply repeating that statement in different words. For instance, the argument that rapists are menaces because they are dangerous doesn't prove a thing: "menaces" are "dangerous" people. Sometimes this fallacy takes the form of "circular reasoning": "He is a liar because he simply isn't telling the truth." Other times it takes the form of defining a word in terms of itself: "Happiness is the state of being happy."

Either/Or Reasoning.   This logical fallacy is a special brand of oversimplification — assuming that an issue has only two sides, that a statement is either true or false, that a question demands either a yes or a no answer, that a problem has only two possible solutions (and only one that's acceptable). "What are we going to do about acid rain? Either we shut down all the factories that cause it, or we just learn to live with it." Any complex situation is likely to have more than two causes, two solutions, or two choices.

Argument from Dubious Authority.   An unidentified authority can be used unfairly to shore up a quaking argument: "According to some of the most knowing scientists in America, smoking two packs a day is as harmless as eating a couple of oatmeal cookies." A reader should also doubt an authority whose expertise lies outside the issue being considered, such as a television personality promoting insurance.

Argument *ad Hominem*.   From the Latin, "against the man," this fallacy consists of attacking an individual's opinion by attacking his or her character. It is widespread in politics: "Sure candidate Smithers advocates this tax deduction. She's married, so it will put money in her pocket!" Or "Carruthers may argue that we need to save the whales, but he's the type who always gets emotional over nothing." Being emotional is no more relevant to a proposal for saving the whales than is membership in a broad category (such as married taxpayers) evidence of an inappropriate personal interest. Joining two such ideas devalues the real issue — the merit of the proposal.

Argument from Ignorance.   This fallacy involves maintaining that because a claim has not been disproved, it has to be accepted: "Despite years of effort, no one has conclusively proved that ghosts don't exist; therefore, we should expect to see them at any time." The converse is also an error — that because a conclusion has not been proved, it should be rejected: "No one has ever shown that there is life on any other planet. Clearly the notion of other living things in the universe is absurd." Demand other evidence that life on other planets is not plausible.

Argument by Analogy.   Writers making this mistake treat a figure of speech (an extended comparison of familiar and unfamiliar items) as though it were evidence to support a claim. In an explanation, an analogy may be useful, setting forth a complex idea in terms of something familiar and easy to imagine. For instance, an analogy between shooting a spacecraft to a distant planet and sinking a golf ball into a hole half a mile away may help readers see the difficulty of the enterprise. But used as evidence, an analogy is logically weak because it dwells only on similarities, not differences — and admitting differences would only weaken the analogy: "People were born free as the birds. It's cruel to expect them to work." Hold on: human society and bird society have more differences than similarities. Because they are alike in one way doesn't mean they're alike in every way.

Bandwagon Argument.   This technique suggests that everyone is joining the group and, if readers don't jump on the bandwagon, they will be left out, perhaps missing out on happiness, success, or a reward. An advertiser may use this fallacy to suggest that those who don't drive a certain car or drink a certain soda won't be part of the "in" crowd.

OTHER ASSIGNMENTS

1. Write a letter to the editor of your newspaper or of a newsmagazine in which you agree or disagree with the publication's editorial stand on a current question or with the recent words or actions of some public figure. Be sure to make clear your reasons for holding your view.

2. Write a short paper in which you express your view on one of the following topics or another that comes to mind. Make clear your reasons for believing as you do.

Bilingual education	Raising the minimum wage
Nonsmokers' rights	Protecting the rainforests
Dealing with date rape	Controlling terrorism
Salaries of professional athletes	Prayer in public schools

3. Write one claim each of substantiation, of evaluation, and of policy for or against censoring pornographic Web sites, and indicate an audience each claim might address effectively. Then list reasons and types of evidence you might need to support one of these claims. Finally, for the same claim, indicate what opposing viewpoints you would need to refute and how you could best do so.

Applying What You Learn: Some Uses of Taking a Stand

In College Courses.   When writing assignments and examination questions ask you to take a stand on a controversy, your responses indicate clearly to your instructor how firmly you grasp the material.

- In a health-care course, you might be asked to criticize this statement: "There's too much science and not enough caring in the modern practice of medicine."

- Your science instructor might ask you to marshal evidence supporting your response to the view that "there's no need to be concerned about carbon dioxide heating up the earth's atmosphere because a warmer climate, by increasing farm production, would be preferable to the one we have now."

- In a criminal justice course, you might be asked to state and defend your opinion on juvenile sentencing; in an economics course, you might be asked to support your choice for the next Nobel laureate.

In the Workplace.   In nearly every professional position you can hold —
lawyer, teacher, nurse, business manager, journalist — you will be invited to
state and support your views about some important matter for the benefit of
others in your profession or the general public.

- Scientists who do original research must persuade the scientific community that their findings are valid, writing and publishing accounts of
  their work in scientific journals for evaluation by their peers.

- Social workers write letters and official documents to persuade courts
  and other agencies that taking a certain action or providing a particular
  service is best for the welfare of their clients.

- In a business with fierce competition, executives must convince their
  CEO that implementing their ideas will result in impressive benefits for
  the company.

In Your Community.   As an active citizen, you may feel compelled to inform and influence the public on matters of concern to all.

- You may want to write a letter to the editor of your local newspaper or
  to your political representative debating a controversial issue faced by
  your community — controlling violence in your schools, funding a new
  drainage system in your neighborhood, enforcing your community's
  leash law.

- You may be called on to represent the tenants in your apartment building by writing a letter of protest to a landlord who wants to raise rents.

- If you are selected to chair a campaign soliciting new members for your
  civic group, you may want to prepare a letter or brochure emphasizing
  all the benefits of membership in order to persuade the recipients to
  join your group.

Chapter 10
Proposing a Solution

If you polluted the air in the 80's,
here's your chance to redeem yourself

Riders wanted.

Responding to an Image

This advertisement appeared as a "spoof ad" on Adbusters, a Web site that advocates a critical eye toward advertisements of all kinds (www.adbusters.org). What is the problem posed by the ad? What techniques are used to make viewers understand the problem? What solution does the ad propose? Is this solution realistic and workable? What is the significance of the "Riders wanted" logo, and how does it affect the credibility of the ad's message? Compare this ad to the Volkswagen ad that appears on page 365, noting the similarities and differences between the two images. How does awareness of Volkswagen's advertising help to make this a more effective spoof?

Sometimes when you learn of a problem such as acid rain, homelessness, or famine, you say to yourself, "Something should be done about that." You can do something constructive yourself—through the powerful and persuasive activity of writing.

Your purpose in such writing, as political leaders and advertisers well know, is to rouse your audience to action. Even in your daily life at college you will find chances to demonstrate this effect. Does some college policy irk you? Would you urge students to attend a rally for a cause or a charity? You can write a letter to your college newspaper or to someone in authority and try to stir your readers to action.

The uses of such writing go far beyond these immediate applications. In Chapter 9, you took a stand and backed it up with evidence. Now go a step further, writing a *proposal*—a recommendation for taking action. If, for instance, you have made the claim "Our national parks are in sorry condition," you might urge readers to act—to write to their representatives in Congress or to visit a national park and pick up trash. Or you might suggest that the Department of the Interior be given a budget increase to hire more park rangers, purchase additional park land to accommodate more visitors, and buy more cleanup equipment. You might also suggest that the department could raise funds through sales of videos of individual parks as well as through increased revenues from visitors drawn to the parks by the videos. The first paper would be a call to immediate action on the part of your readers; the second, an attempt to forge a consensus about what needs to be done.

In making a proposal, you set forth a solution and urge action by using words like *should, ought,* and *must*: "This city ought to have a Bureau of Missing Persons"; "Small private aircraft should be banned from flying closer than one mile to a major commercial airport." Explain the problem fully, and lay out all the reasons you can muster to persuade your readers that your proposal deserves to be implemented.

Learning from Other Writers

The writers of the following two essays propose sensible solutions for pressing problems.

www
For more examples of writing that proposes a solution, visit <www .bedfordstmartins.com/ bedguide>.

As You Read

As you read these essays, ask yourself the following questions:

1. What problem does the writer identify? Does the writer rouse you to want to do something about the problem?
2. What solution does the writer propose? What evidence for the proposed solution does the writer present? Does the writer convince you to agree with this solution?
3. How is the writer qualified to write on this subject?

139

Wilbert Rideau
Why Prisons Don't Work

Wilbert Rideau, editor of the Angolite, *the Louisiana State Penitentiary newsmagazine, offers a voice seldom heard in the debate over crime control — that of the criminal.*

I was among thirty-one murderers sent to the Louisiana State Penitentiary in 1962 to be executed or imprisoned for life. We weren't much different from those we found here, or those who had preceded us. We were unskilled, impulsive, and uneducated misfits, mostly black, who had done dumb, impulsive things — failures, rejects from the larger society. Now a generation has come of age and gone since I've been here, and everything is much the same as I found it. The faces of the prisoners are different, but behind them are the same impulsive, uneducated, unskilled minds that made dumb, impulsive choices that got them into more trouble than they ever thought existed. The vast majority of us are consigned to suffer and die here so politicians can sell the illusion that permanently exiling people to prison will make society safe.

Getting tough has always been a "silver bullet," a quick fix for the crime and violence that society fears. Each year in Louisiana — where excess is a way of life — lawmakers have tried to outdo each other in legislating harsher mandatory penalties and in reducing avenues of release. The only thing to do with criminals, they say, is get tougher. They have. In the process, the purpose of prison began to change. The state boasts one of the highest lockup rates in the country, imposes the most severe penalties in the nation, and vies to execute more criminals per capita than anywhere else. This state is so tough that last year, when prison authorities here wanted to punish an inmate in solitary confinement for an infraction,° the most they could inflict on him was to deprive him of his underwear. It was all he had left.

If getting tough resulted in public safety, Louisiana citizens would be the safest in the nation. They're not. Louisiana has the highest murder rate among states. Prison, like the police and the courts, has a minimal impact on crime because it is a response after the fact, a mop-up operation. It doesn't work. The idea of punishing the few to deter the many is counterfeit because potential criminals either think they're not going to get caught or they're so emotionally desperate or psychologically distressed that they don't care about the consequences of their actions. The threatened punishment, regardless of its severity, is never a factor in the equation. But society, like the incorrigible° criminal it abhors, is unable to learn from its mistakes.

Prison has a role in public safety, but it is not a cure-all. Its value is limited, and its use should also be limited to what it does best: isolating young criminals long enough to give them a chance to grow up and get a grip on their impulses. It is a traumatic experience, certainly, but it should be only a temporary one, not a way of life. Prisoners kept too long tend to embrace the criminal culture, its distorted values and beliefs; they have little choice — prison is their life. There are some prisoners who cannot be returned to society — serial killers, serial rapists, professional hit men, and the like — but

---

infraction: Violation.   **incorrigible:** Incapable of reform.

the monsters who need to die in prison are rare exceptions in the criminal landscape.

Crime is a young man's game. Most of the nation's random violence is 5 committed by young urban terrorists. But because of long, mandatory sentences, most prisoners here are much older, having spent fifteen, twenty, thirty, or more years behind bars, long past necessity. Rather than pay for new prisons, society would be well served by releasing some of its older prisoners who pose no threat and using the money to catch young street thugs. Warden John Whitley agrees that many older prisoners here could be freed tomorrow with little or no danger to society. Release, however, is governed by law or by politicians, not by penal professionals. Even murderers, those most feared by society, pose little risk. Historically, for example, the domestic staff at Louisiana's Governor's mansion has been made up of murderers, hand-picked to work among the chief-of-state and his family. Penologists° have long known that murder is almost always a once-in-a-lifetime act. The most dangerous criminal is the one who has not yet killed but has a history of escalating offenses. He's the one to watch.

Rehabilitation can work. Everyone changes in time. The trick is to influ- 6 ence the direction that change takes. The problem with prisons is that they don't do more to rehabilitate those confined in them. The convict who enters prison illiterate will probably leave the same way. Most convicts want to be better than they are, but education is not a priority. This prison houses 4,600 men and offers academic training to 240, vocational training to a like number. Perhaps it doesn't matter. About 90 percent of the men here may never leave this prison alive.

The only effective way to curb crime is for society to work to prevent the 7 criminal act in the first place, to come between the perpetrator° and crime. Our youngsters must be taught to respect the humanity of others and to handle disputes without violence. It is essential to educate and equip them with the skills to pursue their life ambitions in a meaningful way. As a community, we must address the adverse life circumstances that spawn criminality. These things are not quick, and they're not easy, but they're effective. Politicians think that's too hard a sell. They want to be on record for doing something now, something they can point to at reelection time. So the drumbeat goes on for more police, more prisons, more of the same failed policies.

Ever see a dog chase its tail?   8

Questions to Start You Thinking

Meaning

1. Does Rideau convince you that the belief that "permanently exiling people to prison will make society safe" is an "illusion" (paragraph 1)?

2. According to Rideau, why don't prisons work?

3. What does he propose as solutions to the problem of escalating crime? What other solutions can you think of?

penologist: One who studies prison management and criminal justice.   **perpetrator:** One who is responsible for an action or crime.

Writing Strategies

4. How does Rideau organize his essay? Is his organization easy to follow?

5. What evidence does the author provide to support his assertion that Louisiana's "getting tough" policy has not worked? Does he provide sufficient evidence to convince you? Does he persuade you that action is necessary?

6. What evidence does Rideau give to support his proposals? Does he convince you that they would work? What would make his argument more persuasive?

7. Other than himself, what authorities does Rideau cite? Why do you think he does this?

8. Does the fact that the author is a convicted criminal strengthen or weaken his argument? Why do you think he mentions this fact in his very first sentence?

STUDENT ESSAY

Heather Colbenson
Missed Opportunities

Heather Colbenson's proposal, written for a course in agricultural business, addresses a problem she had encountered personally— the lack of funds to support agricultural programs in rural high schools.

A terrible problem is occurring within some small high schools in Minnesota: the agriculture classes are being reduced or even cut from the curriculum. When agriculture classes are cut, the FFA program is also cut because a student must take an ag class to be in the FFA. At one time the FFA stood for the Future Farmers of America; however, the organization has grown to encompass things other than farming, so it is now called the National FFA Organization, and it has become the largest youth organization in the United States. This is an important organization because it helps students develop leadership skills that they will use to be successful in business and in life. Therefore, the FFA programs in small schools should be saved.

Why would high schools in farming communities drop agriculture classes and the FFA program? One reason is that many colleges require that high school students take specific courses for entry into college. When funding decreases, these courses for college-bound students are seldom cut. Also, students must choose between general education college-prep courses and elective courses such as agriculture. For example, Minnesota colleges now require two years of foreign language. In small schools, like my own, the students could take either foreign language or ag classes. Most students

choose the language classes to fulfill the college requirement. When the students leave the ag classes to take foreign
language, the ag enrollment declines, making it easy for
school administrators to cut ag classes.

   The main reason that small schools are cutting ag pro-   3
grams is that the state has not provided significant funding
for the schools to operate. When schools have to make cuts,
some decide that the agriculture classes are not as important
as other courses--basic education courses such as English,
math, and science and college-prep courses such as foreign
language, calculus, and physics. When there is not enough
money, something has to go, and ag often gets cut.

   If cuts have to be made, why should schools keep their ag   4
courses and the FFA programs? If schools do cut these programs,
students lose many opportunities. The FFA and ag classes are
not just about cows and corn; they teach leadership, teamwork,
and self-motivation. The FFA provides many different ways for
a student to develop skills in these areas through holding
offices, competing in contests, and making friends.

   The main goal of the FFA is leadership development, and   5
one significant benefit of the FFA is the opportunity for
high school students to develop leadership skills. This opportunity is lost if ag classes and FFA organizations are
cut in the schools. Through FFA projects students learn to
identify problems, to research solutions, to formulate plans
to solve problems, and to direct and guide other people in
implementing° the plans. Through these activities, they develop self-confidence and self-motivation. This organization
definitely helped me develop leadership and confidence. When
an FFA program is cut from a school, a major resource of
leadership development is gone because students may never
find out that they can develop the ability to lead. George
Bush, former president of the United States and a former member of the FFA, praises this organization for its leadership
opportunities. If FFA programs are cut, students may not have
other avenues to help them develop these skills.

   Learning teamwork is another benefit of the FFA, and   6
the chance to work as a team is also lost when an ag program
is cut. Of course, students learn teamwork from sports, but

implementing: Putting into effect.

what sport has a team that consists of seventy people, as my
FFA did? When FFA programs are cut, students have fewer opportunities to learn to work cooperatively with other people.

A third advantage of FFA programs is that students dis-   7
cover that they can compete successfully against other students outside of the sports arena. The FFA has competitions
at the local, district, and state levels. If the FFA is cut,
a student may never know the pride of representing his or her
school at all these levels and might never experience the
thrill of competing with people from all over the nation at a
national contest.

A fourth advantage is that FFA offers opportunities for   8
students to explore various careers. FFA activities and competitions deal with livestock, business, sales, horticulture,°
floriculture,° and public speaking. Cutting the program would
result in the lost opportunity of trying different possible
career areas. I might never have found my desire to be a
business major had I not been in the FFA.

A fifth benefit from the FFA is meeting other people. If   9
I had not been in the FFA, one of the greatest losses for me
would have been missing the opportunity to meet other people.
I gained friends from many different schools and states. Now
many of those same friends attend the University of Minnesota
with me. The loss of ag classes and an FFA program would result in a lot of missed opportunities for the students. I believe that there is no other student organization that can
provide the opportunities the FFA does.

With all of these benefits from FFA programs for stu-   10
dents in small high schools, these programs definitely should
be saved. But what can be done to save them? Consolidation°
of programs, fundraising, education, and support are all
things that can very easily keep a program going strong.
First, schools that are having financial trouble can consoli-
date FFA programs. Small schools that have consolidated have
been able to save their ag program, making the chapter
stronger and dividing the cost. A second activity that can
help the financial situation is local fundraising. This is a
great way to keep an FFA program. My chapter sells fruit and

---

horticulture: The science or art of cultivating plants.   **floriculture:** The science or art of cultivating flowering plants.   **consolidation:** The process of merging or uniting separate systems into a whole.

raffle tickets every year to raise money. The school doesn't
pay for any of the activities. Third, the FFA members themselves must educate the administration, teachers, younger
students, and businesspeople of the town as to how the FFA
supports and helps students beyond their increased knowledge
of agriculture. If these people realize the range of benefits
that students receive from the FFA, then they will ensure
that the program remains in the local school. Fourth, FFA
members must support their own program from within. If even
one FFA member says negative things about the FFA, it will
hurt the program; people always remember negative things. Instead, members should share their concerns with other members
and work within the group to change the situation.

 I believe that ag classes and the FFA should remain ||
available for the benefit of students. Small schools do have
financial trouble and do have to make cuts, yet the FFA is
the wrong place to cut because many students would miss out
on opportunities that could very easily change their lives. I
want other students to be members of this great organization
from which I have benefited so much.

Questions to Start You Thinking

Meaning

1. What problem does Colbenson identify? Does she convince you that this is
   an important problem? Why, or why not?

2. What solutions does she propose? Which is her strongest suggestion? Her
   least convincing? Can you think of any other suggestions she might have
   included?

Writing Strategies

3. What kinds of transitions does Colbenson use to lead readers through the
   points she makes in her paper? How effective do you find them?

4. Is her argument easy to follow? Does she provide sufficient evidence?

Learning by Writing

THE ASSIGNMENT: PROPOSING A SOLUTION

In this essay you'll first carefully analyze and explain a specific social, economic, political, civic, or environmental problem—a problem you care
about and strongly wish to see resolved. The problem may be large or small,

*You can complete each of
the steps in this assign-
ment by using the Writing
Guide Software for THE
BEDFORD GUIDE.*

but it shouldn't be trivial. It may affect the whole country or mainly people in your city, campus, or classroom. Show your readers that this problem really exists and that it matters to you and to them. Write for an audience who, once aware of the problem, may be expected to help do something about it. After setting forth the problem, you may want to explain why it exists, as Colbenson does in her essay "Missed Opportunities."

The second thing you are to accomplish in the essay is to propose one or more ways to solve the problem or at least alleviate it. You need to supply evidence that your solution is reasonable and that it can work. Remember that your purpose is to convince your readers that something should be done about the problem.

Some recent papers in which students cogently argued for action include the following:

> Using research studies and statistics, one student argued that using the scores from standardized tests such as the SAT and the ACT as criteria for college admissions is a problem because it favors aggressive students from affluent families. He further argued that the practice of using the scores in this way should be abolished.

> Another argued that one solution to vacation frustration is to turn everything — planning, choosing a location, arranging transportation, reserving lodging — over to a travel agent.

> A third argued that the best solution to the problem of her children's poor education is homeschooling.

GENERATING IDEAS

For more on brainstorming and other strategies for generating ideas, see Ch. 16.

Identify a Problem.   Brainstorm by writing down all the possible topics that come to mind. Then star those that seem to have the most potential. Here are a few questions to help ideas start flowing:

DISCOVERY CHECKLIST

___ Can you recall any problem that needs a solution? What problems do you meet every day or occasionally? What problems concern people near you?

___ What conditions in need of improvement have you observed on television or in your daily activities? What action is called for?

___ What problems have you heard discussed recently on campus or in the classroom?

___ What problems are discussed in the newspaper or a newsmagazine such as *Time, Newsweek,* or *U.S. News & World Report?*

For more on brainstorming, see pp. 260–62.

Think about Solutions.   Once you've chosen a problem, brainstorm — alone or with classmates — for possible solutions. Some problems, such as

Facing the Challenge: Proposing a Solution

The major challenge writers face as they draft a proposal is to develop a detailed and convincing solution. Finding solutions is much harder than finding problems. Convincing readers that you have found a reasonable, workable solution is harder still. For example, suppose you propose the combination of a rigorous exercise program and a low-fat diet as a solution for obesity. While these solutions seem reasonable and workable to you, readers who have lost weight and then gained it back might point out that their main problem is not losing weight but maintaining weight loss over time. To account for their concerns and enhance your credibility, you might revise your solution to focus on defining realistic long-term goals and developing strategies for sticking to an exercise program. For instance, you might recommend that friends join a health club together, so that they can encourage each other to participate, or that they walk together two or three times a week.

To develop a realistic solution that fully addresses a problem and satisfies the concerns of readers, consider questions such as these:

- How might the problem affect different groups of people?
- What range of concerns are your readers likely to have?
- What realistic solution addresses readers' concerns about *all* aspects of the problem?

WWW
To practice considering your readers, visit <www .bedfordstmartins.com/ bedguide>.

reducing international tensions, present no easy solutions. Still, give some thought to any problem that seriously concerns you, even if it has thwarted teams of experts. Sometimes a solution will reveal itself to a novice thinker, and even a small contribution to a partial solution is worth offering.

Both the *causes* of the problem and the *effects* of not solving it can contribute to a persuasive paper. Try also to *analyze* it by breaking it into smaller pieces — subproblems that might be solved one at a time. Try a little *comparison* and *contrast* to gain a sense of how effective and useful a promising solution would be: Has this solution been tried before? How well did it work then? Is it more or less likely to be successful now? Finally, *evaluate* how urgent this problem is. Does something need to be done right now, or should you look for long-range solutions, which may take more time to implement?

For more on causes and effects, see pp. 316–18 and Ch. 8. For more on analysis, see pp. 307–10.

For more on comparison and contrast, see pp. 314–16 and Ch. 7. For more on evaluation, see Ch. 11.

Consider Your Readers.   Readers need to believe that your problem is real and your solution is feasible. If you are addressing your classmates, maybe they haven't thought about the problem before. Try to discover ways to make it personal for them, to show that it affects them and deserves their attention. Here are some questions to ask yourself about your readers:

- Who are your readers? How would you describe them?
- Why should your readers care about this problem? Does it affect their health, conscience, or pocketbook?

- Have they ever expressed any interest in the problem? If so, what has triggered their interest?
- Do they belong to any organization or segment of society that makes them especially susceptible to — or uninterested in — this problem?
- What attitudes about the problem do you share with your readers? Which of their assumptions or values that differ from yours will affect how they view your proposal?

For more on evidence, see Ch. 3.

Gather Evidence. To show that the problem really exists, you'll need evidence and examples. If you feel that further research in the library will help you know more about the problem you want to solve, now is the time to do it.

PLANNING, DRAFTING, AND DEVELOPING

For more on developing a thesis, see pp. 271–75. For strategies for planning, drafting, and developing, see Chs. 17, 18, and 19.

Start with Your Proposal. A basic approach is to state your proposal in a sentence that can act as your thesis: "The legislature should pass a law allowing couples to divorce without having to go to court." From such a statement, the rest of the argument may start to unfold, often falling naturally into a simple two-part shape:

1. *A claim that a problem exists.* This part explains the problem and supplies evidence of its significance.
2. *A claim that something ought to be done about it.* This part proposes a solution to the problem.

You can make your proposal more persuasive by including some or all of the following elements:

Knowledge or experience that qualifies you to propose a solution (your experience as a player or a coach, for example, can help establish your credibility as an authority on Little League)

Values, beliefs, or assumptions that have caused you to feel strongly about the need for action

An estimate of the resources — money, people, skills, material — required to implement the solution (perhaps including what is readily available now and what else needs to be obtained)

Step-by-step actions that need to be taken to achieve your solution

An estimate of the time needed to implement the solution

Possible obstacles or difficulties that may need to be overcome

Reasons your solution is better than others that have been proposed or tried already

Controls or quality checks that could monitor how your solution is proceeding

Any other evidence that shows that your suggestion is practical, reasonable in cost, and likely to be effective

Following is the informal outline that Heather Colbenson used as she wrote her essay "Missed Opportunities." Note the kinds of evidence she chose to include and the order she chose for organizing that evidence.

For more on outlines, see pp. 279– 84.

Thesis: FFA programs in small schools should be saved.

1. Reasons FFA programs are being cut
   –College requirements
   –Decreased funds

2. Reasons FFA programs should not be cut: benefits of FFA
   –Leadership training
   –Teamwork
   –Competition
   –Career exploration
   –Meeting people

3. Suggestions for saving FFA programs
   –Consolidation
   –Fundraising
   –Education
   –Support from within

You can increase the likelihood that your proposal will be accepted in two ways. First, state your proposal by claiming that a problem exists. Then, begin your claim that something should be done about it with a simple and inviting suggestion. For example, a claim that national parks need better care might begin by suggesting that readers head for such a park and personally size up the situation.

To propose a solution persuasively, you must show that you understand a problem well enough to suggest solutions, while addressing specific audience needs. Considering these ideas in columns can help you see them differently than you do when you compose a draft. After drafting your ideas in one file, open a new file, go to the Format menu and choose "Columns," and then click on "3." Label the first column "Problems." Next, create two more columns (in general, click on "Break," choose "Column break," and click "OK"). Head the second column "Solutions" and the third "Readers' Objections." Now return to your draft file, using it to copy and paste your ideas into the appropriate column in your new file. Add points as needed so that you move logically from problem to solution and answer readers' objections point by point. When you are satisfied that your columns show reasonable progress from problem to solution, go back to your draft to reorder your points more effectively.

WRITING WITH A COMPUTER

Imagine Your Readers' Objections.   Perhaps you can think of objections your readers might raise — reservations about the high cost, the complexity, or the workability of your plan, for instance. You can persuade your readers by anticipating an objection that might occur to them and laying it to rest.

For pointers on documenting sources, see E2 in the "Quick Editing Guide."

Cite Sources Carefully.   When you collect ideas and evidence from outside sources, you need to document your evidence — that is, tell where you found everything. Check with your instructor on the documentation method he or she wants you to use. You may also want to identify sources as you introduce them to assure a reader that they are authoritative.

```
According to Newsweek correspondent Josie Fair, . . .

As 2000 census figures indicate, . . .

In his biography FDR: The New Deal Years, Davis
reports . . .

While working as a Senate page in the summer of 1999, I
observed . . .
```

REVISING AND EDITING

For more revising and editing strategies, see Ch. 20.

As you revise, concentrate on a clear explanation of the problem and solid supporting evidence for the solution. Keep your purpose of convincing your readers uppermost in your thoughts. Be sure to make your essay coherent and its parts clear for your readers.

Reorganize for Unity and Coherence.   In drafting her essay, Heather Colbenson encountered problems with organization and coherence. Following are paragraphs 2 and 3 from her first draft:

```
    Why would high schools in farming communities drop
agriculture classes and the FFA program? Small schools are
cutting ag programs because the state has not provided sig-
nificant funding for the small schools to operate. The small
schools have to make cuts, and some small schools are decid-
ing that the agriculture classes are not as important as
other courses. Some small schools are consolidating to re-
ceive more aid. Many of these schools have been able to save
their ag program.
    Many colleges are demanding that students have two
years of foreign language. In small schools, like my own,
the students could take either foreign language or ag
classes. Therefore, students choose language classes to fill
```

the college requirement. When the students leave the ag
classes to take foreign language, the number of students
declines, which makes it easier for school administrators
to cut ag classes.

As she read over her draft, Colbenson realized that she was really talking about the two primary reasons FFA programs are being cut, but she had not made that clear on paper for her readers. She decided to use transitional phrases to make her point clear and to tie her ideas together explicitly, so she added "One reason" and "The main reason." Then she decided to place the main reason, decreased funds, last for emphasis. As she worked further, she realized that her first reason was not actually college requirements, as she had stated, but the competition between college-prep courses and other courses when money is limited. She revised her second paragraph to make this point clear. As she looked at her comment about consolidation, she realized it did not fit at the end of the paragraph explaining cuts made because of inadequate funding. This point was a way to save ag programs, not a reason they were being cut. For unity, she moved the point about consolidation to the last section of her essay, which consists of suggestions to save FFA programs.

Her revised paper was more forcefully organized and more coherent, making it easier for readers to follow. The bridges between ideas were now on paper, not just in her mind. Colbenson was also able to eliminate unnecessary words and, in general, improve the paper's style and precision of expression.

For strategies for achieving coherence, see pp. 296–99.

Be Reasonable.   Exaggerated claims for your solution will not persuade your readers. Don't be afraid to express your own reasonable doubts about the completeness of your solution. On the other hand, you may be tempted to oversimplify the problem so that the solution seems very likely to apply. If necessary, rethink both the problem and the solution.

For more on errors in reasoning, see pp. 134–36.

Exchanging Written Reactions

Exchange with another student the papers you both have written for an assignment in this chapter. Read each other's draft. Then take turns sharing first reactions — positive as well as negative. After this first exchange, take your partner's draft home for a day or two. Before your next meeting, write a review letter to your partner in which you thoughtfully critique the draft and suggest revisions. It will help the writer if you mark the draft as you comment, pointing out any problems with the organization, support, and so forth. Exchange letters during your next meeting, and discuss your experiences. What did you learn about proposing solutions? About writing? About peer editing?

FOR GROUP LEARNING

In looking back over your draft once more, consider these questions:

REVISION CHECKLIST

___ Does your introduction invite the reader into the discussion?

___ Have you made the problem clear? Have you made it relevant to readers?

___ Have you clearly outlined the steps necessary to solve the problem?

___ Have you demonstrated the benefits of your solution?

___ Have you considered other possible solutions before rejecting them in favor of your own?

___ Have you anticipated the doubts readers may have about your solution?

___ Do you come across as a well-meaning, reasonable writer willing to admit that you don't know everything? If you sound preachy, have you overused your *shoulds* and *musts*?

___ Have you avoided promising that your solution will do more than it can possibly do? Have you made believable predictions for the success of your plan?

FOR PEER RESPONSE

For general questions for a peer editor, see pp. 323–24.

Ask several classmates or friends to review your proposal and solution, answering questions such as these about proposals:

- What is your overall reaction to this proposal? Does it make you want to go out and do something about the problem?

- Are you convinced that the problem is of concern to you? If not, why not?

- Are you persuaded that the writer's solution is workable?

- Restate what you understand to be the proposal's major points:

  Problem
  Proposal
  Explanation of proposal
  Procedure
  Advantages
  Disadvantages
  Response to other solutions
  Recommendation

- Has the writer persuasively argued for the advantages of the proposed solution over other solutions? List any additional solutions you think the writer should refute.

- Has the writer paid enough attention to readers and their concerns?

- If this were your paper, what is the one thing you would be sure to work on before handing it in?

After you have revised your proposal, edit and proofread it. Check carefully for problems with grammar, word choice, punctuation, and mechanics—and then correct any problems you find. When editing a paper in which you propose a solution, make sure your sentence structure helps you make your points clearly and directly. Don't let yourself slip into the passive voice, a grammatical construction that represents things as happening without any obvious agent: "The problem should be remedied by spending more money on prevention." It should be obvious in every sentence who should take action: "The dean of students should remedy the problem by spending more money on prevention."

Here are some questions to get you started editing and proofreading:

For more editing and proofreading strategies, see Ch. 20.

EDITING CHECKLIST

___ Is it clear what each pronoun refers to? Is any *this* or *that* ambiguous? Does each pronoun agree with (match) its antecedent?	A4
___ Is your sentence structure correct? Have you avoided writing fragments and run-on sentences?	A6, A7
___ Do your transitions and other introductory elements have commas after them, if these are needed?	C1
___ Have you spelled and capitalized everything correctly, especially names of people and organizations?	D1, D2
___ Have you documented your sources as directed by your teacher?	E2

For more help, turn to the dark-blue-edged pages, and find the "Quick Editing Guide" section noted here.

OTHER ASSIGNMENTS

1. If in Chapter 9 you followed the assignment and took a stand, now write a few additional paragraphs extending that paper, going on to propose a solution that argues for action. You may find it helpful to brainstorm with classmates first.

2. Write a memo to your supervisor at work in which you propose an innovation (related to procedures, schedules, policies, or similar matters) that could benefit your department or company.

3. Choose from the following list a practice that seems to you to represent an inefficient, unethical, unfair, or morally wrong solution to a problem. In a few paragraphs, give reasons for your objections. Then propose a better solution:

    Censorship
    Corporal punishment for children
    Laboratory experiments on animals
    Genetic engineering
    State lotteries
    Dumping of wastes in the ocean

Applying What You Learn: Some Uses of Proposals

In College Courses.   Writing a proposal will be required in many of your courses. Often it will be a plan you must submit for approval before you go ahead with implementing a solution.

- Students embarking on a research project may be required to submit to an adviser or a committee a proposal that sets forth what they intend to investigate and how they will conduct their study.

- In social science courses, you may examine a current issue and propose a solution to the proliferation of guns, the disclosure of adoption records, the rising costs of prescription drugs, prison overcrowding, or racial profiling.

- Students who object to a grade can file a grievance proposing that the grade be changed. Like writers of persuasive essays, they state a claim and supply evidence in support of it.

In the Workplace.   Proposals frequently are written to suggest new projects, recommend changes in procedure, solve personnel problems, or purchase new equipment.

- An office manager might use a proposal as a means to promote harmony with co-workers, first discussing with the staff a certain problem — poor morale, a conflict between smokers and nonsmokers — and then writing a proposal to outline the solution on which the group has agreed.

- When a company decides to build a new building or renovate an existing one, the architect submits a proposal outlining the plans for the client's approval, and then contractors submit bids proposing to complete the project for a certain cost.

- Every job application is a proposal. Applicants propose that an employer hire them and support that proposal by selecting the best possible evidence for their résumés and letters or applications.

In Your Community.   Every day we encounter proposals for solutions — in editorials, in books, in public service announcements, in political debate. When you offer a thoughtful proposal on an issue crucial to your community, you challenge others to think.

- You might write a letter to your church board proposing that your congregation embark on a building fund drive to expand your overcrowded fellowship hall. Your proposal would include evidence of the need for more space, the cost of adding on to the structure, ways of raising the money, and a time frame for completing the project.

- In a speech to your local service club, you might inform them about the drop-out rate at your local high school and ask members to donate their time to work with at-risk teens.

- As volunteer director of your neighborhood art center, you might write a grant proposal asking for funds for a series of children's workshops. Your proposal would have to explain the need for the workshops, the benefits for the children and the neighborhood, the plan for the workshop activities, and the way each dollar would be spent.

Chapter 11

Evaluating

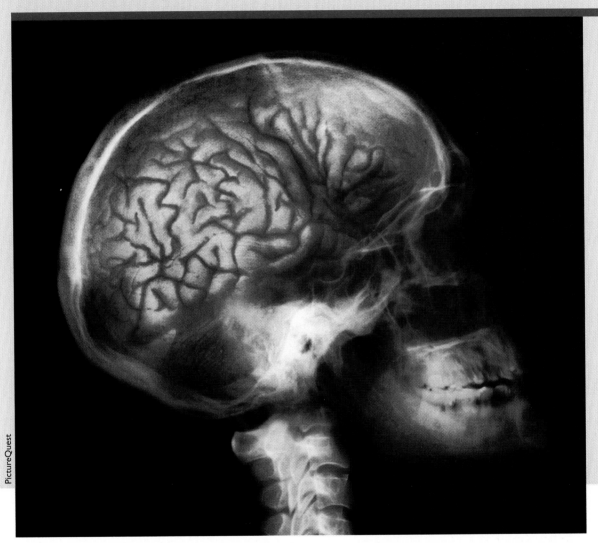

PictureQuest

Responding to an Image

When you evaluate, you use specific criteria to assess the object or image being evaluated and then try to convey your assessment to a particular audience in a credible way. In this image, what details can you discern? What areas are highlighted? What criteria for evaluation would a doctor use to assess this image? What function would evaluation serve for a doctor?

Evaluating means judging. You do it when you decide what candidate to vote for, pick which camera to buy, recommend a new restaurant to your friends. All of us pass judgments—often snap judgments—as we move through a day's routine. A friend asks, "How was that movie you saw last night?" and you reply, "Terrific—don't miss it" or maybe "Pretty good, but it had too much blood and gore for me."

But to *write* an evaluation calls for you to think more critically. As a writer you first decide on *criteria*, or standards for judging, and then come up with evidence to back up your judgment. Your evaluation zeroes in on a definite subject that you inspect carefully in order to reach a considered opinion. The subject might be a film, a book, a sports team, a group of performers, a product, a body of research: the possibilities are endless.

Learning from Other Writers

Here are evaluations by a professional writer and by a student.

WWW
For more examples of evaluative writing, visit <www.bedfordstmartins.com/bedguide>.

As You Read

As you read these essays, ask yourself the following questions:

1. Do you consider the writer qualified to evaluate the subject he or she chose? What biases and prejudices might the writer bring to the evaluation?
2. What criteria for evaluation does the writer establish? Are these reasonable standards for evaluating the subject?
3. What is the writer's assessment of the subject? Does the writer provide sufficient evidence to convince you of his or her evaluation?

Bill McKibben

The Frog Factor

This is a revealing and important book, and you should begin by ignoring the subtitle. Something tells me it wasn't the author's choice: in fact, he's done a remarkably sober and meticulous° job of following a story that's been misreported in almost every newspaper and on every TV station in the country. By book's end, it remains largely unclear what causes frog deformities and exactly how worried we should be about them—but we've instead been treated to a remarkable inside look at science trying to grapple with horribly complicated real-world problems.

In the summer of 1995, eight junior high school students on a field trip 2 discovered a small pond on a Minnesota farm where a great many leopard

Bill McKibben reviews William Souder's book A Plague of Frogs: The Horrifying True Story *in the March 2000* Washington Monthly, *establishing criteria for good investigative journalism up front and then evaluating Souder's treatment of the story.*

---

meticulous: Extremely careful attention to detail.

157

frogs were missing their hind legs. They called the state government, stories began to appear in the newspapers, and soon Minnesota's environmental agency had a map showing similar reports from almost every county in the state. Other such sites began to show up across the Great Lakes region; a Canadian researcher announced that the same trend was evident in Quebec. What did it all mean? No one knew for sure, because no one knew if deformed frogs were rare, or what might cause the deformities, or if that unknown agent might harm humans as well. It was a scientific puzzle, and a particularly difficult one. A pond is filled with water; it's hard to break down that water into its thousands of different compounds and figure out if one of them is, in fact, a poison.

And it's here that William Souder, a freelance journalist living in the region where the first frogs were found, really rolls up his sleeves and goes to work. Instead of "covering" the story with a few calls to bureaucrats, he digs in for the long haul, traveling to a long series of small scientific meetings, talking almost daily with the principal investigators, and watching as the science develops.   3

Though the book is not judgmental, it's abundantly clear whom he respects and whom he doesn't. The state bureaucracy clearly manages to mishandle the case at almost every turn; one lesson this book teaches is that, at least in what amounts to an epidemiological° investigation, you can have too much decentralization. You really want people for whom such an outbreak is not a once-in-a-lifetime event. The EPA comes off a little better, though its penchant for chasing trendy topics is clear. And unknown federal agencies like the National Institute of Environmental Health Science come off better yet.   4

The star players, though, are individual scientists, and the real drama comes as they face off against each other with their competing theories. From the start, Souder writes, there are two broad schools: those who think some chemical, most likely from a pesticide, lies at the root of the deformities; and those who think it's a parasite that has entered the frogs and caused their limbs to malform. The two theories represent two different worldviews: in the first, people are carelessly damaging all that lies around them; in the second, nature is a robust place where stuff simply happens all the time.   5

The researchers come together for scientific meetings that clarify the battlelines — and Souder makes it clear that at least some of the divisions come down to personalities. The chief advocate of the parasite position, Stanley Sessions, seems as arrogant and unpleasant a person as you would care to meet. And yet, as the story drags on, his case seems more persuasive. In fact, most Americans who were following the story probably thought it came to an end last spring when Sessions and a Stanford student published papers in *Science* demonstrating a strong parasite connection.   6

But as Souder convincingly demonstrates, that didn't really end the debate. There's plenty of evidence that doesn't fit the parasite theory, especially a huge set of Canadian data showing deformed frogs in agricultural areas and   7

epidemiological: Relating to the branch of medicine dealing with the cause and control of disease in populations.

healthy ones elsewhere. Apparently ultraviolet light plays a role in damaging at least some species; hence the erosion of the ozone layer might be a villain. The truth is, we don't know yet what is deforming frogs, and we don't know yet why amphibians in general are in decline, and we don't know when we will know. The science is still developing, and as Souder points out, "science as it is actually practiced in the everyday world is like a collection of medieval fiefdoms. Agencies and independent academics live and work in walled enclaves, among which communication and cooperation is possible, but often strained. Scientists, it turns out, suffer the same human foibles as everyone else. They're driven by ambition, by money, by ego, and by the perverse impulse to succeed amid the wreckage of someone else's failure."

One conclusion you could draw from that description is that scientists 8 never really figure out anything. But that would be wrong—with enough work, they usually do, even when the problems are horrendously complicated. The best example is global warming, which in 1990 was at the same battling-theories stage that frog research currently finds itself in. But climatologists, well-funded and pushed by national governments around the globe, figured out a way to organize their efforts and, by 1995, generate a consensus. (And in fact the one conclusive part of the frog story is that certain species of high-elevation toads have been killed off by global warming, which has transformed the Central American cloud forests where they lived.) The public, and certainly Congress, may still be confused by global warming, but scientists speak with confidence about it—their warnings of immediate peril are clear and unmistakable.

Other controversies remain unresolved. The frog case is one part of 9 the growing global concern over endocrine disruptors, chemicals that mimic° hormones and may disrupt reproductive systems, a concern that will eventually be better understood by science. Similar research battles are now erupting over the safety of genetically modified foods. "Eventually," of course, may come too late, and it almost certainly would make sense to take precautions now on the chance that such chemicals or techniques might be harmful. But at the very least, one hopes there are other clear-eyed journalists working as hard as Souder. For these are the most important kind of investigations going on in our world, endlessly more important than the investigations that transfix Washington so regularly. That almost no one bothers to do the work of really covering them is a kind of journalistic crime.

Questions to Start You Thinking

Meaning

1. Why does McKibben begin his review by telling readers they should "[ignore] the subtitle" of Souder's book? Why does he believe the subtitle wasn't chosen by the author?

2. In paragraph 7, McKibben quotes Souder's comparison of the practice of science in the real world to "a collection of medieval fiefdoms." What does Souder mean by that? Is it an effective analogy?

mimic: Show the characteristics of; imitate.

3. According to McKibben, what controversy has science resolved? What unresolved controversy does he mention in paragraph 9? Why do you think McKibben mentions this particular controversy?

Writing Strategies

4. What is McKibben's judgment of *A Plague of Frogs*? What criteria does he use to come to this conclusion?

5. Where in the essay do you find McKibben's support for his judgment? What kinds of support does he use?

6. How much of the essay does McKibben give over to summarizing Souder's book? Is this sufficient for his purposes?

7. Does McKibben address weaknesses in Souder's book? Does this strengthen or weaken the credibility of his judgment?

STUDENT ESSAY

Clay McCuistion
Coffee Odyssey

Writing for The University Daily Kansan, *a University of Kansas student newspaper, features editor Clay McCuistion evaluates six coffee shops according to an explicit set of standards.*

Six cups of cappuccino. Three hours. 1

That was the task I set for myself Tuesday evening on 2 a whirlwind tour of late-night coffee shops in downtown Lawrence. I'd spent time in a couple of them, but perhaps I was missing the very best atmosphere, the very best group of people, or the very best cup of coffee. Where was that elusive° location where diverting conversation, potent caffeinated beverages, and quick service combined to provide the perfect java experience?

In one evening, I decided to sample all the java emporiums in the Massachusetts Street area. I would have the same 3 drink--a small cappuccino--at each. This is the account of my evening's travels. The different shops are not rated in any numerical system. Instead, I've assigned each emporium a descriptive adjective encapsulating° the essence of my experience there. I've also included the preparation time for each cup of cappuccino--after all, if one has to wait two hours for the perfect cup of coffee, it's not so perfect.

Bourgeois Pig, 6 East 9th St.
I began here at 7:45 p.m. with high expectations. I'd heard 4

elusive: Difficult to describe or capture.   **encapsulating:** Summarizing.

the name of this combination coffee shop and bar bandied
about and was looking forward to experiencing the ambience.
The inside of the shop was small, but the bar area was attractive, and the bartender/barista sported a pompadour,
beard, AND sideburns. The cappuccino was the most expensive
of the night--$2.75 for a small cup. Kudos to the music se-
lection though, which included Neil Young, the Beatles, and
Bruce Springsteen.

The coffee looked exquisite, with beautiful light-brown   5
foam, and was served in a stylish little black mug. But once
I actually drank the coffee, I tasted bitter grounds in the
brew, which gave it a distressing° texture.

"You won't get better than this," the server told me   6
after passing me the cup.

I certainly hoped I would.   7
Descriptive adjective: Gritty
Preparation time: One minute and 15 seconds

Java Dive, 10 East 9th St.
This shop was brightly lit, cleanly furnished, and stuffed   8
with prepubescent-looking undergrads.

That's also why it was disturbing.   9

Coffee shops, at least in this reporter's mind, aren't   10
meant to have bright paintings on the walls and quiet, reserved studying taking place. Cigarette smoke is supposed to
billow across the room, choking anyone who dares to inhale
deeply. The tasteful, smoke-free Java Dive just seemed way
too normal.

While waiting for my cup of cappuccino (the longest wait   11
of any shop I visited in the evening), I ran across Kansan
sports columnist Chris Wristen, who was there for some coffee
and study. The Dive is Wristen's shop of choice for the same
reasons it unsettled me. For some reason, he likes a quiet,
positive atmosphere in which to do his homework. The coffee
itself was pleasant and foamy--an entirely competent cup.

Wristen wished me luck, and I moved on.   12
Descriptive adjective: Perky
Preparation time: Three minutes and 30 seconds

distressing: Causing concern and anxiety.

Henry's, 11 East 8th St.

My coffee shop of choice. I pledged I wouldn't give it pref-   13
erential treatment, however--Henry's would have to undergo
the same tests as other shops.

But even to the critical eye, Henry's offers a nice com-   14
bination of style and substance. Chatters can chat, students
can study, and the strange old men can regale each other with
strange, half-remembered anecdotes. Exemplary baristas brew
their concoctions with the concentration of fine artists, and
mismatched furniture litters the shop's cozy interior. Plus,
lots of people I know go there.

The coffee was the smoothest I'd had to that point, a   15
pleasant blending of the espresso and milk necessary for a
good cappuccino, topped with the thickest layer of foam yet.

Buzzing from the caffeine and bored with conventional   16
note taking, I spent much of my time in the store writing
notes about the brands of cigarettes customers were smoking.
I spent a good deal of time speaking with Stan Handshy, Erie
sophomore (who happened to be smoking Marlboro lights). He
was drinking straight black coffee from a mug the size of a
backyard swimming pool.

"I don't like to bastardize my coffee," he told me.   17

I nodded. It was time to go.   18

Descriptive adjective: Eclectic

Preparation time: One minute and 45 seconds

Cafe Nova, 8th St. and New Hampshire

The new kid in town, this cyber café contained few people   19
when I dropped by at about 9:30. The inside of the café was
nice, however, and my cappuccino there was served in the only
transparent glass mug I saw during the night.

The drink tasted oddly nutty, but not unpleasantly so. I   20
took a sip and looked around.

The cafe contained six Internet-ready computers, free   21
for customers' use. Generic alternative rock music played at
a low volume. Lamps on the tables were iMac-translucent. The
place only lacked regular customers--an obvious crowd to define it. This unassuming business had much potential.

Descriptive adjective: Translucent

Preparation time: Two minutes and 5 seconds

Java Break, 17 East 7th St.

This is the coffee shop you should go to if you want to feel   22
cool. Of all the shops I visited, the Break--more than any
other--reeked of alterna-hipness. There was an odd assortment
of rickety furniture, old concert posters on the walls, and
cases full of tattered paperbacks.

My coffee was produced more quickly here than anywhere   23
else--probably because the shot of espresso already had been
made. It was hot, foamy, and beginning to be indistinguish-
able from every other cup of coffee I'd had.

Multiple rooms were the Break's main drawback. A visitor   24
couldn't instantly see who was there--one had to walk around
the three different rooms and endure the cold stares of those
who wanted to be left alone. The shop also attracts a younger
crowd--thanks both to the coolness factor I mentioned and
being open 24 hours a day.

Still, the Java Break epitomizes° everything a college   25
town coffee shop should be--from servers dressed all in black
to nervous freshmen trying to concentrate on psychology homework. It's a testament to the store that this carefully cultivated atmosphere managed to percolate through my caffeine-
addled brain at all.

Descriptive adjective: Groovy
Preparation time: 30 seconds

La Prima Tazza, 638 Massachusetts St.

A pleasant end to a night full of caffeinated hyperness.   26

I was rattled by the time I entered the store. It was   27
10:30, and five cups of charged cappuccino were blazing their
way through my system. The experiment, such as it was, needed
to end. Right there. La Prima Tazza was the last open shop I
could find in the downtown area. As it was, the brightly lit
and spotlessly clean store soothed my frayed nerves.

I ordered my sixth and final cup. I sampled it and nod-   28
ded agreeably as instrumental jazz played over the store's
speakers. The coffee-flavored fuzz coating the inside of my
mouth distracted me a bit, but La Prima Tazza delivered
wholly competent brew.

epitomizes: Provides a representative or typical example of something.

Three other customers--working on math homework--were   29
in the store. I sipped on my cappuccino and smiled. I had
survived the night. I had survived the coffee. I had
survived crowds of angst-ridden twentysomethings. But most importantly, I'd seen a cross-section of late-night coffee culture
in Lawrence.

Had I learned anything?   30

My favorite coffee house was still Henry's--the   31
diverse group of people and furnishings there defined my
perfect hangout. The Java Break came in a close second,
however, and with its youthful vigor would have no doubt
been my favorite as a high schooler. The other shops were
pleasant enough, in their own ways, but the entertainment
and atmosphere of Henry's and the Java Break set them
apart.

But had I learned anything else? Anything really   32
important?

Absolutely. Drinking six cups of cappuccino within three   33
hours is insane.

Descriptive adjective: Pristine

Preparation time: One minute and 30 seconds

Questions to Start You Thinking

Meaning

1. What is the purpose of McCuistion's "coffee odyssey"?

2. How does he rate each of the coffee houses? Are his criteria useful? Are they effective?

3. Does McCuistion embark on his tour with any preconceived expectations? If so, where in the essay does he mention them? How do these preconceptions affect the credibility of his evaluation?

Writing Strategies

4. Look at how McCuistion formats his essay. What purpose do the divisions serve? Would the essay be more or less effective using a traditional format?

5. How would you characterize the tone of McCuistion's essay? Find words and phrases that contribute to the tone. How does his tone add to or detract from the purpose of his essay?

6. What evidence does McCuistion provide to support each of his evaluations? Do you find his evidence convincing?

7. Is McCuistion's conclusion effective? How else might he end his essay?

Learning by Writing

THE ASSIGNMENT: WRITING AN EVALUATION

Pick a subject to evaluate—one you have personal experience with and feel competent to evaluate. This might be a movie, a TV program, a piece of music, an artwork, a new product, a government agency, or anything else you can think of. Then in a thoughtful essay, analyze your subject and evaluate it. You will need to determine specific criteria for evaluation and make them clear to your readers. In writing your evaluation, you will have a twofold purpose: (1) to set forth your assessment of the quality of your subject and (2) to convince your readers that your judgment is reasonable.

> You can complete each of the steps in this assignment by using the *Writing Guide Software for* THE BEDFORD GUIDE.

Among the lively and instructive student-written evaluations we've seen recently are these:

> A music major evaluated several works by American composer Aaron Copland and found Copland a trivial and imitative composer "without a tenth of the talent or inventiveness that George Gershwin or Duke Ellington had in his little finger."

> A student planning a career in business management evaluated a computer firm in which he had worked one summer. His criteria were efficiency, productivity, appeal to new customers, and employee satisfaction.

> A student from Brazil, who had seen firsthand the effects of industrial development in the Amazon rainforest, evaluated the efforts of the U.S. government to protect the ozone layer, comparing them with the efforts of environmentalists in her own country.

GENERATING IDEAS

Find Something to Evaluate.   Try using *brainstorming* to list as many possible topics as you can think of. Select the ones with most potential—the ones that are most familiar or easiest to find out about. Then try *freewriting,* setting down ideas about the topics as fast as they come to mind. From the results of these two techniques, choose one subject for your essay.

> For more strategies for finding ideas, see Ch. 16.

Gather Information.   You'll want to spend time finding material to help you develop a judgment. You may recall a program on television or hunt for an article to read. You might observe a performance or a sports team. Perhaps an interview or conversation would reveal what others think.

Establish Your Criteria.   Jot down criteria, standards to apply to your subject based on the features of the subject worth considering. How well, for example, does a popular entertainer score on musicianship, onstage manner, rapport with the audience, selection of material, originality? In evaluating the desirability of Atlanta as a home for a young careerist, you might

Developing a Consensus

Meet with your writing group to discuss the subject you plan to evaluate, and see whether the group can help you arrive at a sound judgment of it. The other group members will need to see what you're evaluating or hear your detailed report about it. If possible, pass around a product or a course syllabus, show a photograph of artwork, or play a tape of a piece of music. If you are evaluating a short literary work or an idea expressed in a reading, you might want to read that work aloud. Ask your listeners to explain the reasons for their own evaluations. Maybe they'll suggest criteria or evidence that hadn't occurred to you.

ask: Does it provide an ample choice of decent-paying entry-level positions in growth firms? Any criterion you use to evaluate has to fit your subject, your audience, and your purpose. Ample entry-level jobs might not matter to an audience of retirees.

For more on comparing and contrasting, see Ch. 7.

Try Comparing and Contrasting.   Often you can readily size up the worth of a thing by setting it next to another of its kind. (When you *compare,* you point to similarities; when you *contrast,* you note differences.) To be comparable, of course, your two subjects need to have plenty in common. The quality of a Harley Davidson motorcycle might be judged by contrasting it with a Honda but not with a Sherman tank.

For example, if you are writing a paper for a film history course, you might compare and contrast the classic German horror movie *The Cabinet of Dr. Caligari* with the classic Hollywood movie *Frankenstein,* concluding that *Caligari* is the more artistic film. In planning the paper, you might make two columns in which you list the characteristics of each film:

	CALIGARI	FRANKENSTEIN
Sets and lighting	Dreamlike and impressionistic	Realistic, but with heavy Gothic atmosphere
	Sets deliberately angular and distorted	Gothic sets
	Deep shadows that throw figures into relief	In climax: a night scene, torches highlighting monster's face

And so on, point by point. By jotting down each point and each bit of evidence side by side, you can outline your comparison and contrast with great efficiency. Once you have listed them, decide on a possible order for the points.

For more on short definitions, see pp. 305–06.

Try Defining Your Subject.   Another technique for evaluating is to define your subject, indicating its nature so clearly that your readers can easily dis-

Facing the Challenge: Evaluating

The major challenge writers face when they write evaluations is to make clear to their readers the criteria they have used to arrive at their opinion. While you may not be an expert in any field, you should never underestimate your powers of discrimination. When writing a review of a movie, for example, you may tend toward simply summarizing the story of the film and saying whether you like it or not. However, for your review to be useful to readers who are wondering whether to see the movie, you need to go beyond these comments. For example, you might find a movie's special effects, exotic sets, and rollicking plot effective but wish that the characters had seemed more believable. Based on these criteria, you might come up with the thesis, or overall opinion, that the movie may not be realistic but is extremely entertaining and well worth seeing.

Once you've chosen a topic, use the following questions to help you clarify and apply standards for evaluating it:

- What features or standards do you plan to use as criteria for evaluating your topic?
- How could you briefly explain each of the criteria for a reader?
- What judgment or evaluation about your topic do these criteria support?

After identifying your criteria, you can examine each in turn. Explaining your criteria will ensure that you move beyond a mere summary to an opinion or judgment that you can justify to your readers.

WWW
To practice establishing and testing criteria, visit <www.bedfordstmartins .com/bedguide>.

tinguish it from others of its kind. In defining, you help your readers understand your subject — its structure, its habitat, its functions. In evaluating a classic television show such as *Roseanne* or *The Mary Tyler Moore Show*, you might want to do some *extended* defining, discussing the nature of sitcoms over the years, their techniques, their views of women, their effects on the audience. This kind of defining isn't the same as writing a *short definition*, such as you'd find in a dictionary, because your purpose is not simply to explain but to judge. You might ask, What is the nature of my subject? What qualities make my subject unique, unlike others of its sort?

Develop a Judgment.   In the end, you will have to come to a decision: Is your subject good, worthwhile, significant, exemplary, preferable — or not? Most writers find themselves coming to a judgment gradually as they explore their subjects and develop criteria.

To close in on a promising subject, you might ask yourself a few questions:

DISCOVERY CHECKLIST

___ What criteria do you plan to use in making your evaluation? Are they clear and reasonably easy to apply?

___ What evidence can back up your judgments?

___ Would comparing or contrasting help in evaluating your subject? If so, with what might you compare or contrast your subject?

___ What specific qualities define your subject, setting it apart from all the rest of its class?

PLANNING, DRAFTING, AND DEVELOPING

For more on thesis statements, see pp. 271–75.

Remember Your Purpose. Reflect a moment: What is your purpose in this evaluation? What main point do you wish to make? Work on stating a thesis that summarizes your main point, or try writing a paragraph that sums up the purpose of your evaluation.

Consider Your Criteria. Many writers find that a list of specific criteria gives them confidence and provokes ideas. Consider making a chart with three columns — criteria, evidence, and judgment — and filling it in to help focus your thinking.

For more on outlining, see pp. 279–84.

Develop an Organization. You might want to make your main point at the beginning, then demonstrate it through evidence (possibly comparison and contrast but definitely specific examples and details), and finally return to it in your closing. Organizing differently, you might open by wondering, "How good a film is *Gladiator*?" or "Is Keynes's theory of inflation still valuable, or is it hopelessly out of date?" — raising a question that your paper will answer. You then consider the evidence, one piece at a time, and conclude with your overall judgment. You might try both patterns of organiza-

FOR PEER RESPONSE

For general questions for a peer editor, see pp. 323–24.

Enlist the advice of a classmate or friend as you determine your criteria for evaluation and your judgment. Ask your peer editor to answer questions like these about your evaluation:

- What is your overall reaction to this essay? Does the writer make you agree with his or her evaluation?

- When you finish the essay, can you tell exactly what the writer thinks of the subject?

- Can you tell what criteria the writer is using for evaluation?

- Does the writer give you sufficient evidence for his or her judgment? Put stars wherever more evidence is needed.

- What audience does the writer seem to have in mind?

- Would you recommend any changes in the essay's organization?

- If this were your paper, what is the one thing you would be sure to work on before handing it in?

After you have written a draft of your evaluative essay, you will need to consider how well you have linked specific support to your judgments. Scroll through the draft and highlight **each judgment or opinion with bold type**. Then go back to the beginning of the draft and scroll through it again, this time highlighting *all facts and evidence with italics*. First examine the pattern of bold and italic type. Can you see a direct relationship between your **judgments** and the *evidence* you provide to support your claims? Are your claims in bold linked to your support in italics? Then quickly skim the bold and italic points. Do you need to modify your judgments or revise your support? Do you need to add more support at any points or move sentences around so that your support is more closely linked to your judgments? Writing an evaluation is not simply about being right: connecting your claims with your evidence makes your evaluation persuasive and interesting.

WRITING WITH A COMPUTER

tion (or a different one altogether) and see which works better for your subject and purpose. Most writers find that an outline — even a rough list — helps them keep track of points to make.

If you intend to compare and contrast your subject with something else, one way to arrange the points is *subject by subject*: discuss subject A, and then discuss subject B. For a longer comparison, a better way to organize is *point by point*, applying each point first to one subject and then to the other.

REVISING AND EDITING

Be Fair. Make your judgments reasonable, not extreme. A reviewer can find fault with a film and still conclude that it is worth seeing. There's nothing wrong, of course, with passing a fervent judgment ("This is the trashiest excuse for a play I have ever suffered through"), but consider your readers and their likely reactions. Read some reviews in your local newspaper or watch some movie critics on television to see how they balance their judgments.

For more revising and editing strategies, see Ch. 20.

In thinking critically about your draft, you might find this checklist handy:

REVISION CHECKLIST

___ Is the judgment you pass on your subject unmistakably clear?

___ Have you given your readers evidence to support each point you make?

___ Have you been fair? If you are championing something, have you deliberately skipped over any of its disadvantages or faults? If you are condemning your subject, have you omitted any of its admirable traits?

___ Have you anticipated and answered readers' possible objections?

___ If you compare one thing with another, do you look consistently at the same points in both?

For more on comparison and contrast, see pp. 314–16 and Ch. 7.

For more editing and proofreading strategies, see Ch. 20.

After you have revised your evaluation, edit and proofread it. Check carefully for problems with grammar, word choice, punctuation, and mechanics—and then correct any problems you find. Pay attention to sentences in which you describe the subject of your evaluation, making them as precise and useful as possible. If you have used comparisons or contrasts within your evaluation, make sure these are clear: don't lose your readers in a thicket of vague pronouns or confusing references.

Here are some questions to help you start editing and proofreading your paper:

For more help, turn to the dark-blue-edged pages, and find the "Quick Editing Guide" section noted here.

EDITING CHECKLIST

— Is the reference of each pronoun clear? Does each pronoun agree   **A4**
    with (match) its antecedent?

— Is it clear what each modifier in a sentence modifies? Have you   **B1**
    created any dangling or misplaced modifiers, especially in descriptions
    of your subject?

— Have you used parallel structure wherever needed, especially in lists   **B2**
    or comparisons?

OTHER ASSIGNMENTS

1. Write an evaluation of a college course you have taken or are now taking. Analyze its strengths and weaknesses. Does the instructor present the material clearly, understandably, and interestingly? Can you confer with the instructor if you need to? Is there any class discussion or other feedback? Are the assignments pointed and purposeful? Is the textbook helpful, readable, and easy to use? Does this course give you your money's worth?

For more on responding to literature, see Ch. 13.

2. Here are two poems on a similar theme. Read them critically, and decide which seems to you the better poem. Then, in a brief essay, set forth your evaluation. Some criteria to apply might be the poet's choice of concrete, specific words that appeal to the senses and his awareness of his audience.

Putting in the Seed
ROBERT FROST (1874–1963)

You come to fetch me from my work tonight
When supper's on the table, and we'll see

If I can leave off burying the white
Soft petals fallen from the apple tree
(Soft petals, yes, but not so barren quite,
Mingled with these, smooth bean and wrinkled pea),
And go along with you ere you lose sight
Of what you came for and become like me,
Slave to a springtime passion for the earth.

How Love burns through the Putting in the Seed
On through the watching for that early birth
When, just as the soil tarnishes with weed,
The sturdy seedling with arched body comes
Shouldering its way and shedding the earth crumbs.

Between Our Folding Lips
T. E. BROWN (1830–1897)

Between our folding lips
God slips
An embryon life, and goes;
And this becomes your rose.
We love, God makes: in our sweet mirth
God spies occasion for a birth.
Then is it His, or is it ours?
I know not — He is fond of flowers.

3. Visit a restaurant, a museum, or a tourist attraction, and write an evaluation of it for others who might consider a visit. Or evaluate a magazine you do not often read, one of the essays in this textbook, or a proposal under consideration at work or in your local community. Be sure to specify your criteria for evaluation.

Applying What You Learn: Some Uses of Evaluating

In College Courses.   In writing assignments and on exams, you'll be asked over and over to evaluate. Evaluation demonstrates to your instructor your sound understanding and considered opinion of a topic.

- Speech pathology students might be asked to consider the long-standing controversy that rages in education for the deaf by describing and then evaluating three currently disputed teaching methods — oral/aural, signing, and a combination of the two.

- Students of language and linguistics might be asked to evaluate Skinner's behaviorist theory of articulation therapy.

- Students often are asked to write comments to evaluate their instructors and courses; outside class, students on some campuses are invited to write comments for a survey to evaluate their campus facilities or student services.

In the Workplace.   Every executive or professional needs to evaluate. This kind of critical thinking is a constant in every sort of work and is the basis for evaluative writing, whether it be a report, a letter, a memo, or a review of the arts.

- Political commentators and newspaper editors evaluate the state of the economy, the actions of the administration or Congress, the decisions of the Supreme Court, and the merits of proposed legislation.

- Agencies such as police departments, civil defense units, rescue squads, or the Red Cross evaluate their performance in crisis situations in an attempt to refine and perfect responses.

- Teachers evaluate and document student performance for individual student files or for assessment reports to administrators, local boards, or state agencies.

In Your Community.   Familiar kinds of written evaluation abound in our daily lives as well. As citizens of a larger community, we are called upon to evaluate issues of concern and make our judgments known.

- In a posting to an electronic discussion group, you might explain your evaluation of the topic and also of the comments of other members of the group.

- Friends, peers, or co-workers will sometimes ask you to write a letter of recommendation. Whether the letter is a reference for a job or a commendation for an award, you will be evaluating relevant characteristics of performance or merit.

- Family or friends planning a vacation may want to hear your judgment of the places you have visited — restaurants, back-packing trails, bed-and-breakfast inns.

Chapter 12
Reading Critically

Responding to an Image

The images shown here were photographed on the streets of New York City. Spend several minutes examining each image. What is the product, service, or issue it appears to promote? What visual techniques does it employ? What is its apparent audience? Now examine the six images as a total package. What is the effect of seeing so many promotional images together, all displayed in approximately the same size and shape and from the vantage point of the passer-by?

173

"A shut book," according to a saying, "is only a block of paper." So is an open book, until a reader interacts with it. Like flints that strike against one another and cause sparks, readers and writers provoke one another. An involved reader may put down the book to ponder, pick it up again, jot notes, highlight, leaf backward for a second glance, fidget, nod approvingly, or frown. Such a reader interacts visibly with the printed page. But another reader may sit quietly, hardly moving a muscle, and yet also be interacting, deeply involved. Effective reading is active, not passive, reading.

Because the act of reading is highly personal, what readers take away from reading is as varied as their interactions with the printed page. Each reader, like each visitor to a city, has different interests and experiences and so comes away with different responses and insights. For example, when your class discusses an essay or a poem, you may be surprised by the range of insights reported by other readers. If you missed some of their insights when you read alone, remember that other students may be equally surprised by what you see. By using critical reading strategies, all of you can go beyond personal response to interpret more analytically and objectively.

Often you look to other writers — in books or magazines — to stimulate your ideas by suggesting a topic to write about, providing information about it, or helping you explain it or back it up with evidence. Sometimes you read because you want to test ideas; sometimes reading changes your ideas. Sometimes you carry on a mental debate with the writer; sometimes you analyze what a writer says to understand it better or to explain it to other people. In your college classes, you will read for several reasons, but most of your reading should be focused and analytical — in other words, critical.

Learning from Other Writers

WWW
For more examples of writing from critical reading, visit <www .bedfordstmartins.com/ bedguide>.

In the following examples of writing based on critical reading, each writer has read a piece that takes a critical stance on a controversial issue. After explaining the ideas presented, the writers actively engage with what they have read through a combination of analysis, synthesis, and evaluation.

As You Read

As you read these essays, ask yourself the following questions:

1. What reading does the author examine? How does the author identify and present this reading?

2. What information does the author learn from reading? How does she or he use that information in the essay?

3. What original insight does the author reach as a result of reflecting on what she or he has read?

Ellen Goodman
Kids, Divorce, and the Myth

This is what it comes down to in the world of divorce: irreconcilable° differences.

I'm not talking just about the conflicts between husbands and wives. I'm talking about the contradictory ways in which our entire culture views the breakup of a marriage.

When the marriage of a friend, a son, or a sister shatters, we wish this husband or wife another shot at happiness. We believe in the possibility of a second chance.

Yet, if they have children, we have an equal and opposite wish. We wish the children a chance to grow up with both parents in a stable home.

Not that long ago, when the divorce statistics first began to rise, many Americans comforted themselves with the belief that parents and children shared the same perspective. A child in an unhappy home would surely know it, surely suffer from it. What was right for parents — including divorce — was right for children.

But today that seems like a soothing or perhaps self-serving myth.

One of the myth-busters is Judith Wallerstein, who has been studying the children of divorce for over twenty-five years. Her latest book about *The Unexpected Legacy of Divorce* is written about and for the offspring of splintered families, children who carry the family rupture into their adulthood.

This psychologist has followed 131 children of 80 California families, a small and not-so-random sample of the one million children whose parents divorce each year. Today a quarter of all adults under forty-four come from divorced homes, and Wallerstein takes a handful of these children to show in rich detail the way divorce was and remains a life-transforming event.

Her book echoes with the laments° of their tribe. These are adults who spent childhood negotiating between two parents and two homes. Some were emotionally abandoned, others were subject to the crazy postdivorce years. Some still wait for disaster, and others are stronger for the struggle.

But as the elder to their tribe, Wallerstein makes one central and challenging point: "The myth that if the parents have a poor marriage the children are going to be unhappy is not true."

She says bluntly, "Children don't care if parents sleep in separate beds if the household runs well and if the parenting holds up." A good enough marriage, a marriage without violence or martyrdom° or severe disorder, will do for the children.

But if it will not do for the parents, then families face that irreconcilable difference: "The central moral dilemma of divorce which we have not been willing to acknowledge is that in many families what may benefit the parents may not benefit the children."

1 *Ellen Goodman, well-known columnist for* 2 *the* Boston Globe, *analyzes the views presented by Judith* 3 *Wallerstein in* The Unexpected Legacy of Divorce *and ex-* 4 *plores the implications of her finds for future* 5 *generations.*

6

7

8

9

10

11

12

irreconcilable: Incapable of compromise.   laments: Expressions of grief.   martyrdom: Extreme suffering.

175

Indeed, divorce may be the solution for the parents' troubles and the 13
cause of the children's troubles. "If children had the vote," she writes, "almost all would vote to maintain their parents' marriage."

Not surprisingly, this study has raised hackles among the divorced who 14
hear a new spin on the guilty adage: "stay together for the sake of the children." But Wallerstein is actually suggesting something much more subtle than that. And more intractable.°

Even as the advocate of the children, she agrees that "no one has the 15
right to tell an unhappy woman to give up her chance at love," nor does anyone "have the moral right" to tell a troubled man "to stay put."

We can tell them the hard road ahead and offer guidelines, but short of 16
granting every child a happily married set of parents, what can reconcile the differences?

Indeed Wallerstein herself includes a comparative interview with the 17
offspring of an unhappy intact marriage. Was it better for him than divorce? she asks the man she calls Gary. "Of course," he answers.

But as an adult Gary now sees things with the same complexity of our 18
entire society. "I have no idea how unhappy my parents were or whether they had regrets," he says. "After all, there are a lot of other things in life besides kids. I would have liked to see them both happier with their lives. Now that I'm an adult, I feel terribly sorry for both of them."

So divorce remains at the intersection — the collision point — between 19
our belief in the pursuit of happiness and our desire in protecting children. We pass along another unexpected, unresolved legacy to the next generation.

Questions to Start You Thinking

Meaning

1. According to Goodman, what are the contradictory views our culture takes of divorce?

2. What is the myth Goodman refers to in paragraph 6? How is it "self-serving"? How does Judith Wallerstein's research debunk this myth?

3. Goodman moves beyond Wallerstein's finding that children prefer an unhappy family that remains intact, saying the issue is more "subtle" and "intractable" than that (paragraph 14). What complexity does Wallerstein raise? How does her interview with Gary illustrate her point?

4. What does Goodman conclude after reading Wallerstein's book? What is the thesis of her essay?

Writing Strategies

5. Where does Goodman tell us the title and author of the reading to which she refers? Is the placement effective?

6. How much of Goodman's essay is direct quotation? Is this amount enough? Too much?

7. Which ideas are Goodman's, and which are Wallerstein's? How much of Goodman's essay is the presentation of Wallerstein's ideas?

intractable: Hard to manage.

8. Other than quotation marks, how does Goodman let the reader know which are her own thoughts and comments and which are Wallerstein's? Do you find any places where it is unclear whose ideas Goodman is presenting? If so, how might such a passage be handled more clearly?

STUDENT ESSAY

Ryan Miday

Times Series Delved Successfully into Race

The New York Times' six-week series on race this past summer, "How Race Is Lived, in America," demonstrated that it is possible to better understand the dynamic of race in individual lives. Progress was made from two things. First, it had adequate resources, such as institutional support--front-page coverage--and committed staff members; and second, it moved away from a discourse° at the policy level to exploring the subtleties° of race in the day to day experience of Americans across the racial spectrum told by the actors themselves. To construe° it as a success, however, would miss the series' point--that somehow the issue of race could be concluded or even understood fully. Nevertheless, the important point here is that the series illustrated that progress on America's race problem is possible.

Appearing on the Charlie Rose Show, the assistant editor of the series explained that the purpose of the series was to delve into the "silence" of race. Most people either do not talk about race; or if they do, they make it impersonal by objectifying it, warding off any personal identification with it or involvement in it. The silence represents a murky, obscure place, a distant locale occupied by race but covered by layers of deep rooted beliefs, often stereotypes; those layers in turn often mask race to the participants and observer. For an entire year, the reporters engaged the actors in their daily lives. What the Times series revealed was what surfaced from constantly probing those beliefs and experiences otherwise circumscribed by race.

One article, "The Minority Quarterback," for example, told the story of a white football player, Marcus Jacoby,

Ryan Miday, a student at Columbia University, critiques a New York Times *series on race, considering its strengths and limitations and then drawing conclusions about its effectiveness in raising awareness of race.*

1

2

3

---

discourse: Formal discussion of a subject in speech or writing.   **subtleties:** Finely drawn distinctions.   **construe:** Interpret.

"crossing the tracks" to play quarterback for Southern University in Louisiana, a football powerhouse among black colleges. Southern was 94 percent black. Having a white quarterback on the team, which had one other white player on the seventy-man squad, the punter, did not go over well with the team or the community. Jacoby suddenly realized he had a new race on and off the football field.

During the first recruitment meeting with Southern's   4
head football coach, who was black, Mr. Jacoby's father asked the coach, "How are you going to protect my son?" Jacoby was unconcerned; he wanted to play football. After receiving the good news about being signed, Jacoby called his girlfriend to talk about it. Her mother responded, "The niggers over there will kill you. There are bullets flying all over the place. It's a war zone." Getting on the phone, the girlfriend said, "Marcus, I don't want you to call me again."

Jacoby became the starting quarterback as a freshman.   5
But after their second loss, Jacoby recalled, "I heard the entire stadium booing me." Needless to say, losing was bad enough for Southern, but losing with a white quarterback was simply intolerable. The mother of quarterback prospect Sam George remembered, "One lady had a megaphone and she was screaming, 'Get that white honky out of there!'"

Jacoby was the starting quarterback during most of his   6
first two years. He had a highly successful first season; in the second year, he won the Bayou Classic's most valuable player and then won the Heritage Bowl in Atlanta, capping an 11-1 season that earned Southern the black national championship. Entering his junior year, Jacoby quit football and Southern. He was hounded by the press, asking why he left. He told them he was burned out; he never cited race. As a white male, Jacoby's brief experience with his race at Southern was difficult and unique--most whites never encounter such experiences. Jacoby, however, was able to quit the game, unlike others whose race determines a permanent location on the other side of America's tracks.

While beneficial in understanding race relations, the   7
series was not without its limitations. The most significant was that it reflected the prevailing black/white paradigm.°

paradigm: Model or pattern.

It renders everything surrounding race predominately about blacks and whites. Consequently, it makes difficult recognizing and understanding how race is experienced by other ethnic minority groups, such as Native Americans, Asian Americans, or Latinos.

The series was not intended to provide answers or direction on the issue of race. Rather, the series intended to show how race is experienced in people's daily lives. Through the actors' daily lives, it did make clear that, because there is such a heavy emotional and visceral° import to the issue, talking about it, moving through prejudices, and coming to an understanding of it is difficult. Also, it showed how many situations involving race are inherently ambiguous; that is, one person may engage or react differently from the next. The difficulties here render the rhetoric about being tired of the issue of race in America shallow and selfish. A sustained introspection on America's identity is thus needed to improve upon the profound misunderstandings mediated by race between Americans.

The <u>Times</u> series illustrated how devoting a sufficient amount of time, energy, and resources can prove worthwhile in furthering the understanding of race in America. By engaging the actors over the course of a year, the series was able to reveal what surfaces from breaking some of the "silence" around this issue. Only from this type of commitment can the silence be broken, moving toward a deeper understanding of the meaning of race in individuals' day to day experiences.

Questions to Start You Thinking

Meaning

1. What is the topic of the *New York Times* series that Miday examines? According to a *Times* assistant editor, what was the purpose of the series?
2. What significant limitation in the *Times* series does Miday identify?
3. What reasons does Miday give for commending the *Times* on this series?

Writing Strategies

4. Is Miday's introductory paragraph effective? What makes it effective or ineffective? How might Miday strengthen his introduction?
5. Miday states in paragraph 8 that the intention of the *Times* series is to "show how race is experienced in people's daily lives." How well does the anecdote about Marcus Jacoby fulfill this goal?

visceral: Instinctive.

6. What other examples from the series does Miday provide? Would his essay be stronger if he included more examples from the articles?

7. What types of appeal do you find in this essay? Where are they located? Are they effectively placed?

Learning by Writing

THE ASSIGNMENT: READING CRITICALLY

You can complete each of the steps in this assignment by using the *Writing Guide Software for THE BEDFORD GUIDE.*

For more on reading literally and analytically, see Ch. 2.

This assignment invites you to use critical reading strategies to analyze a text on an interesting topic and then to write an essay based on your critical analysis. To read critically, you will need to engage actively with the text on both literal and analytical levels and arrive at a well-reasoned conclusion about it. In your paper, you will then present to your readers the text itself, your analysis, and your conclusion.

Critical reading is different from other types of reading you may do. When you read a telephone book, you quickly skim a list of names to find the one whose phone number you need. When you read the sports page in the newspaper, you probably hunt for the key plays of a football game or a tennis match. When you read a novel for pleasure, you want to find out what happens to the characters in the story. But reading critically to study a text requires critical thinking skills. First, you read on the *literal level* to comprehend and be able to apply the information in a passage. Then you must go further and read on an *analytical level,* analyzing, synthesizing, and evaluating what you read. Both levels are necessary for a thorough critical reading.

We have seen many thoughtful papers written in response to this assignment:

One student read George Orwell's classic essay "Shooting an Elephant" and agreed with Orwell that governments sometimes act unwisely simply to save face. He analyzed Orwell's view, agreed with Orwell's position, and drew parallels between imperial Great Britain and contemporary governments.

Another student read a startling article claiming that the funeral profession reflects our culture. After analyzing the article, she discovered she agreed with the author. She wrote an essay explaining the author's position in order to share her new insights with others.

Another read an editorial on the need to reform political campaign funding. He was so convinced by the editorial's argument and so outraged by the evidence provided that he wrote an essay to share the information with his classmates and to try to convince them that campaign reform is necessary.

GENERATING IDEAS

How will you find ideas for this assignment? Try reading a variety of materials first — maybe one essay, one book chapter, one magazine article, one Internet source. See what piques your interest or looks promising for a meaty analysis, even if you don't fully understand it on first reading. Here are suggestions for unlocking the potential hidden in a good text.

For more on generating ideas, see Ch. 16.

Log Your Reading.   For several days keep a log of articles that you find in newspapers, in magazines, in essay collections from the library, or on the Internet. Try skimming a variety of pieces first — whatever engages you and challenges you to think seriously. Record the author, title, and source for each promising piece so that you can easily find it again. Briefly note the subject and point of view as well, so that your log identifies a variety of possibilities.

Skim and Sample.   As you begin your search for promising material, you can't afford the luxury of reading word for word. Skim, skip, and sample ideas. Try reading just the first two and the last two paragraphs of each article; those paragraphs will probably alert you to the writers' main points. When you look into books, skim through the first chapter and the last, and study the table of contents. If an article or a book looks interesting, you can spend more time later analyzing it critically.

Look for Meaty Pieces.   Start in the library, and spur your thinking by browsing through current magazines such as the *Atlantic Monthly, Harper's, New Republic, Commentary, Ms.,* and *Esquire.* Locate special-interest magazines — such as *Architectural Digest* or *Black History Monthly* — on subjects that engage you. Check the editorials and op-ed columns in your local newspaper or in the *New York Times* or the *Wall Street Journal.* Avoid *People,* the *National Enquirer,* or other periodicals written primarily to entertain. Also check the Internet. Search for articles on a subject of interest to you (for example, the effects of poverty on children, computer addiction, street talk, or Asian American authors). Be sure that the articles you find are meaty, not superficial, and are written to inform and convince, not to entertain or amuse.

Recall Something You Have Already Read.   What have you read lately that started you thinking? Consider drawing on a recent reading — a chapter in a humanities textbook, an article assigned in a sociology course, a research study for a biology course.

Keep a Reading Journal.   Begin responding to your reading as you identify especially promising pieces. For each reading, briefly record the subject, the writer's stand or thesis, and your initial reaction. Do you agree or disagree? Are you persuaded, skeptical, or baffled?

For more on keeping a reading journal, see pp. 17–18.

Choose a Promising Piece.   Once you have sampled various readings, look back over your pool of options and your reading journal. Which selection most interests you? Which of your reflections would most interest your readers? For which entry do you clearly have ideas of your own to add, either in agreement or disagreement? That's the one to develop. You may want to discuss your options with your classmates or your instructor before you proceed.

For more on literal and analytical reading, see Ch. 2.

Read Critically.   Once you select a thought-provoking piece, read it slowly and carefully, giving yourself plenty of time to think. Read first on the literal level, so that you are aware of the information and can both comprehend and apply it. Then read on the analytical level, scrutinizing, synthesizing, and evaluating information. Don't just soak up opinions and information; carry on a mental dialogue with the writer. Criticize. Wonder. Argue back. Demand evidence to be convinced.

Ask questions as you read. You can think of this process as a conversation with the author of the reading or with yourself, if that makes more sense. The following checklist includes questions designed to get you started as a critical reader:

DISCOVERY CHECKLIST

___ *What problems and issues does the author raise?* Does the writer present only one main issue or several related points?

___ *What is the author's purpose?* Is it to explain or inform? To persuade? To amuse? In addition to the overall purpose of the piece, is the author trying to accomplish some other agenda?

___ *Where do you agree, and where do you disagree?* Where do you want to start talking back to the piece, whether that's to say "Yeah, right!" or "I don't think so!"?

___ *How does this piece relate to your own life?* Does it connect to your own experiences or thoughts? Have you encountered anything similar? Is the topic or approach personally intriguing to you?

___ *What is the author assuming or taking for granted?* Do these assumptions make the argument weak or biased?

Annotate the Text.   One of the best ways to engage fully with a piece is to "talk back" by writing notes directly on the page. Obviously, if the piece appears in a book or periodical that you don't own, you'll need to make a photocopy; if it's an Internet source, you'll need to make a printout. You can underline key points, make checks and stars by ideas you agree or disagree with, and jot down questions or comments in the margins. The exact system doesn't matter: just try to come up with one that you'll understand later. For her essay, student Kelly Grecian decided to analyze an article called "Why Men Fear Women's Teams" by Kate Rounds from the January–February 1991 issue of *Ms.* She annotated a key passage in the article like this:

different case from
individual sports

By contrast, women's professional (team) sports have failed   *key point*
spectacularly. Since the mid-seventies, every professional league—
✓ softball, basketball, and volleyball—has gone belly-up. In 1981, after a
four-year struggle, the Women's Basketball League (WBL), backed by   *bitter tone*

example
backs up
point
sports promoter Bill Byrne, folded. The league was drawing fans in a
number of cities, but the sponsors weren't there, TV wasn't there, and
✓ nobody seemed to miss the spectacle of a few good women fighting for
a basketball.   *our team never got*
                                              these either

Something
I know
about!
Or a (volleyball,) for that matter. Despite the success of (bikini)—*Why does she call it this?*
volleyball, an organization called MLV (Major League Volleyball) bit the   *2nd example*
dust in March of 1989 after nearly three years of struggling for
sponsorship, fan support, and television exposure. [As with pro
basketball, there was a man behind women's professional volleyball,] real   *She's suspicious of men*
estate investor Robert (Bat) Batinovich. Batinovich admits that, unlike
oh, great   court volleyball, beach volleyball has a lot of "visual T&A mixed into it." ←

credential
What court volleyball does have, according to former MLV executive
director Lindy Vivas, is strong women athletes. Vivas is assistant   *seems like*
                                                                      these are only
                                                                      two options
volleyball coach at San Jose State University. "The United States in
Why do
guys
always
think
we're
weak
and
prissy?
general," she says, "has problems dealing with women athletes and   *good*
strong, aggressive females. The perception is you have to be more   *quote*
aggressive in team sports than in golf and tennis, which aren't contact
sports. Women athletes are looked at as masculine and get the stigma of ←
being gay."

As you annotate and interact with the text, you can deepen your reading by
asking questions such as these:

- *Is the author credible?* What are his or her credentials? Is the writer an expert in the field? Can you trust the writer to verify information presented?

- *Can you analyze the author's writing strategies?* Where does the author
  state the thesis? How is this thesis developed? Where does the author
  rely on evidence from others or refute others' ideas?

- *How is the text organized?* Where does one point end and another begin?
  How are ideas connected? Is the organization easy to follow? Does it
  seem appropriate?

- *Do you understand every important word and idea?* If not, do you need to read
  more carefully or go to an outside source (such as a dictionary or reference
  book)? Or do you think that the author has not explained sufficiently?

- *What is the author's tone?* How do the words and examples reveal the author's attitude toward the topic? Does the tone indicate the author's
  biases or assumptions?

WWW

To practice summarizing an author's main point, visit <www .bedfordstmartins.com/ bedguide>.

Facing the Challenge: Critical Reading

The major challenge writers face when they write from critical reading is to move from summary to critical analysis. Your active reading provides the foundation necessary to understand a selection so that you can summarize its main points for your readers. It also will help you avoid misrepresenting your sources in your paper—attacking authors for beliefs they never expressed. However, you will need to move beyond the foundation of summarizing a reading to analyzing it critically—providing your own opinions and evidence rather than simply reporting someone else's argument.

To make sure that you can move from explaining a reading's main points to analyzing them, complete the following five-part exercise:

- Locate the author's thesis, or main point, and state it in your own words in a sentence or two.
- Go through the article, paragraph by paragraph, and summarize or "nutshell" the main point made in each paragraph in a sentence or two. Leave several lines of blank space after each of your summaries.
- Locate the author's conclusion, and sum it up.
- In the blank space after your summary of each paragraph, list any evidence the author provides to support that point.
- Finally, write out your own response to each main point, clarifying whether you agree or disagree with the author's interpretation.

Don't be afraid to challenge the opinions expressed in an article or a book: skepticism is often the foundation of critical thinking and reading. But remain respectful of the opinions of others; take the time to understand the points they have made and the arguments and evidence they have provided to support those points.

For more on evaluating evidence, see pp. 27–28.

For more on facts and opinions, see pp. 25–27.

For more on logical fallacies, see pp. 134–36.

- *What evidence is presented?* Does the author include facts, data, statistics, expert opinions, or personal experiences and observations? Is this evidence accurate, relevant, and sufficient?

- *Which statements are facts that can be verified by observation, firsthand testimony, or research? Which are opinions? Does one or the other dominate the piece?*

- *Does the author use logical fallacies or misuse language?* Do you spot any "fighting words," leaps of logic, or other signs that the author's case is not as sound as it should be?

PLANNING, DRAFTING, AND DEVELOPING

For more strategies for planning, drafting, and developing, see Chs. 17, 18, and 19.

Decide What Point You Want to Make.   Before you begin writing, reflect and then read the article again. What conclusions have you drawn so far? What point do you want to make? Do you have what you need to make that point?

Determine an Order for Your Ideas.   You may start your draft with a quotation from your reading or with a summary of your reading, followed by your own view. You may decide to use a relevant anecdote, a comment about the author, or a personal account of the article's effect on you. If you are not sure how to organize your ideas, you might number them, write a formal outline, or try several drafts, each organized differently. Conclude your piece by referring to your main point, not by introducing a new idea.

For more strategies for openings, see pp. 291–92.

Borrow Honestly.   Acknowledge fully and honestly your debt to the writer from whom you borrow anything—a quotation, information, an idea. Not to do so is to lay yourself open to the serious charge of *plagiarism*, using someone else's words or ideas and failing to cite the source. Identify any source of an idea or quotation right away, as soon as you write it in your journal or your notes. Carry that acknowledgment into your first and subsequent drafts.

For pointers on documenting sources, see E2 in the "Quick Editing Guide" (the dark-blue-edged pages).

QUOTING.   When an author expresses an idea so incisively, so brilliantly, or so memorably that you want to reproduce those words exactly, quote them word for word. Direct quotations add life, color, and authority. Be sure to quote exactly, including punctuation and capitalization, and use an ellipsis mark—three dots (. . .)—to indicate where you leave out any of the original wording. Select the words you quote carefully; leave out wording that doesn't relate to your point, but do not distort the author's meaning. For example, if a reviewer calls a movie "a perfect example of poor directing and inept acting," you cannot quote this comment as "perfect . . . directing and . . . acting."

For more on punctuating quotations and using ellipsis marks, see C3 in the "Quick Editing Guide."

NUTSHELLING.   Also called *summarizing*, nutshelling is a useful way to deal with a whole paragraph or section of a work when you're interested in only the section's general point. Rather than quoting word for word, and without doing violence to an idea, you put it in a nutshell: you express its main sense in your own words and tell where you got the idea. A summary or nutshell is generally much shorter than the original; it expresses only the most important ideas in the original. Ellen Goodman, in paragraph 8 of "Kids, Divorce, and the Myth," sums up Judith Wallerstein's research plan: "This psychologist has followed 131 children of 80 California families, a small and not-so-random sample of the one million children whose parents divorce each year."

PARAPHRASING.   The technique of paraphrasing involves restating an author's ideas in your own words. Unlike a nutshell or summary, a paraphrase is generally about the same length as the original; it expresses every idea in the original but in your words. You have to be careful not to let the author's words slip in. If a source says, "President Wilson called an emergency meeting of his cabinet to discuss the new crisis," and you say, "The president called his cabinet to hold an emergency meeting to discuss the new crisis,"

WRITING WITH A COMPUTER

Using a computer file as an electronic note card can help you gather the key ideas from any source you read. Electronic note cards make it easy to identify a source, to take notes from it, and then to copy and paste that electronic information into a writing file, quickly synthesizing your reading.

Besides recording information from readings, annotate these computerized notes with your own thinking by devising a system of "text talking." Experiment with using different fonts, type sizes, colors, and type styles (such as bold, italics, and underlining) to distinguish the exact wording of sources, your paraphrases into your own words, and your comments and analysis. Develop your own system based on word-processing functions that are easy and logical for you. You can also move your notes around, grouping, reorganizing, and analyzing them before you actually write about them. When you start composing your draft in a new computer file, you can quickly and easily copy and paste ideas from your electronic note cards into a working draft of your essay. At this point be sure to return your annotation signals to the correct format.

your words are too close to the source. One option is to quote the original, though it doesn't seem worth quoting word for word. Or, better, you could write: "Summoning his cabinet to an emergency session, Wilson laid out the challenge before them."

How do you paraphrase another writer's thoughts? We suggest you do the following:

1. Read the original passage over a couple of times. Underline key parts, or jot them down.
2. Without looking at the passage, try to state its gist — the main point it makes, the main sense you remember, and the major supporting points.
3. Then go back and reread the original passage one more time, making sure you stated its meaning faithfully. Revise your paraphrase as necessary.
4. Check your paraphrase to be sure that you have not slipped in words from the original and paraphrased too closely.

REVISING AND EDITING

For more revising and editing strategies, see Ch. 20.

If you reread the text and discover new insights or drastically rearrange your ideas, cosmetic changes to your draft may not be enough: you may have to revise thoroughly. In looking back over your paper, you might consider the following questions:

REVISION CHECKLIST

___ Have you emphasized the significant points in the work you read?

___ Have you gone on to develop your own ideas and insights?

___ Do you see any place where a lively quotation might interrupt a monotonous passage?

___ Have you used any direct quotations where a nutshell or a paraphrase would serve better?

___ Do you identify clearly anything borrowed from another source?

___ Is the order of your ideas easy to follow?

___ Do you have enough details and examples to back up your assertions?

As you revise, pay special attention to coherence so that all the parts of your essay — quotations, ideas from the reading, your own points — are tied together. Check for transitions from your source's ideas to your own opinions and for connections between ideas. Revise any mechanical and repetitious transitions, and delete any interesting but irrelevant information that does not belong in the paper.

For more strategies for achieving coherence, see pp. 296–99.

After you have revised your essay, edit and proofread it. Check carefully for problems with grammar, word choice, punctuation, and mechanics — and then correct any problems you find.

For more editing and proofreading strategies, see Ch. 20.

Here are some questions to get you started when editing and proofreading your paper:

EDITING CHECKLIST

___ Have you used the present tense where you need it? Have you used the past tense where you need it? Do you move smoothly between your dominant verb tense and any different tense used in your reading? **A1**

___ Do you know what the subject of each sentence is? Does each verb agree with its subject? **A2**

___ Have you correctly punctuated your quotations from your reading? **C3**

___ Have you spelled and capitalized everything correctly, especially the names of the writer and the text you are analyzing? **D1, D2**

___ Have you documented your sources as directed by your instructor? **E2**

For more help, turn to the dark-blue-edged pages, and find the "Quick Editing Guide" section noted here.

Let a friend or classmate read your draft and suggest how to present both the reading and your analysis more clearly. For a paper in which you write from reading, ask your peer editor to answer questions such as these:

- What is the major insight the writer shares from his or her reading?

- Does this paper make you want to read the original source?

- How effective are the quotations the writer uses? Does the writer introduce them smoothly? Would any be more effective as nutshells or paraphrases?

- Are there parts of the essay where you're not sure whether you are reading the writer's ideas or the source's ideas? Underline any such places.

- Has the writer shared enough of his or her own ideas?

- At any point, do you need additional examples or explanations? Put a check by such places.

- If this were your paper, what is the one thing you would be sure to work on before handing it in?

FOR PEER RESPONSE

For general questions for a peer editor, see pp. 323–24.

**FOR GROUP
LEARNING**

Discussing Your Reading

If all students in your class are asked to analyze a specific reading selection, meet with your writing group, and appoint a moderator to run a discussion of everyone's reaction to the reading. Here are some questions you might ask each group member:

- What did you like about this reading?
- What problems did you have with the reading? What didn't you understand that someone else might explain?
- What do you believe is the author's purpose?
- What main point does the author make?
- Where do you disagree with or doubt the author?
- What does the author do especially well? What could be done better?
- What did you find out from this reading that you didn't know before?

OTHER ASSIGNMENTS

1. Using the critical reading strategies discussed in this chapter, analyze one of the essays in *A Writer's Reader* (Chs. 23–27). Write an essay in which you first give the reader an account of the information in the essay (through quotation, nutshell, or paraphrase) and then add your own insights and ideas. Or you may organize the essay point by point, explaining the reading and adding insights for each point.

2. Instead of analyzing something you have read, apply the critical strategies to something that you hear — a lecture, a television or radio commentary, or a conversation. Or apply them to something that you see — a photograph, a cartoon, a graphic, or an ad on a billboard, in a magazine, or on the Internet. Describe what you have heard or seen, analyze it, and then add your own insights and evaluation.

For advice on reading visual material, see Ch. 22.

3. Analyze two history books' or two newspapers' accounts of a celebrated event — the writing of the Declaration of Independence, the bombing of Hiroshima, a natural disaster, a political event, or any event you wish to read more about. Try to find one recent source and one at least thirty years old. Write an essay in which you identify and account for the differences between the two versions.

Applying What You Learn: Some Uses of Writing from Critical Reading

In College Courses.   You will write from reading almost daily during college. Your instructors will ask you to conduct research, assimilate information, clarify your thoughts, and demonstrate knowledge of what you have read.

- Many instructors will encourage you to read and then write by asking you to keep a notebook or journal of your reading. Literature students are often required to keep a reading log, and sociology or psychology students may be asked to keep a journal of supplementary readings.

- Writing about your reading on tests and examinations will allow you to demonstrate mastery of the course material, whether textbooks, handouts, or outside reading assignments.

- Most instructors ask you to read about a subject specific to your course and report your conclusions based upon your research. In an economics course, you might examine the status of women in the job market; in art, the reaction of minerals to heat when firing clay glazes; in education, the impact of interactive television on curriculum in rural areas.

In the Workplace.   The necessity of writing from reading carries forward into many jobs and professions. Many specialists, from physicists to zoologists, publish articles for others in their field, sharing what they know. Such exchanges of information involve actively reading, writing, and writing about reading.

- Often articles in journals such as *American Journal of Sociology, PMLA, Foreign Affairs,* or *Journal of Comparative Behavior* begin with a short review of previous research.

- Popular magazines and newspapers publish reviews of other people's writing in book reviews, commentaries, or editorials. Some publications, such as *Book Review Digest,* consist entirely of book reviews or summaries.

- Summaries of difficult writing are published to aid both consumers and professionals. Insurance policies often include a summary of provisions and restrictions; an abstract may precede a professional article in a journal or substitute for it in a database; simplified summaries of complex tax codes assist tax return preparers.

In Your Community.   You will constantly be asked to make informed judgments about current issues affecting your community — day care, crime prevention, funding for public projects. Reading for information and synthesizing it will help you form your own opinion.

- A study of abuses in nursing-home care can provide ammunition for a letter appealing for higher standards for the nursing home in your community.

- As a member of a task force exploring bilingual education for your local school district, you would thoroughly research the pros and cons before writing your policy recommendation.

- Summarizing relevant studies of wetlands for your environmental group's brochure or Web site would help alert your community to the need to protect such areas.

PART THREE

Special Writing Situations

Introduction

Much of the writing you'll do while you are in college will fall into one of the categories covered in Part Two. However, three common situations that you're likely to encounter will call for specialized forms of writing — writing about literature, writing for the workplace, and writing for assessment.

In college English and humanities classes, you'll write papers about literature. You may need to write a personal response, a synopsis, a paraphrase, a review, a comparison and contrast, or — most common in college — a literary analysis. Chapter 13 provides brief advice on writing a synopsis or a paraphrase of a literary work. It concentrates on the literary analysis, explaining how to analyze a piece of literature and how to develop a coherent interpretation and present it persuasively.

Whether you are working while you attend college or looking forward to a career once you finish, you will need to use your writing skills in the workplace. You may need to write a business letter to straighten out a bill or lodge a complaint. You may need to write memos and e-mail as part of your current job or to write a résumé and letter of application when you apply for a new position. Chapter 14 offers recommendations and samples for workplace writing.

Finally, as a student you'll face testing situations in which you must demonstrate your knowledge of a subject as well as your proficiency in writing, often constrained by a time limit. Writing essay examinations, short-answer quizzes, impromptu essays, and portfolio entries requires you to use special skills — reading carefully, planning globally, composing quickly, and proofreading independently. Chapter 15 gives valuable tips on how not only to survive but also to thrive in such situations.

Chapter 13

Responding to Literature

As countless readers know, reading fiction gives pleasure and delight. Whether you are reading Stephen King or Stephen Crane, you can be swept up into an imaginative world where you journey to distant lands and meet exotic people. You may also meet characters like yourself and encounter familiar as well as new ways of viewing life. By sharing the experiences of literary characters, you gain insight into your own problems and become more tolerant of others.

More often than not, a writing assignment in a literature or humanities course will require you to read closely a literary work (short story, novel, play, or poem), divide it into its elements, explain its meaning, and support your interpretation with evidence from the work. The analysis is not an end in itself; its purpose is to illuminate the meaning of the work, to help you and others understand it better.

There are certain basic ways of writing about literature, each with its own purpose. We emphasize the *literary analysis,* which requires you to analyze, interpret, and evaluate what you read. We also offer an example of synopsis. A brief glossary introduces literary terms.

Literary Analysis

LEARNING FROM OTHER WRITERS

In a composition course, Jonathan Burns was given an assignment to write a literary analysis of "The Lottery," a provocative short story by Shirley Jackson. Read this story yourself, and understand its meaning. Then read on to see what Jonathan Burns made of it.

Shirley Jackson
The Lottery

The morning of June 27th was clear and sunny, with the fresh warmth of 1
a full-summer day; the flowers were blossoming profusely and the grass
was richly green. The people of the village began to gather in the square, between the post office and the bank, around ten o'clock; in some towns there
were so many people that the lottery took two days and had to be started on
June 26th, but in this village, where there were only about three hundred
people, the whole lottery took less than two hours, so it could begin at ten
o'clock in the morning and still be through in time to allow the villagers to
get home for noon dinner.

The children assembled first, of course. School was recently over for the 2
summer, and the feeling of liberty sat uneasily on most of them; they
tended to gather together quietly for a while before they broke into boister-
ous play, and their talk was still of the classroom and the teacher, of books
and reprimands. Bobby Martin had already stuffed his pockets full of stones,
and the other boys soon followed his example, selecting the smoothest and
roundest stones; Bobby and Harry Jones and Dickie Delacroix—the villagers pronounced his name "Dellacroy"—eventually made a great pile of
stones in one corner of the square and guarded it against the raids of the
other boys. The girls stood aside, talking among themselves, looking over
their shoulders at the boys, and the very small children rolled in the dust or
clung to the hands of their older brothers or sisters.

Soon the men began to gather, surveying their own children, speaking 3
of planting and rain, tractors and taxes. They stood together, away from the
pile of stones in the corner, and their jokes were quiet and they smiled
rather than laughed. The women, wearing faded house dresses and sweaters,
came shortly after their menfolk. They greeted one another and exchanged
bits of gossip as they went to join their husbands. Soon the women, standing by their husbands, began to call to their children, and the children came
reluctantly, having to be called four or five times. Bobby Martin ducked
under his mother's grasping hand and ran, laughing, back to the pile of
stones. His father spoke up sharply, and Bobby came quickly and took his
place between his father and his oldest brother.

The lottery was conducted—as were the square dances, the teenage 4
club, the Halloween program—by Mr. Summers, who had time and energy
to devote to civic activities. He was a round-faced, jovial man and he ran the
coal business, and people were sorry for him, because he had no children
and his wife was a scold. When he arrived in the square, carrying the black
wooden box, there was a murmur of conversation among the villagers, and
he waved and called, "Little late today, folks." The postmaster, Mr. Graves,
followed him, carrying a three-legged stool, and the stool was put in the
center of the square and Mr. Summers set the black box down on it. The villagers kept their distance, leaving a space between themselves and the stool,

and when Mr. Summers said, "Some of you fellows want to give me a hand?" there was a hesitation before two men, Mr. Martin and his oldest son, Baxter, came forward to hold the box steady on the stool while Mr. Summers stirred up the papers inside it.

The original paraphernalia for the lottery had been lost long ago, and 5 the black box now resting on the stool had been put into use even before Old Man Warner, the oldest man in town, was born. Mr. Summers spoke frequently to the villagers about making a new box, but no one liked to upset even as much tradition as was represented by the black box. There was a story that the present box had been made with some pieces of the box that had preceded it, the one that had been constructed when the first people settled down to make a village here. Every year, after the lottery, Mr. Summers began talking again about a new box, but every year the subject was allowed to fade off without anything's being done. The black box grew shabbier each year; by now it was no longer completely black but splintered badly along one side to show the original wood color, and in some places faded or stained.

Mr. Martin and his oldest son, Baxter, held the black box securely on the 6 stool until Mr. Summers had stirred the papers thoroughly with his hand. Because so much of the ritual had been forgotten or discarded, Mr. Summers had been successful in having slips of paper substituted for the chips of wood that had been used for generations. Chips of wood, Mr. Summers had argued, had been all very well when the village was tiny, but now that the population was more than three hundred and likely to keep on growing, it was necessary to use something that would fit more easily into the black box. The night before the lottery, Mr. Summers and Mr. Graves made up the slips of paper and put them in the box, and it was then taken to the safe of Mr. Summers's coal company and locked up until Mr. Summers was ready to take it to the square next morning. The rest of the year, the box was put away, sometimes one place, sometimes another; it had spent one year in Mr. Graves's barn and another year underfoot in the post office, and sometimes it was set on a shelf in the Martin grocery and left there.

There was a great deal of fussing to be done before Mr. Summers declared the lottery open. There were the lists to make up — of heads of families, heads of households in each family, members of each household in each family. There was the proper swearing-in of Mr. Summers by the postmaster, as the official of the lottery; at one time, some people remembered, there had been a recital of some sort, performed by the official of the lottery, a perfunctory, tuneless chant that had been rattled off duly each year; some people believed that the official of the lottery used to stand just so when he said or sang it, others believed that he was supposed to walk among the people, but years and years ago this part of the ritual had been allowed to lapse. There had been, also, a ritual salute, which the official of the lottery had had to use in addressing each person who came up to draw from the box, but this also had changed with time, until now it was felt necessary only for the official to speak to each person approaching. Mr. Summers was very good at all this; in his clean white shirt and blue jeans, with one hand resting carelessly on the black box, he seemed very proper and important as he talked interminably to Mr. Graves and the Martins.

Just as Mr. Summers finally left off talking and turned to the assembled 8 villagers, Mrs. Hutchinson came hurriedly along the path to the square, her sweater thrown over her shoulders, and slid into place in the back of the crowd. "Clean forgot what day it was," she said to Mrs. Delacroix, who stood next to her, and they both laughed softly. "Thought my old man was out back stacking wood," Mrs. Hutchinson went on, "and then I looked out the window and the kids was gone, and then I remembered it was the twenty-seventh and came a-running." She dried her hands on her apron, and Mrs. Delacroix said, "You're in time, though. They're still talking away up there."

Mrs. Hutchinson craned her neck to see through the crowd and found 9 her husband and children standing near the front. She tapped Mrs. Delacroix on the arm as a farewell and began to make her way through the crowd. The people separated good-humoredly to let her through; two or three people said, in voices just loud enough to be heard across the crowd, "Here comes your Missus, Hutchinson," and "Bill, she made it after all." Mrs. Hutchinson reached her husband, and Mr. Summers, who had been waiting, said cheerfully, "Thought we were going to have to get on without you, Tessie." Mrs. Hutchinson said, grinning, "Wouldn't have me leave m'dishes in the sink, now, would you, Joe?" and soft laughter ran through the crowd as the people stirred back into position after Mrs. Hutchinson's arrival.

"Well, now," Mr. Summers said soberly, "guess we better get started, get 10 this over with, so's we can go back to work. Anybody ain't here?"

"Dunbar," several people said. "Dunbar, Dunbar."   11

Mr. Summers consulted his list. "Clyde Dunbar," he said. "That's right. 12 He's broke his leg, hasn't he? Who's drawing for him?"

"Me, I guess," a woman said, and Mr. Summers turned to look at her. 13 "Wife draws for her husband," Mr. Summers said. "Don't you have a grown boy to do it for you, Janey?" Although Mr. Summers and everyone else in the village knew the answer perfectly well, it was the business of the official of the lottery to ask such questions formally. Mr. Summers waited with an expression of polite interest while Mrs. Dunbar answered.

"Horace's not but sixteen yet," Mrs. Dunbar said regretfully. "Guess I 14 gotta fill in for the old man this year."

"Right," Mr. Summers said. He made a note on the list he was holding. 15 Then he asked, "Watson boy drawing this year?"

A tall boy in the crowd raised his hand. "Here," he said. "I'm drawing 16 for m'mother and me." He blinked his eyes nervously and ducked his head as several voices in the crowd said things like "Good fellow, Jack," and "Glad to see your mother's got a man to do it."

"Well," Mr. Summers said, "guess that's everyone. Old Man Warner 17 make it?"

"Here," a voice said, and Mr. Summers nodded.   18

A sudden hush fell on the crowd as Mr. Summers cleared his throat and   19
looked at the list. "All ready?" he called. "Now, I'll read the names — heads
of families first — and the men come up and take a paper out of the box.
Keep the paper folded in your hand without looking at it until everyone has
had a turn. Everything clear?"

The people had done it so many times that they only half listened to the   20
directions; most of them were quiet, wetting their lips, not looking around.
Then Mr. Summers raised one hand high and said, "Adams." A man disen-
gaged himself from the crowd and came forward. "Hi, Steve," Mr. Summers
said, and Mr. Adams said, "Hi, Joe." They grinned at one another humor-
lessly and nervously. Then Mr. Adams reached into the black box and took
out a folded paper. He held it firmly by one corner as he turned and went
hastily back to his place in the crowd, where he stood a little apart from his
family, not looking down at his hand.

"Allen," Mr. Summers said. "Anderson. . . . Bentham."   21

"Seems like there's no time at all between lotteries anymore," Mrs.   22
Delacroix said to Mrs. Graves in the back row. "Seems like we got through
with the last one only last week."

"Time sure goes fast," Mrs. Graves said.   23

"Clark. . . . Delacroix."   24

"There goes my old man," Mrs. Delacroix said. She held her breath   25
while her husband went forward.

"Dunbar," Mr. Summers said, and Mrs. Dunbar went steadily to the box   26
while one of the women said, "Go on, Janey," and another said, "There she
goes."

"We're next," Mrs. Graves said. She watched while Mr. Graves came   27
around from the side of the box, greeted Mr. Summers gravely, and selected
a slip of paper from the box. By now, all through the crowd there were men
holding the small folded papers in their large hands, turning them over and
over nervously. Mrs. Dunbar and her two sons stood together, Mrs. Dunbar
holding the slip of paper.

"Harburt. . . . Hutchinson."   28

"Get up there, Bill," Mrs. Hutchinson said, and the people near her   29
laughed.

"Jones."   30

"They do say," Mr. Adams said to Old Man Warner, who stood next to   31
him, "that over in the north village they're talking of giving up the lottery."

Old Man Warner snorted. "Pack of crazy fools," he said. "Listening to   32
the young folks, nothing's good enough for *them*. Next thing you know,
they'll be wanting to go back to living in caves, nobody work anymore, live
that way for a while. Used to be a saying about 'Lottery in June, corn be
heavy soon.' First thing you know, we'd all be eating stewed chickweed and
acorns. There's *always* been a lottery," he added petulantly. "Bad enough to
see young Joe Summers up there joking with everybody."

"Some places have already quit lotteries," Mrs. Adams said.   33

"Nothing but trouble in *that*," Old Man Warner said stoutly. "Pack of   34
young fools."

"Martin." And Bobby Martin watched his father go forward. "Over-   35
dyke. . . . Percy."

"I wish they'd hurry," Mrs. Dunbar said to her older son. "I wish they'd   36
hurry."

"They're almost through," her son said.   37

"You get ready to run tell Dad," Mrs. Dunbar said.   38

Mr. Summers called his own name and then stepped forward precisely   39
and selected a slip from the box. Then he called, "Warner."

"Seventy-seventh year I been in the lottery," Old Man Warner said as he   40
went through the crowd. "Seventy-seventh time."

"Watson." The tall boy came awkwardly through the crowd. Someone   41
said, "Don't be nervous, Jack," and Mr. Summers said, "Take your time, son."

"Zanini."   42

After that, there was a long pause, a breathless pause, until Mr. Sum-   43
mers, holding his slip of paper in the air, said, "All right, fellows." For a
minute, no one moved, and then all the slips of paper were opened. Suddenly, all the women began to speak at once, saying, "Who is it?" "Who's
got it?" "Is it the Dunbars?" "Is it the Watsons?" Then the voices began to
say, "It's Hutchinson. It's Bill." "Bill Hutchinson's got it."

"Go tell your father," Mrs. Dunbar said to her older son.   44

People began to look around to see the Hutchinsons. Bill Hutchinson   45
was standing quiet, staring down at the paper in his hand. Suddenly, Tessie
Hutchinson shouted to Mr. Summers, "You didn't give him time enough to
take any paper he wanted. I saw you. It wasn't fair!"

"Be a good sport, Tessie," Mrs. Delacroix called, and Mrs. Graves said,   46
"All of us took the same chance."

"Shut up, Tessie," Bill Hutchinson said.   47

"Well, everyone," Mr. Summers said, "that was done pretty fast, and   48
now we've got to be hurrying a little more to get done in time." He consulted his next list. "Bill," he said, "you draw for the Hutchinson family. You
got any other households in the Hutchinsons?"

"There's Don and Eva," Mrs. Hutchinson yelled. "Make *them* take their   49
chance!"

"Daughters draw with their husbands' families, Tessie," Mr. Summers   50
said gently. "You know that as well as anyone else."

"It wasn't *fair*," Tessie said.   51

"I guess not, Joe," Bill Hutchinson said regretfully. "My daughter draws   52
with her husband's family, that's only fair. And I've got no other family except the kids."

"Then, as far as drawing for families is concerned, it's you," Mr. Sum-   53
mers said in explanation, "and as far as drawing for households is concerned, that's you, too. Right?"

"Right," Bill Hutchinson said.   54

"How many kids, Bill?" Mr. Summers asked formally.   55

"Three," Bill Hutchinson said. "There's Bill, Jr., and Nancy, and little 56 Dave. And Tessie and me."

"All right, then," Mr. Summers said. "Harry, you got their tickets back?" 57

Mr. Graves nodded and held up the slips of paper. "Put them in the box, 58 then," Mr. Summers directed. "Take Bill's and put it in."

"I think we ought to start over," Mrs. Hutchinson said, as quietly as she 59 could. "I tell you it wasn't *fair*. You didn't give him time enough to choose. *Every*body saw that."

Mr. Graves had selected the five slips and put them in the box, and he 60 dropped all the papers but those onto the ground, where the breeze caught them and lifted them off.

"Listen, everybody," Mrs. Hutchinson was saying to the people around 61 her.

"Ready, Bill?" Mr. Summers asked, and Bill Hutchinson, with one quick 62 glance around at his wife and children, nodded.

"Remember," Mr. Summers said, "take the slips and keep them folded 63 until each person has taken one. Harry, you help little Dave." Mr. Graves took the hand of the little boy, who came willingly with him up to the box. "Take a paper out of the box, Davy," Mr. Summers said. Davy put his hand into the box and laughed. "Take just *one* paper," Mr. Summers said. "Harry, you hold it for him." Mr. Graves took the child's hand and removed the folded paper from the tight fist and held it while little Dave stood next to him and looked up at him wonderingly.

"Nancy next," Mr. Summers said. Nancy was twelve, and her school 64 friends breathed heavily as she went forward, switching her skirt, and took a slip daintily from the box. "Bill, Jr.," Mr. Summers said, and Billy, his face red and his feet overlarge, nearly knocked the box over as he got a paper out. "Tessie," Mr. Summers said. She hesitated for a minute, looking around defiantly, and then set her lips and went up to the box. She snatched a paper out and held it behind her.

"Bill," Mr. Summers said, and Bill Hutchinson reached into the box and 65 felt around, bringing his hand out at last with the slip of paper in it.

The crowd was quiet. A girl whispered, "I hope it's not Nancy," and the 66 sound of the whisper reached the edges of the crowd.

"It's not the way it used to be," Old Man Warner said clearly. "People 67 ain't the way they used to be."

"All right," Mr. Summers said. "Open the papers. Harry, you open little 68 Dave's."

Mr. Graves opened the slip of paper and there was a general sigh 69 through the crowd as he held it up and everyone could see that it was blank. Nancy and Bill, Jr., opened theirs at the same time, and both beamed and laughed, turning around to the crowd and holding their slips of paper above their heads.

"Tessie," Mr. Summers said. There was a pause, and then Mr. Summers 70 looked at Bill Hutchinson, and Bill unfolded his paper and showed it. It was blank.

"It's Tessie," Mr. Summers said, and his voice was hushed. "Show us her 71 paper, Bill."

Bill Hutchinson went over to his wife and forced the slip of paper out of 72 her hand. It had a black spot on it, the black spot Mr. Summers had made the night before with the heavy pencil in the coal-company office. Bill Hutchinson held it up, and there was a stir in the crowd.

"All right, folks," Mr. Summers said. "Let's finish quickly." 73

Although the villagers had forgotten the ritual and lost the original 74 black box, they still remembered to use stones. The pile of stones the boys had made earlier was ready; there were stones on the ground with the blowing scraps of paper that had come out of the box. Mrs. Delacroix selected a stone so large she had to pick it up with both hands and turned to Mrs. Dunbar. "Come on," she said. "Hurry up."

Mrs. Dunbar had small stones in both hands, and she said, gasping for 75 breath, "I can't run at all. You'll have to go ahead and I'll catch up with you."

The children had stones already, and someone gave little Davy Hutchin- 76 son a few pebbles.

Tessie Hutchinson was in the center of a cleared space by now, and she 77 held her hands out desperately as the villagers moved in on her. "It isn't fair," she said. A stone hit her on the side of the head.

Old Man Warner was saying, "Come on, come on, everyone." Steve 78 Adams was in the front of the crowd of villagers, with Mrs. Graves beside him.

"It isn't fair, it isn't right," Mrs. Hutchinson screamed, and then they 79 were upon her.

Questions to Start You Thinking

Meaning

1. Where does this story take place? When?

2. How does this lottery differ from what we usually think of as a lottery? Why would people conduct a lottery such as this?

3. What does this story mean to you?

Writing Strategies

4. Can you see and hear the people in the story? Do they seem to be real or based on fantasy? Who is the most memorable character to you?

5. Are the events believable? Does the ending shock you? Is it believable?

6. Is this story realistic, or is Jackson using these events to represent something else?

For Burns's synopsis of "The Lottery," see p. 217. For more on writing a summary (nutshelling), see p. 185.

For examples of annotated passages, see pp. 18 and 183.

For more on literal and critical reading, see Chs. 2 and 12.

As Jonathan Burns read "The Lottery," he was carried along quickly to the startling ending. After the immediate impact of the story wore off, Burns reread it, savoring some of the details he had missed during his first reading. Then he wrote a summary or *synopsis* of "The Lottery" to get a clear fix on the literal events in the story.

But Burns knew that he could not write a good analysis without reading the story closely, marking key points in the text. By rereading *at least* three times, he could check his interpretations and be sure that evidence from the story supported his claims. When you analyze a complex work of literature, allow time for several close readings, each for a different reason.

Read to Comprehend.   Read for the literal meaning, an overall idea of what happens to whom, where, when, and why. Get all the facts straight — the setting, the events of the plot, the characters and what they say and do. Be sure you understand all the vocabulary, especially in titles and in poems.

Read to Interpret.   Read critically to understand the meaning of the story or poem beyond the literal level. Mark the sections and analyze the parts. Read with an eye for what you seek in the work — theme, character, style, symbol, form. Make notes, put any hard parts into your own words, or read aloud to yourself. What does the literary work mean? What does it imply? What does it help you understand about the human condition? What insights can you apply to your own life?

Read to Evaluate.   Read to assess the soundness and plausibility of what the author says. Are the words and tone appropriate for the purpose and audience? Does the author achieve his or her purpose? Is it a worthwhile purpose?

Jonathan Burns knew he had to analyze the important elements — such as setting, character, and tone — in "The Lottery" to understand the story well enough to write about it. He immediately thought of the undertone of violence in the story but decided that the undertone was so subtle that writing about it would be difficult. Then he considered writing about the especially memorable characters, Mr. Summers and Old Man Warner. And then there was Tessie Hutchinson; he could hear her screams as the stones hit her. But he could not think of much to say except the vague statement that they were memorable. All of a sudden, he hit on the surprise ending. How did Jackson manipulate all the details to generate such a shock?

To begin to focus his thinking, he brainstormed for possible essay titles having to do with the ending, some serious, others flippant: Death Comes as a Surprise, The Unsuspected Finish, Patience of the Devil. He chose the straightforward title "The Hidden Truth." After reviewing his notes, Burns realized that Jackson uses characterization, symbolism, and ambiguous description to build up to the ending. He listed details from the story under those three headings in the informal plan he made for his paper:

Title: The Hidden Truth
Thesis: In "The Lottery" Shirley Jackson effectively crafts a shock ending.
1. Characterization that contributes to the shock ending
  –The children of the village
  –The adults of the village
  –Conversations among the villagers
2. Symbols that contribute to the shock ending
  –The stones
  –The black box
3. Language that contributes to the shock ending
  –The word "lottery"
  –Comments
    –"clean forgot"
    –"wish they'd hurry"
    –"It isn't fair."
  –Actions
  –Relief
  –Suspense

For more on organizing ideas and outlining, see pp. 275–84.

Then he drafted the following introduction:

For more on introductions, see pp. 291–92.

Unsuspecting, the reader follows Shirley Jackson's softly flowing tale of a rural community's timeless ritual, the lottery. Awareness of what is at stake--the savage murder of one random member--comes slowly, only becoming clear toward the last fraction of the story. No sooner does the realization set in than the story is over. It is a shock ending.

What created so great a shock as the reader experiences after reading "The Lottery"? Shirley Jackson takes great care in producing this effect, using elements such as language, symbolism, and characterization to lure the reader into not anticipating what is to come.

With his synopsis, his plan, his copy of the story, and this beginning of a draft, Burns revised the introduction and wrote the following essay.

For Jonathan Burns's synopsis, see pp. 217–18.

STUDENT ESSAY

Jonathan Burns

The Hidden Truth: An Analysis of Shirley Jackson's "The Lottery"

It is as if the first stone thrown strikes the reader as well as Mrs. Hutchinson. And even though there were signs of the stoning to come, somehow the reader is taken by surprise

at Tessie's violent death. What factors contribute to the
shock ending to "The Lottery"? On closer examination of the
story, the reader finds that through all events leading up to
the ending, Shirley Jackson has used unsuspicious characteri-
zations, unobtrusive symbolism, and ambiguous descriptions to
achieve so sudden an impact.

By all appearances, the village is a normal place with   2
normal people. Children arrive at the scene first, with
school just over for the summer, talking of teachers and
books, not of the fact that someone will die today (195). And
as the adults show up, their actions are just as stereotypical: the men talk of farming and taxes, while the women gossip (195). No trace of hostility, no sense of dread in anyone: death seems very far away here.

The conversations between the villagers are no more omi-   3
nous. As the husbands draw slips of paper for their families,
the villagers make apparently everyday comments about the
seemingly ordinary event of the lottery. Mr. Summers is regarded as a competent and respected figure, despite the fact
that his wife is "a scold" (195). Old Man Warner brags about
how many lotteries he's seen and rambles on criticizing other
towns that have given up the tradition (198-99). The characters' comments show the crowd to be more a closely knit community than a murderous mob.

The symbols of "The Lottery" seem equally ordinary. The   4
stones collected by the boys (195) are unnoticed by the
adults and thus seem a trivial detail. The reader thinks of
the "great pile" (195) as children's entertainment, like a
stack of imaginary coins rather than an arsenal. Ironically,
no stones are ever thrown during the children's play, and no
violence is seen in the pile of stones.

Similarly, Jackson describes the box and its history in   5
great detail, but there seems nothing unusual about it. It is
just another everyday object, stored away in the post office
or on a shelf in the grocery (196). Every other day of the
year, the box is in plain view but goes virtually unnoticed.
The only indication that the box has lethal consequences is
that it is painted black (196), yet this is an ambiguous detail, as a black box can also signify mystery or magic, mysti-
cal forces that are sometimes thought to exist in any lottery.

In her ambiguous descriptions, Jackson refers regularly   6
to the village's lottery and emphasizes it as a central ritual for the people. The word <u>lottery</u> itself is ironic, as it
typically implies a winning of some kind, like a raffle or
sweepstakes. It is paralleled to square dances and to the
teenage club, all under the direction of Mr. Summers (195),
activities people look forward to. There is no implied difference between the occurrences of this day and the festivi-
ties of Halloween: according to Jackson, they are all merely
"civic activities" (195). Equally ambiguous are the people's
emotions: some of the villagers are casual, such as Mrs.
Hutchinson, who arrives late because she "'clean forgot'"
what day it is (197), and some are anxious, such as Mrs.
Dunbar, who repeats to her son, "'I wish they'd hurry,'"
without any sign of the cause of her anxiety (199). With
these descriptive details, the reader finds no threat or
malice in the villagers, only vague expectation and
congeniality.

Even when it becomes clear that the lottery is something   7
no one wants to win, Jackson presents only a vague sense of
sadness and mild protest. The crowd is relieved that the
youngest of the Hutchinsons, Davy, doesn't draw the fatal
slip of paper (200). One girl whispers that she hopes it
isn't Nancy (200), and when the Hutchinson children discover
they aren't the winners, they beam with joy and proudly display their blank slips (200). It's like a theatrical scene,
with growing suspense and excitement apparent only when the
victim is close to being identified. And when Tessie is revealed to be the winner of the lottery (201), she merely
holds her hands out "desperately" and repeats, "'It isn't
fair'" (201).

With a blend of character, symbolism, and description,   8
Shirley Jackson paints an overall portrait of a gentle-
seeming rural community, apparently no different from any
other. The tragic end is sudden only because there is no
recognition of violence beforehand, despite the fact that
Jackson has provided the reader with plenty of clues in the
ample details about the lottery and the people. It is a
haunting discovery that the story ends in death, even though
such is the truth in the everyday life of <u>all</u> people.

Questions to Start You Thinking

Meaning

1. What is Burns's thesis?

2. What major points does he use to support his thesis? What specific elements of the story does he include as evidence to support his interpretation?

Writing Strategies

3. How does this essay differ from a synopsis, a summary of the events of the plot? (For a synopsis of "The Lottery," see pp. 217–18.)

4. Does Burns focus on the technique of the short story or on its theme?

5. Is his introduction effective? Compare and contrast it with the first introduction he drafted (p. 203). What did he change? Which version do you prefer?

6. Why does he explain characterization first, symbolism second, and description last? Would discussing these elements in a different order have made much difference in his essay?

7. Is his conclusion effective?

8. How does he tie his ideas together as he moves from paragraph to paragraph? How does he keep the focus on ideas and technique instead of plot?

ANALYZING THE ELEMENTS OF LITERATURE: A GLOSSARY OF TERMS

Every field — scuba diving, gourmet cooking, engineering — has its own vocabulary. Literary analysis is no different. Before you can write a successful literary analysis, you must be familiar with the elements of fiction, poetry, and drama and with the specialized terms critics and scholars use to talk about those elements. We list a few of the elements in this handy glossary of terms.

Setting.   Setting refers to the time and place of events. The season, the weather, and the people in the background may be part of the setting. The setting often helps establish a literary work's *mood* or *atmosphere,* the emotional climate that a reader senses. Shirley Jackson describes the setting in the first sentence of "The Lottery": "The morning of June 27th was clear and sunny, with the fresh warmth of a full-summer day; the flowers were blossoming profusely and the grass was richly green" (paragraph 1).

Characters.   Characters are imagined people. The author lets you know what they are like through their actions, speech, thoughts, attitudes, and background. Sometimes a writer also tells you about physical characteristics or names or relationships with other people.

In "The Lottery," the initial description of Mr. Summers introduces the official of the lottery as someone with "time and energy to devote to civic activities. He was a round-faced, jovial man and he ran the coal business, and people were sorry for him, because he had no children and his wife was a scold" (paragraph 4). What he says also suggests that he is in charge of the situation and doesn't want any slip-ups: "'Little late today, folks'" (paragraph 4); "'Thought we were going to have to get on without you, Tessie'" (paragraph 9); "'Well, now, . . . guess we better get started, get this over with, so's we can go back to work'" (paragraph 10).

Plot.   Plot is the arrangement of the events of the story—what happens to whom, where, when, and why. If the events follow each other logically and if they are in keeping with what the author tells us about the characters, the plot is *plausible,* or believable. Although the ending of "The Lottery" at first may shock readers, the author uses *foreshadowing,* hints to help readers understand future events or twists in the plot. Looking back, readers can see numerous clues that Tessie and the other villagers are nervous and hesitant about the lottery, not the usual reaction of people who expect someone to win money, a car, or a vacation.

The *protagonist,* or main character, is placed in a dramatic situation of *conflict* with some other person or group of people, the *antagonist.* In "The Lottery," a reader might see Tessie Hutchinson as the protagonist, the villagers as the antagonist, and the dramatic situation as Tessie's joining the group waiting for the lottery. *Conflict* consists of two forces attempting to conquer each other or resisting being conquered. It is not merely any vaguely defined turmoil in a story. *External conflicts* are conflicts outside an individual—between two people, between a person and a group (Tessie Hutchinson versus the villagers), between two groups (those who support the lottery and those who want to do away with it), or even between a character and his or her environment. *Internal conflicts* are those within an individual, between two opposing forces or desires (such as reason versus emotion, or fear versus hope in each villager as the slips of paper are drawn). The *central conflict* of a story is the primary conflict for the protagonist that propels and accounts for the action of the story. What is the central conflict for Tessie?

Events of the plot *complicate* the conflict (Tessie arrives late, Bill Hutchinson draws the slip with the black spot for his family, Tessie claims it wasn't fair) and lead to the climax, the moment at which the outcome is inevitable (Tessie draws the slip with the black dot). The outcome itself is the *resolution,* or conclusion (the villagers stone Tessie Hutchinson). Some contemporary stories let events unfold without any apparent plot—action and change occur inside the characters.

Point of View.   Point of view is the angle from which a story is told. Who is the *narrator:* Who tells the story? Through whose eyes are the events perceived? It might be the author, or it might be some character in the story. If a character, what part does he or she play, and what limits does the author place on that character's knowledge? Is the character aware of everything that is going on, or is he or she an outsider? Three often-used points of view are those of a *first-person narrator* (*I*) who is the *speaker* telling the story; a *third-person narrator* (*he* or *she*) who is a major participant in the action (often the protagonist); and a *third-person narrator* who is an observer, not a participant. The point of view may be *omniscient* (told through several characters' eyes), *limited omniscient* (told through one character's eyes), or *objective* (not told through any character's eyes). The point of view in "The Lottery" is that of a third-person objective narrator seemingly looking on and reporting what occurs without knowing what any of the characters are thinking. Why do you think Shirley Jackson chose this point of view for "The Lottery"? How would the story be different if it were told from Tessie's point of view? From Mr. Summers's? From Old Man Warner's?

Theme.   Theme is a main idea or insight a work contains. It is the author's observation about life, society, or human nature. Sometimes you can sum up a theme in a sentence: "Emotional changes often manifest themselves physically" or "Human beings cannot live without illusion." In a complex work, however, a theme may be implied and difficult to discern. Some works have more than one theme, and they may be stated in various ways.

To state a theme, find an important subject in the story and ask yourself, What does the author say about this subject? Details from the story itself should support your statement of theme, and your theme should account for the details in the story. Be careful not to confuse a subject or topic of a story with a theme. "The Lottery" treats several important subjects: the unexpected, scapegoating, people's inhumanity to one another, outmoded rituals, victims of society, hostility, violence, death. One theme of the story might be stated as "People are selfish, always looking out for number one."

Imagery.   Images are words or groups of words that refer to any sense experience: seeing, hearing, smelling, tasting, touching, or feeling. In "The Lottery," Shirley Jackson uses many images to help readers visualize what happens. The flowers bloom "profusely" and the grass is "richly green" (paragraph 1). The stones the children gather are smooth and round (paragraph 2). When Mr. Summers speaks, a "hush" comes over the crowd (paragraph 19). Mrs. Dunbar is "gasping for breath" as the villagers move toward Tessie (paragraph 75).

Figures of Speech.   Figures of speech are lively or fresh expressions that vary the expected sequence of words or their sense. Some of the most common types of figurative language are the *simile*, a comparison using *like* or *as*; the *metaphor*, an implied comparison; and *personification*, the attribution of human qualities to inanimate or nonhuman creatures or things. In "The Lottery," Bobby Martin, Harry Jones, and Dickie Delacroix *guard* their pile of stones "against the *raids* of the other boys" (paragraph 2).

Symbols.   Symbols are tangible objects, visible actions, or characters that hint at meanings beyond themselves. In "The Lottery," a story filled with symbols, the black box suggests outdated tradition, the past, resistance to change, evil, cruelty, and more.

Irony. Irony results from readers' sense of some discrepancy. A simple kind of irony, *sarcasm*, occurs when you say one thing but mean the opposite: "I just love scrubbing the floor." In literature, an *ironic situation* sets up a wry contrast or incongruity. In "The Lottery," actions of evil cruelty and horror take place on a bright sunny June day in an ordinary village. *Ironic dialogue* occurs when a character says one thing but the audience or reader is aware of another meaning. When someone mentions talk of giving up the lottery, Old Man Warner snorts, " 'Next thing you know, they'll be wanting to go back to living in caves' " (paragraph 32). He implies that without the lottery the villagers would return to a more primitive way of life. His comment is ironic because the reader is aware that this lottery is a primitive ritual. A story has an *ironic point of view* when we sense a difference between the author and the narrator or the character through whose eyes the story is perceived; Shirley Jackson, for instance, clearly does not condone the actions of the villagers, no matter what the reason.

LEARNING BY WRITING

The Assignment: Analyzing a Literary Work. For this assignment, you are to be a literary critic — analyzing, interpreting, and evaluating a literary selection for your classmates. Your purpose is to deepen their understanding because you will have devoted time and effort to digging out the meaning and testing it with evidence from the work itself. Even if they too have studied the work carefully, you will try to convince them that your interpretation is valid.

Write an essay interpreting one or more aspects of a literary work that intrigues you or expresses a worthwhile meaning. Your instructor may want to approve your selection. After careful analysis of the literary work, you will become the expert critic, explaining the meaning you discern, supporting your interpretation with evidence from the work, and evaluating the effectiveness of the literary elements used by the author and the significance of the theme.

You cannot include everything about the work in your paper, so you should focus on one element (such as character, setting, or theme) or the interrelationship of two or three elements (as Jonathan Burns did when he analyzed characterization, symbolism, and description in his interpretation of the surprise ending of "The Lottery"). Although a summary, or *synopsis*, of the plot and characterization is a good beginning point, retelling the story is not a satisfactory literary analysis.

Here are instances of college writers who successfully responded to this type of assignment:

> One writer who was a musician analyzed the credibility of Sonny as a musician in James Baldwin's "Sonny's Blues" — his attitudes, actions, struggles, relationship with his instrument and with other musicians — and concluded that Sonny is a believable character.

www
For more help with creating a Web project devoted to a particular literary work, visit <www.bedfordstmartins.com/bedguide>.

Another demonstrated how the rhythm, rhymes, and images of Adrienne Rich's poem "Aunt Jennifer's Tigers" mesh to convey the poem's theme of tension between a woman's artistic urge and societal constraints.

A psychology major concluded that the relationship between Hamlet and Claudius in Shakespeare's *Hamlet* is in many ways representative of the tension, jealousy, and misunderstanding between stepsons and stepfathers.

Finding a Subject.   Read several literary works until you find two or three you like. You might start with a favorite author or a favorite short story among those you have read for this course. Next, reread the two or three works that interest you to select one to concentrate on. Choose the one that strikes you as especially significant — realistic or universal, moving or disturbing, believable or shocking — with a meaning that you wish to share with your classmates.

For more on analysis, see pp. 307–10.

Generating Ideas.   Analyzing a literary work is the first step in interpreting meaning and evaluating literary quality. As you read the work you have selected, identify its elements and analyze them as Jonathan Burns did in his paper on "The Lottery." Then focus on *one* significant element or a cluster of related elements. When you write your interpretation, restrict your discussion to that element or cluster.

For a glossary of literary terms, see pp. 206–09.

We provide three checklists to guide you in studying different types of literature. Each of these analytical models is an aid to understanding; it is *not* an organizational outline for writing about literature. The first checklist focuses on short stories and novels, but because thinking about your reaction to the work and about setting, characters, and theme is also important for poems or plays, some of the questions can help you analyze almost any kind of literary work.

DISCOVERY CHECKLIST

Analyzing a Short Story or a Novel

___ What is your reaction to the story? Jot it down.

___ Who is the *narrator* — not the author, but the one who tells the story?

___ What is the *point of view?*

___ What is the *setting* (time and place)? What is the *atmosphere* or *mood?*

___ How does the *plot* unfold? Write a synopsis, or summary, of the events in time order, including relationships among those events.

___ What are the *characters* like? Describe their personalities and traits based on their actions, speech, habits, and so on. Who is the *protagonist?* The *antagonist?* Do any characters change? Are the changes believable? Do the characters have clear motivation for what they do?

—— How would you describe the story's *style*, or use of language? Is the style informal or conversational? Is it formal? Does the story use any dialect or foreign words?

—— What are the *external conflicts* and the *internal conflicts*? What is the *central
conflict*? Express the conflicts using the word *versus*, such as "dreams versus
reality" or "the individual versus society."

—— What is the *climax* of the story? Is there any *resolution*?

—— Are there important *symbols*? What might they mean?

—— What does the *title* of the story mean?

—— What are the *themes* of the story? Are they universal (applicable to all people
everywhere at all times)? State your interpretation of the main theme. How
is this theme related to your own life?

—— What other literary works or experiences from life does the story make you
think of? Jot them down.

When looking at a poem, you should consider both the elements specific to poetry and the elements poetry has in common with other genres, as
the following checklist suggests.

DISCOVERY CHECKLIST

Analyzing a Poem

—— What is your reaction to the poem? Jot it down.

—— Who is the *speaker* — not the author, but the one who narrates?

—— Is there a *setting*? How does it relate to the meaning of the poem? What
mood or emotional *atmosphere* does the setting suggest?

—— Can you put the poem into your own words — paraphrase it?

—— What is striking about the language of the poem? Identify any unusual
words or words used in an unusual sense. Look for *archaic* words (words no
longer commonly used) and *repetition* of words. Consider the *connotations* of
important words (the suggestions conjured by the words: *house* has a different connotation from *home*, although both may refer to the same place). Is
the level of language colloquial or formal? Does the poem use irony? What
kind of figurative language is used: *imagery, metaphor, personification*?

—— Is the poem *lyric* (expressing emotion) or *narrative* (telling a story)?

—— What is the structure of the poem? How is it divided? Does it consist of *couplets* (two consecutive rhyming lines) or *quatrains* (units of four lines) or
some other units? How do the beginning and the end relate to each other
and to the poem as a whole?

—— Does the poem use *rhyme* (words that sound alike)? If so, how does the
rhyme contribute to the meaning?

—— Does the poem have *rhythm* (regular meter or beat, patterns of accented and
unaccented syllables)? How does the rhythm contribute to the meaning?

—— What does the *title* of the poem mean?

____ What is the major *theme* of the poem? How does this underlying idea unify the poem? How is it related to your own life?

____ What other literary works or experiences from life does the poem make you think of? Jot them down.

A play is written to be seen and heard, not read. When you analyze a play, you may ask what kind of play it is and how it would appear onstage, as the following checklist suggests.

DISCOVERY CHECKLIST

Analyzing a Play

____ What is your reaction to the play? Jot it down.

____ Is the play a *tragedy* (a serious drama that arouses pity and fear in the audience and usually ends unhappily with the death or downfall of the *tragic hero*) or a *comedy* (drama that aims primarily to amuse and that usually ends happily)?

____ What is the *setting* of the play? What is its *mood?*

____ In brief, what happens? Summarize each act of the play.

____ What are the characters like? Who is the *protagonist?* What *antagonist* opposes the main character? Are there *foil characters* (those who contrast with the main character and reveal his or her traits)? Which characters are in conflict? Do any of the characters change?

____ Which speeches seem especially significant?

____ What is the plot? Identify the *exposition,* the background information needed to understand the story. Determine the main *external* and *internal* conflicts. What is the *central conflict?* What events *complicate* the central conflict? How are these elements of the plot spread throughout the play?

____ What is the *climax* of the play? Is there a *resolution* to the action?

____ What does the *title* mean?

____ Can you identify any *dramatic irony,* words or actions of a character that carry meaning unperceived by the character but evident to the audience?

____ What is the major *theme* of the play? Is it a universal idea? How is this theme related to your own life?

____ What other literary works or experiences from life does the play make you think of? Jot them down.

As you write your analysis, don't worry about impressing your readers with your brilliance. Though you need a critical vocabulary, use only terms that you understand. Regard your readers as friends in whose company you are discussing something already familiar to all of you, though they have not studied the work as carefully as you have. Your purpose is to explain the work's deeper meaning, which your readers may not be aware of after only a cursory reading. This assumption will help you determine how much evidence from the work you need to include and will save you a lot of wordy summarizing.

Planning, Drafting, and Developing.   After you have determined the major element or cluster of elements that you intend to focus on, go through the work again to find all the passages that relate to your main point. Mark them or take notes as you find them. It's a good idea to put these relevant passages on note cards or in a computer file, along with the page references. If you use any quotations, quote them exactly.

For more on planning, drafting, and developing, see Chs. 17, 18, and 19.

DEVELOP YOUR THESIS.   Begin writing by trying to express the main point you want to convey in a thesis statement that identifies the literary work and the author. Suppose you start with a tentative thesis on the theme of "The Lottery":

For more on thesis statements, see pp. 271–75.

> In "The Lottery," Shirley Jackson reveals the theme.

But this statement is too vague, so you decide to rewrite it to be more precise:

> In "The Lottery" by Shirley Jackson, the theme is tradi-
> tion.

This thesis is better, but the statement of the theme is not yet clear or precise. In her narrative, what does Jackson imply about tradition? You try several other ways of expressing your idea:

> In "The Lottery" by Shirley Jackson, one of the major
> themes is that outmoded traditions can be harmful.

You used the qualifier *one of* to indicate that this theme is not the only one in the story, but the rest of the thesis is vague. What does "outmoded" mean? How are the traditions harmful?

> In "The Lottery" by Shirley Jackson, one of the major
> themes is that traditions that have lost their meaning
> can cause otherwise normal people to act abnormally
> without thinking.

This is a better thesis, but it may change as you start writing the analysis. You might decide to go beyond interpretation of Jackson's ideas to an evaluation of what she says:

> In "The Lottery," Shirley Jackson reveals the tragic
> theme that traditions that have lost their meaning can
> cause otherwise normal people to act abnormally without
> thinking.

In this thesis the word *tragic* indicates your evaluation of Jackson's observation of the human condition. Or you might say this:

```
In "The Lottery," Shirley Jackson effectively uses sym-
bolism and irony to reveal the theme that traditions that
have lost their meaning can cause otherwise normal people
to act abnormally without thinking.
```

When planning and organizing your essay, focus on ideas, not events; take care not to merely retell the story. One way you might maintain that focus is to analyze your thesis, dividing it into parts. The thesis just presented could be divided into (1) use of symbolism to reveal theme and (2) use of irony to reveal theme. If you are writing about character change, you might divide the information into the character's original traits or attitudes, the events that cause the change, and the character's new traits or attitudes.

For a story that shows character change, see "The Story of an Hour," pp. 219–21.

For more on introductions, see pp. 291–92.

INTRODUCE YOUR ESSAY.   As you start your analysis, be sure your beginning is tied to your main point. If you are uncertain how to begin, try one of these openings:

- Focus on the universality of the character (pointing out that most people might feel as Tessie in "The Lottery" did and shout "'It isn't fair, it isn't right'" if their name were drawn).
- Focus on the universality of the theme (discussing briefly how traditions seem to be losing their meaning in modern society).
- Quote a striking line from the work ("and then they were upon her" or "'Lottery in June, corn be heavy soon'").
- Start with a statement of what the work is about, with your reaction to the work when you read it, with a parallel personal experience, or with a comment about a technique that the writer uses.
- Begin with a "Have you ever?" question to draw the reader into your interpretation.

For more on citing a literary work, see E2 in the "Quick Editing Guide" (the dark-blue-edged pages).

SUPPORT YOUR INTERPRETATION.   In the body of your analysis, include information that supports your interpretation — descriptions of setting and character, summaries of events, quotations of important dialogue, and other specific evidence from the story. Cite the page numbers (for prose) or line numbers (for poetry) where details can be found in the work. Integrate details from the story with your own comments and ideas.

For a list of transitions showing logical connections, see p. 297.

Keep the focus on ideas, not events, by using transition markers that refer to character traits and personality change, not those that refer to time. Say "Although Mr. Summers was . . ." instead of "At the beginning of the story Mr. Summers was . . . ." Write "Tessie became . . ." instead of "After that Tessie was . . ." State "The villagers in 'The Lottery' changed . . . ," not "On the next page . . ."

CONCLUDE YOUR ESSAY.   When you reach the end, don't just stop writing. Use the same techniques you use for introductions—anecdote, personal experience, comment on technique, quotation—to provide a sense of finality and closing for your readers. Refer to or reaffirm your thesis. Often an effective conclusion ties in directly with the introduction.

For more on conclusions, see pp. 293–94.

Revising and Editing.   Here are some questions to consider as you shape your draft:

For more revising and editing strategies, see Ch. 20.

REVISION CHECKLIST

___ Have you clearly identified the literary work and the author near the beginning of the analysis?

___ Is your main point clear? Does everything in the paper relate to your main point?

___ Have you focused on one element or a limited number of related elements in your analysis? Have you organized your analysis according to these ideas rather than events?

___ Do your transitions focus on ideas, not on plot or time sequence? Do they guide readers easily from one section or sentence to the next?

___ Are your interpretations supported by evidence from the literary work? Do you need to add details, dialogue, action, or description to support your interpretation? Are the details that you use relevant to the points of analysis, or are they just interesting sidelights?

___ Have you woven the details from the work smoothly into your text? Have you cited the correct page or line numbers for the details from the work? Have you properly used quotation marks and citations instead of lifting language and sentence structure from the work itself?

___ Do you understand all the words and literary terms you use?

___ Have you tried to share your insights into the meaning of the work with your readers, or have you slipped into trying to impress them?

After you have revised your literary analysis, edit and proofread it. Check carefully for problems with grammar, word choice, punctuation, and mechanics—and then correct any problems you find. Make sure that all of your quotations and references to the work are introduced smoothly and are woven into your own discussion. Here are some questions to get you started editing and proofreading your paper:

For more editing and proofreading strategies, see Ch. 20.

EDITING CHECKLIST

___ Have you used the present tense for events in the literary work and for comments about the author's presentation?   A1

___ Have you used quotation marks correctly whenever you give the exact words of the literary work?   C3

___ Have you used correct documentation style to identify each page (or line) to which you refer?   E2

For more help, turn to the dark-blue-edged pages, and find the "Quick Editing Guide" section noted here.

FOR PEER RESPONSE

For general questions for a peer editor, see pp. 323–24.

Ask one of your classmates to read your draft, considering how effectively you have analyzed the literary work and presented your analysis. Ask your peer editor to answer specific questions such as these:

- What is your first reaction to the literary analysis?

- In what ways does the analysis add to your understanding of the literary work? In what ways does it add to your insights into life?

- Does the introduction make you want to read the rest of the analysis? What changes would you suggest to strengthen the opening?

- Is the main point clear? Does the writer provide sufficient evidence from the work to support that point? Put stars wherever additional evidence is needed. Is there anything in the analysis that does not belong? Put a check mark by any irrelevant information.

- Does the writer go beyond summarizing the plot to analyze elements, interpret meaning, and evaluate literary merit? If not, how might the writer revise?

- Is the analysis organized by ideas instead of events? What changes in organization would you suggest?

- Do the transitions guide you smoothly from one point to the next? Do the transitions focus on ideas, not on time or position in the story? Note any places where the writer might add transitions.

- If this were your paper, what is the one thing you would be sure to work on before handing it in?

Strategies for Writing about Literature: Synopsis and Paraphrase

LEARNING FROM OTHER WRITERS: SYNOPSIS

For more on nutshelling (summarizing) and paraphrasing, see pp. 185–86.

In your literature courses you will often be asked to write synopses of short stories and novels and to paraphrase poems. Both are valuable to you as a writer because they require you to get the chronology straight and to pick out the significant events and details. Synopsis and paraphrase also help you relate the parts of a work to each other and to the themes of the work. Both assignments require you to dig out the literal level of the work.

A *synopsis* is a summary of the plot of a narrative — a short story, a novel, a play, or a narrative poem. It describes the first level of meaning, the literal layer. It condenses the story to only the major events and the most significant details. You do not include your own interpretation, but you summarize the work in your own words, taking care not to lift language or sentence structure from the work itself. Like a synopsis, a *paraphrase* conveys the meaning of the original piece of literature and the relationships of its parts in your own words. A paraphrase, however, converts the original poetry to your own prose or the original prose to your own words in a passage about as long as the original.

In preparation for writing his literary analysis of "The Lottery"—to make sure he had the sequence of events clear—Jonathan Burns wrote the following synopsis of the story.

For "The Lottery," see pp. 195–201.

STUDENT EXAMPLE

Jonathan Burns
A Synopsis of "The Lottery"

Around ten o'clock on a sunny June 27, the villagers   1
gathered in the square for a lottery, expecting to be home in
time for lunch. The children came first, glad that school was
out for the summer. The boys romped and gathered stones, the
girls talked quietly in small groups, and the little ones
hovered near their brothers and sisters. Then the men came,
followed by the women. When parents called, the children came
reluctantly.

Mr. Summers, who always conducted the town lottery,   2
arrived with the black wooden box and set it on the three-
legged stool that Mr. Graves had brought out. The villagers
remained at a distance from these men and didn't respond when
Mr. Summers asked for help. Finally, Mr. Martin and his son
held the shabby black box as Mr. Summers mixed the papers in
it. Although the townspeople had talked about replacing the
box, they never had, but they had substituted paper slips for
the original wooden chips. To prepare for the drawing, they
listed the members of every household and swore in Mr. Summers. Although they had dropped many aspects of the original
ritual, the official still greeted each person individually.

Tessie Hutchinson rushed into the square, telling her   3
friend Mrs. Delacroix she had almost forgotten what day it
was. Then she joined her husband and children.

When Mr. Summers asked if everyone was present, he was   4
told that Clyde Dunbar was absent because of a broken leg but
that his wife would draw for the family. Summers noted that
the Watson boy was drawing for his mother and checked to see
if Old Man Warner was present.

The crowd got quiet. Mr. Summers reminded everybody of   5
what they were to do and began to call the names in alphabetical order. People in the group joked nervously as the names
were called. Mrs. Delacroix and Mrs. Graves commented on how
fast time had passed since the last lottery, and Old Man
Warner talked about how important the lottery was to the villagers. When Mr. Summers finished calling the roll, there was
a pause before the heads of households opened their slips.
Everybody wondered who had the special slip of paper, who had
won the lottery. They discovered it was Bill Hutchinson. When
Tessie complained that the drawing hadn't been done fairly,
the others told her to be a "good sport."

Mr. Graves put five slips into the box, one for each   6
member of Bill Hutchinson's family. Tessie kept charging un-
fairness. The children drew first, then Tessie, then Bill.
The children opened their slips, smiled broadly, and held
blank pieces of paper over their heads. Bill opened his and
it was blank too. Tessie wouldn't open hers; Bill had to do
it for her. Hers had a black spot on it.

Mr. Summers urged the villagers to complete the process   7
quickly. They picked up stones, even little Davy Hutchinson,
and started throwing them at Tessie, as she kept screaming,
"It isn't fair, it isn't right." Then they stoned her.

Questions to Start You Thinking

Meaning

1. Does this synopsis help you understand the story better?
2. Why isn't a synopsis as interesting as a short story?
3. Can you tell from this synopsis whether Burns understands Jackson's story beyond the literal level?

Writing Strategies

4. Does Burns retell the story accurately and clearly? Does he get the events in correct time order? Does he show the relationships of the events to each other and to the whole? How?
5. Does Burns select the details necessary to indicate what happened in "The Lottery"? Why do you think he omits certain details?
6. Are there any details, comments, or events that you would add to his synopsis? Why, or why not?
7. How does this synopsis differ from Burns's literary analysis (p. 203–05)?

LEARNING BY WRITING: SYNOPSIS

The Assignment: Writing a Synopsis of a Story by Kate Chopin. Whenever you have trouble understanding a story or have a lot of stories to read, you may benefit from writing a synopsis so that you can easily review a story's specifics. Keep your synopsis of the plot true to the original, using accurate details in time order. Condensing five pages to a few hundred words forces you to focus on the most important details in the story and the sequence of events. This focus often leads you to a statement of theme.

Kate Chopin was a nineteenth-century American writer whose female characters search for their own identity and for freedom from domination and oppression. For practice, write a synopsis of two hundred to three hundred words of Chopin's short story "The Story of an Hour." Consider the following questions to help you get started:

DISCOVERY CHECKLIST

___ What are the major events and details of the story?

___ In what time order do events take place?

___ How are the parts of the story related (without adding your own opinions or interpretations)?

___ Which of the author's words might be most useful to add in quotation marks?

Kate Chopin
The Story of an Hour

Knowing that Mrs. Mallard was afflicted with a heart trouble, great care was 1
taken to break to her as gently as possible the news of her husband's death.

It was her sister Josephine who told her, in broken sentences, veiled 2
hints that revealed in half concealing. Her husband's friend Richards was
there, too, near her. It was he who had been in the newspaper office when
intelligence of the railroad disaster was received, with Brently Mallard's
name leading the list of "killed." He had only taken the time to assure himself of its truth by a second telegram, and had hastened to forestall any less
careful, less tender friend in bearing the sad message.

She did not hear the story as many women have heard the same, with a 3
paralyzed inability to accept its significance. She wept at once, with sudden,
wild abandonment, in her sister's arms. When the storm of grief had spent
itself she went away to her room alone. She would have no one follow her.

There stood, facing the open window, a comfortable, roomy armchair. 4
Into this she sank, pressed down by a physical exhaustion that haunted her
body and seemed to reach into her soul.

She could see in the open square before her house the tops of trees that   5
were all aquiver with the new spring life. The delicious breath of rain was in
the air. In the street below a peddler was crying his wares. The notes of a distant song which someone was singing reached her faintly, and countless
sparrows were twittering in the eaves.

There were patches of blue sky showing here and there through the   6
clouds that had met and piled one above the other in the west facing her
window.

She sat with her head thrown back upon the cushion of the chair, quite   7
motionless, except when a sob came up into her throat and shook her, as a
child who has cried itself to sleep continues to sob in its dreams.

She was young, with a fair, calm face, whose lines bespoke repression   8
and even a certain strength. But now there was a dull stare in her eyes,
whose gaze was fixed away off yonder on one of those patches of blue sky. It
was not a glance of reflection, but rather indicated a suspension of intelligent thought.

There was something coming to her and she was waiting for it, fearfully.   9
What was it? She did not know; it was too subtle and elusive to name. But
she felt it, creeping out of the sky, reaching toward her through the sounds,
the scents, the color that filled the air.

Now her bosom rose and fell tumultuously. She was beginning to recog-   10
nize this thing that was approaching to possess her, and she was striving to
beat it back with her will—as powerless as her two white slender hands
would have been.

When she abandoned herself a little whispered word escaped her   11
slightly parted lips. She said it over and over under her breath: "Free, free,
free!" The vacant stare and the look of terror that had followed it went from
her eyes. They stayed keen and bright. Her pulses beat fast, and the coursing
blood warmed and relaxed every inch of her body.

She did not stop to ask if it were not a monstrous joy that held her. A   12
clear and exalted perception enabled her to dismiss the suggestion as trivial.

She knew that she would weep again when she saw the kind, tender   13
hands folded in death; the face that had never looked save with love upon
her, fixed and gray and dead. But she saw beyond that bitter moment a long
procession of years to come that would belong to her absolutely. And she
opened and spread her arms out to them in welcome.

There would be no one to live for during those coming years; she would   14
live for herself. There would be no powerful will bending her in that blind
persistence with which men and women believe they have a right to impose
a private will upon a fellow creature. A kind intention or a cruel intention
made the act seem no less a crime as she looked upon it in that brief moment of illumination.

And yet she had loved him—sometimes. Often she had not. What did   15
it matter! What could love, the unsolved mystery, count for in face of this
possession of self-assertion which she suddenly recognized as the strongest
impulse of her being.

"Free! Body and soul free!" she kept whispering.   16

Josephine was kneeling before the closed door with her lips to the   17
keyhole, imploring for admission. "Louise, open the door! I beg; open the
door—you will make yourself ill. What are you doing, Louise? For heaven's
sake open the door."

"Go away. I am not making myself ill." No; she was drinking in a very   18
elixir of life through that open window.

Her fancy was running riot along those days ahead of her. Spring days,   19
and summer days, and all sorts of days that would be her own. She breathed
a quick prayer that life might be long. It was only yesterday she had thought
with a shudder that life might be long.

She arose at length and opened the door to her sister's importunities.   20
There was a feverish triumph in her eyes, and she carried herself unwittingly
like a goddess of Victory. She clasped her sister's waist, and together they descended the stairs. Richards stood waiting for them at the bottom.

Someone was opening the front door with a latchkey. It was Brently   21
Mallard who entered, a little travel-stained, composedly carrying his grip-
sack and umbrella. He had been far from the scene of the accident, and did
not even know there had been one. He stood amazed at Josephine's piercing
cry; at Richards's quick motion to screen him from the view of his wife.

But Richards was too late.   22

When the doctors came they said she had died of heart disease—of joy   23
that kills.

LEARNING BY WRITING: PARAPHRASE

The Assignment: Writing a Paraphrase of a Poem.   When you study poetry, you can benefit from paraphrasing—that is, expressing the content of a
poem in your own words without adding your opinions or interpretations.
You may write your paraphrase in the margin of the poem or in a notebook.
Writing a paraphrase forces you to divide the poem into logical sections, to
figure out what the poet says in each section, and to discern the relationships
of the parts. After you have paraphrased a poem, you should find it easier to
state its theme—its main idea or insight—in a sentence or two.

For more on paraphras-
ing, see pp. 185–86.

Consider the following questions to help you get started:

DISCOVERY CHECKLIST

___ What are the major sections of the poem? What does the poet say in each
     section?

___ How are the sections of the poem related?

___ Are there any words whose meanings you don't know? Are there any words
     used in a special sense, different from the usual meanings? What do those
     words mean in the context of the poem?

___ Does the poet use images to create sensory pictures? Is figurative language,
     such as similes or metaphors, used to create comparisons? How do these
     contribute to the meaning?

Other Assignments for Writing about Literature

For more on writing a comparison and contrast essay, see Ch. 7.

1. Use a poem, a play, or a novel instead of a short story to write the literary analysis assigned in this chapter (p. 209).

2. Write an essay comparing and contrasting a literary element in two or three short stories or poems.

3. Paraphrase "The Road Not Taken" or "Richard Cory," poems included with the next two assignments. Express the content of the poem in your own words, paying attention to the sections of the poem and their relationships. Make sure you figure out what all the words mean and how any images or figures of speech contribute to the meaning.

4. Read the following poem by Robert Frost (1874–1963). Then write an essay in which you use a paraphrase of this poem as a springboard for your thoughts on a fork in the road of your life — a decision that made a big difference for you.

   The Road Not Taken

   Two roads diverged in a yellow wood,
   And sorry I could not travel both
   And be one traveler, long I stood
   And looked down one as far as I could
   To where it bent in the undergrowth;

   Then took the other, as just as fair,
   And having perhaps the better claim,
   Because it was grassy and wanted wear;
   Though as for that the passing there
   Had worn them really about the same,

   And both that morning equally lay
   In leaves no step had trodden black.
   Oh, I kept the first for another day!
   Yet knowing how way leads on to way,
   I doubted if I should ever come back.

   I shall be telling this with a sigh
   Somewhere ages and ages hence:
   Two roads diverged in a wood, and I —
   I took the one less traveled by,
   And that has made all the difference.

For more on writing a comparison and contrast essay, see Ch. 7.

5. Read the following poem by Edwin Arlington Robinson (1869–1935). Have you known and envied someone similar to Richard Cory, someone who everyone else thought had it all? What happened to him or her? Did you discover that your impression of this individual was wrong? Write a personal response essay in which you compare and contrast the person you knew with Richard Cory. This assignment requires

you to analyze the poem as well as draw on your own experience and
knowledge.

Richard Cory

Whenever Richard Cory went down town,
We people on the pavement looked at him:
He was a gentleman from sole to crown,
Clean favored, and imperially slim.

And he was always quietly arrayed,
And he was always human when he talked;
But still he fluttered pulses when he said,
"Good-morning," and he glittered when he walked.

And he was rich — yes, richer than a king —
And admirably schooled in every grace:
In fine, we thought that he was everything
To make us wish that we were in his place.

So on we worked, and waited for the light,
And went without the meat, and cursed the bread;
And Richard Cory, one calm summer night,
Went home and put a bullet through his head.

6. Write a critical essay analyzing a song, a movie, or a television program.
   Because you won't have a written text in front of you, you probably will
   need to hear the work or view it more than once to pull out the specific
   evidence necessary to support your interpretation.

For more about visual representations, see Ch. 22. For more on analysis, see pp. 307–10.

Chapter 14
Writing in the Workplace

Most of the world's workplace communication takes place in writing. Although a conversation or telephone message may be forgotten or ignored, a letter or memorandum (memo) is a physical thing that sits on a desk, calling for some action and providing a permanent record of business dealings.

Personnel managers, the people who do the hiring in large corporations, tend to be keenly interested in applicants who can write clearly, accurately, and effectively. A survey conducted at Cornell University asked business executives to rate in importance the qualities they would like their employees to possess. Skill in writing was ranked in fourth place, ahead of managerial skill and skill in analysis, suggesting the practical value of a writing course.

In this chapter, we first outline some general guidelines for workplace writing and then show you four kinds likely to prove useful — letters, memoranda, electronic mail, and résumés.

Guidelines for Writing in the Workplace

Good workplace writing succeeds in achieving a clear purpose. To be effective, you need to know your purpose, remember your audience, use an appropriate tone, and present your information carefully. When you write to a business, your writing represents you; when you write as part of your job, your writing represents your company as well.

KNOW YOUR PURPOSE

Your purpose, or reason for writing, helps you select and arrange information; it gives you a standard against which to measure your final draft. Most likely, you will want to create a certain response in your readers, informing them about something or motivating them to take a specific action.

DISCOVERY CHECKLIST

___ Do you want to inform? (For example, do you want to make an announcement, keep your readers posted on a developing situation, explain a specialized piece of knowledge, or reply to a request?)

___ Do you want to motivate some action? (For example, do you want a question answered, a wrong corrected, a certain decision made, or a personnel director to hire you?)

___ When your readers are finished reading what you've written, what do you want them to think? What do you want them to do?

KEEP YOUR AUDIENCE IN MIND

Consider everything in your workplace writing from your readers' point of view. After all, your purpose is not to express your ideas but to have your readers act on them, even if the action is simply to notice that you are on top of the situation. If you do not know the person to whom you are writing, make some educated guesses based on what you know about her or his position or company. Here are some questions to consider about your readers:

DISCOVERY CHECKLIST

___ What do your readers already know about the subject? Are they experts in the field? Have they been kept up to date on the situation?

___ What do your readers need to know? What information do they expect you to provide? What information do they need before they can take action?

___ What can you assume about your readers' priorities and expectations? Are they busy executives, with stacks of mail to weed through? Are they conscientious administrators who will appreciate your attention to detail?

___ What is most likely to motivate your readers to take the action you want?

Especially in letters and memoranda where the purpose is to motivate, it's useful to focus on how "you, the reader" will benefit instead of focusing on what "I, the writer" would like.

"I" ATTITUDE   Please send me the form so that I can process your order.

"YOU" ATTITUDE   So that you can receive your shipment promptly, please send me the form.

USE AN APPROPRIATE TONE

Tone is the quality of writing that reveals your attitude toward your topic and your readers. If you show your readers that you respect them, their intelligence, and their feelings, they in turn are far more likely to view you and your message favorably. Most workplace writing today ranges from the informal to the slightly formal. Gone are the extremely formal phrases that once dotted business correspondence: *enclosed herewith, be advised that, pursuant to the stated request.* At the other extreme, however, slang, overfriendliness, and a too casual style might cast doubts on your seriousness or credibility. Strive for a relaxed and conversational style, using simple sentences, familiar words, and the active voice.

> TOO CASUAL I hear that thing with the new lackey is a definite go.
>
> TOO FORMAL This office stands informed that the administration's request for supplementary personnel has been honored.
>
> APPROPRIATE I understand that a new office assistant has been hired.

In all your business writing, be courteous and considerate. If you are writing to complain, remember that your reader may not be the one who caused the problem — and you are more likely to win your case with courtesy than with sarcasm or insults. When delivering bad news, remember that your reader may interpret a bureaucratic response as coldness and lack of sympathy. And if you have made a mistake or done something wrong, acknowledge it. When you reread your writing to check for tone, here are some questions you can consider:

REVISION CHECKLIST

___ Have you avoided slang terms and extremely casual language?

___ Have you avoided unnecessarily formal or sophisticated words?

___ Are your sentences of a manageable length?

___ Have you used the active voice ("I am sending it") rather than the passive voice ("It is being sent")?

___ Does anything you've written sound blaming or accusatory?

___ Do you hear a friendly, considerate, competent person behind your words?

___ Have you asked someone else to read your writing to check for tone?

PRESENT INFORMATION CAREFULLY

In business, time is money: time wasted reading irrelevant, poorly written material is money wasted. To be effective, your business writing should be concise, clear, and well organized.

Concise writing shows that you respect your readers' time. In most cases, if a letter, memo, or résumé is longer than a page or two, it's too long.

You might need to find a better way to present the information, or you might need to cut unneeded information or details.

Clear writing ensures that the information you convey is accurate, complete, and unambiguous. Put the most important information in a prominent spot (usually at the beginning). Let your readers know exactly what you want them to do — politely, of course. If you have a question, ask it. If you want something, request it.

Well-organized writing helps readers move through it quickly and easily. Every piece of business correspondence should be written so that it can be skimmed. Make sure the topic of the document is absolutely clear from the very beginning, usually the first paragraph of a letter or the subject line of a memorandum. Use a conventional format that your readers will expect (see Figures 14.2 and 14.4 later in this chapter). Break information into easily processed chunks; order these chunks logically and consistently. Finally, use topic sentences and headings (when appropriate) to label each chunk of information and to give your readers an overview of your document.

As you work to make your own business writing clear, concise, and orderly, here are some useful questions to consider:

REVISION CHECKLIST

___ Have you kept your letter, memo, or résumé to a page or two?

___ Have you cut all deadwood and wordiness?

___ Have you scrutinized every word to ensure that it can't be misinterpreted? Have you supplied all the background information readers need?

___ Have you emphasized the most important part of your message? Will readers know what you want them to do?

___ Have you used a consistent and logical order? Have you followed a conventional format?

___ If appropriate, have you included labels and headings?

The sample workplace communication in Figure 14.1 illustrates how successful workplace writing combines attention to purpose, audience, tone, and presentation.

For more revising and editing strategies, see Ch. 20.

Business Letters

Organizations use business letters to correspond with outside parties — either individual people or other organizations. Business letters are used to request and provide information, motivate action, respond to requests, and sell goods and services. Because letters become part of the permanent record, they can be referred to later to determine exactly who said what and when. You should keep a copy of every letter you write, a printout as well as a backup on disk.

For advice on job application letters, see pp. 236–38.

INTERLINK SYSTEMS, INC.

TO: All Employees
FROM: Erica Xiang *EX*
SUBJECT: Changes in employee benefits
DATE: October 21, 2001

Each fall the Human Resources group looks closely at the company's health insurance benefits to make certain that we are providing an excellent level of coverage in a way that makes economic sense. To that end, we have made some changes to our plan, effective January 1, 2002. Let me outline the three major changes.

1. We are pleased to be able to offer employees the opportunity, through a **Flexible Spending Account**, to pay for dependent care and unreimbursed health expenses on a pre-tax basis, a feature that can result in considerable savings. I will distribute additional information on this benefit at our staff meeting tomorrow, October 22, at 10:30 A.M. I will be available immediately after the meeting to answer any specific questions.

2. Those of you who have taken advantage of our **vision care benefit** in the past know that it offers significant help in paying for eye exams, eyeglasses, and contact lenses. The current plan will change slightly on January 1. Employees and covered dependents will be eligible to receive up to $50 each year toward the cost of a routine eye exam and up to $100 every two years toward the cost of eyeglasses or contact lenses. If you see a provider within our health insurance network, you will pay only $10 per office visit.

3. We at Interlink Systems feel strongly that our health insurance benefits are excellent, but as you know, the cost of such plans continues to rise every year. In the interest of maintaining excellent coverage for our employees, we will raise our **employee contribution**. Starting January 1, we are asking employees with single coverage to contribute $12.50 per pay period toward the cost of medical insurance, and employees who cover dependents to contribute $40 per pay period. Even with this increase, the amount the company asks its employees to contribute towards the premiums (about 8%) is significantly less than the nationwide average of 30%.

Please contact me if you have questions or concerns about the changes that I have outlined in this memo. You can reach me at x462 or at exiang@interlink.net.

Figure 14.1   Sample Workplace Communication

Uses standard format to identify readers, writer, topic, and date

Explains purpose, noting reader's priority

Previews clear organization in blocks

Uses friendly tone to note new benefit for employees

Offers assistance

Introduces benefit change with positive background

Presents increased cost carefully, noting coverage quality and high employer contribution

Offers more help

Supplies contact information

A good business letter is brief—limited to one page if at all possible. It supplies whatever information the reader needs, no more. Because they are so brief, business letters are often judged on the basis of small details—grammar, punctuation, format, appearance, and openings and closings.

FORMAT FOR BUSINESS LETTERS

The format of business letters is fairly well established by convention. Except where noted, leave one line of extra space between elements; in very short letters, it's acceptable to leave additional space before the inside address.

See the sample letters on pp. 231 and 237.

Return Address.   This is your address or the address of the company for which you are writing. Use no abbreviations except the two-letter postal abbreviation for the state. A return address is not needed on preprinted letterhead stationery that already provides this information.

Date.   This goes on the first line after the return address, without an extra line of space above. Spell out the month, and follow it by the day, a comma, and the year.

Inside Address.   This is the address of the person to whom you are writing. Begin with the full name of the person and his or her title (*Mr., Ms., Dr., Professor*); when addressing a woman who does not have a professional title, use *Ms.* unless you know for certain that she prefers *Miss* or *Mrs.* The second line should identify the position the person holds (if any), and the third line should name the organization (if you are writing to one). If you don't know the name of the person who will read your letter, it is acceptable to start with the name of the position, department, or organization. Use no abbreviations in the address except the two-letter postal abbreviation for the state.

Salutation.   Skip a line, and then type *Dear* followed by the person's title and last name; end the line with a colon. If you don't know the name of the person who will read your letter, it is acceptable to use the position that person holds (*Dear Editor*) or the name of the organization (*Dear Angell's Bakery*) in place of a name.

Body.   This is your message. Leave one line of space between paragraphs, and begin each paragraph even with the left margin (no indentations). Paragraphs should generally be no longer than seven or eight typed lines.

Closing.   Leave one line of space after the last paragraph, and then use a conventional closing followed by a comma: *Sincerely, Sincerely yours, Respectfully yours, Yours truly.*

Typed Name with Position.   Leave four lines of space after the closing, and type your name in full, even if you will sign only your first name. Do not include a title before your name. If you are writing on behalf of an organization, you can include your position on the next line.

Signature.   After you have printed the letter, sign your name in the space between the closing and the typed name. Unless you have established a personal relationship with the person to whom you are writing, use both your first and last names. Do not include a title before your name.

Abbreviations at End.   Abbreviations after your typed name can communicate additional information about the letter. If you send a copy to someone other than the person addressed, use *cc:* followed by the name of the person or organization who will receive a copy. If the letter is accompanied by another document in the same envelope, use *Enc.* or *Enclosure.* If the letter has been typed by someone other than the person who wrote and signed it, the writer's initials are given in capital letters, followed by a slash and the initials of the typist in lowercase letters: *VW/dbw.* Leave at least two lines of extra space between the typed name and any abbreviations; put each abbreviation on a separate line.

Two standard formats specify the placement of these elements on the page. To correctly align a letter using *modified block style* (see Figure 14.2), you need to imagine a line running down the center of the page from top to bottom. The return address, date, closing, signature, and typed name are placed so that the left side of each aligns with this center line. The *full block style* is generally used only on letterhead stationery that includes the name and address of the organization. Omit typing the return address, and align all the elements at the left margin.

There are also two standard formats for envelopes. The U.S. Postal Service recommends a format that uses all capital letters, standard abbreviations, and no punctuation; this style makes the information on the envelope easier for the Postal Service to scan and process. However, this format may not be acceptable in all situations; it is always safe to use a conventional envelope format (see Figure 14.3).

Finally, remember that the physical appearance of a business letter is very important.

- Use 8½-by-11-inch bond paper, with matching envelopes.
- Single-space and use an extra line of space to separate paragraphs and the different elements of the letter. Use only one side of the page.
- Leave margins of at least one inch on both sides; try to make the top and bottom margins fairly even, although you may have to have a larger bottom margin if your letter is very short.
- Pay careful attention to grammar, punctuation, and mechanics. Your readers will.

1453 Illinois Avenue
Miami, FL 33133
January 26, 2001

Customer Service Department
Fidelity Products, Inc.
1192 Plymouth Avenue
Little Rock, AK 72210

Dear Customer Service Representative:

I recently purchased a VCR stand (Model XAR) from your company. I have been unable to assemble it because the instructions are unclear. These instructions not only are incomplete (step 6 is missing) but are accompanied by diagrams so small and dark that it is impossible to distinguish the numbers for the different pieces.

Please send me usable instructions. If I do not receive improved instructions in the next fourteen days, I will return my VCR stand to the store where I purchased it and request a full refund.

I have used your TV and video equipment for more than ten years and have been very satisfied, so I was particularly surprised and disappointed to find that you produce such an inferior item. If you continue to pay little attention to the needs of your customers, I will consider purchasing the products of other companies.

Thank you for your attention to these concerns.

Sincerely,

James Winter

James Winter

Figure 14.2 Letter Using Modified Block Style

Memoranda

A *memorandum* (*memo* for short) is a form of communication used within a company to request or exchange information, to make announcements, and to confirm what has passed in conversation. Generally, the topic is quite narrow and should be apparent to the reader in a single glance. Memos tend to be written in the first person (*I* or *we*) and can range from the very infor-

Figure 14.3
Envelope Formats

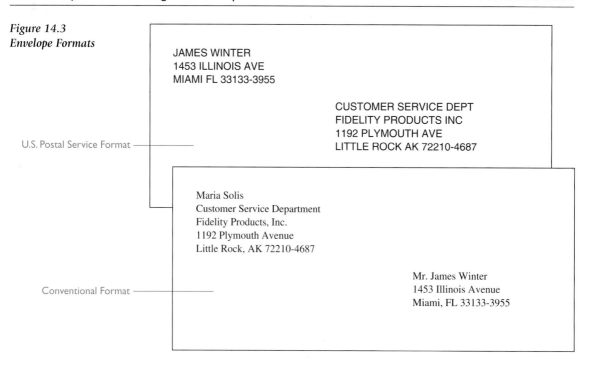

U.S. Postal Service Format

Conventional Format

mal (if written to a peer) to the extremely formal (if written to a high-ranking superior on an important matter). Memos are frequently used to convey information to large groups — an entire team, department, or organization. Most memos are short, but the memo format can also be used to convey proposals and reports; when they are long, good memos freely use headings, subheadings, lists, and other features that are easy to scan. (For a sample memo, see Figure 14.4.)

FORMAT FOR MEMORANDA

Although every organization has its own format for memos, the heading generally consists of a series of lines with clear labels (followed by colons).

Date:	(date on which memo is sent)
To:	(person or persons to whom it is primarily addressed)
cc:	(names of anyone else who receives a copy)
From:	(name of the writer)
Subject: *or* Re:	(concise, accurate statement of the memo's topic)

The subject line often determines whether the memo is read or not. (The old-fashioned abbreviation *Re:* for *regarding* is still used, but we recommend the more common *Subject*.) Accurately summarize the topic in very few words ("Agenda for 12/10 meeting with Ann Kois," "Sales estimates for new product line").

Figure 14.4
Memorandum

memorandum

Date: February 8, 2001

To: Edward Copply, Director, Product Support

cc: Justin Blake

From: Maria Solis, Customer Service Supervisor   *MS*

Subject: Customer dissatisfaction with instructions for Model XAR

As I mentioned in our conversation of January 30, the Customer Service Department has recently received many letters and phone calls regarding the instructions for assembling our new VCR stand, Model XAR. Customers find these instructions confusing and often ask us to arrange a refund. (A copy of the instructions is attached.)

After examining the letters in our files, I've concluded that customers have two specific concerns. The first concern is that the written instructions skip words and entire steps. If you look at the attached copy, you will notice that there is no step 6 and that step 3 reads "Connect the to leg one." The second concern is that the drawings are too dark. Customers complain that dark shading obscures the numbers and makes it difficult to determine where one section begins and the other ends.

The number of calls and letters we're getting suggests that these poor instructions are creating frustration and resentment among both our loyal customers and first-time buyers. In most cases, the customers who contact us are satisfied when we send them a photocopied set of the corrected instructions we've created here in Customer Service, but I feel strongly that the instructions sent out with the product should be improved.

I know that you're planning to review and revise the entire line of product information sheets and instructions, Ed. I recommend that the instructions for Model XAR be put at the top of the list.

Please let me know if I can provide further information.

Enclosure

Electronic Mail

Electronic mail (*e-mail* for short) is popular in business settings because it is easy, speedy, and convenient, combining immediacy with the permanence of letters and memos. It is commonly used both within organizations and between organizations and outside parties. However, letters and memos are often still preferred for formal, official correspondence.

Because it seems so conversational, e-mail may not be polished like other written messages. People who correspond regularly through e-mail tend to forgive one another's infelicities; however, you should remember that your e-mail messages are a part of the official record and have no guarantee of privacy. You may feel that you are having a confidential chat with a trusted friend or colleague, but the chat can be intercepted, recorded on other computers, and distributed either in print or over a network.

FORMAT FOR E-MAIL

The headings for e-mail are predetermined by the systems that generate and transmit it; these almost universally use a standard memo format. The computer will prompt you to enter information in the header lines: *To:*, *cc:*, and *Subject:*, for example. Then you simply type your message. The person receiving your message sees your header information as well as a *From* line that gives your name.

E-mail is a flexible form with a wide range of acceptable practices. Many e-mail messages will be read and responded to while displayed on the computer screen. If possible, keep messages short. If a message runs long, make it easy to navigate by stating at the beginning what it covers and by using clear headings and noticeable dividers (extra space between sections, for example).

Résumés and Application Letters

The most important business correspondence you write may be the résumé and letter you use to apply for a job. Direct, persuasive, correct prose can help you stand out above the crowd.

RÉSUMÉS

In a résumé, you present yourself as someone who has the qualifications needed to excel at a job, someone who will be an asset to the organization. Job seekers often have multiple copies of a single résumé on hand to include with all their applications, but you may want to customize your résumé for each job you apply for if you can easily print out attractive copies.

Although a résumé is a highly formatted document, it also allows a wide variety of decisions about style, organization, and appearance. In this section, we describe a typical résumé, but many formats are acceptable. Unless you have a great deal of relevant work experience, your résumé should be no longer than one page. The standard résumé consists of a heading and labeled sections that detail your experience and qualifications. Within each section, use brief, pointed phrases and clauses rather than complete sentences. Use action verbs (*supervised, ordered, maintained*) and the active voice whenever possible. Highlight labels with underlining, boldface, or a larger type size. Arrange information on the page so that it is pleasing to the eye; use the best paper and clearest printer you can. (For an example of a résumé, see Figure 14.5.)

Figure 14.5   Résumé

Anne Cahill
402 Pigeon Hill Road
Windsor, CT 06095
(860) 555-5763
acahill@mediaone.com

Objective	Position as Registered Nurse in pediatric hospital setting
Education	**University of Connecticut**, Storrs, CT. Bachelor of Science, Major in nursing, May 2000. GPA: 3.5.
	Manchester Community Technical College, Manchester, CT. Associate degree in occupational therapy, May 1995. GPA: 3.3.

Work Experience

9/95–present **Certified Occupational Therapy Assistant**, Johnson Memorial Hospital, Stafford Springs, CT
• Assist children with delayed motor development and cerebral palsy to develop skills for the activities of daily life

9/93–9/95 **Nursing Assistant**, Woodlake Healthcare Center, Tolland, CT
• Assisted geriatric residents with activities of daily living
• Provided support to nursing staff in treating acute care patients

9/91–9/93 **Cashier**, Stop and Shop Supermarket, Vernon, CT
• Responsible for training newly hired cashiers

Clinical Internships **St. Francis Hospital**, Hartford CT
• Student Nurse, Maternity and Postpartum, spring 2000

Hartford Hospital, Hartford, CT
• Student Nurse, Pediatrics, fall 1999

Visiting Nurse and Community Health, Mansfield, CT
• Student Nurse, Community, spring 1999

Manchester General Hospital, Manchester, CT
• Student Nurse, Medical-Surgical, fall 1998

Computer Skills
• Proficient with Microsoft Office, Database, and Windows 98 applications
• Working knowledge of Lotus 1-2-3
• Internet research skills

Activities
• Student Union Board of Governors, U of CT, class representative
• Intramural soccer

References Available upon request

Heading.   The heading is generally centered (or otherwise pleasingly aligned) on the page with separate lines for your name; street address; city, state, and zip code; phone number; and e-mail address.

Employment Objective.   This optional section allows personnel officers to see at a glance your priorities and goals. Try to sound confident and eager but not pompous or presumptuous.

Education.   This section is almost always included, generally first. For each postsecondary school you've attended, specify the name of the institution, your major, your date of graduation (or expected graduation), and your grade point average (if it reflects well on you). You can also mention any awards, honors, or relevant course work.

Experience.   In this key section of the résumé, list each job separately with the most recent one first. You can include both full-time and part-time jobs. For each, give the name of the organization, your position, your responsibilities, and the dates you held the job. If you were involved in any unusual projects or were responsible for any important developments, describe them. Highlight details that show relevant work experience and leadership ability. Minimize information about jobs or responsibilities that are unconnected to the job for which you're applying.

Skills.   If your special skills (data processing, technical drawing, knowledge of a foreign language) aren't obvious from the descriptions of your education and work experience, you can list them.

Interests.   You can specify either professional interests and activities (*Member of Birmingham Bricklayers Association*) or personal pursuits (*skiing, hiking, needlepoint*) showing that you are dedicated and well-rounded.

References.   If a job advertisement requests references, give them. Always contact your references in advance to make sure they will be willing to give you a good recommendation. For each person, give the name, his or her organization and position, and the organization's address and phone number. If references have not been requested, you can simply note "Available on request."

APPLICATION LETTERS

For general guidelines for business letters, see pp. 227–30.

When writing a letter applying for a job, you should follow all the guidelines for writing other business letters. Remember that your immediate objective is to obtain an interview. As you compete against other candidates, your letter and résumé are all the employer has to judge you on.

If you're responding to an advertisement, read it critically. What qualifications are listed? Ideally, you should have all the required qualifications, but if you lack one, try to find something in your background that compensates, some similar experience in a different form. What else can you tell about the organization or position from the ad? How does the organization represent itself? (If you're unfamiliar with the organization and you can't glean much about it from the ad, check the company's Web site.) How does the ad describe the ideal candidate? As a team player? A dynamic individual? If you feel that you are the person this organization is looking for, you'll want to portray yourself this way in your letter.

Figure 14.6
Application Letter

402 Pigeon Hill Road
Windsor, CT 06095
July 8, 2001

Sheryl Sullivan
Director of Nursing
Center for Children's Health and Development
St. Francis Hospital and Medical Center
114 Woodland Street
Hartford, CT 06105

Dear Ms. Sullivan:

I am writing to apply for the full-time position as a pediatric nurse at the Center for Children's Health and Development at St. Francis Hospital, which was advertised on the Eastern Connecticut Health Network Web site. I feel that my varied clinical experiences and my desire to work with children ideally suit me to the job. In addition, I am highly motivated to grow and succeed in the field of health care.

I have worked for the past five years as a certified occupational therapy assistant. In this capacity, I help children with delayed motor function acquire the skills necessary to achieve as high a level of independence as possible. While working as a COTA, I attended nursing school with the ultimate goal of becoming a pediatric nurse. My varied clinical experiences as a student nurse and my previous experience as a nurse's aide in a geriatric center have exposed me to many types of care. I feel that these experiences have helped me to become a well-rounded caregiver; they also, however, have reinforced my belief that my skills and talents are best suited to working with children.

I believe that I would be a strong addition to the medical team at the Children's Center. My clinical experiences have prepared me to deal with a wide range of situations. In addition, I am dedicated to maintaining and enhancing the well-being of children. I am enclosing proof of my recent certification as a Registered Nurse in the state of Connecticut. Please write to me at the address above or via e-mail, or call me at (860) 555-5763. Thank you for your consideration. I look forward to hearing from you.

Sincerely,

Anne Cahill

Anne Cahill

Enclosures

In your letter, you want to spark your readers' interest, convince them that you're a qualified and attractive candidate, and motivate them to grant you an interview. Whenever possible, address your letter to the person responsible for screening applicants and setting up interviews; you may need to call the organization to find out this person's name. In the first paragraph, identify the job, indicate how you heard about it, and summarize your qualifications. In the second paragraph, expand on your qualifications, highlighting key information on your résumé and supplementing it with additional details, if necessary. At this point, you need to show your readers that you're a better candidate than the other applicants. In the third paragraph, restate your interest in the job, ask for an interview, and let your prospective employer know how to reach you. (For a sample application letter, see Figure 14.6.)

Chapter 15
Writing for Assessment

Most college writing is done for assessment — that is, most of the papers you hand in are eventually evaluated and graded. But some college writing tasks exist *only* as methods of assessment: they are designed not to help you expand your writing skills (or content knowledge in other courses) but to allow you to demonstrate that you have mastered them. You often need to do such writing on the spot — a quiz to finish in twenty minutes, a final exam to complete in a few hours, an impromptu essay to dash off in one class period. How do you discover and shape your ideas in a limited time?

In this chapter we provide tips for three types of in-class writing that are commonly used for assessment — the essay exam, the short-answer exam, and the timed writing assignment. We also discuss an assessment tool that is becoming more common — the writing portfolio. A portfolio is simply a collection of writing samples, but it takes careful thinking and effective writing to create one that adequately demonstrates your strengths as a writer.

Essay Examinations

In many courses an essay exam is the most important kind of in-class writing. Instructors believe that such writing shows that you haven't just memorized a batch of material but that you have examined it critically and can clearly communicate your thoughts about it to someone else.

PREPARING FOR THE EXAM

Some instructors favor open-book exams, in which you bring your books and perhaps your notes to class for reference. In an open-book exam, ability to memorize and recall is less important than ability to reason and to select what matters most. On the other hand — if the exam will be closed book — it's a good idea to fix in your memory any vital names, dates, and definitions. But when you review, don't clutter your mind with random details. Instead, look for the main ideas or themes in each textbook chapter. Then ask yourself: What do these main ideas have to do with each other? How might they be combined? What conclusions can I draw from all the facts?

A good way to prepare for any exam, whether the books are to be closed or open, is to imagine questions you might be asked and then plan answers. If your instructor has supplied sample questions, you can pattern new questions after them.

LEARNING FROM ANOTHER WRITER

To start looking at techniques for answering *any* exam question, let's take one concrete example. A final exam in developmental psychology posed this question:

> What evidence indicates innate factors in perceptual organization? You might find it useful to recall any research that shows how infants perceive depth and forms.

In response, David Ian Cohn sat back in his chair for five minutes and thought over the reading he'd done for the course. What perception research had he heard about that used babies for subjects? He jotted down ideas, crossed out a couple of weak ones, and drew lines linking ideas that went together. Then he took a deep breath and wrote this straightforward answer:

For an illustration of linking, see p. 276.

> Research on infants is probably the best way to demonstrate that some factors in perceptual organization are innate. As the cliff box experiment shows, an infant will avoid what looks like a drop-off, even though its mother calls it and even though it can feel glass covering the drop-off area. The same infant will crawl to the other end of the box, which appears (and is) safe. Apparently, infants do not have to be taught what a cliff looks like.
>
> Psychologists have also observed that infants are aware of size constancy. They recognize a difference in size between a 10 cm box at a distance of one meter and a 20 cm box at a distance of two meters. If this phenomenon is not innate, it is at least learned early, for the subjects of the experiment were infants of sixteen to eighteen months.
>
> When shown various patterns, infants tend to respond more noticeably to patterns that resemble the human face than to those that appear random. This seemingly innate recognition helps the infant identify people (such as its mother) from less important inanimate objects.
>
> Infants also seem to have an innate ability to match sight with sound. When simultaneously shown two television screens, each depicting a different subject, while being played a tape that sometimes matched one screen and sometimes the other, infants looked at whichever screen matched what they heard—not always, but at least twice as often.

Questions to Start You Thinking

Meaning

1. What is the main idea of Cohn's answer?

2. If you were the psychology instructor, how could you immediately see that Cohn had thoroughly dealt with the question and only with the question?

Writing Strategies

3. In what places is Cohn's answer concrete and specific, not vague and general?

4. Suppose he had tacked on a concluding sentence: "Thus I have conclusively proved that there are innate factors in perceptual organization, by citing much evidence showing that infants definitely can perceive depth and forms." Would that sentence have strengthened his answer?

GENERATING IDEAS

When you are seated in the classroom, beginning your race with the clock, resist the temptation to start scribbling. First read over all the questions on the exam carefully. If you are offered a choice, just cross out any questions you are *not* going to answer so you don't waste time on them by mistake. And if you don't understand what a question calls for, ask your instructor right away.

Plan a Concrete Answer.   Few people can dash off an excellent essay exam answer without first taking time to plan. Instructors prefer answers that are concrete and specific rather than those that stay up in the clouds of generality. David Cohn's answer to the psychology question cites evidence all the way through — particular experiments in which infants were subjects. A little time taken to generate concrete examples — as Cohn did — will be time wisely spent.

Organize around the Question.   Instructors also prefer answers that are organized and coherent rather than rambling. To write such answers, most of us need to plot some direction to follow before we begin. Often a question will contain directive words that help you define your task: *evaluate, compare, discuss, explain, describe, summarize, trace the development of.* You can put yourself on the right track if you incorporate a form of such a word in your first sentence.

QUESTION	Define romanticism, citing its major characteristics and giving examples of each.
ANSWER	Romanticism is defined as . . .
ANSWER	Romanticism is a complex concept, difficult to define. It . . .

PLANNING: RECOGNIZING TYPICAL EXAM QUESTIONS

Most exam questions fall into types. If you can recognize them, you will know how to organize and begin to write. Here are examples.

For more on explaining cause and effect, see Ch. 8 and pp. 316–18.

The Cause and Effect Question.   These questions usually mention *causes* and *effects*.

> What were the immediate causes of the stock market crash of 1929?

> Describe the principal effects on the economy that commonly result from a low prime rate of interest.

For more on comparing and contrasting, see Ch. 7 and pp. 314–16.

The Compare or Contrast Question.   This popular type of question calls on you to point out similarities (comparing), discuss differences (contrasting), or do both, in the process explaining not one subject but two. Be sure to pay attention to both subjects, paralleling the points you make about each, giving both equal space.

> Compare and contrast *iconic memory* and *eidetic imagery*. (1) Define the two terms, indicating the ways in which they differ, and (2) state the way or ways in which they are related or alike.

After supplying a one-sentence definition of each term, a student proceeded first to contrast and then to compare, for full credit.

> Iconic memory is a picturelike impression that lasts for only a fraction of a second in short-term memory. Eidetic imagery is the ability to take a mental photograph, exact in detail, as though its subject were still present. But iconic memory soon disappears. Unlike an eidetic image, it does not last long enough to enter long-term memory. IM is common; EI is unusual: very few people have it. Both iconic memory and eidetic imagery are similar, however: both record visual images, and every sighted person of normal intelligence has both abilities to some degree.

A question of this kind doesn't always use the words *compare* and *contrast*.

> Signal at least three differences between Copernicus's and Kepler's models of the solar system. In what respects was Kepler's model an improvement on that of Copernicus? [*contrast and show superiority*]

> Distinguish between agnosia and receptive aphasia. In what ways are the two conditions similar? [*contrast and then compare*]

> Briefly explain the duplex theory of memory. What are the main differences between short-term memory and long-term memory? [*contrast only*]

The Demonstration Question.   This kind of question gives you a statement and asks you to back it up.

Demonstrate the truth of Freud's contention that laughter may contain elements of aggression.

In other words, you are asked to explain Freud's claim and supply evidence to support it. You might refer to crowd scenes you have experienced, analyze a joke or a scene in a TV show, or use examples from your reading.

The Discussion Question.   A discussion question may tempt an unwary writer to shoot the breeze.

> Discuss three events that precipitated Lyndon B. Johnson's withdrawal from the 1968 presidential race.

This question looks like an open invitation to ramble about Johnson and Vietnam, but it isn't. Try rewording the question to help you focus your discussion: "Why did President Johnson decide not to seek another term? Analyze the causes and briefly explain each."

Sometimes a discussion question won't announce itself with the word *discuss*, but with *describe* or *explain* or *explore*.

> Describe the national experience following passage of the Eighteenth Amendment. What did most Americans learn from it?

Provided you know that the Eighteenth Amendment (Prohibition) banned the sale, manufacture, and transportation of alcoholic drinks and that it was finally repealed, you can discuss its effects — or perhaps the reasons for its repeal.

The Divide or Classify Question.   Sometimes you are asked to slice the subject into sections, sort things into kinds, or break the idea, place, person, or process into its parts.

For more on division and classification, see pp. 310–12.

> Identify the ways in which each inhabitant of the United States uses, on the average, 1,595 gallons of water a day. How and to what degree might each person cut down on this amount?

For a start, you would divide up water use into several parts — drinking, cooking, bathing, washing cars, and so on. Then after that division, you would give tips for water conservation and tell how effective each is.

> What different genres of film did King Vidor direct? Name at least one outstanding example of each kind.

This classification question asks you to sort films into categories — possibly comedy, war, adventure, mystery, musical, western.

The Definition Question.   When you write an extended definition, illustrate it with an example.

For more on definition, see pp. 305–07.

> Explain the three dominant styles of parenting — *permissive, authoritarian-restrictive,* and *authoritative.*

This question calls for a trio of definitions. The next, however, asks you to explain a single method and give examples.

> Define the Stanislavsky method of acting, citing outstanding actors who have followed it.

For more on taking a stand and evaluating, see Chs. 9 and 11.

The Evaluation Question.   This favorite calls on students to think critically and to present an argument.

> Present and evaluate the most widely accepted theories to account for the disappearance of the dinosaurs.

> Evaluate *one* of the following suggestions, giving reasons for your judgments:
>
> a. Cities should stop building highways to the suburbs and instead build public monorail systems.
> b. Houses and public buildings should be constructed to last no longer than twenty years.

Other argument questions might begin "Defend the idea of . . ." or "Show weaknesses in the concept of . . ." or otherwise call on you to take a stand.

The Respond to the Comment or Quotation Question.   A question might supply a statement for close reading, asking you to test the writer's opinion against what you know.

> Discuss the following statement: high-minded opposition to slavery was only one cause, and not a very important one, of the animosity between North and South that in 1861 escalated into civil war.

Carefully read the statement a few times, and then jot down contrary or supporting evidence.

> Was the following passage written by Gertrude Stein, Kate Chopin, or Tillie Olsen? On what evidence do you base your answer?
>
> > She waited for the material pictures which she thought would gather and blaze before her imagination. She waited in vain. She saw no pictures of solitude, of hope, of longing, or of despair. But the very passions themselves were aroused within her soul, swaying it, lashing it, as the waves daily beat upon her splendid body. She trembled, she was choking, and the tears blinded her.

The passage is taken from a story by Kate Chopin. If you were familiar with Chopin, who specializes in physical and emotional descriptions of impassioned women, you would know this answer, and you might point to language (*swaying, lashing*) that marks it as hers.

For more on process analysis, see pp. 312–14.

The Process Analysis Question.   Often you can spot this kind of question by the word *trace:*

> Trace the stages through which a bill becomes a federal law.

> Trace the development of the medieval Italian city-state.

Both questions want you to tell how something occurs or occurred. In brief, you divide the process into steps and detail each step. The other type of process analysis, the "how-to" variety, is called for in this question:

> An employee has been consistently late for work, varying from fifteen minutes to a half hour daily. This employee has been on the job only five months but shows promise of learning skills that your firm needs badly. How would you deal with this situation?

The Imaginative Question.   Sometimes an instructor will throw in a question that at first glance might seem bizarre. On second glance, you may see that the question reaches deep.

> Imagine yourself to be a trial lawyer in 1921, charged with defending Nicola Sacco and Bartolomeo Vanzetti, two anarchists accused of murder. Argue for their acquittal on whatever grounds you can justify.

This question calls on a prelaw student to show familiarity with a famous case (which ended with the execution of the defendants). In addition, it calls for knowledge of the law and of trial procedure. Such a question might be fun to answer; moreover, in being asked to imagine a time, a place, and dramatic circumstances, you might learn something.

DRAFTING: THE ONLY VERSION

When the clock on the wall is ticking away, generating ideas and shaping an answer often take place at the same time. If you can do your preliminary work right on the exam sheet, you will save time: annotate questions, underline important points, scribble short definitions. Write reminders that you will notice while you work: TWO PARTS TO THIS QUES.! or GET IN EXAMPLE OF ABORIGINES. To make sure that you include all necessary information without repetition, you might jot down a brief, informal outline. This was David Cohn's outline for his answer on his psychology exam:

For David Cohn's complete answer, see p. 240.

> Thesis: Research on infants is probably the best way to demonstrate that some factors in perceptual organization are innate.
> Cliff box—kid fears drop despite glass, mother, knows shallow side safe
> Size constancy—learned early if not intrinsic
> Shapes—infants respond more/better to face shape than nonformed
> Match sound w/ sight—2 TVs, look twice as much at right one

Budget Your Time.   When you have two or more essay questions to answer, block out your time at least roughly based on the points or minutes your instructor allots to each. Give extra minutes to a complicated question (such as one with several parts). Then pace yourself as you write. For example, make a little schedule so you'll know that at 10:30 it's time to wrap up question 2 and move on.

Begin with the Easy Questions.   Many students find that it helps their morale to start with the question they feel best able to answer. Unless your instructor specifies that you have to answer the questions in their given order, why not skip around? Just make sure you clearly number each answer or label the item as your instructor does. Then begin each answer in such a way that the instructor will immediately recognize which question you're answering. If the task is "Compare and contrast the depression of the 1930s with the recession of the 1970s," an answer might begin in this way:

> Compared to the paralyzing depression that began in 1929, the recession of the 1970s seems like a bad case of measles.

For more on thesis statements, see pp. 271–75. For David Cohn's complete answer, see p. 240.

Try Stating Your Thesis at the Start.   Some students make their opening sentence a thesis statement — a sentence that immediately makes clear the main point. Then they proceed in the rest of the answer to back up that statement. Stating a clear thesis often makes good sense; you'll be less likely to ramble, and your instructor will know right away what you're talking about. That's how David Cohn opens his answer to the psychology question. An easy way to get started is to turn the question into a declarative statement and use it to begin an answer.

> QUESTION
> Can adequate reasons for leasing cars and office equipment, instead of purchasing them, be cited for a two-person partnership?

> ANSWER
> I can cite at least four adequate reasons for a two-person partnership to lease cars and office equipment. For one thing, under present tax laws, the entire cost of a regular payment under a leasing agreement may be deducted. . . .

Stick to the Point of the Question.   You may be tempted to throw into your answer everything you have learned in the course. But to do so defeats the purpose of the examination — to put your knowledge to use, not to parade it. Answer by selecting *what matters* from what you know, at the same time shaping it.

Answer the Whole Question.   Often a question will have two parts.

> Name the most common styles of contemporary architecture and then evaluate one of them.

When the dragon of a question has two heads, make sure you cut off both.

Stay Specific.   Pressed for time, some exam takers think, "I haven't got time to get specific here. I'll just sum up this idea in general." That's a mistake. Every time you throw in a large, general statement ("The Industrial

Revolution was beneficial for the peasant"), take time to include specific examples ("In Dusseldorf, as Taine tells us, the mortality rate from starvation among displaced Prussian farmworkers now dropped from a peak of almost 10 percent a year").

Leave Room to Revise.   Give yourself room for second thoughts by writing on only one side of the page in your examination booklet and skipping every other line. Then later, should you wish to add words or sentences or even a whole paragraph, you can do so with ease.

REVISING: REREADING AND PROOFING

If you have paced yourself, you'll have at least a few minutes left for looking over your work. Check how clear your ideas are and how well they hang together. Add sentences wherever you think new ones are needed. If you recall an important point, you can add a paragraph on a blank left-hand page. Just draw an arrow indicating where it goes.

Naturally, errors occur more often when you write under pressure than when you have time to proofread and edit carefully. On an exam, what you say and how forcefully you say it matter most. Still, no instructor will object to careful corrections. You can easily add words with carets (^):

foreign

Israeli ^ policy

Or you can neatly strike out a word by drawing a line through it.

When you receive your paper or blue book back and you look it over, you might learn more about writing essay exams if you consider these questions:

REVISION CHECKLIST

___ Did you answer the whole question, not just part of it?

___ Did you stick to the point, not throw in unrequested information?

___ Did you make your general statements clear by citing evidence or examples?

___ Does your answer sprawl, or is it focused?

___ Did you inflate your answer with hot air, or did you stay close to earth, giving plenty of facts, examples, and illustrations?

___ Did you proofread for omissions and lack of clarity?

___ On what question or questions do you feel you did a good job that satisfies you, no matter what grade you received?

___ If you had to write this exam over again, how would you now go about the job?

Short-Answer Examinations

The *short-answer exam* may call on you to identify names or phrases from your reading, in a sentence or a few words.

> Identify the following: Clemenceau, Treaty of Versailles, Maginot line, Dreyfus affair.

You might answer the question as follows:

> <u>Georges Clemenceau</u> — This French premier, nicknamed The Tiger, headed a popular coalition cabinet during World War I and at the Paris Peace Conference demanded stronger penalties against Germany.

For more about writing definitions, see pp. 305–07.

Writing a short identification is much like writing a short definition. Be sure to mention the general class to which a thing belongs.

> <u>Treaty of Versailles</u> — pact between Germany and the Allies that . . .
> <u>Maginot line</u> — fortifications that . . .

If you do so, you won't lose points for writing an answer like this, which fails to make clear the nature of the thing being identified:

> <u>Maginot line</u> — The Germans went around it.

Timed Writings

Many composition instructors, to give you experience in writing on demand, assign impromptu essays to be written in class. For such writings, your time is limited (usually forty-five minutes to an hour), the setting is controlled (usually you're at a desk and not allowed to use a dictionary or a spell checker), and you can't choose your own subject. The purpose of timed writings is to test your writing skills, not to see how much information you can recall.

Though this rapid-fire type of writing seems a lot different from the leisurely think-plan-draft-revise method of composing, your usual methods of writing can serve you well, even used in a hurry.

Budget Your Time.   For an in-class essay, if you have forty-five minutes to write, a good rule of thumb is to spend ten minutes preparing, thirty minutes writing, and five minutes rereading and making last-minute changes. Take care not to spend so much time thinking and planning that you must rush through getting your ideas down on paper in an essay — the part you will be graded on.

Choose Your Topic Wisely.   For on-the-spot writing, the trick is to make the topic your own. If you have a choice at all, choose the one you know the most about, not the one you think will impress your readers. They'll be most impressed by logical argument and solid evidence. If you have to write on a broad abstract subject (say, a world problem that affects many people), bring it down to something personal, something you have observed or experienced. Have you witnessed traffic jams, brownouts, or condos ruining beaches? Then write about increased population, using these examples.

Think and Plan before You Write.   Despite your limited time, read the instructions and the topics or questions carefully, choose your topic thoughtfully, restrict it to something you know about, form a main idea for focus, and jot down the major divisions for development. If a good hook for the introduction or conclusion occurs to you, make a note of it. Just don't spend so much time on planning that you can't finish the essay.

Don't Try to Be Perfect.   No one expects extemporaneous essays to read as smoothly as reports written over several weeks. You can't polish every sentence or remember the exact word for every spot. And never waste time recopying. Devote your time to the more important parts of writing.

Save Time to Proofread.   The last few minutes when you read over your work and correct glaring errors may be the best-spent minutes of all. Cross out and make corrections neatly. Use asterisks (*), arrows, and carets (∧). Especially check for the following:

For more on making corrections, see E1 in the "Quick Editing Guide" (the dark-blue-edged pages).

- omitted letters (*-ed* or *-s*)
- added letters (develop*e*)
- inverted letters (rec*ie*ve)
- wrong punctuation (a comma instead of a period)
- omitted apostrophes (*dont* instead of *don't*)
- omitted words ("She going" instead of "She *is* going")
- wrong words (*except* instead of *accept*)
- misspelled words (*mispelled*)

TYPES OF TOPICS

Often you can expect the same types of questions or topics for in-class writings as for essay exams. If you know how to organize those recognizable types, you can do well. Just remember to look for the key words and do what they say.

For common types of exam questions, see pp. 242–45.

What were the *causes* of World War I?

Compare and contrast the theories of capitalism and socialism.

Define civil rights.

Thinking Fast

To practice planning quickly for timed writing or tests, brainstorm as a class to explore approaches to writing on the sample topics provided in this chapter. Select one class member (or three, in turn) to record ideas on the board. Devote exactly ten minutes of discussion per topic to these key parts of a successful response:

- possible thesis sentences
- possible patterns of organization
- possible kinds and sources of evidence

Expect a wide range of ideas. Spend the last part of class evaluating those ideas.

If you are given a general subject on which thousands of diverse students can write, add your own personal twist. But again, pay attention to key words.

Analyze a problem in education that is *difficult to solve*.

Discuss ways to cope with stress.

Standardized tests often ask you to respond to a short passage, testing not only your writing ability but also your reading comprehension.

Thomas Jefferson stated, "If a nation expects to be ignorant and free, in a state of civilization, it expects what never was and never will be." *How* is his comment *relevant* to education today?

Writing for Portfolio Assessment

The writing portfolio has become a popular method of assessment for college classes. Portfolio courses typically emphasize revision and reflection — the ability to identify and discuss your choices, strengths, or learning processes. In such a course, you'll need to save all your drafts and notes, keep track of your choices and changes, and near the end of the term select and submit your best writing.

A writing portfolio is a collection of pieces of writing that represent the writer's best work. Collected over time and across projects, a portfolio showcases a writer's talent, hard work, and ability to make thoughtful choices about content and presentation. For a single course, the portfolio is usually due at the end of the term and includes pieces you have written and revised for that course. Most portfolios ask for some kind of accompanying introduction (usually some form of self-assessment or rationale) addressed to readers, who might be teachers, supervisors, evaluators, parents, or classmates.

UNDERSTANDING PORTFOLIO ASSESSMENT

The portfolio is a method of evaluation and teaching that shapes the whole course from beginning to end. For example, your portfolio course will probably emphasize responses to your writing—from your classmates and your instructor—but not necessarily grades on your separate papers. The portfolio method attempts to shift attention to the writing process itself—to discovery, planning, drafting, peer response, revision, editing—and to give time for your skills to develop before the writing "counts" and the portfolio itself is graded.

The portfolio method is flexible, but you will need to read your instructor's syllabus and assignment sheets carefully and listen well in class to determine what kind of portfolio you'll be expected to keep. Below are a few of the typical types of portfolios, and more than one might be used in a single course.

A Writing Folder.   Students are asked to submit all drafts, notes, outlines, scribbles, doodles, and messy pages—in short, all writing done for the course, whether finished or unfinished. Students may also be asked to select from the folder two or three of their most promising pieces to revise for a "presentation portfolio." The folder is usually not accompanied by a reflective introduction or cover letter.

A Learning (or Open) Portfolio.   Students are free to submit a variety of materials that have contributed to their learning. They may even be free to determine the contents, organization, and presentation of the portfolio. A learning portfolio for a composition class might include photos or other nonprint objects collected to demonstrate learning.

A Closed Portfolio.   Students must turn in assignments that are specified by the instructor, or their options for what to include may be limited.

A Midterm Portfolio.   The portfolio is given a trial run at midterm, or the midterm grade is determined by one or two papers that are submitted for evaluation, perhaps accompanied by a brief self-assessment.

A Final or Presentation Portfolio.   The portfolio is evaluated at the end of the course, after it has been revised, edited, and polished to presentation quality.

A Modified or Combination Portfolio.   The student has some choice, but not unlimited choice, in what to include. For example, the instructor may ask for three entries that demonstrate certain features or parts of the course.

Find out when your course begins what kind of portfolio your instructor has in mind. Here's one likely scenario. You are required to submit a modified or combination portfolio—one that contains, for example, three revised papers (out of the five or six required papers). You decide, late in the term, which three papers to include or where to concentrate on revision and editing. You also may be asked to reflect on what those choices say about you as a writer, to demonstrate your own learning in the course, or to explain the decisions you made in the process of writing a paper. Here are some typical questions your instructor, the syllabus, or assignment sheets may answer:

- How many papers should you include in the portfolio?
- Do all these papers need to be revised? If so, what level of revision is expected?
- How much of the course grade is determined by the portfolio grade? Are the portfolio entries graded separately, or does the entire portfolio receive one grade?
- May you include papers written for other courses?
- May you include entries other than texts or documents — such as photographs, videos, maps, disks with downloaded Web pages, or other visual aids?
- Should you preface the portfolio with a cover letter?
- Does each entry need a separate cover sheet?
- What is expected in your introduction: Description? Explanation? Reflection? Self-assessment?

TIPS FOR KEEPING A PORTFOLIO

Keep Everything, and Stay Organized.   Don't throw anything away! Keep all your notes, lists, drafts, outlines, clusters, responses from readers, photocopied articles, and references for works cited. If you have your own computer, *back up everything* to a disk. If you use the computer lab, save your work to a disk, and keep an extra blank disk in your backpack. Use a system to organize everything. Invest in a good folder with pockets, and label the contents of each pocket. Include the drafts, notes, outlines, and peer review forms for each assignment.

Manage Your Time.   The portfolio isn't due until the end of the course (or at midterm), but planning ahead will save you time and frustration. For example, as your instructor returns each of your assignments with comments, make some changes in response to those suggestions while the ideas are fresh. If you don't understand or know how to approach one of your instructor's comments, ask right away — at the end of class or during office hours that same week. Make notes about what you think you want to do. Then, even if you want to let a paper simmer, you will have both a plan and some fresh insight when you work on it again.

Practice Self-Assessment.   For complex activities, it's important to your improvement to step back and evaluate your own performance. Maybe you have great ideas but find it hard to organize them. Maybe you write powerful thesis statements but run out of things to say in support of them. Don't wait until the portfolio cover letter is due to begin tracking your learning or assessing your strengths, weaknesses, or preferences.

You can practice self-assessment from the first day of class. For example, after reviewing your class syllabus carefully, write one or two paragraphs about how you think you will do in this course. Which assignments or activities do you expect to do well on, and why? Which may be hard for you, and why? In addition, for each paper you share with peers or hand in, write a journal entry about what you think the paper does well and what it still needs. Keep track, in a log or journal, of the process you go through to plan, research, or draft each paper—where you get stuck and where things click.

For more on keeping a journal, see pp. 265–66.

Choose the Entries Carefully.   If you can select what to include, consider your choices in light of what the course has emphasized. Of course, you want to select pieces your evaluator will think are "the best," but also consider which ones show the most promise or potential and which ones you might want to revisit. Which drafts show creativity, insight, or an unusual approach to the assignment? Which show variety—different purposes, audiences, or voices? Which show depth—your ability to do thorough research or stay with a topic for several weeks? Also consider the order of the entries—which piece might work best first or last, and how the placement of each entry affects the whole.

Write a Strong Reflective Introduction or Cover Letter.   Your introduction—usually a self-assessment in the form of a cover letter, a statement, or a description for each of your entries—could be the most important text you write all semester. Besides introducing readers to your collection of writing and portraying you as a student writer, it explains your choices in putting the portfolio together and demonstrates that you can evaluate the strengths and weaknesses of your work and your writing process. For many portfolio-based courses, the reflective introduction or cover letter is the "final exam," testing what you've learned about good writing, about readers' needs, and about the importance of details—in this case, the details of a careful self-presentation.

If your instructor has not assigned a reflective introduction or cover letter, it could be that you've been asked to assemble course materials for a writing folder and not a portfolio. But it also could be that descriptions of your process or your choices are expected to appear throughout the portfolio—perhaps at the end or perhaps in brief introductions to each portfolio entry. Here are some questions you can ask about writing a reflective introduction or cover letter:

___ Who will read the cover letter in this portfolio?

___ What qualities of writing will your reader value?

___ Will the reader suggest changes or evaluate your work?

___ What will the outcome of the reading be? How much can you influence the outcome?

___ What do you want to emphasize about your writing? What are you proud of? What have you learned? What did you have trouble with?

___ How can you present your writing ability in the best light?

If your reader or evaluator is also your classroom instructor, look back over his or her responses on your returned papers, and review the course syllabus and assignment sheets. What patterns do you see in your instructor's concerns or directions? What information could you give a friend about your instructor's expectations — or pet peeves? Use what you've learned about your instructor's values as a reader to compose a convincing, well-developed introductory statement or cover letter for your portfolio.

For more on appeals, see pp. 29–30.

If your readers or evaluators are unknown, ask your instructor to give you as much information as possible so that you can decide which logical, ethical, or emotional appeals might be most effective. Although you won't know your readers personally, it's safe to assume that they will be trained in portfolio assessment and will share many of your instructor's ideas about good writing. If your college writing program has guidelines or grading criteria, consult them, too.

How long should your introduction or cover letter be? Check with your instructor, but regardless of length, develop your ideas or support your claims as in any effective piece of writing. If you are asked to write a letter, follow the format for a business letter: include the date, a salutation, and a closing.

In the reflective introduction, you might try some of the following (but don't try to use all of them):

- Discuss your best entry and why it is your best.
- Detail your revisions — the improvements and changes that you want readers to notice.
- Review everything included, touching on the strengths of each.
- Outline the writing and revising process that you used for one or more of your entries.
- State what the portfolio illustrates about you as a writer, student, researcher, or critical thinker.
- Acknowledge your weaknesses, but show how you've worked to overcome them.
- Acknowledge your reader-respondents and their influence on your portfolio pieces.

- Reflect on what you've learned about writing, reading, and other topics of the course.

- Lay the groundwork for a positive evaluation of your work.

Polishing the Final Portfolio.   From the first page to the last, your portfolio should be ready for public presentation, a product you can take pride in or show to others. Besides careful editing and proofreading, think about creative ways to give your portfolio a final distinctive feature. For example, consider having the portfolio bound at your local copy shop, adding a colorful cover or illustrations, or including a table of contents or a running header. Although a cheerful cover will not make up for weak writing or careless editing, readers will value the extra effort you put into the final product.

PART FOUR

*A Writer's
Strategies*

Introduction

The following seven chapters constitute a manual offering in-depth advice on writing strategies. The word *strategy* may remind you of warfare: in the original Greek sense of the word, it is a way to win a battle. Writing a college paper, you'll probably agree, is a battle of a kind. In this manual you'll find an array of small weapons to use — and perhaps some heavy artillery.

Here are techniques you can learn, methods you can follow, good practices you can observe. The first five chapters offer a wealth of suggestions for approaching each of the stages of the writing process: generating ideas, planning, drafting, developing, and revising and editing. In Part Two, each stage was covered for each assignment, and relevant strategies were mentioned briefly. Here, each stage of the writing process gets a full chapter, and the strategies for each are explained and illustrated more fully. The last two chapters here offer advice on strategies of increasing importance — designing your own document and understanding visual representations.

No strategy will appeal to every writer, and no writer uses every one for every writing task. Consider this part of the book a reference guide or instruction manual. Turn to it when you need more help, when you're curious, or when you'd like to enlarge your repertoire of writing skills. We can't tell you which of the ideas and techniques covered in these pages will work for you, but we can promise that if you try some of them, you'll be rewarded.

Chapter 16
Strategies for Generating Ideas

For most writers, the hardest part of writing comes first—confronting a blank sheet of paper. Fortunately, you can do much to get ready for that moment. Many of the tested techniques that follow may strike you as far-out, even silly, but all have worked for some writers—both professionals and students—and some may work for you. This chapter suggests two types of devices—methods for finding ideas for your writing and strategies for getting ready to write.

Finding Ideas

For more help with finding ideas, use the *Writing Guide Software for THE BEDFORD GUIDE.*

Learning to write is learning what questions to ask yourself. When you begin to write, you need to start the ideas flowing. Sometimes ideas appear quickly on the paper or screen. But at other times you can think of the strategies in this chapter as your arsenal of idea generators. These strategies are useful at any point in the writing process when you find your flow of ideas drying up or when you need additional evidence. If one doesn't work for a particular writing task, try another.

BRAINSTORMING

A *brainstorm* is a sudden insight or inspiration, and *brainstorming* is free association for stimulating a chain of ideas. When you brainstorm, you start with a word or phrase to launch your thoughts in some direction. For a set length of time—say, ten or fifteen minutes—put the conscious, analytical part of your mind on hold as you scribble a list of ideas as rapidly as possible, writing down whatever comes to mind with no editing or going back. Then look over the often surprising results.

Brainstorming can be a group activity. In the business world, brainstorming is a common strategy to fill a specific need — a name for a product, a corporate emblem, a slogan for an advertising campaign. You can try group brainstorming with a few other students or your entire class. Members of the group sit facing one another. They designate one person as the recorder to take down on paper or a chalkboard whatever suggestions the others offer. If the suggestions fly too thick and fast, the secretary jots down the best one in the air at that moment. For several minutes, people call out ideas. Then they look over the recorder's list in hopes of finding useful results.

You might brainstorm on your own to find a specific topic for a paper, to generate an illustration or example as you are writing, or to come up with a title for a finished paper. When Martha Calbick's instructor assigned a paper ("Demonstrate from your own experience that the invention of the computer has significantly changed our lives"), Calbick went home and brainstormed. First, she wrote the word *computer* at the top of a sheet of paper. Then she set her alarm to sound in fifteen minutes and began to scribble single words or phrases. The first thing she recalled was how her kid brother sits by the hour playing games on the computer. The first recollection quickly led, by free association, to several more.

> Computer
> My kid bro. thinks computers are for kids
> Always trading games with other kids — software pirates
> In 3rd grade they teach programming
> Hackers
> Some get rich
> Ed's brother-in-law — wrote a program for accountants
> Become a programmer? big future?
> Guided missiles
> Computers in subway stations — print tickets
> Banks — shove in your plastic card
> A man lucked out — deposited $100 — computer credited him with $10,000
> Computers print out grades
> My report card showed a D instead of a B — big fight to correct it
> Are we just numbers now?

When her alarm rang, Calbick stopped and took a break. When she returned to her desk, she went through her list, crossing out ideas that did not interest her. She didn't know much about her brother's games or about missiles. She circled the question "Are we just numbers now?" It looked promising. Maybe some of the rest of her list might express that very idea, such as the mindlessness of the computer that had credited the man with $10,000. She continued brainstorming, adding notes to the list. "Dealing with computers isn't dealing with people," she wrote next to the circled question. From her rough list, an idea was beginning to emerge.

Calbick later wrote a paper on the effect of computer errors, focusing on the simple computer error in her high school office that had momentarily robbed her of a good grade. She recalled how time-consuming it had been to have that error corrected. She mentioned other computer errors, including the man who had struck it rich at the bank. Her conclusion was a wry complaint about computerized society: "A computer knows your name and number, but it doesn't know who you are."

You can see how brainstorming typically works and how it helps you personalize a topic and break it down into specifics. Whenever you try brainstorming, you might follow these bits of advice:

1. *Start with a key word or phrase*—one that will head your thoughts in the direction you wish to pursue. If you are trying to find a topic, begin with a general word or phrase. If you are searching for an example to fill out a paragraph in progress, use a specific word or phrase.
2. *Set a time limit.* Ten to fifteen minutes is long enough: brainstorming can be strenuous.
3. *Write rapidly.* Jot down any words, thoughts, phrases, or short sentences that surface. Keep your entries brief. Put them in a list so that you can scan them quickly later.
4. *Don't stop.* Don't worry about misspelling, repetition, absurdity, or irrelevance. Write down whatever comes into your head, as fast as your pen will go, even if the ideas seem crazy or far-out. Don't judge, don't arrange: just produce. If your mind goes blank, keep your pencil moving, even if you only repeat what you've just written.

When you finish, circle or check anything that suggests directions you may wish to pursue. If anything looks useless or uninteresting, scratch it out. You can now do some conscious organizing. Are any of the thoughts related? Can you group them? If so, maybe such a group of ideas will suggest a topic.

■ Exercise

Brainstorming

From the following list, choose a subject that interests you, that you know something about, and that you'd like to learn more about—in other words, a subject that you might like to write a paper on. Then brainstorm for ten minutes.

travel	fear	exercise
dieting	dreams	automobiles
family	television	sports
advertisements	animals	education

Now look over your brainstorming list, and circle anything that looks as if it might work well as a topic for a paper. How well did this brainstorming exercise work for you? Can you think of any variations that would make it more useful?

Group Brainstorming

Working with a small group of your classmates — or with the entire class — choose one subject from the list on page 262 that each person knows something about. Brainstorm about it individually for ten minutes. Then compare and contrast the brainstorming lists of everyone in the group. Although the group began with the same subject, each writer's treatment will be unique because of differences in experience and perspective. What does this exercise tell you about group brainstorming as a strategy for generating topics for writing?

FOR GROUP LEARNING

FREEWRITING

To tap your unconscious by *freewriting,* you simply write without stopping for fifteen or twenty minutes, trying to keep words pouring forth. Unlike brainstorming, you write a series of sentences, not a list. The sentences don't have to be grammatical or coherent or stylish; just keep them flowing. When you have just the beginning of an idea, freewriting can help open it up and show you what it contains.

Generally, freewriting is most productive if it has an aim — for example, finding a topic, a purpose, or a question you want to answer. Martha Calbick wrote her topic at the top of a page — "How life in the computer age seems impersonal" — and then explored her rough ideas.

For Calbick's brainstorming, see p. 261.

> Computers — so how do they make life impersonal? You push in your plastic card and get some cash. Just a glassy screen. No human teller behind a window. When the computer says you have no money left in your account, that's terrible, frightening. Worse than when a person won't cash your check. At least the person looks you in the face, maybe even smiles. Computers make mistakes, too. That story in the paper about a man — in Utica — who deposited $100.00 to his account and the computer misplaced a decimal point and said he had put in $10,000.

The result, as you can see, wasn't polished prose. It was full of false starts and little asides to herself. Still, in twenty minutes she produced a paragraph that served as a springboard for her finished essay.

If you want to try freewriting, here's what you do:

1. *Write a sentence or two at the top of your page or computer screen* — the idea you plan to develop by freewriting.

2. *For at least ten minutes, write steadily without stopping.* Express whatever comes to mind, even "I have nothing to say about any subject in the universe." If your mind goes blank, write "My mind is blank" until some new thought floats into view.

3. *Don't censor yourself.* Don't cross out false starts, misspellings, or grammatical errors. Don't worry about closing gaps between ideas or finding perfect words.

4. *Feel free to explore.* Your initial sentences can serve as a rough guide, but they shouldn't be a straitjacket. If you find yourself straying from your original idea, a change in direction may be valuable.

5. *Prepare yourself*—if you want to. While you wait for the moment when your pencil starts racing, it may be worth asking yourself some of these questions:

> What interests you about this topic? What aspects of it do you most care about?
>
> What do you recall about this topic from your own experience? What do you know about it that the next person doesn't?
>
> What have you read about it? Observed about it? Heard about it from someone else?
>
> How might you feel about this topic if you were someone else (a parent, an instructor, a person from another country)?

At the very least, your freewriting session may give you something to expand and develop. You can poke at the parts that look most interesting to see if they will further unfold. Here are a few questions you might ask:

> What do you mean by that?
>
> If that is true, what then? So what?
>
> What other examples or evidence does this statement call to mind?
>
> What objections might your reader raise to this?
>
> How might you answer them?

■ Exercise

Freewriting

Edit one of your brainstorming lists by circling interesting ideas, deleting irrelevant or repetitious items, and grouping related ideas. Select one significant idea you can explore further, put that idea at the top of a piece of paper or your computer screen, and freewrite about it for fifteen minutes. Share your freewriting with your classmates.

WRITING WITH A COMPUTER

Invisible writing is a kind of freewriting done on a word processor. After typing your topic at the beginning of a file, darken or turn off your monitor so that you cannot read what's on the screen. Then freewrite. If you feel uneasy, try to relax and concentrate on the ideas. After ten minutes, turn the monitor back on, scroll to the beginning, and read what you have written.

KEEPING A JOURNAL

Journal writing offers rich rewards to anyone who engages in it every day or several times a week. All you need is a notebook, a writing implement, and a few minutes for each entry, and you can write anywhere. For the faithful journal keeper, a journal is a mine studded with priceless nuggets — thoughts and observations, reactions and revelations that are yours for the taking. When you write, you can rifle your well-stocked journal freely — not only for writing topics, but for insights and material.

For ideas about keeping a reading journal, see pp. 17–18.

Poet Sylvia Plath found keeping a journal quite worthwhile. Uncommonly sensitive and colorful, her entries exhibit the freedom and frankness of a writer who was writing for only her own eyes. The following passage from *The Unabridged Journals of Sylvia Plath* (New York: Anchor, 2000) contrasts the happy fantasy world she inhabited as a child with the harsher realities of college life:

> After being conditioned as a child to the lovely never-never land of magic, of fairy queens and virginal maidens, of little princes and their rosebushes, of poignant bears and Eeyore-ish donkeys, [. . .] of the magic wand, [. . .] of the Hobbit and the dwarves, gold-belted with blue and purple hoods [. . .] all this I knew, and felt, and believed. All this was my life when I was young. To go from this to the world of grown-up reality. [. . .] To feel the sex organs develop and call loud to the flesh; to become aware of school, exams (the very words as unlovely as the sound of chalk shrilling on the blackboard), bread and butter, marriage, sex, compatibility, war, economics, death, and self. What a pathetic blighting of the beauty and reality of childhood. Not to be sentimental, as I sound, but why the hell are we conditioned into the smooth strawberry-and-cream Mother-Goose-world, Alice-in-Wonderland fable, only to be broken on the wheel as we grow older and become aware of ourselves as individuals with a dull responsibility in life? [. . .] To learn snide and smutty meanings of words you once loved, like "fairy." [. . .] To go to college fraternity parties where a boy buries his face in your neck or tries to rape you if he isn't satisfied with burying his fingers in the flesh of your breast.

Like Plath, to write a valuable journal you need only the honesty and the willingness to set down what you *genuinely think and feel*. No one will criticize how you spell, punctuate, organize your ideas, or express yourself.

Reflective Journal Writing.   What do you write in your journal? When you make an entry, put less emphasis on recording what happened, as in a diary, than on *reflecting* about what you do or see, hear or read, learn or believe. A journal records your thoughts, for an audience of one: yourself. Here you can explore dreams, try out ideas, vent fears and frustrations. An entry can be a list or an outline, a paragraph or a full-blown essay, a poem or a letter you don't intend to send, even a page of brainstorming. Describe a person or a place, set down a conversation, or record any insights into your actions or those of others. Make comparisons. Record images. Critique the last movie or television show you watched. What are your pet peeves? What do you treasure? What are your religious convictions or moral dilemmas? Have you had an interesting dream or daydream? What would the world — or our country — be like if you were in charge?

For more on responding to reading, see Ch. 2.

Responsive Journal Writing.   Sometimes you *respond* to something in particular — to the reading you've been doing for an assignment, to classroom discussions, to a movie, to a conversation or observation. This type of journal entry is more focused than the reflective entry. Faced with a long paper to write, you might assign *yourself* a response journal. Then when the time comes to write your paper, you will have plenty of material to quarry. In *A Writer's Reader* we have included responsive journal prompts at the end of each selection to help you focus some of your entries.

Warm-Up Journal Writing.   You can also use your journal to explore your thoughts in preparation for an assignment. You can group ideas, scribble outlines, sketch beginnings, try out introductions, capture stray thoughts, record relevant material. Of course what starts out as a quick warm-up comment on an essay you've read (or a responsive journal entry) may turn into the draft of a paper. In other words, don't let the categories we've given straitjacket you. A journal can be just about anything you want it to be, and the best journal is the one that's most useful to *you*.

■ Exercise

Journal Writing

Keep a journal for at least a week. Each day record your thoughts, feelings, and reactions. You may include some events but reflect on what happens and respond to what you read. Try at least one of the responsive prompts following a selection in *A Writer's Reader*. At the end of the week, bring your journal to class, select the entry you like best, and read it aloud to your classmates.

WRITING WITH A COMPUTER

Keeping an e-journal is as simple as creating a file and recording entries by date or subject. If used well, your e-journal may progress into a very useful writing space where you record ideas, feelings, impressions, images, memories, quotations, and any other writing you wish. You also will quickly notice how easy it is to copy and paste inspiring parts of e-mail, interesting quotations from Web pages, or even digitized images and sounds into your e-journal. Just be sure that you identify the source of material that you copy so that you won't later confuse it with your original writing. As your e-journal grows, you will develop a ready supply of "seeds" and support for your writing assignments.

ASKING A REPORTER'S QUESTIONS

Journalists, assembling facts to write the story of a news event, ask themselves six simple questions — the five *W*'s and an *H*:

Who? Where? Why?

What? When? How?

In the *lead*, or opening paragraph, of a good news story, where the writer tries to condense the whole story into a sentence or two, you will find simple answers to all six questions.

> A giant homemade fire balloon [*what*] startled residents of Costa Mesa [*where*] last night [*when*] as Ambrose Barker, 79, [*who*] zigzagged across the sky at nearly 300 miles per hour [*how*] in an attempt to set a new altitude record [*why*].

Later in the news story, the reporter will add details, using the six basic questions to generate more about what happened and why.

For your college writing you can use these six questions in a similar manner to generate specific details for your essays. Your topic may not be the spectacular narrative of a fire balloon's flight, but you will find these questions just as helpful as the reporter does. They can help you explore the significance of a childhood experience, analyze what happened at some moment in history, or investigate a campus or neighborhood problem. If you are using the six basic questions with a topic that is not based on your personal experience, you may have to do some reading or interviewing to answer some of the questions. Take, for example, the topic of the assassination of John F. Kennedy, and notice how each question can lead to further questions.

Who was John F. Kennedy? What kind of person was he? What was his background? What kind of president was he? Who else was with him when he was killed? Who was nearby? Who do most people believe shot him?

What happened to Kennedy — exactly? What was he doing? What events led up to the assassination? What happened during the assassination itself? Was anyone else hurt? What happened to Kennedy immediately after the shots? What did the people around him do? What did the media representatives do? What did everyone across the country do? What happened in the next forty-eight hours? Ask someone who remembers this event what he or she did on hearing about the assassination.

Where was Kennedy assassinated? The city? The street? Where was he going? Was the route announced beforehand? What kind of vehicle was Kennedy riding in? Where was he sitting? Where were the other passengers sitting? Where did the shots likely come from? Where did the shots hit Kennedy? Where did Kennedy die?

When was he assassinated — the day, month, year, time? When did Kennedy decide to go to this city? When — precisely — were the shots fired? When did he die? When was a suspect arrested?

Why was Kennedy assassinated? What are some of the theories of the assassination? What solid evidence is available to explain the assassination? Why has Kennedy's assassination caused so much controversy?

How was Kennedy assassinated? What kind of weapon was used? How many shots were fired? Specifically what caused his death? How can we get at the truth of how and why he was assassinated?

Don't worry if some of the questions go nowhere, seem irrelevant, or lead to repetitious answers. You are trying to gather ideas and material. Later, you'll weed out frivolous and irrelevant points, keeping only those that look promising for your topic.

■ Exercise

Asking a Reporter's Questions

Choose one of the following topics, or use one of your own:

A memorable event in history
An unforgettable event in your life
A concert that you have seen
An accomplishment on campus
An occurrence in your city
An important speech
A proposal for change
A questionable stand someone has taken

For advice on writing a thesis, see pp. 271–75.

Answer the six reporter's questions about the topic. Then write a thesis synthesizing the answers to the six questions into one sentence. Incorporate that thesis sentence into an introductory paragraph for an essay that you might write later.

Getting Ready

Once you have generated a suitable topic and some ideas related to that topic, you are ready to get down to the job of actually writing.

SETTING UP CIRCUMSTANCES

Get Comfortable.   If you can write only with your shoes off or with a can of Orange Crush, set yourself up that way. Some writers need a radio blaring heavy metal; others need quiet. Create an environment that puts you in the mood for writing.

Devote One Special Place to Writing.   When you go to your special place, your mind and body will be ready to settle in for work. Your place may be a desk in your bedroom, the dining room table, or a quiet cubicle in the library — someplace where no one will bother you. It should have good lighting and space to spread out. Try to make it a place where you can leave projects you are working on, where you can keep your pens, paper, computer, dictionary, and other reference materials.

Establish a Ritual. Some writers find that a writing ritual relaxes them and gets them in the mood for writing. You might get a drink, straighten the things on your desk, turn the radio on (or off), and create a new file on the computer.

Relocate. If you're not getting anywhere with your writing, try relocating from the college library to home or from a desk in the den to your bedroom. Try an unfamiliar place — a bowling alley, a restaurant, an airport. The noises around you might motivate you to concentrate hard on your writing.

Reduce Distractions. Most of us can't prevent interruptions, but we can reduce them. If you are expecting your boyfriend to call, call him before you start writing. If you have small children, write when they are asleep or at school. Turn on the answering machine for the telephone. Let people around you know you are serious about writing, and allow yourself to give your full attention to it.

Exhaust Your Excuses. If you, like most writers, are expert at coming up with reasons not to write, you might find that it helps to run out of reasons. Is your room annoyingly jumbled? Straighten it. Sharpen those pencils, throw out that trash, and make that phone call. Then, with your room, your desk, and your mind swept clean, sit down and write.

Yield to Inspiration. Sometimes ideas, images, or powerful urges to write will arrive like sudden miracles. When they come, even if you are taking a shower or getting ready to go to a movie, yield to impulse and write. Your words probably will flow with little exertion.

Write at the Time Best for You. Some people think best early in the morning, others in the afternoon or late at night. Try writing in the small hours when the world is still and your stern self-critic might be asleep, too. Or nap in the afternoon and write from 10:00 P.M. until 2:00 or 3:00 A.M. Writing at dawn or the wee hours, you also will have fewer distractions from other people.

Write on a Schedule. Many writers find that it helps to write at a predictable time of day. This method worked marvels for English novelist Anthony Trollope who would start at 5:30 A.M., write 2,500 words before 8:30 A.M., and then go to his job at the General Post Office. (He wrote more than sixty books.) Even if you can't set aside the same time every day, it may help to decide, "Today from four to five, I'll sit down and write." Or if you get stuck, vary your schedule.

PREPARING YOUR MIND

Discuss Your Plans.   Tell any nearby listener — roommate, student down the hall, spouse, parent, friend — why you want to write this particular paper, what material you'll put into it, how you're going to lay it out. If the other person says, "That sounds good," you'll be encouraged. Even if the reaction is a yawn, you'll have set your own thinking in motion.

Keep a Notebook Handy.   Always have some paper in your pocket or backpack or on the night table to write down good ideas that pop into your mind. Imagination may strike in the checkout line of the supermarket, in the doctor's waiting room, or during a lull on the job.

For more about journals, see pp. 265–66.

Keep a Daily Journal.   Scribbling in a journal about your experiences as a writer can nourish your writing. You might note writing problems you run into (and overcome), ideas for things you'd like to write, reactions to your writing from other people, writing strategies that work well.

Read.   The step from reading to writing is a short one. Even when you're just reading for fun, you start to involve yourself with words. Who knows? You might also hit on something useful for your paper. Or read purposefully. If you have a topic, set out to read and take notes.

Chapter 17
Strategies for Planning

Starting to write often seems a chaotic activity, but you can use the strategies in this chapter to reduce the chaos and create order. For most papers, you will want to focus your writing on a central point or thesis. The first section in this chapter provides guidelines for developing a thesis. To help you sensibly arrange your material, the chapter also includes advice on grouping ideas and on outlining.

Stating and Using a Thesis

Most pieces of effective writing make one main point. All ideas in such essays or articles are unified around that point; that is, all the subpoints and details are relevant to the point. Generally, after you have read an essay, you can sum up the writer's main point in a sentence, even if the author has not stated it explicitly. We call this summary statement a *thesis*.

For more help with stating and using a thesis, use the *Writing Guide Software for THE BEDFORD GUIDE.*

Often the thesis—the writer's main point—will be *explicit*, plainly stated, in the piece of writing itself. In "The Myth of the Latin Woman: I Just Met a Girl Named María" (from *The Latin Deli*, 1993), Judith Ortiz Cofer states her thesis in the last sentence of the first paragraph—"You can leave the Island, master the English language, and travel as far as you can, but if you are a Latina, especially one like me who so obviously belongs to Rita Moreno's gene pool, the Island travels with you." This clear statement, strategically placed, as well as her title helps readers see her main point unmistakably.

In some writing, a thesis may be *implicit*, implied rather than directly stated. In "The Niceness Solution" (from *Beyond Queer*, 1996) Paul Varnell describes an ordinance "banning rude behavior, including rude speech," passed in Raritan, New Jersey. After discussing a 1580 code of conduct, an early effort to require courteous and civil behavior, he identifies four objections to such attempts to limit free speech. He concludes with this sentence: "Sensibly, Raritan Police Chief Joseph Sferro said he would not enforce the new ordinance." Although Varnell does not state his main point in one concise sentence, after you have read his essay you know that he opposes the law passed in New Jersey and any other attempts to legislate "niceness."

The purpose of most academic and workplace writing is to inform, to explain, or to convince, and to achieve any of these purposes you must make your main point crystal clear. A thesis sentence helps you clarify your main idea in your own mind and stay on track as you write. It also helps your readers readily see your point and follow your discussion. Sometimes you may want to imply your thesis, but if you state it explicitly, you ensure that readers cannot miss it.

DISCOVERING YOUR THESIS

It's rare for a writer to develop a clear thesis statement early in the writing process and then write an effective essay that fits it exactly. What you should aim for is a *working thesis* — a statement that can guide you but that you will ultimately refine. Trying to discover and state a working thesis is far less intimidating than trying to find the perfect sentence before you've even written a draft.

Look back over your brainstorming, your freewriting, or your notes, and see if you can generalize from them. Write several tentative thesis sentences. Brainstorm titles: the title is usually a shortened form of the thesis. Freewrite the introduction or conclusion. Write a one-paragraph summary of your paper. Talk with a friend, or tape-record your rambling thoughts about your topic. Whenever an insight occurs, try it out on your peer group or your instructor.

A useful thesis contains not only the *topic* you're writing about but also the *point* you want to make or the *attitude* you intend to take. If you decide to write on the topic "the decline of old-fashioned formal courtesy," you've indicated the area to be explored, but that topic doesn't tell you the point of your paper. If you say, "Old-fashioned formal courtesy is a thing of the past," you are talking in circles. But a working thesis might be "As the roles of men and women have changed in our society, old-fashioned formal cour-

FOR GROUP LEARNING

Identifying Theses

Working in a small group, select five essays from Part Two of this book to read carefully (or your instructor may choose the essays for your group). Then, individually, write out the thesis for each essay. Some thesis sentences are stated outright (explicit), but others are implied (implicit). Compare and contrast the thesis statements that you identified with those your classmates found, and discuss the similarities and differences. How can you account for the differences? Try to agree on a thesis statement for each essay.

tesy toward women has declined." Then you could focus on how changing societal attitudes toward gender roles have caused changes in courtesy. What other thesis sentences might you come up with for this topic?

In some college writing it's easy to let the formal requirements of the assignment distract you from the purpose of writing. For example, if you are going to compare and contrast two local newspapers in their coverage of a Senate election, ask yourself what is the point of that comparison and contrast. A suitable thesis would *not* state that their coverage was different. A satisfactory thesis sentence might be "The *Herald*'s coverage of the Senate elections was more thorough than the *Courier*'s."

■ Exercise

Discovering a Thesis

Generalize about each of the following groups of details to find a working thesis for each group. Then compare and contrast your theses with those of your classmates. What other information would you need to write a good paper on each of these topics? How might the thesis statement change as you write the paper?

1. Cigarettes are expensive.
   Cigarettes can cause fires.
   Cigarettes cause unpleasant odors.
   Cigarettes can cause health problems to the smoker.
   Secondhand smoke from cigarettes can cause health problems.

2. Clinger College has a highly qualified faculty.
   Clinger College has an excellent curriculum in my field.
   Clinger College has a beautiful campus.
   Clinger College is expensive.
   Clinger College has offered me a scholarship.

3. Crisis centers report that date rape is increasing.
   Most date rape is not reported to the police.
   Often the victim of date rape is not believed.
   Sometimes the victim of date rape is blamed or blames herself.
   The effects of date rape stay with a woman for years.

HOW TO STATE A THESIS

Once you have a notion of what your thesis might be, you should try to state it in a way that will be useful to you as you plan and draft your essay. Here are four suggestions for writing a workable thesis statement:

1. *State the thesis sentence exactly.* Use concise, detailed, and down-to-earth language. The statement "There are a lot of troubles with chemical wastes" is too general. Are you going to deal with all chemical wastes, through all of history, all over the world? Are you going to list all the troubles they can cause? Make the statement more specific: "Careless dumping of leftover paint is to blame for a recent outbreak of skin rashes in Atlanta."

2. *State just one central idea in the thesis sentence.* If your paper is to focus on one point, your thesis should state only one main idea. This statement has one idea too many: "Careless dumping of leftover paint has caused a serious problem in Atlanta, and a new kind of biodegradable paint now looks promising." Either the first half or the second would suffice and lead you to a unified essay.

3. *State your thesis positively.* You can usually find evidence to support a positive statement, but you can't prove a negative one. "Medical scientists do not know what causes breast cancer" sounds halfhearted and doesn't seem to lead anywhere. On the other hand, "The causes of breast cancer remain a challenge for medical scientists" might lead to a paper about an exciting quest. Besides, to show that medical scientists are working on the problem would be relatively easy, given an hour of research in a library or on the Internet. To prove that not one medical scientist knows the answer would be very difficult.

4. *Limit your thesis sentence to a statement that is possible to demonstrate.* A thesis sentence should stake out enough territory for you to cover thoroughly within the assigned length and the time available, and no more. In a brief paper, maintaining the thesis "My favorite piece of music is Beethoven's Fifth Symphony" would be difficult because you would need to explain how and why it is your favorite and contrast it with *all* the other musical compositions you know. The statement "For centuries, popular music has indicated vital trends in Western society" wouldn't do either: that thesis could inform a whole encyclopedia of music. "In the past two years, a rise in the number of preteenagers has resulted in a comeback for heavy metal on our local concert scene" sounds much more likely for a brief essay.

Let's try a few more examples of thesis sentences:

"Native American blankets are very beautiful." That vague statement would be hard to demonstrate in a typical assignment of five hundred to eight hundred words.

"Native Americans have adapted to modern civilization." That sounds too large, too unrestricted, unless you plan to write a substantial research paper.

"Members of the Apache tribe are skilled workers in high-rise construction." You could probably find support for that thesis by spending a couple of hours in a library or online.

■ Exercise

Examining Thesis Statements

Discuss each of the following thesis sentences with your classmates. Answer these questions for each:

Is the thesis stated exactly?
Does the thesis state just one idea?

Is the thesis stated positively?
Is the thesis sufficiently limited for a short essay?
How might the thesis be improved?

1. Teenagers should not get married.
2. Cutting classes is like a disease.
3. Students have developed a variety of techniques to conceal inadequate study from their instructors.
4. Older people often imitate teenagers.
5. Violence on television can be harmful to children.
6. I don't know how to change the oil in my car.

HOW TO USE A THESIS

Often a good, clear thesis will suggest an organization for your ideas. Say you plan to write a paper with the thesis "Despite the disadvantages of living in a downtown business district, I wouldn't live anywhere else." That thesis sentence suggests how to organize your essay. You could start with several paragraphs discussing disadvantages of living in the business district, move on to a few paragraphs discussing the advantages, and then close with an affirmation of your fondness for downtown city life.

For more on using a thesis to develop an outline, see pp. 280–81.

A clear thesis will also help keep you on track as you write. Just putting your trial thesis into words can help you stake out your territory. You can refer to it as you select details and as you make connections between sections of the essay.

As you write, however, you don't have to cling to a thesis for dear life. You might begin with the thesis "Because wolves are a menace to people and farm animals, they ought to be exterminated." If further investigation changes your thinking, you can change your thesis to "The wolf, a relatively peaceful animal useful in nature's scheme of things, ought to be protected." The purpose of a thesis statement is to guide you on a quest, not to limit your ideas. You can restate it at any time: as you write, as you revise, as you revise again.

Organizing Your Ideas

When you organize an essay, you select an order for the parts that makes sense and shows your readers how the ideas are connected. If you are describing a place, you might use *spatial organization,* moving from left to right or bottom to top, ordering the details to make it easy for readers to visualize. Mark Twain describes a scene on the Mississippi River by beginning with the dock and moving to the steamboat coming in to the landing and over the broad expanse of the river to the shore on the other side. If you are narrating an event or explaining the steps in a procedure, you would use *chronological or time order*—what happens first, next, and next until the end. If you are explaining an idea or trying to persuade readers, you would use some variation of *logical order*—for example, general to specific, specific to general, least important to most important, cause to effect, or problem to solution. In writing an essay on the effects of the 1997 El Niño, you might select four major consequences, placing the most important one last for emphasis. Following are some techniques to help you select an order for your ideas.

GROUPING YOUR IDEAS

While exploring a topic, you will usually find a few ideas that seem to belong together—two facts on New York traffic jams, four actions of New York drivers, three problems with New York streets. But similar ideas seldom appear together in your list because you did not discover them all at the same time. You'll need to sort your notes into groups, arrange them in sequences. Here are five common ways to work:

1. *Rainbow connections.* List on a sheet of paper all the main points you're going to express. Don't recopy the rest of your material. Use colored pencils to circle with the same color any points that go together. When you write, follow the color code, and deal with related ideas at the same time.

2. *Linking.* Start by making a list of major points, and then draw lines that link related ideas. Number each linked group to identify a sequence for dealing with the ideas. Figure 17.1 illustrates a linked list produced by one writer for an essay to be called "Manhattan Driving." The writer has drawn lines connecting points that go together and has supplied each linked group with a heading. When he writes his draft, each heading will probably inspire a topic sentence to introduce each major division of his essay. One point

Figure 17.1
The linking method for grouping ideas

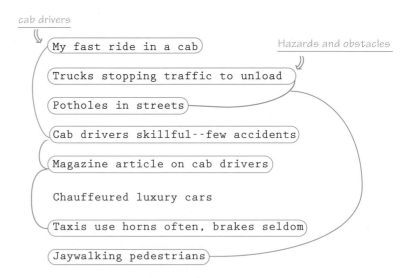

failed to relate to any other: "Chauffeured luxury cars." In the finished paper, he will leave it out.

3. *Solitaire.* Collect notes and ideas on roomy (5-by-8-inch) file cards. To organize, spread out the cards and arrange and rearrange them, as in a game of solitaire. When each idea seems to lead to the next, gather all the cards into a deck in this order. As you write, deal yourself a card at a time and translate its contents into sentences. This technique is particularly helpful when you write about literature or when you write from research.

4. *Slide show.* If you are familiar with presentation software such as Microsoft PowerPoint, consider writing your notes and ideas on "slides" (the software equivalent of blank sheets). When you're done, the program gives you the option of viewing your slides one by one or viewing the entire collection (in Microsoft PowerPoint, choose "View," then "Slide Sorter"). In the slide sorter view, you can shuffle and reshuffle your slides into the most promising order.

5. *Clustering.* Clustering is useful for coming up with ideas, but it is just as valuable as a visual method of grouping those ideas. In the middle of a piece of paper, write your topic in a word or a phrase. Then think of the major divisions into which this topic might be organized. For an essay called "Manhattan Drivers," the major divisions might be the *types* of Manhattan drivers: (1) taxi drivers, (2) bus drivers, (3) truck drivers, (4) drivers of private cars — New Yorkers, and (5) drivers of private cars — out-of-town visitors. Arrange these divisions around your topic on your page and circle them too. Draw lines out from the major topic to the subdivisions. You now have the beginning of a rough plan for an essay. (See Figure 17.2.)

Around each division, make another cluster of points you're going to include — examples, illustrations, facts, statistics, bits of evidence, opinions. Circle each specific item, and connect it to the appropriate type of driver. When you write your paper, you can expand the details into one paragraph for each type of driver.

This technique lets you know where you have enough specific information to make your paper clear and interesting — and where you don't. If one of your subtopics has no small circles around it (such as "bus drivers" in Figure 17.2), you should think of some specific examples to expand it; if you can't, drop it.

■ Exercise

Clustering

Generate clusters for three of the following topics. With your classmates, discuss which one of the three would probably help you write the best paper.

teachers	musicians
Internet sites	civil rights
my favorite restaurants	drug abuse
fast food	good health
leisure-time activities	technology

Figure 17.2
The clustering method for generating ideas

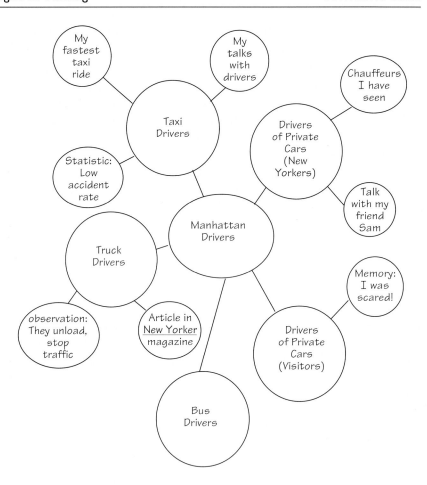

WRITING WITH A COMPUTER

Here are some of the easy computer tools you can use to highlight, categorize, and shape your thinking by graphically distinguishing your points on a screen.

Highlighting

Showing color

Use **bold**, *italics*, underlining

• Adding bullets

1. Numbering

Changing `fonts`

Varying print sizes

Using "Track Changes" or another option to show editing

To use these features for categorizing ideas on a screen, click on their icons on your toolbar or use your menu. You can also create a table or columns to organize your ideas in a separate window to the left of your text.

OUTLINING

A familiar way to organize ideas is to outline. A written outline, whether brief or detailed, shouldn't say *everything* you plan to write in your paper. Think of it as a map that you make before setting out on a journey. It shows where to leave from, where to stop along the way, and where to arrive. If you forget where you are going or what you are trying to say, you can consult it to get back on track. When you turn in your essay, your instructor may request an outline as well, as both a map for readers and a skeletal summary of your material.

How detailed an outline will you need? Some writers like to lay out the job very carefully in advance; others prefer a loose plan. Sometimes an *informal outline* — perhaps just a list of points to make — is enough, especially for familiar material. For complex, unfamiliar information, you'll probably need a more detailed *formal outline* to keep from getting lost. A more detailed plan also might be useful if people tell you your writing isn't well organized and that they can't follow you. On the other hand, if they tell you your writing sounds mechanical, maybe your outline is constricting you.

Informal Outlines.   For in-class writing and brief essays, a short or informal outline, also called a *scratch outline*, may serve your needs. Jot down a brief list of points in the order you plan to make them. This outline is for your eyes only. You can use it to help you get organized, stick to the point, and avoid forgetting good ideas when you write under pressure.

The following informal outline is for a short paper explaining how outdoor enthusiasts can avoid illnesses by treating potentially unsafe drinking water. Its working thesis is "Campers and hikers need to ensure the safety of the water that they drink from rivers or streams." One obvious way to proceed is to list each of the methods for treating water. Then, in the paper, the writer would include details about each method.

Introduction: Treatments for potentially unsafe drinking water

1. Small commercial filter
    —Remove bacteria and protozoa including salmonella and E. coli
    —Use brands convenient for campers and hikers

2. Chemicals
    —Use bleach, chlorine, or iodine
    —Follow general rule: 12 drops per gallon of water

3. Boiling
    —Boil for 5 minutes (Red Cross) to 15 minutes (National Safety Council)
    —Store in a clean, covered container

Conclusion: Using one of three methods of treating water, campers and hikers can
    ensure the safety of water from natural sources.

A simple outline could easily fall into a five-paragraph essay or grow to eight paragraphs — introduction, conclusion, and three pairs of paragraphs

**FOR GROUP
LEARNING**

Outlining

Discuss the formal topic outline on page 282 with some of your classmates or the entire class, considering the following questions:

- Would this outline be useful in organizing an essay?

- How is the organization logical? Is it easy to follow? What are other possible arrangements for the ideas?

- Is this outline sufficiently detailed to develop a paper? Can you spot any gaps in the outline?

- What possible pitfalls would the writer using this outline need to avoid?

in between. You probably won't know until you write the paper exactly how many paragraphs you'll need.

An informal outline can be even briefer than the preceding one. If you were answering an examination question or preparing a very short paper, your outline might be no more than an *outer plan* — three or four phrases jotted down in a list:

> Isolation of region
> Tradition of family businesses
> Growth of electronic commuting

For more on thesis statements, see pp. 271–75.

Often a clear thesis statement will suggest a way to outline. If the thesis contains a plural word (such as *benefits* or *advantages* or *teenagers*), you can make a list of outline headings related to the plural word. If one part of the thesis sentence is subordinate to another (beginning with *because* or *since* or *although*, for instance), you can analyze according to the parts of the sentence. Let's say you are assigned, for an anthropology course, a paper on the people of Melanesia. You decide to focus on the following idea:

> Thesis: Although the Melanesian pattern of family life may look strange to Westerners, it fosters a degree of independence that rivals our own.

Laying out ideas in the same order that they follow in this thesis statement, you might make a short, simple outline like this:

1. Features that appear strange to Westerners
   - A woman supported by her brother, not her husband
   - Trial marriages common
   - Divorce from her children possible for any mother
2. Admirable results of system
   - Wives not dependent on husbands for support
   - Divorce between mates uncommon
   - Greater freedom for parents and children

This informal outline suggests an essay that naturally falls into two parts — features that seem strange and admirable results of the system.

Say you plan to write a "how-to" essay analyzing the process of buying a used car. Your thesis statement might read:

> Thesis: Despite traps that lie waiting for the unwary, preparing yourself before you shop can help you find a good used car.

The key word in this sentence is *preparing,* and you ask yourself *how* the buyer should prepare. What should he or she do before shopping for a used car?

> –Read car magazines and Consumer Reports.
> –Check ads in the newspapers.
> –Make phone calls to several dealers.
> –Talk to friends who have bought used cars.
> –Know what to look and listen for when you test drive.
> –Have a mechanic check it out.

You can start your paper with some horror stories about people who got taken by car sharks and then discuss, point by point, your bits of advice. Of course, you can always change the sequence, add an idea or take one out, or revise your thesis as you go along.

Formal Outlines.   A *formal outline* is an elaborate guide, built with time and care, for a long, complex paper. Because long reports, research papers, and senior theses require so much work, some professors and departments ask a writer to submit a formal outline at an early stage and to include it in the final draft. A formal outline offers the greatest amount of guidance that an outline can give. In a clear, logical way, it spells out where you are going. It shows how ideas relate one to another — which ones are equal and important (*coordinate*) and which are less important (*subordinate*).

When you make a formal outline, you place your thesis sentence at the beginning. Then you list your major points and label them with roman numerals (I, II, III). These points support and develop the main idea of your whole paper. Then you break down these points into divisions with capital letters, indenting them (A, B, C). You subdivide those into divisions with arabic numerals (1, 2, 3), indenting further, and then subdivide those into divisions with small letters (a, b, c), indenting yet again. Align like-numbered or -lettered headings under one another. As indentations go farther in, ideas become more specific. Your outline should continue until fully developed. If you have to subdivide still further, arabic numerals and small letters in parentheses are commonly used, but only extremely complicated projects need that much subdivision. Be sure to cast all headings in parallel grammatical form: phrases or sentences, but not both in the same outline.

For sample formal outlines, see pp. 282–84.

For more on parallelism, see B2 in the "Quick Editing Guide" (the dark-blue-edged pages).

A *formal topic outline* for a long paper about city and small-town drivers might be constructed as follows:

```
               Drivers in Cities and Small Towns
Thesis: Different lifestyles cause city drivers to be
more aggressive than small-town drivers.
   I. Lifestyles of drivers
      A. Fast-paced, stress-filled lifestyle of city drivers
         1. Aggressive
         2. Impatient
         3. Tense
         4. Often frustrated
      B. Slow-paced lifestyle of small-town drivers
         1. Laid-back
         2. Patient
         3. Relaxed
         4. Not easily upset
  II. Resulting behavior as drivers
      A. City drivers
         1. Little consideration for other drivers
            a. Blowing horn
            b. Shouting
            c. Not using proper signals
               (1) Turning across lanes
               (2) Stopping without warning
         2. Disregard for pedestrians
         3. Violation of speed limits
            a. Running red lights
            b. Having many accidents
      B. Small-town drivers
         1. Consideration of other drivers
            a. Driving defensively
            b. Yelling less
            c. Signaling
               (1) Turning
               (2) Stopping
         2. Regard for pedestrians
         3. Attention to speed limits
            a. Observing traffic lights
            b. Having fewer accidents
```

A topic outline may not be thorough enough to help you know what you want to say, how to say it, or how ideas relate. If so, you should consider a *sentence outline*, using complete sentences for the topic headings. Some people use a topic outline as a step in developing a full-blown sentence outline. When topic headings are changed to sentences, relationships between ideas are clearer, and changes in wording are needed, even in the thesis. The sentence outline can clarify what you intend to say and can even help you draft topic sentences and paragraphs, but you cannot be sure how the ideas will fit together until you write the draft itself.

```
                  Drivers in Cities and Small Towns
Thesis: Because of their more stressful lives, city driv-
ers are more aggressive than small-town drivers.
   I. The lives of city drivers are more stress-filled than
      are the lives of small-town drivers.
      A. City drivers are always in a hurry.
         1. They are impatient.
         2. They are often frustrated.
      B. Small-town drivers live slower-paced lives.
         1. They are relaxed.
         2. They are seldom frustrated on the streets.
  II. As a result of the tension they live with constantly,
      city drivers are more aggressive than are small-town
      drivers.
      A. City drivers are aggressive.
         1. They show little consideration for other
            drivers.
            a. They blow their horns often.
            b. They shout at other drivers frequently.
         2. They show little respect for pedestrians.
         3. They do not obey traffic laws.
            a. They do not use proper signals.
            b. They turn across lanes.
            c. They stop without warning.
            d. They speed.
         4. They have many accidents.
      B. Small-town drivers are laid-back.
         1. They are considerate of other drivers.
            a. They drive carefully.
            b. They rarely yell or honk at other drivers.
         2. They show concern for pedestrians.
```

```
3. They obey traffic laws.
   a. They use proper signals.
   b. They turn properly.
   c. They stop slowly.
   d. They speed less.
4. They have fewer accidents.
```

For more on analysis and division, see pp. 307–12.

CAUTION: Some readers and instructors disapprove of categories that contain only one subpoint, reasoning that you can't divide anything into one part (and that's what an outline does — divides or analyzes ideas). Let's say that in an outline on earthquakes you list a 1 without a 2:

```
D. Probable results of an earthquake
   1. Houses stripped of their paint
```

Logically, if you are going to discuss the *probable results* of an earthquake, you need to include more than one result:

```
D. Probable results of an earthquake
   1. Houses stripped of their paint
   2. Foundations cracked
   3. Road surfaces damaged
   4. Bridges collapsed
   5. Water mains broken
```

Not only have you now come up with more points, but you have also placed the most important last for emphasis.

■ Exercise

Outlining

1. Using one of your groups of ideas from the exercises in Chapter 16, construct a formal topic outline that might serve as a guide for an essay.
2. Now turn that topic outline into a formal sentence outline.
3. Discuss both outlines with your classmates and your instructor, bringing up any difficulties you encountered. If you get any better notions for organizing your ideas, change the outline.
4. Write an essay based on your outline.

Chapter 18
Strategies for Drafting

Learning to write well involves learning what key questions to ask yourself: How can I begin this draft? What should I do if I get stuck? How can I flesh out the bones of my paper? How can I end effectively? How can I keep my readers with me? In this chapter we offer advice to get you going and keep you going, drafting the first paragraph to the last.

Making a Start Enjoyable

Some writers find that if they can just start out playfully, they will be hard at work before they know it.

For more help with drafting, use the *Writing Guide Software for* THE BEDFORD GUIDE.

Time Yourself.   Try setting your watch, alarm clock, or egg timer, and vow to finish a page of your draft before the buzzer sounds. Don't stop for anything. If you find yourself writing drivel, just push on. You can cross out later.

Slow to a Crawl.   If speed quotas don't work for you, time yourself to write with exaggerated laziness, completing, say, a sentence every fifteen minutes.

Begin on Scrap Paper.   Some writers feel reluctant to mess up a blank sheet of paper. Try starting on scrap paper, the back of a list, or a small tablet.

Begin Writing the Part You Find Most Appetizing.   Start in the middle or at the end, wherever the thoughts come easily to mind. Novelist Bill Downey points out that writing is different from childhood, "when we were forced to eat our vegetables first and then get our dessert. Writers are allowed to have their dessert first."

For more about stating your purpose in a thesis, see pp. 273–75.

State Your Purpose.   In a sentence or a few lines, set forth what you want your paper to achieve. Are you trying to tell a story? To explain something? To win a reader over to your way of thinking?

Nutshell It.   Write a very terse summary of the paper you want to write. Condense all your ideas into one small, tight paragraph. Later you can expand each sentence until the meaning is clear and all points are adequately supported.

Shrink Your Immediate Job.   Break the writing task into several smaller parts, and do only the first one. Instead of tackling the whole paper, vow to turn out, say, just the first two paragraphs.

Seek a Provocative Title.   Write down a dozen possible titles for your paper, and then decide if any one sounds strikingly good. You can't let such a promising title go to waste, can you?

Tape-Record Yourself.   Talk a first draft into a tape recorder. Then play it back. Then write. Even if you find it hard to transcribe your spoken words, this technique may set your mind in motion.

Imagine You're Giving a Speech.   On your feet, in front of an imaginary cheering crowd, spontaneously utter an opening paragraph. Then — quick! — write it down. Or tape it so you can get it down exactly.

WRITING WITH A COMPUTER

For more advice on document design, see Ch. 21.

As you begin drafting, use your computer to organize your writing. Most word processors (the software in your computer that helps you start a new "page") offer menu options so you can set your margin widths, line spacing, print size, and other aspects of a paper's format and layout. If your teacher has not specified formatting, customize your files to produce pages with one-inch margins and double spacing, using a 12-point font.

Whether you will store your work on disks or on the hard disk of your own computer, a simple file-naming convention and folder system will make it easy for you to keep track of your work. Some students find success with a file system that identifies the course, term, and draft number; others note the paper topic or activity and the draft number in the file name and then store their files in course folders. For example, your first file might be Eng101F2001–1 or Recall–1. When you revise the draft, you would simply create a new file called Eng101F2001–2 or Recall–2. It is wise to duplicate and rename the file before each revision instead of simply rewriting the original file because you or your teacher may wish to look over the process of your revision in stages.

Restarting

When you have to write a long or demanding essay that you can't finish at one sitting, you may return to it only to find yourself stalled. You tromp your starter and nothing happens. Your engine seems reluctant to turn over. Try the following suggestions for getting back on the road.

Take Regular Short Breaks.   Even if you don't feel tired, take a regular break every half hour or so. Get up, walk around the room, stretch, or get a drink of water. Two or three minutes should be enough to refresh your mind.

Change Activities.   When words won't come, do something quite different from writing. Run, walk your dog, cook your favorite meal, or nap. Or reward yourself—after you arrive at a certain point in your labors—with a trip to the vending machine, a phone call to a friend, or a TV show. All the while, your unconscious mind will be working on your writing task.

Switch Instruments.   Do you compose on the computer? Try writing in longhand. If you are a pen user, type for a change. Try writing on note cards or on colored paper.

Reread What You Have Written.   When you return to work, spend a few minutes rereading what you have already written.

Pause in Midstream.   End a writing session by breaking off in midsentence or midparagraph. Just leave a sentence trailing off into space, even if you know what its closing words should be. When you return to your task, you can start writing again immediately.

Leave Hints for How to Continue.   If you're ready to quit, jot down any remaining ideas. Tell yourself what you think might come next, or write the first sentence of the next section. When you come back to work, you will face not a blank wall but rich and suggestive graffiti.

Paragraphing

An essay is written not in large, indigestible lumps but in *paragraphs*—small units, each more or less self-contained, each contributing some new idea in support of the thesis or main point of the essay. Writers dwell on one idea at a time, stating it, developing it, illustrating it with examples or a few facts. Paragraphing effectively means not only telling but also *showing* readers, with plenty of detailed evidence, exactly what you mean.

For more on developing
ideas within paragraphs,
see Ch. 19.

Paragraphing provides signposts to guide your readers through what you say. A paragraph indentation signifies a pause, as if you are taking a breath before moving on. Readers will assume that you're going on to a new idea, a new aspect of your thesis—and that you're going to ask them to think only about that idea for the rest of that paragraph.

Paragraphs can be as short as one sentence or as long as a page. Sometimes the length is governed by the audience, the purpose of the writing, or the medium in which the paragraph appears. News writers, for instance, tend to write in brief, one- or two-sentence paragraphs. Newspaper readers, consuming facts like popcorn, find that short paragraphs allow them to skim an article quickly. College writers, in contrast, should assume their readers' willingness to read through well-developed paragraphs.

The following sections give you some advice on using topic sentences to focus and control *body paragraphs* within an essay. You will also find advice on *opening paragraphs* that draw the reader in and *concluding paragraphs* that wrap up the discussion.

Using Topic Sentences

A *topic sentence* spells out the main idea of a paragraph in the body of an essay. It guides you in your writing and helps direct readers through your prose. When you read a clear explanation or argument, you can easily pick out the topic sentence of a body paragraph, and you know what to expect next. (You can also extend much of the advice on writing topic sentences for paragraphs to writing thesis statements for essays.)

Good topic sentences are interesting, accurate, and limited. They hook readers and give them a way to interpret the rest of the paragraph. The more pointed and lively your topic sentence, the more *interesting* it will be to your readers. "There are many things wrong with television" is dull and vague, but it's a start. Zero in on one specific flaw, and your topic sentence might become "Of all television's faults, the one I dislike most is melodramatizing the news." You can then illustrate your point with two or three melodramatic newscasts. A topic sentence should be *accurate* because it serves as a guide to the rest of the paragraph: if readers think you mean one thing after reading the topic sentence but then think you mean something else after reading the rest of the paragraph, you've got a problem. A topic sentence should be *limited* for the same reason: you don't want to mislead readers about what you intend to cover in a paragraph. If you start off by saying "Seven factors have contributed to the increasing obesity of the average American" but then introduce only one or two of them, you're going to frustrate your readers.

KINDS OF TOPIC SENTENCES

Topic Sentence as First Sentence.   Usually, as in the following example from James David Barber's *The Presidential Character: Predicting Performance in the White House*, 3rd ed. (Englewood Cliffs: Prentice, 1985), the topic sentence appears first in the paragraph, followed by sentences that clarify, illustrate, and support what it says. It is typically a statement but can sometimes be a question, alerting the reader to the topic of the paragraph without giving away the punchline. (In all the following examples, we have put the topic sentences in *italics*.)

> *The first baseline in defining Presidential types is activity-passivity.* How much energy does the man invest in his Presidency? Lyndon Johnson went at his day like a human cyclone, coming to rest long after the sun went down. Calvin Coolidge often slept eleven hours a night and still needed a nap in the middle of the day. In between, the Presidents array themselves on the high or low side of the activity line.

This paragraph moves from the general to the specific. The topic sentence clearly states at the outset what the paragraph is to be about. The second sentence defines *activity-passivity*. The third and fourth sentences, by citing extremes at either end of the baseline, supply illustrations — active Johnson, passive Coolidge. The final sentence makes a generalization that reinforces the central point.

Topic Sentence near the Beginning of Paragraph.   Sometimes the first sentence of a paragraph functions as a transition, linking what is to come with what has gone before. In such a case, the *second* sentence might be the topic sentence. The paragraph quoted here, from "On Societies as Organisms" in *The Lives of a Cell* (New York: Viking, 1974) by physician Lewis Thomas, follows one about insects that ends "and we violate science when we try to read human meanings in their arrangements." The first sentence is transition, and the second is the topic sentence.

> It is hard for a bystander not to do so. *Ants are so much like human beings as to be an embarrassment.* They farm fungi, raise aphids as livestock, launch armies into wars, use chemical sprays to alarm and confuse enemies, capture slaves. The families of weaver ants engage in child labor, holding their larvae like shuttles to spin out the thread that sews the leaves together for their fungus gardens. They exchange information ceaselessly. They do everything but watch television.

Topic Sentence at End of Paragraph.   Occasionally a writer, especially one attempting to persuade the reader to agree, piles detail on detail throughout a paragraph. Then, with a dramatic flourish, the writer *concludes* with the topic sentence, as student Heidi Kessler does in her paper about a contemporary social problem:

> A fourteen-year-old writes to an advice columnist in my hometown newspaper that she has "done it" lots of times and

```
sex is "no big deal." At the neighborhood clinic where my
aunt works, a hardened sixteen-year-old requests her third
abortion. A girl-child I know has two children of her own,
but no husband. A college student in my dorm now finds her-
self sterile from a "social disease" picked up during casual
sexual encounters. Multiply these examples by thousands. It
seems clear to me that women, who fought so hard for sexual
freedom equal to that of men, have emerged from the battle
not as joyous free spirits but as the sexual revolution's
walking wounded.
```

This paragraph moves from the particular to the general—from four examples about individuals to one large statement about American women at the end. By the time you come to the end of the paragraph, you might be ready to accept the conclusion in the topic sentence.

Topic Sentence Implied.   It is also possible to find a perfectly unified, well-organized paragraph that has no topic sentence at all, like the following from "New York" (*Esquire*, July 1960) by Gay Talese:

> Each afternoon in New York a rather seedy saxophone player, his cheeks blown out like a spinnaker, stands on the sidewalk playing "Danny Boy" in such a sad, sensitive way that he soon has half the neighborhood peeking out of windows tossing nickels, dimes, and quarters at his feet. Some of the coins roll under parked cars, but most of them are caught in his outstretched hand. The saxophone player is a street musician named Joe Gabler; for the past thirty years he has serenaded every block in New York and has sometimes been tossed as much as $100 a day in coins. He is also hit with buckets of water, empty beer cans and eggs, and chased by wild dogs. He is believed to be the last of New York's ancient street musicians.

No one sentence neatly sums up the writer's idea. Like most effective paragraphs that do not state a topic sentence, this one contains something just as good—a *topic idea*. The author doesn't allow his paragraph to wander aimlessly. He knows exactly what he wants to achieve—a description of how Joe Gabler, a famous New York street musician, plies his trade. Because Talese keeps this purpose firmly in mind, the main point—that Gabler meets both reward and abuse—is clear to the reader as well.

■ Exercise

Topic Sentences

Discuss each of the following topic sentences with your peer group, answering these questions:

> Will it catch readers' attention?
> Is it accurate?

Is it limited?
How might you develop the idea in the rest of the paragraph?
Can you improve it?

1. Television commercials stereotype people.
2. Living away from home for the first time is hard.
3. It's good for a child to have a pet.
4. A flea market is a good place to buy jewelry.
5. Pollution should be controlled.
6. Everybody should recycle wastes.

Writing an Opening

Even writers with something to say may find it hard to begin. Often they are so intent on writing a brilliant opening that they freeze, unable to write at all. Instead, you can ease your way into the job by simply deciding to set words — any words — on paper, without trying at all for an arresting opening.

A time-honored approach to the opening paragraph is to write it *last*, after you know exactly what direction your essay takes. Some writers like to write a long beginning in the first draft and then cut it down to the most dramatic, exciting, or interesting essentials. Others use the introduction as a summary for themselves and their readers. Whenever you fashion your opening paragraph, your chief aim is to persuade your readers to lay aside their preoccupations and enter the world set forth in your essay.

KINDS OF OPENINGS

Begin with a Story.   Often a simple anecdote can capture your readers' interest and thus serve as a good beginning. Here is how Harry Crews opens his essay "The Car" in *Florida Frenzy* (Gainesville: UP of Florida, 1982):

> The other day, there arrived in the mail a clipping sent by a friend of mine. It had been cut from a Long Beach, California, newspaper and dealt with a young man who had eluded police for fifty-five minutes while he raced over freeways and through city streets at speeds up to 130 miles per hour. During the entire time, he ripped his clothes off and threw them out the window bit by bit. It finally took twenty-five patrol cars and a helicopter to catch him. When they did, he said that God had given him the car and that he had "found God."

Most of us, reading such an anecdote, want to read on. What will the writer say next? What has the anecdote to do with the essay as a whole? Crews has aroused our curiosity.

Introduce Your Subject or Position and Comment on It.   In some essays, the writer introduces a subject and then expands on it, bringing in vital details, as in this opening paragraph by David Morris, from an article entitled "Rootlessness" (*The Utne Reader*, May/June 1990):

> Americans are a rootless people. Each year one in six of us changes residences; one in four changes jobs. We see nothing troubling in these statistics. For most of us, they merely reflect the restless energy that made America great. A nation of immigrants, unsurprisingly, celebrates those willing to pick up stakes and move on: the frontiersman, the cowboy, the entrepreneur, the corporate raider.

After first stating his point baldly, Morris supplies statistics that back up his contention and partially explains the phenomenon he focuses on. This same strategy can be used to challenge readers by opening with a controversial opinion, then backing up the generalization with examples.

Ask a Question.   A well-written essay can begin with a question and answer, as writer James H. Austin begins "Four Kinds of Chance," in *Chase, Chance, and Creativity: The Lucky Art of Novelty* (New York: Columbia UP, 1978):

> What is chance? Dictionaries define it as something fortuitous that happens unpredictably without discernible human intention. Chance is unintentional and capricious, but we needn't conclude that chance is immune from human intervention. Indeed, chance plays several distinct roles when humans react creatively with one another and with their environment.

Beginning to answer the question in the first paragraph leads readers to expect the rest of the essay to continue the answer.

For more on thesis statements, see pp. 271–75.   **End with the Thesis Sentence.**   An effective opening paragraph can end with a statement of the essay's main point. After first capturing your readers' attention with an anecdote or with gripping details or examples, you lead your readers in exactly the direction your essay is to go. Such a thesis statement can be brief, as in this powerful opening of an essay by educator George B. Leonard called "No School?":

> The most obvious barrier between our children and the kind of education that can free their enormous potential seems to be the educational system itself: a vast, suffocating web of people, practices and presumptions, kindly in intent, ponderous in response. Now, when true educational alternatives are at last becoming clear, we may overlook the simplest: no school.

If you find writing an opening paragraph difficult, don't worry about capturing and transfixing your readers; just introduce your idea. Keep it simple. Open with an anecdote, a description, a comparison, a definition, a quotation, a question, or some vital background. Be sure that what you say is relevant to your main point. And don't forget to set forth your thesis.

Writing a Conclusion

The final paragraphs of an essay linger longest in readers' minds. E. B. White's conclusion to "Once More to the Lake" (p. 384) certainly does so. In the essay, White describes his return with his young son to a vacation spot he had loved as a child. At the end of the essay, in an unforgettable image, he remembers how old he really is and realizes the inevitable passing of generations.

> When the others went swimming my son said he was going in, too. He pulled his dripping trunks from the line where they had hung all through the shower and wrung them out. Languidly, and with no thought of going in, I watched him, his hard little body, skinny and bare, saw him wince slightly as he pulled up around his vitals the small, soggy, icy garment. As he buckled the swollen belt, suddenly my groin felt the chill of death.

White's concluding paragraph is a classic example of an effective ending. It begins with a sentence that points back to the previous paragraph and at the same time looks ahead. Then White leads us quickly to his final, chilling insight. And then he stops.

KINDS OF CONCLUSIONS

It's easy to suggest what *not* to do at the end of an essay: don't leave your readers suspended in midair, half expecting you to go on. Don't restate everything you've already said. Don't introduce a brand-new topic that leads away from the point of your essay. And don't signal that the end is near with an obvious phrase like "In conclusion" or "As I have said." In a long, complicated paper, a final terse summation of your main points may help your reader grasp your ideas, but a short paper usually requires either no summary at all or little more than a single sentence or two.

"How *do* you write an ending, then?" you might well ask.

End with a Quotation.   An apt quotation can neatly round out an essay, as literary critic Malcolm Cowley demonstrates at the end of an essay in *The View from Eighty* (New York: Viking, 1980), his discussion of the pitfalls and compensations of old age.

> "Eighty years old!" the great Catholic poet Paul Claudel wrote in his journal. "No eyes left, no ears, no teeth, no legs, no wind! And when all is said and done, how astonishingly well one does without them!"

State or Restate Your Thesis.   In a sharp criticism of American schools, humorist Russell Baker in "School vs. Education" ends by stating his main point, that schools do not educate.

> Afterward, the former student's destiny fulfilled, his life rich with Oriental carpets, rare porcelain, and full bank accounts, he may one day find

himself with the leisure and the inclination to open a book with a curious mind, and start to become educated.

Although you don't want to introduce new topics at the end, you can mention new *implications* of your thesis and discussion, considering "What now?" or "What is the significance of what I have said?" and leaving your readers with one or two provocative thoughts to ponder.

End with a Brief Emphatic Sentence.   For an essay that traces causes or effects, evaluates, or argues, a deft concluding thought can reinforce your main idea. Notice the definite click with which former heavyweight champion Gene Tunney (*The Long Count* [New York: Atheneum, 1969]) closes the door on "The Long Count," an analysis of his two victorious fights with Jack Dempsey, whose boxing style differed markedly from Tunney's own.

> Jack Dempsey was a great fighter — possibly the greatest that ever entered a ring. Looking back objectively, one has to conclude that he was more valuable to the sport or "The Game" than any prizefighter of his time. Whether you consider it from his worth as a gladiator or from the point of view of the box office, he was tops. His name in his most glorious days was magic among his people, and today, twenty years after, the name Jack Dempsey is still magic. This tells a volume in itself. As one who has always had pride in his profession as well as his professional theories, and possessing a fair share of Celtic romanticism, I wish that we could have met when we were both at our unquestionable best. We could have decided many questions, to me the most important of which is whether "a good boxer can always lick a good fighter."
>
> I still say yes.

Stop When the Story Is Over.   Even a quiet ending can be effective, as long as it signals clearly that the essay is finished. Journalist Martin Gansberg simply stops when the story is over in his true account of the fatal beating of a young woman, Kitty Genovese, in full view of residents of a Queens, New York, apartment house. The residents, unwilling to become involved, did nothing to interfere. Here is the last paragraph of his account, "Thirty-eight Who Saw Murder Didn't Call Police" (*New York Times*, 17 Mar. 1964):

> It was 4:25 A.M. when the ambulance arrived to take the body of Miss Genovese. It drove off. "Then," a solemn police detective said, "the people came out."

■ Exercise

Openings and Conclusions

Openings and conclusions frame an essay, contributing to the unity of the whole. The opening sets up the subject and the main idea; the conclusion reaffirms the thesis and rounds off the ideas. Discuss the following with your classmates.

I. Here are two possible beginning paragraphs from a student essay on the importance of teaching children how to swim.

  A. Humans inhabit a world made up of over 70 percent water. In addition to these great bodies of water, we have built millions of swimming pools for sports and leisure activities. At one time or another most people will be faced with either the danger of drowning or the challenge of aquatic recreation. For these reasons, it is essential that we learn to swim. Being a competitive swimmer and a swimming instructor, I fully realize the importance of knowing how to swim.

  B. Four-year-old Carl, curious like most children, last spring ventured out onto his pool patio. He fell into the pool and, not knowing how to swim, helplessly sank to the bottom. Minutes later his uncle found the child and brought him to the surface. Since Carl had no pulse, his uncle immediately administered CPR until the paramedics arrived. Eventually he was revived. During his stay in the hospital, his mother signed him up for beginning swimming classes. Carl was a lucky one. Unlike thousands of other children and adults, he got a second chance.

  1. Which introduction is more effective? Why?
  2. What would the body of this essay consist of? What kinds of evidence would be included?
  3. Write a suitable conclusion for this essay.

II. If you were to read each of the following introductions from professional essays, would you want to read the entire essay? Why?

  A. During my ninth hour underground, as I scrambled up a slanting tunnel through the powdered gypsum, Rick Bridges turned to me and said, "You know, this whole area was just discovered Tuesday." (David Roberts, "Caving Comes into Its Golden Age: A New Mexico Marvel," *Smithsonian* Nov. 1988: 52)

  B. From the batting average on the back of a George Brett baseball card to the interest rate fluctuations that determine whether the economy grows or stagnates, Americans are fascinated by statistics. (Stephen E. Nordlinger, "By the Numbers," *St. Petersburg Times* 6 Nov. 1988: 11)

  C. "What does it look like under there?"
      It was always this question back then, always the same pattern of hello and what's your name, what happened to your eye and what's under there. (Natalie Kusz, "Waiting for a Glass Eye," *Road Song* [New York: Farrar, 1990], rpt. in *Harper's* Nov. 1990)

III. How effective are the following introductions and conclusions from student essays? Could they be improved? If so, how? If they are satisfactory, explain why. What would be an eye-catching yet informative title for each essay?

  A. Recently a friend down from New York astonished me with stories of several people infected—some with AIDS—by stepping on needles washed up on the New Jersey beaches. This is just one incident of pollution, a devastating problem in our society today. Pollution is increasing in our world because of greed, apathy, and Congress's inability to control this problem. . . .

Wouldn't it be nice to have a pollution-free world without medical wastes floating in the water and washing up on our beaches? Without garbage scattered on the streets? With every corporation abiding by the laws set by Congress? In the future we can have a pollution-free world, but it is going to take the cooperation of everyone, including Congress, to ensure our survival on this Planet Earth.

B. The divorce rate has risen 700 percent in this century and continues to rise. More than one out of every two couples who are married end up in divorce. Over one million children a year are affected by divorce in the family. From these statistics it is clear that one of the greatest problems concerning the family today is divorce and the adverse effects it has on our society. . . .

Divorce causes problems that change people for life. The number of divorces will continue to exceed the 700 percent figure unless married couples learn to communicate, to accept their mates unconditionally, and to sacrificially give of themselves.

IV. Choose one of the topics from your brainstorming or freewriting in Chapter 16, and write several — at least three — different introductions with conclusions. Ask your classmates which is the most effective.

Achieving Coherence

Effective writing proceeds in some sensible order, each sentence following naturally from the one before it. Yet even well-organized prose can be hard to read unless it is *coherent*. To make your writing coherent, you can use various devices that tie together words in a sentence, sentences in a paragraph, paragraphs in an essay.

DEVICES THAT CREATE COHERENCE

Transitional Words and Sentences.   You already use transitions every day to help your readers and listeners follow your train of thought. For example, in talking with a friend you might say, "Well, *on the one hand*, a second job would help me save money for tuition. *On the other hand*, I'd have less time to study." But some writers rush through, omitting important links between thoughts. Mistakenly, they assume that connections they see will automatically be clear to their readers. Often just a word, phrase, or sentence of transition inserted in the right place will transform a disconnected passage into a coherent one.

The English language contains many words and phrases that specify connections between or within sentences. The following *transitional markers* are grouped by purpose or the kind of relation or connection they establish.

TO MARK TIME	then, soon, first, second, next, recently, the following day, in a little while, meanwhile, after, later, in the past
TO MARK PLACE OR DIRECTION	in the distance, close by, near, far away, above, below, to the right, on the other side, opposite, to the west, next door
TO SUMMARIZE OR RESTATE	in other words, to put it another way, in brief, in simpler terms, on the whole, in fact, in a word, to sum up, in short, in conclusion, to conclude, finally, therefore
TO RELATE CAUSE AND EFFECT OR RESULT	therefore, accordingly, hence, thus, for, so, consequently, as a result, because of
TO ADD OR AMPLIFY OR LIST	and, also, too, besides, as well, moreover, in addition, furthermore, in effect, second, in the second place, again, next
TO COMPARE	similarly, likewise, in like manner
TO CONCEDE	whereas, on the other hand, with that in mind, still, and yet, even so, in spite of, despite, at least
TO CONTRAST	on the other hand, but, or, however, unlike, nevertheless, on the contrary, conversely, in contrast, instead
TO INDICATE PURPOSE	to this end, for this purpose, with this objective
TO EXPRESS CONDITION	although, though
TO GIVE EXAMPLES OR SPECIFY	for example, for instance, in this case, in particular, to illustrate
TO QUALIFY	for the most part, by and large, with few exceptions, mainly, in most cases, generally, some, sometimes
TO EMPHASIZE	it is true, truly, indeed, of course, to be sure, obviously, without doubt, evidently, clearly, understandably

Occasionally a whole sentence serves as a transition. For example, the first sentence of a new paragraph may hark back to the previous paragraph while simultaneously hinting at the new direction. In this excerpt from an essay by Marsha Traugot about adopting older and handicapped children, the transitional sentence is in italics:

Some exchanges hold monthly meetings where placement workers looking for a match can discuss waiting children or families, and they also sponsor parties where children, workers, and prospective parents meet informally.

And if a match still cannot be made? Exchanges and other child welfare organizations now employ media blitzes as aggressive as those of commercial advertising. . . .

By repeating the key word *match* in her transitional sentence and by inserting the word *still,* Traugot makes clear that what follows will build on what has gone before. At the same time, by making the transitional sentence a rhetorical question, Traugot promises that the new paragraph will introduce fresh material, in this case answering the question.

Transition Paragraphs.   Transitions may be even longer than sentences. In a long and complicated essay, moving clearly from one idea to the next will sometimes require a short paragraph of transition.

> So far, we have been dwelling on the physical and psychological effects of driving nonstop for more than two hundred miles. Now let's reflect on causes. Why do people become addicted to their steering wheels?

Use a transition paragraph only when you sense that your readers might get lost if you don't patiently lead them by the hand. If your essay is short, one question or statement at the beginning of a new paragraph will be enough.

Often, as in the preceding example, a transition paragraph comments on the structure of the essay, looking back and pointing forward. It can also aid your return from one branch of argument to your main trunk. In "Things Unflattened by Science" from *Late Night Thoughts on Listening to Mahler's Ninth Symphony* (New York: Viking, 1983), Lewis Thomas has been complaining that biologists keep expecting medical researchers to come up with quick answers to intractable problems — cancer, schizophrenia, stress. He explains why he doesn't think medical science can solve the problem of stress: "Stress is simply the condition of being human." Now, to turn again to the essay's main idea — what biological problems he would like to see solved — Thomas inserts a transition paragraph.

> But I digress. What I wish to get at is an imaginary situation in which I am allowed three or four questions to ask the world of biomedical science to settle for me by research, as soon as possible. Can I make a short list of top-priority puzzles, things I am more puzzled by than anything else? I can.

In a new paragraph, he continues: "First, I want to know what goes on in the mind of a honeybee," whether a bee is programmed like a robot or can think and imagine, even a little bit. Neatly and effectively, the transition paragraph has led to this speculation and to several paragraphs to come.

Repetitions.   Another way to clarify the relationship between two sentences, paragraphs, or ideas is to repeat a key word or phrase. Such purposeful repetition almost guarantees that readers will understand how all the parts of a passage fit together. Note the repetition of the word *anger* in the following paragraph (italics ours) from *Of Woman Born* (New York: Norton, 1976) by poet Adrienne Rich. In this complex paragraph, the writer explores her relationship with her mother. The repetition holds all the parts together and makes clear the unity and coherence of the paragraph's ideas.

> And I know there must be deep reservoirs of *anger* in her; every mother has known overwhelming, unacceptable *anger* at her children. When I think of the conditions under which my mother became a mother, the impossible expectations, my father's distaste for pregnant women, his hatred of all that he could not control, my *anger* at her dissolves into grief and *anger* for her, and then dissolves back again into *anger* at her: the ancient, unpurged *anger* of the child.

Pronouns.   Because they always refer back to nouns or other pronouns, pronouns serve as transitions by making readers refer back as well. Note how certain pronouns (indicated by italics) hold together the following paragraph by columnist Ellen Goodman:

> I have two friends who moved in together many years ago. *He* looked upon this step as a trial marriage. *She* looked upon it as, well, moving in together. *He* was sure that in a matter of time, after *they* had built up trust and confidence, *she* would agree that marriage was the next logical step. *She*, on the other hand, was thrilled that here at last was a man *who* would never push *her* back to the altar.

Goodman's paragraph contains other transitions, too: time markers like *many years ago, in a matter of time,* and *after;* the marker *on the other hand,* which indicates a contrast; and repetition of synonyms like *trial marriage, marriage,* and *the altar.* All serve the main purpose of transitions — keeping readers on track.

■ Exercise

Identifying Transitions

Go over one of the papers you have already written for this course, and circle all the transitional devices you can detect. Then share your paper with a classmate. Can the classmate find additional transitions? Does the classmate think you need transitions where you don't have any?

Chapter 19
Strategies for Developing

For more help with developing an essay, use the *Writing Guide Software for* THE BEDFORD GUIDE.

How can you spice up your general ideas with the stuff of real life? How can you tug your readers deeper and deeper into your essays until they say, "I see just what you mean"? Well-developed essays have such power because they back up general points with evidence that comes alive for readers. In this chapter we cover giving examples, providing details, defining, dividing and classifying, analyzing a process, comparing and contrasting, and showing cause and effect. You'll find these seven methods of development to be indispensable, whether your purpose in a particular essay is to relate a personal experience, to explain, or to persuade. Although you may choose to use only one method within a single paragraph, a strong essay almost always requires a combination of developmental strategies.

Here are some questions to consider as you develop your ideas more fully:

DISCOVERY CHECKLIST
___ Are any paragraphs only one or two sentences long? Could these be developed more fully?
___ Are your longer paragraphs meaty and interesting to read? Or are they filled with generalizations, repetitions, and wordy phrasings?
___ Is there any point in your essay where you think your readers might have difficulty following you or understanding your meaning? Would more evidence help?
___ Has a peer editor pointed out any ideas that need to be developed more fully?

Giving Examples

An example—the word comes from the Latin *exemplum*, meaning "one thing chosen from among many"—is a typical instance that illustrates a whole type or kind. Giving examples to support a generalization is probably the most often used means of development. Here's an example, from *In Search of Excellence* (New York: Harper and Row, 1982) by Thomas J. Peters and Robert H. Waterman Jr., explaining why America's top corporations are so successful:

> Although he's not a company, our favorite illustration of closeness to the customer is car salesman Joe Girard. He sold more new cars and trucks, each year, for eleven years running, than any other human being. In fact, in a typical year, Joe sold more than twice as many units as whoever was in second place. In explaining his secret of success, Joe said: "I sent out over thirteen thousand cards every month."
>
> Why start with Joe? Because his magic is the magic of IBM and many of the rest of the excellent companies. It is simply service, overpowering service, especially after-sales service. Joe noted, "There's one thing that I do that a lot of salesmen don't, and that's believe the sale really begins *after* the sale—not before. . . . The customer ain't out the door, and my son has made up a thank-you note." Joe would intercede personally, a year later, with the service manager on behalf of his customer. Meanwhile he would keep the communications flowing.

Notice how Peters and Waterman focus on the specific, Joe Girard. They don't write *corporation employees* or even *car salespeople*, but zero in on one particular man to make the point come alive.

| America's top corporations |
| corporation employees |
| car salespeople |
| Joe Girard |

This ladder of abstraction moves from the general—America's top corporations—to a specific person—Joe Girard. The specific example of Joe Girard makes the importance of closeness to the customer *concrete* to readers: he is someone readers can relate to. To check the level of specification in one of your paragraphs or outlines, draw a ladder of abstraction for it. If you haven't gone down to the fourth or fifth level, you are probably being too general and need to add examples. This strategy is also a way to restrict a broad subject to a topic manageable in a short essay.

An example doesn't always have to be a specific individual. Sometimes you can create a picture in your readers' minds of something that they have never encountered before, or you can give an abstraction a recognizable personality and identity. Using this strategy, Jonathan Kozol makes real the plight of illiterate people in our health-care system. The following paragraph is from *Prisoners of Silence: Breaking the Bonds of Adult Illiteracy in the United States* (New York: Continuum, 1980):

> Illiterates live, in more than literal ways, an uninsured existence. They cannot understand the written details on a health insurance form. They cannot read waivers that they sign preceding surgical procedures. Several women I have known in Boston have entered a slum hospital with the intention of obtaining a tubal ligation and have emerged a few days later after having been subjected to a hysterectomy. Unaware of their rights, incognizant of jargon, intimidated by the unfamiliar air of fear and atmosphere of ether that so many of us find oppressive in the confines even of the most attractive and expensive medical facilities, they have signed their names to documents they could not read and which nobody, in the hectic situation that prevails so often in those overcrowded hospitals that serve the urban poor, had ever bothered to explain.

Examples aren't trivial doodads you add to a paragraph for decoration; they are what holds your readers' attention and shows them that your writing makes sense. By using examples, you make your ideas more concrete and tangible. To give plenty of examples is one of the writer's chief tasks.

You may generate examples at any point in the writing process. Begin with your own experience, even with a topic about which you know little — say, the psychology of gift giving. Did you ever know a person who gave large gifts people felt uncomfortable accepting? Why do you suppose the gift giver behaved that way? Was he or she looking for gratitude? A feeling of importance? Power over the recipients? You might also discover examples from conversing with others, from reading, from digging in the library, from browsing on the Web.

Here are some questions to consider when you use examples in your writing:

DISCOVERY CHECKLIST

___ Are your examples relevant to the point you are making?

___ Are your examples the best ones you can think of?

___ Are your examples really specific? Or do they just repeat generalities?

___ From each paragraph, can you draw a ladder of abstraction to at least the fourth level?

■ Exercise

Giving Examples

To help you get in the habit of thinking specifically, fill in a ladder of abstraction for five of the following general subjects. Then share your ladders with classmates and compare and contrast your specifics with theirs. Examples:

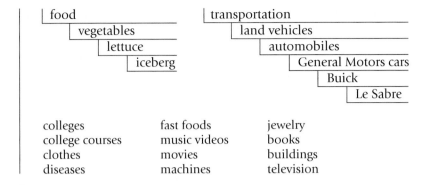

colleges   fast foods   jewelry
college courses   music videos   books
clothes   movies   buildings
diseases   machines   television

Providing Details

In addition to giving examples, you can back up your generalizations by providing convincing details. A *detail* is any specific, concrete piece of information — a fact, a bit of the historical record, your own observation. Details make scenes and images more realistic and vivid for readers. They also convince readers that the writer can make broad assertions with authority.

Mary Harris "Mother" Jones in old age published the story of her life as a labor organizer, *The Autobiography of Mother Jones* (Chicago: Kerr, 1980). In this view of a Pennsylvania coal miner's lot at the end of the nineteenth century, she lends conviction to a general statement with ample evidence from her own experience.

> Mining at its best is wretched work, and the life and surroundings of the miner are hard and ugly. His work is down in the black depths of the earth. He works alone in a drift. There can be little friendly companionship as there is in the factory; as there is among men who build bridges and houses, working together in groups. The work is dirty. Coal dust grinds itself into the skin, never to be removed. The miner must stoop as he works in the drift. He becomes bent like a gnome.
>
> His work is utterly fatiguing. Muscles and bones ache. His lungs breathe coal dust and the strange, damp air of places that are never filled with sunlight. His house is a poor makeshift and there is little to encourage him to make it attractive. The company owns the ground it stands on, and the miner feels the precariousness of his hold. Around his house is mud and slush. Great mounds of culm [the refuse left after coal is screened], black and sullen, surround him. His children are perpetually grimy from playing on the culm mounds. The wife struggles with dirt, with inadequate water supply, with small wages, with overcrowded shacks.

Mother Jones, who was not a learned writer, may have a style heavy with short, simple sentences, but her writing is clear and powerful because of the specific details she uses. She knows the strength of a well-chosen verb: "Coal dust *grinds* itself into the skin." Her opening makes two general statements: (1) "Mining is wretched work," and (2) the miner's life and surroundings are "hard and ugly." Then she supports these generalizations with a barrage of factual evidence. The result is a moving, convincingly detailed portrait of the miner and his family.

N. Scott Momaday ("To the Singing, to the Drums" [*Natural History*, Feb. 1975]) uses many details to describe the scene of the Kiowa celebration of the Gourd Dance on the Fourth of July at Carnegie, Oklahoma.

> The celebration is on the north side. We turn down into a dark depression, a large hollow among trees. It is full of camps and cars and people. At first there are children. According to some centrifugal social force, children function on the periphery. They run about, making festival noises. Firecrackers are snapping all around. We park and I make ready; the girls help me with my regalia. I am already wearing white trousers and moccasins. Now I tie the black velvet sash around my waist, placing the beaded tassels at my right leg. The bandoleer of red beans, which was my grandfather's, goes over my left shoulder, the V at my right hip. I decide to carry the blanket over my arm until I join the dancers; no sense in wrapping up in this heat. There is deep, brick-red dust on the ground. The grass is pale and brittle here and there. We make our way through the camps, stepping carefully to avoid the pegs and guy lines that reach about the tents. Old people, imperturbable, are lying down on cots and benches in the shadows. Smoke hangs in the air. We smell hamburgers, popcorn, gunpowder. Later there will be fried bread, boiled meat, Indian corn.

For more on transitions, see pp. 296–98.

Momaday arranges his vivid details both spatially and chronologically. Notice his spatial transitions: *on the north side, turn down, on the periphery, all around, on the ground, here and there, through the camps, in the shadows, in the air.* Look also at the time markers: *At first, Now, until, Later.* These transitions guide readers through the experience.

Quite different from Momaday's personal details are Paula Gunn Allen's hard facts and objective statistics, heaped up to convince readers that ever since Native Americans began making pacts with the U.S. government, their survival has been threatened.

> Some researchers put our pre-contact population at more than 45 million, while others put it at around 20 million. The U.S. government long put it at 450,000 — a comforting if imaginary figure, though at one point it was put at around 270,000. If our current population is around one million; if, as some researchers estimate, around 25 percent of Indian women and 10 percent of Indian men in the United States have been sterilized without informed consent; if our average life expectancy is, as the best-informed research presently says, 55 years; if our infant mortality rate continues at well above national standards; if our average unemployment for all segments of our population — male, female, young, adult, and middle-aged — is between 60 and 90 percent; if the U.S. government continues its policy of termination, relocation, removal, and assimilation along with the destruction of wilderness, reservation land, and its resources, and severe curtailment of hunting, fishing, timber harvesting, and water-use rights — then existing

tribes are facing the threat of extinction which for several hundred tribal groups has already become fact in the past five hundred years.

Providing details is one of the simplest yet most effective ways of developing ideas. All it takes on your part is close attention and then precise wording to communicate the details to readers. If readers were on the scene, what would they see first? What would they hear, smell, or feel? For a historical account, which small details were most meaningful to you in your reading? Would a bit of research turn up just the right fact or statistic? Remember that effective details have a specific purpose: they must help make your images more evocative or your point more convincing. Every detail should support — in some way — the main idea of your paragraph.

Here are some questions to consider when you use details:

DISCOVERY CHECKLIST

___ Do all your details support your point of view or main idea?

___ Do you have details of sights? Sounds? Tastes? Touch? Smells?

___ Have you included enough details to make your writing clear and interesting?

___ Have you arranged your details in an order that is easy to follow?

■ Exercise

Providing Details

To practice generating and using specific details, brainstorm with classmates or alone on one of the following subjects. Be sure to include details that appeal to all five senses. Group the details in your list (see pp. 276–78), and write a paragraph or two using your specific details. Begin with a statement of the main idea that conveys an interesting message about your subject (not "My grandmother's house was in Topeka, Kansas" but "My grandmother's house was my childhood haven").

the things in my room	an unforgettable game
my grandmother's house	an unusual person
the haunted house	my favorite pet
my graduation	a hospital room
my old car	a high school dance

Defining

Define, from the Latin, means "to set bounds to." You define a thing, a word, or a concept by describing it in such a way that it is distinguished from all similar things. If writers and thinkers don't agree on the meaning of a word or an idea, they can't share knowledge. Scientists in particular take special care to define their terms precisely and accurately. In his article "A

Chemist's Definition of pH," Gessner G. Hawley begins with a brief definition:

> pH is a value taken to represent the acidity or alkalinity of an aqueous solution; it is defined as the logarithm of the reciprocal of the hydrogen-ion concentration of a solution:
>
> $$pH = 1n \frac{1}{[H^+]}$$

If you use a word in a special sense or if you coin a word, you have to explain it or your readers will be lost. Prolific word coiner and social prophet Alvin Toffler in *The Third Wave* (New York: Morrow, 1980) invents (among many others) the word *techno-sphere*, which he defines as follows:

> All societies — primitive, agricultural, or industrial — use energy; they make things; they distribute things. In all societies the energy system, the production system, and the distribution system are interrelated parts of something larger. This larger system is the *techno-sphere*.

In his later book *PowerShift* (New York: Bantam, 1990), Toffler picks up the word *screenie* from Jeffrey Moritz, president of National College Television, and adds his own boundaries to this coined term:

> Moritz uses the term *screenie* to describe this video-drenched generation, which has digested thousands of hours of television, imbibing its "video-logic." To that must be added, for many of them, more hours of interactive video games and, even more important, of work on their own personal computers. They not only follow a different logic, but are accustomed to make the screen do things, thus making them good prospects for the interactive services and products soon to hit the market. Above all, they are accustomed to choice.

Sometimes in writing you stop to define a standard word not often used, to save your readers a trip to the dictionary. Or you may define a familiar but often misunderstood concept. What is intelligence, socialism, HMO, or minimum wage? Whenever you need to indicate the nature of an idea, a thing, a movement, a phenomenon, an organization, you'll find defining a helpful strategy. The more complex or ambiguous the subject, the longer the definition you need to clarify the term for your readers.

Here are some questions to consider when you use definitions:

DISCOVERY CHECKLIST

___ Have you used definitions to help your readers understand the subject matter, not to show off your knowledge?

___ Have you tailored your definition to the needs of your audience?

___ Is your definition specific, clear, and accurate?

___ Would your definition benefit from an example or from details?

■ Exercise

Defining

Write an extended definition (a paragraph or so) of one of the following words. Begin with a one-sentence definition of the word. Then, to expand and clarify your ideas, use some of the strategies discussed in this chapter — examples, details, division and classification, process analysis, comparison and contrast, and cause or effect identification. You may also use *negation* (explaining what something is by stating what it is not). Don't get most of your definition from a dictionary or textbook. Then share your definition with your classmates.

education	abuse	exercise	literacy
privacy	jazz	dieting	success
taboo	rock music	gossip	fear
prejudice	AIDS	ecology	gender

Analyzing

When you *analyze* a subject, you divide it into its parts and then deal with one part at a time. If you took high school chemistry, you probably analyzed water: you separated it into hydrogen and oxygen, its two elements. You've heard many a television commentator analyze the news, telling us what made up an event — who participated, where it occurred, what happened. Analyzing a news event may produce results less certain and clear-cut than analyzing a chemical compound, but the principle is similar — to take something apart for the purpose of understanding it better.

Analysis helps readers understand something complex: they can more readily take in the subject in a series of bites than in one gulp. For this reason, college textbooks do a lot of analyzing: an economics book divides a labor union into its component parts, an anatomy text divides the hand into the bones, muscles, and ligaments that make it up. In your college papers, you might analyze and explain to readers anything from a contemporary subculture (What social groups make up the homeless population of Los Angeles?) to an ecosystem (What animals, plants, and minerals coexist in a rainforest?). Analysis is so useful that you can apply it in many situations: breaking down the components of a subject to classify them, separating the stages in a process to see how it works, or identifying the possible results of an event to project consequences.

In *Cultural Anthropology: A Perspective on the Human Condition* (St. Paul: West, 1987), authors Emily A. Schultz and Robert H. Lavenda briefly but effectively demonstrate by analysis how a metaphor like "the Lord is my shepherd" makes a difficult concept ("the Lord") easy to understand.

For more on division and classification, see pp. 310–12. For more on process analysis, see pp. 312–14. For more on cause and effect, see pp. 316–18.

> The first part of a metaphor, the metaphorical subject, indicates the domain of experience that needs to be clarified (e.g., "the Lord"). The second part of

a metaphor, the metaphorical predicate, suggests a domain of experience which is familiar (e.g., sheep-herding) and which may help us understand what "the Lord" is all about.

Lillian Tsu, a government major at Cornell University, opens her essay "A Woman in the White House" in a similar manner, using analysis to identify major difficulties faced by female politicians in the United States.

The past twenty years have witnessed the rise of several powerful female leaders in world politics. In 1979, Margaret Thatcher became the first female prime minister of Great Britain; in 1986, Corazón Aquino ended a twenty-year dictatorship in the Philippines; and in 1988, Benazir Bhutto became the first woman to head a modern Muslim state when she became the prime minister of Pakistan. However, the success of these women may not translate into the future success of prospective female presidential candidates in the United States. Though these women rose to the top of their respective political ladders, their successes can be categorized as political anomaly or the result of a highly unusual set of circumstances. Although traditionally paternalistic societies like the Philippines and Pakistan and socially conservative states like Great Britain have elected female leaders, particular characteristics of the United States' own electoral system make it unlikely that this country will follow suit and elect a female president. Despite social modernization and the progress of the women's movement, the voters of the United States still lag far behind those of other nations in their willingness to trust in the leadership of a female executive. While the women's movement has succeeded in changing Americans' attitudes as to what roles are socially acceptable for women, female candidates still face a more difficult task in U.S. elections than their male counterparts face. Three factors are responsible for this situation--political socialization, lack of experience, and open discrimination.

Next, Tsu treats these factors in turn, beginning each of the first three sections with a transition phrase emphasizing the difficulties U.S. female candidates face: "One obstacle," "A second obstacle," "A third obstacle." The opening list and the transitions give readers clear direction in a complicated essay, guiding them through the explanation of the three factors to the final section on the implications of the analysis.

When you plan an analysis, you might use a pielike circle with the slices labeled or arrange your subdivisions in a list running from smallest to largest or from least to most important. Make sure that your analysis has a purpose — that it will demonstrate something or tell your readers something they didn't know before. You want to explain your subject, but what about it do you want to explain? For example, you might want to analyze New York City for the purpose of showing its ethnic composition. If so, you might divide the city geographically into neighborhoods — Harlem, Spanish Harlem, Yorkville, Chinatown, Little Italy. If you want to explain New York's social classes, however, you might start with homeless people and work your way up to the cream of society. The way you slice your subject into pieces will depend in part on the point you want to make about it — and the point you end up making will depend in part on how you've sliced it up. As you develop your ideas, you may also find that you have a stronger point to make — that New York City's social hierarchy is oppressive and unstable, for example.

How can you ensure that your readers will be able to follow your thinking as you analyze? Some writers like to start an analysis by telling their readers the subdivisions into which they are going to slice their subject ("The federal government has three branches"). If you invent a name or label for each part you mention, define the terms you use, and clarify with examples, you will also help distinguish each part from all the others. You can make your essay as readable as possible by using transitions — those valuable words and phrases that introduce and connect ideas, leading readers from one part to the next.

For more on transitions, see pp. 296–98.

Here are some questions to consider when you use analysis in your writing:

DISCOVERY CHECKLIST

___ Exactly what will you try to achieve in your analysis?

___ How will you break your subject into parts?

___ How can you make each part clear to your readers?

___ What definitions, details, and examples can help clarify each part of your analysis?

■ Exercise

Analyzing

Analyze one of the following subjects by making a list of its basic parts or elements. Then use your list as the basis for a paragraph or short essay explaining each part. Be sure to identify the purpose or point of your analysis. Compare your analysis with those of others in your class who chose the same subject.

a college   a choir, orchestra, or other musical group
a newspaper   a computer or other technological device
a TV talk show   a basketball, baseball, hockey, or other team
effective teaching   a family
a healthy lifestyle   leadership

Dividing and Classifying

To divide is to break something down into its components. It's far easier to take in a subject, especially a complex subject, one piece at a time. The thing divided may be as concrete as Manhattan (which a writer might divide into neighborhoods) or as abstract as a person's knowledge of art (which the writer might divide into knowledge of sculpture, painting, drawing, and other forms). To classify is to make sense of a complicated and potentially bewildering array of things — works of literature, this year's movies — by sorting them into categories (*types* or *classes*) that you can deal with one at a time. Literature is customarily arranged by genre — novels, stories, poems, plays. Movies might be sorted by audience (movies for children, teenagers, or mature audiences).

These two methods of development are like two sides of the same coin. In theory, any broad subject can be *divided* into components, which can then be *classified* into categories. In practice, it's often difficult to tell where division stops and classification begins.

In the following paragraph from his college textbook *Wildlife Management* (San Francisco: Freeman, 1978), Robert H. Giles Jr. uses division to simplify an especially large, abstract subject: the management of forest wildlife in America. To explain which environmentalists assume which duties and responsibilities, Giles divides forest wildlife management into six levels or areas of concern, arranged roughly from large to small, all neatly explained in fewer than 175 words.

There are six scales of forest wildlife management: (1) national, (2) regional, (3) state or industrial, (4) county or parish, (5) intra-state region, management unit, or watershed, and (6) forest. Each is different. At the national and regional levels, management includes decisions on timber harvest quotas, grazing policy in forested lands, official stance on forest taxation bills, cutting policy relative to threatened and endangered species, management coordination of migratory species, and research fund allocation. At the state or industrial level, decision types include land acquisition, sale, or trade; season setting; and permit systems and fees. At the county level, plans are made, seasons set, and special fees levied. At the intra-state level, decisions include what seasons to recommend, what stances to take on bills not affecting local conditions, the sequence in which to attempt land acquisition, and the placement of facilities. At the forest level, decisions may include some of those of the larger management unit but typically are those of maintenance schedules, planting stock, cutting rotations, personnel employment and supervision, road closures, equipment use, practices to be attempted or used, and boundaries to be marked.

In a textbook lesson on how babies develop, Kurt W. Fischer and Arlyne Lazerson (writing in *Human Development* [New York: Freeman, 1984]) take a paragraph to describe a research project that classified individual babies into three types according to temperament.

> The researchers also found that certain of these temperamental qualities tended to occur together. These clusters of characteristics generally fell into three types — the easy baby, the difficult baby, and the baby who was slow to warm up. The *easy infant* has regular patterns of eating and sleeping, readily approaches new objects and people, adapts easily to changes in the environment, generally reacts with low or moderate intensity, and typically is in a cheerful mood. The *difficult infant* usually shows irregular patterns of eating and sleeping, withdraws from new objects or people, adapts slowly to changes, reacts with great intensity, and is frequently cranky. The *slow-to-warm-up infant* typically has a low activity level, tends to withdraw when presented with an unfamiliar object, reacts with a low level of intensity, and adapts slowly to changes in the environment. Fortunately for parents, most healthy infants — 40 percent or more — have an easy temperament. Only about 10 percent have a difficult temperament, and about 15 percent are slow to warm up. The remaining 35 percent do not easily fit one of the three types but show some other pattern.

When you divide and classify, your point is to make order out of a complex or overwhelming jumble of stuff. Make sure the components and categories you identify are sensible, given your purpose, and follow the same principle of classification or analysis for all categories. For example, if you're trying to discuss campus relations, it makes sense to divide the school population into *instructors, students,* and *support staff*; it would make less sense to divide it into *people from the South, people from the other states,* and *people from overseas.* Also, try to group apples with apples, not with oranges, so that all the components or categories are roughly equivalent. For example, if you're classifying television shows and you've come up with *sitcoms, dramas, talk shows, children's shows, news,* and *cartoons,* then you've got a problem: the last category is probably part of *children's shows.* Finally, check that your final system is simple and easy for your readers to understand. Most people can handle only about seven things at once. If you've got more than six or seven components or categories, perhaps you need to combine or eliminate some.

Here are some questions to consider when you use division or classification:

DISCOVERY CHECKLIST

___ Do you use the most logical principle of division or classification for your purpose?

___ Do you stick to one principle throughout?

___ Have you identified components or categories that are comparable?

___ Have you used the best order for your components or categories?

___ Have you given specific examples for each of your components or categories?

___ Have you made a complex subject more accessible to your readers?

■ Exercise
Dividing and Classifying

For more on brainstorming, see pp. 260–63.

To practice dividing and classifying, choose one or two of the following subjects, and brainstorm for five minutes on each, trying to come up with as many components as you can. With your classmates, create one large list by combining items from all students who chose each subject. Working as a group, take the largest list and try to classify the items on it into logical categories. Feel free to add or change components or categories if you find you've overlooked something.

students	customers	sports	families
teachers	Web sites	vacations	drivers

Analyzing a Process

Analyzing a process — telling step by step how something is or was done or how to do something — is one of the most useful kinds of writing for building an entire essay or a paragraph.

You can analyze an action or a phenomenon — how a skyscraper is built, how a revolution begins, how sunspots form, how to make chili. This strategy can also explain large, long-ago happenings that a writer couldn't possibly have witnessed or complex technical processes that a writer couldn't personally duplicate. Here, for instance, is a paragraph from "The Case for Cloning" (*Time,* 9 Feb. 1998) in which Madeleine Nash describes the process of cloning cells.

> Cloning individual human cells [. . .] is another matter. Biologists are already talking about harnessing for medical purposes the technique that produced the sheep called Dolly. They might, for example, obtain healthy cells from a patient with leukemia or a burn victim and then transfer the nucleus of each cell into an unfertilized egg from which the nucleus has been removed. Coddled in culture dishes, these embryonic clones — each genetically identical to the patient from which the nuclei came — would begin to divide. The cells would not have to grow into a fetus, however. The addition of powerful growth factors could ensure that the clones develop only into specialized cells and tissue. For the leukemia patient, for example, the cloned cells could provide an infusion of fresh bone marrow, and for the burn victim, grafts of brand-new skin. Unlike cells from an unrelated donor, these cloned cells would incur no danger of rejection; patients would be spared the need to take powerful drugs to suppress the immune system.

This paragraph illustrates an *informative* process analysis that sets forth how something happens.

The *directive* or "how-to" process analysis instructs readers how to do something—how to box, invest for retirement, clean a painting—or how to make something—how to draw a map, blaze a trail, set up a computer. In the following example from *The Little Windows Book, 3.1 Edition* (Berkeley: Peachpit, 1992), technical writer Kay Yarborough Nelson uses a directive process description to teach her readers how to use a computer mouse.

> You can use the mouse in three basic ways: by clicking, double-clicking, and dragging.
>
> To select an item on the screen, you can move the mouse pointer to it and click once with the left mouse button. (If you're left-handed, you can change it to the right mouse button, as you'll see in the chapter on customizing Windows.) Selecting an item makes it active, so that you can work with it. For example, you might click on a document's icon so that you could copy or move it.
>
> You can also double-click on an item to make it active and actually start it. To double-click, quickly click twice with the left mouse button. For example, double-clicking on a program's icon will open a window and start the program. . . .
>
> A third way of using the mouse is dragging. To drag, put the mouse pointer on what you want to drag, press and hold the left mouse button down, and then move the mouse.

Notice the care Nelson takes to make each step seem as simple and logical as possible. Her clear divisions (*three basic ways*), unambiguous commands (*move . . . , click . . . , put . . .*), concrete examples (*For example . . .*), and helpful transitions (*a third way, and then*) help guide readers through an unfamiliar process step by step.

Process analyses are wonderful ways to show your readers the inside workings of events or systems, but they can be difficult to follow. Be sure to divide the process into logical steps or stages and to put the steps in a sensible chronological order. Add details or examples wherever your description may become ambiguous or abstract, and use transitions to mark the end of one step and the beginning of the next.

Here are some questions to consider when you use process analysis:

DISCOVERY CHECKLIST

___ Do you thoroughly understand the process you are analyzing?

___ Do you have a good reason to use process analysis at this point in your essay?

___ Have you broken the process down into logical and useful steps?

___ Is the order in which you present these steps the best one possible?

___ Have you used transitions to guide your readers from one step to the next?

■ Exercise
Analyzing a Process

Analyze one of the following processes or procedures as the basis of a paragraph or short essay. Then share your process analysis with classmates. Can they follow your analysis easily? Do they spot anything you left out?

registration for college classes   falling in love
studying for a test   buying a used car
influenza (or another disease)   cloud formation

Comparing and Contrasting

For advice on writing a comparison and contrast essay, see Ch. 7.

Often you can develop a paragraph by setting a pair of subjects side by side, comparing and contrasting them. When you compare, you point out similarities; when you contrast, you discuss differences. Working together, these twin strategies use one subject to clarify another. The dual method works well for a pair of things similar in nature — two cities, two films, the theories of two economists. Because this method shows that you have observed and understood both subjects, college instructors will often ask you to compare and contrast on exams ("Discuss the chief similarities and differences between nineteenth-century French and English colonial policies in West Africa").

In daily life, we compare and contrast to decide which menu item to choose, which car (or other product) to buy, which college course to sign up for. A comparison and contrast can lead to a final evaluation and a decision about which thing is better, but it doesn't have to. In a travel essay, "Venezuela for Visitors" from *Hugging the Shore* (New York: Knopf, 1983), novelist John Updike sees Venezuelan society as polarized. It consists of rich people and Indians, two classes Updike compares and contrasts without choosing between them.

> Missionaries, many of them United States citizens, move among the Indians. They claim that since Western civilization, with all its diseases and detritus, must come, it had best come through them. Nevertheless, Marxist anthropologists inveigh against them. Foreign experts, many of them United States citizens, move among the rich. They claim they are just helping out, and that anyway the oil industry was nationalized five years ago. Nevertheless, Marxist anthropologists are not mollified. The feet of the Indians are very broad in front, their toes spread wide for climbing avocado trees. The feet of the rich are very narrow in front, their toes compressed by pointed Italian shoes. The Indians seek relief from tension in the use of *ebene*, or *yopo*, a mind-altering drug distilled from the bark of the ebene tree and blown into the user's nose through a hollow cane by a colleague. The rich take cocaine through the nose, and frequent mind-altering discotheques, but more customarily imbibe cognac, *vino blanco*, and Scotch, in association with colleagues.

Updike simply sets the two side by side, noting the foreigners among them, the state of their feet, and their drug preferences. By doing so, he throws the two groups into sharp relief.

You can use two basic methods of organization for comparison and contrast — the opposing pattern and the alternating pattern. Using the *opposing pattern*, you discuss all the characteristics or subdivisions of the first subject in the first half of the paragraph or essay and then discuss all the characteristics of the other subject. Using the *alternating pattern*, you move back and forth between the two subjects. This pattern places the specifics close together for immediate comparison and contrast. For example, a writer using the opposing pattern to compare and contrast two brothers would discuss Jim's physical appearance, his personality traits, and his interests and then Jack's appearance, his personality, and his interests — discussing in both parts the same characteristics in the same order. A writer using the alternating pattern would discuss Jim's physical appearance, then Jack's physical appearance; Jim's personality, then Jack's; Jim's interests, then Jack's. Whichever pattern you choose, be sure to cover the same subpoints for each subject and to follow the same order in each part.

For an outline and sample paper using the alternating pattern, see pp. 86–89 and 95.

In the paragraph on page 314 about Venezuelan society, John Updike uses the alternating pattern to compare and contrast rich people and Indians. In the following paragraph, Jacquelyn Wonder and Priscilla Donovan, management consultants, use the opposing pattern of organization to explain the differences in the brains of females and males.

At birth there are basic differences between male and female brains. The female cortex is more fully developed. The sound of the human voice elicits more left-brain activity in infant girls than in infant boys, accounting in part for the earlier development in females of language. Baby girls have larger connectors between the brain's hemispheres and thus integrate information more skillfully. This flexibility bestows greater verbal and intuitive skills. Male infants lack this ready communication between the brain's lobes; therefore, messages are routed and rerouted to the right brain, producing larger right hemispheres. The size advantage accounts for males having greater spatial and physical abilities and explains why they may become more highly lateralized and skilled in specific areas.

For another example using the opposing pattern, see pp. 93–94.

After the topic sentence, "At birth there are basic differences between male and female brains," the authors first explain the development of the female brain and how it accounts for specific thinking styles in females, and then in the last part of the paragraph they explain the development of the male brain and the effects on males' abilities.

Here are some questions to consider when you use comparison and contrast:

DISCOVERY CHECKLIST

___ Is your reason for comparing and contrasting unmistakably clear?

___ Have you chosen the *major* similarities and differences to write about?

—— Have you used the same categories for each item? In discussing each feature, do you always compare or contrast like things?

—— Have you used the best possible arrangement, given your subject and the point you're trying to make?

—— If you are making a judgment between your subjects, have you treated both fairly?

—— Have you avoided a boringly mechanical, monotonous style ("On one hand, . . . now on the other hand")?

■ Exercise

Comparing and Contrasting

Write a paragraph or two in which you compare and contrast the subjects in one of the following pairs:

baseball and football (or basketball)
living in an apartment and living in a house
two cities or towns you are familiar with
two musicians
communicating by telephone and e-mail
watching a sports event on television and in person

Identifying Causes and Effects

For advice on writing a cause and effect essay, see Ch. 8.

From the time we are children, we ask why. Why can't I go out and play? Why is the sky blue? Why did my goldfish die? Our seeking causes and effects continues into adulthood, so it's natural that explaining causal relationships is a commonly used method of development. To use cause and effect successfully, you must think about the subject critically, gather evidence, draw judicious conclusions, and show relationships clearly.

In the following paragraph from "What Pop Lyrics Say to Us" (*New York Times*, 24 Feb. 1985), Robert Palmer speculates on the causes that led young people to turn to rock music for inspiration, as well as the effects of their expectations on the musicians of the time.

> By the late '60's, the peace and civil rights movement were beginning to splinter. The assassinations of the Kennedys and Martin Luther King had robbed a generation of its heroes, the Vietnam War was escalating despite the protests, and at home, violence was on the rise. Young people turned to rock, expecting it to ask the right questions and come up with answers, hoping that the music's most visionary artists could somehow make sense of things. But rock's most influential artists—Bob Dylan, the Beatles, the Rolling Stones—were finding that serving as the conscience of a generation exacted a heavy toll. Mr. Dylan, for one, felt the pressures becoming unbearable, and wrote about his predicament in songs like "All Along the Watchtower."

Instead of focusing on causes *or* effects, often writers trace a *chain* of cause and effect relationships, as Charles C. Mann and Mark L. Plummer do in "The Butterfly Problem" *(Atlantic Monthly,* Jan. 1992).

> More generally, the web of species around us helps generate soil, regulate freshwater supplies, dispose of waste, and maintain the quality of the atmosphere. Pillaging nature to the point where it cannot perform these functions is dangerously foolish. Simple self-protection is thus a second motive for preserving biodiversity. When DDT was sprayed in Borneo, the biologists Paul and Anne Ehrlich relate in their book *Extinction* (1981), it killed all the houseflies. The gecko lizards that preyed on the flies ate their pesticide-filled corpses and died. House cats consumed the dying lizards; they died too. Rats descended on the villages, bringing bubonic plague. Incredibly, the housefly in this case was part of an intricate system that controlled human disease. To make up for its absence, the government was forced to parachute cats into the area.

Here are some questions to consider when you identify causes and effects:

DISCOVERY CHECKLIST

____ Is your use of cause and effect clearly tied to the overall point you're trying to make?

____ Have you identified actual causes? Can you find evidence to support them?

____ Have you identified actual effects, or are they conjecture? If conjecture, are they logical results? Can you find evidence to support them?

____ Have you judiciously drawn conclusions concerning causes and effects? Have you avoided fallacies, such as hasty generalization and stereotyping?

____ Have you presented your points clearly and logically, so that your readers can follow them easily?

For more on logical fallacies, see pp. 134–36.

■ Exercise

Identifying Causes and Effects

1. Identify some of the *causes* of *five* of the following. Discuss possible causes with your classmates.

failing an exam	stage fright	losing a job
an automobile accident	losing/winning a game	losing weight
poor health	stress	going to college
good health	getting a job	getting a scholarship

2. Identify some of the *effects* of *five* of the following. Discuss possible effects with your classmates.

an insult	dieting	divorce
a compliment	speeding	traveling to another country
learning to read	winning the lottery	drinking while driving

3. Identify some of the *causes and effects* of *one* of the following. You may need to do a little research in the library or in a textbook to identify the chain of causes and effects for the event. How might you use what you have discovered as part of an essay? Discuss your findings with your classmates.

the e-commerce boom	the AIDS virus
the Vietnam War	recycling
the Bosnian conflict	FDA approval of RU 486
the discovery of atomic energy	the uses of solar energy
a U.S. Supreme Court decision on abortion	the hole in the ozone layer
	racial tension

Chapter 20

Strategies for Revising and Editing

G ood writing is rewriting. When Ernest Hemingway was asked what made him rewrite the last page of the novel *A Farewell to Arms* thirty-nine times, he replied, "Getting the words right." His comment reflects the care that serious writers take in revising their work. In this chapter we provide strategies for revising and editing — ways to rethink muddy ideas and emphasize important ones, to rephrase obscure passages and restructure garbled sentences. Our advice applies not only to rewriting whole essays but also to rewriting sentences and paragraphs. In addition, we give you tips for editing and proofreading grammar, spelling, punctuation, and mechanics.

Re-viewing and Revising

Revision means "seeing again" — discovering again, conceiving again, shaping again. It is not something you do only after you complete a paper. Rather, it is an integral aspect of the total writing process; it may occur at any and all stages of the process, and most writers do a lot of it. *Macro revising* is making large, global, or fundamental changes that affect the overall direction or impact of writing. Macro revising involves rhetorical aspects of writing, such as purpose, organization, and audience. On the other hand, *micro revising* is paying attention to the details. It involves the language aspects of writing — sentences, words, punctuation, grammar — including ways to create emphasis and eliminate wordiness.

319

REVISING FOR PURPOSE

For more help with revising, use the *Writing Guide Software for THE BEDFORD GUIDE.*

When you revise for purpose, you make sure that your writing really accomplishes whatever you want it to do. If your goal is to create an interesting profile of a person, have you done that? If you want to persuade your readers to take a certain course of action, have you succeeded? Of course, the purpose of your final essay may be different from your purpose when you began writing, especially for complex projects that evolve over time or for assignments that you begin without clear direction. To revise for purpose, try to step back from your writing and see it as other readers will. Concentrate on what's actually in your paper, not what you assume is there.

For more on thesis statements, see pp. 271–75.

At this point you'll probably want to revise your working thesis statement (if you've developed one) or create a thesis sentence (if you haven't). Scrutinize your tentative statement of your main idea. Consider whether each part of the essay directly relates to it, whether each part develops and supports it, and whether everything it promises is carried out. If you find passages that don't relate to the thesis or that contradict it, you have two options: revise the thesis, or revise the essay.

Here are some helpful questions about revising for purpose:

REVISION CHECKLIST

___ Do you know exactly what you want your essay to accomplish? Can you put it in one sentence: "In this paper I want to . . ."?

___ Is your thesis stated outright anywhere in the essay? If not, have you provided clues so that your readers will know precisely what it is?

___ Does every part of the essay work to achieve the same goal?

___ Have you tried to do too much? Does your coverage of your topic seem too thin? If so, how might you reduce the scope of your essay?

___ Does your essay say everything that needs to be said? Is everything — ideas, connections between ideas, supporting evidence — on paper, not just in your head?

___ In writing the essay, have you changed your mind, rethought your assumptions, made a discovery? Does anything now need to be recast?

___ Do you have enough evidence? Is every point developed fully enough to be clear? To be convincing?

REVISING FOR AUDIENCE

An essay is successful only if it succeeds with its particular audience, and what works with one audience can fall flat with another. Visualize one of your readers poring over the essay, sentence by sentence, reacting to what you have written. What expressions do you see on that reader's face? Where does he or she have trouble understanding? Where have you hit the mark?

Your organization, your selection of details, your word choice, and your tone all affect your readers, so you should pay special attention to these aspects.

Here are some helpful questions about revising with your audience in mind:

REVISION CHECKLIST

____ Who will read this essay?

____ Does the essay tell them what they want to know rather than what they probably know already?

____ Are there any places where readers might go to sleep? If so, can such passages be shortened or deleted or livened up?

____ Does the opening of the essay mislead your readers by promising something that the essay never delivers?

____ Do you unfold each idea in enough detail to make it both clear and interesting? Would readers appreciate more detailed evidence?

____ Have you anticipated questions readers might ask?

____ Where might readers raise serious objections? How might you anticipate these objections and answer them?

____ Have you used any specialized or technical language that your readers might not understand? If so, have you worked in brief definitions?

____ What is your attitude toward your readers? Are you chummy, angry, superior, apologetic, condescending, preachy? Should you revise to improve your attitude? Ask your peers for an opinion.

____ Will your readers be convinced that you have told them something worth knowing?

REVISING FOR STRUCTURE

When revising for structure, you make sure that the order of your ideas and the arrangement of material is as effective as possible. You may have all the ingredients of a successful essay — but they may be a jumbled, confusing mess.

In a well-structured essay, each paragraph, sentence, and phrase fulfills a clear function. Are your opening and closing paragraphs relevant, concise, and interesting? Is everything in each paragraph on the same topic? Are all ideas adequately developed? Are the paragraphs arranged in the best possible order? Finally, review each place where you lead readers from one idea to the next to be certain that the transition is clear and painless.

For more on paragraphs, topic sentences, and transition, see Ch. 18.

An outline can be useful for diagnosing a draft that you suspect doesn't quite make sense. Instead of using outlining to plan, now you want to show what you've succeeded in getting on paper. Start by finding the topic sentence of each paragraph in your draft (or creating one, if necessary) and listing them in order. Label the sentences *I., II., A., B.,* and so on to indicate the

For more on using outlining for planning, see pp. 279–84.

logical relationships of ideas in your essay. Do the same with the supporting details under each topic sentence, labeling them also with letters and numbers and indenting appropriately. Now look at the outline. Does it make sense on its own, without the essay to explain it? Would any different order or arrangement be more effective? Does any section look thin and need more evidence? Are the connections between parts in your head but not on paper? Maybe too many ideas are jammed into too few paragraphs. Maybe you don't include as many specific details and examples as you need. Work on the outline until you get it into strong shape, and then rewrite the essay to follow it.

Here are some helpful questions about revising for structure:

REVISION CHECKLIST

___ Does your introduction set up the whole essay? Does it both grab readers' attention and hint at what is to follow?

___ Does the essay fulfill all that you promise in your opening?

___ Would any later passage make a better beginning?

___ Is your thesis clear early in the essay? If explicit, is it given a position of emphasis?

___ Do the paragraph breaks seem logical?

___ Is the main idea of each paragraph clear? Have you used a topic sentence in every paragraph?

___ Is the main idea of each paragraph fully developed? Where might you need more details or evidence to be convincing?

___ Within each paragraph, is each detail or piece of evidence relevant to the topic sentence? If you find a stray bit, should you omit it altogether or move it to another paragraph?

___ Are all the ideas directly relevant to the main point of the essay?

___ Would any paragraphs make more sense in a different order?

___ Does everything follow clearly? Does one point smoothly lead to the next? Would transitions help make the connections clearer?

___ Does the conclusion follow from what has gone before, or does it seem arbitrarily tacked on?

WRITING WITH A COMPUTER

E-mail can be an efficient way for writers and readers to exchange drafts. You can either copy and paste a document into the e-mail message or attach a document. Sometimes copying the draft into the message will remove some formatting, such as italics or bold, but this process usually works well and avoids spreading computer viruses. If you want to preserve the formatting of a document and believe your reader has compatible word-processing software, you may attach the document instead.

WORKING WITH A PEER EDITOR

Of course, there's no substitute for having another person go over your writing. Most college assignments ask you to write for an audience of your classmates, but even if your essay is written for a different group (the town council or readers of the *New Yorker*, for example), having a classmate read over your essay is a worthwhile revision strategy. To get all you can as a writer from a peer review, you need to play an active part in the discussion of your work:

- Ask your readers questions.
- Be open to new ideas — for focus, organization, details, or additional material.
- Use what's helpful, but trust yourself as the author.

To be a helpful, supportive peer editor, try to offer honest, intelligent feedback, not judgment.

- Look at the big picture: purpose, focus, clarity, coherence, organization, support.
- When you identify strengths and weaknesses, be specific, noting examples.
- Answer the writer's questions, and also use the questions supplied throughout this book to concentrate on essentials, not details.

As a writer, you can ask your peer editor to begin with your specific questions or use applicable questions from the following general checklist:

FIRST QUESTIONS FOR A PEER EDITOR
What is your first reaction to this paper?
What is this writer trying to tell you?
What are this paper's greatest strengths?
Does it have any major weaknesses?
What one change would most improve the paper?

QUESTIONS ON MEANING
Do you understand everything? Is the draft missing any information that
     you need to know?
Does this paper tell you anything you didn't know before?
Is the writer trying to cover too much territory? Too little?
Does any point need to be more fully explained or illustrated?
When you come to the end, has the paper delivered what it promised?
Could this paper use a down-to-the-ground revision?

QUESTIONS ON ORGANIZATION
Has the writer begun in a way that grabs your interest and quickly draws
     you into the paper's main idea? Or can you find, at some point later in
     the paper, a better possible beginning?
Does the paper have one main idea, or does it juggle more than one?
Would the main idea stand out better if anything were removed or added?

WRITING WITH A COMPUTER

One of the simplest ways to work with another person's help is to start by saving your file with a new title. Consider adding a "+" and your peer editor's initials to the file name to help you keep track of different drafts. When you and your peer exchange texts, you may each want to use all capitals for the comments you make within each other's drafts. The capitalized comments will then be easy to distinguish from the original text.

Some word processors also offer more advanced editing systems, such as "Track Changes" in your Tools menu. This resource allows peer editors to highlight possible changes in your draft using underlining, color differences, and strikeouts. With this feature, you can easily see your reader's suggestions, and you can track suggestions from several readers.

QUESTIONS ON ORGANIZATION (continued)

Might the ideas in the paper be more effectively arranged? Do any ideas belong together that now seem too far apart?

Can you follow the writer's ideas easily? Does the paper need transitions? If so, at what places?

Does the writer keep to one point of view — one angle of seeing?

Does the ending seem deliberate, as if the writer meant to conclude at this point? Or does the writer seem merely to have run out of gas? If so, how might the writer strengthen the conclusion?

QUESTIONS ON WRITING STRATEGIES

Do you feel that this paper addresses you personally?

Do you dislike or object to any statement the writer makes or any wording the writer uses? Is the problem word choice, tone, or inadequate support to convince you? Should the writer keep or change this part?

Does the draft contain anything that distracts you or seems unnecessary?

Do you get bored at any point? How might the writer make you want to keep reading?

Is the language of this paper too lofty and abstract? If so, where does the writer need to come down to earth and get specific?

Do you understand all the words the writer uses? Are there any specialized words whose meanings need to be clearer?

Stressing What Counts

An ineffective writer treats all ideas as equals. An effective writer decides what matters most and shines a bright light on it. You can't emphasize merely by underlining things, by putting them in "quotation marks," or by throwing them into CAPITAL LETTERS. Such devices soon grow monotonous, stressing nothing at all. This section offers suggestions for how to emphasize things that count.

STATING FIRST OR LAST

The most emphatic positions in an essay, a paragraph, or a sentence are the beginning and the end.

Stating First.   In an essay, you might start with what matters most. Writing an economics paper on the consequences of import quotas (such as the number of foreign cars allowed into a country), Donna Waite began by summing up her findings.

> Although an import quota has many effects, both for the nation imposing the quota and for the nation whose industries must suffer from it, I believe that the most important effect is generally felt at home. A native industry gains a chance to thrive in a marketplace of lessened competition.

Waite's paper goes on to illustrate her general observation with evidence.

A paper that takes a stand or makes a proposal might open with the writer's position.

> Our state's antiquated system of justices of the peace is inefficient.

> The United States should place a human observer in temporary orbit around the planet Mars.

The body would set forth the writer's reasons for holding that view, and probably the writer would hammer the claim or thesis again at the end.

In a single sentence, as in an essay, you can stress things at the start. Consider the following unemphatic sentence:

> When Congress debates the Hall-Hayes Act removing existing protections for endangered species, as now seems likely to occur on May 12, it will be a considerable misfortune if this bill should pass, since the extinction of many rare birds and animals would certainly result.

The coming debate and its probable date take up the start of the sentence. The writer might have made better use of this emphatic position:

> The extinction of many rare birds and animals would certainly follow passage of the Hall-Hayes Act.

Now the writer stresses what he most fears — dire consequences. (In another sentence, he might add the date of the debate and his opinion that passage would be a misfortune.)

Stating Last.   To place an idea last can throw weight on it. One way to assemble your ideas in an emphatic order is to proceed from least important to most important. This order is dramatic: it builds up and up. In papers on import quotas and justices of the peace, however, big dramatic buildups might look artificial and contrived. Still, in an essay on how city parks lure shoppers and visitors to the city, the thesis sentence — summing up the whole point of the essay — might stand at the very end: "For the inner city, improved city parks will bring about a new era of prosperity." Giving all the evidence first and leading up to the thesis at the end is particularly effective in editorials and informal persuasive essays.

A sentence that uses climactic order, suspending its main point until the end, is a *periodic* sentence. Notice how novelist Julian Green builds to his point of emphasis.

> Amid chaos of illusions into which we are cast headlong, there is one thing that stands out as true, and that is — love.

Cutting and Whittling

Like pea pickers who throw out dirt and pebbles, good writers remove needless words that clog their prose. One of the chief joys of revising is to watch 200 paunchy words shrink to a svelte 150. To see how saving words helps, let's first look at some wordiness. In what she imagined to be a gracious style, a New York socialite once sent this dinner invitation to Hu Shi, the Chinese ambassador:

> O learned sage and distinguished representative of the numerous Chinese nation, pray deign to honor my humble abode with your noble presence at a pouring of libations, to be followed by a modest evening repast, on the forthcoming Friday, June Eighteenth, in this Year of the Pig, at the approximate hour of eight o'clock, Eastern Standard Time. Kindly be assured furthermore, O most illustrious sire, that a favorable reply at your earliest convenience will be received most humbly and gratefully by the undersigned unworthy suppliant.

In reply, the witty diplomat sent this telegram:

> CAN DO. HU SHI.

Hu Shi's reply disputes a common assumption — that the more words an idea takes, the more impressive it will seem. Most good contemporary writers know that the more succinctly they can state an idea, the clearer and more forceful it will be.

Cut the Fanfare.   Why bother to announce that you're going to say something? Cut the fanfare. We aren't, by the way, attacking the usefulness of transitions that lead readers along.

For more on transitions, see pp. 296–98.

WORDY   As far as getting ready for winter is concerned, I put antifreeze in my car.

REVISED   To get ready for winter, I put antifreeze in my car.

WORDY   The point should be made that . . .
Let me make it perfectly clear that . . .
In this paper I intend to . . .
In conclusion I would like to say that . . .

Be Direct.   The phrases *on the subject of, in regard to, in terms of, as far as . . . is concerned,* and their ilk often lead to wind.

WORDY   He is more or less a pretty outstanding person in regard to good looks.

REVISED   He is strikingly handsome.

Words can also tend to abound after *There is* or *There are*.

WORDY   There are many people who dislike flying.

REVISED   Many people dislike flying.

Use Strong Verbs.   Forms of the verb *be* (*am, is, are, was, were*) followed by a noun or an adjective can make a statement wordy. Such weak verbs can almost always be replaced by active verbs.

WORDY   The Akron game was a disappointment to the fans.

REVISED   The Akron game disappointed the fans.

Use Relative Pronouns with Caution.   When a clause begins with a relative pronoun (*who, which, that*), you often can whittle it to a phrase.

WORDY   Venus, which is the second planet of the solar system, is called the evening star.

REVISED   Venus, the second planet of the solar system, is called the evening star.

Cut Out Deadwood.   The more you revise, the more shortcuts you'll discover. Try reading the sentences below without the words in *italics*.

Howell spoke for the sophomores, and Janet *also spoke* for the seniors.

He is *something of* a clown but *sort of the* lovable *type*.

As a major in *the field of* economics, I plan to concentrate on *the area of* international banking.

The decision as to whether *or not* to go is up to you.

Cut Descriptors.   Adjectives and adverbs are often dispensable. Contrast these two versions:

WORDY   Johnson's extremely significant research led to highly important major discoveries.

REVISED   Johnson's research led to major discoveries.

Be Short, Not Long.   While a long word may convey a shade of meaning that a shorter synonym doesn't, in general shun a long word when you can pick a short one. Instead of *the remainder,* write *the rest;* instead of *activate, start* or *begin;* instead of *adequate* or *sufficient, enough.* Look for the right word — one that wraps an idea in a smaller package.

WORDY   Andy has a left fist that has a lot of power in it.

REVISED   Andy has a potent left.

By the way, it pays to read. From reading, you absorb words like *potent* and set them to work for you.

Here is a list of questions to use in slimming your writing:

REVISION CHECKLIST

___ Are you direct and straightforward?

___ Do you announce an idea before you utter it? If so, consider chopping out the announcement.

___ Can you recast any sentence that begins *There is* or *There are?*

___ Can you substitute an active verb wherever you use a form of the verb *be* (*is, was, were*)?

___ Can you reduce to a phrase any clause beginning with *which, who,* or *that?*

___ Have you used too many adjectives and adverbs?

___ Do you see any long words where short words would do?

John Martin, a business administration major, wrote the following economics paper to fulfill the assignment "Briefly discuss a current problem in international trade. Venture an opinion or propose a solution." You can see the thoughtful cuts and condensations that Martin made with the help of his English instructor and his peer editor. His large changes — macro revisions — are highlighted in the margin. Both these macro revisions and his smaller micro revisions are marked in the text. Following the edited draft you'll find the paper as he resubmitted it — in fewer words.

FIRST DRAFT

Japan's Closed Doors: Should the U.S. Retaliate?

State problem more clearly for readers

~~There is currently a~~ ^Aserious problem ^{is}brewing in ~~the world of~~ international trade.~~which may turn out to be a~~

a cliché to cut ————→

~~real tempest in a teapot, so to speak.~~ According to the

latest National Trade Estimates report, several ~~of the~~
~~countries that the~~ U.S. [trading partners] ~~has been doing business with~~
deserve to be condemned for ~~what the report has charac-~~
~~terized as~~ "unfair trade practices." The government has
said it will use the report to single out ~~specific~~
countries ~~which it is then going to go ahead and~~ [to] punish
under the Super 301 provisions of the trade law.

The Super 301 section ~~of the trade law~~ requires
Carla Hills, ~~who is~~ the U.S. trade representative, to
[attack] ~~try to get rid of~~ what she [calls] ~~has officially designated to~~
~~be~~ "priority unfair practices." She will ~~be~~ slash~~ing~~ at
the ~~whole~~ web of impediments ~~and obstacles~~ that have
[American] ~~slowed down or~~ denied ~~the various products of the~~
~~many United States~~ firms [fast] ~~much~~ access to Japanese markets.

Rework paragraph to move more directly to point about Japan

same as impediments

Some American businesspeople would ~~like to~~ take aim
at Japan immediately. However, Clyde Prestowitz, ~~who is~~ a
former Commerce Department official, ~~seriously~~ doubts
that ~~in the last analysis~~ it would be [wise to] ~~a good idea to come~~
~~out and~~ name Japan [for] ~~to feel the terrible effects of~~ retaliation under Super 301[:] ~~in view of the fact that in his~~
~~opinion,~~ "It's hard to negotiate with guys you are calling cheats." No doubt ~~there are~~ many other observers ~~who~~
share his view.

Move paragraph to follow background

~~It is important for the reader to note here that for~~
~~a long time, longer than anyone can remember,~~ Japan has
[long] been the ~~leading~~ prime candidate for a dose of Super 301.

Strengthen paragraph focus by opening with the point

Over the past decade, ~~there have been many years of nego-~~ ~~tiations and battering by different~~ [have battered] industry groups [with] at the unyielding doors of ~~the~~ Japanese markets, ~~which have~~ ~~yielded~~ some successes, but have ~~pretty much~~ failed ~~mis-~~ ~~erably~~ to [make them swing wide.] ~~dent the invisible trade barriers that stand~~ ~~looming between us and the Japanese markets, preventing~~ ~~the free access of U.S. goods to Japanese consumers. As~~ ~~far as the~~ [The] U.S. trade deficit with Japan ~~is concerned, it~~ ~~was somewhat~~ more than $50 billion last year, ~~and it~~ shows ~~very~~ little sign of [improving] ~~getting significantly much better~~ this year.

~~Evidently it is the task of the~~ [The] administration [has] to try to [help] ~~pave the way for~~ U.S. exports ~~to~~ wedge their way into the protected Japanese markets while keeping ~~it~~ ~~firmly~~ in mind that the interests of both ~~the United~~ [nations] ~~States and Japan~~ call for [stronger] ~~strengthening of the~~ economic and military ties. ~~that bind both countries into a sphere~~ ~~of friendly relationship. It is my personal conclusion~~ [If] ~~that if~~ the administration goes ahead, ~~with this,~~ it will ~~certainly~~ need to plan ~~ahead for the future~~ carefully.

State opinion more clearly to achieve paper's purpose

REVISED VERSION

Japan's Closed Doors: Should the U.S. Retaliate?

A serious problem is brewing in international trade. According to the latest National Trade Estimates report, several U.S. trading partners deserve to be condemned for "unfair trade practices." The government has said it will use the report to single out countries to punish under the Super 301 provisions of the trade law.

The Super 301 section requires Carla Hills, the U.S. trade representative, to attack what she calls "priority unfair practices." She will slash at the web of impediments that have denied American firms fast access to Japanese markets.

Japan has long been the prime candidate for a dose of Super 301. Over the past decade, industry groups have battered at the unyielding doors of Japanese markets, with some success, but have failed to make them swing wide. The U.S. trade deficit with Japan, more than $50 billion last year, shows little sign of improving this year.

Some American businesspeople would take aim at Japan immediately. However, Clyde Prestowitz, a former Commerce Department official, doubts that it would be wise to name Japan for retaliation under Super 301: "It's hard to negotiate with guys you are calling cheats." No doubt many other observers share his view.

The administration has to try to help U.S. exports wedge their way into protected Japanese markets while keeping in mind that the interests of both nations call for stronger economic and military ties. If the administration goes ahead, it will need to plan carefully.

Editing and Proofreading

Editing means correcting and refining grammar, punctuation, and mechanics. Don't edit and proofread too soon. In your early drafting, don't fret over the correct spelling of an unfamiliar word; the word may be revised out in a later version. If the word stays in, you'll have time to check it later. After you have revised, however, you are ready to refine and correct. Proofreading means taking a final look at your paper to check correctness and to catch spelling or word-processing errors. In college, good editing and proofreading can make the difference between a C and an A. On the job, it may help you get a promotion. Readers, teachers, and bosses like careful writers who take time to edit and proofread.

As you edit, whenever you are in doubt as to whether a word or construction is correct, you should consult a good reference handbook. Learn the grammar conventions you don't understand so you can spot and eliminate problems in your own writing. Practice until you easily recognize major errors such as fragments and comma splices. Ask for assistance from a peer editor or a tutor in the writing center if your campus has one. Use the "Quick Editing Guide" at the end of this book to get you started (look for the pages with dark blue edges). It provides a brief overview of troubling grammar, style, punctuation, and mechanics problems typically found in college writing. For each problem, the "Quick Editing Guide" supplies definitions, examples, and a checklist to help you tackle the problem. Here is an editing checklist that gives you an overview of the problems explained there, along with the section letter and number:

EDITING CHECKLIST

Common and Serious Problems in College Writing

For more help, turn to the dark-blue-edged pages, and find the "Quick Editing Guide" section noted here.

Grammar Problems

—— Have you used the correct form for all verbs in the past tense?   A1
—— Do all verbs agree with their subjects?   A2
—— Have you used the correct case for all pronouns?   A3
—— Do all pronouns agree with their antecedents?   A4
—— Have you used adjectives and adverbs correctly?   A5
—— Have you avoided writing sentence fragments?   A6
—— Have you avoided writing comma splices or fused sentences?   A7

Sentence Problems

—— Does each modifier clearly modify the appropriate sentence element?   B1
—— Have you used parallel structure where necessary?   B2

Punctuation Problems

—— Have you used commas correctly?   C1
—— Have you used apostrophes correctly?   C2
—— Have you punctuated quotations correctly?   C3

Mechanics Problems

—— Have you used capital letters correctly?   D1
—— Have you spelled all words correctly?   D2

Format Problems

—— Have you used correct manuscript form?   E1
—— Have you used correct documentation style?   E2

Careful proofreading is especially important because most errors in writing occur unconsciously and easily become habits. If you have never looked closely at the spelling of *environment,* you may never have noticed the second *n.* Split-second inattention or a break in concentration can also cause errors. Because the mind works faster than the pencil (or the word processor), when you are distracted by someone talking or a telephone ringing, you may omit a word or put in the wrong punctuation.

The very way our eyes work also leads to errors. When you read normally, you usually see only the shells of words — the first and last letters. You fix your eyes on the print only three or four times per line or less. To proofread effectively, you must look at the individual letters in each word and the punctuation marks between words without sliding over the individual symbols. Proofreading requires time and patience, but it is a skill you can develop.

TIPS FOR PROOFREADING

1. Realize that *all* writers make mistakes as they put ideas on paper. Making mistakes isn't bad — but not taking time to find and correct them is.
2. Let a paper sit several days, overnight, or at least a few hours before proofreading it.
3. Budget enough time to proofread thoroughly.
4. Read what you have written very slowly, looking at every word and every letter so that you see what you have actually written, not what you think is there.
5. Read your paper aloud. Speaking forces you to slow down and see more, and sometimes you will hear a mistake you haven't seen.
6. Read the essay backward. This will force you to look at each word because you won't get caught up in the flow of ideas.
7. Use a dictionary or a spell checker whenever you can.
8. Double-check for your own habitual errors (such as leaving off *-s* or *-ed* or putting in unnecessary commas).
9. Read your essay several times, focusing each time on a specific area of difficulty (once for spelling, once for punctuation, once for a problem that recurs in your writing).
10. Ask someone else to read your paper and tell you if it is free of errors. But take pride in your own work. *Don't* let someone else do it for you.

Spell checkers are handy tools, but they aren't foolproof. They can't tell you that you've used *their* when you meant *there, affect* when you meant *effect,* or *won* when you meant *own.* Grammar checkers also can alert you to many types of sentence problems, but you have to reason through the suggestions carefully. As the writer, you, not the software, should always have the final word.

WRITING WITH A COMPUTER

Proofreading in Pairs

Select a passage, from this textbook or elsewhere, that is about one hundred words long. Type up the passage, intentionally adding ten errors in grammar, spelling, punctuation, or capitalization. Swap passages with a classmate; proofread, then check each other's work against the originals. Share your proofreading strategies.

■ Exercise

Editing and Proofreading

Read the following passage carefully. Assume that the organization of the paragraph is satisfactory, but look for ten errors in the paragraph. Find these mistakes in sentence structure, grammar, spelling, punctuation, and capitalization, and correct them. After you have corrected the passage, discuss with your classmates the changes you have made and your reasons for making those changes.

> Robert Frost, one of the most popular American poets. He was born in San Francisco in 1874, and died in Boston in 1963. His family moved to new England when his father died in 1885. There he completed highschool and attended colledge but never graduate. Poverty and problems filled his life. He worked in a woolen mill, on a newspaper, and on varous odd jobs. Because of ill health he settled on a farm and began to teach school to support his wife and children. Throughout his life he dedicated himself to writing poetry, by 1915 he was in demand for public readings and speaking engagements. He was awarded the Pulitzer Prize for poetry four times-in 1924, 1931, 1937, and 1943. The popularity of his poetry rests in his use of common themes and images, expressed in everyday language. Everyone can relate to his universal poems, such as "Swinging on Birches" and "Stopping by Woods on a Snowy Evening." Students read his poetry in school from seventh grade through graduate school, so almost everyone recognize lines from his best-loved poems. America is proud of it's son, the homespun poet Robert Frost.

Chapter 21
Strategies for Designing Your Document

Whether the document you prepare is an essay, a research paper, or a business letter, creating an effective design for it helps you achieve your purpose and meet the expectations of your audience. Through your own reading, you may have noticed that you respond differently to documents depending upon their appearance. For example, which of the two newspapers in Figure 21.1 seems more appealing to you?

If you prefer *USA Today*, you're like many Americans — you like the look of a colorful, casual newspaper and may even consider it easier to read. But if someone asked which of the two newspapers seems more credible or trustworthy, many would say the *Wall Street Journal*. Its closely typed text, narrow columns, limited number of pictures, and serious black-and-white graphs and charts create a look more "respectable" than that of the open, friendly *USA Today* with its abundant pictures, colored graphics, and playful tone. As you can see, the same features that make the *Wall Street Journal* seem more credible than *USA Today* may also make it less inviting to read. Like other newspapers, however, the *Wall Street Journal* freely uses headlines, short paragraphs, white space, page numbers, and other visual markers that help the reader determine the structure of the text at a glance and decide where to plunge in. Without such visual markers, the pages of the *Wall Street Journal* would provide the reader few pathways into its content.

Occasionally, college students are assigned a composition that looks and reads like a newspaper. But most of the papers you will write are not as visually complex as the *Wall Street Journal* or *USA Today*. Instead of calling for visual markers like multiple columns, headlines, and graphs, your teacher will most likely expect to see double-spacing, one-inch margins, numbered pages, and indented block quotations. Many of these visual markers are typical features of college compositions. Figure 21.2 shows two pages — the first page and the list of sources — of a typical college composition that follows the guidelines of the Modern Language Association (MLA).

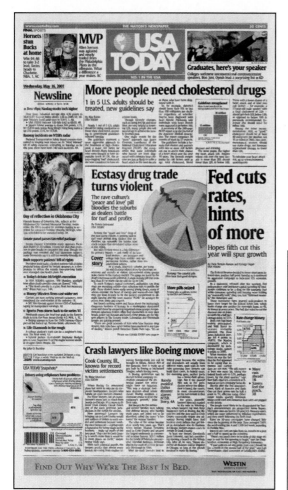

Figure 21.1
Front pages of USA Today *and the* Wall Street Journal

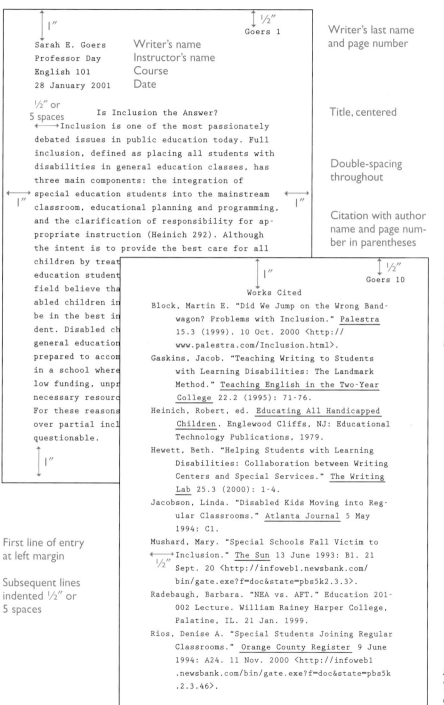

1"

↕ ½"
Goers 1

Sarah E. Goers
Professor Day
English 101
28 January 2001

Writer's name
Instructor's name
Course
Date

Writer's last name
and page number

½" or
5 spaces   Is Inclusion the Answer?

Title, centered

Inclusion is one of the most passionately
debated issues in public education today. Full
inclusion, defined as placing all students with
disabilities in general education classes, has
three main components: the integration of
special education students into the mainstream
classroom, educational planning and programming,
and the clarification of responsibility for appropriate instruction (Heinich 292). Although
the intent is to provide the best care for all
children by treat
education student
field believe tha
abled children i
be in the best i
dent. Disabled ch
general education
prepared to accom
in a school where
low funding, unpr
necessary resourc
For these reasons
over partial incl
questionable.

1"

1"

1"

Double-spacing
throughout

Citation with author
name and page num-
ber in parentheses

List of works cited on a
separate page

1"

↕ ½"
Goers 10

Works Cited
Block, Martin E. "Did We Jump on the Wrong Band-
    wagon? Problems with Inclusion." Palestra
    15.3 (1999). 10 Oct. 2000 <http://
    www.palestra.com/Inclusion.html>.
Gaskins, Jacob. "Teaching Writing to Students
    with Learning Disabilities: The Landmark
    Method." Teaching English in the Two-Year
    College 22.2 (1995): 71-76.
Heinich, Robert, ed. Educating All Handicapped
    Children. Englewood Cliffs, NJ: Educational
    Technology Publications, 1979.
Hewett, Beth. "Helping Students with Learning
    Disabilities: Collaboration between Writing
    Centers and Special Services." The Writing
    Lab 25.3 (2000): 1-4.
Jacobson, Linda. "Disabled Kids Moving into Reg-
    ular Classrooms." Atlanta Journal 5 May
    1994: C1.
Mushard, Mary. "Special Schools Fall Victim to
    Inclusion." The Sun 13 June 1993: B1. 21
    Sept. 20 <http://infoweb1.newsbank.com/
    bin/gate.exe?f=doc&state=pbs5k2.3.3>.
Radebaugh, Barbara. "NEA vs. AFT." Education 201-
    002 Lecture. William Rainey Harper College,
    Palatine, IL. 21 Jan. 1999.
Rios, Denise A. "Special Students Joining Regular
    Classrooms." Orange County Register 9 June
    1994: A24. 11 Nov. 2000 <http://infoweb1
    .newsbank.com/bin/gate.exe?f=doc&state=pbs5k
    .2.3.46>.

½"

Centered heading

List alphabetized by
author's last name

First line of entry
at left margin

Subsequent lines
indented ½" or
5 spaces

Figure 21.2
The first page and Works
Cited page of a student
research paper in MLA
format

Understanding Four Basic Principles of Document Design

Four key principles of document design will help you to produce effective documents in and out of the classroom. Use the following questions based on these principles to help you plan an appropriate design for your college papers or other documents:

DISCOVERY CHECKLIST

___ Who are your readers? What are their key concerns? How might your document design highlight their concerns?

___ What form or genre do readers expect? What features do readers see as typical characteristics of that form?

___ What problems or constraints will your readers face? How can your document design help to address these constraints?

___ What is the purpose of your document? How can your document design help you to achieve this purpose?

PRINCIPLE 1: KNOW YOUR READERS

For questions to help identify your readers, see p. 321.

Whether you are writing an essay for class or preparing an entirely different type of document, identifying your audience is a good first step toward creating an effective design. For most papers that you write in a first-year composition course, your primary reader is your teacher and your secondary readers include your peers. For some assignments, you might be asked to include other readers as well.

For more on purpose and audience, see pp. 12–14.

Suppose you've written a paper explaining the benefits of a longer school year to a real-world audience. An audience of concerned parents would have different concerns than an audience of community leaders or of school officials or teachers. Teachers, for example, would need to be assured that their paychecks would keep pace with the longer work year. The school board would need to be convinced that the increased costs of teacher salaries, building operations, and transportation would pay off in higher student achievement. And other community leaders might want to know how such a move might affect community safety, traffic congestion, and seasonal employment rates.

In deciding how best to design your document, you might consider how to highlight the key concerns of your particular audience, perhaps using headings, white space, and variations in type style. You might also consider whether your audience is likely to read carefully every word of your argument or to skim it for key points. Perhaps visuals such as tables, graphs, or diagrams would help you to make information more accessible. Thinking about such issues as you plan and draft means you'll have a better chance of reaching your audience.

PRINCIPLE 2: SATISFY YOUR READER'S EXPECTATIONS

When you think about a newspaper, a particular type of publication comes to mind because the newspaper is a familiar *genre*, or form. As Figure 21.3 shows, almost all newspapers share a set of defined features, such as a masthead, headlines, pictures with captions, and articles arranged in columns of text. Even if specific details of the form vary, both publications are still recognized as newspapers. Similarly, *Forbes* and *Mademoiselle* both belong to the genre of the magazine: both feature glossy pages, articles arranged in columns, quotes pulled from the text and set in larger type, and many color and black-and-white photographs. Despite their significantly different content, the two magazines share a common genre identification, as Figure 21.4 illustrates.

For samples of workplace genres, see Ch. 14.

Like the newspaper and the magazine, the college composition paper can be thought of as a genre. Readers, including your teacher and your peers, have expectations about what topics are appropriate for such documents, how they should be written, and how they should look. Check your course syllabus to see whether your instructor has supplied specific guidelines for document design.

For advice about a general format for papers, see E1 in the "Quick Editing Guide" (the dark-blue-edged pages).

Usually your readers expect your paper to be word-processed and its pages numbered. Other conventions may also be expected. Some teachers want you to include a cover page with your name, the title of your paper, your course number and section, the date, and perhaps other information. Others may prefer that you follow the Modern Language Association (MLA) paper format, simply supplying a four-line identifier at the top left of the first page along with a centered title. Some teachers will ask you to include your name or a shortened title with the page number at the top or bottom of each page. Unless your teacher encourages unusual or creative formatting, don't experiment too much with the appearance of a college paper.

For sample pages from an MLA paper, see Figure 21.2 on p. 337.

Although you should follow carefully any specific guidelines that your instructor supplies, genre features are somewhat flexible. For example, you might use a larger, bolded font for your paper title or use underlining or boldface to set off your subheadings. Perhaps you might want to separate your page numbers from the rest of the page with a horizontal line, or insert a little extra white space between your paragraphs. Any of these features could help to make your standard paper distinctive and easier for your teacher to read.

Masthead   Photograph

Figure 21.3
Common features in newspaper design

Caption

Headline

Text columns

Headline   Masthead

Photograph

Caption

Text columns

Quote pulled from the text

Photograph

Text columns

Figure 21.4
Common features in magazine design: page spread from Forbes, April 2, 2001 (top) and Mademoiselle, October 1999 (bottom)

Text columns

Photograph

Quote pulled from the text

PRINCIPLE 3: CONSIDER YOUR READER'S CONSTRAINTS

Your teacher has probably requested that you print your paper in a crisp, black 12-point-size type, double-spaced, on one side of a white sheet of paper with one-inch margins. You also may be asked to reprint a paper if you use a nearly empty toner cartridge. Before accusing your teacher of being overly picky, remember that your teacher may read and grade compositions in batches of a hundred or more. Papers that follow the standard format are easier on the eyes than those in other formats. In addition, in order to grade your paper, your teacher needs sufficient margin space for comments. If you try to save paper by using a smaller font, narrower margins, or single spacing, the paper may be not only more difficult to read but also harder for your teacher to grade.

When you address readers besides your teacher, they too will read your document under some constraints. Some may read your document on a computer screen if it arrives as an e-mail attachment. Others may need to skim a text's main points quickly during the morning commute or sort through a stack of résumés before lunch. Just as you want to produce a well-written paper that addresses your reader's information needs, you also want to produce a usable, readable paper — one that the reader can readily absorb regardless of constraints. Don't let poor document design interfere with the effectiveness of your text.

PRINCIPLE 4: REMEMBER YOUR PURPOSE

For more on purpose, see pp. 12–14 and 320.

Like most writers, you have a particular theme, argument, or point of view in mind that you want to convey to your readers. As you consider your readers, their expectations for your text, and the conditions under which they will be reading it, your challenge is to take your readers' needs and expectations into account and to write convincingly. Good document design is no substitute for a clear and well-organized essay, but it can help you achieve your purpose or reason for writing. The rest of this chapter will explain how to use document design to enhance the message you are trying to convey.

Creating an Effective Design for Your Document

When you design a document, you use tools such as typography, white space, headings, repetition, and visuals. Although you may not be used to thinking about design issues, you already make design choices whenever you type something in your word processor. *Typography* refers to the appearance of typeset letters on a page. When you put something in boldface type, use all capital letters, or change type size, you are making a typographic choice. Such choices can make your document clearer and more attractive, but inappropriate use or overuse of an option can clutter your work. What follows are guidelines for making effective design choices so that your document achieves your purpose and appeals to your audience.

CHOOSING FONTS

Current word-processing software allows you to change typefaces, commonly called *fonts*, to increase readability, achieve special effects, add emphasis, or set a particular tone in your writing. Figure 21.5 shows the same sentence written in four different 12-point fonts: Times New Roman, Courier New, Arial, and Comic Sans MS. Although the examples are all written in the same point size, notice that the typefaces occupy different amounts of horizontal space on the page.

Serif or Sans Serif Fonts.   Times New Roman and Courier New are called *serif* fonts. A serif font has small tails, or serifs, at the ends of the letters. Arial and Comic Sans MS, in contrast, are categorized as *sans serif*—without serifs. These fonts have solid, straight lines and no serifs at the tips of the letters. You can see the difference between a serif and sans serif font in these examples:

Times New Roman (serif) B b C c   Arial (sans serif) B b C c

Sans serif fonts have a clean look, but they are less readable than serif fonts, especially in long passages. If you look over your local newspaper, you may notice a combination of serif and sans serif fonts. Typically, sans serif fonts are used for headlines and other display type, such as advertisements and "pull quotes" (interesting quotations that are "pulled out" of an article and printed in larger text to catch the reader's attention). On the other hand,

Times New Roman	An estimated 40 percent of young children have an imaginary friend.
Courier New	An estimated 40 percent of young children have an imaginary friend.
Arial	An estimated 40 percent of young children have an imaginary friend.
Comic Sans MS	An estimated 40 percent of young children have an imaginary friend.

Figure 21.5
Space occupied by different typefaces

Figure 21.6
Sans serif heading used
with serif body font.
Source: Kiplinger's,
February 2000

Watching TV with a Critical Eye

By second grade, kids have figured out, often from personal experience, that the toys they see in commercials don't always measure up in real life. Children this age are old enough to get into more sophisticated discussions about fact and opinion. [. . .]

most newspapers choose serif fonts for their article (or "body") text. In fact, Times New Roman, which is the default font on many word processors, is used by and named after the *New York Times*. Other common serif fonts include Palatino and New Century Schoolbook. A combination of fonts can provide the maximum readability and emphasis, as Figure 21.6 shows.

If you decide to combine two different fonts, keep these points in mind:

- Serif and sans serif fonts can be combined in the same document, though document designers recommend using only one of each.
- For further emphasis, you may vary the type size or type style, such as italics or bold, for each font.

For more on typefaces in visual images, see pp. 366–69.

Novelty Fonts.   For college writing, professional writing, and most writing you will do as a member of your community, novelty fonts are inappropriate. Comic Sans MS is a novelty font, as are *Brush Script* and **Tempus Sans**. While these casual, playful typefaces may suit some writing situations, novelty fonts can set the wrong tone for your paper, especially if your subject matter is either very technical or very serious.

For example, if you are writing a paper about the death penalty, Comic Sans MS might suggest that readers don't need to take your arguments seriously or that you lack respect for a serious subject. Figure 21.7 shows two versions of the same text—one set in Times New Roman, which is appropriate for an academic setting, and the other set in Comic Sans MS, which generally is not. In academic or other serious writing, stick with standard fonts that are familiar to readers and that convey a professional demeanor.

Italics.   When you *italicize* a word or a passage, you call the reader's attention to it.

- Use italics for book, film, or software titles.
    My favorite novel is *Wuthering Heights.*
- Use italics for foreign words.
    My Finnish grandmother called me *Kultani* ("my golden one").

Times New Roman	*Comic Sans MS*
The United States and the Death Penalty	The United States and the Death Penalty
The death penalty is legal in thirty-eight states, but nine of those states have not executed any death-row prisoners in the past twenty years ("Capital Punishment Statistics"). By early November 2000, eleven states had invoked the death penalty. Texas had the most executions—thirty-four—more than three times as many as Oklahoma's eleven ("USA Executions 2000").	The death penalty is legal in thirty-eight states, but nine of those states have not executed any death-row prisoners in the past twenty years ("Capital Punishment Statistics"). By early November 2000, eleven states had invoked the death penalty. Texas had the most executions—thirty-four—more than three times as many as Oklahoma's eleven ("USA Executions 2000").

Figure 21.7   Identical text set in two fonts
Sources: "Capital Punishment Statistics." Bureau of Justice Statistics. 13 February 2001. U.S. Dept of Justice. 20 March 2001. <www.ojp.usdoj.gov/bjs/cp.htm>. "USA Executions 2000." Rick Halperin. Death Penalty News & Updates. 21 March 2001. 22 March 2001. <www.smu.edu/deathpen/exec00.html>.

- Use italics for a new technical or scientific term the first time you use it, and also provide a definition for the reader. After that, use regular type without emphasis.

> AIDS patients monitor their levels of *helper T-cells* because these cells detect antigens in the body and activate other cells to fight the antigens. Because HIV destroys helper T-cells, this information indicates the status of a patient's immune system.

In a text, *italicized words* appear lighter in weight than nonitalicized words. This lightness, coupled with the slant of the letters, makes italics unsuitable for sustained reading. Use italics for emphasis, not for large blocks of text.

Boldface Type.   Boldface type is suitable for emphasis only. Too much boldface produces the "raisin bread" effect, a random scattering of dark spots across a light page, illustrated in Figure 21.8.

This random scattering of boldface raisins in your text encourages the reader to "hear" the words as emphasized, creating in a choppy and unnatural rhythm. Many teachers expect you to choose emphatic words, not to rely on boldface type for emphasis in academic papers. In other documents, be selective about using boldface, highlighting only words that you want the reader to see or "hear" with emphasis added. In general, reserve boldface

Figure 21.8
The raisin-bread effect
produced by too much
boldface

Treating Carpal Tunnel Syndrome

Physicians **generally** suggest one of **three** methods of treating patients with carpal tunnel syndrome. **First,** reducing the amount of repeated **wrist** movement **can** allow the median nerve to heal. **This** can be accomplished by changing habits or **positions** or by using a wrist **splint**. . . .

---

type primarily for headings, for key points in a list of reasons or factors, or for other similar uses.

> **The first reason is longevity.**   People are living longer today, so Social Security funds need to stretch to accommodate these longer lives.

> **The second reason is inflation.**   Dollars paid into the system in 1980 are not worth as much today, and interest on the fund has not kept pace with the growing need for the dollars.

PREPARING LISTS

Lists can make information in your document easily accessible for readers. Lists are easiest to read when they are displayed rather than integrated.

INTEGRATED LIST   Movies are rated by the film rating board of the Classification and Rating Administration (CARA) based on several criteria, including these: overall theme, use of language, presence of violence, presence of nudity and sexual content, and combined use of these elements in the context of an individual film.

DISPLAYED LIST   Movies are rated by the film rating board of the Classification and Rating Administration (CARA) based on several criteria, including these:
- overall theme
- use of language
- presence of violence
- presence of nudity and sexual content
- combined use of these elements in the context of an individual film

Bulleted List.   One type of displayed list uses a mark called a *bullet* to set off a fragment of information. The most common bullet is the small round one often available in a word processor's bulleted list function (•).

Use a bulleted list to enumerate steps, reasons, or items, especially when the order isn't significant, as in this example:

Controversy surrounding the 2000 presidential election climaxed in Florida, where several balloting issues converged.

- A controversial Palm Beach County ballot was blamed for several thousand votes possibly cast in error for a third-party candidate, Pat Buchanan.

- A Florida law triggered a statewide ballot recount when the votes for the two main candidates were separated by less than 1 percent.

- Outstanding absentee ballots had to be counted to determine which candidate had received the most votes.

Numbered List.   Another type of displayed list, the numbered list, can emphasize the importance of sequence, especially in activity plans, how-to advice, instructional writing, or other process descriptions. Here is a simplified sequence of activities for making an article of clothing:

1. Select your pattern and fabric.
2. Lay out the pattern and pin it to the fabric, paying careful attention to the arrows and grain lines.
3. Cut out the fabric pieces following the outline of the pattern.
4. Sew the garment together following the pattern's step-by-step instructions.

USING WHITE SPACE STRATEGICALLY

White space is just that: space within a document that is free of text. Areas of blank space give the eye a rest and can frame important information. As a design device, white space allows you to place emphasis where it is needed and to guide the reader's progress through your document.

For more about white space in visual images, see p. 364. For sample workplace documents using white space, see Ch. 14.

For sample pages from an academic paper, see p. 337.

If you have already written college papers, you have probably used white space to assist your readers. For example, one-inch margins and double spacing provide some respite for the reader's eyes. When you indent the first lines of all your paragraphs, the extra white space helps the reader differentiate one paragraph from the next. Indenting an extended quotation sets it off and marks it as a special kind of text. As you can see in Figure 21.9, white space is crucial to the appearance of your papers.

The single-spaced example on the top of Figure 21.9 is much too cramped. Besides interfering with readers' ability to keep their place in the text, the closely spaced lines and lack of white space might intimidate readers. When all of the text elements are close together and look fairly uniform, finding a place to enter can feel like trying to merge onto a congested freeway. Some readers may give up if they don't see openings where they can easily jump in and begin to navigate your text.

The double-spaced example on the bottom is less cramped than the single-spaced version. The title is close enough to the text to introduce it but not so close as to create congestion for the reader. The double-spaced body text is easy to read, as is the indented block quotation. Finally, the para-

Figure 21.9
Single-spaced and double-spaced versions of the same text. For sources, see Figure 21.7.

Single-spaced

The United States and the Death Penalty

The death penalty is legal in thirty-eight states, but nine of those states have not executed any death-row prisoners in the past twenty years ("Capital Punishment Statistics"). By early November 2000, eleven states had invoked the death penalty. Texas—had the most executions—thirty-four—more than three times as many as Oklahoma's eleven ("USA Executions 2000").

Six of the 29 states that had executed criminals since 1977—Florida, Louisiana, Missouri, Texas, Virginia, and Georgia—conducted 70 percent of all the executions. Geographically, executions are highly concentrated in Southern states ("Capital Punishment Statistics").

When it was reintroduced in 1976, the death penalty was subject to federal standards to a greater extent than had been the case before 1972 ("Capital Punishment Statistics").

Double-spaced

The United States and the Death Penalty

The death penalty is legal in thirty-eight states, but nine of those states have not executed any death-row prisoners in the past twenty years ("Capital Punishment Statistics"). By early November 2000, eleven states had invoked the death penalty. Texas had the most executions—thirty-four—more than three times as many as Oklahoma's eleven ("USA Executions 2000").

Six of the 29 states that had executed criminals since 1977—Florida, Louisiana, Missouri, Texas, Virginia, and Georgia—conducted 70 percent of all the executions. Geographically, executions are highly concentrated in Southern states ("Capital Punishment Statistics").

When it was reintroduced in 1976, the death penalty was subject to federal standards to a greater extent than had been the case before 1972 ("Capital Punishment Statistics").

graph indentation gives the reader a visual indication of where a new idea begins. Overall, the reader can see a place to jump in—a little bit of breathing room within the text. On the other hand, watch what happens when a writer uses too much white space in a paper, as in Figure 21.10.

If you simply separate sections of your paper by hitting the Enter key an extra time or two—especially if your paper is double-spaced—you will add too much white space between sections, which may interfere with your readers' perception of your paper as a cohesive unit. In Figure 21.10, the extra white space after the title and around the quotation interrupts the natural

---

The United States and the Death Penalty

The death penalty is legal in thirty-eight states, but nine of those states

have not executed any death-row prisoners in the past twenty years ("Capi-

tal Punishment Statistics"). By early November 2000, eleven states had in-

voked the death penalty. Texas had the most executions—thirty-four—

more than three times as many as Oklahoma's eleven ("USA Executions

2000").

Six of the 29 states that had executed criminals since 1977—Florida,
Louisiana, Missouri, Texas, Virginia, and Georgia—conducted 70 percent of all the executions. Geographically, executions are highly concentrated in Southern states ("Capital Punishment Statistics").

When it was reintroduced in 1976, the death penalty was subject to federal

standards to a greater extent than had been the case before 1972 ("Capital

Punishment Statistics").

Figure 21.10
Text with too much white space. For sources, see Figure 21.7.

flow of the paper because the reader's eye must leap over a gap to get to the next part of the text. This trapped white space functions only to prevent the reader's eye from making natural connections within the text.

USING HEADINGS AND ALIGNMENT

The visual markers in your document can help your reader navigate. Headings and subheadings show a document's hierarchy, and appropriate alignment guides the reader's eye.

Heading Levels.   The relative size and prominence of the section headings indicate how a document is organized and which sections are most important. Headings also name the sections so that readers know where they are and where they are going. Though headings are often unnecessary in short essays, they can provide a useful pathway through complex documents such as research papers, lab reports, business proposals, and Web-based documents.

Use typographical elements to distinguish clearly between levels of headings and subheadings within your document. Once you decide what a major section (or *level-one*) heading should look like—boldfaced and italicized, for example—be consistent throughout your document. Be consistent with minor section headings as well. In this textbook, you'll notice that all of the major headings within a chapter are set like this:

Level-One Heading   [17-point, boldfaced, italicized, in color]

Level-two and level-three headings are set like this:

LEVEL-TWO HEADING   [12-point, capitalized, boldfaced]

Level-Three Heading   [10-point, boldfaced]

Each of these styles is used consistently through the book in order to offer readers visual cues to both content and organization. The headings differ from each other and from the main text in size, style, and—for the level-one headings—color. Differentiating headings in such ways makes your text easier to read and easier to use whether your reader is scrutinizing every word or scanning only key points.

If your instructor asks you to follow the guidelines of a particular style, you may have less flexibility in formatting headings. For example, MLA does not recommend headings or discuss their formatting. On the other hand, the American Psychological Association (APA) illustrates five levels of headings, all in the same regular font style and size as the body text but varying capitalization, placement (centered or left), and underlining to distinguish the levels.

For more on MLA style, see E2 in the "Quick Editing Guide," consult the MLA Handbook for Writers of Research Papers, or go to <www.mla.org/style>. For more on APA style, consult the Publication Manual of the American Psychological Association or <www.apastyle.org>.

Heading Consistency.   The headings in your document should be brief, clear, and informative. The four most common styles of headings are *-ing* phrases, noun phrases, questions, and imperative sentences. Effective writers maintain consistent parallel phrasing, regardless of the style they choose. In other words, if you write a level-one heading as an *-ing* phrase, make certain that all of the level-one headings that follow are also *-ing* phrases.

Here are some examples of each style of heading:

For more on parallelism, see B2 in the "Quick Editing Guide" (the dark-blue-edged pages).

-ING PHRASES

Using the College Catalog

Choosing Courses

Declaring a Major

NOUN PHRASES

The Benefits of Electronic Commerce

The Challenges of Electronic Commerce

The Characteristics of the E-Consumer

QUESTIONS

What Is Hepatitis C?

Who Is at Risk?

How Is Hepatitis C Treated?

IMPERATIVE SENTENCES

Initiate Your IRA Rollover

Learn Your Distribution Options

Select New Investments

Heading Alignment.   Besides being consistently styled and phrased, headings should also be consistently placed. MLA guidelines recommend centering the document's title but offer no suggestions for headings. While you might be tempted to center all of your headings, doing so may introduce nonfunctional white space that detracts from the effectiveness of your paper. Instead, rely on the graphic designer's principle of alignment: each element should be aligned with at least one other item, rather than having an alignment all its own.

But centering *is* an alignment, you might protest. Indeed, centering all of your headings and subheadings should create a uniform alignment throughout your paper. Except in cases of coincidence, however, each centered heading will be of a different length and thus will have a different alignment, as you can see in Figure 21.11, top.

In contrast, in Figure 21.11, bottom, the headings are positioned at the left margin (or "flush left," as the designers call it) to create a strong line down the left side of the page. This line helps keep the reader's eye moving downward and forward through the paper. The indented paragraphs also line up with each other, creating another strong alignment on the page. The text itself is left justified — that is, it lines up along the left margin.

In Figure 21.12, the text in the top section is left justified; the text in the middle section is right justified; and the text in the bottom section is fully justified, running out to both the left and right margins.

Much of the time you will use both left-justified text and left-justified headings in your document. Right-justified text is rare in a college paper, except for special elements such as running headers and footers (discussed p. 353). Some people like the tidy look of fully justified text, but you should use it with caution. The computer justifies text by adding extra white space between words and by hyphenating words that don't fit on a line; both of these techniques make text more difficult to read. Many teachers prefer left justification only and no automatic hyphenation, as the MLA guidelines advise.

USING REPETITION PURPOSEFULLY

Though common in poetry and in technical writing, verbal repetition is frowned upon in most academic writing. *Visual* repetition, on the other hand, can be helpful to a reader. If you were driving along a freeway and the

Figure 21.11   Centered headings (no strong alignment) compared with left-justified title, headings, and text (strong alignment). Source: "The Progressive Party Platform of 1912." From National Party Platforms 1840–1964. *Kirk H. Porter and Donald Bruce Johnson, comps. U of Illinois P., 1966. 175–78.*

The Progressive Party Platform of 1912

The Rule of the People

The National Progressive party, committed to the principles of government by a self-controlled democracy expressing its will through representatives of the people, pledges itself to secure such alterations in the fundamental law of the several States and the United States as shall insure the representative character of the government.

In particular, the party declares for direct primaries for the nomination of State and National officers; for nationwide preferential primaries for candidates for presidency; for the direct election of the United States Senators by the people; and we urge on the States the policy of the short ballot, with responsibility to the people secured by the initiative, referendum and recall.

Amendment of Constitution

The Progressive party, believing that a free people should have the power from time to time to amend their fundamental law so as to adapt it progressively to the changing needs of the people, pledges itself to provide a more easy and expeditious method of amending the Federal Constitution. . . .

Equal Suffrage

The Progressive party, believing that no people can justly claim to be a true democracy which denies political rights on account of sex, pledges itself to the task of securing equal suffrage to men and women alike.

The Progressive Party Platform of 1912

The Rule of the People

The National Progressive party, committed to the principles of government by a self-controlled democracy expressing its will through representatives of the people, pledges itself to secure such alterations in the fundamental law of the several States and the United States as shall insure the representative character of the government.

In particular, the party declares for direct primaries for the nomination of State and National officers; for nationwide preferential primaries for candidates for presidency; for the direct election of the United States Senators by the people; and we urge on the States the policy of the short ballot, with responsibility to the people secured by the initiative, referendum and recall.

Amendment of Constitution

The Progressive party, believing that a free people should have the power from time to time to amend their fundamental law so as to adapt it progressively to the changing needs of the people, pledges itself to provide a more easy and expeditious method of amending the Federal Constitution. . . .

Equal Suffrage

The Progressive party, believing that no people can justly claim to be a true democracy which denies political rights on account of sex, pledges itself to the task of securing equal suffrage to men and women alike.

familiar navigation signs — the green and white rectangles — suddenly changed to purple triangles, you might wonder whether you had strayed into a different country. Similarly, if the font or alignment suddenly changes in a paper, the reader immediately asks: What is this new navigational cue? What am I expected to do now?

To avoid disorienting readers, you can repeat one or two fonts throughout your paper to sustain a clean and uncluttered look. Consistent headings and subheadings throughout a document also serve as a kind of roadmap to

---

The Progressive Party Platform of 1912

The Rule of the People

The National Progressive party, committed to the principles of government by a self-controlled democracy expressing its will through representatives of the people, pledges itself to secure such alterations in the fundamental law of the several States and the United States as shall insure the representative character of the government.

In particular, the party declares for direct primaries for the nomination of State and National officers; for nationwide preferential primaries for candidates for presidency; for the direct election of the United States Senators by the people; and we urge on the States the policy of the short ballot, with responsibility to the people secured by the initiative, referendum and recall.

Amendment of Constitution

The Progressive party, believing that a free people should have the power from time to time to amend their fundamental law so as to adapt it progressively to the changing needs of the people, pledges itself to provide a more easy and expeditious method of amending the Federal Constitution. . . .

Equal Suffrage

The Progressive party, believing that no people can justly claim to be a true democracy which denies political rights on account of sex, pledges itself to the task of securing equal suffrage to men and women alike.

Figure 21.12   Centered title with left, right, and full justification of text. For source, see Figure 21.11.

---

guide the readers' progress. Another simple design strategy is the use of running, or repeated, headers and footers. A *running header* is any information that appears consistently at the top of each page of your document. Check the top of this page and the few after or before it to see what sort of information is included in this book's running header. Figure 21.13 illustrates the type of header required in MLA style. Some writers use a *running footer*, which appears consistently at the bottom of each page of a document. As either part of the header or the footer, writers sometimes include information such as the document title, its file name, or a distinctive graphic. Once you create a running header or footer, your word processor can automatically insert it on each page with the page number, if you've selected that option, or with the date.

Fallon 2

Claremont's third message is that activism is needed to combat this

terrorism and hatred, and he provides clear models for activism. . . .

*Figure 21.13
Sample running header in MLA style*

Using Visuals to Reinforce Your Content

Some documents that you write may benefit from the addition of graphs, diagrams, maps, photographs, or other materials that add visual interest and also convey information or reinforce your point. Visual materials should be appropriate for your purpose and your audience, not used as decoration.

ADDING VISUALS

When could your document benefit from visuals? To answer this question, think about the ways in which visual material can support your point.

- To illustrate a trend or relationship — the number of school-aged children who use the Internet or the ratio of men to women at your college — create a chart or graph in a spreadsheet and include it in your paper.
- To discuss a conflict in a certain geographical area, supply a map.
- To clarify the stages or steps in a process, include a diagram.
- To illustrate an autobiographical essay, scan an image of yourself as a baby or at some important moment in your life.

In an essay arguing for increased funding for alternative energy sources, one writer used the graph in Figure 21.14 to illustrate the high demand for residential heating oil in New England one winter.

Regional Residential Heating Oil Prices

Figure 21.14
A graph showing the high demand for residential heating oil in New England from October 1999 to March 2000.
Source: Energy Information Administration/State Energy Office Data
<www.eia.doe.gov/pub/ oil_gas/petroleum/ presentations/2000/ senate022400/ senate022400.htm>

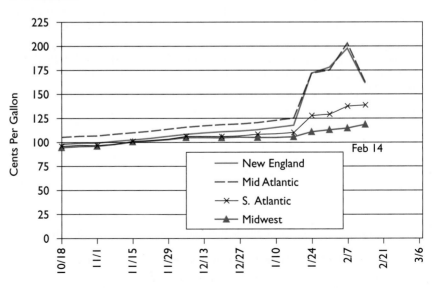

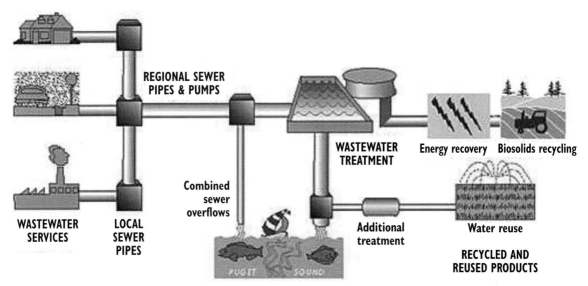

Figure 21.15   A diagram showing the process of wastewater treatment in King County, Washington. Source: King County, Washington, Department of Natural Resources Wastewater Treatment Division <dnr.metrokc .gov/wtd/ntf/link.htm>

Another student, examining the wastewater treatment process in King County, Washington, included the diagram in Figure 21.15 in her paper.

CREDITING SOURCES

If you include visual materials from another source, printed or electronic, credit that source in your essay. Be sure to ask permission, if required, to use an image so that you don't risk violating the copyright. If you download an image from the Web, check the site for its guidelines for the use of images. Follow these guidelines, asking permission if necessary and giving credit to the owner of the copyright. If you are uncertain about whether you can use an image from a source, check with your teacher.

For more on the MLA documentation style, see E2 in the "Quick Editing Guide" (the dark-blue-edged pages).

ARRANGING VISUALS AND TEXT IN YOUR DOCUMENT

Using visuals can create problems in *layout,* the arrangement of text and graphics on a page. Here are some guidelines for ensuring that your layout is effective and appropriate for your purpose and audience.

Integration of Visuals and Text.   Keep in mind that you are including the visual as support for an idea and that your reader will make better sense of the graph, chart, diagram, or photograph if you provide a context for it. In an introductory sentence, you should give your reader this information:

- The number or letter of the visual (for example, Figure 6)
- Its location (on page 9, in section 3)

- Its content
- The point that it helps you to make

Also supply a label with your visual to identify its topic and number.

Placement and Alignment of the Visual. Keep your reader's needs in mind. Placing the visual close to the related discussion will make your document easier to follow. Readers can get easily distracted if they must flip from the body of your text to an appendix, for example. If your headings and text are aligned at the left margin to sustain a strong forward flow through the document, you may not want to disrupt the flow by centering your visuals. Let your eye be the judge.

Balance between Visuals and Text. The visuals should support, not overshadow, the content of your paper. Try to strike a balance between the size of any single graphic or image and related chunks of text. Though your reader's eye should be drawn to the visual, try to give it an appropriate — rather than excessive — share of the page layout.

Consider the following questions as you design your document:

DOCUMENT DESIGN CHECKLIST

___ Does your document design meet your readers' needs and acknowledge their constraints?

___ Does your document design help to achieve your purpose, or reason for writing? Does it help emphasize your key points and demonstrate a clear organization?

___ Have you used appropriate fonts, or typefaces, in your document? Do you use boldface and italic type sparingly for emphasis? Have you used displayed lists when appropriate to call out information?

WRITING WITH A COMPUTER

As a genre, the college composition has certain typical visual features, such as double spacing, one-inch margins, and left-justified text. You can easily apply these features to your papers by creating a template to use for all papers with the same specifications.

First, format your paper the way you want it to look. Then, create a template that you can access any time you create a new document. Depending on your word processor, you will follow a sequence like the following:

1. Create a duplicate copy of your formatted file.
2. Delete all of the text in the document.
3. Save this file as a document template.
4. Give the template a name, such as "English paper" or "Paper form."

The format for this paper will be stored in a folder for document templates. The template will be called whatever you named it when you saved it. When you create a new file, this template will be among your choices. You won't have to recreate the format every time; simply select the template.

___ Does the white space in your document work strategically, calling attention to or linking certain portions of text rather than creating gaps between textual elements?

___ Do your headings, subheadings, and alignment provide your reader with clear and purposeful navigational cues?

___ Have you used repeated elements, such as running headers or footers, that increase visual coherence?

___ Have you used visuals to reinforce the content in your document? Does your layout integrate the visuals using appropriate placement, sizing, and alignment?

___ Have you secured any permission needed to use copyrighted material? Have you credited the source of each visual?

■ Exercises

1. Experiment with the fonts that are available on your computer. Using a paragraph or two from a recent paper, go through the font list to see how your sentences look in each of the fonts available to you. Test different sizes, as well as the bold and italic versions. How readable is each font?

2. Look at a bulletin board, literature rack, magazine display, or other location where many different examples of printed material are displayed. Identify several different uses of fonts to establish a mood or convey a message. Select one example that you find particularly effective, and explain how the font helps to convey the desired mood or message to the audience.

3. Using your favorite search engine (AltaVista or Yahoo!, for example), locate an online example of a research paper or report. (The keywords "research paper" or "research report" should return several examples.) Or find a technical or government report in the library. Read the abstract or introduction to get an idea of the author's message, and then quickly skim the report in order to answer the following questions:

   a. What is the purpose of the report?
   b. Who is the intended audience or reader? How can you tell?
   c. In what ways did the author use document design strategies to address the reader's needs and constraints?
   d. What document design decisions did the author make to get his or her own point across?
   e. What design revisions would you recommend to the author? How might these changes improve the reading experience of the intended audience?

4. Assemble several different documents that you are reading or might read — perhaps a textbook, a newspaper, a magazine, a brochure, a catalog, or a campus publication. Examine the design of each document carefully, considering which aspects of the design seem effective or ineffective in achieving the writer's purpose and meeting the reader's needs.

Chapter 22

Strategies for Understanding Visual Representations

On a street-corner billboard, two sets of footprints mark an otherwise pristine sandy beach. One set of footprints has obviously been made by someone wearing pointed-toe dress shoes; the other set was left behind by a barefoot, carefree beach bum. The billboard gets us to associate the advertiser's light beer with a barefoot walk on the beach and the competitor's light beer with tight shoes and business dinners. All of these associations come directly from the humorous picture because the billboard has no text other than the beer company's logo.

Other billboards on this corner advertise such diverse commodities as fast food, Internet services, and the radiology department at a local hospital. Thousands of drivers pause at this intersection to wait out a red light — a captive audience for aggressive and compelling visual representations. It's a good location for a beer advertisement: on the way home from work, just minutes from their front doors, drivers who see that ad begin mentally kicking off their shoes and leaving the day behind. Obviously, the beer manufacturer hopes these tired workers will remember its brand — the light beer that promises barefoot relaxation — the next time they buy beer.

The specific images on these billboards change with time, but images are a constant and persistent presence in our lives. The sign atop a taxi invites us to try the new ride at a local tourist attraction. A celebrity sporting a milk moustache smiles from the side of a city bus, accompanied by the familiar question, "Got milk?" The lettering on a pickup truck urges us to call for a free landscaping estimate. On television, video, and the Web, advertising images surround us, trying to shape our opinions about everything from personal hygiene products to snack foods to political candidates.

Advertisements are not the only visual representations that affect us. Cartoons, photographs, drawings, paintings, logos, graphics, and other two-dimensional media originate from a variety of sources with a variety of purposes, all working to evoke responses. The critical skills you develop for analyzing these still images also apply to other types of visual representations, including television commercials, films, and stage productions. We can't help but notice visual images, and whether we respond with a smile or a frown, one thing is certain: visuals help to structure our views of reality.

Using Strategies for Visual Analysis

Begin a visual analysis by conducting a *close reading* of the image. Like a literal and critical reading of a written text, a close reading of an image involves careful, in-depth examination of the advertisement, photograph, cartoon, artwork, or other visual representation. Your close reading should focus on the following three levels of questions:

- What is the big picture? What is the source of the image? What is its purpose? What audience does it address?

- What characteristics of the image can you observe? What story does the image tell? What people or animals appear in the image? What are the major elements of the image? How are they arranged?

- How can you interpret what the image suggests? What feeling or mood does it create? What is its cultural meaning? What are the roles of any signs, symbols, or language that it includes? What is the image about?

The rest of the chapter explains these three levels of visual analysis in more detail. You may discover that your classmates respond differently to some images than you do. Your personal, cultural background and your experiences may influence how you interpret the meaning of an image. If you plan to write about the image you analyze, take notes or use your journal to record your observations and interpretations. Be sure to include a copy of the image, if one is available, when you solicit peer review of your essay or submit it to your teacher.

For more on literal and critical reading of texts, see Ch. 2. For a checklist for analyzing images, see p. 373.

Seeing the Big Picture

Begin your close reading of an image by discovering what you can about its source and its overall composition. Use the following checklist to help you find out as much as you can about the purpose and audience for the image:

For more on purpose and audience, see pp. 12–14.

DISCOVERY CHECKLIST

___ If the image is an advertisement, when and where did it run?

___ If the image is a photograph, painting, or other work of art, who is the artist? Where has the image been published or exhibited?

___ What was the purpose of the image?

___ What audience was the image aimed at?

This information will add to your understanding of the image. If you include the image in a paper for your class, you will need to cite the source and its "author" or artist, just as you would if you were examining a reading, an article, or a literary work.

Next, examine the overall composition of the image. The photograph in Figure 22.1 will serve as a guide to this process.

PROMINENT ELEMENT

Start with the overall view. Look carefully at the whole image and ask yourself, "Is there one prominent element — object, person, background, writing — in the image that attracts my attention immediately?" Examine that element in detail, and ask yourself how and why that prominent element draws you into the image.

In Figure 22.1, many people would first notice the dark-haired Caucasian girl. Her prominence in the picture can be explained in part by her position at the left side of the photograph, framed by the white porch railing. People who read from left to right and top to bottom — including most Americans and Europeans — also typically read photographs in the same way, which means that the viewer's eye is likely to be drawn into the photograph at the upper left corner. For this reason, artists and photographers often position the key elements of their photographs — the elements they want their viewers to see right away — somewhere in the upper left quadrant of the page. (See Figure 22.2.)

FOCAL POINT

There is another reason the reader's eye might be drawn first to the girl on the left: notice that all of the other children are turned slightly toward her, straining to see the pages of the magazine she is holding. Not only is she positioned so as to provide a focal point for the viewer, but she is also the focal point of action within the photograph.

Now, take a look at the child on the right side of the picture. You may have noticed him first. Or, once you did notice him, you may have been surprised that he didn't attract your attention right away. After all, he provides some contrast within the photograph because he sits apart from the girls, seems to be a little younger, and does not appear to be included in their little group. What's more, he's not wearing any clothes. Still, most people won't notice him first because of the path the eye typically travels within a photograph. Because of the left-to-right and top-to-bottom reading pattern that Americans and Europeans take for granted, most of us view photographs in a Z pattern, as depicted in Figure 22.3. Most viewers would notice the boy last but would pause to look at him, observe that he's naked, and see that he's looking over at the girls. Thus, the bottom right corner of an image becomes a second very important position that a skilled photographer can use to retain the viewers' attention. When you look at the "big picture" in this way, you can see the overall composition of the image, identify its prominent element, and determine its focal point.

Observing the Characteristics of an Image

As you concentrate on the literal reading of a written text, you become aware of the information it presents, you comprehend what it means, and you are able to apply it in relation to other situations. Similarly, your close reading of an image includes observing its *denotative* or literal characteristics. At this stage, you focus on exactly what the image depicts — observing it objectively — rather than probing what it means or signifies.

For more about reading on a literal level, see pp. 19–20. For a checklist for analyzing images, see p. 373.

CAST OF CHARACTERS

Objects.   Examine the condition, colors, sizes, functions, and positions of the objects included in the image. In Figure 22.1, for example, only one object is depicted in the image: a large magazine. Everything else in the image is either a figure or part of the background.

Figures.   Look closely at any figures (men, women, children, animals) in the image. Consider their facial expressions, poses, hairstyles and colors, ages, sexes, ethnicity, possible education, suggested occupations, apparent relationships to each other, and so on.

Figure 22.1 shows four children. There are three girls, approximately eight or nine years of age. Two are Caucasian, and one is African American. The dark-haired Caucasian girl is wearing a colorful bathing suit. Next to her sits a light-haired Caucasian girl, who is wearing shorts and a short-sleeved blue and white flowered T-shirt. The African American girl sitting beside the light-haired girl also has on a colorful print swimsuit. All three appear to be dressed appropriately for the weather. The three girls pore over the magazine held by the dark-haired Caucasian girl. Judging from their facial expressions, they are totally engrossed in the contents of the magazine, as well as a little puzzled. The girls seem to be looking at a picture; the magazine is turned sideways with the spine at the bottom.

Figure 22.1
*Photograph of four children,
Kodak Picture of the Day,
October 22, 2000*

Figure 22.2 (above left)
Photograph divided into quarters

Figure 22.3 (above right)
Z pattern often used to read images

Figure 22.4 (right)
Close-up detail of photograph

The fourth child in the photograph is a smaller Caucasian boy. He sits slightly apart from the girls and seems to be several years younger than they are. His light hair appears damp—we might wonder if he has recently bathed or is perspiring from exertion. Because two of the girls are attired in swimsuits, we might conclude that the boy's hair is damp from swimming. His nakedness reveals a great many details: for example, we can see that his skin is tanned and that he has several small bruises on his legs, probably acquired during normal play. His right leg is crossed over his left, a position that not only hides his genitals but also causes his body to turn slightly away from the girls. His face is turned toward them, however, and he seems to be trying to see what they are looking at. His hands are raised, his eyes are bright, and he's smiling at whatever he is able to see of the magazine.

STORY OF THE IMAGE

Action.   The action shown in an image suggests its "plot" or story, the events surrounding the moment captured in the image. In Figure 22.1, four children are seated on the steps of a house looking at a magazine on a summer day. Because no adults appear in the picture and the children look puzzled, we might assume that they are looking at something they don't understand, possibly something adults might frown on. On the other hand, they are not acting secretive, so this impression may not be accurate.

Background.   The background in an image shows where and when the action takes place. In Figure 22.1, the children are seated on the wooden steps of a blue house. We might conclude that the steps are part of a back porch rather than a front porch because the porch is relatively small and the steps begin immediately: there is no deck and consequently nowhere to sit except on the steps themselves. The top step is painted blue, and the railing is painted white to match the white metal door and window frames. In a few places the paint is chipped or worn away. But these signs of disrepair simply seem to indicate that the house is lived in and comfortable; they are not severe enough to suggest that the occupants are poor. In the windows next to the steps and on the door, we can see the reflections of trees. The children's clothes identify the season as summer.

DESIGN AND ARRANGEMENT

Design.   When you look at the design of an image, you might reflect on both the elements within the image and their organization. For instance, what are the major colors and shapes? How are they arranged? Does the image appear balanced; that is, are light and dark areas arranged symmetrically? Does the image appear organized or chaotic? Is one area of the picture darker (heavier) or brighter (lighter) than other areas? What does the design make you think of—does it evoke a particular emotion, historical period, or memory?

In Figure 22.1, the most prominent shape is the white porch railing that frames the children and draws the viewer's eye in toward the action. The image appears balanced, in that the white door provides the backdrop for the little boy, while the blue siding and white porch railing seem to frame the three girls. Therefore, the image is split down the center, both by the division that separates the figures in the image and by the shapes that make up the background. The girls' brightly colored summer clothing also accentuates the little boy's monochromatic nakedness.

Relationship of Pictorial Elements.   Visual elements may be related to one another or to written material that appears with the image. As you notice such relationships, consider what they tell you. In Figure 22.1, for instance, the three girls are grouped together around the magazine, and the little boy is clearly not part of their group. He is separated physically from the three girls by a bit of intervening space and by the vertical line formed by the doorframe, which splits the background in two. He is further set apart from them by his gender, not to mention the fact that they are clothed and he is not. Moreover, his body is turned slightly away from them. However, his gaze, like the girls', is on the magazine that they are scrutinizing; this element of the picture connects him to the group of girls.

For white space in document design, see pp. 347–49.

Spatiality.   An image may be surrounded by a lot of "white space" — empty space without text or graphics — or it may be "busy" — full of graphic and written elements. White space is effective when it provides relief from an otherwise busy layout or when it directs the reader's eye to key elements of the image. The image in Figure 22.1 does not include any empty space; its shapes and colors guide the viewer's eye.

In contrast, look at the image in Figure 22.5. It specifically uses white space to call attention to the Volkswagen's small size. When this advertisement was produced back in 1959, many American cars were large and heavy. The VW, a German import, provided consumers with an alternative type of vehicle, and the advertising emphasized this contrast.

ARTISTIC CHOICES

Aesthetic Decisions.   Whether an image is a photograph, a drawing, or another form of representation, the artist who composes it makes many aesthetic choices. For example, if the image is a photograph, the photographer might use a close-up, medium, or wide-angle shot to compose it — and also determine the angle of the shot, the lighting, and the use of color.

The picture of the four children in Figure 22.1 is a medium shot and has been taken at the children's eye level. If the photograph were a close-up, only one aspect of the image would be visible. Notice in Figure 22.4 how the meaning of the picture changes when we view the girls' faces as a close-up. We have no way of telling where the picture was taken or what the girls are doing; moreover, by moving in closer, this view completely cuts out the naked little boy. The girls' attentiveness is still apparent, and it is clear that

Figure 22.5
Volkswagen advertisement,
about 1959

they are all attending to the same thing, but we can't tell what this thing is: it could be a soccer game, a worm, or another person.

In contrast, in the Volkswagen ad (Figure 22.5), the white space creates the effect of a long shot taken from below with a telephoto lens. We see the car as it might appear if we were looking down at it through the wrong end

For more about white space, see pp. 347–49.

of a pair of binoculars. This vantage point shrinks the car so that an already small vehicle looks even smaller.

For more on typefaces, see pp. 343–46.

Typefaces.   Many images, especially advertisements, combine image and text, using the typeface to set a particular mood and convey a particular impression. For example, Times New Roman is a commonly used typeface, easy to read, and somewhat conservative, whereas **Comic Sans MS** is considered informal — almost playful — and looks like handwriting. Any printed element included in an image may be trendy or conservative, large or small, in relation to the image as whole. Further, it may be meant to inform, evoke an emotion, or decorate the page.

Look back at Figure 22.5, the 1959 Volkswagen ad. The words "Think small" are printed in a sans serif typeface — spare and unadorned, just like the VW itself. The ad also includes a significant amount of text across the bottom of the page. While this text is too small to read in the reproduction in this book, we assume that it gives details about the VW, perhaps technical specifications, price, or even a rationale for driving a small imported vehicle instead of one of the many large, roomy cars common at the time.

In contrast to the VW ad campaign, the 1959 Oldsmobile marketing strategy promoted a big vehicle, not a small one, as Figure 22.6 illustrates. Here the cars are shown in medium to close-up view to call attention to their length. Happy human figures positioned in and beside the cars emphasize their size, and the cars are painted in bright colors, unlike the VW's serviceable black. The type in the ad, like the other visual elements, reflects and promotes the Oldsmobile's size. The primary writing in the center of the page is large enough to be read in the reproduction here. It introduces the brand name by opening the first sentence with the Oldsmobile '59 logo and praises the cars' expansive size, space, power, and other features. Near the bottom of each car image, however, are a few lines of "fine print" that we cannot read in the reproduction — presumably warnings or technical specifications not directly related to the reasons given for purchasing such a large, modern car.

Other images besides advertisements use type to evoke a mood. For example, the two images in Figure 22.7 illustrate artists' renditions of the moods set by two common typefaces, Courier and Caslon. The Courier typeface resembles the text produced by a typewriter. The artwork in the example consists entirely of "white space" (actually black in the image) and rows of circles with letters inside. The image looks balanced and serious, apparently meant to make us think of an early manual typewriter. Indeed, if we examine the circles closely, we notice that the letters are arranged in the order in which they appear on a typewriter keyboard. Some viewers are likely to interpret the Courier art as a commentary on the historical development of the typeface.

The artwork that illustrates the Caslon typeface includes familiar international symbols — the man and woman icons that appear on public restrooms, a police officer, a drinking fountain — along with symbols that are less familiar to American viewers. The various styles of the Caslon typeface (and the use of some foreign letters) combine to achieve a cheerful, playful,

Figure 22.6
Oldsmobile advertise-
ments, 1959

cluttered look. For viewers, the Caslon art might suggest not only the effects of mixing type styles willy-nilly on the same page but also the potential problems involved in cross-cultural relations.

Just as type can establish a mood or tone, the absence of any written language in an image can also affect how we view that image. Recall Figure 22.1, the photograph of the children sitting on the porch looking at a

Figure 22.7
Artistic use of typefaces:
Courier (top) and
Caslon (bottom)

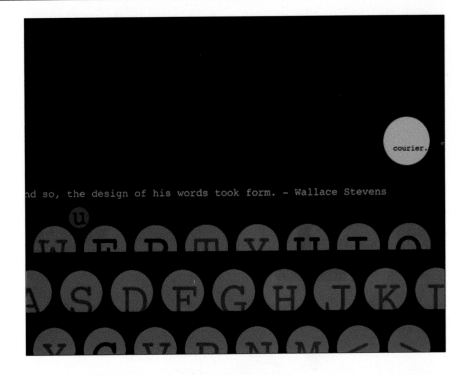

magazine. Because we can't see the magazine's title, we are left to wonder — perhaps with amusement — about what has so engrossed the children. If the title of the magazine — *Sports Illustrated, Wired, Good Housekeeping* — were revealed to us, the photograph might seem less intriguing. By leaving us to speculate about the identity of the magazine, the photographer may keep us looking longer and harder at the image.

Interpreting the Meaning of an Image

When you read a written text on an analytical level, you engage actively with the text. You analyze its parts from different angles, synthesize the material by combining it with related information, and finally evaluate or judge its significance. When you interpret an image, you do much the same, actively questioning and examining what the image *connotes* or suggests, speculating about what it signifies.

For more on reading analytically, see pp. 20–21.

Because interpretation is more personal than observation, this process can reveal deep-seated individual and cultural values. In fact, interpreting an image is sometimes emotional or difficult because it may require you to examine beliefs that you are unaware of holding. You may even become impatient with visual analysis, perhaps feeling that too much is being read into the image. Like learning to read critically, however, learning to interpret images is a valuable skill. When you see an image that attracts you, chances are good that you like it because it upholds strong cultural beliefs. Through close reading of images, you can examine how image makers are able to perpetuate such cultural values and speculate about why — perhaps analyzing an artist's political motivations or an advertiser's economic motivations. When you interpret an image, you go beyond literal observation to examine what the image suggests and what it may mean.

For a checklist for analyzing images, see p. 373.

GENERAL FEELING OR MOOD

To begin interpreting an image, consider what feeling or mood it creates and how it does so. If you are a woman, you probably recall huddling, around age eight or nine, with a couple of "best friends" as the girls do in Figure 22.1. As a result, the interaction in this photograph may seem very familiar and may evoke fond memories. If you are a man, this photograph may call up somewhat different memories. Although eight-year-old boys also cluster in small groups, their motivations may differ from those behind little girls' huddles. Moreover, anyone who was ignored or excluded at a young age may feel a rush of sympathy for the little boy; his separation from the older children may dredge up age-old hurt feelings.

For many viewers, the image may also suggest a mood associated with summer: sitting on the back porch after a trip to the swimming pool, spending a carefree day with friends. This "summer" mood is a particular cultural association related to the summers of childhood. By the time we reach college, summer no longer has the same feeling. Work, summer school, separations, and family responsibilities — maybe even for children like those in the picture — obliterate the freedoms of childhood summer vacations.

SOCIOLOGICAL, POLITICAL, ECONOMIC, OR CULTURAL ATTITUDES

On the surface, the Volkswagen ad in Figure 22.5 is simply an attempt to sell a car. But its message might be interpreted to mean "scale down" — lead a less consumer-oriented lifestyle. If Volkswagen had distributed this ad in the 1970s, it would have been unremarkable — faced with the first energy crisis that adversely affected American gasoline prices, many advertisers used ecological consciousness to sell cars. In 1959, however, energy conservation was not really a concern. Contrasted with other automobile ads of its time, the Volkswagen ad comes across as somewhat eccentric, making the novel suggestion that larger cars are excessively extravagant.

Whereas the Volkswagen ad suggests that "small" refers both to size and affordability, the Oldsmobile ad in Figure 22.6 depicts a large vehicle and implies a large price tag. By emphasizing the Vista-Panoramic view and increased luggage space and by portraying the car near a seashore, the ad leads viewers to think about going on vacation. It thus implies exclusivity — not everyone can afford this car or the activities it suggests.

Sometimes, what is missing from an image is as important as what is included. Viewers of today might readily notice the absence of people of color in the 1959 Oldsmobile ad. An interesting study might investigate what types of magazines originally carried this ad and whether (and if so, how) Oldsmobiles were also advertised in publications aimed at Asian Americans, African Americans, or Spanish-speaking people.

LANGUAGE

Just as you would examine figures, colors, and shapes when you observe the literal characteristics of an image, so you need to examine its words, phrases, and sentences when you interpret what it suggests. Does its language provide information, generate an emotional response, or do both? Do its words repeat a sound or concept, signal a comparison (such as a "new, improved" product), carry sexual overtones, issue a challenge, or offer a definition or philosophy of life? The words that are legible in the Oldsmobile ad in Figure 22.6, for instance, are calculated to associate the car with a leisurely, affluent lifestyle. On the other hand, VW's "Think small" ad in Figure 22.5 turns compactness into a goal, a quality to be desired in a car and, by extension, in life.

Frequently advertisements employ puns or recycle common sayings to get their messages across in a light-hearted way. The Egg Beaters ad in Figure 22.8 shows a round, naked egg weighing itself in a doctor's office. With the

Figure 22.8
Egg Beaters advertisement

punch line "Fat chance," the ad humorously uses a colloquial expression to evoke the concerns of dieters while calling attention to the low-fat, low-cholesterol qualities of egg substitutes. And the product's slogan, centered in yellow at the bottom of the page, uses yet another folksy commonplace, "We're good eggs," to create a friendly tone while further associating the product with good health. In other words, Egg Beaters are "good" eggs, while regular eggs are "bad" because they contain fat and cholesterol.

SIGNS AND SYMBOLS

Signs and symbols, such as product logos, are images or words that communicate key messages. In the Oldsmobile ad in Figure 22.6, the product logo doubles as the phrase that introduces the description of the 1959 model. Sometimes a product logo alone may be enough, as in the Hershey chocolate company's holiday ads that include little more than a single Hershey's Kiss. The shape of the Kiss serves as a logo or symbol for the company.

Similarly, in the Netpliance ad in Figure 22.9, the humorous symbol of the computer nerd — eyeglasses repaired with tape — is used to associate Netpliance computer ownership with computer expertise. Ordinary working folks, fashion models, and even babies — all wearing eyeglasses with taped nosepieces — are elevated by their computer ownership to nerd status, which the ad presents as a desirable goal.

THEMES

The theme of an image is not the same as its plot. When you identify the plot, you identify the story that is told by the image. When you identify the theme, on the other hand, you explain what the image is about. An ad for a diamond ring may tell the story of a man surprising his wife with a ring on their twenty-fifth wedding anniversary, but the advertisement's theme could be sex, romance, longevity, or some other concept. Similarly, the theme of a

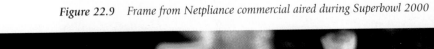

Figure 22.9   *Frame from Netpliance commercial aired during Superbowl 2000*

soft drink ad might be competition, community, compassion, or individualism. A painting of the ocean might be about cheerfulness, fear, or loneliness. Through a close reading, you can unearth clues and details to support your interpretation of the theme and convince others of its merit.

Ask the following questions as you analyze an image or as you prepare to present your analysis in an essay:

VISUAL ANALYSIS CHECKLIST

Seeing the Big Picture

____ What is the source of the image? What is its purpose and audience?

____ What prominent element in the image immediately attracts your attention? How and why does it draw you into the image?

____ What is the focal point of the image? How do the elements of the image direct your attention to this point? What path does your eye follow as you observe the image?

Observing the Characteristics of an Image

____ What objects are included in the image?

____ What figures (people or animals) appear in the image?

____ What action takes place in the image? What is its "plot" or story?

____ What is in the background of the image? Where does the action of the image take place? What kind of place is it?

____ What is the design of the image? What colors and shapes does it include? How are they arranged or balanced? What feeling, memory, or association does the design evoke?

____ How are the pictorial elements related to one another? How are they related to any written material? What do these relationships tell you as a viewer?

____ What is the spatiality of the image? Does the image include a lot of white space, or does it seem cluttered and busy?

____ What aesthetic decisions has the artist made? What type of shot, shot angle, lighting, or color is used?

____ What typefaces are used? What impressions do they convey?

Interpreting the Meaning of an Image

____ What general feeling do you get from looking at the image? What mood does the image create? How does it create this mood?

____ What sociological, political, economic, or cultural attitudes are reflected in the image?

____ What language is included in the image? How does the language function?

____ What signs and symbols can you identify? What role do these play in the image?

____ What theme or themes can you identify in the image?

WWW

For more practice analyzing images, visit <www.bedfordstmartins.com/bedguide>.

■ Exercises

1. Find a print ad that evokes a strong emotional response. Conduct a close reading of the ad, observing its characteristics and interpreting its meaning. Write an essay in which you explain the techniques by which the ad evokes your emotional response. Include a copy of the ad with your essay, and consult others to determine whether they have the same response to the ad.

2. Compile a design notebook. Over the course of several weeks, collect ten or twelve images that appeal to you. You may wish to choose examples of a particular genre, or your teacher may assign a genre or theme. For example, you might select advertisements, portraits, or landscape photographs, or you might choose snack food advertisements from magazines aimed at several different audiences. On the other hand, your collection might revolve around a theme, such as friendship, competition, community, or romance. As you collect these images, "read" each one closely, and write short responses explaining your reactions to the images based on your close readings. At the end of the collection period, choose two or three images. Write an essay in which you compare or contrast them, analyzing how they illustrate the same genre, how they convey a particular theme, or how they appeal to different audiences.

A Writer's Reader

Contents

Introduction: Reading to Write   377

23. Families

E. B. White   Once More to the Lake   379
Amy Tan   Mother Tongue   385
Gerald Early   Black like . . . Shirley Temple?   391
Anna Quindlen   Evan's Two Moms   394
John McPhee   Silk Parachute   397
Noel Perrin   A Part-Time Marriage   400
Stephanie Coontz   Remarriage and Stepfamilies   404

24. Men and Women

Judy Brady   I Want a Wife   412
Scott Russell Sanders   The Men We Carry in Our Minds   415
Emily Prager   Our Barbies, Ourselves   420
Joy Harjo   Three Generations of Native American Women's Birth Experience   423
Dave Barry   From Now On, Let Women Kill Their Own Spiders   428
Deborah Tannen   Women and Men Talking on the Job   431
Nicholas Wade   How Men and Women Think   437

25. Popular Culture

Stephen King   Why We Crave Horror Movies   443
Veronica Chambers   The Myth of Cinderella   446
Phyllis Rose   Shopping and Other Spiritual Adventures in America Today   450
Jay Chiat   Illusions Are Forever   453
Ellen Goodman   How to Zap Violence on TV   456
Mike Males   Public Enemy Number One?   459

26. The Workplace

Joe Robinson   Four Weeks Vacation   467
Steve Olson   Year of the Blue-Collar Guy   473
Jane Smiley   The Case against Chores   476
Katherine S. Newman   *From* No Shame in My Game   479
Ian Bruce   Commercial Fisherman   485
Anne Finnigan   Nice Perks—If You Can Get 'Em   489
Elinor Burkett   Unequal Work for Unequal Pay   495

27. Body Image

Julia Alvarez   I Want to Be Miss América   502
Garry Trudeau   My Inner Shrimp   507
Marisa Kula   Victoria's Not-So-Secret Strategy   510
Alicia Potter   Mirror Image   514
Lisa Jervis   My Jewish Nose   519
Janice Turner   Cutting Edge   524

Introduction: Reading to Write

A Writer's Reader is a collection of thirty-three carefully selected professional essays. We hope, first of all, that you will read these pieces simply for the sake of reading—enjoying and responding to the ideas presented. Good writers read widely, and in doing so, they increase their knowledge of the craft of writing. Second, we hope that you will actively study these essays as solid examples of the situations and strategies explored in *A Writer's Guide*. The authors represented in this reader, experts from varied fields, have faced the same problems and choices you do when you write. You can learn from studying their decisions, structures, and techniques. Finally, we hope that you will find the content of the essays intriguing—and that the essays, along with the questions posed after each one, will give you ideas to write about.

Each chapter in *A Writer's Reader* concentrates on a familiar broad theme—families, men and women, popular culture, the workplace, and body image. In some essays the writers focus on the inner world and write personal experience and opinion papers. In others the authors turn their attention to the outer world and write informational and persuasive essays. Within each chapter, the last two selections are a pair of essays on the same subject. We've provided these pairs so that you can see how different writers use different strategies to address similar issues.

Each chapter in the reader begins with an image, a visual activity, and a Web search activity, all intended to stimulate you to begin to think and write. Each reading selection is preceded by biographical information about the author, placing him or her—and the piece itself—into a cultural and informational context. Following each selection are five Questions to Start You Thinking that consistently cover the same ground: meaning, writing strategies, critical thinking, vocabulary, and comparison and contrast with one or more of the other selections in *A Writer's Reader*. Each paired essay is also followed by a question that asks you about a connection between the essays. After these questions come a couple of journal prompts designed to get your writing juices flowing. Finally, two possible composition assignments make specific suggestions for writing. The first assignment is directed toward your inner world, asking you to draw generally on your personal experience and your understanding of the essay. The second is outer directed, asking you to look outside yourself and write an evaluative or argumentative paper, one that may require further reading or research.

For more on journal writing, see pp. 265–66.

377

Chapter 23
Families

Zack Townsend and His Family / Bruccoli Clark Layman

Responding to an Image

What does the composition of this family photograph suggest to a viewer? Carefully examine the photograph, making thorough notes about the clothing, positions, facial expressions, posture, and other attributes of the people in the photograph. What might these attributes indicate about the occasion? Where do you think this photograph was taken? What kind of family does this photograph portray? Does this family portrait remind you of any others you've seen?

378

E. B. White
Once More to the Lake

E. B. (Elwyn Brooks) White (1899–1985) was born in Mount Vernon, New York. After serving in the army, he graduated from Cornell University and moved to Seattle to work as a reporter. His career led him back to the East Coast, where he joined the staff of the recently established New Yorker *magazine in 1927. For half a century, his satires, poems, and essays helped define that magazine's distinctive style of elegant wit and social comment. He moved to Maine in 1933, and his widely read books for children,* Stuart Little *(1945),* Charlotte's Web *(1952), and* The Trumpet of the Swan *(1970), draw on his life in the country to celebrate life's blend of sadness, happiness, love, and loss. In the following essay, first published in* Harper's *magazine in 1941, White reflects on the experience of returning with his son to a favorite scene from his own childhood.*

AS YOU READ: *Notice what, according to White, changes a person's perspective from childhood to adulthood.*

August 1941

One summer, along about 1904, my father rented a camp on a lake in Maine and took us all there for the month of August. We all got ringworm from some kittens and had to rub Pond's Extract on our arms and legs night and morning, and my father rolled over in a canoe with all his clothes on; but outside of that the vacation was a success and from then on none of us ever thought there was any place in the world like that lake in Maine. We returned summer after summer—always on August 1 for one month. I have since become a salt-water man, but sometimes in summer there are days when the restlessness of the tides and the fearful cold of the sea water and the incessant wind that blows across the afternoon and into the evening make me wish for the placidity of a lake in the woods. A few weeks ago this feeling got so strong I bought myself a couple of bass hooks and a spinner and returned to the lake where we used to go, for a week's fishing and to revisit old haunts.

I took along my son, who had never had any fresh water up his nose and   2
who had seen lily pads only from train windows. On the journey over to the
lake I began to wonder what it would be like. I wondered how time would
have marred this unique, this holy spot—the coves and streams, the hills
that the sun set behind, the camps and the paths behind the camps. I was
sure that the tarred road would have found it out, and I wondered in what
other ways it would be desolated. It is strange how much you can remember
about places like that once you allow your mind to return into the grooves
that lead back. You remember one thing, and that suddenly reminds you of
another thing. I guess I remembered clearest of all the early mornings, when
the lake was cool and motionless, remembered how the bedroom smelled of
the lumber it was made of and of the wet woods whose scent entered
through the screen. The partitions in the camp were thin and did not extend
clear to the top of the rooms, and as I was always the first up I would dress
softly so as not to wake the others, and sneak out into the sweet outdoors
and start out in the canoe, keeping close along the shore in the long shadows
of the pines. I remembered being very careful never to rub my paddle against
the gunwale° for fear of disturbing the stillness of the cathedral.

The lake had never been what you would call a wild lake. There were   3
cottages sprinkled around the shores, and it was in farming country although the shores of the lake were quite heavily wooded. Some of the cottages were owned by nearby farmers, and you would live at the shore and
eat your meals at the farmhouse. That's what our family did. But although it
wasn't wild, it was a fairly large and undisturbed lake and there were places
in it that, to a child at least, seemed infinitely remote and primeval.

I was right about the tar: it led to within half a mile of the shore. But   4
when I got back there, with my boy, and we settled into a camp near a farmhouse and into the kind of summertime I had known, I could tell that it was
going to be pretty much the same as it had been before—I knew it, lying in
bed the first morning smelling the bedroom and hearing the boy sneak quietly out and go off along the shore in a boat. I began to sustain the illusion
that he was I, and therefore, by simple transposition, that I was my father.
This sensation persisted, kept cropping up all the time we were there. It was
not an entirely new feeling, but in this setting it grew much stronger. I seemed
to be living a dual existence. I would be in the middle of some simple act, I
would be picking up a bait box or laying down a table fork, or I would be saying something and suddenly it would be not I but my father who was saying
the words or making the gesture. It gave me a creepy sensation.

We went fishing the first morning. I felt the same damp moss covering   5
the worms in the bait can, and saw the dragonfly alight on the tip of my rod
as it hovered a few inches from the surface of the water. It was the arrival of
this fly that convinced me beyond any doubt that everything was as it always
had been, that the years were a mirage, and that there had been no years.
The small waves were the same, chucking the rowboat under the chin as we

gunwale: Upper edge of the side of a boat.

fished at anchor, and the boat was the same boat, the same color green and the ribs broken in the same places, and under the floorboards the same fresh water leavings and debris — the dead hellgrammite, the wisps of moss, the rusty discarded fishhook, the dried blood from yesterday's catch. We stared silently at the tips of our rods, at the dragonflies that came and went. I lowered the tip of mine into the water, tentatively, pensively dislodging the fly, which darted two feet away, poised, darted two feet back, and came to rest again a little farther up the rod. There had been no years between the ducking of this dragonfly and the other one — the one that was part of memory. I looked at the boy, who was silently watching his fly, and it was my hands that held his rod, my eyes watching. I felt dizzy and didn't know which rod I was at the end of.

We caught two bass, hauling them in briskly as though they were mack- 6
erel, pulling them over the side of the boat in a businesslike manner without any landing net, and stunning them with a blow on the back of the head. When we got back for a swim before lunch, the lake was exactly where we had left it, the same number of inches from the dock, and there was only the merest suggestion of a breeze. This seemed an utterly enchanted sea, this lake you could leave to its own devices for a few hours and come back to, and find that it had not stirred, this constant and trustworthy body of water. In the shallows, the dark, water-soaked sticks and twigs, smooth and old, were undulating in clusters on the bottom against the clean ribbed sand, and the track of the mussel was plain. A school of minnows swam by, each minnow with its small individual shadow, doubling the attendance, so clear and sharp in the sunlight. Some of the other campers were in swimming, along the shore, one of them with a cake of soap, and the water felt thin and clear and unsubstantial. Over the years there had been this person with the cake of soap, this cultist, and here he was. There had been no years.

Up to the farmhouse to dinner through the teeming dusty field, the 7
road under our sneakers was only a two-track road. The middle track was missing, the one with the marks of the hooves and the splotches of dried, flaky manure. There had always been three tracks to choose from in choosing which track to walk in; now the choice was narrowed down to two. For a moment I missed terribly the middle alternative. But the way led past the tennis court, and something about the way it lay there in the sun reassured me; the tape had loosened along the backline, the alleys were green with plantains° and other weeds, and the net (installed in June and removed in September) sagged in the dry noon, and the whole place steamed with midday heat and hunger and emptiness. There was a choice of pie for dessert, and one was blueberry and one was apple, and the waitresses were the same country girls, there having been no passage of time, only the illusion of it as in a dropped curtain — the waitresses were still fifteen; their hair had been washed, that was the only difference — they had been to the movies and seen the pretty girls with the clean hair.

plantains: Common wild plants.

Summertime, oh, summertime, pattern of life indelible° with fade-   8
proof lake, the wood unshatterable, the pasture with the sweetfern and the
juniper forever and ever, summer without end; this was the background,
and the life along the shore was the design, the cottages with their innocent
and tranquil design, their tiny docks with the flagpole and the American flag
floating against the white clouds in the blue sky, the little paths over the
roots of the trees leading from camp to camp and the paths leading back to
the outhouses and the can of lime for sprinkling, and at the souvenir coun-
ters at the store the miniature birchbark canoes and the postcards that
showed things looking a little better than they looked. This was the American family at play, escaping the city heat, wondering whether the newcomers in the camp at the head of the cove were "common" or "nice," wondering whether it was true that the people who drove up for Sunday dinner at
the farmhouse were turned away because there wasn't enough chicken.

It seemed to me, as I kept remembering all this, that those times and   9
those summers had been infinitely precious and worth saving. There had
been jollity and peace and goodness. The arriving (at the beginning of August) had been so big a business in itself, at the railway station the farm
wagon drawn up, the first smell of the pine-laden air, the first glimpse of the
smiling farmer, and the great importance of the trunks and your father's
enormous authority in such matters, and the feel of the wagon under you
for the long ten-mile haul, and at the top of the last long hill catching the
first view of the lake after eleven months of not seeing this cherished body
of water. The shouts and cries of the other campers when they saw you, and
the trunks to be unpacked, to give up their rich burden. (Arriving was less
exciting nowadays, when you sneaked up in your car and parked it under a
tree near the camp and took out the bags and in five minutes it was all over,
no fuss, no loud wonderful fuss about trunks.)

Peace and goodness and jollity. The only thing that was wrong now, re-   10
ally, was the sound of the place, an unfamiliar nervous sound of the outboard motors. This was the note that jarred, the one thing that would sometimes break the illusion and set the years moving. In those other
summertimes all motors were inboard; and when they were at a little distance, the noise they made was a sedative, an ingredient of summer sleep.
They were one-cylinder and two-cylinder engines, and some were make-and-
break and some were jump-spark, but they all made a sleepy sound across
the lake. The one-lungers throbbed and fluttered, and the twin-cylinder ones
purred and purred, and that was a quiet sound, too. But now the campers
all had outboards. In the daytime, in the hot mornings, these motors made
a petulant, irritable sound; at night in the still evening when the afterglow
lit the water, they whined about one's ears like mosquitoes. My boy loved
our rented outboard, and his great desire was to achieve single-handed mastery over it, and authority, and he soon learned the trick of choking it a little
(but not too much), and the adjustment of the needle valve. Watching him I

indelible: Unable to be removed.

would remember the things you could do with the old one-cylinder engine with the heavy flywheel,° how you could have it eating out of your hand if you got really close to it spiritually. Motorboats in those days didn't have clutches, and you would make a landing by shutting off the motor at the proper time and coasting in with a dead rudder. But there was a way of reversing them, if you learned the trick, by cutting the switch and putting it on again exactly on the final dying revolution of the flywheel, so that it would kick back against compression and begin reversing. Approaching a dock in a strong following breeze, it was difficult to slow up sufficiently by the ordinary coasting method, and if a boy felt he had complete mastery over his motor, he was tempted to keep it running beyond its time and then reverse it a few feet from the dock. It took a cool nerve, because if you threw the switch a twentieth of a second too soon you would catch the flywheel when it still had speed enough to go up past center, and the boat would leap ahead, charging bull-fashion at the dock.

We had a good week at the camp. The bass were biting well and the sun   11 shone endlessly, day after day. We would be tired at night and lie down in the accumulated heat of the little bedrooms after the long hot day and the breeze would stir almost imperceptibly outside and the smell of the swamp drift in through the rusty screens. Sleep would come easily and in the morning the red squirrel would be on the roof, tapping out his gay routine. I kept remembering everything, lying in bed in the mornings — the small steamboat that had a long rounded stern like the lip of a Ubangi,° and how quietly she ran on the moonlight sails, when the older boys played their mandolins° and the girls sang and we ate doughnuts dipped in sugar, and how sweet the music was on the water in the shining night, and what it had felt like to think about girls then. After breakfast we would go up to the store and the things were in the same place — the minnows in a bottle, the plugs and spinners disarranged and pawed over by the youngsters from the boys' camp, the Fig Newtons and the Beeman's gum. Outside, the road was tarred and cars stood in front of the store. Inside, all was just as it had always been, except there was more Coca-Cola and not so much Moxie and root beer and birch beer and sarsaparilla. We would walk out with the bottle of pop apiece and sometimes the pop would backfire up our noses and hurt. We explored the streams, quietly, where the turtles slid off the sunny logs and dug their way into the soft bottom; and we lay on the town wharf and fed worms to the tame bass. Everywhere we went I had trouble making out which was I, the one walking at my side, the one walking in my pants.

One afternoon while we were at that lake a thunderstorm came up. It   12 was the revival of an old melodrama that I had seen long ago with childish awe. The second-act climax of the drama of the electrical disturbance over a

---

flywheel: A heavy wheel revolving on a shaft to regulate machinery.   **Ubangi:** People who live near the Ubangi River in the Central African Republic and Zaire. The women traditionally pierce and stretch their lips around flat wooden disks.   **mandolins:** Small stringed instruments often used in ballads and folk music.

lake in America had not changed in any important respect. This was the big scene. The whole thing was so familiar, the first feeling of oppression and heat and a general air around camp of not wanting to go very far away. In midafternoon (it was all the same) a curious darkening of the sky, and a lull in everything that had made life tick; and then the way the boats suddenly swung the other way at their moorings with the coming of a breeze out of the new quarter, and the premonitory° rumble. Then the kettle drum, then the snare, then the bass drum and cymbals, then crackling light against the dark, and the gods grinning and licking their chops in the hills. Afterward the calm, the rain steadily rustling in the calm lake, the return of light and hope and spirits, and the campers running out in joy and relief to go swimming in the rain, their bright cries perpetuating the deathless joke about how they were getting simply drenched, and the children screaming with delight at the new sensation of bathing in the rain, and the joke about getting drenched linking the generations in a strong indestructible chain. And the comedian who waded in carrying an umbrella.

When the others went swimming my son said he was going in, too. He pulled his dripping trunks from the line where they had hung all through the shower and wrung them out. Languidly, and with no thought of going in, I watched him, his hard little body, skinny and bare, saw him wince slightly as he pulled up around his vitals the small, soggy, icy garment. As he buckled the swollen belt, suddenly my groin felt the chill of death. 13

Questions to Start You Thinking

1. CONSIDERING MEANING: How have the lake and the surrounding community, as White depicts them, changed since he was a boy?

2. IDENTIFYING WRITING STRATEGIES: Notice the details White uses to describe life at the lake. How many different sensory experiences do his images evoke? Identify and then analyze at least four memorable images from the essay, explaining what makes each memorable.

3. READING CRITICALLY: White compares the past with the present to show that "there had been no years" since his childhood at the lake (paragraph 5). How does this comparison shape the tone of White's essay? How does the tone change at the end? What is the effect of this sudden change?

4. EXPANDING VOCABULARY: Define *primeval* (paragraph 3), *transposition* (paragraph 4), *hellgrammite* (paragraph 5), *undulating, cultist* (paragraph 6), and *petulant* (paragraph 10). What is White's purpose in using adult words rather than a child's words to look back on his childhood experience?

5. MAKING CONNECTIONS: Both White and Gerald Early in "Black like . . . Shirley Temple?" (pp. 391–93) describe their efforts to please and to draw closer to their children. Whose attempt seems more successful? Why?

---

premonitory: Warning.

Journal Prompts

1. Describe a place that has special meaning for you. Why is it special?

2. Use White's description of a thunderstorm (paragraph 12) as a model to describe a natural event that you have witnessed.

Suggestions for Writing

1. Think of a place you knew as a child and then visited again as an adult. Write an essay explaining how the place had changed and not changed. Use observation and recall to make the place as memorable for your readers as it was for you.

2. How do you think nostalgia—the desire to return to an important and pleasant time in the past—influences the way we remember our own experiences? Use examples from White's essay and from your experience to illustrate your explanation.

Amy Tan
Mother Tongue

Amy Tan *was born in 1952 in Oakland, California, a few years after her parents immigrated to the United States from China. After receiving a B.A. in English and linguistics and an M.A. in linguistics from San Jose State University, Tan worked as a specialist in language development for five years before becoming a freelance business writer in 1981. Tan wrote her first short story in 1985; it became the basis for her first novel,* The Joy Luck Club *(1990), which was a phenomenal bestseller and was made into a movie. Tan's second novel,* The Kitchen God's Wife *(1991), was equally popular. She has also written children's books,* The Moon Lady *(1992) and* The Chinese Siamese Cat *(1994), and edited* Best American Short Stories *(1999). With* The One Hundred Secret Senses *(1995), Tan's ambitious third novel, she returned to familiar themes of familial relationships, loyalty, and ways of reconciling the past with the present. Most recently she published* The Bonesetter's Daughter *(2001). "Mother Tongue" first appeared in* Threepenny Review *in 1990; in this essay, Tan explores the effect her mother's "broken" English—the language Tan grew up with—has had on her life and writing.*

AS YOU READ: *Identify the difficulties Tan says exist for a child growing up in a family that speaks nonstandard English.*

I am not a scholar of English or literature. I cannot give you much more than personal opinions on the English language and its variations in this country or others.

I am a writer. And by that definition, I am someone who has always loved language. I am fascinated by language in daily life. I spend a great deal of my time thinking about the power of language — the way it can evoke an emotion, a visual image, a complex idea, or a simple truth. Language is the tool of my trade. And I use them all — all the Englishes I grew up with.

Recently, I was made keenly aware of the different Englishes I do use. I was giving a talk to a large group of people, the same talk I had already given to half a dozen other groups. The nature of the talk was about my writing, my life, and my book, *The Joy Luck Club*. The talk was going along well enough, until I remembered one major difference that made the whole talk sound wrong. My mother was in the room. And it was perhaps the first time she had heard me give a lengthy speech, using the kind of English I have never used with her. I was saying things like, "The intersection of memory upon imagination" and "There is an aspect of my fiction that relates to thus-and-thus" — a speech filled with carefully wrought° grammatical phrases, burdened, it suddenly seemed to me, with nominalized° forms, past perfect tenses, conditional phrases, all the forms of Standard English that I had learned in school and through books, the forms of English I did not use at home with my mother.

Just last week, I was walking down the street with my mother, and I again found myself conscious of the English I was using, and the English I do use with her. We were talking about the price of new and used furniture and I heard myself saying this: "Not waste money that way." My husband was with us as well, and he didn't notice any switch in my English. And then I realized why. It's because over the twenty years we've been together I've often used that same kind of English with him, and sometimes he even uses it with me. It has become our language of intimacy, a different sort of English that relates to family talk, the language I grew up with.

So you'll have some idea of what this family talk I heard sounds like, I'll quote what my mother said during a recent conversation which I videotaped and then transcribed.° During this conversation, my mother was talking about a political gangster in Shanghai who had the same last name as her family's, Du, and how the gangster in his early years wanted to be adopted by her family, which was rich by comparison. Later, the gangster became more powerful, far richer than my mother's family, and one day showed up at my mother's wedding to pay his respects. Here's what she said in part:

"Du Yusong having business like fruit stand. Like off the street kind. He is like Du Zong — but not Tsung-ming Island people. The local people call putong, the river east side, he belong to that side local people. That man want to ask Du Zong father take him in like become own family. Du Zong father wasn't look down on him, but didn't take seriously, until that man big like become a mafia. Now important person, very hard to inviting him. Chinese way, came only to show respect, don't stay for dinner. Respect for making big celebration, he shows up. Mean gives lots of respect. Chinese

---

wrought: Crafted.   **nominalized:** Made into a noun from a verb.   **transcribed:** Made a written copy of what was said.

custom. Chinese social life that way. If too important won't have to stay too long. He come to my wedding. I didn't see, I heard it. I gone to boy's side, they have YMCA dinner. Chinese age I was nineteen."

You should know that my mother's expressive command of English be- 7 lies° how much she actually understands. She reads the *Forbes* report, listens to *Wall Street Week*, converses daily with her stockbroker, reads all of Shirley MacLaine's books with ease — all kinds of things I can't begin to understand. Yet some of my friends tell me they understand fifty percent of what my mother says. Some say they understand eighty to ninety percent. Some say they understand none of it, as if she were speaking pure Chinese. But to me, my mother's English is perfectly clear, perfectly natural. It's my mother tongue. Her language, as I hear it, is vivid, direct, full of observation and im- agery. That was the language that helped shape the way I saw things, ex- pressed things, made sense of the world.

Lately, I've been giving more thought to the kind of English my mother 8 speaks. Like others, I have described it to people as "broken" or "fractured" English. But I wince when I say that. It has always bothered me that I can think of no way to describe it other than "broken," as if it were damaged and needed to be fixed, as if it lacked a certain wholeness and soundness. I've heard other terms used, "limited English," for example. But they seem just as bad, as if everything is limited, including people's perceptions of the limited English speaker.

I know this for a fact, because when I was growing up, my mother's 9 "limited" English limited *my* perception of her. I was ashamed of her Eng- lish. I believed that her English reflected the quality of what she had to say. That is, because she expressed them imperfectly her thoughts were imper- fect. And I had plenty of empirical evidence to support me: the fact that people in department stores, at banks, and at restaurants did not take her se- riously, did not give her good service, pretended not to understand her, or even acted as if they did not hear her.

My mother has long realized the limitations of her English as well. 10 When I was fifteen, she used to have me call people on the phone to pre- tend I was she. In this guise, I was forced to ask for information or even to complain and yell at people who had been rude to her. One time it was a call to her stockbroker in New York. She had cashed out her small portfolio and it just so happened we were going to go to New York the next week, our very first trip outside California. I had to get on the phone and say in an adolescent voice that was not very convincing, "This is Mrs. Tan."

And my mother was standing in the back whispering loudly, "Why he 11 don't send me check, already two weeks late. So mad he lie to me, losing me money."

And then I said in perfect English, "Yes, I'm getting rather concerned. 12 You had agreed to send the check two weeks ago, but it hasn't arrived."

---

belies: Shows to be false.

Then she began to talk more loudly. "What he want, I come to New 13
York tell him front of his boss, you cheating me?" And I was trying to
calm her down, make her be quiet, while telling the stockbroker, "I can't
tolerate any more excuses. If I don't receive the check immediately, I am
going to have to speak to your manager when I'm in New York next week."
And sure enough, the following week there we were in front of this astonished stockbroker, and I was sitting there red-faced and quiet, and my
mother, the real Mrs. Tan, was shouting at his boss in her impeccable broken English.

We used a similar routine just five days ago, for a situation that was far 14
less humorous. My mother had gone to the hospital for an appointment, to
find out about a benign brain tumor a CAT scan had revealed a month ago.
She said she had spoken very good English, her best English, no mistakes.
Still, she said, the hospital did not apologize when they said they had lost
the CAT scan and she had come for nothing. She said they did not seem to
have any sympathy when she told them she was anxious to know the exact
diagnosis, since her husband and son had both died of brain tumors. She
said they would not give her any more information until the next time and
she would have to make another appointment for that. So she said she
would not leave until the doctor called her daughter. She wouldn't budge.
And when the doctor finally called her daughter, me, who spoke in perfect
English — lo and behold — we had assurances the CAT scan would be
found, promises that a conference call on Monday would be held, and
apologies for any suffering my mother had gone through for a most regrettable mistake.

I think my mother's English almost had an effect on limiting my possi- 15
bilities in life as well. Sociologists and linguists probably will tell you that a
person's developing language skills are more influenced by peers. But I think
that the language spoken in the family, especially in immigrant families
which are more insular, plays a large role in shaping the language of the
child. And I believe that it affected my results on achievement tests, IQ tests,
and the SAT. While my English skills were never judged as poor, compared
to math, English could not be considered my strong suit. In grade school I
did moderately well, getting perhaps B's, sometimes B-pluses, in English and
scoring perhaps in the sixtieth or seventieth percentile on achievement tests.
But those scores were not good enough to override the opinion that my true
abilities lay in math and science, because in those areas I achieved A's and
scored in the ninetieth percentile or higher.

This was understandable. Math is precise; there is only one correct an- 16
swer. Whereas, for me at least, the answers on English tests were always a
judgment call, a matter of opinion and personal experience. Those tests
were constructed around items like fill-in-the-blank sentence completion,
such as, "Even though Tom was _____ , Mary thought he was _____ ." And
the correct answer always seemed to be the most bland combinations of
thoughts, for example, "Even though Tom was shy, Mary thought he was
charming," with the grammatical structure "even though" limiting the cor-

rect answer to some sort of semantic° opposites, so you wouldn't get answers like, "Even though Tom was foolish, Mary thought he was ridiculous." Well, according to my mother, there were very few limitations as to what Tom could have been and what Mary might have thought of him. So I never did well on tests like that.

The same was true with word analogies, pairs of words in which you 17 were supposed to find some sort of logical, semantic relationship — for example, "*Sunset* is to *nightfall* as _____ is to _____ ." And here you would be presented with a list of four possible pairs, one of which showed the same kind of relationship: *red* is to *stoplight, bus* is to *arrival, chills* is to *fever, yawn* is to *boring.* Well, I could never think that way. I knew what the tests were asking, but I could not block out of my mind the images already created by the first pair, "*sunset* is to *nightfall*" — and I would see a burst of colors against a darkening sky, the moon rising, the lowering of a curtain of stars. And all the other pairs of words — *red, bus, stoplight, boring* — just threw up a mass of confusing images, making it impossible for me to sort out something as logical as saying: "A sunset precedes nightfall" is the same as "a chill precedes a fever." The only way I would have gotten that answer right would have been to imagine an associative situation, for example, my being disobedient and staying out past sunset, catching a chill at night, which turns into feverish pneumonia as punishment, which indeed did happen to me.

I have been thinking about all this lately, about my mother's English, 18 about achievement tests. Because lately I've been asked, as a writer, why there are not more Asian Americans enrolled in creative writing programs. Why do so many Chinese students go into engineering? Well, these are broad sociological questions I can't begin to answer. But I have noticed in surveys — in fact, just last week — that Asian students, as a whole, always do significantly better on math achievement tests than in English. And this makes me think that there are other Asian American students whose English spoken in the home might also be described as "broken" or "limited." And perhaps they also have teachers who are steering them away from writing and into math and science, which is what happened to me.

Fortunately, I happen to be rebellious in nature and enjoy the challenge 19 of disproving assumptions made about me. I became an English major my first year in college, after being enrolled as pre-med. I started writing nonfiction as a freelancer the week after I was told by my former boss that writing was my worst skill and I should hone my talents toward account management.

But it wasn't until 1985 that I finally began to write fiction. And at first I 20 wrote using what I thought to be wittily crafted sentences, sentences that would finally prove I had mastery over the English language. Here's an example from the first draft of a story that later made its way into *The Joy Luck*

---

semantic: Relating to the meaning of language.

Club, but without this line: "That was my mental quandary in its nascent°
state." A terrible line, which I can barely pronounce.

Fortunately, for reasons I won't get into today, I later decided I should   21
envision a reader for the stories I would write. And the reader I decided
upon was my mother, because these were stories about mothers. So with
this reader in mind — and in fact she did read my early drafts — I began to
write stories using all the Englishes I grew up with: the English I spoke to
my mother, which for lack of a better term might be described as "simple";
the English she used with me, which for lack of a better term might be described as "broken"; my translation of her Chinese, which could certainly be
described as "watered down"; and what I imagined to be her translation of
her Chinese if she could speak in perfect English, her internal language, and
for that I sought to preserve the essence, but neither an English nor a Chinese structure. I wanted to capture what language ability tests can never reveal: her intent, her passion, her imagery, the rhythms of her speech, and
the nature of her thoughts.

Apart from what any critic had to say about my writing, I knew I had   22
succeeded where it counted when my mother finished reading my book and
gave me her verdict: "So easy to read."

Questions to Start You Thinking

1. CONSIDERING MEANING: What are the Englishes that Tan grew up with?
   What other Englishes has she used in her life? What does each English have
   that gives it an advantage over the other Englishes in certain situations?

2. IDENTIFYING WRITING STRATEGIES: What examples does Tan use to analyze
   the various Englishes she uses? How has Tan been able to synthesize her
   Englishes successfully into her present style of writing fiction?

3. READING CRITICALLY: Although Tan explains that she writes using "all the
   Englishes" she has known throughout her life (paragraph 21), she doesn't
   do that in this essay. What are the differences between the English Tan uses
   in this essay and the kinds she says she uses in her fiction? How does the
   language she uses here fit the purpose of her essay?

4. EXPANDING VOCABULARY: In paragraph 9, Tan writes that she had "plenty of
   empirical evidence" that her mother's "limited" English meant that her
   mother's thoughts were "imperfect" as well. Define *empirical*. What does
   Tan's use of this word tell us about her present attitude toward the way she
   judged her mother when she was growing up?

5. MAKING CONNECTIONS: At the end of her essay, Tan implies that her
   mother's English helped change her perception of the proper ways to communicate and inspired her successful style of writing (paragraph 21). In
   what ways does John McPhee's mother change his perceptions and influence his approach to life in his essay "Silk Parachute" (pp. 397–99)? How
   are Tan's and McPhee's experiences similar?

---

nascent: Beginning; only partly formed.

Journal Prompts

1. Describe one of the Englishes you use to communicate. When do you use it, and when do you avoid using it?

2. In what ways are you a "translator," if not of language, then of current events and fashions, for your parents or other members of your family?

Suggestions for Writing

1. In a personal essay explain an important event in your family's history, using your family's various Englishes or other languages.

2. Take note of and, if possible, transcribe one conversation you have had with a parent or other family member, one with a teacher, and one with a close friend. Write an essay comparing and contrasting the "languages" of the three conversations. How do the languages differ? How do you account for these differences? What do you think would happen if someone used "teacher language" to talk to a friend or used "friend language" in a class discussion or paper?

Gerald Early
Black like . . . Shirley Temple?

Gerald Early, *born in 1952 in Philadelphia, attended the University of Pennsylvania and earned his M.A. and Ph.D. at Cornell University. He now teaches English and is the Merle Kling Professor of Modern Letters at Washington University in St. Louis. Early writes prolifically about various aspects of American culture, from literature to family to sports. Some of his many books include* Tuxedo Junction: Essays on American Culture *(1989),* The Culture of Bruising: Essays on Prizefighting *(1991),* Daughters: On Family and Fatherhood *(1994), and the autobiographical* How the War in the Street Is Won: A Black Poet's Journey into Himself *(1995). He has also edited several books, including* Lure and Loathing: Essays on Race, Identity, and the Ambivalence of Assimilation *(1993) and* The Mohammed Ali Reader *(1998). In this excerpt from an essay entitled "Life with Daughters, or the Cakewalk with Shirley Temple," which was first published in the Winter 1991–1992 issue of* Hungry Mind Review, *Early describes a dilemma he faced when his attempt to influence his daughters backfired.*

AS YOU READ: *Whose opinions seem to influence Early's daughters the most in making decisions about their appearances? Why?*

It was two years ago, the summer that my daughters gave up their Afros and had their hair straightened, that I decided to watch every Shirley Temple film available on video with them. This included nineteen Twentieth

Century Fox films that were made during her heyday° — 1934 to 1938 —
and several short Baby Burlesks.

I am not quite sure why I did this. I do not like Shirley Temple movies. I   2
did not like them much as a child. But my daughters — Linnet, then age ten,
and Rosalind, then age seven — after having seen a colorized version of *Our
Little Girl*, a perfectly wretched Temple vehicle (even Temple herself admits
this in her autobiography), on the Disney channel one evening, very much
wanted to do this summer project. We watched each of the films at least
three times. The project appealed to me because I felt I could share something with my children while exercising parental control. I would seem to
be a kid while retaining my status and authority as father.

Perhaps I associate my children's change in hairstyle with our Shirley   3
Temple phase because so much was made of Temple's hair, her curls, during
her years of stardom. My daughters liked Temple's hair very much.

During the summer that we watched these films together, my relation-   4
ship with my daughters changed. At first I saw the films merely as vehicles
for parental instruction — black parental instruction, I should say, for I had
prepared to give a history of black actors in Hollywood in the 1930s and
provide information on the lives of the black dancer Bill "Bojangles" Robinson, the actress Hattie McDaniel, and some of the other blacks who appeared in Temple films. I was never given much of an opportunity.

"I don't want to hear your old lectures, Daddy," Linnet said. "We want to   5
watch the movies. This isn't school. You make being black seem like a lesson."

When they laughed uproariously at some graceless thing that Stepin   6
Fetchit or Willie Best did, Rosalind turned to me, knowing that I was aghast,
and said:

"Don't worry, we know they aren't real black people."   7

"But do you know what you're laughing at?" I asked, chagrined.°   8

"Yeah," Rosalind said, "clowns, not black people."   9

Eventually, I was told that if all I wanted to do was talk about the   10
movies or analyze them, then I would not be permitted to watch. Besides,
they were more than capable of judging the films themselves. So I grew
quiet as the summer went on. I did not want to be banished.

It was during this summer that they abandoned their Afro hairstyles for   11
good. They had had a hard time of it in school the previous year; their hair
had been the subject of jokes and taunts from both black and white children. Moreover, I suppose they wanted straightened hair like their mother.

When they both burst through the door that evening with their hair   12
newly straightened, beaming, looking for all the world like young ladies, I
was so taken aback in a kind of horror that I could only mutter in astonish-
ment when they asked, "How do you like it?" It was as if my children were
no longer mine, as if a culture that had convinced them they were ugly had
taken them from me. I momentarily looked at my wife as if to say, "This is
your doing. If only you would wear your hair as you did when we first met,
this would not have happened."

heyday: Height of success.   **chagrined:** Dismayed and embarrassed.

My wife's response was, "They wanted their hair straightened and they ₁₃ thought they were old enough for it. Besides, there is no virtue in wearing an Afro. I don't believe in politically correct hair. Who was the last white woman you saw who didn't have something done to her hair? Most white women don't wear their hair the way God put it on their heads. It's been dyed, moussed, permed, teased, spiked, shagged, curled, and coiffed. What do you think, Shirley Temple was born with those curls? I've got news for you. Her mom had to work like heck to get those curls set just right. I want the same privilege to do to my hair what white women can do to theirs. It's my right to self-expression."

Right after this happened, late in the summer, I began to find excuses ₁₄ not to watch the Shirley Temple movies. After about two or three weeks, Linnet, who was particularly upset by my lack of approval, asked me why I would not watch the movies with them anymore. I said that I thought the films were for children, not adults; that I was, in effect, intruding. Besides, I had work to do. Eventually, we got around to her new hairstyle.

"I like my hair like this," she said. "This is the way I want to wear it."   ₁₅

"Do you care if I like it?" I asked.   ₁₆

She paused for a moment. "No," she said, bravely. "I want to wear my ₁₇ hair the way I like."

"To get the approval of other people?" I asked unkindly.   ₁₈

"Well," she said, "a little. I don't like to be called dumb. I don't like to ₁₉ be called ugly. I want to be like everybody else. I wear my hair some for me and some for other people. I don't think I'm Shirley Temple or a white girl, but I want to look like a girl, not like a boy. When you write, Daddy, don't you want approval from other people, too?"

Before the discussion ended, she said, "I wish you would watch the ₂₀ movies with us. It's more fun when you watch, too."

About two weeks later, the weekend before the start of school, I received ₂₁ in the mail a Shirley Temple video we hadn't seen, some early shorts that mimicked adult-genre movies, in which she and the other children went around dressed in diapers. I thought this might make a good truce, and so I brought it to my daughters' room and offered to watch it with them. Just before the video started I made a gesture that surprised even me: I stood above Linnet, bent over, and smelled her hair. It had just been washed and freshly straightened ("touched up," my wife said), and it smelled a bit like shampoo, a bit like pressing oil, and very slightly burned, much like, during my childhood, my mother's, my sisters', my aunts' hair smelled. It was a smell that I had, in some odd way, become fond of because, I suppose, it was so familiar, so distressingly familiar, like home.

Questions to Start You Thinking

1. CONSIDERING MEANING: Why does Early's wife object to "politically correct hair" (paragraph 13)?

2. IDENTIFYING WRITING STRATEGIES: Where in the essay does Early use comparison and contrast? How does the essay's final comparison reveal the author's feelings of ambiguity?

3. READING CRITICALLY: What is Early's purpose in writing this essay? Are the conversations with his children that he includes appropriate to his purpose? Why, or why not?

4. EXPANDING VOCABULARY: What is your definition of *politically correct* (paragraph 13)? Do you think that something like hair can be politically correct or incorrect?

5. MAKING CONNECTIONS: In what ways do both Early and Joy Harjo ("Three Generations of Native American Women's Birth Experience," pp. 423–27) feel powerless to shape their children's lives? Where in each essay does the narrator realize that part of his or her family's history is being repeated?

Journal Prompts

1. Describe some of the hairstyles you have had. What or who influenced those styles?

2. What do you think your current hairstyle "says" about you?

Suggestions for Writing

1. Write an essay recalling a time when you rebelled against your parents with a style of dress or hair. What was the nature of your rebellion? How did your parents react? Was your rebellion "successful"? What is your opinion now of that style?

2. Were you ever influenced by a movie or television show to change your appearance or behavior? Tell the story of this change, and then use examples from your own experience to defend or rebut the notion that movies and television shows have too much influence over viewers.

Anna Quindlen
Evan's Two Moms

Anna Quindlen *was born in 1953 in Philadelphia. After graduating from Barnard College in 1974, she worked briefly as a reporter for the* New York Post *before moving to the* New York Times, *where she wrote the "About New York" column. From 1986 to 1989 Quindlen wrote the syndicated column "Life in the 30s," which drew on her experiences with her family and neighborhood; until 1994, when she left the* Times, *she wrote the syndicated column "Public and Private," which explored more political issues. Quindlen won the Pulitzer Prize for commentary in 1992. In addition to her two collections of columns,* Living Out Loud *(1986) and* Thinking Out Loud *(1993), Quindlen has also written three novels—*Object Lessons *(1991),* One True Thing *(1994), and* Black and Blue *(1998)—and* A Short Guide to a Happy Life *(2000). In "Evan's Two Moms," from* Living Out Loud, *Quindlen emphatically argues that gay marriage should be legalized.*

AS YOU READ: *Identify the main points Quindlen uses to support her position.*

Evan has two moms. This is no big thing. Evan has always had two 1
moms—in his school file, on his emergency forms, with his friends.
"Ooooh, Evan, you're lucky," they sometimes say. "You have two moms." It
sounds like a sitcom, but until last week it was emotional truth without
legal bulwark.° That was when a judge in New York approved the adoption
of a six-year-old boy by his biological mother's lesbian partner. Evan. Evan's
mom. Evan's other mom. A kid, a psychologist, a pediatrician. A family.

The matter of Evan's two moms is one in a series of events over the last 2
year that lead to certain conclusions. A Minnesota appeals court granted
guardianship of a woman left a quadriplegic in a car accident to her lesbian
lover, the culmination of a seven-year battle in which the injured woman's
parents did everything possible to negate the partnership between the two.
A lawyer in Georgia had her job offer withdrawn after the state attorney general found out that she and her lesbian lover were planning a marriage ceremony; she's brought suit. The computer company Lotus announced that the
gay partners of employees would be eligible for the same benefits as
spouses.

Add to these public events the private struggles, the couples who go 3
from lawyer to lawyer to approximate legal protections their straight counterparts take for granted, the AIDS survivors who find themselves shut out of
their partners' dying days by biological family members and shut out of
their apartments by leases with a single name on the dotted line, and one
solution is obvious.

Gay marriage is a radical notion for straight people and a conservative 4
notion for gay ones. After years of being sledgehammered by society, some
gay men and lesbian women are deeply suspicious of participating in an institution that seems to have "straight world" written all over it.

But the rads of twenty years ago, straight and gay alike, have other 5
things on their minds today. Family is one, and the linchpin of family has
commonly been a loving commitment between two adults. When same-sex
couples set out to make that commitment, they discover that they are at a
disadvantage: No joint tax returns. No health insurance coverage for an
uninsured partner. No survivor's benefits from Social Security. None of the
automatic rights, privileges, and responsibilities society attaches to a marriage contract. In Madison, Wisconsin, a couple who applied at the Y with
their kids for a family membership were turned down because both were
women. It's one of those small things that can make you feel small.

Some took marriage statutes that refer to "two persons" at their word 6
and applied for a license. The results were court decisions that quoted the
Bible and embraced circular argument: marriage is by definition the union
of a man and a woman because that is how we've defined it.

No religion should be forced to marry anyone in violation of its tenets,° 7
although ironically it is now only in religious ceremonies that gay people
can marry, performed by clergy who find the blessing of two who love each

---

bulwark: Strong support.   **tenets:** Principles.

other no sin. But there is no secular° reason that we should take a patch-work approach of corporate, governmental, and legal steps to guarantee what can be done simply, economically, conclusively, and inclusively with the words "I do."

"Fran and I chose to get married for the same reasons that any two 8 people do," said the lawyer who was fired in Georgia. "We fell in love; we wanted to spend our lives together." Pretty simple.

Consider the case of *Loving v. Virginia*, aptly named. At the time, sixteen 9 states had laws that barred interracial marriage, relying on natural law, that amorphous° grab bag for justifying prejudice. Sounding a little like God throwing Adam and Eve out of paradise, the trial judge suspended the one-year sentence of Richard Loving, who was white, and his wife, Mildred, who was black, provided they got out of the State of Virginia.

In 1967 the Supreme Court found such laws to be unconstitutional. 10 Only twenty-five years ago and it was a crime for a black woman to marry a white man. Perhaps twenty-five years from now we will find it just as incred-ible that two people of the same sex were not entitled to legally commit themselves to each other. Love and commitment are rare enough; it seems absurd to thwart them in any guise.

Questions to Start You Thinking

1. CONSIDERING MEANING: According to Quindlen, what is unjust about not allowing gay men and lesbians to marry *legally*?
2. IDENTIFYING WRITING STRATEGIES: Quindlen ends her essay with a compari-son of gay marriage and interracial marriage (paragraphs 9 and 10). How does she use this comparison to support her argument? Do you think it is a valid comparison? Why, or why not?
3. READING CRITICALLY: What kinds of appeals does Quindlen use in her essay? How are they appropriate or inappropriate for addressing her opponents' arguments? (See pp. 29–30 in *A Writer's Guide* for an explanation of kinds of appeals.)
4. EXPANDING VOCABULARY: Define *marriage* as Quindlen would define it. How does her definition of the term differ from the one in the dictionary?
5. MAKING CONNECTIONS: What privileges of the majority culture are gay fami-lies, Native American families (Harjo, "Three Generations of Native Ameri-can Women's Birth Experience," pp. 423–27), and Asian American families (Tan, "Mother Tongue," pp. 385–90) sometimes denied?

Journal Prompts

1. In your opinion, is the dictionary definition of *marriage* adequate? If so, how do you think it should be revised? If you think the dictionary defini-tion is fine, defend it against attack.

secular: Relating to nonreligious matters.   **amorphous:** Having no specific shape.

2. Imagine that you have the power to design and create the perfect parents. What would they be like? What criteria would they have to meet to live up to your vision of ideal parents?

Suggestions for Writing

1. Describe the most unconventional family you know. How is this family different from other families? How is it the same?

2. In your opinion, would two parents of the same gender help or hurt a child's development? Write an essay comparing and contrasting the possible benefits and disadvantages of this type of family. Use specific examples — hypothetical or gathered from your own observation or reading — to illustrate your argument.

John McPhee
Silk Parachute

John McPhee *was born in Princeton, New Jersey, and was educated at Princeton University and Cambridge University. He is a staff writer at the* New Yorker *and teaches at Princeton. His books include* A Sense of Where You Are *(1965),* The Headmaster *(1989),* Looking for a Ship *(1990),* Assembling California *(1993),* The Ransom of Russian Art *(1996),* Irons in the Fire *(1997), and* Annals of the Former World *(1998). A prolific writer, McPhee received a Pulitzer Prize in 1999 for general nonfiction, and his work has been nominated for the National Book Award. McPhee also received the Award in Literature from the American Academy of Arts and Letters in 1977. In "Silk Parachute," he remembers his relationship with his mother. Now that she's turning ninety-nine, he passes over memories of childhood struggles and focuses on his mother's many gifts to him, including a silk parachute.*

AS YOU READ: *Determine McPhee's final assessment of his mother's success or failure as a parent.*

When your mother is ninety-nine years old, you have so many memo- 1
ries of her that they tend to overlap, intermingle, and blur. It is extremely difficult to single out one or two, impossible to remember any that exemplify the whole.

It has been alleged that when I was in college she heard that I had 2
stayed up all night playing poker and wrote me a letter that used the word "shame" forty-two times. I do not recall this.

I do not recall being pulled out of my college room and into the church 3
next door.

It has been alleged that on December 24, 1936, when I was five years 4
old, she sent me to my room at or close to 7 P.M. for using four-letter words
while trimming the Christmas tree. I do not recall that.

The assertion° is absolutely false that when I came home from high 5
school with an A-minus she demanded an explanation for the minus.

It has been alleged that she spoiled me with protectionism, because I 6
was the youngest child and therefore the most vulnerable to attack from
overhead — an assertion that I cannot confirm or confute, except to say that
facts don't lie.

We lived only a few blocks from the elementary school and routinely 7
ate lunch at home. It is reported that the following dialogue and ensuing action occurred on January 22, 1941:

"Eat your sandwich." 8

"I don't want to eat my sandwich." 9

"I made that sandwich, and you are going to eat it, Mister Man. You 10
filled yourself up on penny candy on the way home, and now you're not
hungry."

"I'm late. I have to go. I'll eat the sandwich on the way back to school." 11

"Promise?" 12

"Promise." 13

Allegedly, I went up the street with the sandwich in my hand and buried 14
it in a snowbank in front of Dr. Wright's house. My mother, holding back
the curtain in the window of the side door, was watching. She came out in
the bitter cold, wearing only a light dress, ran to the snowbank, dug out the
sandwich, chased me up Nassau Street, and rammed the sandwich down my
throat, snow and all. I do not recall any detail of that story. I believe it to be
a total fabrication.°

There was the case of the missing Cracker Jack at Lindel's corner store. 15
Flimsy evidence pointed to Mrs. McPhee's smallest child. It has been averred
that she laid the guilt on with the following words: "'Like mother, like son'
is a saying so true, the world will judge largely of mother by you." It has
been asserted that she immediately repeated that proverb three times, and
also recited it on other occasions too numerous to count. I have absolutely
no recollection of her saying that about the Cracker Jack or any other controlled substance.

We have now covered everything even faintly unsavory that has been re- 16
ported about this person in ninety-nine years, and even those items are a
collection of rumors, half-truths, prevarications, false allegations, inaccura-
cies, innuendoes, and canards.

This is the mother who — when Alfred Knopf wrote her twenty-two- 17
year-old son a letter saying, "The readers' reports in the case of your manuscript would not be very helpful, and I think might discourage you completely" — said, "Don't listen to Alfred Knopf. Who does Alfred Knopf think

assertion: A positive statement or declaration, usually without support.   **fabrication:**
Something invented or made up.

he is, anyway? Someone should go in there and k-nock his block off." To the best of my recollection, that is what she said.

I also recall her taking me, on or about March 8, my birthday, to the 18 theater in New York every year, beginning in childhood. I remember those journeys as if they were today. I remember *A Connecticut Yankee*. Wednesday, March 8, 1944. Evidently, my father had written for the tickets, because she and I sat in the last row of the second balcony. Mother knew what to do about that. She gave me for my birthday an elegant spyglass, sufficient in power to bring the Connecticut Yankee back from Vermont. I sat there watching the play through my telescope, drawing as many guffaws from the surrounding audience as the comedy on the stage.

On one of those theater days — when I was eleven or twelve — I asked 19 her if we could start for the city early and go out to La Guardia Field to see the comings and goings of airplanes. The temperature was well below the freeze point and the March winds were so blustery that the wind-chill factor was forty below zero. Or seemed to be. My mother figured out how to take the subway to a stop in Jackson Heights and a bus from there — a feat I am unable to duplicate to this day. At La Guardia, she accompanied me to the observation deck and stood there in the icy wind for at least an hour, maybe two, while I, spellbound, watched the DC-3s coming in on final,° their wings flapping in the gusts. When we at last left the observation deck, we went downstairs into the terminal, where she bought me what appeared to be a black rubber ball but on closer inspection was a pair of hollow hemispheres hinged on one side and folded together. They contained a silk parachute. Opposite the hinge, each hemisphere had a small nib. A piece of string wrapped round and round the two nibs kept the ball closed. If you threw it high into the air, the string unwound and the parachute blossomed. If you sent it up with a tennis racket, you could put it into the clouds. Not until the development of the ten-megabyte hard disk would the world ever know such a fabulous toy. Folded just so, the parachute never failed. Always, it floated back to you — silkily, beautifully — to start over and float back again. Even if you abused it, whacked it really hard — gracefully, lightly, it floated back to you.

Questions to Start You Thinking

1. CONSIDERING MEANING: Why does McPhee end his essay with a description of the silk parachute? What is its importance in his memories of his mother?

2. IDENTIFYING WRITING STRATEGIES: How does McPhee use anecdotes to develop his essay? What does each story that he recalls contribute to your impression of his mother?

3. READING CRITICALLY: Which of McPhee's anecdotes are told in passive voice? At what point does he shift to active voice? What is the effect of this shift?

final: A plane's final approach before landing.

4. EXPANDING VOCABULARY: Look at McPhee's use of legal jargon in his essay: *alleged* (paragraphs 2, 4, 6, and 14); *ensuing action* (paragraph 7); *averred* (paragraph 15); and *prevarications, false allegations, innuendoes,* and *canards* (paragraph 16). How do these words affect the tone of the essay? How do they color your impression of the writer? of his mother?

5. MAKING CONNECTIONS: How is McPhee's relationship with his mother similar to Amy Tan's ("Mother Tongue," pp. 385–90)? How is it different? Compare and contrast the two authors' mothers.

Journal Prompts

1. Describe an incident from your childhood. Recall as many sensory details as you can to bring it to life.

2. Write about your favorite childhood toy. Who gave it to you? On what occasion? What finally happened to it?

Suggestions for Writing

1. Recall from your childhood four or five interactions with one of your parents. Decide what qualities these incidents demonstrate in your parent. Write an essay that reveals your parent to the reader.

2. Are there stories about members of your family that have been retold and passed along through the years? Why are these stories repeated? What purpose do they serve? Write an essay in which you explore the value of family stories.

Noel Perrin
A Part-Time Marriage

Noel Perrin *was born in 1927 in New York City. He earned degrees at Williams College, Duke University, and Cambridge University and since 1959 has taught English and environmental studies at Dartmouth College. For all his academic credentials, much of his fame as a writer comes from three volumes of essays on part-time farming—*Second Person Rural *(1980),* Third Person Rural *(1983), and* Last Person Rural *(1991). Perrin's* A Child's Delight *(1997) is a collection of essays celebrating some of his favorite but underappreciated children's books. In the following essay, first published in the* New York Times Magazine *on September 9, 1984, Perrin satirizes the postdivorce behavior of many middle-class couples and proposes a somewhat unusual remedy for the problems that plague modern marriages. In the paired selection that follows, Stephanie Coontz examines the difficulties of forming new stepfamilies and offers her own solutions.*

AS YOU READ: *Identify the problems with marriage that Perrin addresses in his essay.*

When my wife told me she wanted a divorce, I responded like any nor- 1
mal college professor. I hurried to the college library. I wanted to get
hold of some books on divorce and find out what was happening to me.

Over the next week (my wife meanwhile having left), I read or skimmed 2
about twenty. Nineteen of them were no help at all. They offered advice on
financial settlements. They told me my wife and I should have been in
counseling. A bit late for *that* advice.

What I sought was insight. I especially wanted to understand what was 3
wrong with me that my wife had left, and not even for someone else, but
just to be rid of *me*. College professors think they can learn that sort of thing
from books.

As it turned out, I could. Or at least I got a start. The twentieth book was 4
a collection of essays by various sociologists, and one of the pieces took my
breath away. It was like reading my own horoscope.

The two authors had studied a large group of divorced people much like 5
my wife and me. That is, they focused on middle-class Americans of the
straight-arrow persuasion. Serious types, believers in marriage for life. Likely
to be parents — and, on the whole, good parents. Likely to have pillar-of-
the-community potential. But, nevertheless, all divorced.

Naturally there were many different reasons why all these people had 6
divorced, and many different ways they behaved after the divorce. But there
was a dominant pattern, and I instantly recognized myself in it. Recognized
my wife, too. Reading the essay told me not only what was wrong with me,
but also with her. It was the same flaw in both of us. It even gave me a hint
as to what my postdivorce behavior was likely to be, and how I might find
happiness in the future.

This is the story the essay told me. Or, rather, this is the story the essay 7
hinted at, and that I have since pieced together with much observation, a
number of embarrassingly personal questions put to divorced friends, and
to some extent from my own life.

Somewhere in some suburb or small city, a middle-class couple separate. 8
They are probably between thirty and forty years old. They own a house and
have children. The conscious or official reason for their separation is quite
different from what it would have been in their parents' generation. Then, it
would have been a man leaving his wife for another, and usually younger,
woman. Now it's a woman leaving her husband in order to find herself.

When they separate, the wife normally stays in the house they occupied 9
as a married couple. Neither wants to uproot the children. The husband
moves to an apartment, which is nearly always going to be closer to his
place of employment than his house was. The ex-wife will almost certainly
never see that apartment. The husband, however, sees his former house all
the time. Not only is he coming by to pick up the children for visits; if he
and his ex-wife are on reasonably good terms, he is apt to visit them right
there, while she makes use of the time to do errands or to see a friend.

Back when these two were married, they had an informal labor division. 10
She did inside work, he did outside. Naturally there were exceptions: she

gardened, and he did his share of the dishes, maybe even baked bread. But mostly he mowed the lawn and fixed the lawn mower; she put up any new curtains, often enough ones she had made herself.

One Saturday, six months or a year after they separated, he comes to see 11 the kids. He plans also to mow the lawn. Before she leaves, she says, "That damn overhead garage door you got is off the track again. Do you think you'd have time to fix it?" Apartment life makes him restless. He jumps at the chance.

She, just as honorable and straight-arrow as he, has no idea of asking 12 for this as a favor. She invites him to stay for an early dinner. She may put it indirectly — "Michael and Sally want their daddy to have supper with them" — but he is clear that the invitation also proceeds from her.

Provided neither of them has met a really attractive other person yet, 13 they now move into a routine. He comes regularly to do the outside chores, and always stays for dinner. If the children are young enough, he may read to them before bedtime. She may wash his shirts.

One such evening, they both happen to be stirred not only by physical 14 desire but by loneliness. "Oh, you might as well come upstairs," she says with a certain self-contempt. He needs no second invitation; they are upstairs in a flash. It is a delightful end to the evening. More delightful than anything they remember from their marriage, or at least from the later part of it.

That, too, now becomes part of the pattern. He never stays the full 15 night, because, good parents that they are, they don't want the children to get any false hopes up — as they would, seeing their father at breakfast.

Such a relationship may go on for several years, may even be inter- 16 rupted by a romance on one side or the other and then resume. It may even grow to the point where she's mending as well as washing his shirts, and he is advising her on her tax returns and fixing her car.

What they have achieved postdivorce is what their marriage should have 17 been like in the first place. Part-time. Seven days a week of marriage was too much. One afternoon and two evenings is just right.

Although our society is even now witnessing de facto part-time arrange- 18 ments, such as the couple who work in different cities and meet only on weekends, we have no theory of part-time marriage, at least no theory that has reached the general public. The romantic notion still dominates that if you love someone, you obviously want to be with them all the time.

To me it's clear we need such a theory. There are certainly people who 19 thrive on seven-day-a-week marriages. They have a high level of intimacy and they may be better, warmer people than the rest of us. But there are millions and millions of us with medium or low levels of intimacy. We find full-time family memberships a strain. If we could enter marriage with more realistic expectations of what closeness means for us, I suspect the divorce rate might permanently turn downward. It's too bad there isn't a sort of glucose tolerance test for intimacy.

As for me personally, I still do want to get married again. About four days a week. 20

Questions to Start You Thinking

1. CONSIDERING MEANING: How did Perrin's divorce affect him?

2. IDENTIFYING WRITING STRATEGIES: How does Perrin use cause and effect to support the solution he proposes?

3. READING CRITICALLY: What is Perrin's purpose in writing this essay? Do you think he is serious about his proposal for a part-time marriage? What evidence in his essay leads you to your conclusion?

4. EXPANDING VOCABULARY: Notice Perrin's use of the words *straight-arrow*, *pillar-of-the-community* (paragraph 5), *dominant* (paragraph 6), *self-contempt* (paragraph 14), *de facto* (paragraph 18), and *glucose tolerance test* (paragraph 19). How does Perrin's vocabulary fit or challenge your expectations of how a college professor writes? Find other examples to support your answer.

5. MAKING CONNECTIONS: Compare and contrast Perrin's role as a father with that of the father in E. B. White's essay ("Once More to the Lake," pp. 379–84) or in Gerald Early's ("Black like . . . Shirley Temple?," pp. 391–93). How do these fathers interact with their children? How do—or might—their children respond?

Link to the Paired Essay

While Perrin and Stephanie Coontz ("Remarriage and Stepfamilies," pp. 404–09) both discuss a reality of many American families—divorce and remarriage—their essays have very different purposes. Compare and contrast the tones of the two essays. For what purposes might each tone be appropriate? If you as a reader were facing the same problems these writers discuss, how would you respond to the two different tones?

WWW
For useful links to Web sources on topics including *families*, visit <www.bedfordstmartins.com/toplinks>.

Journal Prompts

1. Would you prefer a full- or part-time marriage? Why?

2. Sketch out a theory or a plan for part-time marriage. What elements or rules would be needed to make it successful?

Suggestions for Writing

1. Write an essay explaining how divorce has affected you or those around you.

2. Take a stand on the solution Perrin proposes. In a short essay, agree or disagree with the idea of part-time marriage. Is it a constructive response to problems of marital incompatibility? Why, or why not?

Stephanie Coontz

Remarriage and Stepfamilies

Stephanie Coontz was born in 1944 in Seattle. She attended the University of California at Berkeley and the University of Washington at Seattle and has taught history and women's studies at Evergreen State College in Olympia, Washington, since 1975. Coontz has explored gender roles and the American family in several books, including Women's Work, Men's Property *(with Peta Henderson, 1986),* The Social Origins of Private Life: A History of American Families 1600–1900 *(1988), and* The Way We Never Were: American Families and the Nostalgia Trap *(1992). In this meticulously researched and documented excerpt from* The Way We Really Are: Coming to Terms with America's Changing Families *(1997), Coontz analyzes sociological, psychological, and historical data to urge a reevaluation of traditional assumptions about how "healthy" families are defined and formed. While Noel Perrin ("A Part-Time Marriage," pp. 400–03) uses his personal experience with divorce to call for an expanded definition of marriage as an institution, Coontz uses an analysis of various statistical studies to recommend ways of handling parent-child relationships after a parent has remarried.*

AS YOU READ: *Identify the reasons Coontz gives for the difficulties stepfamilies often encounter. According to Coontz, what are the rewards of forming a healthy stepfamily?*

The contradictory data on stepfamilies also illustrate the problem with 1 sweeping generalizations about family structure. While remarriage tends to reduce stresses associated with economic insecurity, some studies suggest that children in stepfamilies, taken as a whole, have the same added risks for emotional problems as do children in one-parent families; they are actually *more* likely to repeat a grade than children whose mothers have never married. Yet most stepfamilies work quite well. In a recent long-term, ongoing government study, 80 percent of children in stepfamilies were judged to be doing well psychologically — not a whole lot worse than the 90 percent in intact biological families. The large majority of stepparents and children in one national survey rated their households as "relaxed" and "close," while less than one-third described their households as "tense" or "disorganized." Sibling conflict, found in all types of families, was only slightly more frequent in families with stepfathers.[1]

The trouble with generalizing about stepfamilies is that they are even 2 more complicated and varied than other family types because there are so many possible routes to forming them. Kay Pasley and Marilyn Ihinger-Tallman have identified nine "structurally distinct" types of remarried families, depending on the custody and visitation arrangements of each partner, the presence of children from the new marriage, and whether there are children from one or both of the remarried parents' former families. The challenges of blending a new family mount with the complexity of the combinations that are being put together.[2]

There seem to be two pieces of advice we can confidently give to parents [3] considering remarriage. The first is *not* to marry just to find a mother or father for your child. While remarriage may be helpful for single-parent families experiencing economic distress, those with adequate financial resources may find that their children's adjustment and academic performance are initially set back. Many children take longer to adjust to remarriage than to divorce, especially when they are teens.[3]

But the second piece of advice is not to be scared off. Most stepfamilies [4] do well, and a good relationship with a stepparent does appear to strengthen a child's emotional life and academic achievement.[4]

Although stepfamilies create new stresses and adaptive challenges, write [5] researchers Mavis Hetherington and James Bray, they "also offer opportunities for personal growth and more harmonious, fulfilling family and personal relationships." Children gain access to several different role models, get the chance to see their parents in a happier personal situation than in the past, and can benefit from the flexibility they learn in coping with new roles and relations.[5]

The most important thing to grasp about stepfamilies is that they re- [6] quire people to put aside traditional assumptions about how a family evolves and functions. Since the parent-child relationships predate the marriage, each parent and child brings a history of already formed family values, rules, rituals, and habits to the new household. This situation can lead to conflict and misunderstanding. Research does not support the stereotype that children in stepfamilies normally suffer from conflicting loyalties, but there is often considerable ambiguity° about parenting roles and boundaries. For adolescents, the situation can be particularly tense. Their understandable resentment of the newcomer may cause their age-appropriate distancing from the biological parent to proceed too rapidly.[6]

Another major challenge to stepfamilies lies in the fact that traditional [7] gender roles often conflict with the new family structure. As therapists Monica McGoldrick and Betty Carter put it, "if the old rules that called for women to rear children and men to earn and manage the financing are not working well in first-marriage families, which they are not, they have absolutely no chance at all in a system where some of the children are strangers to the wife, and where some of the finances include sources of income and expenditure that are not in the husband's power to control" — for example, alimony or child support.[7]

For stepfamilies to meet the needs of both adults and children, they [8] have to create a new family "culture" that reworks older patterns into some kind of coherent whole, allowing members to mourn losses from the previous families without cutting off those relationships. The main barriers to doing this include leftover conflict from previous marriages, unrealistic

---

ambiguity: Something that is unclear or unspecified.

expectations about instant bonding within the new family, and attempts to reproduce traditional nuclear family norms.[8]

As Lawrence Ganong and Marilyn Coleman point out, stepfamilies that try to function like a first-marriage nuclear family "must engage in massive denial and distortion of reality," pretending that former spouses, with their separate family histories, do not exist and cutting members off from important people or traditions in their life. This is not healthy. Nor is it realistic for the biological parent in the household to expect to have sole control over childrearing decisions. Thus stepfamilies need to have "more permeable° boundaries" than nuclear families usually maintain. And a stepparent-stepchild relationship probably *should* be less emotionally close than a parent-child relationship.[9]

Old-fashioned gender roles pose another problem for stepfamilies. *Stepmother* families have more conflicts, many specialists believe, because both women and men often expect the wife to shoulder responsibility for child care and for the general emotional well-being of the family. A stepmother may therefore try to solve problems between her husband and his children or the children and their biological mother, which sets the stepmother up to be the villain for both the children and the ex-wife. In stepfather families, a woman having trouble with her children may push her new husband to assume a disciplinary role far too early in the marriage, which tends to set back or even derail his developing relationship with the children.[10]

Therapists recommend that stepfamilies be encouraged to see the problems they face as a consequence of their structural complexities, not of ill will or personal inadequacy. Indeed, many of the difficulties may actually be a result of previous strengths in earlier family arrangements — the woman's desire to make relationships work, for example, or the children's strong commitments to older ties and habits. Hetherington found that sons "who were high in self-esteem, assertiveness, and social competence before the remarriage" were most likely to start out being "acrimonious° and negative toward stepfathers." In the long run, though, these boys were especially likely to accept and benefit from a stepfather's addition to the household. Boys who were close to their mothers in the single-parent family tend to resent the establishment of a strong marital alliance in the new stepfamily. Girls are more likely to welcome a close marital relationship, possibly because it serves as a buffer "against the threat of inappropriate intimacy between stepfathers and stepdaughters."[11]

Experts agree that stepfamilies need to develop new norms permitting parental collaboration across household boundaries. They need to facilitate° interactions between children and extended kin on the noncustodial parent's° side of the family. They must let go of romantic fantasies about being able to start over. They also have to become much more flexible about

---

permeable: Able to be passed through; here it means flexible.   **acrimonious:** Bitter.
facilitate: Help to happen.   **noncustodial parent:** The parent who does not have primary custody of a child.

gender roles. The biological parent, whether male or female, should be the primary parent, which means that women must control their tendency to fix everybody's emotional problems and men must control theirs to leave emotional intimacy to women. A new stepfather should resist his wife's desire to have him relieve her of disciplinary duties; similarly, a new wife should resist a husband's pressure to take on maternal roles such as managing schedules, supervising housework, or even making sure the kids remember their lunches on the way to school.[12]

What seems to work best is for a stepparent to initially play the role of 13 camp counselor, uncle, aunt, or even sitter — someone who exercises more adult authority than a friend but is less responsible for direction and discipline than a parent. Behaving supportively toward stepchildren is more effective than trying to exercise control, although stepparents should back up their partners' disciplinary decisions in a matter-of-fact manner and help to keep track of children's whereabouts. Stepparents of adolescents have to recognize that even under the best circumstances, resistance to them is likely to continue for some time. If stepparents understand this reaction as normal, they can control their own natural impulse to feel rejected and to back away.[13]

Parenting in stepfamilies requires a thick skin, a sensitive ear, and a 14 highly developed sense of balance. A successful stepfamily has to tolerate ambiguous, flexible, and often somewhat distant relationships, without allowing any member to disengage entirely. It has to accept a closer relationship between biological parent and child than between stepparent and child without letting that closeness evolve into a parent-child coalition that undermines the united front of the marriage partners. And effective communication skills are even more important in stepfamilies than they are in other kinds of families.[14]

These tasks are challenging, which may be why stepfamilies take longer 15 to come together as a unified team, are more vulnerable to disruption, and often experience renewed turmoil during adolescence. But Jan Lawton, director of the Stepfamily Project in Queensland, Australia, points out that while the divorce rate among remarried families is high in the first two years, it then slows down. After five years, second marriages are more stable than first ones. And researchers have found that even modest, short-term training in communication and problem solving can dramatically increase the stability of stepfamilies.[15]

Notes

1. Barbara Dafoe Whitehead, "Dan Quayle Was Right," *Atlantic Monthly* (April 1993): 71; "School Dropout Rates for Families," *USA Today*, March 15, 1993; "Stepfamilies Aren't Bad for Most Kids," *USA Today*, August 17, 1992: 10; Frank Mott, "The Impact of Father Absence from the Home on Subsequent Cognitive Development of Younger Children," paper delivered at the American Sociological Association, August 1992; Frank F. Furstenberg Jr. and Andrew J. Cherlin, *Divided Families: What Happens to Children When*

Parents Part (Cambridge, Mass.: Harvard University Press, 1991), 89; Andrew J. Cherlin and Frank F. Furstenberg Jr., "Stepfamilies in the United States: A Reconsideration," *Annual Reviews in Sociology* 20 (1994): 372.

2. Kay Pasley and Marilyn Ihinger-Tallman, "Stress and the Remarried Family," *Family Perspectives* 12 (1982): 187.

3. James Bray and Sandra Berger, "Developmental Issues in Stepfamilies Research Project: Family Relationships and Parent-Child Interactions," *Journal of Family Psychology* 7, no. 1 (1993): 86; E. Mavis Hetherington and W. Glenn Clingempeel, *Coping with Marital Transitions: A Family Systems Perspective* (Chicago: Monographs of the Society for Research in Child Development, Serial No. 227, vol. 57, 1992), 205–6; William S. Aquilino, "The Life Course of Children Born to Unmarried Mothers: Childhood Living Arrangements and Young Adult Outcomes," *Journal of Marriage and the Family* 58 (May 1996): 307.

4. E. Mavis Hetherington, "An Overview of the Virginia Longitudinal Study of Divorce and Remarriage with a Focus on Early Adolescence," *Journal of Family Psychology* 7 (1993); Kay Pasley and Marilyn Ihinger-Tallman, *Remarriage and Stepparenting: Current Research and Theory* (New York: Guilford, 1987), 105–9; Bray and Berger, "Developmental Issues in Stepfamilies Research Project," 89.

5. Alan Booth and Judy Dunn, eds., *Stepfamilies: Who Benefits? Who Does Not?* (Hillsdale, N.J.: Lawrence Erlbaum, 1994); Virginia Rutter, "Lessons from Stepfamilies," *Psychology Today* (May–June 1994): 32.

6. Lawrence H. Ganong and Marilyn Coleman, *Remarried Family Relationships* (Thousand Oaks, Calif.: Sage, 1994), 122; Pasley and Ihinger-Tallman, *Remarriage and Stepparenting*, 108; Hetherington and Clingempeel, *Coping with Marital Transitions*, 200–5.

7. Monica McGoldrick and Betty Carter, "Forming a Remarried Family," in McGoldrick and Carter, eds., *The Changing Family Life Cycle: A Framework for Family Therapy*, 3rd ed. (Boston: Allyn and Bacon, 1989).

8. John Visher and Emily Visher, *Therapy with Stepfamilies* (New York: Brunner/Mazel, 1996); McGoldrick and Carter, "Forming a Remarried Family."

9. David Demo and Alan Acock, "The Impact of Divorce on Children," in Alan Booth, ed., 201–2, *Contemporary Families: Looking Forward, Looking Back* (Minneapolis: National Council on Family Relations, 1991); Ganong and Coleman, *Remarried Family Relationships*, 123–37; James Bray and David Harvey, "Adolescents in Stepfamilies: Developmental Family Interventions," *Psychotherapy* 32 (1995): 125; Visher and Visher, *Therapy with Stepfamilies*; McGoldrick and Carter, "Forming a Remarried Family."

10. Lynn White, "Growing Up with Single Parents and Stepparents: Long-Term Effects on Family Solidarity," *Journal of Marriage and the Family* 56, no. 4 (November 1994); Rutter, "Lessons from Stepfamilies," 66; Furstenberg and Cherlin, *Divided Families*, 78; McGoldrick and Carter, "Forming a Remarried Family"; John Visher and Emily Visher, *Old Loyalties, New Ties: Therapeutic Strategies with Stepfamilies* (New York: Brunner/Mazel, 1988).

11. E. Mavis Hetherington, "Presidential Address: Families, Lies, and Videotapes," *Journal of Research on Adolescence* 1, no. 4 (1991): 341, 344.

12. Ganong and Coleman, *Remarried Family Relationships*; James Bray and Sandra Berger, "Noncustodial Father and Paternal Grandparent Relationships in Stepfamilies," *Family Relations* 39 (1990).

13. Mark Fine and Lawrence Kurdek, "The Adjustment of Adolescents in Stepfather and Stepmother Families," *Journal of Marriage and the Family* 54 (1992); Bray and Harvey, "Adolescents in Stepfamilies"; Margaret Crosbie-Burnett and Jean Giles-Sims, "Adolescent Adjustment and Stepparenting Styles," *Family Relations* 43 (October 1994); Hetherington and Clingempeel, *Coping with Marital Transitions*, 10, 200–5; Visher and Visher, *Old Loyalties, New Ties.*

14. McGoldrick and Carter, "Forming a Remarried Family"; Visher and Visher, *Therapy with Stepfamilies*; Nancy Burrell, "Community Patterns in Stepfamilies: Redefining Family Roles, Themes, and Conflict Styles," in Mary Anne Fitzpatrick and Anita Vangelisti, eds., *Explaining Family Interactions* (Thousand Oaks, Calif.: Sage, 1995); Carolyn Henry and Sandra Lovelace, "Family Resources and Adolescent Family Life Satisfaction in Remarried Family Households," *Journal of Family Issues* 16 (1995); Marilyn Coleman and Lawrence H. Ganong, "Family Reconfiguring Following Divorce," in Steve Duck and Julia Wood, eds., *Confronting Relationship Challenges*, vol. 5 (Thousand Oaks, Calif.: Sage, 1995).

15. Rutter, "Lessons from Stepfamilies," 60–62; Phyllis Bronstein, Miriam Frankel Stoll, JoAnn Clauson, Craig L. Abrams, and Maria Briones, "Fathering after Separation or Divorce: Factors Predicting Children's Adjustment," *Family Relations* 43 (October 1994): 478.

Questions to Start You Thinking

1. CONSIDERING MEANING: According to Coontz, what are the traditional expectations about how a family should work that make adjusting to a stepfamily especially difficult? What solutions to these difficulties does Coontz propose?

2. IDENTIFYING WRITING STRATEGIES: Coontz uses cause and effect to explain a stepfamily's problems. Trace the potential causes that she identifies. How effective is the use of cause and effect in Coontz's essay, and why?

3. READING CRITICALLY: Coontz begins her essay by pointing out the logical fallacies of generalizing about stepfamilies. How well does she avoid making generalizations in her own writing?

4. EXPANDING VOCABULARY: In paragraph 8, what does Coontz mean by "family 'culture'"? What does the word *culture* convey that a word like *atmosphere* would not?

5. MAKING CONNECTIONS: Could the solutions that Coontz proposes for stepfamilies' problems be useful for the families in Anna Quindlen's essay ("Evan's Two Moms," pp. 394–96)? Why, or why not?

Link to the Paired Essay

Although Coontz and Noel Perrin ("A Part-Time Marriage," pp. 400–03) explore a similar issue, they use different strategies to develop their different points of view. While Perrin writes about the impact of divorce on a family that is breaking up, Coontz analyzes the new families that form when divorces are followed by second marriages. How are the problems of these two family groups similar? How are they different?

www
For useful links to Web sources on topics including *families*, visit <www .bedfordstmartins.com/ toplinks>.

Journal Prompts

1. Think of a complicated situation or difficult problem in your family or the family of a friend. How was the situation handled?

2. Does Coontz's description of what it takes to have a successful stepfamily seem feasible to you? Why, or why not?

Suggestions for Writing

1. Coontz writes that "parenting in stepfamilies requires a thick skin, a sensitive ear, and a highly developed sense of balance" (paragraph 14). What do you think are the primary requirements of good parenting, whether in step-families or first-marriage families? Drawing from your own experience, write an essay explaining your idea of good parenting.

2. Do you think the family as an institution is deteriorating? Write an essay in which you take a stand—that the family is deteriorating or that the family is not deteriorating—and present evidence to support your position.

Chapter 24
Men and Women

Responding to an Image

Often, a photographer's way of composing a photograph reveals more about its subject than the figures in the picture do. Examine the man and woman in this photograph, particularly noting their arrangement. What internal frames does the photographer seek to emphasize, and what are they framing? What physical characteristics or traits can you describe about the man? What physical characteristics or traits can you describe about the woman? What do you think is the subject of this image, and what elements of the photograph led you to this conclusion?

411

WWW
For an additional Web
Search activity, visit
<www.bedfordstmartins
.com/bedguide>.

Web Search

Use a search engine such as Yahoo! or InfoSeek that locates Web sites rather
than specific documents to find one Web source or publication marketed
for women and one marketed for men. Read a few pages of each, and compare
and contrast the content. How are they similar? How are they different?
Do you think the sources stereotype women and men? How, and for what
reasons?

Judy Brady
I Want a Wife

*Judy Brady was born in 1937 in San Francisco, where she now makes her home.
A graduate of the University of Iowa, Brady has contributed to various publications
and has traveled to Cuba to study class relationships and education. More recently,
she edited the book* 1 in 3: Women with Cancer Confront an Epidemic
*(1991), drawing on her own struggle with the disease. In the following piece,
which has been reprinted frequently since its appearance in* Ms. *magazine in December 1971, Brady considers the role of the American housewife. While she has
said that she is "not a 'writer,'" this essay shows Brady to be a satirist adept at taking a stand and provoking attention.*

AS YOU READ: *Ask yourself why Brady says she wants a wife rather than a husband.*

I belong to that classification of people known as wives. I am A Wife. And,   1
not altogether incidentally, I am a mother.

Not too long ago a male friend of mine appeared on the scene fresh   2
from a recent divorce. He had one child, who is, of course, with his ex-wife.
He is looking for another wife. As I thought about him while I was ironing
one evening, it suddenly occurred to me that I, too, would like to have a
wife. Why do I want a wife?

I would like to go back to school so that I can become economically in-   3
dependent, support myself, and, if need be, support those dependent upon
me. I want a wife who will work and send me to school. And while I am
going to school I want a wife to take care of my children. I want a wife to
keep track of the children's doctor and dentist appointments. And to keep
track of mine, too. I want a wife to make sure my children eat properly and
are kept clean. I want a wife who will wash the children's clothes and keep
them mended. I want a wife who is a good nurturant° attendant to my children, who arranges for their schooling, makes sure that they have an adequate social life with their peers, takes them to the park, the zoo, etc. I want

nurturant: Kind, loving, nourishing.

a wife who takes care of the children when they are sick, a wife who arranges to be around when the children need special care, because, of course, I cannot miss classes at school. My wife must arrange to lose time at work and not lose the job. It may mean a small cut in my wife's income from time to time, but I guess I can tolerate that. Needless to say, my wife will arrange and pay for the care of the children while my wife is working.

I want a wife who will take care of *my* physical needs. I want a wife who will keep my house clean. A wife who will pick up after my children, a wife who will pick up after me. I want a wife who will keep my clothes clean, ironed, mended, replaced when need be, and who will see to it that my personal things are kept in their proper place so that I can find what I need the minute I need it. I want a wife who cooks the meals, a wife who is a *good* cook. I want a wife who will plan the menus, do the necessary grocery shopping, prepare the meals, serve them pleasantly, and then do the cleaning up while I do my studying. I want a wife who will care for me when I am sick and sympathize with my pain and loss of time from school. I want a wife to go along when our family takes a vacation so that someone can continue to care for me and my children when I need a rest and change of scene.

I want a wife who will not bother me with rambling complaints about a wife's duties. But I want a wife who will listen to me when I feel the need to explain a rather difficult point I have come across in my course of studies.

I want a wife who will take care of the details of my social life. When my wife and I are invited out by my friends, I want a wife who will take care of the babysitting arrangements. When I meet people at school that I like and want to entertain, I want a wife who will have the house clean, will prepare a special meal, serve it to me and my friends, and not interrupt when I talk about things that interest me and my friends. I want a wife who will have arranged that the children are fed and ready for bed before my guests arrive so that the children do not bother us. I want a wife who takes care of the needs of my guests so that they feel comfortable, who makes sure that they have an ashtray, that they are passed the hors d'oeuvres, that they are offered a second helping of the food, that their wine glasses are replenished when necessary, that their coffee is served to them as they like it. And I want a wife who knows that sometimes I need a night out by myself.

I want a wife who is sensitive to my sexual needs, a wife who makes love passionately and eagerly when I feel like it, a wife who makes sure that I am satisfied. And, of course, I want a wife who will not demand sexual attention when I am not in the mood for it. I want a wife who assumes the complete responsibility for birth control, because I do not want more children. I want a wife who will remain sexually faithful to me so that I do not have to clutter up my intellectual life with jealousies. And I want a wife who understands that *my* sexual needs may entail more than strict adherence to monogamy. I must, after all, be able to relate to people as fully as possible.

If, by chance, I find another person more suitable as a wife than the wife I already have, I want the liberty to replace my present wife with another one. Naturally, I will expect a fresh, new life; my wife will take the children and be solely responsible for them so that I am left free.   8

When I am through with school and have a job, I want my wife to quit working and remain at home so that my wife can more fully and completely take care of a wife's duties.   9

My God, who *wouldn't* want a wife?   10

Questions to Start You Thinking

1. CONSIDERING MEANING: How does Brady define the traditional role of the wife? Does she think that a wife should perform all of the duties she outlines? How can you tell?

2. IDENTIFYING WRITING STRATEGIES: How does Brady use observation to support her stand? What other approaches does she use?

3. READING CRITICALLY: What is the tone of this essay? How does Brady establish it? Considering the fact that she was writing for a predominantly female — and feminist — audience, do you think Brady's tone is appropriate?

4. EXPANDING VOCABULARY: Why does Brady use such simple language in this essay? What is the effect of her use of such phrases as *of course* (paragraph 2), *Needless to say* (paragraph 3), and *Naturally* (paragraph 8)?

5. MAKING CONNECTIONS: Compare Brady's explanation of the role of wife with Scott Russell Sanders's discussion of the women he observed while growing up ("The Men We Carry in Our Minds," pp. 415–19). What would the women Sanders met at college think of the kind of wife Brady discusses?

Journal Prompts

1. Exert your wishful thinking — describe your ideal mate.

2. Begin with a stereotype of a husband, wife, boyfriend, girlfriend, father, or mother, and write a satirical description of that stereotype.

Suggestions for Writing

1. In a short personal essay, explain what you want or expect in a wife, husband, or life partner. Do your hopes and expectations differ from social and cultural norms? If so, in what way(s)? How has your parents' relationship shaped your attitudes and ideals?

2. How has the role of a wife changed since this essay was written? Write an essay comparing and contrasting the post-2000 wife with the kind of wife Judy Brady claims she wants.

Scott Russell Sanders

The Men We Carry in Our Minds

Scott Russell Sanders *was born in 1945 in Memphis, Tennessee. A graduate of Brown University and Cambridge University, Sanders has taught English at Indiana University since 1971. Although he is the author of novels, short story collections, and more than five children's books, Sanders is best known for his essay collections, including* Paradise of Bombs *(1987),* Staying Put: Making a Home in a Restless World *(1993), and* The Force of Spirit *(2000), for which he won the Lannan Literary Award and the Great Lakes Book Award for personal nonfiction. Sanders has described his writing as "driven by a deep regard for particular places and voices . . . a regard compounded of grief, curiosity, and love." In the following essay, which first appeared in* Milkweed Chronicle *in 1984, Sanders explains how the experience of growing up in a working-class community made it difficult for him to understand the grievances of women from more privileged backgrounds.*

AS YOU READ: *Identify the privileges Sanders associated with being male when he entered college. How did his perception change?*

"This must be a hard time for women," I say to my friend Anneke. 1 "They have so many paths to choose from, and so many voices calling them."

"I think it's a lot harder for men," she replies. 2

"How do you figure that?" 3

"The women I know feel excited, innocent, like crusaders in a just cause. 4 The men I know are eaten up with guilt."

We are sitting at the kitchen table drinking sassafras tea, our hands 5 wrapped around the mugs because this April morning is cool and drizzly. "Like a Dutch morning," Anneke told me earlier. She is Dutch herself, a writer and midwife° and peacemaker, with the round face and sad eyes of a woman in a Vermeer° painting who might be waiting for the rain to stop, for a door to open. She leans over to sniff a sprig of lilac, pale lavender, that rises from a vase of cobalt blue.

"Women feel such pressure to be everything, do everything," I say. "Ca- 6 reer, kids, art, politics. Have their babies and get back to the office a week later. It's as if they're trying to overcome a million years' worth of evolution in one lifetime."

"But we help one another. We don't try to lumber° on alone, like so 7 many wounded grizzly bears, the way men do." Anneke sips her tea. I gave her the mug with owls on it, for wisdom. "And we have this deep-down sense that we're in the *right* — we've been held back, passed over, used —

---

midwife: Someone, usually a woman, who assists in childbirth.   **Vermeer:** Jan Vermeer (1632–1675), Dutch painter known for interior scenes that masterfully portray light and color.   **lumber:** Walk or move with heavy clumsiness.

while men feel they're in the wrong. Men are the ones who've been discredited, who have to search their souls."

I search my soul. I discover guilty feelings aplenty — toward the poor,   8
the Vietnamese, Native Americans, the whales, an endless list of debts — a
guilt in each case that is as bright and unambiguous as a neon sign. But toward women I feel something more confused, a snarl of shame, envy, wary
tenderness, and amazement. This muddle troubles me. To hide my unease I
say, "You're right, it's tough being a man these days."

"Don't laugh." Anneke frowns at me, mournful-eyed, through the sassafras   9
steam. "I wouldn't be a man for anything. It's much easier being the victim. All
the victim has to do is break free. The persecutor has to live with his past."

How deep is this past? I find myself wondering after Anneke has left.   10
How much of an inheritance do I have to throw off? Is it just the beliefs I
breathed in as a child? Do I have to scour memory back through father and
grandfather? Through St. Paul? Beyond Stonehenge° and into the twilit
caves? I'm convinced the past we must contend with is deeper even than
speech. When I think back on my childhood, on how I learned to see men
and women, I have a sense of ancient, dizzying depths. The back roads of
Tennessee and Ohio where I grew up were probably closer, in their sexual
patterns, to the campsites of Stone Age hunters than to the genderless cities
of the future into which we are rushing.

The first men, besides my father, I remember seeing were black convicts   11
and white guards, in the cottonfield across the road from our farm on the
outskirts of Memphis. I must have been three or four. The prisoners wore
dingy gray-and-black zebra suits, heavy as canvas, sodden with sweat. Hatless, stooped, they chopped weeds in the fierce heat, row after row, breathing
the acrid dust of boll-weevil° poison. The overseers wore dazzling white
shirts and broad shadowy hats. The oiled barrels of their shotguns flashed in
the sunlight. Their faces in memory are utterly blank. Of course those men,
white and black, have become for me an emblem of racial hatred. But they
have also come to stand for the twin poles of my early vision of manhood —
the brute toiling animal and the boss.

When I was a boy, the men I knew labored with their bodies. They were   12
marginal farmers, just scraping by, or welders, steelworkers, carpenters; they
swept floors, dug ditches, mined coal, or drove trucks, their forearms ropy
with muscle; they trained horses, stoked furnaces, built tires, stood on assembly lines wrestling parts onto cars and refrigerators. They got up before
light, worked all day long whatever the weather, and when they came home
at night they looked as though somebody had been whipping them. In the
evenings and on weekends they worked on their own places, tilling gardens
that were lumpy with clay, fixing broken-down cars, hammering on houses
that were always too drafty, too leaky, too small.

Stonehenge: Four-thousand-year-old arrangement of enormous stones in southern England, thought to have been used for religious ceremonies and astronomical observations.
boll weevil: A parasitic insect that bores into cotton bolls and ruins crops.

The bodies of the men I knew were twisted and maimed in ways visible 13
and invisible. The nails of their hands were black and split, the hands tat-
tooed with scars. Some had lost fingers. Heavy lifting had given many of
them finicky backs and guts weak from hernias. Racing against conveyor
belts had given them ulcers. Their ankles and knees ached from years of
standing on concrete. Anyone who had worked for long around machines
was hard of hearing. They squinted, and the skin of their faces was creased
like the leather of old work gloves. There were times, studying them, when I
dreaded growing up. Most of them coughed, from dust or cigarettes, and
most of them drank cheap wine or whiskey, so their eyes looked bloodshot
and bruised. The fathers of my friends always seemed older than the mothers. Men wore out sooner. Only women lived into old age.

As a boy I also knew another sort of men, who did not sweat and break 14
down like mules. They were soldiers, and so far as I could tell they scarcely
worked at all. During my early school years we lived on a military base, an arsenal in Ohio, and every day I saw GIs in the guardshacks, on the stoops of
barracks, at the wheels of olive drab Chevrolets. The chief fact of their lives
was boredom. Long after I left the arsenal I came to recognize the sour smell
the soldiers gave off as that of souls in limbo. They were all waiting — for wars,
for transfers, for leaves, for promotions, for the end of their hitch — like so
many braves waiting for the hunt to begin. Unlike the warriors of older tribes,
however, they would have no say about when the battle would start or how it
would be waged. Their waiting was broken only when they practiced for war.
They fired guns at targets, drove tanks across the churned-up fields of the military reservation, set off bombs in the wrecks of old fighter planes. I knew this
was all play. But I also felt certain that when the hour for killing arrived, they
would kill. When the real shooting started, many of them would die. This was
what soldiers were *for*, just as a hammer was for driving nails.

Warriors and toilers: those seemed, in my boyhood vision, to be the 15
chief destinies for men. They weren't the only destinies, as I learned from
having a few male teachers, from reading books, and from watching television. But the men on television — the politicians, the astronauts, the gener-
als, the savvy lawyers, the philosophical doctors, the bosses who gave orders
to both soldiers and laborers — seemed as remote and unreal to me as the
figures in tapestries. I could no more imagine growing up to become one of
these cool, potent creatures than I could imagine becoming a prince.

A nearer and more hopeful example was that of my father, who had es- 16
caped from a red-dirt farm to a tire factory, and from the assembly line to
the front office. Eventually he dressed in a white shirt and tie. He carried
himself as if he had been born to work with his mind. But his body, remembering the early years of slogging work, began to give out on him in his
fifties, and it quit on him entirely before he turned sixty-five. Even such a
partial escape from man's fate as he had accomplished did not seem possible for most of the boys I knew. They joined the army, stood in line for
jobs in the smoky plants, helped build highways. They were bound to work
as their fathers had worked, killing themselves or preparing to kill others.

A scholarship enabled me not only to attend college, a rare enough feat 17 in my circle, but even to study in a university meant for children of the rich. Here I met for the first time young men who had assumed from birth that they would lead lives of comfort and power. And for the first time I met women who told me that men were guilty of having kept all the joys and privileges of the earth for themselves. I was baffled. What privileges? What joys? I thought about the maimed dismal lives of most of the men back home. What had they stolen from their wives and daughters? The right to go five days a week, twelve months a year, for thirty or forty years to a steel mill or a coal mine? The right to drop bombs and die in war? The right to feel every leak in the roof, every gap in the fence, every cough in the engine, as a wound they must mend? The right to feel, when the lay-off comes or the plant shuts down, not only afraid but ashamed?

I was slow to understand the deep grievances of women. This was be- 18 cause, as a boy, I had envied them. Before college, the only people I had ever known who were interested in art or music or literature, the only ones who read books, the only ones who ever seemed to enjoy a sense of ease and grace were the mothers and daughters. Like the menfolk, they fretted about money, they scrimped and made-do. But, when the pay stopped coming in, they were not the ones who had failed. Nor did they have to go to war, and that seemed to me a blessed fact. By comparison with the narrow, ironclad days of fathers, there was an expansiveness,° I thought, in the days of moth- ers. They went to see neighbors, to shop in town, to run errands at school, at the library, at church. No doubt, had I looked harder at their lives, I would have envied them less. It was not my fate to become a woman, so it was eas- ier for me to see the graces. Few of them held jobs outside the home, and those who did filled thankless roles as clerks and waitresses. I didn't see, then, what a prison a house could be, since houses seemed to me brighter, handsomer places than any factory. I did not realize — because such things were never spoken of — how often women suffered from men's bullying. I did learn about the wretchedness of abandoned wives, single mothers, wid- ows; but I also learned about the wretchedness of lone men. Even then I could see how exhausting it was for a mother to cater all day to the needs of young children. But if I had been asked, as a boy, to choose between tending a baby and tending a machine, I think I would have chosen the baby. (Hav- ing now tended both, I know I would choose the baby.)

So I was baffled when the women at college accused me and my sex of 19 having cornered the world's pleasure. I think something like my bafflement has been felt by other boys (and by girls as well) who grew up in dirt-poor farm country, in mining country, in black ghettos, in Hispanic barrios,° in the shadows of factories, in third world nations — any place where the fate of men is as grim and bleak as the fate of women. Toilers and warriors. I re- alize now how ancient these identities are, how deep the tug they exert on men, the undertow of a thousand generations. The miseries I saw, as a boy,

---

expansiveness: Flexibility, openness; also connotes grandness.   **barrios:** Spanish- speaking neighborhoods.

in the lives of nearly all men I continue to see in the lives of many — the body-breaking toil, the tedium, the call to be tough, the humiliating powerlessness, the battle for a living and for territory.

When the women I met at college thought about the joys and privileges 20 of men, they did not carry in their minds the sort of men I had known in my childhood. They thought of their fathers, who were bankers, physicians, architects, stockbrokers, the big wheels of the big cities. These fathers rode the train to work or drove cars that cost more than any of my childhood houses. They were attended from morning to night by female helpers, wives and nurses and secretaries. They were never laid off, never short of cash at month's end, never lined up for welfare. These fathers made decisions that mattered. They ran the world.

The daughters of such men wanted to share in this power, this glory. So 21 did I. They yearned for a say over their future, for jobs worthy of their abilities, for the right to live at peace, unmolested, whole. Yes, I thought, yes yes. The difference between me and these daughters was that they saw me, because of my sex, as destined from birth to become like their fathers, and therefore an enemy to their desires. But I knew better. I wasn't an enemy, in fact or in feeling. I was an ally. If I had known, then, how to tell them so, would they have believed me? Would they now?

Questions to Start You Thinking

1. CONSIDERING MEANING: Why does Sanders call himself an "ally" (paragraph 21) of the women he met in college? Do you agree that he was their ally? Explain.

2. IDENTIFYING WRITING STRATEGIES: How does Sanders use the experiences he recalls to support the stand he takes?

3. READING CRITICALLY: What kinds of appeals — emotional, logical, ethical — does Sanders use in his essay? Are the appeals effective? Why, or why not? (For an explanation of kinds of appeal, see pp. 29–30 in *A Writer's Guide.*)

4. EXPANDING VOCABULARY: What qualities do you associate with "warriors" and "toilers" (paragraph 15)? Are the connotations of these terms generally positive or negative? How does Sanders use these connotations to fit the purpose of his essay?

5. MAKING CONNECTIONS: How do the images of men that Sanders acquired in his childhood differ from the images of women that Julia Alvarez ("I Want to Be Miss América," pp. 502–06) acquired in hers?

Journal Prompts

1. Reflect on some of the men and women you knew as a child. How do they compare to the men and women Sanders remembers from his youth?

2. Do you agree that "it's tough being a man these days" (paragraph 8)? Why, or why not? Role-play: if you are female, take a man's point of view; if you are male, take a woman's point of view.

Suggestions for Writing

1. Recalling your own experience, explain the qualities of an important man you "carry in your mind." Who is this man? How did he help shape your views of what masculinity is?

2. Write an essay explaining whether men's or women's roles are more difficult in today's society. Use examples from your own experience as well as from your knowledge of current events.

Emily Prager

Our Barbies, Ourselves

Emily Prager, *born in 1952, writes fiction featuring a surreal and coldly humorous blend of pop culture slogans and classical allusions. Her novel* Clea and Zeus Divorce *(1987) has been called "a music video in the form of a novel." She is also the author of* A Visit from the Footbinder *(1986),* Eve's Tattoo *(1991), and* Roger Fishbite: A Novel *(1999). A former contributing editor to the* National Lampoon, *she has published essays in the* Village Voice *and* Penthouse *and is now a columnist for the* New York Times. *In the following essay, published in* Interview *magazine in December 1991, Prager analyzes what American culture's infatuation with Barbie tells us about ourselves.*

AS YOU READ: *Identify the gender stereotypes that Prager believes Barbie reinforces and the ones Barbie challenges.*

I read an astounding obituary in the *New York Times* not too long ago. It 1 concerned the death of one Jack Ryan. A former husband of Zsa Zsa Gabor, it said, Mr. Ryan had been an inventor and designer during his lifetime. A man of eclectic° creativity, he designed Sparrow and Hawk missiles when he worked for the Raytheon Company, and, the notice said, when he consulted for Mattel he designed Barbie.

If Barbie was designed by a man, suddenly a lot of things made sense to 2 me, things I'd wondered about for years. I used to look at Barbie and wonder, What's wrong with this picture? What kind of woman designed this doll? Let's be honest: Barbie looks like someone who got her start at the Playboy Mansion. She could be a regular guest on *The Howard Stern Show.* It is a fact of Barbie's design that her breasts are so out of proportion to the rest of her body that if she were a human woman, she'd fall flat on her face.

If it's true that a woman didn't design Barbie, you don't know how 3 much saner that makes me feel. Of course, that doesn't ameliorate° the damage. There are millions of women who are subliminally sure that a

eclectic: Drawing on various sources.   **ameliorate:** Make better.

thirty-nine-inch bust and a twenty-three-inch waist are the epitome of lovability. Could this account for the popularity of breast implant surgery?

I don't mean to step on anyone's toes here. I loved my Barbie. Secretly, I   4
still believe that neon pink and turquoise blue are the only colors in which
to decorate a duplex condo. And like many others of my generation, I've
never married, simply because I cannot find a man who looks as good in
clam diggers° as Ken.

The question that comes to mind is, of course, Did Mr. Ryan design Barbie   5
as a weapon? Because it *is* odd that Barbie appeared about the same time in my
consciousness as the feminist movement — a time when women sought equality and small breasts were king. Or is Barbie the dream date of weapons designers? Or perhaps it's simpler than that: perhaps Barbie is Zsa Zsa if she were
eleven inches tall. No matter what, my discovery of Jack Ryan confirms what I
have always felt: there is something indescribably masculine about Barbie —
dare I say it, phallic. For all her giant breasts and high-heeled feet, she lacks a
certain softness. If you asked a little girl what kind of doll she wanted for
Christmas, I just don't think she'd reply, "Please, Santa, I want a hard-body."

On the other hand, you could say that Barbie, in feminist terms, is defi-   6
nitely her own person. With her condos and fashion plazas and pools and
beauty salons, she is definitely a liberated woman, a gal on the move. And
she has always been sexual, even totemic.° Before Barbie, American dolls
were flat-footed and breastless, and ineffably° dignified. They were created
in the image of little girls or babies. Madame Alexander was the queen of
doll makers in the '50s, and her dollies looked like Elizabeth Taylor in *National Velvet.* They represented the kind of girls who looked perfect in jodhpurs,° whose hair was never out of place, who grew up to be Jackie Kennedy
before she married Onassis. Her dolls' boyfriends were figments of the
imagination, figments with large portfolios and three-piece suits and presidential aspirations, figments who could keep dolly in the style to which
little girls of the '50s were programmed to become accustomed, a style that
spasmed with the '60s and the appearance of Barbie. And perhaps what accounts for Barbie's vast popularity is that she was also a '60s woman: into
free love and fun colors, anticlass, and possessed of a real, molded
boyfriend, Ken, with whom she could chant a mantra.

But there were problems with Ken. I always felt weird about him. He   7
had no genitals, and, even at age ten, I found that ominous. I mean, here
was Barbie with these humongous breasts, and that was O.K. with the toy
company. And then, there was Ken with that truncated,° unidentifiable
lump at his groin. I sensed injustice at work. Why, I wondered, was Barbie
designed with such obvious sexual equipment and Ken not? Why was his
treated as if it were more mysterious than hers? Did the fact that it was
treated as such indicate that somehow his equipment, his essential male-

---

clam diggers: Above-the-ankle pants.   **totemic:** Symbolic.   **ineffably:** Indescribably
or unspeakably.   **jodhpurs:** Wide-hipped pants that fit tightly below the knee; typically
used for riding horses.   **truncated:** Cut short.

ness, was considered more powerful than hers, more worthy of the dignity of concealment? And if the issue in the mind of the toy company was obscenity and its possible damage to children, I still object. How do they think I felt, knowing that no matter how many water beds they slept in, or hot tubs they romped in, or swimming pools they lounged by under the stars, Barbie and Ken could never make love? No matter how much sexuality Barbie possessed, she would never turn Ken on. He would be forever withholding, forever detached. There was a loneliness about Barbie's situation that was always disturbing. And twenty-five years later, movies and videos are still filled with topless women and covered men. As if we're all trapped in Barbie's world and can never escape.

God, it certainly has cheered me up to think that Barbie was designed 8 by Jack Ryan. There's only one thing that could make me happier, and that's if Gorbachev° would come over here and run for president on the Democratic ticket. If they don't want him in Russia, fine. We've got the capitalist system in place, ready to go; all we need is someone to run it.

Gorbachev for president and Barbie designed by a man. A blissful end 9 to 1991.

Questions to Start You Thinking

1. CONSIDERING MEANING: Why was Prager relieved to discover that Barbie was designed by a man?

2. IDENTIFYING WRITING STRATEGIES: What does Prager compare and contrast in this essay?

3. READING CRITICALLY: What is the tone of Prager's essay? Would a more formal tone have strengthened her position? Why, or why not?

4. EXPANDING VOCABULARY: Although Prager uses an informal writing style, she also uses some fairly difficult words and concepts. Locate the vocabulary in the article that seems elevated. Is this diction appropriate to her article? Why, or why not?

5. MAKING CONNECTIONS: To what extent do both Prager and Deborah Tannen ("Women and Men Talking on the Job," pp. 431–36) believe that society's expectations of women, instilled in girlhood, can be damaging? Explain.

Journal Prompts

1. Explain the ways in which women are expected to look like Barbie dolls.

2. Do you agree with Prager that in some ways we are "trapped in Barbie's world" (paragraph 7)? What exactly does she mean?

Suggestions for Writing

1. In a brief personal essay, explain how a childhood toy affected the way you learned to view the world and yourself. How did it encourage you to see yourself?

Gorbachev: Former president of Russia and winner of the Nobel Peace Prize.

2. Write a counterpart to Prager's essay, analyzing the Ken doll, G.I. Joe, or another male play figure as a cultural icon. What problems equivalent to those of Barbie do such figures expose about cultural stereotypes of men?

Joy Harjo
Three Generations of Native American Women's Birth Experience

Joy Harjo *was born in 1951 in Tulsa, Oklahoma, and is of Creek (Muscogee) descent. She studied at the Institute of American Indian Arts, the University of New Mexico, and the Iowa Writers' Workshop, where she earned an M.A. in 1978. Harjo now teaches at the University of New Mexico. A poet, essayist, and screenwriter, she writes primarily about social and spiritual themes in Native American life, especially as they relate to Native American women. Her poems and essays often blend myth with current issues, as in* She Had Some Horses *(1983),* Secrets from the Center of the World *(1989),* In Mad Love and War *(1990),* The Woman Who Fell from the Sky *(1994), and* A Map to the Next World: Poetry and Tales *(2000). Harjo coedited* Reinventing the Enemy's Language: Contemporary Native Women's Writing of North America *(1997), a comprehensive anthology that includes more than eighty writers from nearly fifty nations reflecting on what it means to be a Native American woman at the end of the century. In the following essay, which was first published in the July–August 1991 issue of* Ms., *Harjo compares her own experiences giving birth with those of her mother and daughter, using these stories to argue for a return to a birth experience shaped by traditional Native American values.*

AS YOU READ: *Notice how the women in the essay are affected by the loss of their culture. How does this loss affect men? Are the reactions of men and women different?*

It was still dark when I awakened in the stuffed back-room of my mother-   1
in-law's small rented house with what felt like hard cramps. At seventeen years of age I had read everything I could from the Tahlequah Public Library about pregnancy and giving birth. But nothing prepared me for what was coming. I awakened my child's father and then ironed him a shirt before we walked the four blocks to the Indian hospital because we had no car and no money for a taxi. He had been working with another Cherokee artist silk-screening signs for specials at the supermarket and making $5 a day, and had to leave me alone at the hospital because he had to go to work. We didn't awaken his mother. She had to get up soon enough to fix breakfast for her daughter and granddaughter before leaving for her job at the nursing home. I knew my life was balanced at the edge of great, precarious change and I felt alone and cheated. Where was the circle of women to acknowledge and honor this birth?

It was still dark as we walked through the cold morning, under oaks 2 that symbolized the stubbornness and endurance of the Cherokee people who had made Tahlequah their capital in the new lands. I looked for handholds in the misty gray sky, for a voice announcing this impending miracle. I wanted to change everything; I wanted to go back to a place before childhood, before our tribe's removal to Oklahoma. What kind of life was I bringing this child into? I was a poor, mixed-blood woman heavy with a child who would suffer the struggle of poverty, the legacy of loss. For the second time in my life I felt the sharp tug of my own birth cord, still connected to my mother. I believe it never pulls away, until death, and even then it becomes a streak in the sky symbolizing that most important warrior road. In my teens I had fought my mother's weaknesses with all my might, and here I was at seventeen, becoming as my mother, who was in Tulsa, cooking breakfasts and preparing for the lunch shift at a factory cafeteria as I walked to the hospital to give birth. I should be with her; instead, I was far from her house, in the house of a mother-in-law who later would try to use witchcraft to destroy me.

After my son's father left me I was prepped for birth. This meant my 3 pubic area was shaved completely and then I endured the humiliation of an enema, all at the hands of strangers. I was left alone in a room painted government green. An overwhelming antiseptic smell emphasized the sterility of the hospital, a hospital built because of the U.S. government's treaty and responsibility to provide health care to Indian people.

I intellectually understood the stages of labor, the place of transition, of 4 birth — but it was difficult to bear the actuality of it, and to bear it alone. Yet in some ways I wasn't alone, for history surrounded me. It is with the birth of children that history is given form and voice. Birth is one of the most sacred acts we take part in and witness in our lives. But sacredness seemed to be far from my lonely labor room in the Indian hospital. I heard a woman screaming in the next room with her pain, and I wanted to comfort her. The nurse used her as a bad example to the rest of us who were struggling to keep our suffering silent.

The doctor was a military man who had signed on this watch not for 5 the love of healing or out of awe at the miracle of birth, but to fulfill a contract for medical school payments. I was another statistic to him; he touched me as if he were moving equipment from one place to another. During my last visit I was given the option of being sterilized. He explained to me that the moment of birth was the best time to do it. I was handed the form but chose not to sign it, and am amazed now that I didn't think too much of it at the time. Later I would learn that many Indian women who weren't fluent in English signed, thinking it was a form giving consent for the doctor to deliver their babies. Others were sterilized without even the formality of signing. My light skin had probably saved me from such a fate. It wouldn't be the first time in my life.

When my son was finally born I had been deadened with a needle in 6 my spine. He was shown to me — the incredible miracle nothing prepared me for—then taken from me in the name of medical progress. I fell asleep with the weight of chemicals and awoke yearning for the child I had suffered for, had anticipated in the months proceeding from his unexpected genesis when I was still sixteen and a student at Indian school. I was not allowed to sit up or walk because of the possibility of paralysis (one of the drug's side effects), and when I finally got to hold him, the nurse stood guard as if I would hurt him. I felt enmeshed in a system in which the wisdom that had carried my people from generation to generation was ignored. In that place I felt ashamed I was an Indian woman. But I was also proud of what my body had accomplished despite the rape by the bureaucracy's machinery, and I got us out of there as soon as possible. My son would flourish on beans and fry bread, and on the dreams and stories we fed him.

My daughter was born four years later, while I was an art student at the 7 University of New Mexico. Since my son's birth I had waitressed, cleaned hospital rooms, filled cars with gas (while wearing a miniskirt), worked as a nursing assistant, and led dance classes at a health spa. I knew I didn't want to cook and waitress all my life, as my mother had done. I had watched the varicose veins grow branches on her legs, and as they grew, her zest for dancing and sports dissolved into utter tiredness. She had been born with a caul over her face, the sign of a gifted visionary.

My earliest memories are of my mother writing songs on an ancient Un- 8 derwood typewriter after she had washed and waxed the kitchen floor on her hands and knees. She too had wanted something different for her life. She had left an impoverished existence at age seventeen, bound for the big city of Tulsa. She was shamed in a time in which to be even part Indian was to be an outcast in the great U.S. system. Half her relatives were Cherokee full-bloods from near Jay, Oklahoma, who for the most part had nothing to do with white people. The other half were musically inclined "white trash" addicted to country-western music and Holy Roller fervor. She thought she could disappear in the city; no one would know her family, where she came from. She had dreams of singing and had once been offered a job singing on the radio but turned it down because she was shy. Later one of her songs would be stolen before she could copyright it and would make someone else rich. She would quit writing songs. She and my father would divorce and she would be forced to work for money to feed and clothe four children, all born within two years of each other.

As a child growing up in Oklahoma, I liked to be told the story of my 9 birth. I would beg for it while my mother cleaned and ironed. "You almost killed me," she would say. "We almost died." That I could kill my mother filled me with remorse and shame. And I imagined the push-pull of my life, which is a legacy I deal with even now when I am twice as old as my mother was at my birth. I loved to hear the story of my warrior fight for my breath. The way it was told, it had been my decision to live. When I got older, I realized we were both nearly casualties of the system, the same system flourishing in the Indian hospital where later my son Phil would be born.

My parents felt lucky to have insurance, to be able to have their children 10
in the hospital. My father came from a fairly prominent Muscogee Creek
family. *His* mother was a full-blood who in the early 1920s got her degree in
art. She was a painter. She gave birth to him in a private hospital in Oklahoma City; at least that's what I think he told me before he died at age fifty-
three. It was something of which they were proud.

This experience was much different from my mother's own birth. She 11
and five of her six brothers were born at home, with no medical assistance.
The only time a doctor was called was when someone was dying. When she
was born her mother named her Wynema, a Cherokee name my mother
says means beautiful woman, and Jewell, for a can of shortening stored in
the room where she was born.

I wanted something different for my life, for my son, and for my daugh- 12
ter, who later was born in a university hospital in Albuquerque. It was a
bright summer morning when she was ready to begin her journey. I still had
no car, but I had enough money saved for a taxi for a ride to the hospital.
She was born "naturally," without drugs. I could look out of the hospital
window while I was in labor at the bluest sky in the world. I had support.
Her father was present in the delivery room — though after her birth he disappeared on a drinking binge. I understood his despair, but did not agree
with the painful means to describe it. A few days later Rainy Dawn was presented to the sun at her father's pueblo and given a name so that she will always be recognized as a part of the people, as a child of the sun.

That's not to say that my experience in the hospital reached perfection. 13
The clang of metal against metal in the delivery room had the effect of a
tuning fork reverberating fear in my pelvis. After giving birth I held my
daughter, but they took her from me for "processing." I refused to lie down
to be wheeled to my room after giving birth; I wanted to walk out of there
to find my daughter. We reached a compromise and I rode in a wheelchair.
When we reached the room I stood up and walked to the nursery and demanded my daughter. I knew she needed me. That began my war with the
nursery staff, who deemed me unknowledgeable because I was Indian and
poor. Once again I felt the brushfire of shame, but I'd learned to put it out
much more quickly, and I demanded early release so I could take care of my
baby without the judgment of strangers.

I wanted something different for Rainy, and as she grew up I worked 14
hard to prove that I could make "something" of my life. I obtained two degrees as a single mother. I wrote poetry, screenplays, became a professor, and
tried to live a life that would be a positive influence for both of my children.
My work in this life has to do with reclaiming the memory stolen from our
peoples when we were dispossessed° from our lands east of the Mississippi;
it has to do with restoring us. I am proud of our history, a history so powerful that it both destroyed my father and guarded him. It's a history that
claims my mother as she lives not far from the place her mother was born,
names her as she cooks in the cafeteria of a small college in Oklahoma.

dispossessed: Deprived of ownership.

When my daughter told me she was pregnant, I wasn't surprised. I had 15
known it before she did, or at least before she would admit it to me. I felt
despair, as if nothing had changed or ever would. She had run away from
Indian school with her boyfriend and they had been living in the streets of
Gallup, a border town notorious for the suicides and deaths of Indian
peoples. I brought her and her boyfriend with me because it was the only
way I could bring her home. At age sixteen, she was fighting me just as I had
so fiercely fought my mother. She was making the same mistakes. I felt as if
everything I had accomplished had been in vain. Yet I felt strangely empow-
ered, too, at this repetition of history, this continuance, by a new possibility
of life and love, and I steadfastly stood by my daughter.

I had a university job, so I had insurance that covered my daughter. She 16
saw an obstetrician in town who was reputed to be one of the best. She had
the choice of a birthing room. She had the finest care. Despite this, I once
again battled with a system in which physicians are taught the art of healing
by dissecting cadavers. My daughter went into labor a month early. We both
knew intuitively the baby was ready, but how to explain that to a system in
which numbers and statistics provide the base of understanding? My daughter would have her labor interrupted; her blood pressure would rise because
of the drug given to her to stop the labor. She would be given an unneeded
amniocentesis° and would have her labor induced° — after having it artifi-
cially stopped! I was warned that if I took her out of the hospital so her
labor could occur naturally my insurance would cover nothing.

My daughter's induced labor was unnatural and difficult, monitored by 17
machines, not by touch. I was shocked. I felt as if I'd come full circle, as if I
were watching my mother's labor and the struggle of my own birth. But I
was there in the hospital room with her, as neither my mother had been for
me, nor her mother for her. My daughter and I went through the labor and
birth together.

And when Krista Rae was born she was born to her family. Her father was 18
there for her, as were both her grandmothers and my friend who had flown in
to be with us. Her paternal great-grandparents and aunts and uncles had also
arrived from the Navajo Reservation to honor her. Something *had* changed.

Four days later, I took my granddaughter to the Saguaro forest before 19
dawn and gave her the name I had dreamed for her just before her birth. Her
name looks like clouds of mist settling around a sacred mountain as it begins
to speak. A female ancestor approaches on a horse. We are all together.

Questions to Start You Thinking

1. CONSIDERING MEANING: Summarize Harjo's complaints about her first birth
   experience. How does she feel that her traditional cultural values are damaged by the treatment she received at the hospital? How does she regain
   those values?

---

amniocentesis: A test that extracts and analyzes a small amount of the fluid in which a
fetus is suspended.   **induced:** Forced to start.

2. IDENTIFYING WRITING STRATEGIES: Harjo judges the dominant culture's medical system by contrasting it with the traditions of her Native American heritage. To you, what were the most striking contrasts? Does she convince you that her judgment is correct?

3. READING CRITICALLY: When Harjo compares the experience of giving birth to her son to a "rape" (paragraph 6), how do you respond? Where else does she evoke emotional responses to make her points? How effective for her purpose are these appeals to emotions? (See p. 29 in *A Writer's Guide* for an explanation of emotional appeal.)

4. EXPANDING VOCABULARY: Harjo tells us that her mother "had been born with a caul over her face, the sign of a gifted visionary" (paragraph 7). Define *caul* and *visionary*. Why do you think Harjo provides this detail about her mother?

5. MAKING CONNECTIONS: What family traditions do Harjo and E. B. White ("Once More to the Lake," pp. 379–84) hope to hand down to their children?

Journal Prompts

1. Describe some of the traditions of your family. Which traditions are part of a larger culture, and which are unique to your family?

2. Do you know what your name means? If so, do you think it fits you? If not, can you think of another name for yourself that might better match your personality or identity?

Suggestions for Writing

1. Write an essay describing the cultural traditions of your family. Are there different traditions for women and men? In what ways are you either continuing or breaking these traditions?

2. Harjo says that her "work in this life has to do with reclaiming the memory stolen from our peoples" (paragraph 14). Think of a person you know whose work in life you admire or respect. Drawing examples from reading, observation, or conversation, write an essay in which you describe and analyze this person's lifework. Who benefits from this person's work, and in what way?

Dave Barry

From Now On, Let Women Kill Their Own Spiders

Dave Barry *was born in 1947 in Armonk, New York. According to his own biographical statement, he has been "steadily growing older ever since without ever actually reaching maturity." He attended Haverford College and started his career in journalism at the* Daily Local News *in West Chester, Pennsylvania. He has been* *with the* Miami Herald *since 1983 and won the Pulitzer Prize for commentary in 1988. Barry is the author of numerous books, which include* Babies and Other Hazards of Sex *(1984),* Dave Barry's Complete Guide to Guys *(1995),* Dave Barry Is from Mars and Venus *(1997), and* Dave Barry Turns 50 *(1998). The article "From Now On, Let Women Kill Their Own Spiders" first appeared in the* Miami Herald. *In this piece, Barry pokes fun at miscommunication between men and women. Identifying with both, he laughs at how the sexes inevitably bewilder and infuriate each other.*

AS YOU READ: *Try to discover what Barry is really criticizing.*

From time to time I receive letters from a certain group of individuals 1 that I will describe, for want of a better term, as "women." I have such a letter here, from a Susie Walker of North Augusta, S.C., who asks the following question: "Why do men open a drawer and say, 'Where is the spatula?' instead of, you know, looking for it?"

This question expresses a commonly held (by women) negative stereo- 2 type about guys of the male gender, which is that they cannot find things around the house, especially things in the kitchen. Many women believe that if you want to hide something from a man, all you have to do is put it in plain sight in the refrigerator, and he will never, ever find it, as evidenced by the fact that a man can open a refrigerator containing 463 pounds of as-sorted meats, poultry, cold cuts, condiments, vegetables, frozen dinners, snack foods, desserts, etc., and ask, with no irony whatsoever, "Do we have anything to eat?"

Now I could respond to this stereotype in a snide° manner by making 3 generalizations about women. I could ask, for example, how come your av-erage woman prepares for virtually every upcoming event in her life, includ-ing dental appointments, by buying new shoes, even if she already owns as many pairs as the entire Riverdance troupe. I could point out that, if there were no women, there would be no such thing as Leonardo DiCaprio. I could ask why a woman would walk up to a perfectly innocent man who is minding his own business watching basketball and demand to know if a certain pair of pants makes her butt look too big, and then, no matter what he answers, get mad at him. I could ask why, according to the best scientific estimates, 93 percent of the nation's severely limited bathroom-storage space is taken up by decades-old, mostly empty tubes labeled "moisturizer." I could point out that, to judge from the covers of countless women's maga-zines, the two topics most interesting to women are (1) Why men are all disgusting pigs, and (2) How to attract men.

Yes, I could raise these issues in response to the question asked by Susie 4 Walker of North Augusta, S.C., regarding the man who was asking where the spatula was. I could even ask WHY this particular man might be looking for the spatula. Could it be that he needs a spatula to kill a spider, because,

snide: Sarcastic, especially in a nasty manner.

while he was innocently watching basketball and minding his own business, a member of another major gender — a gender that refuses to personally kill spiders but wants them all dead — DEMANDED that he kill the spider, which nine times out of ten turns out to be a male spider that was minding its own business? Do you realize how many men arrive in hospital emergency rooms every year, sometimes still gripping their spatulas, suffering from painful spider-inflicted injuries? I don't have the exact statistics right here, but I bet they are chilling.

As I say, I could raise these issues and resort to the kind of negativity indulged in by Susie Walker of North Augusta, S.C. But I choose not to. I choose, instead, to address her question seriously, in hopes that, by improving the communication between the genders, all human beings — both men and women, together — will come to a better understanding of how dense° women can be sometimes. 5

I say this because there is an excellent reason why a man would open the spatula drawer and, without looking for the spatula, ask where the spatula is: The man does not have TIME to look for the spatula. Why? Because he is busy thinking. Men are almost always thinking. When you look at a man who appears to be merely scratching himself, rest assured that inside his head, his brain is humming like a high-powered computer, processing millions of pieces of information and producing important insights such as, "This feels good!" 6

We should be grateful that men think so much, because over the years they have thought up countless inventions that have made life better for all people, everywhere. The shot clock in basketball is one example. Another one is underwear-eating bacteria. I found out about this thanks to the many alert readers who sent me an article from *New Scientist* magazine stating that Russian scientists — and you KNOW these are guy scientists — are trying to solve the problem of waste disposal aboard spacecraft, by "designing a cocktail of bacteria to digest astronauts' cotton and paper underpants." Is that great, or what? I am picturing a utopian future wherein, when a man's briefs get dirty, they will simply dissolve from his body, thereby freeing him from the chore of dealing with his soiled underwear via the labor-intensive, time-consuming method he now uses, namely, dropping them on the floor. 7

I'm not saying that guys have solved all the world's problems. I'm just saying that there ARE solutions out there, and if, instead of harping endlessly about spatulas, we allow guys to use their mental talents to look for these solutions, in time, they will find them. Unless they are in the refrigerator. 8

Questions to Start You Thinking

1. CONSIDERING MEANING: What is Barry satirizing in his essay?
2. IDENTIFYING WRITING STRATEGIES: Barry's essay is filled with rhetorical questions. Locate some of these, and consider how he answers them. What evidence does he provide to support his answers? How does this evidence affect his tone? How does it affect meaning?

dense: Slow-witted.

3. READING CRITICALLY: What generalizations about women does Barry make in paragraph 3? How do these serve to support his main point?

4. EXPANDING VOCABULARY: Define *utopian* (paragraph 7). According to Barry, how would underwear-eating bacteria contribute to a utopian future?

5. MAKING CONNECTIONS: Both Barry and Judy Brady ("I Want a Wife," pp. 412–14) use satire, humorously attacking human mistakes and shortcomings in their essays. Compare and contrast their use of satire.

Journal Prompts

1. Put your imagination to work to suggest other inventions — besides underwear-eating bacteria — that would benefit man- (or woman-) kind. Follow Barry's model and have fun.

2. Discuss a conversation you've heard that involved man- or woman-bashing. What was the tone of the conversation? How serious were the participants? What are the effects of such remarks?

Suggestions for Writing

1. Stereotypes can be useful tools in literature, but in real life they may be damaging. Write an essay in which you examine real-life stereotypes. Recall behavior you have both observed and experienced as you develop your essay.

2. Using Barry's essay as a model, write an essay satirizing an issue you find unfair, irritating, or just amusing.

Deborah Tannen
Women and Men Talking on the Job

Deborah Tannen, *born in 1945 in Brooklyn, New York, received her Ph.D. from the University of California at Berkeley in 1979 and is now a University Professor of linguistics at Georgetown University. Tannen believes that it is her "mission" to make academic linguistic research accessible and interesting, as she has done in her many books for the general public about the way people talk to each other. Her books include* That's Not What I Meant! How Conversational Style Makes or Breaks Your Relations with Others *(1986),* You Just Don't Understand: Women and Men in Conversation *(1990), and* I Only Say This Because I Love You: How the Way We Talk Can Make or Break Family Relationships throughout Our Lives *(2001). In* The Argument Culture: Moving from Debate to Dialogue *(1998), Tannen takes a penetrating look at the way Americans argue and the sometimes disastrous consequences that follow. This excerpt is from a longer chapter in* Talking from 9 to 5: How Women's and Men's Conversational Styles Affect Who Gets Heard, Who Gets Credit, and What Gets Done *at Work (1994). Here Tannen focuses on both the causes and effects of some key differences in the way men and women negotiate, present their ideas, and express leadership on the job, while in the paired selection that follows (p. 437), Nicholas Wade addresses broad differences in the ways men and women think.*

AS YOU READ: *Notice what Tannen says accounts for the differences in the ways men and women communicate.*

Negotiating Styles

The managers of a medium-size company got the go-ahead to hire a human-resources coordinator, and two managers who worked well together were assigned to make the choice. As it turned out Maureen and Harold favored different applicants, and both felt strongly about their preferences. Maureen argued with assurance and vigor that the person she wanted to hire was the most creative and innovative, and that he had the most appropriate experience. Harold argued with equal conviction that the applicant he favored had a vision of management that fit with the company's, whereas her candidate might be a thorn in their side. They traded arguments for some time, neither convincing the other. Then Harold said that hiring the applicant Maureen wanted would make him so uncomfortable that he would have to consider resigning. Maureen respected Harold. What's more, she liked and considered him a friend. So she felt that his admission of such strong feelings had to be taken into account. She said what seemed to her the only thing she could say under the circumstances: "Well, I certainly don't want you to feel uncomfortable here; you're one of the pillars of the place. If you feel that strongly about it, I can't argue with that." Harold's choice was hired.

In this case, the decision-making power went not to the manager who had the highest rank in the firm (their positions were parallel) and not necessarily to the one whose judgment was best, but to the one whose arguing strategies were most effective in the negotiation. Maureen was an ardent and persuasive advocate for her view, but she assumed that she and Harold would have to come to an agreement in order to make a decision, and that she had to take his feelings into account. Since Harold would not back down, she did. Most important, when he argued that he would have to quit if she got her way, she felt she had no option but to yield.

What was crucial was not Maureen's and Harold's individual styles in isolation but how their styles interacted — how they played in concert with the other's style. Harold's threat to quit ensures his triumph — when used with someone who would not call his bluff. If he had been arguing with someone who regarded this threat as simply another move in the negotiation rather than as a nonnegotiable expression of deep feelings that had to be respected, the result might have been different. For example, had she said, "That's ridiculous; of course you're not going to quit!" or "If that's how shallow your commitment to this firm is, then we'd be better off without you," the decision might well have gone the other way.

When you talk to someone whose style is similar to yours, you can fairly   4
well predict the response you are going to get. But when you talk to someone whose style is different, you can't predict, and often can't make sense of,
the response. Hearing the reaction you get, if it's not the one you expected,
often makes you regret what you said. Harold later told Maureen that he
was sorry he had used the argument he did. In retrospect he was embarrassed, even a bit ashamed of himself. His retrospective chagrin was like
what you feel if you slam down something in anger and are surprised and
regretful to see that it breaks. You wanted to make a gesture, but you didn't
expect it to come out with such force. Harold regretted what he said precisely because it caused Maureen to back down so completely. He'd known
he was upping the ante° — he felt he had to do something to get them out
of the loop of recycling arguments they were in — but he had not expected it
to end the negotiation summarily; he expected Maureen to meet his move
with a balancing move of her own. He did not predict the impact that per-
sonalizing his argument would have on her. For her part, Maureen did not
think of Harold's threat as just another move in a negotiable argument; she
heard it as a personal plea that she could not reject. Their different approaches to negotiation put her at a disadvantage in negotiating with him.

"How Certain Are You of That?"

Negotiating is only one kind of activity that is accomplished through talk at   5
work. Other kinds of decision making are also based as much on ways of
talking as on the content of the arguments. The CEO of a corporation explained to me that he regularly has to make decisions based on insufficient
information — and making decisions is a large part of his work life. Much of
his day is spent hearing brief presentations following which he must either
approve or reject a course of action. He has to make a judgment in five minutes about issues the presenters have worked on for months. "I decide," he
explained, "based on how confident they seem. If they seem very confident,
I call it a go. If they seem unsure, I figure it's too risky and nix it."

Here is where the rule of competence and the role of communication go   6
hand in hand. Confidence, after all, is an internal feeling. How can you
judge others' confidence? The only evidence you have to go on is circumstantial — how they talk about what they know. You judge by a range of
signs, including facial expression and body posture, but most of all, speech.
Do they hesitate? Do they speak or swallow half their words? Is their tone of
voice declamatory or halting? Do they make bald statements ("This is a winner! We've got to go for it!") or hedge ("Um . . . from what I can tell, I think
it'll work, but we'll never know for sure until we try")? This seems simple
enough. Surely, you can tell how confident people are by paying attention to
how they speak, just as you can tell when someone is lying.

Well, maybe not. Psychologist Paul Ekman has spent years studying   7
lying, and he has found that most people are very sure they can tell when

---

ante: Cost or stakes.

others are lying. The only trouble is, most can't. With a few thus-far inexplicable exceptions, people who tell him they are absolutely sure they can tell if someone is lying are as likely to be wrong as to be right — and he has found this to be as true for judges as for the rest of us.

In the same way, our ability to determine how confident others are is probably quite limited. The CEO who does not take into account the individual styles of the people who make presentations to him will find it difficult, if not impossible, to make the best judgment. Different people will talk very differently, not because of the absolute level of their confidence or lack of it, but because of their habitual ways of speaking. There are those who sound sure of themselves even when inside they're not sure at all, and others who sound tentative even when they're very sure indeed. So being aware of differences in ways of speaking is a prerequisite for making good decisions as well as good presentations.

Feasting on Humble Pie°

Although these factors affecting decision making are the same for men and women, and every individual has his or her own style, it seems that women are more likely to downplay their certainty, men more likely to downplay their doubts. From childhood, girls learn to temper° what they say so as not to sound too aggressive — which means too certain. From the time they are little, most girls learn that sounding too sure of themselves will make them unpopular with their peers. Groups of girls, as researchers who have studied girls at play have found, will penalize and even ostracize a girl who seems too sure she's right. Anthropologist Marjorie Harness Goodwin found that girls criticize other girls who stand out by saying, "She thinks she's cute," or "She thinks she's something." Talking in ways that display self-confidence are not approved for girls. . . .

The expectation that women should not display their own accomplishments brings us back to the matter of negotiating that is so important in the workplace. A man who owned a medium-sized company remarked that women who came to ask him for raises often supported their requests by pointing to a fellow worker on the same level who earned more. He considered this a weak bargaining strategy because he could always identify a different co-worker at that level who earned less. They would do better, he felt, to argue for a raise on the basis of how valuable their own work is to the company. Yet it is likely that many women would be less comfortable "blowing their own horn" than making a claim based on fairness.

Follow the Leader

Similar expectations constrain how girls express leadership. Being a leader often involves giving directions to others, but girls who tell other girls what to do are called "bossy." It is not that girls do not exert influence on their

humble pie: A colloquial expression for having to admit one is wrong.   **temper:** Here used as a verb meaning to moderate.

group — of course they do — but, as anthropologists like Marjorie Harness Goodwin have found, many girls discover they get better results if they phrase their ideas as suggestions rather than orders, and if they give reasons for their suggestions in terms of the good of the group. But while these ways of talking make girls — and, later, women — more likable, they make women seem less competent and self-assured in the world of work. And women who do seem competent and self-assured are as much in danger of being negatively labeled as are girls. After her retirement, Margaret Thatcher was described in the press as "bossy." Whereas girls are ready to stick this label on each other because they don't think any girls should boss the others around, it seems odd to apply it to Thatcher, who, after all, was the boss. And this is the rub: standards of behavior applied to women are based on roles that do not include being boss.

Boys are expected to play by different rules, since the social organization 12 of boys is different. Boys' groups tend to be more obviously hierarchical: someone is one-up, and someone is one-down. Boys don't typically accuse each other of being "bossy" because the high-status boys are expected to give orders and push the low-status boys around. Daniel Maltz and Ruth Borker summarize research by many scholars showing that boys tend to jockey for center stage, challenge those who get it, and deflect challenges. Giving orders and telling the others what to do are ways of getting and keeping the high-status role. Another way of getting high status is taking center stage by telling stories, jokes, and information. Along with this, many boys learn to state their opinions in the strongest possible terms and find out if they're wrong by seeing if others challenge them. These ways of talking translate into an impression of confidence.

The styles typical of women and men both make sense given the context 13 in which they were learned, but they have very different consequences in the workplace. In order to avoid being put in the one-down position, many men have developed strategies for making sure they get the one-up position instead, and this results in ways of talking that serve them well when it comes to hiring and promotion. In relation to the examples I have given, women are more likely to speak in the styles that are less effective in getting recognized and promoted. But if they speak in the styles that are effective when used by men — being assertive, sounding sure of themselves, talking up what they have done to make sure they get credit for it — they run the risk that everyone runs if they do not fit their culture's expectations for appropriate behavior: they will not be liked and may even be seen as having psychological problems.

Both women and men pay a price if they do not behave in ways ex- 14 pected of their gender: men who are not very aggressive are called "wimps," whereas women who are not very aggressive are called "feminine." Men who are aggressive are called "go-getters," though if they go too far, from the point of view of the viewer, they may be called "arrogant." This can hurt them, but not nearly as much as the innumerable labels for women who are thought to be too aggressive — starting with the most hurtful one: bitch.

Even the compliments that we receive are revealing. One woman who 15
had designed and implemented a number of innovative programs was
praised by someone who said, "You have such a gentle way of bringing
about radical change that people don't realize what's happening—or don't
get threatened by it." This was a compliment, but it also hinted at the down-
side of the woman's gentle touch: although it made it possible for her to be
effective in instituting the changes she envisioned, her unobtrusive style en-
sured a lack of recognition. If people don't realize what's happening, they
won't give her credit for what she has accomplished.

Not only advancement and recognition, but hiring is affected by ways of 16
speaking. A woman who supervised three computer programmers mentioned that her best employee was another woman who she had hired over
the objections of her own boss. Her boss had preferred a male candidate, because he felt the man would be better able to step into her supervisory role if
needed. But she had taken a dislike to the male candidate. For one thing, she
had felt he was inappropriately flirtatious with her. But most important, she
had found him arrogant, because he spoke as if he already had the job, using
the pronoun "we" to refer to the group that had not yet hired him.

I have no way of knowing whether the woman hired was indeed the bet- 17
ter of these two candidates, or whether either she or the man was well suited
to assume the supervisory role, but I am intrigued that the male boss was
impressed with the male candidate's take-charge self-presentation, while the
woman supervisor was put off by it. And it seems quite likely that whatever
it was about his way of talking that struck her as arrogant was exactly what
led her boss to conclude that this man would be better able to take over her
job if needed.

Questions to Start You Thinking

1. CONSIDERING MEANING: According to Tannen, what are the key differences
   in the way men and women communicate at work? What are the major
   consequences of these differences?

2. IDENTIFYING WRITING STRATEGIES: Where does Tannen identify the causes
   and the effects of each gender's style of speech in the workplace? How does
   she use this cause-and-effect strategy to make her argument that women are
   at a cultural disadvantage in the workplace?

3. READING CRITICALLY: Tannen supports her argument with evidence she has
   apparently gained from personal interviews as well as with studies by a psychologist, an anthropologist, and other scholars. Why does she draw on this
   wide variety of sources? Is her evidence sufficient to convince you? Why, or
   why not?

4. EXPANDING VOCABULARY: Define *declamatory, halting,* and *circumstantial*
   (paragraph 6). Why does a *declamatory* or *halting* tone provide *circumstantial*
   evidence about a person's level of confidence (paragraph 6)?

5. MAKING CONNECTIONS: Based on Tannen's observations about the differences between the ways men and women talk, how might she respond to

Dave Barry's presentation of interactions between the sexes ("From Now On, Let Women Kill Their Own Spiders, pp. 428–30)? How might she explain the male and female communication styles evident in Barry's examples, such as a woman asking how her pants look or a man asking whether there's anything to eat in the refrigerator?

Link to the Paired Essay

Tannen explains that many of the differences between the way men and women talk are learned as children from their peers, while Nicholas Wade ("How Men and Women Think," pp. 437–40) argues that these differences may actually be the result of differences between male and female brains. Compare and contrast Tannen's and Wade's views.

WWW
For useful links to Web sources on topics including *men and women*, visit <www.bedfordstmartins.com/toplinks>.

Journal Prompts

1. Analyze your own talking or presentation style at work or in the classroom. Does it conform to Tannen's analysis of how men and women talk?

2. What style of verbal presentation is one expected to use at a job interview? If this expectation did not exist, would you choose a different manner of presenting yourself? Explain.

Suggestions for Writing

1. Analyze the way your boss, co-workers, teachers, or classmates talk to you at work or school. How does their way of talking compare with how Tannen suggests they talk?

2. Are gender differences determined by social forces or biological factors? Write an essay in which you take a stand on this issue, drawing on Tannen's and Wade's arguments as well as other evidence to support your position. Be sure to consider and refute the arguments on the other side of the debate.

Nicholas Wade

How Men and Women Think

Nicholas Wade *was born in 1942 in England. Educated at Cambridge, Wade wrote for* Nature *magazine in London before coming to the United States in 1971. He began his U.S. career writing for* Science *magazine before joining the* New York Times *as an editorial writer. Wade is currently the editor of the* New York Times's *Science section and author of the "Method and Madness" column for the* New York Times Magazine. *His several books include* The Ultimate Experiment *(1977),* The Nobel Duel *(1981), and* A World beyond Healing *(1987). He also coedited* The Environment from Your Backyard to the Ocean Floor *(vol. 2 of* The New York Times Book of Science Literacy, *1994) and* The New

York Times Book of Health: How to Feel Fitter, Eat Better, and Live Longer *(1998). "How Men and Women Think" was first published in the* New York Times Magazine *on June 12, 1994. While Deborah Tannen ("Women and Men Talking on the Job," pp. 431–36) believes that behavioral differences between men and women are the result of socialization, Wade suggests that men and women behave differently because of biology.*

AS YOU READ: *Identify the evidence that Wade uses to support his claim that gender differences might have a biological basis.*

The human brain, according to an emerging new body of scientific research, comes in two different varieties, maybe as different as the accompanying physique. Men, when they are lost, instinctively fall back on their inbuilt navigational skills, honed from far-off days of tracking large prey miles from home. Women, by contrast, tend to find their way by the simpler methods of remembering local landmarks or even asking help from strangers.

Men excel on psychological tests that require the imaginary twisting in space of a three-dimensional object. The skill seems to help with higher math, where the topmost ranks are thronged with male minds like Andrew Wiles of Princeton, who proclaimed almost a year ago that he had proved Fermat's Last Theorem° and will surely get around to publishing the proof almost any day now.

Some feminist ideologues° assert that all minds are created equal and women would be just as good at math if they weren't discouraged in school. But Camilla Benbow, a psychologist at Iowa State University, has spent years assessing biases like male math teachers or parents who favor boys. She concludes that boys' superiority at math is mostly innate.°

But women, the new studies assert, have the edge in most other ways, like perceptual speed, verbal fluency, and communications skills. They also have sharper hearing than men, and excel in taste, smell, and touch, and in fine coordination of hand and eye. If Martians arrived and gave job interviews, it seems likely they would direct men to competitive sports and manual labor and staff most professions, diplomacy, and government with women.

The measurement of intellectual differences is a field with a long and mostly disgraceful past. IQ tests have been regularly misused, sometimes even concocted, in support of prevailing prejudices. Distinguished male anatomists used to argue that women were less intelligent because their brains weighed less, neglecting to correct for the strong influence of body weight on brain weight.

The present studies of sex differences are venturing on ground where self-deception and prejudice are constant dangers. The science is difficult

Fermat's Last Theorem: A problem that has been puzzling mathematicians for 350 years. Since this essay first came out, Wiles *has* published the proof.   **ideologues:** People who believe strongly in a certain theory.   **innate:** Present at birth.

and the results prone to misinterpretation. Still, the budding science seems free so far of obvious error. For one thing, many of the field's leading practitioners happen to be women, perhaps because male academics in this controversial field have had their lives made miserable by militant feminists.

For another, the study of brain sex differences does not depend on just   7 one kind of subvertible measure but draws on several different disciplines, including biology and anatomy. As is described in a new book, *Eve's Rib*, by Robert Pool, and the earlier *Brain Sex* by Anne Moir and David Jessel, the foundations of the field have been carefully laid in animal research. Experiments with rats show that exposure in the womb to testosterone indelibly imprints a male pattern of behavior; without testosterone, the rat's brain is female.

In human fetuses, too, the sex hormones seem to mold a male and fe-   8 male version of the brain, each subtly different in organization and behavior. The best evidence comes from girls with a rare genetic anomaly° who are exposed in the womb to more testosterone than normal; they grow up doing better than their unaffected sisters on the tests that boys are typically good at. There's also some evidence, not yet confirmed, that male and female brains may be somewhat differently structured, with the two cerebral hemispheres being more specialized and less well interconnected in men than in women.

If the human brain exists in male and female versions, as modulated in   9 the womb, that would explain what every parent knows, that boys and girls prefer different patterns of play regardless of well-meaning efforts to impose unisex toys on both.

The human mind being very versatile, however, any genetic propensities   10 are far from decisive. In math, for example, the average girl is pretty much as good as the average boy. Only among the few students at the peak of math ability do boys predominate.° Within the loose framework set by the genes, education makes an enormous difference. In Japan, boys exceed girls on the mental rotation tests, just as in America. But the Japanese girls outscore American boys. Maybe Japanese kids are just smarter or, more likely, just better taught, Japan being a country where education is taken seriously and parents and teachers consistently push children to excel.

There are some obvious cautions to draw about the social and political   11 implications that might one day flow from brain sex research. One is that differences between individuals of the same sex often far exceed the slight differences between the sexes as two population groups: "If I were going into combat, I would prefer to have Martina Navratilova° at my side than Robert Reich,"° says Patricia Ireland, president of the National Organization for Women. Even if men in general excel in math, an individual woman could still be better than most men.

---

anomaly: Something that is unlike the general rule.   **predominate:** Be present in greater numbers.   **Martina Navratilova:** World-renowned tennis player, retired as all-time leader among men and women in singles titles.   **Robert Reich:** Former secretary of labor.

On the other hand, if the brains of men and women really are organ- 12
ized differently, it's possible the sexes both prefer and excel at different occupations, perhaps those with more or less competition or social interaction.
"In a world of scrupulous° gender equality, equal numbers of girls and boys
would be educated and trained for . . . all the professions. . . . [Hiring would
proceed] until half of every workplace was made up of men and half,
women," says Judith Lorber in *Paradoxes of Gender*, a new work of feminist
theory. That premise does not hold if there are real intellectual differences
between the sexes; the test of equal opportunity, when all unfair barriers to
women have fallen, will not necessarily be equal outcomes.

Greek mythology tells that Tiresias, having lived both as a man and a 13
woman for some complicated reason, was asked to settle a dispute between
Zeus and Hera as to which sex enjoyed sex more. He replied that there was
no contest — it was ten times better for women. Whereupon Hera struck
him blind for his insolence and Zeus in compensation gave him the gift of
foresight. Like Tiresias, the brain sex researchers are uncovering some impolitic truths, potent enough to shake Mount Olympus some day.

Questions to Start You Thinking

1. CONSIDERING MEANING: According to Wade, why is it difficult to do valid,
   reliable studies of sex differences?

2. IDENTIFYING WRITING STRATEGIES: Wade devotes much of the article to summarizing studies on sex differences. Identify the passages where he summarizes others' research as evidence to support his position.

3. READING CRITICALLY: Although Wade cites many different expert sources as
   evidence to support his argument, he makes a number of claims that he
   does not back up. Reread Wade's essay, noting when he makes a claim without referring to a source. How convincing do you find these claims? Does
   his lack of evidence damage his argument in any way? Why, or why not?

4. EXPANDING VOCABULARY: Define *impolitic* and *potent* (paragraph 13). Why
   are the truths that brain sex researchers are uncovering both "impolitic" and
   "potent"?

5. MAKING CONNECTIONS: How might Nicholas Wade respond to Marisa Kula's
   claim that Victoria's Secret ads are targeted toward a male brain and male
   mentality ("Victoria's Not-So-Secret Strategy," pp. 510–13)? Based on his
   claims about brain sex research, how might Wade explain the differences
   between male and female fantasies and stereotypes about body image?

WWW
For useful links to Web
sources on topics includ-
ing *men and women*, visit
<www.bedfordstmartins
.com/toplinks>.

Link to the Paired Essay

Both Wade and Deborah Tannen ("Women and Men Talking on the Job," pp.
431–36) suggest that no matter what science is able to prove about the cause,

---

scrupulous: Extremely careful.

everyday experience shows us that men and women are different. Why do both authors use common sense and everyday examples to help support the scientific research they cite? Do you find examples from everyday life to be convincing as evidence? Why, or why not?

Journal Prompts

1. Do you have any personality traits or intellectual qualities that you feel are typically associated with the opposite sex? How do you feel about these traits?

2. Drawing on your own experience and observations, do you believe there are significant differences in the way men and women think? If so, do you think these differences are innate or the result of socialization? Explain.

Suggestions for Writing

1. Recall your own experience taking aptitude tests. In your opinion, did these tests accurately measure your abilities — or were they unfair because of gender bias? Write an essay explaining your responses to these tests, offering evidence to support your assessment of their fairness and accuracy.

2. Think of a profession that seems to be dominated by either men or women. Using examples from Wade's and Tannen's essays and your own observations, write an essay that examines the possible causes of a gender imbalance in that field.

Chapter 25
Popular Culture

Keith Haring, *Untitled*, 1987. Lithograph, 11" × 14¾"

Responding to an Image

Mass media is often criticized for neatly packaging "reality" and feeding it back to us—the audience or viewer—in manageable chunks. Comment on this image in light of that criticism. Because this image is very abstract, consisting of some very basic shapes, primary colors, and familiar symbols, consider it in terms of such elements as balance, contrast, and color.

Web Search

Look up a Web page about your favorite television show or a movie of interest to you, and analyze the purpose of the page. For example, is the page trying to attract new viewers or to establish a community of loyal fans? Do you think the Web page achieves its purpose? Why, or why not? Could the producers have achieved this purpose through a medium other than the Internet? Why, or why not?

WWW
For an additional Web Search activity, visit <www.bedfordstmartins.com/bedguide>.

Stephen King
Why We Crave Horror Movies

Stephen King *was born in 1947 in Portland, Maine, attended the University of Maine at Orono, and now lives in Bangor, Maine, where he writes his best-selling horror novels, many of which have been made into popular movies. The prolific King is also the author of screenplays, teleplays, short fiction, essays, e-books, and (under the pseudonym Richard Bachman) novels. His well-known horror novels include* Carrie *(1974),* Firestarter *(1980),* Pet Sematary *(1983),* Misery *(1987),* The Green Mile *(1996),* The Wizard in the Glass *(1997), and* Hearts in Atlantis *(1999). In 2000 he published* On Writing: A Memoir of the Craft. *In the following essay, first published in* Playboy *in December 1981, King draws on his extensive experience with horror to explain the human craving to be frightened.*

AS YOU READ: *Identify the needs that King says horror movies fulfill for viewers.*

I think that we're all mentally ill; those of us outside the asylums only hide it a little better — and maybe not all that much better, after all. We've all known people who talk to themselves, people who sometimes squinch their faces into horrible grimaces when they believe no one is watching, people who have some hysterical fear — of snakes, the dark, the tight place, the long drop . . . and, of course, those final worms and grubs that are waiting so patiently underground.

When we pay our four or five bucks and seat ourselves at tenth-row center in a theater showing a horror movie, we are daring the nightmare.

Why? Some of the reasons are simple and obvious. To show that we can, that we are not afraid, that we can ride this roller coaster. Which is not to say that a really good horror movie may not surprise a scream out of us at some point, the way we may scream when the roller coaster twists through a complete 360 or plows through a lake at the bottom of the drop. And horror movies, like roller coasters, have always been the special province° of the

province: Area.

443

young; by the time one turns forty or fifty, one's appetite for double twists or 360-degree loops may be considerably depleted.

We also go to reestablish our feelings of essential normality; the horror   4
movie is innately conservative, even reactionary. Freda Jackson as the horrible melting woman in *Die, Monster, Die!* confirms for us that no matter how far we may be removed from the beauty of a Robert Redford or a Diana Ross, we are still light-years from true ugliness.

And we go to have fun.   5

Ah, but this is where the ground starts to slope away, isn't it? Because   6
this is a very peculiar sort of fun indeed. The fun comes from seeing others menaced — sometimes killed. One critic suggested that if pro football has become the voyeur's° version of combat, then the horror film has become the modern version of the public lynching.

It is true that the mythic, "fairy-tale" horror film intends to take away   7
the shades of gray. . . . It urges us to put away our more civilized and adult penchant° for analysis and to become children again, seeing things in pure blacks and whites. It may be that horror movies provide psychic relief on this level because this invitation to lapse into simplicity, irrationality, and even outright madness is extended so rarely. We are told we may allow our emotions a free rein . . . or no rein at all.

If we are all insane, then sanity becomes a matter of degree. If your insanity   8
leads you to carve up women like Jack the Ripper or the Cleveland Torso Murderer, we clap you away in the funny farm (but neither of those two amateur-night surgeons was ever caught, heh-heh-heh); if, on the other hand, your insanity leads you only to talk to yourself when you're under stress or to pick your nose on your morning bus, then you are left alone to go about your business . . . though it is doubtful that you will ever be invited to the best parties.

The potential lyncher is in almost all of us (excluding saints, past and   9
present; but then, most saints have been crazy in their own ways), and every now and then, he has to be let loose to scream and roll around in the grass. Our emotions and our fears form their own body, and we recognize that it demands its own exercise to maintain proper muscle tone. Certain of these emotional muscles are accepted — even exalted — in civilized society; they are, of course, the emotions that tend to maintain the status quo° of civilization itself. Love, friendship, loyalty, kindness — these are all the emotions that we applaud, emotions that have been immortalized in the couplets of Hallmark cards and in the verses (I don't dare call it poetry) of Leonard Nimoy.

When we exhibit these emotions, society showers us with positive reinforcement;   10
we learn this even before we get out of diapers. When, as children, we hug our rotten little puke of a sister and give her a kiss, all the aunts and uncles smile and twit and cry, "Isn't he the sweetest little thing?"

---

voyeur: One who takes inordinate pleasure in the act of watching.   **penchant:** Strong inclination.   **status quo:** Existing state of affairs.

Such coveted treats as chocolate-covered graham crackers often follow. But if we deliberately slam the rotten little puke of a sister's fingers in the door, sanctions follow — angry remonstrance° from parents, aunts, and uncles; instead of a chocolate-covered graham cracker, a spanking.

But anticivilization emotions don't go away, and they demand periodic 11 exercise. We have such "sick" jokes as "What's the difference between a truckload of bowling balls and a truckload of dead babies" (You can't unload the truckload of bowling balls with a pitchfork . . . a joke, by the way, that I heard originally from a ten-year-old.) Such a joke may surprise a laugh or a grin out of us even as we recoil, a possibility that confirms the thesis: if we share a brotherhood of man, then we also share an insanity of man. None of which is intended as a defense of either the sick joke or insanity but merely as an explanation of [how] the best horror films, like the best fairy tales, manage to be reactionary, anarchistic, and revolutionary all at the same time.

The mythic horror movie, like the sick joke, has a dirty job to do. It delib- 12 erately appeals to all that is worst in us. It is morbidity unchained, our most base instincts let free, our nastiest fantasies realized . . . and it all happens, fittingly enough, in the dark. For those reasons, good liberals often shy away from horror films. For myself, I like to see the most aggressive of them — *Dawn of the Dead*, for instance — as lifting a trapdoor in the civilized forebrain and throwing a basket of raw meat to the hungry alligators swimming around in that subterranean river beneath.

Why bother? Because it keeps them from getting out, man, it keeps 13 them down there and me up here. It was Lennon and McCartney who said that all you need is love, and I would agree with that.

As long as you keep the gators fed.   14

Questions to Start You Thinking

1. CONSIDERING MEANING: What does King mean when he says that "we're all mentally ill" (paragraph 1)? Is this a serious statement? Why, or why not?

2. IDENTIFYING WRITING STRATEGIES: How does King use analysis to support his argument?

3. READING CRITICALLY: Why do you think King uses the inclusive pronoun *we* so frequently throughout his essay? What effect does the use of this pronoun have on your response to his argument?

4. EXPANDING VOCABULARY: Define *innately* (paragraph 4). What does King mean when he says horror movies are "innately conservative"? Does he contradict himself when he says they are also "reactionary, anarchistic, and revolutionary" (paragraph 11)? Why, or why not?

5. MAKING CONNECTIONS: King argues that watching violence in horror movies provides a kind of release for viewers. How does this argument support or contradict Ellen Goodman's claims about violence on television ("How to Zap Violence on TV," pp. 456–58)?

remonstrance: Objection.

Journal Prompts

1. What is your response to "sick" jokes? Why?
2. Recall a movie that exercised your "anticivilization emotions" (paragraph 11). Describe your state of mind before, during, and after the movie.

Suggestions for Writing

1. What genre of movie do you prefer to watch, and why? What cravings does this type of movie satisfy?
2. Do you agree that "the horror film has become the modern version of the public lynching" (paragraph 6)? Write an argument in which you defend or refute this suggestion, citing examples from King's essay and from your own moviegoing experience to support your position.

Veronica Chambers
The Myth of Cinderella

Veronica Chambers, *born in 1970 in the Canal Zone, Panama, was graduated* summa cum laude *with a B.A. in literary studies from Simon's Rock College in Great Barrington, Massachusetts. She is currently an associate editor at* Newsweek *magazine, where she critiques the social significance of music and electronic media for the Arts and Lifestyle section. Formerly a story editor at the* New York Times Magazine, *she has also been a contributing editor at* Glamour *magazine and a senior associate editor of* Premiere *magazine. She is coauthor of* Poetic Justice: Filmmaking South Central Style *(1993) and a contributor to the* Young Feminist Anthology. *Her freelance writing has appeared in publications such as* Essence, *the* New York Times Book Review, *and* Vogue, *and she was awarded a prestigious research fellowship by the Freedom Forum, which she used to analyze news coverage of Asian and African Americans. Her book* Mama's Girl *(1996) addresses the complexity of African American women and mother-and-daughter relationships. She has also published* Marisol and Magdalena: The Sound of Our Sisterhood *(1998) and* Quinceanera Means Sweet Fifteen *(2001). In this selection, published in* Newsweek *in November 1997, Chambers explores the social and historical significance of a Disney television production of* Cinderella, *in which the fairy-tale heroine is played by an actress of African American descent.*

AS YOU READ: *Identify what Chambers claims attracts young girls to the Cinderella story. What criticism of the story does Chambers have?*

For generations, black women have been the societal embodiment of Cinderella. Like Cinderella, black women (and poor white women, too) have often been relegated to the cooking and the cleaning, watching enviously as the women they worked for lived a more privileged life. Think about *Gone with the Wind*. Wouldn't Scarlett O'Hara have laughed, as the evil stepsisters laughed at Cinderella, if Butterfly McQueen had said that *she* wanted to go to the ball, that *she* wanted to dance with Rhett Butler? For years, the idea of a black girl playing the classic Cinderella was unthinkable. But this Sunday, when Brandy, the eighteen-year-old pop singer, stars in the Disney/ABC presentation of Rodgers and Hammerstein's *Cinderella*, reparations will be made. Finally, a sister is getting to go to the ball.

The casting of Brandy as Disney's latest Cinderella is especially signifi- 2 cant because for many black women, the 1950 animated Disney Cinderella with her blond hair and blue eyes sent a painful message that only white women could be princesses. "It's hard when you don't fit the traditional view of beauty," says Whoopi Goldberg (who plays the prince's mother in the new version). "I've gotten letters from people that say if I'd just get my nose done or if I wasn't so dark, I'd be OK-looking. That's why I love this Cinderella, because Brandy is a beautiful, everyday-looking black girl."

The Disney/ABC twist on *Cinderella* is to take multiracial casting to the 3 never-never-land extreme: while Whoopi is the queen, the king (Victor Garber) is white; Bernadette Peters is the stepmother with one white daughter and one black. Whitney Houston plays the fairy godmother, in a soulful performance reminiscent of Lena Horne's° in *The Wiz*. Jason Alexander is hilarious as the prince's much maligned valet. And who plays the prince? A Filipino actor, Paolo Montalban.

Even in this postfeminist° era, where a Cinderella waiting to be rescued 4 by a prince can be seen as a wimp, the myth still appeals. There are at least a half dozen other movies in the works, including one starring Drew Barrymore, with Anjelica Huston as the wicked stepmother, for Twentieth Century Fox; Tribeca Productions' *Sisterella*; *Cinderella's Revenge* at Sony, and a Whoopi Goldberg project at Trimark.

Disney's politically correct version is sure to spark controversy in the 5 black community. "I'm genuinely bothered by the subliminal message that's sent when you don't have a black Prince Charming," says Denene Millner, author of *The Sistahs' Rules*. "When my stepson who's five looks at that production, I want him to know he can be somebody's Prince Charming." But this *Cinderella* does mirror, unwittingly, a growing loss of faith in black men by many black women. Just as Brandy's Cinderella falls in love with a prince of another color, so have black women begun to date and marry interracially in record numbers. In 1980 there were 27,000 new marriages between black women and white men. By 1990 that number had doubled, to 54,000. While black men still marry outside the race in greater numbers, interracial marriages involving black women are growing at a faster rate. "Some of it is a backlash because there are a lot of women who feel that

---

Lena Horne: Blues singer.   **postfeminist:** Relating to the assumption that the goals of the feminist movement have been achieved and that it is no longer necessary to fight actively for them.

black men have done them wrong," says Pulitzer Prize–winning poet Rita Dove. "It's also a way of taking charge and saying, 'I'm waiting for Prince Charming, but the important thing is that he's charming, not that he's black.'" There's an irony here: for white women the Cinderella myth is about passivity, but for black women it's about actively seeking a partner who's their equal.

With many black women heading households, the issue isn't necessarily 6 about becoming independent. Estelle Farley is a clinical research scientist in Raleigh, North Carolina. In her thirties, Farley says, "[The man I'm looking for] has to have a salary close to what I make or more. I've gone down the road with someone who didn't, and it's not a good road." bell hooks, author of the new book *Wounds of Passion*, is much more blunt. "Keep this in mind, girlfriend," says hooks. "This generation of black women is growing up in a truly integrated pop culture. Most black women under the age of thirty would rather have a rich white man than a poor black man."

Whoopi Goldberg, whose companion is the white actor Frank Langella, 7 has often been under fire for dating white men. "First off, I have dated black men," explains Goldberg. "But a woman with power is a problem for any man, but particularly a black man because it's hard for them to get power. I understand that, but I have to have a life, and that means dating the men that want to date me."

Historically, the struggle for racial equality left little room for black 8 women to indulge in Cinderella fantasies. From Reconstruction° through Jim Crow° and through the civil-rights movement, black women devoted their energies to these struggles while secretly hoping that one day their prince would indeed come. Harvard psychiatrist Dr. Alvin Poussaint remembers that during the 1960s, "many of the black women in the movement used to joke — but it was partly serious — that part of why they were fighting was so black men would be able to get good jobs and they would be able to stay at home like white women and have their men take care of them." Furthermore, in the 1970s, many black women were reluctant to embrace feminism because it seemed that just when it was about to be their turn to be Cinderella, white women were telling them that the fantasy was all wrong. "I think there was always more ambivalence about the women's movement on the part of some black women," says Poussaint. "It meant that they were losing out on their chance to be in this dependent role."

Today Cinderella, for better or worse, is much more accessible to young 9 black women. Disney vice president Anna Perez recalls, "Growing up, I loved fairy tales. But I never thought someone was going to come along and take care of me. It sure didn't happen for my mother, who raised six kids by herself." But Brandy says, "I grew up listening to the Cinderella stories; just because she was white didn't mean that I couldn't live the same dream."

Reconstruction: The period after the Civil War when the South was rebuilding.   **Jim Crow:** Laws that legalized segregation by sanctioning "separate but equal" facilities for whites and blacks.

What gives Cinderella such staying power is the myth's malleability, the 10
many ways in which it continues to be transformed. Author Virginia Hamilton, a MacArthur "genius" award winner, is partial to a plantation myth called
"Catskinella," which appears in her book, *Her Stories*. In this version Cinderella is strong and wily. The prince wants to marry her, but she makes him
wait until she is good and ready. Hamilton says she loves the story because it is
evidence that "when black women were at their most oppressed, they had the
extraordinary imagination to create stories for themselves, about themselves."

For bell hooks, Zora Neale Hurston's classic novel *Their Eyes Were*   11
Watching God is the best Cinderella story going. "Janie rejects her rich husband for Tea Cake, the laborer," hooks says of the book, which Oprah Win-
frey is developing into a movie. "Janie talks about how there is a jewel inside of her. Tea Cake sees that jewel, and he brings it out. Which is very
different from the traditional Cinderella myth of the prince holding the
jewel and you trying to get it from him."

In this latest version of Cinderella, Disney makes a subtle — some might 12
say feeble — attempt to give the myth a slightly more feminist slant. When
they first meet, Cinderella tells the prince that she's not sure she wants to get
to know him. She says, "I doubt if this stranger has any idea how a girl
should be treated." He gives her a knowing look and says, "Like a princess, I
suppose." And she looks at him, with her big brown eyes, and says, "No,
like a *person*. With kindness and respect."

Questions to Start You Thinking

1. CONSIDERING MEANING: What does Chambers say is the difference between
   how black and white women interpret the Cinderella myth?

2. IDENTIFYING WRITING STRATEGIES: How does Chambers use cause and effect
   to explain the relationship between America's history of racism and the appeal of the Cinderella myth to African American women?

3. READING CRITICALLY: Chambers quotes many different women's opinions of
   the Cinderella myth. How do their credentials and opinions help shape the
   essay? Is this strategy effective for the point Chambers is trying to make?
   Why, or why not?

4. EXPANDING VOCABULARY: Define *malleability*. What does Chambers mean
   when she says that the reason the Cinderella myth has remained appealing
   for centuries is its *malleability* (paragraph 10)? What makes the story mal-
   leable?

5. MAKING CONNECTIONS: Would Cinderella as revised by Disney satisfy Ellen
   Goodman's definition of a good television role model for children ("How
   to Zap Violence on TV," pp. 456–58)? Why, or why not?

Journal Prompts

1. What fairy-tale or mythical figure was especially appealing to you as a child?
   Why? In what way — if any — did it shape your expectations of life as an adult?

2. What change in the Cinderella myth does the end of Chambers's essay suggest? Do you see it as a positive change? Why, or why not?

Suggestions for Writing

1. Does the Cinderella myth represent an ideal for you? Why, or why not?
2. Write an essay in which you analyze the influence of a character from popular culture. Is the character a positive or a negative role model? Why?

Phyllis Rose

Shopping and Other Spiritual Adventures in America Today

Phyllis Rose *was born in New York City and earned her B.A. from Radcliffe College in 1964, her M.A. from Yale University in 1965, and her Ph.D. from Harvard University in 1970. A distinguished biographer, Rose's works include* Woman of Letters: A Life of Virginia Woolf *(1978),* Parallel Lives: Five Victorian Marriages *(1983),* Jazz Cleopatra: Josephine Baker in Her Time *(1989),* Writing of Women *(1985), and* The Year of Reading Proust *(1997). She also edited* The Norton Book of Women's Lives *(1996). Currently a professor of English at Wesleyan University, she writes frequently for national nonacademic publications, including the* New York Times Book Review, *the* Sophisticated Traveler, *and* Civilization. *In this essay, which appeared in* Never Say Goodbye *(1991), a collection of American cultural criticism, Rose argues that the American love of shopping transcends simple materialism and actually serves a valuable social function that has little or nothing to do with acquiring goods.*

AS YOU READ: *Try to figure out why Rose says that shopping is a "spiritual adventure."*

Last year a new Waldbaum's Food Mart opened in the shopping mall on Route 66. It belongs to the new generation of superduper-markets open twenty-four hours that have computerized checkout. I went to see the place as soon as it opened and I was impressed. There was trail mix in Lucite° bins. There was freshly made pasta. There were coffee beans, four kinds of tahini,° ten kinds of herb teas, raw shrimp in shells and cooked shelled shrimp, fresh-squeezed orange juice. Every sophistication known to the big city, even goat's cheese covered with ash, was now available in Middletown, Connecticut. People raced from the warehouse aisle to the bagel bin to the coffee beans to the fresh fish market, exclaiming at all the new things. Many

---

Lucite: Hard, transparent plastic.   **tahini:** Sesame paste.

of us felt elevated, graced, complimented by the presence of this food palace in our town.

This is the wonderful egalitarianism° of American business. Was it Andy 2 Warhol° who said that the nice thing about Coke is, no can is any better or worse than any other? Some people may find it dull to cross the country and find the same chain stores with the same merchandise from coast to coast, but it means that my town is as good as yours, my shopping mall as important as yours, equally filled with wonders.

Imagine what people ate during the winter as little as seventy-five years 3 ago. They ate food that was local, long-lasting, and dull, like acorn squash, turnips, and cabbage. Walk into an American supermarket in February and the world lies before you: grapes, melons, artichokes, fennel, lettuce, peppers, pistachios, dates, even strawberries, to say nothing of ice cream. Have you ever considered what a triumph of civilization it is to be able to buy a pound of chicken livers? If you lived on a farm and had to kill a chicken when you wanted to eat one, you wouldn't ever accumulate a pound of chicken livers.

Another wonder of Middletown is Caldor, the discount department 4 store. Here is man's plenty: tennis racquets, panty hose, luggage, glassware, records, toothpaste, Timex watches, Cadbury's chocolate, corn poppers, hair dryers, warm-up suits, car wax, light bulbs, television sets. All good quality at low prices with exchanges cheerfully made on defective goods. There are worse rules to live by. I feel good about America whenever I walk into this store, which is almost every midwinter Sunday afternoon, when life elsewhere has closed down. I go to Caldor the way English people go to pubs: out of sociability. To get away from my house. To widen my horizons. For culture's sake. Caldor provides me too with a welcome sense of seasonal change. When the first outdoor grills and lawn furniture appear there, it's as exciting a sign of spring as the first crocus or robin.

Someone told me about a Soviet émigré° who practices English by de- 5 claiming,° at random, sentences that catch his fancy. One of his favorites is, "Fifty percent off all items today only." Refugees from Communist countries appreciate our supermarkets and discount department stores for the wonders they are. An Eastern European scientist visiting Middletown wept when she first saw the meat counter at Waldbaum's. On the other hand, before her year in America was up, her pleasure turned sour. She wanted everything she saw. Her approach to consumer goods was insufficiently abstract, too materialistic. We Americans are beyond a simple, possessive materialism. We're used to abundance and the possibility of possessing things. The things, and the possibility of possessing them, will still be there next week, next year. So today we can walk the aisles calmly.

It is a misunderstanding of the American retail store to think we go 6 there necessarily to buy. Some of us shop. There's a difference. Shopping has

---

egalitarianism: Equality.   **Andy Warhol:** American artist (1928–1987) known for his depictions of everyday objects, such as soup cans.   **émigré:** A person who has moved to another country permanently.   **declaiming:** Stating loudly.

many purposes, the least interesting of which is to acquire new articles. We shop to cheer ourselves up. We shop to practice decision-making. We shop to be useful and productive members of our class and society. We shop to remind ourselves how much is available to us. We shop to remind ourselves how much is to be striven for. We shop to assert our superiority to the material objects that spread themselves before us.

Shopping's function as a form of therapy is widely appreciated. You 7 don't really need, let's say, another sweater. You need the feeling of power that comes with buying or not buying it. You need the feeling that someone wants something you have — even if it's just your money. To get the benefit of shopping, you needn't actually purchase the sweater, any more than you have to marry every man you flirt with. In fact, window-shopping, like flirting, can be more rewarding, the same high without the distressing commitment, the material encumbrance.° The purest form of shopping is provided by garage sales. A connoisseur° goes out with no goal in mind, open to whatever may come his or her way, secure that it will cost very little. Minimum expense, maximum experience. Perfect shopping.

I try to think of the opposite, a kind of shopping in which the object is 8 all-important, the pleasure of shopping at a minimum. For example, the purchase of blue jeans. I buy new blue jeans as seldom as possible because the experience is so humiliating. For every pair that looks good on me, fifteen look grotesque. But even shopping for blue jeans at Bob's Surplus on Main Street — no frills, bare-bones shopping — is an event in the life of the spirit. Once again I have to come to terms with the fact that I will never look good in Levi's. Much as I want to be mainstream, I never will be.

In fact, I'm doubly an oddball, neither Misses nor Junior, but Misses Pe- 9 tite. I look in the mirror, I acknowledge the disparity between myself and the ideal. I resign myself to making the best of it. I will buy the Lee's Misses Petite. Shopping is a time of reflection, assessment, spiritual self-discipline.

It is appropriate, I think, that Bob's Surplus has a communal dressing 10 room. I used to shop only in places where I could count on a private dressing room with a mirror inside. My impulse then was to hide my weaknesses. Now I believe in sharing them. There are other women in the dressing room at Bob's Surplus trying on blue jeans who look as bad as I do. We take comfort from one another. Sometimes a woman will ask me which of two items looks better. I always give a definite answer. It's the least I can do. I figure we are all in this together, and I emerge from the dressing room not only with a new pair of jeans but with a renewed sense of belonging to a human community.

When a Solzhenitsyn° rants about American materialism, I have to look 11 at my digital Timex and check what year this is. Materialism? Like conformism, a hot moral issue of the fifties, but not now. How to spread the goods, maybe. Whether the goods are the Good, no. Solzhenitsyn, like the visiting scientist who wept at the beauty of Waldbaum's meat counter but

---

encumbrance: Burden.   **connoisseur:** Expert judge of something.   **Solzhenitsyn:** Aleksandr Solzhenitsyn (b. 1918), Russian writer and cultural critic who won the Nobel Prize for literature.

came to covet everything she saw, takes American materialism too material-istically. He doesn't see its spiritual side. Caldor, Waldbaum's, Bob's Surplus — these, perhaps, are our cathedrals.

Questions to Start You Thinking

1. CONSIDERING MEANING: What kind of shopping does Rose claim is most ful-filling? What kind is least fulfilling?

2. IDENTIFYING WRITING STRATEGIES: Identify some of the examples Rose uses to illustrate why Americans shop. How do these examples support her point?

3. READING CRITICALLY: What is the tone of this essay? How does Rose set the tone? Is it appropriate to her purpose? Why, or why not?

4. EXPANDING VOCABULARY: Define *materialism*. What is the difference between "a simple, possessive *materialism*" (paragraph 5) and "American *materialism*" as Rose defines it (paragraph 11)?

5. MAKING CONNECTIONS: Both Rose and Steve Olson ("Year of the Blue-Collar Guy," pp. 473–75) make exaggerated claims about American culture. Com-pare and contrast the effects of the authors' claims. How are the effects simi-lar? How are they different?

Journal Prompts

1. According to your observations, how social is shopping?

2. Do you shop for any reason other than a need to buy particular goods? How do your reasons for shopping compare with those Rose discusses?

Suggestions for Writing

1. Were you ever particularly aware of an abundance or lack of abundance in your life? Using your experience as evidence, explain why you agree or disagree with Rose's claim that Americans are "used to abundance" (para-graph 5).

2. How might an economist respond to Rose's assessment of superstores? Find two expert views on the cause and effect of the superstore phenomenon in American culture. Write an essay that synthesizes your sources' ideas and evaluates whether Rose's enthusiasm is warranted.

Jay Chiat
Illusions Are Forever

Jay Chiat, *born in 1931, is chairman of ScreamingMedia, an Internet company in New York City that builds software for distributing information to corporate intranets and Web sites. He has also founded TBWA/Chiat/Day, one of the ten largest advertising agencies in the world. They create advertising for Apple,*

Everready, Nissan, Kmart, and about a hundred other companies. In "Illusions Are Forever," first published in Forbes, *Chiat explains that advertisers greatly influence how viewers think and feel about human experience. When a consumer imagines what a romantic moment should be like, is that idea formed by the De Beers diamond advertising campaign (or by other media images)?*

AS YOU READ: *Look for the ways in which Chiat says media can affect our perception of truth.*

I know what you're thinking: That's rich, asking an adman to define truth.   1
Advertising people aren't known either for their wisdom or their morals, so it's hard to see why an adman is the right person for this assignment. Well, it's just common sense — like asking an alcoholic about sobriety, or a sinner about piety.° Who is likely to be more obsessively attentive to a subject than the transgressor?°

Everyone thinks that advertising is full of lies, but it's not what you   2
think. The facts presented in advertising are almost always accurate, not because advertising people are sticklers but because their ads are very closely regulated. If you make a false claim in a commercial on network television, the FTC° will catch it. Someone always blows the whistle.

The real lie in advertising — some would call it the "art" of advertising   3
— is harder to detect. What's false in advertising lies in the presentation of situations, values, beliefs, and cultural norms that form a backdrop for the selling message.

Advertising — including movies, TV, and music videos — presents to us a   4
world that is not our world but rather a collection of images and ideas created for the purpose of selling. These images paint a picture of the ideal family life, the perfect home. What a beautiful woman is, and is not. A prescription for being a good parent and a good citizen.

The power of these messages lies in their unrelenting pervasiveness, the   5
twenty-four-hour-a-day drumbeat that leaves no room for an alternative view. We've become acculturated to the way advertisers and other media-makers look at things, so much so that we have trouble seeing things in our own natural way. Advertising robs us of the most intimate moments in our lives because it substitutes an advertiser's idea of what ought to be — What should a romantic moment be like?

You know the De Beers diamond advertising campaign? A clever strat-   6
egy, persuading insecure young men that two months' salary is the appropriate sum to pay for an engagement ring. The arbitrary° algorithm is preposterous, of course, but imagine the fiancée who receives a ring costing only half a month's salary? The advertising-induced insult is grounds for calling

---

piety: Religious devoutness.   **transgressor:** One who violates a law, command, or moral code.   **FTC:** Federal Trade Commission, which regulates trade and protects consumers.   **arbitrary:** Based on preference, not specific criteria or reason.

off the engagement, I imagine. That's marketing telling the fiancée what to feel and what's real.

Unmediated is a great word: It means "without media," without the in-between layer that makes direct experience almost impossible. Media interferes with our capacity to experience naturally, spontaneously, and genuinely, and thereby spoils our capacity for some important kinds of personal "truth." Although media opens our horizons infinitely, it costs us. We have very little direct personal knowledge of anything in the world that is not filtered by media.

Truth seems to be in a particular state of crisis now. When what we watch is patently fictional, like most movies and commercials, it's worrisome enough. But it's absolutely pernicious when it's packaged as reality. Nothing represents a bigger threat to truth than reality-based television, in both its lowbrow and highbrow versions—from *Survivor* to *A&E's Biography*. The lies are sometimes intentional, sometimes errors, often innocent, but in all cases they are the "truth" of a media-maker who claims to be representing reality.

The Internet is also a culprit, obscuring the author, the figure behind the curtain, even more completely. Chat rooms, which sponsor intimate conversation, also allow the participants to misrepresent themselves in every way possible. The creation of authoritative-looking Web sites is within the grasp of any reasonably talented twelve-year-old, creating the appearance of professionalism and expertise where no expert is present. And any mischief maker can write a totally plausible-looking,° totally fake stock analyst's report and post it on the Internet. When the traditional signals of authority are so misleading, how can we know what's for real?

But I believe technology, for all its weaknesses, will be our savior. The Internet is our only hope for true democratization, a truly populist publishing form, a mass communication tool completely accessible to individuals. The Internet puts CNN on the same plane with the freelance journalist and the lady down the street with a conspiracy theory, allowing cultural and ideological pluralism° that never previously existed.

This is good for the cause of truth, because it underscores what is otherwise often forgotten—truth's instability. Truth is not absolute: It is presented, represented, and re-presented by the individuals who have the floor, whether they're powerful or powerless. The more we hear from powerless ones, the less we are in the grasp of powerful ones—and the less we believe that "truth" is inviolable,° given, and closed to interpretation. We also come closer to seeking our own truth.

That's the choice we're given every day. We can accept the very compelling, very seductive version of "truth" offered to us daily by media-makers, or we can tune out its influence for a shot at finding our own individual, confusing, messy version of it. After all, isn't personal truth the ultimate truth?

---

plausible: Credible, believable.   **pluralism:** A state in which minority groups have equal status within society.   **inviolable:** Incapable of being violated or destroyed.

Questions to Start You Thinking

1. CONSIDERING MEANING: According to Chiat, what is truth? How does media affect our perception of truth?

2. IDENTIFYING WRITING STRATEGIES: Reread Chiat's opening paragraph. What kinds of appeals do you find? How does Chiat's use of these appeals in his opening affect the rest of the essay? (See pp. 29–30 in *A Writer's Guide* for an explanation of kinds of appeals.)

3. READING CRITICALLY: Chiat says, "I believe technology, for all its weaknesses, will be our savior" (paragraph 10). On what criteria does Chiat base this evaluation? Explain the effects of the Internet on media that Chiat judges valuable.

4. EXPANDING VOCABULARY: Define *pernicious* (paragraph 8). How are reality-based television programs pernicious? In what ways might other kinds of programs be pernicious?

5. MAKING CONNECTIONS: Chiat says the power of advertising lies in its "unrelenting pervasiveness" (paragraph 5). Does this statement support or conflict with the evidence cited by Ellen Goodman in "How to Zap Violence on TV" (pp. 456–58)?

Journal Prompts

1. Recall a time when someone's version of the truth differed from yours. What caused the differences?

2. To what extent have our perceptions of reality been shaped by advertising? Recall an instance when you or someone you know has based expectations of how life should be on media images.

Suggestions for Writing

1. Do a little research on the media in nineteenth-century America. Then write an essay in which you compare and contrast the democratizing effects of nineteenth-century American newspapers with the media of the twenty-first century. You may want to consider the Internet in your discussion.

2. Watch an episode of *A&E's Biography* or another reality-based television show. In what places might the media-maker's perception of truth have slanted the presentation? Write an essay in which you analyze the ways the program may have selected or interpreted the "truth."

Ellen Goodman

How to Zap Violence on TV

Ellen Goodman, *born in 1941 in Newton, Massachusetts, writes a nationally syndicated column on contemporary American life for the* Boston Globe, *where she is also an associate editor. Before joining the* Globe, *Goodman worked as a researcher,* *reporter, and feature writer for* Newsweek *and the* Detroit Free Press. *With Patricia O'Brien, she has recently coauthored* I Know Just What You Mean: The Power of Friendship in Women's Lives *(2000). Her newspaper columns are collected in* Close to Home *(1979),* Keeping in Touch *(1985),* Making Sense *(1989), and* Value Judgments *(1993). She won a Pulitzer Prize for commentary in 1980. In this article, first published in the* Globe *on February 15, 1996, Goodman addresses the potential connection between violence on television and violent crime in America and suggests a lack of creativity as a larger, more fundamental problem with television entertainment. In the paired selection that follows, Mike Males ("Public Enemy Number One?," pp. 459–64) takes issue with Goodman's assumption that there is a link between television violence and violence in the culture at large.*

AS YOU READ: *Identify the reasons Goodman believes violence on television is a problem.*

Ed Donnerstein is not a cultural coroner. He doesn't believe that you can 1
understand the problem of violence on television by merely doing a
body count. Or a bullet count.

As one of the lead researchers on a study done at . . . [the Santa Barbara] 2
campus of the University of California, he wants to make it perfectly clear
that not all the violence on television is equally harmful, nor are all young
viewers equally harmed.

No, he would not oppose televising *Romeo and Juliet* despite the bodies 3
in the last act. And no, he does not believe that violence on television is the
sole or primary cause of violence in America.

But he says, "We can no longer deny that violence on television con- 4
tributes to the problem." He offers this message slowly and distinctly, as if
trying to be heard over the din.

The *National Television Violence Study* that he and his colleagues labored 5
over for three years was released last week into the middle of heated political debate. It made page 1 just as the telecommunications act became law
with its controversial provision for a V-chip, a device to help parents block
out programs rated too violent. It hit the evening news just as broadcasters
were pondering the president's invitation for a February 29 trip to the White
House woodshed.

Representative Ed Markey, the man with the V-chip on his mind, imme- 6
diately praised the study as a Perry Mason° Moment, the perfect evidence
against an industry in the throes of denial. An NBC executive called the research "ridiculous." *Variety* suggested a lobotomy.°

What the analysis of 2,693 television programs from twenty-three channels 7
showed is that a majority of programs contain what the researchers call "harmful violence." These were programs that posed three distinct threats to public

---

Perry Mason: Fictional crime-solving attorney on television and in books. The guilty person is usually revealed during a courtroom trial.   **lobotomy:** Surgery that removes the
frontal lobe of the brain to make mentally disturbed people less violent but that also
makes them incapable of taking care of themselves.

health: "learning to behave violently, becoming more desensitized to the harmful consequences of violence, and becoming more fearful of being attacked."

"The issue for us," Donnerstein says, "is not just that there was violence but how it was presented." In analyzing the plots, images, and programs, the team asked, what makes violence a public health problem? What contexts should we worry about?

For one thing, violence turns out to do a lot of harm when it looks harmless. One of the lessons children learn watching television is that there are few consequences to the person who commits violence — or to the victim.

In 73 percent of the scenes, the violence went unpunished. In nearly half of the programs with slugfests and shootouts, the victims miraculously never appeared harmed. In 58 percent they showed no pain. In fact, only 16 percent of the programs showed any long-term problems — physical, emotional, or financial.

Add to this "positive" portrayal of negative behavior the fact that children's programs were least likely to show the bad effects of violence and most likely to make it funny. As Donnerstein says, "We're showing children violence that goes unpunished, is unrealistic and humorous."

As for other messages? Only a minuscule 4 percent of violent programs had an antiviolent theme. Or showed any alternative to the gun, the fist, the fight.

It's not surprising that this study is being touted in Washington as a sound basis for rating television violence. After all, if the V-chip is to become what Clinton called the "parents' power chip," we need a ratings system that's more sophisticated than one that counts dead bodies.

Indeed, selling the V-chip to an audience of Virginia parents, Clinton not only quoted the dark facts of the violence research, he promised that "new technologies can put you back in the driver's seat in your life." It's an appeal to parents who want to regain some modest control over the messages coming into their houses and to their children.

But the same *National Television Violence Study* also hints at the limits of a technological fix to what is not really a technological problem.

The portrait that emerges from this analysis, after all, is not just of the television environment. It's a profile of an industry that narrowly equates entertainment with violence. It's a profile of a galaxy of broadcasters, producers, and programmers who have shown more imagination in claiming their programs are harmless than in changing the destructive plots.

The V-chip is a violence block. But the real problem in the television industry is a creative block. Soon we'll have the V-chip. Does anyone know how to get rid of the C-chip?

Questions to Start You Thinking

1. CONSIDERING MEANING: What solutions does Goodman propose to the problem of violence on television? Which solution does Goodman view as the most important?

2. **IDENTIFYING WRITING STRATEGIES:** How does Goodman evaluate the V-chip in her essay? What criteria does she use in her evaluation?

3. **READING CRITICALLY:** How well does Goodman support her assertion that "the real problem in the television industry is a creative block" (paragraph 17)?

4. **EXPANDING VOCABULARY:** Define *desensitized* (paragraph 7). What does it mean to become desensitized to violence? What is the difference between being desensitized and being insensitive?

5. **MAKING CONNECTIONS:** How might Ellen Goodman react to Jay Chiat's explanation of the truth and the falseness of advertising ("Illusions Are Forever," pp. 453–55)? How might Goodman respond to Chiat's assessment of the influence of advertising? What kind of V-chip should there be for the commercials we watch?

Link to the Paired Essay

Goodman and Mike Males ("Public Enemy Number One?" pp. 459–64) take different stands on the issue of television violence. Compare and contrast the two writers' positions. Do they believe violence in the media *causes* real-life violence or simply exists alongside it? Why?

WWW
For useful links to Web sources on topics including *popular culture*, visit <www.bedfordstmartins.com/toplinks>.

Journal Prompts

1. How did you feel when you saw violence in some television shows you've watched recently?

2. How might some people see television violence as giving them permission to act violently?

Suggestions for Writing

1. Is it ever necessary to show violence on television or in a movie? Why, or why not? Write an essay supporting your position.

2. Research media sources to find out what has happened to the V-chip since the publication of Goodman's article. Write an essay that evaluates whether the V-chip has been an effective tool for parents.

Mike Males
Public Enemy Number One?

Mike Males, *born in Oklahoma City in 1950, earned his B.A. in political science from Occidental College in 1972 and is currently finishing his dissertation in social ecology at the University of California at Irvine. A writer whose academic work addresses the correspondence between youth and adult behavior, Males has published articles in* Progressive, Adolescence, *the* Lancet, *the* American Journal of

Public Health, *the* Journal of School Health, *the* New York Times, *the* Los Angeles Times, *and the* Washington Post. *In 1992 and 1996 he received the Project Censored award for articles about America's "war on drugs." A member of the Advisory Board for the California Wellness Foundation, Males is a frequent speaker at conferences on youth behavior and is the author of* Scapegoat Generation: America's War on Adolescents *(1996),* Framing Youth: Ten Myths about the Next Generation *(1999), and* Kids and Guns: How Politicians, Experts, and the Press Fabricate Fear of Youth *(2000). While Ellen Goodman assumes that there is a connection between television violence and violent crime, Males analyzes both media coverage and documented social studies to argue that the economic, social, legal, and domestic violence inflicted on children by adults is far more damaging (and a greater cause of violent crime) than the media representations of violence that children see and hear. This essay was originally published in the news magazine* In Our Times.

AS YOU READ: *Identify what Males says is the main problem with television violence.*

Forget about poverty, racism, child abuse, domestic violence, rape. America, from Michael Medved° to *Mother Jones,*° has discovered the real cause of our country's rising violence: television mayhem, Guns N' Roses, Ice-T, and Freddy Krueger. 1

No need for family support policies, justice system reforms, or grappling with such distressing issues as poverty and sexual violence against the young. Today's top social policy priorities, it seems, are TV lockout gizmos, voluntary restraint, program labeling, and (since everyone agrees these strategies won't work) congressionally supervised censorship. Just when earnest national soul-searching over the epidemic violence of contemporary America seemed unavoidable, that traditional scapegoat — media depravity — is topping the ratings again. 2

What caused four youths to go on a "reign of terror" of beating, burning, and killing in a New York City park in August 1954? Why, declared U.S. Senator Robert Hendrickson, chair of the Juvenile Delinquency Subcommittee, the ringleader was found to have a "horror comic" on his person — proof of the "dangers inherent in the multimillion-copy spate° of lurid comic books that are placed upon the newsstands each month." 3

And what caused four youths to go on a brutal "wilding" spree, nearly killing a jogger in a New York City park in May 1989? Why, Tipper Gore wrote in *Newsweek,* the leader was humming the rap ditty "Wild Thing" after his arrest. Enough said. 4

Today, media violence scapegoating is not just the crusade of censorious conservatives and priggish preachers, but also of those of progressive stripe — from Senator Paul Simon (D-Illinois) and Representative Edward Markey 5

Michael Medved: American film critic.   *Mother Jones:* Magazine advocating liberal viewpoints.   **spate:** Flood.

(D-Massachusetts) to *Mother Jones* and columnist Ellen Goodman. "The average American child," Goodman writes, "sees 8,000 murders and 10,000 acts of violence on television before he or she is out of grammar school." Goodman, like most pundits, expends far more outrage on the sins of TV and rock 'n' roll than on the rapes and violent abuses millions of American children experience before they are out of grammar school.

The campaign is particularly craven° in its efforts to confine the debate   6 to TV's effects on children and adolescents even though the research claims that adults are similarly affected. But no politician wants to tell voters they can't see *Terminator II* because it might incite grownups to mayhem.

Popular perceptions aside, the most convincing research, found in mas-   7 sive, multinational correlational studies° of thousands of people, suggests that, at most, media violence accounts for 1 to 5 percent of all violence in society. For example, a 1984 study led by media-violence expert Rowell Huesmann of 1,500 youth in the United States, Finland, Poland, and Australia found that the amount of media violence watched is associated with about 5 percent of the violence in children, as rated by peers. Other correlational studies have found similarly small effects.

But the biggest question media-violence critics can't answer is the most   8 fundamental one: Is it the *cause*, or simply one of the many *symptoms*, of this unquestionably brutal age? The best evidence does not exonerate celluloid savagery (who could?) but shows that it is a small, derivative influence compared to the real-life violence, both domestic and official, that our children face growing up in '80s and '90s America.

When it comes to the genuine causes of youth violence, it's hard to dis-   9 miss the 51 percent increase in youth poverty since 1973, 1 million rapes, and a like number of violently injurious offenses inflicted upon the young every year, a juvenile justice system bent on retribution against poor and minority youth, and the abysmal neglect of the needs of young families. The Carter-Reagan-Bush eras added 4 million youths to the poverty rolls. The last twenty years have brought a record decline in youth well-being.

Despite claims that media violence is the best-researched social phe-   10 nomenon in history, social sciences indexes show many times more studies of the effects of rape, violence, and poverty on the young. Unlike the indirect methods of most media studies (questionnaires, interviews, peer ratings, and laboratory vignettes), child abuse research includes the records of real-life criminals and their backgrounds. Unlike the media studies, the findings of this avalanche of research are consistent: child poverty, abuse, and neglect underlie every major social problem the nation faces.

And, unlike the small correlations or temporary laboratory effects found   11 in media research, abuse-violence studies produce powerful results: "Eighty-four percent of prison inmates were abused as children," the research agency Childhelp USA reports in a 1993 summary of major findings. Separate stud-

---

craven: Cowardly.   **correlational studies:** Research studies attempting to establish cause-and-effect relationships between events.

ies by the Minnesota State Prison, the Massachusetts Correctional Institute, and the Massachusetts Treatment Center for Sexually Dangerous Persons (to cite a few) find histories of childhood abuse and neglect in 60 to 90 percent of the violent inmates studied — including virtually all death row prisoners. The most conservative study, that by the National Institute of Justice, indicates that some half-million criminally violent offenses each year are the result of offenders being abused as children.

Two million American children are violently injured, sexually abused, or neglected every year by adults whose age averages thirty-two years, according to the Denver-based American Humane Association. One million children and teenagers are raped every year, according to the 1992 federally funded *Rape in America* study of 4,000 women, which has been roundly ignored by the same media outlets that never seem short of space to berate violent rap lyrics.

Sensational articles in *Mother Jones* ("Proof That TV Makes Kids Violent"), *Newsweek* ("The Importance of Being Nasty"), and *U.S. News & World Report* ("Fighting TV Violence") devoted pages to blaming music and media for violence — yet all three ignored this study of the rape of millions of America's children. CNN devoted less than a minute to the study; *Time* magazine gave it only three paragraphs.

In yet another relevant report, the California Department of Justice tabulated 1,600 murders in 1992 for which offenders' and victims' ages are known. It showed that half of all teenage murder victims, six out of seven children killed, and 80 percent of all adult murder victims were slain by adults over age twenty, not by "kids." But don't expect any cover stories on "Poverty and Adult Violence: The Real Causes of Violent Youth," or "Grownups: Wild in the Homes." Politicians and pundits know who not to pick on.

Ron Harris's powerful August 1993 series in the *Los Angeles Times* — one of the few exceptions to the media myopia° on youth violence — details the history of a decade of legal barbarism against youth in the Reagan and Bush years — which juvenile justice experts now link to the late '80s juvenile crime explosion. The inflammatory, punishment-oriented attitudes of these years led to a 50 percent increase in the number of youths behind bars. Youth typically serve sentences 60 percent longer than adults convicted for the same crimes. Today, two-thirds of all incarcerated youth are black, Latino, or Native American, up from less than half before 1985.

Ten years of a costly "get tough" approach to deter youth violence concluded with the highest rate of crime in the nation's history. Teenage violence, which had been declining from 1970 through 1983, doubled from 1983 through 1991. It is not surprising that the defenders of these policies should be casting around for a handy excuse for this policy disaster. TV violence is perfect for their purposes.

This is the sort of escapism liberals should be exposing. But too many shrink from frankly declaring that today's mushrooming violence is the pre-

myopia: Shortsightedness.

dictable consequence of two decades of assault, economic and judicial, against the young. Now, increasingly, they point at Jason, 2 Live Crew, and *Henry: Portrait of a Serial Killer*.

The insistence by such liberal columnists as Goodman and Coleman 18 McCarthy that the evidence linking media violence to youth violence is on par with their linking smoking to lung cancer represents a fundamental misunderstanding of the difference between biological and psychological research. Psychology is not, despite its pretensions, a science. Research designs using human subjects are vulnerable to a bewildering array of confusing factors, many not even clear to researchers. The most serious (but by no means only) weakness is the tendency by even the most conscientious researchers to influence subjects to produce the desired results. Thus the findings of psychological studies must be swallowed with large grains of salt.

Consider a few embarrassing problems with media violence research. 19 First, many studies (particularly those done under more realistic "field conditions") show no increase in violence following exposure to violent media. In fact, a significant number of studies show no effect, or even decreased aggression. Even media-violence critic Huesmann has written that depriving children of violent shows may actually increase their violence.

Second, the definitions of just what constitutes media "violence," let 20 alone what kind produces aggression in viewers, are frustratingly vague. Respected researchers J. Singer and D. Singer found in a comprehensive 1986 study that "later aggressive behavior was predicted by earlier heavy viewing of public television's fast-paced *Sesame Street*." The Parent's Music Resource Center heartily endorsed the band U2 as "healthy and inspiring" for youth to listen to — yet U2's song "Pistol Weighing Heavy" was cited in psychiatric testimony as a key inspiration for the 1989 killing of actress Rebecca Schaeffer.

Third, if, as media critics claim, media violence is the, or even just a, 21 prime cause of youth violence, we might expect to see similar rates of violence among all those exposed to similar amounts of violence in the media, regardless of race, gender, region, economic status, or other demographic differences. Yet this is far from the case.

Consider the issue of race. Surveys show that while black and white 22 families have access to similar commercial television coverage, white families are much more likely to subscribe to violent cable channels. Yet murder arrests among black youth are now twelve times higher than among white, non-Hispanic youth and increasing rapidly. Are blacks genetically more susceptible to television violence than whites? Or could there be other reasons for this pattern — perhaps the 45 percent poverty rates and 60 percent unemployment rates among black teenagers?

And consider also the issue of gender. Girls watch as much violent TV 23 as boys. Yet female adolescents show remarkably low and stable rates of violence. Over the last decade or so, murders by female teens (180 in 1983, 171 in 1991) stayed roughly the same, while murders by boys skyrocketed (1,476 in 1983, 3,435 in 1991). How do the media-blamers explain that?

Finally, consider the issue of locale. Kids see the same amount of violent 24
TV all over, but many rural states show no increases in violence, while in Los
Angeles, to take one example, homicide rates have skyrocketed.

The more media research claims are subjected to close scrutiny, the more 25
their contradictions emerge. It can be shown that violent people do indeed
patronize more violent media, just as it can be shown that urban gang members wear baggy clothes. But no one argues that baggy clothes cause violence.
The coexistence of media and real-life violence suffers from a confusion of
cause and effect: Is an affinity for violent media the result of abuse, poverty,
and anger, or is it a prime cause of the more violent behaviors that just happen to accompany those social conditions? In a 1991 study of teenage boys
who listen to violent music, the University of Chicago's Jeffrey Arnett argues
that "[r]ather than being the cause of recklessness and despair among adolescents, heavy metal music is a reflection of these [behaviors]."

The clamor over TV violence might be harmless were it not for the fact 26
that media and legislative attention are rare, irreplaceable resources. Every
minute devoted to thrashing over issues like violence in the media is one
lost to addressing the accumulating critical social problems that are much
more crucial contributors to violence in the real world. In this regard, the
media-violence crusade offers distressing evidence of the profound decline
of liberalism as America's social conscience, and the rising appeal (even
among progressives) of simplistic Reaganesque answers to problems that
Reaganism multiplied many times over.

Virtually alone among progressives, columnist Carl T. Rowan has ex- 27
pressed outrage over the misplaced energies of those who have embraced
the media crusade and its "escapism from the truth about what makes children (and their parents and grandparents) so violent." Writes Rowan: "I'm
appalled that liberal Democrats . . . are spreading the nonsensical notion
that Americans will, to some meaningful degree, stop beating, raping, and
murdering each other if we just censor what is on the tube or big screen. . . .
The politicians won't, or can't, deal with the real-life social problems that
promote violence in America . . . so they try to make TV programs and
movies the scapegoats! How pathetic!"

Without question, media-violence critics are genuinely concerned about 28
today's pandemic violence. As such, it should alarm them greatly to see
policy-makers and the public so preoccupied with an easy-to-castigate°
media culprit linked by their research to, at most, a small part of the nation's violence — while the urgent social problems devastating a generation
continue to lack even a semblance of redress.°

Questions to Start You Thinking

1. CONSIDERING MEANING: What does Males argue are the major causes of real-
   life violence?

castigate: Punish or blame.   redress: Remedy.

2. **IDENTIFYING WRITING STRATEGIES:** Where does Males use comparison and contrast to support his point that there are many other violent influences on children besides the media? What other techniques does he use? Are these techniques effective?

3. **READING CRITICALLY:** Do you detect a politically liberal bias or a conservative bias in Males's argument? On what evidence do you base your conclusion?

4. **EXPANDING VOCABULARY:** Define *scapegoat, censorious,* and *priggish.* What does Males mean when he says that media violence is the scapegoat (paragraph 2) of "censorious conservatives and priggish preachers" (paragraph 5)?

5. **MAKING CONNECTIONS:** How might Stephen King ("Why We Crave Horror Movies," pp. 443–45) respond to Males's argument that violence on television is a symptom rather than a cause of the escalation of violence in American society?

Linked to the Paired Essay

Males and Ellen Goodman ("How to Zap Violence on TV," pp. 456–58) are part of a national conversation about whether violence on television hurts American children. Locate the points in Males's essay where he specifically mentions Goodman. Does Males represent Goodman's arguments accurately? Why, or why not? How might Goodman respond to Males's accusations?

WWW
For useful links to Web sources on topics including *popular culture,* visit <www.bedfordstmartins.com/toplinks>.

Journal Prompts

1. What was your opinion of the influence of media on real-life violence before you read this essay? Has your opinion changed since reading this essay? Why, or why not?

2. Males explains that many studies of other causes of youth violence do not receive the same publicity as studies of media influences. Why do you think this might be the case?

Suggestions for Writing

1. Write an essay in which you analyze the causes of youth violence. Support your points with your own observations.

2. Males argues that irresponsible government policy is the real cause of the dramatic increase in youth violence and that television, movies, and music are just scapegoats. Within the context of other factors that also influence children, how responsible are the media for real-life violence? Using evidence from both Males and Goodman, write an essay in which you take a stand on this issue.

Chapter 26
The Workplace

© Alberto Ruggieri / The Image Bank

Responding to an Image

List all of the elements in the illustration that comment on how communication is carried out in the workplace. Based on your list, what is the overall mood (general feeling) or theme of the image? Write a caption for the image that captures this mood or theme. What message do you think the artist is trying to convey through color and texture? What advice could you give these two men about workplace communication?

Use a search engine to find Web sites devoted to workplace rights, such as the American Civil Liberties Union site [<www.aclu.org/issues/worker/hmwr.html>], the Privacy Rights Clearinghouse [<www.privacyrights.org/fs/fs7-work.htm>], or the Workplace section of *Advancing Women* e-zine [<www.advancingwomen.com/workplace.html>]. What issues are discussed? Analyze the stand each organization takes on one issue that is important to its members. What kinds of evidence does the Web site use to support the organization's position? Are the arguments convincing? Why, or why not?

WWW
For an additional Web Search activity, visit <www.bedfordstmartins .com/bedguide>.

Joe Robinson
Four Weeks Vacation

Joe Robinson *grew up in California's San Fernando Valley. After receiving a degree in journalism from California State University, Northridge, he moved to London, then returned to Los Angeles and started up a music magazine. Later he became editor and publisher of* Escape *magazine, a successful adventure-travel publication, which continues to be his pastime. In "Four Weeks Vacation," first published in the* Utne Reader, *Robinson scrutinizes the American work ethic and examines how the United States and other countries view vacation time. He asks what is happening to American ideas of self and culture when so many people have so little respite from work.*

AS YOU READ: *Find out why Robinson thinks Americans need more time off and how he thinks they can get it.*

The economy may have boomed in recent years, but most Americans are ready to bust. You don't hear much about that, with the national PR machine breathlessly trumpeting the longest peacetime expansion in U.S. history. But behind the doors of the apartments, ranch houses, and brownstones of the real folks who fuel this economy, there is a different story, one of contraction — lives and family and free time swallowed whole by work without end. Ask most working Americans how things are *really* going and you'll hear stories of burnout and quiet desperation, of fifty- and sixty-hour weeks with no letup in sight. The United States has now passed Japan as the industrialized world's most overworked land. In total hours, Americans work two weeks longer than the Japanese each year, two whole *months* longer than the Germans. On top of that, while Europeans and Australians are able to relieve the grind with four to six weeks of paid vacation each year guaranteed by law, Americans average a paltry nine days off after the first year on the job (and that's totally dependent on the whims of employers). If you need some time to tend to an illness in the family or paint the house,

467

your vacation time is pretty much shot. Forget about Tuscany, Yosemite, or even a few days at a nearby state park.

As a longtime traveler, I first became aware that the United States wasn't number one in everything after encountering far too many Germans, Brits, and Danes gallivanting the globe for five and six weeks a year. (In Denmark two years ago, unions staged a nationwide general strike for a sixth week of vacation and settled for two extra days a year, plus three additional personal days for workers with young children.) We eke out 9.6 days at large U.S. companies after one year, 16 after ten years; at small business operations (where the vast majority of us work these days) it's 8 days after a year, 16 after twenty-five years! But that's only part of the story. There's the drowning number of hours — according to the Families and Work Institute, forty-nine hours is the weekly average for men (and forty-two for women), which adds up to an extra three months on the job each year beyond the alleged forty-hour week.

"The gap between Europe and America seems to be growing," says a baffled Orvar Löfgren, a professor at Lund University in Sweden and author of an excellent history of vacations, *On Holiday* (University of California, 1999). "I'm a bit amazed at this, because Americans love having fun."

Americans started out on a level playing field with Europeans, with a week to two weeks in the '30s, when paid vacations were first introduced, says Löfgren. But "there was a decision made at some stage: Do you want more pay or longer vacations? The unions in Europe went for longer vacations. The state in many European countries was very much concerned that vacations were good for you, that everyone should have holidays, that there should be legislation about vacation time. I don't think the state played the same role in the United States."

After that the Europeans shot ahead of us, adding a week more vacation in the '50s, '60s, and '70s. As a result, Swedes get five weeks off by law, plus another two weeks during the Christmas holidays. And don't forget the paid public holidays, he reminds me, which are far more frequent around the world.

Meanwhile, we are spending more time on the job than in past decades. The husband and wife in a typical U.S. household are now working five hundred more hours a year than they did in 1980, according to Eileen Appelbaum, research director at the Economic Policy Institute. Absenteeism due to job stress has tripled in the past five years. So has the number of people calling in sick who aren't, a phenomenon called "entitlement mentality": Workers are using sick time to take the days off they feel they deserve.

Clearly, we have hit the wall. If we have no time for family and friends, no time to enjoy, explore, refresh, and recreate, no time to think that there could be, should be something more, what exactly do we have?

One tired nation. Estimates are that about half of all U.S. workers suffer from symptoms of burnout. Pam Ammondson, author of *Clarity Quest* (Fireside, 1999), sees the wreckage in her Santa Rosa, California–based Clarity Quest workshops, designed to help people suffering from burnout reclaim their lives: "I see a lot of people who work twelve to fourteen hours a day routinely," she says. "They want to make a change, but they're too tired to know how to do it. *Overwhelmed* is a word they use a lot. . . . We allow downtime for machinery for maintenance and repair, but we don't allow it for the employees."

The health implications of sleep-deprived motorists weaving their way 9 to the office or operating machinery on the job are self-evident. One study conducted by the American Psychosomatic Society found that men age thirty-five to fifty-seven who took annual vacations were 21 percent less likely to die young than nonvacationers and 32 percent less likely to die of coronary heart disease.

We all play our part in this marathon of overwork, seduced by the cul- 10 ture into believing that who we are is what we do. It's this lack of a nonwork identity that allows so many of us to be consumed by the workaholic frenzy. "Americans compared to almost any other society are encouraged to achieve and display identity through labor," explains Mark Liechty, professor of anthropology at the University of Illinois at Chicago. "Most Americans labor to consume and construct the self." In Europe, he points out, there's more of a separation between identity and work; work life is "subordinate° to other kinds of social spheres."

The leading casualty of all this is our time, that commodity° we seemed 11 to have so much of back in sixth grade, when the clock on the wall never seemed to move. Time is the fastener of friendship and family; it gives us the space to explore more than a button on the snooze alarm. Without it, we're a nation of strangers, even to those closest to us — and to ourselves. Families are taking a beating. "People are spending less time with their family," observes Barry Miller, a career counselor at Pace University in New York. "They're not taking the time to rejuvenate and connect with their family members. Intimate relationships are falling apart, their relationships with their children are falling apart."

I used to think that the issue of vacation time was complicated. There's 12 the almost religious stigma° in America against government regulating the private sector, the pressure on runaway consumers to support their shopping habits, and the paranoia that global competitors would outpace our economy if we took half the time off that they do. But they're all just excuses and pretexts that crumble with a hard look at the facts. Business, for instance, can be regulated for the good of the citizenry without jeopardizing profits. Some of the most basic tenets of the working world come out of federal legislation, from Social Security to the minimum wage to the forty-hour week — passed by Congress in 1938 as the Fair Labor Standards Act. Business was dragged kicking and screaming every time, but today these laws enjoy universal support.

Some on the left hold that we don't really want the extra time, because 13 we're too busy consuming goods and running up our credit cards. Yet a

---

subordinate: Less important.   **commodity:** Something of value or advantage.
stigma: A mark of shame or disgrace.

survey by the Families and Work Institute found that 64 percent of Americans *want* to work less, up from 47 percent in 1992. As for the threat of instant economic demise once Americans get real vacations, it doesn't appear that the Swiss or Swedish economies are in danger of immediate collapse. In fact, Löfgren points out that 25 percent of Swedes are able to afford second homes in the countryside.

When I raised the vacation issue in an article six years ago, some irate 14
letter writers predicted that the Asian Tigers — Korea, Thailand, Taiwan — would eat us up if we "gave" any more vacation time. A few economic meltdowns later, we're not too worried about those Tigers anymore. We're blowing away the world's economies and have the lowest unemployment in thirty years. Why are we so insecure? What's the point of being an economic superpower if we don't have time for anything but more work?

Another impediment° to rational discussion in this debate is the idea 15
that employers are giving something away with vacation leave. But it's just the opposite. "In essence, companies get more for their money," says employment counselor Barry Miller. "Not only are they going to get more productive employees, but they're also going to get retention and loyalty. My stepson got a week off for paternity leave from his company. He is so loyal to them, he'll never leave. He has more of a commitment to them because they have an interest in him."

And besides, it's not a giveback so much as a rightful return of a fraction 16
of the hours already burned up by routine fifty-hour weeks. "Within most large companies, the long-hours culture permeates° the way things are done, and the level of stress is high," says Mindy Fried of the Center for Work and Family at Boston College. "People are incredibly burned out." Fried has just released a study showing that flexible hours can help take some of "the steam out of the kettle."

Providing a decent amount of time off also makes good business sense. 17
Employees who are burned out make costly errors, they rack up sick days, they quit or get fired, and companies have to spend extra money to train new employees. SAS Institute, a North Carolina–based software company, has reportedly saved "tens of millions" of dollars in turnover costs with an employee-friendly policy of no overtime and a thirty-five-hour week, according to a study reported in the *New York Times*.

Opponents of a mandated vacation law always trot out the myth that it 18
would hurt productivity. While the United States does rule in productivity, it's not by much compared to Germany, for instance. The difference in output per hour is almost negligible, and Germans manage to do it in two months less work. Think about that one. According to the Bureau of Labor Statistics, from 1992 to 1998, France and Sweden, both five-week-vacation lands, matched or surpassed the annual U.S. increase in output per hour while working vastly fewer hours.

---

impediment: Obstacle.   **permeates:** Spreads through every part of.

Another common misperception is that American business would never   19
accept Euro-style multiweek vacations. Well, it already is. Four-week vacation packages for upper management are routine at major U.S. companies.
And workers with special and highly coveted skills, like high-tech experts,
negotiate lengthy vacation into their contracts. We just need to spread the
wealth.

It's improtant to note that with national legislation, no company will   20
find itself at a disadvantage by establishing humane vacation policies. In
Sweden, for instance, there's no possibility of Volvo gaining a competitive
advantage over Saab by offering less vacation. All employers must follow the
same law. A standardized national system also eliminates the current penalties against people who change jobs, who can't bring the vacation benefits
accrued at their last company to the new one, where they usually have to
start at ground zero again: one or two weeks. In an era when people are
changing jobs as often as cars, this may be one of the best arguments of all
for a national vacation policy.

I'd like to leave it to the free market to work all this out. But the market   21
does what's best for itself — as reflected on the next quarterly report — not
what's best, or even logical, for the long-term health of the human capital
that is its foundation. If six-day weeks and no time off was considered abu-
sive in the nineteenth century and laws were required to make things better,
the situation is equally exploitive today and also requires legislative redress.
Just as we need traffic signs at intersections, we also need them in the workplace, or we'll keep getting run over.

Which brings us to what we must do: amend the Fair Labor Standards   22
Act so that every American who has worked at a job for at least a year gets
three weeks off, increasing to four weeks after three years. That's our policy
at *Escape,* and that's what Work to Live° is pressing for. We're in the middle
of a campaign to gather as many signatures as possible to present to Congress, proving there is an enthusiastic constituency for working to *live,* not
just living to *work.* We want to create a national Internet meeting hall for
supporters of the cause. We're looking for progressive companies to join
with us, as well as activists who can lend their talents to turning this tide of
citizen support into public policy. [. . .]

Courage among politicians is a little like El Niño: It only shows up   23
when heat is applied. That's where we come in. Let's turn up the temperature on candidates, Congress members, and local officials. Send e-mail and
faxes, make phone calls, hit their Web sites, write letters to the editor.

While there's no doubt that we're the home of the brave — a nation   24
ready to work till it drops — can we really be the land of the free when we're
on the chain gang fifty weeks a year? I asked Orvar Löfgren to imagine what
it would be like for him in the American vacation system, no five to seven

---

Work to Live: An e-mail campaign started by *Escape* magazine to petition the U.S. Congress to change the labor laws and increase the length of paid leave.

weeks off, just that long tunnel of eleven and a half months of work every year stretching to the grave. He considered the possibility: "I would think, how could I survive? I would feel claustrophobic. It's a question of priorities. In Europe, vacations have become a basic facet° of the quality of life."

Why not here? We've lost sight in the overwork hysteria of what makes it all worthwhile — the time to enjoy the fruits of our labor. What's the point of it all if there's no time to live but only to exist? Having time for family, friends, exploring, reflecting, hiking — these are the things that give meaning to life. I don't think at the end of our days we're going to be looking back on that great eighty-hour week we pulled back in '99. It's going to be the time playing ball with a kid, snorkeling off Maui, lingering over coffee in a sidewalk café — the time when we had time, the most precious natural resource of all.   25

A wise man once told me that the fear of dying is really just the fear of never having lived.   26

Let's leave no doubt about it. Viva vacations!   27

Questions to Start You Thinking

1. CONSIDERING MEANING: According to Robinson, why do Americans need more vacation time?

2. IDENTIFYING WRITING STRATEGIES: Robinson claims the government should legislate more vacation time for American workers (paragraph 22). Where does he deal with objections to his proposal? Is this the most effective placement? Why, or why not?

3. READING CRITICALLY: Robinson says America is "one tired nation" (paragraph 8). Trace the causal chain that accounts for this fatigue. What effects does Robinson attribute to overwork?

4. EXPANDING VOCABULARY: Define *gallivanting* (paragraph 2). What problem did "Germans, Brits, and Danes gallivanting the globe" make Robinson aware of? What does the use of this word suggest about the author's tone?

5. MAKING CONNECTIONS: What would Judy Brady ("I Want a Wife," pp. 412–14) make of Robinson's claim that four weeks of vacation would make American workers more productive? How might Brady incorporate this information into her essay?

Journal Prompts

1. Would you rather have longer vacations or more money? Why?

2. What was the most expensive item you ever bought? How did you get the money to pay for it? Did you regret buying it, or was it worth the sacrifices you made?

facet: A phase or aspect of something.

Suggestions for Writing

1. America is perceived as a materialistic nation. Is this stereotype accurate? Write an essay in which you use your own observations to define America's national character as materialistic or nonmaterialistic.

2. Robinson asserts that it is a "lack of a nonwork identity that allows so many [Americans] to be consumed by the workaholic frenzy" (paragraph 10). Write an essay in which you consider this question: To what degree do Americans identify themselves with their work?

Steve Olson

Year of the Blue-Collar Guy

Steve Olson *was born in 1946 in Rice Lake, Wisconsin. Unaccompanied by the usual list of degrees, awards, and publications, Olson identified himself simply as "a construction worker" when asked for biographical information. Claiming that he writes "mostly for [him]self," he seems to be speaking for the average American. In the following piece, which appeared as a "My Turn" essay in* Newsweek *on November 6, 1989, Olson strives to honor the dialect and ethic of a group of Americans who are often stereotyped but rarely heard from.*

AS YOU READ: *Identify the stereotypes about blue-collar workers that Olson addresses in his essay.*

While the learned are attaching appropriate labels to the 1980s and speculating on what the 1990s will bring, I would like to steal 1989 for my own much maligned° group and declare it "the year of the blue-collar guy (BCG)." BCGs have been portrayed as beer-drinking, big-bellied, bigoted rednecks who dress badly. Wearing a suit to a cement-finishing job wouldn't be too bright. Watching my tie go around a motor shaft followed by my neck is not the last thing I want to see in this world. But, more to the point, our necks are too big and our arms and shoulders are too awesome to fit suits well without expensive tailoring. Suits are made for white-collar guys.

But we need big bellies as ballast to stay on the bar stool while we're drinking beer. And our necks are red from the sun and we are somewhat bigoted. But aren't we all? At least our bigotry is open and honest and worn out front like a tattoo. White-collar people are bigoted, too. But it's disguised as the pat on the back that holds you back: "You're not good enough so you need affirmative action." BCGs aren't smart enough to be that

maligned: Talked badly about.

cynical. I never met a BCG who didn't respect an honest day's work and a job well done — no matter who did it.

True enough, BCGs aren't perfect. But, I believe this: we are America's 3 last true romantic heroes. When some twenty-first-century Louis L'Amour° writes about this era he won't eulogize the greedy Wall Street insider. He won't commend the narrow-shouldered, wide-hipped lawyers with six-digit unearned incomes doing the same work women can do. His wide-shouldered heroes will be plucked from the ranks of the blue-collar guy. They are the last vestige° of the manly world where strength, skill, and hard work are still valued.

To some extent our negative ratings are our own fault. While we were 4 building the world we live in, white-collar types were sitting on their ever-widening butts redefining the values we live by. One symbol of America's opulent wealth is the number of people who can sit and ponder and comment and write without producing a usable product or skill. Hey, get a real job — make something — then talk. These talkers are the guys we drove from the playgrounds into the libraries when we were young and now for twenty years or more we have endured the revenge of the nerds.

BCGs fidgeted our way out of the classroom and into jobs where, it 5 seemed, the only limit to our income was the limit of our physical strength and energy. A co-worker described a BCG as "a guy who is always doing things that end in the letter 'n' — you know huntin', fishin', workin' . . ." My wise friend is talking energy! I have seen men on the job hand-nail 20 square of shingles (that's 6,480 nails) or more a day, day after day, for weeks. At the same time, they were remodeling their houses, raising children, and coaching Little League. I've seen crews frame entire houses in a day — day after day. I've seen guys finish concrete until 11 P.M., go out on a date, then get up at 6 A.M. and do it all over again the next day.

These are amazing feats of strength. There should be stadiums full of 6 screaming fans for these guys. I saw a forty-year-old man neatly fold a 350-pound piece of rubber roofing, put it on his shoulder and, alone, carry it up a ladder and deposit it on a roof. Nobody acknowledged it because the event was too common. One day at noon this same fellow wrestled a twenty-two-year-old college summer worker. In the prime of his life, the college kid was a 6-foot-3, 190-pound body-builder and he was out of his league. He was on his back to stay in ninety seconds flat.

Great Skilled Workforce

Mondays are tough on any job. But in our world this pain is eased by stories 7 of weekend adventure. While white-collar types are debating the value of reading over watching TV, BCGs are doing stuff. I have honest to God heard these things on Monday mornings about BCG weekends: "I tore out a wall and added a room," "I built a garage," "I went walleye fishing Saturday and

---

Louis L'Amour (1908–1988): Best-selling author of Westerns.   **vestige:** A visible sign left by something vanished or lost.

pheasant hunting Sunday," "I played touch football both days" (in January), "I went skydiving," "I went to the sports show and wrestled the bear." Pack a good novel into these weekends.

My purpose is not so much to put down white-collar people as to stress 8
the importance of blue-collar people to this country. Lawyers, politicians, and bureaucrats are necessary parts of the process, but this great skilled workforce is so taken for granted it is rarely seen as the luxury it truly is. Our plumbing works, our phones work, and repairs are made as quickly as humanly possible. I don't think this is true in all parts of the world. But this blue-collar resource is becoming endangered. Being a tradesman is viewed with such disdain these days that most young people I know treat the trades like a temporary summer job. I've seen young guys take minimum-wage jobs just so they can wear suits. It is as if any job without a dress code is a dead-end job. This is partly our own fault. We even tell our own sons, "Don't be like me, get a job people respect." Blue-collar guys ought to brag more, even swagger a little. We should drive our families past the latest job site and say, "That house was a piece of junk, and now it's the best one on the block. I did that." Nobody will respect us if we don't respect ourselves.

Our work is hard, hot, wet, cold, and always dirty. It is also often very 9
satisfying. Entailing the use of both brain and body there is a product—a physical result of which to be proud. We have fallen from your roofs, died under heavy equipment, and been entombed in your dams. We have done honest, dangerous work. Our skills and energy and strength have transformed lines on paper into physical reality. We are this century's Renaissance men. America could do worse than to honor us. We still do things the old-fashioned way, and we have earned the honor.

Questions to Start You Thinking

1. CONSIDERING MEANING: Why does Olson feel there should be a "Year of the Blue-Collar Guy"? What would be the purpose of such a year?

2. IDENTIFYING WRITING STRATEGIES: How does Olson support his stand by comparing and contrasting the "blue-collar guy" with "white-collar types"?

3. READING CRITICALLY: What kind of appeal—emotional, logical, or ethical—does Olson use when he suggests that blue-collar workers need to do more bragging to their families about the work they do? Is the appeal an effective one? Why, or why not? (For an explanation of appeals, see pp. 29–30 in *A Writer's Guide*.)

4. EXPANDING VOCABULARY: Define *ballast* (paragraph 2), *eulogize* (paragraph 3), *opulent* (paragraph 4), *disdain* (paragraph 8), and *Renaissance men* (paragraph 9). How does Olson's vocabulary compare to one you might expect from a self-professed "blue-collar guy" (paragraph 1)?

5. MAKING CONNECTIONS: Would Olson consider Scott Russell Sanders ("The Men We Carry in Our Minds," p. 415) an ally or a threat to his cause? Why?

Journal Prompts

1. Has a job ever influenced your self-image? When, and how?
2. Does "blue-collar" describe only men? Based on observation or imagination, describe the appearance and leisure activities of a "blue-collar woman."

Suggestions for Writing

1. Identify a group you belong to that you think should have a year of its own (for example, college students, part-time workers, parents), and write an essay taking a stand on why your group deserves such an honor.
2. Have attitudes toward blue-collar workers changed since this essay was published in 1989? Why, or why not? Write an essay in which you respond to this question using information you gather from media sources and current research.

Jane Smiley
The Case against Chores

Jane Smiley *was born in 1949 in Los Angeles, California, and received her B.A. from Vassar College. She earned her M.A., M.F.A., and Ph.D. from the University of Iowa. A contributor to many leading American magazines, Smiley's work has been selected for* Best American Short Stories, The Pushcart Anthology, *and* Best of the Eighties. *The author of many books, her most recent is* Horse Heaven *(2000). Her earlier novel* A Thousand Acres *(1991), retells Shakespeare's* King Lear *in the contemporary Midwest. Besides winning the Pulitzer Prize, National Book Critics Circle Award, and Heartland Award, this novel has been made into a popular film. In this essay, Smiley writes with a light autobiographical touch as she discusses the serious matter of how children should be encouraged to understand work.*

AS YOU READ: *Find the reasons Smiley believes parents should not make their children do chores.*

I've lived in the upper Midwest for twenty-one years now, and I'm here to 1
tell you that the pressure to put your children to work is unrelenting. So far I've squirmed out from under it, and my daughters have led a life of almost tropical idleness, much to their benefit. My son, however, may not be so lucky. His father was himself raised in Iowa and put to work at an early age, and you never know when, in spite of all my husband's best intentions, that early training might kick in.

Although "chores" are so sacred in my neck of the woods that almost no 2
one ever discusses their purpose, I have over the years gleaned some of the

reasons parents give for assigning them. I'm not impressed. Mostly the reasons have to do with developing good work habits or, in the absence of good work habits, at least habits of working. No such thing as a free lunch, any job worth doing is worth doing right, work before play, all of that. According to this reasoning, the world is full of jobs that no one wants to do. If we divide them up and get them over with, then we can go on to pastimes we like. If we do them "right," then we won't have to do them again. Lots of times, though, in a family, that *we* doesn't operate. The operative word is *you*. The practical result of almost every child-labor scheme that I've witnessed is the child doing the dirty work and the parent getting the fun: Mom cooks and Sis does the dishes; the parents plan and plant the garden, the kids weed it. To me, what this teaches the child is the lesson of alienated° labor: not to love the work but to get it over with; not to feel pride in one's contribution but to feel resentment at the waste of one's time.

Another goal of chores: the child contributes to the work of maintaining   3
the family. According to this rationale, the child comes to understand what it takes to have a family, and to feel that he or she is an important, even indispensable member of it. But come on. Would you really want to feel loved primarily because you're the one who gets the floors mopped? Wouldn't you rather feel that your family's love simply exists all around you, no matter what your contribution? And don't the parents love their children anyway, whether the children vacuum or not? Why lie about it just to get the housework done? Let's be frank about the other half of the equation too. In this day and age, it doesn't take much work at all to manage a household, at least in the middle class — maybe four hours a week to clean the house and another four to throw the laundry into the washing machine, move it to the dryer, and fold it. Is it really a good idea to set the sort of example my former neighbors used to set, of mopping the floor every two days, cleaning the toilets every week, vacuuming every day, dusting, dusting, dusting? Didn't they have anything better to do than serve their house?

Let me confess that I wasn't expected to lift a finger when I was growing   4
up. Even when my mother had a full-time job, she cleaned up after me, as did my grandmother. Later there was a housekeeper. I would leave my room in a mess when I headed off for school and find it miraculously neat when I returned. Once in a while I vacuumed, just because I liked the pattern the Hoover made on the carpet. I did learn to run water in my cereal bowl before setting it in the sink.

Where I discovered work was at the stable, and, in fact, there is no house-   5
work like horsework. You've got to clean the horses' stalls, feed them, groom them, tack them up, wrap their legs, exercise them, turn them out, and catch them. You've got to clip them and shave them. You have to sweep the aisle, clean your tack and your boots, carry bales of hay and buckets of water. Minimal horsekeeping, rising just to the level of humaneness, requires many

alienated: Isolated; distant or unfriendly.

more hours than making a few beds, and horsework turned out to be a good preparation for the real work of adulthood, which is rearing children. It was a good preparation not only because it was similar in many ways but also because my desire to do it, and to do a good job of it, grew out of my love of and interest in my horse. I can't say that cleaning out her bucket when she manured in it was an actual joy, but I knew she wasn't going to do it herself. I saw the purpose of my labor, and I wasn't alienated from it.

Probably to the surprise of some of those who knew me as a child, I have 6 turned out to be gainfully employed. I remember when I was in seventh grade, one of my teachers said to me, strongly disapproving, "The trouble with you is you only do what you want to do!" That continues to be the trouble with me, except that over the years I have wanted to do more and more.

My husband worked hard as a child, out-Iowa-ing the Iowans, if such a 7 thing is possible. His dad had him mixing cement with a stick when he was five, pushing wheelbarrows not long after. It's a long sad tale on the order of two miles to school and both ways uphill. The result is, he's a great worker, much better than I am, but all the while he's doing it he wishes he weren't. He thinks of it as work; he's torn between doing a good job and longing not to be doing it at all. Later, when he's out on the golf course, where he really wants to be, he feels a little guilty, knowing there's work that should have been done before he gave in and took advantage of the beautiful day.

Good work is not the work we assign children but the work they want 8 to do, whether it's reading in bed (where would I be today if my parents had rousted me out and put me to scrubbing floors?) or cleaning their rooms or practicing the flute or making roasted potatoes with rosemary and Parmesan for the family dinner. It's good for a teenager to suddenly decide that the bathtub is so disgusting she'd better clean it herself. I admit that for the parent, this can involve years of waiting. But if she doesn't want to wait, she can always spend her time dusting.

Questions to Start You Thinking

1. CONSIDERING MEANING: According to Smiley, why shouldn't children be required to do chores?

2. IDENTIFYING WRITING STRATEGIES: Where does Smiley use recall to support her argument? Is her own experience effective as support? Why, or why not?

3. READING CRITICALLY: Locate the claims Smiley attributes to those who believe chores are "sacred." How does she refute each of these claims? Do you find her argument convincing?

4. EXPANDING VOCABULARY: Define *humaneness* (paragraph 5). What does Smiley mean by "the level of humaneness"? How is "horsekeeping" better preparation for childrearing than doing household chores (paragraph 5)?

5. MAKING CONNECTIONS: What would Ian Bruce ("Commercial Fisherman," pp. 485–88) make of Smiley's argument against chores? Does his idea of meaningful work agree with Smiley's? Do you think he would require his children to do chores? Why, or why not?

Journal Prompts

1. Describe your work ethic. What childhood influences helped shape it?
2. How should chores be divided in a household? How are they divided in yours?

Suggestions for Writing

1. What purpose should work serve in our lives? Is one kind of work more valuable than another? Does work have intrinsic value of its own? Write an essay in which you explore the value and meaning of work.
2. Smiley takes exception with parents who believe they must teach their children good work habits. Choose a commonly accepted practice in childrearing, and defend it or argue against it. Use your personal observations, experience, or expert opinions to support the stand you take in your essay.

Katherine S. Newman
From No Shame in My Game

Katherine S. Newman, *an anthropologist renowned for her research on city life and the working poor, was born in California in 1953 and holds a Ph.D. from the University of California at Berkeley. She taught for many years at Columbia University in New York. Currently she is the Ford Foundation Professor of Urban Studies at the Kennedy School of Government at Harvard University. Her books include* Falling from Grace: Downward Mobility in the Age of Affluence *(1988)*, De-clining Fortunes: The Withering of the American Dream *(1993)*, and No Shame in My Game *(1999)*. The following selection is part of* No Shame in My Game, *which won the Sidney Hillman Book Prize and the Robert F. Kennedy Book Award for the year 2000. In this essay, she discusses the skills involved in a low-wage job at a typical fast-food restaurant and gives an insider's view on what is actually expected of so-called "unskilled" workers.*

AS YOU READ: *Look for the high-level skills Newman credits to fast-food workers.*

Elise has worked the "drive-through" window at Burger Barn for the better part of three years. She is a virtuoso° in a role that totally defeated one of my brightest doctoral students, who tried to work alongside her for a week or two. Her job pays only twenty-five cents above the minimum wage (after five years), but it requires that she listen to orders coming in through a speaker, send out a stream of instructions to co-workers who are preparing the food, pick up and check orders for customers already at the window, and receive money and make change, all more or less simultaneously. She

virtuoso: A person with an exceptional ability.

has to make sure she keeps the sequence of orders straight so that the Big Burger goes to the man in the blue Mustang and not the woman right behind him in the red Camaro who has now revised her order for the third time. The memory and information-processing skills required to perform this job at a minimally acceptable level are considerable. Elise makes the operation look easy, but it clearly is a skilled job, as demanding as any of the dozen better-paid positions in the Post Office or the Gap stores where she has tried in vain to find higher-status employment.

This is not to suggest that working at Burger Barn is as complex as brain 2 surgery. It is true that the component parts of the ballet, the multiple stations behind the counter, have been broken down into the simplest operations. Yet to make them work together under time pressure while minimizing wastage requires higher-order skills. We can think of these jobs as lowly, repetitive, routinized, and demeaning, or we can recognize that doing them right requires their incumbents° to process information, coordinate with others, and track inventory. These valuable competencies are tucked away inside jobs that are popularly characterized as utterly lacking in skill.

If coordination were the only task required of these employees, then ex- 3 perience would probably eliminate the difficulty after a while. But there are many unpredictable events in the course of a workday that require some finesse to manage. Chief among them are abrasive° encounters with customers, who [. . .] often have nothing better to do than rake a poor working stiff over the coals for a missing catsup packet or a batch of french fries that aren't quite hot enough. One afternoon at a Burger Barn cash register is enough to send most sane people into psychological counseling. It takes patience, forbearance, and an eye for the long-range goal (of holding on to your job, of impressing management with your fortitude) to get through some of these encounters. If ever there was an illustration of "people skills," this would be it.

Coping with rude customers and coordinating the many components of 4 the production process are made all the more complex by the fact that in most Harlem Burger Barns, the workers hail from a multitude of countries and speak in a variety of languages. Monolingual Spanish speakers fresh from the Dominican Republic have to figure out orders spoken in Jamaican English. Puerto Ricans, who are generally bilingual, at least in the second generation, have to cope with the English dialects of African Americans. All of these people have to figure out how to serve customers who may be fresh off the boat from Guyana, West Africa, Honduras. The workplace melting pot bubbles along because people from these divergent groups are able to come together and learn bits and snatches of each other's languages — "workplace Spanish" or street English. They can communicate at a very rudimentary° level in several dialects, and they know enough about each other's cultural traditions to be able to interpret actions, practices, dress styles, and

---

incumbents: Holders of an indicated office.   **abrasive:** Rude or antagonistic.   **rudimentary:** Basic.

gender norms in ways that smooth over what can become major conflicts on the street.

In a world where residential segregation is sharp and racial antagonism° 5 no laughing matter, it is striking how well workers get along with one another. Friendships develop across lines that have hardened in the streets. Romances are born between African Americans and Puerto Ricans, legendary antagonists in the neighborhoods beyond the workplace. This is even more remarkable when one considers the competition that these groups are locked into in a declining labor market. They know very well that employers are using race- and class-based preferences to decide who gets a job, and that their ability to foster the employment chances of friends and family members may well be compromised by a manager's racial biases. One can hear in their conversations behind the counter complaints about how they cannot get their friends jobs because — they believe — the manager wants to pick immigrants first and leave the native-born jobless. In this context, resentment builds against unfair barriers. Even so, workers of different ethnic backgrounds are able to reach across the walls of competition and cultural difference.

We are often admonished to remember that the United States is a multi- 6 cultural society and that the workforce of the future will be increasingly composed of minorities and foreigners. Consultants make thousands of dollars advising companies on "diversity training" in order to manage the process of amalgamation. Burger Barn is a living laboratory of diversity, the ultimate melting pot for the working poor. They live in segregated spaces, but they work side by side with people whom they would rarely encounter on the block. If we regard the ability to work in a multiethnic, multilingual environment as a skill, as the consulting industry argues we should, then there is much to recommend the cultural capital acquired in the low-wage workplaces of the inner city.

Restaurant owners are loath to cut their profits by calling in expensive 7 repair services when their equipment breaks down, the plumbing goes out, or the electrical wiring blows. Indeed, general managers are required to spend time in training centers maintained by Burger Barn's corporate headquarters learning how to disassemble the machinery and rebuild it from scratch. The philosophers in the training centers say this is done to teach managers a "ground-up" appreciation for the equipment they are working with. Any store owner will confess, however, that this knowledge is mainly good for holding labor costs down by making it unnecessary to call a repairman every time a milk shake machine malfunctions. What this means in practice is that managers must teach entry-level workers, especially the men (but women as well), the art of mechanical repair and press them into service when the need strikes. Indeed, in one Harlem restaurant, workers had learned how to replace floor-to-ceiling windows (needed because of some bullet holes), a task they performed for well below the prevailing rates of a skilled glazier.

antagonism: Hostility.

Then, of course, there is the matter of money. Burger Barn cash registers 8
have been reengineered to make it possible for people with limited math
abilities to operate them. Buttons on the face of the machine display the
names of the items on the menu, and an internal program belts out the
prices, adds them up, and figures out how much change is due a customer,
all with no more than the push of a finger on the right "pad." Still, the
workers who man the registers have to be careful to account for all the
money that is in the till. Anything amiss and they are in deep trouble: they
must replace any missing cash out of their wages. If money goes missing
more than once, they are routinely fired. And money can disappear for a variety of reasons: someone makes a mistake in making change, an unexpected interloper uses the machine when the main register worker has gone
into the back for some extra mustard packets, a customer changes her mind
and wants to return an item (a transaction that isn't programmed into the
machine). Even though much of the calculation involved in handling funds
is done by computer chips, modest management skills are still required to
keep everything in order.

While this is not computer programming, the demands of the job are 9
nonetheless quite real. This becomes all too clear, even to managers who are
of the opinion that these are "no-skill" jobs, when key people are missing.
Workers who know the secrets of the trade — how to cut corners with the official procedures mandated by the company on food preparation, how to
"trick" the cash register into giving the right amount of change when a mistake has been made, how to keep the orders straight when there are twenty
people backed up in the drive-through line, how to teach new employees
the real methods of food production (as opposed to the official script), and
what to do when a customer throws a screaming fit and disrupts the whole
restaurant — keep the complicated ballet of a fast food operation moving
smoothly. When "experts" disappear from the shift, nothing works the way
it should. When they quit, the whole crew is thrown into a state of near-
chaos, a situation that can take weeks to remedy as new people come "on
line." If these jobs were truly as denuded of skill as they are popularly believed to be, none of this would matter. In fact, however, they are richer in
cognitive complexity and individual responsibility than we acknowledge.

This is particularly evident when one watches closely and over time how 10
new people are trained. Burger Barn, like most of its competitors, has prepared training tapes designed to show new workers with limited literacy
skills how to operate the equipment, assemble the raw materials, and serve
customers courteously. Managers are told to use these tapes to instruct all
new crew members. In the real world, though, the tapes go missing, the VCR
machine doesn't work, and new workers come on board in the middle of the
hamburger rush hour when no one has time to sit them down in front of a
TV set for a lesson. They have to be taught the old-fashioned way — person to
person — with the more experienced and capable workers serving as teachers.

One of my graduate students learned this lesson the hard way. A native 11
of Puerto Rico, Ana Ramos-Zayas made her way to a restaurant in the Do-

minican neighborhood of upper Harlem and put on an apron in the middle of the peak midday demand. Nobody could find the tapes, so she made do by trying to mimic the workers around her. People were screaming at her that she was doing it all wrong, but they were also moving like greased lightning in the kitchen. Ana couldn't figure out how to place the cheese on the hamburger patty so that it fit properly. She tried it one way and then another—nothing came out right. The experienced workers around her, who were all Spanish-speakers, were not initially inclined to help her out, in part because they mistook her for a white girl—something they had not seen behind the counter before. But when they discovered, quite by accident, that Ana was a Latina (she muttered a Spanish curse upon dropping the fifth bun in a row), they embraced her as a fellow migrant and quickly set about making sure she understood the right way to position the cheese.

From that day forward, these workers taught Ana all there was to know 12 about the french fry machine, about how to get a milk shake to come out right, about the difference between cooking a fish sandwich and a chicken sandwich, and about how to forecast demand for each so that the bins do not overfill and force wastage. Without their help, provided entirely along informal lines, Ana would have been at sea. Her experience is typical in the way it reveals the hidden knowledge locked up inside what appears to surface observers (and to many employees themselves) as a job that requires no thinking, no planning, and no skill.

As entry-level employment, fast food jobs provide the worker with expe- 13 rience and knowledge that ought to be useful as a platform for advancement in the work world. After all, many white-collar positions require similar talents: memory skills, inventory management, the ability to work with a diverse crowd of employees, and versatility in covering for fellow workers when the demand increases. Most jobs require "soft skills" in people management, and those that involve customer contact almost always require the ability to placate angry clients. With experience of this kind, Burger Barn workers ought to be able to parlay their "human capital" into jobs that will boost their incomes and advance them up the status ladder.

The fact that this happens so rarely is only partially a function of the 14 diplomas they lack or the mediocre test scores they have to offer employers who use these screening devices. They are equally limited by the popular impression that the jobs they hold now are devoid of value. The fast food industry's reputation for de-skilling its work combines with the low social standing of these inner-city employees to make their skills invisible. Employers with better jobs to offer do recognize that Burger Barn veterans are disciplined: they show up for work on time, they know how to serve the public. Yet if the jobs they are trying to fill require more advanced skills (inventory, the ability to learn new technologies, communication skills), Burger Barn is just about the last place that comes to mind as an appropriate proving ground. A week behind the counter of the average fast food restaurant might convince them otherwise, but employers are not anthropologists out looking for a fresh view of entry-level employment. They operate on the basis of assumptions that are widely shared and have neither the time nor the inclination to seek out the hidden skills that Barn employees have developed.

Perhaps fast food veterans would do better in the search for good jobs if they could reveal that hidden reservoir of human capital. But they are as much the victims of the poor reputation of their jobs as the employers they now seek to impress. When we asked them to explain the skills involved in their work, they invariably looked at us in surprise: "Any fool could do this job. Are you kidding?" They saw themselves as sitting at the bottom of the job chain and the negative valence° of their jobs as more or less justified. A lot of energy goes into living with that "truth" and retaining some sense of dignity, but that effort does not involve rethinking the reputation of their work as skillfree. Hence they are the last people to try to overturn a stereotype and sell themselves to other employers as workers who qualify for better jobs.

I have suggested here that neither the employers nor the job-seekers have got it right. There are competencies involved in these jobs that should be more widely known and more easily built upon as the basis for advancement in the labor market. Yet even if we could work some magic along these lines, the limitations built into the social networks of most low-wage workers in the inner city could make it hard to parlay that new reputation into success.

Questions to Start You Thinking

1. CONSIDERING MEANING: Newman lists numerous high-level skills required of Burger Barn employees. Why, then, do they remain stuck in low-status jobs?

2. IDENTIFYING WRITING STRATEGIES: Identify some of the concrete examples Newman uses to illustrate her points. How do these examples make her essay more readable? More convincing?

3. READING CRITICALLY: What criteria does Newman use to evaluate the skills of Burger Barn workers? What conclusion does she reach?

4. EXPANDING VOCABULARY: Define *amalgamation* (paragraph 6). How is Burger Barn an example of the process of amalgamation? Think of other places where you might find the kind of amalgamation Newman observes in Burger Barn.

5. MAKING CONNECTIONS: What skills might Newman credit to the wife in Judy Brady's essay "I Want a Wife" (pp. 412–14)? How might these skills translate into an office job?

Journal Prompts

1. Newman says fast-food workers are themselves victims of the "negative valence" (paragraph 15) of their low-status jobs. To what degree is confidence in one's ability the cause of advancing in the job market? How does the appearance of self-confidence influence a prospective employer? How does one acquire self-confidence?

valence: Power or capacity to be strong.

2. List the skills required in the jobs you've performed, paid or unpaid. Which skills would look good on your résumé?

Suggestions for Writing

1. What should determine how much a person is paid for doing a job? Supply and demand? Education level? Difficulty? Value to society? Gender? Write an essay in which you explain what should determine the pay for a job. Either defend the status quo or propose different criteria.
2. Using Newman's essay as a model, write an essay that closely examines the competencies required of workers in a job you consider low in status. Suggest how these skills might translate into higher-status jobs.

Ian Bruce
Commercial Fisherman

Ian Bruce's *description of life as an Alaska salmon fisherman is included in a collection of interviews called* Gig: Americans Talk about Their Jobs at the Turn of the Millennium, *produced by the editors of Word.com. Describing his work, Bruce stresses the dangerous aspects of the job, explaining that fishing is a great equalizer: "if you can tie a good knot, you're hired."*

AS YOU READ: *Identify Bruce's reasons for believing that fishing is an important career.*

About eight years ago, I started coming up to Alaska to work in the canneries during the summers. I saw that you could make a decent living on the fishing boats and I guess I was kind of disgusted with this world, you know? I wanted a change. So I moved up here to Kodiak to fish. I worked as a deck hand and then, four years ago, I bought a license that allows me to harvest fish. It costs about fifty grand and it's good for beyond a lifetime. I can will it to my children.

So now I lease a boat. It's just like leasing an office space or something. I'm the captain. It's kind of like the old military where you sort of bought a position. I bought my captain's position when I got my license. I hire a crew, typically college students. They're coveted° because they're real savvy. Much better than a lot of derelicts that you're forced to hire sometimes. They have some sense of personal space. They're generally cleaner.

In the summers, I fish salmon on a forty-foot boat with a quarter-mile-long net. We only catch salmon, none of the by-catch that often makes the press — dolphins and stuff — just pure salmon. The season starts every June. It's an eternal ritual — the salmon come back to the same streams and rivers

coveted: Greatly desired, often with envy.

they were spawned in. And I'm there just waiting for them with a net. It's all highly regulated and the days are long — twenty hours — but it's very easy work. Mostly, you just have to fight the tedium° waiting for the salmon to swim into your nets.

The thing to keep in mind is that the salmon returns here are totally healthy. In fact, that's one of our problems. Alaska's salmon keep coming back in almost obscene numbers. Nature's run amok. It lowers the price. There's only so much canned salmon the world can consume. When was the last time you ate a can of salmon? That's how the ones I catch typically end up — being canned because they come in such a big wallop that they can't be fileted or smoked. You've got to slap it in the can, hope someone buys it. But there's not too many people buying cans of salmon. One bright spot was that scare in Europe — the Mad Cow disease. The British apparently switched straight to canned salmon — something that buoyed us up for a few years, but apparently Mad Cow disease has been solved.   4

Anyway, that's the summertime, salmon. The wintertime is crabs. I fish the snow crabs you get in Sizzler or Red Lobster, which are much more lucrative,° but wintertime fishing is also what earns Alaskan commercial fisherman a place as the most dangerous occupation in America. One out of every hundred of us dies every season. The main reason is that you're isolated and it's incredibly brutal conditions. You spend twenty hours a day working with six hours of sunlight maximum and lots of ice. Most of us die from the capsizing of boats, because any water, any spray that hits the boat, it turns to ice. The boat gets top-heavy — and it's already top-heavy because it's stacked three stories high with thousand-pound crab cages. So then you get a little more spray, high seas, more ice — the boat capsizes. I've lost one good friend this year and an acquaintance that way. And it's a particularly miserable death, because you're trapped in a boat that sometimes floats for hours with an air pocket and you're just sort of waiting for that pocket to disperse. There's been several incidences of the Coast Guard arriving, hearing guys tapping from inside of this capsized boat and not being able to cut open and retrieve them fast enough.   5

All you can do is break the ice. A good five hours a day of any sort of wintertime fishing in Alaska is devoted to just breaking ice off the boats. I use a baseball bat and a big rubber mallet, and when my arms get tired, I just stomp around the decks, breaking the ice.   6

The days typically start around four A.M. I straggle out on deck, after coffee, and it's a numbers game. Each time you pull in your salmon net or you lift up your crab pots isn't that lucrative. You have to do it twenty hours a day. And then it can be lucrative. I have acquaintances that have made eighty thousand bucks in three or four months of work. But twenty hours is a lot of time on a small boat.   7

My job specifically is I fling a little grappling hook that snags a buoy. These buoys are attached to about two hundred feet of line that go straight   8

tedium: Boredom, as brought on by monotony.   lucrative: Profitable.

down to these big giant crab pots at the bottom of the ocean. I thread the line onto an electric coiler that hauls up a pot. I empty the pot and then I watch for another buoy and fling my grappling hook again. The greenhorns— *greenhorn* is the term for people who are new here—they sort the crab, measure the crab, and launch the pot again. When you do that, you have to fling that two hundred feet of line back overboard, and that's another dangerous aspect of the job, because as the line's whizzing overboard, on the far end of it this thousand-pound cage is sinking to the bottom of the Bering Sea, and should you get line tangled around your legs, you're going down.

So it's risky. Actually, it's more than risky—it's a brutal, archaic life. But   9 I like it. When I go out fishing, I'm slipping into a role that humans have always played. It's the eternal hunting party. Five guys go off, you know? And thirty thousand years ago, we went off to score a mammoth. Now we go out to score fish. It's a hunting party—we're hunter-gatherers.

I used to feel left out of this culture. Now, I feel like I'm some throw-   10 back, but that's great. So I'm a throwback, so what? That's my career. I feel sorry for someone who hasn't experienced it. I mean, in Kodiak, particularly in summer, there's this electric feeling—you're in a place that totally has a purpose. It's got a soul. In Kodiak, you fish, and the whole town revolves around you. It might be kind of analogous° to being an auto worker in Detroit during the heyday of car making in America. You're a pillar of the community, even though you're just a blue-collar worker. The whole community revolves around you and your industry. And that's kind of neat. And it's great being in a place that has a very obvious reason to be. I was just down in San Diego, which is where I grew up, and what is actually produced in San Diego? What is its reason to be? Why couldn't whatever is being done there be done in Phoenix or Tucson? Well, Kodiak's reason to be is obvious. It's producing America's seafood.

There's this sort of glorious feel to it—and you know, it's also a very   11 open-minded and liberal feeling. All of the great towns of the Renaissance were maritime towns. And the thing that makes them liberal is because people are forced to have an open mind. Because in fishing there'a a sort of common denominator. If you can tie a good knot, you're hired. It doesn't matter if you're Laotian, Filipino, Portuguese, whatever. And a fishing town is one of the few places in America where a blue-collar worker can feel proud. You are responsible for the whole town. If your job is erased, then the town will be erased. Whereas, if you work in Southern California, you're irrelevant. Who knows what ultimately drives that economy? So there's this wonderful simplicity to your role in the community here.

And here's another thing: you're self-employed. You're no longer a wage   12 earner working the nine-to-five deal. You're an entrepreneur, and you get paid a percentage of the cash. It's profit sharing. Even my deck hands are profit-sharers. And the reason for that is you couldn't pay a person a flat wage high enough to do some of the things this demands.

analogous: Comparable.

The problem is, I don't know what the future is. Some years I make 13 good money, some years I don't. One year my summer earnings doubled in a single afternoon because the Tokyo fish market had a bidding war. And then another summer, they decreased by half because Emperor Hirohito died, and Japan went into some sort of cultural abhorrence° of fish. And Japan's a big market, so there it was. It's unpredictable.

What is predictable is that I'm gonna get busted up eventually. I mean, 14 all my fishing friends have been mangled at least once. The fatality rate is only maybe one percent but the mangling rate is much higher. Hernias, broken collarbones, broken ribs, frostbite, squashed fingers. I myself got a half-inch of my finger chewed up in a coiler and I also have a knee that's bent out of shape. But that's dwelling on the negative. I don't necessarily have to come to a grim end. In ten years, if I keep doing well, I see myself running a boat solely in the summertime, which I always will do. I'll always fish, as long as I physically can. Even if the money dropped out, I'd still fish. I enjoy it so much. I fit the role.

Questions to Start You Thinking

1. CONSIDERING MEANING: How does Bruce justify the risks involved in being a commercial fisherman?

2. IDENTIFYING WRITING STRATEGIES: Bruce weighs the pros and cons of his work. How does he structure his evaluation? Which paragraphs describe appealing aspects of his work? Which describe negative aspects? In what ways do the organization, formality, polish, and other features of this selection reflect its origins as an interview?

3. READING CRITICALLY: In paragraph 10, Bruce says Kodiak is "a place that totally has a purpose." How does he extend this idea in paragraph 11? How is he "responsible for the whole town" (paragraph 11)?

4. EXPANDING VOCABULARY: Define *archaic* (paragraph 9). According to Bruce, how is commercial fishing an archaic life? Why does he find that appealing?

5. MAKING CONNECTIONS: In "The Men We Carry in Our Minds" (pp. 415–19), Scott Russell Sanders remembers men broken by the labor their jobs required and ponders the envy his female classmates hold for men's place in the world. How are Bruce's and Sander's views of men's labor different? In what ways are they similar?

Journal Prompts

1. Bruce calls the mad cow disease scare in Europe a "bright spot" (paragraph 4). Write about other instances of one person's misfortune being another's "bright spot."

2. What difficult jobs can you think of where the satisfaction might outweigh the risks? Would you be willing to take a job like that?

abhorrence: Strong hatred or loathing.

Suggestions for Writing

1. Bruce values Kodiak because its existence depends on the industry located there. On the other hand, he considers many other cities purposeless. Write an essay in which you account for the existence of a specific city or of urban centers in general. Compare and contrast the purpose of the place you choose with the purpose of places like Kodiak or Detroit.

2. Using Bruce's essay as a model, describe a job you know about. Present both its negative and positive aspects. Determine the value inherent in the work, and account for why someone would choose it. If you have not done this work yourself, use observation and conversation to learn about the job.

Anne Finnigan

Nice Perks — If You Can Get 'Em

Anne Finnigan *covers business and consumer issues for* Working Mother *and other magazines. Her article, which accompanied* Working Mother's *survey of the 100 Best Companies for Working Mothers, focuses on the loopholes employees encounter when they try to use the benefits their employers offer. Finnigan identifies three main difficulties faced by workers who want to obtain family-friendly benefits.*

AS YOU READ: *Identify the family-friendly benefits available to employees of the "100 Best" companies and the reasons some employees don't get them.*

You read about them here every year: Companies where you can structure your workday around your child's oboe recital without raising a single managerial eyebrow. Companies that let you work from home — no questions asked. Companies that pick up your dry cleaning, change your oil, even send you home at five o'clock with a hot dinner. You may work for one of those companies, a member of the *Working Mother* 100 Best list. Problem is, even though your company may offer such benefits, they don't seem to be available to you. This year's 100 Best list shows — again — that companies are doing more to accommodate their employees' work/life needs than ever before. They're pushing the envelope with innovative policies and spending hundreds of millions of dollars to make these programs work.

But there's still a long way to go, as the editors of this magazine are reminded each year after publishing the 100 Best list. We get hundreds of letters charging that for every 100 Best working mom who enjoys family-friendly benefits, dozens of others — often in the same company — are still scrambling to meet even the most basic "life" needs. There's the single mom on the swing shift whose company offers child care, but not for anyone working off-peak hours. There are the women working at far-flung satellite

offices who don't have access to the company gym or concierge services at
headquarters; those niceties might as well exist in another galaxy for all the
good they do them. And there's the mom who tries to take advantage of a
company's advertised flextime policies, only to be told by her manager that
he's not approving any such thing.

Why do work/life policies fall short for some employees? There are three 3
reasons. One: No matter what the company says on paper, the corporate culture demands a work-is-your-life commitment. Two: Managers aren't trained
to turn policy into real practice, nor are they rewarded for doing so. And
three: Work/life benefits are distributed inequitably, so that many workers are
left out of the loop — those earning less, those laboring far from headquarters, or those whose jobs, simply by their nature, preclude some benefits.

"Many companies haven't implemented work/life options throughout 4
the entire organization," says Jennifer Chatman, a professor at the University of California at Berkeley's Haas School of Business. "The policies provide a good image and attract employees, but they're not practiced because
people get informally penalized for doing anything that takes away from a
less-than-one-hundred-percent effort."

Here, a look at these three problem areas, the key complaints we've seen 5
in the last year, and information on what some companies are doing to improve the situation.

1. They say it but they don't mean it. Remaking corporate culture can 6
be tougher than turning the *Titanic*. In a big company, it means changing
the minds — and behavior — of tens of thousands of people. That can be especially difficult in a work-is-your-life organization, or one with a rigidly
structured hierarchy° — and the requirements of certain kinds of jobs in
such organizations make it even harder. A Merck employee writes:

> Did you ever interview one field sales rep to see what the stress level is like
> for those of us who don't have a child-care facility on site, or get reimbursed
> for extra hours of child care when our meetings take us away from home for
> a week at a time? Or that when training for field sales, a mother is away
> from home for nearly three months? Management turns a blind eye to these
> issues and replies, "You hired on to this job." Most of us were unaware of
> the seventy- to eighty-hour weeks we were signing on for.

"We're definitely not there yet," Merck spokesperson Maggie Beute re- 7
sponds frankly. "With 36,000 employees in the United States, it's hard to
make sure all managers have great communications skills. As in any large
corporation, not every manager is as excited about these policies as our CEO
is. And individual managers let some people use them but don't let others,
and employees feel they're being treated unfairly." One of the elements at
work: a major culture shift. "Before Raymond Gilmartin joined as CEO, the
organization was very top-down," says Beute. "Now we're supposed to work
face to face, manager to employee."

---

hierarchy: A system in which persons are ranked above one another.

To address this challenge, Merck devised a team brainstorming process 8
in which employees and managers in each unit take up problems like workweeks that have stretched too long or the unavailability of flex. Beute's
group, corporate communications, did this last year. Everyone filled out a
detailed survey on how they worked, and an outside analyst pinpointed
what the unit's problems were and where time could be saved. "A few directors took some of it personally, but it got all of us around a table," says
Beute.

In Beute's case, the process paid off: Her seventy-hour weeks have been 9
cut to fifty, and she works one day a week from home. As important, "when
things get crazy now, I ask for help."

To help workers far from headquarters, Merck is putting computer kiosks 10
at all manufacturing sites, so employees have access to the latest benefits information. Workers with a hard-to-resolve problem can also call a hot line,
staffed by a chief ombudsman and four others. The ombudsmen then call
the manager's manager to see about resolving the problem, Beute says.

The hardest company cultures to change are those that value "face time" 11
above all else. "In these businesses, the attitude is 'your personal life is personal, and you need to be here when I say you need to be here,'" says Rebecca Blank, dean of the University of Michigan's Gerald R. Ford School of
Public Policy. Also challenging: corporate cultures that are designed, 1950s
style, around the idea of a stay-at-home spouse who takes care of all the life
stuff—a pleasant fiction, since more than two-thirds of all U.S. moms are
out in the workplace. Then there's the you-married-the-company kind of
culture, where "once you're hired, you give up any life you used to have outside," as one reader wrote us.

Some kinds of businesses also find it difficult to incorporate work/life 12
practices because of the nature of the work that they do. Enterprises that require employees on site twenty-four hours a day—any kind of manufacturing, for instance—aren't the optimal candidates for work/life benefits like
telecommuting. And those companies that hire large numbers of lower-
income workers have a real challenge helping them meet their child-care
needs affordably.

In other cases, the demands of the job are so intense that they virtually 13
preclude° balance. Take the case of management consultants who can be
away from home four nights out of seven, serving clients in other states. They
may work for a company that has an on-site child-care center and flex—but
to a parent away most of the week, the company isn't likely to feel particularly family-friendly. Certain professions—including law, academia, and finance—also continue to require a fast-track work pace for those who want
to rise to the top. If employees take time off beyond a minimum maternity
leave, "they are labeled 'off-track' very quickly," says Chatman.

2. My manager won't get with the program. An employee's work/life 14
balance stands or falls on her manager's ability to turn policies into work-

preclude: Prevent the possibility of.

able practice. And that ability rests on how well work/life policies are supported from up top. A DuPont employee writes:

> Some of the great things mentioned in your article are just not applicable to most of the workers at DuPont. They are policies that are there in writing, but if I were to need part-time or flextime work, I would be told it wasn't possible. What looks good on paper isn't necessarily true in real life.

"That's one of the hardest issues facing us," admits Claudette Whiting, 15 director of work/life and diversity at DuPont, which has more than eighty sites. "You can have the best programs in place, but you have to educate managers to get them to use them. And you have to know what your employees need." DuPont will spend $200,000 this year to help managers at satellite sites determine how to improve their work/life policies. Another program trains managers in how to put such benefits into practice.

Those sorts of specific steps are virtually mandatory for firms who want 16 to make sure managers understand and use work/life programs. "Probably three quarters of the complaints we hear begin with 'My manager won't let me,'" says Anne Ruddy. "Many of these supervisors are under pressures of their own. It can be tough to persuade them that employees can and should be able to design their own schedule or be trusted to work at home. You've got to teach them."

That's why the best of the 100 Best train their managers extensively and 17 reward them for how much programs like telecommuting and job-sharing get used. Managers are encouraged to be innovative and to focus on what gets done rather than where or how it's done. "Our approach to work/life is common sense," says J. T. (Ted) Childs Jr., vice president of global workforce diversity at IBM, which has been on the 100 Best list for fifteen years. "We want managers to focus on results, not on face time. We don't care how, where, or when the work gets done, but that the results are achieved." These companies also conduct regular employee work/life surveys and make changes based on the feedback they get.

Finally, one of the most effective ways companies can send the message 18 that they mean business about work/life is by having top-level executives practice what they preach. When executives take a paternity or maternity leave or cut out in midafternoon for their kid's softball game, everyone else knows that it's really okay for them to do it too.

3. Workers like me can't get that. Aside from changing the corporate 19 culture and getting managers on board, a company's biggest work/life challenge is to make sure all policies are truly available to all employees, no matter what their level is on the corporate ladder. For a variety of reasons, that rarely happens. One large category of worker who frequently misses out is the blue-collar employee, who is paid by the hour (about two-thirds of all working mothers). "They are compelled to put in overtime under penalty of losing their job if they refuse — and the law is on the company's side," explains Robert Reich, former U.S. Secretary of Labor and professor of social and economic policy at Brandeis University.

The landmark Fair Labor Standards Act of 1938 requires only that a 20
company pay its workers time and a half for each hour of work beyond forty
hours in a single week, Reich says. That leaves these workers with only one
option — trying to convince their company to agree not to order them to
work overtime when spouses, kids, or elderly parents need them at home.
"Some employers do this already, as a means of attracting and keeping good
workers," Reich says. "But other companies have to be prodded." Increasingly, unionized workers are seeking such agreements within formal labor
contracts. "But it's an uphill fight," Reich says. "Less than 8 percent of working women belong to a union."

An employee of Bell Atlantic (called Verizon after its merger with GTE) 21
writes: "Members [of the union group Communications Workers of Amer-
ica] have consistently been assigned mandatory overtime to meet customer
needs. Other items such as flextime, compressed workweeks, and job-
sharing are for management employees only."

Bell Atlantic, on the 100 Best list for its third year, has made the grade by 22
investing in a wide range of family options, from on-site and community-
based child care to flex arrangements like job-sharing. But like many other
companies on the list, Bell Atlantic hasn't been able to make such benefits
available across the board, particularly at sites with unionized hourly employees. Depending on seniority, union workers can receive up to five weeks
of vacation and four excused workdays with pay, and the company's Kids in
the Workplace program provides on-site child care when employees have to
work on holidays. Winning other benefits has proven elusive,° in part because the tight labor market has made it increasingly difficult for Bell Atlantic to find enough workers to fill all the slots they have open.

"We need to have people work overtime," says Sharon Beadle, senior 23
specialist of media relations for Bell Atlantic. "Managers do make an effort
to assign it on a voluntary basis."

"What do you do if you're assigned overtime, but you have to pick up 24
your kid from day care?" responds Linda Kramer, president of the Communications Workers of America Local 1023. "These are stressful jobs, especially for young parents." When one dad had to leave on a few occasions
and was eventually fired, the union took the case to arbitration. The ruling:
The company has the right to schedule mandatory overtime, but also has
the responsibility to accommodate its workers' family issues. The union is
trying to formalize that responsibility in its new contract. But negotiating
work/life balance across the bargaining table is complicated. The adversarial
nature of labor-management relations often results in agreements that are
set in stone, while it can be more desirable to deal with work/life practices
on a case-by-case basis.

Bell Atlantic is currently working to boost the number of supervisors, in 25
the hope that improving the supervisor/worker ratio will help develop more
personal connections. "When I started at Bell thirty years ago, you could go

elusive: Remaining out of reach.

talk to your manager if you had a problem and they'd try to help you work it out — because they knew you," says Kramer. Today, because of corporate cutbacks in the early 1990s, supervisors might have thirty or more employees under them, and their managers might oversee more than 100 — located in different states.

Finding the Solutions

Despite such shortcomings, it's important to note that the 100 Best compa-   26
nies are doing much more for employees than the vast majority of employers. Only 10 percent of U.S. companies offer on-site or near-site child care, according to a survey by Hewitt Associates, a benefits consulting firm; 68 percent of 100 Best companies offer such programs. Flextime, which is an option at 99 percent of the 100 Best companies, is available at only 57 percent of companies in the Hewitt survey.

And some of the 100 Best are ahead of the pack in delivering work/life   27
benefits to lower-income employees, who need them the most — and are least likely to get them. Broadening work/life's base is critical: Recent research by the Families and Work Institute shows that while lower-level workers now have access to some essentials such as job-guaranteed time off for childbirth, other options — like telecommuting, regular flex scheduling, and paid time off to care for a sick child — are still out of reach.

So what will it take to change the workplace for *all* of us? The law of   28
supply and demand may do it. The current worker shortage is giving working mothers increasing clout. And we have a new ally in our quest for balance: Younger workers, who are demanding — and getting — control over their time. The good news is that the adoption of strong work/life practices is fast becoming a bottom-line business necessity.

"It's a golden opportunity," says sociologist Arlie Hochschild, author of   29
The Time Bind and *The Second Shift*, "to get careers designed around family commitments." And in the best of the 100 Best, it's already a reality.

Questions to Start You Thinking

1. CONSIDERING MEANING: According to Finnigan, how successful are the "100 Best" companies in implementing family-friendly policies? What does their success suggest about the availability of such benefits at other companies or other types of jobs?

2. IDENTIFYING WRITING STRATEGIES: How does Finnigan use quotation to support her analysis of family-oriented practices? How does identification of the people she quotes lend credibility to her evidence?

3. READING CRITICALLY: How are the "100 Best" companies trying to resolve the problems with family-friendly policies? What causes their solutions to succeed or fail?

4. EXPANDING VOCABULARY: What are *flextime* (paragraph 2), *face time* (paragraph 11), *telecommuting* (paragraph 12), and *job-sharing* (paragraph 17)? Does Finnigan provide enough context for you to figure out the meaning of these terms? How has her audience influenced her word choice?

5. **MAKING CONNECTIONS:** How might Stephanie Coontz ("Remarriage and Stepfamilies," pp. 404–09) view the family-friendly benefits Finnigan describes? Would they relieve any of the stresses Coontz identifies? Would they increase any other stresses?

Link to the Paired Essay

Both Finnigan and Elinor Burkett ("Unequal Work for Unequal Pay," pp. 495–99) address the increasing shift to family-oriented policies in the workplace. How do their concerns differ? How might Finnigan respond to the concerns raised by Burkett?

WWW
For useful links to Web sources on topics including *the workplace*, visit <www.bedfordstmartins.com/toplinks>.

Journal Prompts

1. How important will a prospective employer's family policies be when you seek a job? In what ways would you expect the importance to vary during different stages of your life?
2. Write about frustrations you've experienced in the workplace.

Suggestions for Writing

1. Taking the point of view of company management, write an essay in which you explore the value of family-friendly policies. Look at both long-range and short-range effects.
2. Finnigan points out that "more than two-thirds of all U.S. moms are out in the workplace" (paragraph 11). Write an essay exploring the effects on the workplace of the shift away from the 1950s-style family. Use reading and your own observations as resources.

Elinor Burkett
Unequal Work for Unequal Pay

Elinor Burkett *taught history before becoming a reporter. She has written for the* New York Times Magazine, The Atlantic Monthly, Rolling Stone, *and* Mirabella. *Her work with the* Miami Herald *has earned her many national and state awards, and she was nominated for a 1991 Pulitzer Prize for journalism. Burkett, who lives in New York, has written several books, including* The Gravest Show on Earth *(1995),* The Right Women *(1998), and* The Baby Boon: How Family-Friendly America Cheats the Children *(2000), from which this selection was taken.* The Baby Boon *was inspired by Burkett's article "Pushing Mommy Off the Track," which appeared in* Mirabella *and recently won the Front Page Award from the Newswomen's Club of New York. In* The Baby Boon, *Burkett questions the fairness of corporations that cater to employees with children.*

AS YOU READ: *Look for ways Burkett feels family-friendly policies affect workers who are not parents.*

Few of the new "family-friendly benefits" have much to do with the lives
of most American workers. In fact, most of the highly touted innova-
tions are entirely irrelevant to them since most workers aren't the kind of
middle-class working mothers who dream up these benefits in the first
place. Look at what the "best" companies — the companies honored by
Working Mother magazine, by *Business Week*, or the Women's Bureau of the
Department of Labor, which actually printed an Honor Roll of well-behaved
corporations — are offering their employees.

Fel-Pro Incorporated is precisely the type of company Americans expect
not to have superb "family" benefits. This is no white-collar corporation
heavy with kid-gloves executives nor a high-tech business packed with professionals and technicians who could move to, say, North Carolina, Boston,
or Silicon Valley with a single phone call. Fel-Pro's twenty-one hundred
employees — 40 percent of them female — manufacture engine gaskets,
sealants, and lubricants in the industrial section of Skokie, Illinois.

But it is a parental heaven, with on-site daycare, a summer camp for
kids at the company's two-hundred-acre park, subsidized in-home childcare for those days when the baby-sitter doesn't show up or a child is ill.
New parents receive a one-thousand-dollar check as a gift for their baby and
two months of unpaid leave. Adoptive parents receive fifteen hundred dollars to help out with the legal bills. Parents of older children can take advantage of a special program that helps them explore college options. And
if their children are outstanding students, they even receive corporate
scholarships.

IBM boasts the nation's most generous family-leave policy, granting parents three years with full benefits. It has spent millions of dollars to help its
employees with childcare, spending five hundred thousand dollars on one
North Carolina daycare center in conjunction with Duke Power, Allstate,
and American Express. Parents can carve out their work schedules any time
from 6:30 A.M. to 10:30 P.M., or opt for a "midday flex."

The largesse of major companies is dramatic. Eli Lilly provides up to ten
thousand dollars in financial aid for adoption. BE&K, one of the nation's
largest building contractors, owns a modular daycare center that it moves
from site to site to provide for the children of construction workers. Stride-
Rite, the shoe manufacturer, allows new parents eight weeks of paid leave
and eighteen weeks more unpaid but with full benefits and job protection.
And Hallmark lends tuition money, interest-free, to parents with five or
more years of service.

When *Working Mother* began its best companies list in 1985, editors say
they could find only thirty companies marginally qualified for the title of
mother-friendly. Now hundreds vie for those slots. According to Hewitt Associates' annual survey of the benefits packages of America's employers, 72
percent allow parents some sort of flexible schedules, 86 percent sponsor a
childcare benefit program, 31 percent provide family-leave benefits that are
more generous than the federal government requires, 25 percent subsidize
adoptions, and a wide array of programs, everything from after-school hot-

lines to family care days, vacation camps, and tuition reimbursement, for the children of their workers, are spreading like wildfire.

Survey after survey confirms that same picture of a family-friendly work- 7 place movement reshaping the nature of work for American parents. A 1998 survey of more than one thousand companies conducted by the Families and Work Institute found that 88 percent of all companies with more than one hundred employees allow parents time off for school functions; 15 percent offer more than twelve weeks of maternity leave, and more than half with some pay; 24 percent award scholarships or other educational assistance to the children of their employees; and 87 percent paid for at least part of the health insurance of their employees' families.

The magazine editors, human resources officers, consultants, and politi- 8 cians who promote these programs, and themselves in the process, argue their value not just on humanistic or moral grounds, but as wise bottom-line decisions. Family-friendliness, they say, pays by promoting loyalty and productivity, reducing absenteeism, tardiness, and turnover, and polishing a company's public image. Such testimonials are legion. The Families and Work Institute presents flow charts and graphs proving that businesses with more "supportive workplaces" have more satisfied employees who are more committed to the success of their employers and more likely to remain on the job. They cite the case of the pharmaceutical giant Johnson & Johnson, where absenteeism plummeted after the introduction of a raft of family programs. Officials at Fel-Pro claim that their turnover rate dropped from between 30 and 40 percent to 10 percent after they opened a company summer camp. Merck reports that it saves three dollars for each dollar it spends on family programs because workers wind up less stressed, less likely to arrive at work late or leave before the end of the workday, to miss work to take care of sick children, or to quit to stay home with the kids. John Fernandez, a Philadelphia management consultant, posits that family-friendly programs can reduce absenteeism by as much as 19 percent and the rate of employee turnover from 8 to 3 percent.

By the time *Business Week* published the results of its first survey of 9 family-friendly corporate America in 1996, Corporate America was in full swoon. "Disbelievers, skeptics, working stiffs, take note," proclaimed the magazine. "Work-family strategies haven't just hit the corporate mainstream — they've become a competitive advantage. . . . It is a phenomenon, in other words, that executives deny at their own risk."

The numbers, however, don't add up, given the demographics of the 10 American workforce. How can turnover and absenteeism drop so precipitously° in response to childcare assistance, family leaves, and scholarships for employees' kids when, according to the Bureau of Labor Statistics, only one-third of the workforce has children at home under the age of eighteen? How can daycare centers account for 50 percent reductions in turnover when only 8 percent of women workers have kids under the age of six? How

precipitously: Steeply.

can a company like Chase Manhattan Bank spend seven hundred thousand dollars a year to run a daycare center in Brooklyn for 110 children and justify the expenditures by citing "return-on-investment" analyses showing savings of $1.5 million in avoided absenteeism alone? Were the parents of those 110 children missing that much work?

Since there are 13 million more working women without kids at home   11
than with kids — 38 million to 25 million — how can corporate America's obsession with family-friendliness possibly be improving morale? Adoption allowances, maternity and paternity leave, childcare, sick kid care, after-school care, and summer camps are entirely irrelevant to them. Those benefits don't do all that much for workers who do have kids, since the vast majority don't adopt, don't seem not to want institutional daycare, and can't take long parental leaves because they can't afford six months without income.

Rather than boosting morale, in fact, the programs are having an oppo-   12
site effect — and for logical reasons. How would you feel if you had no children and worked at Fel-Pro, where employees have access to childcentric benefits worth thousands of dollars more than the benefits you can use? Imagine what it is like to work at the *New York Times*, where parents can claim long unpaid leaves to bond with their children as a right while those without children who ask for unpaid leave to pursue *their* interests, which usually involve writing books, are subject to management whimsy, which often means that their requests are denied.

Consider what state your morale would be in if you, as a nonparent,   13
heard endlessly about your company's concern for employee morale and the balance in their lives, then discovered that the office charged with both was called Work/Family and spent most of its resources referring parents to daycare centers and planning luncheon workshops on parenting. Would you not ask how the morale of the other two-thirds of the workforce was being tended? And think what it would feel like to be on the staff at NationsBank and hear the chief executive officer call the bank a "meritocracy"° when you know that the flexible schedule of the man sitting next to you, or the five thousand dollars in extra benefits of the woman behind you, aren't rewards for meritorious work, but for reproduction.

In today's workplace, childless employees are well-versed in the Ten Com-   14
mandments of workplace etiquette in family-friendly America. They're not yet included in employee handbooks, or posted prominently on bulletin boards alongside flyers about safety or workers' compensation. But they are etched into the experience of virtually every nonparent who works alongside parents.

   1. Thou shalt volunteer to work late so that mothers can leave at 2:00 P.M. to watch their sons play soccer, for a mother's time is more valuable than thine.

meritocracy: A system that bases rewards on ability and performance.

2. Thou shalt never complain when important meetings are broken up at 2:30 by phone calls from children reporting in after school lest thou be considered indifferent to the importance of parental bonding.

3. Thou shalt take thy vacations when no one else wants time off so parents can take theirs during the summer, over Christmas, or on any other school or "family" holiday.

4. Thou shalt not apply the phrase "equal pay for equal work" to thy company's benefits plan, although it offers mothers and fathers thousands of dollars in perks thou can't use.

5. Thou shalt willingly do two jobs for the price of one while mothers are on six-month maternity and parental leaves.

6. Thou shalt never ask for a long leave to write a book, travel, or fulfill thy heart's desire because no desire other than children could possibly be worth thy company's inconvenience.

7. Thou shalt volunteer to take frequent business trips to places like Abilene, Kansas, or Cleveland, Ohio, so that parents can spend their evenings watching *ER* after they put the kids to bed.

8. Thou shalt promote thy "family-friendly" company as a firm that cherishes women because everyone knows that women equals mothers.

9. Thou shalt never utter the words "but that's not my problem" when a parent rushes out the door during the final negotiations of a corporate merger, explaining that he has promised to take the children to the movies.

10. Thou shalt smile graciously when thy co-worker brings her three-year-old to the office and allows him to turn the papers on thy desk into airplanes.

Questions to Start You Thinking

1. **CONSIDERING MEANING:** What are Burkett's objections to the "family-friendly benefits" offered by an increasing number of American companies?

2. **IDENTIFYING WRITING STRATEGIES:** Where does Burkett begin to question the advantages claimed by "family-friendly" advocates? What do her preceding paragraphs describing family benefits contribute to her argument? How successful is this organizational structure?

3. **READING CRITICALLY:** In paragraph 8, Burkett names people who "promote these [family] programs, and themselves in the process." How do advocates of family-friendly programs promote themselves? What evidence does Burkett use to refute the claims of these advocates?

4. **EXPANDING VOCABULARY:** Define *demographics* (paragraph 10). What demographics does Burkett cite that conflict with successes claimed for family-friendly programs?

5. **MAKING CONNECTIONS:** Burkett claims that nonparent workers are treated unequally by policies that grant costly benefits to employees with children. What does Burkett's demographic evidence suggest about the

public perception of minority students? What similarities do you see between this issue and the issue Anna Quindlen takes up in "Evan's Two Moms" (pp. 394–98)?

Link to the Paired Essay

www
For useful links to Web sources on topics including *the workplace*, visit <www.bedfordstmartins.com/toplinks>.

Elinor Burkett and Anne Finnigan ("Nice Perks — If You Can Get 'Em," pp. 489–94) agree that workplace benefits for employees with children are on the rise, but they disagree on the desirability of this trend. Which writer do you find more convincing? Why?

Journal Prompts

1. Describe a practice that you find unfair in your workplace or at school.
2. When you were a child, did you have working or stay-at-home parents? What were some of the advantages or disadvantages?

Suggestions for Writing

1. Do the advantages of family-oriented programs go beyond the financial advantages of increased productivity in the workplace? Write an essay in which you explore the long-term effects of such programs and take a stand on whether they should be expanded or discontinued.
2. Is reproduction rewarded in our society? Should it be? Write an essay that sets forth your own observations. Express your opinion, and then support your stand.

Chapter 27

Body Image

Amanda and Her Cousin Amy, Valdese, NC, © Mary Ellen Mark

Responding to an Image

The girls in this photograph are responding to a "look" they've seen in the media. As objectively as possible, write a detailed description of the girls, including their clothes, hairstyles, facial expressions, posture, and other physical characteristics. What word or short phrase might you use to describe the relationship of each girl with the camera that is pointed at her? Use your descriptions to compare and contrast the two girls, discussing how each girl is (or is not) responding to cultural expectations about body image.

Web Search

Conduct a search on the topic of "body modification" using a search engine, and examine some of the resources you find. (One may be *BME: Body Modification Ezine.*) Evaluate a couple of sites with differing views on body modification to determine their audience and purpose. What issues does each discuss? What kinds of evidence does each use to support or oppose body modifications such as piercing, tattooing, or scarification? Which Web sites are more convincing? more informative? Why?

Julia Alvarez
I Want to Be Miss América

Julia Alvarez *was born in 1950 in New York City, but spent the first ten years of her life in the Dominican Republic. In 1960, her family returned to the United States. She received her B.A. from Middlebury College and her M.F.A. from Syracuse University. Having held positions in various schools and universities, she now teaches English at Middlebury College. Her books include the best-selling* How the Garcia Girls Lost Their Accents *(1991),* In the Time of Butterflies *(1994),* Yo! *(1997), and* In the Name of Salome *(2000). She has also written several books of poetry. In this excerpt from her book of essays,* Something to Declare *(1998), Alvarez describes what's it's like to be an adolescent girl growing up on the fringe of white American culture in the early 1960s.*

AS YOU READ: *Look for ways Alvarez and her sisters try to be more "American."*

As young teenagers in our new country, my three sisters and I searched 1 for clues on how to look as if we belonged here. We collected magazines, studied our classmates and our new TV, which was where we discovered the Miss America contest.

Watching the pageant became an annual event in our family. Once a 2 year, we all plopped down in our parents' bedroom, with Mami and Papi presiding from their bed. In our nightgowns, we watched the fifty young women who had the American look we longed for.

The beginning was always the best part — all fifty contestants came on 3 for one and only one appearance. In alphabetical order, they stepped forward and enthusiastically introduced themselves by name and state. "Hi! I'm! Susie! Martin! Miss! Alaska!" Their voices rang with false cheer. You could hear, not far off, years of high-school cheerleading, pom-poms, bleachers full of moon-eyed boys, and moms on phones, signing them up for all manner of lessons and making dentist appointments.

There they stood, fifty puzzle pieces forming the pretty face of America, 4 so we thought, though most of the color had been left out, except for one, or possibly two, light-skinned black girls. If there was a "Hispanic," she usually looked all-American, and only the last name, López or Rodríguez, often mispronounced, showed a trace of a great-great-grandfather with a dark, curled mustache and a sombrero charging the Alamo. During the initial roll-call, what most amazed us was that some contestants were ever picked in the first place. There were homely girls with cross-eyed smiles or chipmunk cheeks. My mother would inevitably shake her head and say, "The truth is, these Americans believe in democracy—even in looks."

We were beginning to feel at home. Our acute homesickness had 5 passed, and now we were like people recovered from a shipwreck, looking around at our new country, glad to be here. "I want to be in America," my mother hummed after we'd gone to see *West Side Story,* and her four daughters chorused, "OK by me in America." We bought a house in Queens, New York, in a neighborhood that was mostly German and Irish, where we were the only "Hispanics." Actually, no one ever called us that. Our teachers and classmates at the local Catholic schools referred to us as "Porto Ricans" or "Spanish." No one knew where the Dominican Republic was on the map. "South of Florida," I explained, "in the same general vicinity as Bermuda and Jamaica." I could just as well have said west of Puerto Rico or east of Cuba or right next to Haiti, but I wanted us to sound like a vacation spot, not a Third World country, a place they would look down on.

Although we wanted to look like we belonged here, the four sisters, our 6 looks didn't seem to fit in. We complained about how short we were, about how our hair frizzed, how our figures didn't curve like those of the bathing beauties we'd seen on TV.

"The grass always grows on the other side of the fence," my mother 7 scolded. Her daughters looked fine just the way they were.

But how could we trust her opinion about what looked good when she 8 couldn't even get the sayings of our new country right? No, we knew better. We would have to translate our looks into English, iron and tweeze them out, straighten them, mold them into Made-in-the-U.S.A. beauty.

So we painstakingly rolled our long, curly hair round and round, using 9 our heads as giant rollers, ironing it until we had long, shining shanks, like our classmates and the contestants, only darker. Our skin was diagnosed by beauty consultants in department stores as sallow; we definitely needed a strong foundation to tone down that olive. We wore tights even in the summer to hide the legs Mami would not let us shave. We begged for permission, dreaming of the contestants' long, silky limbs. We were ten, fourteen, fifteen, and sixteen—merely children, Mami explained. We had long lives ahead of us in which to shave.

We defied her. Giggly and red-faced, we all pitched in to buy a big tube 10 of Nair at the local drugstore. We acted as if we were purchasing contraceptives. That night we crowded into the bathroom, and I, the most courageous along these lines, offered one of my legs as a guinea pig. When it didn't become gangrenous or fall off as Mami had predicted, we creamed the other seven legs. We beamed at each other; we were one step closer to that runway, those flashing cameras, those oohs and ahhs from the audience.

Mami didn't even notice our Naired legs; she was too busy disapproving 11 of the other changes. Our clothes, for one. "You're going to wear *that* in public!" She'd gawk, as if to say, What will the Americans think of us?

"This *is* what the Americans wear," we would argue back.   12

But the dresses we had picked out made us look cheap, she said, like 13 bad, fast girls — gringas without vergüenza, without shame. She preferred her choices: fuchsia skirts with matching vests, flowered dresses with bows at the neck or gathers where you wanted to look slim, everything bright and busy, like something someone might wear in a foreign country.

Our father didn't really notice our new look at all but, if called upon to 14 comment, would say absently that we looked beautiful. "Like Marilina Monroe." Still, during the pageant, he would offer insights into what he thought made a winner. "Personality, Mami," my father would say from his post at the head of the bed, "Personality is the key," though his favorite contestants, whom he always championed in the name of personality, tended to be the fuller girls with big breasts who gushed shamelessly at Bert Parks. "Ay, Papi," we would groan, rolling our eyes at each other. Sometimes, as the girl sashayed back down the aisle, Papi would break out in a little Dominican song that he sang whenever a girl had a lot of swing in her walk:

> Yo no tumbo caña,
> Que la tumba el viento,
>   Que la tumba Dora
> Con su movimiento!

> ("I don't have to cut the cane,
> The wind knocks it down,
> The wind of Dora's movement
> As she walks downtown.")

My father would stop on a New York City street when a young woman swung by and sing this song out loud to the great embarrassment of his daughters. We were sure that one day when we weren't around to make him look like the respectable father of four girls, he would be arrested.

My mother never seemed to have a favorite contestant. She was an ex- 15 beauty herself, and no one seemed to measure up to her high standards. She liked the good girls who had common sense and talked about their education and about how they owed everything to their mothers. "Tell that to my daughters," my mother would address the screen, as if none of us were there to hear her. If we challenged her — how exactly did we *not* appreciate her? — she'd maintain a wounded silence for the rest of the evening. Until the very end of the show, that is, when all our disagreements were forgotten and we waited anxiously to see which of the two finalists holding hands on that near-empty stage would be the next reigning queen of beauty. How can they hold hands? I always wondered. Don't they secretly wish the other person would, well, die?

My sisters and I always had plenty of commentary on all the contest- 16
ants. We were hardly strangers to this ritual of picking the beauty. In our
own family, we had a running competition as to who was the prettiest of the
four girls. We coveted one another's best feature: the oldest's dark, almond-
shaped eyes, the youngest's great mane of hair, the third oldest's height and
figure. I didn't have a preferred feature, but I was often voted the cutest,
though my oldest sister liked to remind me that I had the kind of looks that
wouldn't age well. Although she was only eleven months older than I was,
she seemed years older, ages wiser. She bragged about the new kind of math
she was learning in high school, called algebra, which she said I would
never be able to figure out. I believed her. Dumb and ex-cute, that's what I
would grow up to be.

As for the prettiest Miss America, we sisters kept our choices secret until 17
the very end. The range was limited — pretty white women who all *really*
wanted to be wives and mothers. But even the small and inane° set of options these girls represented seemed boundless compared with what we
were used to. We were being groomed to go from being dutiful daughters to
being dutiful wives with hymens intact. No stops along the way that might
endanger the latter; no careers, no colleges, no shared apartments with girl-
friends, no boyfriends, no social lives. But the young women on-screen, who
were being held up as models in this new country, were in college, or at least
headed there. They wanted to do this, they were going to do that with their
lives. Everything in our native culture had instructed us otherwise: girls were
to have no aspirations beyond being good wives and mothers.

Sometimes there would even be a contestant headed for law school or 18
medical school. "I wouldn't mind having an office visit with her," my father
would say, smirking. The women who caught my attention were the prodi-
gies° who bounded onstage and danced to tapes of themselves playing original compositions on the piano, always dressed in costumes they had sewn,
with a backdrop of easels holding paintings they'd painted. "Overkill," my
older sister insisted. But if one good thing came out of our watching this
yearly parade of American beauties, it was that subtle permission we all felt
as a family: a girl could excel outside the home and still be a winner.

Every year, the queen came down the runway in her long gown with a 19
sash like an old-world general's belt of ammunition. Down the walkway she
paraded, smiling and waving while Bert sang his sappy song that made our
eyes fill with tears. When she stopped at the very end of the stage and the
camera zoomed in on her misty-eyed beauty and the credits began to appear
on the screen, I always felt let down. I knew I would never be one of those
girls, ever. It wasn't just the blond, blue-eyed looks or the beautiful, leggy
figure. It was who she was — an American — and we were not. We were
foreigners, dark-haired and dark-eyed with olive skin that could never, no
matter the sun blocks or foundation makeup, be made into peaches and
cream.

inane: Silly.   **prodigies:** People with extraordinary talents.

Had we been able to see into the future, beyond our noses, which we 20 thought weren't the right shape; beyond our curly hair, which we wanted to be straight; and beyond the screen, which inspired us with a limited vision of what was considered beautiful in America, we would have been able to see the late sixties coming. Soon, ethnic looks would be in. Even Barbie, that quintessential° white girl, would suddenly be available in different shades of skin color with bright, colorful outfits that looked like the ones Mami had picked out for us. Our classmates in college wore long braids like Native Americans and embroidered shawls and peasant blouses from South America, and long, diaphanous skirts and dangly earrings from India. They wanted to look exotic — they wanted to look like us.

We felt then a gratifying° sense of inclusion, but it had unfortunately 21 come too late. We had already acquired the habit of doubting ourselves as well as the place we came from. To this day, after three decades of living in America, I feel like a stranger in what I now consider my own country. I am still that young teenager sitting in front of the black-and-white TV in my parents' bedroom, knowing in my bones I will never be the beauty queen. There she is, Miss America, but even in my up-to-date, enlightened dreams, she never wears my face.

Questions to Start You Thinking

1. CONSIDERING MEANING: Why is the Alvarez family's ritual of watching the Miss America pageant so important to Alvarez and her sisters?

2. IDENTIFYING WRITING STRATEGIES: What is the thesis of Alvarez's essay? How does she use recall to support her thesis?

3. READING CRITICALLY: How are standards of beauty defined by Alvarez and her family in this essay? What are the effects of those criteria on Alvarez and her sisters? What might the effects be on other ethnic groups?

4. EXPANDING VOCABULARY: In paragraph 5, Alvarez says her family "were the only 'Hispanics'" in a mixed neighborhood. Define *Hispanic*. How do Alvarez's teachers and classmates refer to her? How does she explain to them where she is from?

5. MAKING CONNECTIONS: How might Gerald Early ("Black like . . . Shirley Temple?" pp. 391–93) view the Alvarez family's ritual of watching the Miss America pageant? How did his purpose in watching Shirley Temple movies with his daughters differ from Mr. Alvarez's purpose in watching the pageant with his girls?

Journal Prompts

1. Did you ever feel like an outsider? What did you do to try to belong? What behavior have you observed in others who were trying to fit in?

2. Write about your concept of beauty.

quintessential: Ideal embodiment of.   **gratifying:** Satisfying; pleasing.

Suggestions for Writing

1. Feminists have long decried beauty pageants for objectifying women. Others point to the career successes of past winners and claim beauty pageants open doors to many opportunities. Write an essay supporting one or the other of these views.

2. Write an essay in which you explore the standards of beauty embodied in the Miss America pageant and their effects on women's self-image.

Garry Trudeau
My Inner Shrimp

Garry Trudeau, *born in 1948, was raised in upstate New York and received his B.A. and M.A. from Yale University. The creator of the popular comic strip* Doonesbury, *Trudeau won a Pulitzer Prize in 1975 and in 1994 received the award for best comic strip from the National Cartoonists Society. In the following selection, Trudeau humorously recalls the trials and tribulations of being short as a teenager and reflects on how that experience has served to shape his perceptions of himself and the world around him in adulthood.*

AS YOU READ: *Determine the lifelong impact of Trudeau's delayed growth during his teenage years.*

For the rest of my days, I shall be a recovering short person. Even from 1 my lofty perch of something over six feet (as if I don't know within a micron), I have the soul of a shrimp. I feel the pain of the diminutive, irrespective of whether they feel it themselves, because my visit to the planet of the teenage midgets was harrowing,° humiliating, and extended. I even perceive my last-minute escape to have been flukish, somehow unearned — as if the Commissioner of Growth Spurts had been an old classmate of my father.

My most recent reminder of all this came the afternoon I went hunting 2 for a new office. I had noticed a building under construction in my neighborhood — a brick warren of duplexes, with wide, westerly-facing windows, promising ideal light for a working studio. When I was ushered into the model unit, my pulse quickened: The soaring, twenty-two-foot living room walls were gloriously aglow with the remains of the day. I bonded immediately.

Almost as an afterthought, I ascended the staircase to inspect the loft, 3 ducking as I entered the bedroom. To my great surprise, I stayed ducked: The room was a little more than six feet in height. While my head technically cleared the ceiling, the effect was excruciatingly oppressive. This certainly

harrowing: Extremely disturbing.

wasn't a space I wanted to spend any time in, much less take out a mortgage on.

Puzzled, I wandered down to the sales office and asked if there were any 4 other units to look at. No, replied a resolutely unpleasant receptionist, it was the last one. Besides, they were all exactly alike.

"Are you aware of how low the bedroom ceilings are?" I asked.   5

She shot me an evil look. "Of course we are," she snapped. "There were 6 some problems with the building codes. The architect knows all about the ceilings.

"He's not an idiot, you know," she added, perfectly anticipating my next 7 question.

She abruptly turned away, but it was too late. She'd just confirmed that a 8 major New York developer, working with a fully licensed architect, had knowingly created an entire twelve-story apartment building virtually uninhabitable by anyone of even average height. It was an exclusive high-rise for shorties.

Once I knew that, of course, I couldn't stay away. For days thereafter, as I 9 walked to work, some perverse, unreasoning force would draw me back to the building. But it wasn't just the absurdity, the stone silliness of its design that had me in its grip; it was something far more compelling.° Like some haunted veteran come again to an ancient battlefield, I was revisiting my perilous past.

When I was fourteen, I was the third-smallest in a high school class of 10 one hundred boys, routinely mistaken for a sixth grader. My first week of school, I was drafted into a contingent of students ignominiously° dubbed the "Midgets," so grouped by taller boys presumably so they could taunt us with more perfect efficiency. Inexplicably, some of my fellow Midgets refused to be diminished by the experience, but I retreated into self-pity. I sent away for a book on how to grow tall, and committed to memory its tips on overcoming one's genetic destiny — or at least making the most of a regrettable situation. The book cited historical figures who had gone the latter route — Alexander the Great, Caesar, Napoleon (the mind involuntarily added Hitler). Strategies for stretching the limbs were suggested — hanging from door frames, sleeping on your back, doing assorted floor exercises — all of which I incorporated into my daily routine (get up, brush teeth, hang from door frame). I also learned the importance of meeting girls early in the day, when, the book assured me, my rested spine rendered me perceptibly taller.

For six years, my condition persisted; I grew, but at nowhere near the 11 rate of my peers. I perceived other problems as ancillary,° and loaded up the stature issue with freight shipped in daily from every corner of my life. Lack of athletic success, all absence of a social life, the inevitable run-ins with bullies — all could be attributed to the missing inches. The night I found

---

compelling: Having a powerful and irresistible effect.   **ignominiously:** Intending to cause humiliation.   **ancillary:** Less important.

myself sobbing in my father's arms was the low point; we both knew it was one problem he couldn't fix.

Of course what we couldn't have known was that he and my mother al- 12 ready had. They had given me a delayed developmental timetable. In my seventeenth year, I miraculously shot up six inches, just in time for graduation and a fresh start. I was, in the space of a few months, reborn — and I made the most of it. Which is to say that thereafter, all of life's disappointments, reversals, and calamities° still arrived on schedule — but blissfully free of subtext.°

Once you stop being the butt, of course, any problem recedes, if only to 13 give way to a new one. And yet the impact of being literally looked down on, of being *made* to feel small, is forever. I teaches you how to stretch, how to survive the scorn of others for things that are beyond your control. Not growing forces you to grow up fast.

Sometimes I think I'd like to return to a high-school reunion to surprise 14 my classmates. Not that they didn't know me when I finally started catching up. They did, but I doubt they'd remember. Adolescent hierarchies° have a way of enduring; I'm sure I am still recalled as the Midget I myself have never really left behind.

Of course, if I'm going to show up, it'll have to be soon. I'm starting to 15 shrink.

Questions to Start You Thinking

1. CONSIDERING MEANING: Trudeau says in the first paragraph that he is over six feet tall. Why, then, is he so concerned with height?

2. IDENTIFYING WRITING STRATEGIES: Trudeau opens his essay with an anecdote. How effectively does this anecdote introduce his subject? How does it support his thesis? What other kind of opening could he have used?

3. READING CRITICALLY: How does Trudeau use cause and effect analysis in his essay? Where does he describe short-term effects of being short during his teenage years? Where does he describe long-term effects? Which descriptions do you think have more impact?

4. EXPANDING VOCABULARY: Trudeau writes, "I feel the pain of the diminutive, irrespective of whether they feel it themselves" (paragraph 1). Define *diminutive*. What links Trudeau to this group? How can Trudeau feel pain for people who don't feel it themselves?

5. MAKING CONNECTIONS: Trudeau and Lisa Jervis ("My Jewish Nose," pp. 519–23) both deal with physical traits inherited from their parents. Compare and contrast these two writers' responses to their body images and the ways they cope with them.

---

calamities: Disasters.   **subtext:** Underlying meaning.   **hierarchies:** Systems organized by rank and status.

Journal Prompts

1. What quality did you have in high school or elementary school that you felt identified you in an undesirable way? Have you outgrown it, or are you likely to? What permanent marks has it left?
2. Do you think that people can be drafted into a group against their will? If so, how does this happen? Based on your experience or observation, what might result? If you don't believe that people can be defined by others, how do they resist such definition?

Suggestions for Writing

1. Trudeau claims that "adolescent hierarchies have a way of enduring" (paragraph 14). Write an essay in which you support or refute this statement. Draw upon your own experience or observations to support your stand.
2. Write an essay about someone you know or have observed who deals with circumstances beyond his or her control in an admirable way. Explain the circumstance — a physical abnormality, a disease, a disastrous occurrence — and describe how the person has dealt with it. Consider inner resources the person has drawn upon and the effects of those inner resources on his or her character.

Marisa Kula
Victoria's Not-So-Secret Strategy

Marisa Kula *was born in Honolulu, Hawaii. She studied journalism and women's studies at Northwestern University in Illinois, and she hopes someday to make films with a feminist bent. In the following essay, which first appeared on chickclick.com, Kula examines the catalog of the ubiquitous lingerie store Victoria's Secret and questions whether women are the marketers' intended audience.*

AS YOU READ: *Decide whose fantasies are exploited by the marketers at Victoria's Secret.*

I just can't get enough of the Victoria's Secret catalog — at least that seems to be what the lingerie company thinks. If it's not time for the semi-annual sale or the season sale (basically $2 off everything that was ugly in the last catalog), we're subjected to Victoria's Secret "City" or "Country" themes.

It's a marketing regime that feels like a boot camp in basic "feminine" training and, well, it's not such a great feeling. Not that there's anything wrong with Victoria's Secret's desire to sell underwear. And there's really nothing wrong with the fine, stiletto-heeled line the company walks between salesmanship and pornography. The problem with Victoria's Secret is not what it does but how it does it. And does it. And does it some more.

"Victoria's Secret structures its advertising according to a deeply trou- 3 bling construction of women as sex objects for men," says Joan Callahan, professor of Women's Studies at the University of Kentucky.

The ubiquity° of the endless catalogs, TV commercials, and "fashion 4 show" Webcasts ensures not only [that] adult women will identify Victoria's Secret as a place to buy underwear, but [. . .] that girls will identify Victoria's Secret as being synonymous with being womanly and sexy.

"At the point when girls are really vulnerable and uncertain of who they 5 are, Victoria's Secret is giving them the wrong message about female sexuality," says Natalie Kampen, professor in women's studies at Barnard College, "defining it by the male gaze (what men would like women to be) and determining sexual worth based on whether or not females meet that standard."

Needless to say, your choice of panties is a personal one. As Victoria's 6 Secret supermodel spokeswoman Tyra Banks said in a March 1998 press release, "I wear this lingerie for me. Beautiful lingerie makes me feel more beautiful. It doesn't even matter if I'm the only one who sees it."

If Victoria's Secret is about making women feel great, shouldn't the cata- 7 log represent what females want? Yes. So why [does] a catalog that sells underwear to women [seem] so obviously marketed to men?

"The images [in the catalog] are much more what men's standard of 8 beauty is," agrees Renee Redd, director of the Women's Center at Northwestern University. "The models are not the anorexic type that women tend to idealize. The image of the curvaceous woman is therefore healthier, but the underlying effect is that women are sensing this is what men want. So women want to buy Victoria's Secret mainly because they perceive it's what men like. And women, sadly, are still being taught to please others."

Women are diligent students, apparently. The Victoria's Secret annual re- 9 port is full of facts and figures just as disturbing as the measurements of its models. In 1998 alone, Victoria's Secret catalogs raked in sales of $759 million, leading the industry in profitability and making it the number-one catalog of intimate apparel. And this women-as-men's-sex-objects idea is being glorified around the globe: 406 million Victoria's Secret catalogs were mailed in the United States and abroad in 1998, and within the first six hours of the company's December 1998 Web site launch, Victoria's Secret (which is owned by Intimate Brands Inc.) received orders from thirty-seven countries. A recent Fairchild's survey showed Victoria's Secret had jumped from twenty-sixth to ninth in their 100 "most recognized brands."

"Today, I don't believe there's a country on earth that doesn't know 10 about Victoria's Secret," wrote Leslie H. Wexner, chairman of the Victoria's Secret parent company, Intimate Brands, in the annual report.

That's a good thing?   11

ubiquity: State of being everywhere at once.

"This culture has an absolute obsession with women's bodies, an in-   12
credible focus on women's bodies to the exclusion of everything else," says
Redd. "Female self-esteem is therefore dearly attached to our bodies, how
our bodies look to others. In this case, you could say that women's self-
esteem rests on how attractive they are to men."

And while Victoria's Secret may not have created the standards of female   13
desirability, its mass-marketing of the feminine both nurtures the existing
stereotypes of female sexuality and fertilizes their future growth. Worst of
all, it is a very specific (i.e., noninclusive to women's different body shapes
and sizes) stereotype that is presented as "sexy." Put it this way: Do you look
like a Victoria's Secret model? No? Then you don't look sexy.

"People who have less power socially often come to view themselves   14
through the lenses of people who have more power," says Kampen. "What
happens is that your inner view of yourself is as much subject to power relations as any political debate.

"The Victoria's Secret catalog," she continues, "is playing to the place   15
where men's and women's fantasies are overlapping. Women become com-
plicit° with men, shaping their bodies to be desirable to men, and shaping
their fantasies of their own desirability to the desires of the people with
power, i.e., men."

Even independent marketers agree that Victoria's Secret capitalizes on   16
male fantasies to sell women's panties. "I definitely think the [Victoria's Se-
cret] catalog is geared primarily toward men," says Priya Patel, manager of
business development at Omnicon Group in New York.

"Men like to look at the Victoria's Secret catalog," says Rachel Hayden,   17
from Leo Burnett Company's Marketing Research Association in Chicago.
"They think it's like Playboy Magazine or Penthouse coming to their home
for free."

Interesting, because it is women, not men, who comprise the bulk of   18
Victoria's Secret customers. Managers in Victoria's Secret stores from Los Angeles, New York, Chicago, and Boston all report that their clientele is overwhelmingly female: "I'd say 20 percent, at most, of our customers are men,
and that's a generous estimation," says a Chicago store manager.

"I think it might depend on the store's location, but our clients are usu-   19
ally women shopping alone," agreed a manager of a Victoria's Secret store in
downtown Los Angeles.

These same stores cite the holiday season as the only occasion men   20
prowl around Victoria's Secret in large herds. And catalog purchases are
overwhelmingly made by women. So why are women continuing to patronize a clothing company that, well, continually patronizes them?

"I do think many women purchase Victoria's Secret for themselves,   21
meaning that it makes them feel sexy and better about their bodies," offers

---

complicit: Involved in wrongdoing.

Redd. "But the reason that underwear makes them feel better about themselves is because they think they are pleasing men by wearing it."

Questions to Start You Thinking

1. CONSIDERING MEANING: What strategy does Victoria's Secret use to market its lingerie?

2. IDENTIFYING WRITING STRATEGIES: Where does Kula use quotations from interviews to support her critique of the Victoria's Secret marketing strategy? How does her use of expert opinion affect the tone of her essay?

3. READING CRITICALLY: In paragraph 7, Kula asks a rhetorical question: "So why [does] a catalog that sells underwear to women [seem] so obviously marketed to men?" How does Kula answer this question? What kind of evidence does she use as support?

4. EXPANDING VOCABULARY: In paragraph 20, Kula uses *patronize* twice in the same sentence. Define *patronize*. How do women patronize Victoria's Secret? How does Victoria's Secret patronize them?

5. MAKING CONNECTIONS: Reread Phyllis Rose's description of shopping for blue jeans in "Shopping and Other Spiritual Adventures in America Today" (pp. 450–53, paragraphs 8–10). How could the dressing room in Bob's Surplus serve as therapy for Victoria's Secret customers?

Journal Prompts

1. Do advertising images such as those in Victoria's Secret catalogs set the standard for feminine beauty, or do they merely exploit a pre-existing stereotype for profit?

2. Look over some catalogs other than those for Victoria's Secret. Are there other catalogs that emphasize body image to market their products? What other kinds of fantasy do marketers use? Discuss the various ways different catalogs entice customers to buy.

Suggestions for Writing

1. Think of some women you know personally whom you consider attractively dressed. What standards govern their choice of clothing? Based on conversation and observation, write an essay exploring why women dress as they do and whether male standards of beauty influence their choices.

2. Advocates of dress codes claim that people's behavior is influenced by how they are dressed. Using your own experience, come to some conclusions about the extent to which this claim is true or false. Also find expert opinion to use as support or as counterargument for your claim.

Alicia Potter

Mirror Image

Alicia Potter, *born in 1969,is a freelance writer living in Boston. Her work has appeared in the* Boston Herald, *the* Boston Globe, Family Fun, *and* American Movie Classics *magazine, among others. In 1998, Potter won first-place honors in health writing from the New England Press Association. The following selection first appeared in the* Boston Phoenix. *Readers often hear about women's distorted body images and eating disorders — but what about men's? In "Mirror Image," Potter examines men's attitudes toward their bodies, their desire to be an ideal size, and the role advertising plays in their growing obsession with weight.*

AS YOU READ: *Identify some self-image problems previously attributed to women that men are now experiencing.*

John Updike once compared the male body to a bank account: as long as 1 it's healthy, a man doesn't think much about it. Clearly John Updike never met Emanuel Ward.

Ward has the physique of a star sprinter. His biceps bulge; his calves 2 curve; under his green T-shirt, his stomach no doubt ripples. Yet last summer the twenty-seven-year-old Ward found himself fretting: how would he look in a swimsuit? Maybe not as buff as his buddies, he thought, vowing to step up his gym regimen. "I didn't want to be ashamed," he says.

Not a typical guy thing to say, right? Think again. Being a man these 3 days seems, well, an awful lot like being a woman. For men, more than ever, looks count. In *Vogue* and *Men's Health* alike, modern-day Adonises sell everything from protein powder to Armani cologne. They've got washboard abs, silky skin, nipples so erect they cast shadows. The male torso reigns as the decade's most powerful "crossover image" (appealing to men, women, gays, and straights alike), reports Peter Arnell of the New York advertising agency the Arnell Group.

"It's kind of sad, but sometimes I see a guy on TV who's buff," Ward 4 says, "and if I haven't been working out, I think, Wow! I better get back to the gym." He admits a Hanes underwear ad usually does the trick.

If this is gender equality, then the turning of the tables is not without a 5 surprising, and potentially harmful, set of side effects. As men become more body-conscious, and as advertisers become more shameless about objectifying° the male physique, men are acquiring problems formerly associated with women: eating disorders, body obsessions, low physical self-esteem. One body-image study found that 45 percent of men were dissatisfied with their physiques; women were only slightly less satisfied at 55 percent.

Some women, like Gwynne Reynolds, a twenty-eight-year-old marketing 6 executive, say it's about time. "I think it's only fair that men get a taste of

objectifying: Treating as an object, especially exploitatively.

what it's like to be us," she says. Meanwhile, millions of guys on Stair-Masters are pondering what it means to be a man.

How else to explain the success of the movie *The Full Monty,* a ninety-minute riff on the crisis of the male self-image? The British comedy, about six laid-off steelworkers who put on a strip show despite their considerable physical flaws, has already raked in about $80 million worldwide. Yes, *The Full Monty* was funny, but it revealed more than just flesh.

"You'd better pray that women are more understanding about us," one of the film's characters says. "Anti-wrinkle cream there is, anti-fat bastard cream there is not."

On a busy Monday night at the Boston Body health club, on Boylston Street, the after-five crowd files in to sweat off a weekend's worth of microbrews and pizza. In the weight-training area, a pack of guys grunt and heave like women in labor.

Jay Knudson, twenty-one, is one of them. The six-foot-four, 215-pound law student works out an hour and a half a day, five days a week. "Guys who are working out in their twenties are not doing it so much for their health," he says between biceps curls. "They're doing it for the look."

What look are they shooting for? Currently, two competing body types dominate the pages of *GQ* and *Men's Health.* The first is a slender, sculpted, almost feminine look (think Brad Pitt); the second is a pumped-up but still low-fat physique (think Nicolas Cage). Both images differ greatly from past ideals of male perfection; not so long ago, the manliest men in popular culture were burly, barrel-chested, even hairy. Think of John Wayne in the '40s, Burt Lancaster in the '50s, Steve McQueen in the '60s, Burt Reynolds in the '70s — these guys probably couldn't even point out their deltoids, never mind sculpt them. But this indifference to their appearance only made them sexier.

Then came the '80s, the decade of aerobics, jogging, tofu — and two ubiquitous advertising campaigns featuring male bodies. The Soloflex guy and the Calvin Klein underwear model represented a whole new breed of man. Their bodies, precursors to the Pitt and Cage looks, were hairless and lean, feminized and decidedly self-conscious.

According to Daniel Harris's 1997 book *The Rise and Fall of Gay Culture* (Hyperion), this new body aesthetic had grown partly out of trends in the gay community. For decades, Harris writes, the most attractive gay men had cultivated a slender, more feminized appearance. With the dawn of AIDS in the '80s, however, gay men began to equate a slight physique with sickness, and they flocked to the gym. The perfectionist masculinity of gay gym culture quickly captivated Madison Avenue: think of Marky Mark, smirking in his Y-fronts across billboards and magazine pages. And although Marky himself was a celebrity, most of these ads divorced men's bodies from their personalities in a way that hadn't been done before. Who could name the Soloflex guy? The Diet Coke guy? High school girls could now line their lockers with magazine ads featuring anonymous male physiques as unrealistic as the swimsuit models their male classmates were drooling over.

Meanwhile, men were eyeing those diamond-hard abdominals and 14 thinking that maybe, with enough time in the gym, they too could get cut. The average guy, of course, can no more shape his torso into Marky Mark's than the average gal can whip herself into Cindy Crawford. But suddenly men were presented with a demanding ideal that *seemed* achievable through hard work. And that myth persists. Marcus Schenkenberg, the first man to enter the stratosphere of supermodeldom, has released a new, photo-cluttered biography in which he shares his workout routine with average Joes. His gut-conditioning tip: 650 abdominal crunches a day.

If you're a man and that sounds excessive to you, count yourself lucky. As 15 society demands a fitter body, frowning on every pinch of fat, clinicians sus-pect an increasing number of men are crossing the line into exercise addic-tion. Signs of obsession include feelings of acute anxiety over a missed workout and an urge to make exercise a priority over friends and family. Most trainers recommend working out no more than an hour a day.

But men don't just worry that they are too fat; many worry that they are 16 too thin. Researchers at McLean Hospital [in Belmont, Massachusetts] have just defined a body-image distortion disorder that they liken to "reverse anorexia." Called muscle dysmorphia, the syndrome appears in athletes (both male and female) who, despite being dramatically muscular, are con-vinced that they are too small. Imagine a bodybuilder — 250 pounds, 20-inch biceps, 6 percent body fat — horrified to take his shirt off for fear he looks out of shape.

"What we're seeing now is the same body obsession but in a new form," 17 says Harrison G. Pope Jr., one of the researchers at McLean. "It's coming out in the '90s as a preoccupation with muscularity and size." Indeed, Pope has called muscle dysmorphia "the anorexia of the '90s." That might sound a little alarmist, but Pope says it's no exaggeration. He warns not to under-estimate the power of pop culture, especially Hollywood and the flourishing men's magazine industry (*Men's Health* alone has increased its circulation fivefold, to 1.3 million readers, since its start in 1986).

The pressure on men comes from another direction, too. Women run 18 companies, fly fighter planes, and, yes, pump iron — leaving the boys down-right anxious about the meaning of masculinity. "As androgyny and gender equality increases, it unfortunately becomes very threatening to a lot of men," says Eric Silverman, a DePauw University anthropologist who special-izes in the study of body image. "Suddenly men feel like they need to redi-vide the genders. They need things that are exclusively masculine, even hypermasculine."

For some men, that means more muscle. Indeed, the number of men 19 exercising has increased more than 30 percent since the start of the decade. According to the research firm American Sports Data, last year nine million men belonged to a health club. And on average, they went to the gym eighty-eight days a year. For those keeping score, that was six days more than women.

Pope also adds that steroid use remains high. About one million Ameri-   20
can men have tried the drugs once; up to 6 percent have taken them by age
eighteen.

Indeed, teenage boys are on their way to becoming the next generation   21
of body-conscious men. They avidly lift weights, blend protein shakes, and
buy bodybuilding magazines. "Compare that to when I was in high school
in the 1960s," says Pope. "No one even talked about working out."

[. . .] Of the eight million Americans being treated for eating disorders,   22
one million are men. According [to T. Donald Branum, a psychotherapist
specializing in eating disorders,] men make up about 10 percent of anorex-
ics and about 20 percent of bulimics. Nearly half of binge eaters are men.

Branum, who treats men aged fifteen to sixty-five, reports that many   23
men are ashamed to suffer from a "woman's illness." Indeed, the term "eating disorder" usually conjures the image of a white, surburban teenage girl.
But eating disorders among men were documented in medical journals as
far back as 1649. It's even suspected that Franz Kafka suffered from
anorexia; hence his short story "The Hunger Artist."

Recently, researchers at Massachusetts General Hospital found that gay   24
men face a special risk for eating disorders, particularly bulimia. Like
women, gay men feel undue pressure to adhere to a lean look. "There's a
high level of expectation in my culture," says Boston Body manager Brian
Borrelli, who is gay. "A gay guy's supposed to have neat clothes, a fit body, a
certain sophisticated style. It's easy to take that to the extreme."

Which he did. In high school Borrelli weighed 225 pounds. When he   25
came out in college, he began dieting to fit the gay community's beauty
ideal. He skipped breakfast, grabbed a salad for lunch, and ate soup for dinner. He also ran eight miles a day. In seven months, Borrelli was down to
135 pounds. No one recognized that he was anorexic.

"There was never any help offered to me," he says. "Let's face it, you're   26
not going to be waiting for the T one day and look up and find a sign that
says, 'Are you a white gay man suffering from anorexia?'"

For the most part, eating-disorder research has ignored male sufferers.   27
And many treatment facilities exclude men, although body-image problems
appear to have the same causes in both men and women. Branum reports
that his patients with eating disorders typically grapple with issues of control, anger, and sexuality; food becomes their coping mechanism.

Although Branum doubts a man can develop an eating disorder simply   28
from spending too much time reading GQ, he does believe that a man with
an eating disorder may look to media images to determine physical goals.
He explains, "The man begins to think, 'If I look like that guy in the magazine, then things will be okay inside me.'"

There's another way to look like the people in the magazines, of course, and   29
here, too, men are venturing into women's territory. Rumor has it that the
babes aren't the only ones on *Baywatch* with synthetic chests — yes, David
Hasselhoff's may be fake, too.

Last year men accounted for about 20 percent of all plastic surgeries, ac- 30
cording to the American Academy of Cosmetic Surgery. All told, cosmetic
surgeries on men rose 20 percent from 1994 to 1996, which wasn't too different from the increase for women. Liposuctions for males, though, increased 30 percent, compared to 20 percent for females.

"Women come in waving Victoria's Secret catalogues or *Playboy* clippings 31
and say, 'I want those breasts,'" says Barry Davidson, a Newton plastic surgeon. "Men come in and say, 'I want to get rid of this fat.' Then they grab it."

Michael (not his real name), thirty-four, had been grabbing his waist for 32
years. Even in high school, when he was a skinny five-foot-ten, 150 pounds,
Michael had love handles. He lifted weights and played racquetball five
times a week, but the extra inches wouldn't budge. "Every morning I'd put
on my pants, look in the mirror, and they'd be there," he says. "I just didn't
like the way I looked." Last year, he underwent abdominal liposuction.
While Michael's weight remained at 185 pounds following the operation,
his waist shrank from thirty-four inches to thirty-two inches. The fat he lost
(diluted with saline solution) was enough to fill two two-liter Coke bottles.
"I couldn't be happier," he says of his new waistline. "I guess I'm a vain type
of guy, but if I could afford it, then why the hell not?"

Most abdominal liposuctions cost about three thousand dollars. Just be- 33
cause you can foot the bill doesn't mean you're a guaranteed candidate,
though. Davidson warns that the operation is no substitute for exercise or
dieting. In fact, many plastic surgeons won't operate on someone who has
not first tried traditional weight-loss methods. Age, however, is no barrier;
Davidson operates on men in their early twenties to mid-fifties.

Beyond liposuction, the anatomical possibilities for men border on the 34
bionic. Doctors can lift the flap of skin on the back of the lower leg, insert a
hunk of silicone, and presto: handsome, bulging calves. There are also pec-
toral implants (hello, Mr. Hasselhoff), hair transplants, breast reduction,
and, of course, the very rare but much hyped penis enlargement. Davidson
reports that most men seek surgery to contour hereditary soft spots that exercise can't tone. Love handles, a rounded belly, or excess tissue in the
breasts are common complaints.

The main reason men and women choose surgery is to improve their 35
self-image, reports one study. Beyond that, male patients said that they also
hoped to enhance their careers and to keep up with a peer who's had surgery. It's a desperate scenario: men surreptitiously° checking each other out
at meetings or in the locker room, trying to figure out who had a tummy
tuck or a chin job.

Is this what we're coming to: a silent competition over who's got the 36
firmest pecs?

Questions to Start You Thinking

1. CONSIDERING MEANING: According to Potter, what shift has occurred in
   men's self-image in the last decade? How does she account for this shift?

surreptitiously: Secretively, especially in a sly manner.

2. **IDENTIFYING WRITING STRATEGIES:** How does Potter use interviews to support her claims? Where does she use reading as a resource? Is her use of these sources effective? Why, or why not?

3. **READING CRITICALLY:** Potter says "the turning of the tables is not without a surprising, and potentially harmful, set of side effects" (paragraph 5). What effects does she attribute to objectifying men's bodies? What evidence does she use to support her claim that these effects are potentially harmful?

4. **EXPANDING VOCABULARY:** Define *ubiquitous* (paragraph 12). What resulted from the ubiquity of the Soloflex and Calvin Klein ads? What other ubiquitous ads featuring male bodies can you think of?

5. **MAKING CONNECTIONS:** Compare and contrast the men Potter describes with those described by Dave Barry in "From Now On, Let Women Kill Their Own Spiders" (pp. 428–30). What would Barry have to say about Potter's men?

Journal Prompts

1. Write a description of your own body. Be as objective as possible. Then subjectively evaluate what you have described, and explore what has influenced your opinion.

2. What are the three most startling images you have seen in advertising? What effect did the images have on you? Do you think that impact was their intended purpose?

Suggestions for Writing

1. Potter discusses an area in which gender equality is having some damaging effects. Write an essay in which you evaluate the effects of gender equality in another specific area, such as the workplace. Support your own observations with facts and statistics you gather from research.

2. Write an essay that compares and contrasts media treatment of male and female bodies. Come to your own conclusions about the effects of these depictions on the self-images and expectations of both genders.

Lisa Jervis

My Jewish Nose

Lisa Jervis *was born in 1972 and grew up in New York. She is the editor and publisher of* Bitch: Feminist Response to Pop Culture, *which is self-described as a "print magazine devoted to incisive commentary on our media-driven world." Jervis's writing has appeared in* Ms., *the* San Francisco Chronicle, Salon, *and the* Utne Reader. *She is also coeditor of* Young Wives' Tales: New Adventures in Love and Partnership *(2001). The selection that follows was published in* Body Outlaws *(ed. Ophira Edut; 2000). In this personal account, Jervis addresses how body shape, skin color, and temperament can influence an individual's personal and cultural identification. She considers how the desire to change appearance may be due to common stereotypes (of ethnic, class, and religious backgrounds) but now may extend to avoiding issues like age. By not opting for a nose job, Jervis maintains her identity despite an overwhelming societal pressure to conform to one ideal of beauty.*

AS YOU READ: *Determine exactly why Jervis chooses to leave her nose as is rather than have it "fixed."*

I'm a Jew. I'm not even slightly religious. Aside from attending friends' *bat* 1 *mitzvahs*, I've been to temple maybe twice. I don't know Hebrew; when given the option of religious education, my junior-high self easily chose to sleep in on Sunday mornings. My family skips around the Passover Haggadah to get to the food faster. Before having dated someone from an observant family, I wouldn't have known a *mezuzah* if it bit me on the butt. I was born assimilated.°

But still, I'm a Jew — even though my Jewish identity has very little to 2 do with religion, organized or otherwise. I'm an ethnic Jew of a very specific variety: a godless, New York City–raised, neurotic middle-class girl from a solidly liberal Democrat family, who attended largely Jewish, "progressive" schools that thought they were integrated and nonracist. Growing up, almost everyone around me was Jewish; I was stunned when I found out that Jews make up only two percent of the American population. But what being Jewish meant to me was that on Christmas day my family went out for Chinese food (some years, Indian) and took in the new Woody Allen movie. It also meant that I had a big honkin' nose.

And I still do. By virtue of my class and its sociopolitical trappings, the 3 option of having my nose surgically altered was ever-present. From adolescence on, I've had a standing offer from my mother to get a nose job.

"It's not such a big deal." "Doctors do such individual-looking noses 4 these days, it'll look really natural." "It's not too late, you know," she would say to me for years after I flat-out refused to let someone break my nose, scrape part of it out and reposition it into a smaller, less obtrusive shape. "I'll still pay." As if money were the reason I was resisting.

My mother thought a nose job was a good idea. See, she hadn't wanted 5 one either. But when she was sixteen, her parents demanded that she get that honker "fixed," and they didn't take no for an answer. She insists that she's been glad ever since, although she usually rationalizes that it was good for her social life. (She even briefly dated a guy she met in the surgeon's waiting room: a boxer having his deviated septum corrected.)

Even my father is a believer. He says that without my mother's nose job, 6 my sister and I wouldn't exist, because he never would have gone out with Mom. But I take this with an entire salt lick. My father's a guy who thinks that dressing up means wearing dark sneakers; that pants should be purchased

assimilated: Conforming to the characteristics of a majority group.

every twenty years, and only if the old ones are literally falling apart at the seams; and that haircuts should cost ten dollars and take as many minutes. The only thing he notices about appearances is to say, "You have some crud . . ." as he picks a piece of lint off your sleeve. But he cared about the nose? Whatever.

Even though my mother was happy with her tidy little surgically altered   7 nose, she wasn't going to put me through the same thing, and for that I am truly grateful. I'm also unspeakably glad that her comments stayed far from the "you'd just be so pretty if you did" angle. ("Yours isn't as big as mine was," she would say. "You don't *need* it.") I know a few people who weren't so lucky. Not that they were dragged kicking and screaming to the doctor's office; no, they were coerced and shamed into it. Seems it was their family's decision more than their own — usually older Jewish female relatives: mothers, grandmothers, aunts.

What's the motivation for that kind of pressure? Can it be that for all   8 the strides made against racism and anti-Semitism, Americans still want to expunge° their ethnicity from their looks as much as possible? Were these mothers and grandmothers trying to fit their offspring into a more white, gentile mode? Possibly. Well, definitely. But on purpose? Probably not. Their lust for the button nose is probably more a desire for a typical, "pretty" femininity than for any specific de-ethnicizing. But given the society in which we live, the proximity of white features to the ideal of beauty is no coincidence. I think that anyone who opts for a nose job today (or who pressured her daughter to do so) would say that the reason is to look "better" or "prettier." But when we scratch the surface of what "prettier" means, we find that we might as well be saying "whiter" or "more gentile" (I would add "bland," but that's my personal opinion).

Or perhaps the reason is to become unobtrusive. The stereotypical Jew-   9 ish woman is loud, pushy — qualities that girls really aren't supposed to have. So is it possible that the nose job is supposed to usher in not only physical femininity but a psychological, traditional femininity as well? Ditch the physical and emotional ties to your ethnicity in one simple procedure: Bob your nose, and become feminine in both mind and body. (This certainly seems to be the way it has worked with someone like Courtney Love, although her issue is class more than ethnicity. But it's undeniable that her new nose comes on a Versace-shilling, largely silent persona, in stark contrast to her old messy, outspoken self.)

Thankfully, none of the women I know have become meek and submis-   10 sive from their nose jobs. But *damn*, do they have regrets. One told me it was the biggest mistake of her life; another confessed to wanting her old nose back just a few short years after the surgery. They wish they'd stood up to their families and kept their natural features.

Even though I know plenty of women with their genetically determined   11 schnozzes still intact, women who either refused or never considered surgery, sometimes I still feel like an oddity. From what my mother tells me,

---

expunge: Completely erase.

nose jobs were as compulsory° a rite of passage for her peers as multiple ear-piercings are for mine. Once, when I was still in high school, I went with my mother to a Planned Parenthood fundraiser. It was a cocktail party–type thang in some lovely apartment, with lovely food and drink and a lovely short speech by Wendy Wasserstein. But I was confused: We were at a lefty charity event in Manhattan, and all the women in attendance had little WASP noses. (Most of them were blond, too, but that didn't really register. I guess hair dye is a more universal ritual.)

"Why are there no Jewish women here?" I whispered to my mother. She 12 laughed, but I think she was genuinely shocked. "What do you mean? All of these women are Jewish." And then it hit me: We were wall-to-wall rhinoplasties. And worse, there was no reason to be surprised. These were women my mother's age or older who came of age in the late '50s or before, when anti-Semitism in this country was much more overt than it is today. That kind of surface assimilation was practically the norm for Jews back then, and those honkers were way too, ahem, big a liability on the dating and social scenes. Nose jobs have declined since then. They're no longer in the top five plastic surgery procedures performed, edged out by liposuction and laser skin resurfacing. (I guess now it's more important to be young and trim than gentile, what with societal forces of youth-and-beauty worship replacing post–World War II fear and hatred . . .)

I don't think it's a coincidence that I didn't consider my nose an ethnic fea- 13 ture growing up in New York. I didn't have to, because almost everyone around me had that feature (and that ethnicity) too. It wasn't until I graduated from college and moved to California that I realized how marked I was by my nose and my vaguely ethnic, certainly Jewish appearance. I also then realized how much I liked being marked that way, being instantly recognizable to anyone who knew how to look. I once met another Jewish woman at a conference in California. In the middle of our conversation, she randomly popped out with, "You're Jewish, right?" I replied, "With this nose and this hair, you gotta ask?" We both laughed. I was right: The question was just a formality, and we both knew it.

Living in California, I'm particularly in need of those little moments of 14 recognition. I know that a Jew living in, say, Tennessee might laugh at me for saying this, but there are no Jews in California. I feel conspicuously° Semitic here in a way that I never did anywhere else (not even at my small Ohio liberal arts college — after all, that place was filled with New York Jews). Few of my friends are Jewish, and those random "bagel and lox" references just don't get understood the way I'm used to.

Only once did I feel uneasy about being "identified." At my first job out 15 of college, my boss asked, after I mentioned an upcoming trip to see my family in New York, "So, are your parents just like people in Woody Allen movies?" I wondered if I had a big sign on my forehead reading, "Big Yid

---

compulsory: Required.   **conspicuously:** Attracting special attention.

Here." His comment brought up all those insecurities American Jews can have about our ethnicity that, not coincidentally, Woody Allen loves to play on — and overemphasize for comic effect: Am I *that* Jewish? Is is *that* obvious? I felt conspicuous, exposed. But regardless of that incident, I'm glad I have the sign on my face, even it it's located a tad lower than my forehead.

See, I don't have a whole lot of Jewish heritage to hold on to. My fam- 16 ily's name was changed — it's not as if "Jervis" is particularly gentile, but it sure is a lot less obvious than "Jersowitz," which my grandfather jettisoned before my father can remember. Temple was never a part of my life — I'm an atheist. I don't know what Purim is about. Hell, it takes me a minute to re- member how many candles go in the menorah — and last week I used mine for a candlelight dinner with my husband-to-be, a half-Christian, half- Buddhist Japanese American whose thoughts on God's existence are along the lines of "I don't know, and I don't really care."

But in a larger sense, Judaism is the only identity in which culture and 17 religion are supposedly bound closely: If you're Irish and aren't a practicing Catholic, you can still be fully Irish; being Buddhist doesn't specify a race or an ethnic identity. African Americans can practice any religion, and it doesn't make them any less black. But "Jewish" is a funny ethnicity. Is it a race; is it a set of beliefs? Color doesn't have much to do with it. In fact, the question of whether or not Jews are white can be answered in as many dif- ferent ways as there are people who have an opinion on the topic.

To me, being a Jew is cultural. But for me it's a culture tied only marginally 18 — even hypothetically° — to religion, and mostly to geography (New York Jews are different from California Jews, lemme tell ya) and sensibility/ temperament (hyperintellectual, food-lovin', neurotic, worrywartish, perfec- tionistic). So the question for me is: What happens when Jewish identity be- comes untied from religion? I don't know for sure. And that means I'll grab onto anything I need to keep that identity — including my nose.

Questions to Start You Thinking

1. **CONSIDERING MEANING:** In paragraph 1, Jervis says she is "not even slightly religious." What does being Jewish mean to Jervis? How is her nose symbolic of the distinction between religion and ethnicity?

2. **IDENTIFYING WRITING STRATEGIES:** Find words and phrases Jervis uses that reinforce a strong "New York Jewish" voice in her essay. Why might Jervis choose to emphasize this voice?

3. **READING CRITICALLY:** How does Jervis account for the pressure Jewish families put on their daughters to have nose surgery?

4. **EXPANDING VOCABULARY:** Jervis describes the women at a charity fund- raiser she attends as having "little WASP noses" (paragraph 11). What does the acronym *WASP* mean? Why does Jervis conclude that the women there are "wall to wall rhinoplasties"?

hypothetically: Assumed to exist in theory, if not in actuality.

5. MAKING CONNECTIONS: In paragraph 9, Jervis describes the stereotype of Jewish girls as being "loud, pushy." Based on Deborah Tannen's assessment of the effects of women's assertive behavior on the job ("Women and Men Talking on the Job," pp. 431–36), would Tannen expect Jewish women to be more or less successful than females who typically are less obtrusive? Would Tannen agree with Jervis's causal link between Jewish girls' more assertive natures and their families' pressure on them to have their noses fixed?

Link to the Paired Essay

Jervis and Janice Turner ("Cutting Edge," pp. 524–27) both address the pressure to alter one's natural appearance with cosmetic surgery. How does Jervis's purpose differ from Turner's? Which writer achieves her purpose more effectively? Which piece do you find more convincing? Why?

Journal Prompts

1. Write about a characteristic you have, physical or behavioral, that identifies you with a particular group. How do you feel about this distinction? Why?

2. Are stereotypes ever useful? In what ways are they useful, and in what ways are they not?

Suggestions for Writing

1. Using Jervis's essay as a springboard, write an essay in which you compare and contrast the viewpoints of two or three generations on maintaining or even emphasizing ethnicity. First interview several people who represent different generations of an ethnic group. Use your findings to arrive at a thesis statement, and then support and illustrate your thesis with material from your conversations.

2. Write an essay in which you examine the causes, effects, or both of women opting for plastic surgry. Draw on outside sources to support your analysis.

WWW
For useful links to Web sources on topics including *body image*, visit <www.bedfordstmartins.com/toplinks>.

Janice Turner
Cutting Edge

Janice Turner *wrote "Cutting Edge," an article which examines men's rising interest in plastic surgery, as a news article for the* Toronto Star. *Most men she interviewed decided to undergo cosmetic surgery because they were often judged at work by their appearance. In an uncertain and competitive job market, they turned to cosmetic surgery as a career investment.*

AS YOU READ: *Identify the reasons more men are seeking cosmetic surgery.*

When Joseph hit the big four-oh, he certainly didn't feel old. But he felt 1
he looked old. "To me, I looked very tired," says the Metro business-
man. "And I was getting a decent amount of sleep. I didn't look bad or excessively wrinkled up or that. But it wasn't the way I wanted to look." After a
year of shopping around, Joseph went under the knife. He had his brow
lifted, the skin around his mouth and nose pulled back, his upper eyelids
tucked and some laser skin resurfacing to ease the creases in his lower lids.
And he had it all done at once, for the relatively inexpensive price of $8,000.

A bit young for cosmetic surgery, you think? A little odd for a guy? The 2
answer is a firm no — to both. Today, men account for about a third of all
facial cosmetic surgery done in the United States, up 6 percentage points
since 1990. The bulk of clients are between the ages of forty and sixty.

Stressed out by corporate downsizing, many men are looking for any 3
edge to get or keep their jobs. They view cosmetic surgery as an investment
in their careers. Men are now grappling with the same kind of exacting
beauty standards women have struggled with for decades, observes Shari
Cartwright, a spokesperson for the Illinois-based American Society of Plastic
Reconstructive Surgeons. "Is it a bad thing? When it was just women it was
fine. Perception is reality, in many cases," she adds. "When people look at
you they make an assumption, right or wrong."

The top five most popular procedures sought by men are hair trans- 4
plants, nose work, eyelid work, and scar revision, according to the Washington, D.C.–based American Academy of Facial Plastic and Reconstructive
Surgery, the world's largest association of facial plastic surgeons. The fastest
growing procedures for men are eyelid surgery, liposuction, and facelifts.
[. . .] If you include all cosmetic work — face and body — men account for
roughly 12 percent of all procedures, notes the American Society of Plastic
Reconstructive Surgeons. When it comes to body work, men favor liposuction (face and stomach), and chest reduction.

Men are having things "corrected" as they notice them, according to Dr. 5
Peter Adamson, a Toronto facial plastic surgeon trained in head and neck
surgery, an associate professor at the University of Toronto, and president-
elect of the American Academy of Facial Plastic and Reconstructive Surgery.
Sometimes that's in their twenties or thirties, often it's in their forties and
fifties. "Women have tended to care more about their appearance than men
have," Adamson says. "That's changing, and that's why more and more men
are going further along that spectrum. They're not just dressing in a more
fashion conscious way; they're also using more cosmetics and toiletries."

And they're taking their perceived physical flaws to surgeons. Toronto 6
cosmetic surgeon Dr. William Middleton says men now account for 30 percent of his practice — double that of a year ago. A decade ago, males represented less than 5 percent of his business. And the newcomers aren't necessarily actors, models, or even top executives. They're everyday guys with
fairly everyday looks. "It's obviously out of the closet," says Middleton, who
also has a specialty in head and neck surgery, but does figure surgery as well.
"Men now know it's quite acceptable."

Intense competition in the workplace and on the dating scene appear to   7
be the biggest reasons for the surge. Combine that with a youth-worshiping
society and it's hardly surprising that more male boomers are feeling insecure. As one client told Adamson: "I looked down the (boardroom) table
and I looked like an old lion. I think they're looking to replace the old lion
with a young lion." The aging professional opted for eyelid surgery. "Often
men don't really want to look different," says Adamson. "They just want to
look refreshed."

Joseph, who works in computer marketing and training, says he felt   8
some business pressure. "I was getting older and the workforce was getting
younger," he relates. "My eyelids were saggy and when I would smile I had
deep creases, from my nose to my chin." Of the surgery he says: "It's not the
most pleasant feeling afterward. When you're getting your body cut it's
painful, there's no two ways about it. But the pain was manageable. It wasn't
severe or excessive." Cosmetic surgery, Joseph enthuses, "can do wondrous
things. The growing acceptance, I think that's a good thing. If it makes you
feel better then it's worth it."

Despite greater acceptance, Joseph and other surgery patients inter-   9
viewed for this story still did not want to be identified. They all, however,
said that they had shared their experiences with close friends and family.
The decision to have surgery, notes Joseph, "is a very personal thing." He
points out that it's considered fine for a man to spend money on a car, or
finish his basement. So why shouldn't he be able to put some of his money
into repairing his body's wear and tear? "Getting work done helps you age
how you want to age," he says. "It's not going to turn back that process, but
you can make a difference. You can be more vital and rested. I think it does
increase your confidence, but not to any large degree. I'm still the same person. But when I walk by the mirror I like what I see."

For Bobby, the problem was dark circles under his eyes that had both-   10
ered him since he was a teen. It was a condition that seemed to run in his
family. At the ripe age of twenty-seven, he recently had the fat under his eyes
removed, and the darkness has faded. It cost him $3,000. "A woman can put
on some makeup and hide that kind of thing, but I'd tried that and wasn't
comfortable. I was still self-conscious," says Bobby, who, with short, wavy
hair looks every bit a twentysomething. A couple of his friends are having
hair transplants. No one his age has suggested he was nuts for doing what
he did.

"The bottom line is people don't want to be old and they don't want to   11
grow old," he says. "I think cosmetic surgery among men is going to become
commonplace. To me, it was very exciting." He sees little difference between
his surgery and the guy who goes out and spends thousands of dollars on
new suits. "Now I'm able to put my contact lenses in and go out and know
that no one is going to say, 'Boy, you look tired.' I just feel better about
myself."

Stephen, a man of average looks, has had $16,000 worth of work done   12
over the past four years. First he had his nosed reshaped, then a hair trans-

plant, then flab in his chest removed. "Once you start, you can just continue," says Stephen, who boasts he's a fifty-two-year-old in a twenty-five-
year-old's body. He's delighted with the results, in part because younger
women still find him attractive. "It's the '90s and everything's changed. So
has the philosophy on improving yourself. It's like going to the dentist for
regular checkups. I could see myself at seventy-five going under the knife, no
problem."

Adamson says although more men are having cosmetic surgery, "there's 13
no doubt that women will have a greater psychological imperative than the
majority of men." He sees male interest as an extension of keeping fit and
staying healthy. "The major drive is that people want to have their outer appearance reflect their inner spirit, so that when they see themselves they say,
'Yes, that's me. My body reflects me. This kind of surgery can't in and of itself change their professional or social life, but it can help them indirectly,"
adds Adamson.

Looking good, projecting that current image is crucial today, says Roz 14
Usheroff, a Toronto image and communications consultant who works with
professionals and outplacement firms. "If someone looks outdated, that's
the way it's perceived they think," she says. "You have to look the part. Firms
are looking at the employees as ambassadors. Sure, there needs to be substance, but it's not enough now. It's not just what you say and how you say
it, but how you look as you say it."

More men are realizing their appearance is interfering with what they're 15
trying to convey. "Whether that's good or not, it's realistic," [Usheroff]
says. "A lot of companies are telling men they have to look good. It's not
negotiable — if they want to rise within the ranks, or even stay where they
are. That's still a shock to some of them."

Dr. Art Blouin, an Ottawa clinical psychologist who works with men 16
and body image, says cosmetic surgery, in itself, isn't a bad thing. What can
be troublesome is the intensity with which someone pursues physical perfection. "From a psychological point of view it would probably be healthier
for men to accept their bodies," he says. But he isn't surprised that more
men are dissatisfied with themselves. "Look at the emphasis, culturally, on
attractiveness," he points out. "What we see in the media is a much greater
emphasis on the male physique — and much less on character."

Blouin does find it disturbing that more men are now equating much of 17
their self-worth, both personally and professionally, with their looks. "The
problem is that once you start this type of thing, you may never be satisfied," he says. "The more you look, the worse it gets. The harder you look,
the more you find."

Questions to Start You Thinking

1. CONSIDERING MEANING: According to Turner, why do men increasingly
   seek cosmetic surgery? Which of the reasons Turner cites seem most
   valid to you?

2. **IDENTIFYING WRITING STRATEGIES:** What are some of the journalistic characteristics of Turner's essay, originally a newspaper article? How do these features affect your response as a reader? If Turner added more transitions, for example, how would they change her style?

3. **READING CRITICALLY:** What purpose does Dr. Art Blouin's opinion (paragraphs 16 to 17) serve in Turner's essay? Why does she place it where she does? How does including Blouin's opinion affect the ethical appeal of Turner's essay?

4. **EXPANDING VOCABULARY:** Define *psychological imperative* (paragraph 13). Do you agree that women have a greater psychological imperative to undergo cosmetic surgery than men do? Why or why not?

5. **MAKING CONNECTIONS:** In her essay "Mirror Image" (pp. 514–18), Alicia Potter also reports on men's increasing desire to improve their physical appearance. Compare and contrast the two essays. What causes or effects are mentioned in one essay but not in the other? How do you account for the differences? How do the purposes of the two writers differ?

Linked to the Paired Essay

WWW
For useful links to Web sources on topics including *body image*, visit <www.bedfordstmartins.com/toplinks>.

Both Turner and Lisa Jervis ("My Jewish Nose," pp. 519–23) write about a now commonplace occurrence, cosmetic surgery. Without an unexpected angle, a commonplace topic doesn't have much audience appeal. What unusual angle does each writer use to arouse her audience's interest? How does the writer's angle shape each essay?

Journal Prompts

1. Under what circumstances might you want to have cosmetic surgery? Consider the advantages and disadvantages, both short term and long term. What factors might influence your choice?

2. Recall a time you judged a person based solely on his or her appearance. What conclusions did you come to? How accurate was your initial judgment?

Suggestions for Writing

1. Turner quotes psychologist Art Blouin as saying that in the media there is "a much greater emphasis on the male physique — and much less on character" (paragraph 16). Write an essay in which you agree or disagree with this statement. Support your thesis with examples from different kinds of media, or, if you prefer, narrow your angle to only one kind. Be sure your sampling is representative so your opinion is valid.

2. Cut out an ad or a group of ads, looking closely at the images of men. Does a single standard emerge? If not, what sorts of standards do you find? How realistic are they? What effects might they have on a male audience? On a female audience? Write an essay in which you come to some conclusions about your findings, and use your analysis as evidence to support your thesis.

A Writer's
Research
Manual

Contents

Introduction: The Nature of Research   531

28. Planning and Managing Your Research Project

Planning Your Project   534
   The Assignment: Writing from Sources   534
Generating Ideas and Forming a Research Question   535
   Choosing Your Territory   535
   Taking an Overview   536
   Stating Your Question   537
   Making a Preliminary Search   539
   Using Keywords and Links   539
Managing Your Project   541
   Creating a Schedule   541
   Starting a Working Bibliography   542
   Starting a Research Archive   544
   Keeping Track of Your Electronic Searches   545

29. Finding Sources in the Library, on the Internet, and in the Field

Searching the Library   546
   Using the Online Catalog   547
   Consulting Databases: Periodical Indexes and Bibliographies   552
Using Other Library Resources   555
   Consulting Reference Materials   556
   Locating Special Materials   558
Using the Web for Research   559
   Conducting Advanced Electronic Searches   559
   Finding Online Texts and Discussions   563
Finding Sources in the Field   564
   Interviewing   564
   Observing   565
   Using Questionnaires   565
   Corresponding   568
   Attending Public and Online Events   568

30. Evaluating Sources and Taking Notes

Evaluating Sources   570
   What Is the Purpose?   571
   Who Is the Intended Audience?   572
   Who Is the Author?   573
   Is This a Primary or a Secondary Source?   574
   Who Is the Publisher?   575
   How Sound Is the Evidence?   575

   Is the Source Up-to-Date?   576
   Is the Source Relevant to Your Research?   576
   Are Your Field Sources Useful and Reliable?   576
Taking Notes   577
   Recording Information   577
   Taking Better Notes   578
   Avoiding Plagiarism   579
   Quoting, Paraphrasing, Nutshelling   579

31. Writing Your Research Paper

Planning and Drafting   584
   Moving from Notes to Outline to Draft   584
   Incorporating Source Material: Quoting, Paraphrasing, Nutshelling   588
   Avoiding Plagiarism   592
   Beginning and Ending   595
Revising and Editing   596
Documenting Sources   598
   Citing Sources in Your Text   599
   Listing Sources at the End   599
   Other Assignments   599
Applying What You Learn: Some Uses of Research   600
A Sample Research Paper   601
   Sarah E. Goers, Is Inclusion the Answer?   602

32. Documenting Sources

Citing Sources: MLA Style   616
   Printed Sources: Nonfiction Books   616
   Printed Sources: Literature   618
   Printed Sources: Reference Books and Periodicals   619
   Electronic and Other Nonprint Sources   621
Listing Sources: MLA Style   621
   Books   621
   Parts of Books   624
   Reference Books   625
   Periodicals   625
   Other Printed Sources   627
   Internet and Electronic Sources   627
   Other Nonprint Sources   630
Citing Sources: APA Style   631
   Printed Sources   631
   Other Sources   633
Listing Sources: APA Style   634
   Books   634
   Periodicals   636
   Other Printed Sources   637
   Internet and Electronic Sources   637
   Other Nonprint Sources   639

Introduction:
The Nature of Research

Does cell phone use cause brain tumors?

What steps can law enforcement take to help prevent domestic violence?

How do strict death penalty laws affect crime rates?

Why is baseball exempt from antitrust laws?

You may have asked yourself questions like these. Perhaps you discussed them with your friends, asked a teacher about the subject, or read an article about the issue. In doing so, you were conducting informal research to satisfy your curiosity.

In your day-to-day life, you also conduct practical research to help you make decisions. You may want to buy a wireless phone, consider an innovative medical procedure, or plan a vacation. To become better informed, you may talk with friends, search the Internet, request product information from sales personnel, compare prices, read articles in magazines and newspapers, and listen to commercials. You pull together and weigh as much information as you can, preparing yourself to make a well-informed decision.

When one of your college professors assigns a research paper due in a month or two, you won't be expected to discover the secrets of the spiral nebula. On the other hand, you will find that research isn't merely pasting together information and opinions from other people. Instead, the excitement lies in using research to draw conclusions and arrive at your own fresh view. The key is to start your investigation as professional researchers do — with a research question that you truly want to learn more about. Like a detective, you will need to plan your work but remain flexible, backtracking or jumping ahead if it makes sense to do so. If you meet an insurmountable obstacle, you must turn around, go sideways, or set out in another direction altogether.

Whenever you use research to come to a conclusion based on facts and expert opinions — whether in your personal life, for a college class, or on the job — this research manual will provide you with effective, efficient strategies and procedures.

Chapter 28, "Planning and Managing Your Research Project." This chapter introduces the basics of completing a research assignment, from generating ideas and developing your research question through managing your project with a realistic schedule, a working bibliography, and a research archive.

Chapter 29, "Finding Sources in the Library, on the Internet, and in the Field."   What resources are available to answer your research question? The useful tips in this chapter suggest the best ways to locate promising sources.

Chapter 30, "Evaluating Sources and Taking Notes."   This chapter discusses the critical process of evaluating, or judging, the information you gather in order to select the best evidence for your paper. It provides questions you can use to evaluate library, Internet, and field resources as you conduct your research. It also explains how to take accurate and fruitful notes, whether you quote, summarize, or paraphrase.

Chapter 31, "Writing Your Research Paper."   Here you will learn how to pull together, or synthesize, the information in your sources so that you answer your research question in a readable, trustworthy paper. At the end of the chapter you will find a sample student research paper that integrates library, Internet, and field sources.

Chapter 32, "Documenting Sources."   This chapter explains when and how to cite your sources, illustrating MLA and APA documentation styles.

Chapter 28

Planning and Managing Your Research Project

Writing a research paper is a useful skill, essential not only in an academic community but also in the workplace. Engineers rely on research studies when they write feasibility reports. Health-care workers synthesize research findings to help them decide how to treat patients. Businesses depend on market research to sell their products.

Although research writing is a practical skill — and one you'll draw on for the rest of your life — learning to conduct research efficiently and effectively can be daunting. The Internet, television, books, newspapers, and magazines shower us with facts and figures, statements and reports, views and opinions — some of them half-baked, some revealing and trustworthy. College research requires you to sort through this massive burst of words, distinguishing fact from opinion, off-the-wall claims from expert interpretations.

As you investigate a topic and write a paper based on your findings, you will build valuable skills such as these:

- You'll learn how to find a topic and develop it into a focused and answerable research question.
- You'll draw from a wide range of sources — in the library, on the Internet, and in the field.
- You'll use library, Internet, and field research techniques to complement one another.
- You'll use your sources as evidence to support your own ideas, rather than simply repeating what they say.

- You'll do critical thinking—evaluating, analyzing, and synthesizing ideas.
- You'll learn to cite and list your sources in a form that scholars and professionals follow in writing research reports and articles.

This chapter will help you manage your research project by creating a research schedule, maintaining a working bibliography, and building a research archive. Armed with these skills and tools, you will find yourself prepared to accomplish even the most formidable research task.

Planning Your Project

A research paper is often the most engaging and complex assignment in a course. You may already have learned how to take research notes or how to make a working bibliography, but as we guide you through the research process, we'll pause to explain these special skills. Mastering them, if you haven't done so already, will speed you on your way to completing your assignment and becoming an accomplished research writer.

THE ASSIGNMENT: WRITING FROM SOURCES

Find a topic that intrigues you, and develop a focused research question about it. Answering the question will probably require you to return to writing situations you addressed in Part Two of this book, such as comparing and contrasting, explaining causes and effects, taking a stand, proposing a solution, evaluating, or reading critically. After conducting whatever research is necessary, synthesize the information you assemble to develop your own reasonable answer to the research question. Then write a paper in which you persuasively use a variety of source material to convey your conclusions.

Having a real audience can help you make choices about what to include or exclude as you write your report. If possible, try to use your paper to benefit your campus administration, your employer, or a particular cause or nonprofit group on campus or in your local community. Your final paper, as you will see, will be more than a stack of facts. Reading and digesting the ideas of other writers is just the first step. In the process of writing your paper, you'll also bring your own intelligence to bear on what you have read.

You can anticipate these major stages during your research process:

For advice on scheduling your research project, see pp. 541–42.

THE RESEARCH PROCESS

1. **Choose a general subject.** Your instructor may assign a research topic or suggest some suitable possibilities. If not, choose a general subject that you would like to investigate. (See pp. 535–36.)

2. **Take an overview.** Do a little reading about the subject to see exactly what aspects interest you most. Choose one of these aspects as the topic for your research paper. (See p. 536.)

3. **State your question.** Use your question to identify what you want to find out about your topic. Your question may change as you read more; its purpose is to guide you in your research. (See pp. 537–39.)

4. **Perform a preliminary search.** Survey the library, Internet, or field sources available to answer your question. If necessary, revise your question. (See p. 539.)

5. **Investigate in earnest.** Conduct more research to develop an answer or answers to your research question and to assemble the evidence you'll need to present your ideas persuasively. (See Chs. 29–30.)

6. **Write your paper.** Draft, revise, and edit your paper. Set forth the conclusions you have drawn from your study, giving evidence from your research sources to support your ideas. (See Ch. 31.)

Generating Ideas and Forming a Research Question

What most effectively helps long-term prisoners return to society after they have served their sentences?

How accurately do standardized tests measure intelligence?

What can be done to help homeless families in Miami, Florida?

To define a narrow research question like the examples above, start with your broad interests.

CHOOSING YOUR TERRITORY

To explore, you need a territory—a subject that interests you. Perhaps your work in this very course or in another course will suggest an appropriate territory. A psychology course might encourage you to investigate mental disorders; a sociology course, urban renewal; a geography course, tropical forests.

You'll have an easier time from the start if you can make your territory smaller than "mental disorders" or "urban renewal." "Schizophrenia" and "inner-city housing problems" are smaller territories, easier to explore and to manage as your research leads you to a more focused topic. But if you don't feel you can narrow and define your topic at this point in the process, go ahead and start with a broad subject.

Here are a few questions to help you find a general subject:

DISCOVERY CHECKLIST

___ Can you recall an experience that raises interesting questions or creates unusual associations in your mind?

___ What have you observed recently — perhaps on your way to school or work today — that you could more thoroughly investigate?

___ In a recent conversation with friends or in class, have you encountered any new perspectives you'd like to explore?

___ What problem would you like to solve?

___ What have you read about lately that you'd like to pursue further?

TAKING AN OVERVIEW

Before launching an expedition into a little-known territory, a smart explorer first makes a reconnaissance flight and takes an overview. Having seen the terrain, the explorer then chooses the very spot to set up camp — the point on the map that looks most promising. Research writers do something like that, too. Before committing themselves to a topic, they first get a broad overview to see what parts of the territory look promising and then zero in on one small area that seems most interesting.

Begin in the Library.   How do you take an overview? Say you are looking for preliminary information on inner cities or urban housing developments, schizophrenia or mental illness or (still more general) psychiatry. A good place to start searching is in your college or local library. Most libraries subscribe to many specialized databases (like *Medline, PsycLIT, ERIC,* and the *MLA Bibliography*). Depending on your subject, you will probably be able to familiarize yourself with your topic and get a good feel for the broad range of sources available by beginning your overview here.

For more on electronic searches, see pp. 559–63.   **Go Online.**   You can also spend time on the Internet, visiting Web sites and reading messages posted to newsgroups or Web discussion forums. Web search engines — such as Google, Lycos, and Yahoo! — can lead you to a wide range of suitable Web pages (see p. 562 for URLs). Similarly, the Deja and Forum One Web sites can help you locate newsgroups and mailing lists that deal with your topic (see p. 563 for URLs). The number of sources you can locate on the Internet is vast — and growing daily — so you'll need to exercise discipline when you're online, especially in this early stage of your research.

For more on interviewing, see pp. 564–65 and Ch. 6.   **Talk with Experts.**   Finally, consider discussing your topic with an expert in the field. If you're interested in America's fascination with the automobile, consider meeting with a professor, such as a sociologist or a journalist, who specializes in the area. Or talk with friends or acquaintances who are particularly passionate about their cars. Or spend time at an auto show, carefully observing and talking with the people who attend.

STATING YOUR QUESTION

Once you have zeroed in on part of a territory to explore, you can move from the broad to the specific by asking more definite questions. Ask exactly what you want to find out, and your task will leap into focus. Having begun with a broad interest in social problems in large cities, you might specifically ask, "What happens to teenage runaways on the streets of Manhattan?" Or, if you have started with a general yen to know more about contemporary architecture, your definite question might be "Who in America today is good at designing sports arenas?"

Brainstorm.   You might start with a brainstorming session, jotting down whatever questions come to mind — even useless ones. Then, look over your list for one that appears promising. Your instructor also may have some suggestions, but you will probably be more motivated researching a question you select.

For more on brainstorming, see pp. 260–63.

Size Up Your Question.   Ask these questions as you test for a workable research question:

- Is your question debatable? In other words, does it allow for a range of opinions?
- Is it interesting to you and your readers?
- Is it narrow enough to allow fruitful research?

A workable question should be debatable so that you can support your own view rather than explain something that's generally known and accepted. It should be interesting so that you want to investigate it — and your reader will want to know what you discover. It also needs to be narrow enough to allow for a productive investigation. Many interesting questions are immense and would require years of research, not the few weeks you have.

BROAD QUESTION	How is the climate of the earth changing?
NARROWER QUESTION	How will El Niño affect global climate changes in the next decade?
BROAD QUESTION	Who are the world's best living storytellers?
NARROWER QUESTION	How is Irish step dancing a form of storytelling?
BROAD QUESTION	Why is there poverty?
NARROWER QUESTION	What notable welfare-to-work programs exist in the southeastern United States?

Although you should restrict your topic, a question can be too narrow or too insignificant. If so, it may be impossible to find relevant sources.

TOO NARROW	How did John F. Kennedy's maternal grandfather influence the decisions he made during his first month as president?

A question may also be so narrow that it's uninteresting. Avoid questions that can be answered with a simple yes or no or with a few statistics.

TOO NARROW   Are there more black students or white students in the entering class this year?

BETTER   How does the ratio of black students to white students affect campus relations at our school?

If a single source or two could answer your research question, your paper is likely to be a thin summary, not a true research paper. Instead, ask a question that will lead you to meaty sources and into the heart of a lively controversy. The best research questions ask about issues that other people take seriously and spend time arguing about, issues likely to be of real interest to you and your readers.

Hone Your Question.   Make the wording of your question specific but simple: identify one thing to find out, not several. A well-crafted question will help lead you into your research. Its very phrasing can suggest terms that may be useful as you search databases, the library catalog, or the Web.

QUESTION   What has caused a shortage of low-income housing in northeastern cities?

POSSIBLE SEARCH TERMS   Housing, housing shortage, low-income housing, urban housing

If your question doesn't suggest such leads, try rewording it to make it more concrete and specific.

For more on stating and using a thesis, see pp. 271–75.

Predict an Answer in a Working Thesis.   Some writers find that having not only a question but also an answer in mind makes the research project easier to tackle. At this stage, however, you need to be flexible enough to change your answer or even your question if your research turns up something unexpected.

You can state a proposed answer as a working thesis.

RESEARCH QUESTION   How does a school dress code benefit students?

WORKING THESIS   Instituting a school dress code decreases the incidence of school violence.

Remember that a working thesis is meant to guide your research, not hinder it. If you find that you're not learning anything new, that you're just finding support for what you already thought was the case, then your working thesis has become too dominant, and you're no longer conducting true research. Because of this possibility, some writers prefer to delay formulating a working thesis until they've already done substantial research or even until they begin drafting. Your approach will probably depend on your research assignment, on your instructor's expectations, and on your own work style.

Refine Your Question.   Until you start conducting research, of course, you can't know for certain how fruitful your research question will be. If it doesn't lead you to any definite facts or reliable opinions, if it doesn't start you thinking critically, you'll need to reword it or throw it out and ask a new question. But at the very least, the question you first ask can give you a definite direction in which to start looking.

After you have tentatively stated your question, use these questions to refine it:

RESEARCH CHECKLIST

Questioning Your Question

___ Is the scope of your question appropriate — not too immense and not too narrow? Is your question answerable given the time you have and the word or page limits for your paper?

___ Can you find enough current information about your question?

___ Have you worded your question simply, so that you are seeking just one answer, not several? Have you worded your question concretely and specifically, so that it states exactly what you are looking for?

___ Does your question concern an issue that engages you personally?

MAKING A PRELIMINARY SEARCH

You can quickly test whether your question is likely to lead to an ample research paper by spending an hour or so conducting a fast search at the library. In some ways, this search will be similar to the initial overview you conducted at the beginning of your research process. Your goal then was to discover an interesting aspect of your topic. Your goal now is to determine whether you'll have enough material to address your question and to identify the most fruitful avenues for research.

If your preliminary search turns up such a skimpy list of sources that you won't have much to choose from, or if your first search reveals hundreds of sources, consider asking another question. Try to pick a question that a dozen or twenty available sources focus on. If you need help conducting a reliable search, be sure to ask a librarian for help.

Once you have decided that you can locate enough material to do the job, decide which types of sources to concentrate on. Some research questions require a wide range of sources. Others are better suited to a narrower range, perhaps restricted by date or discipline. Part of your preliminary search should include considering which sources are most likely to yield the best information.

USING KEYWORDS AND LINKS

Keywords are terms or phrases that identify the topics discussed in a research source. As you look for information on the Internet or in databases, you will most likely perform keyword searches. When you enter the keywords into

WWW
To practice using keywords, visit the English Research Room at <www.bedfordstmartins .com/english_research/>.

an electronic search engine (whether in a library catalog or on the Web), the engine will return to you a list of all the sources it can find with that keyword. Knowing how to use keywords to search is a skill useful not only in your research project but also throughout your college career and beyond.

For a list of search engines, see p. 562.

For advanced search strategies, see pp. 559–63.

Finding the best keywords for a particular topic and a particular search engine is essential. Start by using the main terms in your research question. As you conduct your preliminary search, jot down or print out the keywords you use, noting whether they produce too few or too many results. You are likely to find that some keywords work better than others and that certain combinations of keywords produce the best results.

As your keywords lead you to Web sites compiled by specialists or people interested in a particular subject area, you can browse through the information and resources gathered there. These sites often contain *links*—

FOR GROUP LEARNING

Collaborative Research

Conducting research as a group is a complex yet exciting job, one especially common in the workplace. It requires responsible teamwork, clear communication, and full accountability. You might work with a research team in several ways, pooling your research but writing individual papers or collaborating on the entire project. After getting a go-ahead from your instructor, fix a series of deadlines, parcel out the work, and meet faithfully according to a schedule. Everyone must do his or her share of the work. Here is a schedule for full collaboration on an eight-week research project:

- Week One: Each member of the group seeks a topic for the project.

- Week Two: The group meets and agrees on a topic and a research question that they clear with the instructor. Members choose a coordinator to call or e-mail group members in order to keep the project moving.

- Weeks Three and Four: Each member makes a preliminary search and contributes to the group's working bibliography. The group meets to determine responsibilities—who will collect what material for the group's research archive—and all begin work.

- Week Five: Each member continues to collect sources, read, and take notes.

- Week Six: The group meets to evaluate the material collected and to see what else is needed. Members collaborate on a rough plan or outline.

- Week Seven: The group divides up the outline, and each writes part of the draft. Members swap drafts, read them over, and respond.

- Week Eight: The group meets and carefully reviews the combined draft. All write comments and corrections on it. Then one member prepares a polished copy, and the coordinator gives the whole paper one last proofreading.

comprehensive lists of related sites—with information relevant to your research project. These links, in turn, often contain their own lists of related Web pages. By following these connections systematically, you can benefit from the work of others and rapidly expand your own knowledge. Be careful, however, not to look only for information that supports a preconceived notion. Research should be an opportunity to learn more about a topic, to answer an authentic question, not simply to collect evidence that supports what you already think.

Managing Your Project

No matter what your question or where you plan to look for promising material, you will want to manage your project wisely. You will need a schedule to use your time efficiently, a working bibliography to keep track of where you've been and where you still need to go, and a research archive to organize all the varied sources you find—whether photocopies, printouts, or handwritten notes.

CREATING A SCHEDULE

If your instructor doesn't give you a series of deadlines as part of your assignment, set some for yourself. You can be sure that a research paper will require more time than you expect. If you procrastinate and try to toss everything together in a desperate all-night siege, you will not be satisfied with the result. Instead, start with a clear-cut schedule that breaks your project into a series of small tasks.

SAMPLE SCHEDULE

- *Week One:* If you are not assigned a topic, start thinking about an interesting general subject. Take an overview of your topic by searching your library database and the Internet.

- *Week Two:* Begin narrowing your topic to a workable research question. Conduct a preliminary search on your research question. Start your working bibliography and your research archive.

- *Week Three:* Begin your research in earnest. Locate and evaluate your most promising sources. Take notes.

- *Week Four:* Continue narrowing your research, identifying promising sources, evaluating them as you go along, and taking efficient notes.

- *Week Five:* Begin your preliminary outline, and state your thesis. Continue to update your bibliography and research archive, putting your sources in the order in which you think you might use them.

- *Week Six:* Refine your thesis statement. Start your first draft.

WWW
For downloadable sample schedules, visit <www .bedfordstmartins.com/ bedguide>.

- *Week Seven:* Complete your first draft. Begin thinking about ways to revise and improve it. Seek feedback from a peer editor.
- *Week Eight:* Revise and edit your draft. Check that you have used quotations properly and consistently. Carefully go over your documentation. Finally, proofread the entire paper, checking for any errors.

STARTING A WORKING BIBLIOGRAPHY

For help with maintaining a working bibliography, use *Research Assistant HyperFolio*, a software tool available with *The Bedford Guide*.

A working bibliography is a detailed list of the books, articles, and Web sites that you either plan to consult or have consulted. It has two purposes:

It guides your research by recording which sources you've examined and which you intend to examine.

It helps you document or identify the sources you have used by recording detailed information about each source.

Choose a Method for Compiling Your Working Bibliography.   Pick the method that suits you best, the one that you can use most easily and efficiently during the course of your research. Here are some options:

- Note cards, recording one source per card
- Small notebook
- Word-processing program
- Computer database
- Hand-held electronic storage tool

Keep Careful Records.   Whatever method you use, the more carefully you record your tentative sources, the more time you'll save later when you compile a list of the works you actually used and cited. At that point, you'll be grateful to find all the necessary titles, authors, dates, page numbers, and URLs (Internet addresses) at your fingertips — and you'll avoid a frantic, time-consuming trip back to the library.

Start a bibliographic entry for each source you intend to consult. At this point, your information about the source may be incomplete: "Dr. Edward Denu — cardiologist — interview about drug treatments." Later, once you locate a print or Internet source or conduct field research, you'll be able to fill in the complete bibliographical information.

For examples of correct documentation form, see Ch. 32.

Record What You Will Need.   What should each source note in your working bibliography contain? Eventually it should include everything necessary to find the source as well as to write the final list of sources to be placed at the end of your paper.

BOOKS

1. The library call number
2. The author's full name, last name first
3. The book's title, including its subtitle if it has one, underlined or in italics
4. The publication information: place, publisher, year of publication
   (See Figure 28.1.)

PERIODICALS

1. The author's full name, last name first
2. The title of the article, in quotation marks, followed by the name of the publication, underlined or in italics
3. The volume number for a scholarly journal or, in some cases, the issue number
4. The date of the issue
5. The page numbers of the article
   (See Figure 28.2.)

Figure 28.1   *A bibliography card for a book with one author, in MLA style*

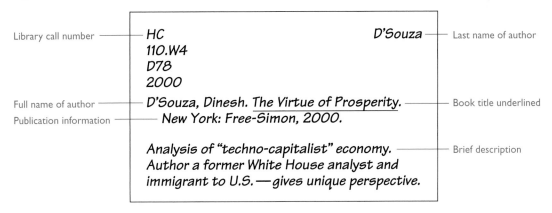

Figure 28.2   *A bibliography source note recorded on a computer for an article in a monthly magazine, in MLA style*

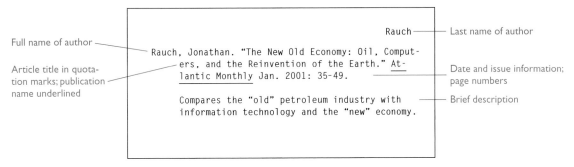

ELECTRONIC SOURCES

1. The author's (or editor's) full name, if identified
2. The title of the site or document
3. The date the source was created or last updated
4. The name of the sponsoring organization (if any)
5. The date you accessed the source
6. The Internet address or URL (Uniform Resource Locator)
   (See Figure 28.3)

FIELD SOURCES

1. The name of the person you interviewed or the setting you observed
2. A descriptive title, such as "Personal interview" or "Telephone interview"
3. The date you conducted the interview or observation
   (See Figure 28.4.)

You may list each item of information separately in your notes, but it is wise at this point to put the information in the correct form for a final bibliography entry in your works cited list. This may seem like a lot of record keeping, but it takes less time to jot down all this information now than to make future trips to the library.

Figure 28.3
A bibliography source note recorded on a computer for an Internet site, in MLA style

```
                                                            MacLeod

MacLeod, David. "Problems Affecting City Economies." 14 Nov. 2000.
    28 Feb. 2001 <http://www3.sympatico.ca/david.macleod/URBECO.htm>.

    Addresses current problems in urban planning.
```

Figure 28.4
A bibliography source note recorded on a computer for a personal interview, in MLA style

```
                                                            Cardone

Cardone, Amy. Personal interview. 28 Feb. 2001.

    Anecdotal evidence. Describes sports injuries in children that she's
    treated.
```

STARTING A RESEARCH ARCHIVE

You can organize information from library, Internet, and field sources by creating a research archive. An *archive* is a place where information is systematically stored. As you locate and evaluate sources, you will accumulate information that you'll want to use later. If you have ever found yourself staring at a pile of books, photocopies, and printouts, wondering which one contained the particular fact or quotation that you wanted to use, you know how important a good organizational system can be. You can use several techniques to create a research archive.

File Paper Copies. To use this method, try to get all important sources in a paper format: photocopy book passages and periodical articles, print out electronic sources, and keep questionnaires and other raw information from your field research. Then put the pages for each source in a different file folder, and label the folder with subject and author. If you take the time to highlight key passages, you'll be able to locate that information even more quickly. Make sure the name of the source and the page number appear on your copy so that you can connect it to the source note in your working bibliography. If necessary, write that information on the photocopy.

Save Computer Files. You can save Web pages, e-mail messages, posts to newsgroups and mailing lists, transcripts of chat sessions, and records from databases to a diskette, a hard drive, or a network drive. Give each file a descriptive name so that you'll be able to locate the information quickly later on. You can also organize the files in different folders or directories, also named so you can easily tell what each contains.

Copy and Take Notes. Regardless of the techniques you use to create your archive, remember two things: copy judiciously and take notes. Some research writers say that copying (either photocopying or saving to a computer file) has done away with the need to take notes. Indeed, judicious copying can save you time as you gather materials. But simply copying everything you read with the vague notion that some of it may be valuable for your essay is likely to waste money and to cost you more time rather than less. Much of the material won't be worth saving. Most important, you won't have digested and evaluated what was on the page; you will merely have copied it. Instead, make it yours by selecting what is essential, highlighting or transcribing it by hand, perhaps nutshelling or paraphrasing it. Then, when you start drafting, you can work from carefully thought-out notes, not spend hours digesting great amounts of copied material.

For more on taking notes, see pp. 577–79.

For more on paraphrasing and nutshelling, see pp. 579–83.

KEEPING TRACK OF YOUR ELECTRONIC SEARCHES

Save Favorites and Bookmarks. You can save the locations of sites on the World Wide Web within your browser so that you can easily locate them again. Microsoft Internet Explorer calls these saved locations *favorites,* while Netscape Navigator calls them *bookmarks.* You can also annotate favorites and bookmarks with your browser and organize them into folders, much as you organize files on a computer.

For help with gathering print and electronic sources, use *Research Assistant HyperFolio,* a software tool available with *The Bedford Guide.*

Save Search Results. If a database or Internet search was particularly fruitful, you can save the results even if you don't have time to locate each relevant source at that moment. Note the keywords or phrases you used to conduct your search, and then repeat the search at a later date. You can also print out the search results or save them to a computer file so you can use them without having to rerun the search.

Chapter 29

Finding Sources in the Library, on the Internet, and in the Field

For more on managing your research project, see Ch. 28.

By now you have narrowed your research question, started your working bibliography, and begun your research archive. Consult your schedule so that you stay on track, and revise it if necessary. This chapter will help you continue your research by using efficient strategies for searching the library, the Web, and the field for relevant sources.

Searching the Library

Your college library is often the best place to begin your search. New technology has made it possible to access many resources — catalogs, indexes, databases, for example — from a computer terminal in your library. Technology has also made it possible to search all of these library resources from home or your dorm room. Although a great deal of the library's information is stored on printed pages, the way it has been for centuries, the tools for locating these pages and, increasingly, the information itself are taking electronic form. Today's researcher needs to be familiar with both the print and electronic worlds.

Your library's home page will very likely be the first and best place to begin your research. There you will find access to a wide variety of resources — from the online catalog, to periodical databases, to online reference material, to guides to the Internet. Your library may also offer tours, online tutorials, or brochures explaining the library's organization and services. (See Figure 29.1 for a sample library home page.) Reference librarians are available to help you answer questions, from specifics such as "What is the GNP of Brazil?" to more general queries such as "Where can I find out about the Brazilian economy?" Before you start looking for sources for your paper, it pays to do a little research on the library itself. The following basic questions about your library can start you off:

RESEARCH CHECKLIST

Investigating Your Library

___ Is there a Web site or pamphlet mapping the library's holdings and resources and explaining its services?

___ Where is the reference desk, and what hours is it open?

___ How do you access the library's catalog?

___ Where are periodicals kept, and how are they arranged?

___ What kinds of indexes or computerized databases are available, and how can you access them?

___ Can you search the catalog or other library databases from your computer at home or from the campus network?

___ Can you use interlibrary loan to order a book or article that the library doesn't have?

USING THE ONLINE CATALOG

A library catalog provides information about the books, periodicals, videos, databases, and other materials owned by a library. A library user can locate them by author, title, or subject. Typically, library catalogs do not provide information about individual articles in periodicals. They do, however, provide you with the periodical's publication information (title, date, publisher, and so on), call number, location, and in some cases availability.

Search by Author, Title, or Subject.   Before you use the catalog, decide what kind of search you are doing:

- Are you looking for the works of a particular author?
- Are you hunting for a particular title?
- Are you searching for what is available on a particular subject?

Use Keyword Searches.   Many online catalogs allow you to enter keywords — terms that identify topics discussed in a source. A keyword search is an easy way to find sources relevant to your topic but can also generate lots of irrelevant titles, especially if the term you enter is a common

For more about keywords, see pp. 539–41.

Figure 29.1
Sample home page from
the Howard University
Libraries

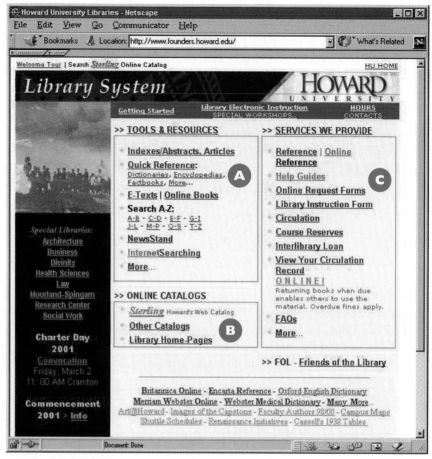

A. Access to databases, reference materials, and Internet guides
B. Access to library holdings (and catalogs for other libraries)
C. Guides to library information and resources

WWW
To practice using key-
words, visit the English
Research Room at
.

one. Once you've found a relevant title, be sure to check the record for alternate search terms. (See Figure 29.2 for an example of the results of an online keyword search and Figure 29.3 for an example of an online record.)
You may also be able to limit a search by the date of publication, a useful
function if you want only current information.

Check for Useful Subject Headings.   For a search by subject, you need to
decide what terms to use. When catalogers put a book into the database,
they assign subject headings from a list of standard terms used by many libraries. Most college libraries catalog their collections according to the *Library of Congress Subject Headings* (LCSH). A researcher can access this list by
consulting a set of large red books that many libraries keep near the catalog
terminals. (See Figure 29.4 for sample entries.) If you have trouble searching

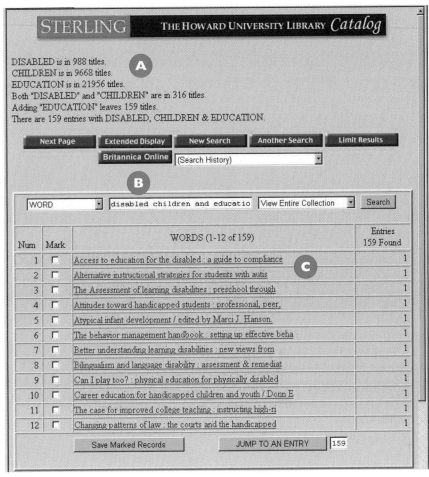

Figure 29.2
General results of a key-word search on "disabled children and education" using an online library catalog

A. Number of results for individual and combined search terms
B. Keyword search window
C. Results screen (linked to full entries)

effectively, you may be using different terms than the catalogers did. For example, catalogers use *developing countries* rather than *third world* and, for continuity, stick to *Afro-American* rather than *African American* and *motion pictures* rather than *movies*.

Sort Your Options.   Once you have done a search, the information in each record you locate can help you decide how to proceed. In addition to the call number or shelf location, the record will identify the author, title, place of publication, and date. Often it will describe what the book contains, how long it is, and which subject headings define its scope. (See Figure 29.3 for an example of an online record.) Though each library presents

Figure 29.3
Specific record selected
from keyword search
results

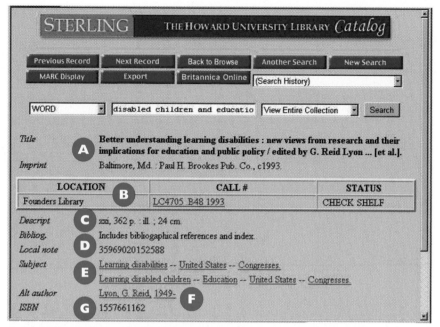

A. Book title, author, and publication information
B. Location and library call number
C. Number of pages, illustrations, height of book
D. Description of bibliography
E. Alternate subject headings (often hyperlinked)
F. Other works by the same author (often hyperlinked)
G. International Standard Book Number (ISBN)

For more on evaluating
sources, see pp. 570–77.

information slightly differently, the elements generally are the same. Use these clues to help you evaluate your sources wisely.

Find Items on the Shelves.   A book's call number is carefully chosen so that books on the same subject end up next to each other on the shelves. College libraries generally use the classification system devised by the Library of Congress. Its call letters and numbers direct you to books and other items grouped in subject areas. Other libraries use the older and more familiar Dewey decimal system, which files items into large categories by number. In either case, it can be fruitful to reserve some of your research time for browsing because you will almost certainly find interesting materials on the shelf next to the ones you found through the catalog. The two common classification systems are outlined here. You may notice that certain subjects aren't clearly included in either system: newer fields, such as computer science, mass communications, and environmental studies, have had to be added to related areas.

Library of Congress classification number — **Human ecology**   *(May Subd Geog)*
[GF1-GF900]
Here are entered works on the relationship of humans to the natural environment. Works on the relationship of humans to their sociocultural environment are entered under Social ecology. Works on the composite of physical, biological, and social sciences concerned with the conditions of the environment and their effects are entered under Environmental sciences. Works on the interrelationships of organisms and their environments, including other organisms, are entered under Ecology.

Used for —— UF   Ecology—Social aspects
Environment, Human
Human environment
Broader topics —— BT   Ecology
Related topics —— RT   Ecological engineering
Human beings—Effect of environment on
Human geography
Nature—Effect of human beings on
Narrower topics —— NT   Community life
Ecofeminism
Hazardous geographic environments
Human settlements
Landscape assessment
Population
Quality of life
Social psychology
Survival skills

Figure 29.4
Entries from the Library of Congress Subject Headings

LIBRARY OF CONGRESS CLASSIFICATION SYSTEM

A   General Works
B   Philosophy, Psychology, Religion
C   Auxiliary Sciences of History
D   History: General and Old World
E   History: America
F   History: America
G   Geography, Anthropology, Recreation
H   Social Sciences
J   Political Science
K   Law
L   Education
M   Music and Books on Music
N   Fine Arts
P   Language and Literature
Q   Science
R   Medicine
S   Agriculture
T   Technology
U   Military Science
V   Naval Science
Z   Library Science

DEWEY DECIMAL CLASSIFICATION SYSTEM

000–009   General Works
100–199   Philosophy
200–299   Religion
300–399   Social Sciences, Government, Customs
400–499   Language
500–599   Natural Sciences
600–699   Applied Sciences
700–799   Fine and Decorative Arts
800–899   Literature
900–999   History, Travel, Biography

Consult Catalogs at Other Libraries.   As more and more colleges and universities make their library catalogs available over the Internet, it will become easier for you to consult them from your home or dorm room. Use these catalogs to find books or other materials that you can borrow through interlibrary loan or by visiting a nearby library. If you're not sure how to access the online catalog at another library, ask a librarian. You may be able to connect directly to other library catalogs via the Internet or through your own library's catalog.

CONSULTING DATABASES: PERIODICAL INDEXES AND BIBLIOGRAPHIES

WWW
To practice consulting databases, visit the English Research Room at <www.bedfordstmartins.com/english_research/>.

Information on current topics is often published first in periodicals rather than in books. Periodicals are journals, magazines, newspapers, and other publications that are issued at regular intervals. Many indexes — guides to the material published within other works — exist to help you locate articles in periodicals. Bibliographies — lists of sources on a particular topic — also can lead you to relevant materials, often those you would never have thought to look up in a catalog.

Print indexes and bibliographies are often kept in the reference area of the library. In electronic form, they can be stored on CD-ROM, on the Internet, or on commercial sites that are accessible only if your library has a subscription. In some cases, you can access an electronic index only from a computer in your library. In other cases, indexes are available on your campus network or the Internet. If you have questions about how to access a particular database, ask a reference or subject-area librarian for help.

Periodical Indexes.   In a periodical index, you'll find every article — listed by author, title, and subject — for the periodicals and the time period covered by the index. The index also includes the source information you'll need to find each article in the library, usually the periodical title, date, issue number, and page numbers. Current electronic indexes may complement or even replace print indexes. For instance, indexes such as *MLA Online, ERIC,* and *PsycLIT* are available in both print and electronic forms.

Electronic indexes — often called periodical databases — are organized as a series of records or entries on a particular item, such as a newspaper or journal article. You can easily and efficiently search for these records using author, title, subject, or keyword. Electronic indexes may include more information on each article than print indexes do, such as a short summary or abstract or even the complete text of the article in question, which you can print out or download for later use. (Electronic indexes cover varying ranges of years. If your subject is historical or draws on early material, you may need to use a print index.)

Each periodical index includes entries for a specific collection of periodicals, so finding the right article is largely a matter of finding the right index. Before you start looking through a periodical index, ask the following questions:

Finding the Right Index

___ Is your subject covered in this index? Does the index cover a broad field or a very specific subject in depth?

___ Does the index cover the time period you're interested in? If the index is electronic, how far back does it go?

___ Does the index cover periodicals written for an expert audience or for a more general audience?

General Indexes.   Several indexes can help you if you're looking for magazine or newspaper articles addressed to the general population.

The *Readers' Guide to Periodical Literature* is available in print, on CD-ROM, and online. (See Figure 29.5 for sample entries.) Because it started publication in 1900, you can use older volumes to locate popular press coverage of events happening at any time in the twentieth century — for example, articles about the bombing of Pearl Harbor (December 1941) published days after the event.

The *New York Times Index* can help you track down that newspaper's coverage of events. Including editions that date back to 1851, this index is useful for historical research.

InfoTrac is a computerized resource that emphasizes materials written for a fairly general audience. (See Figure 29.6 for a sample entry.) It includes the full text of many articles.

NewsBank indexes more than five hundred local U.S. newspapers. Updated monthly, it is available both in print and on CD-ROM for computer searching.

Lexis-Nexis carries mainly full-text articles from newspapers, wire services, and other general-interest publications.

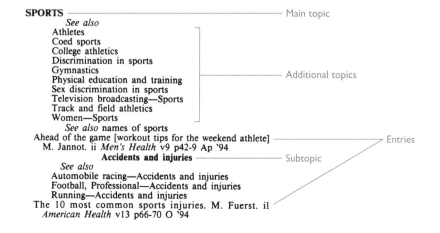

Figure 29.5
Entries from the Reader's Guide to Periodical Literature

Figure 29.6
Search result from InfoTrac index

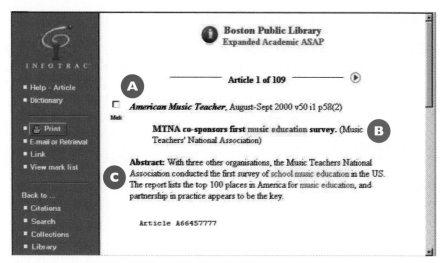

A. Publication name, date, volume number, illustrations, page number, total pages in article
B. Article title and author
C. Abstract summarizing the article

Specialized Indexes.   Discipline-specific indexes include articles that are aimed at a more specialized audience and provide more analysis than articles in popular magazines. If you are looking for literary criticism, research on social issues, or scientific or medical research only summarized or reported in the popular press, turn to indexes such as these:

> *Humanities Index*
>
> *Social Sciences Index*
>
> *Business Periodicals Index*
>
> *PAIS International* (an index focusing on public affairs)

Bibliographies.   When you use a bibliography—a list of sources on a particular topic—you take advantage of the research other people have already done on your subject. Every time you find a good book or article, look at the sources the author draws on; some of these may be useful to you, too. In a full-length book, look for a section at the back labeled "Bibliography" or perhaps called "For Further Reading." If the author has quoted or referred to other works, look for a list called "References" or "Works Cited" at the end of the work. If the book or article uses footnotes or endnotes, check those, too, for possible leads.

Sometimes you may locate a book-length bibliography on your subject. Researchers compile such books based on their research, and they publish them so that other researchers (including you) won't have to duplicate their work. Bibliographies may give citations for a wide variety of materials — including not only books and articles but also films, manuscripts, letters, government documents, and pamphlets — and they will probably lead you to sources that you wouldn't otherwise find.

For example, *Essential Shakespeare* is a bibliography that lists the best books and articles published on each of Shakespeare's works, a wonderful shortcut if you're looking for worthwhile criticism. To find a book-length bibliography, add the word *bibliography* to a subject or keyword search. If you're lucky, such a bibliography will include annotations that describe and evaluate each source.

For more on keyword searches, see pp. 539–41.

Before turning your attention to the wealth of other library and Web resources available, take a moment to assess where you are in your research project. If you have a clear idea of what you have left to accomplish, you will find it easier to stick to your research schedule. And when you reach the final stage, you will be well prepared to write your paper.

RESEARCH CHECKLIST

Managing Your Project

____ Are you on schedule? Do you need to adjust your timetable to give yourself more or less time for any of the stages?

____ Are you using your research question to keep your research on track and to avoid digressions?

____ Are you keeping your materials up-to-date? Are you listing new sources in your working bibliography? Have you labeled and stored new material in your archives?

____ Do you have a clear idea of where you are in the research process?

www
For downloadable sample schedules, visit <www
.bedfordstmartins.com/
bedguide>.

Using Other Library Resources

Many other library resources are available to you beyond what you can access from your library home page. One of the most overlooked resources in the library is its staff. Besides knowing the library better than anyone else, librarians are constantly working with its catalog, reference books, and databases. They are also aware of new additions to the library's collections, sometimes even before those materials are entered into the catalog. If you need help locating materials or want to learn how to use the library catalog or a particular database, consult a librarian.

CONSULTING REFERENCE MATERIALS

The library is also full of useful reference material for your research, including encyclopedias, handbooks, and atlases — many of which are available online through your library's home page. Spending some of your research time in the library, rather than on the Web, can still save you a lot of time and effort in the long run. Remember, the library and all of its resources — whether electronic or print — are specifically designed to help researchers like you to find information as quickly and efficiently as possible.

In any college library the reference collection contains an amazing array of resources. Here you can quickly familiarize yourself with a topic or fine-tune your research by filling in detailed definitions, dates, statistics, or facts. You can look for reference sources related to your topic in the *Guide to Reference Books,* a directory of sources arranged by discipline.

General Encyclopedias.   General encyclopedias are written for readers who aren't specialists, who want an overview of a topic, or who want to find some missing fact. The *New Encyclopaedia Britannica* and *Encyclopedia Americana* are examples of general encyclopedias. These references can give you an overview of your subject and may be especially valuable when you are first casting around for a topic. But when you start investigating more deeply, you will need to go to other sources as well. Encyclopedias generally have an index volume and cross-references to help you find what you need. You can also access many encyclopedias, including the *Encyclopaedia Britannica,* on the Web.

Specialized Encyclopedias.   If you are looking for more specialized information on a topic, these encyclopedias cover a field in much greater depth than general encyclopedias do. The following sampling of titles gives you a sense of the variety of specialized encyclopedias:

> *Dictionary of American History*
> *Encyclopedia of the American Constitution*
> *Encyclopedia of Human Biology*
> *Encyclopedia of Psychology*
> *Encyclopedia of Sociology*
> *Encyclopedia of World Cultures*
> *The Gale Encyclopedia of Science*
> *New Grove Dictionary of Music and Musicians*

Dictionaries.   Libraries have a variety of large and specialized dictionaries. You'll find dictionaries covering foreign languages, abbreviations, and slang as well as dictionaries for the specialized terminology in a particular field, such as *Black's Law Dictionary, Stedman's Medical Dictionary,* or the *Oxford Dictionary of Natural History.* Libraries often have unabridged dictionaries

available on dictionary stands, where you can find the most obscure words
and learn what they mean as well as how to pronounce them.

Handbooks and Companions.   Between encyclopedias and dictionaries
lies a species of reference book in which you will find concise surveys of
terms and topics relating to a specific subject. The articles are generally
longer than dictionary entries but more concise than those found in encyclopedias. Check with a reference librarian to see if specialized handbooks
are available for your topic. The following list suggests the variety available:

> *Blackwell Encyclopaedia of Political Thought*
>
> *Bloomsbury Guide to Women's Literature*
>
> *Dictionary of the Vietnam War*
>
> *Oxford Companion to English Literature*

Statistical Sources.   If numbers are a key type of evidence for your research, you can find sources for statistics in the library and on the Web.

- The *Statistical Abstract of the United States.* Perhaps the most useful single
  compilation of statistics, this resource contains hundreds of tables relating to population, social issues, economics, and so on.

- *Gallup Poll.* Good resources for public-opinion statistics, the surveys
  conducted by the Gallup organization are published in annual volumes,
  in a monthly magazine, and on the Web.

- *<www.census.gov>.* The federal government collects an extraordinary
  amount of statistical data and releases much of it on the Web. Check
  also <www.fedworld.gov> and <www.fedstats.gov> for lists of other government statistics available on the Web.

Atlases.   If your research has a geographical angle, maps and atlases may
be useful. Besides atlases of countries, regions, and the world, others cover
history, natural resources, ethnic groups, and many other special topics.

Biographical Sources.   Directories that list basic information — degrees,
work history, honors, addresses — for prominent people can be very useful
resources. To help you locate biographical sources, you can use tools such as
Biography Index and the *Biographical and Genealogical Master Index*. Biographical resources include the following:

> *American Men and Women of Science*
>
> *The Dictionary of American Biography*
>
> *The Dictionary of National Biography*
>
> *The Dictionary of Scientific Biography*
>
> *Who's Who in Politics*
>
> *Who's Who in the United States*

LOCATING SPECIAL MATERIALS

Your library is likely to have other collections of helpful materials, especially on regional or specialized topics, but you may need to ask about what's available.

Periodicals on Microform.   Most libraries have some of their resources available in microform, especially periodicals. This technology puts a large amount of printed material — for example, two weeks' worth of the *New York Times* — on a durable roll of film (microfilm) that fits into a small box or on a set of plastic sheets the size of index cards (microfiche). The machines used to read microforms often print out full-sized copies of pages.

Primary Materials on Microform.   In addition to newspapers and magazines, many libraries have other primary, or firsthand, material in microform. For example, the *American Culture Series* reproduces books and pamphlets published between 1493 and 1875 along with a good subject index. It is one tool for examining colonial religious tracts or nineteenth-century abolitionist pamphlets without traveling to a museum or rare books collection. The *American Women's Diaries* collection reproduces diaries kept by women living in New England and the South and by pioneer women traveling west, providing rare firsthand glimpses of the past.

Resources from Organizations.   Many groups maintain a Web site where you can go to find information. Your library may also keep a collection of pamphlets and annual reports distributed by companies, trade groups, or professional organizations. If you want to request such materials yourself, the *Encyclopedia of Associations,* organized by subject or group name, or the *United States Government Manual,* listing government agencies, can lead you to useful contacts, especially for field research.

Government Documents.   The federal government of the United States is the most prolific publisher in the world and, in an effort to make information accessible to citizens all over the country, makes an increasing number of documents available on the Web. There are several indexes to government documents, and more and more are available electronically.

- The *Monthly Catalog of United States Government Publications.* This resource is the most complete index to federal documents available.
- The *CIS Index.* This index specializes in congressional documents and includes a handy legislative history index.
- The *Congressional Record Index.* The *Congressional Record,* which reports what happens in Congress each day has indexes of its own.

When most people think of government documents, they may think of congressional hearings, presidential papers, and reports from federal agencies — but the government has published something on practically any topic you can think of. The following sampling of government publications gives you an idea of the kinds of information you can find:

Ozone Depletion, the Greenhouse Effect, and Climate Change

Placement of School Children with Acquired Immune Deficiency

Policy Implications of U.S. Involvement in Bosnia

Small Business and the International Economy

Strengthening Support and Recruitment of Women and Minorities to Positions in Education Administration

Violence on Television

If you plan to use government documents in your research, don't be shy about asking a librarian for help. The documents can be difficult to locate both on the shelves and on the Web.

Using the Web for Research

The Internet contains an enormous and ever-growing amount of information. Unfortunately, because of the sheer bulk of this information, searching for materials that are relevant to your topic can be both too easy and too difficult. Finding information that is actually useful can be time consuming, but understanding a few basic principles can help a great deal.

CONDUCTING ADVANCED ELECTRONIC SEARCHES

Searching the Web is similar to searching library catalogs and databases. Search engines contain millions of records on Web sites, much as a database or library catalog contains records on books, periodicals, or other materials found in a library. Generally, search engines can be searched by broad categories such as *education* or *health* or by keywords, the more specific terms that identify topics discussed in a source.

When you limit your search simply to keywords and broad general categories, however, you may be overwhelmed with information that is not directly related to your research question. For example, Figure 29.7 illustrates a keyword search for sources on *gun control* on Google that produced about 878,000 entries. A keyword search may be ideal if you search for a highly specialized topic, such as training for distance runners. If you search for a more general topic — such as *gun control* — you may turn up seemingly endless lists of results.

Several techniques are available to researchers who want to conduct sophisticated searches of the Web, databases, and library catalogs. Some of these techniques can expand your search, but most researchers want to limit the scope of their searches. By limiting your scope, you are more likely to find results relevant to your research interests. As Figure 29.8 shows, an advanced search produced fewer sources on one aspect of gun control — efforts to improve elementary school safety in Rhode Island by 2002.

WWW
To practice conducting simple and advanced Web searches, visit the English Research Room at <www .bedfordstmartins.com/ english_research/>.

For more on keywords, see pp. 539–41.

Figure 29.7
Results of a keyword search for gun control *using Google, reporting 878,000 entries*

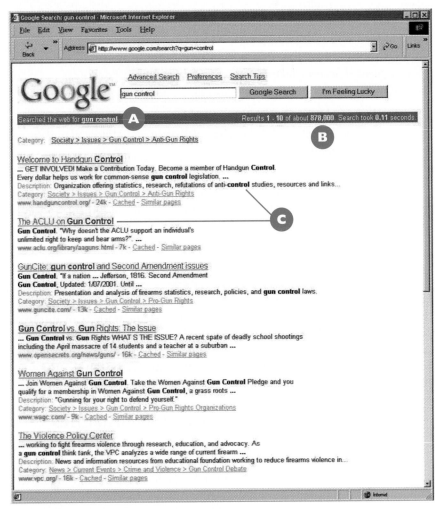

A. Search terms

B. Total number of entries located

C. Highlighted search terms found in entries

Use Wildcards.   Wildcards are symbols that tell the search engine to look for all possible endings to a word. For instance, if you search for the keyword *runner,* you'll get every entry containing that word. But you won't get entries that contain only *run, runs,* or *running.* Using a wildcard symbol such as run*, you can search for all words that begin with *run,* thus increasing the volume of your search results. The most common wildcard symbols are an asterisk (*) for multiple letters, numbers, or symbols and a question mark (?) for single characters.

Search for Exact Phrases.   Researchers often search for an exact phrase, such as *elementary school safety.* Depending on the search site, you may or

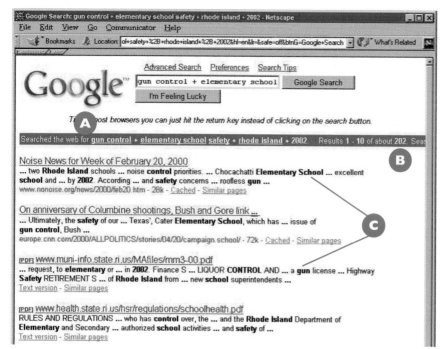

Figure 29.8
Advanced search results on gun control + elementary school safety + rhode island + 2002 *using Google, reporting 202 entries*

A. Search terms
B. Total number of entries located
C. Highlighted search terms found in entries

may not be required to type quotation marks around the phrase. (Follow the advice on the site's help page.)

Conduct Boolean Searches.   A Boolean search, named after the nineteenth-century mathematician George Boole, lets you specify the relationships between your keywords and phrases. Common Boolean search terms include *AND, OR,* and *NOT.* As the terms suggest, *AND* means that all terms must appear in a result. *OR* means that one or more of the terms must appear. And *NOT* means that one or more terms can appear, but another must not.

> `Search for: history AND California`
> Result: all entries containing both *history* and *California*
>
> `Search for: history OR California`
> Result: all entries containing *history* or *California* or both
>
> `Search for: history NOT California`
> Result: all entries containing *history* but not containing *California*
>
> `Search for: history AND California NOT Los Angeles`
> Result: all entries containing *history* and *California* but not containing *Los Angeles*

**WRITING WITH
A COMPUTER**

Leading Internet Search Sites

The best search site is the one you learn to use well. Each of the search tools below uses its own particular phrasing and search designs. In addition to following general search strategies, you should note each site's "search tips" and "help" instructions.

If you are uncertain about your topic, use a directory site like Yahoo!, Magellan, or WebCrawler that begins searches with categories. Next, think of searching like a zoom lens. If you zoom into "no results" or "no pages found," then you can step back and add more information until you start to focus on sites you want to explore. By tinkering with your words, you can improve your searches and locate Web pages with titles and ideas closer to your research goals. This process is much easier than starting with a general prompt and finding thousands of potential sites.

WWW
For links to these and other online resources, visit <www.bedfordstmartins.com/bedguide/>.

SUBJECT CATALOGS, DIRECTORIES, AND GUIDES
Digital Librarian (Margaret Vail Anderson)
Encyclopaedia Britannica's Internet Guide
Google Directory (Open Directory Project)
Librarians' Index to the Internet
Lycos
Michigan Electronic Library
UC Berkeley Internet Sources by Academic Discipline
     <www.lib.berkeley.edu/Collections/acadtarg.html>
Yahoo!

INDEXES WITH CONTENT GATHERED BY COMPUTER "SPIDERS" OR "ROBOTS"
Alta Vista
Excite <www.excite.com/search/>
FAST Search
Go Network
Google
Northern Light Search
Raging Search
Webcrawler

SITES THAT SEARCH MULTIPLE INDEXES AT ONE TIME
Dogpile
Ixquick
Metacrawler
MetaEureka
MetaFind
Search.com
SurfWax

Limit Searches by Publication Information.   Another widely used technique for limiting a search is specifying publication information — often the year of publication. Using publication date as a limiting factor is more useful for databases and library catalogs than on the Web, both because the Web is a more recent development and because most Web search engines can tell you when they indexed a site but not when it was created.

FINDING ONLINE TEXTS AND DISCUSSIONS

You will find that you can locate a variety of material online, ranging from complete texts to conversations among people interested in your topic.

Searching Online Document Collections.   One of the most useful forms of information on the Internet is the online document collection. These collections gather electronic versions of printed texts, often classics on which the copyright has expired. For example, the ambitious *Project Gutenberg* at <promo.net/pg> attempts to provide access to complete literary texts whose copyright has expired. Other leading sites include the *Etext Archives* at <www.etext.org> and the *New Bartleby Digital Library* at <www.bartleby .com>.

Searching Newsgroups and Mailing Lists.   Newsgroups and mailing lists are among the oldest forms of communication on the Internet. Both types of exchange support discussions of particular topics, such as adult education or immigration, among people with a shared interest.

Newsgroups and mailing lists generate an enormous amount of text each day. Some of these lists contain detailed analyses of issues and events by contributors who range from interested members of the general public to acknowledged experts. If you are working on a current issue, consider consulting the archives of newsgroups and mailing lists. Certain Web sites allow you to search for mailing lists and newsgroups — and sometimes for individual messages sent to lists or groups:

Deja.com: <www.deja.com/usenet>

Forum One: <www.forumone.com>

Using Chat.   Chat rooms can be a particularly useful source of information. Major news organizations, such as CNN, use chat to interview public figures or industry leaders in advertised sessions attended by hundreds or even thousands of participants. You can view transcripts of these sessions at <www.cnn.com/chat>. Similarly, major search sites, such as Lycos and Yahoo!, host regular chat sessions on topics including entertainment and finance. Yahoo! also provides transcripts of past sessions.

Finding Sources in the Field

The goal of field research is the same as that of library and Internet research — to gather the information you need to answer your research question and to marshal the evidence you need to present your conclusions persuasively in your research paper. The only difference is where you conduct the research. Many rich, unprinted sources lie beyond the library and the Internet.

If you enjoy meeting and talking with people and don't mind what news reporters call legwork, you may relish obtaining firsthand information. Perhaps you will even investigate matters that few researchers have investigated before. Almost any paper will be enriched by authentic and persuasive field sources. And you'll almost certainly learn more about your topic by going out into the field and developing firsthand knowledge of it. In this section, we focus on field research techniques that have proven most useful for college students.

INTERVIEWING

For more on preparing for an interview, see pp. 72–76.

Interviews — conversations with a purpose — may prove to be your main source of field material. Choose your interview subjects carefully, whenever possible interviewing an expert in the field. Or if you are researching a particular group of people, interview someone who may or may not have any special knowledge of the field but is representative or typical of the group. Regardless of your interview subject, preparation is central to a good interview.

TIPS FOR INTERVIEWING
- Be sure your prospect is willing to be quoted in writing.
- Make an appointment for a day when the person will have enough time — an hour if possible — to have a thorough talk with you.
- Arrive promptly, with carefully thought-out questions to ask.
- Come ready to take notes. If you also want to tape-record the interview, ask permission of the interviewee.
- Really listen. Let the person open up.
- Be flexible, and allow the interview to go in unanticipated directions.
- If a question draws no response, don't persist; just go on to the next question.
- At the end of the interview, be sure to confirm all direct quotations.
- Make additional notes right after the interview to preserve anything you didn't have time to record during the interview.

For more on recording an interview, see pp. 75–76.

Take notes even if you use a tape recorder so that you can remember the interview accurately, distill its most important points, and reconstruct it in your paper. Besides recording key points and quotations, you should note any telling details that might prove useful later—the interviewee's appearance, the setting, the mood, any notable gestures.

If you can't talk to an expert in person, your next best resource may be a telephone interview. Make a phone appointment for a time convenient for both you and your interviewee. A busy person may not be able to give you a half hour of conversation on the spur of a moment, and it is polite to ask for a time when you may call again. Have written questions in hand before you dial so you don't waste the person's time (and yours). Take notes.

Federal regulations, by the way, forbid recording an interview over the phone without notifying the person who is talking that you are recording his or her remarks.

OBSERVING

An observation may well be essential in field research. If you decide to observe a setting such as a business or a school, you will need to make an appointment. As soon as you arrive, identify yourself and your purpose. Some receptionists will insist on identification. You might ask your instructor for a statement on college letterhead declaring that you are a bona fide student doing field research. Follow-up field trips may be necessary if you find gaps in your research or if new ideas occur that you need to test by further observation.

For more on observing, see Ch. 5.

TIPS FOR OBSERVING

- Establish a clear purpose so you know exactly what you want to observe and why.

- Take notes during your observation so that you don't forget important details when you review your findings and incorporate your research into your paper.

- Record facts, telling details, and sensory impressions. Notice the features of the place, the actions or relationships of the people who are there, or whatever relates to the purpose of your observation.

- Consider using a still or video camera if you have equipment available and can operate it without being distracted from the scene you are observing. Some photographs may illustrate your paper, whereas others may help you interpret your observations or remember details while you write.

USING QUESTIONNAIRES

Questionnaires, as you know, are part of contemporary life. You probably filled one out the last time you applied for a job or for college. You may have responded to one in *People* or *Glamour* magazine. As a rule, when researching a particular question, professional pollsters, opinion testers, and survey takers survey thousands of individuals chosen to represent a segment of society or perhaps a broad range of the populace (diversified in geography, income, ethnic background, and education).

Because your surveys will not be this extensive, you should avoid generalizing about your questionnaire responses as if they were unimpeachable facts. It's one thing to say that "many of the students" who filled out a questionnaire on reading habits hadn't read a newspaper in the past month; it's another to claim that this is true of 72 percent of the students at your school — especially when you gave questionnaires only to those who ate in the dining hall the day you were there and half of those students just threw their questionnaires into the trash.

A far more reliable way for you to use questionnaires is to treat them as group interviews: assume that the information you collect from them is representative, use them to build your overall knowledge of the subject, and cull them for interesting or persuasive details or quotations. Use a questionnaire when you want to collect the same type of information from a large number of people, when you're more interested in what a group thinks as a whole than in what a particular individual has to say, or when an interview that would cover all your questions is impractical. (See Figure 29.9 for an example of a student questionnaire.)

TIPS FOR USING A QUESTIONNAIRE

- Ask yourself what you want to discover with your questionnaire. Once you have defined its purpose, thoughtfully invent questions to fulfill it.

- Keep your questionnaire simple. Make it easy and inviting to fill out. Test it on classmates or friends before you distribute it to the group you want to study.

- Ask questions that call for checking alternative answers, marking a simple yes or no, or writing a few words so that responses are easy to tally. It's a good idea to ask for just one piece of information per question.

- When appropriate, ask open-ended questions that call for short written responses. Although these responses will be difficult to tally and fewer people are likely to respond, the answers may supply worthwhile quotations or suggest important issues or factors when you mull over the findings.

- Write unbiased questions that will solicit factual responses. Do not ask, "How religious are you?" Instead ask, "What is your religious affiliation?" and "How often do you attend religious services?" Based on responses to the last two questions, you could report actual numbers and draw logical inferences about the respondents.

- When you get back the completed questionnaires, tally the results. You can simply count short answers ("Republican," "Democrat"), but you will need to classify longer answers into groups or categories. For example, if you asked "What is your goal in life?" you might find that the responses fell into these categories: (1) to make money, (2) to serve hu-

Figure 29.9   A questionnaire asking college students about Internet use

---

QUESTIONNAIRE

Thank you for completing this questionnaire. All information you supply will be kept strictly confidential.

1. What is your age? ____
2. What is your class?
   ____ First year   ____ Junior
   ____ Sophomore   ____ Senior
3. How old were you when you first began using the Internet? ____
4. How do you currently access the Internet? Indicate which of the following statements is true for you.
   ____ With my own computer   ____ Someone I live with has a computer
                                               with Internet access
   ____ I never use a computer   ____ With computers at the library or
                                               university lab
   ____ Other (please specify): _____
5. Approximately how many hours a week do you use the Internet? ____
6. What is your primary reason for using the Internet?
   ____ Personal   ____ School-related   ____ Work-related
7. Indicate all of the ways in which you use the Internet.
   ____ E-mailing
   ____ Recreational Web surfing
   ____ Conducting optional research for a class
   ____ Conducting mandatory research for a class
   ____ Conducting personal research (such as planning travel, evaluating products, or searching for a job)
   ____ Managing your financial accounts
   ____ Visiting chat rooms
   ____ Shopping online
   ____ Posting résumés or job applications
   ____ Designing or posting Web sites
   Other: _____
8. For which of the activities above do you use the Internet most? _____
   _____
9. On a scale of 1 to 5, rate how comfortable you are using the Internet.
   (not very comfortable) 1 2 3 4 5 (very comfortable)
10. Do you feel that you could benefit from further instruction in using the Internet?
    ____ Yes   ____ No   ____ Maybe

---

manity, (3) to travel, (4) to save my soul, (5) other. By classifying, you can group and count similar replies and look for patterns in the responses.

CORRESPONDING

For advice on writing business letters and e-mail messages, see pp. 227–30 and 233–34.

Is there a person whose knowledge or opinions you need but who lives too far away to interview? Do you need information or resources that you might request from large corporations, organizations such as the American Red Cross or the National Wildlife Federation, branches of the military, or offices of the state or federal government? Could an elected official provide what you need? Many organizations and public officials are accustomed to getting requests by mail and may employ public relations officers to answer inquiries like yours. Sometimes they will unexpectedly supply you with a bonus—free brochures, press releases, or other material that they think might interest you. To tap such resources, write a letter, or send an e-mail message.

TIPS FOR CORRESPONDING

- Plan ahead, and allow plenty of time for responses to your requests.
- Make your letter or e-mail message short and polite. Identify yourself, explain what you want to find out, and request what you need. Thank your correspondent for helping you.
- If you want specific information from an individual, send your questionnaire or a short list of pointed questions. If you e-mail your message, insert the questions from your questionnaire into the message.
- Enclose a stamped, self-addressed envelope for a reply by mail. If you are sending an e-mail message, include your e-mail address in the message.

ATTENDING PUBLIC AND ONLINE EVENTS

College organizations frequently bring interesting speakers to campus. Check the schedules of events on bulletin boards and in your campus newspaper. In addition, professionals and special-interest groups sometimes convene for a regional or national conference. These meetings can be fertile sources of fresh ideas for a student researcher. Attending a lecture or professional conference can be an excellent way to begin to learn the language of a discipline.

TIPS FOR ATTENDING EVENTS

- Take notes on the lectures, which are usually given by experts in the field and supply firsthand opinions.
- Ask questions from the audience or corner a speaker or two later for an informal talk.
- Record who attended the lecture or conference, how the audience reacted, or any other background details that could prove useful in writing your paper.
- Depending on the nature of the gathering, a speaker might distribute copies of the paper presented or be willing to send a copy to you. Con-

ferences often publish their proceedings — usually a set of all the lectures delivered — but publication generally takes months or even years after the conference. If the conference does publish proceedings, try looking in the library for proceedings of past conferences.

Be on the lookout, as well, for online discussions — such as the chat sessions sponsored by Web search engines like Yahoo! or Web sites like CNN Online — that are relevant to your research topic. You can participate as an observer or perhaps even ask a question. Remember to use your chat program to record the discussion for later review. You can learn how to record a transcript by consulting the program's online help.

For more on using chat, see p. 563.

Chapter 30

Evaluating Sources and Taking Notes

For more on critical reading, see Chs. 2 and 12.

Locating and collecting information are only two of the many activities involved in writing a research paper. You also have to think critically about what you find. You need to evaluate — in other words judge — your sources, exploring the ideas, opinions, facts, and beliefs they express. You must decide which sources are reliable and relevant to your topic and what information from these sources is most useful for your paper. The ability to evaluate information is an extremely useful skill — one you can apply both in and beyond college.

In this chapter, we will explore strategies for evaluating information and for taking notes. Because these strategies are not necessarily step-by-step activities, you can use them throughout the research and writing processes. As you identify, select, and read sources, you'll use evaluation from start to finish. Taking useful and efficient notes throughout this process will ensure that you are ready when it comes time to write your paper.

Evaluating Sources

WWW
For help with evaluating sources, use *Research Assistant HyperFolio,* a software tool available with *The Bedford Guide.*

Not every source you locate will be equally useful to you. Poor reasoning and strong biases weaken some sources, but many are simply irrelevant to your specific research question. Part of the job of conducting research is thinking critically about sources so that you can select the best evidence for your purposes.

How do you know what evidence is best? Do what experienced researchers do — ask a series of key questions in order to evaluate your sources. The basic questions remain the same whether your source is print or electronic. See Figure 30.1 for a sample evaluation of a Web site.

For evaluating field sources, see pp. 576–77.

RESEARCH CHECKLIST

Evaluating Sources — Print and Electronic

—— What is the purpose of the publication or Web site? Is it to sell a product or service? To inform? To publish new research? To shape opinion about a particular issue or cause?

—— Who is the intended audience? Experts in the field or novices? The general public or people with a particular bias? How does this audience affect the tone and evidence in the source?

—— Who is the author of the source? Does the source provide information about the author's credentials and profession? Can you detect the author's bias or point of view?

—— Is your material a primary source (a firsthand account) or a secondary source (an analysis of primary material)? If it is a secondary source, does it use sound evidence from primary sources? Would you learn more if you looked at the primary source yourself? Is it available?

—— What can you tell about the publisher? Is it a corporation, an organization, or a government agency? Have you heard of this publisher before? Does the publication seem reputable and responsible? If the source is a Web site, what can you find out about its sponsor?

—— What kind of evidence does the source present? Is it reliable, sufficient, and relevant? Does the argument or analysis seem complete, or does it leave many questions unanswered?

—— When was the source published? If it is a Web site, when was it created or last updated? Is the information in the source up-to-date?

—— Is the information in the source directly relevant to your research question? Why should you use this source rather than others?

WHAT IS THE PURPOSE?

Understanding the purpose of a source will help you determine whether it might be useful for your research project. A general reference source in a library serves a much different purpose than a newspaper editorial, a magazine advertisement, or a Web site that promotes a particular product or service. Asking critical questions is crucial: Is the purpose of this source to explain or inform? To persuade? To offer an alternative viewpoint? To sell a product? If you are evaluating electronic posts, what do you know about the newsgroup or mailing list? Does it have a FAQ (Frequently Asked Questions) file available to explain its aims? Identifying the intention of the source can help you determine whether it could supply solid evidence for your paper.

Figure 30.1
Evaluating the purpose,
audience, and bias of a
Web-site home page

A. Identifies group as organization (.org), not school (.edu) or company (.com)

B. Explains purpose of group

C. Uses engaging animal graphics

D. Features news slanted toward animal-lovers and ASPCA activities

E. Offers free newsletter to involve readers

F. Provides links to other animal-oriented Web sites

G. Appeals for support

H. Supplies links to emergency and local help

I. Identifies product sources

J. Provides full contact information

WHO IS THE INTENDED AUDIENCE?

A source written for an audience of experts in a particular field is likely to contain different kinds of information than one written for a general audience. Sources written for technical experts are likely to assume that readers already possess a great deal of background knowledge. These sources typically skip general treatments in favor of detailed discussions tailored to experts. In contrast, sources written for general audiences usually provide background information. For example, for your paper on current treatments for HIV, you might be evaluating an article from a well-known medical journal written by a physician for other physicians. Instead of this article, which discusses the most favorable chemical composition for an effective protease inhibitor, you might be better off beginning with a source that defines *protease inhibitor* and discusses how it helps HIV patients. Think about what kinds of sources might be most helpful for your project.

WHO IS THE AUTHOR?

Make every effort to learn about the author of a source before you use his or her ideas to support a critical point in your paper. Investigate the author's credentials, discover the institutions or organizations with which he or she is affiliated, and explore, if you can, the author's reputation among his or her peers. If your source is a Web site, see whether it provides an e-mail address so you can contact the author. If it is a post to a newsgroup or a mailing list, see what you can tell from the writer's e-mail address and any signature file. Try to make sure that any author you cite is reliable and trustworthy.

Bias.   Consider whether the author's bias affects how he or she presents information and opinions. A *bias* is a preference for a particular side of an issue. Because the vast majority of authors have an opinion on the topic they are writing about, you shouldn't ask whether an author is biased. Instead, ask whether the bias has resulted in a source that treats one side of an issue more favorably than another. To explore for bias, consider the author's overall viewpoint on the topic. What are his or her allegiances? Is the bias hidden or stated? Do you need to look for a balancing viewpoint or approach? Having a strong bias does not mean that everything an author has written is invalid. However, if you recognize such biases early on, you will be better prepared to defend your paper from those who want to challenge your analysis or argument.

Print Credentials.   Where can you find an author's credentials? Look in a book's introduction or preface. Check any biographical note at the beginning or end of a book or article. Ultimately, the best measure of someone's authority is whether his or her work meets the critical demands of other authorities. Do other authors cite the work of your source's author? If your instructor or someone else on campus knows the field, does he or she recognize the author?

Web Credentials.   Learning the credentials of authors of information posted on the Web, on a newsgroup site, or on certain electronic databases can be difficult. If your source is a Web site, look for a link on its home page to information about the author. If no credentials are provided, you might e-mail the author to ask about his or her credentials. If you can't find out anything about the author of a posting, it is best not to use the information.

Publication.　If your source is a weekly newsmagazine like *Time, Newsweek,* or *U.S. News & World Report,* the writer of an article is likely to be a reporter who may not have a famous name and probably is not a world-renowned authority. Such magazines do, however, feature some articles by experts, whose credentials will usually be given in a brief description accompanying the article. All such magazines have a good reputation for checking their facts carefully and presenting a range of opinions. Be aware, however, that some magazines select facts that mirror the opinions of their editors.

Materials with No Author Identified.　If no author is given, as is sometimes the case with newspaper articles and Web sites, try to identify the sponsoring organization or publisher. On a Web site, look for a disclaimer or contact information for the organization on the home page or an "About This Site" page. If a print source doesn't list an author, consider the nature of the publication: Is the article published in a nationally respected newspaper like the *Wall Street Journal* or in a supermarket tabloid? Is the brochure published by a leading organization in its field?

Field Research.　If you are conducting field research, you can sometimes select the authors of your information. If you are investigating the effectiveness of safety standards for infant car seats, for example, a personal interview with a local pediatrician will probably produce different information than an interview with a manufacturer's marketing representative. You can also affect the results of your research by distributing a questionnaire to a certain group of people or by observing a particular setting.

IS THIS A PRIMARY OR A SECONDARY SOURCE?

A *primary source* is a firsthand account written by an eyewitness or a participant. It contains raw data and immediate impressions. A *secondary source* is an analysis of the information contained in one or more primary sources. For example, primary sources for a large fire caused by a gas leak would include the statements of victims and witnesses, the article written by a journalist who was at the scene, and the report of the fire chief in charge of putting out the blaze. If another reporter used those accounts as background for a story on industrial accidents or if a historian used them in a book on urban life, these resulting works would be secondary sources.

For most research papers, you need to use both primary and secondary sources. If you find yourself repeatedly citing a fact or authority as it is quoted in someone else's analysis, go to the primary source of the information itself. For example, statistics can be used by those arguing both sides of an issue: often it's only the interpretation that differs. Going back to the original research or statistics (published as a primary source) will help you to learn where the facts end and the interpretation begins.

WHO IS THE PUBLISHER?

Experienced researchers know that the publisher of a source — the person, organization, government agency, or corporation that prints or electronically distributes a source — plays an important role in shaping its content. Like authors, publishers often have a bias about a particular topic or issue. A corporate publisher, such as Microsoft, which publishes information on one of the largest sites on the Web, is likely to present its own products and services more favorably than those of its competitors. Similarly, political groups, such as the Democratic Party or the National Rifle Association, are likely to publish materials that support policies favored by the organization.

As you evaluate a source, ask critical questions about its publisher. Is a Web site created for commercial purposes, such as selling a product or service? Is it devoted to a particular political cause? Is it developed by a particular organization or government agency? Is a newsgroup or mailing list a general-interest group or one devoted to a particular cause? Is the publisher of a book known for publishing works in a specific field or with a specific political agenda? Does a periodical have a predictable point of view? Commentary in *The Nation*, a magazine with a politically liberal point of view, is likely to give you a different picture of the world than that in the conservative *National Review*.

For an example of how a URL identifies a publisher, see A on p. 572.

Many of these questions are difficult for beginning researchers; consult with a librarian if you need help finding answers. More than other kinds of sources, Web sites and periodicals are likely to reflect a publisher's bias. To learn about the publisher of a Web site, try to locate a disclaimer or a link to "Site Information" or "About This Site." If you are visiting a site sponsored by an organization or agency, look for a mission statement (see Figure 30.1 for an example of a mission statement).

HOW SOUND IS THE EVIDENCE?

The evidence in a source — the information, opinions, and ideas — can tell you a great deal about its reliability and usefulness for your research project. As you evaluate a source, determine whether its evidence is complete, up-to-date, and carefully put together. Identify the thesis, if any, and examine whether it is supported by credible evidence. Think critically about the argument or analysis: Is it convincing? Is there enough evidence to support the claims being made? If the source leaves important questions unanswered, you might do better by looking for another source.

For more on evidence, see pp. 25–28.

IS THE SOURCE UP-TO-DATE?

In general, you should strive to use the most current sources possible. In most fields, new information and discoveries come out every year, so the evidence in a source needs to be up-to-date or at least still timely. If you cite five-year-old procedures for treating AIDS as if they are still used, for example, you'd be wrong. Use older materials when their value has held up over time or when your research focuses on an earlier period.

IS THE SOURCE RELEVANT TO YOUR RESEARCH?

Finally, continue to question whether each of your sources is relevant to your topic, your research question, your thesis, and your claims. An interesting fact or opinion could be just that — interesting. You need facts, opinions, information, and quotations that relate directly to the purpose and audience of your research paper. It's surprisingly easy to waste your time being sidetracked by a persuasive book, article, or Web site on a topic that is only slightly connected to your research.

Why use one source rather than another? Is the information it contains useful for your purposes? Does the source contain strong quotations or hard facts that would be effective in your paper? Does it tackle the subject matter in a relevant way? For one paper, it may be appropriate to use an article from a popular magazine, but for another you may need to cite the research findings published in the scholarly journal article on which the magazine article was based. Remember that you're looking for the best possible sources for your particular purpose. Always ask yourself not only "Will this do?" but also "Would something else be better?"

Consider, as well, how using a source in your paper will affect the future direction of your research. Does the source contain information that challenges your assumptions about the topic? Does it present any strong evidence against your position for which you need to find counterevidence? Does it suggest a new direction that might be more interesting to pursue? It's wise to check in with yourself now and again to make sure you have a clear direction — whether it's the same direction or a completely new one.

ARE YOUR FIELD SOURCES USEFUL AND RELIABLE?

Although the general criteria for evaluating print and electronic sources may also apply to field resources, you might want to ask these questions as well:

RESEARCH CHECKLIST

Evaluating Field Sources

___ Does your source seem biased or prejudiced? If so, is this bias or prejudice so strong that you have to discount some of the source's information?

—— Does your source provide evidence to support or corroborate claims? Have you compared different people's opinions, accounts, or evidence?

—— Is any of your evidence hearsay — one person telling you the thoughts of another or recounting actions that he or she hasn't witnessed? If so, can you support your source's view by comparing it with other evidence?

—— Does your source seem to respond consistently, seriously, and honestly? If a respondent has told you about past events, has time possibly distorted his or her memory?

Each type of field research can also raise particular questions. For example, if you are observing a particular event or setting, are people aware that they are being observed? Often, knowing that they are being observed can change people's behavior. If you have tried to question a random sampling of people, do you feel that they are truly representative? Or, if you have tried to question everyone in a group, have you been thorough enough? It is important for you to think critically about field sources as well as those from the library and the Web.

Taking Notes

Your notes are an extremely important part of the research process because you will use them to transfer information from your sources to your draft. The quality of your notes will contribute to the effectiveness of your paper. As you take notes, think critically about the ideas and facts found in the sources. By selecting information and organizing it for later review, you begin evaluating that information.

RECORDING INFORMATION

As you write your notes, record every fact, idea, and quotation that you might eventually want to use. Make sure your notes are complete and accurate: if you sit down to draft your paper and find you've neglected to jot down that memorable phrase by the most authoritative expert in the field and to make a copy of the source, you'll either have to look it up again or write your paper without it.

For more on organizing a research archive, see pp. 544–45.

Your notes are where you start to analyze and synthesize your sources, turning them into the building blocks for your paper. If you copy down everything you read, exactly as it was written, you not only waste time but also postpone the inevitable. If you want your paper to be a sound analysis or argument based on a variety of reliable sources (and not just a place to show off how many sources you looked up), then sooner or later you're going to have to sit down and separate the useful nuggets in each source from all the rest. Your research notes are the best place to do that. A good research note includes three elements:

1. An *identifier,* usually the last name of the author whose work you're citing, followed by the location of the information — the page number or numbers, an Internet address, or a field source. (You should already have a note in your working bibliography for this source with complete publication information. If not, make one now.)
2. A *subject heading,* some key word or phrase you make up yourself to help you decide where in your paper the information will best fit.
3. The *fact, idea, opinion,* or *quotation* you plan to use in your paper.

You need to record all three elements so that later, when you incorporate your notes into your paper or develop your ideas from multiple sources, you'll have an accurate record of what you found in each source. You'll also know exactly where you found it and be able to cite every source without difficulty.

TAKING BETTER NOTES

Before you begin taking notes, skim through your source to decide what — and how much — you need to record.

Use a Sensible Format.   Many writers find that using note cards or a word-processing program works better than taking notes on sheets of notebook paper. When the time comes to organize the material, they can shuffle and reshuffle cards or computerized notes to arrive at an order that makes most sense to them.

Don't Crowd Your Notes.   Putting two or more ideas on the same card will complicate your task when you organize and draft your paper. If you use a computer to take notes, separate your entries clearly so that you can move them around easily later.

Take Accurate Notes.   Read the entire article or section of a book before beginning to take notes to help you avoid distorting the meaning. Put exact quotations in quotation marks, and take care not to quote something out of context or change the meaning. Double-check all statistics and lists.

For more on research archives, see pp. 544–45.

WRITING WITH A COMPUTER

Working with Your Research Archive

As you build your research archive, you may want to use the computer to create electronic "note cards." For example, you might keep a list of Web sites and the relevant information from them in a computer file that allows you to return to your sources with the click of a mouse. Or you may record information from each source in a separate computer file. Then when you are composing a draft, you can easily keep several files open to copy and paste the source information (with citations) as you weave it into the draft.

Take Thorough Notes.   Don't trust your memory to fill in the blanks. A good rule is to make your notes and citations full enough so that, once they're written, you are totally independent of the source from which they came. That way you'll avoid frantic Internet searches trying to locate a site again or last-minute trips back to the library for a book or periodical you returned weeks ago.

Bristle while You Work.   While reading the material you are collecting, view it a little suspiciously to help you remain critical.

Keep Evaluating.   As you take notes, continue to evaluate what you read. Decide whether the ideas are going to be extremely valuable, fairly valuable, or only a little bit valuable. Some researchers code the top of a note with a star (for great value) or a question mark (for questionable usefulness). Later, when they're organizing their material, they can see what especially stands out and needs emphasis. Others write notes to themselves at the bottom of a card or within the computer file.

Know When to Stop.   How many notes are enough? When you find that your sources are mostly repeating what you've learned from previous sources — and aren't any more authoritative or credible — you have probably done enough reading and note taking.

AVOIDING PLAGIARISM

You have an obligation to the researchers, scholars, and writers who came before you. You repay this obligation by citing your source materials carefully, mentioning the names of all the other writers you get information from. You do so not only for quotations you use but also for ideas, even those you have conveyed in your own words. If a writer fails to acknowledge all sources or uses another writer's words without quotation marks, he or she has *plagiarized*, a very serious offense in academic and business communities. Such a writer is suspected of a theft when he or she may merely have failed to make a debt clear by citing and listing sources, as a good scholar should.

For more on citing sources, see Ch. 32.

QUOTING, PARAPHRASING, NUTSHELLING

When it comes time to draft your paper, you will incorporate your source material in a variety of ways:

- Quoting: transcribing the author's exact words directly from the source
- Paraphrasing: restating the author's ideas fully but in your own words
- Nutshelling: giving a brief summary of the author's main point

WWW
To practice quoting, paraphrasing, and nutshelling, visit <www.bedfordstmartins.com/bedguide/>.

Your notes, too, should be in these three forms — and the form you pick for each bit of information should represent your best guess as to the form you will use in the final paper.

For more on quoting, paraphrasing, and nutshelling, see pp. 588–92.

Deciding whether to quote, paraphrase, or nutshell at the note-taking stage will save you time. A faithful transcription of a long quotation takes much longer than a quick nutshell, so if you know in advance that you intend to use only a nutshell, you might as well save yourself those extra minutes. In addition, weighing each source carefully and deciding how to use it — even while you are reading it — is part of reading critically. The dynamic process of research requires thinking critically about sources and their usefulness, not just taking a source at face value and copying it word for word into your paper. You should always be thinking about how you will use your sources — otherwise, they'll end up using you.

For more on quotations and ellipsis marks, see C3 in the "Quick Editing Guide" (the dark-blue-edged pages).

Quoting.   Quote sparingly, only when doing so adds support and authority to your assertions. If you intend to use a direct quotation, copy the quotation carefully, reproducing the words, spelling, order, and punctuation exactly, even if they're unusual. Go back over what you've written to make sure that you've copied it correctly. Put quotation marks around the material so that when you add it to your paper, you'll remember that it's a direct quotation. (See Figure 30.2 for an example of a note card directly quoting a source.)

Sometimes it doesn't pay to transcribe a long quotation word for word. Parts may fail to serve your purpose, such as transitions, parenthetical remarks, and other information useless to you. If you take out one or more words, indicate the omission in your note by using an ellipsis mark within brackets [. . .].

Paraphrasing.   When paraphrasing, you restate an author's ideas in your own words. A good paraphrase retains the organization, emphasis, and often many of the details of the original passage — so it isn't usually much shorter

---

Children and sports   Leonard 140
  ". . . [in organized sports] children may be subject to intense emotional stress caused by fear and anxiety, concern about physical safety, and doubts about performances and outcomes. This anxiety may emerge if children are ignored, chastised, or made to feel that they are no good. Scanlan and Passer's study of preadolescent male soccer players showed that losing players evidenced more postgame anxiety than winning players. Children who experience anxiety in sport competition may try to avoid failure by shying away from active participation, by developing excuses, or by refusing to try new things." [Good quote!]

Figure 30.2
A sample note card giving a direct quotation from a source

than the original. Even so, paraphrasing is especially helpful when the language of another writer is not particularly memorable, but you want to walk your readers through the points made in the original source. (If you just want to convey the essence of the original, use nutshelling.) When you paraphrase, you aren't judging or interpreting another writer's ideas—you are simply trying to restate them fairly and accurately. Be careful, however, not to hover so close to the author's own words that your paraphrase is merely an echo. (See Figure 30.3 for an example of a note card paraphrasing a source.)

ORIGINAL	"In staging an ancient Greek tragedy today, most directors do not mask the actors."
TOO CLOSE TO THE ORIGINAL	Most directors, in staging an ancient Greek play today, do not mask the actors.
A GOOD PARAPHRASE	Few contemporary directors of Greek tragedy insist that their actors wear masks.

WRITING A GOOD PARAPHRASE

1. Read the entire passage through a few times.
2. Divide the passage into its most important ideas or points either in your mind or by highlighting or annotating the page. Noting three or four points for each paragraph will make the task manageable.
3. Look away from the original source, and restate the first idea in your own words. Summarize the support for this idea. Review the section if necessary.
4. Go on to the next idea, and follow the same procedure. Continue in this way until you reach the last point.
5. Go back and reread the entire original passage one more time, making sure you've conveyed its ideas faithfully but without repeating its words or sentence structure. Revise your paraphrase if necessary.

Figure 30.3   A sample note card paraphrasing the quotation from Leonard's book (Figure 30.2)

Paraphrase about half the length of original passage

Children and sports   Leonard 140

Stress and anxiety on the playing field can result in children backing away from participating in sports because they fear rejection if they perform poorly. This anxiety and stress is a result of the child's fears of being hurt or not being good enough. A study by Scanlan and Passer showing that boys who lose in soccer have more anxiety after losing a game than boys who win confirms these findings.

No interpretation or evaluation of original passage included

Emphasis of original maintained with word choice and order reworked to avoid plagiarism

Subject heading

Reasons for moving to Las Animas	Aaron Sanchez Interview, 3-11-01

Identifier: person interviewed and date

In 1924, my father Octavio and his family (father, mother, four brothers, three sisters) moved to Las Animas because they couldn't make enough money where they were living in New Mexico. The inheritance from his mother's father went to her brothers, and she got nothing. They moved to the Las Animas region, settling in a <u>colonia</u> (labor camp).

Main points clearly broken out

Terse, even fragmentary, notes convey gist of key point in the interview

Figure 30.4   A sample note card nutshelling, or summarizing, a source

Nutshelling.   Sometimes a paraphrase will take more space than you want to spend on it or will disrupt the flow of your own ideas more than is necessary. Often all you need is to convey the main point of a source "in a nutshell." Nutshelling, or summarizing, lets your readers know the most important idea or ideas of a passage by restating them in your own words. This strategy can save a lot of space: a page or more of detailed text can often be distilled into one or two succinct sentences. Be careful, though, that in reducing a long passage down to a brief nutshell you do not distort the original author's meaning or emphasis. Your goal should be to convey as faithfully as possible the meaning of the original. (See Figure 30.4 for an example of a note card nutshelling a source.)

WRITING A GOOD NUTSHELL

1. Read the original passage several times.
2. Without looking back at the passage, state the gist of it, the point it makes, the main sense as you remember it.
3. Go back and reread the original passage one more time, making sure you've conveyed its ideas faithfully. Revise your nutshell if necessary.

Learning to select appropriate quotations and to write useful paraphrases and nutshells takes time and practice. Use the following questions to help you improve your note-taking skills:

RESEARCH CHECKLIST

Taking Notes with Quotations, Paraphrases, and Summaries

___ For each research note, have you identified the source (by the author's last name or an important word from the title) and the exact page? Have you added a subject heading to each note?

___ Have you made a bibliography card or note for each new source you discovered during your reading?

___ Does each note contain only one idea?

___ Have you remained true to the meaning of the original source?

___ Have you quoted sparingly — selecting pointed, striking, short passages?

___ Have you quoted sources exactly? Do you use quotation marks around significant words, phrases, and longer passages from the original sources? Do you use ellipsis marks as needed to show where any words are omitted?

___ Have you taken most notes in your own words — paraphrasing or nutshelling?

___ Have you avoided paraphrasing too close to the source?

Chapter 31
Writing Your Research Paper

Planning and Drafting

You began gathering material from library, Internet, and field sources with a question in mind. By now, if your research has been thorough and fruitful, you know your answer. The moment has come to weave together the material you have gathered. We can vouch for two time-proven methods.

For advice on stating a thesis, see pp. 273–75.

The Thesis Method. Decide what your research has led you to believe. What does it all mean? Sum up that view in a sentence. That sentence is your thesis, the one main idea your paper will demonstrate. You can then start planning and drafting, including only material that supports your thesis, concentrating from beginning to end on making that thesis clear.

For revision strategies, see pp. 319–24.

The Answer Method. Some writers have an easier time if they plunge in and start writing without first stating any thesis at all. If you care to try this method, recall your original research question, and start writing with the purpose of answering it, lining up evidence as you go. You may discover what you want to say as you write. (Note that this method usually requires more revising than the thesis method.)

MOVING FROM NOTES TO OUTLINE TO DRAFT

Your source notes are only the raw material for your research paper. If they are to end up in a readable, unified whole, you need to put them into the proper setting, shaping and finely polishing them. Sometimes you can copy good, thoughtful notes verbatim from note card to first draft. But usually you need to rewrite to fit them in so they don't stand out like boulders in the stream of your prose. Moving from the nuggets of information in your notes to a smooth, persuasive analysis or argument is the most challenging part of the research process — and, ironically, the part on which we can give the least concrete advice. Every writer's habits of mind are different. Nonetheless, you'll probably find yourself cycling again and again through four basic activities:

- Interpreting your sources
- Refining your thesis
- Organizing your ideas
- Putting your thoughts into the form of a draft

Interpreting Your Sources.   On their own, your source notes are only pieces of information. They need your careful interpretation to transform them into effective evidence. As a researcher and writer, you have to think critically about each fact and decide what it means in the context of your paper. Then you have to make sure that the fact itself is strong enough to bear the weight of the claim you're going to base on it. You may find that you need supplemental evidence to shore up an interesting but possibly ambiguous fact.

For more on evidence, see pp. 25–28.

You'll also need to synthesize your sources and evidence, to weave them into a unified whole. If you've been guided throughout your research by a research question or a working thesis, you may find this synthesis fairly easy. You know what the question is; you know what the general answer is; you just need to let the pieces fall into place. If your question or thesis has changed, perhaps because you have unearthed persuasive information somewhat at odds with your original direction, consider these questions:

- Taken as a whole, what does all this information mean?
- What does it actually tell you about your topic?
- What's the most important thing you've learned?
- What's the most important thing you can tell your readers?

Refining Your Thesis.   A thesis is a clear, precise statement of the point you want to make in your paper. It will help you decide what to say and how to say it. If it is clear to your readers, the thesis will help them interpret what you present by letting them know in advance the scope of your paper and your general message.

Explicitly stating your thesis as the first or last sentence in your opening paragraph is only one option. Sometimes you can craft your opening paragraph so that your readers know exactly what your thesis is even though you only imply it. (Check with your instructor if you're unsure whether an implicit thesis statement will be acceptable.)

For more on stating and using a thesis, see pp. 271–75.

For help with organizing sources and ideas, use *Research Assistant Hyper-Folio*, a software tool available with *The Bedford Guide*.

If you haven't developed a thesis yet, now is the time to write one. If you've used a working thesis to guide your research, sharpen and refine it before you start drafting. Later you may need to change it even further, but a clear thesis will guide you in organizing and expressing your ideas.

In your thesis, try to be precise and concrete, and don't claim more than you can demonstrate in your paper. If your paper is argumentative — that is, if you take a stand, propose a solution, or evaluate something — then you should make clear what your stand, solution, or appraisal is.

TOPIC	Americans' attitudes toward sports
RESEARCH QUESTION	Is America obsessed with sports?
THESIS	The national obsession with sports must end.

For more on organizing and developing ideas, see Part Two or Ch. 19.

Organizing Your Ideas.   In writing your paper, it isn't enough simply to describe the steps you took in answering your research question or to string the data together in chronological order. You aren't writing a memoir; you're reporting the significance of what you found out. Put your material together in various combinations until you arrive at an organization that seems engaging and clear — one that fulfills your purpose.

For more on research questions, see pp. 535–41.

If you began with a clear, carefully worded research question, you will not have much difficulty selecting and organizing your evidence to answer it. But research questions often change while you're at work at the library, on the Internet, or in the field. Don't be afraid to ditch an original question that no longer works and to reorganize around a newly formed question. In the long run, you'll save both time and toil.

For more on outlining, see pp. 279–84.

If your material seems to resist taking shape, you may find it helpful to order your ideas by writing an outline. You might arrange your notes, whether cards or computer file entries, in an order that makes sense. Then the sequence of these notes becomes a plan you can follow as you write. Or you can write out an informal or formal outline on paper or on the computer.

For more strategies for drafting, see Ch. 18.

Beginning to Draft.   An outline is a skeleton to which you will add flesh (details). Use the outline as a working plan, but change the subdivisions or the order of the parts if you discover a better way as you draft. When you look over your outline, compare each section with the notes you have on hand for it. If for a certain section you have no notes, or only one note, your research has a gap, so go back to the library, to the Internet, or into the field. Even if everything hasn't fallen into perfect order, start writing anyway. Get something down on paper so that you will have something to revise. And remember that you don't have to start at the beginning; start wherever you feel most comfortable.

As you write, cultivate a certain detachment rather than swaggering in triumph over what you have discovered. Make no exorbitant claims for what you have discovered ("Thus I have shown that day-care centers deserve the trust of parents in the state of Washington"). You have probably not answered your research question for all time; you need not claim to be irrefutable.

Outlining and Organizing Your Draft

Word processors offer an outline planning and drafting tool often found in the View menu. This resource will prompt you to think critically about your organization. You may organize your outline by assigning outline levels to your headings or to individual paragraphs, letting the word processor automatically fashion your ordering into outline form. After you have outlined your text, you can display headings by hiding text, and you can manipulate text while you reorganize your thinking.

WRITING WITH A COMPUTER

Besides using the computer to outline your points, you can use it to develop a personalized system of coding using bold, italics, underlining, color, or other highlighting. Some writers like to organize their ideas around italicized questions, while others like to use bold headings. Some use a color scheme to show pro and con thinking; others highlight their main pro and con points. Think about the features on a computer that you can easily employ to make your ideas more visual and easier to organize.

Try to make the connections between parts of your paper clear. For example, summarizing the previous section of your paper will remind your reader of what you have already said. This strategy is especially handy in a long paper when, after a few pages, readers' memories may need refreshing.

As you write, document all the ideas, facts, summaries, and paraphrases you've drawn from your reading or field research. Right after every such borrowing, you need to refer your readers to the exact source of your material. Citing your sources as you draft saves fuss when you're putting your paper into final form. And it prevents unintentional plagiarism.

If you are following MLA style, note in your draft, right after each borrowed item, the name of the author and the page of the book or article you took it from. If you are quoting a field source, include the date of the interview or lecture and the name of the person speaking, if any. If you're using two or more works by the same author, you need one more detail to tell them apart: shorten the titles — the first word or phrase will do — and include the shortened title with the author's name.

For more on documenting sources, see Ch. 32. For advice on avoiding plagiarism, see pp. 592–94.

```
An assassin outrages us not only by his deed but also by his
unacceptable reason for violence. Nearly as offensive as his
act of wounding President Reagan was Hinckley's explanation
that he fired in order to impress screen star Jodie Foster
(Szasz, "Intentionality," 5).
```

The title in parentheses is short for "Intentionality and Insanity," the title of an article by Thomas Szasz, to distinguish it from another work by Szasz that the writer also cites — *The Myth of Mental Illness*.

When you include a direct quotation in your draft, you might as well save copying time. If your note is in a computer file, you can just copy the passage from the file and paste it right where you want it in your draft file. If it is on a note card, you can just tape the whole card into a handwritten or printed draft. If your draft looks sloppy, who cares?

As you lay the quotation into place, add a few words to introduce it. A brief transition might go something like this: *A more negative view of standardized intelligence tests is that of Harry S. Baum, director of the Sooner Research Center.* Then comes Baum's opinion that IQ tests aren't very reliable. The transition announces why Baum will be quoted—to refute a previous quotation in favor of IQ tests. The transition, brief as it is, tells readers a little about Baum by including his professional title. Knowing that he is a recognized authority would probably make readers willing to accept his expert view.

For more on transitions, see pp. 296–98.

If no transition occurs to you as you are placing a quotation or borrowed idea into your draft, don't sit around waiting for one. A series of slapped-in summaries and quotations makes rough reading, but you can make a marginal or bracketed note that you'll need to add a transition. Keep writing while the spirit moves you along; later, when you rewrite, you can add connective tissue.

INCORPORATING SOURCE MATERIAL: QUOTING, PARAPHRASING, NUTSHELLING

WWW
To practice quoting, paraphrasing, and nut-shelling, visit <www .bedfordstmartins.com/ bedguide/>.

Use Sources (and Don't Let Them Use You).   Sometimes you may end up discussing something that doesn't have much to do with your research question or thesis, perhaps because the material is interesting and you have a heap of it. Once you have written out a note, it's a great temptation to include it in your paper at all costs. Resist. Include only material that answers your research question. A note dragged in by force always sticks out like a pig in the belly of a boa constrictor.

For more on quoting, paraphrasing, and summarizing, see pp. 579–83.

When material fits, consider how to incorporate it. Quoting reproduces an author's exact words. Paraphrasing restates an author's ideas in your own words. Nutshelling extracts the essence of an author's meaning and states it "in a nutshell." You used these methods as you recorded your notes, and now you face the challenge of using them to incorporate your sources into your paper.

Summarize in a Nutshell.   To illustrate how nutshelling can serve you, let's first look at a passage from historian Barbara W. Tuchman. In *The Distant Mirror: The Calamitous Fourteenth Century* (New York: Knopf, 1978), Tuchman sets forth the effects of the famous plague known as the Black Death. In her foreword, she admits that any historian dealing with the Middle Ages faces difficulties. For one, large gaps exist in the recorded information. Here is Tuchman's original wording:

ORIGINAL

A greater hazard, built into the very nature of recorded history, is overload of the negative: the disproportionate survival of the bad side—of evil, misery, contention, and harm. In history this is exactly the same as in the daily newspaper. The normal does not make news. History is made by the documents that survive, and these lean heavily on crisis and calamity, crime and misbehavior, because such things are the subject matter of the documentary process — of lawsuits, treaties, moralists' denunciations, literary satire, papal Bulls. No Pope ever issued a Bull to approve of something. Negative overload can be seen at work in the religious reformer Nicolas de Clamanges, who, in denouncing unfit and worldly prelates in 1401, said that in his anxiety for reform he would not discuss the good clerics because "they do not count beside the perverse men."

Disaster is rarely as pervasive as it seems from recorded accounts. The fact of being on the record makes it appear continuous and ubiquitous whereas it is more likely to have been sporadic both in time and place. Besides, persistence of the normal is usually greater than the effect of disturbance, as we know from our own times. After absorbing the news of today, one expects to face a world consisting entirely of strikes, crimes, power failures, broken water mains, stalled trains, school shutdowns, muggers, drug addicts, neo-Nazis, and rapists. The fact is that one can come home in the evening — on a lucky day — without having encountered more than one or two of these phenomena.

This passage in a nutshell might be summarized as follows:

NUTSHELL

```
Tuchman reminds us that history lays stress on misery and
misdeeds because these negative events attracted notice
in their time and so were reported in writing; just as in
a newspaper today, bad news predominates. But we should
remember that suffering and social upheaval didn't pre-
vail everywhere all the time (xviii).
```

As you can see, this nutshell merely abstracts from the original. Not everything in the original has been preserved — not Tuchman's thought about papal bulls, not the examples such as Nicolas de Clamanges or the modern neo-Nazis. But the gist — the summary of the main idea — echoes Tuchman faithfully.

Before you write a nutshell, or summary, an effective way to sense the gist of a passage is to pare away examples, details, modifiers, offhand remarks, and nonessential points. Following is the original quotation from Tuchman as one student marked it up on a photocopy, crossing out elements she decided to omit from her paraphrase.

~~A greater hazard,~~ built into the ~~very~~ nature of recorded history, is ~~overload of the negative:~~ the disproportionate survival of the bad side — ~~of evil, misery, contention, and harm. In history~~ this is exactly the same as in the daily newspaper. ~~The normal does not make news. History is made by the~~ documents that survive, ~~and these~~ lean heavily on crisis and calamity, crime and misbehavior, because such things are the subject matter of the documentary process — ~~of lawsuits, treaties, moralists' denunciations, literary~~

satire, papal Bulls. ~~No Pope ever issued a Bull to approve of something.~~ ~~Negative overload can be seen at work in the religious reformer Nicolas de~~ ~~Clamanges, who, in denouncing unfit and worldly prelates in 1401, said~~ ~~that in his anxiety for reform he would not discuss the good clerics because~~ ~~"they do not count beside the perverse men."~~

Disaster is rarely as pervasive as it seems from recorded accounts. ~~The~~ ~~fact of being on the record makes it appear continuous and ubiquitous~~ ~~whereas~~ it is more likely to have been sporadic both in time and place. Be sides, persistence of the normal is usually greater than the effect of disturbance, as we know from our own times. ~~After absorbing the news of today,~~ ~~one expects to face a world consisting entirely of strikes, crimes, power fail-~~ ~~ures, broken water mains, stalled trains, school shutdowns, muggers, drug~~ ~~addicts, neo Nazis, and rapists. The fact is that one can come home in the~~ ~~evening—on a lucky day—without having encountered more than one or~~ ~~two of these phenomena.~~

Rewording what was left, she wrote the following nutshell version:

NUTSHELL

```
History, like a daily newspaper, reports more bad than
good. Why? Because the documents that have come down to
us tend to deal with upheavals and disturbances, which
are seldom as extensive and long-lasting as history books
might lead us to believe (Tuchman xviii).
```

In filling her nutshell, the student couldn't simply omit the words she had deleted. The result would have been less readable and still long. She knew she couldn't use Tuchman's very words: that would be plagiarism. To make a good, honest, compact nutshell that would fit smoothly into her research paper, she had to condense the passage into her own words.

Paraphrase in Your Own Words.   Sometimes you want to include more than the essence of a source, restating the details of an author's ideas in your own words as a paraphrase. In the following paraphrase of Tuchman's passage, notice how the writer has put Tuchman's ideas into other words but retained her major points and given her credit for the ideas.

PARAPHRASE

```
Tuchman points out that historians find some distortion
of the truth hard to avoid, for more documentation exists
for crimes, suffering, and calamities than for the events
of ordinary life. As a result, history may overemphasize
the negative. The author reminds us that we are familiar
with this process from our contemporary newspapers, in
```

which bad news is played up as being of greater interest
than good news. If we believed that newspapers told all
the truth, we would think ourselves threatened at all
times by technical failures, strikes, crime, and vio-
lence--but we are threatened only some of the time, and
normal life goes on. The good, dull, ordinary parts of
our lives do not make the front page, and praiseworthy
things tend to be ignored. "No Pope," says Tuchman, "ever
issued a Bull to approve of something." But in truth,
social upheaval did not prevail as widely as we might
think from the surviving documents of medieval life. Nor,
the author observes, can we agree with a critic of the
church, Nicolas de Clamanges, in whose view evildoers in
the clergy mattered more than men of goodwill (xviii).

In this reasonably complete and accurate paraphrase, about three-quarters the length of the original, most of Tuchman's points have been preserved and spelled out fully. The writer doesn't interpret or evaluate Tuchman's ideas — she only passes them on. Paraphrasing enables the writer to emphasize ideas important to her research. It also makes readers more aware of them as support for the writer's thesis than if the whole passage had been quoted directly. But notice that the writer has kept Tuchman's remark about papal bulls as a direct quotation because that statement is short and memorable, and it would be hard to improve on her words.

Often you paraphrase to emphasize one essential point. Here is an original passage from Evelyn Underhill's classic study *Mysticism* (New York: Doubleday, 1990):

ORIGINAL
In the evidence given during the process for St. Teresa's beatification, Maria de San Francisco of Medina, one of her early nuns, stated that on entering the saint's cell whilst she was writing this same "Interior Castle" she found her [St. Teresa] so absorbed in contemplation as to be unaware of the external world. "If we made a noise close to her," said another, Maria del Nacimiento, "she neither ceased to write nor complained of being disturbed." Both these nuns, and also Ana de la Encarnacion, prioress of Granada, affirmed that she wrote with immense speed, never stopping to erase or to correct, being anxious, as she said, to write what the Lord had given her before she forgot it.

Suppose that the names of the witnesses do not matter but that the researcher wishes to emphasize, in fewer words, the celebrated mystic's writing habits. To bring out that point, the writer might paraphrase the passage (and quote it in part) like this:

PARAPHRASE WITH QUOTATION

Evelyn Underhill has recalled the testimony of those who saw St. Teresa at work on The Interior Castle. Oblivious to noise, the celebrated mystic appeared to write in a state of complete absorption, driving her pen "with immense speed, never stopping to erase or to correct, being anxious, as she said, to write what the Lord had given her before she forgot it" (242).

AVOIDING PLAGIARISM

Here is a point we can't stress too strongly: when you write, never lift another writer's words or ideas without giving that writer due credit and transforming them into words of your own. If you do use words or ideas without giving credit, you are plagiarizing. You have seen in this chapter examples of honest nutshelling and paraphrasing. Introducing them into a paper, a writer would clearly indicate that their ideas belong to the originator, Barbara Tuchman or Evelyn Underhill. Now here are a few horrible examples—paraphrases of Tuchman's passage that lift, without thanks, her ideas and even her very words. Finding such gross borrowings in a paper, an instructor might hear the ringing of a burglar alarm. The first example lifts both thoughts and words.

PLAGIARIZED THOUGHTS AND WORDS

For Tuchman's original passage, see pp. 588–89.

Sometimes it's difficult for historians to learn the truth about the everyday lives of people from past societies because of the disproportionate survival of the bad side of things. Historical documents, like today's newspapers, tend to lean rather heavily on crisis, crime, and misbehavior. Reading the newspaper could lead one to expect a world consisting entirely of strikes, crimes, power failures, muggers, drug addicts, and rapists. In fact, though, disaster is rarely so pervasive as recorded accounts can make it seem.

What are the problems here? The phrase "the disproportionate survival of the bad side" is quoted directly from Tuchman's passage (line 2). The series "crisis, crime, and misbehavior" is too close to Tuchman's series "crisis and calamity, crime and misbehavior" (lines 5–6); only the words "and calamity" have been omitted. The words "lead one to expect a world consisting entirely" is almost the same as the original "one expects to face a world consisting entirely" (line 18). The phrase "strikes, crimes, power failures, muggers, drug addicts, and rapists" simply records—and in the same order—six of the ten examples Tuchman provides (lines 18–20). The last sentence in the plagiarized passage ("In fact, though, disaster is rarely so pervasive as recorded accounts can make it seem") is almost the same — and thus too close to the source — as the first sentence of Tuchman's second paragraph ("Disaster is rarely as pervasive as it seems from recorded accounts"). The student who attempted this paraphrase failed to comprehend Tuchman's passage sufficiently to be able to put Tuchman's ideas in his or her own words. Remember that taking useful notes from a source is a process of both writing and understanding what you read.

The second example is a more subtle theft, lifting thoughts but not words.

PLAGIARIZED THOUGHTS

```
It's not always easy to determine the truth about the
everyday lives of people from past societies because bad
news gets recorded a lot more frequently than good news
does. Historical documents, like today's newspapers, tend
to pick up on malice and disaster and ignore flat normal-
ity. If I were to base my opinion of the world on what I
see on the seven o'clock news, I would expect to see
death and destruction around me all the time. Actually,
though, I rarely come up against true disaster.
```

By using the first-person pronoun *I*, this student suggests that Tuchman's ideas are his own. That is just as dishonest as quoting without using quotation marks, as reprehensible as not citing the source of ideas.

The next example fails to make clear which ideas belong to the writer and which belong to Tuchman.

PLAGIARIZED WITH FAULTY CREDIT

```
Barbara Tuchman explains that it can be difficult for
historians to learn about the everyday lives of people
who lived a long time ago because historical documents
tend to record only the bad news. Today's newspapers are
like that, too: disaster, malice, and confusion take up a
lot more room on the front page than happiness and seren-
ity. Just as the ins and outs of our everyday lives go
unreported, we can suspect that upheavals do not really
play so important a part in the making of history as they
seem to do.
```

After rightfully attributing the ideas in the first sentence to Tuchman, the student researcher makes a comparison to today's world in sentence 2. Then in sentence 3, she returns to Tuchman's ideas without giving Tuchman credit. The placement of the final sentence suggests that this last idea is the student's whereas it is really Tuchman's. You can distinguish your ideas from those of your source by using some clear phrase or phrases of transition to introduce (As "Tuchman observes . . .") or conclude (". . . or so Tuchman affirms. In my own view . . .") your paraphrases.

As you write your paper, use ideas and words from your sources carefully, and credit those sources. Rely on quotation marks and other punctuation to show exactly which words come from your sources. Use the questions in the following checklist to help you avoid plagiarizing:

For more on quotation marks, ellipses, and brackets, see C3 in the "Quick Editing Guide" (the dark-blue-edged pages).

RESEARCH CHECKLIST

Avoiding Plagiarism

___ Have you identified the author of material you quote, paraphrase, or summarize? Have you credited the originator of facts and ideas you use?

___ Have you clearly indicated where another writer's ideas stop and yours begin?

___ Have you checked each paraphrase or summary against the original for accuracy? Do you use your own words? Do you avoid wording and sentence structure close to that in the original? Do you avoid misinterpreting or distorting the meaning of the original?

___ Have you checked each quotation against the original for accuracy? Have you used quotation marks for both passages and significant words taken directly from your source?

___ Have you used an ellipsis mark in brackets ([. . .]) to show where you have omitted something from the original? Have you used brackets ([ ]) to indicate your changes or additions in a quotation? Have you avoided distorting the meaning of the original?

■ Exercise

Paraphrasing

Study one of the following passages until you understand it thoroughly. Then, using your own words, write a paraphrase of the passage. Compare and contrast your version with those of your classmates. With their help, evaluate your own version: What are its strengths and weaknesses? Where should it be revised?

PASSAGE 1

Within the next decades education will change more than it has changed since the modern school was created by the printed book over three hundred years ago. An economy in which knowledge is becoming the true capital and the premier wealth-producing resource makes new and stringent demands on the schools for educational performance and educational responsibility. A society dominated by knowledge workers makes even newer—and even more stringent—demands for social performance and social responsibility. Once again we will have to think through what an educated person is. At the same time, how we learn and how we teach are changing drastically and fast—the result, in part, of new theoretical understanding of the learning process, in part of new technology. Finally, many of the traditional disciplines of the schools are becoming sterile, if not obsolescent. We thus also face changes in what we learn and teach and, indeed, in what we mean by knowledge.

— Peter F. Drucker, *The New Realities*

PASSAGE 2

When I look to the future of humanity beyond the twenty-first century, I see on my list of things to come the extension of our inquisitiveness from the objective domain of science to the subjective domain of feeling and memory. Homo sapiens, the exploring animal, will not be content with merely physical exploration. Our curiosity will drive us to explore the dimensions of the mind as vigorously as we explore the dimensions of space and time. For every pioneer who explores a new asteroid or a new planet, there will be another pioneer who explores from the inside the minds of our fellow passengers on planet Earth. It is our nature to strive to explore everything, alive and dead, present and past and future. When once the technology exists to read and write memories from one mind into another, the age of mental exploration will begin in earnest. Instead of admiring the beauties of nature from the outside, we will look at nature directly through the eyes of the elephant, the eagle, and the whale. We will be able, through the magic of science, to feel in our own minds the pride of the peacock and the wrath of the lion. That magic is no greater than the magic that enables me to see the rocking horse through the eyes of the child who rode it sixty years ago.

— Freeman Dyson, *Infinite in All Directions*

BEGINNING AND ENDING

Perhaps you will think of a good beginning and conclusion only after you have written the body of your paper. The head and tail of your paper might simply make clear your conclusion about whatever you have found out. But that is not the only way to begin and end a research paper.

Build to Your Finish.   Depending on the kind of paper you are writing, you might prefer to start out slowly by opening with a clear account of an event to draw your readers into the paper. You could then build up to a strong finish, saving your strongest argument until the end—after you have had the chance to present all the evidence to support your thesis. For example, if your paper argues that American children are being harmed by the national obsession with sports, you might wish to organize your paper something like this:

- Begin with a factual account of a real event, putting you and your reader on the same footing.

- Explore that event's implications to prepare your reader for your view.

- State your thesis (main idea): for example, "The national obsession with sports must end."

- Support your thesis with evidence and well-chosen sources, moving to your strongest argument.
- Then end with a rousing call to action:

```
For the sake of our children and the future of our coun-
try, isn't it time that we put the brakes on America's
sports mania? The youth of America have been sold a false
and harmful bill of goods. Let's stop such madness and
step off the carousel now. We owe that to the children of
America and to ourselves.
```

Sum Up the Findings of Others.　Still another way to begin a research paper is to summarize the work of other scholars. One research biologist, Edgar F. Warner, has reduced this time-tested opening to a formula.

> First, in one or two paragraphs, you review everything that has been said about your topic, naming the most prominent earlier commentators. Next you declare why all of them are wrong. Then you set forth your own claim, and you spend the rest of your paper supporting it.

That pattern may seem cut and dried, but it is clear and useful because it places your research and ideas into a historical and conceptual framework. If you browse in specialized journals in many fields — literary criticism, social studies, sciences — you may be surprised to see how many articles begin this very way. Of course, you don't need to damn every earlier commentator. One or two other writers may be enough to argue with. For example, a student writing on the American poet Charles Olson starts her research paper by disputing two views of him.

```
To Cid Corman, Charles Olson of Gloucester, Massachusetts,
is "the one dynamic and original epic poet twentieth-century
America has produced" (116). To Allen Tate, Olson is "a lo-
quacious charlatan" (McFinnery 92). The truth lies between
these two extremes, nearer to Corman's view.
```

For more strategies for opening and concluding, see pp. 291–94.

Whether or not you have fully stated your view at the beginning, you will certainly need to make it clear in your closing paragraph. A suggestion: before writing the last lines of your paper, read back over what you have already written. Then, without referring to your paper, try to put your view into writing.

Revising and Editing

For more revising and editing strategies, see Ch. 20.

Looking over your draft, you may find your essay changing. Don't be afraid to develop a whole new interpretation, shift the organization, strengthen your evidence, drop a section, or add a new one.

Have a classmate or friend read your draft and suggest how you might make your paper more informative, tightly reasoned, and interesting to read. Ask your peer editor to answer questions such as these about writing from sources:

- What is your overall reaction to this paper?

- What do you understand the research question to be? Does the writer answer that question?

- How effective is the opening? Does it draw you into the paper?

- How effective is the conclusion? Does it merely restate the introduction? Is it too abrupt or too hurried?

- Is the organization logical and easy to follow? Are there any places where the essay is hard to follow?

- Do you know which information is from the writer and which is from the research sources?

- Does the writer need all the quotations he or she has used?

- Do you have any questions about the writer's evidence or the conclusions drawn from the evidence? Point out any areas where the writer has not fully backed up his or her conclusions.

- If this were your paper, what is the one thing you would be sure to work on before handing it in?

FOR PEER RESPONSE

For general questions for a peer editor, see pp. 323–24.

As you revise the draft of your research paper, answering these questions may help you see how to improve your essay:

REVISION CHECKLIST

___ Have you honestly said something, not just heaped facts and statements by other writers that don't add up to anything?

___ Is your thesis (main idea) clear?

___ Have you included only evidence that makes a point? Do all your points support your main idea?

___ Does each new idea or piece of information follow from the one before it? Can you see any stronger order in which to arrange things? Have you provided transitions to connect the parts?

___ Do you need more—or better—evidence to back up any point? If so, where might you find it?

___ Are the words that you quote truly memorable? Are your paraphrases and summaries accurate and clear?

___ Is the source of every quotation, every fact, every idea you have borrowed made unmistakably clear?

WRITING WITH A COMPUTER

Revising a Research Paper

To help you step back from a draft, begin revising by duplicating your file. (Use a command such as Save As or Versions from the File menu.) This step is important because it will enable you to experiment with your work without losing your existing draft. Your software may also have a useful resource such as Track Changes in the Tools menu. By using colors and cross-outs to highlight text and record comments, this resource allows writers to see the changes they make in a text. It can even automatically compare documents so that you can revise freely and then see how much your writing has changed from the previous draft.

After you have revised your research paper, edit and proofread it. Look carefully for problems with grammar, word choice, punctuation, and mechanics — and then correct any problems you may find. Be sure you check your documentation, too — how you identify the sources of quotations and how you list the works you have cited in your paper. Here are some questions to get you started editing and proofreading your paper:

For more help, turn to the dark-blue-edged pages, and find the "Quick Editing Guide" section noted here.

EDITING CHECKLIST	
___ Have you used commas correctly, especially in complicated sentences that quote or refer to sources?	C1
___ Have you punctuated quotations correctly?	C3
___ Have you used capital letters correctly, especially in titles of sources?	D1
___ Have you used correct manuscript form?	E1
___ Have you used correct documentation style?	E2

Documenting Sources

A research paper calls on you to follow special rules in documenting your sources — in citing them as you write and in listing them at the end of your paper. At first, these rules may seem fiendishly fussy, but research papers that follow the rules are easy to read and easy to set into type. The rules also ensure that any interested reader can use complete and accurate source information to look up the original materials.

In humanities courses and the social sciences, most writers of research papers follow the style of the Modern Language Association (MLA) or the American Psychological Association (APA). Your instructor will probably suggest which style to follow; if you are not told, use MLA. The first time you prepare a research paper according to MLA or APA rules, you'll need extra time to look up exactly what to do in each situation.

For more on documenting sources, see Ch. 32.

CITING SOURCES IN YOUR TEXT

When you use a short direct quotation, four lines or fewer, you must put quotation marks around the words you're using from your source and cite the author and page number. For a quotation longer than four lines, indent the entire quotation in your text, without quotation marks, and also note its source. In both cases, you may include the author's name either in the text of the essay — as in the following example of a short quotation — or in parentheses with the page number at the end of the quotation.

For more on punctuation in quotations, see C3 in the "Quick Editing Guide" (the dark-blue-edged pages).

```
Johnson heavily emphasizes the importance of "giving the
child what she needs at the precise moment in her life when
it will do the most good" (23).
```

You also can indicate your source in a terse phrase — "Barbara W. Tuchman believes that . . ." or "According to Tuchman . . ." — and then give the page number in parentheses after your quotation, paraphrase, or summary.

For more on citing sources, see pp. 616–21 (MLA) or pp. 631–34 (APA).

LISTING SOURCES AT THE END

At the very end of a research paper, you list all the sources you have cited — books, articles, Web sites, interviews, and other materials. This list is usually the last thing you write. If your working bibliography includes in each source note all the necessary information, your list of sources will be easy to construct. Simply arrange the works you used in alphabetical order and type the information about each, following the MLA or APA guidelines. The MLA specifies that you call your list "Works Cited"; the APA, "References." Your list should include only the works actually mentioned in your paper. Simply file away any leftovers — notes for sources you haven't used after all — for any future writing about the subject you may do. Resist the temptation to use them to lengthen your list.

For the source information you need to record, see pp. 542–44.

For specific MLA and APA guidelines, see Ch. 32.

OTHER ASSIGNMENTS

Using library, Internet, and field sources, write a research paper on one of the following topics or another that your instructor approves. Proceed as if you had chosen to work on the main assignment described on page 534.

1. Investigate the career opportunities in a line of work that interests you. Include data from interviews conducted with people in the field.
2. Write a paper discussing the progress being made in the prevention and cure of a disease or syndrome, including current data.
3. Discuss recent political or economic changes in another country.
4. Compare student achievement in schools with different characteristics — for example, those with limited or extensive computer access or those with low and high numbers of students who move.

WRITING WITH A COMPUTER

Using Software to Document Sources

Programs such as *Citation, EndNote, Reference Manager,* and *Pro Cite* can help you to build a database of bibliographic information and generate citations in the style required by your instructor. You can also go to <www.mla.org> or <www.apa.org/journals> to get advice and style updates for the MLA and APA documentation styles.

5. Study the growth of telecommuting—people working in their homes and keeping in touch with the main office by phone, fax, and e-mail.
6. Write a portrait of life in your town or neighborhood as it was in the past, using sources such as local library archives, photographs or other visual evidence, articles in the local newspaper, and interviews with long-time residents or a local historian.
7. Write a short history of your immediate family, drawing on interviews, photographs, scrapbooks, old letters, unpublished records, and any other available sources.
8. Study the reasons students today give for going to college. Gather your information from interviews with a variety of students at your college and possibly from questionnaires.
9. Investigate a current trend you have noticed on television, collecting evidence by observing news shows, other programs, or commercials.
10. Write a survey of recent films of a certain kind (such as horror movies, comedies, or love stories), supporting your generalizations with evidence from your film watching.

Applying What You Learn: Some Uses of Research

In College Courses.   In many courses beyond your English course, you will be asked to write papers incorporating library, Internet, and field research.

- Some courses require you to write short papers using a few sources rather than a full research project, but instructors still expect you to use all your research skills—finding, evaluating, and documenting relevant sources or conducting your own field research.
- The more deeply you move into specialized courses for your major, the more independent research and thinking you will do. Some colleges require a long research paper of all seniors to graduate.
- In some courses, you may be asked to prepare a review of the literature or an annotated bibliography on a topic or research question. To do so, you will need to locate, evaluate, and summarize major sources in the field.

In the Workplace.   Many workplaces demand writing based on research to support the development and distribution of their products and services.

- Large companies often maintain their own specialized libraries because information and opinions are worth money and are necessary for decision-making. If you should take an entry-level job at corporate headquarters, don't be surprised to be told, "We're opening a branch office in Sri Lanka, and the V.P. doesn't know a thing about the place. Can you write a report on it—customs, geography, climate, government, state of the economy, political stability, religion, lifestyle, and all that?"

- If you start your own business, plan to spend time investigating print, electronic, and human resources to determine market segment, growth trends, budgeting, strategic planning, and product development.

- At a large city newspaper, reporters and feature writers continually conduct library and Internet research as well as field interviews and surveys. The newspaper's library of clippings on subjects covered in the past (the "morgue") is in constant use.

In the Community.   Research often benefits the community where you live.

- If you oppose a business building a factory in your neighborhood that you think might be environmentally unsound, your research on zoning laws and environmental issues will strengthen your appeal to the local planning commission.

- As a volunteer at the local women's shelter, you may want to persuade board members to open a second facility. Researching other community shelters, citing authoritative sources, and composing your findings into a research report will allow you to argue effectively for your view.

- Research can be a great help when you or an organization intends to purchase something—be it a new kitchen for the community center or a new car for yourself. Knowing where to find sources and how to look at them will help you make balanced, reasoned decisions.

A Sample Research Paper

In her paper "Is Inclusion the Answer?" Sarah E. Goers grapples with the complex topic of equal access to education for disabled students. By drawing on a variety of sources, Goers is able to show both sides of the issue while forming her own conclusions about her topic. As a result, her paper is more than just a compilation of facts or a string of quotations. Goers sets forth a problem that troubles her, she provides evidence to support her concern, and she adds her own thoughts to the facts and ideas she has gleaned from her research.

Writer's last name, followed by page number in small roman numerals, on upper right corner of all pages of outline

"Outline" centered, one inch from top

Main idea stated in thesis

Double-spacing throughout

Sentence outline is a skeleton of the research paper

WWW
For more sample student research papers, visit <www.bedfordstmartins.com/bedguide/>.

Goers i

1"   ½"

Outline

Is Inclusion the Answer?

Thesis: The full inclusion of disabled children into mainstream classrooms may not truly be in the best interest of every student.

I.   The practice and degree of inclusion is debated among many groups.

    a. Current options include full inclusion, partial inclusion, and separate programs.

    b. Teacher organizations feel that disabled students need specialized instruction in separate programs, at least part of the time, to meet their needs.

    c. Opponents of full inclusion fear that it will negatively affect mainstream schools.

    d. Disabled children have equal rights to free public education.

II.   The actual implementation of inclusive practices may have negative consequences.

    a. Without promised federal funding, schools may have to spend general funds on special education, possibly at the expense of other scholastic areas.

    b. General education teachers are often not adequately prepared to accommodate special needs students in their classrooms.

    c. Resources needed for specialized instruction are often inadequate in public schools.

III. Some parents of disabled students and students themselves oppose inclusion.

    a. Children are happy with the services offered by special education schools, and parents don't want their learning disrupted.

    b. Parents fear their children will "fall through the cracks," especially if separate schools close before solid programs are established in general schools.

IV. Pull-out programs have been proposed as a solution.

    a. Students experience the general classroom and also receive specialized instruction.

    b. Pull-out programs are still subject to the same concerns raised by full inclusion.

    c. Disabled students deserve respect for their individual needs.

Writer's last name and page number ½" from top of page

Goers 1

Writer's name

Instructor's name

Course

Date

Title, centered

Sarah E. Goers

Professor Day

English 101

28 January 2001

½" indent (or 5 spaces)

Is Inclusion the Answer?

Opening definition of "inclusion," citing sources in parentheses

Inclusion is one of the most passionately debated issues in public education today. Full inclusion, defined as placing all students with disabilities in general education classes, has three main components: the integration of special education students into the mainstream classroom, educational planning and programming, and the clarification of responsibility for appropriate instruction (Heinich 292). Al-

Thesis established

though the intent of inclusion is to provide the best care for all children by treating both special and general education students equally, some people in the field believe that the full inclusion of disabled children in mainstream classrooms may not be in the best interest of

Brief overview of paper's development following thesis

either type of student. Disabled children will not benefit from a general education program unless the school is prepared to accommodate their needs; if placed in a school where their needs are not met due to low funding, unprepared teachers, or a lack of necessary resources, they most likely will suffer. For these reasons, the merits of full inclusion over partial inclusion or separate programs are questionable.

Double spacing throughout

Although individual children learn differently, students classified as "special needs" require significantly different types of instruction because of their physical, mental, or

Goers 2

emotional state. The degree of differentiated
instruction that they require, and how best to
provide it, is the basis of the ongoing debate
about inclusion. Initially, full inclusion
sounds like a wonderful step toward implementing the democratic belief that all people in
all environments are to be treated as equals.
In her lecture at William Rainey Harper College, however, Barbara Radebaugh explained the
positions of the two major national teacher organizations on this issue.

*Lecturer's name identifies
public address*

The American Federation of Teachers (AFT)
disagrees with full inclusion, believing that
special needs students learn best in separate
programs where they can receive the specialized
instruction their disabilities require. On the
other hand, the National Education Association
(NEA) favors "appropriate inclusion," a less
extreme approach, in which each special needs
student would receive a combination of general
and special education throughout the school day
(Radebaugh). In this way, students would experience the general classroom while still receiving some degree of specialized instruction.

While the teacher organizations debate the
benefits of inclusion in terms of how disabled
students learn best, other groups oppose inclusion because of how the changes might affect
them. At a typical school, if a disabled student were to be placed in general education
classrooms, the school would have to undergo
changes including teacher training and a larger
staff, both to assist the special needs child

Goers 3

and to aid other students' adjustment to an inclusive environment (Block 6-7). Some opponents
of inclusion include the parents of non-learn-
ing disabled students who fear that these
changes will result in less attention for their
own children and thus slow their academic
progress. Other opponents, such as local taxpayers, cite the cost of these changes as reasons against inclusion (Rios).

In response to such arguments, protective
laws have been enacted to ensure disabled persons equal access to appropriate public education, regardless of extra cost or others'
fears. The Education for All Handicapped Children Act of 1975 mandates that schools must
provide free public education to all students
with disabilities. The main tenets of the 1975
legislation declare that all learners with
handicaps between the ages of three and twenty-
one have the right to a free public education
and an individualized education program involving both the school and the parents. Also protecting the disabled is the Individuals with
Disabilities Education Act (IDEA), which calls
for serving children with disabilities in the
least restrictive environment possible, and
Section 504 of the Rehabilitation Act, which
guarantees disabled people access to services
provided by any institution that receives federal funding (Heinich 293).

Society has made great strides in protecting the rights of disabled students, and inclusion theoretically upholds their right to free

No page number needed for one-page article

Point from last paragraph used for transition to new topic

Source establishes histori-cal background

Goers 4

and equal education. There is still concern
about the actual implementation of inclusive
practices, however. In California, for example,
journalist Denise Rios explains a situation
whereby, as more parents opt to place children
with special needs in regular classrooms,
"state and education officials are grappling
with several issues that could affect the future of special education. At the top of their
list is funding." According to Rios, finan-
cially strapped school districts use as much as
25% of their general funds to pay for federally
mandated special education programs. Officials
explain that this high percentage is a result
of the federal government's not fulfilling its
monetary promises, costing local districts in
California about $600 million a year (Rios).
Money must be taken from other scholastic areas
to supplement the lack of funding designated
for special education.

    To help offset the expensive cost of inte-
grating disabled students into the regular
classroom, California officials contend that
the federal government promised to fund 40% of
program costs when federal mandates guarantee-
ing access for special education students were
passed in 1975. However, government contribution has actually averaged only 7% or 8% of
program costs (Rios). While money ideally
should not be an issue when it comes to the
well-being of students, the figures in a situation such as this are troubling. Since special
education may demand a large amount of the

Brief quotation specifies critical issue, followed by paraphrase of source

Facts and data support main point

Goers 5

already tight funds that most districts are working with, schools may be forced to use a high percentage of these limited resources on a minority of students, rather than the entire school. Without proper financial support from the government, money unfortunately does become an issue when it threatens to undermine the well-being of the majority of students.

When inclusive practices are implemented, teachers as well as students are forced to undergo dramatic classroom changes. Teachers feel a great deal of pressure in this debate in that many believe that they are not adequately trained to teach students with disabilities effectively. They are concerned that special needs students will therefore not receive the instruction that they need to succeed, and these teachers may be frustrated by their inability to provide appropriate instruction (Block 7). Without significant help from special education teachers in the regular classroom, teachers fear that inclusion could result in disaster due to their frustrations, lack of appropriate training, and students' distraction levels. Linda Jacobson describes the dilemma of general education instruction: "Because special education teachers often float among classes, regular classroom teachers sometimes are left on their own." She also notes the AFT's criticism of inclusive practices when "teachers are promised resources and training to make inclusion work, but school systems often don't deliver" (Jacobson).

Community College of Baltimore County pro-

Paraphrase of original source, followed by source in parentheses

Only one citation needed for quotations from the same source that appear in sequence in a paragraph

Goers 6

fessor Beth Hewett finds that while teachers
receive information about a specific student's
disability and how to offer fair classroom
treatment, this information is usually only
cursory. She eloquently echoes Jacobson's concerns through firsthand experience:

> Our experiences with these students
> often are frustrating and unsatisfy-
> ing because we do not know enough
> about how to help them. Recognizing
> our limited knowledge and skills in
> helping students with disabilities to
> read and write well, we often floun-
> der and leave teaching situations
> feeling that we have missed a key op-
> portunity to help a student address a
> particular challenge. Many of us
> would welcome rescue through more
> practical knowledge of the problems,
> better training to recognize and deal
> with them, and access to technologi-
> cal tools that address special needs.
> We sense that our students would be
> equally grateful if we were better
> prepared. (Hewett 1-2)

After observing the methods of teachers at
the Landmark Institute, a private postsecondary
institution renowned for its work with learning
disabled students, Jacob Gaskins notes the importance of putting students through a battery
of diagnostic testing and then teaching specifically to these diagnoses in a variety of
modalities. In an institution like Landmark,
with a student/faculty ratio of approximately 3

*Direct quotation longer
than four lines set off from
text without quotation
marks, followed by source
in parentheses*

to 1, teachers are able to tailor their instruction to give students personal attention.
The sheer number of teachers, all of whom have
training specific to all types of learning disabilities, along with access to, and training
in how to use, supplemental learning tools, enables them to meet the wide range of needs and
disabilities they encounter (73). Because these
resources are not often adequately provided in
public schools, however, many teachers wonder
if inclusion is truly beneficial for students
who have disabilities that require specialized
instruction.

Valuable information paraphrased after naming author earlier in paragraph and noting page number of original source in parentheses

Some parents of disabled students and some
disabled students themselves also do not agree
with full inclusion. Mary Mushard explains in
her article, "Special Schools Fall Victim to
Inclusion," that many disabled students prefer
to learn in a special education school because
they like the small class sizes, the nurturing
staff specifically trained to teach special
needs students, the family atmosphere, and the
many available specialized services. The parents of these students do not want to disrupt a
system which their children are happy with and
are afraid that their children will "fall
through the cracks" in the general educational
system. Unfortunately, many special education
schools are being closed due to low enrollment,
mainly because those parents who support inclusion have taken their disabled children out of
special schools and placed them in regular education classes. Among parents who do favor inclusion, some nonetheless worry that the coun-

Goers 8

try is moving away from special education schools too fast for solid special education programs to be established in the general schools (Mushard).

As a solution, pull-out programs--in which disabled students are in the regular classroom for part of the day and special instruction classes for the remainder of the day--have been suggested. In this way, disabled students would have daily classroom instruction as well as one-on-one instruction. These programs offer a compromise to address the concerns of some educators that the individual needs of disabled students would be neglected when they are integrated into the general classroom (Block 7). However, while ensuring that at least part of the students' day will consist of instruction tailored to their needs, these programs do not ensure that the students' time in the general classroom will be productive. These programs are promising, but only to the extent that the students will also be receiving quality instruction in the general classroom; otherwise, they simply shorten the amount of unproductive classroom time. Thus, there is still a need for teacher training and adequate resources to help meet the needs of disabled students when they are not in the special education classes (Urbina).

Despite individual beliefs about which system is best, we can reasonably assume that the majority of society supports efforts to provide all children with the best possible care and education. When considering inclusion,

Possible solution or compromise follows various sides of argument

Writer gives credit to source after summarizing, or nutshelling, the ideas from the source

Electronic sources without page numbers cited only by author

Goers 9

it is necessary to look at the big picture by
considering everyone involved. Unless the
school is adequately prepared to provide proper
services and meet students' individual needs,
inclusion truly may not be the best solution
for disabled students. If we want our children
to be as successful as they possibly can be,
each individual should be assessed and placed
where he or she will learn most effectively,
whether in a general classroom, a special education classroom, or a combination of both.
While many people support inclusion because
they feel that it is wrong to exclude anyone,
they must also look at the potential problems
inclusion may cause. Disabled students should
receive proper respect for their needs without
the intrusion of policy, funding, and what others, particularly those who are uninformed
about the issue, decide they want.

*Conclusion summarizes
main points and restates
thesis*

Goers 10

Works Cited

Block, Martin E. "Did We Jump on the Wrong
    Bandwagon? Problems with Inclusion."
    <u>Palestra</u> 15.3 (1999): 4-10. 10 Oct. 2000
    <http://www.palestra.com/Inclusion.html>.

Gaskins, Jacob. "Teaching Writing to Students
    with Learning Disabilities: The Landmark
    Method." <u>Teaching English in the Two-Year</u>
    <u>College</u> 22.2 (1995): 71-76.

Heinich, Robert, ed. <u>Educating All Handicapped</u>
    <u>Children</u>. Englewood Cliffs, NJ:
    Educational Technology Publications,
    1979.

Hewett, Beth. "Helping Students with Learning
    Disabilities: Collaboration between Writ-
    ing Centers and Special Services." <u>The</u>
    <u>Writing Lab</u> 25.3 (2000): 1-4.

Jacobson, Linda. "Disabled Kids Moving into
    Regular Classrooms." <u>Atlanta Journal</u> 5 May
    1994: C1.

Mushard, Mary. "Special Schools Fall Victim to
    Inclusion." <u>The Sun</u> 13 June 1993: B1. 21
    Sept. 2000 <http://infoweb1.newsbank.com/
    bin/gate.exe?f=doc&state=pbs5k2.3.3>.

Radebaugh, Barbara. "NEA vs. AFT." Education
    201-002 Lecture. William Rainey Harper
    College, Palatine, IL. 21 Jan. 1999.

Rios, Denise A. "Special Students Joining Regu-
    lar Classrooms." <u>Orange County Register</u> 9
    June 1994. 11 Nov. 2000 <http://infoweb1
    .newsbank.com/bin/gate.exe?f=doc&state=
    pbs5k.2.3.46>.

List of works cited on a separate page

List alphabetized by authors' last names

First line of entry at left margin

Subsequent lines indented ½"

For more on citing sources, see Ch. 32.

Goers 11

Urbina, Yolanda. "Full Inclusion of Disabled
    Children in a Regular Classroom." 8 Aug.
    1998. 15 Oct. 2000 <http://www.lgc.edu/
    academic/educatn/yolanda/lai.htm>.

Chapter 32

Documenting Sources

MLA Style   616
APA Style   631

When writers use information from other sources — written or spoken — they must *document* those sources. That is, in the text of their paper they cite, or identify, the exact source (book or article with page number, person interviewed, television program, Web site) for every fact or idea, paraphrased or quoted, from their research. At the end of the paper, they list the sources that were cited. The purpose of citing and listing sources is twofold: (1) to give proper credit to the original writer or speaker and (2) to enable any interested reader to look up a source for further information. The mechanics of documentation may seem fussy, but the obligation to cite and list sources keeps research writers truthful and responsible.

Writers of college research papers most often follow the rules for citing and listing sources from either of two style manuals — one compiled by the Modern Language Association (MLA) and the other by the American Psychological Association (APA). The documentation style of the MLA is generally observed in English composition, literature, history, foreign languages, and other humanities courses. APA documentation style usually prevails in the social sciences and business. If your research takes you into scholarly or professional journals in those special areas, you will probably find that the articles there follow a recognizable style. Other disciplines follow other style manuals: *Scientific Style and Format: The CBE Style Manual for Authors, Editors, and Publishers of the Council of Biology Editors* (1994), for instance, is used in the sciences and medicine.

You need not memorize any of the documentation styles. Instead, you should understand that you will use different styles in different disciplines, and you need to practice using at least one style to become accustomed to scholarly practices. For your composition course, more than likely your instructor will ask you to use the MLA style. The sample paper in Chapter 31 illustrates the use of this style.

This chapter is here for handy reference. We try to tell you no more than you will need to know to write a first-year research paper. Knowing MLA style or APA style will be useful at these moments:

> *Citing while you write.* You'll need to use a documentation style any time you want to document (often on a note card or in your paper) exactly

where you obtained a fact, statistic, idea, opinion, quotation, graph, or chart.

For advice on preparing a list of works cited, see pp. 621–31.

Listing all your sources. You'll need to use a documentation style when you prepare a final bibliography (a list entitled "Works Cited" or "References").

Citing Sources: MLA Style

For a brief overview of MLA style, see E2 in the "Quick Editing Guide" (the dark-blue-edged pages).

The *MLA Handbook for Writers of Research Papers,* Fifth Edition (New York: MLA, 1999) supplies extensive and exact recommendations for citing sources in your paper and then listing them at the end in a section titled "Works Cited." If you want more detailed advice than that given here, you can purchase a copy of the *MLA Handbook* or consult a copy in the reference room of your college library.

PRINTED SOURCES: NONFICTION BOOKS

AUTHOR NOT NAMED IN SENTENCE

To cite a book in the text of your paper, you can place in parentheses the author's last name and the number of the page containing the information cited.

```
At least one critic maintains that Dean Rusk's exposure to
Nazi power in Europe in the 1930s "scarred his mind, leading
him to share Acheson's hostility to appeasement in any form
anywhere" (Karnow 194).
```

AUTHOR NAMED IN SENTENCE

For the sake of readability and transition, you'll sometimes want to mention an author in your text. In this case, put only the page number in parentheses.

```
Morgan claims that one reason we admire Simone de Beauvoir
is that "she lived the life she believed" (58).
```

AUTHOR UNKNOWN

For a source with an unknown author, use the complete title in your sentence or a word or two from the title in parentheses. If a source is sponsored by a corporation or other group, name the sponsor as the author.

```
According to a recent study, drivers are 42% more likely to
get into an accident if they are using a wireless phone
while driving ("Driving Dangerously" 32).
```

LONG QUOTATION

When a quotation is longer than four typed lines, indent the entire quotation one inch or ten spaces. Double-space it, but don't place quotation marks around it. If the quotation is one paragraph or less, begin its first line without any extra paragraph indentation.

```
Cynthia Griffin Wolff comments on Emily Dickinson's incisive
use of language:
           Language, of course, was a far subtler weapon than
           a hammer. Dickinson's verbal maneuvers would in-
           creasingly reveal immense skill in avoiding a
           frontal attack; she preferred the silent knife of
           irony to the strident battering of loud complaint.
           She had never suffered fools gladly. The little
           girl who had written of a dull classmate, "He is
           the silliest creature that ever lived I think,"
           grew into a woman who could deliver wrath and
           contempt with excruciating economy and cunning.
           Scarcely submissive, she had acquired the cool
           calculation of an assassin. (170-171)
```

TWO OR THREE AUTHORS

Include each author's last name either in your text or in the parenthetical citation.

```
Taylor and Wheeler present yet another view (25).
```

MORE THAN THREE AUTHORS

Give the names of all the authors, or use only the last name of the first author listed, followed by the abbreviation *et al.* (Latin for "and others"). Present the source the same way in your list of works cited.

```
In the years between 1870 and 1900, the nation's cities grew
at an astonishing rate, mostly as a result of internal and
international movement of people (Roark et al. 422).
```

MULTIPLE WORKS BY THE SAME AUTHOR

If you cite two or more works by the same author, use an abbreviated title to indicate which one you are citing in your text. In a paper that uses two books by Ann Charters, *Major Writers of Short Fiction* and *The Story and Its Writer,* you would cite them as follows:

```
Having done extensive studies of short fiction, Charters be-
lieves that "the range and quality of the writer's mind are
the only limitations on a story's shape" (Story 3).
```

```
One observer notes the changing tide of short fiction, rep-
resented in part by the flood of magazine fiction which car-
ries with it "stories of real distinction" (Charters, Major
Writers 1408).
```

A MULTIVOLUME WORK

For a work with multiple volumes, provide the author's name and the volume number, followed by a colon and the page number.

```
In ancient times, astrological predictions were sometimes
used as a kind of black magic (Sarton 2: 319).
```

INDIRECT SOURCE

Whenever possible, cite the original source. If that source is unavailable to you (as often happens with published accounts of spoken remarks), use the abbreviation *qtd. in* (for "quoted in") before the secondary source you cite in parentheses.

```
Zill says that, psychologically, children in stepfamilies
most resemble children in single-parent families, even if
they live in a two-parent household (qtd. in Derber 119).
```

PRINTED SOURCES: LITERATURE

NOVEL OR SHORT STORY

Give the page number from your source first. If possible, include further identifying information, such as the section or chapter where the passage can be found in any edition.

```
In A Tale of Two Cities, Dickens describes the aptly named
Stryver as "shouldering himself (morally and physically)
into companies and conversations, that argued well for his
shouldering his way up in life" (110; bk. 2, ch. 4).
```

PLAY

For a verse play, list the act, scene, and line numbers, separated by periods.

```
"Love," Iago says, "is merely a lust of the blood and a per-
mission of the will" (Othello 1.3.326).
```

POETRY

When quoting poetry, add a slash mark to show where each new line begins. Use the word *line* or *lines* in the first reference but only numbers in subsequent references, as in the following examples from William Wordsworth's "The World Is Too Much with Us." The first reference:

```
"The world is too much with us; late and soon / Getting and
spending, we lay waste our powers" (lines 1-2).
```

The subsequent reference:

```
"Or hear old Triton blow his wreathed horn" (14).
```

If a poem has multiple parts, cite the part and line numbers, separated by a period. Do not include the word *line*.

```
In "Ode: Intimations of Immortality," Wordsworth ponders the
truths of human existence, "Which we are toiling all our
lives to find, / In darkness lost, the darkness of the
grave" (8.116-117).
```

A WORK IN AN ANTHOLOGY

For works in an anthology, cite the author of the selection — not the editor of the collection.

```
As Julio Marzán's "The Ingredient" opens, Vincent looks down
on his neighborhood from a rooftop, realizing that "there
was a kind of beauty to the view" (145).
```

PRINTED SOURCES: REFERENCE BOOKS AND PERIODICALS

ARTICLE IN A REFERENCE BOOK

In citing a one-page article from a work with entries arranged alphabetically, include the author's name and omit the page number.

```
One unusual definition of love calls it the force that en-
ables individuals to "understand the separateness of other
people" (Havell).
```

If a reference article is longer than one page, include the page number.

```
Gordon discusses Carver's "implosive" technique of ending
stories just before epiphany (176).
```

If the article is unsigned, identify a brief title in your text or in parentheses.

```
She alienated many feminists with her portraits of women
"who seemed to accept victimization" ("Didion").
```

JOURNAL ARTICLE

Follow the same format used for a nonfiction book, citing author and page number.

```
Arthur seeks a goal "beyond the immediate context of the
narrative" (Mueller 751).
```

MAGAZINE OR NEWSPAPER ARTICLE

In citing a one-page article, include the author's name in your text or in parentheses. Do not include the page number, which will be noted in the list of works cited at the end of the paper.

```
Vacuum-tube audio equipment is making a comeback, with
aficionados praising the warmth and glow from the tubes, as
well as the sound (Patton).
```

When citing articles longer than one page, provide the specific page number or numbers in the parenthetical reference.

```
Some less than perfect means have been used to measure tele-
vision viewership, including a sensor that scans rooms for
"hot bodies" (Larson 69).
```

For an anonymous magazine article, cite the first few words of its title in parentheses. Begin with the word by which it is alphabetized in the list of works cited.

```
In a new take on the concept of "road rage," Newsweek re-
ports that a consortium of businesses in London has called
for a sidewalk speed lane to weed out "dawdlers" ("Speed
Bump").
```

THE BIBLE

Include the version, book, and chapter and verse numbers when referencing a specific quotation.

```
"What He has seen and heard, of that He testifies" (New
American Bible, John 3.32).
```

ELECTRONIC AND OTHER NONPRINT SOURCES

WEB SITE

Treat a Web site as you would a print source, indicating the author (or, if no author, a brief title) in parentheses or in the text. If the source lacks stable pagination, do not include page numbers in your citation.

```
The five-year survival rate for a woman with localized
breast cancer is 93 percent (Bruckheim).
```

ONLINE ARTICLE

You may cite an online article in parentheses or weave it into your paper. No page or paragraph numbers are needed unless supplied online.

```
Robert S. Boynton's article in The Atlantic Monthly Online
explores the recent achievements and popularity of the new
African American intellectuals.
```

INTERVIEW

```
In a recent interview, nutritionist Christina Diaz discussed
how control issues can trigger eating disorders among teens,
especially girls.
```

RECORDING

```
Hearing Yeats reading "The Song of the Old Mother" on tape
sheds new light on the poem.
```

Listing Sources: MLA Style

At the end of your paper, you need to list the sources from which you have cited ideas or information. When you follow the MLA style, title this list "Works Cited" and center the title at the top of a new page. Double-space the list, and alphabetize the entries by authors' last names or, for works with no author, by title. When an entry exceeds one line, indent the following lines one-half inch (or five spaces). Include only those sources actually cited in your paper.

BOOKS

The information about each source is divided into three sections, each followed by a period — author or agency's name (if there is one), title, and publishing information. Give the author's name, last name first, and the title in full as they appear on the title page. (If a work has more than one author, all names after the first are given in normal order.) If the publisher lists more than one city, include just the first. Use just the first name of a publisher with multiple names: not "Holt, Rinehart and Winston," but simply "Holt." Omit initials: for "J. B. Lippincott Co.," simply write "Lippincott." Also omit terms such as *Press, Inc.,* and *Co.,* except when naming university presses. (Use *UP,* as in *Oxford UP.*) You should use the most recent copyright date in your entry.

SINGLE AUTHOR

Lincoln, Kenneth. <u>Men Down West</u>. Santa Barbara, CA: Capra, 1997.

TWO OR THREE AUTHORS

Name the authors in the order in which they are listed on the title page.

Phelan, James R., and Lewis Chester. <u>The Money: The Battle for Howard Hughes's Billions</u>. New York: Random, 1997.

FOUR OR MORE AUTHORS

Give the names of all the authors, or give only the name of the first author listed, followed by *et al.* for "and others." Identify the source in the same way you cite it in the text.

Roark, James L., et al. <u>The American Promise</u>. Boston: Bedford, 1998.

MULTIPLE WORKS BY THE SAME AUTHOR

Use the author's name for the first entry only; for subsequent entries, replace the name with three hyphens and a period. List works alphabetically by title.

Gould, Stephen Jay. <u>Full House: The Spread of Excellence from Plato to Darwin</u>. New York: Harmony, 1996.

---, ed. <u>Questioning the Millennium</u>. New York: Harmony, 1997.

CORPORATE AUTHOR

Cite the name of the organization as author. (The name may reappear as the publisher.)

Student Conservation Association. <u>The Guide to Graduate Environmental Programs</u>. Washington: Island, 1997.

UNKNOWN AUTHOR

Start with the work's title.

The New International Atlas. Chicago: Rand-McNally, 1998.

EDITED BOOK

If your paper focuses on the work or its author, cite the author first.

Marx, Karl, and Frederick Engels. The Communist Manifesto.
    1848. Ed. John E. Toews. Boston: Bedford, 1999.

If your paper focuses on the editor or the edition used, cite the editor first.

Toews, John E., ed. The Communist Manifesto. By Karl Marx
    and Frederick Engels. 1848. Boston: Bedford, 1999.

TRANSLATED WORK

Hoeg, Peter. Tales of the Night. Trans. Barbara Haveland.
    New York: Farrar, 1998.

If your paper focuses on the translation, cite the translator first.

Haveland, Barbara, trans. Tales of the Night. By Peter Hoeg.
    New York: Farrar, 1998.

MULTIVOLUME WORK

To cite the full work, include the number of volumes, followed by *vols.,* after
the title.

Who Built America? Working People and the Nation's Economy,
    Politics, Culture, and Society. 2 vols. New York:
    Worth, 2000.

To cite only one volume, give its number after the title. If you wish, you can
add the total number of volumes after the date.

Ford, Boris, ed. The Age of Shakespeare. New York: Penguin,
    1982. Vol. 2 of The New Pelican Guide to English
    Literature. 8 vols.

EDITION OTHER THAN THE FIRST

Volti, Rudi. Society and Technological Change. 4th ed. New
    York: Worth, 2001.

BOOK IN A SERIES

After the book title, add the series name as it appears on the title page, followed by any series number.

Berlin, Jeffrey B., ed. Approaches to Teaching Mann's Death
        in Venice. Approaches to Teaching World Literature 43.
        New York: MLA, 1992.

PARTS OF BOOKS

When citing part of a book, give the author of the section first; the editor of the book should follow the title. Give the page numbers of the selection after the publication information.

CHAPTER OR SECTION IN A BOOK

Burke, Kenneth. "A Grammar of Motives." The Rhetorical
        Tradition: Readings from Classical Times to the
        Present. Ed. Patricia Bizzell and Bruce Herzberg.
        Boston: Bedford, 2001. 1298-1324.

ESSAY, SHORT STORY, POEM, OR PLAY IN AN EDITED COLLECTION

Sandor, Marjorie. "You with Your Nose in a Book." The Most
        Wonderful Books. Ed. Michael Dorris and Emilie Buch-
        wald. Minneapolis: Milkweed, 1997. 219-21.

TWO OR MORE WORKS FROM THE SAME EDITED COLLECTION

The following examples show citations for articles in the collection *The Beacon Book of Essays by Contemporary American Women,* as well as the citation for the collection itself.

Cisneros, Sandra. "Only Daughter." Martin 10-13.

Martin, Wendy, ed. The Beacon Book of Essays by Contemporary
        American Women. Boston: Beacon, 1996.

Tan, Amy. "Mother Tongue." Martin 32-37.

INTRODUCTION, PREFACE, FOREWORD, OR AFTERWORD

Godwin, Mike. Foreword. High Noon on the Electronic
        Frontier. Ed. Peter Ludlow. Cambridge: MIT, 1996.
        xiii-xvi.

REFERENCE BOOKS

It is not necessary to supply the editor, publisher, or place of publication for well-known references such as *Webster's, The Random House Dictionary, World Book Encyclopedia,* and *Encyclopaedia Britannica.* Omit volume and page numbers when citing an entry from a reference that is arranged alphabetically.

SIGNED DICTIONARY ENTRY

Turner, V. W. "Divination." A Dictionary of the Social
     Sciences. Ed. Julius Gould and William L. Kolb. New
     York: Free, 1964.

UNSIGNED DICTIONARY ENTRY

"Organize." Merriam Webster's Collegiate Dictionary. 1998
     ed.

SIGNED ENCYCLOPEDIA ARTICLE

Binder, Raymond C., et al. "Mathematical Aspects of Physical
     Theories." The New Encyclopaedia Britannica: Macropae-
     dia. 15th ed. 1993.

UNSIGNED ENCYCLOPEDIA ARTICLE

"Solstice." Encyclopaedia Britannica. 15th ed. 1997.

PERIODICALS

ARTICLE FROM A JOURNAL PAGINATED BY ISSUE

For an article from a journal that starts each issue with page 1, provide the issue number as well as the volume number, separated by a period.

Ferris, Lucy. "'Never Truly Members': Andre Dubus's Patriar-
     chal Catholicism." South Atlantic Review 62.2 (1997):
     39-55.

ARTICLE FROM A JOURNAL PAGINATED BY VOLUME

For articles from journals in which page numbers run continuously through all issues of a volume, give only the volume number, year, and page numbers.

Daly, Mary E. "Recent Writing on Modern Irish History: The
     Interaction between Past and Present." Journal of Mod-
     ern History 69 (1997): 512-33.

SIGNED MAGAZINE ARTICLE

Give the month and year of the issue, or its specific date, after the title of the magazine.

```
Morris, Jim. "The FAA Stretched to the Limit." U.S. News &
     World Report 18 Dec. 2000: 46.
```

If the pages for the article are not consecutive, add a + after its initial page.

```
Lemley, Brad. "The Underground Architect." New Age Journal
     Jan.-Feb. 1995: 66+.
```

UNSIGNED MAGAZINE ARTICLE

```
"Speed Bump." Newsweek 11 Dec. 2000: 12.
```

SIGNED NEWSPAPER ARTICLE

If the newspaper has different editions, indicate which edition the article can be found in.

```
Kolata, Gina. "Men and Women Use Brain Differently, Study
     Discovers." New York Times 16 Feb. 1995, natl. ed.:
     A1+.
```

UNSIGNED NEWSPAPER ARTICLE

```
"U.S. Seeks Broader NATO Ties for Russia." Boston Globe 21
     Feb. 1995: 4.
```

SIGNED EDITORIAL

```
Jacoby, Jeff. "When Jerusalem Was Divided." Editorial.
     Boston Globe 8 Jan. 2001: A11.
```

UNSIGNED EDITORIAL

```
"Taking the Initiatives." Editorial. Nation 13 Nov. 2000:
     3-4.
```

PUBLISHED INTERVIEW

```
Kallen, Ben. "Freeing Your Inner Artist." New Age Journal
     Jan.-Feb. 1995: 53+.
```

LETTER TO THE EDITOR

```
Freeland, Edward P. Letter. Atlantic Feb. 1995: 10.
```

REVIEW

Include the words *Rev. of* before the title of the work reviewed.

```
Passaro, Vince. "The Unsparing Vision of Don DeLillo." Rev.
     of Underworld, by Don DeLillo. Harper's Nov. 1997:
     72-75.
```

OTHER PRINTED SOURCES

GOVERNMENT DOCUMENT

Generally, the "author" will be the name of the government and the government agency, separated by periods. If the document names an author or editor, that name may be provided either before the title or after it, if you supply the government agency as author.

```
United States. Bureau of the Census. Statistical Abstract of
     the United States. 117th ed. Washington: GPO, 1997.
```

PAMPHLET

Follow the format for a book.

```
Metropolitan Life Insurance Company. Metlife Dental. New
     York: Metropolitan Life Insurance, 1996.
```

DOCTORAL DISSERTATION

If the dissertation is unpublished, place the title in quotation marks; if published, underline the title as you would a book. Follow the title with the abbreviation *Diss.*

```
Beilke, Debra J. "Cracking Up the South: Humor and Identity
     in Southern Renaissance Fiction." Diss. U of Wisconsin,
     Madison, 1997.
```

PERSONAL LETTER

```
Finch, Katherine. Letter to the author. 15 Jan. 1998.
```

ADVERTISEMENT

```
Marriott. Advertisement. Sports Illustrated 9 Mar. 1998: 37.
```

INTERNET AND ELECTRONIC SOURCES

Here are the basic elements of an Internet or electronic citation:

- Name of the author or editor (if known)
- Title of the site or document

- Date of publication or of latest update
- Name of the sponsoring organization (if any)
- Date on which you accessed the source
- URL (online address), in angle brackets

Because most Internet sources do not have page numbers, these are not required.

PROFESSIONAL OR PERSONAL WEB SITE

If the author's name is unknown, begin with the site title.

EPA Laws and Regulations Page. 6 Mar. 1998. United States
     Environmental Protection Agency. 11 Mar. 1998
     <http://www.epa.gov/epahome/rules.html>.

If no title is available, include a description such as *Home page.*

Watson, Chad J. Home page. 27 Jan. 1998. 10 Mar. 1998
     <http://cc.usu.edu/~slypx/index.html>.

ONLINE SCHOLARLY PROJECT OR REFERENCE DATABASE

For an online source accessed from within a larger scholarly project or reference database, note the author (if any), title of the source, and any editors or translators. Then supply the electronic publication information, including version number (if relevant and available), date of electronic publication or of the latest update, name of the sponsoring organization, your date of access, and the URL.

The Einstein Papers Project. Ed. Robert Schulmann. 9 Nov.
     1997. Boston U. 29 Jan. 1998 <http://albert.bu.edu>.

"Osteoporosis." Britannica Online. Vers. 98.1. Sept. 1997.
     Encyclopaedia Britannica. 10 Mar. 1998 <http://www.eb
     .com:180/cgi-bin>.

ARTICLE IN AN ONLINE PERIODICAL

When citing articles from online journals, magazines, and newspapers, provide information as you would for print articles but end with the date on which you accessed the information and the URL.

Loker, William M. "'Campesinos' and the Crisis of Moderniza-
     tion in Latin America." Journal of Political Ecology
     3.1 (1996). 13 Mar. 1998 <http://www.library.arizona
     .edu/ej/jpe/volume_3/ascii-lokeriso.txt>.

If you are citing an abstract, indicate this before the date of access.

```
Duch, Raymond M., Harvey D. Palmer, and Christopher J.
     Anderson. "Heterogeneity in Perceptions of National
     Economic Conditions." American Journal of Political
     Science 44.4 (2000). Abstract. 9 Jan. 2001
     <http://ajps.org/Frames_Abstract.htm>.
```

AN ONLINE POSTING

For an online posting, begin with the author, the title (the subject line), the words *Online Posting,* the posting date, the access date, and the address. Identify a newsgroup by adding the word *news* before the group's name.

```
Cowan, Cheryl. "Eating Disorders." Online posting. 23 Feb.
     1998. 16 Mar. 1998 <news:alt.arts.ballet>.
```

If the posting is from an e-mail discussion list, add the name of the group or forum (if known) after the posting date. Supply the URL for the group's Web site or the moderator's e-mail address.

```
Royar, Robert D. "Internet Linked Courses." Online posting.
     28 Feb. 1998. Alliance for Computers and Writing. 3
     Mar. 1998 <acw-l@ttacs6.ttu.edu>.
```

E-MAIL

```
Moore, Jack. E-mail to the author. 11 Jan. 2001.
```

PUBLICATION ON CD-ROM

```
Sheehy, Donald, ed. Robert Frost: Poems, Life, Legacy. CD-
     ROM. New York: Holt, 1997.
```

COMPUTER SOFTWARE

```
Electronic Supplements for Real Writing: 1. Interactive Writ-
     ing Software. Diskette. Vers. 1. Boston: Bedford, 1998.
```

MATERIAL ACCESSED THROUGH AN ONLINE SUBSCRIPTION SERVICE

If you find a source through a subscription service (such as America Online) and do not have a URL, cite the keyword or path that you used to find the information.

```
"Echocardiography." Merriam-Webster Medical Dictionary. 13
     Oct. 1995. America Online. 8 June 1999. Keyword: Med-
     ical Dictionary.
```

OTHER NONPRINT SOURCES

AUDIOTAPE OR RECORDING

Begin with the name of the speaker, the writer, or the production director, depending on what you want to emphasize. If the recording is not on a CD, note the format.

Byrne, Gabriel. The James Joyce Collection. Dove Audio, 1996.

Yeats, William Butler. "The Song of the Old Mother." The Poems of William Butler Yeats. Read by William Butler Yeats, Siobhan McKenna, and Michael MacLiammoir. Audio-tape. Spoken Arts, 1974.

TELEVISION OR RADIO PROGRAM

The Windsors: A Royal Family. PBS. WGBH, Boston. 12 Mar. 1995.

"A Dangerous Man: Lawrence after Arabia." Great Performances. Perf. Ralph Fiennes and Siddig el Fadil. PBS. WNET, New York. 6 May 1992.

FILM

Primary Colors. Dir. Mike Nichols. Universal, 1998.

If you wish to emphasize the work of a person connected with the film, start with his or her name.

Nichols, Mike, dir. Primary Colors. Universal, 1998.

PERFORMANCE

Whale Music. By Anthony Minghella. Dir. Anthony Minghella. Perf. Francie Swift. Theater Off Park, New York. 23 Mar. 1998.

A WORK OF ART

Botticelli, Sandro. The Birth of Venus. Uffizi Gallery, Florence.

SPEECH OR LECTURE

Hurley, James. Address. Opening Gen. Sess. Amer. Bar Assn. Convention. Chicago, 17 Jan. 1987.

BROADCAST INTERVIEW

```
Bernstein, Richard. Interview. Fresh Air. WBUR, Boston.
     3 Apr. 2001.
```

PERSONAL INTERVIEW

```
Boyd, Dierdre. Personal interview. 5 Feb. 2001.

Ladner, John. Telephone interview. 20 Oct. 2000.
```

Citing Sources: APA Style

The American Psychological Association (APA) details the style most commonly used in the social sciences in its *Publication Manual*, Fifth Edition (Washington, D.C.: APA, 2001). As in MLA style, APA citations are placed in parentheses in the body of the text.

For advice on preparing an APA list of references, see pp. 634–39.

PRINTED SOURCES

To cite a work in APA style, you usually place in parentheses the author's last name, a comma, and the year the source was published. You must add a page number for a direct quotation from the source and may include one for a paraphrase.

AUTHOR NOT NAMED IN SENTENCE

```
Some experts feel that adolescent boys who bully are not
merely aggressive but are depressed and acting out in an ag-
gressive manner (Pollack, 2000).
```

If you paraphrase ideas from a long work, you can refer to a specific page so that your readers can easily find the reference. Use the abbreviation *p.* (or *pp.*).

```
Dean Rusk's exposure to Nazi power in Europe in the 1930s
seems to have permanently influenced his attitude toward ap-
peasement (Karnow, 1991, p. 194).
```

AUTHOR NAMED IN SENTENCE

If you name the author in your text, give only the date in parentheses.

```
Pollack (2000) contends that boys tend to contain their pain
and sadness for fear of appearing vulnerable and inviting
ridicule.
```

When the author's name appears in the text, put the page number in parentheses after quoted or paraphrased material.

Karnow (1991) maintains that Dean Rusk's exposure to Nazi power in Europe in the 1930s "scarred his mind" (p. 194).

LONG QUOTATION

If you quote forty words or more from your source, indent the whole quotation one-half inch (five spaces) and double-space it unless directed otherwise. Put the author's name, the publication year, and the page number in parentheses following the quotation with no additional period.

At least one critic maintains that Dean Rusk's exposure to Nazi power in Europe in the 1930s permanently influenced his attitude toward appeasement:

> Then came the moment that transformed his life and his thinking. He won a Rhodes scholarship to Oxford. More important, his exposure to Europe in the early 1930s, as the Nazis consolidated their power in Germany, scarred his mind, leading him to share Acheson's hostility to appeasement in any form anywhere. (Karnow, 1991, p. 194)

TWO AUTHORS

List the last names of coauthors in the order in which they appear in the book or article you cite. Join the names with *and* if you mention them in your text and with an ampersand (&) if the citation is in parentheses.

A group's cultural development enhances its chance for survival, providing both physical and psychological protection (Anderson & Ross, 1998).

Anderson and Ross (1998) contend that the development of a group's culture provides both physical and psychological protection.

THREE TO FIVE AUTHORS

Include all the last names in your first reference only. In any later references, use the first author's last name with *et al.* (for "and others"), whether in the text or in parentheses.

The relatively new discipline of conservation biology has developed in response to the accelerating rate at which species are now being lost due to human activities (Purves, Orians, & Heller, 1999).

CORPORATE AUTHOR

There are three signs of oxygen deprivation (American Red Cross, 1984).

GOVERNMENT DOCUMENT

In the first citation in your text, give the full name of the originating agency. If the name is complicated or commonly shortened, you can add an abbreviation in brackets.

Clearly, it is of paramount importance to stop the spread of mosquito-borne diseases (Department of Health and Human Services [DHHS], 1986, p. 25).

In later citations, use just the abbreviation and the date: (DHHS, 1986).

UNKNOWN AUTHOR

Identify the source with a short title and a date.

There are questions people can ask themselves if they suspect their drinking has gotten out of hand (*Alcoholism*, 1986).

MULTIPLE WORKS BY THE SAME AUTHOR

One nuclear energy proponent has insisted on tight controls for the industry (Weinberg, 1972), even calling on utility companies to insure each reactor with their own funds (Weinberg, 1977).

OTHER SOURCES

PERSONAL COMMUNICATIONS

Personal communications — such as personal interviews, letters, telephone conversations, memos, and e-mail — are not included in the reference list. But in the text of your paper, you should include the initials and last name of your source, with the date of the communication.

```
J. T. Moore (personal communication, February 10, 2001) has
specific suggestions for stimulating the local economy.
```

WEB SITE OR OTHER ELECTRONIC DOCUMENT

When possible, treat a Web site or online article as you would treat a print source, indicating the author's name and the date in parentheses.

```
Breast cancer survival rates depend on early detection be-
fore the cancer has a chance to spread (Bruckheim, 1998).
```

For an electronic source with no author named, use the full title of the document in text or include the first word or two of the title in parentheses. When the date is unknown, use "n.d." to indicate "no date." For a source without page numbers, include any information that helps readers to locate quoted material, such as the paragraph number or the appropriate section heading.

```
"Interval training involves alternating short bursts of in-
tense activity with what is called active recovery, which
is typically a less-intense form of the original activity"
(Interval training, n.d., para. 2).
```

Listing Sources: APA Style

In the latest APA style (2001), your list of sources is titled "References" and appears at the end of your paper. The APA guidelines for manuscript preparation instruct you to format entries with a hanging indent: the first line is not indented, while subsequent lines are. Use a hanging indentation of one-half inch, or about five to seven spaces.

Double-space your list, organize it alphabetically by authors' last names, and use only initials for the authors' first and middle names. The year immediately follows the authors' names in parentheses. In book and article titles, capitalize only the first word, proper names, and the first word following a colon. Italicize book titles (or, if your word processing program has no italics function, underline), but use no quotation marks or italics for article titles. Italicize journal names, and capitalize all important words. Use a shortened name for a publisher, but include *Press*. Omit the state name with larger cities.

BOOKS

SINGLE AUTHOR

```
Pollack, W. (2000). Real boys' voices. New York: Random
    House.
```

TWO OR MORE AUTHORS

Anderson, R., & Ross, V. (1998). *Questions of communication.*
    New York: St. Martin's Press.

CORPORATE AUTHOR

American Red Cross. (1984). *Lifesaving: Rescue and water*
    safety. New York: Doubleday.

UNKNOWN AUTHOR

The new international atlas. (1998). Chicago: Rand-McNally.

MULTIPLE WORKS BY THE SAME AUTHOR

Arrange the titles by date, the earliest first.

Gould, S. J. (1996). *Full house: The spread of excellence*
    from Plato to Darwin. New York: Harmony.

Gould, S. J. (Ed.). (1997). *Questioning the millennium.* New
    York: Harmony.

CHAPTER OR SECTION OF A BOOK

Write "In" after the chapter title, followed by the editor's name, the book
title, and the chapter's page numbers.

Shofner, J. H. (1995). Florida's black codes. In L. Dinner-
    stein & K. T. Jackson (Eds.), *American vistas: 1877 to*
    the present (pp. 56-75). New York: Oxford University
    Press.

INTRODUCTION, PREFACE, FOREWORD, OR AFTERWORD

Godwin, M. (1996). Foreword. In P. Ludlow (Ed.), *High noon*
    on the electronic frontier (pp. xiii-xvi). Cambridge:
    MIT Press.

WORK IN AN EDITED COLLECTION

Tollifson, J. (1997). Imperfection is a beautiful thing: On
    disability and meditation. In K. Fries (Ed.), *Staring*
    back (pp. 105-112). New York: Plume-Random.

EDITED BOOK

Bolles, E. B. (Ed.). (1999). *Galileo's commandment: 2,500*
    years of great science writing. New York: W. H. Freeman.

TRANSLATED WORK

Ishinomori, I. (1998). *Japan inc.: Introduction to Japanese economics* (B. Schneiner, Trans.). Berkeley: University of California Press. (Original work published 1986)

REVISED EDITION

Volti, R. (2001). *Society and technological change.* (4th ed.). New York: Worth.

PERIODICALS

ARTICLE FROM A JOURNAL PAGINATED BY ISSUE

Place the issue number in parentheses after the volume. Note that volume numbers are italicized along with the titles of the journals and magazines.

Lipkin, S. N. (1999). Real emotional logic: Persuasive strategies in docudrama. *Cinema Journal, 38*(4), 68-85.

ARTICLE FROM A JOURNAL PAGINATED BY VOLUME

Martin, J. (1997). Inventing sincerity, refashioning prudence: The discovery of the individual in Renaissance Europe. *American Historical Review, 102,* 1309-1342.

MAGAZINE ARTICLE

Lankford, K. (1998, April). The trouble with rules of thumb. *Kiplinger's Personal Finance Magazine, 52,* 102-104.

SIGNED NEWSPAPER ARTICLE

Brody, J. E. (1995, February 21). Health factor in vegetables still elusive. *The New York Times,* p. C1.

UNSIGNED NEWSPAPER ARTICLE

The AMD unveils faster bargain microprocessor. (2001, January 8). *The Boston Globe,* p. C4.

SIGNED EDITORIAL

Kass, R. (1998, March 23). Wanted: An official state janitor. [Editorial.] *The Boston Globe,* p. A15.

UNSIGNED EDITORIAL

```
Taking the initiatives. (2000, November 13). [Editorial.]
     The Nation, 272, 3-4.
```

LETTER TO THE EDITOR

```
Yusuf, S. (2000, November 4). Pakistan's choice [Letter to
     the editor]. Economist, 357, 6.
```

REVIEW

```
Rose, T. (1998, February 24). Blues sisters [Review of the
     book Blues legacies and black feminism: Gertrude "Ma"
     Rainey, Bessie Smith, and Billie Holliday]. Village
     Voice, pp. 139-141.
```

OTHER PRINTED SOURCES

GOVERNMENT DOCUMENT

Start with the name of the agency and then give the date of publication, the title (and author, if any), identifying number, and publisher.

```
U.S. Bureau of the Census. (1997). Statistical abstract of
     the United States (117th ed.). Washington, DC: U.S.
     Government Printing Office.
```

UNPUBLISHED DOCTORAL DISSERTATION

Write out the words "unpublished doctoral dissertation," followed by information about the college that granted the degree.

```
Beilke, D. (1997). Cracking up the South: Humor and identity
     in Southern Renaissance fiction. Unpublished doctoral
     dissertation, University of Wisconsin, Madison.
```

INTERNET AND ELECTRONIC SOURCES

For Internet and electronic sources, provide as much of the following information as available:

- Name of the author or editor (if known)
- Date of publication or of latest update, in parentheses
- Document title, in italics

- Date of retrieval
- URL or online location

For current information on formatting online sources using APA style, visit the official Web site of the APA at <www.apastyle.org>.

NONPERIODICAL WEB DOCUMENT

```
Watkins, C., & Brynes, G. (2001). Anxiety disorders in
     children and adults. Retrieved July 20, 2001, from
     http://www.baltimorepsych.com/anxiety.htm
```

For a chapter or section within a Web site, identify the section as well as the main site.

```
Watkins, C. (2001). Separation anxiety in young children. In
     Anxiety disorders in children and adults (chap. 1). Re-
     trieved July 20, 2001, from http://www.baltimorepsych
     .com/anxiety.htm
```

For a document that is part of a government agency Web site or other large site, identify the sponsoring agency or organization before the URL.

```
United States Department of the Interior. Bureau of Indian
     Affairs. (2001, July). Report on tribal priority allo-
     cations. Retrieved from the Bureau of Indian Affairs
     Web site: http://www.doi.gov/bia/tpa/TPARept.pdf
```

ARTICLE FROM AN ONLINE PERIODICAL

```
Loker, W. M. (1996). "Campesinos" and the crisis of modern-
     ization in Latin America [Electronic version]. Journal
     of Political Ecology, 3, 69-88.
```

Do not include a URL in the citation if the article also appears in a printed journal. Instead, include "Electronic version" in brackets after the title. If there is no print version of the article, include in your retrieval statement your date of access and the URL.

```
Rothfleisch, J. (2001, February). Mid-dermal elastolysis.
     Dermatology Online Journal, 7. Retrieved June 8, 2001,
     from http://dermatology.cdlib.org/DOJvol7num1/
     NYUcases/elastolysis/rothfleisch.html
```

ONLINE NEWSPAPER ARTICLE

Stevenson, R. (2001, July 20). Panel argues for changing so-
      cial security. *New York Times*. Retrieved July 20, 2001,
      from http://www.nytimes.com

E-MAIL (INCLUDING MAILING LISTS)

APA does not recommend including these messages in your reference list, as
they are difficult or impossible for readers to retrieve. Cite them in your text
as personal communications. See pp. 633–34.

COMPUTER SOFTWARE

Microsoft Excel (Version 5.0) [Computer software]. (1993).
      Redmond, WA: Microsoft.

ARTICLE FROM AN INFORMATION SERVICE OR DATABASE

Berger, S. (1995). Inclusion: a legal mandate, an educa-
      tional dream. *Updating School Board Policies, 26*(4),
      1–4. Retrieved February 15, 2001, from ERIC database
      (No. ED386789)

NOTE: If the source is an abstract, include "Abstract" in brackets after the title.

OTHER NONPRINT SOURCES

MUSIC RECORDING

Byrne, G. (1996). *The James Joyce collection* [Cassette].
      Hollywood: Dove Audio.

TELEVISION OR RADIO PROGRAM

Braithwaite, D., & Jimenez, S. (1995). Murder, rape and DNA
      [Television series episode]. In P. Aspell (Executive
      Producer), *Nova*. Boston: WGBH.

MOTION PICTURE

Lustig, B., Molen, G., & Spielberg, S. (Producers). (1993).
      Schindler's List [Motion Picture]. Los Angeles: Universal.

PERSONAL INTERVIEW

APA guidelines omit personal interviews from the reference list because they
do not provide recoverable data. Mention such sources in your paper as personal communications. See pp. 633–34.

A Writer's Handbook

Contents

*Introduction: Grammar, or The Way
Words Work*   *H-3*

33. Grammatical Sentences

  1. Sentence Fragments   H-5

  2. Comma Splices and Fused
     Sentences   H-10

  3. Verbs   H-14

  4. Subject-Verb Agreement   H-31

  5. Pronoun Case   H-36

  6. Pronoun Reference   H-40

  7. Pronoun-Antecedent Agreement   H-44

  8. Adjectives and Adverbs   H-46

  9. Shifts   H-52

34. Effective Sentences

  10. Misplaced and Dangling Modifiers   H-57

  11. Incomplete Sentences   H-60

  12. Mixed Constructions and Faulty
      Predication   H-64

  13. Parallel Structure   H-68

  14. Coordination and Subordination   H-71

  15. Sentence Variety   H-78

35. Word Choice

  16. Appropriateness   H-81

  17. Exact Words   H-86

  18. Bias-Free Language   H-90

  19. Wordiness   H-94

36. Punctuation

  20. End Punctuation   H-96

  21. The Comma   H-98

  22. The Semicolon   H-108

  23. The Colon   H-110

  24. The Apostrophe   H-113

  25. Quotation Marks   H-116

  26. The Dash   H-120

  27. Parentheses, Brackets, and the
      Ellipsis Mark   H-122

37. Mechanics

  28. Abbreviations   H-127

  29. Capital Letters   H-130

  30. Numbers   H-134

  31. Italics   H-136

  32. The Hyphen   H-139

  33. Spelling   H-142

Introduction:
Grammar, or The Way Words Work

Every speaker of English, even a child, commands a grammatical system of tremendous complexity. Take the sentence "A bear is occupying a telephone booth while a tourist impatiently waits in line." In theory, there are nineteen billion different ways to state the idea in that sentence.[1] (Another is "A tourist fumes while he waits for a bear to finish yakking on a pay phone.") How do we understand a unique sentence like that one? For we do understand it, even though we have never heard it before — not in those very same words, not in the very same order.

To begin with, we recognize familiar words and we know their meanings. Just as significantly, we recognize grammatical structures. As we read or hear the sentence, we know that it contains a familiar pattern of *syntax*, or word order, that helps the sentence make sense to us. Ordinarily we aren't even conscious of such an order, but to notice it, all we need do is rearrange the words of our sentence:

> Telephone a impatiently line in waits tourist bear a occupying is a booth while.

The result is nonsense: it defies English grammar. The would-be sentence doesn't follow familiar patterns or meet our expectations of order.

Hundreds of times a day, with wonderful efficiency, we perform tasks of understanding and constructing complex sentences. Why, then, think about grammar in college? Isn't it entirely possible to write well without contemplating grammar at all? Yes. If your innate sense of grammar is reliable, you can write clearly and logically and forcefully without knowing a predicate nominative from a handsaw. Most successful writers, though, have practiced for many years to gain this sense. When you doubt a word or a construction, a glance in a handbook often can clear up your confusion and restore your confidence — just as referring to a dictionary can help your spelling.

The grammatical conventions you'll find in this handbook are not mechanical specifications, but accepted ways in which skilled writers and speakers put words together to convey meaning clearly. The amateur writer can learn by following their example, just as an amateur athlete, artist, or even auto mechanic can learn by watching the professionals.

---

[1] Richard Ohmann, "Grammar and Meaning," *American Heritage Dictionary* (Boston: Houghton, 1979), pp. xxxi–xxxii.

This handbook is divided into the following chapters, which contain complete information on all important rules and conventions of standard written English. Exercises are provided so you can practice putting the information to use.

33 Grammatical Sentences
34 Effective Sentences
35 Word Choice
36 Punctuation
37 Mechanics

Following the handbook are convenient appendices. You can find the first of these, the "Quick Editing Guide," by looking for the dark blue band that runs down the edges of the pages.

QUICK EDITING GUIDE
The "Quick Editing Guide" briefly discusses how to edit the common grammar, style, punctuation, mechanics, and format problems found in college writing. It also contains useful tables, lists, and editing checklists.

A GLOSSARY OF TROUBLEMAKERS
"A Glossary of Troublemakers" lists words and phrases that often trouble writers. Turn here when you have questions about which of two words to use (*affect* or *effect*, for example) or when you're not sure you're using a word correctly.

ANSWERS FOR LETTERED EXERCISES
The "Answers for Lettered Exercises" are excellent tools for self-study. To test yourself on a particular skill, simply answer the lettered exercise sentences in the handbook, and then turn to the answers to see how you did.

Here are some easy ways to find information in *A Writer's Handbook*:

- Use the *table of contents* at the beginning of the handbook (p. H-2). If you were looking for help with quotation marks, for instance, you would first look under the chapter titled "Punctuation." By scanning the list of topics, you would quickly find the section and page number you need (section 25, Quotation Marks, p. H-116).

- Turn to the alphabetically arranged *index* located at the back of the book. Here you will find all of the key terms used in the handbook followed by the exact page that you should turn to.

- For those of you who speak English as a second language, near the back of the book is an *ESL index* listing all the ESL boxes in the handbook.

Chapter 33
Grammatical Sentences

1. Sentence Fragments   H-5
2. Comma Splices and Fused Sentences   H-10
3. Verbs   H-14
4. Subject-Verb Agreement   H-31
5. Pronoun Case   H-36
6. Pronoun Reference   H-40
7. Pronoun-Antecedent Agreement   H-44
8. Adjectives and Adverbs   H-46
9. Shifts   H-52

1 *Sentence Fragments*

A *fragment* lacks a subject or a predicate or both or for some other reason fails to express a complete thought. We all use fragments in everyday speech, where their context and the way they are said make them understandable and therefore acceptable.

> That bicycle over there.

> Good job.

> Not if I can help it.

In writing, fragments like these fail to communicate complete, coherent ideas. Notice how much more effective they are as complete sentences.

complete sentence: A word group that includes both a subject and a predicate and can stand alone

> I'd like to buy that bicycle over there.

> You did a good job sanding the floor.

> Nobody will steal my seat if I can help it.

Some writers purposefully use fragments. For example, advertisers are fond of short, emphatic fragments that command attention, like a series of quick jabs to the head.

> For seafood lovers. Every Tuesday night. All you can eat.

In college writing, though, it is good practice to express your ideas in complete sentences. Besides, complete sentences usually convey more information than fragments — a big advantage in essay writing.

For more on editing for fragments, see A6 in the "Quick Editing Guide."

If you sometimes write fragments without recognizing them, learn to edit your work. Luckily, fragments are fairly easy to correct. Often you can attach a fragment to a neighboring sentence with a comma, a dash, or a colon. Sometimes you can combine two thoughts without adding any punctuation at all.

1a If a fragment is a phrase, link it to an adjoining sentence or make it a complete sentence.

phrase: Two or more related words that work together but may lack a subject, a verb, or both

You have two choices for revising a fragment if it is a phrase: (1) link it to an adjoining sentence using punctuation such as a comma or a colon, or (2) add a subject or a verb to the phrase to make it a complete sentence.

FRAGMENT   Malcolm has two goals in life. *Wealth and power.* [Phrase without verb]

FRAGMENT   Schmidt ended his stories as he mixed his martinis. *With a twist.* [Prepositional phrase without subject or verb]

FRAGMENT   *To stamp out the union.* That was the bosses' plan. [Infinitive phrase without main verb or subject]

FRAGMENT   The students taking the final exam in the auditorium. [Participial phrase without complete verb]

You can make each of these phrases express a complete thought by linking it with a neighboring sentence or by adding the missing element.

REVISED   Malcolm has two goals in life: wealth and power. [A colon links *wealth and power* to *goals*.]

REVISED   Schmidt ended his stories as he mixed his martinis, with a twist. [The prepositional phrase *with a twist* is connected to the main clause with a comma.]

REVISED   To stamp out the union was the bosses' plan. [The infinitive phrase *To stamp out the union* becomes the subject of the sentence.]

REVISED   The students were taking the final exam in the auditorium. [The helping verb *were* completes the verb and thus makes a sentence.]

1b If a fragment is a subordinate clause, link it to an adjoining sentence or eliminate the subordinating conjunction.

subordinate clause: A group of words that contains a subject and a verb but cannot stand alone because it depends on a main clause to help it make sense: Pia, *who plays the oboe,* prefers solitude. (See 14d–14f.)

Some fragments are missing neither subject nor verb. Instead, they are subordinate clauses, unable to express complete thoughts unless linked with main clauses. When you find a subordinating conjunction at the start or in the middle of a word group that looks like a sentence, that word group may be a subordinate clause and not a sentence at all.

FRAGMENT   The new law will stem the tide of inflation. *If it passes.*

FRAGMENT   George loves winter in the mountains. *Because he is an avid skier.*

If you have treated a subordinate clause as a complete sentence, you can correct the problem in one of two ways: (1) you can combine the fragment with a main clause nearby, or (2) you can make the subordinate clause into a complete sentence by dropping the subordinating conjunction.

REVISED   The new law will stem the tide of inflation, if it passes.

REVISED   George loves winter in the mountains. He is an avid skier.

A sentence is not necessarily a fragment just because it opens with a subordinating conjunction. Some perfectly legitimate sentences with both main and subordinate clauses have their conjunctions up front instead of in the middle.

If you leave early, say good-bye.

Because it rained all afternoon, the game was canceled.

> **subordinating conjunction:** A word (such as *because, although, if, when*) used to make one clause dependent on, or subordinate to, another: *Unless* you have a key, we are locked out. (See 14d–14f.)

1c   If a fragment has a participle but no other verb, change the participle to a main verb or link the fragment to an adjoining sentence.

A present participle (the *-ing* form of the verb) can serve as the main verb in a sentence only when it is accompanied by a form of *be* ("Sally *is working* harder than usual"). When a writer mistakenly uses a participle alone as a main verb, the result is a fragment.

FRAGMENT   Jon was used to the pressure of deadlines. *Having worked the night shift at the daily newspaper.*

One solution is to combine the fragment with an adjoining sentence.

REVISED   Jon was used to the pressure of deadlines, having worked the night shift at the daily newspaper.

Another solution is to turn the fragment into a complete sentence by choosing a form of the verb other than the participle.

REVISED   Jon was used to the pressure of deadlines. He *had worked* the night shift at the daily newspaper.

> **participle:** A form of a verb that cannot function alone as a main verb, including present participles ending in *-ing* (*dancing*) and past participles often ending in *-ed* or *-d* (*danced*)

1d   If a fragment is part of a compound predicate, link it with the complete sentence containing the rest of the predicate.

FRAGMENT   In spite of a pulled muscle, Jeremy ran the race. *And won.*

A fragment such as *And won* sounds satisfyingly punchy. Still, it cannot stand on its own because it is part of a compound predicate. You can create a complete sentence by linking the two verbs.

REVISED   In spite of a pulled muscle, Jeremy *ran* the race *and won.*

> **compound predicate:** A predicate consisting of two or more verbs linked by a conjunction: My sister *stopped and stared.*

For advice on punctuating linked phrases and clauses, see 14a.

If you want to keep more emphasis on the second verb, you can turn the fragment into a full clause by adding punctuation and another subject.

REVISED   In spite of a pulled muscle, Jeremy ran the race — and *he* won.

ESL GUIDELINES

verbal: A form of a verb that cannot function alone as a main verb, including infinitives (*to live*), present participles (*living*), and past participles (*lived*)

participle: A form of a verb that cannot function alone as a main verb, including present participles ending in -*ing* (*dancing*) and past participles often ending in -*ed* or -*d* (*danced*)

infinitive: The base form of a verb preceded by *to* (*to go, to play*)

gerund: A form of a verb, ending in -*ing*, that functions as a noun: Lacey likes *playing* in the steel band.

Using Participles, Infinitives, and Gerunds

A *verbal* cannot function as the main verb in a sentence but can function as an adjective, an adverb, or a noun.

Using participles
When used as an adjective, the -*ing* form expresses cause, and the -*ed* and -*d* forms express effect or result.

The movie was *terrifying to the children.* [The movie caused terror.]

The children were *terrified by the movie.* [The movie resulted in terrified children.]

Using verbs with gerunds and infinitives
Some verbs are followed by gerunds, while other verbs are followed by infinitives.

- Verbs that are followed by infinitives include *decide, expect, pretend, refuse,* and *want,* among others.

  My mother decided *to eat* at McDonald's for dinner.

- Verbs that are followed by gerunds include *appreciate, avoid, consider, discuss, enjoy, finish, imagine, practice,* and *suggest,* among others.

  My family enjoys *going* to the beach.

- Some verbs, including *continue, like, love, hate, remember, forget, start,* and *stop,* can be followed by either a gerund or an infinitive.

  I like *going* to the museum, but Nadine likes *to go* to the movies.

NOTE: Some verbs, such as *stop, remember,* and *forget,* have significantly different meanings according to whether they are followed by a gerund or an infinitive.

I stopped *smoking.* [I don't smoke anymore.]

I stopped *to smoke.* [I stopped so that I could smoke.]

- *Used to* (meaning "did in the past") is followed by the basic form of the verb. *Be used to* or *get used to* (meaning "be or become accustomed to") is followed by a gerund.

  I *used to live* in Rio, but now I live in New York. [I lived in Rio in the past.]

  I *am used to living* in New York. [I am accustomed to living in New York.]

  I *got used to living* in New York. [I became accustomed to living in New York.]

■ Exercise 1–1

Eliminating Fragments

Find and eliminate any fragments in the following examples. Some sentences may be correct. Possible revisions for the lettered sentences appear in the back of the book. Example:

> Bryan hates parsnips. And loathes squash.

> Bryan hates parsnips *and* loathes squash.

WWW
For more practice, visit *Exercise Central* at <www.bedfordstmartins.com/bedguide>.

a. Michael had a beautiful Southern accent. Having lived many years in Georgia.

b. Pat and Chris are determined to marry each other. Even if their families do not approve.

c. Jack seemed well qualified for a career in the Air Force. Except for his tendency to get airsick.

d. Lisa advocated sleeping no more than four hours a night. Until she started nodding through her classes.

e. They met. They talked. They fought. They reached agreement.

1. Being the first person in his family ever to attend college. Alex is determined to succeed.

2. Does our society rob children of their childhood? By making them aware too soon of adult ills?

3. Richard III supposedly had the young princes murdered. No one has ever found out what really happened to them.

4. For democracy to function at all, two elements are crucial. An educated populace and a firm collective belief in people's ability to chart their own course.

5. You must take his stories as others do. With a grain of salt.

■ Exercise 1–2

Eliminating Fragments

Rewrite the following paragraph, eliminating all fragments. Explain why you made each change. Example:

> Many people exercise to change their body image. And may become obsessed with their looks. [The second word group is a fragment because it lacks a subject.]

> Many people exercise to change their body image *and* may become obsessed with their looks. [This revised sentence links the fragment to the rest of the sentence.]

Some people assume that only women are overly concerned with body image. However, men often share this concern. While women tend to exercise vigorously to stay slender, men usually lift weights to "bulk up." Because of their desire to look masculine. Both are trying to achieve the "ideal" body form. The muscular male and the waifish female. Sometimes working out begins to interfere with other aspects of life. Such as sleeping, eating regularly, or going to school or work. These are warning signs. Of too much emphasis on physical appearance. Preoccupation with body image may turn a healthy lifestyle into an unhealthy obsession. Many people believe that looking attractive will bring them happiness. Unfortunately, when they become compulsive. Beautiful people are not always happy.

2 *Comma Splices and Fused Sentences*

main clause: A group of words that has both a subject and a verb and can stand alone as a complete sentence: *My sister has a friend.*

For more on editing for comma splices and fused sentences, see A7 in the "Quick Editing Guide."

Splice two ropes, or two strips of movie film, and you join them into one. Splice two main clauses by putting only a comma between them, however, and you get an ungainly construction called a *comma splice.* Here, for instance, are two perfectly good main clauses, each separate, each able to stand on its own as a sentence:

> The detective wriggled on his belly toward the campfire. The drunken smugglers didn't notice him.

Now let's splice those sentences with a comma.

> COMMA SPLICE   The detective wriggled on his belly toward the campfire, the drunken smugglers didn't notice him.

The resulting comma splice makes for difficult reading.

Even more confusing than a comma splice is a *fused* (or *run-on*) *sentence:* two main clauses joined without any punctuation.

> FUSED SENTENCE   The detective wriggled on his belly toward the campfire the drunken smugglers didn't notice him.

Lacking clues from the writer, a reader cannot tell where to pause. To understand the sentence, he or she must halt and reread.

On the following two pages are five simple ways to eliminate both comma splices and fused sentences. Your choice depends on the length and complexity of your main clauses and the effect you want to achieve.

Sentence Parts at a Glance

The *subject* of a sentence identifies some person, place, thing, activity, or idea.

The *predicate* of a sentence includes a verb and makes an assertion about the subject.

An *object* is the target or recipient of the action described by the verb.

A *complement* renames or describes a subject or object.

2a   Write separate complete sentences to correct a comma splice or a fused sentence.

sentence: A word group that includes both a subject and a predicate and can stand alone

COMMA SPLICE   Sigmund Freud has been called an enemy of sexual repression, the truth is that he is not a friend of free love.

FUSED SENTENCE   Sigmund Freud has been called an enemy of sexual repression the truth is that he is not a friend of free love.

Neither sentence yields its meaning without a struggle. To point readers in the right direction, separate the clauses.

REVISED   Sigmund Freud has been called an enemy of sexual repression. The truth is that he is not a friend of free love.

2b   Use a comma and a coordinating conjunction to correct a comma splice or a fused sentence.

coordinating conjunction: A one-syllable linking word (*and, but, for, or, nor, so, yet*) that joins elements with equal or near-equal importance: Jack *and* Jill, sink *or* swim

Is it always incorrect to join two main clauses with a comma? No. If both clauses are of roughly equal weight, you can use a comma to link them — as long as you add a coordinating conjunction after the comma.

COMMA SPLICE   Hurricane winds hit ninety miles an hour, they tore the roof from every house on Paradise Drive.

REVISED   Hurricane winds hit ninety miles an hour, *and* they tore the roof from every house on Paradise Drive.

For advice on coordination, see 14a–14c.

2c   Use a semicolon or a colon to correct a comma splice or a fused sentence.

A semicolon can keep two thoughts connected while giving full emphasis to each one.

COMMA SPLICE   Hurricane winds hit ninety miles an hour, they tore the roof from every house on Paradise Drive.

REVISED   Hurricane winds hit ninety miles an hour; they tore the roof from every house on Paradise Drive.

If the second thought clearly illustrates or explains the first, add it on with a colon.

REVISED   The hurricane caused extensive damage: it tore the roof from every house on Paradise Drive.

Remember that the only punctuation powerful enough to link two main clauses single-handedly is a semicolon, a colon, or a period. A lone comma won't do the job.

EXCEPTION: Certain very short, similar main clauses can be joined with a comma.

Jill runs by day, Tom walks by night.

I came, I saw, I conquered.

Commas are not obligatory with short, similar clauses. If you find this issue confusing, you can stick with semicolons to join all main clauses, short or long.

Jill runs by day; Tom walks by night.

I came; I saw; I conquered.

main clause: A group of words that has both a subject and a verb and can stand alone as a complete sentence: *My sister has a friend.*

subordinate clause: A group of words that contains a subject and a verb but cannot stand alone because it depends on a main clause to help it make sense: Pia, *who plays the oboe,* prefers solitude.

For advice on subordination, see 14d–14f.

2d Use subordination to correct a comma splice or a fused sentence.

If one main clause is more important than the other, or if you want to give it more importance, you can make the less important one a subordinate clause. When you make one clause subordinate, you throw weight on the main clause. In effect, you show your reader how one idea relates to another: you decide which matters more.

FUSED SENTENCE	Hurricane winds hit ninety miles an hour they tore the roof from every house on Paradise Drive.
REVISED	*When hurricane winds hit ninety miles an hour,* they tore the roof from every house on Paradise Drive.
REVISED	Hurricane winds hit ninety miles an hour, *tearing the roof from every house on Paradise Drive.*

2e Use a conjunctive adverb with a semicolon and a comma to correct a comma splice or a fused sentence.

conjunctive adverb: A linking word that can connect independent clauses and show a relationship between two ideas: Armando is a serious student; *therefore,* he studies every day. (See 14.)

If you want to cram more than one clause into a sentence, you may join two clauses with a *conjunctive adverb.* Conjunctive adverbs show relationships such as addition (*also, besides*), comparison (*likewise, similarly*), contrast (*instead, however*), emphasis (*namely, certainly*), cause and effect (*thus, therefore*), or time (*finally, subsequently*). These transitional words and phrases can be a useful way of linking clauses — but only if used with the right punctuation.

COMMA SPLICE	Sigmund Freud has been called an enemy of sexual repression, however the truth is that he is not a friend of free love.

A writer might consider a comma plus the conjunctive adverb *however* enough to combine the two main clauses, but that glue won't hold. Stronger binding is called for.

REVISED	Sigmund Freud has been called an enemy of sexual repression; however, the truth is that he is not a friend of free love.

■ Exercise 2–1

Revising Comma Splices and Fused Sentences

In the following examples, correct each comma splice or fused sentence in two ways and decide which way you believe works best. Be creative: don't correct every one in the same way. Some sentences may be correct as written. Possible revisions for the lettered sentences appear in the back of the book. Example:

WWW
For more practice, visit *Exercise Central* at <www.bedfordstmartins.com/bedguide>.

> The castle looked eerie from a distance, it filled us with nameless fear as we approached.

> The castle looked eerie from a *distance;* it filled us with nameless fear as we approached.

> *Or*

> The castle, *which looked eerie from a distance,* filled us with nameless fear as we approached.

a. We followed the scientist down a flight of wet stone steps at last he stopped before a huge oak door.

b. Dr. Frankenstein selected a heavy key, he twisted it in the lock.

c. The huge door gave a groan it swung open on a dimly lighted laboratory.

d. Before us on a dissecting table lay a form with closed eyes to behold it sent a quick chill down my spine.

e. The scientist strode to the table, he lifted a white-gloved hand.

1. Dr. Frankenstein flung a power switch, blue streamers of static electricity crackled about the table, the creature gave a grunt and opened smoldering eyes.

2. "I've won!" exclaimed the scientist in triumph he circled the room doing a demented Irish reel.

3. The creature's right hand strained, the heavy steel manacle imprisoning his wrist began to creak.

4. Like a staple wrenched from a document, the manacle yielded.

5. The creature sat upright and tugged at the shackles binding his ankles, Frankenstein uttered a piercing scream.

■ Exercise 2–2

Revising Comma Splices and Fused Sentences

Revise the following passage, using subordination, a conjunctive adverb, a semicolon, or a colon to correct each comma splice or fused sentence. You may also write separate complete sentences. Some sentences may be correct. Example:

> English can be difficult to learn, it is full of expressions that don't mean what they literally say.

> English can be difficult to learn because it is full of expressions that don't mean what they literally say.

Have you ever wondered why you drive on parkways and park on driveways, that's about as logical as your nose running while your feet smell! When you stop to think about it, these phrases don't make sense yet we tend to accept them without thinking about what they literally mean we simply take their intended meanings for granted. Think, however, how confusing they are for a person who is just learning the language. If, for example, you have just learned the verb *park*, you would logically assume that a parkway is where you should park your car, of course when most people see a parkway or a driveway they realize that braking on a parkway would be hazardous, while speeding through a driveway will not take them very far. However, our language is full of many idiomatic expressions that may be difficult for a person from another language background to understand. Fortunately, there are plenty of questions to keep us *all* confused, such as why Americans commonly refer to going to work as "punching the clock."

3   *Verbs*

For help editing verbs, see A1 in the "Quick Editing Guide."

Most verbs show action (*swim, eat, sleep, win*). Some verbs indicate a state of being by linking the subject of a sentence with a word that renames or describes it; they are called **linking verbs** (*is, become, seem*). A few verbs work with a main verb to give more information about its action; they are called **helping verbs** or **auxiliary verbs** (*have, must, can*).

VERB FORMS

3a   Use a linking verb to connect the subject of a sentence with a subject complement.

linking verb: A verb (*is, become, seem, feel*) that shows a state of being by linking the sentence subject with a word that renames or describes the subject: The sky *is* blue.

subject complement: A noun, an adjective, or a group of words that follows a linking verb and renames or describes the subject: This plum tastes *ripe*.

By indicating what the subject of a sentence *is* or is *like*, a linking verb creates a sort of equation, either positive or negative, between the subject and its complement. The subject complement can be a noun, a pronoun, or an adjective.

       LV   SC
Julia will *make* a good *doctor*. [Noun]

    LV   SC
Jorge *is* not the *one*. [Pronoun]

           LV   SC
London weather *seems foggy*. [Adjective]

A verb may be a linking verb in some sentences and not in others. If you pay attention to what the verb means, you can usually tell how it is functioning.

I often *grow* sleepy after lunch. [Linking verb with subject complement *sleepy*]

I often *grow* tomatoes in my garden. [Transitive verb with direct object *tomatoes*]

> ## Common Linking Verbs at a Glance
>
> Some linking verbs tell what a noun is, was, or will be.
>
> > *be, become, remain*
> >
> > *grow:* The sky is *growing* dark.
> >
> > *make:* One plus two *makes* three.
> >
> > *prove:* His warning *proved* accurate.
> >
> > *turn:* The weather *turned* cold.
>
> Some linking verbs tell what a noun might be.
>
> > *appear, seem, look*
>
> Most verbs of the senses can operate as linking verbs.
>
> > *feel, smell, sound, taste*

3b   Use helping verbs to add information about the main verb.

Adding a *helping* or *auxiliary verb* to a simple verb (*go, shoot, be*) allows you to express a wide variety of tenses and moods (*am going, did shoot, would have been*). (See 3g–3l and 3n–3p.)

A main verb plus one or more helping verbs is called a *verb phrase*. The parts of a verb phrase need not appear together but may be separated by other words.

> I probably *am going* to France this summer.
>
> You *should* not *have shot* that pigeon.
>
> This change *may* well *have been* seriously *contemplated* by the governor even before the election.

helping verb: A verb added to a main verb to show variations in its action (*do, can, have, will*)

main verb: The verb in a sentence that identifies the central action (*hit, stopped*)

> ## Helping Verbs at a Glance
>
> Of the twenty-three helping verbs in English, fourteen can also function as main verbs:
>
> > be, is, am, are, was, were, being, been
> >
> > do, does, did
> >
> > have, has, had
>
> The other nine can function only as helping verbs, never as main verbs:
>
> > can, could, should, would, may, might, must, shall, will

3c   Use the correct principal parts of the verb.

For the principal parts of many irregular verbs, see A1 and A2 in the "Quick Editing Guide."

The *principal parts* are the forms the verb can take — alone or with helping verbs — to indicate the full range of times when an action or state of being does, did, or will occur. Verbs have three principal parts: the infinitive, the past tense, and the past participle.

The *infinitive* is the simple or dictionary form of the verb (*go, sing, laugh*) or the simple form preceded by *to* (*to go, to sing, to laugh*).

The *past tense* signals that the verb's action is completed (*went, sang, laughed*).

The *past participle* is combined with helping verbs to indicate action occurring at various times in the past or future (*have gone, had sung, will have laughed*). It is also used with forms of *be* to make the passive voice. (See 3m.)

In addition to the three principal parts, all verbs have a present participle, the *-ing* form of the verb (*going, singing, laughing*). The present participle is used to make the progressive tenses. (See 3k and 3l.) It also can modify nouns and pronouns ("the *leaking* bottle"); and, as a gerund, it can function as a noun ("*Sleeping all day* pleases me").

3d   Use *-d* or *-ed* to form the past tense and past participle of regular verbs.

Most verbs in English are *regular verbs:* they form the past tense and past participle in a standard, predictable way. Regular verbs that end in *-e* add *-d* to the infinitive; those that do not end in *-e* add *-ed*.

INFINITIVE	PAST TENSE	PAST PARTICIPLES
(to) smile	smiled	smiled
(to) act	acted	acted

3e   Use the correct forms for the past tense and past participle of irregular verbs.

For the forms of many irregular verbs, see A1 in the "Quick Editing Guide." For the forms of *be* and *have*, see A2 in the "Quick Editing Guide."

The English language has at least two hundred *irregular verbs,* which form their past tense and past participle in some other way than by adding *-d* or *-ed*. Most irregular verbs are familiar to native English speakers and pose no problem.

3f   Use the correct forms of *lie* and *lay* and *sit* and *set*.

By taking two easy steps, you can forever eliminate confusion between *lie* and *lay*. The first is to memorize the principal parts and present participles of both verbs (see the chart on p. H-17).

The second step is to fix in memory that *lie,* in all its forms, is intransitive. *Lie* never takes a direct object: "The island *lies* due east," "Jed *has lain* on

intransitive verb: A verb that is complete in itself and needs no object: The surgeon *paused*.

Forms of *Lie* and *Lay, Sit* and *Set*

lie, lay, lain, lying: recline

PRESENT TENSE		PAST TENSE	
I lie	we lie	I lay	we lay
you lie	you lie	you lay	you lay
he/she/it lies	they lie	he/she/it lay	they lay

PAST PARTICIPLE
lain   (We have *lain* in the sun long enough.)

PRESENT PARTICIPLE
lying   (At ten o'clock he was still *lying* in bed.)

lay, laid, laid, laying: put in place, deposit

PRESENT TENSE		PAST TENSE	
I lay	we lay	I laid	we laid
you lay	you lay	you laid	you laid
he/she/it lays	they lay	he/she/it laid	they laid

PAST PARTICIPLE
laid   (Having *laid* his clothes on the bed, Mark jumped into the shower.)

PRESENT PARTICIPLE
laying   (*Laying* her cards on the table, Lola cried, "Gin!")

sit, sat, sat, sitting: be seated

PRESENT TENSE		PAST TENSE	
I sit	we sit	I sat	we sat
you sit	you sit	you sat	you sat
he/she/it sits	they sit	he/she/it sat	they sat

PAST PARTICIPLE
sat   (I have *sat* here long enough.)

PRESENT PARTICIPLE
sitting   (Why are you *sitting* on that rickety bench?)

set, set, set, setting: place

PRESENT TENSE		PAST TENSE	
I set	we set	I set	we set
you set	you set	you set	you set
he/she/it sets	they set	he/she/it set	they set

PAST PARTICIPLE
set   (Paul has *set* the table for eight.)

PRESENT PARTICIPLE
setting   (Chanh-Duy has been *setting* pins at the Bowl-a-drome.)

transitive verb: A verb that must have an object to complete its meaning: Alan *hit* the ball.

the floor all day." *Lay*, a transitive verb, always requires an object: "*Lay* that pistol down."

The same distinction exists between *sit* and *set*. Usually, *sit* is intransitive: "He *sits* on the stairs." *Set*, on the other hand, almost always takes an object: "He *sets* the bottle on the counter." There are, however, a few easily memorized exceptions. The sun *sets*. A hen *sets*. Gelatin *sets*. You *sit* on a horse. You can *sit* yourself down at a table that *sits* twelve.

■ Exercise 3–1

Using Irregular Verb Forms

WWW
For more practice, visit *Exercise Central* at <www.bedfordstmartins .com/bedguide>.

Underline each incorrectly used irregular verb in the following sentences, and substitute the verb's correct form. Some sentences may be correct. Answers for the lettered sentences appear in the back of the book. Example:

> We have already <u>drove</u> eight hundred miles, and we still have a long way to go to reach Oregon.

> We have already *driven* eight hundred miles, and we still have a long way to go to reach Oregon.

a. In those days, Benjamin wrote all the music, and his sister sung all the songs.
b. After she had eaten her bagel, she drank a cup of coffee with milk.
c. When the bell rung, darkness had already fell.
d. Voters have chose several new representatives, who won't take office until January.
e. Carol threw the ball into the water, and the dog swum after it.

1. He brought along two of the fish they had caught the day before.
2. By the time the sun set, the birds had all went away.
3. Teachers had spoke to his parents long before he stole the bicycle.
4. While the cat laid on the bed, the mouse ran beneath the door.
5. For the past three days the wind has blew hard from the south, but now the clouds have began to drift in.

TENSES

tense: The time when the action of a verb did, does, or will occur

With the *simple tenses* we can indicate whether the verb's action took place in the past, takes place in the present, or will take place in the future. The *perfect tenses* enable us to narrow the timing even further, specifying that the action was or will be completed by the time of some other action. With the *progressive tenses* we can indicate that the verb's action did, does, or will continue.

For advice on consistent verb tense, see 9a.

Studying tenses can improve your writing by making you aware of the variety of verb forms at your disposal and by giving you practice at using them effectively.

> ## Verb Tenses at a Glance
>
> NOTE: The examples show first person only.
>
> SIMPLE TENSES
>
> | *Present* | *Past* | *Future* |
> |---|---|---|
> | I cook | I cooked | I will cook |
> | I see | I saw | I will see |
>
> PERFECT TENSES
>
> | *Present perfect* | *Past perfect* | *Future perfect* |
> |---|---|---|
> | I have cooked | I had cooked | I will have cooked |
> | I have seen | I had seen | I will have seen |
>
> PROGRESSIVE TENSES
>
> | *Present progressive* | *Past progressive* | *Future progressive* |
> |---|---|---|
> | I am cooking | I was cooking | I will be cooking |
> | I am seeing | I was seeing | I will be seeing |
>
> | *Present perfect progressive* | *Past perfect progressive* | *Future perfect progressive* |
> |---|---|---|
> | I have been cooking | I had been cooking | I will have been cooking |
> | I have been seeing | I had been seeing | I will have been seeing |

3g **Use the simple present tense for an action that takes place once, repeatedly, or continuously in the present.**

The simple present tense is the infinitive form of a regular verb plus *-s* or *-es* for the third-person singular.

I like, I go	we like, we go
you like, you go	you like, you go
he/she/it likes, he/she/it goes	they like, they go

Some irregular verbs, such as *go*, form their simple present tense following the same rules as regular verbs. Other irregular verbs, such as *be* and *have*, are special cases for which you should learn the correct forms.

I am, I have	we are, we have
you are, you have	you are, you have
he/she/it is, he/she/it has	they are, they have

You can use the simple present tense for an action that is happening right now ("I *welcome* this news"), an action that happens repeatedly in the present ("Judy *goes* to church every Sunday"), or an ongoing present action ("Wesley *likes* ice cream"). In some cases, if you want to ask a question or intensify the action, use the helping verb *do* or *does* before the infinitive form of the main verb.

I *do think* you should take the job.

Does Christos *want* it?

Besides present action, you can use the simple present for future action: "Football season *starts* Wednesday."

Use the simple present for a general truth, even if the rest of the sentence is in a different tense:

Columbus proved in 1492 that the world *is* round.

Mr. Hammond will argue that people *are* basically good.

3h Use the simple past tense for actions already completed.

For a chart of troublesome irregular verbs, see A1 in the "Quick Editing Guide."

Regular verbs form the past tense by adding *-d* or *-ed* to the infinitive; the past tense of irregular verbs must be memorized.

Jack *enjoyed* the party. [Regular verb]

Akita *went* home early. [Irregular verb]

Although speakers may not always pronounce the *-d* or *-ed* ending clearly, standard written English requires that you add the *-d* or *-ed* to all regular past tense verbs.

| NONSTANDARD | I *use* to wear weird clothes when I was a child. |
| STANDARD | I *used* to wear weird clothes when I was a child. |

In the past tense, you can use the helping verb *did* (past tense of *do*) to ask a question or intensify the action. Use *did* with the infinitive form of the main verb for both regular and irregular verbs.

I went.	I did go.	Why did I go?
You saw.	You did see.	What did you see?
She ran.	She did run.	Where did she run?

3i Use the simple future tense for actions that are expected to happen but have not happened yet.

George *will arrive* in time for dinner.

Will you please *show* him where to park?

To form the simple future tense, add *will* to the infinitive form of the verb.

I will go	we will go
you will go	you will go
he/she/it will go	they will go

You can also use *shall* to inject a tone of determination ("We *shall overcome!*") or in polite questions ("*Shall* we dance?").

The Simple Tenses

Present Tense: base form of the verb (+ *-s* or *-es* for *he, she, it*)

- Use the simple present tense to express general statements of fact or habitual activities or customs. Although it is called "present," this tense is really general or timeless.

    You *make* wonderful coffee.

    Zanetta *goes* to the movies every Sunday afternoon.

- To form negatives and questions, use *do* or *does* + base form.

    Zanetta *does not* (*doesn't*) go to the movies during the week.

    Do you still *make* wonderful coffee?

Past Tense: base form + *-d* or *-ed* for regular verbs

For the past forms of many irregular verbs, see A1 in the "Quick Editing Guide."

- Use the simple past tense to express an action that occurred at a specific time in the past. The specific time may be stated or implied.

    The package *arrived* yesterday.

    They *went* to San Juan for spring break.

- To form negatives and questions, use *did* + base form.

    They *did not* (*didn't*) go to Fort Lauderdale.

    Did the package *arrive* yesterday?

Future Tense: *will* or *be going to* + base form

- Use the simple future tense to express an action that will take place in the future. Also use *will* to imply promises and predictions.

    The students *will study* hard for their exam.

    The students *are going to study* hard for their exam.

    We *will help* you move. [Promise]

    Computers *will* soon *replace* most typewriters. [Prediction]

- To form negatives and questions, use *will* + base form.

    José *will not* (*won't*) *graduate* this year.

    Will computers *replace* typewriters?

NOTE: Use the simple present, not the future, to express future meaning in clauses beginning with *before, after,* or *when*.

> INCORRECT   When my mother *will get* home from work, we will make dinner.
>
> CORRECT   When my mother *gets* home from work, we will make dinner.

Use the simple present to show a future action when other words in the sentence make the future meaning clear.

    The bus *departs* in five minutes.

    We *leave* for Chicago in the morning and *return* next Wednesday.

Although the present tense can indicate future action ("We *go* on vacation next Monday"), most actions that have not yet taken place are expressed in the simple future tense ("Surely it *will snow* tomorrow").

3j   Use the perfect tenses for an action completed at the time of another action.

The present perfect, past perfect, and future perfect tenses consist of a form of the helping verb *have* plus the past participle. The tense of *have* indicates the tense of the whole verb phrase.

The action of a ***present perfect*** verb was completed before the sentence is uttered. Its helping verb is in the present tense: *have* or *has*.

ESL GUIDELINES

For the forms of many irregular verbs, see A1 in the "Quick Editing Guide."

The Perfect Tenses

Present Perfect Tense: *has* or *have* + past participle (*-ed* or *-en* form for regular verbs)

- Use the present perfect tense when an action took place at some unspecified time in the past. The action may have occurred repeatedly.

  I *have traveled* to many countries.

  The dog *has bitten* my aunt twice.

- Use the present perfect tense with *for* and *since* to indicate that an action began in the past, is occurring now, and will probably continue.

  I *have gone* to school with Min and Paolo since fifth grade.

  Soo-Jung *has lived* next door to the Kramers for twelve years.

Past Perfect Tense: *had* + past participle

- Use the past perfect tense to indicate an action was completed in the past before some other past action.

  Josef *had smoked* for many years before he decided to quit.

  We got rid of the dog because he *had bitten* my aunt twice.

- Particularly in speech or informal writing, the simple past may be used instead of the past perfect when the relationship between actions is made clear by a conjunction such as *when, before, after,* or *until*.

  Observers *saw* the place catch fire before it landed.

Future Perfect Tense: *will* + *have* + past participle

- Use the future perfect tense when an action will take place before some time in the future.

  The package *will have* already *arrived* by the time we get home from work.

  By June, the students *will have studied* ten chapters.

I *have* never *been* to Spain, but I *have been* to Oklahoma.

Mr. Grimaldi *has gone* home for the day.

Have you *seen* John Sayles's new film?

You can use the present perfect tense either for an action completed before some other action ("I *have washed* my hands of the whole affair, but I am watching from a safe distance") or for an action begun in the past and still going on ("Max *has worked* in this office for twelve years").

The action of a *past perfect* verb was completed before some other action in the past. Its helping verb is in the past tense: *had.*

The concert *had ended* by the time we found a parking space.

Until I met her, I *had* not *pictured* Jenna as a redhead.

Had you *wanted* to clean the house before Mother arrived?

The action of a *future perfect* verb will be completed by some point (specified or implied) in the future. Its helping verb is in the future tense: *will have.*

The builders *will have finished* the house by June.

When you get the Dutch Blue, *will* you *have collected* every stamp you need?

The store *will* not *have closed* by the time we get there.

3k   Use the simple progressive tenses for an action in progress.

The present progressive, past progressive, and future progressive tenses consist of a form of the helping verb *be* plus the present participle (which is formed by adding *-ing* to the infinitive). The tense of *be* determines the tense of the whole verb phrase.

The *present progressive* expresses an action that is taking place now. Its helping verb is in the present tense: *am, is,* or *are.*

I *am thinking* of a word that starts with *R.*

Is Stefan *babysitting* while Marie *is* off *visiting* her sister?

You can also express future action with the present progressive of *go* plus an infinitive phrase.

I *am going to read* Tolstoy's *War and Peace* someday.

Are you *going to sign up* for Professor Blaine's course on the sixties?

The *past progressive* expresses an action that took place continuously at some time in the past, whether or not that action is still going on. Its helping verb is in the past tense: *was* or *were.*

The old men *were sitting* on the porch when we passed.

Lucy *was planning* to take the weekend off.

The Simple Progressive Tenses

Present Progressive Tense: present tense of *be* + present participle (*-ing* form)

- Use the present progressive tense when an action began in the past, is happening now, and will end at some time in the future.

   The students *are studying* for their exam.

   My sister *is living* with us until she graduates from college.

- You can also use the present progressive tense to show a future action when other words in the sentence make the future meaning clear.

   Nili *is flying* to Pittsburgh on July 8.

NOTE: Linking verbs (such as *be, seem, look*), verbs that express an emotional or mental state (such as *trust, like, guess, realize*), and verbs without action (such as *belong, have, need*) are not generally used in the present progressive tense. For these verbs, use the present tense to express a continuous state.

   INCORRECT   I think I *am liking* you very much.

   CORRECT   I think I *like* you very much.

Past Progressive Tense: *was* or *were* + present participle

- Use the past progressive tense when an action began and continued at a specific time in the past.

   Maria *was watching* the news when I arrived.

   The students *were studying* for their exam all day.

Future Progressive Tense: *will be* + present participle; or present tense of *be* + *going to be* + present participle

- Use the future progressive tense when an action will begin and will continue in the future.

   Hans *will be wearing* blue jeans to the party tonight.

   The students *are going to be studying* until midnight.

The *future progressive* expresses an action that will take place continuously at some time in the future. Its helping verb is in the future tense: *will be.*

They *will be answering* the phones while she is gone.

Will we *be dining* out every night on our vacation?

31 Use the perfect progressive tenses for a continuing action that began in the past.

Use the present perfect progressive, the past perfect progressive, or the future perfect progressive tense for an action that started in the past and did, does, or will continue.

The *present perfect progressive* indicates an action that started in the past and is continuing in the present. Form it by adding the present perfect of *be* (*has been* or *have been*) to the present participle (the *-ing* form) of the main verb.

All morning Fred *has been singing* the blues about his neighbor's wild parties.

Have you *been reading* Uma's postcards from England?

The *past perfect progressive* expresses a continuing action that was completed before another past action. Form it by adding the past perfect of *be* (*had been*) to the present participle of the main verb.

By the time Khalid finally arrived, I *had been waiting* for twenty minutes.

The *future perfect progressive* expresses an action that is expected to continue into the future beyond some other future action. Form it by adding the future perfect of *be* (*will have been*) to the present participle of the main verb.

By 2006 Joanne *will have been attending* school longer than anyone else I know.

The Perfect Progressive Tenses

ESL GUIDELINES

Present Perfect Progressive Tense: *have* or *has been* + present participle (*-ing* form)

- Use the present perfect progressive tense when an action began at some time in the past and has continued to the present. The words *for* and *since* are often used in sentences with this tense.

    She *has been answering* questions all day.

    The students *have been studying* for a long time.

Past Perfect Progressive Tense: *had been* + present participle

- Use the past perfect progressive tense when an action began and continued in the past and then was completed before some other past action.

    We *had been studying* for three hours before we took a break.

    Miguel *had been ringing* the doorbell for five minutes when we got home.

Future Perfect Progressive Tense: *will have been* + present participle

- Use the future perfect progressive tense when an action will continue in the future for a specific amount of time and then will end before another future action.

    The students *will have been studying* for twenty-four hours by the time they take the exam tomorrow.

    The captain *will have been sailing* for ten days when she arrives in Jamaica.

■ Exercise 3–2

Identifying Verb Tenses

Underline each verb or verb phrase and identify its tense in the following sentences. Answers for the lettered sentences appear in the back of the book. Example:

> John is living in Hinsdale, but he prefers Joliet.
>
> John <u>is living</u> [present progressive] in Hinsdale, but he <u>prefers</u> [simple present] Joliet.

a. He has been living like a hunted animal ever since he hacked into the university computer lab to change all of his grades.

b. I have never appeared on a television talk show, and I never will appear on one unless Jerry Springer asks me nicely.

c. James had been at the party for only fifteen minutes when his host suddenly pitched the caterer into the swimming pool.

d. As of next month, I will have been studying karate for six years, and I will be taking the test for my orange belt in July.

e. The dachshund was running at its fastest speed, but the squirrel strolled toward the tree without fear.

1. As of December 1, Ira and Sandy will have been going together for three years.

2. She will be working in her study if you need her.

3. Have you been hoping that Carlos will come to your party?

4. I know that he will not yet have returned from Chicago.

5. His parents had been expecting him home any day until they heard that he was still waiting for the bus.

VOICE

> Intelligent students read challenging books.
>
> Challenging books are read by intelligent students.

These two statements convey similar information, but their emphasis is different. In the first sentence, the subject (*students*) performs the verb's action (*read*); in the second sentence, the subject (*books*) receives the verb's action (*are read*). One sentence states its idea directly, the other indirectly. We say that the first sentence is in the ***active voice*** and the second is in the ***passive voice***.

3m Use the active voice rather than the passive voice.

Verbs in the ***active voice*** consist of principal parts and helping verbs. Verbs in the ***passive voice*** consist of the past participle preceded by a form of *be* ("you *are given*," "I *was given*," "she *will be given*"). Most writers prefer the active to the passive voice because it is clearer and simpler, requires fewer words, and identifies the actor and the action more explicitly.

ACTIVE VOICE   *Sergeants give* orders. *Privates obey* them.

Some writers use a verb in the passive voice when the active voice would be more effective. Normally the subject of a sentence is the focus of the readers' attention. If that subject does not perform the verb's action but instead receives the action, readers may wonder: What did the writer mean to emphasize? Just what is the point?

PASSIVE VOICE   *Orders are given* by sergeants. *They are obeyed* by privates.

The Passive Voice

Passive Voice: form of *be* + past participle (*-ed* or *-en* form for regular verbs)

ESL GUIDELINES

- In a passive voice sentence, the grammatical subject *receives* the action of the verb instead of performing it.

    ACTIVE   The university *awarded* Hamid a scholarship. [The subject (*university*) performs the action of *awarding*.]

    PASSIVE   Hamid *was awarded* a scholarship by the university. [The subject (*Hamid*) receives the action.]

- Often the identity of the action's performer is not important or is understood, and the *by* phrase is omitted.

    PASSIVE   Automobiles are built in Detroit. [It is understood that they are built *by people*.]

- When forming the passive, be careful to use the appropriate tenses of *be* to maintain the tense of the original active sentence.

    ACTIVE   Bongo the clown *entertains* children. [Present tense]

    PASSIVE   Children *are entertained* by Bongo the clown. [Present tense]

    ACTIVE   Bongo the clown *entertained* the children. [Past tense]

    PASSIVE   The children *were entertained* by Bongo the clown. [Past tense]

NOTE: Intransitive verbs are not used in the passive voice.

intransitive verb: A verb that is complete in itself and needs no object: The surgeon *paused.*

    INCORRECT   The plane *was arrived*.

    CORRECT   The plane *arrived*.

NOTE: The future progressive and future perfect progressive tenses are not used in the passive voice.

    INCORRECT   The novel *will be being read* by John.

    CORRECT   John *will be reading* the novel.

Other writers misuse the passive voice to try to lend pomp to a humble truth (or would-be truth). When the airplane needs repairs, the flight attendant tells the passengers, "Slight technical difficulties are being experienced." Some even use the passive voice deliberately to obscure the truth — a contradiction of the very purpose of writing.

You do not need to eliminate the passive voice entirely from your writing. In some contexts the performer of the verb's action in a sentence is unknown or irrelevant. With a passive voice verb, you can simply omit the performer, as in "Many fortunes were lost in the stock market crash of 1929" or "The passive voice is often misused." It's a good idea, though, as you comb through a rough draft, to substitute the active voice for the passive unless you have a good reason for using the passive.

■ **Exercise 3–3**

Using Active and Passive Voice Verbs

Revise the following passage, changing the passive voice to the active voice in each sentence, unless you can justify keeping the passive. Example:

> The Galápagos Islands were reached by many species of animals in ancient times.

> Many species of animals *reached* the Galápagos Islands in ancient times.

The unique creatures of the Galápagos Islands have been studied by many scientists. The islands were explored by Charles Darwin in 1835. His observations led to the theory of evolution, which he explained in his book *On the Origin of Species*. Thirteen species of finches on the islands were discovered by Darwin, all descended from a common stock; even today this great variety of species can be seen by visitors to the islands. Each island species has evolved by adapting to local conditions. A twig is used by the woodpecker finch to probe trees for grubs. Algae on the ocean floor is fed on by the marine iguana. Salt water can be drunk by the Galápagos cormorant, thanks to a salt-extracting gland. Because of the tameness of these animals, they can be studied by visitors at close range.

MOOD

Still another characteristic of verbs is mood. Every verb is in one of three *moods:* the *indicative,* the *imperative,* or the *subjunctive.* The indicative mood is the most common. The imperative mood and subjunctive mood add valuable versatility to the English language.

3n Use the indicative mood to state a fact, to ask a question, or to express an opinion.

The vast majority of verbs in English are in the indicative mood.

FACT   Danika *left* home two months ago.

QUESTION   *Will* she *find* happiness as a belly dancer?

OPINION   I *think* not.

3o   Use the imperative mood to make a request or to give a command or direction.

The understood but usually unstated subject of a verb in the imperative mood is *you*. The verb's form is the infinitive.

REQUEST   Please *be* there before noon. [*You* please be there. . . .]

COMMAND   *Hurry!* [*You* hurry!]

DIRECTION   To reach my house, *drive* east on State Street. [. . . *you* drive east. . . .]

3p   Use the subjunctive mood to express a wish, a requirement, a suggestion, or a condition contrary to fact.

The subjunctive mood is used in a subordinate clause to suggest uncertainty: the action expressed by the verb may or may not actually take place as specified. In any clause opening with *that* and expressing a requirement, the verb is in the subjunctive mood and its form is the infinitive.

> Professor Voegtli requires that every student *deliver* his or her work promptly.

> She asked that we *be* on time for all meetings.

When you use the subjunctive mood to describe a condition that is contrary to fact, use *were* if the verb is *be*; for other verbs, use the simple past tense. Wishes, whether present or past, follow the same rules.

> If I *were* rich, I would be happy.

> If I *had* a million dollars, I would be happy.

> Elissa wishes that Ted *were* more goal-oriented.

> Elissa wished that Ted *knew* what he wanted to do.

For a condition that was contrary to fact at some point in the past, use the past perfect tense.

> If I *had been* awake, I would have seen the meteor showers.

> If Jessie *had known* you were coming, she would have cleaned her room.

Although use of the subjunctive mood has grown scarcer over the years, it still sounds crude to write "If I *was* you. . . ." If you ever feel that the subjunctive mood makes a sentence sound stilted, you can rewrite it, substituting an infinitive phrase.

> Professor Voegtli requires every student *to deliver* his or her work promptly.

ESL GUIDELINES

Conditionals

Conditional sentences usually contain an *if* clause, which states the condition, and a result clause.

- When the condition is true or possibly true in the present or future, use the present tense in the *if* clause and the present or future tense in the result clause. The future tense is not used in the *if* clause.

  If Jane *prepares* her composition early, she usually *writes* very well.

  If Maria *saves* enough money, she *will buy* some new software.

- When the condition is not true in the present, for most verbs use the past tense in the *if* clause; for the verb **be,** use **were.** Use **would, could,** or **might** + infinitive form in the result clause.

  If Carlos *had* a computer, he *would need* a monitor, too.

  If Claudia *were* here, she *could do* it herself.

- When the condition was not true in the past, use the past perfect tense in the *if* clause. If the possible result was in the past, use **would have, could have,** or **might have** + past participle (-*ed* or -*en* form) in the result clause. If the possible result is in the present, use **would, could,** or **might** + infinitive form in the result clause.

  If Claudia *had saved* enough money last month, she *could have bought* new software. [Result in the past]

  If Annie *had finished* law school, she *might* be a successful lawyer now. [Result in the present]

■ Exercise 3–4

Using the Correct Mood of Verbs

Find and correct any errors in mood of verbs in the following sentences. Identify the mood of the incorrect verb as well as of its correct replacement. Some sentences may be correct. Answers for the lettered sentences appear in the back of the book. Example:

> The law requires that each person files a tax return by April 15.

> The law requires that each person *file* a tax return by April 15. [Incorrect *files,* indicative; correct *file,* subjunctive]

a. Dr. Belanger recommended that Juan flosses his teeth every day.

b. If I was you, I would have done the same thing.

c. Tradition demands that Daegun shows respect for his elders.

d. Please attends the training lesson if you plan to skydive later today.

1. If she was slightly older, she could stay home by herself.

2. If they have waited a little longer, they would have seen some amazing things.

3. Emilia's contract stipulates that she works on Saturdays.

4. If James invested in the company ten years ago, he would have made a lot of money.

4 Subject-Verb Agreement

What does it mean for a subject and a verb to agree? Practically speaking, it means that their forms match: plural subjects take plural verbs, third-person subjects take third-person verbs, and so forth. When your subjects and verbs agree, you prevent a mismatch that could distract readers from your message.

For more on editing for subject-verb agreement, see A2 in the "Quick Editing Guide."

4a A verb agrees with its subject in person and number.

Subject and verb agree in person (first, second, or third):

I write my research papers on a typewriter. [Subject and verb in first person]

Eamon writes his research papers on a word processor. [Subject and verb in third person]

Subject and verb agree in number (singular or plural):

Grace has enjoyed college. [Subject and verb singular]

She and Jim have enjoyed their vacation. [Subject and verb plural]

The present tense of most verbs is the infinitive form, with no added ending except in the third-person singular. (See 3g–3l.)

subject: The part of a sentence that names something—a person, an object, an idea, a situation—about which the predicate makes an assertion: The *king* lives.

I enjoy	we enjoy
you enjoy	you enjoy
he/she/it enjoys	they enjoy

Forms of the verb *be* vary from this rule.

verb: A word that shows action (The cow *jumped* over the moon) or a state of being (The cow *is* brown)

I am	we are
you are	you are
he/she/it is	they are

4b A verb agrees with its subject, not with any words that intervene.

My *favorite* of O. Henry's short stories *is* "The Gift of the Magi."

Home sales, once driving the local economy, *have fallen* during the last few months.

A singular subject linked to another noun or pronoun by a prepositional phrase beginning with wording such as *along with, as well as,* or *in addition to* remains a singular subject and takes a singular verb.

My cousin *James* as well as his wife and son *plans* to vote for Levine.

prepositional phrase: The preposition and its object (a noun or pronoun), plus any modifiers: *in the bar, under a rickety table*

4c Subjects joined by *and* usually take a plural verb.

compound subject: A subject consisting of two or more nouns or pronouns linked by *and: My mother and my sister drove home.*

In most cases, a compound subject takes a plural verb.

"Howl" and "Gerontion" are Barry's favorite poems.

Sugar, salt, and fat adversely *affect* people's health.

However, for phrases like *each man and woman* or *every dog and cat,* where the subjects are considered individually, use a singular verb.

Each man and woman in the room *has* a different story to tell.

Use a singular verb for two singular subjects that refer to the same thing.

Lime juice and soda quenches your thirst.

4d With subjects joined by *or* or *nor,* the verb agrees with the part of the subject nearest to it.

Either they or *Max is* guilty.

Neither Swaylhi nor *I am* willing to face the truth.

Subjects containing *not . . . but* follow this rule also.

Not we but *George knows* the whole story.

You can remedy the awkwardness of such constructions by rephrasing.

Either they are guilty or Max is.

Swaylhi and I are unwilling to face the truth.

We do not know the whole story, but George does.

4e Most collective nouns take singular verbs.

collective noun: A singular noun that represents a group of people or items, such as *committee, family, jury, trio*

When a collective noun refers to a group of people acting in unison, use a singular verb.

The *jury finds* the defendant guilty.

When the members act individually, use a plural verb.

The *jury do* not yet *agree* on a verdict.

For more on agreement with collective nouns, see 7e.

If you feel that using a plural verb results in an awkward sentence, re-word the subject so that it refers to members of the group individually.

The *jurors do* not yet *agree* on a verdict.

Count Nouns and Articles

Nouns referring to items that can be counted are called *count* (or *countable*) nouns. Count nouns can be made plural.

> *table, chair, egg*   two *tables*, several *chairs*, a dozen *eggs*

Singular count nouns must be preceded by a *determiner*. The class of words called determiners includes ***articles*** (*a, an, the*), ***possessives*** (*John's, your, his, my,* and so on), ***demonstratives*** (*this, that, these, those*), ***numbers*** (*three, the third,* and so on), and ***indefinite quantity words*** (*no, some, many,* and so on).

> *a* dog, *the* football, *one* reason, *the first* page, *no* chance

ESL GUIDELINES

Noncount Nouns and Articles

Nouns referring to items that cannot be counted are called *noncount* (or *uncountable*) nouns. Noncount nouns cannot be made plural.

For more on using articles with count and noncount nouns, see pp. H-48–49.

INCORRECT   I need to learn more *grammars*.

CORRECT   I need to learn more *grammar*.

- Common categories of noncount nouns include types of ***food*** (*cheese, meat, bread*), ***solids*** (*dirt, salt, chalk*), ***liquids*** (*milk, juice, gasoline*), ***gases*** (*methane, hydrogen, air*), and ***abstract ideas*** including emotions (*democracy, gravity, love*).

- Another category of noncount nouns is ***mass*** nouns, which usually represent a large group of countable nouns, such as *furniture, mail,* and *clothing*.

- The only way to count noncountable nouns is to use a countable noun with them, usually to indicate a quantity or a container.

  > one *piece* of furniture
  >
  > two *quarts* of water
  >
  > an *example* of jealousy

- Noncount nouns are never preceded by an indefinite article; they are often preceded by *some*.

INCORRECT   She gave us *a* good advice.

CORRECT   She gave us good advice.

CORRECT   She gave us *some* good advice.

- When noncount nouns are *general* in meaning, no article is required, but when the context makes them specific (usually in a phrase or a clause after the noun), the definite article is used.

GENERAL   Deliver us from *evil*.

SPECIFIC   The *evil* that humans do lives after them.

4f   Most indefinite pronouns take a third-person singular verb.

indefinite pronoun: A pronoun standing for an unspecified person or thing, including singular forms (*any, each, everyone, no one*) and plural forms (*both, few*): *Everyone is soaking wet.*

The indefinite pronouns *each, either, neither, anyone, anybody, anything, everyone, everybody, everything, one, no one, nobody, nothing, someone, somebody,* and *something* are considered singular and take a third-person singular verb.

> *Someone is bothering* me.

Even when one of these subjects is followed by a phrase containing a noun or pronoun of a different person or number, use a singular verb.

> *Each* of you *is* here to stay.

> *One* of the pandas *seems* dangerously ill.

4g   The indefinite pronouns *all, any,* and *some* use a singular or plural verb depending on their meaning.

For a list of indefinite pronouns, see A4 in the "Quick Editing Guide."

> I have no explanation. *Is any* needed?

> *Any* of the changes considered critical *have* been made already.

> *All is* lost.

> *All* of the bananas *are gone.*

> *Some* of the blame *is* mine.

> *Some* of us *are* Democrats.

For more on agreement with indefinite pronouns, see 7d.

None — like *all, any,* and *some* — takes a singular or a plural verb, depending on the sense in which the pronoun is used.

> *None* of you *is* exempt.

> *None* of his wives *were* blond.

4h   In a subordinate clause with a relative pronoun as the subject, the verb agrees with the antecedent.

subordinate clause: A group of words that contains a subject and a verb but cannot stand alone because it depends on a main clause to help it make sense: *Pia, who plays the oboe,* prefers solitude. (See 14d–14f.)

To determine the person and number of the verb in a subordinate clause whose subject is *who, which,* or *that,* look back at the word to which the pronoun refers. The antecedent is usually (but not always) the noun closest to the relative pronoun.

> I have a roommate *who studies* day and night. [The antecedent of *who* is the third-person singular noun *roommate.* Therefore, the verb in the subordinate clause is third-person singular, *studies.*]

Unfortunately, I bought one of the two hundred new cars *that have* defective upholstery. [The antecedent of *that* is *cars,* so the verb is third-person plural, *have.*]

This is the only one of the mayor's new ideas *that has* any worth. [Here *one,* not *ideas,* is the antecedent of *that.* Thus, the verb in the subordinate clause is third-person singular, *has,* not *have.*]

4i **A verb agrees with its subject even when the subject follows the verb.**

In some sentences, an introductory phrase or a word such as *there* or *here* changes the ordinary subject-verb order so that the subject follows the verb. Remember that verbs agree with subjects and that *here* and *there* are never subjects.

Here *is* a *riddle* for you.

There *are* forty *people* in my law class.

Under the bridge *were* a broken-down *boat and* a worn *tire.*

4j **A linking verb agrees with its subject, not its subject complement.**

When a form of the verb *be* is used to link two or more nouns, the subject is the noun that precedes the linking verb. Nouns that follow the linking verb are subject complements. Make a linking verb agree with the subject of the sentence, not with the subject complement.

Jim is a gentleman and a scholar.

Amy's *parents are* her most enthusiastic audience.

4k **When the subject is a title, use a singular verb.**

When I was younger, *Harry Potter and the Sorcerer's Stone was* my favorite book.

"Memories" sung by Barbra Streisand *is* my aunt's favorite song.

4l **Singular nouns that end in -s take singular verbs.**

Some nouns look plural even though they refer to a singular subject: *measles, logistics, mathematics, electronics.* Such nouns take singular verbs.

The *news is* that *economics has become* one of the most popular majors.

---

relative pronoun: A pronoun (*who, which, that, what, whom, whomever, whose*) that opens a subordinate clause, modifying a noun or pronoun in another clause: The gift *that* I received is very practical.

antecedent: The word to which a pronoun refers: *Lyn* plays golf, and *she* putts well.

linking verb: A verb (*is, become, seem, feel*) that shows a state of being by linking the sentence subject with a word that renames or describes the subject: The sky *is* blue. (See 3a.)

subject complement: A noun, an adjective, or a group of words that follows a linking verb and renames or describes the subject: This plum tastes *ripe.* (See 3a.)

www
For more practice, visit *Exercise Central* at <www.bedfordstmartins.com/bedguide>.

■ **Exercise 4–1**

Making Subjects and Verbs Agree

Find and correct any errors of subject-verb agreement in the following sentences. Some sentences may be correct. Answers for the lettered sentences appear in the back of the book. Example:

> Addressing the audience tonight is the nominees for club president.
>
> Addressing the audience tonight *are* the nominees for club president.

a. For many college graduates, the process of looking for jobs are often long and stressful.

b. Not too long ago, searching the classifieds and inquiring in person was the primary methods of job hunting.

c. Today, however, everyone also seem to use the Internet to search for openings or to e-mail their résumés.

d. My classmates and my cousin sends most résumés over the Internet because it costs less than mailing them.

e. All of the résumés arrives quickly when they are sent electronically.

1. There are many people who thinks that interviewing is the most stressful part of the job search.

2. Sometimes only one person conducts an interview, while other times a whole committee conduct it.

3. Either the interviewer or the committee usually begin by asking simple questions about your background.

4. Making eye contact, dressing professionally, and appearing confident is some of the qualities an interviewer may consider important.

5. After an interview, most people sends a thank-you letter to the person who conducted it.

5 *Pronoun Case*

For advice on editing pronoun case, see A3 in the "Quick Editing Guide."

As you know, pronouns come in distinctive forms. The first-person pronoun can be *I*, or it can be *me, my, mine, we, us, our,* or *ours.* Which form do you pick? It depends on what job you want the pronoun to do.

Depending on a pronoun's function in a sentence, we say that it is in the *subjective case,* the *objective case,* or the *possessive case.* Some pronouns change form when they change case, and some do not. The personal pronouns *I, he, she, we,* and *they* and the relative pronoun *who* have different forms in the subjective, objective, and possessive cases. Other pronouns, such as *you, it, that,* and *which,* have only two forms: the plain case (which serves as both subjective and objective) and the possessive case.

We can pin the labels *subjective, objective,* and *possessive* on nouns as well as on pronouns. Like the pronouns *you, it, that,* and *which,* nouns shift out of their plain form only in the possessive case (*teacher's* pet, the *Joneses'* poodle).

Beware, when you are not sure which case to choose, of the temptation to fall back on a reflexive pronoun (*myself, himself*). If you catch yourself writing, "You can return the form to John or *myself*" or "John and *myself* are in charge," replace the reflexive pronoun with one that is grammatically correct: "You can return the form to John or *me*"; "John and *I* are in charge."

5a Use the subjective case for the subject of a sentence or clause.

Jed and *I* ate the granola.

Who cares?

Maya recalled that *she* played jai alai.

Election officials are the people *who* count.

A pronoun serving as the subject for a verb is subjective even when the verb isn't written but is only implied:

Jed is hungrier than *I* [am].

Don't be fooled by a pronoun that appears immediately after a verb, as if it were a direct object, but that functions as the subject of a clause. The pronoun's case is determined by its role, not by its position.

The judge didn't believe *I* hadn't been the driver.

We were happy to interview *whoever* was running. [Subject of *was running*]

5b Use the subjective case for a subject complement.

When a pronoun functions as a subject complement, it plays essentially the same role as the subject and its case is subjective.

The phantom graffiti artist couldn't have been *he*. It was *I*.

5c Use the subjective case for an appositive to a subject or subject complement.

A pronoun placed in apposition to a subject or subject complement is like an identical twin to the noun it stands beside. It has the same meaning and the same case.

The class *officers* — Ravi and *she* — announced a senior breakfast.

---

subject: The part of a sentence that names something—a person, an object, an idea, a situation—about which the predicate makes an assertion: The *king* lives.

direct object: The target of a verb that completes the action performed by the subject or asserted about the subject: I photographed *the sheriff.*

subject complement: A noun, an adjective, or a group of words that follows a linking verb (*is, become, feel, seem,* or another verb that shows a state of being) and that renames or describes the subject: This plum tastes *ripe.* (See 3a.)

appositive: A word or group of words that adds information about a subject or object by identifying it in a different way: my dog *Rover,* Hal's brother *Fred*

5d Use the objective case for a direct object, an indirect object, the object of a preposition, or a subject of an infinitive.

The custard pies hit *him* and *me*. [Direct object]

Mona threw *us* towels. [Indirect object]

Mona threw towels to *him* and *us*. [Object of a preposition]

We always expect *him* to win. [Subject of an infinitive]

indirect object: A person or thing affected by the subject's action, usually the recipient of the direct object, through the action indicated by a verb such as *bring, get, offer, promise, sell, show, tell,* and *write:* Charlene asked *you* a question.

5e Use the objective case for an appositive to a direct or indirect object or the object of a preposition.

Mona helped us *all*—Mrs. Van Dumont, *him,* and *me.* [*Him* and *me* are in apposition to the direct object *us.*]

Binks gave his favorite *students,* Tom and *her,* an approving nod. [*Her* is in apposition to the indirect object *students.*]

Yelling, the pie flingers ran after *us*—Mona, *him,* and *me.* [*Him* and *me* are in apposition to *us,* the object of the preposition *after.*]

5f Use the possessive case to show ownership.

Possessive pronouns can function as adjectives or as nouns. The pronouns *my, your, his, her, its, our,* and *their* function as adjectives by modifying nouns or pronouns.

My new bike is having *its* first road test today.

For a chart of possessive personal pronouns, see C2 in the "Quick Editing Guide."

Notice that the possessive pronoun *its* does not contain an apostrophe. *It's* with an apostrophe is a contraction for *it is,* as in "*It's* a beautiful day for bike riding."

The possessive pronouns *mine, yours, his, hers, ours,* and *theirs* can discharge the whole range of noun duties, serving as subjects, subject complements, direct objects, indirect objects, or objects of prepositions.

Yours is the last vote we need. [Subject]

This day is *ours.* [Subject complement]

Don't take your car; take *mine.* [Direct object]

If we're honoring requests, give *hers* top priority. [Indirect object]

Give her request priority over *theirs.* [Object of a preposition]

5g Use the possessive case to modify a gerund.

gerund: A form of a verb, ending in *-ing,* that functions as a noun: Lacey likes *playing* in the steel band.

A possessive pronoun (or a possessive noun) is the appropriate escort for a gerund. As a noun, a gerund requires an adjective, not another noun, for a modifier.

Mary is tired of *his griping.* [The possessive pronoun *his* modifies the gerund *griping.*]

I can stand *their being* late every morning but not *his drinking* on the job. [The possessive pronoun *their* modifies the gerund *being;* the possessive pronoun *his* modifies the gerund *drinking.*]

Gerunds can cause confusion when you edit because they look exactly like present participles. Whereas a gerund functions as a noun, a participle often functions as an adjective modifying a noun or pronoun.

Mary heard *him griping* about work. [The participle *griping* modifies the direct object *him.*]

If you are not sure whether to use a possessive or an objective pronoun with a word ending in *-ing,* look closely at your sentence. Which word — the pronoun or the *-ing* word — is the object of your main verb? That word functions as a noun; the other word modifies it.

Mr. Phipps remembered *them* smoking in the boys' room. [Mr. Phipps remembers *them,* those naughty students. *Them* is the object of the verb, so *smoking* is a participle modifying *them.*]

Mr. Phipps remembered *their* smoking in the boys' room. [Mr. Phipps remembers *smoking,* that nasty habit. The gerund *smoking* is the object of the verb, and the possessive pronoun *their* modifies it.]

In everyday speech, the rules about pronoun case apply less rigidly. Someone who correctly asks in conversation, "To whom are you referring?" is likely to sound pretentious. You are within your rights to reply, as did the comic-strip character Pogo Possum, "Youm, that's whom!" Say, if you like, "It's *me,*" but write "It is *I.*" Say, if you wish, "*Who* did he ask to the party?" but write "*Whom* did he ask?"

> **present participle:** A form of a verb ending in *-ing* that cannot function alone as a main verb but can act as an adjective: *Leading* the pack, Michael crossed the finish line.

■ Exercise 5–I

Using Pronouns Correctly

Replace any pronouns that are used incorrectly in the following sentences. (Consider all these examples as written — not spoken — English, and so apply the rules strictly.) Explain why each pronoun was incorrect. Some sentences may be correct. Answers for the lettered sentences appear in the back of the book. Example:

> That is her, the new university president, at the podium.

> That is *she,* the new university president, at the podium. [*She* is a subject complement.]

a. I didn't appreciate you laughing at her and I.

b. Lee and me would be delighted to serenade whomever will listen.

c. The waiters and us busboys are highly trustworthy.

> **WWW**
> For more practice, visit *Exercise Central* at <www.bedfordstmartins .com/bedguide>.

   d. The neighbors were driven berserk by him singing.

   e. Jerry and myself regard you and she as the very people who we wish to meet.

1. Have you guessed the identity of the person of who I am speaking?
2. It was him asking about the clock that started me suspecting him.
3. They — Jerry and her — are the troublemakers.
4. Mrs. Van Dumont awarded the prize to Mona and I.
5. The counterattack was launched by Dusty and myself.

6   *Pronoun Reference*

Look hard at just about any piece of writing — this discussion, if you like — and you'll find that practically every pronoun in it points to some noun. This is the main use of pronouns: to refer in a brief, convenient form to some *antecedent* that has already been named. A pronoun usually has a noun or another pronoun as its antecedent. Often the antecedent is the subject or object of the same clause in which the pronoun appears.

> Josie hit the *ball* after *its* first bounce.

> Smashing into *Greg,* the ball knocked off *his* glasses.

The antecedent also can appear in a different clause or even a different sentence from the pronoun.

> *Josie* hit the *ball* when *it* bounced back to *her.*

> The *ball* smashed into *Greg. It* knocked off *his* glasses.

A pronoun as well as a noun can be an antecedent.

> My *dog* hid in the closet when *she* had *her* puppies. [*Dog* is the antecedent of *she; she* is the antecedent of *her.*]

6a   Name the pronoun's antecedent: don't just imply it.

antecedent: The word to which a pronoun refers: *Lyn* plays golf, and *she* putts well.

When editing, be sure you have identified clearly the antecedent of each pronoun. A writer who leaves a key idea unsaid is likely to confuse readers.

> VAGUE   Ted wanted a Norwegian canoe because he'd heard that *they* produce the lightest canoes afloat.

What noun or pronoun does *they* refer to? Not to *Norwegian,* which is an adjective. We may guess that this writer has in mind Norwegian canoe builders, but no such noun has been mentioned. To make the sentence work, the writer must supply an antecedent for *they.*

CLEAR   Ted wanted a Norwegian canoe because he'd heard that Norway produces [*or* Norwegians produce] the lightest canoes afloat.

Watch out for possessive nouns. They won't work as antecedents.

VAGUE   On William's canoe *he* painted a skull and bones. (For all we know, *he* might be some joker named Gustavo.)

CLEAR   On his canoe William painted a skull and bones.

Adjective Clauses and Relative Pronouns

ESL GUIDELINES

Be sure to use relative pronouns (*who, which, that*) correctly in sentences with adjective clauses.

- Do not omit the relative pronoun when it is the subject within the adjective clause.

INCORRECT   The woman *gave us directions to the museum* told us not to miss the Picasso exhibit.

CORRECT   The woman who *gave us directions to the museum* told us not to miss the Picasso exhibit. [*Who* is the subject of the adjective clause.]

- In speech and informal writing, you can imply (not state) a relative pronoun when it is the object of a verb or preposition within the adjective clause. In formal writing, you should use the relative pronoun.

FORMAL   Jamal forgot to return the book *that I gave him.* [*That* is the object of *gave.*]

INFORMAL   Jamal forgot to return the book *I gave him.* [The relative pronoun *that* is implied.]

FORMAL   This is the box *in which we found the jewelry.* [*Which* is the object of the preposition *in.*]

INFORMAL   This is the box *we found the jewelry in.* [The relative pronoun *which* is implied.]

NOTE: When the relative pronoun is omitted, the preposition moves to the end of the sentence but must not be left out.

- *Whose* is the only possessive form of a relative pronoun. It is used with persons, animals, and things.

INCORRECT   I sat on a chair *that its* legs were wobbly.

CORRECT   I sat on a chair *whose* legs were wobbly.

NOTE: If you are not sure how to use a relative pronoun, try rephrasing the sentence more simply.

I sat on a chair *that had wobbly legs* [or *with wobbly legs*].

6b Give the pronoun *it, this, that,* or *which* a clear antecedent.

Vagueness arises, thick as fog, whenever *it, this, that,* or *which* points to something a writer assumes he or she has said but indeed hasn't. Often the best way out of the fog is to substitute a specific noun or expression for the pronoun.

> VAGUE   I was an only child, and *it* was hard.

> CLEAR   I was an only child, and my solitary life was hard.

> VAGUE   Judy could not get along with her younger brother. *This* is the reason she wanted to get her own apartment.

> CLEAR   Because Judy could not get along with her younger brother, she wanted to get her own apartment.

6c Make the pronoun's antecedent clear.

Confusion strikes if a pronoun seems to point in two or more directions. In such a puzzling situation, more than one antecedent looks possible. Baffled, the reader wonders which the writer means.

> CONFUSING   Hanwei shouted to Kenny to take off his burning sweater.

Whose sweater does *his* mean — Kenny's or Hanwei's? Simply changing a pronoun won't clear up the confusion. The writer needs to revise drastically enough to move the two possible antecedents out of each other's way.

> CLEAR   "Kenny!" shouted Hanwei. "Your sweater's on fire! Take it off!"

> CLEAR   Flames were shooting from Kenny's sweater. Hanwei shouted to Kenny to take it off.

Pronouns referring to nouns of the same gender are particular offenders.

> CONFUSING   Linda welcomed Lee-Ann's move into the apartment next door. Little did she dream that soon she would be secretly dating her husband.

Let meaning show you the way to straighten out the grammatical tangle. If you had written these sentences, you would know which person is the sneak. One way to clarify the antecedents of *she* and *her* is to add more information.

> CLEAR   In welcoming Lee-Ann to the apartment next door, Linda didn't dream that soon her own husband would be secretly dating her former sorority sister.

6d **Place the pronoun close to its antecedent to keep the relationship clear.**

Watch out for distractions that slip in between noun and pronoun. If your sentence contains two or more nouns that look like antecedents to a pronoun, your readers may become bewildered.

CONFUSING   Harper steered his dinghy alongside the cabin cruiser that the drug smugglers had left anchored under an overhanging willow in the tiny harbor and eased it to a stop.

What did Harper ease to a stop? By the time readers reach the end of the sentence, they are likely to have forgotten. To avoid confusion, keep the pronoun and its antecedent reasonably close together.

CLEAR   Harper steered his dinghy into the tiny harbor and eased it to a stop alongside the cabin cruiser that the drug smugglers had left anchored under an overhanging willow.

Never force your readers to stop and think, "What does that pronoun stand for?" You, the writer, have to do this thinking for them.

■ Exercise 6–1

Making Pronoun Reference Clear

Revise each sentence or group of sentences so that any pronoun needing an antecedent clearly points to one. Possible revisions for the lettered sentences appear in the back of the book. Example:

WWW
For more practice, visit *Exercise Central* at <www .bedfordstmartins.com/ bedguide>.

I took the money out of the wallet and threw it in the trash.

I took the money out of the wallet and threw *the wallet* in the trash.

a. I could see the moon and the faint shadow of the tree as it began to rise.

b. Katrina spent the summer in Paris and traveled throughout Europe, which broadened her awareness of cultural differences.

c. Most managers want employees to work as many hours as possible. They never consider the work they need to do at home.

d. I worked twelve hours a day and almost never got enough sleep, but it was worth it.

e. Kevin asked Mike to meet him for lunch but forgot that he had class at that time.

1. Bill's prank frightened Josh and made him wonder why he had done it.

2. Korean students study up to twenty subjects a year, including algebra, calculus, and engineering. Because they are required, they must study them year after year.

3. Pedro Martinez signed a baseball for Chad that he had used in a game.

4. When the bottle hit the windshield, it shattered.

5. My friends believe they are more mature than many of their peers because of the discipline enforced at their school. However, it can also lead to problems.

7   *Pronoun-Antecedent Agreement*

pronoun: A word that stands in place of a noun (*he, him,* or *his* for *Nate*)

A pronoun's job is to fill in for a noun, much as an actor's double fills in for the actor. Pronouns are a short, convenient way for writers to avoid repeating the same noun over and over.

> The sheriff drew a six-shooter; he fired twice.

antecedent: The word to which a pronoun refers: *Lyn* plays golf, and *she* putts well.

In this action-packed sentence, first comes a noun (*sheriff*) and then a pronoun (*he*) that refers back to it. *Sheriff* is the antecedent of *he*.

Just as verbs need to agree with their subjects, pronouns need to agree with the nouns they stand for. A successful writer takes care not to shift number, person, or gender in midsentence ("The *sheriff* and the *outlaw* drew *their* six-shooters; *he* fired twice").

7a   Pronouns agree with their antecedents in person and number.

For more on editing for pronoun-antecedent agreement, see A4 in the "Quick Editing Guide."

A pronoun matches its antecedent in person (first, second, or third) and in number (singular or plural), even when intervening words separate the pronoun and its antecedent.

> FAULTY   All *campers* should bring *your* knapsacks.

Here, noun and pronoun disagree in person: *campers* is third person, but *your* is second person.

> FAULTY   Every *camper* should bring *their* knapsack.

Here, noun and pronoun disagree in number: *camper* is singular, but *their* is plural.

> REVISED   All *campers* should bring *their* knapsacks.

> REVISED   Every *camper* should bring *his or her* knapsack. (See also 7f.)

7b   Most antecedents joined by *and* require a plural pronoun.

compound subject: A subject consisting of two or more nouns or pronouns linked by *and: My mother and my sister drove home.*

A *compound subject* is plural; use a plural pronoun to refer to it.

> *George,* who has been here before, *and Susan,* who hasn't, should bring *their* knapsacks.

If the nouns in a compound subject refer to the same person or thing, they make up a singular antecedent. Use a singular pronoun too.

The *owner and founder* of this camp carries *his* own knapsack everywhere.

7c A pronoun agrees with the closest part of an antecedent joined by *or* or *nor*.

If your subject is two or more nouns (or a combination of nouns and pronouns) connected by *or* or *nor*, look closely at the subject's parts. Are they all singular? If so, your pronoun should be singular.

Neither *Joy nor Jean* remembered *her* knapsack last year.

If *Sam, Arthur, or Dieter* shows up, tell *him* I'm looking for *him*.

If the part of the subject closest to the pronoun is plural, the pronoun should be plural.

Neither *Joy nor her sisters* remembered *their* knapsacks last year.

If you see *Sam, Arthur, or their friends*, tell *them* I'm looking for *them*.

7d An antecedent that is an indefinite pronoun takes a singular pronoun.

Indefinite pronouns are usually singular in meaning, so a pronoun referring to one of them is also singular.

Either of the boys can do it, as long as *he's* on time.

Warn *anybody* who's still in *her* swimsuit that a uniform is required for dinner.

Sometimes the meaning of an indefinite pronoun is plural. To avoid awkwardness, avoid using such a pronoun as an antecedent.

Tell *everyone* in Cabin B that I'm looking for *him*.

This sentence works better if it is phrased differently.

Tell *all the campers* in Cabin B that I'm looking for *them*.

7e Most collective nouns used as antecedents require singular pronouns.

When the members of such a group act as a unit, use a singular pronoun to refer to them.

The *cast* for the play will be posted as soon as the director chooses *it*.

When the group members act individually, use a plural pronoun.

The *cast* will go *their* separate ways when summer ends.

---

indefinite pronoun: A pronoun standing for an unspecified person or thing, including singular forms (*any, each, everyone, no one*) and plural forms (*both, few*): *Everyone is soaking wet.*

For a list of indefinite pronouns, see A4 in the "Quick Editing Guide."

For more on agreement with indefinite pronouns, see 4f and 7f.

collective noun: A singular noun that represents a group of people or items, such as *committee, family, jury, trio*

For more on agreement with collective nouns, see 4e.

7f   **A pronoun agrees with its antecedent in gender.**

If *one of your parents* brings you to camp, invite *him* to stay for lunch.

For more on bias-free language, see 18.

While technically correct (the singular pronoun *he* is used to refer to the singular antecedent *one*), this sentence overlooks the fact that some parents are male, some female. To make sure the pronoun refers to both, a writer has two choices.

If *one of your parents* brings you to camp, invite *him or her* to stay for lunch.

If your *parents* bring you to camp, invite *them* to stay for lunch.

■ **Exercise 7–1**

Making Pronouns and Antecedents Agree

www
For more practice, visit *Exercise Central* at <www.bedfordstmartins.com/bedguide>.

If any nouns and pronouns disagree in number, person, or gender in the following sentences, substitute pronouns that agree with the nouns. If you prefer, strengthen any sentence by rewriting it. Some sentences may be correct. Possible revisions for the lettered sentences appear in the back of the book. Example:

A cat expects people to feed them often.

A *cat* expects people to feed *it* often. *Or*

Cats expect people to feed *them* often.

a. Many architects find work their greatest pleasure.
b. Neither Melissa nor James has received their application form yet.
c. He is the kind of man who gets their fun out of just sipping one's beer and watching his Saturday games on TV.
d. Many a mother has mourned the loss of their child.
e. When one enjoys one's work, it's easy to spend all your spare time thinking about it.

1. All students are urged to complete your registration on time.
2. When a baby doesn't know their own mother, they may have been born with some kind of vision deficiency.
3. Each member of the sorority has to make her own bed.
4. If you don't like the songs the choir sings, don't join them.
5. Young people should know how to protect oneself against AIDS.

8   *Adjectives and Adverbs*

adjective: A word or phrase that describes, or modifies, a noun or a pronoun: The *small brown* cow leaned against the *old* fence.

An adjective's job is to provide information about the person, place, object, or idea named by the noun or pronoun. The adjective typically answers the question Which? or What kind?

Karen bought a *small red* car.

The radios *on sale* are an *excellent* value.

An adverb typically answers the question How? or When? or Where? Sometimes it answers the question Why?

Karen bought her car *quickly.*

The radios arrived *yesterday;* Denis put them *in the electronics department.*

Karen needed her new car *to commute to school.*

The most common problems that writers have with adjectives and adverbs involve mixing them up: sending an adjective to do an adverb's job or vice versa.

> *adverb:* A word or phrase that modifies a verb, an adjective, or another adverb: The cow bawled *loudly.*

> For more on editing adjectives and adverbs, see A5 in the "Quick Editing Guide."

8a Use an adverb, not an adjective, to modify a verb, adjective, or another adverb.

FAULTY   Karen bought her car *quick.*

FAULTY   It's *awful* hot today.

Although an informal speaker might be able to get away with these sentences, a writer cannot. *Quick* and *awful* are adjectives, so they can modify only nouns or pronouns. Adverbs are needed to modify the verb *bought* and the adjective *hot.*

REVISED   Karen bought her car *quickly.*

REVISED   It's *awfully* hot today.

8b Use an adjective, not an adverb, as a subject complement or object complement.

If we write, "Her old car looked awful," the adjective *awful* is a *subject complement:* it follows a linking verb and modifies the subject, *car.* An *object complement* completes the description of a direct object and can be an adjective or a noun, but never an adverb.

> *subject complement:* A noun, an adjective, or a group of words that follows a linking verb (such as *be, am, were, seem, feel*) and renames or describes the subject: This plum tastes *ripe.* (See 3a.)

> *object complement:* A noun, an adjective, or a group of words that renames or describes a direct object: The judges rated Hugo *the best skater.*

Early to bed and early to rise makes a man *healthy, wealthy,* and *wise.* [Adjectives modifying the direct object *man*]

When you are not sure whether you're dealing with an object complement or an adverb, look closely at the word's role in the sentence. If it modifies a noun, it is an object complement and therefore should be an adjective.

The coach called the referee *stupid* and *blind.* [*Stupid* and *blind* are adjectives modifying the direct object *referee.*]

If it modifies a verb, you want an adverb instead.

In fact, though, the ref had called the play *correctly.* [*Correctly* is an adverb modifying the verb *called.*]

ESL GUIDELINES

count noun: A noun with both singular and plural forms that refers to an item that can be counted: *apple, apples*

noncount noun: A noun that cannot be made plural because it refers to an item that cannot be counted: *cheese, salt, air*

The Definite Article (*the*)

- Use *the* with a specific count or noncount noun when both the writer and the reader know what is referred to or when the noun has been mentioned before.

    Did you feed *the* baby? [Both the reader and the writer know which baby is referred to.]

    She got a huge box in the mail. *The* box contained oranges from Florida. [*The* is used the second time the noun (*box*) is mentioned.]

- Use *the* before specific count or noncount nouns when the reader is given enough information to identify what is being referred to.

    The furniture in my apartment is old and faded. [Specific furniture]

- Use *the* before a singular count noun to make a generality.

    The dog has been humans' favorite pet for centuries. [*The dog* here refers to all dogs.]

- Use *the* before some geographical names.

    Collectives: the United States, the United Kingdom

    Groups of Islands: the Bahamas, the Canary Islands

    Large Bodies of Water (except lakes): the Atlantic Ocean, the Dead Sea, the Monongahela River, the Gulf of Mexico

    Mountain Ranges: the Rockies, the Himalaya Mountains

- When plural count nouns are used to name a general group, they are not preceded by an article. When they are used to name a definite or specific group they must be preceded by *the* or another determiner.

    Horses don't eat meat, and neither do *cows*.

    Hal is feeding *the horses* in the barn, and he has already fed *his cows*.

---

subject complement: A noun, an adjective, or a group of words that follows a linking verb (such as *be, am, were, seem, feel*) and renames or describes the subject: This plum tastes *ripe*. (See 3a.)

linking verb: A verb (*is, become, seem, feel*) that shows a state of being by linking the sentence subject with a word that renames or describes the subject: The sky *is* blue. (See 3a.)

8c Use *good* as an adjective and *well* as an adverb.

This sandwich tastes *good*. [The adjective *good* is a subject complement following the linking verb *tastes* and modifying the noun *sandwich*.]

Heloise's skin healed *well* after surgery. [The adverb *well* modifies the verb *healed*.]

Only if the verb is a linking verb can you safely follow it with *good*. Other kinds of verbs do not take subject complements. Instead, they need adverbs to modify them.

FAULTY   That painting came out *good*.

REVISED   That painting came out *well*.

Complications arise when we write or speak about health. It is perfectly correct to say *I feel good,* using the adjective *good* as a subject complement after the linking verb *feel*. However, generations of confusion have nudged the adverb *well* into the adjective category, too. A nurse may speak of "a well baby"; and greeting cards urge patients to "get well" — meaning, "become healthy." Just as *healthy* is an adjective here, so is *well*.

What, then, is the best answer when someone asks, "How do you feel?" If you want to duck the issue, reply, "Fine!" Otherwise, in speech either *good* or *well* is acceptable; in writing, use *good*.

8d   Form comparatives and superlatives of most adjectives with *-er* and *-est* and of most adverbs with *more* and *most*.

Comparatives and superlatives are special adjective and adverb forms that allow us to describe one thing in relation to another. You can put most adjectives into their comparative form by adding *-er* and into their superlative form by adding *-est*.

> The budget deficit is *larger* than the trade deficit.

> This year's trade deficit is the *largest* ever.

We usually form the comparative and superlative of long adjectives with *more* and *most* rather than with *-er* and *-est*, to keep them from becoming cumbersome.

> Our national debt may become *more enormous* over the next few years.

The Indefinite Article (*a, an*)

ESL GUIDELINES

- Use *a* or *an* with a nonspecific, singular count noun when it is not known to the reader or to the writer.

    My brother has *an* antique car. [The car's identity is unknown to the reader.]

    I saw *a* dog in my back yard this morning. [The dog's identity is unknown to the writer.]

- Use the indefinite article (*a, an*) when the noun is mentioned for the first time. Use the definite article (*the*) when the noun is mentioned again.

    I saw *a* car that I would love to buy. *The* car was red and had a leather interior.

- Use *some* or no article instead of *a* or *an* with noncount nouns or plural nouns used in a general sense.

    INCORRECT   I am going to buy *a* furniture for my apartment.

    CORRECT   I am going to buy *some* furniture for my apartment.

    CORRECT   I am going to buy furniture for my apartment.

count noun: A noun with both singular and plural forms that refers to an item that can be counted: *apple, apples*

noncount noun: A noun that cannot be made plural because it refers to an item that cannot be counted: *cheese, salt, air*

For short adverbs that do not end in *-ly,* usually add *-er* and *-est* in the comparative and superlative forms. With all other adverbs, use *more* and *most.* (Also see 8f.)

> The trade deficit grows *fastest* and *most uncontrollably* when exports are down and imports remain high.

For negative comparisons, use *less* and *least* for both adjectives and adverbs.

> Michael's speech was *less interesting* than Louie's.

> Paulette spoke *less interestingly* than Michael.

The comparative and superlative forms of irregular adjectives and adverbs (such as *bad* and *badly*) are also irregular and should be used with special care.

For a chart of comparative forms of irregular adjectives and adverbs, see A5 in the "Quick Editing Guide."

> Tom's golf is *bad,* but no *worse* than George's.

> Tom plays golf *badly,* but no *worse* than George does.

8e Omit *more* and *most* with an adjective or adverb that is already comparative or superlative.

Some words become comparative or superlative when we tack on *-er* or *-est.* Others, such as *top, favorite,* and *unique,* mark whatever they modify as one of a kind by definition. Neither category requires further assistance to make its point. To say "a *more worse* fate" or "my *most favorite* movie" is redundant: "a *worse* fate" or "my *favorite* movie" does the job.

> FAULTY   Lisa is *more uniquely* qualified for the job than any other candidate we have interviewed.

> REVISED   Lisa is *better* qualified for the job than any other candidate we have interviewed.

> REVISED   Lisa is *uniquely* qualified for the job.

Adjectives and Adverbs at a Glance

ADJECTIVES

1. Typically answer the question Which? or What kind?
2. Modify nouns or pronouns

ADVERBS

3. Answer the question How? When? Where? or sometimes Why?
4. Modify verbs, adjectives, and other adverbs

8f   **Use the comparative form of an adjective or adverb to compare two people or things, the superlative form to compare more than two.**

No matter how wonderful something is, we can call it the *best* only when we compare it with more than one other thing. Any comparison between two things uses the comparative form (*better*), not the superlative (*best*).

> FAULTY   Chocolate and vanilla are both good, but I like chocolate *best*.
>
> REVISED   Chocolate and vanilla are both good, but I like chocolate *better*.

Cumulative Adjectives

Cumulative adjectives are two or more adjectives used directly before a noun and not separated by commas or the word *and*.

> She is an *attractive older French* woman.
>
> His *expressive large brown* eyes moved me.

ESL GUIDELINES

Cumulative adjectives usually have a specific order of placement before a noun. Use the following list as a guideline for adjective order, but keep in mind that the order can be varied.

1. Articles or determiners
   a, an, the, some, this, these, his, my, two, several
2. Evaluative adjectives
   beautiful, wonderful, hard-working, distasteful
3. Size or dimension
   big, small, huge, obese, petite, six-foot
4. Length or shape
   long, short, round, square, oblong, oval
5. Age
   old, young, new, fresh, ancient
6. Color
   red, pink, aquamarine, orange
7. Nation or place of origin
   American, Japanese, European, Bostonian, Floridian
8. Religion
   Protestant, Muslim, Hindu, Buddhist, Catholic, Jewish
9. Matter or substance
   wood, gold, cotton, plastic, pine, metal
10. Noun used as an adjective
    telephone (as in *telephone operator*), *computer* (as in *computer software*)

For advice on using commas with adjectives, see 21d.

WWW
For more practice, visit
Exercise Central at
<www.bedfordstmartins
.com/bedguide>.

■ Exercise 8–1

Using Adjectives and Adverbs Correctly

Find and correct any improperly used adjectives and adverbs in the following sentences. Some sentences may be correct. Answers for the lettered sentences appear in the back of the book. Example:

> The deal worked out good for both of us.

> The deal worked out *well* for both of us.

a. Credit card debt is becoming increasing common among college students, who have expenses but do not work full-time.

b. Nearly all credit card companies try to convince you to apply by offering introductory rates that are enticingly low.

c. It then is easy for students to charge many items on different cards and make only the lower minimum payments each month.

d. Unfortunately, when juggling multiple credit cards, many students lose sight of how rapid the debt is accumulating.

e. It is a well idea to charge only as much as you can pay in full each month.

1. A popular trend in television today is voyeurism, or the act of secret watching people as they go about their daily lives.

2. In the late 1990s, the popularity of MTV's *The Real World* sparked increasingly interest in this concept.

3. Music videos and commercials also began to incorporate voyeuristic elements, although, of the two, videos used the technique most frequently.

4. With the millennium came a flood of new "voyeuristic" programs all trying to capitalize more distinctively on the current trend.

5. On the program *Survivor*, contestants were filmed living on a desert island with limited supplies, while viewers at home watched breathless to see how the contestants would behave.

9   *Shifts*

Just as you can view a scene from different vantage points and at different times, you can also consider a subject in a sentence from various positions. If the time or the actor changes, your writing should reflect the change. However, writers sometimes shift point of view unconsciously or unnecessarily, causing ambiguity and confusion for readers. Such shifts are evident in grammatical inconsistencies.

9a   Maintain consistency in verb tense.

tense: The time when the action of a verb did, does, or will occur

When you write a paragraph or an essay, keep the verbs in the same tense unless the time changes.

INCONSISTENT	The driver *yelled* at us to get off the bus, so I *ask* him why, and he *tells* me it *is* none of my business.
CONSISTENT	The driver *yells* at us to get off the bus, so I *ask* him why, and he *tells* me it *is* none of my business. [All verbs are present tense.]
CONSISTENT	The driver *yelled* at us to get off the bus, so I *asked* him why, and he *told* me it *was* none of my business. [All verbs are past tense.]

9b If the time changes, change the verb tense.

Shifts in tense should indicate an actual change in time. If you are writing about something that occurred in the past, use past tense verbs. If you are writing about something that occurs in the present, use present tense verbs. If the time shifts, change the verb tense.

> I *do* not *like* the new television programs this year. The situation comedies *are* too realistic to be amusing, the adventure shows *don't have* much action, and the courtroom dramas *drag* on and on. Last year the television programs *were* different. The sitcoms *were* hilarious, the adventure shows *were* action-packed, and the courtroom dramas *were* fast-paced. I *prefer* last year's reruns to this year's new choices.

The time and the verb tense change appropriately from present (*do like, are, do have, drag*) to past (*were, were, were, were*) back to present (*prefer*), contrasting this year's *present* programming with last year's *past* programming and ending with *present* opinion.

NOTE: When writing papers about literature, the accepted practice is to use present tense verbs to summarize what happens in a story, poem, or play. When discussing other aspects of a work, use present tense for present time, past tense for past, and future tense for future.

> John Steinbeck *wrote* "The Chrysanthemums" in 1937. [Past tense for past time]

> In "The Chrysanthemums," John Steinbeck *describes* the Salinas Valley as "a closed pot" cut off from the world by fog. [Present tense for story summary]

9c Maintain consistency in the voice of verbs.

In most writing, active voice is preferable to passive voice. Shifting unnecessarily from active to passive voice causes confusion for readers.

For more on using active and passive voice, see 3m.

INCONSISTENT	My roommates and I *sit* up late many nights talking about our problems. Grades, teachers, jobs, money, and dates *are discussed* at length.
CONSISTENT	My roommates and I *sit* up late many nights talking about our problems. We *discuss* grades, teachers, jobs, money, and dates at length.

ESL GUIDELINES

Negatives

You can make a sentence negative by using either *not* or another negative adverb such as *seldom, rarely, never, hardly, hardly ever,* or *almost never.*

- With *not:* subject + helping verb + *not* + main verb

    Gina did *not* go to the concert.

    They will *not* call again.

- For questions: helping verb + *n't* (contraction for *not*) + subject + main verb

    Didn't Gina go to the concert?

    Won't [for *Will not*] they call again?

- With a negative adverb: subject + negative adverb + main verb; *or* subject + helping verb + negative adverb + main verb

    My son *seldom* watches TV.

    Jared may *never* see them again.

- With a negative adverb at the beginning of a clause: negative adverb + helping verb + subject + verb

    Not only does Emma play tennis well, but she also excels in golf.

    Never before have I been so happy.

9d Maintain consistency in person.

For more on pronoun forms, see 5 and also A3 in the "Quick Editing Guide."

Person indicates the perspective from which an essay is written. First person (*I, we*) establishes a personal, informal relationship with readers. Second person (*you*) is also informal and personal, bringing the readers into the writing. Third person (*he, she, it, they*) is more formal and objective than the other two persons. In a formal scientific report, first person and second person are seldom appropriate. In a personal essay, using *he, she,* or *one* to refer to yourself sounds stilted. Choose the person appropriate for your purpose and stick to it.

INCONSISTENT   College *students* need transportation, but *you* need a job to pay for the insurance and the gasoline.

CONSISTENT   College *students* need transportation, but *they* need jobs to pay for the insurance and the gasoline.

INCONSISTENT   *Anyone* can go skydiving if *you* have the guts.

CONSISTENT   *Anyone* can go skydiving if *he or she* has the guts.

CONSISTENT   *You* can go skydiving if *you* have the guts.

9e Maintain consistency in the mood of verbs.

For examples of verbs in all three moods, see 3n–3p.

Closely related to shift in person is shift in the mood of the verb, usually from the indicative to the imperative.

| INCONSISTENT | Counselors *advised* the students to register early. Also *pay* tuition on time to avoid being dropped from classes. [Shift from indicative to imperative] |
| CONSISTENT | Counselors *advised* the students to register early. They also *advised* them to pay their tuition on time to avoid being dropped from classes. [Both verbs in indicative] |

9f Maintain consistency in level of language.

Attempting to impress readers, writers sometimes inappropriately use inflated language or slip into slang or informal wording. The level of language should be appropriate to your purpose and your audience throughout an essay.

If you are writing a personal essay, use informal language.

| INCONSISTENT | I felt like a typical tourist. I carried an expensive camera with lots of gadgets I didn't quite know how to operate. But I was in a quandary because there was such a plethora of picturesque tableaus to record for posterity. |

The sudden shift to formal language is inappropriate. The writer could end the passage simply: *But with so much beautiful scenery all around, I just couldn't decide where to start.*

If you are writing an academic essay, use formal language.

| INCONSISTENT | Puccini's final work *Turandot* is set in a China of legends, riddles, and fantasy. Brimming with beautiful melodies, this opera is music drama at its most spectacular. What a hip show! |

The last sentence can be cut to avoid an unnecessary shift in formality.

■ Exercise 9–1

Maintaining Grammatical Consistency

Revise the following sentences to eliminate shifts in verb tense, voice, mood, person, and level of language. Possible revisions for the lettered sentences appear in the back of the book. Example:

> I needed the job at the restaurant, so I tried to tolerate the insults of my boss, but a person can take only so much.

> I needed the job at the restaurant, so I tried to tolerate the insults of my boss, but *I could* take only so much.

a. Dr. Jamison is an erudite professor who cracks jokes in class.

b. The audience listened intently to the lecture, but the message was not understood.

c. Scientists can no longer evade the social, political, and ethical consequences of what they did in the laboratory.

WWW

For more practice, visit *Exercise Central* at <www.bedfordstmartins.com/bedguide>.

d. To have good government, citizens must become informed on the issues. Also, be sure to vote.

e. Good writing is essential to success in many professions, especially in business, where ideas must be communicated in down-to-earth lingo.

1. Our legal system made it extremely difficult to prove a bribe. If the charges are not proven to the satisfaction of a jury or a judge, then we jump to the conclusion that the absence of a conviction demonstrates the innocence of the subject.

2. Before Morris K. Udall, Democrat from Arizona, resigns his seat in the U.S. House of Representatives, he helped preserve hundreds of acres of wilderness.

3. Anyone can learn another language if you have the time and the patience.

4. The immigration officer asked how long we planned to stay, so I show him my letter of acceptance from Tulane.

5. Archaeologists spent many months studying the site of the African city of Zimbabwe, and many artifacts were uncovered.

Chapter 34

Effective Sentences

10. Misplaced and Dangling Modifiers   H-57
11. Incomplete Sentences   H-60
12. Mixed Constructions and Faulty Predication   H-64
13. Parallel Structure   H-68
14. Coordination and Subordination   H-71
15. Sentence Variety   H-78

10 *Misplaced and Dangling Modifiers*

The purpose of a modifier is to give readers additional information. To do so, the modifier must be linked clearly to whatever it is meant to modify. If you wrote, "We saw a stone wall around a house on a grassy hill, beautiful and distant," your readers would be hard put to figure out whether *beautiful* and *distant* modify *wall, house,* or *hill.* When you finish writing, double-check your modifiers—especially prepositional phrases and subordinate clauses—to make sure each one is in the right place.

For more on editing for misplaced or dangling modifiers, see B1 in the "Quick Editing Guide."

10a Keep modifiers close to what they modify.

Misplaced modifiers—phrases and clauses that wander away from what they modify—produce results that are more likely to amuse your readers than to inform them. To avoid confusion, place your modifiers as close as possible to whatever they modify.

modifier: A word (such as an adjective or adverb), phrase, or clause that provides more information about other parts of a sentence: Plays *staged by the drama class* are *always successful.*

MISPLACED   She offered handcrafted toys to all the children in colorful packages. [Does the phrase *in colorful packages* modify *toys* or *children?*]

CLEAR   She offered handcrafted toys in colorful packages to all the children.

MISPLACED   Today we will remove the dishes from the crates that got chipped. [Does the clause *that got chipped* modify *dishes* or *crates?*]

CLEAR   Today we will remove from the crates the dishes that got chipped.

Sometimes when you move a misplaced modifier to a better place, an additional change or two will help you to clarify the sentence.

MISPLACED   Chuck offered cream and sugar to his guests in their coffee.

CLEAR   Chuck offered his guests cream and sugar in their coffee. [When *guests* is made an indirect object, *to* is cut.]

10b Place each modifier so that it clearly modifies only one thing.

A *squinting modifier* is one that looks two ways, leaving the reader uncertain whether it modifies the word before it or the word after it. A good tactic to avoid ambiguity is to place your modifier close to the word or phrase it modifies and away from any others that might cause confusion.

SQUINTING   The best-seller that appealed to Mary *tremendously* bored Marcus.

CLEAR   The best-seller that *tremendously* appealed to Mary bored Marcus.

CLEAR   The best-seller that appealed to Mary bored Marcus *tremendously.*

■ Exercise 10–1

Placing Modifiers

WWW
For more practice, visit *Exercise Central* at <www.bedfordstmartins .com/bedguide>.

Revise the following sentences, which contain modifiers that are misplaced or squinting. Possible revisions for the lettered sentences appear in the back of the book. Example:

Patti found the cat using a flashlight in the dark.

Using a flashlight in the dark, Patti found the cat.

a. The bus got stuck in a ditch full of passengers.
b. He was daydreaming about fishing for trout in the middle of a staff meeting.
c. The boy threw the paper airplane through an open window with a smirk.
d. I reached for my sunglasses when the glare appeared from the glove compartment.
e. High above them, Sally and Glen watched the kites drift back and forth.

1. In her soup she found a fly at one of the best French restaurants in town.
2. Andy learned some tips about building kites from the pages of an old book.
3. Alex vowed to return to the island sometime soon on the day he left it.
4. The fish was carried in a suitcase wrapped in newspaper.
5. The reporters were informed of the crimes committed by a press release.

10c Have something in the sentence for each modifier to modify.

Generally we assume that a modifying phrase at the start of a sentence modifies the subject of the main clause to follow. If we encounter a modifying phrase midway through a sentence, we assume that it modifies something just before or (less often) after it.

> *Feeling tired after the long hike, Jason* went to bed.

> *Alicia, while sympathetic,* was not inclined to help.

Occasionally a writer will slip up by allowing a modifying phrase to dangle. A **dangling modifier** is one that doesn't modify anything in its sentence.

DANGLING   *Noticing a slight pain behind his eyes,* an aspirin seemed like a good idea. [The introductory phrase does not modify *aspirin* or, in fact, anything.]

To correct a dangling modifier, first figure out what noun, pronoun, or noun phrase the modifier is meant to modify, and then make that word or phrase the subject of the main clause.

CLEAR   *Noticing a slight pain behind his eyes,* he decided to take an aspirin.

Another way to correct a dangling modifier is to turn the dangler into a clause that includes the missing noun or pronoun.

DANGLING   Her progress, *although talented,* has been slowed by poor work habits.

CLEAR   *Although she is talented,* her progress has been slowed by poor work habits.

Sometimes rewriting will clarify what the modifier modifies and improve the sentence as well.

CLEAR   *Although talented,* she has been handicapped by poor work habits.

■ Exercise 10–2

Revising Dangling Modifiers

Revise any sentences that contain dangling modifiers. Some sentences may be correct. Possible revisions for the lettered sentences appear in the back of the book. Example:

> Angry at her poor showing, geology would never be Joan's favorite class.

> *Angry at her poor showing, Joan* knew that geology would never be her favorite class.

a. Unpacking the suitcase, a horrible idea occurred to me.

b. After preparing breakfast that morning, the oven might still be left on at home.

c. Trying to reach my neighbor, her telephone was busy.

d. Desperate to get information, my solution was to ask my mother to drive over to check the oven.

e. With enormous relief, my mother's call confirmed that everything was fine.

1. After working six hours, the job was done.

2. Further information can be obtained by calling the specified number.

3. To compete in the Olympics, talent, training, and dedication are needed.

4. Pressing hard on the brakes, the car spun into a hedge.

5. Showing a lack of design experience, the architect advised the student to take her model back to the drawing board.

11 *Incomplete Sentences*

For advice on editing fragments, see I and also A6 in the "Quick Editing Guide."

A fragment fails to qualify as a sentence because it lacks a subject or a predicate or both. However, a sentence can contain these two essentials and still miss the mark. If it lacks some other key element — a crucial word or phrase — the sentence is *incomplete*. Incomplete sentences catch writers most often in two writing situations: comparisons and elliptical constructions.

COMPARISONS

11a Make your comparisons clear by stating fully what you are comparing with what.

INCOMPLETE   Roscoe loves spending time online more than Diane.

What is this writer trying to tell us? Does Roscoe prefer the company of a keyboard to the company of his friend? Or, of these two people, is Roscoe (and not Diane) the online addict? We can't be sure because the writer has not completed the comparison. Adding a word would solve the problem.

REVISED   Roscoe loves spending time online more than Diane *does*.

REVISED   Roscoe loves spending time online more than *with* Diane.

11b When you start to draw a comparison, finish it.

The unfinished comparison is a favorite trick of advertisers — "Our product is better!" — because it dodges the question "Better than what?" A sharp writer (or shopper) knows that any item being compared must be compared *with* something else.

INCOMPLETE	Scottish tweeds are warmer.
REVISED	Scottish tweeds are warmer *than any other fabric you can buy.*

11c Be sure the things you compare are of the same kind.

A sentence that draws a comparison should assure its readers that the items involved are similar enough to compare and should make the terms of the comparison clear and logical.

> INCOMPLETE   The engine of a Ford truck is heavier than a Piper Cub airplane.

What is being compared? Truck engine and airplane? Or engine and engine? Since a truck engine is unlikely to outweigh an airplane, we can guess the writer meant to compare engines. Readers, however, should not have to make the effort to complete a writer's thought.

REVISED	The engine of a Ford truck is heavier than *that of* a Piper Cub airplane.
REVISED	A Ford truck's engine is heavier than a *Piper Cub's.*

In this last example, parallel structure (*Ford truck's* and *Piper Cub's*) helps to make the comparison concise as well as clear.

For more on parallel structure, see 13.

11d To compare an item with others of its kind, use *any other.*

A comparison using *any* shows how something relates to a group without belonging to the group.

> Alaska is larger than *any* country in Central America.

> Bluefish has as much protein as *any* meat.

A comparison using *any other* shows how one member of a group relates to other members of the same group.

> Death Valley is drier than *any other* place in the United States.

> Bluefish has as distinctive a flavor as *any other* fish.

■ Exercise 11–1

Completing Comparisons

Revise the following sentences by adding needed words to any comparisons that are incomplete. (There may be more than one way to complete some comparisons.) Some sentences may be correct. Possible revisions for the lettered sentences appear in the back of the book. Example:

> I hate hot weather more than you.

> I hate hot weather more than you *do. Or*

> I hate hot weather more than *I hate* you.

www
For more practice, visit *Exercise Central* at <www.bedfordstmartins.com/bedguide>.

a. The movie version of *The Brady Bunch* was much more ironic.

b. Taking care of a dog is often more demanding than a cat.

c. I received more free calendars in the mail for 2001 than any year.

d. The crime rate in the United States is higher than Canada.

e. Liver contains more iron than any meat.

1. Driving a sports car means more to Jake than his professors.

2. People who go to college aren't necessarily smarter, but they will always have an advantage at job interviews.

3. I don't have as much trouble getting along with Michelle as Karen.

4. A hen lays fewer eggs than a turtle.

5. Singing is closer to prayer than a meal of Chicken McNuggets.

ELLIPTICAL CONSTRUCTIONS

Robert Frost begins his well-known poem "Fire and Ice" with these lines:

> Some say the world will end in fire, / Some say in ice.

When Frost wrote that opening, he avoided needless repetition by implying certain words rather than stating them. The result is more concise and more effective than a complete version of the same sentence would be:

> Some say the world will end in fire, some say the world will end in ice.

This common writer's tactic produces an ***elliptical construction*** — one that leaves out (for the sake of conciseness) words that are unnecessary but clearly understood by readers. Elliptical constructions can create confusion, however, if the writer gives readers too little information to fill in those missing words accurately.

1 1e **When you eliminate repetition, keep all words that are essential for clarity.**

An elliptical construction saves repeating what a reader already knows, but be sure to omit only words that are stated elsewhere in the sentence. Otherwise, your reader may fill the gap incorrectly.

> INCOMPLETE How can I date her, seeing that she is a senior, I a mere freshman?

This elliptical construction won't work. A reader supplying the stated verb in the last part of the sentence would get "I *is* a mere freshman."

> REVISED How can I date her, seeing that she is a senior and I *am* a mere freshman?

Be sure to state necessary prepositions as well.

> INCOMPLETE The train neither goes nor returns from Middletown.

Readers are likely to fill in an extra *from* after *goes,* to complete the verb's action. Write instead:

REVISED   The train neither goes *to* nor returns from Middletown.

11f In a compound predicate, leave out only verb forms that have already been stated.

Compound predicates are especially prone to incomplete elliptical constructions. Check your verbs especially carefully if they are in different tenses. Be sure that no necessary part is missing.

INCOMPLETE   The mayor never has and never will vote to raise taxes.

REVISED   The mayor never has *voted* and never will vote to raise taxes.

compound predicate: A predicate consisting of two or more verbs linked by a conjunction: My sister *stopped and stared.*

11g If you mix comparisons using *as* and *than,* include both words.

To contrast two different things, we normally use the comparative form of an adjective followed by *than: better than, more than, fewer than.* To show a similarity between two things, we normally sandwich the simple form of an adjective between *as* and *as: as good as, as many as, as few as.* Often we can combine two *than* comparisons or two *as* comparisons into an elliptical construction.

For more on comparative forms, see 8d–8f.

The White House is smaller [than] and newer than Buckingham Palace.

Some executives live in homes as large [as] and as grand as the White House.

If you want to combine a *than* comparison with an *as* comparison, however, an elliptical construction won't work.

INCOMPLETE   The White House is smaller but just as beautiful as Buckingham Palace.

REVISED   The White House is smaller *than* but just *as* beautiful *as* Buckingham Palace.

INCOMPLETE   Some executives live in homes as large and no less grand than the White House.

REVISED   Some executives live in homes *as* large *as* and no less grand *than* the White House.

■ Exercise 11–2

Completing Sentences

Revise the following sentences by adding needed words to any constructions that are incomplete. (There may be more than one way to complete some constructions.) Some sentences may be correct. Possible revisions for the lettered sentences appear in the back of the book. Example:

> President Kennedy should have but didn't see the perils of invading Cuba.

> President Kennedy should have *seen* but didn't see the perils of invading Cuba.

a. Eighteenth-century China was as civilized and in many respects more sophisticated than the Western world.

b. Pembroke was never contacted, much less involved with, the election committee.

c. I haven't yet but soon will finish my term paper.

d. Ron likes his popcorn with butter, Linda with parmesan cheese.

e. George Washington always has been and will be regarded as the father of this country.

1. You have traveled to exotic Tahiti; Maureen to Asbury Park, New Jersey.

2. The mayor refuses to negotiate or even talk to the civic association.

3. Building a new sewage treatment plant would be no more costly and just as effective as modifying the existing one.

4. You'll be able to tell Jon from the rest of the team: Jon wears white Reeboks, the others black high-tops.

5. Erosion has and always will reshape the shoreline.

12 *Mixed Constructions and Faulty Predication*

Sometimes a sentence contains all the necessary parts and still doesn't make sense. The problem may be a discord between two or more parts of the sentence: the writer has combined phrases or clauses that don't fit together (a *mixed construction*) or mismatched a verb and its subject, object, or modifier (*faulty predication*).

12a Link phrases and clauses logically.

phrase: Two or more related words that work together but may lack a subject (as in *will have been*), a verb (*my uncle Zeke*), or both (*in the attic*)

A *mixed construction* results when a writer connects phrases or clauses (or both) that don't work together as a sentence.

> MIXED   In her efforts to solve the tax problem only caused the mayor additional difficulties.

The prepositional phrase *In her efforts to solve the tax problem* is a modifier; it cannot function as the subject of a sentence. The writer, however, has used this phrase as a noun — the subject of the verb *caused*. To untangle the mixed construction, the writer has two choices: (1) rewrite the phrase so that it works as a noun, or (2) use the phrase as a modifier rather than a subject.

> REVISED   Her efforts to solve the tax problem only caused the mayor additional difficulties. [With *in* gone, *efforts* becomes the subject of the sentence.]

> REVISED   In her efforts to solve the tax problem, the mayor created additional difficulties. [The prepositional phrase now modifies the verb *created*.]

To avoid mixed constructions, check the links that join your phrases and clauses — especially prepositions and conjunctions. A sentence, like a chain, is only as strong as its weakest link.

> MIXED   Jack, although he was picked up by the police, but was not charged with anything.

Using both *although* and *but* gives this sentence one link too many. We can unmix the construction in two ways.

> REVISED   Jack was picked up by the police but was not charged with anything.

> REVISED   Although he was picked up by the police, Jack was not charged with anything.

12b Relate the parts of a sentence logically.

Faulty predication refers to a skewed relationship between a verb and some other part of a sentence.

> FAULTY   *The temperature of water freezes* at 32 degrees Fahrenheit.

At first glance, that sentence looks all right. It contains both subject and predicate. It expresses a complete thought. What is wrong with it? The writer has slipped into faulty predication by mismatching the subject and verb. The sentence tells us that *temperature freezes,* when science and common sense tell us it is *water* that freezes. To correct this error, the writer must find a subject and verb that fit each other.

> REVISED   *Water freezes* at 32 degrees Fahrenheit.

Faulty predication also can result from a mismatch between a verb and its direct object.

> FAULTY   Rising costs *diminish college* for many students.

Costs don't *diminish college.* To correct this predication error, the writer must change the sentence so that its direct object follows logically from its verb.

> REVISED   Rising costs *diminish the number of students who can attend college.*

---

clause: A group of related words that includes both a subject and a verb: *The sailboats raced until the sun set.*

preposition: A transitional word (such as *in, on, at, of, from*) that leads into a phrase such as *in the bar, under a rickety table*

conjunction: A linking word that connects words or groups of words through coordination (*and, but*) or subordination (*because, although, unless*)

subject: The part of a sentence that names something—a person, an object, an idea, a situation—about which the predicate makes an assertion: The *king* lives.

predicate: The part of a sentence that makes an assertion about the subject involving an action (Birds *fly*), a relationship (Birds *have feathers*), or a state of being ("Birds *are warm-blooded*)

verb: A word that shows action (The cow *jumped* over the moon) or a state of being (The cow *is brown*)

direct object: The target of a verb that completes the action performed by the subject or asserted about the subject: I photographed *the sheriff.*

Subtler predication errors result when a writer uses a linking verb to forge a false connection between the subject and a subject complement.

linking verb: A verb (*is, become, seem, feel*) that shows a state of being by linking the sentence subject with a word that renames or describes the subject: The sky *is* blue. (See 3a.)

subject complement: A noun, an adjective, or a group of words that follows a linking verb and renames or describes the subject: This plum tastes *ripe*. (See 3a.)

FAULTY   *Industrial waste* has become *an important modern priority.*

Is it really *waste* that has become a *priority*? Or is it *solving the problems caused by careless disposal of industrial waste*? A writer who says all that, though, risks wordiness. Why not just replace *priority* with a closer match for *waste*?

REVISED   *Industrial waste* has become a *modern menace.*

Predication errors tend to plague writers who are too fond of the passive voice. Mismatches between a verb and its subject, its object, or another part of the sentence are easier to avoid when the verb is active than when it is passive.

For more on using active and passive voice, see 3m.

FAULTY   The idea of giving thanks for a good harvest *was not done* first by the Pilgrims.

REVISED   The idea of giving thanks for a good harvest *did not originate* with the Pilgrims.

12c Avoid starting a definition with *when* or *where*.

A definition, like any other phrase or clause, needs to fit grammatically with the rest of the sentence.

FAULTY   Dyslexia is when you have a reading disorder.

REVISED   Dyslexia is a reading disorder.

FAULTY   A lay-up is where a player dribbles close to the basket and then makes a one-handed, banked shot.

REVISED   To shoot a lay-up, a player dribbles in close to the basket and then makes a one-handed, banked shot.

12d Avoid using *the reason is because* . . .

Anytime you start an explanation with *the reason is,* what follows *is* should be a subject complement: an adjective, a noun, or a noun clause. *Because* is a conjunction; it cannot function as a noun or adjective.

FAULTY   *The reason* Gerard hesitates *is because* no one supported him two years ago.

REVISED   *The reason* Gerard hesitates *is simple*: no one supported him two years ago.

REVISED   *The reason* Gerard hesitates *is that* no one supported him two years ago.

REVISED   *The reason* Gerard hesitates *is his lack of support* two years ago.

Mixed Constructions, Faulty Predication, and Subject Errors

Mixed constructions result when phrases or clauses are joined even though they do not logically go together. Combine clauses with either a coordinating conjunction or a subordinating conjunction, never both.

> INCORRECT   *Although* baseball is called "the national pastime" of the United States, *but* football is probably more popular.
>
> CORRECT   *Although* baseball is called "the national pastime" of the United States, football is probably more popular.
>
> CORRECT   Baseball is called "the national pastime" of the United States, *but* football is probably more popular.

Faulty predication results when a verb and its subject, object, or modifier do not match. Do not use a noun as both the subject of the sentence and the object of a preposition.

> INCORRECT   *In my neighborhood has* several good restaurants.
>
> CORRECT   *My neighborhood has* several good restaurants.
>
> CORRECT   *In my neighborhood, there are* several good restaurants.

Also avoid these common errors involving subjects of clauses.

- Do not omit *it* used as a subject. A subject is required in all English sentences except imperatives.

> INCORRECT   *Is* interesting to visit museums.
>
> CORRECT   *It is* interesting to visit museums.

- Do not repeat the subject of a sentence with a pronoun.

> INCORRECT   *My brother-in-law, he* is a successful investor.
>
> CORRECT   *My brother-in-law* is a successful investor.

ESL GUIDELINES

For more on conjunctions, see 14a–14c.

coordinating conjunction: A one-syllable linking word (*and, but, for, or, nor, so, yet*) that joins elements with equal or near-equal importance: Jack *and* Jill, sink *or* swim

subordinating conjunction: A word (such as *because, although, if, when*) used to make one clause dependent on, or subordinate to, another: *Unless* you have a key, we are locked out.

■ **Exercise 12–1**

Correcting Mixed Constructions and Faulty Predication

Correct any mixed constructions and faulty predication you find in the following sentences. Possible revisions for the lettered sentences appear in the back of the book. Example:

> The storm damaged the beach erosion.
>
> The storm worsened the beach erosion. *Or*
>
> The storm damaged the beach.

a. The cost of health insurance protects people from big medical bills.

b. In his determination to prevail helped him finish the race.

c. The AIDS epidemic destroys the body's immune system.

WWW

For more practice, visit *Exercise Central* at <www.bedfordstmartins.com/bedguide>.

    d. The temperatures are too cold for the orange trees.

    e. A recession is when economic growth is small or nonexistent and unemployment increases.

    1. The opening of the new shopping mall should draw out-of-town shoppers for years to come.

    2. The reason the referendum was defeated was because voters are tired of paying so much in taxes.

    3. In the glacier's retreat created the valley.

    4. A drop in prices could put farmers out of business.

    5. The researchers' main goal is cancer.

13   *Parallel Structure*

You use *parallel structure*, or parallelism, when you create a series of words, phrases, clauses, or sentences with the same grammatical form. The pattern created by the series — its parallel structure — emphasizes the similarities or differences among the items, whether things, qualities, actions, or ideas.

> My favorite foods are roast beef, apple pie, and linguine with clam sauce.

> Louise is charming, witty, intelligent, and talented.

> Jeff likes to swim, ride, and run.

> Dave likes movies that scare him and books that make him laugh.

For more on editing for parallel structure, see B2 in the "Quick Editing Guide."

Each series is a perfect parallel construction, composed of equivalent words: nouns in the first example, adjectives in the second, verbs in the third, and adjective clauses in the fourth.

13a   In a series linked by a coordinating conjunction, keep all elements in the same grammatical form.

coordinating conjunction: A one-syllable linking word (*and, but, for, or, nor, so, yet*) that joins elements with equal or near-equal importance: Jack *and* Jill, sink *or* swim

A coordinating conjunction cues your readers to expect a parallel structure. Whether your series consists of single words, phrases, or clauses, its parts should balance one another.

AWKWARD The puppies are *tiny, clumsily bumping* into each other, *and cute.*

Two elements in this series are parallel one-word adjectives (*tiny, cute*), but the third, the verb phrase *clumsily bumping,* is inconsistent.

PARALLEL   The puppies are *tiny, clumsy, and cute.*

Don't mix verb forms in a series. Avoid, for instance, pairing a gerund and an infinitive.

For more on coordination, see 14a–14c.

AWKWARD Plan a winter vacation if you like *skiing and to skate.*

PARALLEL   Plan a winter vacation if you like *skiing and skating.*

PARALLEL   Plan a winter vacation if you like *to ski and to skate.*

In a series of phrases or clauses, be sure that all elements in the series are similar in form, even if they are not similar in length.

AWKWARD   The fight in the bar happens *after the two lovers have their scene together* but *before the car chase.* [The clause starting with *after* is not parallel to the phrase starting with *before.*]

PARALLEL   The fight in the bar happens *after the love scene* but *before the car chase.*

AWKWARD   You can take the key, or don't forget to leave it under the mat. [The declarative clause starting with *You can* is not parallel to the imperative clause starting with *don't forget.*]

PARALLEL   You can *take the key,* or you can *leave it* under the mat.

13b In a series linked by correlative conjunctions, keep all elements in the same grammatical form.

When you use a correlative conjunction, follow each part with a similarly structured word, phrase, or clause.

AWKWARD   I'm looking forward *to either attending* Saturday's wrestling match *or to seeing* it on closed-circuit TV. [*To* precedes the first part of the correlative conjunction (*to either*) but follows the second part (*or to*).]

PARALLEL   I'm looking forward *either to attending* Saturday's wrestling match *or to seeing* it on closed-circuit television.

AWKWARD   Take my advice: try *neither to be first nor last* in the lunch line. [*To be* follows the first part of the correlative conjunction but not the second part.]

PARALLEL   Take my advice: try to be *neither first nor last* in the lunch line.

correlative conjunction: A pair of linking words (such as *either/or, not only/but also*) that appear separately but work together to join elements of a sentence: *Neither* his friends *nor* hers like pizza.

13c Make the elements in a comparison parallel in form.

A comparative word such as *than* or *as* cues the reader to expect a parallel structure. This makes logical sense: to be compared, two things must resemble each other, and parallel structure emphasizes this resemblance.

For more on comparisons, see 11a–11d and 11g.

AWKWARD   Philip likes *fishing* better than *to sail.*

PARALLEL   Philip likes *fishing* better than *sailing.*

PARALLEL   Philip likes *to fish* better than *to sail.*

AWKWARD   *Maintaining* railway lines is as important to our public transportation system as *to buy* new trains.

PARALLEL   *Maintaining* railway lines is as important to our public transportation system as *buying* new trains.

13d Reinforce parallel structure by repeating rather than mixing lead-in words.

Parallel structures are especially useful when a sentence contains a series of clauses or phrases. For example, try to precede potentially confusing clauses with *that, who, when, where,* or some other connective, repeating the same connective every time. To do so not only helps you to keep your thoughts in order but helps readers to follow them with ease.

> No one in this country needs a government *that* aids big business at the expense of farmers and laborers, *that* ravages the environment in the name of progress, or *that* slashes budgets for health and education.

Repeating an opening phrase can accomplish the same goal in a series of parallel sentences, as this graceful example shows.

> The Russian dramatist is one who, walking through a cemetery, does not see the flowers on the graves. The American dramatist is one who, walking through a cemetery, does not see the graves under the flowers.

Sometimes the same lead-in word won't work for all elements in a series. In such cases you may be able to preserve a parallel structure by changing the order of the elements to minimize variation.

> AWKWARD   The new school building is large but not very comfortable, and expensive but unattractive.
>
> PARALLEL   The new school building is large and expensive, but uncomfortable and unattractive.

■ Exercise 13–1

Making Sentences Parallel

WWW
For more practice, visit *Exercise Central* at <www.bedfordstmartins.com/bedguide>.

Revise the following sentences by substituting parallel structures for awkward ones. Possible revisions for the lettered sentences appear in the back of the book. Example:

> In the Rio Grande Valley, the interests of conservationists, government officials, and those trying to immigrate collide.
>
> In the Rio Grande Valley, the interests of conservationists, government officials, and immigrants collide.

a. The border separating Texas and Mexico marks not only the political boundary of two countries, but it also is the last frontier for some endangered wildlife.

b. In the Rio Grande Valley, both local residents and the people who happen to be tourists enjoy visiting the national wildlife refuges.

c. The tall grasses in this valley are the home of many insects, birds, and there are abundant small mammals.

d. Two endangered wildcats, the ocelot and another called the jaguarundi, also make the Rio Grande Valley their home.

e. Many people from Central America are desperate to immigrate to the United States by either legal or by illegal means.

1. Because the land along the Rio Grande has few human inhabitants and the fact that the river is often shallow, many illegal immigrants attempt to cross the border there.

2. To capture illegal immigrants more easily, the U.S. government has cut down tall grasses, put up fences, and the number of immigration patrols has been increased.

3. For illegal immigrants, crossing the border at night makes more sense than to enter the United States in broad daylight, so the U.S. government has recently installed bright lights along the border.

4. The ocelot and the jaguarundi need darkness, hiding places, and to have some solitude if they are to survive.

5. Neither the immigration officials nor have wildlife conservationists been able to find a solution that will protect both the U.S. border and these endangered wildcats.

14 *Coordination and Subordination*

When you write, you can use coordination and subordination to bring out the relationships between your ideas. Coordination clarifies the connection between thoughts of equal importance; subordination shows how one thought affects another. Often, conjunctions—words that link groups of words and connect them in sense—specify these relationships. Together, coordination and subordination will help you produce sentences, paragraphs, and essays that function as a coherent whole.

14a Coordinate clauses or sentences that are related in theme and equal in importance.

The car skidded for a hundred yards. It crashed into a brick wall.

These two clauses make equally significant statements about the same subject, a car accident. Because the writer has indicated no link between the sentences, we can only guess that the crash followed from the skid; we cannot be sure.

Suppose we join the two with a conjunction.

The car skidded for a hundred yards, and it crashed into a brick wall.

Now the sequence is clear: first the car skidded, then it crashed. That's coordination.

clause: A group of related words that includes both a subject and a verb: *The sailboats raced until the sun set.*

sentence: A word group that includes both a subject and a predicate and can stand alone

compound predicate: A predicate consisting of two or more verbs linked by a conjunction: My sister *stopped and stared.*

Another way to coordinate the two clauses is to combine them into a single sentence with a compound predicate.

The car skidded for a hundred yards and crashed into a brick wall.

Now the connection is so clear we can almost hear screeching brakes and crunching metal.

Once you decide to coordinate two clauses, there are three ways you can do it: with a conjunction, with a conjunctive adverb, or with punctuation.

coordinating conjunction: A one-syllable linking word (*and, but, for, or, nor, so, yet*) that joins elements with equal or near-equal importance: Jack *and* Jill, sink *or* swim

1. Join two main clauses with a coordinating conjunction.

UNCOORDINATED	Ari does not want to be placed on your mailing list. He does not want a salesperson to call him.
COORDINATED	Ari does not want to be placed on your mailing list, nor does he want a salesperson to call him.
COORDINATED	Ari does not want to be placed on your mailing list or called by a salesperson.

conjunctive adverb: A linking word that can connect independent clauses and show a relationship between two ideas: Armando is a serious student; *therefore,* he studies every day.

2. Join two main clauses with a semicolon and a conjunctive adverb. Conjunctive adverbs show relationships such as addition (*also, besides*), comparison (*likewise, similarly*), contrast (*instead, however*), emphasis (*namely, certainly*), cause and effect (*thus, therefore*), or time (*finally, subsequently*).

UNCOORDINATED	The guerrillas did not observe the truce. They never intended to.
COORDINATED	The guerrillas did not observe the truce; furthermore, they never intended to.

For more on semicolons and colons, see 22 and 23.

3. Join two main clauses with a semicolon or a colon.

UNCOORDINATED	The government wants to negotiate. The guerrillas prefer to fight.
COORDINATED	The government wants to negotiate; the guerrillas prefer to fight.
UNCOORDINATED	The guerrillas have two advantages. They know the terrain, and the people support them.
COORDINATED	The guerrillas have two advantages: they know the terrain, and the people support them.

14b Coordinate clauses only if they are clearly and logically related.

Whenever you hitch together two sentences, make sure they get along. Will the relationship between them be evident to your readers?

FAULTY	The sportscasters were surprised by Easy Goer's failure to win the Kentucky Derby, but it rained on Derby day.

The writer has not included enough information for the reader to see why these two clauses are connected.

COORDINATED   The sportscasters were surprised by Easy Goer's failure to win the Kentucky Derby; *however, he runs poorly on a muddy track,* and it rained on Derby day.

Have you chosen a coordinating conjunction, conjunctive adverb, or punctuation mark that accurately reflects this relationship?

FAULTY   The sportscasters all expected Easy Goer to win the Kentucky Derby, and Sunday Silence beat him.

Because *and* implies that both clauses reflect the same assumptions, which is not the case, the writer should choose a conjunction that expresses difference.

COORDINATED   The sportscasters all expected Easy Goer to win the Kentucky Derby, *but* Sunday Silence beat him.

Coordinating and Subordinating Words at a Glance

Coordinating Conjunctions

and, but, for, nor, or, so, yet

Correlative Conjunctions

as . . . as	just as . . . so	not only . . . but also
both . . . and	neither . . . nor	whether . . . or
either . . . or	not . . . but	

Common Conjunctive Adverbs

accordingly	finally	likewise	otherwise
also	furthermore	meanwhile	similarly
anyway	hence	moreover	still
as	however	nevertheless	then
besides	incidentally	next	therefore
certainly	indeed	nonetheless	thus
consequently	instead	now	undoubtedly

Common Subordinating Conjunctions

after	even if	since	when
although	even though	so	whenever
as	how	so that	where
as if	if	than	wherever
as soon as	in order that	that	while
as though	once	though	why
because	provided that	unless	
before	rather than	until	

Relative Pronouns

that	what	who	whom
which	whatever	whoever	whomever
whose			

14c Coordinate clauses only if they work together to make a coherent point.

When a writer strings together several clauses in a row, often the result is excessive coordination. Trying to pack too much information into a single sentence can make readers dizzy, unable to pick out which points really matter.

> EXCESSIVE   Easy Goer was the Kentucky Derby favorite, and all the sportscasters expected him to win, but he runs poorly on a muddy track, and it rained on Derby day, so Sunday Silence beat him.

What are the main points in this passage? Each key idea deserves its own sentence so that readers will recognize it as important.

> REVISED   Easy Goer was the Kentucky Derby favorite, and all the sportscasters expected him to win. However, he runs poorly on a muddy track, and it rained on Derby day; so Sunday Silence beat him.

Excessive coordination also may result when a writer uses the same conjunction repeatedly.

> EXCESSIVE   Phil was out of the house all day, so he didn't know about the rain, so he went ahead and bet on Easy Goer, so he lost twenty bucks, so now he wants to borrow money from me.

> REVISED   Phil was out of the house all day, so he didn't know about the rain. He went ahead and bet on Easy Goer, and he lost twenty bucks. Now he wants to borrow money from me.

For advice on subordination, see 14d.

One solution to excessive coordination is subordination: making one clause dependent on another instead of giving both clauses equal weight.

■ Exercise 14–1

Using Coordination

www
For more practice, visit *Exercise Central* at <www.bedfordstmartins.com/bedguide>.

Revise the following sentences, adding coordination where appropriate and removing faulty or excessive coordination. Possible revisions for the lettered sentences appear in the back of the book. Example:

> The wind was rising, and leaves tossed on the trees, and the air seemed to crackle with electricity, and we knew that a thunderstorm was on the way.

> The wind was rising, leaves tossed on the trees, and the air seemed to crackle with electricity. We knew that a thunderstorm was on the way.

a. Professional poker players try to win money and prizes in high-stakes tournaments. They may lose thousands of dollars.

b. Poker is not an easy way to make a living. Playing professional poker is not a good way to relax.

c. A good "poker face" reveals no emotions. Communicating too much information puts a player at a disadvantage.

d. Hidden feelings may come out in unconscious movements. An expert poker player watches other players carefully.

e. Poker is different from most other casino gambling games, for it requires skill and it forces players to compete against each other, and other casino gambling pits players against the house, so they may win out of sheer luck, but skill has little to do with winning those games.

1. The rebels may take the capital in a week. They may not be able to hold it.

2. If you want to take Spanish this semester, you have only one choice. You must sign up for the 8 A.M. course.

3. Peterson's Market has raised its prices. Last week tuna fish cost $.89 a can. Now it's up to $1.09.

4. Joe starts the morning with a cup of coffee, which wakes him up, and then at lunch he eats a chocolate bar, so that the sugar and caffeine will bring up his energy level.

5. The *Hindenburg* drifted peacefully over New York City. It exploded just before landing.

14d Subordinate less important ideas to more important ideas.

Subordination is one of the most useful of all writing strategies. By subordinating a less important clause to a more important one, you show your readers that one fact or idea follows from another or affects another. You stress what counts, thereby encouraging your readers to share your viewpoint — an important goal, whatever you are writing.

When you have two sentences that contain ideas in need of connecting, you can subordinate one to the other in any of the following three ways.

1. Turn the less important idea into a subordinate clause by introducing it with a subordinating conjunction.

Jason has a keen sense of humor. He has an obnoxious, braying laugh.

From that pair of sentences, readers don't know what to feel about Jason. Is he likable or repellent? The writer needs to decide which trait matters more and to emphasize it.

Although Jason has a keen sense of humor, he has an obnoxious, braying laugh.

This revision makes Jason's sense of humor less important than his annoying hee-haw. The less important idea is stated as a subordinate clause opening with *Although,* and the more important idea is stated as the main clause.

The writer could reverse the meaning by combining the two ideas the other way around:

Although Jason has an obnoxious, braying laugh, he has a keen sense of humor.

That version makes Jason sound fun to be with, despite his mannerism.

> **subordinating conjunction:** A word (such as *because, although, if, when*) used to make one clause dependent on, or subordinate to, another: *Unless* you have a key, we are locked out.
>
> For a list of subordinating words, see p. H-73.

Which of Jason's traits to emphasize is up to the writer. What matters is that, in both combined versions of the original two separate sentences, the writer takes a clear stand by making one sentence a main clause and the other a subordinate clause.

2. Turn the less important idea into a subordinate clause by introducing it with a relative pronoun such as *who, which,* or *that.*

Jason, *who has an obnoxious, braying laugh,* has a keen sense of humor.

Jason, *whose sense of humor is keen,* has an obnoxious, braying laugh.

3. Turn the less important idea into a phrase.

Jason, *a keen humorist,* has an obnoxious, braying laugh.

Despite his obnoxious, braying laugh, Jason has a keen sense of humor.

relative pronoun: A pronoun (*who, which, that, what, whom, whomever, whose*) that opens a subordinate clause, modifying a noun or pronoun in another clause: The gift *that* I received is very practical.

phrase: Two or more related words that work together but may lack a subject (as in *will have been*), a verb (*my uncle Zeke*), or both (*in the attic*)

main clause: A group of words that has both a subject and a verb and can stand alone as a complete sentence: *My sister has a friend.*

14e Express the more important idea in the main clause.

Sometimes a writer accidentally subordinates a more important idea to a less important idea and turns the sentence's meaning upside down.

FAULTY SUBORDINATION　Although the heroism of the Allied troops on D-Day lives on in spirit, many of the World War II soldiers who invaded Normandy are dead now.

This sentence is factually accurate. Does the writer, however, really want to stress death over life? This is the effect of putting *are dead now* in the main clause and *lives on* in the subordinate clause. Recognizing a case of faulty subordination, the writer can reverse the two clauses.

REVISED　Although many of the World War II soldiers who invaded Normandy are dead now, the heroism of the Allied troops on D-Day lives on in spirit.

subordinate clause: A group of words that contains a subject and a verb but cannot stand alone because it depends on a main clause to help it make sense: Pia, *who plays the oboe,* prefers solitude.

14f Limit the number of subordinate clauses in a sentence.

Often the result of cramming too much information into one sentence, excessive subordination strings so many ideas together that readers may not be able to pick out what matters.

EXCESSIVE SUBORDINATION　Debate over the Strategic Defense Initiative (SDI), which was originally proposed as a space-based defensive shield that would protect America from enemy attack, but which critics have suggested amounts to creating a first-strike capability in space, has to some extent focused on the wrong question.

In revising this sentence, the writer needs to decide which are the main points and turn each one into a main clause. Lesser points can remain as subordinate clauses, arranged so that each gets appropriate emphasis.

REVISED   Debate over the Strategic Defense Initiative (SDI) has to some extent focused on the wrong question. The plan was originally proposed as a space-based defensive shield that would protect America from enemy attack. Critics have suggested, however, that it amounts to creating a first-strike capability in space.

■ Exercise 14–2

Using Subordination

Revise the following sentences, adding subordination where appropriate and removing faulty or excessive subordination. Possible revisions for the lettered sentences appear in the back of the book. Example:

Some playwrights like to work with performing theater companies. It is helpful to hear a script read aloud by actors.

Some playwrights like to work with performing theater companies *because* it is helpful to hear a script read aloud by actors.

a. Cape Cod is a peninsula in Massachusetts. It juts into the Atlantic Ocean south of Boston. The Cape marks the northern turning point of the Gulf Stream.

b. The developer had hoped the condominiums would sell quickly. Sales were sluggish.

c. Tourists love Italy. Italy has a wonderful climate, beautiful towns and cities, and a rich history.

d. At the end of Verdi's opera *La Traviata,* Alfredo has to see his beloved Violetta again. He knows she is dying and all he can say is good-bye.

e. I usually have more fun at a concert with Rico than with Morey. Rico loves music. Morey merely tolerates it.

1. Although we occasionally hear horror stories about fruits and vegetables being unsafe to eat because they were sprayed with toxic chemicals or were grown in contaminated soil, the fact remains that, given their high nutritional value, these fresh foods are generally much better for us than processed foods.

2. English has become an international language. Its grammar is filled with exceptions to the rules.

3. Some television cartoon shows have become cult classics. This has happened years after they went off the air. Examples include *Rocky and Bullwinkle* and *Speed Racer.*

4. Although bank customers have not yet begun to shift their money out of savings accounts, the interest rate on NOW accounts has gone up.

5. Violetta gives away her money. She bids adieu to her faithful servant. After that she dies in her lover's arms.

15 *Sentence Variety*

sentence: A word group that includes both a subject and a predicate and can stand alone

Most writers rely on some patterns more than others to express ideas directly and efficiently, but sometimes they combine sentence elements in unexpected ways to emphasize ideas and to surprise readers.

15a Normal Sentences

main clause: A group of words that has both a subject and a verb and can stand alone as a complete sentence: *My sister has a friend.*

In a *normal sentence,* a writer puts the subject before the verb at the beginning of the main clause. This pattern is the most common in English because it expresses ideas in the most straightforward manner.

Most college *students* today *want* interesting classes.

15b Inverted Sentences

In an *inverted sentence,* a writer inverts or reverses the subject-verb order to emphasize an idea in the predicate.

NORMAL   *My peers are uninterested* in reading.

INVERTED   How *uninterested* in reading *are my peers*!

15c Cumulative Sentences

In a *cumulative sentence,* a writer piles details at the end of a sentence to help readers visualize a scene or understand an idea.

They came walking out in heavily brocaded yellow and black costumes, the familiar "toreador" suit, heavy with gold embroidery, cape, jacket, shirt and collar, knee breeches, pink stockings, and low pumps.
                    — Ernest Hemingway, "Bull Fighting a Tragedy"

15d Periodic Sentences

The positions of emphasis in a sentence are the beginning and the end. In a *periodic sentence,* a writer suspends the main clause for a climactic ending, emphasizing an idea by withholding it until the end.

Leaning back in his chair, shaking his head slowly back and forth, frustrated over his inability to solve the quadratic equation, Franklin scowled.

Types of Sentences at a Glance

Simple Sentences

Any sentence that contains only one main clause is a *simple sentence,* even if it includes modifiers, objects, complements, and phrases in addition to its subject and verb.

┌─────────────────── MAIN CLAUSE ───────────────────┐
Even amateur stargazers can easily locate the Big Dipper in the night sky.

A simple sentence may have a compound subject (*Fred and Sandy*) or a compound verb (*laughed and cried*). Sometimes the subject of a simple sentence is not stated but is clearly understood, as is *you* in the command "Run!"

Compound Sentences

A *compound sentence* consists of two or more main clauses joined by a coordinating conjunction such as *and, but,* or *for* or by a semicolon. Sometimes the semicolon is followed by a conjunctive adverb such as *however, nevertheless,* or *therefore.*

For lists of coordinating conjunctions and conjunctive adverbs, see p. H-73.

                                        MAIN CLAUSE
┌──────────── MAIN CLAUSE ────────────┐ ┌────────┐
I would like to accompany you, but I can't.

┌──── MAIN CLAUSE ────┐   ┌──────── MAIN CLAUSE ────────┐
My car broke down; therefore, I missed the first day of class.

Complex Sentences

A *complex sentence* consists of one main clause and one or more subordinate clauses.

For lists of subordinating words, see p. H-73.

        MAIN   SUBORDINATE
┌──── CLAUSE ────┐ ┌──── CLAUSE ────┐
I will be at the airport when you arrive.

In some sentences, the relative pronoun linking the subordinate clause to the main clause is implied rather than stated.

  MAIN   SUBORDINATE
CLAUSE ┌──── CLAUSE ────┐
I know [that] you saw us.

Compound-Complex Sentences

A *compound-complex sentence* shares the attributes of both a compound sentence (two or more main clauses) and a complex sentence (at least one subordinate clause).

      MAIN   SUBORDINATE   SUBORDINATE   MAIN
┌── CLAUSE ──┐ ┌──── CLAUSE ────┐ ┌── CLAUSE ──┐ ┌──── CLAUSE ────┐
I'd gladly wait until you're ready; but if I do, I'll miss the boat.

■ **Exercise 15–1**

www
For more practice, visit
Exercise Central at <www
.bedfordstmartins.com/
bedguide>.

Increasing Sentence Variety

Revise the following passage, adding sentence variety to create interest, emphasize important ideas, and strengthen coherence.

We are terrified of death. We do not think of it, and we don't speak of
death. We don't mourn in public. We don't know how to console a grieving
friend. In fact, we have eliminated or suppressed all the traditional rituals surrounding death.

The Victorians coped with death differently. Their funerals were elaborate.
The yards of black crepe around the hearse, hired professional mourners, and
its solemn procession leading to an ornate tomb is now only a distant memory. They wore mourning jewelry. They had a complicated dress code for the
grieving process. It governed what mourners wore, and it governed how long
they wore it. Many of these Victorian rituals may seem excessive or even mor-
bid to us today. The rituals served a psychological purpose in helping the living
deal with loss.

Chapter 35

Word Choice

16. Appropriateness   H-81
17. Exact Words   H-86
18. Bias-Free Language   H-90
19. Wordiness   H-94

16 *Appropriateness*

When you talk to people face to face, you can gauge how they are reacting to what you say. Often their responses guide your tone of voice and your choice of words: if your listener chuckles at your humor, you go on being humorous; if your listener frowns, you cut the comedy and speak more seriously.

When you write, you cannot gauge your readers' reactions as easily because you cannot see them. Instead, you must imagine yourself in their place, probably focusing most closely on their responses when you revise.

16a Choose a tone appropriate for your topic and audience.

Like a speaker, a writer may come across as friendly or aloof, furious or merely annoyed, playful or grimly serious. This attitude is the *tone* of the piece of writing, and, like the tone of the speaking voice, it strongly influences the audience's response. A tone that seems right to a reader conveys your awareness of and concern for how the reader may react. If you ignore or are unaware of your reader, then your tone will be inappropriate. For instance, taking a humorous approach to a disease such as cancer or AIDS probably would yield an inappropriate tone. The reader, not finding the topic funny, is likely to reject what you say.

To help you convey your tone, you may use sentence length, level of language, vocabulary, and other elements of style. You may choose formal or informal language, colorful or bland words, coolly objective words, or words loaded with emotional connotations ("You pig!" "You angel!").

16b Choose a level of formality appropriate for your tone.

Being aware of the tone you want to convey to your audience helps you choose words that are neither too formal nor too informal. By *formal* language, we mean the impersonal language of educated persons, usually written. In general, formal language is marked by relatively long and complex sentences and by a large, often esoteric, vocabulary. It doesn't use contractions (such as *doesn't*), and the writer's attitude toward the topic is serious.

Informal language more closely resembles ordinary conversation. Its sentences tend to be relatively short and simple. Informal language is marked by common words and may include contractions, slang, and references to everyday objects and activities (cheeseburgers, T-shirts, CDs). It may address the reader as *you,* and the writer may use *I.*

The right language for most college essays lies somewhere between formal and informal. If your topic and your tone are serious (say, for an expository paper on the United Nations), then your language is likely to lean toward formality. If your topic is not weighty and your tone is light and humorous (say, for a narrative paper about giving your dog a bath), then your language can be informal.

■ Exercise 16–1

Choosing an Appropriate Tone and Level of Formality

www
For more practice, visit *Exercise Central* at <www.bedfordstmartins .com/bedguide>.

Revise the following passages to ensure that both the tone and the level of formality are appropriate for the topic and audience. Example:

> I'm sending you this letter because I want you to meet with me and give me some info about the job you do.

> I'm writing to inquire about the possibility of an informational interview about your profession.

1. Dear Senator Crowley:
   I think you've got to vote for the new environmental law, so I'm writing this letter. We're messing up forests and wetlands — maybe for good. Let's do something now for everybody who's born after us.
   Thanks,
   Glenn Turner

2. The new Holocaust Museum in Washington, D.C., is a great museum dedicated to a real bad time in history. It's real hard not to get bummed out by the stuff on show. Take it from me, it's an experience you'll never forget.

3. Dear Elaine,
   I am so pleased that you plan on attending the homecoming dance with me on Friday. It promises to be a gala event, and I am confident that we will enjoy ourselves immensely. I understand a local recording act by the name of Acid Bunny will be providing the musical entertainment. Please call me at your earliest convenience to let me know when I should pick you up.
   Sincerely,
   Bill

16c Choose common words instead of jargon.

Whatever your tone and your level of formality, certain types of language are best avoided when you write an essay. *Jargon* is the name given to the specialized vocabulary used by people in a particular field. Nearly every academic, professional, and even recreational field—music, carpentry, the law, computer programming, sports—has its own jargon. In baseball, retired pitcher Dennis Eckersley once said that when he faced a dangerous batter, he would think: "If I throw him *the heater,* maybe he *juices it out* on me" (emphasis added). Translation: "If I throw him a fastball, he might hit a home run."[1]

To a specialist addressing other specialists, jargon is convenient and necessary. Without technical terms, after all, two surgeons could hardly discuss a patient's anatomy. To an outsider, though, such terms may be incomprehensible. If your writing is meant (as it should be) to communicate information to your readers and not to make them feel excluded or confused, you should avoid unnecessary jargon.

Commonly, we apply the name *jargon* to any private, pretentious, or needlessly specialized language. Jargon can include not only words but ways of using words. Some politicians and bureaucrats like to make nouns into verbs by tacking on suffixes like *-ize.*

> JARGON   The government intends to *privatize* federal land.
>
> CLEAR   The government intends to *sell* federal land to *private buyers.*

Although *privatize* implies merely "convert to private ownership," usually its real meaning is "sell off"—as might occur were a national park to be auctioned to developers. *Privatize* thus also can be called a *euphemism,* a pleasant term that masks an unpleasant meaning (see 16d).

Besides confusing readers, jargon is likely to mislead them. Recently, technology has made verbs of the familiar nouns *access, boot,* and *format* and has popularized *interface, x amount of, database,* and *parameters.* Such terms are useful to explain technical processes; but when thoughtlessly applied to nontechnical ideas, they can obscure meaning.

> JARGON   A democracy needs the electorate's *input.*
>
> CLEAR   A democracy needs the electorate *to vote and to express its views to elected officials.*

Here's how to avoid needless jargon:

1. Beware of choosing any trendy new word when a perfectly good old word will do.
2. Before using a word ending in *-ize, -wise,* or *-ism,* count to ten. This will give you time either to think of a clearer alternative or to be sure that none exists.

---

[1] Quoted by Mike Whiteford, *How to Talk Baseball* (New York: Dembner, 1983) 51.

3. Avoid the jargon of a special discipline — say, psychology or fly-fishing — unless you are writing of those matters and you know for sure that your reader is familiar with them. If you're writing for general readers about some field in which you are an expert — for instance, explaining the fundamentals of hang gliding — define any specialized terms. Even if you're addressing fellow experts, use plain words and you'll rarely go wrong.

■ Exercise 16–2

Avoiding Jargon

Revise the following sentences to eliminate the jargon. If you see a need to change a sentence extensively, go ahead. If you can't tell what a sentence means, decide what it might mean, and rewrite it so that its meaning is clear. Possible revisions for the lettered sentences appear in the back of the book. Example:

> The proximity of Mr. Fitton's knife to Mr. Schering's arm produced a violation of the integrity of the skin.

> Mr. Fitton's knife cut Mr. Schering's arm.

a. Everyone at Boondoggle and Gall puts in face time at the holiday gatherings to maximize networking opportunities.

b. This year, in excess of fifty nonessential employees were negatively impacted by Boondoggle and Gall's decision to downsize effective September 1.

c. The layoffs made Jensen the sole point of responsibility for telephone interface in the customer service department.

d. The numerical quotient of Jensen's telephonic exchanges increased by a factor of three post-downsizing, yet Jensen received no addition fiscal remuneration.

e. Jensen was not on the same page with management re her compensation, so she exercised the option to terminate her relationship with Boondoggle and Gall.

1. The driver education course prepares the student for the skills of handling a vehicle on the highway transportation system.

2. We of the State Department have carefully contexted the riots in Lebanon intelligencewise and, after full and thorough database utilization, find them abnormalling rapidly.

3. In the heart area, Mr. Pitt is a prime candidate-elect for intervention of a multiple bypass nature.

4. Engaging in a conversational situation with God permits an individual to maximally interface with God.

5. The deer hunters number-balance the ecological infrastructure by quietizing x amount of the deer populace.

16d Use euphemisms sparingly.

Euphemisms are plain truths dressed in attractive words, sometimes hard facts stated gently. To say that someone *passed away* instead of *died* is a common euphemism — useful and humane, perhaps, in breaking terrible news to an anxious family. In such shock-absorbing language, an army that *retreats makes a strategic withdrawal*, a person who is *underweight* turns *slim*, and an acne medication treats not *pimples* but *blemishes*. Even if you aren't prone to using euphemisms in your own writing, be aware of them when you read, especially when collecting evidence from biased sources and official spokespersons.

16e Avoid slang in formal writing.

Slang, especially when new, can be colorful ("She's not playing with a full deck"), playful ("He's wicked cute!"), and apt (*ice* for diamonds, a *stiff* for a corpse). The trouble with most slang, however, is that it quickly comes to seem as old and wrinkled as the Jazz Age's favorite exclamation of glee, *twenty-three skidoo!* To be understood in the classroom and out of it, your best bet is to stick to Standard English. Seek words that are usual but exact, not the latest thing, and your writing will stay young longer.

■ Exercise 16–3

Avoiding Euphemisms and Slang

Revise the following sentences to replace euphemisms with plainer words and slang with Standard English. Possible revisions for the lettered sentences appear in the back of the book. Example:

> Some dude ripped off my wallet, so I am currently experiencing a negative cash flow.
>
> *Someone stole* my wallet, so I am now *in debt.*

a. Our security forces have judiciously thinned an excessive number of political dissidents.
b. At three hundred bucks a month, the apartment is a steal.
c. The soldiers were victims of friendly fire during a strategic withdrawal.
d. Churchill was a wicked good politician.
e. The president's health-care plan was toast; there was no way that Congress would approve it.

1. To bridge the projected shortfall between collections and expenditures in next year's budget, the governor advocates some form of revenue enhancement.

2. The course was a joke; the prof passed everyone and didn't even grade the stuff we turned in.

3. Saturday's weather forecast calls for extended periods of shower activity.

4. The caller to the talk-radio program sounded totally wigged out.

5. We anticipate a downturn in economic vitality.

17 *Exact Words*

What would you think if you read in a newspaper that a certain leading citizen is a *pillow of the community*? Good writing depends on more than good grammar. Just as important are knowing what words and phrases mean and using them precisely.

17a Choose words for their connotations as well as their denotations.

The *denotation* of a word is its basic meaning—its dictionary definition. *Excited, agitated,* and *exhilarated* all denote a similar state of physical and emotional arousal. When you look up a word in a dictionary or thesaurus, the synonyms you find have been selected for their shared denotation.

The *connotations* of a word are the shades of meaning that set it apart from its synonyms. You might be *agitated* by the prospect of exams next week, but *exhilarated* by your plans for a vacation afterward. When you choose one out of several synonyms, you base your choice on connotation.

Paying attention to connotation helps a writer to say exactly what he or she intends, instead of almost but not quite.

> IMPRECISE   Advertisers have given light beer a macho image by showing football players *sipping* the product with *enthusiasm.*
>
> REVISED   Advertisers have given light beer a macho image by showing football players *guzzling* the product with *gusto.*

17b Avoid clichés.

A *cliché* is a trite expression, once vivid or figurative but now worn out from too much use. If a story begins, "It was a dark and stormy night," then its author is obviously using dull, predictable words. Clichés abound when writers and speakers try hard to sound vigorous and colorful but don't trouble themselves to invent anything vigorous, colorful, and new.

If you read newspapers, you are familiar with these ready-made constructions. A strike is usually settled after a *marathon bargaining session* that *narrowly averts a walkout,* often *at the eleventh hour.* Fires customarily *race* and *gut.* Some writers use clichés to exaggerate, but the writer to whom everything is *fantastic* or *terrific* arouses a reader's suspicion that it isn't.

No writer can entirely avoid clichés or avoid echoing colorful expressions first used by someone else. You need not ban from your writing all proverbs ("It takes a thief to catch a thief"), well-worked quotations from Shakespeare ("Neither a borrower nor a lender be"), and other faintly dusty wares from the storehouse of our language. "Looking for a needle in a haystack" may be a time-worn phrase, yet who can put that idea any more memorably?

When editing your writing, you will usually recognize any really annoying cliché if you feel a sudden guilty desire to surround an expression with quotation marks, as if to apologize for it. You might also show your papers to friends, asking them to look for anything trite. As you go on in college, your awareness of clichés will grow with reading. The more you read, the easier it is to recognize a cliché on sight, for you will have met it often before. If one turns up in your writing, try replacing it with something more vivid and original.

COMMON CLICHÉS

above and beyond the call of duty	make a long story short
add insult to injury	neat as a pin
beyond a shadow of a doubt	nutty as a fruitcake
The bottom line is . . .	old as the hills
burn one's bridges	on the brink of disaster
burn the midnight oil	pay through the nose
busy as a beaver (or a bee)	piece of cake
But that's another story.	point with pride
come hell or high water	pull the wool over someone's eyes
cool as a cucumber	sell like hotcakes
cream of the crop	a sheepish grin
dressed fit to kill	since the dawn of time
easy as taking candy from a baby	skating on thin ice
feeling on top of the world	a skeleton in the closet
few and far between	a sneaking suspicion
golden years	stab me in the back
greased lightning	stick out like a sore thumb
hands-on learning experience	sweet as honey
hard as a rock	That's the way the ball bounces.
honest as the day is long	through thick and thin
In conclusion, I would like to say . . .	tip of the iceberg
in my wildest dreams	too little and too late
last but not least	tried but true
little did I dream	

17c Use idioms in their correct form.

Every language contains *idioms,* or *idiomatic expressions:* phrases that, through long use, have become standard even though their construction may defy logic or grammar. Many idiomatic expressions require us to choose the right preposition. To pause *for* a minute is not the same as to

ESL GUIDELINES

In, On, At: Prepositions of Location and Time

The prepositions *in, on,* and *at* are frequently used to express location.

> Elaine lives *in* Manhattan *at* a swanky address *on* Fifth Avenue.

- *In* means "within" or "inside of" a place, including geographical areas, such as cities, states, countries, and continents.

  > I packed my books *in* my backpack and left to visit my cousins *in* Canada.

- Where *in* emphasizes *location* only, *at* is often used to refer to a place when a specific *activity* is implied: *at the store* (to shop), *at the office* (to work), *at the theater* (to see a play), and so on.

  > Angelo left his bicycle *in* the bike rack while he was *at* school.

- *On* means "on the surface of" or "on top of" something and is used with floors of buildings and planets. It is also used to indicate a location *beside* a lake, river, ocean, or other body of water.

  > The service department is *on* the fourth floor.

  > We have a cabin *on* Lake Michigan.

In, on, and *at* can all be used in addresses. *In* is used to identify a general location, such as a city or neighborhood. *On* is used to identify a specific street. *At* is used to give an exact address.

> We live *in* Boston *on* Medway Street.

> We live *at* 20 Medway Street.

- *In* and *at* can both be used with the verb *arrive*. *In* indicates a large place, such as a city, state, country, or continent. *At* indicates a smaller place, such as a specific building or address. (*To* is never used with *arrive*.)

- Alanya arrived *in* Alaska yesterday, and Sanjei will arrive *at* the airport soon.

The prepositions *in, on,* and *at* are also used in many time expressions.

- *In* indicates the span of time during which something occurs or a time in the future; it is also used in the expressions *in a minute* (meaning "shortly") and *in time* (meaning "soon enough"). *In* is also used with seasons, months, and periods of the day.

  > He needs to read this book *in* the next three days. [During the next three days]

  > I'll meet you *in* the morning *in* two weeks. [Two weeks from now]

- *On* is used with the days of the week, with the word *weekend*, and in the expression *on time* (meaning "punctually").

  > Let's have lunch *on* Friday.

- *At* is used in reference to a specific time on the clock as well as a specific time of the day (*at night, at dawn, at twilight*).

  > We'll meet again next Monday *at* 2:15 P.M.

pause *in* a minute. We work *up* a sweat while working *out* in the gym. We argue *with* someone but *about* something, *for* or *against* it.

For some idioms we must know which article to use before a noun — or whether to use any article at all. We can be *in motion,* but we have to be *in the swim.* We're occasionally in *a tight spot* but never in *a trouble.* Certain idioms vary from country to country: in Britain, a patient has an operation *in hospital;* in America, *in the hospital.* Idioms can involve choosing the right verb with the right noun: we *seize* an opportunity, but we *catch* a plane.

When you're at work on a paper, the dictionary can help you choose the appropriate idiom. Look up *agree* in *The American Heritage Dictionary,* for

---

To, For: Indirect Objects and Prepositions

These sentences mean the same thing:

> I sent the president a letter.

> I sent a letter to the president.

ESL GUIDELINES

In the first sentence, *the president* is the **indirect object:** he or she receives the direct object (*a letter*), which was acted on (*sent*) by the subject of the sentence (*I*). In the second sentence, the same idea is expressed using a **prepositional phrase** beginning with *to.*

- Some verbs can use either an indirect object or the preposition *to: give, send, lend, offer, owe, pay, sell, show, teach,* and *tell.* Some verbs can use either an indirect object or the preposition *for: bake, build, buy, cook, find, get,* and *make.*

  > I paid *the travel agent* one hundred dollars.

  > I paid one hundred dollars *to the travel agent.*

  > Margarita cooked *her family* some chicken.

  > Margarita cooked some chicken *for her family.*

- Some verbs cannot have an indirect object; they must use a preposition. The following verbs must use the preposition *to: describe, demonstrate, explain, introduce,* and *suggest.*

INCORRECT	Please explain me indirect objects.
CORRECT	Please explain indirect objects *to me.*

- The following verbs must use the preposition *for: answer* and *prepare.*

INCORRECT	He prepared me the punch.
CORRECT	He prepared the punch *for me.*

- Some verbs must have an indirect object; they cannot use a preposition. The following verbs must have an indirect object: *ask* and *cost.*

INCORRECT	Sasha asked a question to her.
CORRECT	Sasha asked her a question.

indirect object: A person or thing affected by the subject's action, usually the recipient of the direct object, through the action indicated by a verb such as *bring, get, offer, promise, sell, show, tell,* and *write:* Charlene asked *you* a question.

preposition: A transitional word (such as *in, on, at, of, from*) that leads into a phrase such as *in the bar, under a rickety table*

instance, and you will find *agree to, agree with, agree on,* and *agree that* illustrated with sentence examples that make clear just where and when each combination is appropriate. You can then pick the idiom that belongs in the sentence you are working on.

■ Exercise 17–1

Selecting Words

Revise the following passage to replace inappropriate connotations, clichés, and faulty idioms. Example:

> The Mayan city of Uxmal is a common tourist attraction. The ruins have stood alone in the jungle since time immemorial.

> The Mayan city of Uxmal is a *popular* tourist attraction. The ruins have stood alone in the jungle since *ancient times.*

We spent the first day of our holiday in Mexico arguing around what we wanted to see on our second day. We finally agreed to a day trip out to some Mayan ruins. The next day we arrived on the Mayan city of Uxmal, which is as old as the hills. It really is a sight for sore eyes, smack dab in a jungle stretching as far as the eye can see, with many buildings still covered in plants and iguanas moving quickly over the decayed buildings. The view from the top of the Soothsayer's Temple was good, although we noticed storm clouds gathering in the distance. The rain held up until we got off of the pyramid, but we drove back to the hotel in a lot of rain. After a day of sightseeing, we were so hungry that we could have eaten a horse, so we had a good meal before we turned in.

www
For more practice, visit *Exercise Central* at <www.bedfordstmartins.com/bedguide>.

18   *Bias-Free Language*

The connotations of the words we use reveal our attitudes — our likes and dislikes, our preferences and prejudices. A *brat* is quite different from a *little angel,* a *station wagon* from a *limousine.*

Thoughtful writers try to avoid harmful bias in language. They respect their readers and don't want to insult them, make them angry, or impede communication. You may not be able to eliminate discrimination from society, but you can eliminate discriminatory language in your writing. Be on the lookout for words that insult or stereotype individuals or groups by gender, age, race, ethnic origin, sexual preference, or religion.

18a   To eliminate sexist language, use alternatives that make no reference to gender.

Among the prime targets of American feminists in the 1960s and 1970s was the male bias built into the English language. Why, they asked, do we talk about *prehistoric man, manpower,* and *the brotherhood of man,* when by *man* we mean the entire human race? Why do we focus attention on the gender of an accomplished woman by calling her a *poetess* or a *lady doctor*? Why does a letter to a corporation have to begin "Gentlemen:"?

Early efforts to provide alternatives to sexist language often led to awkward, even ungrammatical solutions. To substitute "Everyone prefers their own customs" for "Everyone prefers *his* own customs" is to replace sexism with bad grammar. How then can we as sensitive writers minimize the sexist constraints that the English language places in our path? Although there are no perfect solutions, we can be aware of the potholes and try to steer around them as smoothly as possible.

18b Avoid terms that include or imply *man*.

We all know from experience that the most obvious way to neuter *man* or a word starting with *man* is to substitute *human*. The result, however, is often clumsy.

> SEXIST   Mankind has always been obsessed with man's inhumanity to man.
>
> NONSEXIST   *Humankind* has always been obsessed with *humans'* inhumanity to *other humans*.

Adding *hu-* to *man* alleviates sexism but weighs down the sentence. Usually you can find a more graceful solution.

> REVISED   *Human beings* have always been obsessed with *people's* cruelty to one another.

Similarly, when you face a word that ends with *-man*, you need not simply replace that ending with *-person*. Take a different approach: think about what the word means and find a synonym that is truly neutral.

> SEXIST   Did you leave a note for the mailman?
>
> REVISED   Did you leave a note for the *mail carrier*?

The same tactic works for designations with a male and a female ending, such as *steward* and *stewardess*.

> SEXIST   Ask your steward [or stewardess] for a pillow.
>
> REVISED   Ask your *flight attendant* for a pillow.

18c Use plural instead of singular forms.

Another way to avoid sexist language is to use the plural rather than the singular (*they* and *their* rather than *he* and *his*). This strategy may also avoid the unintentional stereotype implied by a single individual standing for a large and diverse group.

> SEXIST   Today's student values his education.
>
> REVISED   Today's students value *their* education.
>
> STEREOTYPE   The Englishman drives on the left-hand side of the road.
>
> REVISED   *English drivers* use the left-hand side of the road.

18d Where possible, omit words that denote gender.

You can make your language more bias-free by omitting pronouns and other words that needlessly indicate gender.

SEXIST   For optimal results, there must be rapport between a stockbroker and his client, a teacher and her student, a doctor and his patient.

REVISED   For optimal results, there must be rapport between stockbroker and *client*, teacher and *student*, doctor and *patient*.

You should also be careful to treat men and women equally in terms of description or title.

SEXIST   I now pronounce you man and wife.

REVISED   I now pronounce you *husband* and wife.

SEXIST   Please page Mr. Pease, Mr. Mankodi, and Susan Brillantes.

REVISED   Please page Mr. Pease, Mr. Mankodi, and *Ms.* Brillantes.

18e Avoid condescending labels.

A responsible writer does not call women *chicks, coeds, babes, woman drivers,* or any other names that imply that they are not to be taken seriously. Nor should an employee ever be referred to as a *girl* or *boy*. Avoid any terms that put down individuals or groups because of age (*old goat, the grannies*), race or ethnic background (*Indian giver, Chinaman's chance*), or disability (*amputee, handicapped*).

CONDESCENDING   The girls in the office bought Mr. Baart a birthday cake.

REVISED   The *administrative assistants* bought Mr. Baart a birthday cake.

CONDESCENDING   My neighbor is just an old fogy.

REVISED   My neighbor *has old-fashioned ideas.*

When describing any group, try to use the label or term that the members of that group prefer. While the preferred label is sometimes difficult to determine, the extra effort will be appreciated.

POSSIBLY OFFENSIVE   Alice is interested in learning about Oriental culture.

REVISED   Alice is interested in learning about *Asian* culture.

18f Avoid implied stereotypes.

Sometimes a stereotype is linked to a title or designation indirectly. Aside from a few obvious exceptions such as *mothers* and *fathers*, never assume that all the members of a group are of the same gender.

STEREOTYPE	Pilots have little time to spend with their wives and children.
REVISED	Pilots have little time to spend with their *families*.

Sometimes we debase individuals or groups by assigning a stereotypical descriptor to them. Be alert for these widespread biases, whether negative or positive.

STEREOTYPE	Roberto isn't very good at paying his rent on time, which doesn't surprise me because he is from Mexico.
REVISED	Roberto isn't very good at paying his rent on time.
STEREOTYPE	I assume Ben will do very well in medical school because his parents are Jewish.
REVISED	I assume Ben will do very well in medical school.

18g Use *Ms.* for a woman with no other known title.

Comparable to *Mr.* for a man, *Ms.* is easier to use than either *Miss* or *Mrs.* for someone whose marital status you don't know. Now that many married women are keeping their original last names, either professionally or in all areas of their lives, *Ms.* is often the best choice even for someone whose marital status you do know. However, if the woman to whom you are writing holds a doctorate, a professional office, or some other position with a title, use that title rather than *Ms.*

Ms. Jane Doe, Editor   Dear Ms. Doe:
Professor Jane Doe, Department of English   Dear Professor Doe:
Senator Jane Doe, Washington, D.C.   Dear Senator Doe:

■ Exercise 18–1

Avoiding Bias

Revise the following sentences to eliminate bias words. Possible revisions for the lettered sentences appear in the back of the book. Example:

> A fireman needs to check his equipment regularly.

> *Firefighters* need to check *their* equipment regularly.

a. Our school's extensive athletic program will be of particular interest to Black applicants.

b. The new physicians on our staff include Dr. Scalia, Anna Baniski, and Dr. Throckmorton.

c. A Native American, Joni believes in the healing properties of herbal remedies.

d. Philosophers have long pondered whether man is innately evil or innately good.

e. The diligent researcher will always find the sources he seeks.

WWW
For more practice, visit *Exercise Central* at <www.bedfordstmartins.com/bedguide>.

1. Simon drinks like an Irishman.
2. The television crew conducted a series of man-on-the-street interviews on the new tax proposal.
3. Whether the president of the United States is a Democrat or a Republican, he will always be a symbol of the nation.
4. Like most Asian Americans, Soon Li excels at music and mathematics.
5. Dick drives a Porsche because he likes the way she handles on the road. He gets pretty upset at the little old ladies who slow down traffic.

19 *Wordiness*

For strategies for cutting extra words, see Ch. 20.

Conciseness takes more effort than wordiness, but it pays off in clarity. The following list contains common words and phrases that take up more room than they deserve. Each has a shorter substitute. This checklist can be useful for self-editing, particularly if you ever face a strict word limit, as in an article for a college newspaper where space is tight, a laboratory report that you must squeeze into a standard worksheet, or an assignment limited to six hundred words.

WINDY WORDS AND PHRASES

WORDY	CONCISE
adequate enough	adequate
a period of a week	a week
approximately	about
area of, field of	[Omit.]
arrive at an agreement, conclude an agreement	agree
as a result of	because
at an earlier point in time	before, earlier
at a later moment	after, later
join together	join
kind of, sort of, type of	[Omit.]
large in size, large-sized	large
a large number of	many
lend assistance to	assist, aid, help
merge together	merge
numerous	many
on a daily basis	daily
other alternatives	alternatives
past experience, past history	experience, history
persons of the female gender	women
persons of the Methodist faith	Methodists
pertaining to	about, on
plan ahead for the future	plan
prior to	before
put an end to, terminate	end
rarely ever, seldom ever	rarely, seldom

refer back to	refer to
repeat again	repeat
resemble in appearance	look like
similar to	like
subsequent to	after
sufficient amount of	enough
sufficient number (or amount) of	enough
true facts	facts, truth
until such time	until
utilize, make use of	use
very	[Omit unless you need it.]
whether or not, as to whether	whether

■ Exercise 19–1

Eliminating Wordiness

Revise the following passage to eliminate wordiness. Example:

> At this point in time, a debate pertaining to freedom of speech is raging across our campuses.

> A debate *about* freedom of speech is raging across our campuses.

www

For more practice, visit *Exercise Central* at <www.bedfordstmartins.com/bedguide>.

  The media in recent times have become obsessed with the conflict on campuses across the nation between freedom of speech and the attempt to protect minorities from verbal abuse. Very innocent remarks or remarks of a humorous nature, sometimes taken out of context, have got a large number of students into trouble for the violation of college speech codes. Numerous students have become very vocal in attacking these "politically correct" speech codes and defending the right to free speech. But is the campaign against the politically correct really pertaining to freedom of speech, or is it itself a way in which to silence debate? Due to the fact that the phrase "politically correct" has become associated with liberal social causes and sensitivity to minority feelings, it now carries a very extraordinary stigma in the eyes of conservatives. It has become a kind of condemnation against which no defense is possible. To accuse someone of being politically correct is to refute their ideas before hearing their argument. The attempt to silence the members of the opposition is a dangerous sign of our times and suggests that we are indeed in the midst of a cultural war.

Chapter 36
Punctuation

20. End Punctuation   H-96
21. The Comma   H-98
22. The Semicolon   H-108
23. The Colon   H-110
24. The Apostrophe   H-113
25. Quotation Marks   H-116
26. The Dash   H-120
27. Parentheses, Brackets, and the Ellipsis Mark   H-122

20 *End Punctuation*

Three marks can signal the end of a sentence: the period, the exclamation point, and the question mark.

20a Use a period to end a declarative sentence, a directive, or an indirect question.

Most English sentences are *declarative,* meaning simply that they make a statement. No matter what its topic, a declarative sentence properly ends with a period.

> Most people on earth are malnourished.

A period is also used after a *directive,* a statement telling someone to do something.

> Please send a check or money order with your application.

Some readers are surprised to find a period, not a question mark, at the end of an *indirect question.* But an indirect question is really a kind of declarative sentence: it states that a question was asked or is being asked.

> The counselor asked Marcia why she rarely gets to class on time.

> I wonder why Roland didn't show up.

If those sentences were written as *direct questions,* they would require a question mark.

> The counselor asked, "Marcia, why do you rarely get to class on time?"

> Why, I wonder, didn't Roland show up?

20b   Use a period after most abbreviations.

A period within a sentence shows that what precedes it has been shortened.

> Dr. Hooke's plane arrived in Washington, D.C., at 8:00 P.M.

The names of most organizations (YMCA, PTA), countries (USA, UK), and people (JFK, FDR) are abbreviated without periods. Other abbreviations, such as those for academic degrees and designations of time, use periods. When an abbreviation with periods ends a sentence, follow it with just one period, not two.

For more on abbreviating names, see 28e.

> Darius hopes to do graduate work at UCLA after receiving his B.A.

20c   Use a question mark to end a direct question.

> How many angels can dance on the head of a pin?

The question mark comes at the end of the question even if the question is part of a longer declarative sentence.

For advice on punctuating indirect quotations and questions, see 25a. For examples of indirect questions, see 20a.

> "What'll I do now?" Marjorie wailed.

You can use a question mark, also, to indicate doubt about the accuracy of a number or date.

> Aristophanes, born in 450(?) B.C., became the master comic playwright of Greece's Golden Age.

Often the same purpose can be accomplished more gracefully in words:

> Aristophanes, born around 450 B.C., became the master comic playwright of Greece's Golden Age.

In formal writing, avoid using a question mark to express irony or sarcasm: *her generous (?) gift.* If your doubts are worth including, state them directly: *her meager but highly publicized gift.*

20d   Use an exclamation point to end an interjection or an urgent command.

An exclamation point signals strong, even violent, emotion. It can end any sentence that requires unusually strong emphasis.

> We've struck an iceberg! We're sinking! I can't believe it!

It may mark the short, emphatic structure known as an ***interjection.***

> Oh, no! Fire!

Or it may indicate an urgent directive.

> Hurry up! Help me!

interjection: A word or expression (oh, alas) that inserts an outburst of feeling at the beginning, middle, or end of a sentence

Because most essays appeal to readers' reason more than to their passions, you will rarely need this punctuation mark in expository writing.

■ Exercise 20–I

Using End Punctuation

www
For more practice, visit
Exercise Central at
<www.bedfordstmartins
.com/bedguide>.

Where appropriate, correct the end punctuation in the following sentences. Give reasons for any changes you make. Some sentences may be correct. Answers for the lettered sentences appear in the back of the book. Example:

Tom asked Cindy if she would be willing to edit his research paper?

Tom asked Cindy if she would be willing to edit his research paper. [Not a direct question]

a. The question that still troubles the community after all these years is why federal agents did not act sooner?

b. We will ask him if he will help us build the canoe.

c. I wonder what he was thinking at the time?

d. One man, who suffered a broken leg, was rescued when he was heard screaming, "Help me. Help me."

e. If the suspect is convicted, will lawyers appeal the case?

1. What will Brad and Emilia do if they can't have their vacations at the same time.

2. When a tree falls in a forest, but no one hears it, does it make a sound.

3. If you have a chance to see the new Ang Lee film, you should do so. The acting is first-rate!

4. What will happen next is anyone's guess.

5. On what day does the fall term begin.

21 | *The Comma*

For more on comma
usage, see C1 in the
"Quick Editing Guide."

Speech without pauses would be hard to listen to. Likewise, writing without commas would make hard reading. Like a split-second pause in conversation, a well-placed comma helps your readers to catch the train of your thought. It keeps them, time and again, from stumbling over a solid block of words or drawing an inaccurate conclusion.

Consider the following sentence:

Lyman paints fences and bowls.

From this statement, we can deduce that Lyman is a painter who works with both a large and a small brush. But add commas and the portrait changes:

Lyman paints, fences, and bowls.

Now Lyman wields a paintbrush, a sword, and a bowling ball. What we learn about his activities depends on how the writer punctuates the sentence.

2Ia   Use a comma with a coordinating conjunction to join two main clauses.

Main clauses joined by a coordinating conjunction also need a comma. The comma comes after the first clause, right before the conjunction.

> The pie whooshed through the air, and it landed in Lyman's face.

> The pie whooshed with deadly aim, but the agile Lyman ducked.

If your clauses are short and parallel in structure, you may omit the comma.

> Spring passed and summer came.

> They urged but I refused.

Or you may keep the comma. It can lend your words a speechlike ring, throwing a bit of emphasis on your second clause.

> Spring passed, and summer came.

> They urged, but I refused.

CAUTION: Don't use a comma with a coordinating conjunction that links two phrases or that links a phrase and a clause.

> FAULTY   The mustangs galloped, and cavorted across the plain.
> REVISED   The mustangs galloped and cavorted across the plain.

2Ib   Use a comma after an introductory clause, phrase, or word.

> *Weeping,* Lydia stumbled down the stairs.

> *Before that,* Arthur saw her reading an old love letter.

> *If he knew who the writer was,* he didn't tell.

Placed after any such opening word, phrase, or subordinate clause, a comma tells your reader, "Enough preliminaries: now the main clause starts."

EXCEPTION: You need not use a comma after a single introductory word or a short phrase or clause if there is no danger of misreading.

> *Sooner or later* Lydia will tell us the whole story.

---

main clause: A group of words that has both a subject and a verb and can stand alone as a complete sentence: *My sister has a friend.*

coordinating conjunction: A one-syllable linking word (*and, but, for, or, nor, so, yet*) that joins elements with equal or near-equal importance: *Jack and Jill, sink or swim*

phrase: Two or more related words that work together but may lack a subject (as in *will have been*), a verb (*my uncle Zeke*), or both (*in the attic*)

clause: A group of related words that includes both a subject and a verb: *The sailboats raced until the sun set.*

WWW
For more practice, visit
Exercise Central at
<www.bedfordstmartins
.com/bedguide>.

■ Exercise 21–1

Using Commas

Add any necessary commas to the following sentences, and remove any commas that do not belong. Some sentences may be correct. Answers for the lettered sentences appear in the back of the book. Example:

> Your dog may have sharp teeth but my lawyer can bite harder.

> Your dog may have sharp teeth, but my lawyer can bite harder.

a. Farmers around the world tend to rely on just a few breeds of livestock so some breeds are disappearing.

b. Older breeds of livestock are often less profitable, for they have not been genetically engineered to grow quickly.

c. For instance modern breeds of cattle usually grow larger, and produce more meat and milk than older breeds.

d. In both wild and domestic animals genetic diversity can make the animals resistant to disease, and parasites so older breeds can give scientists important information.

e. Until recently, small organic farmers were often the only ones interested in raising old-fashioned breeds but animal scientists now support this practice as well.

1. During the summer of the great soybean failure Larry took little interest in national affairs.

2. Unaware of the world he slept and grew within his mother's womb.

3. While across the nation farmers were begging for mortgages he swam without a care.

4. Neither the mounting agricultural crisis, nor any other current events, disturbed his tranquillity.

5. In fact you might have called him irresponsible.

21c Use a comma between items in a series.

When you list three or more items, whether they are nouns, verbs, adjectives, adverbs, or entire phrases or clauses, separate them with commas.

> Country ham, sweet corn, and potatoes weighted Grandma's table.

> Joel prefers music that shakes, rattles, and rolls.

> In one afternoon, we climbed the Matterhorn, voyaged beneath the sea, and flew on a rocket through space.

Notice that no comma *follows* the final item in the series.

NOTE: Some writers omit the comma *before* the final item in the series. This custom may throw off the rhythm of a sentence and, in some cases, obscure the writer's meaning. Using the comma in such a case is never wrong; omitting it can create confusion.

> I was met at the station by my cousins, brother and sister.

Are these people a brother-and-sister pair who are the writer's cousins or a group consisting of the writer's cousins, her brother, and her sister? If they are in fact more than two people, a comma would clear up the confusion.

> I was met at the station by my cousins, brother, and sister.

21d Use a comma between coordinate adjectives but not between cumulative adjectives.

Adjectives that function independently of each other, even though they modify the same noun, are called *coordinate adjectives.* Set them off with commas.

> Ruth was a clear, vibrant, persuasive speaker.

> Life is nasty, brutish, and short.

CAUTION: Don't use a comma after the final adjective before a noun.

> FAULTY   My professor was a brilliant, caring, teacher.
>
> REVISED   My professor was a brilliant, caring teacher.

To check whether adjectives are coordinate, apply two tests. Can you rearrange the adjectives without distorting the meaning of the sentence? (*Ruth was a persuasive, vibrant, clear speaker.*) Can you insert *and* between them? (*Life is nasty and brutish and short.*)

If the answer to both questions is yes, the adjectives are coordinate. Removing any one of them would not greatly affect the others' impact. Use commas between them to show that they are separate and equal.

NOTE: If you choose to link coordinate adjectives with *and* or another conjunction, omit the commas.

> New York City is huge and dirty and beautiful.

Cumulative adjectives work together to create a single unified picture of the noun they modify. Remove any one of them and you change the picture. No commas separate cumulative adjectives.

> Ruth has two small white poodles.

> Who's afraid of the big bad wolf?

If you rearrange cumulative adjectives or insert *and* between them, the effect of the sentence is distorted (*two white small poodles; the big and bad wolf*).

■ **Exercise 21–2**

Using Commas

Add any necessary commas to the following sentences, remove any commas that do not belong, and change any punctuation that is incorrect. Some sentences may be correct. Answers for the lettered sentences appear in the back of the book. Example:

> Mel has been a faithful hard-working consistent pain in the neck.
>
> Mel has been a faithful, hard-working, consistent pain in the neck.

a. Mrs. Carver looks like a sweet, little, old lady, but she plays a wicked electric guitar.

b. Her bass player, her drummer and her keyboard player all live in the same retirement community.

c. They practice individually in the afternoon, rehearse together at night and play at the community's Saturday night dances.

d. The Rest Home Rebels have to rehearse quietly, and cautiously, to keep from disturbing the other residents.

e. Mrs. Carver has organized the group, scheduled their rehearsals, and acquired back-up instruments.

1. When she breaks a string, she doesn't want her elderly crew to have to grab the guitar change the string and hand it back to her, before the song ends.

2. The Rest Home Rebels' favorite bands are U2, Matchbox 20 and Lester Lanin and his orchestra.

3. They watch a lot of MTV because it is fast-paced colorful exciting and informative and it has more variety than soap operas.

4. Just once, Mrs. Carver wants to play in a really, huge, sold-out, arena.

5. She hopes to borrow the community's big, white, van to take herself her band and their equipment to a major, professional, downtown, recording studio.

21e Use commas to set off a nonrestrictive phrase or clause.

modifier: A word (such as an adjective or adverb), phrase, or clause that provides more information about other parts of a sentence: Plays *staged by the drama class* are *always successful.*

A *nonrestrictive modifier* adds a fact that, while perhaps interesting and valuable, isn't essential. You could leave it out of the sentence and still make good sense. When a word in your sentence is modified by a nonrestrictive phrase or clause, set off the modifier with commas before and after it.

> Potts Alley, *which runs north from Chestnut Street,* is too narrow for cars.
>
> At the end of the alley, *where the street fair was held last summer,* a getaway car waited.

A *restrictive modifier* is essential. Omit it and you significantly change the meaning of both the modified word and the sentence. Such a modifier is called *restrictive* because it limits what it modifies: it specifies this place, person, action, or whatever, and no other. Because a restrictive modifier is part of the identity of whatever it modifies, no commas set it off from the rest of the sentence.

> They picked the alley *that runs north from Chestnut Street* because it is close to the highway.

> Anyone *who robs my house* will regret it.

Leave out the modifier in that last sentence — writing *Anyone will regret it* — and you change the meaning from potential robbers to all humankind.

NOTE: Use *that* to introduce (or to recognize) a restrictive phrase or clause. Use *which* to introduce (or to recognize) a nonrestrictive phrase or clause.

> The food *that I love best* is chocolate.

> Chocolate, *which I love,* is not on my diet.

21f Use commas to set off nonrestrictive appositives.

Like the modifiers discussed in 21e, an *appositive* can be either restrictive or nonrestrictive. If it is nonrestrictive — if the sentence still makes sense when the appositive is omitted or changed — then set it off with commas before and after.

> My third ex-husband, *Hugo,* will be glad to meet you.

> We are bringing dessert, *a blueberry pie,* to follow dinner.

If the appositive is restrictive — if you can't take it out or change it without changing your meaning — then include it without commas.

> Of all the men I've been married to, my ex-husband *Hugo* is the best cook.

appositive: A word or group of words that adds information about a subject or object by identifying it in a different way: my dog *Rover,* Hal's brother *Fred*

■ Exercise 21–3

Using Commas

Add any necessary commas to the following sentences, and remove any commas that do not belong. You may have to draw your own conclusions about what the writer meant to say. Some sentences may be correct. Possible revisions for the lettered sentences appear in the back of the book. Example:

> Jay and his wife the former Laura McCready were high school sweethearts.

> Jay and his wife, the former Laura McCready, were high school sweethearts.

a. We are bringing a dish vegetable lasagna, to the potluck supper.

b. I like to go to Central Bank, on this side of town, because this branch tends to have short lines.

c. The colony, that the English established at Roanoke disappeared mysteriously.

d. If the base commanders had checked their gun room where powder is stored, they would have found that several hundred pounds of gunpowder were missing.

e. Brazil's tropical rain forests which help produce the air we breathe all over the world, are being cut down at an alarming rate.

1. The aye-aye which is a member of the lemur family is threatened with extinction.

2. The party, a dismal occasion ended earlier than we had expected.

3. Secretary Stern warned that the concessions, that the West was prepared to make, would be withdrawn if not matched by the East.

4. Although both of Don's children are blond, his daughter Sharon has darker hair than his son Jake.

5. Herbal tea which has no caffeine makes a better after-dinner drink than coffee.

For punctuation with a conjunctive adverb, see 22b.

conjunctive adverb: A linking word that can connect independent clauses and show a relationship between two ideas: Armando is a serious student; *therefore*, he studies every day. (See 14.)

parenthetical expression: An aside to readers or a transitional expression such as *for example* or *in contrast*

2lg Use commas to set off conjunctive adverbs.

When you drop a conjunctive adverb into the middle of a clause, set it off with commas before and after it.

Using lead paint in homes has been illegal, *however,* since 1973.

Builders, *indeed,* gave it up some twenty years earlier.

2lh Use commas to set off parenthetical expressions.

Use a pair of commas around any parenthetical expression or any aside from you to your readers.

Home inspectors, *for this reason,* sometimes test for lead paint.

Cosmic Construction never used lead paint, *or so their spokesperson says,* even when it was legal.

2li Use commas to set off a phrase or clause expressing contrast.

It was Rudolph, *not Dasher,* who had a red nose.

EXCEPTION: Short contrasting phrases beginning with *but* need not be set off by commas.

It was not Dasher but Rudolph who had a red nose.

21j Use commas to set off an absolute phrase.

The link between an absolute phrase and the rest of the sentence is a comma, or two commas if the phrase falls in midsentence.

> *Our worst fears drawing us together,* we huddled over the letter.

> Luke, *his knife being the sharpest,* slit the envelope.

absolute phrase: An expression, usually a noun followed by a participle, that modifies an entire clause or sentence and can appear anywhere in the sentence: The stallion pawed the ground, *chestnut mane and tail swirling in the wind.*

■ **Exercise 21–4**

Using Commas

Add any necessary commas to the following sentences, and change any punctuation that is incorrect. Answers for the lettered sentences appear in the back of the book. Example:

> The officer a radar gun in his hand gauged the speed of the passing cars.

> The officer, a radar gun in his hand, gauged the speed of the passing cars.

a. The university insisted however that the students were not accepted merely because of their parents' generous contributions.

b. This dispute in any case is an old one.

c. It was the young man's striking good looks not his acting ability that first attracted the Hollywood agents.

d. Gretchen learned moreover not to always accept as true what she had read in textbooks.

e. The hikers most of them wearing ponchos or rain jackets headed out into the steady drizzle.

1. The lawsuit demanded furthermore that construction already under way be halted immediately.

2. It is the Supreme Court not Congress or the president that ultimately determines the legality of a law.

3. The judge complained that the case was being tried not by the court but by the media.

4. The actor kneeling recited the lines with great emotion.

5. Both sides' patience running thin workers and management carried the strike into its sixth week.

21k Use commas to set off a direct quotation from your own words.

When you briefly quote someone, distinguish the source's words from yours with commas (and, of course, quotation marks). When you insert an explanation into a quotation (such as *he said*), set that off with commas.

> Shakespeare wrote, "Some are born great, some achieve greatness, and some have greatness thrust upon them."

"The best thing that can come with success," commented the actress Liv Ullmann, "is the knowledge that it is nothing to long for."

For advice on using punctuation marks with quotations, see 25g–25i; for advice on using quotation marks, see 25a–25d and C3 in the "Quick Editing Guide."

Notice that the comma always comes *before* the quotation marks.

EXCEPTION: Do not use a comma with a very short quotation or one introduced by *that*.

Don't tell me "yes" if you mean "maybe."

Jules said that "Nothing ventured, nothing gained" is his motto.

linking verb: A verb (*is, become, seem, feel*) that shows a state of being by linking the sentence subject with a word that renames or describes the subject: The sky *is* blue. (See 3a.)

Don't use a comma with any quotation that is run into your own sentence and that reads as part of it. Often such quotations are introduced by linking verbs.

Her favorite statement at age three was "I can do it myself."

Shakespeare originated the expression "my salad days, when I was green in judgment."

21l Use commas around *yes* and *no*, mild interjections, tag questions, and the name or title of someone directly addressed.

YES AND NO	*Yes,* I would like to own a Rolls-Royce, but, *no,* I didn't order one.
INTERJECTION	*Well,* don't blame it on me.
TAG QUESTION	It would be fun to ride in a Silver Cloud, *wouldn't it*?
DIRECT ADDRESS	Drive us home, *James*.

21m Use commas to set off dates, states, countries, and addresses.

On June 6, 1979, Ned Shaw was born.

East Rutherford, New Jersey, seemed like Paris, France, to him.

His family moved to 11 Maple Street, Middletown, Ohio.

NOTE: Do not use a comma between a state and a zip code: *Bedford, MA 01730.*

■ Exercise 21–5

Using Commas

Add any necessary commas to the following sentences, remove any commas that do not belong, and change any punctuation that is incorrect. Some sentences may be correct. Answers for the lettered sentences appear in the back of the book. Example:

When Alexander Graham Bell said "Mr. Watson come here, I want you" the telephone entered history.

When Alexander Graham Bell said, "Mr. Watson, come here, I want you," the telephone entered history.

a. César Chávez was born on March 31 1927, on a farm in Yuma, Arizona.

b. Chávez, who spent years as a migrant farmworker, told other farm laborers "If you're outraged at conditions, then you can't possibly be free or happy until you devote all your time to changing them."

c. Chávez founded the United Farm Workers union and did indeed, devote all his time to changing conditions for farmworkers.

d. Robert F. Kennedy called Chávez, "one of the heroic figures of our time."

e. Chávez, who died on April 23, 1993, became the second Mexican American to receive the highest civilian honor in the United States, the Presidential Medal of Freedom.

1. Yes I was born on April 14 1973 in Bombay India.

2. Move downstage Gary, for Pete's sake or you'll run into Mrs. Clackett.

3. Vicki my precious, when you say, "great" or "terrific," look as though you mean it.

4. Perhaps you have forgotten darling that sometimes you make mistakes, too.

5. Well Dotty, it only makes sense that when you say, "Sardines!," you should go off to get the sardines.

21n Do not use a comma to separate a subject from its verb or a verb from its object.

FAULTY   The athlete driving the purple Jaguar, was Jim Fuld. [Subject separated from verb]

REVISED   The athlete driving the purple Jaguar was Jim Fuld.

FAULTY   The governor should not have given his campaign manager, such a prestigious appointment. [Verb separated from direct object]

REVISED   The governor should not have given his campaign manager such a prestigious appointment.

21o Do not use a comma between words or phrases joined by correlative or coordinating conjunctions.

Be careful not to divide a compound subject or predicate unnecessarily with a comma.

FAULTY   Neither Peter Pan, nor the fairy Tinkerbell, saw the pirates sneaking toward their hideout. [Compound subject]

REVISED   Neither Peter Pan nor the fairy Tinkerbell saw the pirates sneaking toward their hideout.

subject: The part of a sentence that names something—a person, an object, an idea, a situation—about which the predicate makes an assertion: The *king* lives.

verb: A word that shows action (The cow *jumped* over the moon) or a state of being (The cow *is* brown)

direct object: The target of a verb that completes the action performed by the subject or asserted about the subject: I photographed *the sheriff.*

correlative conjunction: A pair of linking words (such as *either/or, not only/but also*) that appear separately but work together to join elements of a sentence: *Neither* his friends *nor* hers like pizza.

*coordinating conjunc-
tion:* A one-syllable linking word (*and, but, for, or,
nor, so, yet*) that joins elements with equal or
near-equal importance:
Jack *and* Jill, sink *or* swim

FAULTY   The chickens clucked, and pecked, and flapped their wings.
          [Compound predicate]

REVISED   The chickens clucked and pecked and flapped their wings.

21p Do not use a comma before the first or after the last item in a series.

FAULTY   We had to see, my mother's doctor, my father's lawyer, and my
          dog's veterinarian, in one afternoon.

REVISED   We had to see my mother's doctor, my father's lawyer, and my
          dog's veterinarian in one afternoon.

21q Do not use a comma to set off a restrictive word, phrase, or clause.

For an explanation of
restrictive modifiers, see
21e.

A restrictive modifier is essential to the definition or identification of whatever it modifies; a nonrestrictive modifier is not.

FAULTY   The fireworks, that I saw on Sunday, were the best I've ever seen.

REVISED   The fireworks that I saw on Sunday were the best I've ever seen.

21r Do not use commas to set off indirect quotations.

For more on quoting
someone's exact words,
see 25a–25c.

When *that* introduces a quotation, the quotation is indirect and requires
neither a comma nor quotation marks.

FAULTY   He told us that, we shouldn't have done it.

REVISED   He told us that we shouldn't have done it.

This sentence also would be correct if it were recast as a direct quotation, with a comma and quotation marks.

FAULTY   He told us that, "You shouldn't have done it."

REVISED   He told us, "You shouldn't have done it."

22 *The Semicolon*

A semicolon is a sort of compromise between a comma and a period: it creates a stop without ending a sentence.

*coordinating conjunc-
tion:* A one-syllable linking word (*and, but, for, or,
nor, so, yet*) that joins elements with equal or
near-equal importance:
Jack *and* Jill, sink *or* swim

22a Use a semicolon to join two main clauses not joined by a coordinating conjunction.

Suppose, having written one statement, you want to add another that is
closely related in sense. You decide to keep them both in a single sentence.

Shooting clay pigeons was my mother's favorite sport; she would smash them for hours at a time.

A semicolon is a good substitute for a period when you don't want to bring your readers to a complete stop.

By the yard life is hard; by the inch it's a cinch.

NOTE: When you join a subordinate clause to a main one or join two statements with a coordinating conjunction, you can generally use just a comma. Use a semicolon instead to avoid confusion when long, complex clauses include internal punctuation.

22b Use a semicolon to join two main clauses that are linked by a conjunctive adverb.

You can use a conjunctive adverb to show a relationship between clauses such as addition (*also, besides*), comparison (*likewise, similarly*), contrast (*instead, however*), emphasis (*namely, certainly*), cause and effect (*thus, therefore*), or time (*finally, subsequently*). When the second of two statements begins with (or includes) a conjunctive adverb, you can join it to the first statement with a semicolon.

conjunctive adverb: A linking word that can connect independent clauses and show a relationship between two ideas: Armando is a serious student; *therefore,* he studies every day. (See 14.)

Bert is a stand-out player; *indeed,* he's the one hope of our team.

We yearned to attend the concert; tickets, *however,* were hard to come by.

Note in the second sentence that the conjunctive adverb falls within the second main clause. No matter where the conjunctive adverb appears, the semicolon is placed between the two clauses.

For punctuation with conjunctive adverbs within clauses, see 21g.

22c Use a semicolon to separate items in a series that contain internal punctuation or that are long and complex.

The semicolon is especially useful for setting off one group of items from another. More powerful than a comma, it divides a series of series.

The auctioneer sold clocks, watches, and cameras; freezers of steaks and tons of bean sprouts; motorcycles, cars, speedboats, canoes, and cabin cruisers; and rare coins, curious stamps, and precious stones.

If the writer had used commas in place of semicolons in that sentence, the divisions would have been harder to notice.

Commas are not the only internal punctuation that warrants the extra force of semicolons between items.

The auctioneer sold clocks and watches (with or without hands); freezers of steaks and tons of bean sprouts; trucks and motorcycles (some of which had working engines); and dozens of smaller items.

www

For more practice, visit *Exercise Central* at <www.bedfordstmartins .com/bedguide>.

■ Exercise 22–1

Using Semicolons

Add any necessary semicolons to the following sentences, and change any that are incorrectly used. Some sentences may be correct. Answers for the lettered sentences appear in the back of the book. Example:

> They had used up all their money, they barely had enough left for the train trip home.

> They had used up all their money; they barely had enough left for the train trip home.

a. By the beginning of 1993, Shirley was eager to retire, nevertheless, she agreed to stay on for two more years.

b. In 1968 Lyndon Johnson abandoned his hopes for reelection; because of fierce opposition from within his own party.

c. The committee was asked to determine the extent of violent crime among teenagers, especially those between the ages of fourteen and sixteen, to act as a liaison between the city and schools and between churches and volunteer organizations, and to draw up a plan to significantly reduce violence, both public and private, by the end of the century.

d. The leaves on the oak trees near the lake were tinged with red, swimmers no longer ventured into the water.

e. The football team has yet to win a game, however, the season is still young.

1. Although taking the subway is slow, it is still faster than driving to work.

2. When the harpist began to play; the bride and her father prepared to walk down the aisle.

3. The Mariners lost all three games to Milwaukee, worse yet, two star players were injured.

4. There was nothing the firefighters could do; the building already had been consumed by flames.

5. Chess is difficult to master; but even a small child can learn the basic rules.

phrase: Two or more related words that work together but may lack a subject (as in *will have been*), a verb (*my uncle Zeke*), or both (*in the attic*)

23   *The Colon*

A colon introduces a further thought, one added to throw light on a first. In using it, a writer declares: "What follows will clarify what I've just said."

Some writers use a capital letter to start any complete sentence that follows a colon; others prefer a lowercase letter. Both habits are acceptable.

Whichever you choose, be consistent. A phrase that follows a colon always begins with a lowercase letter.

23a   Use a colon between two main clauses if the second exemplifies, explains, or summarizes the first.

Like a semicolon, a colon can join two sentences into one. The chief difference is this: a semicolon says merely that two main clauses are related; a colon says that the second clause gives an example or explanation of the point made in the first clause. You can think of a colon as an abbreviation for *that is* or *for example*.

> She tried everything: she scoured the library, made dozens of phone calls, wrote letters, even consulted a lawyer.

main clause: A group of words that has both a subject and a verb and can stand alone as a complete sentence: *My sister has a friend.*

23b   Use a colon to introduce a list or a series.

A colon can introduce a word, a phrase, or a series as well as a second main clause. Sometimes the introduction is made stronger by *as follows* or *the following*.

> The dance steps are as follows: forward, back, turn, and glide.

> Engrave the following truth upon your memory: a colon is always constructed of two dots.

When a colon introduces a series of words or phrases, it often means *such as* or *for instance*. A list of examples after a colon need not include *and* before the last item unless all possible examples have been stated.

> On a Saturday night many kinds of people crowd our downtown area: drifters, bored senior citizens, college students out for a good time.

23c   Use a colon to introduce an appositive.

A colon can introduce an appositive when the colon is preceded by a main clause.

> I have discovered the key to the future: plastics.

appositive: A word or group of words that adds information about a subject or object by identifying it in a different way: my dog *Rover*, Hal's brother *Fred*

23d   Use a colon to introduce a long or comma-filled quotation.

Sometimes you can't conveniently introduce a quoted passage with a comma. Perhaps the quotation is too long or heavily punctuated; perhaps your prefatory remarks demand a longer pause. In either case, use a colon.

> God told Adam and Eve: "Be fruitful, and multiply, and replenish the earth, and subdue it."

23e Use a colon when convention calls for it.

AFTER A SALUTATION Dear Professor James:
Dear Account Representative:

BIBLICAL CITATIONS Genesis 4:7 [The book of Genesis, chapter four, seventh verse]

BOOK TITLES *Convergences: Essays on Art and Literature*
AND SUBTITLES *In the Beginning: Creation Stories from around the World*

SOURCE REFERENCES Welty, Eudora. *The Eye of the Story.* New York: Random, 1978.

TIME OF DAY 2:02 P.M.

23f Use a colon only at the end of a main clause.

main clause: A group of words that has both a subject and a verb and can stand alone as a complete sentence: *My sister has a friend.*

In a sentence, a colon always follows a clause, never a phrase. Avoid using a colon between a verb and its object, between a preposition and its object, and before a list introduced by *such as.* Any time you are in doubt about whether to use a colon, first make sure that the preceding statement is a complete sentence. Then you will not litter your writing with unnecessary colons.

FAULTY My mother and father are: Bella and Benjamin.

REVISED My mother and father are Bella and Benjamin.

FAULTY Many great inventors have changed our lives, such as: Edison, Marconi, and Glutz.

REVISED Many great inventors have changed our lives, such as Edison, Marconi, and Glutz.

REVISED Many great inventors have changed our lives: Edison, Marconi, Glutz.

Use either *such as* or a colon. You don't need both.

■ Exercise 23–1

Using Colons

www
For more practice, visit *Exercise Central* at <www.bedfordstmartins.com/bedguide>.

Add, remove, or replace colons wherever appropriate in the following sentences. Where necessary, revise the sentences further to support your changes in punctuation. Some sentences may be correct. Possible revisions for the lettered sentences appear in the back of the book. Example:

Yum-Yum Burger has franchises in the following cities; New York, Chicago, Miami, San Francisco, and Seattle.

Yum-Yum Burger has franchises in the following cities: New York, Chicago, Miami, San Francisco, and Seattle.

a. The Continuing Education Program offers courses in: building and construction management, engineering, and design.

b. The interview ended with a test of skills, taking messages, operating the computer, typing a sample letter, and proofreading documents.

c. The sample letter began, "Dear Mr. Rasheed, Please accept our apologies for the late shipment."

d. If you go to the beach this summer, remember these three rules: wear plenty of sunscreen, eat plenty of fruit to replace lost fluids, and avoid exposure during the hottest hours of the day.

e. These are my dreams, to ride in a horse-drawn sleigh, to fly in a small plane, to gallop down a beach on horseback, and to cross the ocean in a sailboat.

1. In the case of *Bowers v. Hardwick,* the Supreme Court decided that: citizens had no right to sexual privacy.

2. He ended his speech with a quotation from Homer's *Iliad,* "Whoever obeys the gods, to him they particularly listen."

3. Professor Bligh's book is called *Management, A Networking Approach.*

4. George handed Cynthia a note, "Meet me after class under the big clock on Main Street."

5. Rosa expected to arrive at 4.10, but she didn't get there until 4.20.

24   *The Apostrophe*

Use apostrophes for three purposes: to show possession, to indicate an omission, and to add an ending to a number, letter, or abbreviation.

For advice on editing for apostrophes, see C2 in the "Quick Editing Guide."

24a To make a singular noun possessive, add -'s.

The *plumber's* wrench left grease stains on *Harry's* shirt.

Add -'s even when your singular noun ends with the sound of *s.*

Felix's roommate enjoys reading *Henry James's* novels.

Some writers find it awkward to add -'s to nouns that already end in an -*s,* especially those of two syllables or more. You may, if you wish, form such a possessive by adding only an apostrophe.

The Egyptian king *Cheops'* death occurred more than two thousand years before *Socrates'.*

24b To make a plural noun ending in -*s* possessive, add an apostrophe.

A *stockbrokers'* meeting combines *foxes'* cunning with the noisy chaos of a *boys'* locker room.

Possessive Nouns and Plural Nouns

Both plural nouns and possessive nouns often end with *-s*. *Plural* means more than one (two *dogs*, six *friends*), but *possessive* means ownership (the *dogs'* biscuits, my *friends'* cars). If you can substitute the word *of* for the *-s* and apostrophe (the biscuits *of* the dogs, the cars *of* my friends), you need the plural possessive with an apostrophe after the *-s*. If you cannot substitute *of*, you need the simple plural with no apostrophe (the *dogs* are well fed, my *friends* have no money for gas).

24c **To make a plural noun not ending in *-s* possessive, add *-'s*.**

Nouns such as *men, mice, geese,* and *alumni* form the possessive case the same way as singular nouns: with *-'s*.

What effect has the *women's* movement had on *children's* literature?

24d **To show joint possession by two people or groups, add an apostrophe or *-'s* to the second noun of the pair.**

I left my *mother and father's* house with our *friends and neighbors'* good wishes.

If the two members of a noun pair possess a set of things individually, add an apostrophe or *-'s* to each noun.

Men's and *women's* marathon records are improving steadily.

24e **To make a compound noun possessive, add an apostrophe or *-'s* to the last word in the compound.**

For more on plurals of compound nouns, see p. H-143.

A compound noun consists of more than one word (*commander in chief, sons-in-law*); it may be either singular or plural.

The *commander in chief's* duties will end on July 1.

Esther does not approve of her *sons-in-law's* professions.

24f **To make an indefinite pronoun possessive, add *-'s*.**

Indefinite pronouns such as *anyone, nobody,* and *another* are usually singular in meaning, so they form the possessive case the same way as singular nouns: with *-'s*. (See 24a.)

What caused the accident is *anybody's* guess; but it appears to be *no one's* fault.

24g To indicate the possessive of a personal pronoun, use its possessive case.

The personal pronouns are irregular; each has its own possessive form. No possessive personal pronoun contains an apostrophe. Resist the temptation to add an apostrophe or -'s.

NOTE: *Its* (no apostrophe) is always a possessive pronoun.

> I retreated when the Murphys' German shepherd bared *its* fangs.

It's (with an apostrophe) is always a contraction.

> *It's* [It is] not our fault.

personal pronoun: A pronoun (*I, me, you, it, he, we, them*) that stands for a noun that names a person or thing: Mark awoke slowly, but suddenly *he* bolted from the bed.

For a chart of possessive personal pronouns, see C2 in the "Quick Editing Guide."

24h Use an apostrophe to indicate an omission in a contraction.

> *They're* [They are] too sophisticated for me.
> Pat *didn't* [did not] finish her assignment.
> Americans grow up admiring the Spirit of *'76* [1776].
> *It's* [it is] nearly eight *o'clock* [of the clock].

24i Use an apostrophe to form the plural of an abbreviation and of a letter, word, or number mentioned as a word.

ABBREVIATION	Do we need I.D.'s at YMCA's in other towns?
LETTER	How many *n*'s are there in *Cincinnati*?
WORD	Try replacing all the *should*'s in that list with *could's*.
NUMBER	Cut out two 3's to sew on Larry's shirt.

For advice on italicizing a letter, word, or number named as a word, see 31e.

EXCEPTION: To refer to the years in a decade, add *-s* without an apostrophe.

> The 1980s differed greatly from the 1970s.

■ Exercise 24–1

Using the Apostrophe

Correct any errors in the use of the apostrophe in the following sentences. Some sentences may be correct. Answers for the lettered sentences appear in the back of the book. Example:

> Youd better put on you're new shoes.
>
> *You'd* better put on *your* new shoes.

WWW
For more practice, visit *Exercise Central* at <www.bedfordstmartins .com/bedguide>.

a. Joe and Chucks' fathers were both in the class of 53.

b. They're going to finish their term papers as soon as the party ends.

c. It was a strange coincidence that all three womens' cars broke down after they had picked up their mothers-in-law.

d. Don't forget to dot you're *is* and cross you're *ts*.

e. Mario and Shelley's son is marrying the editor's in chief's daughter.

1. The Hendersons' never change: their always whining about Mr. Scobee farming land thats rightfully their's.

2. Its hard to join a womens' basketball team because so few of them exist.

3. I had'nt expected to hear Janice' voice again.

4. Don't give the Murphy's dog it's biscuit until it's sitting up.

5. Isnt' it the mother and fathers' job to teach kid's to mind their *ps* and *qs*?

25 *Quotation Marks*

For more on editing quotation marks, see C3 in the "Quick Editing Guide."

Quotation marks always come in pairs: one at the start and one at the finish of a quoted passage. In the United States, the double quotation mark (") is preferred over the single one (') for most uses. Use quotation marks to set off quoted or highlighted words from the rest of your text.

> "Injustice anywhere is a threat to justice everywhere," wrote Martin Luther King Jr.

25a Use quotation marks around direct quotations from another writer or speaker.

You can enrich the content, language, and authority of your writing by occasionally quoting a source whose ideas support your own. When you do this, you owe credit to the quoted person. If you use his or her exact words, enclose them in quotation marks.

For more on quoting, paraphrasing, and summarizing, see pp. 185–86.

For capitalization with quotation marks, see 29j.

For punctuation of direct and indirect quotations, see 21r.

> Anwar al-Sadat reflected the Arab concept of community when he said, "A man's village is his peace of mind."

In an indirect quotation, you report someone else's idea without using his or her exact words. Do not enclose an indirect quotation in quotation marks. Do, however, name your source, and accurately present what the source said.

> Anwar al-Sadat asserted that a person's community provides a sense of well-being.

Direct and Indirect Quotations

Avoid the problems that arise when a direct quotation (someone else's exact words) is changed into an indirect quotation (someone else's idea reported without using his or her exact words).

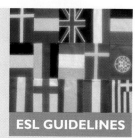

ESL GUIDELINES

- Be sure to change the punctuation and capitalization. You also may need to change the verb tense.

  DIRECT QUOTATION   Pascal said, "The assignment is on Chinua Achebe, the Nigerian writer."

  INDIRECT QUOTATION   Pascal said that the assignment was on Chinua Achebe, the Nigerian writer.

- If the direct quotation is a question, you must change the word order in the indirect quotation.

  DIRECT QUOTATION   Jean asked, "How far is it to Boston?"

  INDIRECT QUOTATION   Jean asked how far it was to Boston.

NOTE: Use a period, not a question mark, with questions in indirect quotations.

- Very often, you must change pronouns when using an indirect quotation.

  DIRECT QUOTATION   Antonio said, "I think you are mistaken."

  INDIRECT QUOTATION   Antonio said that he thought I was mistaken.

25b Use single quotation marks around a quotation inside another quotation.

Sometimes a source you are quoting quotes someone else or puts a word or words in quotation marks. When that happens, use single quotation marks around the internal quotation (even if your source used double ones), and put double quotation marks around the larger passage that you are quoting.

"My favorite advice from Socrates, 'Know thyself and fear all women,'" said Dr. Blatz, "has been getting me into trouble lately."

25c Instead of using quotation marks, indent a quotation of more than four lines.

Suppose you are writing an essay about Soviet dissidents living in the United States. You might include a paragraph like this:

In a 1978 commencement address at Harvard University,
Aleksandr Solzhenitsyn made this observation:

> I have spent all my life under a Communist regime,
> and I will tell you that a society without any ob-
> jective legal scale is a terrible one indeed. But
> a society with no other scale but the legal one is
> not quite worthy of man either.

Merely indenting the quoted passage shows that it is a direct quotation. You need not frame it with quotation marks. Simply double-space above and below the passage, indent it ten spaces from the left margin, and double-space the quoted lines.

Follow the same practice if you quote more than three lines of a poem.

Phillis Wheatley, the outstanding black poet of colonial
America, expresses a sense that she is condemned to write in
obscurity and be forgotten:

> No costly marble shall be reared,
>   No Mausoleum's pride--
> Nor chiselled stone be raised to tell
>   That I have lived and died.

For advice on capitals and quotations, see 29j.

Notice that not only the source's words but her punctuation, capitalization, indentation, and line breaks are quoted exactly.

25d In dialogue, use quotation marks around a speaker's words, and mark each change of speaker with a new paragraph.

Randolph gazed at Ellen and sighed. "What extraordinary beauty."

"They are lovely," she replied, staring at the roses, "aren't they?"

25e Use quotation marks around the titles of a speech, an article in a newspaper or magazine, a short story, a poem shorter than book length, a chapter in a book, a song, and an episode of a television or radio program.

For advice on italicizing or underlining titles, see 31a and the chart on p. H-137.

The article "An Updike Retrospective" praises "Solitaire" as the best story in John Updike's collection *Museums and Women*.

In Chapter 5, "Expatriates," Schwartz discusses Eliot's famous poem "The Love Song of J. Alfred Prufrock."

25f   Avoid using quotation marks to indicate slang or to be witty.

INADVISABLE   Liza looked like a born "loser," but Jerry was "hard up" for company.

REVISED   Liza looked like a born loser, but Jerry was hard up for company.

Stick your neck out. If you really want to use those words, just go ahead. Otherwise, reword the sentence.

Some writers assume that, by placing a word in quotation marks, they wax witty and ironic.

INADVISABLE   By the time I finished all my chores, my "day off" was over.

REVISED   By the time I finished all my chores, my day off was over.

No quotation marks are needed after *so-called* and other words with similar meaning.

FAULTY   Call me "a dreamer," but I believe we can win.

REVISED   Call me a dreamer, but I believe we can win.

25g   Put commas and periods inside quotation marks.

A comma or a period always comes before quotation marks, even if it is not part of the quotation.

We pleaded, "Keep off the grass," in hope of preserving the lawn.

For more on commas with quotations, see 21k.

25h   Put semicolons and colons outside quotation marks.

We said, "Keep off the grass"; they still tromped onward.

25i   Put other punctuation inside or outside quotation marks depending on its function in the sentence.

Parentheses that are part of the quotation go inside the quotation marks. Parentheses that are your own, not part of the quotation, go outside the quotation marks.

We said, "Keep off the grass (unless it's artificial turf)."

They tromped onward (although we had said, "Keep off the grass").

If a question mark, exclamation point, or dash is part of the quotation, place it inside the quotation marks. Otherwise, place it after the closing quotation marks.

She hollered, "Fire!"

Who hollered "Fire"?

Don't close a sentence with two end punctuation marks, one inside and one outside the quotation marks. If the quoted passage ends with a dash, exclamation point, question mark, or period, you need not add any further end punctuation. If the quoted passage falls within a question asked by you, however, it should finish with a question mark, even if that means cutting other end punctuation (*Who hollered "Fire"?*).

■ Exercise 25–1

Using Quotation Marks

www
For more practice, visit *Exercise Central* at <www.bedfordstmartins .com/bedguide>.

Add quotation marks wherever they are needed in the following sentences, and correct any other errors. Answers for the lettered sentences appear in the back of the book. Example:

> Annie asked him, Do you believe in free will?

> Annie asked him, "Do you believe in free will?"

a. What we still need to figure out, the police chief said, is whether the victim was acquainted with his assailant.

b. A skillful orator, Patrick Henry is credited with the phrase Give me liberty or give me death.

c. I could hear the crowd chanting my name — Jones! Jones! — and that spurred me on, said Bruce Jones, the winner of the 5,000-meter race.

d. The video for the rock group Guns and Roses' epic song November Rain is based on a short story by Del James.

e. After the Gore/Bush election debacle of 2000, *Time* essayist Lance Morrow predicts, The memory of the 2000 post-election chadfest will revive an angry energy in 2004, which will produce the biggest voter turnout in history.

1. That day at school, the kids were as "high as kites."

2. Notice, the professor told the class, Cassius's choice of imagery when he asks, Upon what meat doth this our Caesar feed, / That he is grown so great?

3. "As I was rounding the bend," Peter explained, "I failed to see the sign that said Caution: Ice.

4. John Cheever's story The Swimmer begins with the line It was one of those midsummer Sundays when everyone sits around saying, I drank too much last night.

5. Who coined the saying Love is blind?

26 *The Dash*

A *dash* is a horizontal line used to separate parts of a sentence — a more dramatic substitute for a comma, semicolon, or colon. To type a dash, hit your hyphen key twice.

26a Use a dash to indicate a sudden break in thought or shift in tone.

The dash signals that a surprise is in store: a shift in viewpoint, perhaps, or an unfinished statement.

> Ivan doesn't care which team wins — he bet on both.

> I didn't pay much attention to my parents' accented speech — at least not at home.

26b Use a dash to introduce an explanation, an illustration, or a series.

When you want a preparatory pause without the formality of a colon, try a dash.

> My advice to you is simple — stop complaining.

You can use a dash to introduce an appositive that needs drama or contains commas.

> Longfellow wrote about three young sisters — grave Alice, laughing Allegra, and Edith with golden hair — in "The Children's Hour."

appositive: A word or group of words that adds information about a subject or object by identifying it in a different way: my dog *Rover,* Hal's brother *Fred*

26c Use dashes to set off an emphatic aside or parenthetical expression from the rest of a sentence.

> It was as hot — and I mean *hot* — as the Fourth of July in Death Valley.

> If I went through anguish in botany and economics — for different reasons — sociology was even worse.

parenthetical expression: An aside to readers or a transitional expression such as *for example* or *in contrast*

26d Avoid overusing dashes.

Like a physical gesture of emphasis — a jab of a pointing finger — the dash becomes meaningless if used too often. Use it only when a comma, a colon, or parentheses don't seem strong enough.

For more on dashes compared with commas, see 21, and with parentheses, see 27a–27b.

> EXCESSIVE   Algy's grandmother — a sweet old lady — asked him to pick up some things at the store — milk, eggs, and cheese.

> REVISED   Algy's grandmother, a sweet old lady, asked him to pick up some things at the store: milk, eggs, and cheese.

■ **Exercise 26–1**

Using the Dash

Add, remove, or replace dashes wherever appropriate in the following sentences. Some sentences may be correct. Possible answers for the lettered sentences appear in the back of the book. Example:

WWW
For more practice, visit *Exercise Central* at <www.bedfordstmartins .com/bedguide>.

Stanton had all the identifying marks, boating shoes, yellow slicker, sunblock, and an anchor, of a sailor.

Stanton had all the identifying marks — boating shoes, yellow slicker, sunblock, and an anchor — of a sailor.

a. I enjoy going hiking with my friend John — whom I've known for fifteen years.

b. Pedro's new boat is spectacular: a regular seagoing Ferrari.

c. The Thompsons devote their weekends to their favorite pastime, eating bags of potato chips and cookies beside the warm glow of the television.

1. The sport of fishing — or at least some people call it a sport — is boring, dirty — and tiring.

2. At that time, three states in the Sunbelt, Florida, California, and Arizona, were the fastest growing in the nation.

3. LuLu was ecstatic when she saw her grades, all A's!

27 Parentheses, Brackets, and the Ellipsis Mark

Like quotation marks, parentheses (singular, *parenthesis*) work in pairs. So do brackets. Both sets of marks usually surround bits of information added to make a statement perfectly clear. An ellipsis mark is a trio of periods inserted to show that some information has been cut.

PARENTHESES

27a Use parentheses to set off interruptions that are useful but not essential.

FDR (as people called Franklin D. Roosevelt) won four presidential elections.

In fact, he occupied the White House for so many years (1933 to mid-1945) that babies became teenagers without having known any other president.

The material within the parentheses may be helpful, but it isn't essential. Without it, the sentences would still make good sense. Use parentheses when adding in midsentence a qualifying word or phrase, a helpful date, or a brief explanation — words that, in conversation, you might introduce in a changed tone of voice.

27b Use parentheses around letters or numbers indicating items in a series.

Archimedes asserted that, given (1) a lever long enough, (2) a fulcrum, and (3) a place to stand, he could move the earth.

You need not put parentheses around numbers or letters in a list that you set off from the text by indentation.

■ **Exercise 27–1**

Using Parentheses

Add, remove, or replace parentheses wherever appropriate in the following sentences. Some sentences may be correct. Possible answers for the lettered sentences appear in the back of the book. Example:

www
For more practice, visit
Exercise Central at
<www.bedfordstmartins
.com/bedguide>.

> The Islamic fundamentalist Ayatollah Khomeini — 1903–1989 — was described as having led Iran forward into the fifteenth century.

> The Islamic fundamentalist Ayatollah Khomeini (1903–1989) was described as having led Iran forward into the fifteenth century.

a. Our cafeteria serves the four basic food groups: white — milk, bread, and mashed potatoes — brown — mystery meat and gravy — green — overcooked vegetables and underwashed lettuce — and orange — squash, carrots, and tomato sauce.

b. The hijackers will release the hostages only if the government, 1, frees all political prisoners and, 2, allows the hijackers to leave the country unharmed.

c. When Phil said he works with whales (as well as other marine mammals) for the Whale Stranding Network, Lisa thought he meant that his group lures whales onto beaches.

1. The new pear-shaped bottles will hold 200 milliliters, 6.8 fluid ounces, of lotion.

2. World War I, or "The Great War," as it was once called, destroyed the old European order forever.

3. The Internet is a mine of fascinating, and sometimes useless, information.

BRACKETS

Brackets, those open-ended typographical boxes, work in pairs like parentheses. They serve a special purpose: they mark changes in quoted material.

27c **Use brackets to add information or to make changes within a direct quotation.**

A quotation must be quoted exactly. If you add or alter a word or a phrase in a quotation from another writer, place brackets around your changes. If you add ellipsis marks to signal an omission in a quotation, the Modern Language Association (MLA) suggests that you also place brackets around them. Most often the need for such changes arises when you weave into your own prose a piece of someone else's.

For advice on quoting, paraphrasing, and summarizing, see pp. 185–86.

Suppose you are writing about James McGuire's being named chairman of the board of directors of General Motors. In your source, the actual words are these: "A radio bulletin first brought the humble professor of philosophy the astounding news." But in your paper, you want readers to know the professor's identity. So you add that information, in brackets.

> "A radio bulletin first brought the humble professor of philosophy [James McGuire] the astounding news."

Be careful never to alter a quoted statement any more than you have to. Every time you consider an alteration, ask yourself: Do I really need this word-for-word quotation, or should I paraphrase?

27d Use brackets around *sic* to indicate an error in a direct quotation.

When you faithfully quote a statement that contains an error, follow the error with a bracketed *sic* (Latin for "so" or "so the writer says").

> "President Ronald Reagan foresaw a yearly growth of 29,000,000,000 [*sic*] in the American populace."

Of course, any statement as incorrect as that one is not worth quoting. Usually you're better off paraphrasing an error-riddled passage than pointing out its weaknesses.

THE ELLIPSIS MARK

27e Use the ellipsis mark to signal that you have omitted part of a quotation.

Occasionally you will want to quote just those parts of a passage that relate to your topic. It's all right to make judicious cuts in a quotation, as long as you acknowledge them. To do this, use the *ellipsis mark:* three periods with a space between each one (. . .).

Let's say you are writing an essay, "Today's Children: Counselors on Marital Affairs." One of your sources is Marie Winn's book *Children without Childhood* (New York: Penguin, 1984), in which you find this passage:

> Consider the demise of sexual innocence among children. We know that the casual integration of children into adult society in the Middle Ages included few sexual prohibitions. Today's nine- and ten-year-olds watch pornographic movies on cable TV, casually discourse about oral sex and sadomasochism, and not infrequently find themselves involved in their own parents' complicated sex lives, if not as actual observers or participants, at least as advisers, friendly commentators, and intermediaries.

You want to quote Winn's last sentence but omit some of its detail. If you use an ellipsis mark within a sentence and add brackets as MLA suggests, leave a space before and after the brackets.

For more on brackets, see 27c.

"Today's nine- and ten-year-olds [. . .] not infrequently find themselves involved in their own parents' complicated sex lives, [. . .] at least as advisers, friendly commentators, and intermediaries."

If the ellipsis mark concludes your sentence, place a period after the second bracket without leaving a space.

"Consider the demise of sexual innocence [. . .]. Today's nine- and ten-year-olds [quotation continues as in preceding example]."

27f   Avoid using the ellipsis mark at the beginning or end of a quotation.

Even though the book *Children without Childhood* continues after the quoted passage, you don't need an ellipsis mark at the end of your quotation. Nor do you ever need to begin a quotation with three dots. Save the ellipsis mark for words or sentences you omit *inside* whatever you quote.

Anytime you decide to alter a quotation, with an ellipsis mark or with brackets, ask yourself whether the quoted material is still necessary and still effective. If you plan to cut more than one or two sections from a quotation, think about paraphrasing instead.

For more on quoting, paraphrasing, and summarizing, see pp. 185–86.

■ Exercise 27–2

Using Brackets and the Ellipsis Mark

The following are two hypothetical passages from original essays. Each one is followed by a set of quotations. Paraphrase or adapt each quotation, using brackets and ellipsis marks, and splice it into the essay passage.

1. ESSAY PASSAGE

Most people are willing to work hard for a better life. Too often, however, Americans do not realize that the desire for more possessions leads them away from the happiness they hope to find. Many people work longer and longer hours to earn more money and as a result have less time to devote to family, friends, and activities that are truly important. When larger houses, sport-utility vehicles, and wide-screen TVs fail to bring them joy, they find even more things to buy and work even harder to pay for them. This cycle can grind down the most optimistic American. The only solution is to realize how few material possessions people absolutely need to have.

QUOTATIONS

a. Only when he has ceased to need things can a man truly be his own master and so really exist.

— Anwar al-Sadat

b. I like to walk amidst the beautiful things that adorn the world; but private wealth I should decline, or any sort of personal possessions, because they would take away my liberty.

— George Santayana

c. To live content with small means; to seek elegance rather than luxury, and refinement rather than fashion; to be worthy, not respectable and wealthy, not rich; to study hard, think quietly, talk gently, act frankly; to listen to stars and birds, to babes and sages, with open heart; to bear all cheerfully, do all bravely, await occasions, hurry never. In a word, to let the spiritual, unbidden and unconscious, grow up through the common. This is to be my symphony.

— William Henry Channing

2. ESSAY PASSAGE

Every human life is touched by the natural world. Before the modern industrial era, most people recognized the earth as the giver and supporter of existence. Nowadays, with the power of technology, we can (if we choose) destroy many of the complex balances of nature. With such power comes responsibility. We are no longer merely nature's children, but nature's parents as well.

QUOTATIONS

a. The overwhelming importance of the atmosphere means that there are no longer any frontiers to defend against pollution, attack, or propaganda. It means, further, that only by a deep patriotic devotion to one's country can there be a hope of the kind of protection of the whole planet, which is necessary for the survival of the people of other countries.

— Anthropologist Margaret Mead

b. The survival of our wildlife is a matter of grave concern to all of us in Africa. These wild creatures amid the wild places they inhabit are not only important as a source of wonder and inspiration but are an integral part of our natural resources and of our future livelihood and well-being.

— Former president of Tanzania Julius Nyerere

Chapter 37

Mechanics

28. Abbreviations   H-127
29. Capital Letters   H-130
30. Numbers   H-134
31. Italics   H-136
32. The Hyphen   H-139
33. Spelling   H-142

28   *Abbreviations*

Abbreviations enable a writer to include certain necessary information in capsule form. In your writing, limit abbreviations to those that are common enough for readers to recognize, or add an explanation so that a reader does not have to stop and ask, "What does this mean?"

If ever you're unsure about whether to abbreviate a word, remember: when in doubt, spell it out.

28a   Use abbreviations for some titles with proper names.

Abbreviate the following titles:

Mr. and Mrs. Hubert Collins   Dr. Martin Luther King Jr.
Ms. Martha Reading   St. Matthew

Write out other titles in full, including titles that are unfamiliar to readers of English, such as *M.* (for the French *Monsieur*) or *Sr.* (for the Spanish *Señor*).

General Douglas MacArthur   Senator Dianne Feinstein
President George W. Bush   Professor Shirley Fixler

Spell out most titles that appear without proper names.

FAULTY   Tomás is studying to be a dr.

REVISED   Tomás is studying to be a doctor.

When an abbreviated title (such as an academic degree) follows a proper name, set it off with commas.

Alice Martin, C.P.A., is the accountant for Charlotte Cordera, Ph.D.

Lucy Chen, M.D., and James Filbert, D.D.S., have moved to new offices.

An academic degree that appears without a proper name can be abbreviated, but it is not set off with commas.

My brother has a B.A. in economics.

Avoid repeating different forms of the same title before and after a proper name. You can properly refer to a doctor of dental surgery as either *Dr. Jane Doe* or *Jane Doe, D.D.S.*, but not as *Dr. Jane Doe, D.D.S.*

28b Use *a.m., p.m.,* B.C., A.D., and $ with numbers.

9:05 a.m.   3:45 p.m.   2000 B.C.   A.D. 1066

The words for pinpointing years and times are so commonly abbreviated that many writers have forgotten what the letters stand for. In case you are curious: *a.m.* means *ante meridiem,* Latin for "before noon"; *p.m.* means *post meridiem,* "after noon." A.D. is *anno domini,* Latin for "in the year of the Lord" — that is, since the official year of Jesus' birth. B.C. stands for "before Christ." You may also run into alternative designations such as B.C.E., "before the common era."

For exact prices that include cents and for amounts in the millions, use a dollar sign with figures (*$17.95, $10.52, $3.5 billion*).

Avoid using an abbreviation with wording that means the same thing: write *$1 million,* not *$1 million dollars.* Write *9:05 a.m.* or *9:05 in the morning,* not *9:05 a.m. in the morning.*

28c Avoid abbreviating names of months, days of the week, units of measurement, or parts of literary works.

Many references that can be abbreviated in citations should be spelled out when they appear in the body of an essay.

NAMES OF MONTHS AND DAYS OF THE WEEK

FAULTY   After their meeting on 9/3, they did not see each other again until Fri., Dec. 12.

REVISED   After their meeting on September 3 [*or* the third of September], they did not see each other again until Friday, December 12.

UNITS OF MEASUREMENT

FAULTY   It would take 10,000 lbs. of concrete to build a causeway 25 ft. × 58 in. [*or* 25' × 58"].

REVISED   It would take 10,000 pounds of concrete to build a causeway 25 feet by 58 inches.

PARTS OF LITERARY WORKS

FAULTY   Von Bargen's reply appears in vol. 2, ch. 12, p. 187.

REVISED   Von Bargen's reply appears in volume 2, chapter 12, page 187.

FAULTY   Leona first speaks in act 1, sc. 2.

REVISED   Leona first speaks in act 1, scene 2 [*or* the second scene of act 1].

28d Use the full English version of most Latin abbreviations.

Unless you are writing for an audience of ancient Romans, translate Latin abbreviations into English and spell them out whenever possible.

For the use of *sic* to identify an error, see 27d.

COMMON LATIN ABBREVIATIONS

ABBREVIATION	LATIN	ENGLISH
et al.	*et alia*	and others, and other people, and the others (people)
etc.	*et cetera*	and so forth, and others, and the rest (things)
i.e.	*id est*	that is
e.g.	*exempli gratia*	for example, such as

Latin abbreviations are acceptable, however, for source citations and for comments in parentheses and brackets.

28e Use abbreviations for familiar organizations, corporations, and people.

Most sets of initials that are read as letters do not require periods between the letters (CIA, JFK, UCLA). You will not be wrong if you insert periods (C.I.A., J.F.K., U.C.L.A.), as long as you are consistent.

A set of initials that is pronounced as a word is called an *acronym* (NATO, AIDS, UNICEF) and never has periods between letters.

To avoid misunderstanding, write out an organization's full name the first time you mention it, followed by its initials in parentheses. Then, in later references, you can rely on initials alone. (With very familiar initials, such as FBI or CBS, you need not give the full name.)

28f Avoid abbreviations for countries.

When you mention the United States or another country, give its full name, unless the name is repeated so often that it would weigh down your paragraph.

The president will return to the United States [*not* U.S.] on Tuesday from a trip to the United Kingdom [*not* U.K.].

EXCEPTION: Although it is not advisable to use *U.S.* as a noun, you can use it as an adjective: *U.S. Senate, U.S. foreign policy.* For other countries, find an alternative: *British ambassador.*

■ **Exercise 28–1**

Using Abbreviations

WWW

For more practice, visit *Exercise Central* at <www.bedfordstmartins .com/bedguide>.

Substitute abbreviations for words and vice versa wherever appropriate in the following sentences. Correct any incorrectly used abbreviations. Answers for the lettered sentences appear in the back of the book. Example:

> Please return this form to our office no later than noon on Wed., Apr. 7.

> Please return this form to our office no later than noon on *Wednesday, April 7.*

a. At 7:50 p.m. in the evening on election day, the media first awarded Florida to Al Gore, only to reverse that statement and declare George W. Bush the president a few hours later.

b. Biology lectures are only ninety mins. long because lab sessions immediately follow them.

c. Prof. James has office hours on Mon. and Tues., beginning at 10:00 a.m.

d. Emotional issues, e.g., abortion and capital punishment, cannot be settled easily by compromise.

e. The red peppers are selling for three dollars and twenty-five cents a lb.

1. Hamlet's famous soliloquy comes in act three, sc. one.

2. A.I.D.S. has affected people throughout U.S. society, not just gay men and IV-drug users.

3. Mister Robert Glendale, a C.P.A. accountant, is today's lucky winner of the daily double.

4. The end of the cold war between the U.S. and the Soviet Union complicated the role of the U.N. and drastically altered the purpose of N.A.T.O.

5. The salmon measured thirty-eight in. and weighed twenty-one lbs.

29 *Capital Letters*

For advice and a useful chart on capitalization, see D1 in the "Quick Editing Guide."

The main thing to remember about capital letters is to use them only with good reason. If you think a word will work in lowercase letters, you're probably right.

29a Capitalize proper names and adjectives made from proper names.

Proper names designate individuals, places, organizations, institutions, brand names, and certain other distinctive things.

Miles Standish	University of Iowa
Belgium	a Volkswagen
United Nations	a Xerox copier

Any proper name can have an adjective as well as a noun form. The adjective form too is capitalized.

Australian beer   a Renaissance man
Shakespearean comedy   Machiavellian tactics

29b   Capitalize a title or rank before a proper name.

Now in her second term, Senator Wilimczyk serves on two committees.

In his lecture, Professor Jones analyzed fossil evidence.

Titles that do not come before proper names generally are not capitalized.

Ten senators voted against the missile research appropriation.

Jones is the department's only full professor.

EXCEPTION: The abbreviation of an academic or professional degree is capitalized, whether or not it accompanies a proper name. The informal name of a degree is not capitalized.

Dora E. McLean, M.D., also holds a B.A. in music.

Dora holds a bachelor's degree in music.

29c   Capitalize a family relationship only when it is part of a proper name or when it substitutes for a proper name.

Do you know the song about Mother Machree?

I've invited Mother to visit next weekend.

I'd like you to meet my aunt, Emily Smith.

29d   Capitalize the names of religions, their deities, and their followers.

Christianity   Muslims   Jehovah   Krishna
Islam   Methodists   Allah   the Holy Spirit

29e   Capitalize proper names of places, regions, and geographic features.

Los Angeles   the Black Hills   the Atlantic Ocean
Death Valley   Big Sur   the Philippines

Do not capitalize *north, south, east,* or *west* unless it is part of a proper name (*West Virginia, South Orange*) or refers to formal geographic locations.

Drive south to Chicago and then east to Cleveland.

Jim, who has always lived in the South, likes to read about the Northeast.

A common noun such as *street, avenue, boulevard, park, lake,* or *hill* is capitalized when part of a proper name.

Meinecke Avenue   Hamilton Park   Lake Michigan

29f Capitalize days of the week, months, and holidays, but not seasons or academic terms.

During spring term, by the Monday after Passover, I have to choose between the January study plan and junior year abroad.

29g Capitalize historical events, periods, and documents.

Black Monday   the Roaring Twenties
the Civil War [*but* a civil war]   Magna Carta
the Holocaust [*but* a holocaust]   Declaration of Independence
the Bronze Age   Atomic Energy Act

29h Capitalize the names of schools, colleges, departments, and courses.

West End School, Central High School [*but* elementary school, high school]

Reed College, Arizona State University [*but* the college, a university]

Department of History [*but* history department, department office]

Feminist Perspectives in Nineteenth-Century Literature [*but* literature course]

29i Capitalize the first, last, and main words in titles.

For advice on using quotation marks and italics for titles, see 25e and 31a.

When you write the title of a paper, book, article, work of art, television show, poem, or performance, capitalize the first and last words and all main words in between. Do not capitalize articles (*a, an, the*), coordinating conjunctions (*and, but, for, or, nor, so, yet*), or prepositions (such as *in, on, at, of, from*) unless they come first or last in the title or follow a colon.

ESSAY	"Once More to the Lake"
NOVEL	*Of Mice and Men*
VOLUME OF POETRY	*Poems after Martial*
POEM	"A Valediction: Of Weeping"
BALLET	*Swan Lake*

29j **Capitalize the first letter of a quoted sentence.**

For advice on punctuating quotations, see 25g–25i.

Oscar Wilde wrote, "The only way to get rid of a temptation is to yield to it."

Only the first word of a quoted sentence is capitalized, even when you break the sentence with words of your own.

"The only way to get rid of a temptation," wrote Oscar Wilde, "is to yield to it."

If you quote more than one sentence, start each one with a capital letter.

"Art should never try to be popular," said Wilde. "The public should try to make itself artistic."

If the quoted passage blends in with your sentence, be sure to present every detail of your source accurately.

Oscar Wilde wrote that "The only way to get rid of a temptation is to yield to it."

■ **Exercise 29–1**

Using Capitalization

Correct any capitalization errors you find in the following sentences. Some sentences may be correct. Answers for the lettered sentences appear in the back of the book. Example:

www
For more practice, visit *Exercise Central* at <www.bedfordstmartins.com/bedguide>.

"The quality of mercy," says Portia in Shakespeare's *The Merchant Of Venice,* "Is not strained."

"The quality of mercy," says Portia in Shakespeare's *The Merchant of Venice,* "is not strained."

a. At our Family Reunion, I met my Cousin Sam for the first time, as well as my father's brother George.

b. I already knew from dad that his brother had moved to Australia years ago to explore the great barrier reef.

c. I had heard that uncle George was estranged from his Mother, a Roman catholic, after he married an Atheist.

d. She told George that God created many religions so that people would not become Atheists.

e. When my Uncle announced that he was moving to a Continent thousands of miles Southwest of the United States, his Mother gave him a bible to take along.

1. My Aunt, Linda McCallum, received her Doctorate from one of the State Universities in California.

2. After graduation she worked there as Registrar and lived in the San Bernardino valley.

3. She has pursued her interest in Hispanic Studies by traveling to South America from her home in Northeastern Australia.

4. She uses her maiden name — Linda McCallum, Ph.D. — for her nonprofit business, Hands across the Sea.

5. After dinner we all toasted grandmother's Ninetieth Birthday and sang "For She's A Jolly Good Fellow."

30 *Numbers*

When do you write out a number (*twenty-seven*) and when do you use figures for it (27)? Unless your essay relies on statistics, you'll want in most cases to use words. Figures are most appropriate in contexts where readers are used to seeing them, such as times and dates (*11:05 P.M. on March 15*).

30a In general, write out a number that consists of one or two words, and use figures for longer numbers.

Short names of numbers are easily read (*ten, six hundred*); longer ones take more thought (*two thousand four hundred eighty-seven*). So for numbers of more than a word or two, use figures.

Two hundred fans paid twenty-five dollars apiece for that shirt.

A frog's tongue has 970,580 taste buds, but a human's has six times as many.

EXCEPTION: For multiples of a million or more, use a figure plus a word.

The earth is 93 million miles from the sun.

For examples, see Figures at a Glance on p. H-135.

30b Use figures for most addresses, dates, decimals, fractions, parts of literary works, percentages, exact prices, scores, statistics, and times.

Using figures is mainly a matter of convenience. If you think words will be easier for your readers to follow, you can always write out a number.

For more on the plurals of figures (6's, 1960s), see 24i.

30c Use words or figures consistently for numbers in the same category throughout a passage.

Switching back and forth between words and figures for numbers can be distracting to readers. Choose whichever form suits like numbers in your passage, and use that form consistently for all numbers in the same category.

Of the 276 representatives who voted, 97 supported a 25 percent raise, while 179 supported a 30 percent raise over five years.

Figures at a Glance

ADDRESSES	4 East 74th Street; also, One Copley Place, 5 Fifth Avenue
DATES	May 20, 1992; 450 B.C.; also, Fourth of July
DECIMALS	98.6° Fahrenheit; .57 acre
FRACTIONS	3½ years ago; 1¾ miles; also, half a loaf, three-fourths of voters surveyed
PARTS OF LITERARY WORKS	volume 2, chapter 5, page 37; act 1, scene 2 (*or* act I, scene ii)
PERCENTAGES	25 percent; 99.9 percent; also, 25%, 99.9%
EXACT PRICES	$1.99; $200,000; also, $5 million, ten cents, a dollar
SCORES	a 114–111 victory; a final score of 5 to 3
STATISTICS	men in the 25–30 age group; odds of 5 to 1 (*or* 5–1 odds); height 5'7"; also, three out of four doctors
TIMES	2:29 P.M.; 10:15 tomorrow morning; also, half past four, three o'clock (always with a number in words)

30d   **Write out a number that begins a sentence.**

Readers recognize a new sentence by its initial capital; however, you can't capitalize a figure. When a number starts a sentence, either write it out or move it deeper into the sentence. If a number starting a sentence is followed by other numbers in the same category, write them out, too, unless doing so makes the sentence excessively awkward.

> Five percent of the frogs in our aquarium ate sixty-two percent of the flies.

> Ten thousand people packed an arena built for 8,550.

■ **Exercise 30–1**

Using Numbers

Correct any inappropriate uses of numbers in the following sentences. Some sentences may be correct. Answers for the lettered sentences appear in the back of the book. Example:

> As Feinberg notes on page 197, a delay of 3 minutes cost the researchers 5 years' worth of work.

> As Feinberg notes on page 197, a delay of *three* minutes cost the researchers *five* years' worth of work.

a. If the murder took place at approximately six-twenty P.M. and the suspect was ½ a mile away at the time, he could not possibly have committed the crime.

WWW
For more practice, visit *Exercise Central* at <www.bedfordstmartins.com/bedguide>.

b. A program to help save the sea otter transferred more than eighty animals to a new colony over the course of 2 years; however, all but 34 otters swam back home again.

c. 1 percent or less of the estimated fifteen to twenty billion pounds of plastic discarded annually in the United States is recycled.

d. The 1983 Little League World Series saw the Roosters beat the Dusters ninety-four to four before a throng of seven thousand five hundred and fifty.

e. In act two, scene nine, of Shakespeare's *The Merchant of Venice,* Portia's 2nd suitor fails to guess which of 3 caskets contains her portrait.

1. *Fourscore* means 4 times 20; a *fortnight* means 2 weeks; and a *brace* is two of anything.

2. 50 years ago, traveling from New York City to San Francisco took approximately 15 hours by plane, 50 hours by train, and almost 100 hours by car.

3. The little cottage we bought for fifty-five thousand dollars in the nineteen-seventies may sell for $2,000,000 today.

4. At 7 o'clock this morning the temperature was already ninety-seven degrees Fahrenheit.

5. Angelica finished volume one of Proust's *Remembrance of Things Past,* but by the time she got to page forty of volume two, she had forgotten the beginning and had to start over.

31   *Italics*

Italic type — as in this line — slants to the right. Slightly harder to read than perpendicular type, it is usually saved for emphasis or for special use of a word or phrase. In handwriting or typewriting, indicate italics by underlining.

31a   Italicize the titles of magazines, newspapers, and long literary works (books, pamphlets, plays); the titles of films; the titles of paintings and other works of art; the titles of long musical works (operas, symphonies); the titles of CDs and record albums; and the names of television and radio programs.

We read the story "Araby" in James Joyce's book *Dubliners.*

The Broadway musical *My Fair Lady* was based on Shaw's play *Pygmalion.*

The names of the Bible (King James Version, Revised Standard Version), the books of the Bible (Genesis, Matthew), and other sacred books (the Koran, the Rig-Veda) are not italicized.

Italics at a Glance

TITLES

MAGAZINES AND NEWSPAPERS
Ms.   the *London Times*

LONG LITERARY WORKS
The Bluest Eye (a novel)   *The Less Deceived* (a collection of poems)

FILMS
Psycho   *Crouching Tiger, Hidden Dragon*

PAINTINGS AND OTHER WORKS OF ART
Four Dancers (a painting)   *The Thinker* (a sculpture)

LONG MUSICAL WORKS
Aïda   Handel's *Messiah*

CDS AND RECORD ALBUMS
Crash   *Disciplined Breakdown*

TELEVISION AND RADIO PROGRAMS
Will and Grace   *All Things Considered*

OTHER WORDS AND PHRASES

NAMES OF AIRCRAFT, SPACECRAFT, SHIPS, AND TRAINS
the *Orient Express*   the *Challenger*

A WORD OR PHRASE FROM A FOREIGN LANGUAGE IF IT IS NOT IN EVERYDAY USE
The Finnish sauna ritual uses a *vihta,* a brush made of fresh birch branches tied together.

A LETTER, NUMBER, WORD, OR PHRASE WHEN YOU DEFINE IT OR REFER TO IT AS A WORD
Two neon *5*'s on the door identified the café's address.

What do you think *fiery* is referring to in the second line?

When you give a synonym or a translation — a definition of just one or two words — italicize the word being defined and put the definition in quotation marks.

> The word *orthodoxy* means "conformity."
>
> *Trois, drei,* and *tres* are all words for "three."

For titles that need to be placed in quotation marks, see 25e.

31b Italicize the names of ships, boats, trains, airplanes, and spacecraft.

The launching of the Venus probe *Magellan* was a heartening success after the *Challenger* disaster.

31c Italicize a word or phrase from a foreign language if it is not in everyday use.

Gandhi taught the principles of *satya* and *ahimsa:* truth and nonviolence.

Foreign words that are familiar to most American readers need not be italicized. (Check your dictionary to see which words are considered familiar.)

I prefer provolone to mozzarella.

31d Italicize a word when you define it.

The rhythmic, wavelike motion of the walls of the alimentary canal is called *peristalsis.*

31e Italicize a letter, number, word, or phrase used as a word.

George Bernard Shaw pointed out that *fish* could be spelled *ghoti: gh* as in *tough, o* as in *women,* and *ti* as in *fiction.*

Watching the big red *8* on a basketball player's jersey, I recalled the scarlet letter *A* worn by Hester Prynne.

31f Use italics sparingly for emphasis.

When you absolutely *must* stress a point, use italics. In most cases, the structure of your sentence, not a typographical gimmick, should give emphasis where emphasis is due.

He suggested putting the package *under* the mailbox, not *into* the mailbox.

People living in affluent countries may not be aware that *forty thousand children per day* die of starvation or malnutrition.

■ **Exercise 31–1**

Using Italics

Add or remove italics as needed in the following sentences. Some sentences may be correct. Answers for the lettered sentences appear in the back of the book. Example:

Hiram could not *believe* that his parents had seen *the Beatles'* legendary performance at Shea Stadium.

Hiram could not believe that his parents had seen the Beatles' legendary performance at Shea Stadium.

a. Does "avocado" mean "lawyer" in Spanish?

www
For more practice, visit *Exercise Central* at <www.bedfordstmartins.com/bedguide>.

b. During this year's *First Night* celebrations, we heard Verdi's Requiem and Monteverdi's Orfeo.

c. You can pick out some of the best basketball players in the *NBA* by the 33 on their jerseys.

d. It was fun watching the passengers on the Europa trying to dance to *Blue Moon* in the midst of a storm.

e. In one episode of the sitcom "Seinfeld," Kramer gets a job as an underwear model.

1. *Eye* in French is *oeil,* while *eyes* is *yeux.*

2. "Deux yeux bleus" means "two blue eyes" in French.

3. Jan can never remember whether Cincinnati has three n's and one t or two n's and two t's.

4. My favorite comic bit in "The Pirates of Penzance" is Major General Stanley's confusion between "orphan" and "often."

5. In Tom Stoppard's play "The Real Thing," the character Henry accuses Bach of copying a *cantata* from a popular song by *Procol Harum.*

32 *The Hyphen*

The hyphen, that Scotch-tape mark of punctuation, is used to join words and to connect parts of words.

32a Use hyphens in compound words that require them.

Compound words in the English language take three forms:

1. Two or more words combined into one (*crossroads, salesperson*)
2. Two or more words that remain separate but function as one (*gas station, high school*)
3. Two or more words linked by hyphens (*sister-in-law, window-shop*)

Compound nouns and verbs fall into these categories more by custom than by rule. When you're not sure which way to write a compound, refer to your dictionary. If the compound is not listed in your dictionary, write it as two words.

Use a hyphen in a compound word containing one or more elements beginning with a capital letter.

Bill says that, as a *neo-Marxist* living in an *A-frame* house, it would be politically incorrect for him to wear a Mickey Mouse *T-shirt.*

There are exceptions to this rule: unchristian, for one. If you think a compound word looks odd with a hyphen, check your dictionary.

32b Use a hyphen in a compound adjective preceding a noun but not following a noun.

Jerome, a devotee of *twentieth-century* music, has no interest in the classic symphonies of the *eighteenth century.*

I'd like living in an *out-of-the-way* place better if it weren't so far *out of the way.*

In a series of hyphenated adjectives with the same second word, you can omit that word (but not the hyphen) in all but the last adjective of the series.

Julia is a lover of eighteenth-, nineteenth-, and twentieth-century music.

The adverb *well,* when coupled with an adjective, follows the same hyphenation rules as if it were an adjective.

It is *well known* that Tony has a *well-equipped* kitchen, although his is not as *well equipped* as the hotel's.

Do *not* use a hyphen to link an adverb ending in *-ly* with an adjective.

FAULTY   The sun hung like a newly-minted penny in a freshly-washed sky.

REVISED   The sun hung like a newly minted penny in a freshly washed sky.

32c Use a hyphen after the prefixes *all-, ex-,* and *self-* and before the suffix *-elect.*

Lucille's *ex-husband* is studying *self-hypnosis.*

This *all-important* debate pits Senator Browning against the *president-elect.*

Note that these prefixes and suffixes also can function as parts of words that are not hyphenated (*exit, selfish*). Whenever you are unsure whether to use a hyphen, check a dictionary.

32d Use a hyphen in most cases if an added prefix or suffix creates a double vowel, triple consonant, or ambiguous pronunciation.

It is also acceptable to omit the hyphen in the case of a double *e: reeducate.*

The contractor's *pre-estimate* did not cover any *pre-existing* flaws in the house.

The recreation department favors the *re-creation* of a summer program.

32e Use a hyphen in spelled-out fractions and compound whole numbers from twenty-one to ninety-nine.

When her sister gave Leslie's age as six and *three-quarters,* Leslie corrected her: "I'm six and *five-sixths!*"

The fifth graders learned that *forty-four* rounds down to forty while *forty-five* rounds up to fifty.

32f **Use a hyphen to indicate inclusive numbers.**

The section covering the years 1975-1980 is found on pages 20-27.

32g **Use a hyphen to break a word between syllables at the end of a line.**

Although many readers will prefer that you turn off your word processor's automatic hyphenation function, using it will require that you check the word divisions it generates. Words are divided as they are pronounced, by syllables. Break a hyphenated compound at its hyphen and a nonhyphenated compound between the words that make it up. If you are not sure where to break a word, check your dictionary.

FAULTY   Bubba hates to be called an-
           ti-American.

REVISED   Bubba hates to be called anti-
           American.

Don't split a one-syllable word, even if keeping it intact makes your line come out a bit too short or too long.

FAULTY   I'm completely drench-
           ed.

REVISED   I'm completely drenched.

■ **Exercise 32–1**

Using Hyphens

Add necessary hyphens and remove incorrectly used hyphens in the following sentences. Some sentences may be correct. Answers for the lettered sentences appear in the back of the book. Example:

Her exhusband works part-time as a short order cook.

Her *ex-husband* works part-time as a *short-order* cook.

WWW
For more practice, visit *Exercise Central* at <www.bedfordstmartins.com/bedguide>.

a. The strong smelling smoke alerted them to a potentially life threatening danger.

b. Burt's wildly-swinging opponent had tired himself out before the climactic third round.

c. Tony soaked his son's ketchup and mustard stained T shirt in a pail of water mixed with chlorine bleach.

d. The badly damaged ship was in no condition to enter the wide-open waters beyond the bay.

e. Tracy's brother in law lives with his family in a six room apartment.

1. Do you want salt-and-pepper on your roast beef sandwich?
2. Health insurance companies should not be allowed to exclude people on account of preexisting conditions.
3. Heat-seeking missiles are often employed in modern day air-to-air combat.
4. *The Piano* is a beautifully-crafted film with first-rate performances by Holly Hunter and Harvey Keitel.
5. Nearly three fourths of the money in the repair and maintenance account already has been spent.

33 *Spelling*

For advice on spelling and for useful spelling lists, see D2 in the "Quick Editing Guide."

English spelling so often defies the rules that many writers wonder if, indeed, there *are* rules. You probably learned to spell — as most of us did — mainly by memorizing. By now you remember that there's a *b* in *doubt* but not in *spout*. You know that the same sound can have several spellings, as in *here, ear, pier, sneer,* and *weird*. You are resigned to pronouncing *ou* differently in *four, round, ought,* and *double*. Still, like most people, you may have trouble spelling certain words.

How many times have you heard someone say "ath-uh-lete" for *athlete* or "gov-er-ment" for *government*? Get the pronunciation right and you realize that the spelling has to be *arctic* (not *artic*), *perform* (not *preform*), *surprise* (not *suprise*), and *similar* (not *similiar*). The trouble is that careful pronunciation is only sometimes a reliable guide to English spelling. Knowing how to pronounce *psychology, whistle, light, gauge,* and *rhythm* doesn't help you spell them. How, then, are you to cope? You can proofread carefully and use your spell checker. You can refer to lists of commonly misspelled words and of **homonyms,** words that sound the same, or almost the same, but are spelled differently. You can also follow the spelling rules and advice about spelling skills included in this section.

33a Follow spelling rules.

Fortunately, a few rules for spelling English words work most of the time. Learning them, and some of their exceptions, will give you a sturdy foundation on which to build.

***EI* or *IE*?**   The best way to remember which words are spelled *ei* and which ones *ie* is to recall this familiar jingle:

I before *e* except after *c*,

Or when sounded like *a*, as in *neighbor* and *weigh*.

Niece, believe, field, receive, receipt, ceiling, beige, and *freight* are just a few of the words you'll be able to spell easily once you learn that rule. Then memorize a few of the exceptions:

counterfeit	foreign	kaleidoscope	protein	seize
either	forfeit	leisure	science	weird
financier	height	neither	seismograph	

Also among the rule breakers are words in which *cien* is pronounced "shen": *ancient, efficient, conscience, prescience.*

Plurals.   Here are six useful rules:

1. To form the plural of most common nouns, add *-s*. If a noun ends in *-ch, -sh, -s,* or *-x,* form its plural by adding *-es.*

attack, attacks	umbrella, umbrellas
boss, bosses	zone, zones
sandwich, sandwiches	trellis, trellises
tax, taxes	crash, crashes

2. To form the plural of a common noun ending in *-o,* add *-s* if the *-o* follows a vowel and *-es* if it follows a consonant.

radio, radios	video, videos
hero, heroes	potato, potatoes

3. To form the plural of a common noun ending in *-y,* change the *y* to *i* and add *-es* if the *y* follows a consonant. Add only *-s* if the *y* follows a vowel.

baby, babies	sissy, sissies
toy, toys	day, days

4. To form the plural of a proper noun, add *-s* or *-es.* Proper nouns follow the same rules as common nouns, with one exception: a proper noun never changes its spelling in the plural form.

Mary Jane, Mary Janes	Dr. Maddox, the Maddoxes
Professor Jones, the Joneses	Saturday, Saturdays

5. To form the plural of a compound noun, add *-s* or *-es* to the chief word or to the last word if all the words are equal in weight.

brother-in-law, brothers-in-law	actor-manager, actor-managers
aide-de-camp, aides-de-camp	tractor-trailer, tractor-trailers

6. Memorize the plural forms of nouns that diverge from these rules. Certain nouns have special plurals. Here are a few:

alumna, alumnae	man, men
alumnus, alumni	medium, media
child, children	mouse, mice
goose, geese	self, selves
half, halves	tooth, teeth
leaf, leaves	woman, women

Suffixes. The *-s* added to a word to make it plural is one type of *suffix,* or tail section. Suffixes allow the same root word to do a variety of jobs, giving it different forms for different functions.

1. Drop a silent *e* before a suffix that begins with a vowel.

   move, mover, moved, moving   argue, arguer, argued, arguing

   EXCEPTION: If the *e* has an essential function, keep it before adding a suffix that begins with a vowel. In *singe,* for instance, the *e* changes the word's pronunciation from "sing" to "sinj." If you dropped the *e* in *singeing,* it would become *singing.*

   singe, singed, singeing   tiptoe, tiptoed, tiptoeing

2. Keep a silent *e* before a suffix that begins with a consonant.

   move, movement   hope, hopeless

   EXCEPTION: In a word ending in a silent *e* preceded by a vowel, sometimes (but not always) drop the *e.*

   argue, argument   true, truly

3. Change a final *y* to *i* before a suffix if the *y* follows a consonant but not if the *y* follows a vowel.

   cry, crier, cried   joy, joyous, joyful
   happy, happiest, happily   pray, prayed, prayer
   hurry, hurried

   EXCEPTION: Keep the *y* whenever the suffix is *-ing.*

   hurry, hurrying   pray, praying

   Drop a final *y* before the suffix *-ize.*

   deputy, deputize   memory, memorize

4. Double the final consonant of a one-syllable word before a suffix if (1) the suffix starts with a vowel *and* (2) the final consonant follows a single vowel.

   sit, sitter, sitting   rob, robbed, robbery

   Don't double the final consonant if it follows two vowels or another consonant.

   fail, failed, failure   stack, stacking, stackable

   Don't double the final consonant if the suffix starts with a consonant.

   top, topless   cap, capful

5. Double the final consonant of a word with two or more syllables if (1) the suffix starts with a vowel *and* (2) the final consonant follows a

single vowel *and* (3) the last syllable of the stem is accented once the suffix is added.

   commit, committed, committing   rebut, rebuttal
   regret, regretted, regrettable

Don't double the final consonant if it follows more than one vowel —

   avail, available   repeat, repeating

— or if it follows another consonant —

   accent, accented   depend, dependence

— or the suffix starts with a consonant —

   commit, commitment   jewel, jewelry

— or, when the suffix is added, the final syllable of the stem is unaccented.

   confer, conference (*but* conferred)   travel, traveler

Prefixes.   The main point to remember when writing a word with a *prefix* (or nose section) is that the prefix usually does not alter the spelling of the root word it precedes.

For advice on using a hyphen with a prefix, see 32c and 32d.

   dis + appear = disappear   mis + understand = misunderstand
   dis + satisfied = dissatisfied   with + hold = withhold
   mis + step = misstep   un + necessary = unnecessary

33b Develop spelling skills.

Besides becoming familiar with the rules in this chapter, you can use several other tactics to teach yourself to be a better speller.

   1. *Use mnemonic devices.* To make unusual spellings stick in your memory, invent associations. Using such mnemonic devices (tricks to aid memory) may help you with whatever troublesome spelling you are determined to remember. *Weird* behaves *weirdly.* Rise ag*ain*, Brit*ain*! One *d* in *dish*, one in *radish.* Why isn't *mathe*matics like *athle*tics? You write a *letter* on station*ery.* Any silly phrase or sentence will do, as long as it brings tricky spellings to mind.

   2. *Keep a record of words you misspell.* Buy yourself a little notebook in which to enter words that invariably trip you up. Each time you proofread a paper you have written and each time you receive one back from your instructor, write down any words you have misspelled. Then practice pronouncing, writing, and spelling them out loud until you have mastered them.

   3. *Check any questionable spelling by referring to your dictionary.* Keep a dictionary at your elbow as you write. In matters of spelling, that good-as-gold book is your best friend. Use it to check words as you come up with them and to double-check them as you proofread and edit your work.

4. *Learn commonly misspelled words.* To save you the trouble of looking up every spelling bugbear, the "Quick Editing Guide" has a list of words frequently misspelled (see D2). This list will serve to review our whole discussion of spelling, for it contains the trickiest words we've mentioned. Checkmark those that give you trouble—but don't stop there. Spend a few minutes each day going over them. Pronounce each one carefully or have a friend read the list to you. Spell every troublesome word out loud; write it ten times. Your spelling will improve rapidly.

■ Exercise 33–1

Spelling

www
For more practice, visit
Exercise Central at
<www.bedfordstmartins
.com/bedguide>.

For helpful spelling lists,
see D2 in the "Quick
Editing Guide."

Edit the following passage to correct misspelled words.

> The rapid growth of teknology threatens to altar traditional practice in the music bizness.

> The rapid growth of *technology* threatens to *alter* traditional practice in the music *business*.

With technology that inables us to download music from the Internet and the increasing availability of acess to the online world, the face of the music industry is rapidly changing. Musicians and their label companys are afraid that, since music can be downloaded free of charge, people will no longer by cds. This issue was brought to a head when some musicains, including the rock group Metallica, sued Napster, a popular online music community, for copyright enfringement. Although Napster was found innocent of these charges, many people predict that soon all of these companys will begin charging for downloads to increase thier own prophet, despite profesing a committment to providing music free of charge. Perhaps this is merely a cynical asumption; however, many people are downloading all the music they can today, rather than waiting for tommorrow.

Appendix

Quick Editing Guide

A. Editing for Common Grammar Problems   A-3
B. Editing to Ensure Effective Sentences   A-12
C. Editing for Common Punctuation Problems   A-14
D. Editing for Common Mechanics Problems   A-17
E. Editing for Common Format Problems   A-23

Editing and proofreading are needed at the end of the writing process be-cause writers — *all* writers — find it difficult to write error-free sentences the very first time they try. Sometimes as a writer you pay more attention to

WRITING WITH A COMPUTER

Computers can help you edit in several ways. Grammar checkers will catch some errors, but you always need to consider the grammar checker's sugges-tions carefully before accepting them. For example, a grammar checker cannot always correctly identify the subject or verb in a sentence. As a result, it may question whether a sentence is complete or whether its subject and verb agree, even when the sentence is correct. Grammar checkers also are likely to miss certain problems such as misplaced modifiers, faulty parallelism, possessives without apostrophes, or incorrectly positioned commas. On the other hand, most grammar checkers do a good job of spotting problems with adjectives and adverbs, such as confusing *good* and *well*.

You can also use your word processor to search for your own typical edit-ing problems. Begin by keeping track of your mistakes so that you can de-velop an "error hit list." You then may be able to figure out how to use your software's Find and Replace capacity to edit quickly for some of these prob-lems. For instance, you might search for all instances of *each* (always singular) or *few* (always plural), and check to see if all the verbs agree.

The computer can also help you read your draft more closely. For ex-ample, you can automatically isolate each sentence so that you are less likely to skip over sentence errors. Make a copy of the draft you want to work on, and select the Replace function in your software's Edit menu. Ask the software to find every period in the file, and then replace it with a period and two re-turns. This change will create a version with each sentence separated by sev-eral spaces so that you can easily check every one for fragments, comma splices, or other sentence problems.

what you want to say than to how you say it. Sometimes you inaccurately remember spelling or grammar or punctuation. At other times you are distracted by something happening around you, or you simply make keyboarding errors. Once you are satisfied that you have your ideas down on paper, you should make sure that each sentence and word is concise, clear, and correct.

This "Quick Editing Guide" provides an overview of troubling grammar, style, punctuation, and mechanics problems typical of college writing. Certain common errors in Standard Written English are like red flags to careful readers: they send the message that the writer is either ignorant or careless. Use the editing checklist below to check your paper for these problems; additional editing checklists in each section help you focus on and correct specific errors in your writing.

For editing and proof-reading strategies, see pp. 331–34.

EDITING CHECKLIST

Common and Serious Problems in College Writing

Grammar Problems

___ Have you used the correct form for all verbs in the past tense?	A1
___ Do all verbs agree with their subjects?	A2
___ Have you used the correct case for all pronouns?	A3
___ Do all pronouns agree with their antecedents?	A4
___ Have you used adjectives and adverbs correctly?	A5
___ Have you avoided writing sentence fragments?	A6
___ Have you avoided writing comma splices or fused sentences?	A7

Sentence Problems

___ Does each modifier clearly modify the appropriate sentence element?	B1
___ Have you used parallel structure where necessary?	B2

Punctuation Problems

___ Have you used commas correctly?	C1
___ Have you used apostrophes correctly?	C2
___ Have you punctuated quotations correctly?	C3

Mechanics Problems

___ Have you used capital letters correctly?	D1
___ Have you spelled all words correctly?	D2

Format Problems

___ Have you used correct manuscript form?	E1
___ Have you used correct documentation style?	E2

A *Editing for Common Grammar Problems*

A1 Check for correct past tense verb forms.

The *form* of a verb, the way it is spelled and pronounced, can change to show its *tense* — the time when its action did, does, or will occur (whether it is in the past, the present, or the future). In other words, a verb about something in the present will often be spelled and pronounced differently than a verb about something in the past.

> **verb:** A word that shows action (The cow *jumped* over the moon) or a state of being (The cow *is* brown)

PRESENT   Right now, I *watch* only a few minutes of television each day.

PAST   Last month, I *watched* television shows every evening.

Many writers fail to use the correct form for past tense verbs for two different reasons, depending on whether the verb is regular or irregular. ***Regular verbs*** are verbs whose forms follow standard rules; they form the past tense by adding *-ed* or *-d* to the end of the present tense form: *watch/watched, look/looked, hope/hoped.* Check all regular verbs in the past tense to be sure you have used one of these endings.

FAULTY   I *ask* my brother for a loan yesterday.

CORRECT   I *asked* my brother for a loan yesterday.

FAULTY   Nicole *finish* her English essay.

CORRECT   Nicole *finished* her English essay.

TIP: If you say the final *-d* sound when you talk, you may find it easier to add the final *-d* or *-ed* when you write past tense regular verbs.

Irregular verbs do not follow standard rules to make their different forms. There is no way to predict what the past tense forms will look like, so they have to be memorized: *eat/ate, see/saw, get/got.* Irregular verbs can also use different forms for the past tense and the past participle: "She *ate* the whole pie; she *has eaten* two pies this week." The most troublesome irregular verbs are actually very common, so if you make the effort to learn the correct forms for the past tense and past participle, you will quickly improve your writing.

> **participle:** A form of a verb that cannot function alone as a main verb, including present participles ending in *-ing* (*dancing*) and past participles often ending in *-ed* or *-d* (*danced*)

FAULTY   My cat *laid* on the tile floor to take her nap.

CORRECT   My cat *lay* on the tile floor to take her nap.

FAULTY   I *have swam* twenty laps every day this month.

CORRECT   I *have swum* twenty laps every day this month.

For a chart showing the forms of many irregular verbs, see pp. A-4–A-5.

TIP: In your college papers, follow convention by using the present tense, not the past, when you describe the work of an author or the events in a literary work.

FAULTY   In "The Lottery," Shirley Jackson *revealed* the power of tradition. As the story *opened,* the villagers *gathered* in the square.

CORRECT   In "The Lottery," Shirley Jackson *reveals* the power of tradition. As the story *opens,* the villagers *gather* in the square.

EDITING CHECKLIST

Past Tense Verb Forms

___ Have you identified the main verb in the sentence?

___ Is the sentence about the past, the present, or the future? Does the verb reflect this sense of time?

___ Is the verb regular or irregular?

___ Have you used the correct form to express your meaning?

Principal Parts of Common Irregular Verbs

INFINITIVE	PAST TENSE	PAST PARTICIPLE
be	was	been
become	became	become
begin	began	begun
blow	blew	blown
break	broke	broken
bring	brought	brought
burst	burst	burst
catch	caught	caught
choose	chose	chosen
come	came	come
do	did	done
draw	drew	drawn
drink	drank	drunk
drive	drove	driven
eat	ate	eaten
fall	fell	fallen
fight	fought	fought
freeze	froze	frozen
get	got	got, gotten
give	gave	given
go	went	gone
grow	grew	grown
have	had	had
hear	heard	heard
hide	hid	hidden
know	knew	known

(continued)

INFINITIVE	PAST TENSE	PAST PARTICIPLE
lay	laid	laid
lead	led	led
let	let	let
lie	lay	lain
make	made	made
raise	raised	raised
ride	rode	ridden
ring	rang	rung
rise	rose	risen
run	ran	run
say	said	said
see	saw	seen
set	set	set
sing	sang	sung
sit	sat	sat
slay	slew	slain
slide	slid	slid
speak	spoke	spoken
spin	spun	spun
stand	stood	stood
steal	stole	stolen
swim	swam	swum
swing	swung	swung
teach	taught	taught
tear	tore	torn
think	thought	thought
throw	threw	thrown
wake	woke, waked	woken, waked
write	wrote	written

For the forms of irregular verbs not on this list, consult your dictionary. (Some dictionaries list principal parts for all verbs, some just for irregular verbs.)

A2   Check for correct subject-verb agreement.

The *form* of a verb, the way it is spelled and pronounced, can change to show *number*—whether the subject is singular (one) or plural (more than one). It can also change to show *person*—whether the subject is *you* or *she,* for example.

SINGULAR	Our instructor *grades* every paper carefully.
PLURAL	Most instructors *grade* tests using a standard scale.
SECOND PERSON	You *write* well-documented research papers.
THIRD PERSON	She *writes* good research papers, too.

verb: A word that shows action (The cow *jumped* over the moon) or a state of being (The cow *is* brown)

subject: The part of a sentence that names something—a person, an object, an idea, a situation—about which the predicate makes an assertion: The *king* lives.

For a chart showing the forms of many irregular verbs, see pp. A-4–A-5.

A verb must match (or *agree with*) its subject in terms of number and person. For regular verbs (those that follow a standard rule to make the different forms), this rule causes problems only in the present tense. Regular verbs have two present-tense forms: one that ends in *-s* or *-es* and one that does not. Only the subjects *he, she, it,* and singular nouns use the verb form that ends in *-s* or *-es.*

I like	we like
you like	you like
he/she/it likes	they like

The verbs *be* and *have* do not follow the *-s/no -s* pattern to form the present tense; they are irregular verbs, so their forms must be memorized. The verb *be* is also irregular in the past tense.

indefinite pronoun: A pronoun standing for an unspecified person or thing, including singular forms (*any, each, everyone, no one*) and plural forms (*both, few*): *Everyone is soaking wet.*

Problems in agreement often occur when the subject is difficult to find, is an indefinite pronoun, or is confusing for some other reason. In particular, make sure that you have not left off any *-s* or *-es* endings and that you have used the correct form for irregular verbs.

FAULTY	Jim *write* his research papers on a computer.
CORRECT	Jim *writes* his research papers on a computer.

FAULTY	The students *has* difficulty understanding the assignment.
CORRECT	The students *have* difficulty understanding the assignment.

FAULTY	Every one of the cakes *were* sold at the church bazaar.
CORRECT	Every one of the cakes *was* sold at the church bazaar.

EDITING CHECKLIST

Subject-Verb Agreement

___ Have you correctly identified the subject and the verb in the sentence?
___ Is the subject singular or plural? Does the verb match?
___ Have you used the correct form of the verb?

Forms of *Be* and *Have*

THE PRESENT TENSE OF *BE*

I am	we are
you are	you are
he/she/it is	they are

THE PAST TENSE OF *BE*

I was	we were
you were	you were
he/she/it was	they were

THE PRESENT TENSE OF *HAVE*

I have	we have
you have	you have
he/she/it has	they have

THE PAST TENSE OF *HAVE*

I had	we had
you had	you had
he/she/it had	they had

A3 Check for correct pronoun case.

Depending on the role a pronoun plays in a sentence, it is said to be in the *subjective case, objective case,* or *possessive case.* Use the subjective case if the pronoun is the subject of a sentence, the subject of a subordinate clause, or a subject complement (after a linking verb). Use the objective case if the pronoun is a direct or indirect object of a verb or the object of a preposition. Use the possessive case to show possession.

SUBJECTIVE	*I* will argue that our campus needs more parking.
OBJECTIVE	This issue is important to *me.*
POSSESSIVE	*My* argument will be quite persuasive.

There are many types of pronouns, but only some change form to show case. The personal pronouns *I, you, he, she, it, we,* and *they* and the relative pronoun *who* each have at least two forms.

There are two frequent errors in pronoun case. First, writers often use the subjective case when they should use the objective case — sometimes because they are trying to sound formal and correct. Instead, choose the correct form for a personal pronoun based on its function in the sentence.

FAULTY	My company gave my husband and *I* a trip to the Cayman Islands.
CORRECT	My company gave my husband and *me* a trip to the Cayman Islands.
FAULTY	The argument occurred because my uncle and *me* had different expectations.
CORRECT	The argument occurred because my uncle and *I* had different expectations.
FAULTY	Jack is taller than *me.*
CORRECT	Jack is taller than *I.*

Pronoun Cases at a Glance

SUBJECTIVE	OBJECTIVE	POSSESSIVE
I	me	my, mine
you	you	your, yours
he	him	his
she	her	hers
it	it	its
we	us	our, ours
they	them	their, theirs
who	whom	whose

---

pronoun: A word that stands in place of a noun (*he, him,* or *his* for *Nate*)

subject: The part of a sentence that names something—a person, an object, an idea, a situation—about which the predicate makes an assertion: The *king* lives.

subject complement: A noun, an adjective, or a group of words that follows a linking verb (such as *be, am, were, seem, feel*) and renames or describes the subject: This plum tastes *ripe.*

object: The target or recipient of the action of a verb: Some geese bite *people.*

gerund: A form of a verb, ending in *-ing*, that functions as a noun: Lacey likes *playing* in the steel band.

A second common error with pronoun case involves gerunds. Whenever you need a pronoun to modify a gerund, use the possessive case.

FAULTY   Our supervisor disapproves of *us* talking in the hallway.

CORRECT   Our supervisor disapproves of *our* talking in the hallway.

EDITING CHECKLIST

Pronoun Case

___ Have you identified all the pronouns in the sentence?
___ Is each one functioning as a subject, an object, or a possessive?
___ Given the function of each, have you used the correct form?

A4   **Check for correct pronoun-antecedent agreement.**

pronoun: A word that stands in place of a noun (*he, him,* or *his* for Nate)

The *form* of a pronoun, the way it is spelled and pronounced, changes depending on how it is used in a particular sentence. The form can change to show *number*—whether the subject is singular (one) or plural (more than one). It can change to show *gender*—masculine or feminine, for example. It can also change to show *person*—first (*I, we*), second (*you*), or third (*he, she, it, they*).

SINGULAR   My brother took *his* coat and left.

PLURAL   My brothers took *their* coats and left.

MASCULINE   I talked to Steven before *he* had a chance to leave.

FEMININE   I talked to Stephanie before *she* had a chance to leave.

In most cases, a pronoun refers to a specific noun or pronoun mentioned nearby; that word is called the pronoun's *antecedent.* The connection between the pronoun and the antecedent must be clear so that readers know what the pronoun means in the sentence. One way to make this connection clear is to ensure that the pronoun and the antecedent match (or *agree*) in number and gender.

Indefinite Pronouns at a Glance

ALWAYS SINGULAR			ALWAYS PLURAL
anybody	everyone	no one	any
anyone	everything	nothing	both
anything	much	one (of)	few
each (of)	neither (of)	somebody	many
either (of)	nobody	someone	several
everybody	none	something	

A common error in pronoun agreement is using a plural pronoun to refer to a singular antecedent. This error often crops up when the antecedent is difficult to find, when the antecedent is an indefinite pronoun, or when the antecedent is confusing for some other reason. When editing for pronoun-antecedent agreement, look carefully to find the correct antecedent, and then make sure you know whether it is singular or plural. Make the pronoun match its antecedent.

FAULTY   Each of the boys in the Classic Club has *their* own rebuilt car.

CORRECT   Each of the boys in the Classic Club has *his* own rebuilt car.

> [The word *each*, not *boys*, is the antecedent. *Each* is an indefinite pronoun and is always singular, so any pronoun referring to it must be singular as well.]

FAULTY   Everyone in the meeting had *their* own cell phone.

CORRECT   Everyone in the meeting had *his or her* own cell phone.

> [*Everyone* is an indefinite pronoun that is always singular, so any pronoun referring to it must be singular as well.]

FAULTY   Neither Juanita nor Paula has received approval of *their* financial aid yet.

CORRECT   Neither Juanita nor Paula has received approval of *her* financial aid yet.

> [*Neither Juanita nor Paula* is a compound subject joined by *nor*. Any pronoun referring to it must agree with only the nearer part of the compound. In other words, *her* needs to agree with *Paula*, which is singular.]

Indefinite pronouns as antecedents are troublesome when they are grammatically singular but create a plural image in the writer's mind. Fortunately, most indefinite pronouns are either always singular or always plural.

EDITING CHECKLIST

Pronoun-Antecedent Agreement

___ Have you identified the antecedent for each pronoun?

___ Is the antecedent singular or plural? Does the pronoun match?

___ Is the antecedent masculine, feminine, or neuter? Does the pronoun match?

___ Is the antecedent in the first, second, or third person? Does the pronoun match?

A5   Check for correct adjectives and adverbs.

Adjectives and *adverbs* describe or give more information about (*modify*) other words in a sentence. Many adverbs are formed by adding *-ly* to adjectives: *simple, simply; quiet, quietly*. Because adjectives and adverbs resemble

---

Comparison of Irregular Adjectives and Adverbs

	POSITIVE	COMPARATIVE	SUPERLATIVE
ADJECTIVES	good	better	best
	bad	worse	worst
	little	less, littler	least, littlest
	many, some, much	more	most
ADVERBS	well	better	best
	badly	worse	worst
	little	less	least

---

one another, writers sometimes mistakenly use one instead of the other. To edit, find the word that the adjective or adverb modifies. If that word is a noun or pronoun, use an adjective. (An adjective typically describes which or what kind.) If that word is a verb, adjective, or another adverb, use an adverb. (An adverb typically describes how, when, where, or why.)

FAULTY   Kelly ran into the house *quick*.

CORRECT   Kelly ran into the house *quickly*.

FAULTY   Gabriela looked *terribly* after her bout with the flu.

CORRECT   Gabriela looked *terrible* after her bout with the flu.

Adjectives and adverbs that have similar comparative and superlative forms can also cause trouble. Always ask whether you need an adjective or an adverb in the sentence, and then use the correct word.

FAULTY   His scar healed so *good* that it was barely visible.

CORRECT   His scar healed so *well* that it was barely visible.

EDITING CHECKLIST

Adjectives and Adverbs

___ Have you identified which word the adjective or adverb modifies?
___ If the word modified is a noun or pronoun, have you used an adjective?
___ If the word modified is a verb, adjective, or adverb, have you used an adverb?
___ Have you used the correct comparative or superlative form?

A6 **Check for any sentence fragments.**

subject: The part of a sentence that names something—a person, an object, an idea, a situation—about which the predicate makes an assertion: The *king* lives.

A complete sentence is one that has a subject, has a predicate, and can stand on its own. A *sentence fragment* lacks a subject, a predicate, or both, or for some other reason fails to convey a complete thought. It cannot stand on its own as a sentence.

Although they are used frequently in advertising and fiction, fragments are usually ineffective in college writing because they do not communicate coherent thoughts. To edit for fragments, examine each sentence carefully to make sure that it has a subject and a verb and that it expresses a complete thought. To correct a fragment, you can make it into a complete sentence by adding a missing part or by dropping an unnecessary subordinating conjunction. You can also join it to a complete sentence nearby, if that would make more sense.

FAULTY	Roberto has two sisters. Maya and Leeza.
CORRECT	Roberto has two sisters, Maya and Leeza.
FAULTY	The children going to the zoo.
CORRECT	The children were going to the zoo.
CORRECT	The children going to the zoo were caught in a traffic jam.
FAULTY	Last night when we saw Cameron Diaz's most recent movie.
CORRECT	Last night we saw Cameron Diaz's most recent movie.

> **predicate:** The part of a sentence that makes an assertion about the subject involving an action (Birds *fly*), a relationship (Birds *have feathers*), or a state of being (Birds are *warm-blooded*)
>
> **subordinating conjunction:** A word (such as *because, although, if, when*) used to make one clause dependent on, or subordinate to, another: *Unless* you have a key, we are locked out.

EDITING CHECKLIST

Fragments

___ Does the sentence have a subject?

___ Does the sentence have a complete verb?

___ If the sentence contains a subordinate clause, does it contain a clause that is a complete sentence too?

___ If you find a fragment, can you link it to an adjoining sentence, eliminate its subordinating conjunction, or add any missing element?

A7   Check for any comma splices or fused sentences.

A complete sentence has a subject and a predicate and can stand on its own. When two sentences are joined together to form one sentence, each sentence within the larger one is called a *main clause*. However, there are rules for joining main clauses, and when writers fail to follow these rules, they create serious sentence errors — comma splices or fused sentences. A *comma splice* is two main clauses joined with only a comma. A *fused sentence* is two main clauses joined with no punctuation at all.

> **subject:** The part of a sentence that names something — a person, an object, an idea, a situation — about which the predicate makes an assertion: The *king* lives.
>
> **predicate:** The part of a sentence that makes an assertion about the subject involving an action (Birds *fly*), a relationship (Birds *have feathers*), or a state of being (Birds are *warm-blooded*)

COMMA SPLICE	I went to the mall, I bought a new CD by my favorite group.
FUSED SENTENCE	I went to the mall I bought a new CD by my favorite group.

To find comma splices and fused sentences, examine each sentence to be sure it is complete. If it has two main clauses, make sure they are joined

main clause: A group of words that has both a subject and a verb and can stand alone as a complete sentence: *My sister has a friend.*

coordinating conjunction: A one-syllable linking word (*and, but, for, or, nor, so, yet*) that joins elements with equal or near-equal importance: Jack *and* Jill, sink *or* swim

subordinating conjunction: A word (such as *because, although, if, when*) used to make one clause dependent on, or subordinate to, another: *Unless* you have a key, we are locked out.

correctly. If you find a comma splice or fused sentence, correct it in one of these four ways, depending on which makes the best sense:

ADD A PERIOD	I went to the mall. I bought a new CD by my favorite group.
ADD A SEMICOLON	I went to the mall; I bought a new CD by my favorite group.
ADD A COMMA AND A COORDINATING CONJUNCTION	I went to the mall, and I bought a new CD by my favorite group.
ADD A SUBORDINATING CONJUNCTION	I went to the mall where I bought a new CD by my favorite group.

EDITING CHECKLIST

Comma Splices and Fused Sentences

___ Can you make each main clause a separate sentence?

___ Can you link the two main clauses with a comma and a coordinating conjunction?

___ Can you link the two main clauses with a semicolon or, if appropriate, a colon?

___ Can you subordinate one clause to the other?

modifier: A word (such as an adjective or adverb), phrase, or clause that provides more information about other parts of a sentence: Plays *staged by the drama class* are *always successful.*

B *Editing to Ensure Effective Sentences*

B I Check for any misplaced or dangling modifiers.

For a sentence to be clear, the connection between a modifier and the thing it modifies must be obvious. Usually, a modifier should be placed right before or right after the sentence element it modifies. If the modifier is placed too close to some other sentence element, it is a *misplaced modifier.* If there is nothing in the sentence that the modifier can logically modify, it is a *dangling modifier.* Both of these errors cause confusion for readers—and they sometimes create unintentionally humorous images. As you edit, be sure that a modifier is placed directly before or after the word modified and that the connection between the two is clear.

MISPLACED	George found some leftover chicken when he visited in the refrigerator.
CORRECT	George found some leftover chicken in the refrigerator when he visited.
	[In the faulty sentence, *in the refrigerator* seems to modify George's visit. Obviously the chicken is in the refrigerator, not George.]

DANGLING   Looking out the window, the clouds were beautiful.

CORRECT   Looking out the window, I saw that the clouds were beautiful.

CORRECT   When I looked out the window, the clouds were beautiful.

[In the faulty sentence, *looking out the window* should modify *I*, but *I* is not in the sentence. The modifier is left without anything logical to modify — a dangling modifier. To correct this, the writer has to edit so that *I* is in the sentence.]

EDITING CHECKLIST

Misplaced and Dangling Modifiers

—— What is each modifier meant to modify? Is the modifier as close as possible to that sentence element? Is any misreading possible?

—— If a modifier is misplaced, can you move it to clarify the meaning?

—— What noun or pronoun is a dangling modifier meant to modify? Can you make that word or phrase the subject of the main clause? Or can you turn the dangling modifier into a clause that includes the missing noun or pronoun?

B2   Check for parallel structure.

A series of words, phrases, clauses, or sentences with the same grammatical form are said to be *parallel.* Using parallel form for elements that are parallel in meaning or function helps readers grasp the meaning of a sentence more easily. A lack of parallelism can confuse readers: at the very least, it will distract and annoy them.

To use parallelism, put nouns with nouns, verbs with verbs, and phrases with phrases. Parallelism is particularly important in a series, with correlative conjunctions, and in comparisons using *than* or *as.*

> **correlative conjunction:** A pair of linking words (such as *either/or, not only/but also*) that appear separately but work together to join elements of a sentence: *Neither* his friends *nor* hers like pizza.

FAULTY   I like to go to Estes Park for skiing, ice skating, and to meet interesting people.

CORRECT   I like to go to Estes Park to ski, to ice skate, and to meet interesting people.

FAULTY   The proposal is neither practical, nor is it innovative.

CORRECT   The proposal is neither practical nor innovative.

FAULTY   A parent should have a few firm rules rather than having many flimsy ones.

CORRECT   A parent should have a few firm rules rather than many flimsy ones.

Take special care to reinforce parallel structures by repeating articles, conjunctions, prepositions, or lead-in words as needed.

AWKWARD   His dream was that he would never have to give up his routine enjoyments but he would still find time to explore new frontiers.

PARALLEL   His dream was that he would never have to give up his routine enjoyments but *that* he would still find time to explore new frontiers.

EDITING CHECKLIST

Parallel Structure

___ Are all the elements in a series in the same grammatical form?
___ Are the elements in a comparison parallel in form?
___ Are the articles, conjunctions, or prepositions between elements repeated rather than mixed or omitted?
___ Are lead-in words repeated as needed?

C *Editing for Common Punctuation Problems*

C1 Check for correct use of commas.

The *comma* is a punctuation mark indicating a pause. By setting some words apart from others, commas help clarify relationships; they prevent the words on the page and the ideas they represent from becoming a meaningless jumble. Here are some of the most important conventional uses of commas.

1. Use a comma before a coordinating conjunction (*and, but, for, or, so, yet, nor*) joining two main clauses in a compound sentence.

   The discussion was brief, *so* the meeting was adjourned early.

2. Use a comma after an introductory word or word group unless it is short and cannot be misread.

   After the war, the North's economy developed rapidly.

3. Use commas to separate the items in a series of three or more items.

   The chief advantages will be *speed, durability,* and *longevity.*

4. Use commas to set off a modifying clause or phrase if it is nonrestrictive — that is, if it can be taken out of the sentence without significantly changing the meaning of the sentence.

   Good childcare, *which is difficult to find,* should be provided by the employer.

   Good childcare *that is reliable and inexpensive* is the right of every employee.

5. Use commas to set off an appositive, an expression that comes directly after a noun or pronoun and renames it.

   Sheri, *my sister,* has a new job as an events coordinator.

appositive: A word or group of words that adds information about a subject or object by identifying it in a different way: my dog *Rover,* Hal's brother *Fred*

6. Use commas to set off parenthetical expressions, conjunctive adverbs, and other interrupters.

The proposal from the mayor's commission, however, will not be feasible.

EDITING CHECKLIST

Commas

___ Have you added a comma between two main clauses joined by a coordinating conjunction?

___ Have you added commas needed after introductory words or word groups?

___ Have you separated items in a series with commas?

___ Have you avoided putting commas before the first item in a series or after the last?

___ Have you used commas before and after each nonrestrictive phrase or clause?

___ Have you avoided using commas around a restrictive word, phrase, or clause?

___ Have you used commas to set off appositives, parenthetical expressions, conjunctive adverbs, and other interrupters?

parenthetical expression: An aside to readers or a transitional expression such as *for example* or *in contrast*

conjunctive adverb: A linking word that can connect independent clauses and show a relationship between two ideas: Armando is a serious student; *therefore*, he studies every day.

C2   Check for correct use of apostrophes.

An *apostrophe* is a punctuation mark that either shows possession (*Sylvia's*) or indicates that one or more letters have intentionally been left out to form a contraction (*didn't*). Because apostrophes are easy to overlook, writers often omit a necessary apostrophe, use one where it is not needed, or put the apostrophe in the wrong place. Remember that an apostrophe is never used to create the possessive form of a pronoun; use the possessive pronoun form instead.

FAULTY	*Mikes* car was totaled in the accident.
CORRECT	*Mike's* car was totaled in the accident.
FAULTY	The principles of the *womens'* liberation movement are still controversial to some people.
CORRECT	The principles of the *women's* liberation movement are still controversial to some people.
FAULTY	The dog wagged *it's* tail happily.
CORRECT	The dog wagged *its* tail happily.
FAULTY	*Its* raining.
CORRECT	*It's* raining.
FAULTY	Che *did'nt* want to stay at home and study.
CORRECT	Che *didn't* want to stay at home and study.

Possessive Personal Pronouns at a Glance

PERSONAL PRONOUN	POSSESSIVE CASE
I	my, mine
you	your, yours (*not* your's)
he	his
she	her, hers (*not* her's)
it	its (*not* it's)
we	our, ours (*not* our's)
they	their, theirs (*not* their's)
who	whose (*not* who's)

EDITING CHECKLIST

Apostrophes

___ Have you used an apostrophe to show that letters have been left out in a contraction?

___ Have you used an apostrophe to create the possessive form of a noun?

___ Have you used the possessive case — rather than an apostrophe — to show that a pronoun is possessive?

___ Have you used *it's* correctly (to mean *it is*)?

C3 **Check for correct punctuation of quotations.**

When you quote the exact words of a person you have interviewed or a source you have read, make sure that you enclose those words in quotation marks.

> Derek is straightforward when asked about how his work is received in the local community: "My work is outside the mainstream. Because it's controversial, it's not easy for me to get exposure."

If your source is quoting someone else (a quotation within a quotation), put your subject's words in quotation marks and the words he or she is quoting in single quotation marks. Always put commas and periods inside the quotation marks; put semicolons and colons outside.

Substitute an ellipsis mark (. . .) — three spaced dots — for any words you have omitted from the middle of a direct quotation. If you are following MLA style, place the ellipsis mark inside brackets ([. . .]) to show that you, not the original writer, have added it. If the ellipsis mark comes at the end of a sentence, add another period to conclude the sentence. You don't need an ellipsis mark to show the beginning or ending of a quotation that is clearly incomplete.

```
"The importance of what women athletes wear can't be
underestimated," Rounds claims. "Beach volleyball, which
is played [. . .] by bikini-clad women, rates network
coverage" (44).
```

Common errors in punctuating quotations include leaving out necessary punctuation marks or putting them in the incorrect place or sequence.

FAULTY   In the comic book *The Uncanny X-Men*, Magneto championed
            his fellow mutants, "people slaughtered wholesale for no more
            reason than" . . . "the presence in their DNA of an extra special
            gene".

CORRECT   In the comic book *The Uncanny X-Men*, Magneto championed
            his fellow mutants, "people slaughtered wholesale for no more
            reason than [. . .] the presence in their DNA of an extra special
            gene."

EDITING CHECKLIST

Punctuation with Quotations

___ Are the exact words quoted from your source enclosed in quotation marks?

___ Are commas and periods placed inside closing quotation marks?

___ Are colons and semicolons placed outside closing quotation marks?

___ Have you used an ellipsis mark (and brackets in MLA style) to show where
any words are omitted from the middle of a quotation?

D Editing for Common Mechanics Problems

D1 Check for correct use of capital letters.

Capital letters are used in three general situations: to begin a new sentence;
to begin names of specific peoples, places, dates, and things (proper nouns);
and to begin important words in titles. Writers sometimes use capital letters
where they are not needed, such as for emphasis, or fail to use capital letters
where they are needed.

FAULTY   During my Sophomore year in College, I took World Literature,
            Biology, History, Psychology, and French — courses required for a
            Humanities Major.

CORRECT   During my sophomore year in college, I took world literature, bi-
            ology, history, psychology, and French — courses required for a
            humanities major.

EDITING CHECKLIST

Capitalization

___ Have you used a capital letter at the beginning of each complete sentence, including sentences that are quoted?

___ Have you used capital letters for proper nouns and pronouns?

___ Have you avoided using capital letters for emphasis?

___ Have you used a capital letter for each important word in a title, including the first word and the last word?

Capitalization at a Glance

Capitalize the following:

THE FIRST LETTER OF A SENTENCE, INCLUDING A QUOTED SENTENCE
She called out, "Come in! The water's not cold."

PROPER NAMES AND ADJECTIVES MADE FROM THEM
Marie Curie   Cranberry Island
Smithsonian Institution   a Freudian reading

RANK OR TITLE BEFORE A PROPER NAME
Ms. Olson   Professor Santocolon

FAMILY RELATIONSHIP ONLY WHEN IT SUBSTITUTES FOR OR IS PART OF A PROPER NAME
Grandma Jones   Father Time

RELIGIONS, THEIR FOLLOWERS, AND DEITIES
Islam   Orthodox Jew   Buddha

PLACES, REGIONS, AND GEOGRAPHIC FEATURES
Palo Alto   the Berkshire Mountains

DAYS OF THE WEEK, MONTHS, AND HOLIDAYS
Wednesday   July   Labor Day

HISTORICAL EVENTS, PERIODS, AND DOCUMENTS
the Boston Tea Party   the Middle Ages   the Constitution

SCHOOLS, COLLEGES, UNIVERSITIES, AND SPECIFIC COURSES
Temple University   Introduction to Clinical Psychology

FIRST, LAST, AND MAIN WORDS IN TITLES OF PAPERS, BOOKS, ARTICLES, WORKS OF ART, TELEVISION SHOWS, POEMS, AND PERFORMANCES
The Decline and Fall of the Roman Empire

D2 Check spelling.

Misspelled words are difficult to spot in your own writing. You usually see what you think you wrote, and often pronunciation or faulty memory may interfere with correct spelling. When you proofread for spelling, check especially for words that sound alike but are spelled differently (*accept* and *except*, for example), words that are spelled differently than they are pronounced, words that do not follow the basic rules for spelling English words (*judgment*, for example), and words that you habitually confuse and misspell.

For a list of commonly confused words, see p. A-20. For a list of commonly misspelled words, see pp. A-21–A-23.

EDITING CHECKLIST

Spelling

—— Have you checked for the words you habitually misspell?

—— Have you checked for commonly confused or misspelled words?

—— Are you familiar with the standard spelling rules, including their exceptions?

—— Have you checked a dictionary for any words you are unsure about?

WRITING WITH A COMPUTER

If you know which words you habitually misspell, you can use your word processor's Search or Find functions to locate all instances and check their spelling. Consider keeping track of misspelled words in your papers for a few weeks so you can take advantage of this feature to simplify your editing.

Spell checkers offer a handy alternative to the dictionary, but you need to be aware of their limitations. A spell checker compares the words in your text with the words listed in its dictionary, and it highlights words that do not appear there. (The size of computer spelling dictionaries varies greatly, but most contain fewer entries than a typical college-level dictionary in book form.) A spell checker cannot help you spell words that its dictionary does not contain, including most proper nouns. Spell checkers ignore one-letter words; for example, they will not flag a typographical error such as *s truck* for *a truck*. Nor will they highlight words that are misspelled as different words, such as *except* for *accept, to* for *too*, or *own* for *won*. Always check the spelling in your text by eye *after* you've used your spell checker.

Grammar checkers may note some commonly confused words, but they often do this even when you have used the correct form. Use a dictionary to decide whether to accept the grammar checker's suggestion.

COMMONLY CONFUSED HOMONYMS

accept (v., receive willingly); **except** (prep., other than)

Mimi could *accept* all of Lefty's gifts *except* his ring.

affect (v., influence); **effect** (n., result)

If the new rules *affect* us, what will be their *effect?*

allusion (n., reference); **illusion** (n., fantasy)

Any *allusion* to Norman's mother may revive his *illusion* that she is up-stairs, alive, in her rocking chair.

capital (adj., uppercase; n., seat of government); **capitol** (n., government building)

The *Capitol* building in our nation's *capital* is spelled with a *capital C.*

cite (v., refer to); **sight** (n., vision or tourist attraction); **site** (n., place)

Did you *cite* Mother as your authority on which *sites* feature the most interesting *sights?*

complement (v., complete; n., counterpart); **compliment** (v. or n., praise)

For Lee to say that Sheila's beauty *complements* her intelligence may or may not be a *compliment.*

desert (v., abandon); **dessert** (n., end-of-meal sweet)

Don't *desert* us by leaving before *dessert.*

elicit (v., bring out); **illicit** (adj., illegal)

By going undercover, Sonny should *elicit* some offers of *illicit* drugs.

formally (adv., officially); **formerly** (adv., in the past)

Jane and John Doe-Smith, *formerly* Jane Doe and John Smith, sent cards *formally* announcing their marriage.

led (v., past tense of *lead*); **lead** (n., a metal)

Gil's heart was heavy as *lead* when he *led* the mourners to the grave.

principal (n. or adj., chief); **principle** (n., rule or standard)

The *principal* problem is convincing the media that our school *principal* is a person of high *principles.*

stationary (adj., motionless); **stationery** (n., writing paper)

Hubert's *stationery* shop stood *stationary* until a flood swept it down the river.

their (pron., belonging to them); **there** (adv., in that place); **they're** (contraction of *they are*)

Sue said *they're* going over *there* to visit *their* aunt.

to (prep., toward); **too** (adv., also or excessively); **two** (n. or adj., numeral: one more than one)

Let's not take *two* cars to town — that's *too* many unless Lucille and Harry are coming *too.*

who's (contraction of *who is*); **whose** (pron., belonging to whom)

Who's going to tell me *whose* dog this is?

your (pron., belonging to you); **you're** (contraction of *you are*)

You're not getting *your* own way this time!

COMMONLY MISSPELLED WORDS

absence
academic
acceptable
accessible
accidentally
accommodate
achievement
acknowledgment
acquaintance
acquire
address
advertisement
advice
advise
aggravate
aggressive
aging
allege
all right
all together (all in
    one group)
a lot
already
although
altogether (entirely)
amateur
analysis
analyze
answer
anxiety
appearance
appetite
appreciate
appropriate
arctic
argument
ascent
assassinate
assistance
association
athlete
athletics
attendance
audience
average
awkward
basically
beginning

believe
beneficial
benefited
breath (noun)
breathe (verb)
bureaucracy
business
calendar
careful
casualties
category
cemetery
certain
changeable
changing
characteristic
chief
choose (present tense)
chose (past tense)
climbed
column
coming
commitment
committed
comparative
competition
conceive
condemn
congratulate
conscience
conscientious
conscious
consistent
controlled
criticism
criticize
curiosity
curious
deceive
decision
defendant
deficient
definite
dependent
descendant
describe
description
desirable

despair
desperate
develop
development
device (noun)
devise (verb)
diary
difference
dilemma
dining
disappear
disappoint
disastrous
discipline
discussion
disease
dissatisfied
divide
doesn't
dominant
don't
drunkenness
efficiency
eighth
either
embarrass
entirety
environment
equipped
especially
exaggerate
exceed
excel
excellence
exercise
exhaust
existence
experience
explanation
extremely
familiar
fascinate
February
fiery
financial
foreign
foresee
forth

(continued)

COMMONLY MISSPELLED WORDS *(continued)*

forty
forward
fourth (number four)
frantically
fraternities
friend
fulfill
gaiety
genealogy
generally
genuine
government
grammar
grief
guarantee
guard
guidance
harass
height
heroes
herring
humorous
illiterate
illogical
imitation
immediately
incredible
indefinite
independence
indispensable
infinite
influential
intelligence
intentionally
interest
interpret
interrupt
irrelevant
irresistible
irritable
island
its (possessive)
it's (it is, it has)
jealousy
judgment
knowledge
laboratory
led (past tense of *lead*)
library

license
lightning
literature
loneliness
loose (adjective)
lose (verb)
lying
magazine
maintenance
marriage
mathematics
medicine
miniature
mischievous
misspell
muscle
mysterious
necessary
neither
niece
ninety
ninth
noticeable
notorious
nuclear
nucleus
numerous
obstacle
occasionally
occur
occurrence
official
omission
omitted
opinion
opportunity
originally
outrageous
paid
pamphlet
panicky
parallel
particularly
pastime
peaceable
perceive
performance
permanent
permissible

persistence
personnel
persuade
physical
playwright
possession
possibly
practically
precede
predominant
preferred
prejudice
prevalent
privilege
probably
procedure
proceed
professor
prominent
pronounce
pronunciation
pursue
quantity
quiet
quite
quizzes
realize
rebelled
recede
receipt
receive
recipe
recommend
reference
referring
regrettable
relevance
relief
relieve
religious
remembrance
reminisce
reminiscence
repetition
representative
resistance
restaurant
review
rhythm

ridiculous	supersede	unnoticed
roommate	suppress	until
sacrifice	surprise	useful
safety	suspicious	usually
scarcely	technical	valuable
schedule	technique	vengeance
secretary	temperature	vicious
seize	tendency	view
separate	therefore	villain
siege	thorough	warrant
similar	thoroughbred	weather
sincerely	though	Wednesday
sophomore	thought	weird
source	throughout	whether
specifically	tragedy	who's (who is)
sponsor	transferred	whose (possessive
strategy	traveling	of *who*)
strength	truly	withhold
stretch	twelfth	woman
succeed	tyranny	women
successful	unanimous	
suddenness	unnecessary	

E *Editing for Common Format Problems*

EI Check for correct manuscript form.

In case you have received no particular instructions for the form of your paper, here are some general, all-purpose specifications.

For more on document design, see Ch. 21.

GENERAL MANUSCRIPT STYLE FOR COLLEGE ESSAYS, ARTICLES, AND REPORTS

1. If you use a word processor, pick a conventional, easy-to-read type-face such as Courier, Times New Roman, Helvetica, or Palatino. Make sure you have a fresh cartridge in your printer. If you handwrite your paper, make sure your handwriting is legible.

2. Print in black ink if you use a computer. Use dark blue or black ink if you write by hand.

3. Write or print on just one side of standard letter-size bond paper ($8\frac{1}{2}$ inches by 11 inches). If you handwrite your paper, use $8\frac{1}{2}$-by-11-inch paper with smooth edges (not torn from a spiral-bound notebook).

4. For a paper without a separate title page, place your name, your in-structor's name, the number and section of the course, and the date in the

preposition: A transitional word (such as *in, on, at, of,* or *from*) that leads into a phrase

coordinating conjunction: A one-syllable linking word (*and, but, for, or, nor, so, yet*)

article: The word *a, an,* or *the*

upper left or right corner of the first page, each item on a new line. (Ask whether your instructor has a preference for which side.) Double-space and center your title. Don't underline the title, don't put it in quotation marks or use all capital letters, and don't put a period after it. Capitalize the first and last words, the first word after a colon or semicolon, and all other words except prepositions, coordinating conjunctions, and articles. Double-space between the title and the first line of your text. (Most instructors do not require a title page for short college papers. If your instructor does request one but doesn't give you any guidelines, see number 1 under Additional Suggestions for Research Papers, below.)

5. Number your pages consecutively, including the first page. For a paper of two or more pages, use a running header — that is, put your last name in the upper right corner of each sheet along with the page number. Do not type the word *page* or the letter *p* before the number, and do not follow the number with a period or parenthesis.

6. Leave ample margins — at least an inch — left and right, top and bottom.

7. If you use a word processor, double-space your manuscript; if you handwrite, use wide-ruled paper or skip every other line.

8. Indent each new paragraph five spaces or one-half inch.

For more about citing sources, see E2.

9. Long quotations should be double-spaced like the rest of your paper but indented from the left margin — ten spaces (one inch) if you're following MLA (Modern Language Association) guidelines, five (one-half inch) if you're using APA (American Psychological Association) guidelines. Put the source citation in parentheses immediately after the final punctuation mark of the block quotation.

10. Label all illustrations, and made sure they are bound securely to the paper.

11. Staple the paper in the top left corner, or use a paper clip as MLA advises. Don't use any other method to secure the pages unless one is recommended by your instructor.

12. For safety's sake and peace of mind, make a copy of your paper, and back up your file.

ADDITIONAL SUGGESTIONS FOR RESEARCH PAPERS

For research papers, the format is the same as recommended in the previous section, with the following additional specifications.

1. The MLA guidelines do not recommend a title page. If your instructor wants one, type the title of your paper, centered and double-spaced, about a third of the way down the page. Then go down two to four more lines and type your name, then the instructor's name, the number and

section of the course, and the date, each on a separate line and double-spaced.

2. Do not number your title page; number your outline, if you submit one with your paper, with small roman numerals (i, ii, iii, and so on). Number consecutively all subsequent pages in the essay, including your "Works Cited" or "References" pages, using arabic numerals (1, 2, 3, and so on) in the upper right corner of the page.

3. Double-space your works cited or references list, if you have one.

HOW TO MAKE A CORRECTION

Before you produce your final copy, make any large changes in your draft, edit and proofread carefully, and run your spell checker. When you give your paper a last once-over, however, don't be afraid to make small corrections in pen. In making such corrections, you may find it handy to use certain symbols used by printers and proofreaders.

A transposition mark (⌐⌐) reverses the positions of two words or two letters:

```
The nearby star Tau Ceti closely resmebles our sun.
```

Close-up marks (⌒) bring together the parts of a word accidentally split. A separation mark (|) inserts a space where one is needed:

```
The nearby star Tau Ceti closely re sembles our|sun.
```

To delete a letter or a punctuation mark, draw a line with a curlicue through it:

```
The nearby star Tau Ceti closely ressembles our sun.
```

When you insert a word or letter, use a caret (∧) to indicate where the insertion belongs:

```
                                      s
The nearby star Tau Ceti closely reembles our sun.
                                    ∧
```

The symbol ¶ before a word or a line means "start a new paragraph":

```
But lately, astronomers have slackened their efforts to

study dark nebulae.¶That other solar systems may support

life as we know it makes for still another fascinating

speculation.
```

To make a letter lowercase, draw a slanted line through it. To make a letter uppercase, put three short lines under it:

```
i read it for my History class.
```

You can always cross out a word neatly, with a single horizontal line, and write a better one over it.

```
                              closely
    The nearby star Tau Ceti somewhat resembles our sun.
```

Finally, if a page has many handwritten corrections on it, print or write it over again.

E2   Check for correct documentation style.

When you paraphrase or quote directly from a magazine article, book, literary work, Web site, or other resource, you need to cite, or identify, your source. Correctly and systematically documenting your sources indicates your intellectual honesty by acknowledging your debt to other writers. It also helps readers who want to find out more about your assertions or to look at your sources.

The Modern Language Association (MLA) recommends a documentation style often required in papers for English classes. When you use MLA style, you briefly identify each source in your essay by putting the author's last name and the page number (or line number for poetry) in parentheses after each direct quotation or paraphrase.

```
When "The Lottery" begins, the reader thinks of the
"great pile of stones" (Jackson 195) as children's
entertainment.
```

If you identify the writer in your own sentence, you do not need to repeat the name in parentheses.

```
The speaker in Robinson's poem describes Richard Cory as
"richer than a king" (line 9), an attractive man who
"fluttered pulses when he said, / 'Good-morning.'" (7-8).
```

If you use only one source in your paper, identify it at the beginning of your essay. Then just give page or line numbers in parentheses after each quotation or paraphrase.

On a page at the end of your paper, fully identify the author, title, and publication information for all of the sources you have used in an alphabetical list called "Works Cited." The following examples illustrate the MLA formats for common types of sources, showing the sequence and punctuation for presenting this information. (Some sources require more complicated citations. For these, consult a research guide or the current *MLA Handbook for Writers of Research Papers*.)

BOOK
    Period   Title of book   Period   Publisher (shortened name)   Comma

Tan, Amy. The Joy Luck Club. New York: Ballantine, 1989. —— Period

Author's name   Underlined   City of publication   Colon   Year of publication

ESSAY, STORY, OR POEM IN A BOOK   Title of essay

Talvi, Silja J. A. "Marked for Life: Tattoos and the
        Redefinition of Self." Body Outlaws. Ed. Ophira — Editor's name
        Edut. Seattle: Seal, 2000. 211-18. —— Page numbers of the selection

Title of book

MAGAZINE ARTICLE   Title of article

Lipsky, David. "War and Peace: A Year in the Life of the
        New West Point." Rolling Stone 25 Nov. 1999: 73-85.

Title of magazine   Date of publication

JOURNAL ARTICLE   Title of journal article

Zhao, Jensen J. "The Chinese Approach to International
        Business Negotiation." Journal of Business Communi-
        cation 37 (2000): 209-37.   Title of journal

Volume number   Page numbers of the article

WEB SITE   Site title (author unknown)   Date of publication or latest update

Pathology Mission Statement. 27 Sept. 1999. U. of
        Massachusetts Medical School. 18 July. 2001. — Date of access
Name of   <http://www.umassmed.edu/pathology/>.
sponsoring
organization   URL

Appendix

A Glossary of Troublemakers

For advice on spelling, see 33. For advice on wordiness, see Ch. 20.

Usage refers to the way in which writers customarily use certain words and phrases, including matters of accepted practice or convention. This glossary lists words and phrases whose usage may trouble writers. Not every possible problem is listed — only some that frequently puzzle students. Look over this brief list; refer to it when you don't remember the preferred usage.

a, an   Use *an* only before a word beginning with a vowel sound. "*An* asp can eat *an* egg *an* hour." (Note that some words, such as *hour* and *honest*, open with a vowel sound even though spelled with an *h.*)

above   Using *above* or *below* to refer back or forward in an essay is awkward and may not be accurate. Less awkward alternatives: "the *preceding* argument," "in the *following* discussion," "on the *next* page."

accept, except   *Accept* is a verb meaning "to receive willingly"; *except* is usually a preposition meaning "not including." "This childcare center *accepts* all children *except* those under two." Sometimes *except* is a verb, meaning "to exempt." "The entry fee *excepts* children under twelve."

advice, advise   *Advice* is a noun, *advise* a verb. When someone *advises* you, you receive *advice.*

affect, effect   Most of the time, the verb *affect* means "to act on" or "to influence." "Too much beer can *affect* your speech." *Affect* can also mean "to put on airs." "He *affected* an Oxford accent." *Effect*, a noun, means "a result": "Too much beer has a numbing *effect.*" But *effect* is also a verb, meaning "to bring about." "Pride *effected* his downfall."

agree to, agree with, agree on   *Agree to* means "to consent to"; *agree with*, "to be in accord." "I *agreed to* attend the New Age lecture, but I didn't *agree with* the speaker's views." *Agree on* means "to come to or have an understanding about." "Chuck and I finally *agreed on* a compromise: the children would go to camp but not overnight."

ain't   Don't use *ain't* in writing; it is nonstandard English for *am not, is not (isn't)*, and *are not (aren't)*.

a lot   Many people mistakenly write the colloquial expression *a lot* as one word: *alot*. Use *a lot* if you must, but in writing *much* or *a large amount* is preferable. See also *lots, lots of, a lot of.*

already, all ready   *Already* means "by now"; *all ready* means "set to go." "At last our picnic was *all ready*, but *already* it was night."

altogether, all together   *Altogether* means "entirely." "He is *altogether* mistaken." *All together* means "in unison" or "assembled." "Now *all together* — heave!" "Inspector Trent gathered the suspects *all together* in the drawing room."

among, between   *Between* refers to two persons or things; *among*, to more than two. "Some disagreement *between* the two countries was inevitable. Still, there was general harmony *among* the five nations represented at the conference."

amount, number   Use *amount* to refer to quantities that cannot be counted or to bulk; use *number* to refer to countable, separate items. "The *number* of people you want to serve determines the *amount* of ice cream you'll need."

an, a   See *a, an.*

and/or   Usually use either *and* or *or* alone. "Tim *and* Elaine will come to the party." "Tim *or* Elaine will come to the party." If you mean three distinct options, write, "Tim *or* Elaine, *or both*, will come to the party, depending on whether they can find a babysitter."

ante-, anti-   The prefix *ante-* means "preceding." *Antebellum* means "before the Civil War." *Anti-* most often means "opposing": *antidepressant*. It needs a hyphen in front of *i* (*anti-inflationary*) or in front of a capital letter (*anti-Marxist*).

anybody, any body   When *anybody* is used as an indefinite pronoun, write it as one word: "*Anybody* in his or her right mind abhors murder." Because *anybody* is singular, do not write "Anybody in *their* right mind." (See 7d.) *Any body*, written as two words, is the adjective *any* modifying the noun *body*. "Name *any body* of water in Australia."

anyone, any one   *Anyone* is an indefinite pronoun written as one word. "Does *anyone* want dessert?" The phrase *any one* consists of the pronoun *one* modified by the adjective *any* and is used to single out something in a group: "Pick *any one* of the pies — they're all good."

anyplace   *Anyplace* is colloquial for *anywhere* and should not be used in formal writing.

anyways, anywheres   These nonstandard forms of *anyway* and *anywhere* should not be used in writing.

as   Sometimes using the subordinating conjunction *as* can make a sentence ambiguous. "*As* we were climbing the mountain, we put on heavy sweaters." Does *as* here mean "because" or "while"? Whenever using *as* would be confusing, use a more specific term instead, such as *because* or *while*.

as, like   Use *as, as if*, or *as though* rather than *like* to introduce clauses of comparison. "Dan's compositions are tuneful, *as* [not *like*] music ought to be." "Jeffrey behaves *as if* [not *like*] he were ill." *Like*, because it is a preposition, can introduce a phrase but not a clause. "My brother looks *like* me." "Henrietta runs *like* a duck."

as to   Usually this expression sounds stilted. Use *about* instead. "He complained *about* [not *as to*] the cockroaches."

at   See *where at, where to*.

bad, badly   *Bad* is an adjective; *badly* is an adverb. Following linking verbs (*be, appear, become, grow, seem, prove*) and verbs of the senses (*feel, look, smell, sound, taste*), use the adjective form. "I feel *bad* that

we missed the plane." "The egg smells *bad*." (See 8a, 8b.) The adverb form is used to modify a verb or an adjective. "The Tartans played so *badly* they lost to the last-place team whose *badly* needed victory saved them from elimination."

being as, being that   Instead of "*being as* I was ignorant of the facts, I kept still," write "*Because* I was ignorant" or "*Not knowing* the facts."

beside, besides   *Beside* is a preposition meaning "next to." "Sheldon enjoyed sitting *beside* the guest of honor." *Besides* is an adverb meaning "in addition." "*Besides*, he has a sense of humor." *Besides* is also a preposition meaning "other than." "Something *besides* shyness caused his embarrassment."

between, among   See *among, between*.

between you and I   The preposition *between* always takes the objective case. "Between *you* and *me* [not *I*], Joe's story sounds suspicious." "Between *us* [not *we*], what's going on between Chris and *her* [not *she*] is unfathomable."

but that, but what   "I don't know *but what* [or *but that*] you're right" is a wordy, imprecise way of saying "Maybe you're right" or "I believe you're right."

can, may   Use *can* to indicate ability. "Jake *can* bench-press 650 pounds." *May* involves permission. "*May* I bench-press today?" "You *may*, if you *can*."

capital, capitol   A *capital* is a city that is the center of government for a state or country. *Capital* can also mean "wealth." A *capitol* is a building in which legislators meet. "Who knows what the *capital* of Finland is?" "The renovated *capitol* is a popular tourist attraction."

center around   Say "Class discussion *centered on* [or *revolved around*] her paper." In this sense, the verb *center* means "to have one main concern" — the way a circle has a central point. (Thus, to say a discussion centers *around* anything is a murky metaphor.)

cite, sight, site   *Cite*, a verb, means "to quote from or refer to." *Sight* as a verb means "to see or glimpse"; as a noun it means "a view, a spectacle." "When the police officer *sighted* my terrier running across the playground, she *cited* the leash laws." *Site*, a noun, means "location." "Standing and weeping at the *site* of his childhood home, he was a pitiful *sight*."

climatic, climactic *Climatic*, from *climate*, refers to meteorological conditions. Saying "climatic conditions," however, is wordy — you can usually substitute "the climate": "*Climatic* conditions are [or "The *climate* is"] changing because of the hole in the ozone layer." *Climactic*, from *climax*, refers to the culmination of a progression of events. "In the *climactic* scene the hero drives his car off the pier."

compare, contrast *Compare* has two main meanings. The first, "to liken or represent as similar," is followed by *to*. "She *compared* her room *to* a jail cell." In its second meaning, *compare* means "to analyze for similarities and differences" and is generally followed by *with*. "The speaker *compared* the American educational system *with* the Japanese system."

Contrast also has two main meanings. As a transitive verb, taking an object, it means "to analyze to emphasize differences" and is generally followed by *with*. "The speaker *contrasted* the social emphasis of the Japanese primary grades *with* the academic emphasis of ours." As an intransitive verb, *contrast* means "to exhibit differences when compared." "The sour taste of the milk *contrasted* sharply *with* its usual fresh flavor."

complement, compliment *Compliment* is a verb meaning "to praise" or a noun meaning "praise." "The professor *complimented* Sarah on her perceptiveness." *Complement* is a verb meaning "to complete or reinforce." "Jennifer's experiences as an intern *complemented* what she learned in her education class."

could care less This is nonstandard English for *couldn't care less* and should not be used in writing. "The cat *couldn't* [not *could*] *care less* about which brand of cat food you buy."

could of *Could of* is colloquial for *could have* and should not be used in writing.

couple of Write "a *couple of* drinks" when you mean two. For more than two, say "a *few* [or *several*] drinks."

criteria, criterion *Criteria* is the plural of *criterion*, which means "a standard or requirement on which a judgment or decision is based." "The main *criteria* for this job are attention to detail and good computer skills."

data *Data* is a plural noun. Write "The data *are*" and "*these* data." The singular form of *data* is *datum* —

rarely used because it sounds musty. Instead, use *fact, figure,* or *statistic*.

different from, different than *Different from* is usually the correct form to use. "How is good poetry *different from* prose?" Use *different than* when a whole clause follows. "Violin lessons with Mr. James were *different than* I had imagined."

don't, doesn't *Don't* is the contraction for *do not*, and *doesn't* is the contraction for *does not*. "They *don't* want to get dressed up for the ceremony." "The cat *doesn't* [not *don't*] like to be combed."

due to *Due* is an adjective and must modify a noun or pronoun; it can't modify a verb or an adjective. Begin a sentence with *due to* and you invite trouble: "*Due to rain*, the game was postponed." Write instead, "*Because of rain*." *Due to* works after the verb *be*. "His fall was *due to* a banana peel." There, *due* modifies the noun *fall*.

due to the fact that A windy expression for *because*.

effect, affect See *affect, effect*.

either Use *either* when referring to one of two things. "Both internships sound great; I'd be happy with *either*." When referring to one of three or more things, use *any one* or *any*. "*Any one* of our four counselors will be able to help you."

et cetera, etc. Sharpen your writing by replacing *et cetera* (or its abbreviation, *etc.*) with exact words. Even translating the Latin expression into English ("and other things") is an improvement, as in "high-jumping, shot-putting, and other field events."

everybody, every body When used as an indefinite pronoun, *everybody* is one word. "Why is *everybody* on the boys' team waving his arms?" Because *everybody* is singular, it is a mistake to write, "Why is *everybody* waving *their* arms?" (See 7d.) *Every body* written as two words refers to separate, individual bodies. "After the massacre, they buried *every body* in *its* [not *their*] own grave."

everyone, every one Used as an indefinite pronoun, *everyone* is one word. "*Everyone* has *his or her* own ideas." Because *everyone* is singular, it is incorrect to write, "*Everyone* has *their* own ideas." (See 7d.) *Every one* written as two words refers to individual, distinct items. "I studied *every one* of the chapters."

except, accept See *accept, except*.

expect In writing, avoid the informal use of *expect* to mean "suppose, assume, or think." "I *suppose* [not *expect*] you're going on the geology field trip."

fact that This is a wordy expression that, nearly always, you can do without. Instead of "*The fact that* he was puny went unnoticed," write, "That he was puny went unnoticed." "Because [not *Because of the fact that*] it snowed, the game was canceled."

farther, further In your writing, use *farther* to refer to literal distance. "Chicago is *farther* from Nome than from New York." When you mean additional degree, time, or quantity, use *further*: "Sally's idea requires *further* discussion."

fewer, less *Less* refers to general quantity or bulk; *fewer* refers to separate, countable items. "Eat *less* pizza." "Salad has *fewer* calories."

field of In a statement such as "He took courses in *the field of* economics," leave out *the field of* and save words.

firstly The recommended usage is *first* (and *second*, not *secondly*; *third*, not *thirdly*; and so on).

former, latter *Former* means "first of two"; *latter*, "second of two." They are an acceptable but heavy-handed pair, often obliging your reader to back-track. Your writing generally will be clearer if you simply name again the persons or things you mean. Instead of writing, "The *former* great artist is the master of the flowing line, while the *latter* is the master of color," write, "Picasso is the master of the flowing line, while Matisse is the master of color."

further, farther See *farther, further*.

get, got *Get* has many meanings, especially in slang and colloquial use. Some, such as the following, are not appropriate in formal writing:

To start, begin: "Let's start [not *get*] painting."

To stir the emotions: "His frequent interruptions finally started annoying [not *getting to*] me."

To harm, punish, or take revenge on: "She's going to take revenge on [not *get*] him." Or better, be even more specific about what you mean. "She's going to spread rumors about him to ruin his reputation."

good, well To modify a verb, use the adverb *well*, not the adjective *good*. "Jan dives *well* [not *good*]." Linking verbs (*be, appear, become, grow, seem, prove*) and verbs of the senses (such as *feel, look, smell, sound, taste*) call for the adjective *good*. "The paint job looks *good*." *Well* is an adjective used only to refer to health. "She looks *well*" means that she seems to be in good health. "She looks *good*" means that her appearance is attractive. (See 8b, 8c.)

hanged, hung Both words are the past tense of the verb *hang*. *Hanged* refers to an execution. "The murderer was *hanged* at dawn." For all other situations, use *hung*. "Jim *hung* his wash on the clothesline to dry."

have got to In formal writing, avoid using the phrase *have got to* to mean "have to" or "must." "I *must* [not *have got to*] phone them right away."

he, she, he or she Using *he* to refer to an indefinite person is considered sexist; so is using *she* with traditionally female occupations or pastimes. However, the phrase *he or she* can seem wordy and awkward. For alternatives, see 18.

herself See *-self, -selves*.

himself See *-self, -selves*.

hopefully *Hopefully* means "with hope." "The children turned *hopefully* toward the door, expecting Santa Claus." In writing, avoid *hopefully* when you mean "it is to be hoped" or "let us hope." "*I hope* [not *Hopefully*] the posse will arrive soon."

if, whether Use *whether*, not *if*, in indirect questions and to introduce alternatives. "Father asked me *whether* [not *if*] I was planning to sleep all morning." "I'm so confused I don't know *whether* [not *if*] it's day or night."

imply, infer *Imply* means "to suggest"; *infer* means "to draw a conclusion." "Maria *implied* that she was too busy to see Tom, but Tom *inferred* that Maria had lost interest in him."

in, into *In* refers to a location or condition; *into* refers to the direction of movement or change. "The hero burst *into* the room and found the heroine *in* another man's arms."

infer, imply See *imply, infer*.

in regards to Write *in regard to*, *regarding*, or *about*.

inside of, outside of As prepositions, *inside* and *outside* do not require *of*. "The students were more interested in events *outside* [not *outside of*] the building than those *inside* [not *inside of*] the classroom." In formal writing, do not use *inside of* to refer to time or *outside of* to mean "except." "I'll finish the assignment *within* [not *inside of*] two hours." "He told no one *except* [not *outside of*] a few friends."

irregardless   *Irregardless* is a double negative. Use *regardless.*

is because   See *reason is because, reason . . . is.*

is when, is where   Using these expressions results in errors in predication. "Obesity *is when* a person is greatly overweight." "Biology *is where* students dissect frogs." *When* refers to a point in time, but *obesity* is not a point in time; *where* refers to a place, but *biology* is not a place. Write instead, "Obesity is the condition of extreme overweight." "Biology is a laboratory course in which students dissect frogs." (See 12c.)

its, it's   *Its* is a possessive pronoun, never in need of an apostrophe. *It's* is a contraction for *it is.* "Every new experience has *its* bad moments. Still, *it's* exciting to explore the unknown." (See 24g.)

it's me, it is I   Although *it's me* is widely used in speech, don't use it in formal writing. Write "It is I," which is grammatically correct. The same applies to other personal pronouns. "It was *he* [not *him*] who started the mutiny." (See 5.)

kind of, sort of, type of   When you use *kind, sort,* or *type* — singular words — make sure that the sentence construction is singular. "That *type* of show *offends* me." "Those *types* of shows *offend* me." In speech, *kind of* and *sort of* are used as qualifiers. "He is *sort of* fat." Avoid them in writing. "He is *rather* [or *somewhat* or *slightly*] fat."

latter, former   See *former, latter.*

lay, lie   The verb *lay,* meaning "to put or place," takes an object. "*Lay* that pistol down." *Lie,* meaning "to rest or recline," does not. "*Lie* on the bed until your headache goes away." Their principal parts are *lay, laid, laid* and *lie, lay, lain.* (See 3f.)

less, fewer   See *fewer, less.*

liable, likely   Use *likely* to mean "plausible" or "having the potential." "Jake is *likely* [not *liable*] to win." Save *liable* for "legally obligated" or "susceptible." "A stunt man is *liable* to injury."

lie, lay   See *lay, lie.*

like, as   See *as, like.*

likely, liable   See *liable, likely.*

literally   Don't sling *literally* around for emphasis. Because it means "strictly according to the meaning of a word (or words)," it will wreck your credibility if you are speaking figuratively. "Professor Gray *literally* flew down the hall" means that Gray traveled on wings. Save *literally* to mean that you're reporting a fact. "Chemical wastes travel on the winds, and the skies *literally* rain poison."

loose, lose   *Loose,* an adjective, most commonly means "not fastened" or "poorly fastened." *Lose,* a verb, means "to misplace" or "to not win." "I have to be careful not to *lose* this button — it's so *loose.*"

lots, lots of, a lot of   Use these expressions only in informal speech. In formal writing, use *many* or *much.* See also *a lot.*

mankind   This term is considered sexist by many people. Use *humanity, humankind, the human race,* or *people* instead.

may, can   See *can, may.*

media, medium   *Media* is the plural of *medium* and most commonly refers to the various forms of public communication. "Some argue that, of all the *media,* television is the worst for children."

might of   *Might of* is colloquial for *might have* and should not be used in writing.

most   Do not use *most* when you mean "almost" or "nearly." "*Almost* [not *Most*] all of the students felt that Professor Chartrand should have received tenure."

must of   *Must of* is colloquial for *must have* and should not be used in writing.

myself   See *-self, -selves.*

not all that   *Not all that* is colloquial for *not very;* do not use it in formal writing. "The movie was *not very* [not *not all that*] exciting."

number, amount   See *amount, number.*

of   See *could of, might of, must of, should of.*

O.K., o.k., okay   In formal writing, do not use any of these expressions. *All right* and *I agree* are possible substitutes.

one   Like a balloon, *one,* meaning "a person," tends to inflate. One *one* can lead to another. "When *one* is in college, *one* learns to make up *one's* mind for *oneself.*" Avoid this pompous usage. Whenever possible, substitute *people* or a more specific plural noun. "When *students* are in college, *they* learn to make up their minds for *themselves*."

ourselves   See *-self, -selves.*

outside of, inside of   See *inside of, outside of.*

percent, per cent, percentage   When you specify a number, write *percent* (also written *per cent*). "Nearly 40 *percent* of the listeners responded to the offer." The only time to use *percentage*, meaning "part," is with an adjective, when you mention no number. "A high *percentage* [or *a large percentage*] of listeners responded." *A large number* or *a large proportion* sounds better yet.

phenomenon, phenomena   *Phenomena* is the plural of *phenomenon*, which means "an observable fact or occurrence." "Of the many mysterious supernatural *phenomena*, clairvoyance is the strangest *phenomenon* of all."

precede, proceed   *Precede* means "to go before or ahead of"; *proceed* means "to go forward." "The fire drill *proceeded* smoothly; the children *preceded* the teachers onto the playground."

principal, principle   *Principal* means "chief," whether used as an adjective or as a noun. "According to the *principal*, the school's *principal* goal will be teaching reading." Referring to money, *principal* means "capital." "Investors in high-risk companies may lose their *principal*." *Principle*, a noun, means *rule* or *standard*. "Let's apply the *principle* of equality in hiring."

proved, proven   Although both forms can be used as past participles, *proved* is recommended. Use *proven* as an adjective. "They had *proved* their skill in match after match." "Try this *proven* cough remedy."

quote, quotation   *Quote* is a verb meaning "to cite, to use the words of." *Quotation* is a noun meaning "something that is quoted." "The *quotation* [not *quote*] next to her yearbook picture fits her perfectly."

raise, rise   *Raise*, meaning "to cause to move upward," is a transitive verb and takes an object. *Rise*, meaning "to move up (on its own)" is intransitive and does not take an object: "I *rose* from my seat and *raised* my arm."

rarely ever   *Rarely* by itself is strong enough. "George *rarely* [not *rarely ever*] eats dinner with his family."

real, really   *Real* is an adjective, *really* an adverb. Do not use *real* to modify a verb or another adjective, and avoid overusing either word. "*The Ambassadors* is a *really* [not *real*] fine novel." Even better: "*The Ambassadors* is a fine novel."

reason is because, reason . . . is   *Reason . . . is* requires a clause beginning with *that*. Using *because* is nonstandard. "The *reason* I can't come *is that* [not *is because*] I have the flu." It is simpler and more direct to write, "I can't come because I have the flu." (See 12d.)

rise   See *raise, rise.*

-self, -selves   Don't use a pronoun ending in *-self* or *-selves* in place of *her, him, me, them, us,* or *you.* "Nobody volunteered but Jim and *me* [not *myself*]." Use the *-self* pronouns to refer back to a noun or another pronoun and to lend emphasis. "*We* did it *ourselves*." "Sarah *herself* is a noted musician."

set, sit   *Set*, meaning "to put or place," is a transitive verb and takes an object. *Sit*, meaning "to be seated," is intransitive and does not take an object. "We were asked to *set* our jewelry and metal objects on the counter and *sit* down." (See 3f.)

shall, will; should, would   The helping verb *shall* formerly was used with first-person pronouns. It is still used to express determination ("We *shall* overcome") or to ask consent ("*Shall* we march?"). Otherwise, *will* is commonly used with all three persons. "I *will* enter medical school in the fall." *Should* is a helping verb that expresses obligation; *would*, a helping verb that expresses a hypothetical condition. "I *should* wash the dishes before I watch TV." "He *would* learn to speak English if you *would* give him a chance."

she, he or she   See *he, she, he or she.*

should of   *Should of* is colloquial for *should have* and should not be used in writing.

sight   See *cite, sight, site.*

since   Sometimes using *since* can make a sentence ambiguous. "*Since* the babysitter left, the children have been watching television." Does *since* here mean "because" or "from the time that"? If using *since* might be confusing, use an unambiguous term (*because, ever since*).

sit   See *set, sit.*

site   See *cite, sight, site.*

sort of See *kind of, sort of, type of.*

stationary, stationery *Stationary,* an adjective, means "fixed, unmoving." "The fireplace remained *stationary* though the wind blew down the house." *Stationery* is paper for letter writing. To spell it right, remember that *letter* also contains *-er.*

suppose to Write *supposed to.* "He was *supposed to* read a novel."

sure *Sure* is an adjective, *surely* an adverb. Do not use *sure* to modify a verb or another adjective. If by *sure* you mean "certainly," write *certainly* or *surely* instead. "He *surely* [not *sure*] makes the Civil War come alive."

than, then *Than* is a conjunction used in comparisons; *then* is an adverb indicating time. "Marlene is brainier *than* her sister." "First crack six eggs; *then* beat them."

that, where See *where, that.*

that, which Which pronoun should open a clause —*that* or *which*? If the clause adds to its sentence an idea that, however interesting, could be left out, then the clause is nonrestrictive. It should begin with *which* and be separated from the rest of the sentence with commas. "The vampire, *which* had been hovering nearby, leaped for Sarah's throat."

If the clause is essential to your meaning, it is restrictive. It should begin with *that* and should not have commas around it. "The vampire *that* Mel brought from Transylvania leaped for Sarah's throat." The clause indicates not just any old vampire but one in particular. (See 21e.)

Don't use *which* to refer vaguely to an entire clause. Instead of "Jack was an expert drummer in high school, *which* won him a college scholarship," write "Jack's skill as a drummer won him . . ." (See 6b.)

that, who, which, whose See *who, which, that, whose.*

themselves See *-self, -selves.*

then, than See *than, then.*

there, their, they're *There* is an adverb indicating place. *Their* is a possessive pronoun. *They're* is a contraction of *they are.* "After playing tennis *there* for three hours, Lamont and Laura went to change *their* clothes because *they're* going out to dinner."

to, too, two *To* is a preposition. *Too* is an adverb meaning "also" or "in excess." *Two* is a number. "Janet wanted to go *too,* but she feared she was *too* sick to travel in the car for *two* days. Instead, she went *to* bed."

toward, towards *Toward* is preferred in the United States, *towards* in Britain.

try and Use *try to.* "I'll *try to* [not *try and*] attend the opening performance of your play."

type of See *kind of, sort of, type of.*

unique Nothing can be *more unique, less unique,* or *very unique. Unique* means "one of a kind." (See 8e.)

use to Write *used to.* "Jeffrey *used to* have a beard, but now he is clean-shaven."

wait for, wait on *Wait for* means "await"; *wait on* means "to serve." "While *waiting for* his friends, George decided to *wait on* one more customer."

well, good See *good, well.*

where, that Although speakers sometimes use *where* instead of *that,* you should not do so in writing. "I heard on the news *that* [not *where*] it got hot enough to fry eggs on car hoods."

where at, where to The colloquial use of *at* or *to* after *where* is redundant. Write "*Where* were you?" not "*Where* were you *at*?" "I know *where* she was rushing [not *rushing to*]."

whether See *if, whether.*

which, that See *that, which.*

who, which, that, whose *Who* refers to people, *which* to things and ideas. "Was it Pogo *who* said, 'We have met the enemy and he is us'?" "The blouse, *which* was lime green, accented her dark skin." *That* refers to things but can also be used for a class of people. "The team *that* increases sales the most will get a bonus." Because *of which* can be cumbersome, use *whose* even to refer to things. "The mountain, *whose* snowy peaks were famous world over, was covered by fog." See also *that, which.*

who, whom *Who* is used as a subject, *whom* as an object. In "*Whom* do I see?" *Whom* is the object of *see.* In "*Who* goes there?" *Who* is the subject of "goes." (See also 5a.)

who's, whose   *Who's* is a contraction for *who is* or *who has.* "*Who's* going with Phil?" *Whose* is a possessive pronoun. "Bill is a conservative politician *whose* ideas are unlikely to change."

whose, who, which, that   See *who, which, that, whose.*

will, shall   See *shall, will; should, would.*

would, should   See *shall, will; should, would.*

would of   *Would of* is colloquial for *would have* and should not be used in writing.

you   *You,* meaning "a person," occurs often in conversation. "When *you* go to college, *you* have to work hard." In writing, use *one* or a specific, preferably plural noun. "When *students* go to college, *they* have to work hard." But see *one* for some cautions. And see 18c.

your, you're   *Your* is a possessive pronoun; *you're* is the contraction for *you are.* "*You're* lying! It was *your* handwriting on the envelope."

yourself, yourselves   See *-self, -selves.*

Appendix

Answers for Lettered Exercises

EXERCISE 1–1 ELIMINATING FRAGMENTS, p. H-9

Suggested revisions:

a. Michael had a beautiful Southern accent, having lived many years in Georgia.
b. Pat and Chris are determined to marry each other, even if their families do not approve.
c. Jack seemed well qualified for a career in the Air Force, except for his tendency to get airsick.
d. Lisa advocated sleeping no more than four hours a night until she started nodding through her classes.
e. Complete Sentences

EXERCISE 2–1 REVISING COMMA SPLICES AND FUSED SENTENCES, p. H-13

Suggested revisions:

a. We followed the scientist down a flight of wet stone steps. At last he stopped before a huge oak door.
We followed the scientist down a flight of wet stone steps, until at last he stopped before a huge oak door.
b. Dr. Frankenstein selected a heavy key; he twisted it in the lock.
Dr. Frankenstein selected a heavy key, which he twisted in the lock.
c. The huge door gave a groan; it swung open on a dimly lighted laboratory.
The huge door gave a groan and swung open on a dimly lighted laboratory.
d. Before us on a dissecting table lay a form with closed eyes. To behold it sent a quick chill down my spine.
Before us on a dissecting table lay a form with closed eyes; beholding it sent a quick chill down my spine.
e. The scientist strode to the table and lifted a white-gloved hand.
The scientist strode to the table; he lifted a white-gloved hand.

EXERCISE 3–1 USING IRREGULAR VERB FORMS, p. H-18

a. In those days, Benjamin wrote all the music, and his sister *sang* all the songs.
b. Correct
c. When the bell *rang*, darkness had already *fallen*.
d. Voters have *chosen* several new representatives, who won't take office until January.
e. Carol threw the ball into the water, and the dog *swam* after it.

EXERCISE 3–2 IDENTIFYING VERB TENSES, p. H-26

a. has been living: present perfect progressive; hacked: simple past; change: simple present **b.** have never appeared: present perfect; never will appear: simple future; asks: simple present **c.** had been: past perfect; pitched: simple past **d.** will have been studying: future perfect progressive; will be taking: future progressive **e.** was running: past progressive; strolled: simple past

EXERCISE 3–4 USING THE CORRECT MOOD OF VERBS, p. H-30

a. Dr. Belanger recommended that Juan *floss* his teeth every day. (Incorrect *flosses*, indicative; correct *floss*, subjunctive)
b. If I *were* you, I would have done the same thing. (Incorrect *was*, indicative; correct *were*, subjunctive)
c. Tradition demands that Daegun *show* respect for his elders. (Incorrect *shows*, indicative; correct *show*, subjunctive)
d. Please *attend* the training lesson if you plan to skydive later today. (Incorrect *attends*, indicative; correct *attend*, imperative)

EXERCISE 4–1 MAKING SUBJECTS AND VERBS AGREE, p. H-36

a. For many college graduates, the process of looking for jobs *is* often long and stressful.

A-37

b. Not too long ago, searching the classifieds and inquiring in person *were* the primary methods of job hunting.

c. Today, however, everyone also *seems* to use the Internet to search for openings or to e-mail *his or her* résumés.

d. My classmates and my cousin *send* most résumés over the Internet because it costs less than mailing them.

e. All of the résumés *arrive* quickly when they are sent electronically.

EXERCISE 5–1   USING PRONOUNS CORRECTLY, p. H-39

a. I didn't appreciate *your* laughing at her and *me.* (*Your* modifies the gerund *laughing; me* is an object of the preposition *at.*)

b. Lee and *I* would be delighted to serenade *whoever* will listen. (*I* is a subject of the verb phrase *would be delighted; whoever* is the subject of the clause *whoever will listen.*)

c. The waiters and *we* busboys are highly trustworthy. (*We* is a subject complement.)

d. The neighbors were driven berserk by *his* singing. (The gerund *singing* is the object of the verb *driven;* the possessive pronoun *his* modifies *singing.*)   *Or*
Correct as is. (*Him* is the object of the verb *driven; singing* is a participle modifying *him.*)

e. Jerry and *I* regard you and *her* as the very people *whom* we wish to meet. (*I* is a subject of the verb *regard; her* is a direct object of the verb *regard; whom* is the object of the infinitive *to meet.*)

EXERCISE 6–1   MAKING PRONOUN REFERENCE CLEAR, p. H-43

Suggested revisions:

a. As the moon began to rise, I could see the faint shadow of the tree.

b. While she spent the summer in Paris, Katrina broadened her awareness of cultural differences by traveling throughout Europe.

c. Most managers want employees to work as many hours as possible. They never consider the work their employees need to do at home.

d. Working twelve hours a day and almost never getting enough sleep was worth it.

e. Kevin asked Mike to meet him for lunch but forgot that Mike had class at that time.   *Or*
Kevin forgot that he had class at the time he asked Mike to meet him for lunch.

EXERCISE 7–1   MAKING PRONOUNS AND ANTECEDENTS AGREE, p. H-46

Suggested revisions:

a. Correct

b. Neither Melissa nor James has received an application form yet.   *Or*

Melissa and James have not received their application forms yet.

c. He is the kind of man who gets his fun out of just sipping his beer and watching his Saturday games on TV.

d. Many a mother has mourned the loss of her child.   *Or*
Many mothers have mourned the loss of their children.

e. When you enjoy your work, it's easy to spend all your spare time thinking about it.   *Or*
When one enjoys one's work, it's easy to spend all one's spare time thinking about it.

EXERCISE 8–1   USING ADJECTIVES AND ADVERBS CORRECTLY, p. H-52

a. Change *increasing* to *increasingly.*   b. Correct.   c. Change *lower* to *lowest.*   d. Change *rapid* to *rapidly.*   e. Change *well* to *good.*

EXERCISE 9–1   MAINTAINING GRAMMATICAL CONSISTENCY, p. H-55

Suggested revisions:

a. Dr. Jamison is an erudite professor who tells amusing anecdotes in class. (Formal) *Or* Dr. Jamison is a funny teacher who cracks jokes in class. (Informal)

b. The audience listened intently to the lecture but did not understand the message.

c. Scientists can no longer evade the social, political, and ethical consequences of what they do in the laboratory.

d. To have good government, citizens must become informed on the issues. Also, they must vote.

e. Good writing is essential to success in many professions, especially in business, where ideas must be communicated clearly.

EXERCISE 10–1   PLACING MODIFIERS, p. H-58

Suggested revisions:

a. The bus full of passengers got stuck in a ditch.

b. In the middle of a staff meeting, he was daydreaming about fishing for trout.

c. With a smirk, the boy threw the paper airplane through an open window.

d. When the glare appeared, I reached for my sunglasses from the glove compartment.

e. Sally and Glen watched the kites high above them drift back and forth.

EXERCISE 10–2   REVISING DANGLING MODIFIERS, p. H-59

Suggested revisions:

a. As I was unpacking the suitcase, a horrible idea occurred to me.

b. After preparing breakfast that morning, I might have left the oven on at home.

c. Although I tried to reach my neighbor, her telephone was busy.

d. Desperate to get information, I asked my mother to drive over to check the oven.

e. I felt enormous relief when my mother's call confirmed that everything was fine.

EXERCISE 11–1 COMPLETING COMPARISONS, p. H-61

Suggested revisions:

a. The movie version of *The Brady Bunch* was much more ironic *than the television show*.

b. Taking care of a dog is often more demanding than *taking care of* a cat.

c. I received more free calendars in the mail for the year 2001 than *I have for* any other year.

d. The crime rate in the United States is higher than *it is in* Canada.

e. Liver contains more iron than any *other* meat.

EXERCISE 11–2 COMPLETING SENTENCES, p. H-63

Suggested revisions:

a. Eighteenth-century China was as civilized *as* and in many respects more sophisticated than the Western world.

b. Pembroke was never contacted *by,* much less involved with, the election committee.

c. I haven't yet *finished* but soon will finish my term paper.

d. Ron likes his popcorn with butter; Linda *likes hers* with parmesan cheese.

e. Correct

EXERCISE 12–1 CORRECTING MIXED CONSTRUCTIONS AND FAULTY PREDICATION, p. H-67

Suggested revisions:

a. Health insurance protects people from big medical bills.

b. His determination to prevail helped him finish the race.

c. AIDS destroys the body's immune system.

d. The temperatures are too low for the orange trees.

e. In a recession, economic growth is small or nonexistent, and unemployment increases.

EXERCISE 13–1 MAKING SENTENCES PARALLEL, p. H-70

Suggested revisions:

a. The border separating Texas and Mexico marks not only the political boundary of two countries but also the last frontier for some endangered wildlife.

b. In the Rio Grande Valley, both local residents and tourists enjoy visiting the national wildlife refuges.

c. The tall grasses in this valley are the home of many insects, birds, and small mammals.

d. Two endangered wildcats, the ocelot and the jaguarundi, also make the Rio Grande Valley their home.

e. Many people from Central America are desperate to immigrate to the United States by either legal or illegal means.

EXERCISE 14–1 USING COORDINATION, p. H-74

Suggested revisions:

a. Professional poker players try to win money and prizes in high-stakes tournaments; however, they may lose thousands of dollars.

b. Poker is not an easy way to make a living, and playing professional poker is not a good way to relax.

c. A good "poker face" reveals no emotions, for communicating too much information puts a player at a disadvantage.

d. Hidden feelings may come out in unconscious movements, so an expert poker player watches other players carefully.

e. Poker is different from most other casino gambling games, for it requires skill and it forces players to compete against each other. Other casino gambling pits players against the house, so they may win out of sheer luck, but skill has little to do with winning those games.

EXERCISE 14–2 USING SUBORDINATION, p. H-77

Suggested revisions:

a. Cape Cod is a peninsula in Massachusetts that juts into the Atlantic Ocean south of Boston, marking the northern turning point of the Gulf Stream.

b. Although the developer had hoped the condominiums would sell quickly, sales were sluggish.

c. Tourists love Italy because it has a wonderful climate, beautiful towns and cities, and a rich history.

d. At the end of Verdi's opera *La Traviata,* Alfredo has to see his beloved Violetta again, even though he knows she is dying and all he can say is good-bye.

e. I usually have more fun at a concert with Rico than with Morey because Rico loves music while Morey merely tolerates it.

EXERCISE 16–2 AVOIDING JARGON, p. H-84

Suggested revisions:

a. Everyone at Boondoggle and Gall attends holiday gatherings in order to meet and socialize with potential business partners.

b. This year, more than fifty employees lost their jobs after Boondoggle and Gall's decision to reduce their number of employees by September 1.

c. The layoffs left Jensen in charge of all telephone calls in the customer service department.

d. Jensen was responsible for handling three times as many telephone calls after the layoffs, yet she did not receive any extra pay.

e. Jensen and her managers could not agree on a fair compensation, so she decided to quit her job at Boondoggle and Gall.

EXERCISE 16–3   AVOIDING EUPHEMISMS AND SLANG, p. H-85

Suggested revisions:

a. Our security forces have arrested many political dissidents.

b. At three hundred dollars a month, the apartment is a bargain.

c. The soldiers were accidentally shot by members of their own troops while they were retreating.

d. Churchill was an excellent politician.

e. The president's health-care plan was doomed; Congress would not approve it.

EXERCISE 18–1   AVOIDING BIAS, p. H-93

Suggested revisions:

a. Our school's extensive athletic program will be of interest to *many* applicants.

b. The new physicians on our staff include Dr. Scalia, *Dr. Baniski,* and *Dr. Throckmorton.*

c. Joni believes in the healing properties of herbal remedies.

d. Philosophers have long pondered whether *humans are* innately evil or innately good.

e. *Diligent researchers* will always find the sources *they* seek.

EXERCISE 20–1   USING END PUNCTUATION, p. H-98

a. The question that still troubles the community after all these years is why federal agents did not act sooner. [Not a direct question]

b. Correct

c. I wonder what he was thinking at the time. [Not a direct question]

d. One man, who suffered a broken leg, was rescued when he was heard screaming, "Help me! Help me!" [Urgent directive]

e. Correct

EXERCISE 21–1   USING COMMAS, p. H-100

a. Farmers around the world tend to rely on just a few breeds of livestock, so some breeds are disappearing.

b. Correct

c. For instance, modern breeds of cattle usually grow larger and produce more meat and milk than older breeds.

d. In both wild and domestic animals, genetic diversity can make the animals resistant to disease and parasites, so older breeds can give scientists important information.

e. Until recently, small organic farmers were often the only ones interested in raising old-fashioned breeds, but animal scientists now support this practice as well.

EXERCISE 21–2   USING COMMAS, p. H-102

a. Mrs. Carver looks like a sweet little old lady, but she plays a wicked electric guitar.

b. Her bass player, her drummer, and her keyboard player all live in the same retirement community.

c. They practice individually in the afternoon, rehearse together at night, and play at the community's Saturday night dances.

d. The Rest Home Rebels have to rehearse quietly and cautiously to keep from disturbing the other residents.

e. Correct

EXERCISE 21–3   USING COMMAS, p. H-103

Suggested revisions:

a. We are bringing a dish, vegetable lasagna, to the potluck supper.

b. I like to go to Central Bank on this side of town because this branch tends to have short lines.

c. The colony that the English established at Roanoke disappeared mysteriously.

d. If the base commanders had checked their gun room, where powder is stored, they would have found that several hundred pounds of gunpowder were missing.

e. Brazil's tropical rain forests, which help produce the air we breathe all over the world, are being cut down at an alarming rate.

EXERCISE 21–4   USING COMMAS, p. H-105

a. The university insisted, however, that the students were not accepted merely because of their parents' generous contributions.

b. This dispute, in any case, is an old one.

c. It was the young man's striking good looks, not his acting ability, that first attracted the Hollywood agents.

d. Gretchen learned, moreover, not to always accept as true what she had read in textbooks.

e. The hikers, most of them wearing ponchos or rain jackets, headed out into the steady drizzle.

EXERCISE 21–5   USING COMMAS, p. H-106

a. César Chávez was born on March 31, 1927, on a farm in Yuma, Arizona.

b. Chávez, who spent years as a migrant farmworker, told other farm laborers, "If you're outraged at conditions, then you can't possibly be free or happy until you devote all your time to changing them."

c. Chávez founded the United Farm Workers union and did, indeed, devote all his time to changing conditions for farmworkers.

d. Robert F. Kennedy called Chávez "one of the heroic figures of our time."

e. Correct

EXERCISE 22–1   USING SEMICOLONS, p. H-110

a. By the beginning of 1993, Shirley was eager to retire; nevertheless, she agreed to stay on for two more years.

b. In 1968 Lyndon Johnson abandoned his hopes for reelection because of fierce opposition from within his own party.

c. The committee was asked to determine the extent of violent crime among teenagers, especially those between the ages of fourteen and sixteen; to act as a liaison between the city and schools and between churches and volunteer organizations; and to draw up a plan to significantly reduce violence, both public and private, by the end of the century.

d. The leaves on the oak trees near the lake were tinged with red; swimmers no longer ventured into the water.

e. The football team has yet to win a game; however, the season is still young.

EXERCISE 23–1   USING COLONS, p. H-112

Suggested revisions:

a. The Continuing Education Program offers courses in building and construction management, engineering, and design.

b. The interview ended with a test of skills: taking messages, operating the computer, typing a sample letter, and proofreading documents.

c. The sample letter began, "Dear Mr. Rasheed: Please accept our apologies for the late shipment."

d. Correct

e. These are my dreams: to ride in a horse-drawn sleigh, to fly in a small plane, to gallop down a beach on horseback, and to cross the ocean in a sailboat.

EXERCISE 24–1   USING THE APOSTROPHE, p. H-115

a. Joe's and Chuck's fathers were both in the class of '53.

b. Correct

c. It was a strange coincidence that all three women's cars broke down after they had picked up their mothers-in-law.

d. Don't forget to dot your *i*'s and cross your *t*'s.

e. Mario and Shelley's son is marrying the editor in chief's daughter.

EXERCISE 25–1   USING QUOTATION MARKS, p. H-120

a. "What we still need to figure out," the police chief said, "is whether the victim was acquainted with his assailant."

b. A skillful orator, Patrick Henry is credited with the phrase "Give me liberty or give me death."

c. "I could hear the crowd chanting my name — 'Jones! Jones!' — and that spurred me on," said Bruce Jones, the winner of the 5,000-meter race.

d. The video for the rock group Guns and Roses' epic song "November Rain" is based on a short story by Del James.

e. After the Gore/Bush election debacle of 2000, *Time* essayist Lance Morrow predicts, "The memory of the 2000 post-election chadfest will revive an angry energy in 2004, which will produce the biggest voter turnout in history."

EXERCISE 26–1   USING THE DASH, p. H-121

Suggested revisions:

a. I enjoy going hiking with my friend John, whom I've known for fifteen years.

b. Pedro's new boat is spectacular — a regular seagoing Ferrari.

c. The Thompsons devote their weekends to their favorite pastime — eating bags of potato chips and cookies beside the warm glow of the television.

EXERCISE 27–1   USING PARENTHESES, p. H-123

Suggested revisions:

a. Our cafeteria serves the four basic food groups: white (milk, bread, and mashed potatoes), brown (mystery meat and gravy), green (overcooked vegetables and underwashed lettuce), and orange (squash, carrots, and tomato sauce).

b. The hijackers will release the hostages only if the government (1) frees all political prisoners and (2) allows the hijackers to leave the country unharmed.

c. Correct

EXERCISE 28–1   USING ABBREVIATIONS, p. H-130

a. At 7:50 p.m. [*or* 7:50 in the evening] on election day, the media first awarded Florida to Al Gore, only to reverse that statement and declare George W. Bush the president a few hours later.

b. Biology lectures are only ninety *minutes* long because lab sessions immediately follow them.

c. *Professor* James has office hours on Monday and Tuesday, beginning at 10:00 a.m.

d. Emotional issues, *for example*, abortion and capital punishment, cannot be settled easily by compromise.

e. The red peppers are selling for *$3.25* a pound.

EXERCISE 29–1   USING CAPITALIZATION, p. H-133

a. At our family reunion, I met my cousin Sam for the first time, as well as my father's brother George.

b. I already knew from Dad that his brother had moved to Australia years ago to explore the Great Barrier Reef.

c. I had heard that Uncle George was estranged from his mother, a Roman Catholic, after he married an atheist.

d. She told George that God created many religions so that people would not become atheists.

e. When my uncle announced that he was moving to a continent thousands of miles southwest of the United States, his mother gave him a Bible to take along.

EXERCISE 30–1   USING NUMBERS, p. H-135

a. If the murder took place at approximately 6:20 p.m. and the suspect was *half* a mile away at the time, he could not possibly have committed the crime.

b. A program to help save the sea otter transferred more than eighty animals to a new colony over the course of *two* years; however, all but *thirty-four* otters swam back home again.

c. *One percent* or less of the estimated *15* to *20* billion pounds of plastic discarded annually in the United States is recycled.

d. The 1983 Little League World Series saw the Roosters beat the Dusters *94–4* before a throng of *7,550.*

e. In act II, scene ix, of Shakespeare's *The Merchant of Venice,* Portia's *second* suitor fails to guess which of *three* caskets contains her portrait.

EXERCISE 31–1   USING ITALICS, p. H-138

a. Does *avocado* mean "lawyer" in Spanish?

b. During this year's First Night celebrations, we heard Verdi's *Requiem* and Monteverdi's *Orfeo.*

c. You can pick out some of the best basketball players in the NBA by the *33* on their jerseys.

d. It was fun watching the passengers on the *Europa* trying to dance to "Blue Moon" in the midst of a storm.

e. In one episode of the sitcom *Seinfeld,* Kramer gets a job as an underwear model.

EXERCISE 32–1   USING HYPHENS, p. H-141

a. The strong-smelling smoke alerted them to a potentially life-threatening danger.

b. Burt's wildly swinging opponent had tired himself out before the climactic third round.

c. Tony soaked his son's ketchup- and mustard-stained T-shirt in a pail of water mixed with chlorine bleach.

d. Correct

e. Tracy's brother-in-law lives with his family in a six-room apartment.

ACKNOWLEDGMENTS (continued from p. iv)

Tim Chabot, "Take Me Out to the Ball Game, but Which One?" Reprinted with the permission of the author.

Veronica Chambers, "The Myth of Cinderella," from *Newsweek* (November 3, 1997). Copyright © 1997 by Newsweek, Inc. Reprinted by permission. All rights reserved.

Jay Chiat, "Illusions Are Forever," from *Forbes* (October 2, 2000). Copyright © 2000 by Forbes, Inc. Reprinted by permission of Forbes ASAP Magazine.

Yun Yung Choi, "Invisible Women." Reprinted with the permission of the author.

Heather Colbenson, "Missed Opportunities." Reprinted with the permission of the author.

Stephanie Coontz, "Remarriage and Stepfamilies," from *The Way We Really Are.* Copyright © 1997 by Stephanie Coontz. Reprinted with the permission of HarperCollins Publishers, Inc.

Harry Crews, excerpt from "The Car," from *Florida Frenzy* (Gainesville: University Press of Florida, 1982). Copyright © 1982 by Harry Crews. Reprinted with the permission of the author.

Freeman Dyson, excerpt from *Infinite in All Directions.* Copyright © 1988 by Freeman Dyson. Reprinted with the permission of HarperCollins Publishers, Inc.

Gerald Early, "Black like . . . Shirley Temple?" from *Harper's* (February 1992). Copyright © 1992 by *Harper's.* Reprinted with the permission of the author.

Anne Finnigan, "Nice Perks — If You Can Get 'Em" from *Working Mother* (October 2000). Copyright © 2000 by Working Woman Network, Inc. Reprinted with permission.

Kurt M. Fischer and Arlyne Lazerson, excerpt from *Human Development.* Copyright © 1984 by W. H. Freeman and Company. Reprinted with permission.

Robert Frost, "Putting in the Seed" and "The Road Not Taken" from *The Poetry of Robert Frost,* edited by Edward Connery Lathem. Copyright 1916, 1969 by Henry Holt and Company. Reprinted with the permission of Henry Holt and Company, LLC.

Sarah E. Goers, "Is Inclusion the Answer?" Reprinted with the permission of the author. This selection includes an excerpt from Beth Hewett, "Helping Students with Learning Disabilities: Collaboration between Writing Centers and Special Services," from *The Writing Lab* 25.3 (2000).

Ellen Goodman, "Kids, Divorce, and the Myth," from *The Boston Globe Online* (September 28, 2000). Copyright © 2000 by The Boston Globe Newspaper Co. / Washington Post Writers Group. Reprinted with permission. "How to Zap Violence on TV," from *The Boston Globe* (February 1996). Copyright © 1996 by Ellen Goodman. Reprinted with permission.

Lin Haire-Sargeant, "You Are the Detective." Reprinted with the permission of the author.

Joy Harjo, "Three Generations of Native American Women's Birth Experience," from *Ms.* (July / August 1991). Copyright © 1991 by *Ms.* Reprinted with the permission of the author and *Ms.*

Suzan Shown Harjo, "Last Rites for Indian Dead" from the *Los Angeles Times* (September 16, 1989). Copyright © 1989 by Suzan Shown Harjo. Reprinted with permission.

Shirley Jackson, "The Lottery," from *The Lottery and Other Stories.* Copyright © 1948, 1949 by Shirley Jackson. Copyright renewed © 1976, 1977 by Laurence Hyman, Barry Hyman, Mrs. Sarah Webster, and Mrs. Joanne Schnurer. Reprinted with the permission of Farrar, Straus & Giroux, LLC.

Lisa Jervis, "My Jewish Nose," from *Body Outlaws,* edited by Ophira Edut. Copyright © 2000. Reprinted with the permission of Seal Press.

Stephen King, "Why We Crave Horror Movies." Copyright © by Stephen King. Reprinted with permission.

Monica Yant Kinney, "Mining for Humor," from *Notre Dame University Alumni Magazine* (2000). Copyright © 2000 by Monica Yant Kinney. Reprinted with the permission of the author.

Dawn Kortz, "Listen." Reprinted with the permission of the author.

William Severini Kowinski, "Kids in the Mall: Growing Up Controlled," from *The Malling of America: An Inside Look at the Great Consumer Paradise.* Copyright © 1985 by William Severini Kowinski. Reprinted with the permission of HarperCollins Publishers, Inc.

Marisa Kula, "Victoria's Not-So-Secret Strategy," from chickclick .com (September 27, 1999). Copyright © 1999. Reprinted with permission.

Mike Males, "Public Enemy Number One?" from *In These Times* (September 23, 1993). Reprinted with permission.

Charles C. Mann and Mark L. Plummer, "The Butterfly Problem," from *The Atlantic Monthly* (January 1992). Copyright © 1992 by Charles C. Mann. Reprinted with permission.

Clay McCuistion, "Coffee Odyssey," from *The University Daily Kansan* (University of Kansas). Reprinted with the permission of the author.

Bill McKibben, "The Frog Factor," from *The Washington Monthly Online* (March 2000). Copyright © 2000 by The Washington Monthly. Reprinted with permission.

John McPhee, "Silk Parachute," from *The New Yorker* (1997). Copyright © 1997 by John McPhee. Reprinted with the permission of the author. All rights reserved.

Sandy Messina, "Footprints: The Mark of Our Passing." Reprinted with the permission of the author.

Ryan Miday, "*Times* Series Delved Successfully into Race," from *Columbia Daily Spectator* (September 22, 2000). Reprinted with permission.

N. Scott Momaday, "To the Singing, To the Drums" (excerpt), from *Natural History* (February 1975). Copyright © 1975 by the American Museum of Natural History. Reprinted with permission.

Madeleine Nash, excerpt from "The Case for Cloning," from *Time* (February 9, 1998). Copyright © 1998 by Time, Inc. Reprinted by permission.

Katherine S. Newman, excerpt from *No Shame in My Game: The Working Poor in the Inner City.* Copyright © 1999 by Katherine S. Newman. Reprinted with the permission of Alfred A. Knopf, a division of Random House, Inc.

Steve Olson, "Year of the Blue-Collar Guy," from *Newsweek* (November 6, 1989). Copyright © 1989 by Steve Olson. Reprinted with the permission of the author.

Noel Perrin, "A Part-Time Marriage," from *The New York Times Magazine* (September 9, 1984). Copyright © 1984 by The New York Times Company. Reprinted with permission.

Sylvia Plath, excerpt from "Northhampton," from *The Journals of Sylvia Plath,* edited by Ted Hughes and Francis McCullough. Copyright © 1982 by Ted Hughes and Francis McCullough. Reprinted with the permission of Doubleday, a division of Random House, Inc.

Alicia Potter, "Mirror Image," from the *Boston Phoenix* (December 4–11, 1997). Copyright © 1997 by The Phoenix Media/Communication Group. All rights reserved.

Emily Prager, "Our Barbies, Ourselves," from *Interview* (December 1991). Copyright © 1991 by Emily Prager. Reprinted with the permission of *Interview*.

Anna Quindlen, "Evan's Two Moms," from *The New York Times* (February 5, 1992). Copyright © 1992 by The New York Times Company. Reprinted with permission.

Wilbert Rideau, "Why Prisons Don't Work," from *Time* (March 21, 1994). Copyright © 1994 by Time, Inc. Reprinted with permission.

Joe Robinson, "Four Weeks Vacation," from *The Utne Reader* #101 (Sept / Oct 2000). Reprinted with the permission of the author.

Phyllis Rose, "Shopping and Other Spiritual Adventures in America Today," from *Never Say Goodbye* (New York: Doubleday, 1991). Copyright © 1991 by Phyllis Rose. Reprinted with the permission of The Wylie Agency, Inc.

Scott Russell Sanders, "The Men We Carry in Our Minds," from *Milkweed Chronicle* (1984). Copyright © 1984 by Scott Russell Sanders. Reprinted with the permission of the Virginia Kidd Agency, Inc.

Robert G. Schreiner, "What Is a Hunter?" Reprinted with the permission of the author.

Jane Smiley, "The Case against Chores," from *Harper's* (June 1995). Copyright © 1995 by Harper's Magazine Foundation. Reprinted with the permission of *Harper's*.

Tom Standage, "The Victorian Internet," from *The Victorian Internet: The Remarkable Story of the Telegraph and the Nineteenth Century's On-Line Pioneers.* Copyright © 1998 by Tom Standage. Reprinted with the permission of Walker and Company.

Amy Tan, "Mother Tongue," from *Threepenny Review* (1990). Copyright © 1990 by Amy Tan. Reprinted with permission.

Deborah Tannen, "Women and Men Talking on the Job," from *Talking from 9 to 5.* Copyright © 1994 by Deborah Tannen. Reprinted with the permission of HarperCollins Publishers, Inc.

Garry Trudeau, "My Inner Shrimp," from *The New York Times Magazine* (March 31, 1997). Copyright © 1996 by The New York Times Company. Reprinted with permission.

Lillian Tsu, excerpt from "A Woman in the White House," from *Cornell Political Forum* (1997). Copyright © 1997 by Lillian Tsu. Reprinted with the permission of the author.

Janice Turner, "Cutting Edge," from *The Toronto Star* (1996). Reprinted with the permission of Toronto Star Newspapers Limited.

John Updike, excerpt from "Venezuela for Visitors," from *Hugging the Shore.* Originally published in *The New Yorker.* Copyright © 1983 by John Updike. Reprinted with the permission of Alfred A. Knopf, a division of Random House, Inc.

Nicholas Wade, "How Men and Women Think," from *The New York Times Magazine* (June 12, 1994). Copyright © 1994 by The New York Times Company. Reprinted with permission.

Thaddeus Watulak, "Affirmative Action Encourages Racism," from *Johns Hopkins Newsletter* (March 26, 1998). Copyright © 1998 by Johns Hopkins University. Reprinted with permission.

E. B. White, "Here Is New York," from *Here Is New York.* Copyright 1949 by E. B. White. Reprinted with the permission of HarperCollins Publishers, Inc. "Once More to the Lake," from *Essays of E. B. White.* Copyright 1944 by E. B. White. Reprinted with the permission of Mr. Joel White.

Art and Photograph Credits

Figure 2.1: Figure adapted from *Taxonomy of Educational Objectives, Handbook I: Cognitive Domain* by Benjamin S. Bloom, et al. © 1956 McKay.

Page 35: Photograph copyright © 2001: Whitney Museum of American Art. Photography by Geoffrey Clements.

Page 51: John Storey / TimePix.

Page 65: © William Coupon.

Page 81: Reprinted with special permission of King Features Syndicate.

Page 100: Courtesy of Nikolai Fine Art, New York.

Page 117: Courtesy of The Body Shop International PLC.

Page 138: Image courtesy of www.adbusters.org.

Page 156: PictureQuest.

Page 173: © 2000 Saul Metnick of panOptic.

Figures 21.1 and 21.3: Front page, *USA TODAY.* Copyright *USA TODAY.* Reprinted with permission. Front page, *Wall Street Journal.* Reprinted by permission of *The Wall Street Journal,* © 2001 Dow Jones & Company, Inc. All rights reserved worldwide.

Figure 21.4: Front cover, *Forbes.* Reprinted by permission of *Forbes Magazine* © 2001 Forbes Inc. Article "The Best Lover He's Ever Had" © Lisa Carver, photo © Michael Edwards. Both the article and the photo originally appeared in *Mademoiselle.*

Figure 21.14: Courtesy of the Energy Information Administration.

Figure 21.15: Courtesy of the King County Wastewater Treatment Division.

Figure 22.1: © Merrilee Giegerich.

Figure 22.5: Courtesy of Volkswagen of America.

Figure 22.6: Courtesy of Leo Burnett USA.

Figure 22.7: Courier Typeface. Becky Carpenter / Razorfish Studios, www.rsub.com. Caslon Typeface. Ryan McGinness / Razorfish Studios, www.rsub.com.

Figure 22.8: Egg Beaters Ad. © 2000 Beatrice Foods.

Figure 22.9: Courtesy of Netpliance. Creative Director: James Mikus; Director: Albert Watson.

Page 378: From *A TRUE LIKENESS* (Columbia, S.C.; Bruccoli Clark Layman 1986) by permission of The Estate of Richard Samuel Roberts.

Page 411: Elliott Erwitt / Magnum.

Page 442: © The Estate of Keith Haring.

Page 466: Alberto Ruggieri / The Image Bank.

Page 501: © Mary Ellen Mark.

Figure 29.1: Howard University library home page. Text and artwork copyright © 2000 Howard University. All rights reserved.

Figure 29.2: Keyword search, Howard University library. Text and artwork copyright © 2000 Howard University.

Figure 29.3: Online record, Howard University library. Text and artwork copyright © 2000 Howard University.

Figure 29.4: Courtesy of the Library of Congress.

Figure 29.5: *Reader's Guide to Periodical Literature* © 2001 The H. W. Wilson Company. Material reproduced with permission of the H. W. Wilson Company.

Figure 29.6: Reprinted by permission of the Gale Group.

Figures 29.7 and 29.8: © Google, Inc.

Figure 30.1: Courtesy of The American Society for the Prevention of Cruelty to Animals.

Index

Abbreviations, H-97, H-115, H-127–29
Absolute phrases, H-105
Acronyms, H-129
Active voice, H-26–27
Address, forms of, H-93, H-127–28
Addresses, commas in, H-106
Ad hominem, argument, 135
Adjective clauses, ESL guidelines for, H-41
Adjectives, H-46–51
    capitalization of, H-130–31
    checking for, using a computer, 62
    comparatives and superlatives of, H-49–51, A-10
    editing guide for, A-9–10
    ESL guidelines for, H-51
    revising, 327–28
Adverbs, H-46–51. *See also* Conjunctive adverbs
    checking for, using a computer, 62
    comparatives and superlatives of, H-50–51, A-10
    editing guide for, A-9–10
    revising, 327–28
Advertisements, 343, 358–59, 365–66, 365 (fig.), 367 (fig.), 370, 371 (fig.), 372 (fig.)
"Affirmative Action Encourages Racism" (Watulak), 121–23
Agreement
    pronoun-antecedent, H-44–46, A-8–9
    subject-verb, H-31–35, A-5–6
Alignment, 351, 356
Allen, Paula Gunn, 304–05
Allness, 134
Alvarez, Julia, 502
    "I Want to Be Miss América," 502–06
American Memory (online archive), 379
American Psychological Association (APA) style, 350, 598, 599, 600, 615, 631
    citing sources, 631–34
    listing sources, 599, 634–39
Analogy, 135

Analytical skills, 19 (fig.), 20–21
Analyzing
    critical reading and, 19 (fig.), 20–21, 180, 182, 183, 202–03
    critical thinking and, 23–24, 23 (fig.)
    development strategies using, 306–09, 312–13
    process analysis and, 312–13
    proposals and, 147
    visuals and, 259
    writing and, 33
Annotation, text, 18, 182–84, 186
Annual reports, in libraries, 558
Answer method, and research papers, 584
Antagonist, 207
Antecedents of pronouns, H-40–46
APA. *See* American Psychological Association
Apostrophes, H-113–15, A-15–16
Appeals, 29–30, 131–32, 254
Application letters, 234, 236–38, 237 (fig.)
Applying information, in critical reading, 16, 19–20, 19 (fig.)
Appositive, H-37, H-38, H-103, H-111, H-121, A-14–15
Appropriateness of words, H-81–85
Archive, research, 544–45, 578
Arguments
    ad hominem, 135
    by analogy, 135
    bandwagon, 135–36
    from dubious authority, 135
    from ignorance, 135
Articles (grammar), A-24
    definite, ESL guidelines for, H-48
    indefinite, ESL guidelines for, H-49
    with nouns, ESL guidelines for, H-33
"Art of Eating Spaghetti, The" (Baker), 36–38
Assessment, 239–55
    drafting and, 245–47
    essay examinations and, 239–40
    generating ideas for, 241
    group learning activity for, 250

planning for, 242–45
of portfolios, 250–55
preparing for, 239–40
revising, 247
revision checklist for, 247
short-answer examinations 248
timed writings and, 248–50
types of exam questions and, 242–44
Assignments, 33
    causes and effects, 108–09, 115
    comparing and contrasting, 90, 97–98
    evaluating, 165, 170–71
    interviewing a subject, 72, 79
    observation, 57–58, 62–63
    opinion (taking a stand), 124–25, 136
    proposals, 145–46, 153–54
    reading critically, 180, 188
    recall, 43, 48–49
    research project, 534–35, 599
    writing about literature, 209–12, 219, 222–23
    writing a research paper, 599
Atlases, in libraries, 557
Atmosphere, 206
Audience (readers), 12–13
    appeals to, 29–30, 131–32
    causes and effects and, 108
    designing a document and, 338–42
    evaluations and, 167
    evidence and, 27–28
    opinion (taking a stand) essay and, 124, 127–28
    proposals and, 147–48, 150
    revising for, 320–21
    source evaluation and, 571–73, 572 (fig.)
    tone of writing and, H-81
    writing about literature and, 212
    writing in the workplace and, 225, 226–27, 238
Austin, James H., 292
Authorship, of sources, 573–74
Autobiography of Mother Jones, The (Jones), 303–04
Auxiliary (helping) verbs, H-14, H-15

I-1

Backgrounds, 362 (fig.), 363
Baker, Russell, 46, 293–94
    "The Art of Eating Spaghetti,"
        36–38
Bandwagon argument, 135–36
Barber, James David, 289
Barry, Dave, 428–29
    "From Now On, Let Women Kill
        Their Own Spiders," 429–30
Be (verb), A-6
Begging the question, 134
Beginnings (openings), 77, 82, 241,
        291–92, 325, 595–96, 604. *See
        also* Introductions
Beston, Henry, 59
Bias, in sources, 570, 573, 575
Bias-free language, H-90–93
Bible, H-112, H-136
Bibliographies
    in libraries, 552, 554–55
    working, 542–44, 543 (fig.), 544
        (fig.)
Biographical sources, 557
"Black like . . . Shirley Temple?"
        (Early), 391–93
Bloom, Benjamin S., 16
Boldface type, 169, 278, 342, 345–46,
        346 (fig.), 349
Bookmarks for Web sites, 545
Books
    citing, 616–19 (MLA), 631–33
        (APA)
    listing as sources, 621–25 (MLA),
        634–36 (APA)
    source notes for, 542–43, 543 (fig.)
Boolean searches, 561
Brackets, H-122, H-123–24, A-16–17
Brady, Judy, 412
    "I Want a Wife," 412–14
Brainstorming
    comparing and contrasting and, 90
    critical reading and, 202
    evaluating and, 165
    generating ideas using, 260–62
    group learning activity and, 250,
        261, 263
    interviews and, 72
    observation and, 58
    opinion (taking a stand) essay and,
        125
    proposals and, 146
    recall and, 44
    research questions and, 537
    stating a thesis and, 272
    timed writings and, 250

Browsers, Web, 545
Bruce, Ian, 485
    "Commercial Fisherman," 485–88
Bulleted lists, 346–47
Burkett, Elinor, 495
    "Unequal Work for Unequal Pay,"
        496–99
Burns, Jonathan (student writer),
        202–03, 209
    "The Hidden Truth: An Analysis of
        Shirley Jackson's 'The Lottery,'"
        203–05
    "A Synopsis of 'The Lottery,'"
        217–18
Business letters, 234, 227–30, 231
        (fig.)
    envelopes for, 230, 232 (fig.)
    format for, 229–30
    guidelines for writing, 224–27
Business writing. *See* Workplace,
        writing in
"Butterfly Problem, The" (Mann and
        Plummer), 317

Calbick, Martha (student writer),
        261–63
Call numbers, 550–51
Cameras, and field research, 565
Capitalization, H-110–11, H-118,
        H-130–33, A-17–18
"Car, The" (Crews), 291
"Case against Chores, The" (Smiley),
        476–78
"Case for Cloning, The" (Nash), 312
Case of pronouns, H-36–39
Catalogs, library, 546, 555, 562
    searching online, 547–52, 549
        (fig.), 550 (fig.), 559, 563
    subject headings in, 548–49, 551
        (fig.)
Categorizing ideas. *See* Organizing
        information
Causality. *See* Causes and effects
Cause and effect questions, 242
Causes and effects, 34, 96, 100–16
    applications of, 115–16
    assignments on, 108–09, 115
    computers and, 113
    as development strategy, 316–17
    discovery checklists for, 109, 317
    editing checklist for, 114
    facing the challenge, 110
    generating ideas for, 109–11
    group learning activity on, 115
    peer response checklist for, 114

planning, drafting, and developing
        of, 111–12
    proposals and, 147
    revising and editing of, 112–13
    revision checklist for, 113
CD-ROMs, 552
    library resources on, 552, 553
    listing as source, 629 (MLA)
Central conflict, 207
Chabot, Tim (student writer), 94
    "Take Me Out to the Ball Game, but
        Which One?" 86–89
Chambers, Veronica, 446
    "The Myth of Cinderella," 446–49
Characters, 206–07
Chat rooms, 545, 563, 569
Checklists. *See also* Discovery
        checklists; Editing checklists;
        Research checklists; Revision
        checklists
    document design, 356
    visual analysis, 373
"Chemist's Definition of pH, A"
        (Hawley), 306
Chiat, Jay, 454–55
    "Illusions Are Forever," 455–56
Choi, Yun Yung (student writer), 108,
        111, 112
    "Invisible Women," 105–08, 112
Chopin, Kate, 244
    "The Story of an Hour," 219–21
Chronological order, 276, 304
Citation (software), 600
Citing sources, 599, 600, 616–21
        (MLA), 631–34 (APA), A-26–27
Claims, 126–28, 575
Classification. *See also* Organizing
        information
    development strategy, 310–12
Clauses, H-65, H-70, H-79
    coordination of, H-71–74
    main, H-10, H-76, H-78, H-79,
        H-112, A-112
    punctuation of, H-99, H-102–03,
        H-104, H-108–09, H-109, H-111,
        H-112, A-14–15
    subordination of, H-74, H-75–77,
        H-79
Clichés, H-86–87
Climax, 207
Close reading, 359
Clustering ideas, 277, 278 (fig.)
CNN Online, 569
"Coffee Odyssey" (McCuistion),
        160–64

Cognitive activity, 16

Coherence
  drafting and, 296–98
  revising for, 187

Cohn, David Ian (student writer), 240–41, 245, 246

Colbenson, Heather (student writer), 146, 149, 150–51
  "Missed Opportunities," 142–45

Collaboration. *See* Group learning activities

Collaborative research, 540

Collective interview, 78

Collective nouns, H-32, H-45

College courses, applications of learning in
  causes and effects and, 115–16
  comparing and contrasting and, 98–99
  evaluation and, 171
  interviewing and, 80
  observation and, 63–64
  opinion (taking a stand) essay and, 136
  proposals and, 154
  reading critically and, 188–89
  recalling experience for, 49
  research and, 531, 533, 600
  writing assignments in, 7, 14, 194

Colons, H-11, H-110–12, H-119, A-16–17

Color, in document design, 350, 361

Column format, 149

Commas, H-10–12, H-98–108, H-119, H-127–28, A-14–15, A-16–17

Comma splices, H-10–12, A-11–12

"Commercial Fisherman" (Bruce), 485–88

Community, applications of learning in
  causes and effects and, 116
  comparing and contrasting and, 98–99
  evaluation and, 171
  interviewing and, 80
  observation and, 64
  opinion (taking a stand) essay and, 137
  proposals and, 154–55
  reading critically and, 189
  recalling experience for, 50
  research and, 601

Comparatives, H-49–51, A-10

Compare or contrast questions, 241–42

Comparing and contrasting, 13–14, 33, 81–99, 273
  applications of, 98–99
  assignments on, 90, 97–98
  computers and, 92
  as development strategy, 314–16
  discovery checklists for, 91, 315–16
  editing checklist for, 97
  evaluating and, 166, 168
  facing the challenge and, 91
  generating ideas for, 90–93
  group learning activity for, 96
  organization in, 93–95, 314–15
  peer response checklist for, 94
  planning, drafting, and developing in, 93–96
  proposals and, 147
  revising and editing and, 96–97
  revision checklist for, 97
  transitions in, 96

Comparisons (grammar), 208, H-60–61, H-69

Complements, H-10, H-14, H-37, H-66, A-7

Complete sentences, H-5

Compound adjectives, H-140

Compound-complex sentences, H-79

Compound nouns, H-114

Compound predicates, H-7–8, H-63, H-72

Compound sentences, H-79

Compound subjects, H-32, H-79

Compound verbs, H-79

Compound words, H-139

Comprehending, in critical reading, 16, 19, 19 (fig.)

Comprehension, reading for, 202

Computers. *See also* Writing with a computer
  annotating with, 186
  business letters and, 227
  causes and effects and, 113
  comparing and contrasting and, 92
  document design and, 356
  document sources using, 600
  drafting with, 286, 587, A-1
  editing with, A-1, A-19
  evaluating and, 169
  formatting manuscripts with, 113, 131, 149, 286
  grammar checkers on, A-1, A-19
  grouping ideas using, 277
  Internet search sites and, 562
  interviewing and, 75
  invisible writing and, 264

journal keeping with, 266

note taking and, 186

observation and, 62

opinion (taking a stand) essay and, 131

organizing ideas using, 278, 587

outlining and organizing a draft using, 587

proofreading and, 333

proposals and, 149

reading critically and, 186

recall and, 44

research archive on, 545, 578

research papers and, 587, 598, 600

revising with, 322, 324, 598

spell checkers on, 333, A-19

working bibliography using, 542

Computer software, listing as a source, 629 (MLA), 639 (APA)

Conclusions (endings), 82, 215, 293–94, 326, 596, 612

Conditional sentences, ESL guidelines for, H-30

Conferences, and field research, 568–69

Conflict, 207

Conjunctions, H-65, H-73, A-11, A-12, A-14–15. *See also* Coordinating conjunctions; Correlative conjunctions; Subordinating conjunctions

Conjunctive adverbs, H-12, H-72, H-79, H-104, H-109, A-15

Connotations of a word, H-86

Consensus, 166

Consistency, grammatical, H-52–55

Contractions, H-115, A-15–16

Contrast, phrase expressing, H-104

Contrasting. *See* Comparing and contrasting

Conversation, writing from. *See also* Interviewing
  comparing and contrasting and, 93
  evaluating and, 165

Coontz, Stephanie, 404
  "Remarriage and Stepfamilies," 404–07

Coordinate adjectives, H-101

Coordinating conjunctions, H-11, H-68–69, H-72, H-73, H-79, H-99, H-107–08, A-12, A-14–15, A-24

Coordination (grammar), H-71–74

Correlative conjunctions, H-69, H-73, H-107–08, A-13

Correspondence. *See* Electronic mail; Letters
Count nouns, H-33, H-49
Countries
    abbreviations for, 129
    commas for, in addresses, H-106
Cover letters, to writing portfolios, 253–54
Cowley, Malcolm, 293
Credibility, 183
Crews, Harry, 291
Criteria, and evaluating, 157, 165–66, 168
Critical reading. *See* Reading critically
Critical thinking, 8–9, 33
    process of, 22–30, 23 (fig.)
    research and, 534, 570
Cultural Anthropology: A Perspective on the Human Condition (Schultz and Lavenda), 307–08
Cultural attitudes, and visuals, 369, 370
Cummings, William K., 93–94
Cumulative adjectives, H-101
    ESL guidelines for, H-51
Cumulative sentences, H-78
Cutting, in revision, 326–31
"Cutting Edge" (Turner), 525–27

Dangling modifiers, H-59, A-12–13
Dashes, H-120–21
Databases
    library research using, 536, 546, 552–55, 559, 563
    listing material from, 628 (MLA), 639 (APA)
    recording research sources using, 542, 545, 600
Dates, commas for, H-106
Declarative sentences, H-96
Defining
    development strategies and, 305–06
    evaluating and, 166–67
Definite articles, ESL guidelines for, H-48
Definition questions, 243–44
Definitions, H-66
    in exam answers, 248
    italics for, 345
    in opinion essays, 130
Deja (Web site), 563
Demonstration questions, 242–43
Denotations of a word, H-86
Designing a document, 335–56, A-23–24. *See also* Format
    checklist for, 356–57

computers and, 356
creating an effective design, 342–53
discovery checklist for, 338
fonts in, 343–46, 343 (fig.), 344 (fig.), 345 (fig.), 346 (fig.)
headings and alignment in, 349–51, 352 (fig.), 353 (fig.)
lists in, 346–47
magazine design features, 339, 340 (fig.)
newspaper design features, 335, 336 (fig.), 339, 340 (fig.)
principles of, 338–42
repetition in, 351–53
research paper design features, 337 (fig.), 601–14
visuals in, 354–57, 354 (fig.), 355 (fig.)
Details, use of, 47, 50, 59, 82, 303–05
Developing, 11
    analyzing and, 306–09
    causes and effects and, 111–12
    causes and effects in, 316–17
    comparing and contrasting and, 93–96, 314–16
    defining and, 305–06
    details and, 303–05
    discovery checklists for, 300, 302, 305, 306, 309, 311–12, 313, 315–16, 317
    dividing and classifying and, 310–12
    evaluation and, 168–69
    examples in, 301–02
    interviews and, 76–78
    observation and, 59
    opinion (taking a stand) essay and, 130–32
    process analysis and, 312–13
    proposals and, 148–50
    reading critically and, 184–86
    recall and, 45–46
    strategies for, 300–18
    writing about literature and, 213–15
Dewey decimal classification system, 550, 551
Diagrams, 339, 355, 355 (fig.)
Dialogue
    ironic, 209
    quotation marks for, H-118
Diaries, 45, 265
Dictionaries, H-89–90, H-145
    in libraries, 556–57
    listing as a source, 625

Direct address, H-106
Directive, 313
Directives, H-96
Direct objects, H-37, H-38, H-107
Direct questions, H-96
Direct quotations, H-105–06, H-116, H-123–24
    ESL guidelines for, H-117
Discovery checklists
    analyzing, 309
    causes and effects, 109, 317
    comparing and contrasting, 91, 315–16
    defining, 306
    designing a document, 338
    details, 305
    developing and, 300, 302, 305, 306, 309, 311–12, 313, 315–16, 317
    dividing and classifying, 311–12
    evaluating, 167–68
    examples, 302
    interviews, 72–73
    observation, 58
    opinion (taking a stand) essay, 129
    process analysis, 313
    proposals, 146
    reading critically, 182
    recall, 44
    research question, 536
    writing about literature, 210–12, 219, 221
    writing in the workplace and, 225
    writing portfolio, 254
Discussion questions, 241, 243
Distant Mirror, The (Tuchman), 588–91
Divide or classify questions, 243
Division, and development strategies, 310–12
Doctoral dissertation, 627, 637
Document collections, online, 563
Document design. *See* Designing a document
Documenting sources, 598–600, 615–31 (MLA), 631–39 (APA), A-26–27. *See also* American Psychological Association (APA) style; Modern Language Association (MLA) style
    drafting and, 587–88
    working bibliography for, 542–44, 543 (fig.), 544 (fig.)
Documents, government
    citing (APA), 633
    indexes to, 558

library research using, 558–59
listing as sources, 627 (MLA), 637
    (APA)
Donovan, Priscilla, 315
Drafting, 11, 586–88
    causes and effects and, 111–12
    coherence and, 296–98
    comparing and contrasting and,
        93–96
    computers and, 286, 587, A-2
    conclusions and, 293–94
    evaluating and, 168–69
    exam answers and, 245–47
    incorporating source material
        during, 588–94
    interviews and, 76–78
    notes used in, 584–85
    observation and, 59
    openings and, 291–92
    opinion (taking a stand) essay and,
        130–32
    outlining and, 586
    paragraphing and, 287–88
    plagiarism avoidance in, 592–94
    proposals and, 148–50
    reading critically and, 184–86
    recall and, 45–46
    research archive and, 578
    restarting and, 287
    starting, 285–86
    strategies for, 285–99
    topic sentences and, 288–91
    writing about literature and,
        213–15
Dubious authority, reasoning from,
    135

Early, Gerald, 391
    "Black like . . . Shirley Temple?"
        391–93
Economic attitudes, and visuals, 370
Editing, 12. See also Proofreading;
        Revising
    causes and effects and, 112–13
    checklist for, 332
    clichés and, H-87
    comparing and contrasting, 96–97
    computers for, 62, 333
    evaluation and, 169–70
    interviews and, 78–79
    observation, 61–62
    opinion (taking a stand) essay and,
        132–33
    proposals and, 150–53
    reading critically and, 186–87

recall and, 46–48
research paper and, 598
spell checkers and, 333, A-19
strategies for, 331–34
writing about literature and, 215
writing portfolio and, 255
Editing checklists
    adjectives and adverbs, A-10
    apostrophes, A-16
    capitalization, A-18
    causes and effects, 114
    commas, A-15
    comma splices or fused sentences,
        A-12
    common and serious problems in
        college writing, 332, A-2
    comparing and contrasting, 97
    evaluating, 170
    interviews, 79
    misplaced and dangling modifiers,
        A-13
    observation, 62
    opinion (taking a stand) essay, 133
    parallel structure, A-14
    past tense, A-4
    pronoun-antecedent agreement, A-9
    pronoun case, A-8
    proposals, 153
    punctuation with quotations, A-17
    reading critically, 187
    recall, 48
    research papers, 598
    sentence fragments, A-11
    spelling, A-19
    subject-verb agreement, A-6
    writing about literature, 215
Editing guide, A-1–27
    effective sentences, A-12–14
    format problems, A-23–27
    grammar problems, A-2–12
    mechanics problems, A-17–23
    punctuation problems, A-14–17
Editorials, listing as sources, 626
    (MLA), 636–37 (APA)
Educational Policies in Crisis: Japanese
        and American Perspectives
        (Cummings), 93–94
Effects, 96, 110. See also Causes and
        effects
Either/or reasoning, 134–35
Electronic mail (e-mail)
    evaluating sources using, 574
    field research using, 568
    listing as a source, 629 (MLA), 639
        (APA)

mailing lists for, 563
research archive for, 545
revising using, 322
writing in the workplace using,
    233–34
Electronic research. See Internet;
    World Wide Web (WWW)
Electronic sources
    citing, 621 (MLA), 634 (APA)
    evaluating, 570–77
    listing as source, 627–29 (MLA)
        637–39 (APA)
    research checklist for, 571
    source notes on, 542, 544, 544
        (fig.)
    tracking, 545
Ellipsis marks, H-122, H-124–25,
    A-16–17
Elliptical constructions, H-62–63
E-mail. See Electronic mail
Emotional appeal, 29, 131, 254
Emphasis
    capitals for, A-17–18
    italics for, H-138
    revising and, 325–26
Encyclopedias
    in libraries, 556
    listing as source, 625 (MLA)
Endings (conclusions), 82, 215,
    293–94, 326, 596, 612
EndNote (software), 600
End punctuation, H-96–98, H-120
Envelopes, 230, 232 (fig.)
ERIC, 536, 552
ESL guidelines
    adjective clauses and relative
        pronouns, H-41
    conditionals, H-30
    count nouns and articles, H-33
    cumulative adjectives, H-51
    definite articles, H-48
    direct and indirect quotations, H-117
    indefinite articles, H-49
    indirect objects and prepositions,
        H-89
    mixed constructions, faulty
        predication, and subject errors,
        H-67
    negatives, H-54
    noncount nouns and articles, H-33
    participles, infinitives, and gerunds,
        H-8
    passive voice, H-27
    perfect progressive tenses, H-25
    perfect tenses, H-22

ESL guidelines (*cont.*)
  prepositions of location and time,
    H-88
  simple progressive tenses, H-24
  simple tenses, H-21
Essay examinations, 239–47
  drafting and, 245–47
  example of answer on, 240–41
  generating ideas for, 241
  planning for, 242–45
  preparing for, 239–40
  revising, 247
  revision checklist for, 247
  types of questions on, 242–44
Etext Archives, 563
Ethical appeal, 30, 131, 254
Euphemisms, H-85
Evaluating, 33, 34, 156–72
  applications of, 171–72
  assignments on, 165, 170–71
  cognitive activity and, 16, 20–21
  computers and, 169
  critical reading and, 19 (fig.),
    20–21, 202–03
  critical thinking and, 23 (fig.), 24
  discovery checklist for, 167–68
  editing checklist for, 170
  facing the challenge, 167
  generating ideas in, 165–67
  group learning activity and, 166
  interview material and, 76
  peer response checklist for, 168
  planning, drafting, and developing
    in, 168–69
  revising and editing in, 169–70
  revision checklist for, 169
  of sources, 570–77, 579
Evaluation, claims of, 127, 128
Evaluation questions, 241, 244
"Evan's Two Moms" (Quindlen),
    395–96
Evidence, 25–27
  appeals to readers with, 29–30
  opinion (taking a stand) and, 125,
    128–30
  proposals and, 148
  reading critically and, 184
  research sources and, 533, 575
  testing, 27–28, 129–30
  writing about literature and, 209
Examinations, 239–47
  drafting and, 245–47
  essay examinations, 239–40
  example of answer on, 240–41
  generating ideas for, 241

planning for, 242–45
preparing for, 239–40
revising, 247
revision checklist for, 247
short-answer examinations, 248
timed writings, 248–50
types of questions on, 242–44
Example, proof by, 134
Examples, 129, 301–02
Exclamation points, H-97–98, H-120
Expectations of readers, 339
Experience, recalling. *See* Recall,
    writing from
Experts
  research using, 531, 536, 565, 568
  testimony from, 26–27, 129, 132
External conflicts, 207

Facing the challenge
  causes and effects, 110
  comparing and contrasting, 91
  evaluating, 167
  interviewing, 72
  observation, 57
  opinion (taking a stand), 125
  proposals, 147
  reading critically, 184
  recall, 43
Facts
  evidence and, 25–26, 28, 129
  observation and, 565
  reading critically and, 184
  research and, 531, 577, 578
Fallacies, logical, 134–36, 184
Faulty predication, H-65–66
  ESL guidelines for, H-67
Favorites (bookmarks), 545
Fiction. *See* Literature, writing about
Field research, 533, 564–69, 574. *See
    also* Research
  checklist for, 576–77
  citing, 544, 621 (MLA), 631 (APA)
  conferences, lectures, and other
    events and, 568–69
  interviews and, 564–65
  letters used in, 568
  listing as source, 631 (MLA), 639
    (APA)
  observations and, 565, 577
  questionnaires and, 565–67, 567
    (fig.), 574
  source evaluation in, 574, 576–77
  source notes on, 544, 544 (fig.)
Figures (numbers), H-134–35
Figures of speech, 208

Films, listing as source, 630 (MLA),
    639 (APA)
Finnigan, Anne, 489
  "Nice Perks — If You Can Get 'Em,"
    489–94
First-person narrator, 208
Fischer, Kurt W., 311
Flashbacks, 45
Focal point, 360–61, 362 (fig.)
Follow-up, in reading, 17
Fonts, 343–46, 343 (fig.), 344 (fig.),
    345 (fig.), 346 (fig.), 352–53,
    366–69, 368 (fig.)
"Footprints: The Mark of Our Passing"
    (Messina), 54–56, 58–59
Foreshadowing, 207
Formal language, H-55, H-81–82,
    H-85
Formal outlines, 281–84. *See also*
    Outlines and outlining
Format. *See also* Designing a
    document
  for business letters, 229–30, 231
    (fig.)
  computers and, 113, 131, 149, 278,
    286, 356
  for electronic mail, 234
  manuscript, 337 (fig.) A-23–26
  for memoranda, 232, 233 (fig.)
  questionnaires, 566
  sample research paper, 337 (fig.),
    601–14
Forms of address, H-93, H-127–28
Forum One (Web site), 536, 563
"Four Kinds of Chance" (Austin), 292
"Four Weeks Vacation" (Robinson),
    467–72
Fragments, sentence, H-5–8, A-10–11
Free association, 91
Freewriting
  comparing and contrasting and, 91
  evaluating and, 165
  generating ideas and, 263–64
  recall and, 44–45
  stating a thesis and, 272
"Frog Factor, The" (McKibben), 157–59
"From Now On, Let Women Kill Their
    Own Spiders" (Barry), 429–30
Frost, Robert, 222, H-62
Full block style, for business letters,
    230
Fused sentences, H-10–12, A-11–12
Future perfect progressive tense, H-19,
    H-25
  ESL guidelines for, H-25

Future perfect tense, H-19, H-22–23
  ESL guidelines for, H-22
Future progressive tense, H-19, H-23, H-24
  ESL guidelines for, H-24
Future tense, H-19, H-20–22
  ESL guidelines for, H-21

Gallup Poll, 557
Gansberg, Martin, 294
Gender
  language and, H-90–91, H-92
  pronoun-antecedent agreement and, H-46, A-8
Generating ideas, 10
  brainstorming and, 260–62
  causes and effects and, 109–11
  comparing and contrasting and, 90–93
  computers and, 264, 266
  for essay exams, 241
  evaluating and, 165–67
  freewriting and, 263–64
  group learning activity for, 263
  interviews and, 72–76
  journal keeping and, 265–66, 270
  observation and, 58–59
  opinion (taking a stand) essay and, 125–26
  preparing for, 268–70
  proposals and, 146–48
  reading critically and, 180–84, 270
  recall and, 44
  reporter's questions and, 267–68
  for research project, 535–41
  setting up for, 268–70
  strategies for, 260–70
  writing about literature and, 210–11
Genre (form), 339
Gerund, H-38–39, A-8
  ESL guidelines for, H-8
Giles, Robert H., Jr., 310–11
Goers, Sarah E. (student writer), 600–14
Goodman, Ellen, 185, 299, 456–57
  "How to Zap Violence on TV," 457–58
  "Kids, Divorce, and the Myth," 175–76
Google, 536, 559, 560 (fig.), 561 (fig.)
Government documents. *See* Documents, government
Grammar checkers, A-1, A-19
Grammar problems
  adjectives and adverbs, A-9–10

apostrophes, A-15–16
capitalization, A-17–18
comma splices and fused sentences, A-11–12
comma usage, A-14–15
editing checklist for, A-2
homonyms, A-20
misplaced or dangling modifiers, A-12–13
parallel structure, A-13–14
past tense verb forms, A-3–5
pronoun-antecedent agreement, A-8–9
pronoun case, A-7–8
sentence fragments, A-10–11
spelling, A-19–23
subject-verb agreement, A-5–6
Graphics, 354–57, 354 (fig.), 355 (fig.)
Graphs, 338, 354, 354 (fig.)
Grecian, Kelly (student writer), 182–83
Grouping ideas, 276–77
Group interview, 78
Group learning activities
  brainstorming and, 250, 261, 263
  causes and effects and, 115
  collaborative research and, 540
  comparing and contrasting and, 96
  evaluating and, 166
  interviewing and, 78
  observation and, 62
  opinion (taking a stand) essay and, 127
  outlining and, 280
  peer editing, 46
  proofreading in pairs, 334
  proposals and, 151
  reading aloud in, 62
  reading critically and, 188
  thesis identification and, 272
  timed writings and, 250
Guide to Reference Books, 556

Handbooks, in libraries, 557
Harjo, Joy, 423
  "Three Generations of Native American Women's Birth Experience," 423–27
Harjo, Suzan Shown
  "Last Rites for Indian Dead," 118–20
Have (verb), A-6
Hawley, Gessner G., 306

Headings
  in document design, 339, 349–51, 352 (fig.), 353 (fig.)
  in outlines, 587
Helping (auxiliary) verbs, H-14, H-15
"Here Is New York" (White), 52–54
"Hidden Truth, The: An Analysis of Shirley Jackson's 'The Lottery'" (Burns), 203–05
Home pages of libraries, 546–47, 548 (fig.)
Homonyms, H-142, A-19–20
"How Men and Women Think" (Wade), 438–40
"How-to" process analysis, 313
"How to Zap Violence on TV" (Goodman), 457–58
Human Development (Fischer and Lazerson), 311
Hunger of Memory (Rodriguez), 45–46
Hyphens, H-139–41

Ideas, organizing, 586. *See also* Generating ideas; Organizing information
Idioms, H-87–90
"Illusions Are Forever" (Chiat), 455–56
Illustrations, 354–57, 354 (fig.), 355 (fig.)
Imagery, 208
Images. *See also* Visuals
  observation and, 59–60
  recalling an experience and, 59
  responding to, 35, 51, 65, 81, 100, 117, 138, 156, 173, 378, 411, 442, 466, 501
Imaginative questions, 245
Imperative mood, H-28, H-29
Inclusive numbers, H-141
Incomplete sentences, H-60–63
Indefinite articles, ESL guidelines for, H-49
Indefinite pronouns, H-34, H-45, H-114, A-6, A-8
Indexes, 546, 553–54
  electronic, 552
  government documents, 558
  periodicals, 552, 553 (fig.)
  research checklist for, 553
  Web, 562
Indicative mood, H-28–29
Indirect objects, H-38, H-89
Indirect questions, H-96
Indirect quotations, H-108
  ESL guidelines for, H-117

Infinitives, H-16, H-31
    ESL guidelines for, H-8
Informal language, H-55, H-82
Informal outlines, 279–81. *See also*
    Outlines and outlining
InfoTrac, 553, 554 (fig.)
In Search of Excellence (Peters and
    Waterman), 301
Interjections, H-97–98, H-106
Interlibrary loans, 552
Internal conflicts, 207
Internet, 533, 536. *See also* Electronic
    mail; Electronic sources; World
    Wide Web (WWW)
    chat rooms on, 563, 569
    newsgroups and mailing lists on,
        563
    search sites on, 562
    search techniques for, 539–40,
        559–63
Interpretation
    reading and, 202
    of sources, 585
    supporting, 214
Interviewing, 33, 65–80
    applications of, 80
    assignments using, 72, 79
    brainstorming on, 72
    citing, 544, 621 (MLA), 633 (APA)
    computers and, 75
    conducting a collective interview,
        78
    discovery checklist for, 72–73
    editing checklist for, 79
    facing the challenge, 73
    field research using, 564–65, 574
    generating ideas for, 72–76
    group learning activity for, 78
    letter requesting, 238
    listing as source, 631 (MLA), 639
        (APA)
    observation during, 74–75
    peer response checklists for, 74, 77
    planning, drafting, and developing,
        76–78
    preparing questions for, 74
    questionnaires and, 566–67
    recording information during,
        75–76, 564–65
    revising and editing, 78–79
    revision checklist for, 78–79
    setting up, 73
    source notes on, 544, 544 (fig.)
    by telephone, 75, 565
Intransitive verbs, H-16

Introductions, 203, 214. *See also*
    Beginnings (openings)
    to writing portfolios, 253–54
Introductory words with comma,
    A-14–15
Inverted sentences, H-78
"Invisible Women" (Choi), 105–08, 111
Invisible writing, 264
Ironic dialogue, 209
Ironic situations, 209
Irony, 209
Irregular adjectives, H-50, A-10
Irregular adverbs, H-50, A-10
Irregular verbs, H-16–18, A-3–5
"Is Inclusion the Answer?" (Goers),
    602–14
Issues, taking a stand on. *See* Opinion
Italics, 169, 278, 344–45, 587,
    H-136–38
It's, its (pronoun), A-15–16
"I Want a Wife" (Brady), 412–14
"I Want to Be Miss América" (Alvarez),
    502–06

Jackson, Shirley, 206, 208
    "The Lottery," 195–201, 206–07,
        208–09
Jargon, H-83–84
Jervis, Lisa, 519–20
    "My Jewish Nose," 520–23
Jones, Mary Harris ("Mother"), 303–04
Journals. *See also* Periodicals
    computers and, 266
    generating ideas with, 58–59,
        265–66, 270
    reading and, 17–18, 181
    writing and, 45, 49, 126, 265–66,
        270
Judgment, in evaluating, 167, 169

Kessler, Heidi (student writer),
    289–90
Key words, in brainstorming, 262
Keyword searches, 539–41
    in library catalogs, 547–48, 549
        (fig.), 555
    on the Web, 555, 559–61, 560
        (fig.), 561 (fig.)
"Kids, Divorce, and the Myth"
    (Goodman), 175–76, 185
"Kids in the Mall: Growing Up
    Controlled" (Kowinski), 101–05
King, Stephen, 443
    "Why We Crave Horror Movies,"
        443–45

Kinney, Monica Yant, 77
    "Mining for Humor," 66–68
Knowing information, in critical
    reading, 16, 19, 19 (fig.)
Kortz, Dawn (student writer)
    "Listen," 68–71
Kowinski, William Severini
    "Kids in the Mall: Growing Up
        Controlled," 101–05
Kozol, Jonathan, 301–02
Kula, Marisa, 510
    "Victoria's Not-So-Secret Strategy,"
        510–13

Labels, condescending, H-92
Language
    bias-free, H-90–93
    evidence and, 26–27
    level of, H-55, H-81–82
    sexist, H-90–93
    in visuals, 367–69, 370–71
"Last Rites for Indian Dead" (Harjo),
    118–20
Latin abbreviations, H-128, H-129
Lavenda, Robert H., 307–08
Lazerson, Arlyne, 311
Lectures, and field research, 568–69
Leonard, George B., 292
Letters
    application, 236–38
    business, 227–30
    field research and, 568
Letters to the editor, listing as source,
    626 (MLA), 637 (APA)
Levels, heading, 349–50, 587
Lexis-Nexis, 553
Librarians, 547, 552, 555, 559, 575
Libraries, 533. *See also* Library research
    atlases in, 557
    bibliographies in, 554–55
    biographical sources in, 557
    classification systems of, 550–51
    databases in, 536, 546, 552–55
    dictionaries in, 556–57
    encyclopedias in, 556
    government documents in, 558–59
    handbooks and companions in,
        557
    home pages of, 546–47, 548 (fig.)
    indexes in, 552–55, 553 (fig.), 554
        (fig.)
    interlibrary loans and, 552
    microforms in, 558
    reference materials in, 556–59
    research project and, 536

special collections in, 558–59
statistical sources in, 557
Library catalogs, 547–52, 555
    searching, 540–41, 547–52, 549
        (fig.), 550 (fig.)
    subject headings in, 548–49, 551
        (fig.)
Library of Congress classification
    system, 550–51
Library of Congress online archive,
    379
Library of Congress Subject Headings
    (LCSH), 548, 551 (fig.)
Library research, 546–59. *See also*
    Research; Research project
    keywords and links in, 547–48, 549
        (fig.), 550 (fig.)
    online catalogs in, 547–52
    overview before starting, 536
    research checklist for, 547
Limited omniscient point of view, 208
Linking ideas, 276–77, 276 (fig.)
Linking verbs, H-14, H-15, H-35, H-48,
    H-66
Links, online, 539–41
"Listen" (Kortz), 68–71
Lists, 346–47
Literal level, in reading, 19–20, 180
Literal skills, in critical reading, 19–20,
    19 (fig.)
Literary analysis, 194
Literature, citing, 618–19
Literature, writing about, 194–223
    assignments, 209–10, 219, 222–23
    critical reading in, 202
    discovery checklists for, 210–11,
        211–12, 219, 221
    editing checklist for, 215
    evaluating in, 202–03
    generating ideas in, 210–11
    glossary of terms for, 206–09
    paraphrase and, 216–17, 221
    peer response checklist for, 216
    planning, drafting, and developing
        in, 213–15
    revising and editing, 215
    revision checklist for, 215
    strategies for, 216–21
    synopsis and, 202, 216–17
Little Windows Book, The (Nelson), 313
Lives of a Cell, The (Thomas), 289
Location, prepositions of, ESL
    guidelines for, H-88
Logical appeal, 29, 131, 254
Logical fallacies, 129, 134–36, 184

Logical order, 276
Logos, 367 (fig.), 372
Long Count, The (Tunney), 294
"Lottery, The" (Jackson), 195–201,
    206–07, 208–09
Lycos, 536, 563

McCuistion, Clay (student writer)
    "Coffee Odyssey," 160–64
McKibben, Bill
    "The Frog Factor," 157–59
McPhee, John, 397
    "Silk Parachute," 397–99
Magazines. *See also* Periodicals
    common design features of, 339,
        340 (fig.)
Magellan, 562
Mail, electronic. *See* Electronic mail
Main clauses, H-10, H-12, H-76, H-78,
    H-79, H-99, H-112, A-11–12
Main verbs, H-15
Males, Mike, 459–60
    "Public Enemy Number One?"
        460–64
Mann, Charles C., 317
Manuscript form, A-23–26
    APA style, 634
    MLA style, 337 (fig.), 338, 339, 350,
        351, 353
Maps, 354, 557
Martin, John (student writer), 328–31
Mass nouns, H-33
MedLine, 536
Memoranda (memos), 224, 231–32,
    233 (fig.)
    format for, 232
    guidelines for writing, 224–27
"Men We Carry in Our Minds, The"
    (Sanders), 415–19
Messina, Sandy (student writer),
    58–59
    "Footprints: The Mark of Our
        Passing," 54–56
Metaphor, 208, 307–08
Microforms, 558
Miday, Ryan (student writer)
    "*Times* Series Delved Successfully
        into Race," 177–79
"Mining for Humor" (Kinney), 66–68,
    77
"Mirror Image" (Potter), 514–18
Misplaced modifiers, H-57–59,
    A-12–13
"Missed Opportunities" (Colbenson),
    142–45, 146, 149, 150–51

Mixed constructions, H-64–65
    ESL guidelines for, H-67
MLA. *See* Modern Language
    Association (MLA) style
MLA Bibliography, 536
*MLA Handbook for Writers of Research
    Papers*, 616
MLA Online, 552
Mnemonic devices, H-145
Modern Language Association (MLA)
    style, 543 (fig.), 544 (fig.), 599,
        600, H-123, A-26–27
    citing sources, 587, 616–21
    format for paper, 337 (fig.), 338,
        339, 350, 351, 353
    listing sources, 599, 621–31
    source notes, 543 (fig.), 544 (fig.)
Modified block style, in business
    letters, 230, 231 (fig.)
Modifiers, H-57–59, H-102, A-12–13
    checking for, using a computer, 62
    dangling, H-59, A-12–13
    misplaced, H-57–59, A-12–13
    nonrestrictive, H-102–03, A-14–15
    restrictive, H-103, H-108, A-15
    squinting, H-58
Momaday, N. Scott, 304
Mood (atmosphere), 206, 369–70
Mood (verbs), H-28–30, H-54–55
Moritz, Jeffrey, 306
Morris, David, 292
"Mother Tongue" (Tan), 385–90
"My Inner Shrimp" (Trudeau), 507–09
"My Jewish Nose" (Jervis), 520–23
Mysticism (Underhill), 591–92
"Myth of Cinderella, The"
    (Chambers), 446–49

Narration, 45
Narrator, 207–08
Nash, Madeleine, 312
Negatives, ESL guidelines for, H-54
Nelson, Kay Yarborough, 313
New Bartleby Digital Library, 563
Newman, Katherine S., 479
    No Shame in My Game, 479–84
News
    causes and effects and, 115
    reporter's questions (five W's and
        an H) and, 45, 92–93, 267–68
NewsBank, 553
Newsgroups, 536, 545, 563, 573
Newspapers
    articles in, 45, 574
    citing, 620 (MLA)

Newspapers (*cont.*)
design of, 335, 336 (fig.), 339, 340 (fig.)
listing as source, 626 (MLA), 636 (APA)
"New York" (Talese), 290
New York Times Index, 553
"Niceness Solution, The" (Varnell), 271–72
"Nice Perks — If You Can Get 'Em" (Finnigan), 489–94
Noncount nouns, H-33, H-49
Nonfiction books, citing, 616–18
Nonprint sources
citing, 621 (MLA), 634 (APA)
listing as sources, 627–31 (MLA), 637–39 (APA)
Nonrestrictive modifiers, H-102–03, A-14–15
Non sequitur, 134
Normal sentences, H-78
Northern Farm (Beston), 59
"No School?" (Leonard), 292
No Shame in My Game (Newman), 479–84
Note cards, format of, 578
Notes
elements of, 577–78
examinations and, 239
preparing for writing with, 270
stating a thesis and, 272
writing from sources using, 586, 587
Note taking
computers and, 44, 186, 578
format, 578
generating ideas from, 59
incorporating source material from, 584–85, 588
interviewing and, 75–76, 564–65
nutshelling (summarizing) and, 580, 582, 582 (fig.)
observation and, 565
paraphrasing and, 580–81, 581 (fig.)
plagiarism avoidance and, 579, 587
quotations and, 580, 580 (fig.)
reading and, 186
research and, 577–83
research archive and, 545
research checklist for, 582–83
working bibliography and, 542–44, 543 (fig.), 544 (fig.)
Nouns
ESL guidelines for, H-33
plural, H-35, H-113–14

Novels. *See also* Literature, writing about
analyzing, 210–11
Novelty fonts, 344, 345 (fig.)
Number (grammar), H-44, A-5–6, A-8
Numbered lists, 347
Numbers, H-128, H-134–35, H-140–41
Nutshelling (summarizing), 185, 286, 545
plagiarism avoidance in, 590, 594
reading critically and, 185
research and, 545, 579, 582, 582 (fig.)
research checklist for, 582–83
writing from sources using, 588–90, 592

Object, H-10, A-7
Object complements, H-47
Objective nouns, H-37
Objective point of view, 208
Objective pronoun case, H-37, H-38, A-7
Observation, writing from, 33, 51–64
applications of, 63–64
assignments on, 57–58, 62–63
computers and, 62
critical thinking and, 27
discovery checklist for, 58
editing checklist for, 61–62
evaluating and, 165
facing the challenge, 57
field research using, 58, 565, 577
generating ideas in, 58–59
group learning activity for, 62
imagery and, 59
interviewing and, 74–75
note taking in, 59
organizing information in, 60
peer response checklist for, 61
planning, drafting, and developing in, 60
purpose in, 60
revising and editing in, 60–61
revision checklist for, 61
Observation sheet, 59
Of Woman Born (Rich), 298–99
Olson, Charles, 596
Olson, Steve, 473
"Year of the Blue-Collar Guy," 473–75
"Once More to the Lake" (White), 293, 379–84

Online library catalogs, 546
searching, 547–52, 549 (fig.), 550 (fig.)
subject headings in, 548–49
Online research. *See* Internet; World Wide Web (WWW)
"On Societies as Organisms" (Thomas), 289
Open-book examinations, 239–40. *See also* Examinations
Openings (beginnings), 77, 82, 241, 291–92, 325, 595–96, 604. *See also* Introductions
Opinion (taking a stand), 117–37, 139
appeals to readers in, 131–32
applications of, 136–37
assignments on, 124–25, 136
beginning essays with, 292
computers and, 131
discovery checklist for, 129
editing checklist for, 133
evaluating and, 157
evidence and, 128–30
facing the challenge, 125
generating ideas for, 125–29
group learning activity and, 127
logical fallacies and, 134–36
peer response checklist for, 133
planning, drafting, and developing, 130–32
purpose of, 118
revising and editing, 132–33
revision checklist for, 132
Organizations, information from, 558
Organizing information, 82, 275–84. *See also* Outlines and outlining
causes and effects and, 111–12
comparing and contrasting and, 92, 93–96, 314–16
computers for, 277, 278
details and, 304
dividing and classifying in, 310–12
essay examinations and, 241
evaluating and, 168–69
grouping ideas, 276–77
observation and, 60
opinion (taking a stand) essay and, 130
planning and, 275–84
point by point, 94–95, 169
reading critically and, 183, 185
research archive and, 544–45
subject by subject, 93–94, 169
writing a research paper and, 586

writing in the workplace and, 227
writing portfolio and, 252
"Our Barbies, Ourselves" (Prager),
    420–22
Outlines and outlining, 279–84
    causes and effects and, 111
    comparing and contrasting and,
        95
    computers for, 587
    drafting and, 586–87
    evaluating and, 169
    formal, 281–84
    group learning activity for, 280
    informal, 279–81
    planning with, 279–84
    revising and, 321
    sample, 203, 279, 280, 281, 282,
        283–84, 602–03
    sentence, 283–84, 602–03
Oversimplification, 134
Overviews, and research projects, 536

Paragraphs
    drafting, 287–88
    revising, 322
    transition, 298
Parallel structure, H-66–70, A-13–14
Paraphrasing
    plagiarism avoidance in, 592–94
    quotations mixed with, 591–92
    reading critically and, 185–86
    research and, 545, 579, 580–81,
        581 (fig.)
    research checklist for, 582–83
    writing about literature and,
        216–17, 221
    writing from sources using, 588,
        590–92
Parentheses, H-122–23
Parenthetical expressions, H-104,
    H-121, A-15
Participles, H-7, A-3
    ESL guidelines for, H-8
"Part-Time Marriage, A" (Perrin),
    401–03
Passive voice, H-26–28, H-66
    ESL guidelines for, H-27
Past participles, H-16
Past perfect progressive tense, H-19,
    H-24–25
    ESL guidelines for, H-25
Past perfect tense, H-19, H-22–23
    ESL guidelines for, H-22
Past progressive tense, H-19, H-23
    ESL guidelines for, H-24

Past tense, 84, H-16, H-20, H-30,
    A-3–4
    ESL guidelines for, H-21
Peer editors, 46, 61, 323–24
Peer response checklists
    causes and effects, 114
    comparing and contrasting, 94
    conversation, 74, 77
    evaluating, 168
    interviewing, 74, 77
    observation, 61
    opinion (taking a stand) essay, 133
    proposals, 152
    reading critically, 187
    recall, 48
    writing about literature, 216
    writing from research, 597
Perfect progressive tense, H-24–25
    ESL guidelines for, H-25
Perfect tenses, H-22–23, H-30
    ESL guidelines for, H-22
Periodicals
    citing, 620 (MLA)
    electronic, 628–29 (MLA), 638
        (APA)
    generating ideas and, 181
    indexes to, 552–54
    listing as sources, 625–27 (MLA),
        628–29 (MLA), 636–37 (APA)
    source notes for, 542, 543, 543
        (fig.)
    as sources for research papers, 575
Periodic sentences, H-78
Periods, H-96–97, H-119, H-120,
    A-16–17
Perrin, Noel, 400
    "A Part-Time Marriage," 401–03
Person (grammar), H-31, H-44, H-54,
    A-5–6
Personal communications, citing, 633
    (APA)
Personal pronouns, H-115, A16
Personification, 208
Peters, Thomas J., 301
Photocopying, and research, 545
Photographs, 354, 364, 565
Phrases, H-6
Plagiarism, 185, 579, 587, 592–94
Planning, 10
    causes and effects and, 111–12
    comparing and contrasting and,
        93–96, 273
    computers and, 278
    evaluating and, 168–69
    for exam questions, 242–45, 249

grouping ideas and, 276–77
group learning activities and, 272,
    280
interviews and, 76–78
observation and, 59
opinion (taking a stand) essay and,
    130–32
organizing ideas in, 275–84
outlining and, 279–84
for a proposal, 148–50
reading critically and, 184–86
recall and, 45–46
strategies for, 271–84
thesis statement in, 271–75
writing about literature and,
    213–15
Plath, Sylvia, 265
Plausibility, 207
Plays. *See also* Literature, writing
    about
    analyzing, 210–11
Plot
    of images, 363
    of stories, 207, 216
Plummer, Mark L., 317
Plurals
    apostrophes and, H-113–15
    bias-free language using, H-91
    formation of, H-143
    spelling of, H-143
Poems
    analyzing, 211–12
    paraphrasing, 221
Point of view, 207–08
Policy, claims of, 127, 128
Political attitudes, and visuals, 370
Portfolios, 252–55
    discovery checklist for, 254
    tips for keeping, 252–55
Possessive nouns, H-37
Possessive pronouns, H-37, H-38–39,
    A-7, A-15–16
Possessives (grammar), H-113–15,
    A-15–16
Post hoc ergo propter hoc, 134
Potter, Alicia, 514
    "Mirror Image," 514–18
PowerShift (Toffler), 306
Prager, Emily, 420
    "Our Barbies, Ourselves," 420–22
Predicates, H-10, A-11
Prefixes, H-140, H-145
Prepositional phrase, H-31
Prepositions, H-65, H-89, A-24
Present participles, H-39

Present perfect progressive tense, H-19, H-24–25
  ESL guidelines for, H-25
Present perfect tense, H-19, H-22–23
  ESL guidelines for, H-22
Present progressive tense, H-19, H-23
  ESL guidelines for, H-24
Present tense, H-17–20
  ESL guidelines for, H-21
  with literary work, A-3–4
Presidential Character, The: Predicting Performance in the White House (Barber), 289
Primary sources, 574–75
Prisoners of Silence: Breaking the Bonds of Adult Illiteracy in the United States (Kozol), 302
Problems, writing about. *See* Proposals
Proceedings, conference, 569
Process analysis, 244–45, 312–13
Pro Cite (software), 600
Product logos, 367 (fig.), 372
Progressive tenses, H-18, H-19, H-23–24
  ESL guidelines for, H-24
Project. *See* Research projects
Project Gutenberg, 563
Pronouns, H-44, A-7–8.
  antecedent agreement and, H-44–46, A-8–9
  antecedents of, H-40–43
  case, H-36–39, A-7–8
  indefinite, H-34, H-45, H-114, A-6, A-8
  possessive case of, A-7, A-16
  reference, H-40–43
  relative, H-34–35, H-41, H-73, H-76
  revising, 327
  transitions and, 299
Proof by example, 134
Proofreading, 12, 47, 97, 113, 133, 170, 215, A-1–2
  computers and, 333
  exam questions and, 249
  group learning activity for, 334
  observation essay and, 61
  research paper and, 598
  spell checkers and, 333, A-19
  strategies for, 332–34
  symbols for, A-25–26
  tips for, 333
  writing portfolio and, 255

Proper names, H-127–28, H-130–31, H-143, A-17–18
Proposals, 34, 49, 64, 138–55
  applications of, 154–55
  assignments on, 145–46, 153–54
  computers and, 149
  critical thinking and, 94
  discovery checklist for, 146
  editing checklist for, 153
  facing the challenge, 147
  generating ideas for, 146–48
  group learning activity and, 151
  peer response checklist for, 152
  planning, drafting, and developing, 148–50
  revising and editing, 150–53
  revision checklist for, 152
Protagonist, 207
PsycLIT, 536, 552
Publication Manual (American Psychological Association), 631. *See also* American Psychological Association (APA) style
"Public Enemy Number One?" (Males), 460–64
Publishers, evaluating in sources, 575
Pull quotes, 343
Punctuation, H-96–126, A-14–17. *See also individual punctuation marks*
Purpose
  comparing and contrasting and, 91, 92, 96
  document design and, 342
  drafting and, 286
  evaluating and, 165, 168
  observation and, 60
  opinion (taking a stand) and, 118
  reading process and, 17
  revising for, 320
  source evaluation and, 571
  writing in the workplace and, 224, 225
  writing process and, 13–14

Question marks, H-96–97, H-120
Questionnaires, 565–67, 567 (fig.), 574
Questions. *See also* Examinations
  beginning essays with, 292
  direct, H-96, H-123–24
  evaluation with, 168
  indirect, H-96
  interviewing with, 74, 565
  opinion (taking a stand) essay and, 125–26

for reporters (five *W*'s and an *H*), 45, 92–93, 267–68
  research papers and, 531, 537–39
  selecting a research subject using, 535–36
Quindlen, Anna, 394
  "Evan's Two Moms," 395–96
Quizzes, 239. *See also* Examinations
Quotation marks, 578, 580, 599, H-116–20, A-16–17
Quotations, 566, 607, 609
  capitalization in, H-133, A-18
  concluding essays with, 293
  direct, H-105–06, H-116
  double checking, 77–78
  in exam questions, 244
  indirect, H-108
  interviewing and, 76, 77, 564
  literary critiques and, 215
  paraphrasing mixed with, 591–92
  plagiarism avoidance and, 592–94
  punctuation of, H-111, H-116–20, H-125, A-16–17
  reading critically and, 185, 187
  research and, 578, 579, 580, 580 (fig.)
  research checklist for, 582–83
  style of, 599
  transitions with, 588
  writing from sources using, 587–88, 591–92

Radio program, listing as source, 630 (MLA), 639 (APA)
Readers. *See* Audience (readers)
Readers' Guide to Periodical Literature, 553, 553 (fig.)
Reading, 15–21
  comparing and contrasting and, 93
  process of, 15–21
  writing and, 8–9
Reading aloud, 62
Reading critically, 15, 33, 34, 173–89, 270
  applications of, 188–89
  assignments for, 180, 188
  computers and, 186
  discovery checklist for, 182
  editing checklist for, 187
  evaluating and, 165
  facing the challenge, 184
  generating ideas in, 180–84, 270
  group learning activity on, 188

literal and analytical reading skills in, 19–20, 19 (fig.)

peer response checklist for, 187

planning, drafting, and developing in, 184–86

revising and editing and, 186–87

revision checklist for, 186–87

Reading journal, 17–18, 181

Recall, writing from, 10, 33, 35–50

applications of, 49–50

assignments on, 43, 48–49

computers and, 44

discovery checklist for, 44

editing checklist for, 48

evaluating and, 165

facing the challenge, 43

freewriting and, 44–45

generating ideas and, 44

group learning activity for, 46

peer response checklist for, 48

planning, drafting, and developing in, 45–46

reading critically and, 181

revising and editing in, 46–47

revision checklist for, 47

Recording

evidence, 129

an interview, 75–76, 564, 565

notes, 577–78, 579–83, 580 (fig.), 581 (fig.), 582 (fig.)

online searches, 545

Reference books

citing, 619–20 (MLA)

in libraries, 556–57

listing as source, 625 (MLA)

Reference Manager (software), 600

"References" (list of sources), 554, 599, 634 (APA). *See also* "Works Cited" (list of sources)

References, in résumés, 236

Reflective introductions, 253–55

Reflective journal writing, 265–66

Regular verbs, H-16, A-3, A-5–6

Relative pronouns, H-34–35, H-73, H-76

ESL guidelines for, H-41

revising, 327

"Remarriage and Stepfamilies" (Coontz), 404–07

Repetition, H-62, H-70

document design and, 351–53

transitions using, 298–99

Reporter's questions (five *W*'s and an *H*), 45, 92–93, 267–68

Rereading, and drafting, 287

Research, 531. *See also* Field research; Library research

applications of, 600–01

collaborative, 540

skills in, 533–34

Research archive, 544–45, 578

Research checklists

evaluating field sources, 576–77

evaluating print and electronic sources, 571

finding the right index, 553

library research, 547

managing your project, 555

note taking, 582–83

plagiarism avoidance, 594

research questions, 539

Research papers, 531, 533, 584–614. *See also* Research projects

format, 337 (fig.), 601–14, A-23–26

planning and drafting, 584–96

sample, 601–14

skills needed for, 533–34

Research projects

choosing a subject for, 535–36

collaborative research in, 540

discovery checklist for, 536

evaluating sources in, 570–77

generating ideas for, 535–36

group learning activity for, 540

managing, 541–45, 555

overview before starting, 536

plagiarism avoidance in, 579

planning, 534–35

preliminary search in, 539–41

research question, 537–39

sample research paper, 601–14

schedule for, 541–42, 555

skills needed for, 533–34

taking notes for, 577–83, 580 (fig.), 581 (fig.), 582 (fig.)

working bibliography for, 542–44, 543 (fig.), 544 (fig.)

Research question, 531, 537–39, 586

keywords based on, 540

research checklist for, 539

stating, 537–39

Responsive journal writing, 266

Restarting, 287

Restrictive modifiers, H-103, H-108, A-15

Résumés, 234–36, 235 (fig.)

Reviewing, 151, 240, 319–24

Revising, 11–12. *See also* Editing

audience and, 320–21

causes and effects and, 112–13

checklists for, 320, 322, 328, 597

comparing and contrasting and, 96–97

computers and, 322, 324, 598

cutting and whittling in, 326–31

evaluation and, 169–70

exam answers, 247

interviews and, 78–79

macro, 319

micro, 319

observation and, 61–62

opinion (taking a stand) essay and, 132–33

peer editors and, 323–24

proposals and, 150–53

purpose and, 320

reading critically and, 186–87

recall and, 46–48

research papers and, 596–98

strategies for, 319–34

stressing what counts in, 324–25

structure and, 321–22

writing about literature and, 215

Revision checklists

audience, 321

causes and effects, 113

comparing and contrasting and, 97

cutting and whittling, 328

evaluating, 169

exam answers, 247

interviews, 78–79

observation, 61

opinion (taking a stand) essay, 132

proposals, 152

purpose, 320

reading critically, 186–87

recall, 47

research paper, 597

structure, 322

writing about literature, 215

writing in the workplace, 226, 227

Rich, Adrienne, 298–99

Rideau, Wilbert

"Why Prisons Don't Work," 140–41

Robinson, Edwin Arlington, 223

Robinson, Joe, 467

"Four Weeks Vacation," 467–72

Rodriguez, Richard, 45–46

"Rootlessness" (Morris), 292

Rose, Phyllis, 450

"Shopping and Other Spiritual Adventures in America Today," 450–53

Rounds, Kate, 182–83

Running header, 353, 353 (fig.)

Run-on (fused) sentences, H-10–12, A-11–12

Salutations, H-112
Sanders, Scott Russell, 415
  "The Men We Carry in Our Minds," 415–19
Sans serif fonts, 343–44, 344 (fig.)
Sarcasm, 209
Scene, observing. *See* Observation, writing from
Schedules
  for collaborating on research, 540
  for research projects, 541–42
  for writing, 269
"School vs. Education" (Baker), 293–94
Schreiner, Robert G. (student writer), 46, 47
  "What Is a Hunter?" 39–42
Schultz, Emily A., 307–08
Scope of a paper, 92–93
Scratch outline, 279. *See also* Outlines and outlining
Search engines, 536, 559–63
Searches
  keywords in, 539–41, 555, 559–61, 560 (fig.), 561 (fig.)
  in online library catalogs, 540, 547–52, 549 (fig.), 550 (fig.)
  on the Web, 539–41, 545, 555, 559–63, 560 (fig.), 561 (fig.)
Secondary sources, 574–75
Self-assessment, 253
Semicolons, H-11, H-12, H-72, H-79, H-108–09, H-119, A-12, A-16–17
Sentence fragments, H-5–8, A-10–11
Sentence outlines, 283–84, 602–03.
  See also Outlines and outlining
Sentences, H-11
  adjectives and adverbs in, H-46–51, A-9–10
  comma splices in, H-10–12, A-11–12
  comparisons in, H-60–62
  consistency in, H-52–55
  coordination and subordination in, H-71–77
  effective, H-57–80
  elliptical constructions in, H-62–63
  faulty predication in, H-65–66
  fragments, H-5–8, A-10–11
  fused, H-10–12, A-11–12
  grammatical, H-5–56
  incomplete, H-60–63

mixed constructions in, H-64–65
modifiers in, H-57–59, A-12–13
normal, H-78
number beginning, H-135
parallel structure in, H-68–70, A-13–14
parts of, H-10
pronoun-antecedent agreement in, H-44–46, A-8–9
pronoun case in, H-36–39, A-7–8
pronoun reference in, H-40–43
shifts in, H-52–55
subject-verb agreement in, H-31–35, A-5–6
types of, H-79
variety in, H-78–79
verbs in, H-14–36, A-3–5
Series
  parallel structure in, H-68–70, A-13–14
  punctuation of, H-100–01, H-108, H-109, H-111, H-122–23, A-14–15
Serif fonts, 343–44, 345 (fig.)
Setting, 206
"Shopping and Other Spiritual Adventures in America Today" (Rose), 450–53
Short-answer examinations, 248
Short stories. *See also* Literature, writing about
  analyzing, 210–11
"Silk Parachute" (McPhee), 397–99
Simile, 208
Simple future tense, H-19, H-20–22
Simple past tense, H-19, H-20, A-3–4
Simple present tense, H-19–20
Simple sentences, H-79
Simple tenses, H-18, H-19–22
  ESL guidelines for, H-21
Skimming, 17, 181
Slang, H-85, H-119
Smiley, Jane, 476
  "The Case against Chores," 476–78
Sociological attitudes, and visuals, 370
Software, listing as a source, 629 (MLA), 639 (APA)
Solitaire technique, 277
Solutions, proposing. *See* Proposals
Sources. *See also* Documenting sources
  audience and, 572–73
  authorship issues and, 573–74
  citing, 599, 616–21 (MLA), 631–34 (APA), A-26–27 (MLA)
  crediting, 355

evaluating, 570–77, 572 (fig.) 579
incorporating in a paper, 588–92
interpreting, 585
listing at the end, 599, 621–31 (MLA), 634–39 (APA)
nutshelling (summarizing) of, 582, 582 (fig.), 588–90
opinion (taking a stand) essay and, 132
paraphrasing, 580–81, 581 (fig.), 588, 590–92
primary, 574–75
proposals and, 150
purpose of, 571
research archive and, 544–45
research checklist for, 571
research skills and, 533
quoting, 579, 580, 580 (fig.)
sample "Works Cited," 613–14
secondary, 574–75
of visuals, 355
working bibliography of, 542–44, 543 (fig.), 544 (fig.)
Space, in document design, 339, 347–49, 348 (fig.), 364, 365–66, 365 (fig.)
Spatiality, in visuals, 364
Spatial organization, 275–76, 304
Spell checker software, 333, A-19
Spelling, H-142–46
  checking, 47, A-19–23
  commonly confused homonyms, A-20
  commonly misspelled words, H-146, A-21–23
  rules for, H-142–45
  skills in, H-145–46
Squinting modifiers, H-58
Standage, Tom
  "The Victorian Internet," 82–85
Standard English, H-85
Standardized tests, 250
States in addresses, commas for, H-106
Statistical Abstract of the United States, 557
Statistics
  sources of, 557
  using, 26, 28, 129, 304–05, 575
Stereotypes, H-92–93
"Story of an Hour, The" (Chopin), 219–21
Strategies, 259
  designing a document, 335–56
  developing, 300–18
  drafting, 285–99

generating ideas, 260–70
planning, 271–84
reviewing and revising, 319–24
understanding visual
representations, 358–74
Structure, revising for, 321–22
Style manuals for documentation,
615. *See also* American
Psychological Association (APA)
style; Modern Language
Association (MLA) style
Subject complements, H-14, H-37,
H-47, H-48, H-66, A-7
Subject headings, 548–49, 551 (fig.),
578
Subjective nouns, H-37
Subjective pronoun case, H-37, A-7
Subjects (grammar), H-10, H-107,
A-6
ESL guidelines for, H-67
Subjects (in writing)
for an assignment, 90, 210
for interviews, 72
for research projects, 534–36
Subject-verb agreement, H-31–35,
A-5–6
Subjunctive mood, H-28, H-29
Subordinate clauses, H-6–7, H-34–35,
H-76–77, H-79, H-99
Subordinating conjunctions, H-7,
H-73, H-75, A-11, A-12
Subordination (grammar), H-12,
H-71, H-74, H-75–77
Substantiation, claims of, 127, 128
Subtitles, H-112
Suffixes, H-144–45
Summarizing. *See* Nutshelling
Superlatives, H-49–51, A-10
Survey questionnaires, 565–67, 567
(fig.), 574
Symbols, 208–09
proofreading, A-25–26
understanding, in visuals, 366–67,
367 (fig.), 372
Synopsis, 202, 216–17
"Synopsis of 'The Lottery,' A" (Burns),
217–18
Syntax, H-3
Synthesis, 33
cognitive activity and, 16, 20
critical reading and, 19 (fig.), 20
critical thinking and, 23 (fig.), 24

Table format, 113, 339
Tag questions, H-106

"Take Me Out to the Ball Game, but
Which One?" (Chabot), 86–89,
94
Taking a stand, 117–37, 139
appeals to readers in, 131–32
applications of, 136–37
assignments on, 124–25, 136
beginning essays with, 292
computers and, 131
discovery checklist for, 129
editing checklist for, 133
evaluating and, 157
evidence and, 128–30
facing the challenge, 125
generating ideas for, 125–29
group learning activity and, 127
logical fallacies and, 134–36
peer response checklist for, 133
planning, drafting, and developing,
130–32
purpose of, 118
revising and editing, 132–33
revision checklist for, 132
Talese, Gay, 290
Tan, Amy, 385
"Mother Tongue," 385–90
Tannen, Deborah, 431–32
"Women and Men Talking on the
Job," 432–36
Tape recorders, 75, 286, 564–65
Telephone interviewing, 75, 544, 565
Television program, listing as source,
630 (MLA), 639 (APA)
Templates, 356
Tense (verbs), 104, H-18–25,
H-52–53, A-3–4
ESL guidelines for, H-21, H-22,
H-24, H-25
Testing. *See also* Examinations
of evidence, 27–28, 129–30
Theme
of visuals, 372–73
of writing, 208
Thesis, 596, 604
causes and effects and, 110
concluding with restatement of,
293–94
developing, 213–14
in essay answers, 246
proposals with, 148
refining, 585–86
source evaluation and, 575, 576
statements of, 95
stating, 271–75, 293–94, 586, 596,
602

using, 275
working, 272–73, 538
Thesis method, and research, 584
Thesis sentences, 213–14, 246, 272,
273–74, 275, 280, 586, 602
"Things Unflattened by Science"
(Thomas), 298
Thinking critically. *See* Critical
thinking
Third-person narrator, 208
Third Wave, The (Toffler), 306
"Thirty-eight Who Saw Murder Didn't
Call Police" (Gansberg), 294
Thomas, Lewis, 289, 298
"Three Generations of Native
American Women's Birth
Experience" (Harjo), 423–27
Time
abbreviations for, H-128
prepositions of, ESL guidelines for,
H-88
punctuation and, H-106, H-112,
H-128
verb tense and changes in, H-53
Timed writings, 248–50
Time issues, 269
in brainstorming, 262
in drafting, 285
exams and, 245, 248
in freewriting, 263
writing portfolio and, 252
Time order, 276
"*Times* Series Delved Successfully into
Race" (Miday), 177–79
Titles of individuals, H-127–28, H-131
Titles of works, 272, 286, 604, H-35,
H-112, H-118, H-132, H-136,
H-137, A-17–18
Toffler, Alvin, 306
Tone (writing), 183, 226, H-81–82,
H-121
Topic outlines, 282–83
Topic sentences, 128
drafting, 288–91
kinds of, 289–90
"To the Singing, to the Drums"
(Momaday), 304
Transitional markers, 214
Transition paragraphs, 298
Transitions, 96, 187, 214, 296–98,
588, 606
Transitive verbs, H-18
Traugot, Marsha, 297–98
Trudeau, Garry, 507
"My Inner Shrimp," 507–09

Tsu, Lillian (student writer), 308
Tuchman, Barbara, 588–91, 592–94
Tunney, Gene, 294
Turner, Janice, 524
  "Cutting Edge," 525–27
Twain, Mark, 275
Type style, in document design, 339
Typography, 342–43, 366–69, 368
  (fig.)

Unabridged Journals of Sylvia Plath, The
  (Plath), 265
Underhill, Evelyn, 591–92
Underlining, 324, 587
"Unequal Work for Unequal Pay"
  (Burkett), 496–99
Updike, John, 315

Varnell, Paul, 271–72
"Venezuela for Visitors" (Updike), 315
Verbal, H-8
Verb phrases, H-15
Verbs, H-14–35, H-107, A-3
  ESL guidelines for, H-21, H-22,
    H-24, H-25, H-27, H-30
  irregular, H-16–18, A-3–5
  main, H-15
  mood and, H-28–30
  past tense, 84, H-16, H-20, H-30,
    A-3–4
  present tense with literary work,
    A-3–4
  principal parts of, H-16, A-4–5
  revising, 327
  subject-verb agreement, H-31–35,
    A-5–6
  tenses of, H-18–25
  voice of, H-26–28
"Victorian Internet, The" (Standage),
  82–85
"Victoria's Not-So-Secret Strategy"
  (Kula), 510–13
Video cameras, and field research, 565
View from Eighty, The (Cowley), 293
Visual analysis, 359, 373
Visuals. *See also* Images
  artistic choices in, 364–69, 365
    (fig.), 367 (fig.), 368 (fig.)
  design and arrangement of, 363–64
  discovery checklist for, 360
  document design and, 354–57, 354
    (fig.), 355 (fig.)
  focal point in, 360–61, 362 (fig.)
  language in, 367–69, 370–71
  levels of analysis of, 359

meaning of, 369–73, 371 (fig.), 372
  (fig.)
observing characteristics of image
  in, 361–69, 362 (fig.)
prominent element in, 360, 362
  (fig.)
seeing the big picture with, 359–61
story of the image in, 363
strategies for understanding,
  358–74
visual analysis checklist, 373
Voice (grammar), H-26–28

Wade, Nicholas, 437–38
  "How Men and Women Think,"
    438–40
Waite, Donna (student writer), 325
Warm-up journal writing, 266
Warner, Edgar F., 596
Waterman, Robert H., Jr., 301
Watulak, Thaddeus (student writer),
  126, 128
  "Affirmative Action Encourages
    Racism," 121–23
Web. *See* World Wide Web (WWW)
WebCrawler, 562
"What Is a Hunter?" (Schreiner),
  39–42
White, E. B., 379
  "Here Is New York," 52–54
  "Once More to the Lake," 293,
    379–84
White space, 339, 347–49, 348 (fig.),
  364, 365–66, 365 (fig.)
Whittling, in revision, 326–31
"Why Men Fear Women's Teams"
  (Rounds), 182–83
"Why Prisons Don't Work" (Rideau),
  140–41
"Why We Crave Horror Movies"
  (King), 443–45
Wildcards, in Web searches, 560
Wildlife Management (Giles), 310–11
"Woman in the White House, A"
  (Tsu), 308
"Women and Men Talking on the Job"
  (Tannen), 432–36
Wonder, Jacquelyn, 315
Word choice, H-81–95
  appropriateness in, H-81–85
  bias-free language and, H-90–93
  clichés and, H-86–87
  exactness in, H-86–90
  idioms and, H-87–90
  wordiness and, H-94–95

Word division, H-141
Wordiness, H-94–95
Word processing. *See* Computers
Working bibliography, 542–44, 543
  (fig.), 544 (fig.)
Working thesis, 272–73, 538
Workplace applications of learning
  causes and effects and, 116
  comparing and contrasting and,
    98–99
  evaluation and, 171–72
  interviewing and, 80
  observation and, 64
  opinion (taking a stand) essay and,
    137
  proposals and, 154
  reading critically and, 189
  recalling experience and, 49–50
  research and, 601
Workplace, writing in, 228 (fig.),
  234–38
  application letters, 236–38, 237
    (fig.)
  audience and, 225
  business letters, 227–30, 231 (fig.)
  discovery checklists for, 225
  electronic mail, 233–34
  guidelines for, 224–27
  memoranda, 231–32, 233 (fig.)
  presenting information in, 226–27
  purpose in, 225
  résumés, 234–36, 235 (fig.)
  revision checklists for, 226, 227
  tone in, 226
"Works Cited" (list of sources), 554,
  599, 613–14, 621 (MLA)
World Wide Web (WWW). *See also*
  Internet
  authorship issues on, 573–74
  bookmarks on, 545
  citing sites on, 621 (MLA), 634
    (APA)
  databases on, 552–55
  document collections on, 563
  documenting sources on, 544, 544
    (fig.), 620 (MLA), 627–29
    (MLA), 634 (APA), 637–38
    (APA)
  encyclopedias on, 556
  evaluating sources on, 571, 572
    (fig.), 573–74
  government documents on, 558–59
  library catalogs on, 547–52
  library home pages on, 546–47,
    548 (fig.)

listing as source, 628 (MLA), 638 (APA)
organizations and, 558
publishers of sites on, 575
research archive of sites on, 544–45
research using, 559–63
saving search results, 545
search activities on, 379, 412, 443, 467, 502
search sites on, 562
search strategies on, 539–41, 545, 555, 559–63, 560 (fig.), 561 (fig.)
statistical data on, 557
Writer's strategies, 259
designing a document, 335–56
developing, 300–18
drafting, 285–99
generating ideas, 260–70
planning, 271–84
reviewing and revising, 319–24
understanding visual representations, 358–74

Writing, 7–14. *See also* Causes and effects; Comparing and contrasting; Evaluating; Interviews and interviewing; Literature, writing about; Observation, writing from; Opinion (taking a stand); Proposals; Reading, writing from; Recall, writing from; Writing for assessment; Writing with a computer
mechanics of, H-127–46
process of, 9–14
Writing for assessment, 239–55
drafting and, 245–47
essay examinations and, 239–40
generating ideas for, 241
group learning activity for, 250
planning for, 242–45
portfolio assessment, 252–55
preparing for, 239–40
revising in, 247

revision checklist for, 247
sample exam answer, 240
short-answer examinations and, 248
timed writings and, 248–50
types of exam questions and, 242–44
Writing group. *See* Group learning activities
Writing portfolio, 252–55
discovery checklist for, 254
tips for keeping, 252–55
types of, 251–52
Writing with a computer, 44, 62, 74, 92, 113, 131, 149, 169, 186, 227, 266, 278, 286, 322, 324, 356, 562, 578, 587, 598, 600, A-1, A-19. *See also* Computers

Yahoo! 536, 562, 563, 569
"Year of the Blue-Collar Guy" (Olson), 473–75

Proofreading Symbols

Use these standard proofreading marks when making minor corrections in your final draft. If extensive revision is necessary, type or print out a clean copy.

Symbol	Meaning
∿	Transpose
≡	Capitalize
/	Lowercase
#	Add space
⌢	Close up space
℘	Delete
⌣ (stet marks)	Stet (undo deletion)
∧	Insert
⊙	Insert period
⋏	Insert comma
;/	Insert semicolon
:/	Insert colon
⌄	Insert apostrophe
⌄ ⌄	Insert quotation marks
|=|	Insert hyphen
¶	New paragraph
no ¶	No new paragraph

Correction Symbols

Many instructors use these abbreviations and symbols to mark errors in student papers. Refer to this chart to find out what they mean.

Boldface numbers refer to sections of the handbook and the "Quick Editing Guide."

abbr	faulty abbreviation **28**	*om*	omitted word **11**
ad	misuse of adverb or adjective **8, A5**	*p*	error in punctuation **20–27, C**
agr	faulty agreement **4, 7, A2, A4**	*⌃;*	comma **21, C1**
appr	inappropriate language **9f, 16, 18**	*no ,*	no comma **21n–r, C1**
awk	awkward	*;*	semicolon **22**
cap	capital letter **29, D1**	*:*	colon **23**
case	error in case **5, A3**	*⌄*	apostrophe **24, C2**
coord	faulty coordination **14a–c**	*" "*	quotation marks **25, C3**
cs	comma splice **2, A7**	*. ? !*	period, question mark, exclamation point **20**
dm	dangling modifier **10c, B1**	*– ( ) [ ] . . .*	dash, parentheses, brackets, ellipsis **26–27**
exact	inexact language **17**	*par, ¶*	new paragraph **E1**
frag	sentence fragment **1, A6**	*pass*	ineffective passive **3m**
fs	fused sentence **2, A7**	*ref*	error in pronoun reference **6, A4**
gl	see Glossary of Troublemakers	*rev*	revise
gr	grammar **1–9, A**	*sp*	misspelled word **33, D2**
hyph	error in use of hyphen **32**	*sub*	faulty subordination **14d–f**
inc	incomplete construction **11**	*t*	error in verb tense **3g–l, 9a–b, A1**
irreg	error in irregular verb **3e–f, A1**	*v*	voice **3m, 9c**
ital	italics (underlining) **31**	*vb*	error in verb form **3a–f, A1, A2**
lc	use lowercase letter **29, D1**	*w*	wordy **19**
mixed	mixed construction **12**	*//*	faulty parallelism **13, B2**
mm	misplaced modifier **10a–b, B1**	*⌃*	insert **E1**
mood	error in mood **3n–p, 9e**	*x*	obvious error
ms	manuscript form **E1**	*#*	insert space
nonst	nonstandard usage **16, 17**	*⌣*	close up space **E1**
num	error in use of numbers **30**		

Directory to MLA Documentation Models

CITING SOURCES

PRINTED SOURCES: NONFICTION BOOKS
Author not named in sentence, 616
Author named in sentence, 616
Author unknown, 616
Long quotation, 617
Two or three authors, 617
More than three authors, 617
Multiple works by the same author, 617
A multivolume work, 618
Indirect source, 618

PRINTED SOURCES: LITERATURE
Novel or short story, 618
Play, 618
Poetry, 619
A work in an anthology, 619

PRINTED SOURCES:
REFERENCE BOOKS AND PERIODICALS
Article in a reference book, 619
Journal article, 620
Magazine or newspaper article, 620
The Bible, 620

ELECTRONIC AND OTHER NONPRINT SOURCES
Web site, 621
Online article, 621
Interview, 621
Recording, 621

LISTING SOURCES

BOOKS
Single author, 622
Two or three authors, 622
Four or more authors, 622
Multiple works by the same author, 622
Corporate author, 622
Unknown author, 623
Edited book, 623
Translated work, 623
Multivolume work, 623
Edition other than the first, 623
Book in a series, 624

PARTS OF BOOKS
Chapter or section in a book, 624
Essay, short story, poem, or play in an edited collection, 624
Two or more works from the same edited collection, 624
Introduction, preface, foreword, or afterword, 624

REFERENCE BOOKS
Signed dictionary entry, 625
Unsigned dictionary entry, 625
Signed encyclopedia article, 625
Unsigned encyclopedia article, 625

PERIODICALS
Article from a journal paginated by issue, 625
Article from a journal paginated by volume, 625
Signed magazine article, 626
Unsigned magazine article, 626
Signed newspaper article, 626
Unsigned newspaper article, 626
Signed editorial, 626
Unsigned editorial, 626
Published interview, 626
Letter to the editor, 626
Review, 627

OTHER PRINTED SOURCES
Government document, 627
Pamphlet, 627
Doctoral dissertation, 627
Personal letter, 627
Advertisement, 627

INTERNET AND ELECTRONIC SOURCES
Professional or personal Web site, 628
Online scholarly project or reference database, 628
Article in an online periodical, 628
An online posting, 629
E-mail, 629
Publication on CD-ROM, 629
Computer software, 629
Material accessed through an online subscription service, 629

OTHER NONPRINT SOURCES
Audiotape or recording, 630
Television or radio program, 630
Film, 630
Performance, 630
A work of art, 630
Speech or lecture, 630
Broadcast interview, 631
Personal interview, 631

Directory to APA Documentation Models

CITING SOURCES

PRINTED SOURCES
Author not named in sentence, 631
Author named in sentence, 631
Long quotation, 632
Two authors, 632
Three to five authors, 632
Corporate author, 633
Government document, 633
Unknown author, 633
Multiple works by the same author, 633

OTHER SOURCES
Personal communications, 633
Web site or other electronic document, 634

LISTING SOURCES

BOOKS
Single author, 634
Two or more authors, 635
Corporate author, 635
Unknown author, 635
Multiple works by the same author, 635
Chapter or section of a book, 635
Introduction, preface, foreword, or afterword, 635
Work in an edited collection, 635

Edited book, 635
Translated work, 636
Revised edition, 636

PERIODICALS
Article from a journal paginated by issue, 636
Article from a journal paginated by volume, 636
Magazine article, 636
Signed newspaper article, 636
Unsigned newspaper article, 636
Signed editorial, 636
Unsigned editorial, 637
Letter to the editor, 637
Review, 637

OTHER PRINTED SOURCES
Government document, 637
Unpublished doctoral dissertation, 637

INTERNET AND ELECTRONIC SOURCES
Nonperiodical Web document, 638
Article from an online periodical, 638
Online newspaper article, 639
E-mail (including mailing lists), 639
Computer software, 639
Article from an information service or database, 639

OTHER NONPRINT SOURCES
Music recording, 639
Television or radio program, 639
Motion picture, 639
Personal interview, 639

Index to ESL Guidelines

a, an. See Articles.

Addresses, prepositions with, H-88

Adjective clauses, using with relative pronouns, H-41

Adjectives, H-51

arrive, prepositions with, H-88

Articles, H-33, H-48, H-49, H-51

at, as preposition of location and time, H-88

be going to, to form future tense, H-21

be used to, H-8

be, H-24, H-27

Capitalization, with direct and indirect quotations, H-117

Conditional sentences, H-30

could, to form conditional sentences, H-30

Count nouns, H-33, H-48, H-49

Cumulative adjectives, H-51

Definite articles. *See* Articles.

Demonstratives, and count nouns, H-33

Determiners, H-33, H-51

Direct quotations, H-117

-ed form of verb, H-21, H-22, H-27, H-30

-en form of verb. *See -ed* form of verb.

Faulty predication, H-67

for, prepositional phrases beginning with, H-89

Future perfect progressive tense, H-25

Future perfect tense, H-22

Future progressive tense, H-24

Future tense, H-21

Gerunds, H-8

get used to, H-8

have, to form different verb tenses, H-22

if, in conditional sentences, H-30

in, as preposition of location and time, H-88

in a minute, H-88

in time, H-88

Indefinite articles. *See* Articles.

Indirect objects, use of prepositions compared with, H-89

Indirect quotations, H-117

Infinitives, H-8

-ing form of verb, H-8, H-24, H-25

Intransitive verbs, and passive voice, H-27

it, used as a subject, H-67

Mass nouns, H-33

might, to form conditional sentences, H-30

Mixed constructions, H-67

Modifiers, H-67

Negatives, forming, H-21, H-54

Noncount nouns, H-33, H-48, H-49

not, to form negatives, H-54

Numbers, and count nouns, H-33

on, as preposition of location and time, H-88

on time, H-88

Participles, H-8

Passive voice, H-27

Past participle, to form different verb tenses, H-22, H-27, H-30

Past perfect progressive tense, H-25

Past perfect tense, H-22

Past progressive tense, H-24

Past tense, H-21

Perfect progressive tenses, H-25

Perfect tenses, H-22

Possessives, and count nouns, H-33

Prepositional phrases, H-89

Prepositions, use of indirect objects compared with, H-89

Present participle, to form different verb tenses, H-24, H-25

Present perfect progressive tense, H-25

Present perfect tense, H-22

Present progressive tense, H-24

Present tense, H-21

Pronouns, with direct and indirect quotations, H-117

Punctuation, with direct and indirect quotations, H-117

Questions, forming, H-21, H-54, H-117

Relative pronouns, using with adjective clauses, H-41

Simple progressive tenses, H-24

Simple verb tenses, H-21

some, and noncount nouns, H-33, H-49

Subject errors, H-67

Tenses (verb), H-21, H-22, H-24, H-25

that, using with adjective clauses, H-41

the. See Articles.

to, prepositional phrases beginning with, H-89

Uncountable nouns. *See* Noncount nouns.

used to, H-8

Verb tenses, H-21, H-22, H-24, H-25

Verbals, H-8

which, using with adjective clauses, H-41

who, using with adjective clauses, H-41

will, to form future tenses, H-21, H-22, H-24, H-25

Word order, with direct and indirect quotations, H-117

would, to form conditional sentences, H-30

A Guide to the Handbook

33. GRAMMATICAL SENTENCES   H-5

1. Sentence Fragments **frag**   H-5
a. Phrases, H-6
b. Subordinate clauses, H-6
c. With *having* or another participle, H-7
d. Compound predicates, H-7
   ESL Guidelines: Using Participles, Infinitives, and Gerunds, H-8

2. Comma Splices and Fused Sentences **cs/fs**   H-10
a. Repair by separating sentences, H-11
b. Use a comma and a coordinating conjunction, H-11
c. Use a semicolon or a colon, H-11
d. Use subordination, H-12
e. Use a conjunctive adverb, H-12

3. Verbs **vb**   H-14

VERB FORMS   H-14
a. Linking verbs, H-14
b. Helping verbs, H-15
c. Principal parts, H-16
d. Regular verbs, H-16
e. Irregular verbs, H-16
f. *Lie* and *lay*/*sit* and *set*, H-16

TENSES   H-18
g. Simple present, H-19
h. Simple past, H-20
i. Simple future, H-20
   ESL Guidelines: The Simple Tenses, H-21
j. Present, past, and future perfect, H-22
   ESL Guidelines: The Perfect Tenses, H-22
k. Present, past, and future progressive, H-23
   ESL Guidelines: The Simple Progressive Tenses, H-24
l. Present perfect progressive, past perfect progressive, and future perfect progressive, H-24
   ESL Guidelines: The Perfect Progressive Tenses, H-25

VOICE   H-26
m. Active/Passive, H-26
   ESL Guidelines: The Passive Voice, H-27

MOOD   H-28
n. Indicative, H-28
o. Imperative, H-29
p. Subjunctive, H-29
   ESL Guidelines: Conditionals, H-30

4. Subject-Verb Agreement **agr**   H-31
a. Person and number, H-31
b. Intervening words, H-31
c. Subjects with *and*, H-32
d. Subjects with *or* or *nor*, H-32
e. Collective nouns, H-32

   ESL Guidelines: Count Nouns and Articles, Noncount Nouns and Articles, H-33
f. Indefinite pronouns, H-34
g. *All*, *any*, and *some*, H-34
h. Subordinate clause, H-34
i. Subject following verb, H-35
j. Linking verbs, H-35
k. Titles, H-35
l. Singular nouns that end in *-s*, H-35

5. Pronoun Case **case**   H-36
a. Subjects, H-37
b. Subject complements, H-37
c. Appositives to subjects, H-37
d. Objects, H-38
e. Appositives to objects, H-38
f. Possessive case, H-38
g. With gerunds, H-38

6. Pronoun Reference **ref**   H-40
a. Implied antecedents, H-40
   ESL Guidelines: Adjective Clauses and Relative Pronouns, H-41
b. Antecedents of *it*, *this*, *that*, or *which*, H-42
c. Ambiguous reference, H-42
d. Keep pronoun close to its antecedent, H-43

7. Pronoun-Antecedent Agreement **agr**   H-44
a. Person and number, H-44
b. Antecedents joined by *and*, H-44
c. Antecedents joined by *or* or *nor*, H-45
d. Indefinite pronouns, H-45
e. Collective nouns, H-45
f. Gender, H-46

8. Adjectives and Adverbs **ad**   H-46
a. Adverbs to modify a verb, adjective, or adverb, H-47
b. Adjectives as subject or object complements, H-47
   ESL Guidelines: The Definite Article (*the*), H-48
c. *Good* and *well*, H-48
d. Form of comparatives and superlatives, H-49
   ESL Guidelines: The Indefinite Article (*a*, *an*), H-49
e. Redundant comparatives and superlatives, H-50
f. Use of comparatives and superlatives, H-51
   ESL Guidelines: Cumulative Adjectives, H-51

9. Shifts **shift**   H-52
a. Tense, H-52
b. Time, H-53
c. Voice, H-53
   ESL Guidelines: Negatives, H-54
d. Person, H-54
e. Mood, H-54
f. Level of language, H-55

34. EFFECTIVE SENTENCES   H-57

10. Misplaced and Dangling Modifiers **mm/dm**   H-57
a. Misplaced modifiers, H-57
b. Squinting modifiers, H-58
c. Dangling modifiers, H-59

11. Incomplete Sentences **inc**   H-60

COMPARISONS   H-60
a. Make full comparisons, H-60
b. Finish comparisons, H-60
c. Compare things of the same kind, H-61
d. Use *any other*, H-61

ELLIPTICAL CONSTRUCTIONS   H-62
e. Words essential for clarity, H-62
f. In a compound predicate, H-63
g. With *as* and *than*, H-63

12. Mixed Constructions and Faulty Predication **mixed**   H-64
a. Mixed construction, H-64
b. Faulty predication, H-65
c. Definitions with *when* or *where*, H-66
d. *The reason is because*, H-66
   ESL Guidelines: Mixed Constructions, Faulty Predication, and Subject Errors, H-67

13. Parallel Structure **//**   H-68
a. Coordinating conjunction, H-68
b. Correlative conjunction, H-69
c. Comparisons, H-69
d. Repeating words, H-70

14. Coordination and Subordination **coord/sub**   H-71
a. Uses of coordination, H-71
b. Faulty coordination, H-72
c. Excessive coordination, H-74
d. Uses of subordination, H-75
e. Faulty subordination, H-76
f. Excessive subordination, H-76

15. Sentence Variety **var**   H-78
a. Normal sentences, H-78
b. Inverted sentences, H-78
c. Cumulative sentences, H-78
d. Periodic sentences, H-78

35. WORD CHOICE   H-81

16. Appropriateness **appr**   H-81
a. Tone, H-81
b. Level of formality, H-81
c. Jargon, H-83